T0142056

Lecture Notes of the Institute for Computer Sciences, Social Informatics and Telecommunications Engineering 491

The LNICST series publishes ICST's conferences, symposia and workshops.
LNICST reports state-of-the-art results in areas related to the scope of the Institute.
The type of material published includes

- Proceedings (published in time for the respective event)
- Other edited monographs (such as project reports or invited volumes)

LNICST topics span the following areas:

- General Computer Science
- E-Economy
- E-Medicine
- Knowledge Management
- Multimedia
- Operations, Management and Policy
- Social Informatics
- Systems

Md. Shahriare Satu · Mohammad Ali Moni ·
M. Shamim Kaiser · Mohammad Shamsul Arefin
Editors

Machine Intelligence and Emerging Technologies

First International Conference, MIET 2022
Noakhali, Bangladesh, September 23–25, 2022
Proceedings, Part II

 Springer

Editors
Md. Shahriare Satu (ID)
Noakhali Science and Technology University
Noakhali, Bangladesh

M. Shamim Kaiser (ID)
Jahangirnagar University
Dhaka, Bangladesh

Mohammad Ali Moni (ID)
The University of Queensland
St. Lucia, QLD, Australia

Mohammad Shamsul Arefin (ID)
Daffodil International University
Dhaka, Bangladesh

Chittagong University of Engineering
and Technology
Chattogram, Bangladesh

ISSN 1867-8211   ISSN 1867-822X (electronic)
Lecture Notes of the Institute for Computer Sciences, Social Informatics
and Telecommunications Engineering
ISBN 978-3-031-34621-7   ISBN 978-3-031-34622-4 (eBook)
https://doi.org/10.1007/978-3-031-34622-4

This Springer imprint is published by the registered company Springer Nature Switzerland AG
The registered company address is: Gewerbestrasse 11, 6330 Cham, Switzerland

Preface

Machine intelligence is the practice of designing computer systems to make intelligent decisions based on context rather than direct input. It is important to understand that machine intelligence relies on a huge volume of data. On the other hand, the emerging technology can be termed as a radically novel and relatively fast-growing technology characterized by a certain degree of coherence that persists over time and with the potential to exert a significant impact on the socio-economic domain which is observed in terms of the composition of actors, institutions, and patterns of interactions among those, as well as the associated knowledge production processes.

To that end, the 1st International Conference on Machine Intelligence and Emerging Technologies (MIET 2022) provided an opportunity to engage researchers, academicians, industry professionals, and experts in the multidisciplinary field and to share their cutting-edge research results gained through the application of Machine Learning, Data Science, Internet of Things, Cloud Computing, Sensing, and Security. Researchers in the relevant fields were invited to submit their original, novel, and extended unpublished works at this conference.

The conference was hosted by Noakhali Science and Technology University (NSTU), Sonapur, Noakhali, 3814, Bangladesh. Support for MIET 2022 came from the IEEE Computer Society Bangladesh Chapter, Center for Natural Science and Engineering Research (CNSER), University Grant Commission (UGC) Bangladesh, Agrani Bank Limited, Mercantile Bank Limited, Union Bank Limited, Globe Pharmaceuticals Limited, EXIM Bank Limited and Janata Bank Limited. The papers presented at MIET 2022 covered theoretical and methodological frameworks for replicating applied research. These articles offer a representative cross-section of recent academic progress in the study of AI and IT's wide-ranging applications. There are five main categories that the accepted papers cover: (1) imaging for disease detection; (2) pattern recognition and NLP; (3) biosignals and recommendation systems for well-being; (4) network, security, and nanotechnology; and (5) emerging technologies for society and industry. The five MIET 2022 streams received a total of 272 entries from writers in 12 different nations. There was one round of double-blind review performed on all articles, and each was read by at least two experts (one of whom was the managing chair). In the end, 104 full papers from authors in 9 countries were accepted for presentation at the conference after a thorough review procedure in which reports from the reviewers and the track chairs on the various articles were considered. All 104 papers that were presented physically at MIET 2022 are included in this volume of the proceedings. All of us on the MIET 2022 committee are indebted to the committee members' tireless efforts and invaluable contributions. Without the hard work and dedication of the MIET 2022 Program Committee members in assessing the conference papers, we would not have had the fantastic program that we had. The success of MIET 2022 is due to the hard work of many people and the financial backing of our kind sponsors. We'd like to give particular thanks to Springer Nature and the rest of the Springer LNICST and EAI team for their support of our work. We'd like to extend our appreciation to the Springer and EAI teams for their tireless efforts in managing the publishing of this volume. Finally, we'd like to express our gratitude to everyone who has helped us prepare for MIET 2022 and contributed to it in any way.

November 2022

Md. Shahriare Satu
Mohammad Ali Moni
M. Shamim Kaiser
Mohammad Shamsul Arefin

Organization

International Advisory Committee

Ali Dewan	Athabasca University, Canada
Amir Hussain	Edinburgh Napier University, UK
Anirban Bandyopadhyay	National Institute for Materials Science, Japan
Anton Nijholt	University of Twente, The Netherlands
Chanchal K. Roy	University of Saskatchewan, Canada
David Brown	Nottingham Trent University, UK
Enamul Hoque Prince	York University, Canada
Jarrod Trevathan	Griffith University, Australia
Joarder Kamruzzaman	Federation University, Australia
Kanad Ray	Amity University, India
Karl Andersson	Luleå University of Technology, Sweden
Kenichi Matsumoto	Nara Institute of Science and Technology, Japan
M. Julius Hossain	European Molecular Biology Laboratory, Germany
Md. Atiqur Rahman Ahad	University of East London, UK
Mohammad Tariqul Islam	Universiti Kebangsaan Malaysia, Malaysia
Manzur Murshed	Federation University, Australia
Mukesh Prasad	University of Technology Sydney, Australia
Ning Zhong	Maebashi Institute of Technology, Japan
Pranab K. Muhuri	South Asian University, India
Saidur Rahman	Sunway University, Malaysia
Saifur Rahman	Virginia Tech Advanced Research Institute, USA
Shariful Islam	Deakin University, Australia
Stefano Vassanelli	University of Padova, Italy
Suresh Chandra Satapathy	KIIT Deemed to be University, India
Syed Ishtiaque Ahmed	University of Toronto, Canada
Upal Mahbub	Qualcomm Inc., USA
V. R. Singh	National Physical Laboratory, India
Yang Yang	Maebashi Institute of Technology, Japan
Yoshinori Kuno	Saitama University, Japan
Zamshed Chowdhury	Intel Corporation, USA

National Advisory Committee

A. B. M. Siddique Hossain	AIUB, Bangladesh
A. Z. M. Touhidul Islam	RU, Bangladesh

Abu Sayed Md. Latiful Hoque	BUET, Bangladesh
Dibyadyuti Sarkar	NSTU, Bangladesh
Hafiz Md. Hasan Babu	DU, Bangladesh
Kaushik Deb	CUET, Bangladesh
Firoz Ahmed	NSTU, Bangladesh
Kazi Muheymin-Us-Sakib	DU, Bangladesh
M. Lutfar Rahman	DIU, Bangladesh
M. M. A. Hashem	KUET, Bangladesh
M. Rizwan Khan	UIU, Bangladesh
M. Sohel Rahman	BUET, Bangladesh
Md. Liakot Ali	BUET, Bangladesh
Md. Mahbubur Rahman	MIST, Bangladesh
Md. Sazzad Hossain	UGC, Bangladesh
Mohammod Abul Kashem	DUET, Bangladesh
Mohammad Hanif	NSTU, Bangladesh
Mohammad Kaykobad	BRACU, Bangladesh
Mohammad Mahfuzul Islam	BUET, Bangladesh
Mohammad Salim Hossain	NSTU, Bangladesh
Mohammad Shahidur Rahman	SUST, Bangladesh
Mohammad Shorif Uddin	JU, Bangladesh
Mohd Abdur Rashid	NSTU, Bangladesh
Mozammel Huq Azad Khan	EWU, Bangladesh
Muhammad Quamruzzaman	CUET, Bangladesh
Munaz Ahmed Noor	BDU, Bangladesh
Nasim Akhtar	CSTU, Bangladesh
Newaz Mohammed Bahadur	NSTU, Bangladesh
S. I. Khan	BRACU, Bangladesh
Subrata Kumar Aditya	SHU, Bangladesh
Suraiya Pervin	DU, Bangladesh
Syed Akhter Hossain	CUB, Bangladesh

Organizing Committee

General Chairs

Pietro Lió	University of Cambridge, UK
A. B. M. Shawkat Ali	CQUniversity, Australia
Nazmul Siddique	University of Ulster, UK

General Co-chairs

Ashadun Nobi	NSTU, Bangladesh
Mohammad Ali Moni	University of Queensland, Australia
Mufti Mahmud	Nottingham Trent University, UK

TPC Chairs

Ashikur Rahman Khan	NSTU, Bangladesh
M. Shamim Kaiser	JU, Bangladesh
Mohammad Shamsul Arefin	DIU, Bangladesh

TPC Co-chairs

Md. Amran Hossain Bhuiyan	NSTU, Bangladesh
Md. Zahidul Islam	IU, Bangladesh

Track Chairs

Fateha Khanam Bappee	NSTU, Bangladesh
M. Shamim Kaiser	JU, Bangladesh
Nazia Majadi	NSTU, Bangladesh
Rashed Mustafa	CU, Bangladesh
Moahammad Jamshed Patwary	IIUC, Bangladesh
Md. Atiqur Rahman Ahad	University of East London, UK
Yusuf Sulistyo Nugroho	Universitas Muhammadiyah Surakarta, Indonesia
Mohammad Ali Moni	University of Queensland, Australia
Md. Amran Hossain Bhuiyan	NSTU, Bangladesh
Firoz Mridha	AIUB, Bangladesh
Ashik Iftekher	Nikon Corporation, Japan
Mohammad Shamsul Arefin	DIU, Bangladesh
Syful Islam	NSTU, Bangladesh

General Secretary

S. M. Mahabubur Rahman	NSTU, Bangladesh

Joint Secretaries

Md. Auhidur Rahman	NSTU, Bangladesh
Md. Iftekharul Alam Efat	NSTU, Bangladesh
Mimma Tabassum	NSTU, Bangladesh

Technical Secretary

Koushik Chandra Howlader   North Dakota State University, USA

Organizing Chair

Md. Shahriare Satu   NSTU, Bangladesh

Organizing Co-chairs

A. Q. M. Salauddin Pathan   NSTU, Bangladesh
Md. Abidur Rahman   NSTU, Bangladesh

Finance Subcommittee

Main Uddin   NSTU, Bangladesh
Md. Javed Hossain   NSTU, Bangladesh
Md. Omar Faruk   NSTU, Bangladesh
Md. Shahriare Satu   NSTU, Bangladesh

Keynote Selection Subcommittee

A. R. M. Mahamudul Hasan Rana   NSTU, Bangladesh
Nazia Majadi   NSTU, Bangladesh

Special Session Chairs

Md. Kamal Uddin   NSTU, Bangladesh
Zyed-Us-Salehin   NSTU, Bangladesh

Tutorials Chairs

Dipanita Saha   NSTU, Bangladesh
Sultana Jahan Soheli   NSTU, Bangladesh

Panels Chair

Falguny Roy   NSTU, Bangladesh

Workshops Chair

Nishu Nath   NSTU, Bangladesh

Proceeding Publication Committee

Md. Shahriare Satu	NSTU, Bangladesh
Mohammad Ali Moni	University of Queensland, Australia
M. Shamim Kaiser	JU, Bangladesh
Mohammad Shamsul Arefin	DIU, Bangladesh

Industrial Session Chairs

Apurba Adhikhary	NSTU, Bangladesh
Tanvir Zaman Khan	NSTU, Bangladesh

Project and Exhibition Chairs

Dipok Chandra Das	NSTU, Bangladesh
Rutnadip Kuri	NSTU, Bangladesh

Publicity Chair

Muhammad Abdus Salam	NSTU, Bangladesh

Kit and Registration Chairs

K. M. Aslam Uddin	NSTU, Bangladesh
Md. Bipul Hossain	NSTU, Bangladesh

Venue Preparation Subcommittee

Md. Habibur Rahman	NSTU, Bangladesh
Md. Shohel Rana	NSTU, Bangladesh
Md. Hasnat Riaz	NSTU, Bangladesh

Accommodation and Food Management Subcommittee

Kamruzaman	NSTU, Bangladesh
Md. Mamun Mia	NSTU, Bangladesh
Subrata Bhowmik	NSTU, Bangladesh

Public Relation Chairs

Md. Al-Amin	NSTU, Bangladesh
Tasniya Ahmed	NSTU, Bangladesh

Award Chair

Md. Abul Kalam Azad   NSTU, Bangladesh

International Guest Management Subcommittee

Iftakhar Parvez   NSTU, Bangladesh
Tonmoy Dey   NSTU, Bangladesh
Trisha Saha   NSTU, Bangladesh

Web Masters

Md. Jane Alam Adnan   NSTU, Bangladesh
Rahat Uddin Azad   NSTU, Bangladesh

Graphics Designers

Mohit Sarkar   NSTU, Bangladesh
Shamsun Nahar Needhe   Hezhou University, China

Technical Program Committee

A. K. M. Mahbubur Rahman	IUB, Bangladesh
A. S. M. Sanwar Hosen	JNU, South Korea
A. A. Mamun	JU, Bangladesh
A. F. M. Rashidul Hasan	RU, Bangladesh
Abdul Kader Muhammad Masum	IIUC, Bangladesh
Abdul Kaium Masud	NSTU, Bangladesh
Abdullah Nahid	KU, Bangladesh
Abdur Rahman Bin Shahid	Concord University, USA
Abdur Rouf	DUET, Bangladesh
A. B. M. Aowlad Hossain	KUET, Bangladesh
Adnan Anwar	Deakin University, Australia
Ahmed Imteaj	Florida International University, USA
Ahmed Wasif Reza	EWU, Bangladesh
Ahsanur Rahman	NSU, Bangladesh
Alessandra Pedrocchi	Politecnico di Milano, Italy
Alex Ng	La Trobe University, Australia
Anindya Das Antar	University of Michigan, USA
Anirban Bandyopadhyay	NIMS, Japan
Antesar Shabut	Leeds Trinity University, UK

Antony Lam	Mercari Inc., Japan
Anup Majumder	JU, Bangladesh
Anupam Kumar Bairagi	KU, Bangladesh
Arif Ahmad	SUST, Bangladesh
Asif Nashiry	JUST, Bangladesh
A. S. M. Kayes	La Trobe University, Australia
Atik Mahabub	Concordia University, Canada
Aye Su Phyo	Computer University Kalay, Myanmar
Azizur Rahman	City University of London, UK
Babul Islam	RU, Bangladesh
Banani Roy	University of Saskatchewan, Canada
Belayat Hossain	Loughborough University, UK
Boshir Ahmed	RUET, Bangladesh
Chandan Kumar Karmakar	Deakin University, Australia
Cosimo Ieracitano	University Mediterranea of Reggio Calabria, Italy
Cris Calude	University of Auckland, New Zealand
Derong Liu	University of Illinois at Chicago, USA
Dewan Md. Farid	UIU, Bangladesh
Dipankar Das	RU, Bangladesh
Duong Minh Quan	University of Da Nang, Vietnam
Eleni Vasilaki	University of Sheffield, UK
Emanuele Ogliari	Politechnico di Milano, Italy
Enamul Hoque Prince	York University, Canada
Ezharul Islam	JU, Bangladesh
Farah Deeba	DUET, Bangladesh
Fateha Khanam Bappee	NSTU, Bangladesh
Francesco Carlo Morabito	Mediterranean University of Reggio Calabria, Italy
Gabriela Nicoleta Sava	University POLITEHNICA of Bucharest, Romania
Giancarlo Ferregno	Politechnico di Milano, Italy
Golam Dastoger Bashar	Boise State University, USA
H. Liu	Wayne State University, USA
Habibur Rahman	IU, Bangladesh
Hishato Fukuda	Saitama University, Japan
Imtiaz Mahmud	Kyungpook National University, South Korea
Indika Kumara	Jheronimus Academy of Data Science, The Netherlands
Iqbal Hasan Sarkar	CUET, Bangladesh
Joarder Kamruzzaman	Federation University, Australia
John H. L. Hansen	University of Texas at Dallas, USA
Jonathan Mappelli	University of Modena, Italy

Joyprokash Chakrabartty	CUET, Bangladesh
Kamruddin Md. Nur	AIUB, Bangladesh
Kamrul Hasan Talukder	KU, Bangladesh
Kawsar Ahmed	University of Saskatchewan, Canada
K. C. Santosh	University of South Dakota, USA
Khan Iftekharuddin	Old Dominion University, USA
Khondaker Abdullah-Al-Mamun	UIU, Bangladesh
Khoo Bee Ee	Universiti Sains Malaysia, Malaysia
Lamia Iftekhar	NSU, Bangladesh
Linta Islam	Jagannath University, Bangladesh
Lu Cao	Saitama University, Japan
Luca Benini	ETH, Switzerland
Luca Berdondini	IIT, Italy
Luciano Gamberini	University of Padova, Italy
M. Tanseer Ali	AIUB, Bangladesh
M. Firoz Mridha	AIUB, Bangladesh
M. Julius Hossain	EMBL, Germany
M. M. Azizur Rahman	Grand Valley State University, USA
M. Tariqul Islam	Universiti Kebangsaan, Malaysia
Mahfuzul Hoq Chowdhury	CUET, Bangladesh
Mahmudul Kabir	Akita University, Japan
Manjunath Aradhya	JSS S&T University, India
Manohar Das	Oakland University, USA
Marzia Hoque Tania	University of Oxford, UK
Md. Badrul Alam Miah	UPM, Malaysia
Md. Faruk Hossain	RUET, Bangladesh
Md. Fazlul Kader	CU, Bangladesh
Md. Manirul Islam	AIUB, Bangladesh
Md. Saiful Islam	CUET, Bangladesh
Md. Sanaul Haque	University of Oulu, Finland
Md. Shirajum Munir	Kyung Hee University, South Korea
Md. Whaiduzzaman	Queensland University of Technology, Australia
Md. Abdul Awal	KU, Bangladesh
Md. Abdur Razzak	IUB, Bangladesh
Md. Abu Layek	Jagannath University, Bangladesh
Md. Ahsan Habib	MBSTU, Bangladesh
Md. Al Mamun	RUET, Bangladesh
Md. Amzad Hossain	NSTU, Bangladesh
Md. Golam Rashed	RU, Bangladesh
Md. Hanif Seddiqui	CU, Bangladesh
Md. Hasanul Kabir	IUT, Bangladesh
Md. Hasanuzzaman	DU, Bangladesh

Md. Kamal Uddin	NSTU, Bangladesh
Md. Mahfuzur Rahman	Queensland University of Technology, Australia
Md. Murad Hossain	University of Turin, Italy
Md. Nurul Islam Khan	BUET, Bangladesh
Md. Obaidur Rahman	DUET, Bangladesh
Md. Raju Ahmed	DUET, Bangladesh
Md. Rakibul Hoque	DU, Bangladesh
Md. Saiful Islam	Griffith University, Australia
Md. Sanaul Rabbi	CUET, Bangladesh
Md. Shamim Ahsan	KU, Bangladesh
Md. Shamim Akhter	SUB, Bangladesh
Md. Sipon Miah	IU, Bangladesh
Md. Ziaul Haque	NSTU, Bangladesh
Mehdi Hasan Chowdhury	City University of Hong Kong, China
Michele Magno	ETH, Switzerland
Milon Biswas	University of Alabama at Birmingham, USA
Min Jiang	Xiamen University, China
Mohammad Abu Yousuf	JU, Bangladesh
Mohammad Hammoudeh	Manchester Metropolitan University, UK
Mohammad Mehedi Hassan	King Saud University, KSA
Mohammad Motiur Rahman	MBSTU, Bangladesh
Mohammad Nurul Huda	UIU, Bangladesh
Mohammad Osiur Rahman	CU, Bangladesh
Mohammad Zoynul Abedin	Teesside University, UK
Mohiuddin Ahmed	Edith Cowan University, Australia
Monirul Islam Sharif	Google, USA
Monjurul Islam	Canberra Institute of Technology, Australia
Muhammad Mahbub Alam	IUT, Bangladesh
Muhammed J. Alam Patwary	IIUC, Bangladesh
Nabeel Mohammed	NSU, Bangladesh
Nahida Akter	UNSW, Australia
Nashid Alam	Aberystwyth University, UK
Nasfikur Rahman Khan	University of South Alabama, USA
Nelishia Pillay	University of Pretoria, South Africa
Nihad Karim Chowdhury	CU, Bangladesh
Nilanjan Dey	JIS University, India
Noushath Shaffi	College of Applied Sciences, Oman
Nur Mohammad	CUET, Bangladesh
Nursadul Mamun	University of Texas at Dallas, USA
Omaru Maruatona	Aiculus Pty Ltd, Australia
Omprakash Kaiwartya	Nottingham Trent University, UK
Osman Ali	NSTU, Bangladesh

Paolo Massobrio	University of Genova, Italy
Partha Chakraborty	Cumilla University, Bangladesh
Paul Watters	La Trobe University, Australia
Phalguni Gupta	IIT Kanpur, India
Pranab Kumar Dhar	CUET, Bangladesh
Rahma Mukta	UNSW, Australia
Ralf Zeitler	Venneos GmbH, Germany
Ramani Kannan	Universiti Teknologi PETRONAS, Malaysia
Rameswar Debnath	KU, Bangladesh
Rashed Mustafa	CU, Bangladesh
Risala Tasin Khan	JU, Bangladesh
Rokan Uddin Faruqui	CU, Bangladesh
Roland Thewes	Technical University of Berlin, Germany
Ryote Suzuki	Saitama University, Japan
S. M. Rafizul Haque	Canadian Food Inspection Agency, Canada
S. M. Riazul Islam	Sejong University, South Korea
S. M. Abdur Razzak	RUET, Bangladesh
Saiful Azad	Universiti Malaysia Pahang, Malaysia
Saifur Rahman	University of North Dakota, USA
Sajal Halder	RMIT, Australia
Sajib Chakraborty	Vrije Universiteit Brussel, Belgium
Sajjad Waheed	MBSTU, Bangladesh
Samrat Kumar Dey	BOU, Bangladesh
Sayed Asaduzzaman	University of North Dakota, USA
Sayed Mohsin Reza	University of Texas at El Paso, USA
Sazzadur Rahman	JU, Bangladesh
Shafkat Kibria	SUST, Bangladesh
Shahidul Islam Khan	IIUC, Bangladesh
Shahriar Badsha	University of Nevada, USA
Shamim A. Mamun	JU, Bangladesh
Shanto Roy	University of Houston, USA
Sharmin Majumder	Texas A&M University, USA
Silvestro Micera	Scuola Superiore Sant'Anna, Italy
Surapong Uttama	Mae Fah Luang University, Thailand
Syed Md. Galib	JUST, Bangladesh
Syful Islam	NSTU, Bangladesh
Tabin Hassan	AIUB, Bangladesh
Tamal Adhikary	University of Waterloo, Canada
Tarique Anwar	Macquarie University, Australia
Tauhidul Alam	LSU Shreveport University, USA
Tawfik Al-Hadhrami	Nottingham Trent University, UK
Themis Prodomakis	University of Southampton, UK

Thompson Stephan	M. S. Ramaiah University of Applied Sciences, India
Tianhua Chen	University of Huddersfield, UK
Tingwen Huang	Texas A&M University, Qatar
Tomonori Hashiyama	University of Electro-Communications, Japan
Touhid Bhuiyan	DIU, Bangladesh
Tushar Kanti Saha	JKKNIU, Bangladesh
Wladyslaw Homenda	Warsaw University of Technology, Poland
Wolfgang Maas	Technische Universität Graz, Austria
Yasin Kabir	Missouri University of Science and Technology, USA
Yusuf Sulistyo Nugroho	Universitas Muhammadiyah Surakarta, Indonesia
Zubair Fadlullah	Lakehead University, Canada

Contents – Part II

Network, Security and Nanotechnology

Emerging Technologies for Society and Industry

Contents – Part I

Bio Signals and Recommendation Systems for Wellbeing

Diagnosis and Classification of Fetal Health Based on CTG Data Using Machine Learning Techniques

Md. Monirul Islam[1]([✉])(iD), Md. Rokunojjaman[2](iD), Al Amin[3],
Md. Nasim Akhtar[4], and Iqbal H. Sarker[5](iD)

[1] Department of Computer Science and Engineering, University of Information
Technology and Sciences (UITS), Dhaka 1212, Bangladesh
monir.duet.cse@gmail.com, monirul.islam@uits.edu.bd
[2] Department of Computer Science and Mathematics,
Bangladesh Agricultural University, Mymensingh 2202, Bangladesh
[3] Department of Computer Science and Technology,
Chongqing University of Technology, Banan District, Chongqing, China
[4] Department of Computer Science and Engineering,
Dhaka University of Engineering and Technology, Gazipur 1707, Bangladesh
drnasim@duet.ac.bd
[5] Department of Computer Science and Engineering,
Chittagong University of Engineering and Technology, Chittagong 4349, Bangladesh
iqbal@cuet.ac.bd

Abstract. Cardiotocograms (CTGs) is a simple and inexpensive way
for healthcare providers to monitor fetal health, allowing them to take
step to lessen infant as well as mother died. The technology operates by
emitting ultrasound pulses and monitoring the response, revealing information such as fetal heart rate (FHR), fetal movements, uterine contractions, and more. Knowing the state of fetal, doctors and patients can take
necessary steps in a time. Machine learning can play a vital role in this
field. In this paper, we classified the state of fetal including normal state,
suspect state, pathological state on the fetal disease dataset using seven
machine learning model named AdaBoost (AdB), Random Forest (RF),
K- nearest Neighbors (K-NN), Support Vector Machine (SVM), Gradient
Boosting Classifier (GBC), Decision Tree Classifier (DTC), and Logistic
Regression (LR). To validate the experimental task, we used several performance metrics containing accuracy, precision, recall, and F1-score. We
also used a scaling technique named standard scalar for doing an unbiased dataset. Among the classification models, GCB outperforms the
best by achieving the accuracy 95%, precision (for normal 96%, suspect
85%, pathological 97%), recall (for normal 98%, suspect 78%, pathological 94%), and F1-score (for normal 97%, suspect 81%, pathological 96%).
Although, RF, SVM, and K-NN perform better precision (100%) in the
class of pathological state only.

© ICST Institute for Computer Sciences, Social Informatics and Telecommunications Engineering 2023
Published by Springer Nature Switzerland AG 2023. All Rights Reserved
Md. S. Satu et al. (Eds.): MIET 2022, LNICST 491, pp. 3–16, 2023.
https://doi.org/10.1007/978-3-031-34622-4_1

Keywords: Fetal Health classification · Machine learning based classification · CTG Dataset · Scaling

1   Introduction

Pregnancy refers a woman to being a mother which is extremely exciting and pleasurable. During pregnancy, a fetal starts the journey in the woman's womb which is transferred to a baby after a period of time. The importance of fetal growth and development in producing a healthy kid with a healthy mother cannot be overstated. Each trimester, a medical practitioner recommends several laboratory tests where Cardiotocogram (CTG) is one of them. In clinical evaluations, CTG testing is frequently used to catch the health and status of the fetus in the uterus. Both uterine contractions (UC), CTG signals fetal heart rate (FHR) are considered to monitor prenatal. For predicting the fetus's health, a computer technology called machine learning is going to play an adequate act in the medical industry recently.

CTG is a system that monitors heart rate and fetal activity, also uterine contractions, on the core principle of fetal heartbeats per minute (BPM), which is collected through the use of an ultrasonic transducer positioned on the mother's abdomen and assist the doctor in determining if the fetus is fit and active during and before delivery. Predicting or identifying the fetus's health is extremely crucial, which can prevent and reduce the risk of perinatal mortality. There are three classes for classifying the CTG test reports: suspect, normal, or pathological by the FHR, variation of the FHR, decelerations, and accelerations [13]. Health researchers are focusing on developing an automatic CTG translation, but the outcomes have yet to predict suspicious fetal abnormalities. In the meantime, a dynamic technology called machine learning also performed well for diagnosis, analyzing, and predicting fetus nature in many conditions. Several machine learning algorithms or models have been applied in many works. Supervised Learning Techniques are more commonly utilized than Unsupervised Learning Techniques when reasoning an instance with known labels that aid inaccurate prediction. For instance, SVM, Decision Tree, Naïve Bayes, and KNN classifiers are applied as the supervised learning approach [9]. Furthermore, when compared to traditional CTG, a significant decrease in maternal deaths occurs with the use of automated CTG, with such a relative risk ratio of 0.20 and a confidence level of 95 percent. However, because this study includes information of medium quality, more research is needed to determine the influence of CTG on perinatal outcomes [5]. On that note, Chinnaiyan et al. [3] did a review of the different processes of machine learning for accurate diagnosis and prognosis of abdominal disorders with a low amount of occurrences. Using learning methodologies, a reliable and efficient healthcare support structure can play a vital role in progressing diagnosis accuracy as well as lessening diagnosis time. Machine learning algorithms have been proven to reduce human effort while also producing more accurate outcomes.

As a result, several researchers began to use various ML algorithms to anticipate the state of the fetus in the mother's belly. The major contribution of this paper is as follows:

- We develop seven different machine learning models for a best classification considering performance classifiers like (precision, recall, F1score) as well as a scaling called standard scaling for biased data which can identify pathologically, suspicious and high-risk fetuses accurately with a greater accuracy.
- We diagnose and classify the fetal heart rate condition using 21 attributes including uterine constructions, fetal movement, prolonged decreased and so on.
- We also find out the comparison among all the performance metrics and define the best model for classifying the fetal state.

This paper has been divided into some parts as follows. Section explains the literature review and Sect. 3 shows the methodology, Results along with discussion are discussed in Sect. 4. Section 5 conclude the paper.

2 Literature Review

We commence considering the risk of the fetus after 30 years of CTG brightly appearing. Through, the predictive capability is currently limited, but there is plenty of room for improvement. Recent studies show a significant improvement in fetal abnormality detection and prediction based on CTG data in the first trimester of pregnancy. According to Noor et al. [9], K-NN, Linear SVM, Nave Bayes, Decision Tree (J48), Ada Boost, Bagging, as well as Stacking were used to analyze and categorize the data set with supervised Machine Learning. The final step is to create Bayesian networks and compare them to the other classifier. When all classifiers are compared, the Ada Boost with Random Forest sub-model has the higher precision (94.7%) with k = 10. Further, the study can apply other learning methods and well dataset for getting a cutting edge accuracy. Dutta et al. [4] conducted another study to determine the accuracy of ML algorithm approaches using CTG data in detecting high-risk fetuses. They gathered data from a machine learning repository and processed it using SMOTE and hyper parameter adjustment of the training dataset to minimize the model's difficulty and oversampled unbalanced CTG data, respectively. They classified the fetal condition using five different machine learning techniques: SVC, DT, RF, KNN, and Linear SVC. Overall, they got a standard accuracy in each algorithms but need little improvement on their size of dataset and the robustness of accuracy. Imran Molla et al. [6] published a paper that shows a CTG data categorization system that uses a RF method. To distinguish abnormal as well as suspicious condition of the fetus, the performance of the random forest classifier accelerates three separate performance classifier measures: Recall, Precision, and F-measure. This paper gets the classification accuracy of 94.8% and classifier performance has also been evaluated which are 0.948. In fine, random forest performed well with limited accuracy which need to be increased further.

Additionally, there are also two works that evaluate the effect of different factors analyzed by machine learning algorithms such as RF, support vector machine, multi-layer perceptron as well as KNN through CTG data to predict the health state of the fetus, and another that compares a classification model for identifying the outcome of the cardiotocographic inspection based on CFS Subset assessment, Chi-Square, and Info Gain for the best feature which correlated to each other. Both evaluated matrix of precision, Recall, F-Measure, Accuracy but second one also evaluated MCC, ROC, PRC [8, 12].

A research done by Ramla, M. et al. [14], where they took out a classified dataset consist of normal, suspicious and pathologic attribute and applied couple of algorithms named Classification and Regression (CART) and GINI index to classify the status. GINI index achieved the highest accuracy which is 90.12%, while CART achieved 88.87%. Since, the accuracy is not prominent, boosting techniques and using statistical approach can be next drive to get greater accuracy further. They concentrated on the evolutionary multi-objective genetic algorithm (MOGA) and classification based on association (CBA) for extracting essential elements influencing fetal death utilizing CTG assessment of fetal evaluation based on feature value in those proposed investigations. The seven existing classification models named LR, SVM, RF, DT, KNN, GNB and XGBoost are used which achieved 86%, 79%, 91%, 94%, 92%, 92% and 83% for WDS feature and 86%, 79%, 91%, 94%, 92%, 92% and 83% for RDS feature in the both work except CBA 83% in the second work respectively. RF and eXtreme Gradient Boosting performed well for both, where DT, RF, GNB, SVM are also played well for the first work. The imbalanced data accused for getting low accuracy which can be a better solution in the future for this both work. Those work conducted by Piri, Jayashree et al. [10, 11]. They built a prediction method with an assistive e-Health application that both pregnant women along with practitioners can use to compare performance using Accuracy, F1-Score, and AUC measures in this study. Boosted Decision Tree, Averaged Perceptron, Bayes Point Machine, Decision Jungle, Decision Forest, Locally-Deep SVM, Neural Network, LR, and SVM were among the nine binary classification models they used. The highest accuracy achieved Decision Forest which was 89.5% in test and 87.5% in real [2].

Based on the early works related to several machine learning techniques, different classifiers, statistical approaches, hybrid techniques for getting higher accuracy and better performance, we focused to apply many machine learning algorithms in a large number of CTG updated dataset for predicting or classifying fetal status with a peak accuracy, Precision, Recall along with F1-Score after consider the gap of previous works.

3   Methodology

Figure 1 exhibits a detailed block diagram of the methodology. It exhibits the methodology graphically which describes the work procedure. We used pre-processing, scaling steps then applied several machine learning models. After performing the machine learning model, we classified the target variables as normal, suspect and pathological. Finally, We have found out the prediction of categorical output.

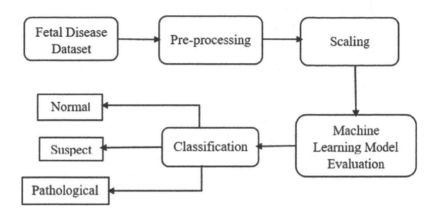

Fig. 1. Block Diagram of the proposed methodology.

3.1 Dataset Narration

We applied fetal dataset in this paper which is got in kaggle platform [1]. It contains 2126 records of attributes obtained from CTG tests, which were divided into 3 classes by 3 adept gynecologist like 1st for normal, 2nd for suspect and 3rd for pathological. There are also 20 independent variables and 1 target variable. Table 1 displays the sample of the utilized dataset. Table 2 discusses the description of the dataset.

Table 1. Dataset sample

Bval	astv	mvs	pal	mvl	HW	Hmi	Hma	hnp	hnz	Hmo	Hmea	Hme	Hvar	Hte	FH
120	73	0.5	43	2.4	64	62	126	2	0	120	137	121	73	1	2
132	17	2.1	0	10.4	130	68	198	6	1	141	136	140	12	0	1
133	16	2.1	0	13.4	130	68	198	5	1	141	135	138	13	0	1
134	16	2.4	0	23	117	53	170	11	0	137	134	137	13	1	1

3.2 Preprossessing

The reason for data prepping is to make the training/testing process more efficient by transforming and resizing the full dataset appropriately. Preparing the machine learning models for training is essential. During pre-processing phase, outliers are eliminated and the parameters are scaled to a comparable range. In the preprocessing step, we checked the hidden relationship among all attributes. We checked null value, correlation, hitmap, etc. Table 3 shows the short information of dataset.

Table 2. Dataset description where hist is histogram, W is width, Mo is mode, Me is mean, Var is variance and Tend is tendency.

Attribute	Description
Bval	FHR baseline (beats per minute)
acce	The count of accelerations for every second
fm	The count of fetal activity for every second
uc	The digit of uterine contractions for each second
ld	The digit of light decelerations for each second
sd	The count of acute deferments for each second
pd	Digit of extended lateness for each second
astv	It stands for abnormal short term variability (STV)
mvs	STV mean value
pal	% of abnormal long term variability (LTV) in time
mvl	LTV mean value
hw	W hist about fetal
hmi	Min hist about fetal
hma	Max hist of fetal
hnp	Digit of hist peaks
hnz	Count of hist zeros
hmo	Mo of hist
hmea	Me of hist
hme	Med of hist
hvar	Var of hist
hte	Tend of hist
FH	1 (Normal), 2 (Suspect) and 3 (Pathological)

Table 3. Information of class-wise data

Null values	Shape	Value counts (Target variable)
False	(2126, 22)	1.0 → 1655 2.0 → 295 3.0 → 176

3.3   Scaling

Feature scaling is nothing but a method which is used to normalize the thoroughness of free data stuff. As a result, the dataset is relatively unbiased. It is also cognizant as data normalization in data processing as well as is often conducted during the data preparation. In our datasets, the attributes- Bval, hmax, hmin, hw, hmod, hmea, hmed are unbiased with another independent features. It is important in machine learning algorithms for getting the accuracy correctly. In this paper, we used standard scalar. It standardizes datasets. The standard scalar works according to the 5 no equation and the values of the dataset are converted to standard form. Standardization is done by dividing the subtraction of any data and the average value of that variable by their standard deviation. After scaling, the feature variables are look like Table 4.

$$X\_new = \frac{X_i - X_{mean}}{StandardDeviation} \tag{1}$$

Table 4. Sample Data after Scaling

Bval	Hme	Hvar
−0.03088439	−0.00624416	−0.2004807
−0.1325256	0.13203796	−0.23499819
0.68060404	0.96173066	−0.51113811
0.68060404	0.8925896	−0.51113811
0.88388645	0.47774325	−0.61469058

3.4 Machine Learning Classifier

We used 7 machine learning models [15] for classifying the fetus state to protect the maternal and baby death rate.

A RF is a meta criterion that applies averaging to promulgate predicted accuracy as well as manage over-fitting by fitting a number of decision tree classifiers on various sub-samples of the dataset.

An AdB classifier is a meta-estimator that commences by fitting a classifier on the main dataset, then suitable additional copies of the classifier on the same dataset with the weights of badly classified examples altered, allowing subsequent classifiers to focus more on tough scenarios.

K-NN algorithm works by implementing the k-nearest neighbors vote.

GBC builds an additive model step by step, allowing the minimization of any differentiable loss function.

The support vector machine approach is applicable to classification and regression issues. The data points are separated by a hyperplain in this procedure, and the kernel defines the shape of the hyperplain.

Although the name has the word regression, logistic regression is actually a classification algorithm. In logistical regression, we predict multinomial class. When the prediction class is more than two, it is called the multinomial class. Our dataset has multiple classes.

Both classification and regression problems can be solved with the DTC algorithm. The used hyper parameter of all models utilized in this work is shown in Table 5.

Table 5. Used Hyper parameter of all models

Model	Parameters
SVM	Kernel = rbf
GBC	Learning rate is 0.1
RF	n_estimators=10, maximum depth = 5, random state is 0
AdaBoost	n_estimators is 150, learning rate is 1
Logistic Regression	Penalty = l2
K-NN	n_neighbors = 5, metric = 'euclidean'
DTC	Criterion = gini, Splitter = best

3.5   Classification

In this section, we used 7 classification models to categorize the fetal health state like normal, suspect, and pathological. Figure 2 shows comparison of accuracy of all algorithms. GBC is in the first position, DTC is in the second position, Rf is in the third position, K-NN and SVM are in the fourth position, and AdB along

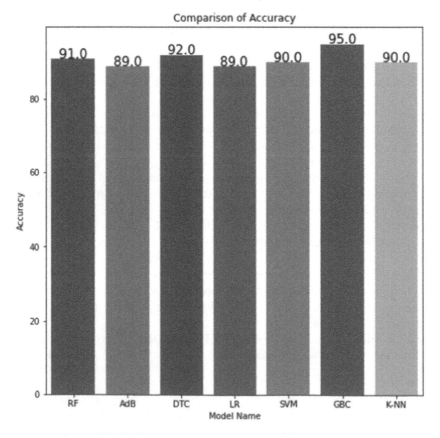

Fig. 2. Comparison of accuracy of all models.

with LR is in the fifth position by achieving 95%, 92%, 91%, 90% and 89% of accuracy respectively.

4 Result and Discussion

We used Python programming in google colab for data analysis to categorize the fetal health state. The tool is quite useful for analysis and it is the virtual version of Jupyter notebook. We take the 20:80 ratio as test train splitting for all models.

4.1 Performance Metrics

As for performance metrics, we used accuracy, precision, recall, and f1 score for analysis of the models. All these are calculated from confusion matrix. Table 6 shows a confusion matrix.

Table 6. Confusion Matrix

	Predicted Yes	Predicted No
Actual Yes	$T_r(+)$	$F(-)$
Actual No	$F(+)$	$T_r(-)$

In Table 6, $T_r(+)$ is true positive, $F(-)$ is false negative, $F(+)$ is false positive, and $T_r(-)$ is true negative. The mathematical equation of all metrics is as follows:

$$Accuracy = \frac{\sum_{i=1}^{n} (T_r(+) + T_r(-))}{\sum_{i=1}^{n} ((T_r(+) + T_r(-) + F(+) + F(-))} \qquad (2)$$

$$Precision = \frac{\sum_{i=1}^{n} T_r(+)}{\sum_{i=1}^{n} (T_r(+) + F(+))} \qquad (3)$$

$$Recall = \frac{\sum_{i=1}^{n} T_r(+)}{\sum_{i=1}^{n} (T_r(+) + F(-)} \qquad (4)$$

$$F1 - score = \frac{2 \times Precision \times Recall}{Precision + Recall} \qquad (5)$$

4.2 Experimental Analysis

Figure 3 shows the confusion matrix of all algorithms. Here, we show the confusion matrix of all models during the experimental demonstration. As we know that we can find out the performance metrics from the confusion matrix like classwise precision, recall, f1-score, and overall accuracy of a model. As an example, we can calculate the performance metrics of gradient boosting classifier shown in

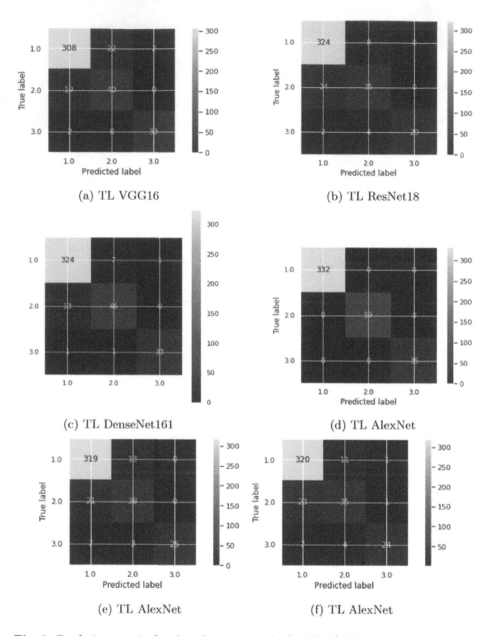

Fig. 3. Confusion matrix for classification model, a) AdB, b) RF, c) GBC, d) DTC, e) SVM, f) KNN

3. e), accuracy $= (324 + 45 + 33)/(324 + 7 + 1 + 13 + 45 + 0 + 1 + 1) = 0.95$, precision for 1st class $= (324)/(324 + 1 + 13) = 0.96$, recall for 1st class $= (324)/(324 + 7 + 1) = 0.98$, and F1-score for 1st class $= (2 \times (0.96 \times 0.98)/(0.96 + 0.98) = 0.97$ and thus for other classes.

Table 7 shows the performance metrics of all classification models for fetal health state. According to accuracy metric, GBC's score is highest of 95% than all others. In the second place, DTC places as getting 92%. RF is in the third by 91%, K-NN and SVM are in the fourth by 90%, and AdB and LR get the fifth position by 89% in the accuracy scale respectively. In this paper, GBC performs better than others models. Because we know that GBC is an example of ensemble learning. Ensemble learning entails constructing a strong model from a group of lesser models. Gradient boosting approaches, which learn from each weak learner repeatedly to produce a strong model. The label variable has three classes. Among them, pathological class is very serious issue for fetal disease. K-NN, SVM, and RF achieve the 100% precision of performance metrics.

Table 7. Performance metrics analysis where A = Accuracy, P = Precision, R = Recall, F1 = F1-score.

Model	Class	P (%)	R (%)	F1 (%)	A (%)
AdB	Normal	94	93	93	89
	Suspect	65	68	66	
	Pathological	94	94	94	
DTC	Normal	94	96	95	92
	Suspect	75	66	70	
	Pathological	94	94	94	
GBC	Normal	96	98	97	95
	Suspect	85	78	81	
	Pathological	97	94	96	
K-NN	Normal	91	98	95	90
	Suspect	74	54	63	
	Pathological	100	74	85	
LR	Normal	93	95	94	89
	Suspect	71	66	68	
	Pathological	83	69	75	
RF	Normal	93	98	95	91
	Suspect	74	59	66	
	Pathological	100	83	91	
SVM	Normal	92	96	94	90
	Suspect	70	64	67	
	Pathological	100	71	83	

Figure 4 shows the graphical representation of Table 7. In the performance metrics are colored by blue-colored for precision, red-colored for recall, green-colored for F1-score, and purple-colored for accuracy respectively. In GBC model, accuracy is highest. There are three types of label variables normal, suspect, and pathological. Among these, the pathological class is a major concern for fetal illness. K-NN, SVM, and RF reach performance metric precision of 100%.

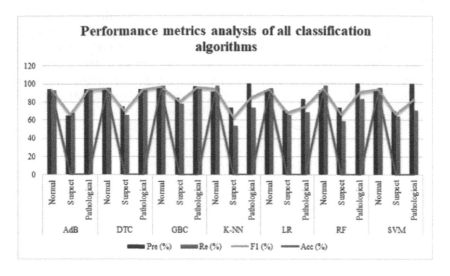

Fig. 4. Performance metrics analysis of all classification algorithms

4.3   Comparison Result

Several works have been conducted in recent years to classify fetal disease states. Researchers are working to discover a better solution to the problem. Table 8 shows an examination and comparison of our proposed model with an existing similar study.

Table 8. The comparison result of the proposed model with existing works

SN	Sources	Model	Accuracy
01	[9]	Ada Boost with sub-model Random Forest	94.7
02	[6]	Random Forest	94.8
03	[11]	DTC	94
04	[2]	DTC	89.5
05	[12]	RF	93.74
06	[7]	Naive Bayesian classifier with firefly algorithm	86.55
07	[14]	CART	90.12
08	Proposed	GBC	95

In a brief, many researchers have been using classification techniques in their works. The classification techniques using machine learning are used in the medical sector. This is helpful for the physicians for classifying the various diseases on time, accurate diagnosis and it is also less expensive. This work would be facilitated for the doctors to taking proper decisions and avoid human mistakes.

5 Conclusion and Future Works

Knowing the state of fetal, doctors and patients can take necessary steps on time. Machine learning plays a vital role in this field. In this paper, we classified the state of fetal including normal state, suspect state, pathological state on the fetal disease dataset using seven machine learning models named AdB, RF, K-NN, SVM, GBC, DTC, and LR. We employed many performance indicators to verify the experimental task, including accuracy, precision, recall, and F1-score. For performing an unbiased dataset, we also employed a scaling approach called a standard scalar. This work would be benefitted the patients and doctors to take the proper decision on time to lessen the unwanted situations created during a baby's birth. Since the used classifiers techniques can classify the fetus state properly. In future, we will apply deep learning, transfer learning on huge fetus records.

References

1. Fetal health dataset. Technical report. https://www.kaggle.com/andrewmvd/fetal-health-classification
2. Akbulut, A., Ertugrul, E., Topcu, V.: Fetal health status prediction based on maternal clinical history using machine learning techniques. Comput. Methods Progr. Biomed. **163**, 87–100 (2018)
3. Chinnaiyan, R., Alex, S.: Machine learning approaches for early diagnosis and prediction of fetal abnormalities. In: 2021 International Conference on Computer Communication and Informatics (ICCCI), pp. 1–3. IEEE (2021)
4. Dutta, P., Paul, S., Majumder, M.: Intelligent smote based machine learning classification for fetal state on cardiotocography dataset (2021)
5. Grivell, R.M., Alfirevic, Z., Gyte, G.M., Devane, D. Antenatal cardiotocography for fetal assessment. Cochrane Database Systemat. Rev. (9) (2015)
6. Imran Molla, M.M., Jui, J.J., Bari, B.S., Rashid, M., Hasan, M.J.: Cardiotocogram data classification using random forest based machine learning algorithm. In: Md Zain, Z., et al. (eds.) Proceedings of the 11th National Technical Seminar on Unmanned System Technology 2019. LNEE, vol. 666, pp. 357–369. Springer, Singapore (2021). https://doi.org/10.1007/978-981-15-5281-6_25
7. Kadhim, N.J.A., Abed, J.K.: Enhancing the prediction accuracy for cardiotocography (ctg) using firefly algorithm and naive bayesian classifier. In: IOP Conference Series: Materials Science and Engineering, vol. 745, p. 012101. IOP Publishing (2020)
8. Mehbodniya, A., et al.: Fetal health classification from cardiotocographic data using machine learning. Expert Syst. **39**, e12899 (2021)
9. Noor, N.F.M., Ahmad, N., Noor, N.M.: Fetal health classification using supervised learning approach. In: 2021 IEEE National Biomedical Engineering Conference (NBEC), pp. 36–41. IEEE (2021)

10. Piri, J., Mohapatra, P.: Exploring fetal health status using an association based classification approach. In: 2019 International Conference on Information Technology (ICIT), pp. 166–171. IEEE (2019)
11. Piri, J., Mohapatra, P., Dey, R.: Fetal health status classification using moga-cd based feature selection approach. In: 2020 IEEE International Conference on Electronics, Computing and Communication Technologies (CONECCT), pp. 1–6. IEEE (2020)
12. Prasetyo, S.E., Prastyo, P.H., Arti, S.: A cardiotocographic classification using feature selection: a comparative study. JITCE (J. Inf. Technol. Comput. Eng.) 5(01), 25–32 (2021)
13. Rahmayanti, N., Pradani, H., Pahlawan, M., Vinarti, R.: Comparison of machine learning algorithms to classify fetal health using cardiotocogram data. Procedia Comput. Sci. **197**, 162–171 (2022)
14. Ramla, M., Sangeetha, S., Nickolas, S.: Fetal health state monitoring using decision tree classifier from cardiotocography measurements. In: 2018 Second International Conference on Intelligent Computing and Control Systems (ICICCS), pp. 1799–1803. IEEE (2018)
15. Sarker, I.H.: Machine learning: algorithms, real-world applications and research directions. SN Comput. Sci. **2**(3), 1–21 (2021)

Epileptic Seizure Prediction Using Bandpass Filtering and Convolutional Neural Network

Nabiha Mustaqeem$^{(\boxtimes)}$, Tasnia Rahman ,
Jannatul Ferdous Binta Kalam Priyo , Mohammad Zavid Parvez ,
and Tanvir Ahmed

Department of Computer Science and Engineering, BRAC University,
Dhaka, Bangladesh
{nabiha.mustaqeem,tasnia.rahman,
jannatul.ferdous.binta.kalam.priyo}@g.bracu.ac.bd,
{zavid.parvez,tanvir.ahmed}@bracu.ac.bd

Abstract. The paper proposes a generalized approach for epileptic seizure prediction rather than a patient-specific approach. The early diagnosis of seizures may assist in reducing the severity of damage and can be utilized to aid in the treatment of epilepsy patients. Developing a patient-independent model is more challenging than a patient-specific model due to the EEG variability across patients. Our objective is to predict seizure accurately by detecting the pre-ictal state that occurs prior to a seizure. We have used the "CHB-MIT Scalp EEG Dataset" for our research and implemented the research work using Butterworth Bandpass Filter and simple 2D Convolutional Neural Network to differentiate pre-ictal and inter-ictal signals. We have achieved accuracy of 89.5%, sensitivity 89.7%, precision 89.0% and AUC, the area under the curve is 89.5% with our proposed model. In addition, we have addressed several researchers' seizure prediction models, sketched their core mechanism, predictive effectiveness, and compared them with ours.

Keywords: Bandpass filter · Chronic neurological disorder · Convolutional neural network · CHB-MIT Scalp EEG Dataset · Deep learning · Epilepsy · Generalized model · Prediction · Seizure

1 Introduction

Seizures have different signs and symptoms depending on the type. Not every seizure is epileptic. Epileptic seizures, in contrast to other types of seizures, are triggered because of the dysfunction in the brain; causing electrical storms in the brain. These aberrant electrical signals might be localized to a certain area of the brain or they can be more widespread [21]. Generalized seizures, focal seizures, and epileptic spasms are three forms of epileptic seizures. A neurologist can classify seizure/epilepsy types based on a patient's medical history, EEG results, and other supporting data [14].

Multichannel recordings of electrical activity produced by groups of neurons in a brain are made from scalp EEG recordings. EEG electrodes are placed on a patient's scalp to record scalp EEG signals, or electrodes can be implanted into the brain to monitor intracranial EEG signals [2]. Neuronal activity in the scalp EEG is constrained in its occurrence and features because of the principles of EEG generation. Any time a seizure occurs, the brain's electrical activity changes rapidly, and this can be detected in scalp EEG recordings as a sudden redistribution of spectral shifts [17].

The epileptic seizure prediction process mainly includes dataset collection, pre-processing of data, feature extraction, classification, and post-processing of all parts of the epileptic seizure prediction process to validate the result [19]. As a first step in using EEG data to diagnose an illness or interpret brain activity for neuropsychological testing, one needs to use spectral information or extract the features from the raw data [1]. The raw data that we get from the EEG tests cannot be used for diagnosing because it is difficult to interpret the data [9]. Preprocessing EEG data is necessary because the signals picked up by the scalp are not always precise representations of the brain's signals and the signals tend to be noisy, which might mask weak EEG signals. Moreover, blinking or muscle movement may taint data and distort images [23]. The noise is removed in this stage from the EEG signal to enhance the signal-to-noise ratio. Artifacts are eliminated from the primary signal to identify the artifact-free signal. To filter the data in this procedure, band-pass filter is used [9]. In this study, we present comprehensive findings of EEG data using the freely accessible "CHB-MIT Scalp EEG Database" [4]. Developing a model that has a generalized approach with high accuracy for epileptic seizure is the goal of this study. For this rather than counting all the features, we have extracted the features using the foremost significance and preprocess EEG signals accordingly using Butterworth Bandpass Filter. Afterwards, we have used automated feature extraction instead of traditional handcrafted feature extraction and utilized CNN to classify the data to differentiate the pre-ictal and the inter-ictal state. Our approach aims to assist people in predicting Epileptic Seizure in its earliest stages, so that when the initial stage, pre-ictal, is detected, patients and others can take necessary precautions to avoid or prepare for the final stage of Epileptic Seizure, and to assist the patient in dealing with it.

2   Background

2.1   Epileptic Seizure

Numerous researchers [5,11,13,15,18] have analyzed the association between EEG synchronization patterns and seizures, indicating that the pre-ictal state, ictal state, inter-ictal state, and post-ictal state may be distinguished.

(i) Pre-ictal State: This is the period of time before the seizure; typically, 30 to 90 min before the onset of the seizure. Mood swings, anxiety, feeling lightheaded, trouble sleeping, difficulty staying focused, experiencing a sense of déjà vu, nausea, and headache are some of the symptoms that might occur. It is not always visible. Alterations in the basic signals are used to predict seizures. To be therapeutically effective in a warning system, a pre-ictal condition must be detected early enough to reduce time spent in false alarm [6].

(ii) Ictal State: A shift in electroencephalogram (EEG) data that occurs during a seizure is referred to as the ictal state. This is the state of seizure itself. In this state, the person's brain experiences an electrical storm. Until the brain stimulation stops, the autonomic nervous system controls movements that tend to continue rapidly and rhythmically.

(iii) Inter-ictal State: This state is the interval between the onsets of two consecutive seizures. The quantity of cortical area, epileptogenic neurons, and seizure length may all be varied in the same person.

(iv) Post-ictal State: This is the final state, the typically lengthy period of recovery after a seizure has occurred. The length of time it takes for a person to recover to normal depends on the severity, type, and location of the seizure in their brain.

2.2 EEG Signals

In diagnostic and therapeutic uses, the electroencephalogram (EEG) has been widely utilized to capture the electrical activity of the human brain. Multichannel recordings of electrical activity produced by groups of neurons in a brain are made from scalp EEG recordings. Due to its low cost and non-invasive nature, EEG is an extensively utilized noninvasive neuro-diagnostic tool globally. In 1929, Hans Berger, a German psychiatrist, devised EEG, a non-invasive functional imaging technology for gaining a better understanding of the brain that enables clinicians to establish a neurological diagnosis and plan future neurosurgical operations [10].

EEG electrodes are placed on a patient's scalp to record scalp EEG signals, or electrodes can be implanted into the brain to monitor intracranial EEG signals. A patient's scalp is considered to be divided into four different lobes- frontal, parietal, temporal, and occipital. The EEG electrodes are placed in those parts of the crown of the skull. The numbers and names of these channels are employed in the data analysis. Neuronal activity evident in the scalp EEG is constrained in its occurrence and features because of the principles of EEG generation. For example, the left hemispheric frontal lobe is represented in the channel "FP1 - F7". This is how we may identify the kind of seizure, such as Localized, Myclonic, or Generalized, as well as its severity. Any time a seizure occurs, the brain's electrical activity changes rapidly, and this can be detected in scalp EEG recordings as a sudden redistribution of spectral shifts. EEG results may suggest seizure activity was not happening at the time of the test, if they appear normal.

2.3 Butterworth Bandpass Filter

Noise and artifacts contaminate measurements in the area of brain research, one of the most challenging issues. Examples of such sources include background noise, instrument noise, and internal signal sources that aren't relevant to the experiment. Noise may either conceal or complicate the accurate analysis of the intended signal. However, if the signal and interference are situated in discrete spectral parts of the spectrum, it may be possible to boost the SNR by applying a filter to the data.

The Butterworth Bandpass filter is one of the most used frequency domain filters, also known as the maximally flat filter. Throughout its bandpass, it is a form of Active Filter that has a reasonably flat frequency response. Because the filter has a strong frequency roll-off feature, a magnitude function that changes monotonically with frequency, and a more linear phase response in the passband when compared to other traditional filters, it is more efficient.

Digital Butterworth filters and Low pass Butterworth filters are two examples of Butterworth filter types. Increasing the Butterworth filter order brings the wall response and filter closer together, which in turn brings up the number of cascaded stages in the design. This filter is to attenuate noise, remove artifacts and enhance target activity, making EEG recording analysis more accurate and precise. This filter aims to keep the unique frequency of the signal, and the information received from the clean EEG signal can be utilized for therapeutic applications, such as the detection of epilepsy, coma, brain damage and stroke amongst other things [1].

2.4   Convolutional Neural Network (CNN)

Neural networks are mathematical models that store knowledge via the use of brain-inspired learning mechanisms. Similar to the brain, the neural networks are composed of several neurons which are connected through numerous connections. In a variety of applications, neural networks have been used to simulate unknown relationships between various parameters using a huge number of samples [22]. Additionally, neural networks are increasingly being applied in medicinal applications. A Neural Network's fundamental input layer, an output layer and one or more hidden layers are all components of architecture.

3   Related Works

Numerous researchers [5, 11, 13, 15, 18] have presented seizure prediction algorithms using deep learning and machine learning techniques to distinguish between distinct stages of epileptic seizure states which can be helpful in treating the seizures at different stages, and predicting the onset of the seizure. Mormann et al., [8] reviewed the seizure prediction systems from the 1970s s to 2006 and examined the crucial problems associated with the epileptic seizure prediction technique. Gadhoumi et al., [3] provided a thorough discussion of appropriate methodologies for the epileptic seizure prediction, as well as a thorough analysis of the statistical significance of the forecast's findings. Kuhlmann et al., offered a concise overview of current advances in the field of epileptic seizure prediction in a newly published paper [6].

The use of Convolutional Neural Network (CNN) is prevalent in predicting a typical seizure in many researches [9,11,13,18] following preprocessing for feature extraction from EEG data. Troung et al., detected epileptic episodes, utilizing EEG and 13-layer depth CNN with the accuracy rate of 88 percent [15]. Qin et al. [13], extracted the EEG characteristics and identified states using CNN and SVM algorithms in another study with an accuracy of 86.25 percent using this approach. The sensitivity (i.e., the probability of detection) is taken into account while measuring classification performance. Ozcan et al. [11], classified the EEG data with 89% accuracy using CNN, whose findings were reported in NeuroImage. Using a CNN architecture with six convolutional layers, Khan et al. [5], were able to extract features from EEG wavelets with 87.8% sensitivity rate. Usman [9] demonstrated using Butterworth bandpass filters that the CHB-MIT scalp EEG dataset has 90.8% specificity and 92.7% average sensitivity, followed by STFT.

In this study, we present comprehensive findings of EEG data using freely accessible "CHB-MIT Scalp EEG Database" [4]. Developing a model that has high accuracy and the low false alarm rate for epileptic seizure is the goal of this study. For this rather than counting all the features, we will extract the features using the foremost significance and preprocess raw EEG signals using Butterworth Bandpass Filter. Afterwards, we will use automated feature extraction instead of traditional handcrafted feature extraction to utilize CNN, along with several functions to classify the data to distinguish the pre-ictal and the inter-ictal signals. To predict the onset of epileptic seizures by detecting the pre-ictal state is crucial to prevent an oncoming seizure or to minimize the seizure-related harm from occurring.

4 Proposed Model

4.1 Data Acquisition

Our initial objective was to search for and retrieve publicly accessible EEG databases. Despite the fact that there are only a few open-access scalp EEG databases available, we will use the CHB-MIT Scalp EEG Database [4] from Children's Hospital Boston.

4.2 CHB-MIT Scalp EEG Dataset

The database contains scalp electroencephalograms of twenty-three patients with intractable focal epilepsy, nine of whom are men and seventeen of whom are women. Each case contains nine to twenty-four EDF files compiled from continuous EEG waves from the patients. Digitalized EEG signals contained in EDF files have exactly one-hour length. The bulk of files contain 23 channels in total. The data has a resolution of 16 bits and 256 samples per second sampling rate. This dataset contains a total of 198 seizures. It is possible to locate recordings labeled "chb_n", with the nth sample for the suitable subject denoted by the number n (Table 1).

Table 1. The CHB-MIT EEG DATASET description. GENDER: Female(F) AND Male(M)

Case	Gender	Age	Number of seizure(s)
chb01	F	11	7
chb02	M	11	3
chb03	F	14	7
chb04	M	22	4
chb05	F	7	5
chb06	F	1.5	10
chb07	F	14.5	3
chb08	M	3.5	5
chb09	F	10	4
chb10	M	3	7
chb11	F	12	3
chb12	F	2	40
chb13	F	3	12
chb14	F	9	8
chb15	M	16	20
chb16	F	7	10
chb17	F	12	3
chb18	F	18	6
chb19	F	19	3
chb20	F	6	8
chb21	F	13	4
chb22	F	9	3
chb23	F	7	7

4.3   Observations on Raw EDF Files

The International 10 to 20 systems of EEG electrode placements and nomenclature were employed in order to obtain the EEG recordings. These groups of electrodes, which are twenty-one in number, are positioned on the scalp. In addition to the 21 electrodes of the 10–20 system, which is widely used around the world, it is also feasible to employ intermediate 10% electrode sites. The CHB-MIT Dataset [4] is comprised of a total of 23 channels: "FP1-F7", "FP2-F4", "F7-T7", "P3-O1", "P7-T7", "T7-P7", "T7-FT9", "F4-C4", "FP2-F8", "FP1-F3", "P7-O1", "F8-T8", "F3-C3", "T8-P8", "C3-P3", "FT9-FT10", "T8-P8", "P8-O2", "P4-O2", "CZ-PZ", "FT10-T8", "FZ-CZ". It shows the central, parietal, frontal, frontal polar, occipital, and occipital-temporal relationships. Cases chb01-chb11 and chb23 all had 23 channels, as determined by analyzing the dataset. Up to five "dummy" signals (marked as "-") were inserted between EEG readings in some situations, including chb12-chb19 and chb20-chb22, although these "dummy" signals can be ignored. While evaluating the dataset, it is discovered that channels in chb11-chb23 are altered many times. Channels between chb12 and chb23 have been altered at least three times. When the channels are changed, the difference between one electrode and a weighted average of electrodes in it's proximity changes as well.

4.4 Preprocessing

The CHB-MIT Scalp EEG dataset [4] contains the raw EDF files, both the seizure and non-seizure of a total of 23 pediatric patients, that were recorded using 23–31 channels. In our study, we decided to work with the first 10 patients having 55 seizure files and with 18 common channels due to the generalization approach in our model. For preprocessing our data, we concatenate the pre-ictal/ictal signals as 30 min and we refer to them as pre-ictal signals for each patient's seizure [12]. After delimiting the pre-ictal signals, the remainder of the recording of the seizure files is referred to as the inter-ictal signals Fig. 1. The pre-ictal and inter-ictal signals are split into 5s signals without overlapping for binary classification trials [23]. We used an 8:2 ratio to train and test the data. Since we have two categories of data, we used binary classification. To achieve generalization, we used all patients' inter-ictal and pre-ictal data for training and individual patient data for testing.

4.5 2D CNN

In our proposed 2D CNN Model Fig. 2, we have kept the input shape the same as our sample size (18, 1280) to begin with in the input layer. Except for input and output layers, our proposed model consists of 4 convolution layers with a (ReLU) activation function. After every convolution layer there is a Batch Normalization layer which normalizes the output of the conv2d layer and then a 2D max-pooling layer. Each convolution layer has the kernel size of (3, 3). We decided to use a Global Average Pooling (GAP) that constructs a feature map for each classification task's associated category. We also used two FC/dense layers. The output layer uses Sigmoid activation function for binary classification. Layers that are completely linked are prone to overfitting. So, the Sigmoid activation function in the output layer is also called a logistic function that is suitable for our proposed CNN model since we are using binary classification of data. We employed a dropout rate of 0.4 to set the activations of completely linked layers to zero randomly during training. It has enhanced generalization capacity and helps to reduce overfitting.

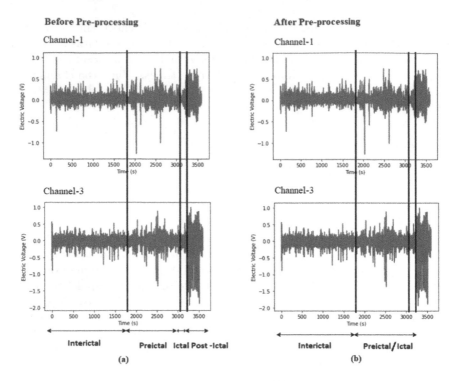

Fig. 1. Raw Signal Data of chb02_19 seizure file (a) and Filtered Data of chb02_19 seizure file (b)

5   Results

5.1   Evaluation Methods

Our work employs four evaluation criteria to assess algorithm performance: Accuracy, Sensitivity, area under the curve (AUC), and Precision Table 2.

5.2   Justification of 5s Trials

We have already stated that we conducted 5s trials of the inter-ictal and pre-ictal states, but to ensure that we obtain superior findings with 5s trials, we cross-checked our accuracy and sensitivity evaluation metrics with 2.5s and 10s trials as well. After comparison, we get an average accuracy of 78.3% and a sensitivity of 75.8% for 10s trials, which has 11.2% and 13.9% less accuracy and sensitivity than 5s trials, respectively. Additionally, we attain an average accuracy of 82.6% and a sensitivity of 58.9% for 2.5s trials, which is 6.9% and 30.8% lower than the accuracy and sensitivity of 5s trials, respectively Fig. 3.

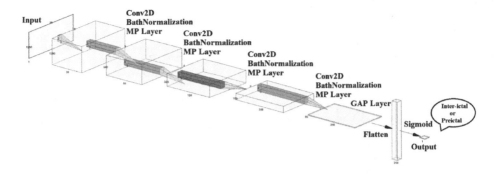

Fig. 2. CNN Model Implementation

Table 2. Patient wise Performance Evaluation of our proposed method

Patient No.	Accuracy	Sensitivity	AUC	Precision
01	0.92	0.94	0.92	0.93
02	0.89	0.88	0.90	0.89
03	0.90	0.91	0.88	0.87
04	0.90	0.87	0.87	0.90
05	0.89	0.89	0.89	0.90
06	0.88	0.92	0.91	0.91
07	0.89	0.87	0.90	0.93
08	0.90	0.89	0.89	0.89
09	0.90	0.91	0.90	0.85
10	0.89	0.89	0.89	0.83
Average	0.895	0.897	0.895	0.890

Table 3. Comparison with previous work

Method	Patients	Seizures	Channels	Feature Extraction	Classifier	Sensitivity (%)	Accuracy (%)
Truong et al. [16]	13	59	23–31	Automated	2D CNN	89.1	–
Wang et al. [20]	7	42	23–31	Automated	Dilated 3D CNN	85.8	80.5
Ozcan et al. [11]	16	77	23–31	Spectral power, Statistical moments, Hjorth parameters	3D CNN	85.71	–
Liu et al. [7]	2	12	23–31	Automated	Multi-view CNN	91.5	85.5
This work	10	55	18	Automated	2D CNN	89.7	89.5

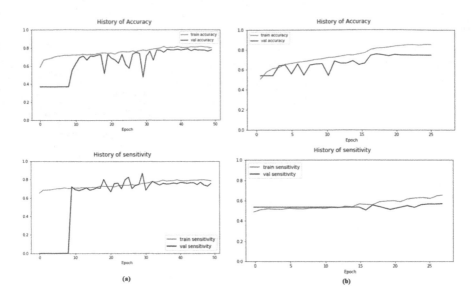

Fig. 3. Visualization of Accuracy and Sensitivity of CNN Model for a Window of 10s (a), and a window of 2.5s (b)

5.3 Comparison Results

Since our goal is to propose a study that is both simple and effective at predicting seizures, we attempted to analyze our model's performance in comparison to four other prior works Table 3. The major goal of our study was generalization of seizure prediction instead of patient based approach, so we considered the common 18 channels unlike Wang [20], Truong [16], Ozcan [11], Liu [7] who considered all channels. The idea of selecting the common channels has improved our evaluation metrics considerably. Our proposed technique is suitable since no patient-specific engineering has been done available at a particular stage. We trained the entire dataset, and tested on each patient for generalizing the proposed model. We considered the mean of the evaluation metrics for the performance of our proposed model. Ozcan [11], Truong [16] have also proposed a generalized approach for predicting seizure of individual patients. However, Liu [7]and Wang [20] have proposed patient-specific models.

Our 2D CNN Model, like Wang [20], has a GAP layer, but unlike Ozcan [11], Truong [16], and Liu [7], does not include any flatten layer. In addition to dropout layers, Liu [7] employs the $\ell 2$ regularizer to prevent the model from overfitting; However, we overcame overfitting using GAP. We reduced the number of parameters in the model by using the GAP layer, which helps to reduce overfitting and improves performance. GAP layers perform a more drastic reduction in dimension, reducing a tensor with dimensions H× W× D to dimensions 1×1× D. One dimensional GAP block accepts a two-dimensional tensor (data point channels) and computes the average of all values (data points) for each channel. GAP has reduced the amount of parameters, resulting in a model that is shallow and quick enough for real-time use. Additionally, to train very deep neural networks we used batch normalization techniques such as Truong [16]. It standardizes inputs to each mini-batch layer. It has resulted in a significant reduction in the number of training epochs necessary for deep networks to be trained. However, Wang [20] , Ozcan [11], and Liu [7] did not utilize a normalizing procedure. The layer normalizes its output during testing by taking the mean and standard deviation of batches it encountered during training are calculated as a moving average.

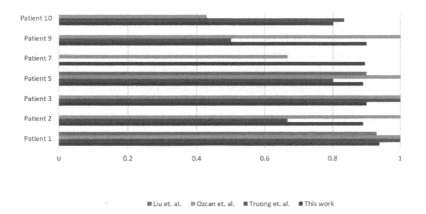

Fig. 4. Sensitivity comparisons for individual patients among Ozcan et al., Truong et al., Liu et al., and this work

In our study, the GAP layer is followed by two fully connected layers with ReLU activation function. A Softmax function, on the other hand, with only one FC layer with is implemented in Wang's proposed model [20]. Truong [16] used two fully-connected layers using the sigmoid activation. A fully connected layer in Liu's multi-view CNN has a different activation function than a convolutional layer, and that activation function is Tanh. Only Wang [20] has used the activation function in the FC layer similar to our study. However, due to using different activation functions, the sensitivity and accuracy of the papers have affected and varied accordingly. In our study, the output layer uses Sigmoid Activation function instead of the typical Softmax function unlike Wang [20], Ozcan [11]. Truong [16]uses the Sigmoid Activation function like us. In Liu [7], they utilized stochastic gradient descent to optimize the model; in this case, we used Adam's optimizer. While Liu [7] utilized two convolutional layers, we used four. Due to a shortage of training data, initially, Liu [7] presented five convolutional layers comprised multi-view CNN that was susceptible to over-fitting, reduced CNN architecture, to address this problem, with just two convolutional layers was employed afterwards. Truong [16] utilized scalp EEG data without using any de-noising procedures other than the removal of the power line noise.

They converted the raw EEG data to a 2D matrix with frequency and time axes using the Short-Time Fourier Transform. They efficiently reduced the power line noise in the frequency domain by removing components at 47–53 Hz and 97–103 Hz, as well 0 Hz at the DC component. Ozcan [11] eliminated power line noise and harmonics 60 Hz for his proposed model, by using frequency ranges 57–63 Hz and 117–123 Hz, which are not often employed in spectral power calculations. A0 Hz, the DC component was likewise eliminated. We used BB for de-noising of scalp EEG.

Although our paper has worked with 10 patients, but adequate data was generated from these patients, and the GAP layer has reduced our overfitting significantly. According to Liu [7], there were only two individuals in the scalp database who had acceptable pre-ictal and inter-ictal sections. Even in the lack of training data for a complicated multi-view CNN model, they concluded that 5 convolutional layers are vulnerable to over-fitting when used in the absence of training data, so they used two convolutional layers. They believe that the classifier is unable to correctly separate the data points in the new space based on the retrieved attributes because the classifier does not have enough information. We figured out that instead of using handcrafted feature extraction, we opted for an automated feature extraction process unlike Ozcan [11]. Ozcan [11] considered preserving the picture's spatial structure while analyzing the characteristics gathered from the EEG data. Seizures were successfully predicted utilizing cascade CNN and LSTM networks, using the multi-color image series acquired from multi-channel EEG data, and this was done without involving the patient. We have shown the comparison of the common patients' sensitivity metrics with ours in Fig. 4.

6   Conclusion

Rather than focusing on a single patient, the paper's goal was to provide a generalized solution that may be applied to many patients. In this paper we pre-processed the raw EEG signals using Butterworth bandpass, and then used automated feature extraction, CNN, to detect the pre-ictal state and differentiate pre-ictal and inter-ictal signals to predict the onset of the epileptic seizure. We provided the data of 10 patients for the model and confirmed that they had an average accuracy of 89.7% and average sensitivity of 89.5%. Although the accuracy percentages we obtained from our training models were statistically significant, there is still opportunity for improvement. In the future, we hope our findings will assist scientists in better understanding the role that model interpretation plays in predicting behavior patterns and find real-world solutions for the seizure prediction.

References

1. Butterworth filter design, equations and calculations. https://www.elprocus.com/butterworth-filter-formula-and-calculations/
2. Steven, C., Obsorne, P., Joseph, I.: Who Gets Epilepsy? Epilepsy Foundation. Kernel description (2013). https://www.epilepsy.com/learn/about-epilepsy-basics/who-getsepilepsy
3. Gadhoumi, K., Lina, J.M., Mormann, F., Gotman, J.: Seizure prediction for therapeutic devices: a review. J. Neurosci. Methods **260**, 270–282 (2016). https://doi.org/10.1016/j.jneumeth.2015.06.010
4. Goldberger, A.L., et al.: PhysioBank, PhysioToolkit, and PhysioNet: components of a new research resource for complex physiologic signals. Circulation **101**(23), E215-20 (2000)
5. Khan, H., Marcuse, L., Fields, M., Swann, K., Yener, B.: Focal onset seizure prediction using convolutional networks. IEEE Trans. Biomed. Eng. (2017). https://doi.org/10.1109/TBME.2017.2785401
6. Kuhlmann, L., Lehnertz, K., Richardson, M., Schelter, B., Zaveri, H.: Seizure prediction - ready for a new era. Nat. Rev. Neurol. **14** (2018). https://doi.org/10.1038/s41582-018-0055-2
7. Liu, C.L., Xiao, B., Hsaio, W.H., Tseng, V.S.: Epileptic seizure prediction with multi-view convolutional neural networks. IEEE Access **7**, 170352–170361 (2019). https://doi.org/10.1109/ACCESS.2019.2955285
8. Mormann, F., Andrzejak, R.G., Elger, C.E., Lehnertz, K.: Seizure prediction: the long and winding road. Brain **130**(2), 314–333 (2007). https://doi.org/10.1093/BRAIN/AWL241
9. Muhammad Usman, S., Khalid, S., Aslam, M.H.: Epileptic seizures prediction using deep learning techniques. IEEE Access **8**, 39998–40007 (2020). https://doi.org/10.1109/ACCESS.2020.2976866
10. Nall, R.: What you should know about seizures (2021). https://www.healthline.com/health/seizures
11. Ozcan, A.R., Erturk, S.: Seizure prediction in scalp EEG using 3D convolutional neural networks with an image-based approach. IEEE Trans. Neural Syst. Rehabil. Eng. **27**(11), 2284–2293 (2019). https://doi.org/10.1109/TNSRE.2019.2943707
12. Parvez, M.Z., Paul, M.: Seizure prediction using undulated global and local features. IEEE Trans. Biomed. Eng. **64**(1), 208–217 (2017). https://doi.org/10.1109/TBME.2016.2553131
13. Qin, Y., Zheng, H., Chen, W., Qin, Q., Han, C., Che, Y.: Patient-specific seizure prediction with scalp EEG using convolutional neural network and extreme learning machine. In: 2020 39th Chinese Control Conference (CCC), pp. 7622–7625 (2020). https://doi.org/10.23919/CCC50068.2020.9189578
14. Stafstrom, C., Carmant, L.: Seizures and epilepsy: an overview for neuroscientists. Cold Spring Harbor Perspect. Med. **5**, a022426–a022426 (2015). https://doi.org/10.1101/cshperspect.a022426
15. Truong, N.D., et al.: Convolutional neural networks for seizure prediction using intracranial and scalp electroencephalogram. Neural Netw. **105**, 104–111 (2018). https://doi.org/10.1016/j.neunet.2018.04.018
16. Truong, N.D., Nguyen, A.D., Kuhlmann, L., Bonyadi, M.R., Yang, J., Kavehei, O.: A generalised seizure prediction with convolutional neural networks for intracranial and scalp electroencephalogram data analysis (2017). https://doi.org/10.48550/arXiv.1707.01976

17. Usman, S.M., Khalid, S., Akhtar, R., Bortolotto, Z., Bashir, Z., Qiu, H.: Using scalp EEG and intracranial EEG signals for predicting epileptic seizures: Review of available methodologies. Seizure **71**, 258–269 (2019). https://doi.org/10.1016/j.seizure.2019.08.006

18. Usman, S.M., Khalid, S., Bashir, Z.: Epileptic seizure prediction using scalp electroencephalogram signals. Biocybern. Biomed. Eng. **41**(1), 211–220 (2021). https://doi.org/10.1016/j.bbe.2021.01.001, https://www.sciencedirect.com/science/article/pii/S0208521621000024

19. Viglione, S., Walsh, G.: Proceedings: epileptic seizure prediction. Electroencephalogr. Clin. Neurophysiol. **39**(4), 435–436 (1975). http://europepmc.org/abstract/MED/51767

20. Wang, Z., Yang, J., Sawan, M.: A novel multi-scale dilated 3D CNN for epileptic seizure prediction. In: 2021 IEEE 3rd International Conference on Artificial Intelligence Circuits and Systems (AICAS), pp. 1–4 (2021). https://doi.org/10.1109/AICAS51828.2021.9458571

21. Epilepsy and seizures: Provoked seizures, seizure disorder, and more. https://www.webmd.com/epilepsy/guide/understanding-seizures-and-epilepsy/

22. Yu, D., et al.: Deep convolutional neural networks with layer-wise context expansion and attention. In: Interspeech, pp. 17–21 (2016). https://doi.org/10.21437/Interspeech.2016-251

23. Zhang, Y., Guo, Y., Yang, P., Chen, W., Lo, B.: Using scalp EEG and intracranial EEG signals for predicting epileptic seizures: review of available methodologies. IEEE J. Biomed. Health Inf. **24**(2), 465–474 (2019). https://doi.org/10.1109/JBHI.2019.2933046

Autism Spectrum Disorder Detection from EEG Through Hjorth Parameters and Classification Using Neural Network

Zahrul Jannat Peya[1]([✉]) [ID], Bipasha Zaman[1], M. A. H. Akhand[1] [ID],
and Nazmul Siddique[2] [ID]

[1] Department of Computer Science and Engineering, Khulna University of Engineering and
Technology, Khulna-9203, Bangladesh
jannat.kuet@gmail.com, akhand@cse.kuet.ac.bd
[2] School of Computing, Engineering and Intelligent Systems, Ulster University, Londonderry,
Northern Ireland, UK
nh.siddique@ulster.ac.uk

Abstract. Autism spectrum disorders (ASD) are a collection of neurodevelop-mental disorders. Even though ASD has no cure, early detection and interven-tion can help developing language, behavior, and communication skills. Research shows that ASD can be diagnosed from brain signals, particularly electroen-cephalography (EEG) where the brain activity is recorded over time as an EEG signal from humans' scalp and then used to study neuropsychiatric disorders. This study investigates the classification performance of the Neural Networks (NN) model with Hjorth features namely activity, mobility, and complexity extracted from EEG signals through selected channels using the XGBoost algorithm. The classification accuracy is 80% using all 19 channels of EEG data whereas the accuracy of the model using activity, mobility and complexity reached 100% with selected channels. Hjorth parameter-based NN model with channel selection seems to be promising that improves the computation complexity significantly.

Keywords: Autism Spectrum Disorders (ASD) · Electroencephalography (EEG) · Hjorth Parameters · Neural Networks (NN)

1 Introduction

Autism spectrum disorders (ASD) [1] are a collection of neurological diseases marked by a lack of verbal and nonverbal communication as well as repetitive stereotypical behaviors. Children with ASD experience symptoms like social communication and social interaction deficiencies. Very often autistic children show repetitive patterns of behavior or activities [1]. Children with ASD may not look when someone points to a thing like a flying airplane because they lack joint attention. Many autistic children experience language difficulties and echolalia, in which they repeat words or phrases instead of speaking normally [2].

© ICST Institute for Computer Sciences, Social Informatics and Telecommunications Engineering 2023
Published by Springer Nature Switzerland AG 2023. All Rights Reserved
Md. S. Satu et al. (Eds.): MIET 2022, LNICST 491, pp. 31–40, 2023.
https://doi.org/10.1007/978-3-031-34622-4_3

In roughly 20% of children with ASD, inattention, impulsivity, and hyperactivity are important symptoms [3]. In South Asia, one out of every 160 children is thought to have ASD [4]. ASD affects about 2 out of 1000 children in Bangladesh, according to the Bangabandhu Sheikh Mujib Medical University (BSMMU). In metropolitan areas, the disease is more prevalent than in rural areas. There is mounting evidence that these early interventions can assist children with ASD in improving their living.

Nowadays, detecting ASD is a major consideration. There are various methods for detecting ASD. A screening strategy [5] is ideal for ASD detection since it is a cost-effective way for primary health care providers to identify patients that require additional specialist treatment. Screening aids in determining whether further specialized study by doctors is required. As ASD is a neurodevelopmental disorder usually reflected in brain signals, therefore, detecting ASD directly from brain signals would be more authentic. Among the widely used non-invasive neuroimaging techniques for brain function analysis are Magnetic Resonance Imaging (MRI) [6], functional MRI (fMRI) [6, 7], electroencephalography (EEG) [8–10], and magnetoencephalography (MEG) [11]. Because EEG has a high temporal resolution and is more accessible than other brain signals, it is being identified as a potential diagnostic tool for assessing brain activity.

EEG [12] is regarded as a realistic and effective signal for ASD detection among various brain signals since it has numerous advantages over other approaches for examining brain activity. They are also effective for diagnosing and monitoring brain activity because they exhibit pathological, physiological, and metabolic alterations in the brain and possibly other sections of the body, in addition to functional changes [13]. Therefore, EEG is employed as a useful indicator of ASD.

Several studies reported in the literature used EEG signals for ASD detection [14–16]. EEG signal was used as a clinical tool in assessing abnormal brain growth where an SVM was deployed as a classifier [14]. The prognosis of the clinical diagnosis of ASD using the EEG signals was accurate for children as early as 3 months old. Pearson's Correlation Coefficient (PCC) was used in [15] where EEG data from the 19 channels were converted into two-dimensional images to employ CNN. An accuracy of 100% was achieved using Resnet of CNN. Alturki et al. [16] employed discrete wavelet transform to decompose EEG signal into its sub-bands, extracted five statistical features from the sub-bands, and used four classifiers for diagnosing neurological disorders.

Research shows that the accuracy of classifiers largely depends on the quality of the features extracted from the EEG signals. A brief account of feature descriptors and extraction methods is provided in [17]. In pursuit of such quality features, new feature descriptors based on Hjorth parameters to be extracted from EEG signals are proposed [18]. The first three derivatives of EEG signal, i.e., mobility, activity, and complexity, are the most commonly utilized Hjorth parameters. Banerjee et al. [19] used the Hjorth parameters as features of electrooculogram signals and classified them with ensemble classifiers, which achieved an average accuracy of 90.96%. Elamir et al. [20] used Hjorth parameters as features extracted from three physiological signals, namely EEG, EMG, and GSR, and employed three supervised classifiers (KNN, SVM, Decision Tree) for emotion classification (arousal and valence) that achieved an accuracy of 93.2%. Mehmood et al.[21] used Hjorth parameters as features extracted from EEG signals and classified them by SVM for emotion recognition. This method showed an accuracy of 70%. Prakash et al. [22] has also used Hjorth parameters as features for automatic detection of sleep from single channel EEG signals. Bagging Classifier is used in this work for classification.

This research will investigate the pertinence of Hjorth parameters as features to be used for ASD detection from EEG signals. EEG data were collected from 19 channels for 25 patients at resting-state. The three main Hjorth parameters, i.e., activity, mobility, and complexity, values were calculated for all channels of EEG signals. The feature extracted from EEG data were fed into the Neural Network (NN) model, which allowed classification for ASD and control participants. A channel selection has been applied using XGBoost algorithm to select a subset of channels with higher information content suitable for classification. Finally obtained classification accuracies of Hjorth parameters were compared with and without channel selection.

The remaining part of the paper is structured as follows: The methodology is described in detail in Sect. 2. Sections 3 and 4 present the experimental outcomes and discussion, respectively. The conclusion is presented in Section 5.

2   ASD Diagnosis Using Hjorth Parameters from EEG

This study aims to investigate NN based ASD detection method from EEG signals. Hjorth parameter-based feature extraction is employed in this research to exploit the performance of the NN-model. Three features defined by activity, mobility, and complexity are extracted from EEG signals. Another facet of the EEG signal-based ASD detection method is channel selection. Hence, the XGBoost algorithm is used to select the information-rich channels out of 19 channels. The proposed methodology is presented in Fig. 1. The different steps in the methodology are described in the following sections.

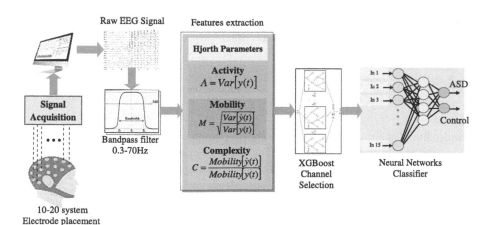

Fig. 1. Proposed ASD diagnosis system through Hjorth parameters and NN.

2.1 EEG Data Preparation

EEG is a powerful modality representing brain signals corresponding to various mental states and activities. Therefore, EEG signals are used for the diagnosis and monitoring of neuropsychiatric disorders. The standard 10–20 scheme of electrode placement on the scalp is used for EEG signal recording [23]. The layout of the standard 10–20 electrode placement is shown in Fig. 2.

2.2 Feature Extraction Using Hjorth Parameters

Hjorth parameters are time-domain parameters that are often utilized to construct feature descriptors from physiological signals such as EEG. It was first introduced by Hjorth [18]. The Hjorth Parameters are called activity, mobility, and complexity. Since they may be specified using first and second derivatives, these are also known as normalized slope descriptors.

Activity: Activity is the first parameter of the Hjorth parameter set. It is a measurement of the mean power of the signal that also represents the frequency domain surface of the power spectrum. Activity is defined by the following equation:

$$Activity = var (y (t)) \tag{1}$$

where y(t) is the signal itself, activity is the variance (mean power) of that signal and var(y(t)) denotes the biased variance of signal y(t) of length N with the mean value of t and it is given by

$$var (y (t)) = \frac{\sum_{t=1}^{N} (y (t) - \overline{y})}{N} \tag{2}$$

Mobility: The second parameter mobility is an estimate of the mean frequency representing the proportion of standard deviation of the power spectrum. Mobility is defined by the following equation.

$$Mobility = \sqrt{\frac{var (\frac{dy(t)}{dt})}{var (y(t))}} \tag{3}$$

Complexity: The third parameter of the Hjorth parameter set is complexity. It provides an estimate of the signal's bandwidth. The value of complexity converges to 1 if the signal is similar. Complexity is defined by the following equation:

$$\frac{Mobility (\frac{dy(t)}{dt})}{Mobility (y(t))} \tag{4}$$

These three parameters are calculated for the dataset. Each channel contains one value of activity, mobility, and complexity individually. So, each subject has 19 values of activity, 19 values of mobility, and 19 values of complexity.

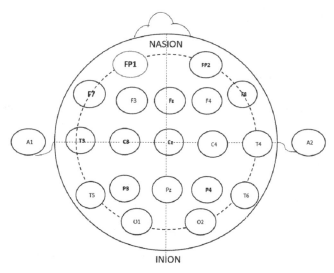

Fig. 2. Standard 10–20 system of electrode placement on the scalp for EEG recording.

2.3 Channel Selection Using XGboost Algorithm

XGBoost [24] stands for extreme Gradient Boosting and represents the premier machine learning toolkit for regression, classification, and ranking tasks. In this research, XGBoost is used to select the more information-rich channels from 19 channels of the dataset. At first, XGBoost is applied to the activity feature set. After applying this channel number is reduced to 10 channels from 19 channels. Similarly, after applying XGBoost to the mobility and complexity feature sets, 14 channels and 12 channels are selected respectively.

Table 1. The architecture of the neural network used for classification

Layer (Type)	Output Shape	Param#
dense (Dense)	(None, 15)	300
dense_1 (Dense)	(None, 4)	64
dense_2 (Dense)	(None, 2)	10

2.4 Classification Using Neural Network

Neural networks (NN) [25, 26] are layered interconnected neural computing models that function similarly to neurons in the human brain. An NN model with a single hidden layer with a sufficient number of neurons is capable of modeling any non-linear system. In this study, a simple three layered NN is considered for classification. Extracted features from EEG signals (i.e., activity, mobility, and complexity) with and without selected channels are passed into the NN model. Table 1 shows the parameters of the NN architecture used in this study.

3 Experimental Studies

The experimental results of the proposed ASD detection system are presented here. Classification performance was analyzed with and without channel selection.

3.1 Experimental Data

This study uses an EEG dataset collected from Villa Santa Maria Institute, Italy [27]. The 19-channel EEG data system was used to collect EEG signals from 15 (3 female, 12 male) ASD subjects and 10 (6 female, 4 male) controlled subjects. The age ranges of the subjects were 7 to 14 years and 7 to 12 years for the ASD and control subjects respectively. A bandpass filter of 0.3–70 Hz was applied to filter the EEG signals.

3.2 Experimental Setup

The algorithm is implemented using Anaconda. A Windows 10 OS platform-based PC (Processor of 8th Generation Intel® Core™ i5 – 8265U CPU @ 1.60 GHz, 1.80 GHz, 4 GB RAM) was used for the simulation experiments. For the training-testing protocol, 20 cases were used for the training set and 5 cases were used for the testing set. The available set of libraries such as Keras, Pandas, Sklearn, NumPy, Os, Tesorflow, Matplotlib and pyplot was used for the Neural Networks.

3.3 Experimental Result and Analysis

For each participant's channels, activity, mobility, and complexity features were calculated. Then feature extracted EEG data was passed to NN for classifying the ASD and control subjects. XGBoost algorithm was applied to the features for selecting the important channels individually. From 19 channels, it selects 10 channels for activity features. Similarly, 14 channels and 12 channels are picked separately after applying XGBoost for the mobility and complexity feature sets. Figure 3 shows the accuracy comparison between activity, mobility, and complexity before channel selection. According to the figure, for activity, train accuracy reached 95% after 400 epochs and test accuracy reached 80% after 100 epochs. For mobility, train accuracy fluctuates up to 200 epochs and then reached 100%. On the other hand, test accuracy reached 80% after 200 epochs. For complexity, train accuracy reached 95% after 400 epochs and test accuracy reached 80% after 200 epochs. So, the performance of mobility feature is better than activity and complexity. Figure 4 shows the accuracy comparison of activity, mobility and complexity after channel selection. After performing channel selection using XGBoost, 10 channels are selected for activity, 14 channels are selected for mobility and similarly, 12 channels are selected for complexity. For activity, test accuracy reaches to 100% with 10 channels since it was 80% before. For mobility and complexity test accuracy reaches 100% with 14 channels and 12 channels respectively since it was 80% before for both

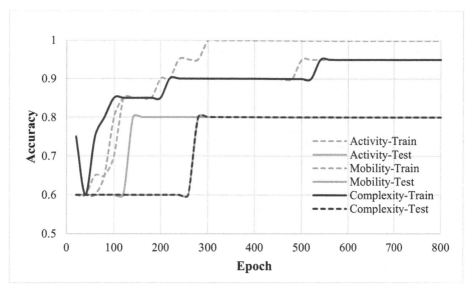

Fig. 3. Accuracy curve of activity, mobility, and complexity of 19-channel EEG data for epoch varying up to 800.

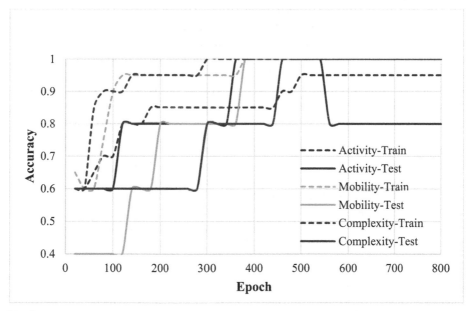

Fig. 4. Accuracy curve of activity, mobility, and complexity of selected channel EEG data (10 channels for activity, 14 channels for mobility, 12 channels for complexity) for epoch varying up to 800.

cases. So, the accuracy is increased with a reduced number of channels for activity, mobility, and complexity. So, the channel selection method seems to be promising.

Accuracy comparison of activity, mobility and complexity before and after channel selection is shown in Table 2. At first accuracy for 19 channels is computed individually for activity, mobility, and complexity. After channel selection using XGBoost, accuracy is again computed to make a comparison. For activity, using 19 channels the accuracy is 80% and the F1 score is 86%. After channel selection, 10 channels are selected and the accuracy is 100% with F1 score of 86%. Again, for mobility, the accuracy is 80% using 19 channels with F1 score of 86%. After channel selection, 14 channels are picked for accuracy and this time the accuracy is 100% with an F1 score of 100%. So, the accuracy is increased. Then for complexity, the accuracy is gained at 80% using 19 channels with F1 score of 86%. After channel selection, 12 channels are selected and the accuracy is 100% with an F1 score of 100%. This time also, the accuracy is increased. The number of channels and overall data decreased significantly after the channel selection is applied.

4   Discussion

The proposed method detects ASD using the Hjorth parameter and NN. Along with this method, XGBoost is used to reduce the number of channels of EEG data. By using the channel selection method, a significant reduction of number of channels, i.e., approximately 50%–66% is achieved. This method selects 10 channels for activity, 14 channels for mobility, and 12 channels for complexity. The amount of data is huge for 19 channels contributing to the features set with high computational cost. The reduction of the number of channels has direct impact on the data reduction leading to significant reduction of computational cost. This will enable designing a simple and efficient EEG-based ASD detection system. It also ensures an accuracy of 100%. This is a relatively high accuracy for early detection of ASD.

Table 2. Accuracy comparison of activity, mobility, and complexity before and after channel selection.

Feature	Without Channel Selection (i.e., 19 Channels)			With Selected Channels			
	Train Set Accuracy	Test Set Accuracy	F1 Score	No. of Channels	Train. Set Accuracy	Test Set Accuracy	F1 Score
Activity	95%	80%	86%	10	95%	100%	86%
Mobility	100%	80%	86%	14	100%	100%	100%
Complexity	95%	80%	86%	12	100%	100%	100%

5 Conclusion

The performance of machine learning model-based detection of ASD depends on the technique used for feature extraction from EEG signals. This research presents the use of Hjorth parameters employed for feature extraction from EEG signals, which are used in the machine learning model for ASD detection. Another facet of the EEG signal-based ASD detection approach is channel selection. This research also reports a channel reduction method using XGBoost after feature extraction. Neural Network is used as a classifier in this research. Channel reduction is performed for activity, mobility, and complexity individually. Application of both Hjorth parameters and XGBoost has resulted in channel reduction and accuracy improvement as well as a reduced amount of data, which again improves the overall computational complexity. A future extension of this research would be to apply this approach to large data sets.

References

1. Johnson, C.P., Myers, S.M.: Identification and evaluation of children with autism spectrum disorders. Pediatrics **120**(5), 1183–1215 (2007). https://doi.org/10.1542/peds.2007.2361
2. Roberts, J.M.A.: Echolalia and comprehension in autistic children. J. Autism Dev. Disord. **19**(2), 271–281 (1989). https://doi.org/10.1007/BF02211846
3. Tonge, B.J., Brereton, A.: Autism spectrum disorders. Aust. Fam. Physician. **40**(9), pp. 7–11, 2011, [Online]. Available: https://www.racgp.org.au/download/documents/AFP/2011/September/201109tonge.pdf
4. Hasan, M.S.: ASD and its Care in Bangladesh. The Daily Star, 25th Aug 2021 (2021)
5. Vladimir, V.F.: Autism screening in children: using the social communication questionnaire in South Africa". Gastron. ecuatoriana y Tur. local. **1**(69), 5–24 (1967)
6. Ha, S., Sohn, I.-J., Kim, N., Sim, H.J., Cheon, K.-A.: Characteristics of brains in autism spectrum disorder: structure, function and connectivity across the lifespan. Exp. Neurobiol. **24**(4), 273–284 (2015). https://doi.org/10.5607/en.2015.24.4.273
7. Sólon, A., Rosa, A., Craddock, R.C., Buchweitz, A., Meneguzzi, F.: NeuroImage: Clinical identification of autism spectrum disorder using deep learning and the ABIDE dataset. NeuroImage Clin. **17**, 16–23 (2018). https://doi.org/10.1016/j.nicl.2017.08.017
8. Korik, A., Sosnik, R., Siddique, N., Coyle, D.: 3D hand motion trajectory prediction from EEG mu and beta bandpower. In: Brain-Computer Interfaces: Lab Experiments to Real-World Applications, vol. 228, 1st edn., pp. 71–105. Elsevier B.V. (2016)
9. Korik, A., Sosnik, R., Siddique, N., Coyle, D.: Imagined 3D hand movement trajectory decoding from sensorimotor EEG rhythms. In: 2016 IEEE International Conference System Man, Cybernatics SMC 2016 – Conference Proceedings, pp. 4591–4596 (2017). https://doi.org/10.1109/SMC.2016.7844955
10. Korik, A., Sosnik, R., Siddique, N., Coyle, D.: Decoding imagined 3D hand movement trajectories from EEG: evidence to support the use of mu, beta, and low gamma oscillations. Front. Neurosci. **12**(MAR), 1–16 (2018). https://doi.org/10.3389/fnins.2018.00130
11. Aoe, J., et al.: Automatic diagnosis of neurological diseases using MEG signals with a deep neural network. Sci. Rep. **9**(1), 1–9 (2019). https://doi.org/10.1038/s41598-019-41500-x
12. Ibrahim, S., Djemal, R., Alsuwailem, A.: Electroencephalography (EEG) signal processing for epilepsy and autism spectrum disorder diagnosis. Biocybern. Biomed. Eng. **38**(1), 16–26 (2018). https://doi.org/10.1016/j.bbe.2017.08.006

13. Sanei, S.: EEG/MEG signal processing. Hindawi Publ. Corp. Comput. Intell. Neurosci. Artic. ID 97026 **2007**, 2 (2007). https://doi.org/10.1155/2007/97026
14. Bosl, W.J., Tager-Flusberg, H., Nelson, C.A.: EEG analytics for early detection of autism spectrum disorder: a data-driven approach. Sci. Rep. **8**(1), 1–20 (2018). https://doi.org/10.1038/s41598-018-24318-x
15. Peya, Z.J., Akhand, M.A.H., Ferdous Srabonee, J., Siddique, N.: EEG based autism detection using CNN through correlation based transformation of channels' data. In: 2020 IEEE Region 10 Symposium, TENSYMP 2020, 2020, no. June, pp. 1278–1281. https://doi.org/10.1109/TENSYMP50017.2020.9230928
16. Alturki, F.A., AlSharabi, K., Abdurraqeeb, A.M., Aljalal, M.: Eeg signal analysis for diagnosing neurological disorders using discrete wavelet transform and intelligent techniques. Sensors **20**(9), 2505 (2020). https://doi.org/10.3390/s20092505
17. Rizon, M.M.M.: Feature extraction methods for human emotion recognition using eeg – a study. In: Conference Malaysia-Japan International Symposium Advance Technology, no. July 2017 (2007)
18. Hjorth, B.: EEG analysis based on time domain properties. Electroencephalogr. Clin. Neurophysiol. **29**(3), 306–310 (1970). https://doi.org/10.1016/0013-4694(70)90143-4
19. Banerjee, A., Pal, M., Datta, S., Tibarewala, D.N., Konar, A.: Eye movement sequence analysis using electrooculogram to assist autistic children. Biomed. Signal Process. Control **14**(1), 134–140 (2014). https://doi.org/10.1016/j.bspc.2014.07.010
20. Elamir, M.M., Al-atabany, W., Eldosoky, M.A.: Emotion recognition via physiological signals using higher order crossing and Hjorth parameter. Res. J. Life Sci. Bioinform. Pharm. Chem. Sci. **5**(2), 839–846 (2019). https://doi.org/10.26479/2019.0502.63
21. Mehmood, R.M., Lee, H.J.: EEG based emotion recognition from human brain using Hjorth parameters and SVM. Int. J. Bio-Science Bio-Technology **7**(3), 23–32 (2015). https://doi.org/10.14257/ijbsbt.2015.7.3.03
22. Prakash, A., Roy, V.: An automatic detection of sleep using different statistical parameters of single channel EEG signals. Int. J. Signal Process. Image Process. Pattern Recognit. **9**(11), 335–344 (2016). https://doi.org/10.14257/ijsip.2016.9.10.32
23. Misra, U.K., Kalita, J.: Clinical Electroencephalography E-Book. Elsevier Health Sciences (2018)
24. Chen, T., Guestrin, C.: XGBoost: A scalable tree boosting system. In: Proceedings ACM SIGKDD International Conference Knowledge Discovery Data Mining, vol. 13–17-Aug, pp. 785–794 (2016). https://doi.org/10.1145/2939672.2939785
25. Siddique, N., Adeli, H.: Computational Intelligence: Synergies of Fuzzy Logic, Neural Networks and Evolutionary Computing. John Wiley and Sons, Chichester, UK (2013)
26. Cross, S., Harrison, R.F., Kennedy, R.L.: Introduction to neural networks. The Lancet **346**(8982), 1075–1079 (1995). https://doi.org/10.1016/S0140-6736(95)91746-2
27. Grossi, E., Olivieri, C., Buscema, M.: Diagnosis of autism through EEG processed by advanced computational algorithms: a pilot study. Comput. Methods Programs Biomed. **142**, 73–79 (2017). https://doi.org/10.1016/j.cmpb.2017.02.002

A Review on Heart Diseases Prediction Using Artificial Intelligence

Rehnuma Hasnat[1], Abdullah Al Mamun[2], Ahmmad Musha[1], and Anik Tahabilder[3]([✉])

[1] Department of Electrical and Electronic Engineering, Pabna University of Science and Technology, Pabna, Bangladesh
rehnumahasnat@gmail.com, mushaxyz@gmail.com
[2] Faculty of Engineering and Technology, Multimedia University, Melaka, Malaysia
mamun130203@gmail.com
[3] Department of Computer Science, Wayne State University, Detroit, MI, USA
tahabilderanik@gmail.com

Abstract. Heart disease is one of the major concerns of this modern world. The insufficiency of the experts has made this issue a bigger concern. Diagnosing heart diseases at an early stage is possible with Artificial Intelligence (AI) techniques, which will lessen the needed number of experts. This paper has initially discussed different kinds of heart diseases and the importance of detecting them early. Two popular diagnosis systems for collecting data and their working function are then highlighted. Different types of Model architectures in the corresponding field are described. Firstly, the Support Vector Machine (SVM) machine learning algorithm is described, and secondly, popular deep learning model architecture such as Convolutional Neural Network (CNN), Recurrent Neural Network (RNN), Long Short-Term Memory (LSTM), etc. are highlighted to detect heart disease. Finally, discussion, comparison, and future work are described. This article aims to clarify AI's present and future state in medical technology to predict heart diseases.

Keywords: Artificial Intelligence · Heart Diseases · Deep Learning · CNN · RNN

1 Introduction

Among all non-communicable diseases, heart diseases are the number 1 cause of death. Many people die of heart diseases every year, even before getting any medical treatment. The Conventional methods of diagnosis of heart diseases are time-consuming and expert-dependent. Sometimes it is not even possible to get experts' advice and treatment. That is why early detection of heart failure is a significant concern. With advanced artificial intelligence (AI) technology, early detection of heart failure is possible, which will also change the conventional method of detecting heart diseases and make it less human-dependent.

Globally, Cardiovascular Disease (CVD) is one of the leading causes of death. 17.5 million deaths were reported worldwide due to CVD in 2012, which is 31% of

Md. S. Satu et al. (Eds.): MIET 2022, LNICST 491, pp. 41–54, 2023.
https://doi.org/10.1007/978-3-031-34622-4_4

all deaths in the following year. Of these, Coronary Artery Disease (CAD) took about 7.4 million lives [1]. Atherosclerosis is the reason why CAD is initialized. It causes an inflammatory reaction to the vessel wall [2]. Also, 20% of patients who have coronary heart disease (CHD) meet the requirements of clinical depression, and few depressive symptoms are experienced by about 40% of them. CHD is associated with a noticeably advanced risk of adverse events along with deaths and Myocardial infarction (MI) in a consistent manner [3]. By 2030, an estimation has shown that people aged 60 years and above will increase by 56%, which is 1.5 billion from 901 million. Even it is anticipated that the number will double by 2050, which is almost 2.1 billion. The increased number of aged populations will create health care and economic issues [4].

When people grow older, the cardiovascular system becomes frail day by day [5]. Furthermore, the arteries and the left ventricle's muscle wall thicken when we get old, which results in reducing the compliance of blood vessels of the arteries. Thus it affects the general activities of a healthy heart, which leads to arrhythmia [6]. Therefore, arrhythmia is also considered a significant heart disease because it shows an unusual heartbeat rhythm, sometimes harmless and censorious.

Before using deep learning technology to predict cardiovascular diseases (CVD) machine learning technologies were used. Though the accuracies of those proposed models were not satisfactory, it leads to today's deep learning technology to predict heart diseases and give proper treatment in real-time. For many data mining and Machine Learning (ML) methods, Bayes rules or Naive Bayes is the basis. B. Szymanski et al. [7] in 2006 presented a model using the kernel in SUPANOVA to diagnose heart disease. 83.7% prediction of that model was correct. An intelligent Heart Diseases Prediction System using three classifiers was developed by A. Rajkumar et al.[8] in 2010. The three classifiers were Naïve Bayes, which gave 52.33% accuracy, Decision List, which provided 52% accuracy and KNN, which showed 45.67% accuracy. Data mining is another application that got much attention in the medical sector. It can estimate the success of medical treatment by comparing. In 2011 Heart Diseases Prediction System (HDPS) was introduced, which used only ANN (Artificial Neural Network). That model can classify heart diseases based on 13 different attributes [9]. Milan Kumari et al.[10] in 2011 proposed data mining classification techniques that contained Decision Tree, Support Vector Mechanism (SVM), Artificial Neural Network (ANNs) and RIPPER classifier, which was analyzed on CVD (Cardio Vascular Diseases) dataset. Accuracy of Decision Tree, SVM, ANNs and RIPPER were 79.05%, 84.12%, 80.06% and 81.08%, respectively. M. Anbarasi et al. [11] in 2010 used the Genetic Algorithm technique to predict heart diseases, which were inspired by natural genetic and natural selection. Naïve Bayes, Classification with clustering and Decision Tree were three classifiers used for the detection of heart diseases of patients. For the experiment, the Weka data mining tool was used. In that experiment, the Decision Tree has the highest construction time and accuracy than others.

A systemic literature search of recent papers was performed of studies AI in heart diseases analysis. The search subheadings and terminologies such as "heart diseases prediction", "Artificial Intelligence in heart diseases", "Echocardiogram report analysis using deep learning", "Heart failure prediction", "Phonocardiogram report analysis using deep learning" were used. A manual search of bibliography lists was performed for additional literature.

This paper has been organized into sections. Firstly, in Sect. 2, a short review of commonly used diagnosis systems to detect heart disease is discussed. Section 3 describes model architectures to predict the heart disease technique using artificial intelligence (AI). Then in Sect. 4, an overview of related papers is given in Table 1. Finally, the discussion and conclusion are given in Sect. 5.

2 Commonly Used Diagnosis Techniques

The experts use mainly the two most common diagnosis systems to analyze heart abnormalities. In this paper, the discussed models to predict heart diseases with artificial intelligence (AI) also used these two most common diagnosis methods [12]. Short descriptions of these two methods are given in the following section.

2.1 ECG

The ECG (electrocardiogram), a noninvasive test, which is generally used by professionals to record patients' heart activities. Healthcare professionals generally use an ECG to observe or decide arrhythmia, heart attack, chest pain because of blocked or narrowed arteries, and check certain heart diseases treatment such as pacemaker activity. Doctors review information recorded by the ECG machine to detect any heart abnormalities, including heart rhythm, heart rate, heart attack, inadequate oxygen and blood supply to the heart, and structural abnormalities [13]. But visually analyzing recorded EGC reports takes much time; moreover, the manual analysis may vary from one person to another.

In Fig. 1, a basic ECG signal structure has been shown. P wave and PR segment represent electrical depolarization of the heart. It is an essential part of an ECG. The period from the beginning of the P wave to the beginning of the QRS complex is called PR interval. Here the QRS complex is ventricular depolarization. After QRS and before the start of the T wave, the isoelectric period is called ST-segment [14]. When there are any abnormalities of the heart, they can be detected from the ECG signal analysis. An automated ECG explanation can remarkably improve quality, lower cost and increase cardiologists' making proper and faster diagnoses with trained deep learning classifiers. A Madani et al. in 2018 developed a deep learning classifier model for prediction tasks in cardiology, which was a data-efficient model. That model showed 94.4% accuracy for 15-view still-image echocardiographic view classification and binary left ventricular hypertrophy classification, an accuracy of 91.2% was achieved [15]. Kwon et al. [16] in 2018 showed in their paper that a deep learning-based model could predict HD (Heart Diseases) from ECG more perfectly than any other model, which can help diagnose any HD. Advanced AI technology can extract information about the heart condition from the ECG signal. It would make the early detection of heart failure possible.

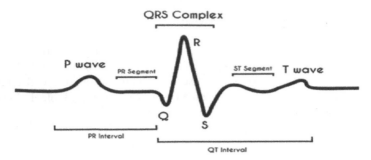

Fig. 1. Representation of EEG Signal.

2.2 PCG

The PCG (phonocardiogram) is another test; doctors can detect any heart abnormalities by analyzing its signal. The PCG records the sound of the heart because of the blood flow rate. The mechanical activity of the heart is reflected by PCG. It evaluates the heart murmurs' frequency and magnitude and analyzes if any kind of arrhythmia is present. In a word, it examines for any change in diastolic and systolic heart sound. Mainly the heart makes two murmurs, 1st one is indicated as S1, which is timing to QPS complex, and the 2nd one means a systolic pause in the heart's regular function [17] used by professionals. An additional sound will never be considered as a healthy heart. In the case of CHF (Congestive Heart Failure), there is a 3rd sound heard. But a PCG recording may vary from one expert to another; that is why a doctor can never be sure about CHF only from PCG [18]. With the recent advancements of artificial intelligence, experts can analyze any abnormalities of the heart quickly. The traditional method for the identification of abnormal PCG signals requires two steps classification and feature extraction. Samanta et al. [19] in 2018 obtained 82.57% accuracy using features extracted from four-channel PCG signals. From the PCG signal, that model extracts five different features from the time and frequency domain. H. Li et al. [20] in 2020 introduced a framework that can bring out multi-domain features of PCG with deep learning features to detect CAD. That framework achieved an accuracy of 90.43%, a sensitivity of 93.67%, and 83.36% specificity. Detection of heart diseases from PCG signals with the help of deep learning can create new possibilities in the medical field. Many lives can be saved by early detecting heart failure, which could provide proper treatment at the right time.

3 Model Architecture

Nowadays, Artificial Intelligence (AI) is a general non-technical term that signifies the use of a computer framework of intelligent behavior with minimum human work. AI alludes to different types of Machine Learning (ML) and many types of Deep Learning (DL). AI could help us detect CVD early, which is a key point to decrease the fatality rate due to CVD. If we can apply all the modern AI technology in the medical sector, especially in cardiology, it is possible to decrease the fatality rate due to CVD. ML is categorized as unsupervised learning and supervised learning. In supervised learning, a function is generated that replicates an output by deducing from training data. Training data is put together with nominal vectors or numerical vectors, which would be the properties for the corresponding output and input data. The training process is considered as regression when the output data is continuous. The process is regarded as a classification if the output data value is categorized. In comparison to supervised learning, unsupervised learning does not consider output data. It hypothesizes a function that describes the unlabeled input data structure. Unsupervised learning includes many other solutions that sum up and describe the data's main features [21]. In recent years most popular classification and regression algorithms for ML are Support Vector Regression (SVR) and Artificial Neural Network (ANN), and the regression of specific problems has shown superior performance [22].

3.1 SVM

SVM was initially developed in the 1960s, and then it was refined again in the 1990s. It is becoming a more popular supervised machine learning model that uses both classification and regression problems. It is powerful and different from other machine learning algorithms [23].

The objective of the SVM algorithm is to create the best line or decision boundary (hyperplane) in an N-dimensional space. For finding the best line, the line is chosen, which is the maximum distance between the classes. And that hyperplane can separate n-dimensional space into class [24].

K. Tan et al. [25] proposed a model using two algorithms which were SVM and genetic algorithm. That gained an accuracy of 85.81% with co-relation and 85.48% without co-relation for heart disease classification. M. Chala Beyene et al. [26] suggested a model that predicts and analyzes heart diseases with data mining techniques, SVM, naïve Bayes and J48. It gave superior quality results, which were helpful for reducing the cost and improving the quality of service. W. Dai et al. [27] used 5 different algorithms, including SVM, to predict hospitalization because of heart diseases. That model showed an accuracy of 82% and a false alarm rate of 30%.

3.2 Deep Learning

Conventional ML techniques had their boundaries in processing raw forms of natural data. It needed careful domain experts and engineering to transform the raw data with the help of a designed feature extractor that gives an acceptable feature vector or representation. But a machine can independently find the representation needed for detection or classification of raw data with the help of representation learning, a set of methods. The representation learning method with multiple layers of representation is known as Deep Learning (DL) method.

Significant advances have been made with the help of DL, which has restricted the path of AI technology development [28]. DL in current years has set a remarkable new shift in ML. The basic structures of DL are well established in traditional Neural networks. But DL is the reason why we can use many concealed neurons and layers, generally more than two, which is an architectural development with a training model.

In the medical sector, the creation of an automated feature set has many benefits that are without any human engagement [29].

CNN. One form of deep learning is Convolutional Neural Network (CNN). CNN is now widely used in image processing, even though it is getting a lot of attention in the medical field. CNN can process multiple array data. Many data are in the form of various array-like volumetric images or videos are in 3D, audio spectrums or images are in 2D, sequence and signals, including language, are in 1D. Biological images are segmented with the help of CNN [27]. Prearranged kernels are not used by CNN; it learns locally attached neurons which means data-specific kernels [29]. With the CNN method's help, we can segment ECG report automatically without human assistance, which can be time-saving and more accurate. CNN could be applied to combine the 8 leads ECG recordings into a 2-dimensional matrix. This method is named Leads Convolutional Neural Network (LCNN) in this convolutional kernels' sliding range confined with the agreement of the rule that 1 filter is unable to share by individual leads of ECG recordings. Though the ECG classification accuracy increases with this method the application is restricted by the demand of multi-lead inputs [30]. We can use multiple hidden layers to examine the recorded ECG signal perfectly.

N. Gawande et al. [31] used CNN for the classification of different heart diseases, which showed 99.46% of accuracy. U. Acharya et al. [5] proposed a deep CNN model to classify ECG signals into normal and Congestive Heart Failure (CHF) classes. That model showed satisfactory results with a specificity of 99.01%, sensitivity 98.87% and accuracy of 98.97%. Ö. Yıldırım et al. [32] presented a new approach to detect cardiac arrhythmia based on long-time ECG signals. That model got an accuracy of 91.33%. W. Yin et al. [30] introduced a CNN-based system that applies the impulse radio ultra-wideband radar data for extra details. The model was designed for arrhythmia detection that gains an accuracy of 88.89%. S. Sudarsanan et al. [17] used a CNN model to classify heart sound between abnormal and normal. That proposed model achieved an accuracy of 97% and was helpful for the clinician for detecting any abnormalities in heart sound in real-time. By modifying the CNN-based model, it is possible to detect any kind of heart disease early. This can change the traditional method of detecting heart disease and open a new era of deep learning in the medical sector.

RNN. Recurrent Neural Network (RNN) was created in the early' 80s, but we realized their real potential in recent years. Because of the invention of LSTM (Long Short-Term Memory) and the improvement of computational power with a massive amount of data, RNN has come in front. RNN is mainly a class of ANN (Artificial Neural Network) which is specialized for temporal data. The OF-RNN (end-to-end deep learning algorithm framework) could precisely detect myocardial infarction (MI). There are 3 function layers inside them. This is a great model for analyzing MI from images with a high accuracy rate [33]. With the help of RNN we can analyze ECG of the heart, and which could be very helpful for diagnosing many heart diseases like MI.

F. Ma et al. [34] in 2017 applied RNN to model sequential Electronic Health Records (EHR) data, which provided robust and accurate representations of patients' diagnoses, including prediction tasks for heart diseases. N. Pillai et al. [35] in 2019 used the RNN classifier ensemble, which can include non-identical base classifier into classifier ensembles models for classification problems. A. N. Shihab et al. [36] in 2021 proposed an

IOT based system that receives the information of the human body heartbeat rate. When the raw signals are taken into the input layer by the system architecture, the hidden layer differentiates the signal with the help of RNN and LSTM.

LSTM. LSTM is an artificial RNN architecture. It can process both single data points (such as images) and a sequence of data (such as video or speech). RNN's have trouble with short-time memory. The RNNs face difficulties carrying information from previous time steps to the next steps for a long sequence. LSTM can remind the info for a long time. So, LSTM is a special type of RNN. LSTM is very useful for modeling clinical data. A long line of research into RNNs for sequence learning, Hochreiter & Schmidhuber in 1997, first introduced LSTM [37].

This special kind of RNN is also very helpful in the medical sector. LSTM is very effective for modeling clinical data. Z. Lipton [37] in 2016 showed that multivariate time series of clinical measurements could be classified accurately by LSTM. L. Wang et al. [38] combined convolution net architecture and LSTM network to establish a diagnosis system network structure that can automatically detect CHF. G. Maragatham et al. [39] in 2019 proposed a model that was LSTM based on detecting heart failure early. LSTM model showed better performance compared to usual methods such as multilayer perceptron (MLP), support vector machine (SVM), K-nearest neighbor (KNN), and logistic regression.

4   An Overview of Related Work

In recent years many authors have given some models to predict heart diseases in real-time. With the help of these papers, many issues have been solved and more research are going on. However, some problems need to be solved. In the following Table 1, some recent papers are discussed in brief. Here A: Accuracy, R: Recall/Sensitivity, S: Specificity.

Table 1. Summary of recent works on artificial intelligence for detecting heart diseases.

Reference, (year)	Sector	Model(s)	Objective	Dataset	Result
K. Tan et al [25], (2009)	Iris, Diabetes, Breast cancer, Heart Disease, Hepatitis	SVM and genetic algorithm	Attribute selection in data mining	UCI machine learning reposi- tory	A: 84.07%
R. Chitra et al. [40], (2013)	Cardiovascular Diseases	CNN and SVM	Development of an intelligent cardiovascular diseases prediction system	270 patients database from University of California, Irvine C.A	A: 85%, R: 83%, S: 87% for CNN A: 82%, R: 85.5%, S: 77.5% for SVM
W. Dai et al. [27], (2014)	Heart Diseases	AdaBoost	To predict hospitalization because of heart diseases	Electronic Health Record (EHR)	A: 82%

(continued)

Table 1. (*continued*)

Reference, (year)	Sector	Model(s)	Objective	Dataset	Result
E. Choi et al. [41], (2016)	Heart Failure	RNN	Improve a model to predict initial diagnosis of heart failure	3884 HF cases from EHR	AUC: 88.3%
J. Tan et al. [42], (2017)	Coronary artery Disease	CNN	Detection of coronary artery disease from ECG signals	PhysioNet	A: 99.85%
C. Xu et al. [33], (2017)	Myocardial Infarction (MI)	RNN	Detect pixel-level MI areas via DL	25 2D images, 43 apical, 37 mid-cavity and 34 basal short axis image datasets for 114 subjects using gadolinium agents	A: 94.35%
D. Li et al. [43], (2018)	Heart Failure	RNN	automatic staging of heart failure in real-time and dynamically	Chest Pain Centers (CPCs) of Shanxi Academy of Medical Sciences	A: 97.6%, R: 96.3%, S: 97.4% for 2s duration A: 96.2%, R: 95.7% S: 94.3% for 5s duration
U.R. Acharya et al. [44], (2018)	Congestive heart failure	CNN	Early detection of congestive heart failure	NSRDB/BIDMC Fantasia/BIDMC	A: 98.97%, R: 99.01%, S: 98.87%
N. Gawande et al. [31], (2018)	Arrhythmia	CNN	Classification of arrhythmic heart diseases using CNN	MIT-BIH	A: 99.46%
S. Sanchez-Martinez et al. [45] (2018)	Heart Failure	Threshold	Heart failure characterization from echocardiographic variables with preserved ejection function	University Hospital of Wales (UK), Scuola di Medicina of Eastern Piedmont University (Italy), Università degli Studi di Perugia (Italy) and Oslo University Hospital (Norway)	R: 71%
Yildirim et al. [32], (2018)	Arrhythmias	CNN	Detection of 17 types of arrhythmias from ECG signal	MIT-BIH	A: 91.33%
E. Ebrahimzadeh et al. [46], (2018)	Paroxysmal Atrial Fibrillation (PAF)	KNN, SVM, NN	Prediction of PAF from the variability of heart rate	106 data from 53 pairs of ECG for training	R: 100% S: 95.55% A: 98.21%
S. Oh et al. [4] (2018)	Arrhythmia	CNN and LSTM	Detection of common arrhythmias precisely on Electrocardiogram screening	MIT-BIT	A: 98.10%, R: 97.50%, S: 98.70%
O. Deperlioglu et al. [47], (2018)	Cardiovascular Diseases	CNN	Classification of heart sound from phonocardiogram	PASCAL	A: 97.9%

(*continued*)

Table 1. (*continued*)

Reference, (year)	Sector	Model(s)	Objective	Dataset	Result
Samanta et al. [19], (2018)	Coronary Artery Diseases (CAD)	ANN	PCG signal-based CAD detection method	PhysioNet	A: 82.57%
A. Madani et al. [15], (2018)	Heart Diseases	CNN and GAN	Automated diagnosis of cardiac diseases	Institutional Review Board (IRB) at the University of California, San Francisco (UCSF)	A: 94.4%
I. Mohapatra et al. [48], (2019)	Heart Failure	Dual-Tree Complex Wavelet Transfer (DTCWT)	Cardiac failure detection	MIT-BIH NSR	A: 96.6%
K. Kusonose et al. [49], (2019)	Myocardial Infarction (MI)	CNN	Improved detection of Regional Wall Motion Abnormalities	1200 short-axis echo videos of 400 patients who had gone through angiography and echo	AUC: 90–97%
U. Baloglu et al. [50], (2019)	Myocardial Infarction (MI)	CNN	Detection of MI automatically from 12 lead electrocardiogram signal	Physiobank (PTB)	A: 99.00%
M. Gjoreski et al. [18], (2020)	Chronic heart failure (CHF)	Random Forest	CHF detection from heart sound	PhysioNet 2016	A: 92.9%
S. Khade et al. [51], (2019)	Heart Failure	SVM	Detect heart failure using deep learning	FANATASIA on PhysioNetBank	A: 84%
T. Hoang et al. [52], (2019)	Premature Ventricular Contraction (PVC)	CNN	Detection of PVC using tensor based method	12 lead ECG signals from St. Petersburg Arrhythmias	A: 90.84%, R:78.60%, S:99.86%
L. Bouny et al. [53], (2020)	Arrhythmia	CNN	Better performance of heart disease diagnosis from ECG signal	MIT-BIH	A: 99.57%
S. Sudarsanan et al. [17], (2020)	Cardiovascular diseases	CNN	Classification of heart sound to abnormal and normal sound from phonocardiogram signals	Databases of 5 with 3126 heart records in a time range from 5s to 120s	A: 97%
K. Kusunose et al [54], (2020)	Ejection fraction	CNN	Accurately analyzing ECG data	340 patients with 5 standard views and 10 images in a cycle. Total 17000 labeled images	A:98.1%

5   Discussion

From the above review, it is observed that analyzing ECG or PCG signals with the help of advanced AI technology can help detect any heart disease like arrhythmia, heart failure, congestive heart failure, myocardial infarction, etc. By advancing in the AI sector, the reports' observation errors can be reduced at a high rate. If we can analyze and detect any kind of heart abnormalities at a primary stage, the mortality rate due to cardiovascular disease can also be lessened. With the help of SVM, which is a supervised ML technology, we can classify ECG signals. S. Khade et al. [51] proposed a model that is based on SVM, which gives an accuracy of 84%. R. Chitra et al. [40] showed different results between CNN and SVM and improved a model for heart disease analysis. ML methods give us less accuracy than DL. CNN methods have a great future in the study of ECG and PCG signals. Models developed using CNN, their accuracy, sensitivity, and specificity rate was more than 90%. S. Sanchez-Martinez et al. [45] proposed a model using an unsupervised ML algorithm, which gave 71% of the true positive result, which is not so good enough for medical analysis as we need perfect analysis in the medical sector. D. Li et al. [43] improved a model based on RNN and CNN with accuracy, sensitivity, and specificity over 90%, which was a satisfactory result.

Here Fig. 2 illustrates the comparison between different type of approaches of machine learning and deep learning by different authors.

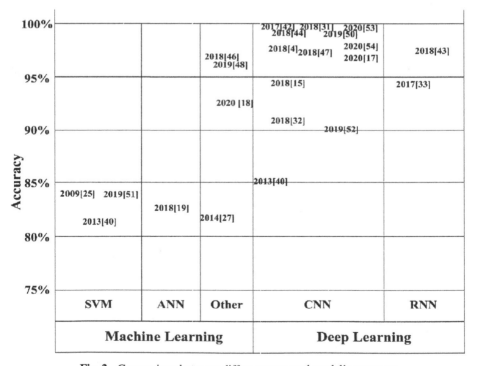

Fig. 2. Comparison between different proposed model's accuracy.

Nowadays, the expert number of doctors in cardiovascular diseases is very insufficient in proportion to patients. With the help of a developed CVD detection model, the reliability of expert doctors will also be lessened. People who are at high risk of CVD or who have CVD need early detection, or we cannot change the present scenario. Suppose development in AI technology for the CVD sector is possible. In that case, it will also be helpful for the growth of the economy because a vast amount of healthy population can contribute to the economic growth. Because of the traditional healthcare method, a large number of heart attacks cause death even before they get any treatment. In the future, with the help of digitalized healthcare monitoring, we can detect heart failure before it gets serious. Digitally analyzed data would be preferable and helpful to the doctors. Even in the distant future, we would monitor CVD patients and monitor their heart health without going to the doctor. The traditional healthcare system would face a huge change.

To reach human-level classification performance, deep learning needs a massive amount of data. Because of privacy law, differing standards across the healthcare industry, and the lack of medical system integration, medical data is less accessible in comparison with other sectors of computer vision. Medical image labeling is complicated, and it needs the time of medical experts, which make it costly than other computer vision task. Medical data hold metadata that is not relevant for the classification work, which leads to lower than optimal performance of deep learning model if the model cannot filter out those additional data [55].

But using a high-quality image with proper labeling can lessen the number of cases needed to create a DL model. K. Kusunose et al. [54] in 2020 proposed a model for analyzing ECG data, which was clinically feasible and accurate. That model was CNN-based, which showed an excellent accuracy of 98.1%, which means CNN could be very successful in the view classification. A system was proposed by W. Yin et al. [30] in 2016, which used the impulse radio ultra-wideband radar data as extra information to assist the classification of ECG in the slight motion state. J. Kown et al. [16] in 2018 validated and developed a model for HD using only the result of ECG. Deep learning was used to derive a model with high performance. A deep learning-based model to predict heart diseases is more accurate than any other machine learning model.

6 Conclusion

In this article, a short review of AI technology to classify and predict heart diseases is discussed. The above study shows that CNN-based models have shown a great success rate compared to other models. If a sufficient amount of dataset is available, lessening the limitation for detecting heart diseases using deep learning could be possible. A deep learning method to detect any heart diseases has a great possibility in the near future, which will reduce the mortality rate.

References

1. Lih, O.S., et al.: Comprehensive electrocardiographic diagnosis based on deep learning. Artif. Intell. Med. **103**, 101789 (2020). https://doi.org/10.1016/j.artmed.2019.101789

2. Maximilian Buja, L., McAllister, H.A.: Coronary artery disease: pathologic anatomy and pathogenesis. Cardiovasc. Med. 593–610 (2007). https://doi.org/10.1007/978-1-84628-715-2_25
3. Ye, S., et al.: Behavioral mechanisms, elevated depressive symptoms, and the risk for myocardial infarction or death in individuals with coronary heart disease: the regards (reason for geographic and racial differences in stroke) study. J. Am. Coll. Cardiol. 61, 622–630 (2013). https://doi.org/10.1016/j.jacc.2012.09.058
4. Oh, S.L., Ng, E.Y.K., Tan, R.S., Acharya, U.R.: Automated diagnosis of arrhythmia using combination of CNN and LSTM techniques with variable length heart beats. Comput. Biol. Med. 102, 278–287 (2018). https://doi.org/10.1016/j.compbiomed.2018.06.002
5. Acharya, U.R., Fujita, H., Lih, O.S., Hagiwara, Y., Tan, J.H., Adam, M.: Automated detection of arrhythmias using different intervals of tachycardia ECG segments with convolutional neural network. Inf. Sci. (Ny) 405, 81–90 (2017). https://doi.org/10.1016/j.ins.2017.04.012
6. Chow, G.V., Marine, J.E., Fleg, J.L.: Epidemiology of arrhythmias and conduction disorders in older adults. Clin. Geriatr. Med. 28, 539–553 (2012). https://doi.org/10.1016/j.cger.2012.07.003
7. Szymanski, B., Embrechts, M., Sternickel, K., Han, L., Ross, A., Zhu, L.: Using efficient SUPANOVA kernel for heart disease diagnosis. Intell. Eng. Syst. through Artif. Neural Netw. 16, 305–310 (2010) https://doi.org/10.1115/1.802566.paper46
8. Rajkumar, A., Reena, G.S.: Diagnosis of heart disease using datamining algorithm. Glob. J. Comput. Sci. Technol. 10, 38–43 (2010)
9. Shafique, U., Majeed, F., Qaiser, H., Mustafa, I.U.: Data mining in healthcare for heart diseases. Int. J. Innov. Appl. Stud. 10, 1312 (2016)
10. Kumari, M., Godara, S.: Comparative study of data mining classification methods in cardiovascular disease prediction. Int. J. Comput. Sci. Trends Technol. 2, 304–308 (2011)
11. Anbarasi, M., Anupriya, E., Sriman Narayana Iyenger, N.Ch.: Enhanced prediction of heart disease with feature subset selection using genetic algorithm. Int. J. Eng. Sci. Technol. 2, 5370–5376 (2010)
12. Heart disease - Diagnosis and treatment - Mayo Clinic
13. Addison, P.S.: Wavelet transforms and the ECG: a review. Physiol. Meas. 26, R155–R199 (2005). https://doi.org/10.1088/0967-3334/26/5/R01
14. Dupre, A., Vincent, S., Iaizzo, P.A.: Basic ECG theory, recordings, and interpretation. Handb. Card. Anatomy, Physiol. Devices, pp. 191–201 (2005) https://doi.org/10.1007/978-1-59259-835-9_15
15. Madani, A., Ong, J.R., Tibrewal, A., Mofrad, M.R.K.: Deep echocardiography: data-efficient supervised and semi-supervised deep learning towards automated diagnosis of cardiac disease. npj Digit. Med. 1, 1–11 (2018). https://doi.org/10.1038/s41746-018-0065-x
16. Kwon, J.M., Kim, K.H., Jeon, K.H., Park, J.: Deep learning for predicting in-hospital mortality among heart disease patients based on echocardiography. Echocardiography 36, 213–218 (2019). https://doi.org/10.1111/echo.14220
17. Sudarsanan, S., Aravinth, J.: Classification of heart murmur using CNN. In: Proceedings of the 5th International Conference Communication Electronic System ICCES 2020, pp. 818–822 (2020). https://doi.org/10.1109/ICCES48766.2020.09138059
18. Gjoreski, M., Gradisek, A., Budna, B., Gams, M., Poglajen, G.: Machine learning and end-to-end deep learning for the detection of chronic heart failure from heart sounds. IEEE Access 8, 20313–20324 (2020). https://doi.org/10.1109/ACCESS.2020.2968900
19. Samanta, P., Pathak, A., Mandana, K., Saha, G.: Classification of coronary artery diseased and normal subjects using multi-channel phonocardiogram signal. Biocybern. Biomed. Eng. 39, 426–443 (2019). https://doi.org/10.1016/j.bbe.2019.02.003

20. Li, H., et al.: A fusion framework based on multi-domain features and deep learning features of phonocardiogram for coronary artery disease detection. Comput. Biol. Med. **120**, 103733 (2020). https://doi.org/10.1016/j.compbiomed.2020.103733

21. Lee, J.G., et al.: Deep learning in medical imaging: general overview. Korean J. Radiol. **18**(4), 570–584 (2017). https://doi.org/10.3348/kjr.2017.18.4.570

22. Drucker, H., Surges, C.J.C., Kaufman, L., Smola, A., Vapnik, V.: Support vector regression machines. Adv. Neural Inf. Process. Syst. **1**, 155–161 (1997)

23. Wang, Y., Zhang, F., Chen, L.: An approach to incremental SVM learning algorithm. In: Proceedings - ISECS International Colloquium Computing Communication Control Management CCCM 2008. 1, pp. 352–354 (2008). https://doi.org/10.1109/CCCM.2008.163

24. Kecman, V.: Support vector machines – an introduction 1 basics of learning from data. StudFuzz. **177**, 1–47 (2005)

25. Tan, K.C., Teoh, E.J., Yu, Q., Goh, K.C.: A hybrid evolutionary algorithm for attribute selection in data mining. Expert Syst. Appl. **36**, 8616–8630 (2009). https://doi.org/10.1016/j.eswa. 2008.10.013

26. Chala Beyene, M.: Survey on prediction and analysis the occurrence of heart disease using data mining techniques. Int. J. Pure Appl. Math. **118**, 165–173 (2020)

27. Dai, W., Brisimi, T.S., Adams, W.G., Mela, T., Saligrama, V., Paschalidis, I.C.: Prediction of hospitalization due to heart diseases by supervised learning methods. Int. J. Med. Inform. **84**, 189–197 (2015). https://doi.org/10.1016/j.ijmedinf.2014.10.002

28. Lecun, Y., Bengio, Y., Hinton, G.: Deep learning. Nature **521**, 436–444 (2015). https://doi. org/10.1038/nature14539

29. Rav, D., Wong, C., Deligianni, F., Berthelot, M., Andreu-Perez, J., Lo, B.: Deep learning for health informatics. IEEE J. Biomed. Health Inform. **21**(1), 1–18 (2017). https://doi.org/10. 1109/JBHI.2016.2636665

30. Yin, W., Yang, X., Zhang, L., Oki, E.: ECG monitoring system integrated with IR-UWB radar based on CNN. IEEE Access. **4**, 6344–6351 (2016). https://doi.org/10.1109/ACCESS.2016. 2608777

31. Gawande, N., Barhatte, A.: Heart diseases classification using convolutional neural network. In: Proceedings 2nd International Conference Communication Electronics Systems. ICCES 2017, pp. 17–20 (2018) https://doi.org/10.1109/CESYS.2017.8321264

32. Yıldırım, Ö., Pławiak, P., Tan, R.S., Acharya, U.R.: Arrhythmia detection using deep convolutional neural network with long duration ECG signals. Comput. Biol. Med. **102**, 411–420 (2018). https://doi.org/10.1016/j.compbiomed.2018.09.009

33. Xu, C., et al.: Direct detection of pixel-level myocardial infarction areas via a deep-learning algorithm. Lect. Notes Comput. Sci. (including Subser. Lect. Notes Artif. Intell. Lect. Notes Bioinformatics). **10435** LNCS, 240–249 (2017). https://doi.org/10.1007/978-3-319-66179-7_28

34. Ma, F., You, Q., Chitta, R., Sun, T., Zhou, J., Gao, J.: Dipole: diagnosis prediction in healthcare via attention-based bidirectional recurrent neural networks. arXiv. 1903–1911 (2017)

35. Pillai, N.S.R., Bee, K.K.: Prediction of heart disease using Rnn algorithm. Int. Res. J. Eng. Technol. (IRJET) **6**, 4452–4458 (2019)

36. Shihab, A.N., Mokarrama, M.J., Karim, R., Khatun, S., Arefin, M.S.: An iot-based heart disease detection system using rnn. Adv. Intell. Syst. Comput. **1200** AISC 535–545 (2021). https://doi.org/10.1007/978-3-030-51859-2_49

37. Lipton, Z.C., Kale, D.C., Elkan, C., Wetzel, R.: Learning to diagnose with LSTM recurrent neural networks. In: 4th International Conference Learning Represent ICLR 2016 - Conference Track Proceedings, pp. 1–18 (2016)

38. Wang, L., Zhou, X.: Detection of congestive heart failure based on LSTM-based deep network via short-term RR intervals. Sensors **19**(7), 1502 (2019). https://doi.org/10.3390/s19071502

39. Maragatham, G., Devi, S.: LSTM model for prediction of heart failure in big data. J. Med. Syst. **43**(5), 1–13 (2019). https://doi.org/10.1007/s10916-019-1243-3
40. Chitra, R.: Heart disease prediction system using supervised learning classifier. Bonfring Int. J. Softw Eng. Soft Comput. **3**, 01–07 (2013). https://doi.org/10.9756/bijsesc.4336
41. Choi, E., Schuetz, A., Stewart, W.F., Sun, J.: Using recurrent neural network models for early detection of heart failure onset. J. Am. Med. Informatics Assoc. **24**, 361–370 (2017). https://doi.org/10.1093/jamia/ocw112
42. Tan, J.H., et al.: Application of stacked convolutional and long short-term memory network for accurate identification of CAD ECG signals. Comput. Biol. Med. **94**, 19–26 (2018). https://doi.org/10.1016/j.compbiomed.2017.12.023
43. Li, D., Li, X., Zhao, J., Bai, X.: Automatic staging model of heart failure based on deep learning. Biomed. Signal Process. Control. **52**, 77–83 (2019). https://doi.org/10.1016/j.bspc.2019.03.009
44. Acharya, U.R., et al.: Deep convolutional neural network for the automated diagnosis of congestive heart failure using ECG signals. Appl. Intell. **49**(1), 16–27 (2018). https://doi.org/10.1007/s10489-018-1179-1
45. Sanchez-Martinez, S., et al.: Machine learning analysis of left ventricular function to characterize heart failure with preserved ejection fraction. Circ. Cardiovasc. Imaging **11**, e007138 (2018). https://doi.org/10.1161/CIRCIMAGING.117.007138
46. Ebrahimzadeh, E., Kalantari, M., Joulani, M., Shahraki, R.S., Fayaz, F., Ahmadi, F.: Prediction of paroxysmal atrial fibrillation: a machine learning based approach using combined feature vector and mixture of expert classification on HRV signal. Comput. Methods Programs Biomed. **165**, 53–67 (2018). https://doi.org/10.1016/j.cmpb.2018.07.014
47. Deperlioğlu, Ö.: Classification of segmented phonocardiograms by convolutional neural networks. BRAIN. Broad Res. Artif. Intell. Neurosci. **10**, 5–13 (2019)
48. Mohapatra, I., Pattnaik, P., Mohanty, M.N.: Cardiac failure detection using neural network model with dual-tree complex wavelet transform. Springer Singapore (2019). https://doi.org/10.1007/978-981-13-2182-5_9
49. Kusunose, K., et al.: A deep learning approach for assessment of regional wall motion abnormality from echocardiographic images. JACC Cardiovasc. Imaging. **13**, 374–381 (2020). https://doi.org/10.1016/j.jcmg.2019.02.024
50. Baloglu, U.B., Talo, M., Yildirim, O., Tan, R.S., Acharya, U.R.: Classification of myocardial infarction with multi-lead ECG signals and deep CNN. Pattern Recognit. Lett. **122**, 23–30 (2019). https://doi.org/10.1016/j.patrec.2019.02.016
51. Khade, S., Subhedar, A., Choudhary, K., Deshpande, T., Kulkarni, U.: A System to detect heart failure using deep learning techniques. Int. Res. J. Eng. Technol. **6**, 384–387 (2019)
52. Hoang, T., Fahier, N., Fang, W.C.: Multi-leads ECG premature ventricular contraction detection using tensor decomposition and convolutional neural network. In: BioCAS 2019 - Biomedical Circuits Systems Conference Proceedings, pp. 1–4 (2019). https://doi.org/10.1109/BIOCAS.2019.8919049
53. Bouny, L.E., Khalil, M., Adib, A.: An end-to-end multi-level wavelet convolutional neural networks for heart diseases diagnosis. Neurocomputing **417**, 187–201 (2020). https://doi.org/10.1016/j.neucom.2020.07.056
54. Kusunose, K., Haga, A., Inoue, M., Fukuda, D., Yamada, H., Sata, M.: Clinically feasible and accurate view classification of echocardiographic images using deep learning. Biomolecules **10**, 1–8 (2020). https://doi.org/10.3390/biom10050665
55. Khamis, H., Zurakhov, G., Azar, V., Raz, A., Friedman, Z., Adam, D.: Automatic apical view classification of echocardiograms using a discriminative learning dictionary. Med. Image Anal. **36**, 15–21 (2017). https://doi.org/10.1016/j.media.2016.10.007

Machine Learning Models to Identify Discriminatory Factors of Diabetes Subtypes

Shahriar Hassan[1,2]([⊠]) [iD], Tania Akter[1] [iD], Farzana Tasnim[1] [iD],
and Md. Karam Newaz[1] [iD]

[1] Department of Computer Science and Engineering, Gono Bishwabidyalay,
Dhaka, Bangladesh
shahriar.hassan303@gmail.com
[2] Department of Computer Science and Engineering,
Bangladesh University of Engineering and Technology, Dhaka, Bangladesh

Abstract. Diabetes Mellitus is a chronic illness that can be defined by high glucose levels in the blood due to its outreach cells in the body. Numerous efforts were happened to detect diabetes however most works were not considered critical factors of diabetes. In this study, proposed machine learning model creates various diabetes subtypes and pinpoints discriminating features. First, we gathered Pima Indians diabetic dataset (PIDD) and Sylhet Diabetes Hospital Datasets (SDHD) from the University of California Irvine (UCI) machine learning repository. Then, only diabetes records were extracted, and created some subtypes from both datasets using k-means clustering and silhouette method. These subtypes data were balanced employing Random Over-Sampling (ROS) and Synthetic Minority Over-sampling Technique (SMOTE). Then, we employed various classifiers such as Decision Tree (DT), K-Nearest Neighbor (KNN), Naïve Bayes (NB), Random Forest (RF), Support Vector Machine (SVM), Gradient Boosting (GB), Adaboost (AdaB), Extreme Gradient Boosting (XGB), Multi-Layer Perceptron (MLP) and Logistic Regression (LR) into the subtypes of PIDD, SDHD, and their balanced datasets. In this case, RF showed the best performance for SMOTE dataset of PIDD subtypes. In addition, LR provided the best performance for ROS dataset of SDHD subtypes. Then, Local Interpretable Model-Agnostic Explanations (LIME) was employed to identify discriminatory factors of these diabetes subtypes by ranking their features.

Keywords: Diabetes · K-means Clustering · Machine Learning · Classification · LIME · Discriminatory Factors

1 Introduction

Diabetes is a metabolic, chronic situation that is a result of insulin hormone resistance in the body due to a malfunctioning pancreas. Most of the foods

© ICST Institute for Computer Sciences, Social Informatics and Telecommunications Engineering 2023
Published by Springer Nature Switzerland AG 2023. All Rights Reserved
Md. S. Satu et al. (Eds.): MIET 2022, LNICST 491, pp. 55–67, 2023.
https://doi.org/10.1007/978-3-031-34622-4_5

are converted into sugar and directly released it to the bloodstream. In this circumstances, human body faces many difficulties to produce energy from different types of foods. Therefore, the glucose level is increased in the blood which causes this disease [12]. Various factors such as genetical, irregular lifestyles, and environmental issues are also responsible to happen this disease. According to World Health Organization (WHO), around 8.5% adults (i.e., in 2014) were suffering in diabetes worldwide. Almost 48% deaths in the world were happened in 2019 due to diabetes [https://www.who.int/news-room/fact-sheets/detail/diabetes][Accessed: 16-May-2022]. Moreover, the prevalence of diabetes was found 4% in 1995 according to the International Diabetes Federation (IDF). However, it was increased into 5% in 2000 and 9% from 2006 to 2010. Besides, this prevalence will be reached 13% by 2030 [9,16]. Therefore, these issues are making diabetes as a global concern day by day.

Diabetes causes various types of disabilities in human body like coma, renal failure, retinal malfunction, pathological beta cell loss in the pancreas, cardiovascular and vascular diseases, impotence, joint problem, muscle mass reduction, ulcer, and pathogenic effects on immunity [3,7]. While this disease is not completely cured, proper diagnosis is required to prevent the progression of this disease. However, detecting diabetes at its early-stages is a difficult task because it consists of various large, heterogeneous, and multidimensional characteristics [10]. Therefore, numerous reasons are associated to happen this disease [5,7]. If we can explore several subtypes of diabetes and can interpret the factors differentiating those subtypes, it can be more easier to understand how this disease happens and which treatments are required to mitigate the effects of diabetes.

Machine learning enables systems to train them using existing instances and improve its performance without explicit programming [1,4,17,19]. This techniques are widely used to investigate various harmful diseases more efficiently [2]. There were happened numerous works to detect diabetes at early stages [7,11,18]. Hasan et al. [6] proposed a robust model for early-stage prediction of diabetes. They investigated these records using outlier rejection, missing value imputation, data standardization, and feature selection methods. Then, DT, KNN, RF, AdaB, NB, XGB and MLP were employed into diabetes dataset considering K-fold cross-validation. Reddy et al. [14] proposed a machine learning model that employed different classifiers such as SVM, KNN, LR, NB, GB, and RF into diabetes instances. In that work, RF showed the highest 98.48% Accuracy, 98.00% Precision, 95.57% Recall, 97.73% F-Measure, and 97.78% Area under Receiver Operating Characteristic Curve (AUROC). Patel et al. [13] represented a diabetes prediction system that used multiple machine learning techniques to diagnose diabetes. In that work, MLP and Radial Basis Function Network (RBFN) showed the maximum specificity of 95.00% and 98.72%, respectively. Also, RBFN provided the best 98.80% accuracy using 10-fold cross-validation. Rony et al. [16] employed Linear Discriminant Analysis (LDA), KNN, SVM, and RF into diabetes dataset. In that case, RF outperformed other classifiers by providing the maximum accuracy of 87.66% for detecting diabetes at early stage. However, most of those works were not considered any diabetes subtypes for investigating this disease more precisely.

In this work, we gathered only diabetes records from PIDD and SDHD, UCI machine learning repository. Several diabetes subtypes were generated using K-means clustering method from both of these datasets. Then, we balanced subtypes of both datasets and applied DT, KNN, NB, RF, SVM, GB, AdaB, XGB, MLP and LR to investigate them. In this case, RF showed more stable results for PIDD subtypes and LR provided more sound outcomes for SDHD subtypes. Then, some discriminatory factors were determined using LIME analysis based on the best classifiers of PIDD and SDHD subtypes. These insights can be helped physicians to plan medications and take preventive measures. The following are the work's most important contributions:

- This model extracted diabetic subtypes and classifies these groups more accurately.
- It employed various data analytic methods such as clustering, normalization, data balancing into diabetes subtypes to generate more significant outcomes.
- This model determines several discriminatory factors which is more useful to understand different characteristics of the disease.

The remainder of the text is structured as follows: Sect. 2 presents the methodological steps to investigate diabetes and determine discriminatory factors. The experimental results and discuss its impacts are provided briefly in Sect. 3. Also, Sect. 4 summarizes this research and offers some recommendations for future study to enhance this model and get better results.

2   Materials and Methods

This section provides a brief description about working datasets, proposed diabetes subtype detection model, and evaluation metrics as follows.

2.1   Dataset Description

In this work, we collected PIDD [22] and SDHD [8] from the UCI machine learning repository. PIDD represents 768 female patients whose ages were at least 21 years old. In addition, it contains 268 diabetic patients and 500 non-diabetic people of Pima Indians near Phoenix, Arizona. It consists of eight attributes where all of its features are numeric. Instead, SDHD contains 520 records including 16 features from Sylhet Diabetes Hospital, Sylhet, Bangladesh. It represents data of 192 female and 328 male subjects. In addition, it has 314 diabetes and 186 normal people. All features of this dataset are categorical. Table 1 describes individual features of PIDD and SDHD.

2.2   Proposed Model for Detecting Diabetes Subtypes

This section briefly described how proposed model generates diabetes subtypes and further extracts several discriminatory factors. They are useful to distinguish individual characteristics of diabetes. The overall process of automatic diabetes subtype detection is briefly given in Fig. 1.

Table 1. Description of Diabetes Dataset's Features: (a) PIDD (b) SDHD

PIDD		
Attributes	Types	Values
Pregnancies	Numeric	0–17
Glucose	Numeric	0–199
Blood Pressure	Numeric	0–122
Skin Thickness	Numeric	0–99
Insulin	Numeric	0–846
BMI	Numeric	0–67.1
Diabetes Pedigree Function	Numeric	0.08–2.42
Age	Numeric	21–81
Outcome	Binary	0, 1

SDHD		
Attributes	Types	Values
Age	Numeric	1.20–65
Sex	Category	Male, Female
Polyuria	Binary	Yes, No
Polydipsia	Binary	Yes, No
Sudden Weight Loss	Binary	Yes, No
Weakness	Binary	Yes, No
Polyphagia	Binary	Yes, No
Genital Thrush	Binary	Yes, No
Visual Blurring	Binary	Yes, No
Itching	Binary	Yes, No
Irritability	Binary	Yes, No
Delayed Healing	Binary	Yes, No
Partial Paresis	Binary	Yes, No
Muscle Stiffness	Binary	Yes, No
Alopecia	Binary	Yes, No
Obesity	Binary	Yes, No
Class	Category	Positive, Negative

(a)   (b)

- **Data Preprocessing:** In this step, we gathered only diabetes instances of PIDD and SDHD datasets. The number of rows reduced to 268 and 320 for PIDD and SDHD datasets respectively. There were not found any missing values in SDHD. However, we found some outliers in PIDD. There are several zero values in different columns: 2 in BMI, 138 in Insulin, 2 in Glucose, 16 in Blood Pressure and 88 in Skin Thickness column. Then, we replaced them with a random number in the range of that column. Besides, we converted all categorical values of SDHD into an integer to properly manipulate their values by different machine learning models.
- **Apply K-means Clustering Method:** K-means clustering method is used to generate several clusters in a dataset which characterizes by the similarity within similar clusters and the dissimilarity among different clusters [21]. In this work, we applied k-means clustering method [1] into diabetes records of PIDD and SDHD and generated various clusters. Each cluster was identified as diabetes subtype.
- **Silhouette Analysis:** Silhouette analysis [20] is used to interpret and validate the quality of clusters. It evaluates each cluster's data consistency and estimation of the detachment gap. This method calculates the range of each cluster from −1 to +1. In this work, diabetes records of PIDD and SDHD were fitted with k-means method through changing the values of k from 2 to

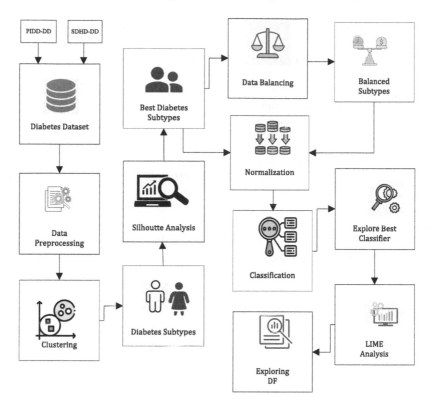

Fig. 1. Proposed Diabetes Subtype Model

10 in each iteration. Then, Silhouette method is produced scores based on subtype labels in each iteration (i.e., k = 2 to 10). In this case, we identified the best clusters/subtypes for PIDD and SDHD based on their highest silhouette scores respectively.

- **Data Balancing:** We explored the best subtypes from the diabetes records of PIDD and SDHD. However, these subtype datasets were highly imbalanced with the majority and minority clusters. To produce better outcomes, it is needed to balance these subtypes. Therefore, we applied ROS into PIDD and SDHD subtypes which created randomly duplicate samples from minority classes with replacement. Again, SMOTE generated more synthetic data to increase instances of the minority class in similar subtypes.

- **Normalization:** Normalization is a scaling technique that helps to reduce redundancy and change the values of numeric columns in the dataset using a common scale. In this work, primary, ROS, and SMOTE diabetes subtypes of PIDD and SDHD were normalized by scaling and translating each feature individually between zero and one.

– **Classification:** After normalization process, different extensively used classifiers such as DT, KNN, NB, RF, SVM, GB, AdaB, XGB, MLP and LR were implemented into primary, ROS and SMOTE diabetes subtypes. Then, they produced significant results to classify individual subtypes of this disease. We have choosen these classifiers as they are proven to provide great performance in classifying diabetes data in the existing works [6,14,16]. However, the best classifier was identified by justifying their performance based on several evaluation metrics such as accuracy, F1-Score, and AUROC.

– **Exploring Significant Features:** Finally, LIME [15] approach was explored high significant features using best performing classifier. This explanation is generated by learning a simpler model (i.e., linear classifier). It generates an interpretation for a single test instance and works in local fidelity. Moreover, it can be used to identify globally important features for a model [15]. To determine important features of PIDD and SDHD subtypes, we manipulated all diabetes instances and averaged the results. Therefore, we identified discriminatory factors of diabetes subtypes by calculating their frequencies.

2.3   Evaluation Metrics

In order to evaluate the performance of different classifiers, a number of evaluation metrics like Accuracy, F1-Score, and AUROC are used. However, these metrics are manipulated using true positive (TP), true negative (TN), false positive (FP) and false negative (FN) values which are described as follows:

– **Accuracy** is calculated the ratio of the total population to the sum of the TP and TN.

$$\text{Accuracy} = \frac{TP + TN}{TP + FN + FP + TN} \tag{1}$$

– **F1-Score** accumulates the precision and recall and manipulates the harmonic mean of them.

$$\text{F-Measure} = 2 \times \frac{\text{precision} \times \text{recall}}{\text{precision} + \text{recall}}$$
$$= \frac{TP}{TP + \frac{1}{2}(FP + FN)} \tag{2}$$

– **AUROC** measures how well true positive values are separated from false positive values.

$$\text{AUROC} = \frac{\text{TP rate} + \text{TN rate}}{2} \tag{3}$$

3 Experimental Results and Discussion

In this experiment, all works are carried out with Jupyter Notebook version 6.1.4 using Python. To generate and identify different clusters, we employed k-means clustering method and calculated Silhouette scores for different values of k using scikit-learn library. Then, we applied ROS and SMOTE methods to balance these primary subtypes of PIDD and SDHD using imbalanced-learn library. Also, we normalized primary and balanced subtypes using scikit-learn preprocessing package. Individual classifiers such as DT, KNN, NB, RF, SVM, GB, AdaB, XGB, MLP, and LR were used to classify different subtype groups following 10-fold cross-validation. In this case, all these classifiers were implemented using scikit-learn library. Finally, LIME was utilized to interpret discriminatory factors for classifying diabetes subtypes employing lime library.

In Fig. 2, we notice the silhouette score for different k-values (ranging from 2 to 10) in both PIDD and SDHD. We obtained the best score (0.15 and 0.53) with k = 2 and identified two subtypes from both datasets (see Fig. 2b and 2a). Therefore, we generated two diabetes subtypes (i.e., Subtype-1 and Subtype-2) of PIDD and SDHD for considering k = 2 best silhouette score.

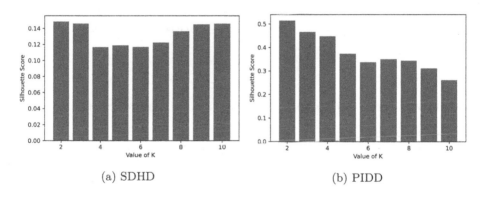

(a) SDHD   (b) PIDD

Fig. 2. Silhouette scores for individual clusters at various K values.

3.1 Performance of Individual Classifiers

Table 2 shows the experimental results of different classifiers for primary and its balanced subtype datasets (i.e., ROS subtypes, SMOTE subtypes) of PIDD. We used several evaluation metrices like Accuracy, F1-Score and AUROC to justify our findings. All classifiers were generated their results above 90%. In PIDD subtypes, RF outperformed other classifiers with respect to accuracy (99.63%), F1-Score (99.63%) and AUROC (99.98%). Again, this classifier achieved the highest accuracy (99.31%) and XGB gave the best F1-Score (99.33%) for ROS subtypes of PIDD. In addition, RF, SVM and LR provided 100% AUROC for these subtypes. Besides, DT, RF, and AdaB represented the maximum accuracy (99.66%) and F1-Score (99.66%) for SMOTE subtypes of PIDD. In the same subtypes, RF and LR showed the highest AUROC (100.00%) to detect diabetes. Above these results, we observed that RF was the most stable classifier to detect different subtypes of diabetes. In addition, DT, GB, XGB, and LR provided almost close results to RF. On the other hand, different classifiers gave better results for balanced subtypes (specially for SMOTE subtypes).

Table 2. Experimental Results for PIDD Subtypes and its Balanced Subtypes

Classifiers	PIDD Subtypes			ROS Subtypes			SMOTE Subtypes		
	Accuracy	F1-Score	AUROC	Accuracy	F1-Score	AUROC	Accuracy	F1-Score	AUROC
DT	99.26	99.26	99.29	99.29	99.29	99.29	**99.66**	**99.66**	99.67
KNN	96.30	96.44	99.81	97.86	97.91	99.77	98.62	98.60	99.95
NB	95.19	95.19	99.67	95.71	95.71	99.80	93.15	93.15	99.01
RF	99.63	99.63	99.98	99.31	99.31	**100.00**	**99.66**	**99.66**	**100.00**
SVM	97.04	96.98	99.77	96.06	96.36	**100.00**	98.97	98.99	99.95
GB	99.26	99.26	99.56	99.29	98.21	99.48	99.64	99.63	99.64
AdaB	98.89	98.89	99.29	99.29	98.21	99.29	99.64	99.63	99.67
XGB	99.26	99.26	99.29	99.29	99.33	99.29	**99.66**	**99.66**	99.67
MLP	97.78	97.41	99.95	98.21	98.21	99.90	98.20	98.20	99.95
LR	98.15	98.15	99.95	98.93	98.93	**100.00**	99.29	99.28	**100.00**

Table 3. Experimental Results for SDHD Subtypes and its Balanced Subtypes

Classifiers	SDHD Subtypes			ROS Subtypes			SMOTE Subtypes		
	Accuracy	F1-Score	AUROC	Accuracy	F1-Score	AUROC	Accuracy	F1-Score	AUROC
DT	94.38	91.72	94.54	96.44	96.67	96.67	97.91	98.59	98.61
KNN	95.63	92.73	95.85	93.78	93.74	97.54	95.81	95.91	98.17
NB	90.63	86.64	97.85	93.78	94.20	99.11	93.02	93.13	97.00
RF	97.5	94.90	99.39	98.44	98.29	99.45	97.44	97.97	99.74
SVM	66.56	66.56	99.87	61.11	61.11	99.94	86.25	86.25	99.47
GB	96.88	95.06	99.05	97.56	97.58	99.53	97.67	97.73	99.65
AdaB	98.13	96.81	98.55	98.00	97.98	99.36	97.91	97.91	99.07
XGB	97.19	95.42	98.82	97.78	97.73	99.42	98.14	98.18	99.55
MLP	80.31	82.19	92.78	94.00	95.56	99.66	96.51	95.58	98.92
LR	99.06	98.95	99.07	**99.56**	**99.56**	**99.96**	97.44	97.44	99.63

Then, Table 3 shows the outcomes of individual classifiers for primary and its balanced subtype datasets (i.e., ROS dataset, SMOTE dataset) of SDHD. In primary SDHD subtypes, LR outperformed other classifiers with respect to accuracy (99.06%) and F1-Score (98.95%). Besides, SVM gave the highest AUROC (99.87%) in the same subtypes. In case of ROS subtypes for SDHD, LR achieved highest accuracy (99.56%), F1-Score (99.56%), and AUROC (99.96%). Again, XGB generated the best accuracy (98.14%) and DT provided the maximum F1-Score (98.59%) for SMOTE subtypes of SDHD. However, RF showed the highest AUROC (99.74%) in the same subtypes. Finally, it is observable that LR provided the highest accuracy (99.56%), F1-Score (99.56%) and AUROC (99.96%) for ROS subtypes. However, all classifiers are also provided better outcomes in balanced subtypes than primary subtypes of SDHD.

3.2 Interpretation of Discriminatory Factors

We applied LIME on both PIDD and SDHD subtypes with their best performing classifiers. In this work, this method is used to identify features for which various classifiers were achieved best results. In addition, we determined several discriminatory factors within individual subtypes (see Fig. 3 and 4). Different positive coefficients against features were used to provide positive impact on classifying their subtypes. On the other hand, negative coefficients are denied the impact of features in classification.

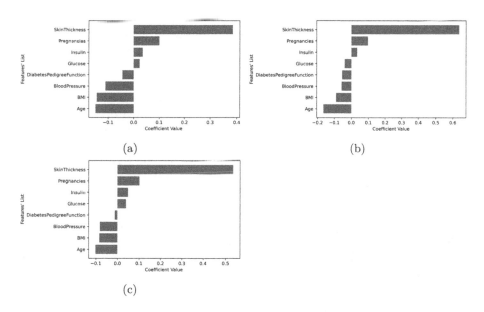

Fig. 3. LIME Coefficient Analysis using best performing RF classifier for (a) PIDD, its balanced (b) ROS, and (c) SMOTE dataset

In Fig. 3, we find different features in the same order for primary, ROS and SMOTE subtype datasets of PIDD. SkinThickness (Triceps skin-fold thickness) was the most important feature to distinguish two subtypes. In this case, SkinThickness less than 50 (mm) was indicated as most common features in Subtype-1. Besides, SkinThickness more than 50 (mm) to 99 (mm) was denoted

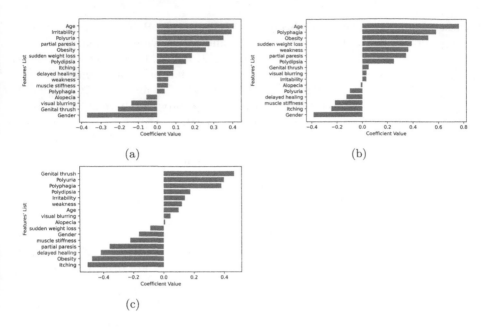

Fig. 4. LIME Coefficient Analysis using best performing LR classifier for (a) primary, (b) ROS, and (c) SMOTE generated Diabetes subtypes for SDHD Dataset.

as most general feature in Subtype-2. Then, pregnancies (Number of times pregnant) is considered as the second most important discriminatory factor in this work. Again, the number of pregnancy less than 8 was most common factor in Subtype-1. In addition, the number of pregnancy more than 8 to 17 was most common in Subtype-2. Then, Insulin (2-h serum insulin (mu U/ml)) and Glucose (Plasma glucose concentration 2 h in an oral glucose tolerance test) were found as the next important discriminatory features. In PIDD subtypes, we did not include Glucose as a discriminatory feature here. In this case, the Insulin levels less than 290 (mu U/ml) was found as the mostly notable factor in Subtype-1. For ROS subtypes of PIDD, Insulin levels more than 290 (mu U/ml) to 846 (mu U/ml) was considered as the mostly visible factor in Subtype-2. Again, Age is considered as the least impact factor to discriminating individual subtypes.

In Fig. 4, we observed some differences in discriminatory features for primary, ROS and SMOTE subtype dataset of SDHD. In this case, 'Age' is the most important feature found in primary SDHD subtypes and ROS subtypes. However, 'Age' is also considered as a discriminatory factor in SMOTE dataset of SDHD. Besides, it is found as less importance for SMOTE dataset. For SDHD subtypes and its oversampled subtype datasets, the range of ages from 16 to 45 was represented as common feature for Subtype-2. Instead, ages greater than 45 to 90 was esteemed as the general feature for Subtype-1. For both ROS and SMOTE subtypes, 'Genital thrush' was referred to as an important feature though it is not an important feature for SDHD subtypes. Also, it was the most important discriminating factor for SMOTE subtypes. Further, patients with no "Genital thrush" was categorized as Subtype-1 and patients having "Genital thrush" was categorized as Subtype-2. In the analysis of other features, we found some significant features in all of these subtypes such as 'Irritability', 'Polydipsia', 'weakness', and 'Polyphagia'. On the other hand, 'Gender' and 'Alopecia' are considered as some least important features. However, 'partial paresis', 'obesity', and 'sudden weight loss' are the most significant discriminatory factor for SDHD subtypes and ROS subtypes. Also, 'delayed healing', 'Itching', and 'muscle stiffness' are found as the most discriminatory factors for SDHD subtypes to identify diabetes subtypes.

Many works were happened on PIDD and SDHD to identify diabetes at early stage [11,13,14]. Along with historical records investigation, many medical images and clinical samples were continuously used to know about this disease. In the field of artificial intelligence, [6,16,18] were used to investigate the best way to detect diabetes and ensure proper treatment policy more precisely. Different researchers were tried to enrich their models by improving classification accuracy to identify proper cases. However, diabetes is a metabolic disease that does not happened in a single ways. Individual subtypes of diabetes are expressed different characteristics of diabetes more precisely. Also, they are helpful to identify proper treatments because of their specific symptoms and discriminatory factors. Besides, they are required to deeply understand type-2 diabetes. However, most of the existing works did not consider this issues properly. And so, a comparative analysis with the existing work based on classification performance was not rational to include here.

4   Conclusion and Future Work

In this work, we gathered diabetes records from PIDD and SDHD and generated significant number of subtypes using clustering technique. Then, these subtypes were balanced and applied different classifiers to identify which subtypes are better. In PIDD, RF provided the highest 99.66% accuracy for SMOTE subtypes. On the other hand, LR showed the best 99.56% accuracy for ROS subtypes for SDHD. Then, different features were visualized to identify discriminatory factors of the subtypes. The rapid identification of diabetes is useful to prepare proper treatment plans for preventing serious effects of this disease. This work can be used as a complementary tool to diagnosis diabetes effectively. However, PIDD and SDHD are not contained more diabetes instances to investigate about this disease. In future work, we will investigate instances from multiple diabetes databases and integrate more advanced techniques to get better insights for conducting this disease.

References

1. Akter, T., et al.: Improved transfer-learning-based facial recognition framework to detect autistic children at an early stage. Brain Sci. 11(6), 734 (2021)

2. Akter, T., Ali, M.H., Satu, M.S., Khan, M.I., Mahmud, M.: Towards autism sub-type detection through identification of discriminatory factors using machine learning. In: Mahmud, M., Kaiser, M.S., Vassanelli, S., Dai, Q., Zhong, N. (eds.) BI 2021. LNCS (LNAI), vol. 12960, pp. 401–410. Springer, Cham (2021). https://doi.org/10.1007/978-3-030-86993-9_36

3. American Diabetes Association: Diagnosis and classification of diabetes mellitus. Diab. Care **32**(Supplement_1), S62–S67 (2009)

4. Bala, M., Ali, M.H., Satu, M.S., Hasan, K.F., Moni, M.A.: Efficient machine learning models for early stage detection of autism spectrum disorder. Algorithms **15**(5), 166 (2022)

5. Fazakis, N., Kocsis, O., Dritsas, E., Alexiou, S., Fakotakis, N., Moustakas, K.: Machine learning tools for long-term type 2 diabetes risk prediction. IEEE Access **9**, 103737–103757 (2021)

6. Hasan, M.K., Alam, M.A., Das, D., Hossain, E., Hasan, M.: Diabetes prediction using ensembling of different machine learning classifiers. IEEE Access **8**, 76516–76531 (2020)

7. Howlader, K.C., et al.: Machine learning models for classification and identification of significant attributes to detect type 2 diabetes. Health Inf. Sci. Syst. **10**(1), 1–13 (2022)

8. Islam, M.M.F., Ferdousi, R., Rahman, S., Bushra, H.Y.: Likelihood prediction of diabetes at early stage using data mining techniques. In: Gupta, M., Konar, D., Bhattacharyya, S., Biswas, S. (eds.) Computer Vision and Machine Intelligence in Medical Image Analysis. AISC, vol. 992, pp. 113–125. Springer, Singapore (2020). https://doi.org/10.1007/978-981-13-8798-2_12

9. Klass, L.: Machine learning-definition and application examples. Spotlight Metal (2018)

10. Krishnan, R., et al.: Early detection of diabetes from health claims. In: Machine Learning in Healthcare Workshop, NIPS, pp. 1–5 (2013)

11. Malik, Sumbal, Harous, Saad, El-Sayed, Hesham: Comparative Analysis of Machine Learning Algorithms for Early Prediction of Diabetes Mellitus in Women. In: Chikhi, Salim, Amine, Abdelmalek, Chaoui, Allaoua, Saidouni, Djamel Eddine, Kholladi, Mohamed Khireddine (eds.) MISC 2020. LNNS, vol. 156, pp. 95–106. Springer, Cham (2021). https://doi.org/10.1007/978-3-030-58861-8_7

12. Mujumdar, A., Vaidehi, V.: Diabetes prediction using machine learning algorithms. Procedia Comput. Sci. **165**, 292–299 (2019). https://doi.org/10.1016/j.procs.2020.01.047, https://www.sciencedirect.com/science/article/pii/S1877050920300557

13. Patel, S., et al.: Predicting a risk of diabetes at early stage using machine learning approach. Turk. J. Comput. Math. Educ. (TURCOMAT) **12**(10), 5277–5284 (2021)

14. Reddy, D.J., et al.: Predictive machine learning model for early detection and analysis of diabetes. Mater. Today: Proc. (2020)

15. Ribeiro, M.T., Singh, S., Guestrin, C.: "Why should i trust you?": explaining the predictions of any classifier. In: Proceedings of the 22nd ACM SIGKDD International Conference on Knowledge Discovery and Data Mining, pp. 1135–1144. KDD 2016, Association for Computing Machinery, New York, USA (2016). https://doi.org/10.1145/2939672.2939778

16. Rony, M.A.T., Satu, M.S., Whaiduzzaman, M., et al.: Mining significant features of diabetes through employing various classification methods. In: 2021 International Conference on Information and Communication Technology for Sustainable Development (ICICT4SD), pp. 240–244. IEEE (2021)

17. Satu, M.S.: COVID-hero: machine learning based COVID-19 awareness enhancement mobile game for children. In: Mahmud, M., Kaiser, M.S., Kasabov, N., Iftekharuddin, K., Zhong, N. (eds.) AII 2021. CCIS, vol. 1435, pp. 321–335. Springer, Cham (2021). https://doi.org/10.1007/978-3-030-82269-9_25

18. Shahriare Satu, M., Atik, S.T., Moni, M.A.: A novel hybrid machine learning model to predict diabetes mellitus. In: Uddin, M.S., Bansal, J.C. (eds.) Proceedings of International Joint Conference on Computational Intelligence. AIS, pp. 453–465. Springer, Singapore (2020). https://doi.org/10.1007/978-981-15-3607-6_36

19. Satu, M.S., et al.: TClustVID: a novel machine learning classification model to investigate topics and sentiment in COVID-19 tweets. Knowl. Based Syst. **226**, 107126 (2021)

20. Shutaywi, M., Kachouie, N.N.: Silhouette analysis for performance evaluation in machine learning with applications to clustering. Entropy **23**(6), 759 (2021)

21. Sinaga, K.P., Yang, M.S.: Unsupervised k-means clustering algorithm. IEEE Access **8**, 80716–80727 (2020)

22. Smith, J.W., Everhart, J.E., Dickson, W., Knowler, W.C., Johannes, R.S.: Using the ADAP learning algorithm to forecast the onset of diabetes mellitus. In: Proceedings of the Annual Symposium on Computer Application in Medical Care, p. 261. American Medical Informatics Association (1988)

Analysis of Hand Movement from Surface EMG Signals Using Artificial Neural Network

S. A. Ahsan Rajon(✉), Mahmudul Hasan Abid, Niloy Sikder, Kamrul Hasan Talukder, Md. Mizanur Rahman, Md. Shamim Ahsan, Abu Shamim Mohammad Arif, and Abdullah-Al Nahid

Khulna University, Khulna-9208, Bangladesh
ahsan.rajon@gmail.com

Abstract. Fatal accidents are an inseparable part of life which often costs us loss of limbs especially hands and legs and turns any of our body asset into a burden to the family, as well as the society. The only solution to such misfortune is to facilitate the human with a new taste of living a happy life by having an artificial arm or leg that would be functional enough to have the everyday life activities smoother. The only way to make any artificial organ functional is to mimic its working from the remaining part of the organ or from the other similar organ more efficiently which is achieved by successfully and more intelligently extracting the features from biomedical signals especially from electromyogram (EMG) signals. This paper analyzes and detects various hand movements from surface EMG signals for six classes using a state-of-the-art Machine Learning scheme. This paper also presents an overview of the contemporary research on hand movement detection using EMG signals. The main contribution of this paper is the application of Convolutional Neural Network (CNN) in selection of the features from EMG signals along with some data preprocessing schemes including Fast Fourier Transform (FFT). The proposed approach has been applied to the available EMG dataset and demonstrates better accuracy along with computational simplicity than most existing schemes.

Keywords: Hand Movement Detection · Prosthesis · Feature Selection · Convolutional Neural Network · Deep Learning

1 Introduction

The craving for living a normal life for any person who has lost a hand or leg due to any accident or illness is the use of artificial limbs. Even though an artificial hand or leg can never be as perfect as that of the real limb, technology is dedicated to turn the leg or hand to the best function possible. These prosthetic devices recognize the movement intentions through the electrical activity of the muscles from the remaining arm or leg using surface biomedical signals. The recognized activity is then communicated to the prosthetic hand/leg which may function on the basis of the communicated command. An intelligent interface performs this recognition and manipulation from muscle activity to prosthetic activity performance which varies because of several potent body factors.

The most undeniable truth is to get older and thus often the fate turns into becoming paralyzed because of stroke or other complexities. In such touching situations, the solution resides in mimicking the movements from opposite limbs to the disabled limbs. For these purposes it is crucial to identify the desired movement exactly. Surface EMG signals are widely used in analyzing the electrical activity of various organs of the human body. Different movement produces different patterns of EMG signals which can be differentiated, identified and consequently applied to the interface between the human body and prosthetic organs or even to robotic limbs.

A number of available researchers are focusing on the feature detection and analysis of human motion, especially aimed at replicating the actions of disabled people. In [1], authors investigated two dynamic factors (within orientation and between orientations) of EMG pattern recognition, where they employed twelve intact-limbed along with one bilateral trans-radial (below-elbow) amputee. Here they have considered six classes. They utilized wavelet transform based features, time domain features, Discrete Fourier Transform based features, Time Domain Power Spectral Descriptors etc. for feature extraction while a Support Vector Machine (SVM) classifier was used to classify the data. In [2], a set of ECG signals has been classified using machine learning in algorithm along with the feature selections. Partitioning data based on event-related synchronization and movement-related cortical potential features and then applying Independent Component Analysis spatial filter with Automatic Artifact Removal and Rhythm Isolation constituted feature vector construction was applied in [2]. Umut and Centik [3] utilized a set of machine learning algorithms along with digital signal processing techniques to classify periodic leg movement. They also found that Multilayer Perceptron Algorithm provides 91.87% accuracy on an average. Conventional Machine Learning techniques have solved numerous problems. However they are largely dependent on hand-crafted features. In [4] Alex et al. proposed a convolutional neural network in a novel way to solve natural image classification problems. Recently, this method has also been utilized in many fields including [5].

In [6] Phinyomark, Khushaba and Scheme evaluated Classification of hand and finger movements of both physically fit and amputee subjects with 26 discriminating features and 08 groups of combined features and recommended 2 novel sets of EMG features.

Naik et al. [7] applied independent component analysis to separate muscle activity from different muscles and classified using backpropagation neural networks with 3 inputs and 4 outputs for three types of hand gestures. Most of these schemes are computationally complex and thus often real time implementation suffers.

A summary of prominent researches on hand movement recognition has been presented in Table 1. In the table, a comparison on the methods and applied and type of subject classification for hand movement analysis has been incorporated.

This paper analyzes and detects various hand movements from surface EMG signals for six classes using a state-of-the-art Machine Learning scheme. This paper also presents an overview of the contemporary research on hand movement detection using EMG signals. The main contribution of this paper is the application of Convolutional Neural Network (CNN) in selection of the features from EMG signals along with data preprocessing schemes including Fast Fourier Transform (FFT).

Table 1. Summary of researches on hand movement recognition

Authors	Ref	Year	Average accuracy rates	Subject Classification		Methods										Remarks
				Single	Multi	Wavelet transform	PCA	Self-organizing feature map	Multilayer perceptron	correlation features	LDA classifier	ANN	SVM	KNN	Deep learning	
Chu et al.	[8]	2006	96.5	✓		✓	✓	✓	✓							Multilayer perceptron
Tang et al.	[9]	2012	89%	✓						✓	✓					
Sapsanis et al.	[10]	2013	85%	✓			✓									Relief algorithm
Isakovic et al.	[11]	2014	62.76%	✓			✓									piecewise quadratic classifier
Mane et al.	[12]	2015	93%	✓		✓						✓				
Ruangpaisarn and Jaiyen	[13]	2015	94.64%	✓									✓	✓		Singular value decomposition
Atzori et al.	[14]	2016	86.10%	✓								✓	✓		✓	
Angari et al.	[15]	2016	94%	✓						✓			✓			
Gu et al.	[16]	2017	81.36%	✓			✓					✓				AdaBoost with Linear discriminant Analysis, Random Forest
Martinez et al.	[17]	2019	91.98%	✓					✓				✓			Autoregressive model
Tsinganos et al.	[18]	2018	71.24		✓										✓	Decision trees
Jafarzadeh et al.	[19]	2019	91.26%		✓	✓						✓			✓	Uses raw EMG signals
Côté et al.	[20]	2019	83.64%		✓										✓	
Rabin et al.	[21]	2020	84.12%	✓	✓		✓								✓	Uses DM

The paper is organized into four sections. In this section, the implication of the research along with a brief overview of the recent research has been presented. Section 2 presents an overview of the methodology including preprocessing techniques and utilization of the Deep Neural Network based classifier model. Section 3 describes various aspects of our research findings based on different performance measurement criteria and at last, the paper is concluded in Sect. 4.

2 Methodology

This experiment performs classification of hand movement based on supervised manner. The overall methodology of the experiment has been illustrated in Fig. 1. In general, after appropriate preprocessing, the entire dataset is split into learning and testing datasets. The most crucial part includes finding out the appropriate and best features for classifying the data with best accuracy efficiently. After hyper-model tuning, data is fed to model fit which also grabs the testing data. Performance is evaluated based on the model classification accuracy.

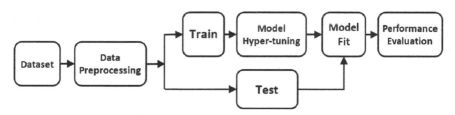

Fig. 1. Steps of applied framework

The dataset used in the research is obtained from [10, 22]. The line interface were eliminated in the dataset by applying a Butterworth band-pass filter considering low and high cutoff at 15 Hz respectively along with a notch filter at 50 Hz [10, 22]. The dataset used in the proposed system contains 5000 attributes. The six classes considered includes: a) Spherical (used to hold spherical objects, b) Tip (holding small objects) c) Palmar (grasping with palm facing the object), d) Lateral (holding flat, thin objects, e) Cylindrical (holding cylindrical objects and f) Hook (supporting a heavy object) [10, 22]. The frequency of each class of this dataset has been presented through the following pie chart presented in Fig. 2. This figure shows that all the classes contain similar amount of sample which indicates the dataset is balanced.

The obtained dataset is used for both training and testing in part. However, new information domain has been formed using the time domain original signal and its frequency domain variant. Finally, this time domain and frequency domain signal has been converted into feature image. To extract frequency domain information Fast Fourier Transform (FFT) has been applied on the original time domain signal.

Fourier Transformation (FT) is a well-known tool to extract frequency spectrums from corresponding time domain signal. An FT can extract frequency-domain information from both the periodic and non-periodic signals in continuous or discrete time.

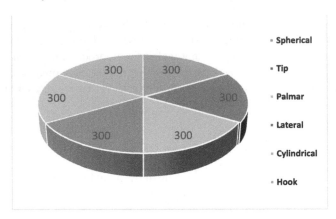

Fig. 2. Statistical distribution of utilized dataset

A periodic signal can be represented as a summation of many sinusoidal signals with corresponding amplitude and phase [23]. The basic operation of the FT involves finding the specific frequencies that carry the most information of the time-domain signal and representing it over a range of frequencies. The process highlights certain frequencies that are containing relevant information along with those caused by noise, giving us a clear visualization on which frequencies to focus on and which to filter out. The resultant frequency-domain signal can be reverted back to the time domain by performing an Inverse Fourier Transform (IFT). By using FT, a complex signal structure can be decomposed into simpler parts very easily to facilitate further analysis. There are multiple variants of FT, two of the most used methods are Discrete Fourier Transform (DFT) and Fast FFT. The DFT operates by expanding a periodic signal into a series of sine and cosine waves of distinct frequencies known as a Discrete Fourier Series (DFS). A periodic signal $\tilde{x}(p)$ with a period P can be defined as

$$\tilde{x}(p) = \tilde{x}(p + mP) \tag{1}$$

where $m = 1, 2, \ldots, N$

Now, the DFS of (1) can be written as

$$\tilde{X}(p) = \sum_{p=0}^{P-1} \tilde{x}(p) W_P^{mp} \tag{2}$$

here $\tilde{X}(p)$ is a periodic signal having period P in the frequency domain and W_P^{mp} is the Twiddle Factor. Using DFT the frequency spectrum of (2) can be defined as

$$X(p) = \sum_{p=0}^{P-1} x[p] \times e^{\frac{-2\pi m}{P} pi} \tag{3}$$

[24]. The execution time, complexity and processing power required to execute a program heavily depend on the number of multiplications involved in the operation. The

basic algorithm of the DFT requires P^2 multiplications to perform an FT on a signal, whereas FFT requires only $Plog_2(P)$. FFT reduces the number of multiplications by separating the even and odd samples of the series before performing the DFT operation and using the symmetric properties of the Twiddle Factor. From (3), the FFT of the signal $\tilde{x}(p)$ can be written as

$$X(p) = \sum_{p=0}^{P-1} x[2p] \times e^{\frac{-\pi m}{P}pi} + \sum_{p=0}^{P-1} x[2p+1] \times e^{\frac{-\pi m}{P}pi} \qquad (4)$$

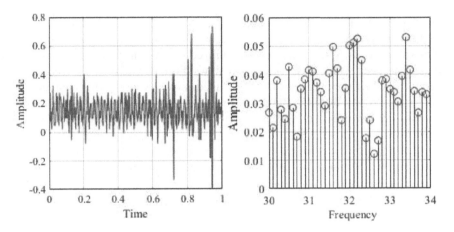

Fig. 3. (a) Original Signal and (b) frequency domain representation.

In Fig. 3(a) shows the original EMG signal in time domain Fig. 3(b) represents the frequency domain representation of the signal.

2.1 Classifier Model

For the classification purposes, the study utilized a DNN approach specifically promising Convolutional Neural network (CNN). Conventional classifier generally depends on the handcrafted local feature set. The outcome of this kind of classifier model largely depends on judicial selection of the features. However, CNN model scratch out the local features from the available data in a global nature. This feature sets are collected utilizing a mathematical tool named as kernel. A kernel is basically a m × n matrix which is convolved with the original data. The value of the kernels are selected using a particular distribution. Zero-padding techniques are utilized to overcome the border effect. Pooling operation has been operated for down sampling (Fig. 4).

In the above model, the original feature image is scanned utilizing a kernel of size 3 × 3. Here, 32 channels are produced in first layer which provide an output of 32 channels. After the first layer kernel of similar size is again utilized to produce second layer of 32 channels and third layer with 64 channels. Too many features might over-trained a

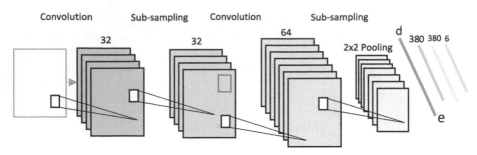

Fig. 4. Proposed Workflow

model. After the third layer, pooling operation has been performed with a kernel of size 2 × 2. After this layer, consecutively a few dense layers have been utilized. As this model performs as a classifier, the last dense layer utilized six neurons with softmax activation function. This layer with softmax activation allows this model to work as a conventional classifier. To reduce the overall loss, the output errors are propagated to the initial layer utilizing back-propagation algorithm. To find the appropriate weight and bias values, an Adam optimization algorithm has been utilized. The overall model is hyper-tuned up-to 100 epochs.

The last layer (f) is considered as classification layer as it consists softmax activation function. By the convention of CNN, the (f-1) layer will also be a dense layer. Consider x_l^{f-1} layer be the output of each neuron of layer $(f-1)$ where $l \in \{1, \ldots \ldots \ldots, k\}$, here $k = 360$. Then, the weight and bias function of softmax layer can be represented as

$$x_p^f = w^f * x_l^{f-1} + b^f, \text{ where, } l \in \{1, 2, \ldots \ldots \ldots, 6\}.$$

The last layer of a CNN model can be represented as,

$$S_p = \frac{e^{x_p^f}}{(e^{x_1^f} + e^{x_2^f} + \ldots \ldots \ldots \ldots + e^{x_6^f})}$$

Utilizing the above equation, a loss value of the overall model is calculated by the following equation

$$L_p = -\ln(S_p)$$

Finally, the predicted class is calculated as

$$P = arg \ min(L_p)$$

3   Results and Discussions

Confusion matrix presents a two dimensional visualization which demonstrates the performance of a classifier. A confusion matrix whose diagonal element shows the maximum value with all other non-diagonal elements as zero resembles the best performance out of any classifier. From the confusion matrix in Fig. 5, we see that the best classification is achieved for Tip classes with an accuracy of 93% while for the palmar class it was misclassified as lateral for 16 percent cases yielding 67% accuracy for the worst classification. The cylindrical, spherical and hook classification possess approximately 89%, 80% and 78% respectively. The confusion matrix also shows that, among the 6 classes, only 61 confusion did arise, which definitely resembles better performance in terms of complexity and time.

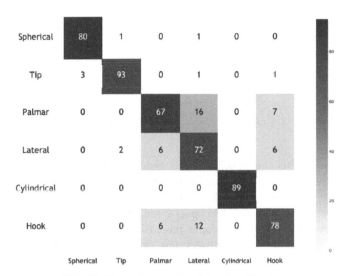

Fig. 5. Confusion matrix of the classification

The performance of the Confusion Matrix is also verified by a t-SNE graph presented in Fig. 6. t-SNE is a dimension reduction technique mostly used for data visualization of large dimensional data. The two dimensional t-SNE information of the dataset used has been presented in Fig. 6. The pink color used in Fig. 6 represents the Hook class, which is mostly concentrated into the center. With a few exceptions, most of the sphere class (Red) is placed at the outermost region. Most typically distributed information includes the Palm class as indicated by the blue color.

From Fig. 7(a) it is evident that proposed scheme achieves a training accuracy very close to 100% after nearly 30 epochs. Starting with uprising accuracy, the testing reaches a nearly steady state of 95% after 30 epochs. That is, after training for 35 epochs the model approaches, while for the testing it shows a minimum loss for 10 to 35 epochs and the outcome deteriorates slowly afterwards. Since the performance of the test accuracy doesn't exceed the training accuracy, the system is over trained. F-Measure is a variant of accuracy measurement which considers both the precision and recall scores. Figure 7(c) shows that the training F measure reaches to maximum (100%) while the test F measure varies from 70 to 80. It is also interesting that, after nearly 30 epochs, both the train and test F measure maintain a constant difference between them. The Matthews Correlation Coefficient (MCC) is a performance metric which is bounded into a region of −1 to 1. After nearly 30 epochs the test MCC curve for the training score reaches 1 while

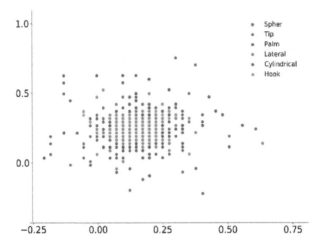

Fig. 6. T-SNE plot of the classification (Color figure online)

the test MCC measure is almost 0.7 after the same number of epochs. It is noteworthy that none of the values is subzero found in the study as shown in the bottom left image of Fig. 7(d). The Kullback-Leibler divergence is another loss measurement parameter. Figure 7(e) shows that after around 35 epochs, the KLL value for train scheme touches almost 0. However, the test KLL value is increasing for the Test scheme resulting an increase in an increase in the gap between test and train KLL value. The topmost left point of the ROC curve represents that the classifier is perfect. The ROC curve of our proposed scheme presented in Fig. 7(f) is close to the topmost point.

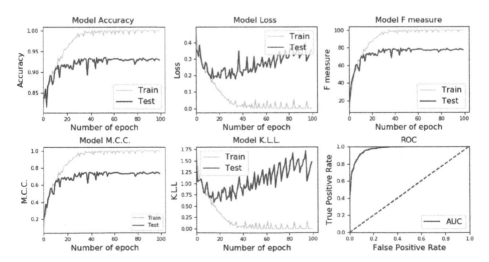

Fig. 7. Performance analysis of proposed scheme

4 Conclusion

This research aims to classify and analyze the hand movement activity with an aim to identify the specific patterns using surface electromyogram signals. In order to attain accuracy in identification and analysis hybridization of state-of-art methodologies have been applied based on machine learning. Focusing on Fast Fourier Transform in pre-processing of the data, for classifying the six classes in consideration, the Convolutional Neural Network has been used. Experimental results show that, proposed system provides reasonably good performance. Future works may be dedicated to finding the optimal set of pre-processing and classification schemes and finding a better feature set.

References

1. Khushaba, R.N., Al-Timemy, A., Kodagoda, S., Nazarpour, K.: Combined influence of fore-arm orientation and muscular contraction on EMG pattern recognition. Expert Syst. Appl. 154–161 (2016)
2. Alomari, M.H., Samaha, A., Al Kamha, K.: Automated classification of L/R hand movement EEG signals using advanced feature extraction and machine learning. (IJACSA) Int. J. Adv. Comput. Sci. Appl. 4(6) (2013)
3. Umut, E., Çentik, G.: Detection of periodic leg movements by machine learning methods using polysomnographic parameters other than leg electromyography. Hindawi Publishing Corporation, Computational and Mathematical Methods in Medicine (2016)
4. Zhai, X., Jelfs, B., Chan, R.: Tin C. Self-Recalibrating Surface EMG Pattern Recognition for Neuroprosthesis Control Based on Convolutional Neural Network. Front. Neurosci. (2017)
5. Hu, Y., Wong, Y., Wei, W., Du, Y., Kankanhalli, M.: A novel attention-based hybrid CNN-RNN architecture for sEMG-based gesture recognition. PLOS ONE (2018)
6. Phinyomark, A., Khushaba, R.N., Scheme, E.: Feature extraction and selection for myoelectric control based on wearable EMG sensors. Sensors (2018)
7. Naik, G., Kant Kumar, R.D., Pal Singh, V., Palaniswami, M.: Hand gestures for HCI using ICA of EMG, HCSNet (2006)
8. Chu, J.U., Moon, I., Mun, M.S.: A real-time EMG pattern recognition system based on linear-nonlinear feature projection for a multifunction myoelectric. IEEE Trans. Biomed. Eng. (2006)
9. Tang, X., Liu, Y., Lv, C., Sun, D.: Hand motion classification using a multi-channel surface electromyography sensor. Sensors (2012)
10. Sapsanis, C., Georgoulas, G., Tzes, A.: EMG based classification of basic hand. In: 2013 21st Mediterranean Conference (2013)
11. Isakovic, M.S., Miljkovic, N., Popovic, M.B.: Classifying sEMG-based hand. In: 2014 22nd Telecommunications Forum Telfor (TELFOR) (2014)
12. Mane, S.M., Kambli, R.A., Kazi, F.S., Singh, N.M.: Hand motion recognition from single channel surface EMG using wavelet artificial neural network. Procedia Comput. Sci. (2015)
13. Ruangpaisarn, Y., Jaiyen, S.: SEMG signal classification using SMO algorithm. In: 7th International Conference on Information Technology and Electrical Engineering (ICITEE) (2015)
14. Atzori, M., Cognolato, M., Müller, H.: Deep learning with convolutional neural networks applied to electromyography data: a resource for the classification of movements for prosthetic hands. Front. Neurorobot. 10, 9 (2016)

15. Al-Angari, H.M., Kanitz, G., Tarantino, S., Cipriani, C.: Distance and mutual information methods for EMG feature and channel subset selection for classification of hand movements. Biomed. Signal Process. Control (2016)
16. Gu, Z., Zhang, K., Zhao, W., Luo, Y.: Multi-Class classification for basic hand movements. Technical Report (2017)
17. Ramírez-Martínez, D., Alfaro-Ponce, M., Pogrebnyak, O., Aldape-Pérez, M., Argüelles-Cruz, A.J.: Hand movement classification using burg reflection coefficients. Sensors (2019)
18. Tsinganos, P., Cornelis, B., Cornelis, J., Jansen, B., Skodras, A.: Deep learning in EMG-based gesture recognition. PhyCS (2018)
19. Jafarzadeh, M., Hussey, D., Tadesse, Y.: Deep learning approach to control of prosthetic hands with electromyography signals. In: 2019 IEEE International Symposium on Measurement and Control in Robotics (ISMCR). Houston, Texas, USA (2019)
20. Côté-Allard, U., Fall, C.L., Drouin, A., Campeau-Lecours, A., Gosselin, C., Glette, K.: Deep learning for electromyographic hand gesture signal classification using transfer learning. IEEE Trans. Neural Syst. Rehab. Eng. (2019)
21. Rabin, N., Kahlon, M., Malayev, S., Ratnovsky, A.: Classification of human hand movements based on EMG signals using nonlinear dimensionality reduction and data fusion techniques. Expert Syst. Appl. (2020)
22. Sapsanis, C., Georgoulas, G., Tzes, A., Lymberopoulos, A.: Improving EMG based classification of basic hand movements using EMD. In: 35th Annual International Conference of the IEEE Engineering in Medicine and Biology Society 13 (EMBC 13) (2013)
23. Huang, W., MacFarlane, D.L.: Fast Fourier Transform and MATLAB Implementation. The University of Texas at Dallas. Dr. Duncan L, MacFarlane (2006)
24. Sikder, N., Nahid, B.A., Islam, M.M.M.: Fault Diagnosis of Motor Bearing Using Ensemble Learning Algorithm with FFT-based Preprocessing (2019)
25. Sapsanis, C., Georgoulas, G., Tzes, A.: EMG based classification of basic hand movements based on time-frequency features. In: 21th IEEE Mediterranean Conference on Control and Automation (MED 13), June 25–28, pp. 716–722 (2013)
26. Larraz, E.L., Birbaumer, N., Murguialday, A.R.: A hybrid EEG-EMG BMI improves the detection of movement intention in cortical stroke patients with complete hand paralysis. In: Annual International Conference of the IEEE Engineering in Medicine and Biology Society. IEEE Engineering in Medicine and Biology Society (2018)
27. Tigra, W., Navarro, B., Cherubini, A., Gorron, X., Gélis, A.: A novel EMG interface for individuals with tetraplegia to pilot robot hand grasping. In: IEEE Transactions on Neural Systems and Rehabilitation Engineering, Institute of Electrical and Electronics Engineers (2018)
28. Krizhevsky, A., Sutskever, I., Hinton, G.: Imagenet classification with deep convolutional neural networks. Adv. Neural Info. Process. Sys. (2012)

Design and Implementation of a Drowsiness Detection System Up to Extended Head Angle Using FaceMesh Machine Learning Solution

Jafirul Islam Jewel⬤, Md. Mahabub Hossain$^{(\boxtimes)}$ ⬤, and Md. Dulal Haque⬤

Department of Electronics and Communication Engineering, Hajee Mohammad Danesh Science and Technology University, Dinajpur, Bangladesh
im.mahabub@gmail.com

Abstract. Drowsiness of drivers is a severe problem for safe driving in Bangladesh. Drowsiness and fatigue are the major contributing causes of accidents on the road. In this paper, we proposed a design of a system to detect drowsiness of drivers up to an extend angle position of the head of the driver while driving, and notify them. The awakeness of the driver is also detected during driving mode. The range of the multiple angles of head position using FaceMesh machine learning solution have been shown for determining the detection drowsiness. Moreover, different positions of the face are calculated to detect the drowsiness of the driver with 97.5% accuracy in straight face position, as well as the response time of the system is calculated that is around 3 s. We have found out that our proposed system is less complex in design, low cost and performs better than related contemporary works.

Keywords: Drowsiness Detection · Awakeness Detection · FaceMesh Algorithm · Machine Learning · Safe Driving

1 Introduction

New technological innovations in the field of system automation and the internet of things (IoT) are in high demand for the solution of many fundamental issues in our daily lives for the ease and security of many people's life activities in various aspects [1–3]. On long-distance journeys, the driver's drowsiness is considered one of the major reasons for vehicle accidents. In particular, on long night journeys in our country, drivers are forced to drive for a long time restlessly. This results in the tiredness and drowsiness of drivers, ultimately causing serious accidents. In developed countries, drivers have driven vehicles for a long time, though they have their own slots for driving. As a consequence, drivers suffer from drowsiness, which causes unwanted situations [4, 5]. According to the Road Safety Foundation (RSF) findings, at least 6,284 people were died and 7,468 were bad wounded in road casualty in Bangladesh in 2021 [6]. The early detection of a driver's drowsiness may solution to avoid any possible road accident. Drowsy drivers exhibit many signs, such as repetitive yawning, repeatedly eye closure, and frequent changing

Md. S. Satu et al. (Eds.): MIET 2022, LNICST 491, pp. 79–90, 2023.
https://doi.org/10.1007/978-3-031-34622-4_7

the lanes of the street [7]. For developing countries like Bangladesh, there is a potential demand to develop a low-cost technology that can be used cost effectively for all kinds of people for the early detection of drowsiness of drivers. The early stage detection of drowsiness will prevent accidents significantly caused by it. The main goal is to develop a system that can observe the driver most accurately as well as efficiently during driving and can determine in real-time when the driver gets drowsy [8]. With the reading of facial expressions, eye blinking, and how they blink, a system model can be trained to determine whether the driver is sleeping or not. The technology uses an algorithm with a large amount of data for training [9]. With a lot of data about driver facial expressions, it gives the system an idea about different types of eyes and facial patterns, whether the driver gets drowsy or not, which is sufficient enough to avoid road accidents due to driver drowsiness [10]. Some researchers have attempted to address such concerns. Their methods perform well in their own way, but have several drawbacks. The major drawback is the failure to detect the driver's head positions at sufficient angles. Some of them only detect straight head angles, and their algorithms yield increased power costs.

In this paper,

- We have overcome these limitations by introducing a cost-effective design of a drowsiness detector to detect using the FaceMesh algorithm up to an extended angle position of the head of the driver while driving and notify them.
- The awakeness of the driver is also detected during driving mode with utilizing low power and fast response time compared to others.
- We design a less comples and low cost drowsiness detection system.

Some technical challenges are still exist in our proposed system. It is really challenging task to find out the drowsiness in night or the perfromance may be decrease in low light. Also, if the condition of the road is not good then the vibrator shows little less performance, but that is tolarable. Using IR or night vison camera may solve the first issue easily and driving on the good conditioned highways, vibration problem may be overcome significantly.

The rest of the paper is sectioned as follows: discussion on some of the relevant works is presented in Sect. 2. Section 3 represents the proposed design and methodology, Sect. 4 contains the outcome and discussion, and Sect. 5 depicts the conclusion and potentiality of the system.

2 Related Work

Much work has already been done in this field. Zhu et al. reported a convolution neural network (CNN) based wearable electroencephalographic (EEG) method for the detection of drowsiness in divers. They have implemented the warning method by collecting data from the wearable EEG. A neural network including inception module has a classification accuracy of 95.59%, while the AlexNet module has a classification accuracy of 94.68% [11]. Drowsiness detection using EEG is highly accurate, though it is intrusive. Although an eye-tracking-based approach to detection appears appealing, the system, which consists of a high-speed camera and a complex algorithm, is difficult to implement. Quddus et al. have proposed a method to use the eye images directly from the camera, omitting expensive eye tracking modules. A recurrent neural network (RNN) is utilized in their model to detect drowsiness. Two different approaches were introduced in their study. The first one is the R-LSTM-based approach, which gives 82% accuracy, and the second is the G-LSTM-based approach, which gives 97% accuracy [12]. A model consisting of four deep learning (DL) models—Alex Net, ResNet, VGG-Face Net, and Flow ImageNet—was proposed by Dua et al. Four different features were considered to find the drowsiness signs of the driver. Their model obtained the accuracy of around 85% in detecting the drowsiness of a subject [13]. Histogram of Oriented Gradient (HOG) features were introduced by Bakheet, S. et al. to implement a robust, compact model to detect the driver's drowsiness. This approach achieved a detection accuracy of 85% [14]. Salman et al. introduced Ensemble Convolutional Neural Networks to detect a driver's drowsiness. To train the detection model, eye blinking, nodding, and yawning were taken into account to train the detection model. For the dataset, YawDD was used. In their study, ECNN achieved an F1 score of 0.935 [15]. A comparison of early studies is shown in Table 1. Kundinger et al. designed a drowsiness detection model with smart wearables. This model processes the heart rate of the driver using an integrated machine learning classifier. The study is also applicable to modern day auto pilot driving systems. Authors have utilized physiological data which are collected from the wearable wrist devices for drowsiness detection. For older participants, this model showed superior results compared to younger participants. Summarizing the work, this model was found to achieve an accuracy of 82.72% in detecting the driver's drowsiness [16].

Table 1. Comparison of related literature

Ref.	Year	Dataset	Model	Accuracy
[11] Zhu et al	2021	Open BCI	EEG based on convolution neural network	95.59%
[12] Quddus et al	2021	User Data	Recurrent Neural Network (RNN)	97%
[13] Dua et al	2021	NTHU driver drowsiness standard video datasets	CNN	85%
[14] Bakheet et al	2021	NTHU-DDD	Histogram of Oriented Gradient	85.62%
[15] Salman et al	2021	YawDD	CNN	F1 = 0.935
[16] Kundinger et al	2021	NA	Integrated Machine Learning	82.72%
Our proposed system		Real time face data	MediaPipe Face Mesh	97.5%

3 Methodology

The proposed design of the drowsiness detection (DD) system is represented in Fig. 1(a). The functional work flow for both the drowsiness as well as yawn detection techniques is depicted in Fig. 1(b). Facial input is always read in real time by the camera. The FaceMesh algorithm processes the real-time face data, and the microcontroller and microprocessor components perform the necessary activities. The microcontroller and microprocessor

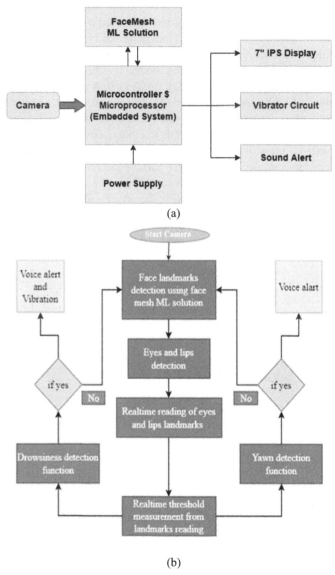

(a)

(b)

Fig. 1. (a) Proposed design of the drowsiness detection (DD) system and (b) the functional work flow.

are powered by an external power supply at all times. The Media Pipe FaceMesh machine learning (ML) function is a 468-face landmark solution that works on the CPU. The 468 facial landmarks are depicted on a map along with their placements on the face. The filtered landmarks on the face and real-time facial position are displayed on 7" IPS monitors. The vibration of the motor is controlled by the vibrator motor circuit in response to signals received from Facemesk. The Sound Box amplifies the related audio impulses.

The camera collects in real time the driver's face data. A sound alert in conjunction with a seat belt vibrator is used; this will activate if drivers keep their eyes closed for at least 3 s. Figure 2 shows the integration of the system with the driver. The driver will sit in the driving position, the device will be set in front of the driver, and the alarming vibrator is integrated with the seat belt.

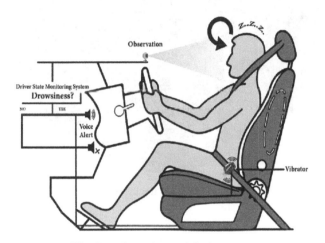

Fig. 2. Driver view and device setup.

Our camera always takes real-time face video of the driver. Using the FaceMesh ML solution, our system always generates face landmarks to detect eyes and lip movements. It can calculate the threshold using generated landmarks. Driver closes his eyes for at least 3 s, the drowsiness detection function will run and it will give a voice alert alongside seatbelt vibration. If the driver only yawns, then the yawn detection function will run and turn on the voice alert, as shown in the Fig. 1(b). On the other hand, if the above conditions are not fulfilled, the FaceMesh ML solution will run continuously. In this study, the media pipe face mesh was used. Even on using of different devices, it has 468 real-time 3D facial landmarks.

The solution includes the Facial Transform which is a module that connects the dots between the estimation of facial landmark and the applications of augmented reality. It constructs a metric in 3D space and employs the facial landmark screen positions to estimate a face transform inside that space. Among the common 3D primitives present in the face transform data, a face position transformation matrix and a triangular face mesh in important. A lightweight statistical analysis approach, called procrustes analysis is employed to power the logic, which is robust, performant, and portable. On top of the

ML model inference, the analysis runs on the CPU and has a small speed and memory footprint. We have used a new library named "Media Pipe". Media Pipe brings heavy AI models to embedded systems and smartphones, utilizing various model optimization techniques. Media Pipe's face mesh is a 468-face landmark solution [17]. A map of the 468 facial landmarks with their corresponding positions on Fig. 3.

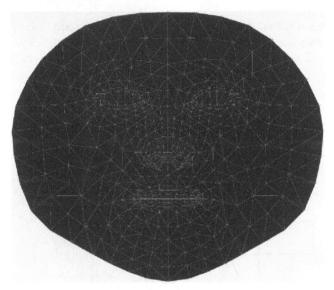

Fig. 3. The numbers of the facial key points

3.1 Machine Learning Pipeline

The machine learning (ML) pipeline used in this study consists of two deep neural network models in real-time that cooperate: a detector that computes face positions on the full image and a model of 3D face landmark which acts on those locations and employs regression to prognosticate an approximation of the 3D field [18]. Correct cropping of the face significantly reduces the requirement for typical data augmentations such affine transformations, which include rotation, translation, and scale modifications. This results in less consistency in the data and more variation between data points. Additionally, it permits the network to concentrate most of its efforts on improving coordinate prediction accuracy. Additionally, facial landmarks detection based cropping was included to our pipeline in an earlier frame, and the face detector model is only employed to delocalize the face in cases where the landmark model failed to detect its presence.

3.2 Models Used in This Study

Blaze Face detection model [19], a compact and effective face detector model that functions well on both Low-end and High-end based processors, has been utilized for face detection. It runs at a pace of 200–1000 + FPS on flagship devices. A lightweight feature extraction network built on a GPU-friendly anchor technique derived from Single Shot MultiBox Detector (SSD) and an enhanced tie resolution strategy in place of non-maximum suppression are used in the model's backend. [20].

3D facial landmarks are another name for the face landmark model. The 3D landmark coordinates on synthetic rendered data is predicted by the network while simultaneously predicting 2D semantic contours on annotated real-world data via transfer learning. Along with the Face Landmark Model, it is used a model for focusing on the important facial features. This model requires more computation but predicts landmarks more accurately around the eyes, irises, and mouth. Among other things, it makes it possible for AR puppeteering and cosmetics.

The Facial Landmark Model employs a single camera to locate facial landmarks in screen coordinate space; the Horizontal and Vertical coordinates are conventional screen coordinates, while the Z coordinate is related to the Horizontal coordinate under the weak perspective projection camera model. Despite being suitable for some applications, this format does not support all augmented reality (AR) features, such as matching a virtual 3D object with a recognized face. The Face Transform module transforms a detected face into a standard 3D object by leaving the screen coordinate space and entering metric 3D space. When the landmark model can no longer detect the presence of a face, it is intended to be able to project the finished 3D scene back into screen coordinate space using a perspective viewpoint while keeping the location of the face landmarks.

4   Results

The implementation of the proposed system in terms of experimental setup and hardware configuration as well as real time output have been described in this section. The proposed system has been tested in terms of user angle that indicates how many angle the system cover to takes its input, and distance which measures how far the system captures input from a driver. Then the response time has been measured.

4.1   Hardware Arrangement and Experimental Setting

The Raspberry Pi 4.0 was employed as the central control unit for the system. In order to experiment the project, several modules such as a vibrator, camera module, speaker, and touch display were used. Figure 4 depicts the system's experimental setup and implementation. All the components in the setup are connected by different types of male and female cables. The Fig. 4 shows the setup of our device. It doesn't need any extra cable or need not join any cable for the setup. Different parts can be separated and reassemble easily. It showa the less complexity of design. Most of parts buys from the local market and price are lower than others available divices, it makes the device less expensive.

Figure 5(a) represents the different angle of driver head position and yawn of the driver also. Figure 5(b) shows the measurement procedure of determining the maximum angle position of the driver. Both eyes of the driver were positioned with the camera at zero-degree (0°) angle. When the driver turned his head at maximum 80° angle to the

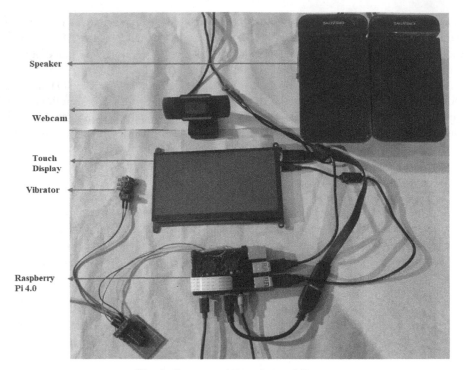

Fig. 4. System and Experimental Setup.

right side, the camera could be able to accurately detect at least his left eye. On the other hand, when the driver rotated his head at maximum 80° angle to the left side, the camera could be able to accurately detect at least his right eye. The angle cover of the device based on eyes are tabulated in Table 2.

Table 2. Angle covered by this device.

Angle (Left)	Detection	Angle (Right)	Detection
0°	Yes	0°	Yes
40°	Yes	40°	Yes
60°	Yes	60°	Yes
80°	Yes	80°	Yes

We trail 20 times for each position and then calculate the mathematical average of the response time using following equation.

$$Avg = \sum_{i=1}^{n=20} \frac{T_i}{n} \tag{1}$$

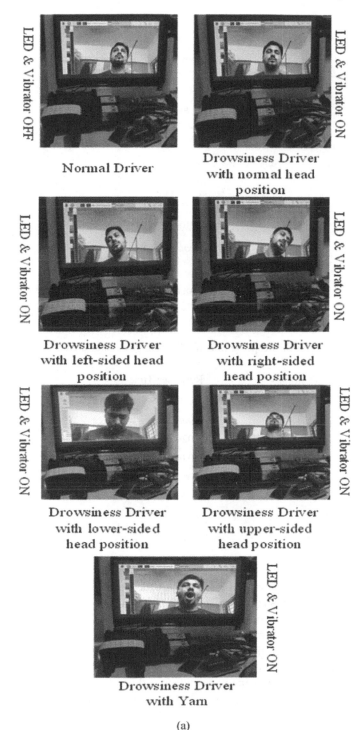

(a)

Fig. 5. (a) Different driver angle view of experiment, and (b) measurement procedure.

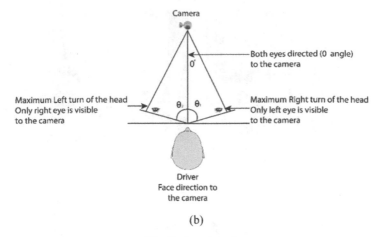

(b)

Fig. 5. (*continued*)

After calculating the average for each position, we get the response time almost 3 s. Average time for each position is tabulated in Table 3.

Table 3. Response time for different position of driver.

Position	Response Time
1	3.02s
2	3.05s
3	3.02s
4	3.03s
5	3.00s
6	3.04s
7	3.02s
Average	3.02S

The average response time is 3.02 s. It means the alarm and vibrators are activated after detecting the drowsiness of the driver. 3.02 s is not a big time in real world and both the alarm and vibrator start warning together can make aware the driver about drowsiness. Driver can get back the safe mode of driving within this few time that ensure the safe drive in a vehicle. Moreover, the designed system was tested 80 times, where it showed 78 times positive feedback which indicated 97.5% accuracy of the system.

If we can train the model using more videos and images of the drowsiness as well as more features like body language, facial expression of drivers, which will make the system more intelligent for the real environment, then the system will response more quickly and provide more accuracy.

5 Conclusions

The proposed design of the system can find the drowsiness of driver during driving mode in a short time. FaceMesh technique is used to determine the eye and facial expression of the driver and after calculating the different face point, this system take a decision that the drowsiness is detected or not. Average 3.02 s response time has been achieved during several test. It is minimal and a vibrator is response quickly to aware the drive about the driving mode. Most of the components are connected by cables that give the permission to separate the parts and reassemble easily. In future, this drowsiness detection system can be implemented by a cloud-based system and proper monitoring system in integrated to observe the activities of driver.

Acknowledgement. This study was supported and funded by the Institute of Research and Training (IRT), Hajee Mohammad Danesh Science and Technology University, Dinajpur-5200, Bangladesh.

References

1. Rahman, M.F., Hossain, M.M.: Implementation of robotics to design a sniffer dog for the application of metal detection. In: Proceedings of International Conference on Trends in Computational and Cognitive Engineering. Springer, Singapore (2021)
2. Kaimujjaman, M., Islam, M.M., Mahmud, R., Sultana, M., Mahabub, M.M.: Digital FM transceiver design and construction using microcontroller and I 2 C interfacing techniques. Int. J. Recent Technol. Eng 8(5) (2020)
3. Hossain, M.S., Waheed, S., Rahman, Z., Shezan, S., Hossain, M.M.: Blockchain for the security of internet of things: a smart home use case using Ethereum. Int. J. Recent Technol. Eng 8(5), 4601–4608 (2020)
4. Zhang, G., Yau, K.K., Zhang, X., Li, Y.: Traffic accidents involving fatigue driving and their extent of casualties. Accid. Anal. Prev. 87, 34–42 (2016)
5. Maulina, D., Irwanda, D.Y., Sekarmewangi, T.H., Putri, K.M.H., Otgaar, H.: How accurate are memories of traffic accidents? Increased false memory levels among motorcyclists when confronted with accident-related word lists. Transportation research part F: traffic psychology and behaviour 80, 275–294 (2021)
6. Perilous roads in Bangladesh; 6,284 killed in 2021: RSF, UNB news, published on January 08 (2020)
7. Albadawi, Y., Takruri, M., Awad, M.: A review of recent developments in driver drowsiness detection systems. Sensors 22, 2069 (2022)
8. Ji, Q., Zhu, Z., Lan, P.: Real-time nonintrusive monitoring and prediction of driver fatigue. IEEE Trans. Veh. Technol. 53(4), 1052–1068 (2004)
9. You, F., Li, Y.H., Huang, L., Chen, K., Zhang, R.H., Xu, J.M.: Monitoring drivers' sleepy status at night based on machine vision. Multimedia Tools and Applications 76(13), 14869-14886 (2017)
10. Dong, Y., Hu, Z., Uchimura, K., Murayama, N.: Driver inattention monitoring system for intelligent vehicles. A review. IEEE transactions on intelligent transportation systems 12(2), 596–614 (2010)
11. Zhu, M., Chen, J., Li, H., Liang, F., Han, L., Zhang, Z.: Vehicle driver drowsiness detection method using wearable EEG based on convolution neural network. Neural Comput. Appl. 33(20), 13965–13980 (2021). https://doi.org/10.1007/s00521-021-06038-y

12. Quddus, A., Zandi, A.S., Prest, L., Comeau, F.J.: Using long short-term memory and con-volutional neural networks for driver drowsiness detection. Accid. Anal. Prev. **156**, 106107 (2021)
13. Dua, M., Singla, R., Raj, S., Jangra, A.: Deep CNN models-based ensemble approach to driver drowsiness detection. Neural Comput. Appl. **33**(8), 3155–3168 (2021)
14. Bakheet, S., Al-Hamadi, A.: A framework for instantaneous driver drowsiness detection based on improved HOG features and naïve Bayesian classification. Brain Sci. **11**(2), 240 (2021)
15. Salman, R.M., Rashid, M., Roy, R., Ahsan, M.M., Siddique, Z.: Driver Drowsiness Detection Using Ensemble Convolutional Neural Networks on YawDD. arXiv preprint arXiv:2112. 10298 (2021)
16. Kundinger, T., Riener, A., Bhat, R.: Performance and acceptance evaluation of a driver drowsiness detection system based on smart wearables. In: 13th International Conference on Automotive User Interfaces and Interactive Vehicular Applications, pp. 49–58 (2021)
17. Singh, A.K., Kumbhare, V.A., Arthi, K.: Real-time human pose detection and recognition using MediaPipe. In: International Conference on Soft Computing and Signal Processing, pp. 145–154 (2021)
18. Feng, Y., Wu, F., Shao, X., Wang, Y., Zhou, X.: Joint 3d face reconstruction and dense alignment with position map regression network. In: Proceedings of the European conference on computer vision (ECCV), pp. 534–551 (2018)
19. Brar, D.S., Kumar, A., Mittal, U., Rana, P.: Face detection for real world application. In: 2021 2nd International Conference on Intelligent Engineering and Management (ICIEM), pp. 239–242 (2021 Apr 28)
20. Bazarevsky, V., Kartynnik, Y., Vakunov, A., Raveendran, K., Grundmann, M.: BlazeFace. Sub-millisecond Neural Face Detection on Mobile GPUs. arXiv:1907.05047 (2019)

Fuzziness Based Semi-supervised Deep Learning for Multimodal Image Classification

Abeda Asma[1], Dilshad Noor Mostafa[1], Koli Akter[1], Mufti Mahmud[2,3,4] (iD),
and Muhammed J. A. Patwary[1,2(✉)] (iD)

[1] Department of CSE, International Islamic University Chittagong,
Chittagong, Bangladesh
mjap@iiuc.ac.bd, jamshed_cse_cu@yahoo.com

[2] Department of Computer Science, Nottingham Trent University, Clifton Lane,
Nottingham NG118NS, UK

[3] Medical Technologies Innovation Facility, Nottingham Trent University,
Clifton Lane, Nottingham NG118NS, UK

[4] Computing and Informatics Research Center, Nottingham Trent University,
Clifton Lane, Nottingham NG118NS, UK
mufti.mahmud@ntu.ac.uk

Abstract. Predicting a class or label of text-aided image has practical application in a range of domains including social media, machine learning and medical domain. Usually, supervised learning model is used to make such predictions where labeled data is mandatory, which is time consuming and required manual help. Classification of images are accomplished on visual features only by utilizing deep learning. Employing semi-supervised learning is a viable answer to these issues that needs a few label sample to classify huge unlabeled samples. The paper suggests a novel semi-supervised deep learning method based on fuzziness, called (FSSDL-MIC) for multimodal image classification to tackle the challenge of web image classification. For the first time in this scenario, we integrate Multilayer perceptron for textual features and MobileNetV2 for visual features to create a multimodal paradigm. Using data from PASCAL VOC'07, experiments have revealed that the proposed framework achieves significant improvement and outperforms modern techniques for multimodal image categorization. We also see a positive impact of low fuzzy sample when final model trained with visual features only.

Keywords: Semi-supervised Learning · Deep Learning · Fuzziness · Multimodal learning

1 Introduction

Image classification is the process of analyzing an image and categorizing it into different classes based on its features. With the advancement of technology the collection of images has been increased. These images can be categorized into

Md. S. Satu et al. (Eds.): MIET 2022, LNICST 491, pp. 91–105, 2023.
https://doi.org/10.1007/978-3-031-34622-4_8

two part e.g. labeled and unlabeled. The standard method for multimodal image categorization is supervised learning approach, which necessitates the collection of sufficient labeled instances, which is problematic.

For image classification M.Guillaumin et al. [1] proposed a SSV learning strategy to achieve the data included in the text with unlabelled images using Multiple Kernel Learning (MKL) and Least-Squares Regression (LSR) model. They used an MKL classifier for integrating image information and the keywords, then used LSR to retain using a visual feature classifier depending on the output of MKL classifier and labeled data. In [2], the authors proposed an approach that combines Refinement of tags, Graph based SSV Learning and SVR, to handle the issues in image classification effectively. In [3], the authors have presented a way to improve image classification by combining textual tags. To improve the visual feature classification, they created DPFG to display multi-model association and fuses textual and visual information for multimodal examples that are easily obtained from the web. To learn both labeled and unlabeled samples, they proposed a 3 step SSV learning process: MKL+RSL+SVM. Finally, they used DPGF+RLS+SVM to address the poorly supervised case in which noisy class labels are obtained from image tags (Fig. 1).

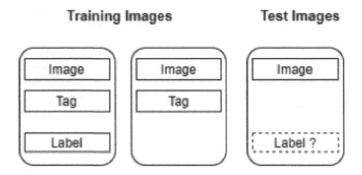

Fig. 1. Multi-modal semi-supervised classification: a high-level overview

In this research we have tried to classify images among twenty classes. In the dataset every image has its own unique label. Our contributions in this research are as follows:

1. A novice fuzziness based semi-supervised deep learning approach- (FSS-DLMIC) has been proposed for multimodal image classification.
2. Multilayer Perceptron Learning has been introduced to extract the textual aspects of the images and MobilenetV2 has been introduced to extract the visual characteristics of the images with greater accuracy rate.
3. Through an empirical observation, we analyze the proposed model on a benchmark dataset and show in what manner the introducing attention might enhance classification performance.

The remaining sections of the paper are organized as follows: The second portion explains the scope of the study as well as a literature review. Section 3 discusses the proposed methodology in depth. Section 4 describes the experimental setup which include Development Environment, datasets and features extraction. The outcomes of the experiments are discussed in detail in Sect. 6. Finally, Our general findings, as well as our future work plans are included in the concluding section.

2 Literature Review

In this Chapter, we analyze the most relevant articles on different image classification approaches, multimodal image classification and fuzzy set theory.

In relation to this topic, MJA Patwary et al. [4] investigated the divide and conquer approach, a novel component of SSV technique, to improve classifier performance. Additionally, it was discovered that the augmentation substantially depended on the basic classifier's accuracy, with the greatest outcomes being attained when the precision was between 70% and 80%.

MJA Patwary et al. [5] established a beginner approach by integrating low-fuzziness patterns. The findings of the trials conducted during the whole study showed that using a fuzziness calculation model to asses each sample's fuzziness had a considerable positive influence on SSL correctness.

MJA Patwary et al. [6] have presented a multi-modal learning system for gesture recognition [7] of the bedridden patient. They have used a RGBDT video database of a hospital of Denmark to conduct the research. The results of the research shows that their method outperforms other existing supervised learning algorithms.

Guillaumin et al. [1] proposed an semi-supervised strategy to achieve the information included in the text with unlabeled images using Multiple Kernel Learning (MKL) and Least-Squares Regression (LSR) model. Using PASCAL VOC 2007 and MIR Flickr datasets, they compared the result with other state-of-the-art algorithm and achieved significant improvement. Some issues with this approach are- Tags from images on internet websites (Flickr) likely to be incorrect. Train MKL classifier using a few labeled samples is not reliable at all. LSR model is time-consuming and also breaks the symmetry of visual feature matrix.

Xie et al. [2] proposed an approach that Combine Image Tag Refinement (TR), Graph-Based Learning (by adopting global and local consistency method), and Support Vector Regression, to handle the issues in [1] effectively. They proposed TR+GSSL+SVR approach scored superior performance over MKL+LSR approach [1] using the same datasets. Their result shows PASCAL VOC'07 datasets achieved MAP score 0.422 (where MKL+LSR achieved 0.367) and MIR Flickr datasets achieved 0.406 (Where MKL+LSR achieved 0.366) for 50 positive and negative labeled samples.

Luo et al. [8] proposed an algorithm for extracting shared subspace by combining Multi-Task Learning Algorithm and Manifold Regularization. Using same datasets as [1] they compared the result with some proposed MTL approach and SSL image classification algorithms. Where for most of the classes their method performs better and achieved mAP of 0.41 for both datasets using 50 positive and negative labels.

MJA Patwary et al. [9] Proposed a strategy to decrease HOG features when identifying person from pictures. To calculate the edge ratio of each feature, they employed difference of Gaussian [10]. Then, features with a low edge ratio are removed using a threshold. The linear SVM was then used to classify the selected features. Using INRIA dataset they find the proposed strategy decrease the dimension of the HOG features with 93.47% success rate.

Gong et al. [11] employed Curriculum Learning approach with multimodality (MMCL) by exploring the reliability and discriminability of unlabeled images in order to generate a sequence logically according to difficulty level of classifying unlabeled images. They compared the proposed MMCL method with two other methods and observed that the MMCL carry more image data, also evaluates the difficulty level more better than both NoCL and SMCL method.

Cai et al. [12] proposed Graph-oriented strategy to combine heterogeneous features that learns weight for different feature modalities also learns the common class label of image. To assess the efficiency of the strategy, they compared it with five related recent approaches using five different benchmark datasets and their approach scored 98% accuracy on average and converges very fast on all datasets.

Zhang et al. [13] Proposed an Active Learning method to select high information contents and high-confident unlabeled data that assign pseudo-label data for feature learning using CNN. Using CIFAR-10 datasets compared existing CEAL method with proposed Tri-CEAL method, which results better generalization performance [14] over CEAL (Tri-CEAL 75% where CEAL 70%). In term of error rate, Tri-CEAL is more reliable as it shows less error rate than CEAL for pseudo-label assignments.

3 Methodology

3.1 Proposed Work

In this study our projected methodology is the commencing semi-supervised deep learning model constructed considering text based image classification and it's final target is to train a classifier with image features only. Using a few labeled images with huge number of unlabeled samples resulting out to a positive feedback contrast to rival methods.

1) Multimodal Model: For multimodal concept we combine **Multilayer perceptron (MLP)** and top layer of **MobileNetV2** with global average pooling. MLP is classified as a feed forward neural network since inputs are combined in a weighted sum with starting weights and then applied to the activation function Rectified Linear Unit (ReLU). To train the neurons in the MLP a back propagation learning strategy is utilized. ReLU function, $f(x) = \max(0, x)$. A group of Google researchers recently released MobileNetV2, a classification model based on neural network design, the TensorFlow-Slim Image Classification Library includes it.

In this model textual features are used to train multilayer perceptron and visual features are used to train mobilNet-V2. We utilized the softmax function in the output layer for classification using testing set which has visual features only. The architecture of our proposed multimodal model is outline in Fig. 2:

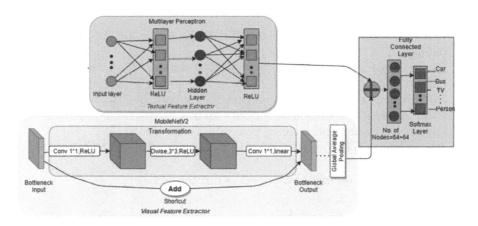

Fig. 2. Our proposed multimodal model architecture

2) Semi-Supervised Learning: The strategy of semi-supervised learning incorporates both supervised and unsupervised technique. Supervised learning approach build with labeled samples that needs manual expertise which is consuming time and high-priced. Further, Unsupervised approach build with unlabeled data which is easily found in real life uses. And that's why researchers invented semi-supervised technique [15] where a few labeled sample are used to classify huge amount of unlabeled sample. In our work we firstly used label image to train the model and after prediction low fuzzy sample added in training set then retrain the model. By classifying these pictures we can use these images for various purposes [16].

3) Fuzziness based Divide and Conquer Strategy: To handle uncertainty, a fresh approach based on divide-and-conquer tactic has been used in fuzziness. There were three levels of fuzziness in the testing data: low, medium, high. The dataset then separated into two groups. Low fuzzy examples then added to the initial training set then it was re-taught. We offer a new technique for multimodal image classification using fuzziness and deep learning with semi-supervised.

4) Proposed Algorithm: Based on early studies from [5], we expanded the algorithm and projected a novel methodology (Algorithm 1) for multimodal image classification applying MLP+MobilnetV2.

Algorithm 1 FSSDL-MIC

Input: Dataset(Text+image)
Output: Improvement of accuracy with visual features and labeling the unlabeled images.

1. Create a training(Tn) and testing(Tt) dataset by randomly dividing the dataset.
2. Divide the training set, Tn, into labeled dataset Tn(L) and unlabeled dataset, Tt(U).
3. Build text and image model and concatenate both as C.
4. Using a training algorithm, train the classifier C, based on Tn(L)
5. Obtain the testing and training precision Tnacc, Ttacc
6. For each sample in Tn(U), obtain the fuzzy vector Fi $=(x_1),(x_2),......, f(x_n)$ by classifier C.
7. Determine each sample's fuzziness F(v) in the Tn(U) by

$$F(v) = -1/n \sum_{i=1}^{n} (x_i \log x_i + (1 - x_i) \log(1 - x_i)) \tag{1}$$

8. Calculate the low fuzziness Tn(U)low.
9. Obtain a new training set by adding low fuzzy sample Tn'=Tn (L) U Tn(U)low.
10. Using the provided training algorithm, retrain a new classifier C' with Tn'.
11. Note the accuracy of training and testing TnaccF, TtaccF by classifier C' with Tn'.

Our proposed method's schematic diagram is shown in Fig. 3.

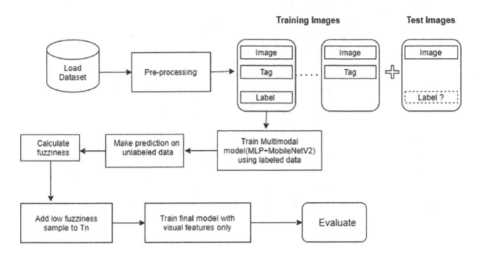

Fig. 3. Methodology of our proposed algorithm

4 Experimental Setup

4.1 Integrated Development Environments (IDE)

To implement the proposed method, we have used Google Colaboratory platform. A computer configured with an Intel Core i5–2.4 GHz CPU, 8 GB of RAM, and Windows 10 64-bit operating system served as the platform for the experiments.

4.2 Datasets and Features Extraction

We performed our experiment on a benchmark dataset PASCAL VOC 2007 [17] which is an object detection dataset collected from Kaggle. The dataset contains 9,963 images from 20 classes. All the 9963 images were annotated for each of the classes. There are 24,640 annotated objects in 9,963 photos. The images comes with text tags. Total 804 tags for 9587 images were downloaded from Flickr and remaining images were presumed to have a complete nonappearance of text-tags. Typical train-test-split is used, where the training and testing set include 5,011 and 4,952 images respectively.

4.3 Data Preprocessing

Preprocessing Textual Features: To represent the tags associated with images, we used a binary vector $T = (t_1,...,t_n)$. where t_n is the total number of tags. t_i encodes $(t_i = 1)$ as the presence of that tag in the image where $(t_i = 0)$ denotes the absence of that tag in the image.

Preprocessing Visual Features: At the beginning of preprocessing, we read the annotation file for each image which is in the XML format, we parse the file and get the object position inside the image, crop the image according to position of the entity. Then we resize those images into (160,160) because our feature extractor model, MobileNetV2 requires (160,160,3) as input image. The pixel values of the photos are scaled by dividing 127.5 in order to minimize the computational complexity of classifier model training. We enhanced the photos by 20° rotation and horizontal flipping in order to boost the quantity of images.

Combining Text and Image Data: After getting the text and image data, we combined those side by side, where both text and image represent the same class data. Fitting the data into the combined text and image model, we obtained the textual features and visual features.

4.4 Multimodal Model

Two concurrent systems-one for extracting visual information and the other for obtaining textual features-combine to generate the multimodal model. We utilize a Multilayer Perceptron model to extract text from the vectors and a pre-trained MobilenetV2 model to extract visual attributes. After that, the features from both modalities are integrated to generate a combined representation, which is then processed via a Softmax layer for classification. We consider 3 sorts of model on the basis of their features:

(i) **Textual feature based model (Multilayer Perceptron):** To classify textual features, a feed-forward neural network-Multilayer Perceptron (MLP) is used, where data flows through a sequence of layers. MLP consists of fully connected layers where the input layer represents the feature vector that contains text. Three layers with dense (64,32,64) and ReLU activation function were used to extract textual features.

(ii) **Image Model (MobileNetV2):** To extract visual features, we first instantiated a MobileNetV2 model that was already pre-loaded with ImageNet-trained weights. To prevent updating the weights of the layers, we made the entire model non-trainable. We used the network which do not contain the classification layers on top, that makes it suitable for extraction of features. The model requires (160, 160, 3) images as input. The feature generator converts each image of (160, 160, 3) into the $(5 \times 5 \times 1280)$ block of features. To make estimation from the block of features, (5×5) spatial-locations were taken, via Global Average Pooling 2D layer for converting the features into single 1280 element-vectors. We applied a Dense layer for converting the features into prediction.

(iii) **Multimodal MLP-MobileNetV2 Model:** To implement the multimodal model we concatenate the outputs of text model and image model. To do this, we kept the last layer of both text and image model dense 64 thus producing a combined output of dense 64 using ReLU activation function. Finally applied Softmax activation function on the fully connected layer (Table 1).

Table 1. List of Hyper parameters

ACTIVATION FUNCTION (HIDDEN LAYER)	ReLU
ACTIVATION FUNCTION (OUTPUT LAYER)	Softmax
DROPOUT	0.2
LEARNING RATE	0.001
BATCH SIZE	32
LOSS FUNCTION	Categorical crossentropy
OPTIMIZER	Adam

4.5   Fuzziness Calculation

The multimodal classifier gives a fuzzy vector outputr Fi $= (x_1), (x_2), (x_3), \ldots\ldots,$ (x_n). We utilized the prediction values over the unlabeled test samples to compute the fuzziness and divided them into 3 categories based on the degree of fuzziness in each sample: low fuzzy-samples, medium fuzzy-samples, and high fuzzy-samples. Several methods have been proposed for determining the fuzziness of a fuzzy set.

To evaluate the level of fuzzy event's degree of fuzziness, we have used the equation from [5] -

$$F(v) = -1/n \sum_{i=1}^{n} (x_i \log x_i + (1 - x_i) \log(1 - x_i)) \qquad (2)$$

Where,
n represents the no. of classes
x_i represents the quantity of associativity for i-th class

After Calculating fuzziness for each sample we got a list of fuzziness. The samples with low fuzziness from the fuzziness list are transferred into testing set to training dataset in order to retrain them. Finally, using the new training set trained the final model- MobilenetV2 using the visual features only.

5   Result and Discussion

In this segment, we discuss about proposed method's experimental results and compare the result with other approaches. To evaluate the performance, we measure Average Precision (AP) and mean Average Precision (mAP).

Table 2 represents the first set of experimental results, a comparison between the classification performance (AP and mAP) using the tags and the visual features for each of the classes. For visual features, we have used MobileNetV2 in the visual kernel, and for textual features, we have used Multilayer Perceptron in the text/tag kernel.

Table 2. Comparison between different multimodal semisupervised image classification methods and proposed FSSD-MIC method

Class Names	MKL+LSR [1]	DPGF [3]	FSSDL-MIC
aeroplane	0.879	0.886	**0.89**
bicycle	0.655	0.721	**0.92**
bird	0.763	0.785	**0.90**
boat	0.756	**0.76**	0.71
bottle	0.315	0.343	**0.83**
bus	0.713	**0.747**	0.74
car	0.775	0.803	**0.88**
cat	0.792	0.836	**0.86**
chair	0.462	0.475	**0.68**
cow	0.627	0.664	**0.75**
diningtable	0.414	0.542	**0.84**
dog	0.746	**0.767**	0.75
horse	0.846	**0.859**	0.82
motorbike	0.762	0.763	**0.91**
person	0.846	**0.855**	0.79
Pottedplant	0.48	0.493	**0.87**
sheep	0.677	0.741	**0.79**
sofa	0.443	0.526	**0.69**
train	0.861	0.888	**0.90**
Tvmonitor	0.527	0.597	**0.87**
Mean	0.667	0.703	**0.80**

We observed that proposed approach outperform most of the classes and achieves a higher mAP score. The method scored lower AP score than the DPGF approach [3] only for five classes out of twenty classes but with a microscopic difference (the differences for boat, bus, dog, horse and person classes are 0.05, 0.007, 0.017, 0.03 and 0.06 respectively). Remarkably, the classifier obtained 80% accuracy by merging textual and visual features which outperforms MKL+LSR method [1] by 14% and DPGF method [3] by 10% on PASCAL VOC 2007 dataset.

Figure 4 demonstrates the comparison of the proposed FSSDL-MIC approach with MKL+LSR and DPGF. All categories' AP scores are displayed, and green boxes highlight several categories where the FSSDL-MIC performs lower than the baselines.

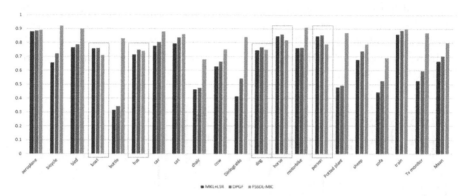

Fig. 4. Histogram to compare different approaches based on textual+visual features

Table 3. Comparison between the AP scores using 50 positive and negative labeled data

CLASS NAME	MKL+LSR [1]	TR+GSSL+SVR [2]	MRMTL-SVM+CoTR [8]	DPGF [3]	FSSDL-MIC
AEROPLANE	.59	.64	.62	.70	**.94**
BICYCLE	.32	.44	.31	.48	**.94**
BIRD	.37	.38	.33	.44	**.85**
BOAT	.51	.52	.54	.61	**.95**
BOTTLE	.15	.14	.20	.20	**.73**
BUS	.27	.42	.36	.49	**.97**
CAR	.50	.54	.55	.53	**.72**
CAT	.36	.43	.39	.50	**.91**
CHAIR	.30	.32	.41	.38	**.70**
COW	.11	.27	.21	.22	**.89**
DINING TABLE	.25	.27	.31	.38	**.97**
DOG	.33	.34	.33	.34	**.83**
HORSE	.63	.69	.62	.71	**.98**
MOTORBIKE	.38	.47	.45	.55	**1.00**
PERSON	.70	.69	**.73**	.65	.41
PLOTTED PLANT	.21	.26	.24	.23	**.90**
SHEEP	.21	.33	.28	.34	**.90**
SOFA	.19	.22	.27	.20	**.83**
TRAIN	.61	.69	.62	.74	**.94**
TV MONITOR	.25	.27	.31	.38	**.97**
MEAN AP	.36	.42	.41	.45	**.84**

In Table 3, we report the findings using 50 randomly selected positive and negative labeled data for each class. For only one class at a time, we select positive and negative samples at random. To avoid multi-label classification problem different labeled samples are picked for each classes. We noticed our method visibly outperforms all previous semi-supervised methods. One exception is the "Person" class, where our method receives a lower AP score than other methods, although the difference is just 0.24. Our method also achieved 0.839 of mAP scores, which indicates significant improvement on the classification results than other classifiers, the mAP score increases by 38% from DPGF+RLS+SVM, 41% from TR+GSSL+SVR, 42% from MRMTL-SVM+CoTR and 47% from MKL+LSR on PASCAL VOC 2007.

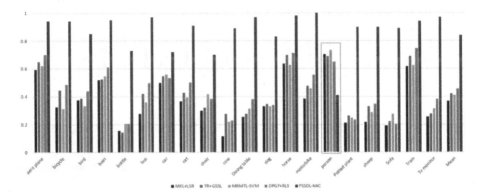

Fig. 5. Histogram to compare different approaches based on visual features only.

Figure 5, shows the performance, or AP and mAP scores, for each class using the four approaches that were compared: MKL+LSR, TR+GSSL+SVR, MRMTL-SVR+CoTR, and DPGF+RLS+SVM. For each class, we use 50 labelled data that are positive and 50 labelled data that are negative. The "person" class where the FSSDL-MIC performs worse than the baselines is highlighted in green, and the AP scores for all classes are displayed.

The performance of the combined model: MLP and MobileNetV2 have made tremendous progress in this research. If we analyze the outcomes of both models, they indicate that textual characteristics can enhance the effectiveness of visual classifiers. Additionally, calculating fuzziness and retraining the low fuzzy samples enhances the performance of the classifier.

Finally, we verified how accurate our model can make prediction for various random photographs downloaded from the internet and captured by camera. Figure 6 illustrates that our model can properly anticipate most of the images.

Fig. 6. Prediction of our model on some random example images

6 Conclusion and Future Work

In today's world, the number of image data is increasing exponentially and with that, the need of image classification is also increasing parallelly. In this research, we tried to classify images into twenty categories by combining Multilayer Perceptron Learning and MobilenetV2. We also calculated the fuzziness for achieving better accuracy. The result demonstrates that, the suggested strategy outperforms state-of-the-art algorithm. We found the Average Precision for most of the class is significantly high using Multi-modal Fuzzy Semi Supervised Deep Learning approach and scored Mean Average Precision 0.80 for the textual and visual classifier and 0.84 for visual classification only. In future, we intend to add automatic caption generation for unlabeled images. Besides predicting the class of the images we will try to label the image with tags, also with short details of the image. Simultaneously, we will test our model on several datasets and evaluate its performance.

References

1. Guillaumin, M., Verbeek, J., Schmid, C.: Multimodal semi-supervised learning for image classification. In: 2010 IEEE Computer Society Conference on Computer Vision and Pattern Recognition, pp. 902–909. IEEE (2010)
2. Xie, W., Lu, Z., Peng, Y., Xiao, J.: Graph-based multimodal semi-supervised image classification. Neurocomputing **138**, 167–179 (2014)
3. Xie, L., Pan, P., Yansheng, L.: Markov random field based fusion for supervised and semi-supervised multi-modal image classification. Multimedia Tools Appl. **74**(2), 613–634 (2015)
4. Patwary, M.J., Wang, X.-Z.: Sensitivity analysis on initial classifier accuracy in fuzziness based semi-supervised learning. Inf. Sci. **490**, 93–112 (2019)
5. Patwary, M.J., Wang, X.Z., Yan, D.: Impact of fuzziness measures on the performance of semi-supervised learning. Int. J. Fuzzy Syst. **21**(5), 1430–1442 (2019)
6. Patwary, M.J., Cao, W., Wang, X.Z., Haque, M.A.: Fuzziness based semi-supervised multimodal learning for patient's activity recognition using RGBDT videos. Appl. Soft Comput. **120**, 108655 (2022)
7. Osman, A.B., et al.: Examining mental disorder/psychological chaos through various ML and DL techniques: a critical review. Ann. Emerg. Technol. Comput. (AETiC) **6**, 61–71 (2022)
8. Luo, Y., Tao, D., Geng, B., Xu, C., Maybank, S.J.: Manifold regularized multitask learning for semi-supervised multilabel image classification. IEEE Trans. Image Process. **22**(2), 523–536 (2013)
9. Patwary, M.J.A., Parvin, S., Akter, S.: Significant HOG-histogram of oriented gradient feature selection for human detection. Int. J. Comput. Appl. **132**(17) (2015)
10. Alam, M.S.B., Patwary, M.J., Hassan, M.: Birth mode prediction using bagging ensemble classifier: a case study of Bangladesh. In: 2021 International Conference on Information and Communication Technology for Sustainable Development (ICICT4SD), pp. 95–99. IEEE (2021)
11. Gong, C., Tao, D., Maybank, S.J., Liu, W., Kang, G., Yang, J.: Multi-modal curriculum learning for semi-supervised image classification. IEEE Trans. Image Process. **25**(7), 3249–3260 (2016)
12. Cai, X., Nie, F., Cai, W., Huang, H.: eterogeneous image features integration via multi-modal semi-supervised learning model. In:Proceedings of the IEEE International Conference on Computer Vision, pp. 1737–1744 (2013)
13. Zhang, Y., Yan, S.: Semi-supervised active learning image classification method based on tri-training algorithm. In: 2020 IEEE International Conference on Artificial Intelligence and Information Systems (ICAIIS), pp. 206–210. IEEE (2020)
14. Hossain, S., Zahid Hasan, M., Patwary, M.J.A., Uddin, M.S.: An expert system to determine systemic lupus erythematosus under uncertainty. In: Uddin, M.S., Bansal, J.C. (eds.) Proceedings of International Joint Conference on Advances in Computational Intelligence. AIS, pp. 117–130. Springer, Singapore (2021). https://doi.org/10.1007/978-981-16-0586-4_10
15. Karim, S., Akter, N., Patwary, M.J.: Predicting autism spectrum disorder (ASD) meltdown using fuzzy semi-supervised learning with NNRW. In: 2022 International Conference on Innovations in Science, Engineering and Technology (ICISET), pp. 367–372. IEEE (2022)

16. Kowsher, M., Alam, M.A., Uddin, M.J., Ahmed, F., Ullah, M.W., Islam, M.R.: Detecting third umpire decisions & automated scoring system of cricket. In: 2019 International Conference on Computer, Communication, Chemical, Materials and Electronic Engineering (IC4ME2), pp. 1–8. IEEE (2019)
17. Everingham, M., Van Gool, L., Williams, C.K., Winn, J., Zisserman, A.: The pascal visual object classes (VOC) challenge. Int. J. Comput. Vision **88**(2), 303–338 (2010)

Human Emotion Recognition from Facial Images Using Convolutional Neural Network

Saima Sultana$^{(\boxtimes)}$, Rashed Mustafa ,
and Mohammad Sanaullah Chowdhury

Department of Computer Science and Engineering, University of Chittagong,
Chittagong, Bangladesh
saimasultanaoman@gmail.com, rashed.m@cu.ac.bd

Abstract. Recognizing human emotions from facial images has drawn widespread attention in different kinds of applications. Detecting emotions from face has become one of the important research areas as it has a significant impact on the area of emotional communication between people and machines. The goal of this project is to develop a convolutional neural network-based face emotion identification system through the analysis of facial expressions. Convolution Neural Network also known as CNN has been recognized as the best algorithm for image classification. To begin the implementation of our system, each image was subjected to a pre-processing method as part of the image processing procedure. Then, the Convolution, Pooling, and Dropout layers work on the pre-processed image to extract its features. For classification of the image, a fully connected layer with a classifier is used here. To achieve a better performance, we have implemented our system using different optimizers, classifiers, and deep learning techniques. The entire dataset from the Facial Emotion Recognition FER-2013 with Kaggle was used to test the model. Using the FER-2013 dataset, the assessed performance displays the greatest training and testing accuracy, which are, respectively, 77 and 68%. This method aids in categorizing the seven emotions-angry, disgusted, fearful, happy, neutral, sad, and surprised from facial images.

Keywords: Convolution Neural Network · Convolution · RELU · Pooling layer · Fully connected layer · facial emotion · Optimizers

1 Introduction

Emotion is a psychological situation which implies to different conditions of mind. Recognizing and understanding emotions are very common and necessary skills in our daily communication and in day to day life social workings. Human being is well capable of recognizing emotions by observing the behavior and actions of a person. But a computer or any machine cannot do it easily, perfectly or accurately. Hence, we have conducted this research to build a system

© ICST Institute for Computer Sciences, Social Informatics and Telecommunications Engineering 2023
Published by Springer Nature Switzerland AG 2023. All Rights Reserved
Md. S. Satu et al. (Eds.): MIET 2022, LNICST 491, pp. 106–120, 2023.
https://doi.org/10.1007/978-3-031-34622-4_9

that makes a computer capable to do the same. To realize a more natural and intelligent human-machine interaction, recognition of emotions has been studied widely in current decades, and it attracted more and more researchers' attention [11,18,19,29]. Generally, people can realize the emotional states of others if they are happy, sad, surprise or anger, using facial expressions [1], behavior, pose, Speech [31] and vocal tone. But facial expression is the most precise to recognize emotions from faces' expressions. Facial Emotion Recognition is a progressing research field where huge kind of progressions are happening day by day such as character translation systems [4], device to human interaction in industries [16]. Apart from this, the paper focus to input images of emotional faces from datasets, image preprocessing, survey and review various facial extraction features, learning algorithm of Convolutional Neural Network Model and Classifications of seven kind of human emotions (sad, angry, happy, neutral, surprise, fear, disgust) and so on.

The goal of the research was to develop a system that enables recognizing seven types of emotions from a person's face. The objective was achieved by training a model using machine learning techniques utilizing FER dataset from "kaggle" site. Finally, improvement of testing accuracy has been compared to other existing techniques and keeping up a better or an equivalent recognition rate for each class will also be addressed. The aims and objective of this research are identified as finding out the limitations of the existing methods that have been built regarding this topic, developing Facial Emotion Recognition System which can take a facial image file as an input, can recognize it and can classify this into seven types of classes such as angry, fearful, disgust, happy, neutral, surprise and sad with improving accuracy of individual class compared to other existing system. The classification of numerous sorts of emotions is the goal of our study, thus it is obvious that there is still room for new machine learning models to be created or for existing models to be improved in order to achieve greater accuracy when categorizing multiple types of emotions. In this study, we used the Convolutional Neural Network (CNN) and computer vision to construct an integrated machine learning model that can fill the research gap left by earlier works.

The contribution of this research paper is to develop and train a Convolutional Neural Network (CNN) Model, which can achieve respectable accuracy metrics and the capability of classifying image samples. The novel contribution related to this research is to implement a Convolutional Neural Network architecture which trains the model with adequate data, and to export the model with the highest accuracy metric. The significant contribution of our work is: We have shown comparison of performance among different optimizers and among different activation functions. We have applied deep learning approaches here. We have splitted our dataset into different ratio and experimented so that we can gain the best accuracy comparing with them.

The organization of the next chapters are, Sect. 2 will provide some background knowledge and works that have been conducted so far on this field. Section 3 describes the methodology that we have applied to design our proposed model and how we have deal with our datasets. Section 4 shows the experimental tools and environment. Section 5 shows the results and comparison with other approaches. Section 6 concludes the research by showing the future scope of the research.

2   Related Work

This is a very common and important research on facial emotion recognition which has been conducting for a long time. There was always a space to improve in every research. And, so there are many more opportunity with regard this topic. Let us discuss about some research works done in facial expression recognition and their limitations that can be solved-

Akash Saravanan et al. [25] worked on a CNN model with six convolutional layers Model. The previously described training data set, which consists of 28,000 occurrences over seven distinct classes, is used to carry out the task. 80 percent of the data set is utilized for training, while the remaining 20 percent is used for testing. They used CNN model using six convolutional layers and achieved 60% accuracy. Based on the results, it is clear that the classification accuracy of CNN model algorithm is worthy than other algorithms. However, they used six convolution layers which makes the model somewhat complex while dealing with tha dataset.

Shima Alizadeh et al. [3] have applied a hybrid feature strategy and with this feature, they merged raw pixel data with Histogram of Oriented Gradients (HOG) characteristics to train an unique CNN model. They made use of a variety of strategies to lessen the overfitting of the models. These methods include batch normalization and dropout. They employed cross validation to determine the optimal hyper-parameters. They also present how the different layers of a network visualizes in order to show a facial feature learning by CNN model. The best shallow model has given 55% accuracy while working on the validation set and 54% on the test set. They didn't use their model working with color image which didn't allow them to investigate the working efficiency of pre-trained models such as VGGNet [26] or AlexNet [12] for facial emotion recognition.

Nithya Roopa. S et al. [23] In this work, investigation on various datasets have occurred and training of the datasets were explored so that they can be able to train the model to recognize facial expressions. Inception Net is used for recognizing the expressions with the dataset of FERC (Facial Expression Recognition Challenge) from Kaggle and Karolinska Directed Emotional Faces datasets. Here, while using Inception Net v3 Model, the final outcome of this model becomes 35%. The low accuracy of this model makes it less reliable than the others as it performs with low predictive possible solutions,

Hanh Phan-Xuan, [21] developed a Field-Programmable Gate Arrays (FPGA) architecture to recognize expressions using CNN in order to lower computational costs through hardware parallelism. Here, a deep learning model has been used in this situation. Using that method, posed-emotion dataset (FER2013) was trained. The dataset FERC-2013 carries 28,709 training examples and the publics testing set consists of 3589 examples. They gained their training accuracy 60.5% and testing accuracy 60.4%.

Shan Li and Weihong Deng, [16] has applied a CNN-RNN architectured model to train each input static images. There was also a use of the Acted Facial Expressions in the Wild (AFEW), deal with gradient problem.

Ninad, Mehendale et al. [18] have applied a unique technique, Facial Emotion Recognition using Convolutional Neural Network, divided into two sections. First one was to remove background of pictures and the second section focused on facial feature vector extraction. They were able to classify five types of expressions e using expression vector. They used 70% of 10,000 dataset images for training and the remaining 30% for testing. Overall, 25 iterations occurred with different sets of data in training set.

Considering the above literature review, we can think of a improvement in expression classification. Here, some limitations are found in the feature extraction part and also in classification part that are performed in a separate way. In these works, we can see that, some of works are limited to classify five types of emotions, some are complicated in their system model and carries less accuracy with less number of image set than ours. Therefore, we worked here to overcome some problems and to recognise successfully seven type of emotions from a large number of image dataset. Without prior knowledge these works can not be done properly. In case of CNN, model of a multi layer neural network doesn't depend upon prior knowledge and shows a better performance. We have worked with a previously experimented dataset [21] and implemented with this model to make more potential.

3   Methodology

In this section, we are set to represent the methodology that we are following to build our model. It also includes the system events flow charts and the deep learning [17,28] method which is going to be implemented. Figure 1 shows the pipeline of the whole system.

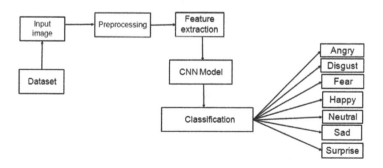

Fig. 1. The pipeline of the proposed solution

According to Fig. 1, at first, images are loaded from dataset and these images are preprocessed. This preprocessing technique converts all the raw data of images to the mathematical format. Then the features of the images starts extracting. After feature extraction, the work of doing prediction is done by CNN model. Here, a CNN architecture has been used by the suggested system. CNN, a deep learning system with the ability to distinguish between each image in the dataset. Generally, CNN is used where image analyses, segmentations and classifications are needed. According to the prediction, emotion classification is occurred.

3.1   Dataset

The first step of emotion recognition from face image is image acquisition which is very important and complicated because of differences in size and color of the human face from one to another. We can capture image from camera or we can collect a large number of image from internet. Except this, there are several datasets of face images with age label for emotion recognition. Sometimes, there are found several types of output for the same input because of different environment states in the process of acquisition such as lighting effect, different positioning and split of distance.

There are several datasets available what are used in the research field of recognizing emotions. In this paper, we have used FERC-2013 datasets [7, 20] from kaggle. All the images are categorized with based on their facial expressions. These are in seven category such as angry, disgust, fear, happy, neutral, sad and surprise. Here, there are 3,589 instances in the testing set, which is used to evaluate the model's performance, and 28,709 samples in the training set. Figure 2 shows a sample of dataset of FER-2013 [7, 20].

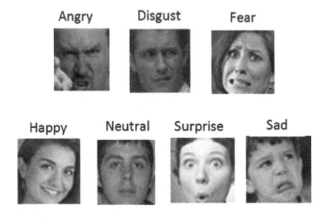

Fig. 2. Sample images used in Dataset

3.2   Preprocessing

Pre-processing is a very fundamental and an important part in emotion recognition system to reduce noise of the image, and prepare the faces' images for the better feature extraction. It may not improve the information of image but it helps us to get accurate result. Preprocessing of image are generally involved with removing low frequency and background noises, with the normalization of the intensity of each input image, removing lighting reflection. The images are normalized so that the differences can be eliminated and can get improved image of face. The steps of pre-processing an image has been illustrated in Fig. 3.

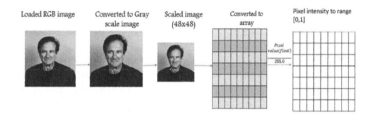

Fig. 3. Preprocessing of an image

In Fig. 3, we presented three images of a person where image localization is done. First image is an input image, second one is in the form of gray scaled image and the third one is scaled image with dimension 48×48. The image is converted to an array carrying pixel values. Before being divided by 255.0 to get a value between 0 and 1, each pixel value is converted to a float.

Preprocessing of images is one of the step of enhancing data image prior to image processing. The technique include image resize, erosion, dilation, cropping and noise reduction etc. The captured image contains many parts of the face not only the region of interest for that its necessary to implement main step which is localization of face to isolate the face region from the rest of the acquired image.

3.3   Convolutional Neural Network

Convolutional Neural Networks are inspired by the human brain [5,14]. A hierarchical neural network model was proposed by a researcher named Fukushima in 1980. This model took inspiration from the concepts of the Complex cells and Simple cells in the human brain. By learning about the shapes of objects it was able to recognize patterns. Convolutional Neural Network was introduced in a research paper by Le Cun et al. in 1998 [13]. A Convolutional Neural Network mainly has two major components. The feature extraction part and the Hidden Layers or Fully Connected Layers which supports classifications.

Feature Extraction. In the feature extraction part, 3 activities are performed. Convolution, Pooling, and Flattening. Convolution is a mathematical operation which is performed on the image matrix using one or more kernels or filters. To perform some operations like detecting edge can be done while there is performed a convolution with different filters on an image. After every Convolution process, the ReLU (Rectified Linear Unit) procedure is applied. To minimize the bulk of the data, pooling layers are utilized, then parameters are decreased in number, which is helpful when the image is too large. Max pooling is generally preferred when dealing with computer vision because it produces better results. The purpose of Max pooling is to target the highest value of the rectified feature map. Flattening is the process of converting the matrix into a linear array so that it can be provided as input for the nodes of the fully connected layers in the neural network.

Classification. Here, hidden layer uses a softmax activation function for providing the probability of each target class over all possible target classes. Dropout [27] is used in neural networks mainly to minimize overfitting. It works on training data to prevent co-adaptations which are in complex format. The Fully Connected layer is a traditional Multi-Layer. The output layer of this Perceptron layer has a softmax activation function. The Fully Connected layer's primary goal is to use these characteristics to divide the input picture into several groups depending on the training dataset.

The architecture of our proposed model has been shown in Fig. 4.

In Fig. 4, we can see the main model consists of 8 2D convolutional layers. The input form was 48 * 48 * 1 because all of the input photos were reshaped to 48*48 and made into grayscale images. These convolutional layers employed filters with values of 32, 64, 128, 256, 512, 728, and 1024. The kernel was also 3*3 in size. But there were also utilized 4 Batch Normalization layers, MaxPooling layers, and dropout layers. The model was constructed in the output layer using the Flatter layer and the Dense layer.

An activation function, Rectified Linear Unit (ReLU) in each and every convolution layer is used the which is shown in Eq. (1).

$$ReLU(y) = max(0, y) \tag{1}$$

As an activation function in the output layer, Softmax has been applied which is shown in Eq. (2).

$$Softmax(y) = \frac{e^i}{\sum\limits_{j} e^j} \tag{2}$$

4   Experimental Setup

We used Python as a programming language to implement our system. Some libraries such as numpy, pandas, matpotlib, keras are used. Functions (activation function, layers, utils, callback, optimizers) are loaded from keras. This model

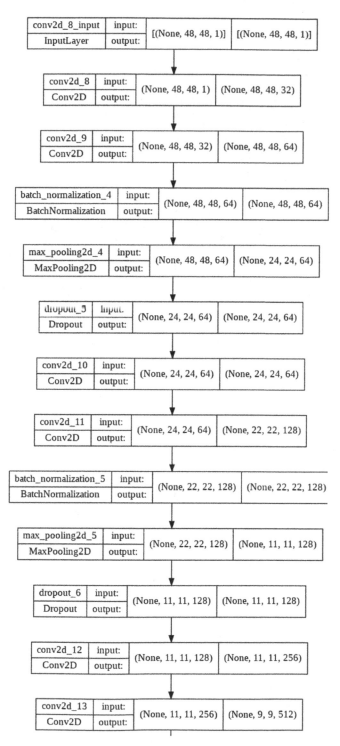

Fig. 4. The architecture of our model

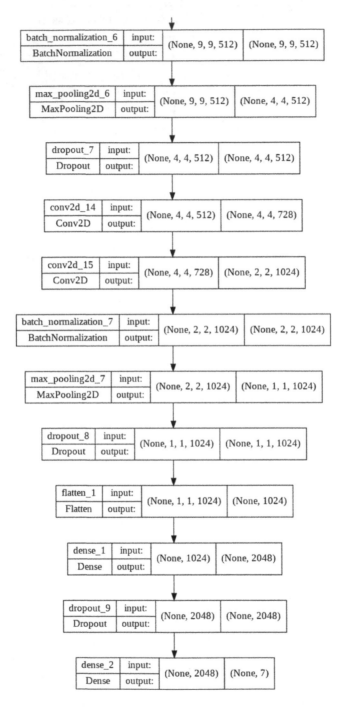

Fig. 4. (*continued*)

was trained using multiple activation functions such as relu, sigmoid and softmax. Different optimizers like adam, adamax, adadelta, adagrad, sgd nadam also used in training. Comparing all these, best performance result founded when softmax activation function, and adam optimizer.

Table 1 shows the tools used in experiment to implement this system

Table 1. Experimental Tools

Type	Name	Descriptions
Hardware Requirement	Laptop	Name: HP pavilion G series Processor: AMD A4-3300M APU with Radeon™ HD Graphics, 1.90 GHz RAM: 4.00 GB System Type: 64-bit operating system
Software Requirement	Operating system	Microsoft windows 10
	Programming Language	Python
	Software	Spyder Anaconda 3 (Python 3.7)
	Library	Keras 2.2.4, Tensorflow 1.15.0

5   Result and Discussion

5.1   Compare to the Result of Different Activation Functions and Optimizers

As stated before, we have used CNN model for classification in our Experiment. In case of checking accuracy, we have trained our model using three different classifiers. These are Softmax, Relu, and Sigmoid. We have applied several optimizers including Adam, Adamax, Adadelta, Adagrad, Nadam, RMSProp, and SGD. The accuracy for these different classifiers are stated below in Table 2 and Table 3.

Table 2. Classification using Adam, Adamax, Adadelta, and Adagrad optimizer

Activation Function	Optimizer							
	Adam		Adamax		Adadelta		Adagrad	
	Training	Testing	Training	Testing	Training	Testing	Training	Testing
Softmax	77%	68%	74.82%	55.2%	64.71%	53.17%	50.52%	46.82%
ReLU	39.64%	61.86%	13.88%	14.74%	46.87%	26.16%	49.31%	21.29%
Sigmoid	47.25%	36.55%	74.92%	55.14%	55.55%	43.22%	31.33%	28.82%

According to Table 2 and Table 3, we can see among these three classifiers, the best accuracy is observed using the "Softmax" classifier.

Figure 5 shows the learning curve of our model.

According to the learning curve, we can see the model loss was initially above 20. After starting the training, the loss also started to reduce and it became close to zero later after training.

Table 3. Classification using Nadam, RMSProp, and SGD optimizer

Activation Function	Optimizer					
	Nadam		RMSProp		SGD	
	Training	Testing	Training	Testing	Training	Testing
Softmax	59.21%	51.57%	49.79%	46.30%	70.96%	52.42%
ReLU	52.82%	44.83%	36.39%	26.29%	62.2%	59.45%
Sigmoid	55.27%	52.77%	33.25%	29.45%	61.11%	51.93%

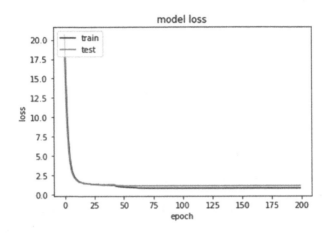

Fig. 5. Training vs testing loss curve

Generally the prediction outcomes that we get on a classification problem are summarized with a confusion matrix. Count values are used to summarize and break down the number of corrections or inaccurate predictions by class.

Based on the confusion matrix shown in Fig. 6, our model can predict most of the correct categories of an unknown dataset.

5.2 Compare to Different Model

Using same FER dataset, we have trained some machine learning approaches [6] i.e., Support Vector Machine (SVM) [24], Random Forest, Gradient Boosting [14], K Nearest Neighbor (KNN), Decision Tree Classifier, etc. we made a comparison implementing with these models and proposed model that is shown in Table 4.

This comparison table may demonstrate that the suggested model's performance cannot be outperformed by that of other models because it outperformed them in terms of accuracy, precision, recall, and f1-score. After putting our suggested model to the test, we evaluated how it performed against other models based on the literature review. To compare two standard approaches for detec-

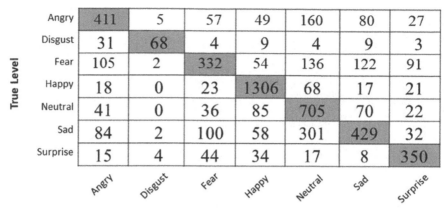

Predicted Level

Fig. 6. Confusion matrix

Table 4. Comparison of performance among Machine learning Models

Model	Accuracy	Precision	Recall	F1-Score
SVM	30.96%	31.22%	30.96%	30.95%
Random Forest	44.90%	48.80%	44.90%	42.05%
Gradient Boosting	39.22%	37.89%	39.22%	36.30%
KNN	31.29%	30.97%	31.28%	29.77%
Decision Tree	29.35%	29.44%	29.35%	29.37%
Proposed Model	68%	66%	64%	65%

tion, Support Vector Machine (SVM) [8] and another CNN network [15] were used.

After testing the model we proposed, we have compared the performance of our model to the existing models based on the literature review. We chose two conventional methods, Support Vector Machine (SVM) [8] along with another CNN network [15] to make a detection comparison. We implemented these models using FER2013 database and made a comparison taking accuracy metric obtained when testing on this same database. Hence, we made an analysis on some same standard deep learning methods such as inception model, shallow model, CNN with Histogram of Oriented Gradients (HOG) features. The performance of these models and our proposed model has shown in Table 5.

On regarding CNN methods, Akash Saravanan et al., [25] used a CNN model using 6 convolutional layers, and achieved 60% accuracy. Shima et al. [3] used a CNN model using 14 layers with HOG features where a SVM classifier is in the termination part of pipeline and achieved 62.4%. Again, they experimented shallow model and achieved 55%. Nithya Roopa. S et al., [23] used inception model on FER and Karolinska Directed Emotional Faces (KDEF) dataset. They

Table 5. Comparison of the proposed method with existing method

Reference	Method	Dataset	Accuracy
[25]	CNN with 6 Convolutional layers	FERC-2013	60%
[3]	i) CNN with 14 convolutional layers + HOG Features ii) Shallow model	FERC-2013	i) 62.4% ii) 55%
[23]	Inception Model	FERC-2013+KDEF	39%
[21]	CNN with 3 convolutional layers	FERC-2013	60.4%
[9]	SVM	FERC-2013	59.8%
Proposed Method	CNN with 8 convolutional layers	FERC-2013	68%

achieved 39%. Hanh Phan-Xuan, [21] used CNN model with 3 convolutional layers and 60.3% has achieved. A. Horseman [9] used SVM method, achieved 59.8%. They used the entire FER database as a result for testing and training. Therefore, using the identical set of data, our model is not significantly different from their model. In our model, we used 8 2D convolutional layers on FERC-2013 dataset. Again in the FER dataset, there are 28,709 files were used for training, The system was tested using 3,589 files. The best testing accuracy recorded throughout the last 200 epochs is 68%. 77% accuracy was the best for both training and testing. The average testing accuracy became 68% respectively. In Table 5, The recommended approach is the best available, as it overcomes these conventional methods and left the SVM [9] behind.

6   Conclusion

The development of a system for identifying emotions from face photographs is the goal of this study. In order to categorize the emotions, we have suggested a combined approach based on deep learning and computer vision. This study looked into how to classify facial expressions in a way that would meet opportunities and approaches. The Convolutional Neural Network method proves itself to be more worthwhile and efficient compared to other machine learning techniques. The model we proposed achieves a high accuracy value on the FER dataset. As the dataset carries data that were larger in amount with huge variation, it can help the model to observe the features and characteristics of the classes in more efficient ways. The future work in this research should be improving the performance of the proposed system, improving real time validation, the dataset can also be increased to make prediction more accurate, by bringing change with the addition of more classes. Our system can be made better using different classifiers such as sigmoid and ReLU with different optimizers and also be applied BRBES [2, 10, 22, 30] to develop integrated models [32].

References

1. Ahmed, T.U., Jamil, M.N., Hossain, M.S., Andersson, K., Hossain, M.S.: An integrated real-time deep learning and belief rule base intelligent system to assess facial expression under uncertainty. In: 2020 Joint 9th International Conference on Informatics, Electronics & Vision (ICIEV) and 2020 4th International Conference on Imaging, Vision & Pattern Recognition (icIVPR), pp. 1–6. IEEE (2020)
2. Alharbi, S.T., Hossain, M.S., Monrat, A.A.: A belief rule based expert system to assess autism under uncertainty. In: Proceedings of the World Congress on Engineering and Computer Science, vol. 1 (2015)
3. Alizadeh, S., Fazel, A.: Convolutional neural networks for facial expression recognition (2017)
4. Chowdhury, R.R., Hossain, M.S., ul Islam, R., Andersson, K., Hossain, S.: Bangla handwritten character recognition using convolutional neural network with data augmentation. In: 2019 Joint 8th International Conference on Informatics, Electronics & Vision (ICIEV) and 2019 3rd International Conference on Imaging, Vision & Pattern Recognition (icIVPR), pp. 318–323. IEEE (2019)
5. Darwin, C.: The Expression of the Emotions in Man and Animals. University of Chicago Press, Chicago (2015)
6. Fumo, D.: Types of machine learning algorithms you should know. Towards Data Sci. **15** (2017)
7. Goodfellow, I.J., et al.: Challenges in representation learning: a report on three machine learning contests. In: Lee, M., Hirose, A., Hou, Z.-G., Kil, R.M. (eds.) ICONIP 2013. LNCS, vol. 8228, pp. 117–124. Springer, Heidelberg (2013). https://doi.org/10.1007/978-3-642-42051-1_16
8. Gunes, H., Schuller, B.: Categorical and dimensional affect analysis in continuous input: current trends and future directions. Image Vis. Comput. **31**(2), 120–136 (2013)
9. Horseman, A.: SVM for facial expression recognition. A demonstrate project using SVM (2007)
10. Kabir, S., Islam, R.U., Hossain, M.S., Andersson, K.: An integrated approach of belief rule base and deep learning to predict air pollution. Sensors **20**(7), 1956 (2020)
11. Ko, B.C.: A brief review of facial emotion recognition based on visual information. Sensors **18**(2), 401 (2018)
12. Krizhevsky, A., Sutskever, I., Hinton, G.E.: ImageNet classification with deep convolutional neural networks. In: Advances in Neural Information Processing Systems, vol. 25 (2012)
13. Latha, C.P., Priya, M.: A review on deep learning algorithms for speech and facial emotion recognition. APTIKOM J. Comput. Sci. Inf. Technol. **1**(3), 92–108 (2016)
14. LeCun, Y., Bottou, L., Bengio, Y., Haffner, P.: Gradient-based learning applied to document recognition. Proc. IEEE **86**(11), 2278–2324 (1998)
15. Li, F., Ma, J., Huang, D.: MFCC and SVM based recognition of Chinese vowels. In: Hao, Y., et al. (eds.) CIS 2005. LNCS (LNAI), vol. 3802, pp. 812–819. Springer, Heidelberg (2005). https://doi.org/10.1007/11596981_118
16. Li, S., Deng, W.: Deep facial expression recognition: a survey. IEEE Trans. Affect. Comput. **13**(3), 1195–1215 (2020)
17. Liliana, D.Y.: Emotion recognition from facial expression using deep convolutional neural network. In: Journal of Physics: Conference Series, vol. 1193, p. 012004. IOP Publishing (2019)

18. Mehendale, N.: Facial emotion recognition using convolutional neural networks (FERC). SN Appl. Sci. **2**(3), 1–8 (2020)
19. Mohammadpour, M., Khaliliardali, H., Hashemi, S.M.R., AlyanNezhadi, M.M.: Facial emotion recognition using deep convolutional networks. In: 2017 IEEE 4th International Conference on Knowledge-based Engineering and Innovation (KBEI), pp. 0017–0021. IEEE (2017)
20. Otroshi-Shahreza, H.: Frame-based face emotion recognition using linear discriminant analysis. In: 2017 3rd Iranian Conference on Intelligent Systems and Signal Processing (ICSPIS), pp. 141–146. IEEE (2017)
21. Phan-Xuan, H., Le-Tien, T., Nguyen-Tan, S.: FPGA platform applied for facial expression recognition system using convolutional neural networks. Procedia Comput. Sci. **151**, 651–658 (2019)
22. Raihan, S., Zisad, S.N., Islam, R.U., Hossain, M.S., Andersson, K.: A belief rule base approach to support comparison of digital speech signal features for Parkinson's disease diagnosis. In: Mahmud, M., Kaiser, M.S., Vassanelli, S., Dai, Q., Zhong, N. (eds.) BI 2021. LNCS (LNAI), vol. 12960, pp. 388–400. Springer, Cham (2021). https://doi.org/10.1007/978-3-030-86993-9_35
23. Roopa, N.: Emotion recognition from facial expression using deep learning. Int. J. Eng. Adv. Technol. (IJEAT) (2019). ISSN 2249–8958
24. Sajja, T.K., Kalluri, H.K.: Gender classification based on face images of local binary pattern using support vector machine and back propagation neural networks. Adv. Modell. Anal. B **62**(1), 31–35 (2019). https://iieta.org/journals/ama_b
25. Saravanan, A., Perichetla, G., Gayathri, D.K.S.: Facial emotion recognition using convolutional neural networks (2019)
26. Simonyan, K., Zisserman, A.: Very deep convolutional networks for large-scale image recognition. arXiv preprint arXiv:1409.1556 (2014)
27. Toumi, T., Zidani, A.: From human-computer interaction to human-robot social interaction. arXiv preprint arXiv:1412.1251 (2014)
28. Voulodimos, A., Doulamis, N., Doulamis, A., Protopapadakis, E.: Deep learning for computer vision: a brief review. Comput. Intell. Neurosci. **2018** (2018)
29. Zadeh, M.M.T., Imani, M., Majidi, B.: Fast facial emotion recognition using convolutional neural networks and Gabor filters. In: 2019 5th Conference on Knowledge Based Engineering and Innovation (KBEI), pp. 577–581. IEEE (2019)
30. Zisad, S.N., Chowdhury, E., Hossain, M.S., Islam, R.U., Andersson, K.: An integrated deep learning and belief rule-based expert system for visual sentiment analysis under uncertainty. Algorithms **14**(7), 213 (2021)
31. Zisad, S.N., Hossain, M.S., Andersson, K.: Speech emotion recognition in neurological disorders using convolutional neural network. In: Mahmud, M., Vassanelli, S., Kaiser, M.S., Zhong, N. (eds.) BI 2020. LNCS (LNAI), vol. 12241, pp. 287–296. Springer, Cham (2020). https://doi.org/10.1007/978-3-030-59277-6_26
32. Zisad, S.N., Hossain, M.S., Hossain, M.S., Andersson, K.: An integrated neural network and SEIR model to predict COVID-19. Algorithms **14**(3), 94 (2021)

Emotion Recognition from Brain Wave Using Multitask Machine Learning Leveraging Residual Connections

Rumman Ahmed Prodhan[1], Sumya Akter[1], Muhammad Bin Mujib[1], Md. Akhtaruzzaman Adnan[1], and Tanmoy Sarkar Pias[2(✉)]

[1] University of Asia Pacific, Dhaka 1205, Bangladesh
adnan.cse@uap-bd.edu
[2] Virginia Tech, Blacksburg, VA 24061, USA
tanmoysarkar@vt.edu

Abstract. Emotions have a significant influence on both our personal and professional lives. Images, videos, and brain signals can all be used to identify emotion. Electroencephalography (EEG), which is used to determine the state of the human brain, can also be used to recognize emotion. However, emotion recognition from EEG is a complex problem by nature, yet it is more dependable than other emotion detection methods. Despite the efforts of numerous researchers in the past to increase performance to identify emotion more correctly, they were unable to do so. This paper proposes a deep learning strategy to recognize human emotions better using EEG data from the DEAP dataset. We leverage multitask machine learning to improve performance by using the capability of residual connections. Most studies concentrated solely on valence and arousal, which are directly related to emotion but incapable of fully comprehending the emotional state. To detect emotion better, we consider valence, arousal, dominance, liking, and familiarity in this experiment. The results demonstrated that the proposed technique can accurately predict emotions with an accuracy of 96.85%, 97.10%, 97.19%, 97.03%, and 95.24% for 2 class classification and for 3 class classification 95.92%, 96.02%, 96.63%, 96.08%, 95.39% for valence, arousal, dominance, liking, and familiarity respectively.

Keywords: Emotion Recognition · DEAP · EEG · FFT · Multitask Learning · Residual Connection · CNN · Deep Learning

1 Introduction

Emotion is a feeling or experience associated with a particular event or situation. Some emotions are positive such as happiness, love, and joy. Others are negative, such as sadness, anger, and fear. It is tough to understand a person's emotional state. Emotion recognition is the ability to identify and understand the emotions expressed by people with the help of mathematical models.

© ICST Institute for Computer Sciences, Social Informatics and Telecommunications Engineering 2023
Published by Springer Nature Switzerland AG 2023. All Rights Reserved
Md. S. Satu et al. (Eds.): MIET 2022, LNICST 491, pp. 121–136, 2023.
https://doi.org/10.1007/978-3-031-34622-4_10

Electroencephalography (EEG) is a technique that measures the brain's electrical activity [14]. The EEG signal can be used to determine the electrical activity associated with various emotions.

The DEAP dataset [17] is a large, publicly accessible dataset containing EEG signals that have been used in various research on emotion recognition [13,18,29]. This dataset has five labels: valence, arousal, dominance, liking, and familiarity. The other authors [11,19] mainly focused on arousal and valence, which indicate emotions, but the other three labels are also essential to identify emotions. Dominance, which is part of human emotion, indicates how much a person feels empowered or helpless. Liking indicates how much a person likes or dislikes something. Familiarity could help to understand how much a person is familiar with something. These labels are interconnected and could give a more accurate representation of a person's emotional state. The proposed work tried to detect emotions more precisely by classifying them into three classes.

In 1971, Paul Ekman introduced seven universal facial expressions [8] by which a person generally expresses their emotion. This study chooses a three-class classification because it will give eight basic emotions in three classes, which is better than a two-class classification. These eight emotions are closer to Paul Ekman's seven universal emotions. But recognizing emotion is a complex task. The deep learning approach is popular for different types of intricate tasks, like, vehicle recognition [24], gender recognition [25], ECG analysis [5], and computer vision [26]. Thus in this study, the authors use a deep learning technique called a multitask learning model, where the model is trained on multiple tasks simultaneously and optimizes multiple loss functions simultaneously. The assumption is that tasks share some common structure or are related somehow, so learning how to solve one task can help learn how to solve the others. The proposed model uses this technique to learn each level (valence, arousal, dominance, liking, and familiarity) to analyze how the levels work together more efficiently and effectively.

Significant contributions of this paper:

- For the first time, we have applied multitask learning in all five labels of the DEAP dataset.
- We divide the five labels of the DEAP dataset into 2 and 3 classes for practical applications.
- We have used a 1D-CNN with residual connections for increased performance.

2   Literature Review

There has been a lot of study on emotion recognition using EEG signal processing. Many public datasets for emotion recognition are available, which include DEAP [17], SEED [3], LUMED [1], DREAMER [16], MAHNOB-HCI [27], and AMIGOS [21]. Among the public datasets, the DEAP dataset is the most used. That is why the DEAP dataset is adopted in this research. The contributions of prior research that have used the DEAP dataset are discussed in Table 1. This section consists of a detailed review of some important recent experiments on

EEG signals for emotion recognition. For effective classification of emotions, several factors play an important role, such as different feature extraction methods, modeling techniques, and working labels.

2.1 Feature Extraction Method

It has been found that several different techniques are used for feature extraction from the EEG signal. There are mainly three [22] types of features: Time-domain features, Frequency-domain features, and Time-Frequency domain features that can be used for extracting the EEG signal. Various time-domain features like differential entropy (DE) [7,9,30], Hjorth [10], and sample entropy are used and achieve good accuracy in working on valence and arousal emotion labels. Frequency domain features like power spectral density (PSD) [9,10] are also used. Time-Frequency domain features like DWT [19] are also described in several research papers. Many researchers used multiple features like Garg et al. [11] used wavelet transform and statistical measures features in their work. The fast Fourier transform [13,19] is mostly used for feature extraction in recent times. In this paper, the author uses the FFT feature extraction technique.

2.2 Modeling Technique

Different type of modeling techniques is observed in emotion recognition from the EEG field. Convolution Neural Network (CNN) and Long Short-Term Memory (LSTM) models are frequently used and achieve outstanding accuracy. Other approaches are also used in this field.

CNN-Based Approach. Islam et al. [15] demonstrated a CNN model with the help of Pearson's correlation coefficient (PCC) feature. Their model has two protocols. One is used to identify two levels of emotion; the other is used to demonstrate three levels of emotional arousal and valence. They reached an accuracy of 78.22% in valence and 74.92% in arousal when applied to two classes. They also achieve an accuracy of 70.23% in valence and 70.25% in arousal when applied to a three-class classification. Gao et al. [10] proposed a multi-feature fusion network based CNN model that performs better when an SVM classifier is used. To assess the method, they used a leave-one-subject-out experiment on the DEAP dataset and achieved 80.52% in valence and 75.22% in arousal emotion labels. Hasan et al. [13] proposed a CNN model for two and eight classes. They used FFT as the feature extraction method and achieved 96.63% in valence and 96.17% in arousal across two classes of classification. They also achieved 93.83% in valence and 93.7% in arousal across eight class classifications. Yin et al. [30] suggested a method that combined GCNN and LSTM. Their fusion model worked in a subject-dependent experiment and reached an accuracy of 90.45% in valence and 90.60% in arousal labels.

LSTM-Based Approach. Garg et al. [11] work with four emotion labels and obtain an accuracy of 83.85%, 84.89%, 84.37%, and 80,72% on arousal, valence, dominance, and liking, respectively, by using a merged LSTM model. All labels are classified independently and could not achieve higher accuracy. Ma et al. [20] proposed a network called the MM-ResLSTM method for emotion recognition. Their multimodal residual LSTM model achieved an accuracy of 92.87% in arousal and 92.30% in valence. Only two emotion labels, arousal, and valence are classified in their work. Anubhav et al. [4] used a Long-Short-Term Memory (LSTM) based model to assess PSD over the 32 channels of the DEAP dataset. Their model can only work on valence and arousal working labels and achieved 94.69% accuracy for valence and 93.13% accuracy for arousal labels.

Other Approaches. Fang et al. [9] categorized emotions into five classes using Multi-Feature Deep Forest (MFDF) as a classifier. PSD and DE are used as input features for their proposed MFDF method. Their model obtained a total accuracy of 71.05% on the valence and arousal labels. Tan et al. [28] used spiking neural networks (SNN) in their short-term emotion recognition framework. However, they only work on valence and arousal emotion labels. Their achieved accuracy is 78.97% in arousal and 67.76% in valence labels. Lie et al. [18] used an end-to-end MLF-CapsNet framework, which can perform on raw EEG signals. Their frameworks achieve an accuracy of 98.31% on arousal, 97.97% on valence, and 98.32% on dominance labels.

The above discussion shows that most researchers worked on two essential emotion labels (valence and arousal). Only a few covered three or four emotion labels from the DEAP dataset with two classes. Two-class classification can only detect four emotions at a time which is not satisfactory for detecting exact emotions. To overcome this problem, this study uses a 1D-CNN using the residual connection and multitask learning in which all five labels are learned simultaneously. Also, to recognize emotions more precisely, a three-class classification is used.

3   Dataset

The DEAP dataset is a multimodal dataset mainly used for analyzing the effective states of humans. The dataset team selected 120 music videos with a one-minute duration. The overview of the DEAP dataset is shown in Table 2.

In the DEAP dataset, there are a .bdf file for each participant and all of them are recorded with 48 channels 512 Hz. This dataset is recorded in two different places. The data of participants 1–22 are recorded in Twente, and 23–32 are recorded in Geneva.

The DEAP dataset also contains preprocessed files that are downsampled 128 Hz. There are two downsampled zips available in the DEAP dataset. The preprocessed python zip is used for this study, which has 32 files in .dat format. Each .dat file represents a single participant. There are 2 arrays available. The data array has 40 trials, 40 channels, and 8064 data. There are 32 EEG channels out of the previously mentioned 40 channels. The duration of each trial is 63 s. That is why the data is $128 \times 63 = 8064$.

Table 1. Overview of the literature review on emotion recognition from DEAP Dataset

Research	Year	Feature extraction	Modeling technique	No. of class	Label	Performance
Xun wu et al. [29]	2022	Functional Connectivity Network	DCCA	2 class	Valence, Arousal	Arousal: 85.34%, Valence: 86.61%
Cui et al. [7]	2022	DE	DE-CNN-BiLSTM	2 class	Valence, Arousal	Arousal: 94.86%, Valence: 94.02%
Ghosh et al. [12]	2021	Maximally Informative Dimension	MI maximization	2 class, 3 class	Valence, Arousal, Dominance	Avg Arousal and Valence: 82%(Two class), Avg Arousal and Valence: 72% (Three class), Dominance: 95.87%
Islam et al. [15]	2021	PCC	CNN	2 class 3 class	Valence, Arousal	Valence: 78.22%, Arousal: 74.92%
Fang etel. [9]	2021	PSD, DE	MFDF	5-class	Valence, Arousal,	Avg Arousal and Valence:71.05%
Tan et al. [28]	2021	Handcrafted features	SNN	2 class	Valence, Arousal	Arousal: 78.97%, Valence: 67.76%
Gao et al. [10]	2021	PSD, Hjorth	CNN	2 class	Valence, Arousal	Valence: 80.52%, Arousal: 75.22%
Hasan et al. [13]	2021	FFT	CNN	2 class, 8 class	Valence, Arousal	Valence: 96.63%, Arousal: 96.17%(2 class), Valence: 93.83%, Arousal: 93.79% (8 class)
Yin et al. [30]	2021	DE	GCNN, LSTM	2 class	Valence, Arousal	Valence: 90.45%, Arousal: 90.60%
Lie et al. [18]	2020	Frequency domain feature	MLF-CapsNet	2 class	Valence, Arousal, Dominance	Valence: 97.97%, Arousal: 98.31%, Dominance: 98.32%
Y. Luo et al. [19]	2020	DWT, FFT	SNN	2 class	Arousal, Valence, Dominance, Liking	Arousal: 74%, Valence: 78%, Dominance: 80%, Liking: 86.27%
Anubhav et al. [4]	2020	Raw EEG	LSTM	2 class	Arousal, Valence	Valence: 94.69%, Arousal: 93.13%
Garg et al. [11]	2019	Wavelet, Statistical measures,	LSTM	2 class	Valence, Arousal, Dominance, Liking	Valence: 84.89% Arousal: 83.85% Dominance: 84.37% Liking: 80.72%
Ma et al. [20]	2019	Wavelet	MMResLSTM	2 class	Arousal, Valence	Arousal: 92.87%, Valence: 92.30%

Table 2. Overview of the DEAP Dataset

Dataset type	Multimodal
Subjects	32
Number of Videos	40
Number of EEG Channels	32
Labels	Valance, Arousal, Dominance, Liking and Familiarity
Original sample rate	512 Hz
Preprocessed downsampled rate	128 HZ
Rating Values	Between 1 and 9 in floating number (Valance, Arousal, Dominance and Liking) Between 1 and 5 in integer number (Familiarity)

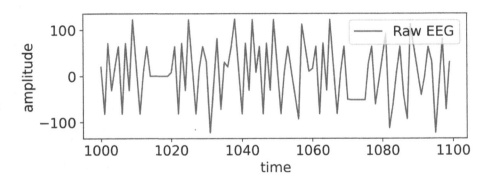

Fig. 1. Raw EEG data segment of a subject from the DEAP dataset

A participant's dat file from the preprocessed Python folder is plotted in Fig. 1. This is what the EEG signals look like for each participant. The label array has 40 trials and 4 labels that are valence, arousal, dominance, and liking. Familiarity is missing in this label. In the participant rating file, all participant's ratings for each trial are available. Familiarity along with valence, arousal, dominance, and liking is also available in this file. Familiarity is missing for participants 2, 15, and 23. For this study, familiarity is added with the remaining 29 .dat files.

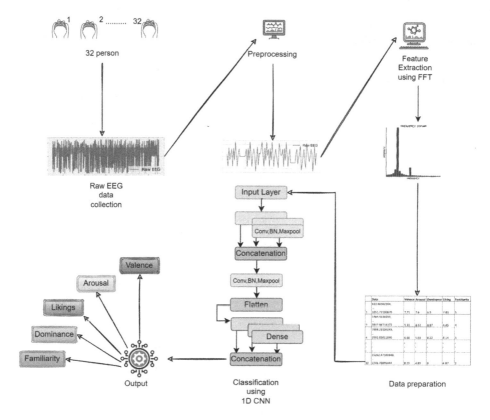

Fig. 2. Complete workflow diagram of emotion recognition from DEAP dataset using multitask CNN

4   Methodology

Figure 2 illustrates a comprehensive summary of EEG data analysis. Firstly, the raw EEG data is collected. Then various data preprocessing techniques are applied. After that, the feature extraction step uses FFT to partition the preprocessed data. Then data preparation is done by applying labeling and normalization to all five labels of emotion. Finally, the 1D CNN uses those data to train the model with multitask learning to classify the emotions more accurately.

4.1   Preprocessing

The EEG signals are downsampled 128 Hz from the 512 Hz. Eye artifacts are removed using a blind source separation technique [2]. A bandpass frequency filter is applied with 4.0–45.0Hz. According to the common reference, the data is averaged. As the EEG data is recorded in 2 different locations, the EEG channels are reordered following the Geneva order. Each trial's data is broken down into 60 s and a 3-second pre-trial baseline. Afterward, the pre-trial segment is removed. Also, the trials are reordered to experiment of the video order from the presentation order.

4.2   Feature Extraction

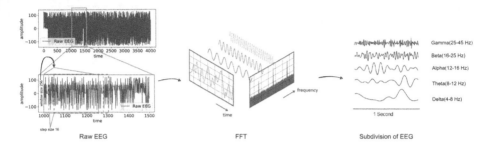

Fig. 3. Feature extraction: Decomposing the raw EEG into sub-bands using FFT

Feature extraction is essential to minimize the loss of valuable signals, reduce overfitting, and reduce complexity for implementation. Generally, instead of using raw data [4], using any feature extraction technique could provide better results for classification. In this study, the author uses frequency-domain features [6], which are mainly used to decompose signal data into subbands shown in Fig. 3. For EEG features extraction Wavelet transform (WT), fast Fourier transform (FFT), Equivocator methods (EM), etc., are primarily used. The fast Fourier transform is used from these feature extraction methods to the EEG signals. FFT is an algorithm for calculating a sequence's discrete Fourier transform or inverse discrete Fourier transform. The discrete Fourier transform (DTF) can be written like the following:

$$x[k] = \sum_{n=0}^{N-1} x[n]e^{\frac{-j2\pi kn}{N}} \tag{1}$$

Here, n is the size of the domain. To calculate the DFT of a discrete signal x[n], multiplication of each of its values by e power to some function of n should be done. Then the summation of the results obtained for a given n should be taken. The complexity of calculating the DFT of a signal is $O(N^2)$. As the name suggests, the fast Fourier transform (FFT) is significantly faster than DFT. FFT reduces the complexity from $O(N^2)$ to $O(NlogN)$.

In this study, 14 EEG channels are selected. These are Fp1, AF3, F3, F7, FC1, P3, PO3, Fp2, Fz, F4, F8, C4, P4, and PO4. 5 bands are selected. These are Delta (4–8 Hz), Theta (8–12 Hz), Alpha (12–16 Hz), Beta (16–25 Hz), and Gamma (25–45 Hz). Windows size is 256, the step size is 16, and the sample rate is 128 hz.

4.3 Data Preparation

After applying FFT each EEG file contains 19520 rows and 4 columns. Here familiarity is missing. Familiarity is available on the participant ratings file. Each preprocessed EEG file is converted into a dataframe. From the participant ratings files, there are 9 columns. 4 columns are dropped except the 5 label columns. Then both dataframe are merged on 4 common labels (valence, arousal, dominance, and liking), and thus familiarity is added.

Then, the data is ready to feed into the CNN model. Now, the EEG file contains 19520 rows and 5 columns. After dividing 19520 rows by 8, the training consists of 17114 rows which are 87.5%, and testing consists of 2406 rows which are 12.5%. This is done for all 29 files as 2, 15, and 23 don't have familiarity. So, the data are split into training and testing following 87.5% and 12.5% respectively.

For valence, arousal, dominance, and liking the label array contains floating values from 1 to 9. But the rating of 9 is poor compared to other ratings. That is why the author converted 9 into 8.99 for better handling calculation. As the difference between 9 and 8.99 is very low, it does not have any impact.

For binary classification, each label is divided into 2 categories except familiarity which is divided into 5 categories. For valence, arousal, dominance, and liking 1–4.9 are divided into 1 category, and 5–8.9 are divided into another category. For familiarity, every individual integer ranging from 1 to 5 is selected as a category.

For 3 class classification, each label is divided into three categories except familiarity, which is divided into five categories like previously. For valence, arousal, dominance, and liking 1–3.66 are divided into category 1, 3.67–6.33 are divided into category 2, and 6.34–8.99 are divided into category 3. The labels are categorized using categorical functions. The EEG data are normalized using the standard scalar techniques. The DEAP dataset has 2D arrays but it is converted into 3D using reshape function as our model takes 3D data as input.

4.4 CNN Model Structure

Before creating the model, all the necessary processing is completed. In the proposed model shown in Fig. 4, a 1D-CNN has been used with hidden layers, which can be changed to affect the accuracy. The 1D-CNN is popular for signal processing, recognizing sensor data [23] etc. The proposed model uses multitask learning on the residual connection on the DEAP dataset. Initially, the model is converted from sequential to functional for implementing the residual connection, which is a type of skip connection. As the proposed model uses multitask learning, the concatenated value is passed into five different output layers for valence, arousal, dominance, liking, and familiarity, respectively.

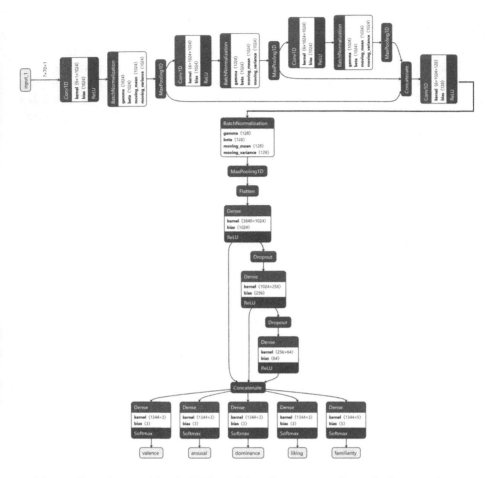

Fig. 4. Complete multitask CNN model architecture with residual connections

5   Experiment and Result Analysis

In this study, two different approaches are used to identify emotions clearly. One is the conventional binary classification method for multitasking learning on all four labels: valence, arousal, dominance, and liking, except familiarity, which is classified into five classes. Another approach is a 3 class classification method for multitask learning. Like previously, here all the 4 labels are divided into 3 classes except familiarity. The same 1D-CNN shown in Fig. 4 is used for both classification methods. For improving the accuracy, residual connections are used.

Table 3 shows the training and testing accuracies. It shows that there is a around 3 percent discrepancy between training and testing accuracy. For the proposed model, the author experimented with increasing the batch size to 1024 or decreasing the batch size to 32. Batch size 256 is selected as it has the best

Table 3. Result summary for two class and three class classification

Type	Valence		Arousal		Dominance		Liking		Familiarity	
	Train	Test	Train	Test	Train	Test	Train	Test	Train	Test
2-Class	99.75	96.85	99.70	97.10	99.76	97.19	99.74	97.03	99.59	95.24
3-Class	99.59	95.92	99.59	96.02	99.67	96.63	99.59	96.08	99.57	95.39

test accuracy and test loss. After each dense layer, dropout is used to reduce overfitting. Dropout is experimented with by changing from 0.1 to 0.5. Dropout 0.2 is selected as it reduces overfitting the most. The convolutional filter size is experimented with, by changing from 1024 to 64. Convolutional filter size 1024 is selected for providing the best accuracy. For running the proposed model, the author uses google colab, and the selected language is python. All the improvements after every epoch have been saved to google drive.

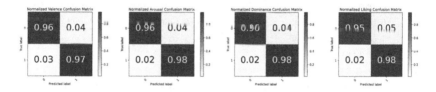

Fig. 5. Confusion matrix for binary classification

Figure 5 shows the confusion matrix for 2 class classifications for valence, arousal, liking, and dominance with normalization. The confusion matrix shows the summary of the prediction results where the number of correct and incorrect predictions are summarized and broken down into each class. It represents that the proposed model performs consistently across both classes for every label.

Figure 6 shows the confusion matrix for 3 class classifications for valence, arousal, liking, and dominance labels with normalization. The proposed model performs notably well across all three classes.

In Fig. 7, the confusion matrix for familiarity is shown. The left one is from two label classification model and the right one is from three label classification model. The proposed model performs well for all five classes of familiarity.

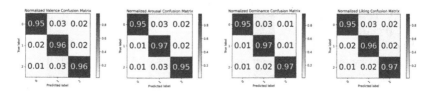

Fig. 6. Confusion matrix for three label classification

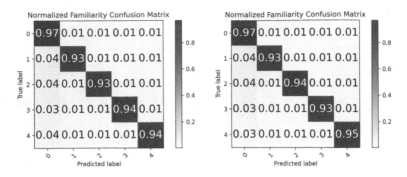

Fig. 7. Confusion matrix for familiarity from two label classification (left) and three label classification (right) model

Table 4. Performance report of two class and three label classification

Label	Three label Classification Report				Two Label Classification Report			
	Classes(score)	Precision	Recall	F1	Classes(score)	Precision	Recall	F1
Valence	0 (1–3.66)	0.95	0.95	0.95	0 (1–4.9)	0.96	0.96	0.96
	1 (3.67–6.33)	0.96	0.96	0.96	1 (5–8.9)	0.97	0.97	0.97
	2 (6.34–8.99)	0.96	0.96	0.96	-	-	-	-
Arousal	0 (1–3.66)	0.95	0.95	0.95	0 (1–4.9)	0.96	0.96	0.96
	1 (3.67–6.33)	0.97	0.97	0.97	1 (5–8.9)	0.98	0.98	0.98
	2 (6.34–8.99)	0.96	0.95	0.96	-	-	-	-
Dominance	0 (1–3.66)	0.96	0.95	0.96	0 (1–4.9)	0.96	0.96	0.96
	1 (3.67–6.33)	0.97	0.97	0.97	1 (5–8.9)	0.98	0.98	0.98
	2 (6.34–8.99)	0.97	0.96	0.97	-	-	-	-
Liking	0 (1–3.66)	0.95	0.95	0.95	0 (1–4.9)	0.96	0.95	0.95
	1 (3.67–6.33)	0.96	0.96	0.96	1 (5–8.9)	0.98	0.98	0.98
	2 (6.34–8.99)	0.97	0.97	0.97	-	-	-	-
Familiarity	0 (1)	0.96	0.97	0.97	0 (1)	0.96	0.97	0.97
	1 (2)	0.94	0.93	0.94	1 (2)	0.95	0.93	0.94
	2 (3)	0.93	0.94	0.93	2 (3)	0.93	0.93	0.93
	3 (4)	0.95	0.93	0.94	3 (4)	0.95	0.94	0.94
	4 (5)	0.95	0.95	0.95	4 (5)	0.95	0.94	0.95

Table 4 represents the classification report for the proposed model in 2 and 3 classes. It is designed to measure the model's effectiveness by displaying the precision, recall, and fl score.

In Fig. 8, the change of training accuracy and loss for 2 and 3 class classification with every epoch are shown respectively for all 5 labels. Initially, valence has more loss compared to the other 4 labels. However, it has been adjusted after 40 epochs. The proposed model gets a rapid increase in accuracy and a decrease in the loss in the first 20 epochs. Then from 21 to 60 epochs, the model

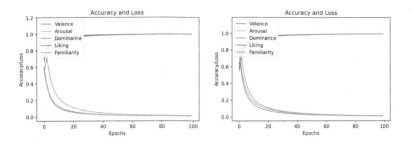

Fig. 8. Training accuracy and loss for two label (left figure) and three label (right figure) classification

gets a subtle increase and decrease in accuracy and loss. After 60 epochs the improvement of accuracy and loss is relatively low.

Table 5. Comparing our result with state-of-the-art

No.	Modeling technique	No. of class	Working label	Accuracy (Avg.)
1	CNN [13]	2-Class, 8-Class	Valence, arousal	96.40% (two class), 93.81% (eight class)
2	LSTM [4]	2-Class	Valence, arousal	93.91%
3	SNN [19]	2-Class	Arousal, Valence, Dominance, Liking	79.57%
4	MFDF [9]	5-Class	Valence, Arousal	71.05%
5	**Proposed Model: Multitask CNN**	**2-Class, 3-Class**	**Valence, Arousal, Dominance, Liking, Familiarity**	**96.68% (2-Class), 96.01% (3-Class)**

Table 5 shows result comparisons for the best modeling techniques on the DEAP dataset. Hasan et al. [13] achieved the best accuracy by using a 1D-CNN model on valence and arousal. In 2 class proposed model slightly outperformed their model while training on 5 labels simultaneously. Anubhav et al. [4] used LSTM for 2-class classification on valence and arousal. The proposed model exceeds their accuracy by 3%. Y. Luo et al. [19] used SNN for 2-class classification on 4 labels. The proposed model outperforms their accuracy by 17%. Fang et al. [9] uses MFDF for 5-class classification on valence, and arousal with the selected 23 participants. Proposed model surpasses their accuracy by 25%. The proposed Multitask CNN model achieved average testing accuracy of 96.68% for 2 class classification and 96.01% for 3 class classification, which is the highest compared to all other models mentioned in Table 5.

6   Conclusion

The proposed model uses multitask learning using 1D CNN to learn all 5 labels of emotions from EEG signals of the DEAP dataset. The model achieved an average accuracy of 96.68% for 2 classes and 96.01% for 3 classes. It can recognize emotions more accurately compared to existing works in the benchmark activities shown in Table 5. The result demonstrated that multitask learning using the CNN model can achieve the state of the art performance, which illustrated that valence, arousal, dominance, liking, and familiarity all are interconnected to recognize emotion from EEG signals. However, in this study, the data are split vertically. So the model is subject-dependent as it is trained and tested on the same subjects. In the future, the author wants to work on subject independent emotion recognition from EEG signals while making the model more lightweight and accurate.

Data and code availability. The used DEAP dataset is available on their official website. The code used in this study is available on github. The code is written in python using google colab.

References

1. Loughborough University EEG based Emotion Recognition Dataset (LUMED). https://www.dropbox.com/s/xlh2orv6mgweehq/LUMED_EEG.zip?dl=0. Accessed 11 Apr 2022
2. Emotions in social psychology: essential readings. https://www.worldcat.org/title/emotions-in-social-psychology-essential-readings/oclc/44425388
3. SEED dataset. https://bcmi.sjtu.edu.cn/home/seed/. Accessed 12 Apr 2022
4. Anubhav, Nath, D., Singh, M., Sethia, D., Kalra, D., Indu, S.: An efficient approach to EEG-based emotion recognition using LSTM network. In: 2020 16th IEEE International Colloquium on Signal Processing Its Applications (CSPA), pp. 88–92 (2020). https://doi.org/10.1109/CSPA48992.2020.9068691
5. Apu, M.R.H., Akter, F., Lubna, M.F.A., Helaly, T., Pias, T.S.: ECG arrhythmia classification using 1D CNN leveraging the resampling technique and gaussian mixture model. In: 2021 Joint 10th International Conference on Informatics, Electronics Vision (ICIEV) and 2021 5th International Conference on Imaging, Vision Pattern Recognition (icIVPR), pp. 1–8 (2021). https://doi.org/10.1109/ICIEVicIVPR52578.2021.9564201
6. Boonyakitanont, P., Lek-uthai, A., Chomtho, K., Songsiri, J.: A review of feature extraction and performance evaluation in epileptic seizure detection using EEG. Biomed. Sig. Process. Control **57**, 101702 (2020). https://doi.org/10.1016/j.bspc.2019.101702. https://www.sciencedirect.com/science/article/pii/S1746809419302836
7. Cui, F., Wang, R., Ding, W., Chen, Y., Huang, L.: A novel DE-CNN-BiLSTM multi-fusion model for EEG emotion recognition. Mathematics **10**(4) (2022). https://doi.org/10.3390/math10040582. https://www.mdpi.com/2227-7390/10/4/582
8. Ekman, P.: Universals and cultural differences in facial expressions of emotion. Nebr. Symp. Motiv. **19**, 207–283 (1971)

9. Fang, Y., Yang, H., Zhang, X., Liu, H., Tao, B.: Multi-feature input deep forest for EEG-based emotion recognition. Frontiers Neurorob. **14** (2021). https://doi.org/10.3389/fnbot.2020.617531. https://www.frontiersin.org/article/10.3389/fnbot.2020.617531
10. Gao, Q., Yang, Y., Kang, Q., Tian, Z., Song, Y.: EEG-based emotion recognition with feature fusion networks. Int. J. Mach. Learn. Cybern. (2021). https://link.springer.com/article/10.1007/s13042-021-01414-5#:
11. Garg, A., Kapoor, A., Bedi, A.K., Sunkaria, R.K.: Merged LSTM model for emotion classification using EEG signals. In: 2019 International Conference on Data Science and Engineering (ICDSE), pp. 139–143 (2019). https://doi.org/10.1109/ICDSE47409.2019.8971484
12. Ghosh, S.M., Bandyopadhyay, S., Mitra, D.: Nonlinear classification of emotion from EEG signal based on maximized mutual information. Exp. Syst. Appl. **185**, 115605 (2021). https://doi.org/10.1016/j.eswa.2021.115605. https://www.sciencedirect.com/science/article/pii/S0957417421010046
13. Hasan, M., Rokhshana-Nishat-Anzum, Yasmin, S., Pias, T.S.: Fine-grained emotion recognition from EEG signal using fast Fourier transformation and CNN. In: 2021 Joint 10th International Conference on Informatics, Electronics Vision (ICIEV) and 2021 5th International Conference on Imaging, Vision Pattern Recognition (icIVPR), pp. 1–9 (2021). https://doi.org/10.1109/ICIEVicIVPR52578.2021.9564204
14. Hassan, R., Hasan, S., Hasan, M.J., Jamader, M.R., Eisenberg, D., Pias, T.: Human attention recognition with machine learning from brain-EEG signals. In: 2020 IEEE 2nd Eurasia Conference on Biomedical Engineering, Healthcare and Sustainability (ECBIOS), pp. 16–19 (2020). https://doi.org/10.1109/ECBIOS50299.2020.9203672
15. Islam, M.R., et al.: EEG channel correlation based model for emotion recognition. Comput. Biol. Med. **136**, 104757 (2021). https://doi.org/10.1016/j.compbiomed.2021.104757. https://www.sciencedirect.com/science/article/pii/S0010482521005515
16. Katsigiannis, S., Ramzan, N.: Dreamer: a database for emotion recognition through EEG and ECG signals from wireless low-cost off-the-shelf devices. IEEE J. Biomed. Health Inform. **22**(1), 98–107 (2018). https://doi.org/10.1109/JBHI.2017.2688239
17. Koelstra, S., et al.: DEAP: a database for emotion analysis; using physiological signals. IEEE Trans. Affect. Comput. **3**(1), 18–31 (2012). https://doi.org/10.1109/T-AFFC.2011.15
18. Liu, Y., et al.: Multi-channel EEG-based emotion recognition via a multi-level features guided capsule network. Comput. Biol. Med. **123**, 103927 (2020). https://doi.org/10.1016/j.compbiomed.2020.103927. https://www.sciencedirect.com/science/article/pii/S0010482520302663
19. Luo, Y., et al.: EEG-based emotion classification using spiking neural networks. IEEE Access **8**, 46007–46016 (2020). https://doi.org/10.1109/ACCESS.2020.2978163
20. Ma, J., Tang, H., Zheng, W.L., Lu, B.L.: Emotion recognition using multimodal residual LSTM network. In: Proceedings of the 27th ACM International Conference on Multimedia, MM 2019, pp. 176–183. Association for Computing Machinery, New York (2019). https://doi.org/10.1145/3343031.3350871
21. Miranda-Correa, J.A., Abadi, M.K., Sebe, N., Patras, I.: AMIGOS: a dataset for affect, personality and mood research on individuals and groups. IEEE Trans. Affect. Comput. **12**(2), 479–493 (2021). https://doi.org/10.1109/TAFFC.2018.2884461

22. Nath, D., Anubhav, A., Singh, M., Sethia, D., Kalra, D., Sreedevi, I.: A comparative study of subject-dependent and subject-independent strategies for EEG-based emotion recognition using LSTM network, pp. 142–147 (2020). https://doi.org/10.1145/3388142.3388167

23. Pias, T.S., Eisenberg, D., Fresneda Fernandez, J.: Accuracy improvement of vehicle recognition by using smart device sensors. Sensors 22(12) (2022). https://doi.org/10.3390/s22124397

24. Pias, T.S., Eisenberg, D., Islam, M.A.: Vehicle recognition via sensor data from smart devices. In: 2019 IEEE Eurasia Conference on IOT, Communication and Engineering (ECICE), pp. 96–99 (2019). https://doi.org/10.1109/ECICE47484.2019.8942799

25. Pias, T.S., Kabir, R., Eisenberg, D., Ahmed, N., Islam, M.R.: Gender recognition by monitoring walking patterns via smartwatch sensors. In: 2019 IEEE Eurasia Conference on IOT, Communication and Engineering (ECICE), pp. 220–223 (2019). https://doi.org/10.1109/ECICE47484.2019.8942670

26. Sarif, M.M., Pias, T.S., Helaly, T., Tutul, M.S.R., Rahman, M.N.: Deep learning-based Bangladeshi license plate recognition system. In: 2020 4th International Symposium on Multidisciplinary Studies and Innovative Technologies (ISMSIT), pp. 1–6 (2020). https://doi.org/10.1109/ISMSIT50672.2020.9254748

27. Soleymani, M., Lichtenauer, J., Pun, T., Pantic, M.: A multimodal database for affect recognition and implicit tagging. IEEE Trans. Affect. Comput. 3(1), 42–55 (2012). https://doi.org/10.1109/T-AFFC.2011.25

28. Tan, C., Šarlija, M., Kasabov, N.: NeuroSense: short-term emotion recognition and understanding based on spiking neural network modelling of spatio-temporal EEG patterns. Neurocomputing 434, 137–148 (2021). https://doi.org/10.1016/j.neucom.2020.12.098. https://www.sciencedirect.com/science/article/pii/S0925231220320105

29. Wu, X., Zheng, W.L., Lu, B.L.: Investigating EEG-based functional connectivity patterns for multimodal emotion recognition (2020). https://doi.org/10.48550/ARXIV.2004.01973

30. Yin, Y., Zheng, X., Hu, B., Zhang, Y., Cui, X.: EEG emotion recognition using fusion model of graph convolutional neural networks and LSTM. Appl. Soft Comput. 100, 106954 (2021). https://doi.org/10.1016/j.asoc.2020.106954. https://www.sciencedirect.com/science/article/pii/S1568494620308929

Emotion Recognition from EEG Using Mutual Information Based Feature Map and CNN

Mahfuza Akter Maria[1], A. B. M. Aowlad Hossain[2] (iD), and M. A. H. Akhand[1](✉) (iD)

[1] Department of Computer Science and Engineering, Khulna University of Engineering and Technology, Khulna, Bangladesh
maria2007518@stud.kuet.ac.bd, akhand@cse.kuet.ac.bd
[2] Department of Electronics and Communication Engineering, Khulna University of Engineering and Technology, Khulna, Bangladesh
aowlad0403@ece.kuet.ac.bd

Abstract. Emotion is the fundamental trait of human beings, and brain signal is the most prospectus for emotion recognition. Electroencephalography (EEG) is a preferable brain signal for recognizing emotions. Extracting features from EEG signals is an essential part of this emotion recognition. Recently, EEG channel connectivity features have been widely used in emotion recognition. Automatic emotion recognition (ER) from EEG is a challenging computational intelligence or machine learning task due to the inherited complexity of EEG signals. The aim of the study is to analyze mutual information (MI) based connectivity measures for feature extraction from EEG signals and classify emotions using deep learning. At a glance, this study investigated MI and its two variants, Normalized MI (NMI) and Partial MI (PMI), for connectivity feature extraction from EEG; and then Convolutional Neural Network was employed for emotion classification from these features. Experimental results confirm the effectiveness of PMI based ER method while compared with related methods on a benchmark EEG dataset.

Keywords: Emotion · Electroencephalography · Feature Extraction · Convolutional Neural Network · Mutual Information · Partial Mutual Information

1 Introduction

Humans are innately emotional, and brain signals are the best tools for recognizing such emotions. Emotion or mental state is a psycho-physiological process which is activated by a person's conscious or subconscious perception of an object or event. It often has a strong impact on personality and disposition, temperament, mood, motivation [1]. One can express emotions either vocally (using emotional language and voice tones) or nonverbally, including the use of body language or facial expressions. Most commonly, modalities such as facial images [2], speech [3], and gestures [4] can be used to identify emotions. However, these approaches to recognition are not ubiquitous and have low recognition accuracy because they depend on the person's age, appearance, culture,

Md. S. Satu et al. (Eds.): MIET 2022, LNICST 491, pp. 137–150, 2023.
https://doi.org/10.1007/978-3-031-34622-4_11

language, and habits. [5]. Besides, humans can express fake emotions using facial expressions or voices. On the other hand, the brain is regarded as the place where emotional activities are evoked [6], so the true emotions can be reflected through brain signals. Consequently, researchers are eager to reveal the neural mechanism behind emotions to develop a recognition system that reflects individuals' real emotions.

Electroencephalography (EEG) is a preferable brain signal for emotion recognition. EEG is inexpensive, fast, portable, non-invasive and easy to use [7] in comparison to alternative neuroimaging methods like positron emission tomography [8], functional magnetic resonance imaging [9]. EEG is a technique for capturing the electrical impulses generated by neuronal activities of the brain through its small sensors (i.e., EEG channels) attached to the brain. It is anticipated that these signals will provide comprehensive information about the emotional process. EEG based emotion recognition is being explored in recent studies [6, 10–16] due to its prospect to use in different areas like entertainment, virtual worlds, e-learning, instant messaging, online games and e-healthcare applications [11].

Automatic emotion recognition (ER) from EEG signals is a challenging computational intelligence or machine learning (ML) task due to the inherited complexity of EEG signals. These signals are non-stationary, nonlinear as well as temporal asymmetry in type in the microvolt range [13]. Since the signals also represent other components of perceptual experience in addition to emotion, the task of ER from EEG is complex. Additionally, there are individual variances in EEG patterns, which makes it more challenging to derive meaningful emotion-related representations from raw EEG signals. Hence, processing the raw EEG signals is a vital task to recognize emotions using any ML method [12].

Pioneer studies considered different ML methods to classify emotions using features extracted from individual EEG channels [14, 15]. Liu et al. [14] used support vector machine (SVM) to recognize discrete emotions (e.g., happiness, sadness) from power spectral density (PSD) features. EEG data's time-frequency features produced by the multivariate synchrosqueezing transform were used by Mert and Akan [15] to categorize emotions between the high and low state of Arousal and Valence using fully connected neural network.

Several ML based ER works considered features based on connectivity between EEG channels [6, 12, 16]. By evaluating the brain activity dependencies, such as causal relationship and coactivation, these connectivity features investigate the relationship between several brain areas. In comparison to traditional EEG features, these features offer information on the functioning of the brain from a different angle [12]. There are numerous methods that can calculate connectivity features for every pair of EEG electrode (i.e., channel) and construct a connectivity matrix; the constructed connectivity matrix or connectivity feature map (CFM) is a two-dimensional (2D) matrix those are used by a ML method for classification. For example, in [6], Pearson correlation coefficient (PCC), mutual information (MI) and phase coherence connectivity were used individually for CFM preparation, and SVM was used for classification. Wang et al. [17] also used SVM for emotion classification, where Normalized MI (NMI) was used for connectivity feature extraction. Recently, Chao et al. [18] used maximal information coefficient (MIC) for connectivity feature extraction, principal component analysis network (PCANet) based deep learning model also used for deep feature extraction from MIC feature and both features were classified with SVM. Moon et al. [12] used convolutional neural network (CNN) for classification but used phase locking value (PLV), PCC and transfer entropy to measure connectivity.

The aim of this study is to analyze MI based connectivity measures for feature extraction from EEG signals and classify emotions using deep learning. The mutual dependency between the two variables is measured by MI. It measures the amount of information regarding one random variable that is gained by observing the other random variable. In case of ER using EEG, MI-defined connectivity records physiologically relevant features of the brain network. NMI and Partial MI (PMI) are two variants of MI. Several existing methods considered MI and NMI, those are closed in nature. On the other hand, PMI has a significant difference from MI and NMI, and it considers signals from three channels and measures shared information between two signals given the information of a third signal [19]. Therefore, connectivity feature extraction using PMI and its performance comparison with MI and NMI might be interesting; those are the aims of this study. The major contributions of this study are summarized as follows:

- Construction of 2D connectivity feature maps (i.e., CFMs) from EEG using three MI based methods: MI, NMI and PMI.
- Emotion recognition on the basis of Valence and Arousal classification from constructed CFMs using CNN model.

The remainder of this paper is divided into the following sections. Section 2 contains the overall emotion recognition process that includes data preprocessing, extracting features from the data and classification. In Sect. 3, the experimental setup, results, and comparison with other studies on emotion recognition are described. At last, Sect. 4 concludes the paper.

2   Emotion Recognition from EEG Using MI Based Feature Map and CNN

Emotion recognition (ER) from EEG signals can be summed up in three steps: Preprocessing the signals, feature extraction and identifying emotions using these features. The proposed MI based Emotion Recognition (MIER) system is depicted in Fig. 1.

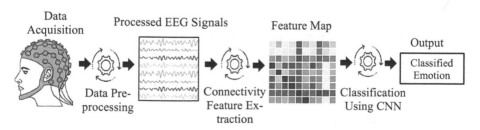

Fig. 1. The Framework of Proposed Emotion Recognition from EEG.

where MI and its variants were considered for feature extraction and then CNN was used for classifying emotions using those features. The following subsections briefly describe the major steps of MIER.

2.1 Benchmark Dataset and Preprocessing

Preprocessing is common to work with EEG signals which includes filtering the signals, removing artifacts etc. The Database for Emotion Analysis Using Physiological Signals (DEAP) [1], one of the largest EEG datasets for ER, was used in this study. It includes EEG and peripheral physiological signals of 32 participants (i.e., subjects) where 40 emotional music videos were used as stimuli. Additionally, the database has subjective scores that characterize the emotional states brought on by seeing the movies in terms of their levels of Valence, Arousal, Liking, and Dominance. This study employed preprocessed EEG signals from the database which was downsampled to 128 Hz, EOG artifacts were removed, and a band-pass frequency filter was applied from 4.0 to 45.0 Hz. There were 40 channels total, of which 32 were for EEG signals and the remaining channels for peripheral physiological inputs. The EEG channels were rearranged in the preprocessed version of the dataset so that they are all in the Geneva order as follows: Fp1, AF3, F3, F7, FC5, FC1, C3, T7, CP5, CP1, P3, P7, PO3, O1, Oz, Pz, Fp2, AF4, Fz, F4, F8, FC6, FC2, Cz, C4, T8, CP6, CP2, P4, P8, PO4, O2.

In the dataset, the length of the signal was 63 s. The first 3 s data were the pre-trial baseline which were removed, and the last 60 s data were processed for this study. Filtering was applied to this data to extract Gamma (30-50Hz) frequency band, and the filtering was performed with an open-source toolbox EEGLAB [20]. In order to increase samples for training, the EEG signals were segmented. An ideal segmentation time window size is 3–12 and 3–10 s that preserves the key information of Valence and Arousal levels, respectively, as demonstrated by Candra et al. [21]. For this experiment EEG signals were segmented using an 8-s sliding time window with an overlap of 4 s. Thus, there were 14 segments for the total 60 s duration. Total segments for a single participant were 14×32 (channel) $\times 40$ (video).

In the dataset, the ratings for Valence and Arousal were 1 to 9. Binary (High vs. Low) classification of both Valence and Arousal was performed in this study. Here High was regarded as positive emotion and Low was regarded as negative emotion and this was also followed by the study [22]. For this classification, the Valence and Arousal ratings higher than 4.5 were considered to be High Valence (HV) and High Arousal (HA), otherwise regarded as Low Valence (LV) and Low Arousal (LA), respectively.

2.2 MI Based Connectivity Feature Map (CFM) Construction

The feature extraction technique transforms inputs to new dimensions which are different (linear, non-linear, directed etc.) combinations of the inputs. Basic MI and its two variants, NMI and PMI, were investigated in this study for CFM construction.

Mutual Information (MI). How much information about one random variable may be learned from observing another is measured as MI. The following is the definition of MI between two random variables, X and Y:

$$MI(X, Y) = H(X) + H(Y) - H(X, Y) \tag{1}$$

In this case, H stands for Shannon entropy [23]. The marginal entropies of X and Y are $H(X)$ and $H(Y)$, respectively, while $H(X,Y)$ is their joint entropy. MI is symmetric and nonnegative. The range of MI's value is 0 to ∞. If $MI(X,Y) = 0$, then X and Y are independent. If $MI(X,Y) > 0$, then X and Y are dependent.

Since MI is based on probability distributions, its key benefit is its ability to identify high order correlations, if any exist. For this, it is independent of any particular data model. However, as it lacks directional information, it cannot detect causal relationship.

Normalized MI (NMI). As $MI(X, Y)$ does not typically have definite upper bounds it is sometimes better to normalize this measure such that $MI(X, Y) \in [0, 1]$. In NMI, $MI(X, Y)$ is normalized by $H(X) + H(Y)$ to provide a value ranging from 0 (independence) and 1 (strong dependence), with the equation represented as:

$$NMI(X, Y) = \frac{MI(X, Y)}{H(X) + H(Y)} = \frac{H(X) + H(Y) - H(X, Y)}{H(X) + H(Y)} = 1 - \frac{H(X, Y)}{H(X) + H(Y)} \tag{2}$$

Partial MI (PMI). It is an update of MI with an additional variable. The amount of shared information between X and Y is estimated by MI. It does not specify if connectivity between these two variable is direct or indirect, therefore it is unclear if the shared information is the consequence of a third variable (Z) that influences both X and Y. This problem is addressed by PMI, which measures the information that X and Y share while excluding the possibility that Z influences both X and Y. If X, Y and Z are three random variable, then PMI is determined by:

$$PMI(X, Y|Z) = H(X, Z) + H(Z, Y) - H(Z) - H(X, Z, Y) \tag{3}$$

When Z is independent of X or Y, $H(X,Z,Y) = 0$ and PMI degenerates into MI. PMI may either increase or reduce the value of MI. For jointly distributed discrete random variables X, Y, and Z, it is constant that $PMI(X,Z,Y) \geq 0$. For calculating probability that is required to calculate entropy, the fixed bin histogram approach was followed. The number of bins selected for all the calculations is 10.

CFM Construction. Here, the variables are signals from individual EEG channels. The MI and NMI work with two variables, whereas PMI works with three variables. The CFM created with MI and NMI features has 32 rows and 32 columns for 32 EEG electrodes. Thus, the connectivity matrix is 32 by 32 in size. According to Fig. 2, the matrix's element at position (X, Y) represents the connectivity or interconnection of the EEG signals acquired from the Xth channel and Yth channels. The values of location (X,X) or (Y,Y) were set to zero, as these are not information between two different channels. The CFM is equivalent to a graph's adjacency matrix, where the connectivity features act as edge weights and the EEG channels serve as nodes.

The connectivity features from three channels calculated by PMI can be represented as Fig. 3. Here, the rows represent channel Z, and columns represent all combinations of channel pair X and Y. Thus, a total of 496 combinations from 32 channels exist, and the size of the feature map is 32 × 496. As each channel data were segmented into 14 segments, so there were 14 (segment) × 40 (video) × 32 (subject) = 17,920 connectivity feature map for a single connectivity method.

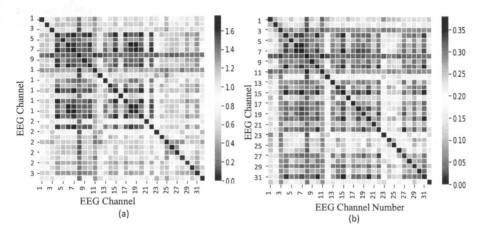

Fig. 2. Sample Connectivity Feature Map (CFM) using (a) MI and (b) NMI.

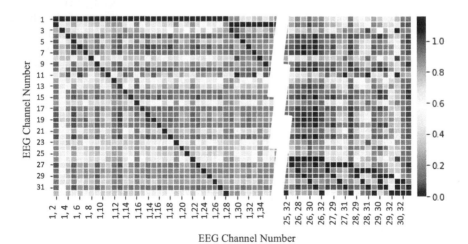

Fig. 3. Example of a PMI Connectivity Feature Map (CFM). Initial and Last Portions of the CFM are Displayed for Better Visualization.

2.3 Classification Using Convolutional Neural Network (CNN)

The most successful classifier for 2D data among the many DL techniques is CNN, which may implicitly extract relevant features [24]. Since the constructed CFMs are in 2D, CNN was chosen as a suitable classifier. An input layer, several convolutional-subsampling layers, a flatten layer, a fully connected layer, and an output layer make up the basic components of a CNN architecture. The first operation of a CNN is convolution performed on the input (matrix, image or map) with its kernel, which generate a new convolved matrix. Preceding subsampling operation will downsize the convolved matrix with important features. Pooling operation lets the computation proceed faster. After one or more convolutional-subsampling operations, through a fully connected layer, the output layer categorizes the given 2D matrix as input of the CNN.

Three convolutional layers, two max-pooling layers, flatten layer, and a dense layer and an output layer make up the CNN architecture employed in this study. Figure 4 depicts the proposed CNN's architecture.

Every convolution layer used kernels of size 3×3 and stride was set to 1. Rectified linear unit (ReLU) was used as activation function. The numbers of filters were 32, 64 and 128 for the 1st, 2nd and 3rd convolution layers respectively. To preserve the information from the pixels of a corner of the input image, same convolution (padding $= 1$) was used for all the convolution layers. Figure 4 clearly shows how many filters, strides, and padding are included in each layer.

Two max-pooling layers was used after the 1st and 3rd convolution layers. The 2×2 sized kernels with stride 2 were used in every pooling layer. After each max-poling layer, batch normalization was used to accelerate the model training.

After convolution and pooling operation the feature map was flattened to a single column vector and was fed to the dense layer. The dense layer and output layer's respective neuron counts were set at 128 and 2 and the dense layer is accompanied by a 25% dropout to decrease network complexity. In the output layer, the "Sigmoid" activation function was applied.

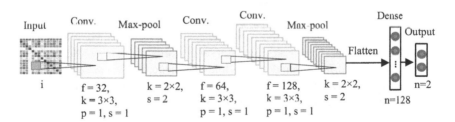

i = Input Size (32×32 for MI and NMI, 32×496 for PMI); f = Numbers of Filters; k = Kernel Size; p = Padding; s = Stride; n = Numbers of Neurons.

Fig. 4. The proposed CNN model's architecture for recognizing emotions.

3 Experimental Studies

The experimental results of this MIER system for CFMs created with MI, NMI and PMI individually are described in this section. The method's performance is evaluated using the test set recognition accuracy. The results are compared with those from other currently used and widely acknowledged approaches in the literature to validate the performance of this system.

3.1 Experimental Setup

The CNN was trained using the Adam algorithm [25], and the loss function was binary cross-entropy. Learning rate and batch size in CNN were set to 0.00001 and 32. A 5 fold Cross Validation (CV) was applied where 20% of the available data were reserved as testing set by turn. From 80% training set data, 10% was used as validation set, and 70% was used to update the model. We also considered the Training–Test split as 80% and 20%. Two deep learning frameworks, Keras and Tensorflow, available in Python, were used for implementing the CNN model for the classification process. The training was performed using the GPU of Google Colaboratory.

3.2 Experimental Results and Comparison

Figures 5–6 show model's loss and accuracy curves on training and validation sets for Valence and Arousal classification for a sample run.

The training was performed for three different models up to 200 epochs for CFMs using MI, NMI and PMI. According to Fig. 5(a) and Fig. 6(a), loss convergence for PMI is faster than MI and NMI for both Valance and Arousal. Similarly, accuracy improvement for PMI is faster than MI and NMI, as seen in Fig. 5(b) as well as Fig. 6(b) for Valance and Arousal, respectively. For MI and NMI, validation loss starts to increase from near 100 and 150 epochs. The accuracy curves also reflect the issues showing stability after that epochs. In the case of PMI, the validation loss gradually increases for both Valence and Arousal after 50 epochs, and there is no significant improvement in the accuracy after that. The figures clearly revealed the significant performance of PMI over MI and NMI.

Table 1 shows the test set accuracies on Valence and Arousal for MI, NMI and PMI CFMs which were measured for best validation set performance. The test set accuracies were measured in two different modes. In 5 fold CV mode, the test set accuracy is the average of five individual runs considering 20% data as test sets in turn. From the table, it is observed that the performance of MI and NMI are competitive in both modes. In 5 fold CV, accuracies are 87.14% and 87.95% on Valence classification and 87.59% and 88.18% on Arousal classification for MI and NMI, respectively. On the other hand, PMI method achieved more accuracies than the other two methods (i.e., MI and NMI) on both the 5 fold CV and the Training-Test split for both Valance and Arousal classification. The achieved Training-Test split accuracies for PMI are 89.34% and 89.70% for Valance and Arousal classification, respectively.

The classification performance of the three best models that used MI, NMI and PMI features is presented in Table 2 as confusion matrixes. The last column of each confusion matrix, represents the accuracy of individual classes of Low and High. The overall accuracy of the classification is shown in the last row of the last column which is the same as in Table 1 in the case of the Train-Test split.

Table 3 compares the Valance and Arousal classification accuracies of the proposed emotion recognition with related exiting studies on the DEAP dataset. The Table also

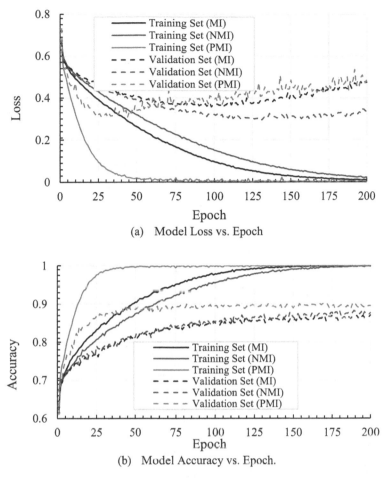

(a)   Model Loss vs. Epoch

(b)   Model Accuracy vs. Epoch.

Fig. 5. Model Loss and Accuracy on Training and Validation Sets for Valence Classification

presents feature map construction, classification method and Train-Test selection mode. Exiting studies considered different methods for feature map constructions, including MI and NMI. The pioneer methods considered SVM for classification and classification accuracies are around 70% [17, 26]. The recent studies considered different DL methods (e.g., CNN, LSTM) and showed better performance than ML based methods. For the proposed method, accuracies with PMI are considered as it showed better than MI and NMI. The table shows that this MIER method outperforms existing MI-based methods of [17, 18, 26] and competitive with [27]. It is notable that the data set consideration in [27] is different from other studies; in the method, Valance classification was divided into two groups for LA and HA. Similarly, Arousal classification was separated into two groups for LV and HV. Since tasks were divided into four with smaller similar samples in [27], its better performance in several cases is logical. The proposed method has shown competitive performance with recent methods with other different connectivity features and DL methods. The proposed approach has shown superior than the recent study of

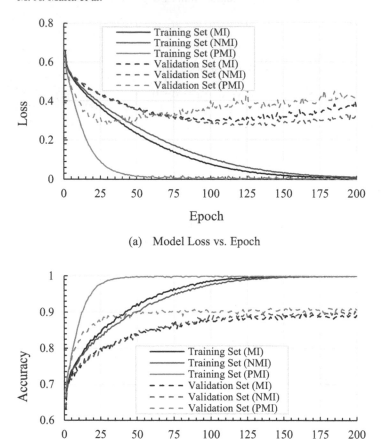

(a)   Model Loss vs. Epoch

(b)   Model Accuracy vs. Epoch.

Fig. 6. Model Loss and Accuracy on Training and Validation Sets for Arousal Classification.

[13] with PCC for feature maps and CNN for classification. For Valence and Arousal, the method [13] attained classification accuracy rates of 78.22% and 74.92%, respectively. On the other hand, proposed method (with PMI and CNN) achieved accuracies of 89.34% (for Valence) and 89.70% (for Arousal) in Train-Test split mode. Finally, the proposed method with PMI is better than MI / NMI based methods and shows a good EEG-based emotion recognition method.

Table 1. Test set classification accuracy using different connectivity feature map methods.

Connectivity Feature Map Method	Test Set Accuracy	
	5 Fold CV	Training and Test Sets Split as 80% and 20%
MI	87.14% (Valence) 87.59% (Arousal)	87.53% (Valence) 88.03% (Arousal)
NMI	87.95% (Valence) 88.18% (Arousal)	88.42% (Valence) 88.81% (Arousal)
PMI	88.89% (Valence) 89.15% (Arousal)	89.34% (Valence) 89.70% (Arousal)

Table 2. Test set confusion matrixes for Valence and Arousal classification.

		Valence				**Arousal**		
		Low	**High**	**Accuracy**		**Low**	**High**	**Accuracy**
MI	L	1054	239	81.51%	L	1089	233	82.37%
	H	208	2083	90.92%	H	196	2066	91.34%
	Overall Accuracy =			87.53%	Overall Accuracy =			88.03%
NMI	L	1046	246	80.96%	L	1054	234	88.83%
	H	169	2123	92.63%	H	167	2129	92.73%
	Overall Accuracy =			88.42%	Overall Accuracy =			88.81%
PMI	L	1065	231	82.18%	L	1122	194	85.26%
	H	151	2137	93.40%	H	175	2093	92.28%
	Overall Accuracy =			89.34%	Overall Accuracy =			89.70%

Table 3. Comparison of Valence and Arousal test set classification accuracies of proposed method with related studies on DEAP dataset.

Work Ref. and Year	Connectivity Feature	Classifier	CV / Train Test Split	Test Set Accuracy
González et al (2017) [26]	MI	SVM	Leave 01 Trial Out CV	67.7% (Valence) 69.6% (Arousal)
Wang et al (2019) [17]	NMI	SVM	80% - 20%	74.41% (Valence) 73.64% (Arousal)
Chao et al (2020) [18]	MIC	SVM	10 Fold CV	70.21% (Valence) 71.85% (Arousal)
Farashi et al (2020) [27]	PLI	SVM	10 Fold CV	72.49($\pm$ 1.40)% (Valence I HA) 81.56($\pm$ 0.70)% (Valence I LA) 80.93($\pm$ 1.31)% (Arousal I HV) 87.17($\pm$ 1.31)% (Arousal I LV)
	MI			67.49($\pm$ 1.31)% (Valence I HA) 88.75($\pm$ 1.30)% (Valence I LA) 74.06($\pm$ 1.78)% (Arousal I HV) 90.31($\pm$ 0.70)% (Arousal I LV)
Moon et al (2018) [16]	PCC	CNN	5 Fold CV	94.44% (Valence)
	PLV			99.72% (Valence)
	PLI			85.03% (Valence)
Luo et al (2020) [28]	PCC	CNN + SAE + DNN	80% - 20%	89.49% (Valence) 92.86% (Arousal)
Jin et al (2020) [29]	PCC	LSTM + MLP	10 Fold CV	98.93% (Valence) 99.10% (Arousal)
Islam et al (2021) [13]	PCC	CNN	95% -5%	78.22% (Valence) 74.92% (Arousal)
Proposed Method	PMI	CNN	5 Fold CV	88.89% (Valence) 89.15% (Arousal)
			80% - 20%	89.34% (Valence) 89.70% (Arousal)

PLI: phase lag index, LSTM: long short-term memory, SAE: sparse autoencoder, DNN: deep neural network, MLP: multilayer perceptron.

4 Conclusions

In this study, basic MI and its two variants Normalized MI (NMI) and Partial MI (PMI) were employed for connectivity feature map (CFM) construction from EEG signals and then CNN was used to recognize emotions from CFM. The use of PMI for CFM construction is the significant contribution of the study with respect to the existing studies. Results of this experiments using the DEAP benchmark EEG dataset revealed the effectiveness of the proposed emotion recognition with PMI outperforming MI and NMI based methods. It is also remarkable that the CNN model work with PMI shows faster convergence than MI or NMI. However, similar to NMI, normalized PMI may be interesting and another alternative exists for further research.

References

1. Koelstra, S., et al.: DEAP: a database for emotion analysis using physiological signals. EEE Transactions on Affective Computing. **3**, 18–31 (2012)
2. Khattak, A., Asghar, M.Z., Ali, M., Batool, U.: An efficient deep learning technique for facial emotion recognition. Multimedia Tools and Applications **81**(2), 1649–1683 (2021). https://doi.org/10.1007/s11042-021-11298-w
3. Morais, E., Hoory, R., Zhu, W., Gat, I., Damasceno, M., Aronowitz, H.: Speech emotion recognition using self-supervised features. In: ICASSP 2022 - 2022 IEEE International Conference on Acoustics, Speech and Signal Processing (ICASSP), pp. 6922–6926 (2022). https://doi.org/10.1109/ICASSP43922.2022.9747870
4. Kessous, L., Castellano, G., Caridakis, G.: Multimodal emotion recognition in speech-based interaction using facial expression, body gesture and acoustic analysis. Journal on Multimodal User Interfaces. **3**, 33–48 (2009). https://doi.org/10.1007/s12193-009-0025-5
5. Liu, X., et al.: Emotion recognition and dynamic functional connectivity analysis based on EEG. IEEE Access. **7**, 143293–143302 (2019). https://doi.org/10.1109/ACCESS.2019.2945059
6. Chen, M., Han, J., Guo, L., Wang, J., Patras, I.: Identifying valence and arousal levels via connectivity between EEG channels. In: 2015 International Conference on Affective Computing and Intelligent Interaction, ACII 2015, pp. 63–69. IEEE (2015). https://doi.org/10.1109/ACII.2015.7344552
7. Moon, S.-E., Lee, J.-S.: Implicit analysis of perceptual multimedia experience based on physiological response: a review. IEEE Trans. Multimedia **19**, 340–353 (2017)
8. Paradiso, S., et al.: Emotions in unmedicated patients with schizophrenia during evaluation with positron emission tomography (2003). https://doi.org/10.1176/appi.ajp.160.10.1775
9. Koelsch, S., Fritz, T., Cramon, D.Y.V., Müller, K., Friederici, A.D.: Investigating emotion with music: An fMRI study. Human Brain Mapping **27**, 239–250 (2006). https://doi.org/10.1002/hbm.20180
10. Hondrou, C., Caridakis, G.: Affective, natural interaction using EEG: sensors, application and future directions. In: Maglogiannis, I., Plagianakos, V., Vlahavas, I. (eds.) Artificial Intelligence: Theories and Applications, pp. 331–338. Springer, Berlin Heidelberg, Berlin, Heidelberg (2012)
11. Alarcão, S.M., Fonseca, M.J.: Emotions recognition using EEG signals: A survey. IEEE Trans. Affect. Comput. **10**, 374–393 (2019). https://doi.org/10.1109/TAFFC.2017.2714671
12. Moon, S.-E., Chen, C.-J., Hsieh, C.-J., Wang, J.-L., Lee, J.-S.: Emotional EEG classification using connectivity features and convolutional neural networks. Neural Netw. **132**, 96–107 (2020). https://doi.org/10.1016/j.neunet.2020.08.009

13. Islam, M.R., et al.: EEG channel correlation based model for emotion recognition. Comput. Biol. Med. **136**, 104757 (2021). https://doi.org/10.1016/j.compbiomed.2021.104757
14. Liu, S., et al.: Study on an effective cross-stimulus emotion recognition model using EEGs based on feature selection and support vector machine. Int. J. Mach. Learn. Cybern. **9**(5), 721–726 (2016). https://doi.org/10.1007/s13042-016-0601-4
15. Mert, A., Akan, A.: Emotion recognition based on time-frequency distribution of EEG signals using multivariate synchrosqueezing transform. Digital Signal Processing. **81**, 106–115 (2018)
16. Moon, S.-E., Jang, S., Lee, J.-S.: Convolutional neural network approach for EEG-based emotion recognition using brain connectivity and its spatial information. In: 2018 IEEE International Conference on Acoustics, Speech and Signal Processing (ICASSP), pp. 2556–2560 (2018). https://doi.org/10.1109/ICASSP.2018.8461315
17. Wang, Z.: Channel selection method for EEG emotion recognition using normalized mutual information. IEEE Access. **7**, 143303–143311 (2019)
18. Chao, H., Dong, L., Liu, Y., Lu, B.: Improved deep feature learning by synchronization measurements for multi-channel EEG emotion recognition. Complexity. 2020 (2020). https://doi.org/10.1155/2020/6816502
19. Niso, G., et al.: HERMES: towards an integrated toolbox to characterize functional and effective brain connectivity. Neuroinformatics **11**(4), 405–434 (2013). https://doi.org/10.1007/s12021-013-9186-1
20. Delorme, A., Makeig, S.: EEGLAB: an open source toolbox for analysis of single-trial EEG dynamics including independent component analysis. Journal of Neuroscience Methods **134**, 9–21 (2004). https://doi.org/10.1016/j.jneumeth.2003.10.009
21. Candra, H., et al.: Investigation of window size in classification of EEG-emotion signal with wavelet entropy and support vector machine. In: 2015 37th Annual International Conference of the IEEE Engineering in Medicine and Biology Society (EMBC), pp. 7250–7253 (2015). https://doi.org/10.1109/EMBC.2015.7320065
22. Islam, M., Ahmad, M.: Virtual image from EEG to recognize appropriate emotion using convolutional neural network. In: 1st International Conference on Advances in Science, Engineering and Robotics Technology (ICASERT), pp. 1–4 (2019). https://doi.org/10.1109/ICASERT.2019.8934760
23. Shannon, C.E.: A mathematical theory of communication. The Bell System Technical Journal. **27**, 379–423 (1948). https://doi.org/10.1002/j.1538-7305.1948.tb01338.x
24. Akhand, M.A.H.: Deep Learning Fundamentals- A Practical Approach to Understanding Deep Learning Methods. University Grants Commission of Bangladesh (2021)
25. Kingma, D.P., Ba, J.: Adam: A Method for Stochastic Optimization (2014)
26. Arnau-González, P., Arevalillo-Herráez, M., Ramzan, N.: Fusing highly dimensional energy and connectivity features to identify affective states from EEG signals. Neurocomputing **244**, 81–89 (2017). https://doi.org/10.1016/j.neucom.2017.03.027
27. Farashi, S., Khosrowabadi, R.: EEG based emotion recognition using minimum spanning tree. Physical and Engineering Sciences in Medicine **43**(3), 985–996 (2020). https://doi.org/10.1007/s13246-020-00895-y
28. Luo, Y., et al.: EEG-based emotion classification using deep neural network and sparse autoencoder. Frontiers in Systems Neuroscience **14** (2020). https://doi.org/10.3389/fnsys.2020.00043
29. Jin, L., Kim, E.Y.: Interpretable cross-subject EEG-based emotion recognition using channel-wise features. Sensors **20** (2020)

A Machine Learning-Based System to Recommend Appropriate Military Training Program for a Soldier

Md Tauhidur Rahman, Raquib Hasan Dewan, Md Abdur Razzak,
Sumaiya Nuha Mustafina⬩, and Muhammad Nazrul Islam⁽✉⁾⬩

Department of Computer Science and Engineering, Military Institute of Science and
Technology, Mirpur Cantonment, Dhaka, Bangladesh
nazrul@cse.mist.ac.bd

Abstract. Each military units have its own branch of service, mission,
and composition. Personnel, equipment, training, and operations are all
critical basic components of each unit. Recommending appropriate soldiers to pursue appropriate military training is a crucial problem for
commanders aiming to increase soldiers' skills. There have been few
studies especially aimed at comprehending the surroundings, challenges,
and needs of military personnel in a unit for their daily official obliga-
tions, and only a handful of the techniques were previously suggested
in a military environment. However, very less attention has been paid
to incorporate machine learning(ML) to select appropriate courses for a
soldier to improve the troop's performance. Therefore, the objective of
this study is to find out the best-performed ML technique by exploring
the existing classifiers. The results demonstrate that when choosing the
right military training for a soldier, the random forest algorithm has the
highest accuracy (95.83%). The random forest algorithm also yields the
greatest AUROC rating, which is 0.972.

Keywords: machine learning · military training · prediction · soldier ·
accuracy

1 Introduction

Units are the core elements of an army consisting of small groups of people,
which can perform tasks independently. At the organizational level, the primary
apprehension should be how best men and materials can be managed within
limited resources. Often there is a requirement of numerous professional and
personal data of the soldiers and group information to select appropriate candidates for suitable military training. The selection of an appropriate course
can build a successful career for a soldier. The selection process for the right
military course candidate requires a long time. In most of the cases, units are
following an age-old manuscript-based system for appropriate course selection

© ICST Institute for Computer Sciences, Social Informatics and Telecommunications Engineering 2023
Published by Springer Nature Switzerland AG 2023. All Rights Reserved
Md. S. Satu et al. (Eds.): MIET 2022, LNICST 491, pp. 151–161, 2023.
https://doi.org/10.1007/978-3-031-34622-4_12

for a specific soldier; while recent research suggested that a soldier's course selection should take into account a variety of elements, including cognitive aptitude, demographic features, and the like [8]. However, very little attention has been paid to find out appropriate military training for a soldier grounding on his/her profile using machine learning techniques. In such circumstances, military personnel may benefit greatly from an automated course selection system.

Selection of a soldier for suitable training is a tremendous job that requires various information such as height, weight, age, PT performance, etc. Different courses have different criteria for selection. For selecting a soldier for an appropriate course these criteria need to be filled up. Thus, it becomes a very difficult task for the higher authority to find out an appropriate course for a soldier. Hence, the automation of selecting appropriate courses is important for the career development of a soldier.

Machine Learning (ML) based technologies are deliberately used in different contexts for predicting results; since ML technology enables software applications to improve their accuracy at result prediction and suggest the best possible solution [12,14,21]. ML techniques can be very useful for recommending appropriate military training programs [23]. However, It has been found that the idea of recommending military courses for a soldier is very recent and related documents are insufficient. For example, Elen and Cato [10] replicated the process of selecting recruits for the Norwegian Naval Special Forces (NFS). They suggested two predictors as valid for NFS training that includes: indications of good mental health and the Rorschach variables [18]. Ronald and Trysha [24] presented a technique for forecasting the future unpredictability of military teams integrating the concept of Ml and neurodynamics.

Therefore, the objective of this study is to find out the best-performed ML technique by exploring the existing classifiers for the selection of appropriate military courses with a view to developing future careers of soldiers. To attain these objectives, we firstly acquired around 600 datasets through questionnaires. After the preprocessing of the data, we have explored Naive Bayes Classifier, Support Vector Machine, Random Forest Classifier, Decision Tree machine learning models; and by analyzing their results we have found the best-performed model that can be used for the selection of appropriate military course.

2   Related Works

To find relevant literature, major scholarly repositories, including Google Scholar, ACM digital library, IEEE Xplore, and Scopus were searched using the keywords like "Military Course", "Military Training", "Military Candidate Selection", and "Machine Learning While Selecting Military Training". Few articles have been conducted emphasizing military training and machine learning connectivity. For example, Marié and Adelai [7] analyzed the learning ability, career-related aspirations or choice, and psychological adaptability of 251 applicants for selecting the operational force of SANDF (South African National Defense Force). They highlighted that psychological adaptability, learning ability, and career-related choice data may be utilized to better choose military recruits for the operational force. Lin et al. [15] presented a set of clinically assessable factors that can be used to identify military personnel having high-risk of committing suicide. Ronald and Trysha [24] proposed a method for predicting the future unpredictability of military teams that combined the idea of neurodynamics with machine learning.

Elen and Cato [10] conducted a replication study to examine how Norwegian Naval Special Forces applicants were chosen. Their findings indicated that Rorschach traits and signs of mental health may be reliable measures of success in NFS training. Forgues [8] looked into the unique cognitive talents and demographic features of applicants for aircrew (Canadian Forces pilot) selection using three aptitude test batteries. As outcome, Forgues found that successful completion of the pilot selection process necessitated applicants' mastery of a variety of skill areas. In another study, Brennan et al. [6] examined the function of the Behavioral Health and Performance Group (BHP) in the evaluation and selection of military aviators.

Again, even though numerous studies were conducted to aid the military segment and the suggested systems were successful in accomplishing their objectives [11,13,22]; there were relatively few studies that were devoted to comprehending the surroundings, issues, and requirements of military soldiers in a unit for their daily official responsibilities. Despite the fact that a number of military management systems exist, but only a few have adopted machine learning techniques. Furthermore, most of the existing systems concentrated on only a few elements of management, while only a small number of the current systems were discovered to be reviewed with active user engagement. Thus, this study concentrates on identifying the needs and obstacles experienced by military people to recommend appropriate courses for a soldier, and building an ML model to meet those needs.

3   Methodology

Support Vector Machine (SVM), Naive Bayes Classifier (NB), Random Forest Classifier (RF), and Decision Tree (DT) were investigated in order to find the best efficient method for identifying courses that qualify as military-eligible. The stages for developing and evaluating machine learning models to select appropriate military training programs are presented in Fig. 1 that includes: data acquisition, data preprocessing, developing prediction models, and evaluating prediction models. The following topics provide a succinct description of the stages:

3.1   Data Acquisition

A dataset containing 600 soldiers' information was acquired through questionnaires. Questionnaires were prepared considering various parameters for the selection of a course including soldier's age, height, weight, number of push up, number of beams, running performance of 1.6 km run, and running performance

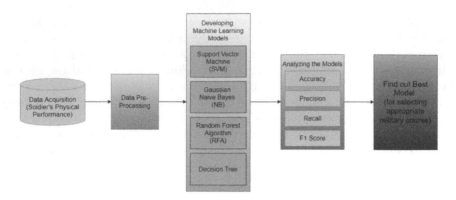

Fig. 1. A methodological overview to predict the appropriate military training/course.

of 3.2 km run. Target features like whether a soldier was eligible for PT, Drill, or Commando course were also collected.

3.2   Data Preprocessing

Data preprocessing is a crucial step in preparing data for the formation of a machine learning model. That includes, for example, data cleaning, data transformation, and feature selection [19]. Data cleaning and transformation approaches are utilized to eliminate outliers data and to standardize data in order to create a model in an easy way [5]. In this research, firstly the necessary libraries were imported for the datasets available in CSV formats. Next, the missing values and noisy data were checked and removed from the datasets. Imputation is used to treat the missing values and retrieve the relevant values. All data containing relevant information along with target feature commando, pt, and drill were prepared for feeding into the prediction models. The dataset was separated into a random train-test split, with 80% (480 instances) of the data being in the train dataset and 20% (120 instances) being in the test dataset.

3.3   Developing Machine Learning Models

Four alternative machine learning (ML) models—Support Vector Machine (SVM), Naive Bayes Classifier (NB), Random Forest Algorithm (RF), and Decision Tree (DT)—were developed to choose the most appropriate military training. Later their performance was evaluated and compared. The train_test_split () function in the sklearn package was used to split the data into train test sets using a python program (Scikit-Learn).

Support Vector Machine (SVM) - Support vector machines are supervised learning models with corresponding learning algorithms that examine data for regression analysis and classification analysis. Each data point in an SVM is plotted in an n-dimensional plane, with a particular coordinate standing in for each feature's value. To separate these data points into two categories, a hyperplane is built. In order to widen the distance between the two groups, SVM applies spatial mappings to these data points. Then, new instances are mapped into the same space and given a category according to where they fall on the gap [1].

Naive Bayes Classifier (NB) - Naive Bayes classifiers are based on the Bayes theorem and make strong (naive) assumptions about the independence of the attributes. Naive Bayes is a probabilistic classifier that gives probabilistic output. Naive Bayes classifiers are highly scalable, requiring only a small amount of training data to estimate classification parameters [3]. A variation of the NB Classifier that supports continuous data and adheres to the Gaussian normal distribution is the Gaussian Naive Bayes classifier [17].

Random Forest Algorithm (RF) - Random Forest is a classifier that averages the results of multiple decision trees on various subsets of a dataset to increase the dataset's predicted accuracy. The more trees there are in the forest, the more accurate it is, and overfitting is avoided [2].

Decision Tree (DT) - Decision Tree is a supervised training method that is most commonly employed to solve classification issues. The inspiration came from the standard tree structure, which consists of a root, nodes, branches, and leaves. Internal nodes contain characteristics of the dataset, branches provide rules for decision making, and the leaf nodes help to reach the conclusion in this tree-structured algorithm [2].

3.4   Analyzing the Models

The train data set was used to construct prediction models, and the accuracy of prediction models was analyzed for the train as well as the test dataset in this experiment. All the models were measured for testing instances in three categories (Commando, PT, and Drill) and the results are showed in terms of accuracy, precision, recall, and f1 score. The result was further analyzed with the ROC-AUC curve and confusion matrix for finding out the best ML model that can be used to predict appropriate military course for a soldier.

4   Results and Evaluation

4.1   Analyzing the Results

Performance was measured for the four developed models (SVM, NB, RF, and DT) for test data and the results are presented in Table 1. We utilize five metrics to assess the predictive models' classification and prediction accuracy through the Confusion Matrix for Multi-class and the Receiver Operating Characteristics (ROC). The confusion matrix can be used to evaluate and assess a multiclass classification model [25] in terms of *accuracy*, which is defined as the proportion of correct predictions out of all instances evaluated [9]; *precision*, which is defined as the proportion of true positives to the total of true positives and false positives; *recall*, which is defined as the proportion of true positives to the total of true positives and false negatives [4]; and the *F1-score*, which is defined as the proportion of true positives to the total number of true positives and false negatives [16]; and the means of ROC graph is another statistic that might be used to evaluate the model's performance that uses visualization, organization, and performance-based classifier selection. The area under the ROC graph, or AUC, represents the likelihood that a randomly chosen positive occurrence will be rated higher than a randomly chosen negative instance. The AUC value runs from 0 to 1.0; hence, a greater value closer to 1.0 indicates practically flawless prediction, whereas values less than 0.5 indicate inadequate or almost failed categorization [20].

Table 1. Performance measures for the developed models for Test Data

Model	Feature	Accuracy	Precision	Recall	F1 Score
SVM	Commando	70.83	72.52	86.84	79.04
	PT	69.17	69.17	100	81.77
	Drill	60	0	0	0
Naive Bayes	Commando	71.67	72.82	88.16	79.76
	PT	83.33	86.20	90.36	88.23
	Drill	83.33	74.14	89.58	81.13
Random Forest	Commando	77.5	78.16	89.47	83.43
	PT	90	92.77	92.77	92.77
	Drill	95.83	97.77	91.67	94.62
Decision Tree	Commando	66.66	71.95	77.63	74.68
	PT	91.67	93.97	93.97	93.97
	Drill	86.67	84.78	81.25	82.98

From Table 1, it can be seen that the highest accuracy was obtained after applying the RF Classifier; which represents that the prediction accuracy of RF is higher than the other models. Though in other classifiers percentage of accuracy, precision, recall, and f1 score are more or less the same but accuracy, precision, and f1 score are higher in RF than NB, SVM, and DT. The accuracy of RF in commando, PT, and drill are 77.5%, 90%, and 95.83% respectively. The accuracy of NB in commando, PT, and drill are 71.67%, 83.33%, and 83.33% accordingly whereas the accuracy for SVM in commando, PT, and drill are 70.83%, 69.17%, and 60% respectively and the accuracy for DT in commando, PT and drill are 66.66%, 91.67%, and 86.67% respectively.

The RF model also showed the best performance considering the other performance measures (precision, recall, and f1 score). For Commando, the RF model's precision, recall, and f1 score were respectively 78.16%, 89.47%, and 83.43%; the SVM model's results were 72.52%, 86.84%, and 79.04%; NB's results were 72.82%, 100%, and 81.77%; and DT's results were 71.95%, 77.63%, and 74.68%.

Again, for PT, RF model had precision, recall and f1 score of 92.77%, 92.77% and 92.77% respectively; and SVM model showed as 69.17%, 100% and 81.77% respectively; whereas NB showed 86.20%, 90.36% and 88.23% respectively; and DT showed as 93.97%, 93.97% and 93.97% respectively.

The result showed that the average accuracy, precision, recall, and f1 score of RF model are higher than other models. As a result, the RF model is the most efficient of the above models for selecting appropriate military courses.

The confusion matrices are presented in Fig. 2, The matrices show in case of commando that RF provides fewer false predictions than other algorithms. In the case of PT, the result shows more accuracy in DT, because out of 120 instances it predicted 10 predictions wrong. In Drill, the accuracy is more and the best prediction can be done with RF algorithms because most test data is within true-negative and true-positive; which shows 95% accuracy of the predicted data.

The ROC-AUC curve presented in Fig. 3 shows the rate of true positive and false positive. In case of SVM the AUROC value is less than 0.5. Therefore, the model will give an unsatisfactory result and failed classification in case of selecting the appropriate course. RF AUROC and NB AUROC values are higher than other models. However, RF outperforms PT in terms of AUROC, with a value of 0.972. In addition, RF performs better in terms of accuracy, precision, recall, and F1 score in all other scenarios.

4.2   Selection of Best ML Models

The study of the results reveals that RF had the best performance for choosing the appropriate military courses. The result is analyzed and the graphical representation of the performances showed that RF will be able to predict the appropriate military course for a soldier.

5   Discussion and Conclusion

Although there have been a number of studies related to ML in Warfare Platforms, ML in Cyber security, ML in Battlefield Healthcare, ML in Defense Combat Training, etc. only a few studies have included Machine Learning algorithms for selecting appropriate military candidates for skillful soldiers. Few studies included artificial intelligence for skill development and building simulation software. While this study fulfills the goal of finding out the best-performed ML technique by exploring the existing classifiers and concluded with accuracy ranging from 60% to 95.83% (as shown in Table 1) for predicting the suitable course of a soldier for future career development. The findings of the study can make a new contribution to research and increase the performance of military training and make skillful soldiers. The finding shows that random forest algorithm gives 95.83% accuracy while selecting appropriate military courses.

There are few limitations to this study. For example, only four ML models were explored in this study. Another drawback is that the dataset used to predict the outcome was compiled by taking into account 5–6 criteria. There might be

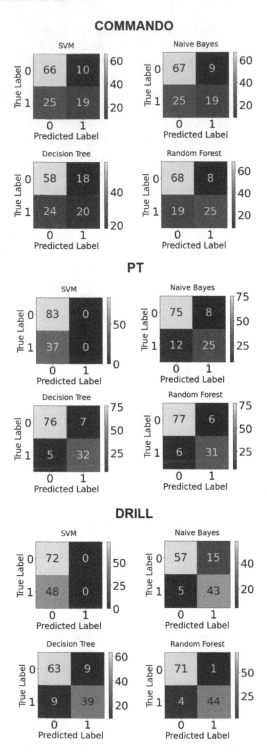

Fig. 2. Confusion matrices of commando, pt, and drill with different classifiers

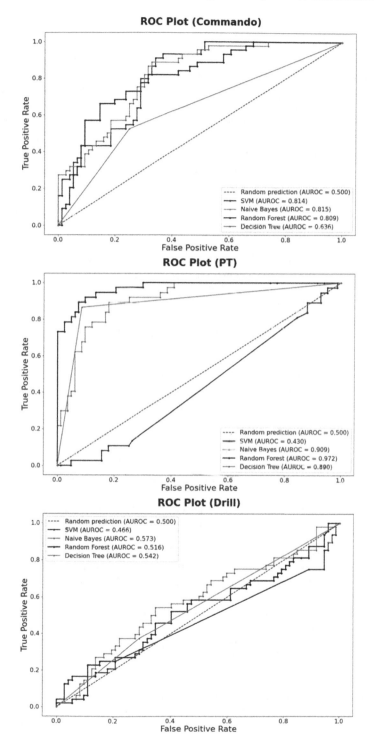

Fig. 3. ROC-AUC curves for different algorithms

more criteria that need to be observed while selecting a suitable course for a soldier. Moreover, the dataset was not adequate to recommend all the major courses for a soldier. To overcome these limitations, other machine learning methods and deep learning approaches may be utilized in the long term to make the prediction outcome better. Larger dataset need to be tested in the future for better accuracy and various criteria need to be included for selecting appropriate courses in future development. The developed model can be incorporated with a web application in the future to provide a real-time application.

In a military unit, selecting the appropriate soldier for the appropriate course is one of the hard task. Hence, this study can recommend the appropriate course by using the best-performed ML model.

References

1. SVM: support vector machine algorithm in machine learning, August 2021. https://www.analyticsvidhya.com/blog/2017/09/understaing-support-vector-machine-example-code/. Accessed 25 Mar 2022
2. Ali, J., Khan, R., Ahmad, N., Maqsood, I.: Random forests and decision trees. Int. J. Comput. Sci. Issues(IJCSI) **9** (2012)
3. Bhavani, V.: Naive Bayes classifier, March 2022. https://devopedia.org/naive-bayes-classifier/. Accessed 21 Apr 2022
4. Buckland, M., Gey, F.: The relationship between recall and precision. J. Am. Soc. Inf. Sci. **45**(1), 12–19 (1994)
5. Chakrabarty, A., Mannan, S., Cagin, T.: Inherently safer design. In: Chakrabarty, A., Mannan, S., Cagin, T. (eds.) Multiscale Modeling for Process Safety Applications, pp. 339–396. Butterworth-Heinemann, Boston (2016). https://doi.org/10.1016/B978-0-12-396975-0.00008-5. https://www.sciencedirect.com/science/article/pii/B9780123969750000085
6. Cox, B.D., Schmidt, L.L., Slack, K.J., Foster, T.C.: Assessment and selection of military aviators and astronauts. In: Aeromedical Psychology, pp. 17–36. CRC Press (2017)
7. De Beer, M., Van Heerden, A.: The psychological coping, learning potential and career preferences profiles of operational force military candidates. J. Psychol. Afr. **27**(1), 33–40 (2017)
8. Forgues, S.: Aptitude testing of military pilot candidates. Ph.D. thesis (2014)
9. García, S., Fernández, A., Luengo, J., Herrera, F.: A study of statistical techniques and performance measures for genetics-based machine learning: accuracy and interpretability. Soft. Comput. **13**(10), 959–977 (2009)
10. Hartmann, E., Grønnerød, C.: Rorschach variables and big five scales as predictors of military training completion: a replication study of the selection of candidates to the naval special forces in Norway. J. Pers. Assess. **91**(3), 254–264 (2009)
11. Islam, M.N., Islam, M.R.U., Islam, S.M.R., Bhuyan, S.A., Hasib, F.: LocSoldiers: towards developing an emergency troops locating system in military operations. In: 2018 4th International Conference on Electrical Engineering and Information & Communication Technology (iCEEiCT), pp. 264–267 (2018). https://doi.org/10.1109/CEEICT.2018.8628089

12. Islam, M.N., Mustafina, S.N., Mahmud, T., Khan, N.I.: Machine learning to predict pregnancy outcomes: a systematic review, synthesizing framework and future research agenda. BMC Pregnancy Childbirth **22**(1), 348 (2022). https://doi.org/10.1186/s12884-022-04594-2

13. Islam, M.N., Oishwee, S.J., Mayem, S.Z., Nur Mokarrom, A., Razzak, M.A., Kabir, A.H.: Developing a multi-channel military application using interactive dialogue model (IDM). In: 2017 3rd International Conference on Electrical Information and Communication Technology (EICT), pp. 1–6 (2017). https://doi.org/10.1109/EICT.2017.8275230

14. Islam, U.I., Haque, E., Alsalman, D., Islam, M.N., Moni, M.A., Sarker, I.: A machine learning model for predicting individual substance abuse with associated risk-factors. Ann. Data Sci. (2022). https://doi.org/10.1007/s40745-022-00381-0

15. Lin, G.M., Nagamine, M., Yang, S.N., Tai, Y.M., Lin, C., Sato, H.: Machine learning based suicide ideation prediction for military personnel. IEEE J. Biomed. Health Inform. **24**(7), 1907–1916 (2020)

16. Lipton, Z.C., Elkan, C., Narayanaswamy, B.: Thresholding classifiers to maximize F1 score. arXiv preprint arXiv:1402.1892 (2014)

17. Majumder, P.: Gaussian Naive Bayes (2020). https://iq.opengenus.org/gaussian-naive-bayes/. Accessed 25 Mar 2022

18. Mihura, J.L., Meyer, G.J., Dumitrascu, N., Bombel, G.: The validity of individual Rorschach variables: systematic reviews and meta-analyses of the comprehensive system. Psychol. Bull. **139**(3), 548 (2013)

19. Nantasenamat, C., Isarankura-Na-Ayudhya, C., Naenna, T., Prachayasittikul, V.: A practical overview of quantitative structure-activity relationship (2009)

20. Narkhede, S.: Understanding AUC-ROC curve. Towards Data Sci. **26**(1), 220–227 (2018)

21. Omar, K.S., Mondal, P., Khan, N.S., Rizvi, M.R.K., Islam, M.N.: A machine learning approach to predict autism spectrum disorder. In: 2019 International Conference on Electrical, Computer and Communication Engineering (ECCE), pp. 1–6 (2019). https://doi.org/10.1109/ECACE.2019.8679454

22. Razzak, M.A., Islam, M.N.: Exploring and evaluating the usability factors for military application: a road map for HCI in military applications. Hum. Fact. Mec. Eng. Defense Saf. **4**(1), 1–18 (2020). https://doi.org/10.1007/s41314-019-0032-6

23. Roy, A., Rahman, M.R., Islam, M.N., Saimon, N.I., Alfaz, M.A., Jaber, A.-A.-S.: A deep learning approach to predict academic result and recommend study plan for improving student's academic performance. In: Karuppusamy, P., Perikos, I., García Márquez, F.P. (eds.) Ubiquitous Intelligent Systems. SIST, vol. 243, pp. 253–266. Springer, Singapore (2022). https://doi.org/10.1007/978-981-16-3675-2_19

24. Stevens, R.H., Galloway, T.L.: Can machine learning be used to forecast the future uncertainty of military teams? J. Defense Model. Simul., 1548512921999112 (2021)

25. Visa, S., Ramsay, B., Ralescu, A.L., Van Der Knaap, E.: Confusion matrix-based feature selection. MAICS **710**, 120–127 (2011)

Integrated Music Recommendation System Using Collaborative and Content Based Filtering, and Sentiment Analysis

Arafat Bin Hossain, Wordh Ul Hasan, Kimia Tuz Zaman,
and Koushik Howlader$^{(\boxtimes)}$

North Dakota State University, Fargo, ND, USA
koushik.howlader@ndsu.edu

Abstract. This paper deals with a comparative analysis between Collaborative Filtering (CF), Content Based Filtering (CB) and Sentiment Analysis to build a recommendation Engine using Spotify Dataset. Using playlist-song association as an implicit feedback for a user, we implemented CF and we applied the Content Based Filtering using song metadata from spotify dataset. Using lyrics from the dataset, we developed a sentiment analysis model, labeled the song to create a novel dataset and use it to suggest songs based on the mood. K performs better for a smaller value of K, but CF improves as K increases. CF improves as K is increased while K works better for a lower value of K. By comparing all results, TF-IDF outperforms SVM and NB in sentiment analysis.

Keywords: Music recommendation · Recommendation engine · Collaborative filtering · Content based filtering · tf-idf · cosine similarity · KNN · Sentiment Analysis · Spotify

1 Introduction

Recommendation Systems are a widely used field of Artificial Intelligence. Recommendation Systems has already driven much research in finding movie recommendations, tourist spot recommendations, music recommendations. Recommendation Systems are primarily developed to cater the needs by helping people navigate through lots of choices when it comes to picking. We have utilized a Recommendation System for generating a playlist for music services like Spotify.

Due to the quantity and diversity of information available online, determining what people want-especially that which aligns with user needs-has proven to be a challenging undertaking. While collaborative recommendation systems seek to recommend items to users whose interests are similar to the given user's, content-based recommendation systems aim to suggest items that the given user has presumably previously enjoyed in the past.

A lot of work has been done in the recommendation field already. Although machine learning (ML) is frequently employed in the development of recommendation systems, it is not the only option. There are numerous approaches to

Md. S. Satu et al. (Eds.): MIET 2022, LNICST 491, pp. 162–172, 2023.
https://doi.org/10.1007/978-3-031-34622-4_13

developing a recommendation system. Simpler ways, for example, when we have little data or need to construct a quick solution. H khan et al. in their work [1] used fuzzy logic to recommend tourist spots. Florent Garcin et al. [2] used the context tree technique to improve news and story recommendations. This technology makes better recommendations based on the user's preferences. As a result, forecast accuracy and recommendation quality have improved.

The collaborative filtering technique is particularly significant in recommendation systems. It solely takes rating data from a large dataset. Different consumers rate 'N' products or behave similarly in CF, hence CF will rate or act similarly on additional items. The CF technique uses log server information about items/user interest to anticipate items/user interest to different active (new) users who would like active (new) user. Bamshad M et al. in their work [3] used collaborative filtering approach on anonymous web usage data. They used a profile aggregation clustering technique but they couldn't solve the cold start problem. Yoon Ho Cho et al. [5] also used collaborative filtering with decision tree mining but the cold start problem persists.

A content-based filtering takes into consideration the user's behavior patterns. It doesn't take into consideration what other users have liked or their behavior is rather focused on the items and builds an item to item relation that generates recommendation based on the fact that if a user likes item a similar item b will be likable by that user. Pal A. et al. in their work [7] showed content based filtering for movie recommendation. In this work they also developed a hybrid model where they used content based and collaborative filtering. Tewari A. S. et al. used content-based filtering for book recommendation in their work [8].

It is possible to categorize and index the songs using the ID3 tag information in compressed digital audio files, which includes the song's title, artist, album, and genre. This is a quick method of making music recommendations [6]. However, if the ID3 tag information in our favorite music collections is incomplete or incorrect, this technique will not work. In this situation, it is feasible to provide music similarity metrics that only use the acoustic signals of music songs when grouping related songs into one category. We compared and employed song mood-based suggestion, collaborative filtering, and content-based filtering for our study. We created a music recommendation system for mood-based recommendations that is based on the sentiment of a lyric.

2   Methodology

In this methodology section of the paper we are going to discuss how we implemented three techniques Content Based Filtering, Collaborative Filtering and Mood Based Filtering using Sentiment Analysis and incorporated them to build a Music Recommendation system. Currently, our existing database has no label for it's sentiment. We will feed a song into the sentiment analysis model and it will return the song with sentiment. Then the database will be updated with the mood of the song. Finally, the recommendation system will suggest some similar mood from this database.

2.1   Content Based Filtering

For Content Based Recommendation we have collected Spotify Songs Dataset containing 18,455 tracks. The Dataset structure is given in Table 1. We have used the same dataset for CF and Sentiment Analysis as well.

Table 1. Spotify Songs dataset structure

track Id	Track identifier produced by Spoitfy
acousticness	Between 0 and 1
danceability	Between 0 and 1
energy	Between 0 and 1
$duration_m s$	Integer that frequently falls between 200k and 300k
valence	Between 0 and 1
popularity	Between 0 and 100
tempo	Float usually between 50 and 150
liveness	Between 0 and 1
loudness	Float usually between -60 and 0
speechiness	Between 0 and 1
mode	0 = Minor, 1 = Major
explicit	One indicates explicit material; zero indicates none
$Track_n ame$	Name of the Track
$Track_a rtist$	Name of the artists that worked on the track
Lyrics	Full lyrics of the track
$Track_a lbum$	Album name the track belongs to
$track_a lbum_r elease_d ate$	Date when the track album was released
$Track_a lbum_i d$	Id of the track generated by spotify
$playlist_n ame$	List of playlists where this song can be found
$Playlist_i d$	Id's of the playlist generated by spotify
Genre	Genre of the track (rock, r&b, pop, edm, latin)
$Playlist_s ubgenre$	Further breakdown of the genre into sub-genre
Language	Language of the tracks

Feature Extraction: The dataset has 25 features. From these 25 features there are 10 features that define how the track sounds. These 10 features have numerical values and solely focus on how the song sounds to our years. These features have nothing to do with what year the song was released, who was the artist, if the song was popular or not, what album or genre the song belongs to.

Table 2. Selected Features

Selected Features	Description
acousticness	Between 0 and 1
danceability	Between 0 and 1
energy	Between 0 and 1
key	Between 0 and 11
valence	Between 0 and 1
tempo	Float usually between 50 and 150
liveness	Between 0 and 1
loudness	Float usually between -60 and 0
speechiness	Between 0 and 1
intrumenlessness	Between 0 and 1

The 10 features are given in Table 2. For our item-to-item content-based filtering we have chosen these ten features to build our model and make recommendations.

Normalization: From the chosen features the domain of the values varies a lot. Some features have a range from 0 to 1 some features have range 0 to 100 and one feature has range -60 to 0. Due to having a wide variety of ranges, we have to scale these to represent from 0 to 1. Because if we do not do this, scaling the features that have range up to 100 will be a dominating bias in the model. This process is called normalization.

Train the Model: For getting the recommendation of a given song we have used an Unsupervised Machine Learning Algorithm. The algorithm we used is called K Nearest Neighbor also known as KNN [10]. Since it is really hard to evaluate if a song is selected by a user the recommendation, we provide will also be liked by the user but the hypothesis that we are using for Item-to-Item content-based filtering is if a user likes a song from a genre the other songs that the user will listen will also belong from the same genre. But here comes another challenge. If there are thousands of songs in the dataset that belong from the same genre but how do we rank among those songs that are more relevant to the user provided the same genre song?

To solve this problem and ranking among the same genre songs we selected the ten parameters in feature extraction. These features are used with KNN models where we use the features to plot points for each track in a ten-dimensional plane. In Fig. 1 we have shown just two features with a two-dimensional plane.

For finding songs relevant to the user selected song, we take data points of that song and calculate the distance between k number of data points. For example, if we give a song from the POP genre, we expect more songs from the pop genre. This will not give us all neighbors from pop rather give us the majority

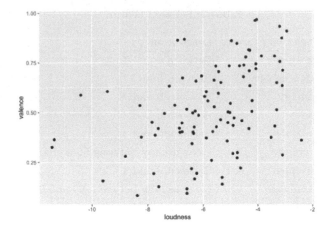

Fig. 1. Loudness feature in X axis and Valence feature on Y Axis.

from pop. If we select K = 3 and the three nearest neighbors are classified as first being pop, second being pop and third being Latin, this results two versus one and votes for pop. And the selected song is also classified as pop. Since we selected a song from pop and the prediction also tells us the song is pop we can select the neighbors given by knn algorithm and serve it as a recommendation to the user. For Calculating the nearest neighbors among all the data plots we used Euclidean distance (Fig. 2).

$$d(\mathbf{p}, \mathbf{q}) = \sqrt{\sum_{i=1}^{n} (q_i - p_i)^2}$$

Fig. 2. Euclidean distance measurement.

2.2   Collaborative Filtering

The Collaborative Filtering (CF) makes item suggestions or forecasts based on the feedback of other users [7]. Both model-based and memory-based algorithms can be used in CF methods. Memory-based algorithms, also known as nearest-neighbor algorithms, look for related users at the same time as they make recommendations using Neighbors and focus on the neighborhood to make recommendations [12]. The nearest neighbor model is usually built using a cosine similarity matrix. The equation in Fig. 3 explains how cosine similarity works.

There is another approach to Recommender System which is called model-based approach trains and models user expectations using data mining or deep learning techniques. Centered on the known model, it then makes a test forecast.

$$\text{similarity} = \cos(\theta) = \frac{\mathbf{A} \cdot \mathbf{B}}{\|\mathbf{A}\|\|\mathbf{B}\|} = \frac{\sum\limits_{i=1}^{n} A_i B_i}{\sqrt{\sum\limits_{i=1}^{n} A_i^2}\sqrt{\sum\limits_{i=1}^{n} B_i^2}},$$

where A_i and B_i are components of vector A and B respectively.

Fig. 3. Euclidean distance measurement.

The final approach, which outperforms all individual versions, blends the two approaches and is dubbed the hybrid method [13–15].

The idea of incorporating CF in a music recommender system is trivial because it is tricky to define what 'rating' means for this context. So, taking implicit feedback by tracking the playlist is one of the approaches. In this project, we have used the playlist dataset of spotify and built a playlist recommender using CF.

- Using the playlist data set, a song-playlist matrix is firstly being created where each column represents a playlist while each row is a particular song.
- The cell value is 1 if a song belongs to a playlist or otherwise it's 0. Using this matrix, a cosine similarity matrix is then created in order to have all possible combinations of two songs and the relative cosine of angle between them along the playlists. To explain mathematically, If the cosine of angle between two songs is small, it means they are close to each other. In other words, in terms of playlist, two songs are similar if they share the same playlist along the dataset and cosine similarity would tend to reflect this notion in a more quantitative manner.
- This csr matrix is then used to train the KNN model.
- If a song is now given, the model will try to find K nearest neighbours of the song by trying to find songs from other similar playlists.

Figure 4 below explains the overall approach we took when applying the CF to the spotify dataset.

2.3 Sentiment Analysis

For Mood based music recommendation we used the same dataset for Content Based filtering. The dataset shown in Fig. 1 is used with the parameter Lyrics being the main focus of our data for mood-based recommendation. For mood based recommendation we used the following methodology.

Data Preprocessing: Before applying any algorithm we need to preprocess its lyrics. The preprocessing steps contain down casing words, split string into words, remove short words, put words into base form, remove stopwords, and remove special annotations.

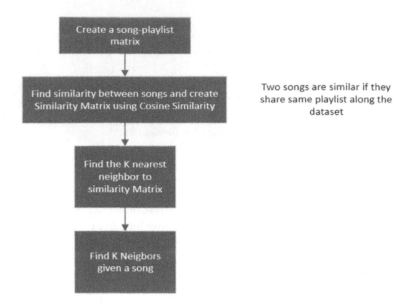

Two songs are similar if they share same playlist along the dataset

Fig. 4. CF Procedural diagram.

Model Selection: Three algorithms have been used to train the model on the dataset: Naive Bayes, SVM and TF-IDF [4]. Since the TF-IDF approach surpassed the other two, we decided upon using this in our work. An overview of how it has been implemented is discussed below.

2.3.3 TF-IDF: Information retrieval and text mining frequently employ the term frequency-inverse document frequency (Tf*idf) machine learning technique, which considers both the frequency of a word (TF) and its inverse document frequency (IDF). There exists TF and IDF scores for each word or term that appears in the text.

The product of a term's TF and IDF scores is the term's TF*IDF weight. Simply put, a text's TF*IDF score (weight) increases with how infrequently it appears in a given text, and vice versa [1] (Fig. 5).

Returning to our TF-IDF now,
TF-IDF is Term Frequency (TF) multiplied by Inverse Document Frequency (IDF)

Terminology

- t — term (word)
- d — document (set of words)
- N — count of corpus
- corpus — the total document set

Term Frequency

tf(t,d) = count of t in d/number of words in d

df(t) = occurrence of t in documents

Document Frequency

df(t) = occurrence of t in documents

Inverse Document Frequency

idf(t) = N/df

idf(t) = log(N/(df + 1))

Finally, tf-idf(t, d) = tf(t, d) * log(N/(df + 1))

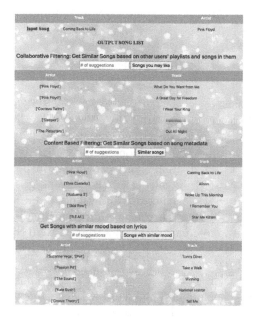

Fig. 5. Web Application.

2.4   Building the Web Application

By combining all the approaches discussed above, we created a python flask based web application which takes a song as input and recommends 3 sets of playlist, one using CF while the other two uses Content Based Filtering and Mood based filtering respectively.

3   Result and Discussion

3.1   Content Based Filtering

For accuracy calculation from the test sets we selected Ten thousand tracks to train the model on. All the tracks have genre labeled on them, but we did not select the genre as a feature to train the model on.

For the accuracy calculation we did five cross validation tests. For each cross validation we tested on 3 different neighbor numbers. We tested for 10 neighbors, 5 neighbors and 3 neighbors.

Table 3. Accuracy KNN Algorithm

Neighbor	Accuracy
10	35%
5	65%
3	83%

For each neighbor we did 100 iterations. For each iteration if the neighbor's majority is from the selected input genre, then the output is given true else its false. From 100 iterations we calculated the percentage of the results. After calculating the percentage for each cross validation, we did mean calculation for each neighbor. The results show if the neighbor number is less the algorithm performs better. But if we increase neighbors Item to Item content-based recommendation does not perform better. For lower neighbor numbers the algorithm performs well.

Table 3 shows the accuracy for each neighbor. For ten neighbors the accuracy is fifteen percent, for five neighbors the accuracy is forty five percent and for three neighbors the accuracy is sixty three percent.

3.2   Collaborative Filtering

We calculated R precision to evaluate the model.R-precision is the number of retrieved relevant tracks divided by the number of known relevant tracks. We have picked 50 random playlists from the dataset. For each playlist, a random song is picked and the song is used in the model to come up with the recommendations of K songs that the model thinks is relevant to the song. After that, we count how many suggestions actually match with the tracks in the original playlist. In this way, we measure the recall to figure out the accuracy of the model.

Furthermore, we repeat the whole process of evaluation explained above for K = 15, 20, 25, 30, 35, 40, 45, 50 in order to see how the model performs with a greater number of suggestions.

Figure 6 shows as we increase the number of K in KNN, the model comes up with more relevant suggestions of the songs and it takes a linear rise in slope

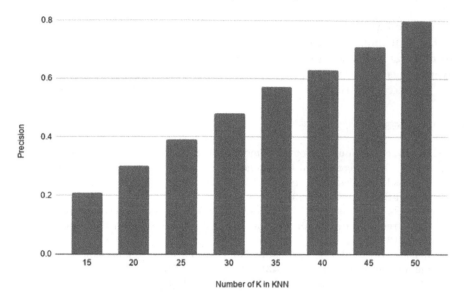

Fig. 6. Precision of KNN vs Number of Neighbour.

reaching almost a precision of 0.8 when asked to suggest 50 songs. It makes sense to use CF and playlist-song matrix to build recommender systems when using spotify dataset because the playlist-song interaction reflects a user item interaction and it works as expected for our experimental setup as well.

3.3 Sentiment Analysis

On the data we have, we used the NB, SVM, and TF-IDF algorithms. TF-IDF had the best performance among the findings we obtained (Table 4).

Table 4. Accuracy Comparison of different models used for Sentiment Analysis

Algorithm	Accuracy
NB	68%
SVM	57%
TF-IDF	78.54%

4 Conclusion

This paper investigates the usefulness of three approaches for building a music recommendation system and provides a quantitative analysis on which approach gives more relevant suggestions of songs. Collaborative Filtering is more stable than CB as it improves with greater K while CB provides more relevant suggestions of songs with lower value of K. Sentiment Analysis can not always provide relevant songs as its feature is conservative on basing the mood of a song by its lyrics. 42 percent of the time, it can end up in giving irrelevant results.

References

1. Khan, H., et al.: Tourist spot recommendation system using fuzzy inference system. In: 2017 13th International Conference on Natural Computation, Fuzzy Systems and Knowledge Discovery (ICNC-FSKD), pp. 1532–1539 (2017). https://doi.org/10.1109/FSKD.2017.8392993
2. Garcin, F., Dimitrakakis, C., Faltings, B.: Personalized news recommendation with context trees. In: Proceedings of the 7th ACM Conference on Recommender Systems (2013)
3. Mobasher, B., Cooley, R., Srivastava, J.: Automatic personalization based on web usage mining. Commun. ACM **43**(8), 142–151 (2000)
4. Satu, M.D, et al.: Short-term prediction of COVID-19 cases using machine learning models. Appl. Sci. **11**(9), 4266 (2021)
5. Cho, Y.H., Kim, J.K., Kim, S.H.: A personalized recommender system based on web usage mining and decision tree induction. Exp. Syst. Appl. **23**(3), 329–342 (2002)
6. ID3 tag. https://www.id3.org. Accessed 04 May 2021
7. Pal, A., Parhi, P., Aggarwal, M.: An improved content based collaborative filtering algorithm for movie recommendations. In: 2017 Tenth International Conference on Contemporary Computing (IC3), pp. 1–3 (2017). https://doi.org/10.1109/IC3.2017.8284357
8. Tewari, A.S., Kumar, A., Barman, A.G.: Book recommendation system based on combine features of content based filtering, collaborative filtering and association rule mining. In: IEEE International Advance Computing Conference (IACC) 2014, pp. 500–503 (2014). https://doi.org/10.1109/IAdCC.2014.6779375
9. Wu, H., Luk, R., Wong, K., Kwok, K.: Interpreting TF-IDF term weights as making relevance decisions. ACM Trans. Inf. Syst. **26**(3) (2008)
10. Howlader, K.C., et al.: Machine learning models for classification and identification of significant attributes to detect type 2 diabetes. Health Inf. Sci. Syst. **10**(1), 1–13 (2022)
11. TF-IDF from scratch in python on real world dataset. https://towardsdatascience.com/tf-idf-for-document-ranking-from-scratch-in-python-on-real-world-dataset-796d339a4089. Accessed 20 Apr 2021
12. Sarwar, B., et al.: Item-based collaborative filtering recommendation algorithms. In: Proceedings of the 10th International Conference on World Wide Web (2001)
13. Ding, Y., Liu, C.: Exploring drawbacks in music recommender systems: the Spotify case (2015)
14. Song, Y., Dixon, S., Pearce, M.: A survey of music recommendation systems and future perspectives. In: 9th International Symposium on Computer Music Modeling and Retrieval, vol. 4 (2012)
15. Hu, Y.: A model-based music recommendation system for individual users and implicit user groups. University of Miami (2014)
16. Music Recommendation System Spotify - Collaborative Filtering. https://hpac.cs.umu.se/teaching/sem-mus-17/Reports/Madathil.pdf. Accessed 15 Apr 2021

A Clustering Based Niching Method for Effectively Solving the 0-1 Knapsack Problem

Md. Meheruzzaman Sarker[iD], Md. Jakirul Islam[(✉)][iD],
and Md. Zakir Hossain[iD]

Department of Computer Science and Engineering, Dhaka University of Engineering
and Technology, Gazipur, Bangladesh
15204055@student.duet.ac.bd, {jakirduet,zakircse}@duet.ac.bd

Abstract. The 0-1 knapsack problem (01-KP) is a NP-hard combinatorial optimization problems (COPs) with several applications. Because of its non-convexity, its search space contains several local and/or global optimum solutions. In this situation, both the classical and metaheuristic global optimization approaches often failed to locate the optimal solution to the 01-KP. Therefore, this research develops a clustering-based niching (CBN) method for maintaining and locating multiple solutions within an optimization run, increasing the possibility of locating the global optimal solution to the 01-KP. To do this, CBN method divides the population individuals into a number of clusters (similar to niches in a biology or ecology system) by measuring the Hamming distance between individuals. During the optimization, the individuals in the formed clusters independently explore different regions of the combinatorial search space in order to find promising solutions. For simplicity, the proposed CBN method is implemented using a modified binary PSO (*lbest*-BPSO) method. The numerical results show that the CBN method is superior than the well-known metaheuristic methods on the basis of solution quality, with a better success rate and average function evaluations, over widely used sets of 0-1 knapsack instance. This guarantees that CBN method is a suitable optimization method for determining the optimal solution to combinatorial optimization problems.

Keywords: Niching method · Clustering · The 0-1 Knapsack problem · Combinatorial optimization · Binary PSO

1 Introduction

Combinatorial optimization problems (COPs) are difficult in that an optimal solution must be found from a finite number of solutions. Many real-world COPs are NP-hard and non-convex in nature, therefore their search space frequently contains several local or global optimum solutions. From a practical standpoint,

Md. S. Satu et al. (Eds.): MIET 2022, LNICST 491, pp. 173–187, 2023.
https://doi.org/10.1007/978-3-031-34622-4_14

174   Md. M. Sarker et al.

developing an effective method capable of identifying as many different solutions as possible enhances the possibility of locating the global optimal solution [1].

The 01-KP is an NP-hard COP, aims to find a subset from a set of items that maximizes total profit by ensuring that the accumulated weights of the selected items does not exceed the knapsack capacity. Since the decision variable depends on the 0 or 1, there are a set of possibilities to get the optimal solution. In the last decades, several number of methaheuristic methods have been developed for the 01-KP. These methods have been developed based on the genetic algorithm (GA) [2,3], ant colony optimization (ACO) [4,5], simulated annealing (SA) [6,7], and binary particle swarm optimization (BPSO) [8,9]. Literature shows that these methods have been developed for locating a single solution for the 01-KP. Note that these methods often trapped in a local optimum because of their low exploration ability [9]. As a result, they often failed to locate the desired (optimal) solution for the strongly correlated 0-1 knapsack instances. To address this issue, niching methods can be used because they can find multiple solutions, increasing the possibility of locating the optimal solution.

Niching methods have the ability to locate more than one solutions within a single run, regardless of whether these solutions are similar or distinct in terms of fitness value [10]. Basically, they divide the population into subpopulations, with each subpopulation simultaneously exploring various portions of the search space. At the end of the run, they gradually converge to the different optimal solutions (local or global) that are situated in the different locations of the search space, as illustrated in Fig. 1.

In the last decades, many researches have been conducted to developed the niching methods which includes fitness sharing [10], clearing [11], crowding [12], speciation-based PSO (SPSO) [13], ring topology-based PSO (RPSO) [14], distance-based locally informed PSO [15], differential evolution (DE) [16], niching GA [17], and niche GSA [18]. Literature shows that these niching methods perform well on low-dimensional continuous optimization problems. Literature shows that most of these niching methods have inherent difficulties, and

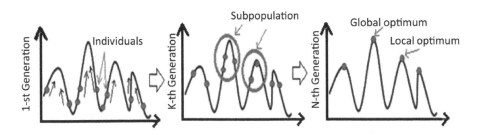

Fig. 1. Optimization procedure of the niching methods. The distribution of populations (a) at the 1st generation (b) k-th generation, and (c) N-th generation, respectively.

thus they cannot directly apply for the 01-KP. For example, the fitness sharing, SPSO, and clearing niching methods define the neighborhood structure according to the Euclidean distance between individuals. A user-defined parameter r (i.e. the niche radius) is employed in these approaches to distribute individuals to each neighborhood. The value of such a parameter is depends on the basis that the optima are uniformly distributed and sufficiently separated from one another in relation to r. In these methods, the predefined value is used for r and it remains constant for all neighborhoods. In fact, the optima may be distributed unevenly, with some being near to each other and others being far apart in relation to the niche radius. In such situations, these niching methods may ignore potential optima in the fitness landscape, drastically degrading their effectiveness.

In the crowding approach, the neighborhood structure is formed by the parents and offspring's during the reproduction stage of the genetic algorithm (GA), and the members with higher fitness value get replaced with the members with lower fitness value. In this method, the construction of niches does not depend on the user-defined parameter, however individuals in a neighborhood may belong to the other niches. For this reason, the obtained niche my be lost due to the replacement behavior of GA. Finally, RPSO method creates neighborhood structures by the PSO population by defining a ring topology structure between particles and their personal best position. In this method, neighborhood members move towards the fittest member. In RPSO, neighborhood structure is based on PSO indices. Therefore, the particles in a neighborhood may escape their neighborhood by moving to fitter neighbors in another neighborhood.

The above shows that the existing continuous niching methods may not be used to find multiple solutions for the 01-KP. Therefore, this research intents to design a new niching approach for the 01-KP. The proposed niching approach creates a subpopulation (niche) from individuals in the population that are similar based on their Hamming distance. Due to the combinatorial nature of the 01-KP, we employ Hamming distance for the similarity measure in this study rather than Euclidean distance, as is common in the niching community. The individuals of each subpopulation individually discover the promising areas of the search space to converge on the best solution of their corresponding search region. In this study, we modify a local best BPSO *lbest-BPSO* to implement the proposed niching approach. As because, the *lbest-BPSO* is simple and straightforward to implement for any combinatorial optimization problem.

The paper is organized in the following way. Section 2 focuses on related works. Section 3 explains the niching method. Section 4 shows experimental results. Section 5 concludes this study.

2   Related Works

The 0-1 knapsack problem is studied since 1896 [28]. This problem consists of n number of items and each item i consists of weight w_i, and profit p_i. The goal of the problem is to choose a subset of items in order to maximize profit while the weight of the selected items not exceeding the knapsack capacity C. To model, we use x_i as a decision variable, where the value of $x_i = 1$ indicates that the item is chosen to put in the knapsack. Formally, this problem can be presented by the following equation:

$$\text{maximize} \sum_{i=1}^{n} p_i x_i$$
$$\text{s. t.} \sum_{i=1}^{n} w_i x_i \leq C, \tag{1}$$
$$\text{where } x_i \in \{0,1\}, \ i = 1, ..., n.$$

Several optimization methods have been developed during the last several decades for the 01-KP. For example, the author of [19] proposed an artificial chemical reaction optimization strategy to tackle the 01-KP. A new repair operator based on the greedy approach and random selection is employed in this method to convert infeasible solutions to feasible solutions. On solving the popular 0-1 knapsack instances, the experimental results confirmed that this strategy outperformed the genetic algorithm and the quantum-inspired evolutionary algorithm. [20] proposes a hybrid cuckoo search algorithm with global harmony search approach for the 01-KP. The drawbacks of the cuckoo search and global harmony search methods were eliminated in this method to efficiently locate the solution of 0-1 knapsack instances. In [21], another hybrid PSO based on the greedy strategy is suggested for the 0-1 Knapsack Problem. This hybrid method introduced two different strategies namely penalty function and greedy to convert infeasible solutions into feasible ones. The experimental results demonstrated the efficiency of this method in tackling the difficult 0-1 knapsack instances. For the same problem, [22] proposes a hybrid BPSO named BPSO-GA. To solve the 01-KP, this technique combines the strengths of BPSO with the genetic algorithm (GA). The OMBO technique is another hybrid optimization approach introduced in [23], in which a Gaussian perturbation strategy is used inside the opposition-based learning monarch butterfly (OBL) optimization to effectively find the optimal solution of the 01-KP.

Some other metaheuristic methods, such as the modified whale method [24], Tissue P system with cell division method [25], U-Shaped transfer function based BPSO [26], and ZBPSO method [8], have recently been proposed for the challenge of solving the 01-KP. All of these methods are designed to find a global optimal solution. However, because they are stochastic, they frequently fail to find the global optimal solution for the strongly correlated 0-1 knapsack instances. To address this issue, this study intents to develop a new niching method which will offer multiple solutions for the 01-KP within a single run. It is obvious that with these solutions, the chance of finding the optimal solution by the proposed CB-NM will be increased. The detail of the CBN method is provided in the following section.

3   The Proposed Clustering Based Niching Method

This section describes the formation of niches for the proposed niching concept, followed by the implementation of the proposed clustering-based niching method.

3.1   Formation of Niches

The formation of niches relies on the clustering and Hamming distance concepts. Clustering splits data or population individuals into groups (sub-populations) where members in the same group are more similar than those in other groups. In clustering, the similarity between individuals are measure in terms of the Euclidean distance: two or more individuals reside to the same cluster when they are "close" according to a given distance. In this study, the proposed niching concept is developed for the 01-KP, which is a combinatorial optimization problem in which the candidate solutions (population individuals) are typically represented by the binary string e.g. "010101". Therefore, this study intends to use the Hamming distance rather than the Euclidean distance as the similarity metric for clustering the population individuals, as because it's commonly used to calculate the distance between two binary strings. This study calculates the Hamming distance between individuals using the following equation:

$$d^{Ham}(\mathbf{x}_i, \mathbf{x}_j) = \sum_{k=1}^{d} l_k; \quad \text{where} \quad l_k = \begin{cases} 1 & \text{if } x_{i,k} = x_{j,k}; i \neq j, \\ 0 & \text{otherwise} \end{cases} \quad (2)$$

where, d is the problem dimension and $\mathbf{x}_i$ and $\mathbf{x}_j$ are two individuals of the population.

For this study, we use a fixed number of population members $(\mathbf{x}_1, \mathbf{x}_2, \ldots, \mathbf{x}_P)$ to optimize the 0-1 knapsack problem. We assume each cluster can hold M individuals. The benefit is that all clusters have almost the same number of members, so they can explore the binary search space comprehensively and find promising solutions. With this assumption, the proposed niching scheme calculates the Hamming distance between X_1 and other individuals $(X_2, \ldots, X_P)$, to form the first cluster. Individuals who have a Hamming distance of zero (0) with X_1 are considered to be members of the first cluster. If the number of members in the first cluster reaches the maximum number of allowed members (M), the proposed method begins forming the second cluster with the remaining individuals. Otherwise, the proposed method attempts to fill the first cluster with individuals who have a Hamming distance of one. If this cluster still remains unfilled, it attempts to fill it with individuals who maintain a Hamming distance of two, and so on. The above concept is described by the flowchart presented in Fig. 2.

In this study, each cluster acts as a niche, and its members are responsible for locating the optimal or near-optimal solution within that niche. Note that all cluster members perform the search operation in parallel. Consequently, they can provide multiple solutions within a single optimization run. The proposed niching scheme then selects the solution that has the highest probability of being the optimal solution for the given problem.

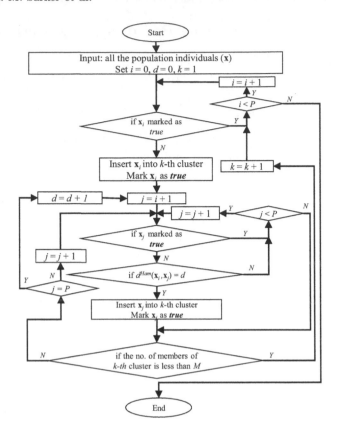

Fig. 2. Flowchart of the proposed Hamming distance based clustering concept.

3.2 Implementation of the Proposed Niching Method

Number of combinatorial optimization methods have been developed which includes BPSO, GA, and ACO. In comparison, the BPSO is simple and easy to implement because it performs optimization based on two simple equations. Therefore, the original BPSO is chosen for this study to implement the proposed niching concept. It should be noted that the original BPSO is unable to find multiple solutions within a single run. Therefore, this study employs the proposed clustering concept in BPSO, which is further described below.

Kennedy and Eberhart designed the original BPSO [29] for the combinatorial optimization problems. It consists of particles that fly throughout the search space to locate the optimal solution. The i-th particle in the iterative process remembers two values: its personal best position $\mathbf{p}_i$ and its global best position $\mathbf{p}_g$. At the k-th iteration, the velocity and position of the i-th particle are modified according to the following two equations

$$\mathbf{v}_i^k = \mathbf{v}_i^k + c_1 r_1^k (\mathbf{p}_i^k - \mathbf{x}_i^k) + c_2 r_2^k (\mathbf{p}_g - \mathbf{x}_i^k) \tag{3}$$

and

$$\mathbf{x}_i^k = \begin{cases} 0 & \text{if } rand() > S(\mathbf{v}_i^k), \\ 1 & \text{otherwise}, \end{cases} \tag{4}$$

respectively, where k denotes the current iteration, $rand()$ generates uniformly distributed random numbers between 0 and 1, c_1 and c_2 are two constants, r_1^k and r_2^k are two random numbers in range $[0,1]$, and $S(\mathbf{v}_i^k)$ represents a sigmoid function. The formula of calculating the value of S is as follows:

$$S(\mathbf{v}_i^k) = \frac{1}{1 + e^{-\mathbf{v}_i^k}}. \tag{5}$$

The above BPSO is designed to obtain a single optimal solution to the combinatorial optimization problem. However, the research aims to obtain multiple solutions for the 01-KP. To achieve this, this study modifies the BPSO by incorporating the proposed Hamming distance based clustering concept described in Sect. 3.1. In the modified BPSO method, we use the notation $\mathbf{x}_{ij}$ and $\mathbf{p}_{ij}$ instead of $\mathbf{x}_i$ and $\mathbf{p}_i$ to represent the position and personal best position of the i-th particle in the j-th cluster, where $j = 1, 2, 3, ...,$. Similarly, we use the notation $\mathbf{p}_{gj}$ instead of $\mathbf{p}_g$ to represent the global best position of the j-th cluster. With these modifications, the modified BPSO updates the value of velocity (v_{ij}) and position (p_{ij}) based on the following equations:

$$\mathbf{v}_{ij}^k = \mathbf{v}_{ij}^k + c_1 r_1^k (\mathbf{p}_{ij}^k - \mathbf{x}_{ij}^k) + c_2 r_2^k (\mathbf{p}_{gj} - \mathbf{x}_{ij}^k) \tag{6}$$

and

$$\mathbf{x}_{ij}^k = \begin{cases} 0 & \text{if } rand() > S(\mathbf{v}_{ij}^k), \\ 1 & \text{otherwise}, \end{cases} \tag{7}$$

where, the value of sigmoid function is calculated using the following equation:

$$S(\mathbf{v}_{ij}^k) = \frac{1}{1 + e^{-\mathbf{v}_{ij}^k}}. \tag{8}$$

In this study, the modified BPSO is used as a niching technique to find multiple optimal or nearly optimal solutions to the 01-KP. This modified BPSO is referred to as the clustering-based niching (CBN) method, which is described by the flowchart in Fig. 3.

According to flowchart in Fig. 3, the proposed CBN method first sets its parameters c_1, c_2, V_{max}, and g. Following that, it randomly initializes the particles' velocity $\mathbf{v}_{ij}$, position, and personal best position. In this case, the value of $\mathbf{v}_{ij}$ is chosen at random from the ranges V_{max} and $-V_{max}$. Similarly, the value of $\mathbf{x}_{ij}$ is chosen at random between 0 and 1. Here, the personal best position p_{ij} is initially set to x_{ij}. Following the initialization phase, the Hamming distance based clustering concept (see Fig. 2) is applied to the particles of CBN method to form the clusters.

The main loop begins immediately after the fitness value calculation stage of the proposed CBN method. The blocks within the dashed lines in Fig. 3 are

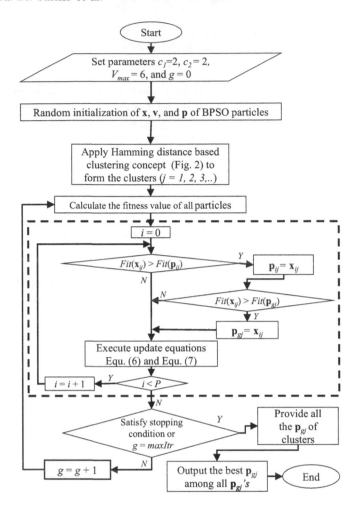

Fig. 3. Flowchart of CBN method.

in responsible of updating the personal best position ($\mathbf{p}ij$), global best position ($\mathbf{p}_{gj}$), velocity ($\mathbf{v}_{ij}$), and position ($\mathbf{x}_{ij}$) of the i-th particle of the j-th cluster. Following that, the proposed method checks for termination conditions. If the termination condition is met, the proposed method returns all global best solutions (p_{gj}) discovered by the particles of the formed clusters. The p_{gj} with the highest fitness value is then chosen as the best solution for the given 0-1 knapsack instances. Otherwise, the proposed algorithm repeats the entire process in order to find the best solution to the 0-1 knapsack problem.

4   Experimental Studies

In this section, three different experiments will be conducted on the weakly and strongly correlated 0-1 knapsack instances [30,31]. These two sets of instances are largely used for the evaluation purpose of combinatorial optimization methods. The first experiment is conducted to find the best value for two parameters, the population size m and the maximum number of iterations ($maxItr$) of CBN method. The second and third experiments compare the proposed niching method to well-known BPSO variants.

In this paper, the solution of the test instances are available in literature. Therefore, we compare the CBN method and the well-known metaheuristic methods over three performance matrices, the average profit ($AvgPft$), standard deviations (SD), success rate (SR), and average function evaluations ($AvgFEs$). Here, the function evaluations referrers to the number of times the objective function is called during an optimization run. The success rate is the percentage of runs that find the global optimum of the given problem.

4.1   Find the Best Value for m and $maxItr$

An experiment is carried out for determining the best values for m and $maxItr$. For this, two weakly correlated 0-1 knapsack instances f_1 and f_5 are chosen from [30] and two strongly correlated instances $Ks20\_a$ and $Ks24\_b$ are chosen from [31]. This experiment is carried out using $m = 40$ to 120 and $c_1 = c_2 = 2$, and $maxItr = 500$ to 2000.

Table 1 shows the success rate obtained by the proposed niching method for four benchmark instances, which are the average value of 30 independent runs. According to this table, the proposed method achieved a 100 percent success rate for two weakly correlated instances (f_1 and f_5) in all cases, indicating that the obtained success rate is independent of m and $maxItr$. The proposed method, on the other hand, achieved a good success rate (SR) when the value of m was set to 120 and the value of $maxItr$ was set to 2000 for two strongly correlated instances Ks_20a and Ks_24b, respectively. According to these, we choose a swarm size of 120 and a maximum number of iterations of 2000 (which are common for both weakly and strongly correlated 0-1 knapsack instances) for the subsequent experiments.

4.2   Results and Discussion

Following the previous section, the proposed CBN method is compared to the BPSO [29], L-BPSO [30], V1-BPSO [32], V2-BPSO [33], and TVT-BPSO [9], respectively. For the experiments, ten weakly and fifteen strongly correlated 0-1 knapsack instances are used in this study. The results of all comparisons are averaged over 30 separate runs. This study considers two termination conditions for the compared methods. They are terminated when the global optimum is found or when the maximum number of iterations is reached. All of the compared methods in this paper are based on BPSO. As a result, we set the value for V_{max}

Table 1. The average SR obtained by the proposed CBN method over 30 runs on f_1, f_5, Ks_20a, and Ks_24b.

Instance	Size	Iterations	Population size(m)		
			40	80	120
f_1	10	500	100	100	100
		1000	100	100	100
		1500	100	100	100
		2000	100	100	100
f_5	15	500	100	100	100
		1000	100	100	100
		1500	100	100	100
		2000	100	100	100
Ks_20a	20	500	50	93.33	**96.67**
		1000	90	100	100
		1500	96.67	100	100
		2000	100	100	100
Ks_24b	24	500	13.33	26.67	50
		1000	43.33	56.67	**86.67**
		1500	53.33	80	**93.33**
		2000	70	**93.33**	**95.61**

$= 6$, $c_1 = c_2 = 2$ for all of the compared methods based on the literature. The best results are highlighted in bold.

Weakly Correlated Instances. Table 2 summarizes the results for the weakly correlated instances. According to this table the CBN method, TVT-BPSO method, and V2-BPSO method obtained the similar results in terms of the average profit ($AvgPft$) and success rate. However, when comparing the results of SR and $AvgFEs$, CBN method is superior since it has a greater SR for 8 out of 10 test instances with fewer $AvgFEs$. This demonstrates that CBN is more accurate and efficient than five well-known metaheuristic methods in weakly correlated 0-1 knapsack instances. In comparison to the proposed CBN method, V1-BPSO obtained the lowest SR and the highest $AvgFEs$ for all the instances except f_9. As a result, this BPSO is neither a reliable nor an efficient method for this set instances.

Strongly Correlated Instances. Table 3 summarizes the results for the strongly correlated 0-1 knapsack instances.

According to Table 3, the proposed CBN method performs well on the strongly correlated instances. Specifically, the proposed CBN method and TVT-BPSO obtained the similar result for the case of Ks_16a, Ks_16b, and Ks_20d. However, the result of $AvgFEs$ for these three instances show that CBN method is superior to TVT-BPSO method in terms of computational complexity. For Ks_16c, Ks_16e, Ks_20a, Ks_20c, and Ks_20e instances, CBN method is superior than the other compared methods in terms of all the three performance matrices $AvgPft$, SR, and $AvgFEs$. This again proves that CBN method is not

Table 2. The results of six different BPSOs on f_1 to f_{10}. The first, second, and third line shows the obtained ($AvgPft$ and SD), SR and $AvgFEs$, respectively.

Instance	Size	Opt. Value	V2-BPSO	BPSO	L-BPSO	V1-BPSO	TVT-BPSO	Proposed
f_3	4	35	35±0	35±0	35±0	34.70±1.32	35±0	35±0
			100	100	100	93.33	100	100
			41	92	45	2712	43	**27**
f_4	4	23	23±0	23±0	22.97±0.18	22.97±0.18	23±0	23±0
			100	100	96.67	96.67	100	100
			41	461	1372	1372	43	**20**
f_9	5	130	130±0	130±0	127.20±5.16	128.40±4.15	130±0	130±0
			100	100	76.67	86.67	100	100
			54.67	1058.67	9373.33	5377.33	56	**38**
f_7	7	107	107±0	103.90±4.28	105.73±1.41	103.53±4.54	107±0	107±0
			100	30	46.67	43.33	100	100
			140	28019	21364	22685	167	202
f_1	10	295	295±0	294.57±1.38	290.77±10.66	281.83±21.11	295±0	295±0
			100	86.67	56.67	26.67	100	100
			413	8556	17429	29369	851	**387**
f_6	10	52	52±0	51.80±0.55	51.63±0.85	51.33±1.15	52±0	52±0
			100	86.67	83.33	66.67	100	100
			180	8556	6973	13469	280	211
f_5	15	481.07	481.07±0	478.10±10.04	474.80±17.01	427.19±39.87	481.07±0	481.07±0
			100	93.33	73.33	16.67	100	100
			1976	4223	10920	33364	14715	**879**
f_2	20	1024	1024±0	1024±0	1002.53±22.32	931.27±53.80	1024±0	1024±0
			100	100	26.67	0	100	100
			6820	3533	29449	40000	31289	**1630**
f_{10}	20	1025	1025±0	1025±0	989.70±36.43	933.07±50.78	1025±0	1025±0
			100	100	13.33	3.33	100	100
			4707	1980	34703	38681	29440	**1597**
f_8	23	9767	9767±0	9766.93±0.37	9766.30±2.59	9757.33±8.03	9766.97±0.18	9767±0.00
			100	96.67	90	20	96.67	100
			11060	6001	6424	32371	36060	**5160**

only a reliable but also a faster optimization method for these test instances. In terms of SR, CBN method outperforms the well-known optimization methods for Ks_16d, Ks_20b, and Ks_24a to Ks_24e. In terms of $AvgFEs$, CBN method is superior than the other compared methods except TVT-BPSO for Ks_16d, Ks_20b, and Ks_24a to Ks_24e.

The convergence behaviour of six optimization methods on the cases ks_16e and Ks_20b is demonstrated in Fig. 4. It can be seen that the CBN method consistently outperformed the other metaheuristic methods on both the weakly (ks_16e) and strongly (Ks_20b) correlated 0-1 knapsack benchmark instances. For both these two instances, V1-BPSO showed worst performance than the other methods.

Table 3. The results of six different BPSOs on Ks_16a to Ks_24e [9,30]. The first, second, third, and fourth line shows the obtained $AvgPft$, SD, SR, and $AvgFEs$.

Instance	Size	Opt. Value	Proposed	TVT-BPSO	S-BPSO	L-BPSO	V1-BPSO	V2-BPSO
Ks_16a	16	7850983	**7850983**	**7850983**	7771152.37	7797246.9	7693936.9	7850983
			±0.00	±0.00	±76092.77	±67539.40	±122910.45	±0.00
			100	100	16.67	26.67	16.67	100
			4848	9252	35263	29888	33775	21676
Ks_16b	16	9352998	**9352998**	**9352998**	9245414.87	9250490.5	7927968	9352998
			±0.00	±0.00	±84778.02	±120292.36	±159529.14	±0.00
			100	100	26.67	26.67	3.33	100
			4483	7835	30153	29907	38725	19859
Ks_16c	16	9151147	**9151147**	9150326.3	9036801.6	9052814.6	8924175	9150326.3
			±0.00	±4495.16	±105374.18	±83568.41	±147544.37	±4495.16
			100	96.67	13.33	16.67	6.67	96.67
			5235	9223	35448	33597	37441	19669
Ks_16d	16	9348889	**9348889**	9347669.2	9271454.97	9294715.1	9188651.2	9347262.6
			±0.00	±3721.96	±69041.39	±52798.58	±95956.06	±4217.41
			100	90	13.33	20	0	86.67
			14666	**13440**	35053	32740	41000	25804
Ks_16e	16	7769117	**7769117**	7768496.13	7693213	7713892.5	7587932.3	7767875.27
			±0.00	±3400.63	±75474.04	±78597.11	±125788.08	±4725.57
			100	96.67	13.33	30	3.33	93.33
			5304	13660	35517	28467	38681	21015
Ks_20a	20	10727049	**10727049**	10724840.5	10669618.5	10692482	10563640	10714666.4
			±0.00	±7523.13	±60759.13	±58716.61	±120918.17	±13060.22
			100	90	26.67	33.33	3.33	43.33
			16095	18976	32543	27853	38672	38615
Ks_20b	20	9818261	**9818261**	9815420.1	9735538.37	9766711.5	9632312.5	9797837.57
			±0.00	±9323.38	±79571.34	±57579.60	±112517.84	±20116.05
			100	90	20	30	0	40
			20428	**18389**	34121	29204	40000	38263
Ks_20c	20	10714023	**10714023**	10712635.8	10615440.8	10688081	10486056	10709990.3
			±0.00	±4077.25	±115323.68	±45556.95	±133805.32	±6230.09
			100	86.67	23.33	36.67	0	60
			10865	19208	32559	26319	40000	36317
Ks_20d	20	8929156	**8929156**	**8929156**	8866124.1	8883763.2	8735162.4	8916392.47
			±0.00	±0.00	±74952.33	±70473.79	±104543.78	±15587.49
			100	100	33.33	43.33	0	53.33
			14843	15155	31507	24383	40000	37295
Ks_20e	20	9357969	**9357969**	9356953.67	9306943.83	9318815.1	9181466.3	9353699.9
			±0.00	±3038.76	±54249.45	±68243.98	±126241.20	±9589.14
			100	66.67	23.33	20	0	56.67
			18950	24236	34183	32973	40000	36537
Ks_24a	24	13549094	**13548269**	13533425.3	13507548.4	13512452	13323723	13499799.43
			±9013.26	±20555.05	±58236.73	±31391.28	±137591.62	±22346.71
			96.67	56.67	36.67	26.67	3.33	0
			62279	**30016**	31949	31051	38796	40000
Ks_24b	24	12233713	**12233281**	12222004.6	12152367.5	12191466	12031295	12182354.87
			±6344.13	±15052.33	±71669.10	±51448.35	±107235.86	±25839.01
			96.67	53.33	16.67	30	0	3.33
			51065	**29381**	36640	30167	40000	39867
Ks_24c	24	12448780	**12448780**	12444104.2	12395398.5	12420325	12255888	12414359.7
			±0.00	±10802	±78169.05	±47375.30	±114864.01	±27122.87
			100	70	36.67	40	3.33	16.67
			49269	**29713**	31723	26820	39008	38471
Ks_24d	24	11815315	**11815315**	11809811.8	11778345.2	11776442	11632527	11776692.07
			±0.00	±9023.92	±58548.76	±59364.89	±128661.51	±21915.93
			100	50	46.67	26.67	0	10
			41082	**32332**	29028	30903	40000	39400
Ks_24e	24	13940099	**13940099**	13937049.8	13914845.7	13904779	13777674	13897801.7
			±0.00	±6653.97	±45334.60	±67627.36	±150279.17	±26691.06
			100	76.67	43.33	43.33	13.33	13.33
			29756	**28019**	30343	25769	35296	39533

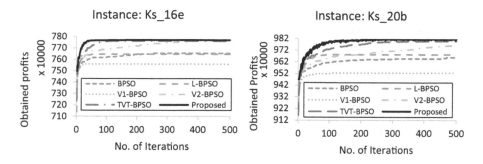

Fig. 4. Comparing the convergences of six different optimization methods on the benchmark instances ks_16e and Ks_20b.

5   Conclusion

This paper proposed a clustering based niching method to effectively solving the 01-KP. This method can offer multiple (both local and global) solutions as oppose to the traditional metaherustic optimization methods within a single optimization run. By doing this, the chance of locating the global optimal solution is increased. The robustness of the CBN method is verified by conducting two different experiments using ten weakly correlated and fifteen strongly correlated 0-1 knapsack instances. Experiment results demonstrate that the developed CBN method is better than the well-known metaheuristic methods in respect of solution quality and efficiency. This proves that the CBN method is a robust method for obtaining the optimal solution to the 0-1 knapsack instances.

In future, the proposed CBN method will be evaluated over the real-life COPs such as structural topology optimization problem.

References

1. Li, J.P., Balazs, M.E., Parks, G.T., Clarkson, P.J.: A species conserving genetic algorithm for multimodal function optimization. Evol. Comput. **10**(3), 207–234 (2002)
2. Soukaina, L., Mohamed, N., Hassan, E., Boujemâa, A.: A hybrid genetic algorithm for solving 0/1 knapsack problem. In: Proceedings of the International Conference on Learning and Optimization Algorithms: Theory and Applications, pp. 1–6 (2018)
3. Lim, T.Y., Al-Betar, M.A., Khader, A.T.: Taming the 0/1 knapsack problem with monogamous pairs genetic algorithm. Exp. Syst. Appl. **54**, 241–50 (2016)
4. Zhang, S., Liu, S.: A discrete improved artificial bee colony algorithm for 0–1 knapsack problem. IEEE Access **7**, 104982–104991 (2019)
5. Alzaqebah, A., Abu-Shareha, A.A.: Ant colony system algorithm with dynamic pheromone updating for 0/1 knapsack problem. Int. J. Intell. Syst. Appl. **10**(2), 9–17 (2019)

6. Moradi, N., Kayvanfar, V., Rafiee, M.: An efficient population-based simulated annealing algorithm for 0–1 knapsack problem. Eng. Comput. **5**, 1–20 (2021)
7. Zhan, S.H., Zhang, Z.J., Wang, L.J., Zhong, Y.W.: List-based simulated annealing algorithm with hybrid greedy repair and optimization operator for 0–1 knapsack problem. IEEE Access **6**, 54447–54458 (2018)
8. Sun, W.Z., Zhang, M., Wang, J.S., Guo, S.S., Wang, M., Hao, W.K.: Binary particle swarm optimization algorithm based on Z-shaped probability transfer function to solve 0–1 knapsack problem. IAENG Int. J. Comput. Sci. **48**(2) (2021)
9. Islam, M.J., Li, X., Mei, Y.: A time-varying transfer function for balancing the exploration and exploitation ability of a binary PSO. Appl. Soft Comput. **59**, 182–196 (2017)
10. Goldberg, D.E., Richardson, J.: Genetic algorithms with sharing for multimodal function optimization. In: Genetic Algorithms and Their Applications: Proceedings of the Second International Conference on Genetic Algorithms, pp. 41–49. Lawrence Erlbaum, Hillsdale (1987)
11. Pétrowski, A.: A clearing procedure as a niching method for genetic algorithms. In: Proceedings of IEEE International Conference on Evolutionary Computation. pp. 798–803. IEEE (1996)
12. Mahfoud, S.W.: Niching methods for genetic algorithm. Ph.D. thesis, University of Illinois (1995)
13. Parrott, D., Li, X.: Locating and tracking multiple dynamic optima by a particle swarm model using speciation. IEEE Trans. Evol. Comput. **10**(4), 440–58 (2006)
14. Li, X.: Niching without niching parameters: particle swarm optimization using a ring topology. IEEE Trans. Evol. Comput. **14**(1), 150–169 (2010)
15. Lynn, N., Suganthan, P.N.: Distance based locally informed particle swarm optimizer with dynamic population size. In: Proceedings of the 18th Asia Pacific Symposium on Intelligent and Evolutionary Systems, pp. 577–587 (2015)
16. Chen, Z.G., Zhan, Z.H., Wang, H., Zhang, J.: Distributed individuals for multiple peaks: a novel differential evolution for multimodal optimization problems. IEEE Trans. Evol. Comput. **24**(4), 708–19 (2019)
17. Ueno, A., Hagita, N., Takubo, T.: A niching genetic algorithm including an inbreeding mechanism for multimodal problems. In: Zin, T.T., Lin, J.C.-W., Pan, J.-S., Tin, P., Yokota, M. (eds.) Genetic and Evolutionary Computing. AISC, vol. 387, pp. 71–80. Springer, Cham (2016). https://doi.org/10.1007/978-3-319-23204-1_9
18. Haghbayan, P., Nezamabadi-Pour, H., Kamyab, S.: A niche GSA method with nearest neighbor scheme for multimodal optimization. Swarm Evol. Comput. **35**, 78–92 (2017)
19. Truong, T.K., Li, K., Xu, Y., Ouyang, A., Nguyen, T.T.: Solving 0–1 knapsack problem by artificial chemical reaction optimization algorithm with a greedy strategy. J. Intell. Fuzzy Syst. **28**(5), 2179–86 (2015)
20. Feng, Y., Wang, G.G., Gao, X.Z.: A novel hybrid cuckoo search algorithm with global harmony search for 0–1 knapsack problems. Int. J. Comput. Intell. Syst. **9**(6), 1174–1190 (2016)
21. Nguyen, P.H., Wang, D., Truong, T.K.: A new hybrid particle swarm optimization and greedy for 0–1 knapsack problem. Indonesian J. Electric. Eng. Comput. Sci. **1**(3), 411–418 (2016)
22. Wang, J., Liu, J., Pan, J.-S., Xue, X., Huang, L.: A hybrid BPSO-GA algorithm for 0-1 knapsack problems. In: Krömer, P., Alba, E., Pan, J.-S., Snášel, V. (eds.) ECC 2017. AISC, vol. 682, pp. 344–351. Springer, Cham (2018). https://doi.org/10.1007/978-3-319-68527-4_37

23. Feng, Y., Wang, G.G., Dong, J., Wang, L.: Opposition-based learning monarch butterfly optimization with Gaussian perturbation for large-scale 0–1 knapsack problem. Comput. Electric. Eng. **67**, 454–68 (2018)
24. Abdel-Basset, M., El-Shahat, D., Sangaiah, A.K.: A modified nature inspired metaheuristic whale optimization algorithm for solving 0–1 knapsack problem. Int. J. Mach. Learn. Cybern. **10**(3), 495–514 (2019)
25. Ye, L., Zheng, J., Guo, P., Pérez-Jiménez, M.J.: Solving the 0–1 knapsack problem by using tissue p system with cell division. IEEE Access **7**, 66055–66067 (2019)
26. Mirjalili, S., Zhang, H., Mirjalili, S., Chalup, S., Noman, N.: A novel U-shaped transfer function for binary particle swarm optimisation. In: Nagar, A.K., Deep, K., Bansal, J.C., Das, K.N. (eds.) Soft Computing for Problem Solving 2019. AISC, vol. 1138, pp. 241–259. Springer, Singapore (2020). https://doi.org/10.1007/978-981-15-3290-0_19
27. Williamson, D.P., Shmoys, D.B.: The Design of Approximation Algorithms. Cambridge University Press (2011)
28. Mathews, G.B.: On the partition of numbers. In: Proceedings of the London Mathematical Society, vol. s1–28, no. (1), pp. 486–490 (1896)
29. Kennedy, J., Eberhart, R.C.: A discrete binary version of the particle swarm algorithm. In: Proceedings of the IEEE International Conference on Systems, Man, and Cybernetics, pp. 4104–4108 (1997). https://doi.org/10.1109/ICSMC.1997.637339
30. Bansal, J., Deep, K.: A modified binary particle swarm optimization for knapsack problems. Appl. Math. Comput. **218**, 11042–11061 (2012)
31. Wang, L., Yang, R., Xu, Y., Niu, Q., Pardalos, P., Fei, M.: An improved adaptive binary Harmony Search algorithm. Inf. Sci. **232**, 58–87 (2013)
32. Liu, J., Yang, R., Sun, S.: The analysis of binary particle swarm optimization. J. Nanjing Univ. (Nat. Sci.) **47**, 504–514 (2011)
33. Mirjalili, S., Lewis, A.: S-shaped versus V-shaped transfer functions for binary particle swarm optimization. Swarm Evol. Comput. **9**, 1–14 (2013)

Assorted, Archetypal and Annotated Two Million (3A2M) Cooking Recipes Dataset Based on Active Learning

Nazmus Sakib[1]($\boxtimes$), G. M. Shahariar[2], Md. Mohsinul Kabir[1],
Md. Kamrul Hasan[1], and Hasan Mahmud[1]

[1] Islamic University of Technology (IUT), Gazipur, Bangladesh
nazmussakib009@gmail.com, sshibli745@gmail.com,
{mohsinulkabir,hasank,hasan}@iut-dhaka.edu
[2] Bangladesh University of Engineering and Technology, Dhaka, Bangladesh

Abstract. Cooking recipes allow individuals to exchange culinary ideas and provide food preparation instructions. Due to a lack of adequate labeled data, categorizing raw recipes found online to the appropriate food genres is a challenging task. Utilizing the knowledge of domain experts to categorize recipes could be a solution. In this study, we present a novel dataset of two million culinary recipes labeled in respective categories leveraging the knowledge of food experts and an active learning technique. So, we collect the recipes from the RecipeNLG dataset [1]. We employ three human experts whose trustworthiness score is higher than 86.667% to categorize 300K recipe by their Named Entity Recognition (NER) and assign it to one of the nine categories: bakery, drinks, non-veg, vegetables, fast food, cereals, meals, sides and fusion. Finally, we categorize the remaining 1900K recipes using Active Learning method with a blend of Query-by-Committee and Human In The Loop (HITL) approaches. There are more than two million recipes in our dataset, each of which is categorized and has a confidence score linked with it. For the 9 genres, the Fleiss Kappa score of this massive dataset is roughly 0.56026. We believe that the researchers can use this dataset to perform various machine learning and NLP tasks. The dataset will be available upon publication: https://tinyurl.com/3zu4778y.

Keywords: Natural Language Processing (NLP) · Named Entity Recognition (NER) · Dataset Annotation · Active Learning · Machine Learning · Human-in-the-loop (HITL)

1 Introduction

A recipe is a text that is used when cooking or baking food that specifies the cooking method, the items required, and how to use them. Recipes allow individuals to make new dishes without having to watch a demonstration. One maybe familiar with the basics of food preparation, but the preparation of certain meals, such as Sushi and Baklava, have unique procedures that must be learned before

© ICST Institute for Computer Sciences, Social Informatics and Telecommunications Engineering 2023
Published by Springer Nature Switzerland AG 2023. All Rights Reserved
Md. S. Satu et al. (Eds.): MIET 2022, LNICST 491, pp. 188–203, 2023.
https://doi.org/10.1007/978-3-031-34622-4_15

they can be properly cooked. Even if a person has a large number of ingredients in their refrigerator, making some recipes can be challenging. A recipe can save a lot of his time by instructing him on how to prepare the food, which ingredients to use, how to prepare them, and any nutritional information that may be relevant. A person may even find a recipe on the internet for a dish that he or she has never heard of before. As recipes describe a set of rules for cooking food in an informal way, there is no strict rule of how these texts should be structured. The same recipe may appear in many journals and multiple periodicals in different representations, but are actually the same in outcome. Recipes can also be organized by nation or continent [1,9]. In this skewed circumstance, if the meal is evaluated in a certain genre, it can allow consumers to make an informed choice based on their interests and tastes [24]. It is also worth noting that, while each meal (depending on its ingredients) may fall into a specific genre, each dish has the capacity to stand alone or fall into another. A salad, for example, can be a salad, a side dish, a main meal, or a dessert. The same holds true for a main course.

There is a surge of interest in using culinary recipe datasets for deep learning research [16]. This is because culinary recipes include a wealth of data that can be utilized to train deep learning models. There are, however, a scarcity of publicly available culinary recipe datasets appropriate for training deep learning models. The RecipeNLG dataset [1] alleviate this issue by including both culinary recipes and named entities of more than 2 million food items. The corpus includes culinary recipes from various sources such as cookbooks, blogs, and recipe websites. It is regarded as the first publicly accessible dataset of culinary recipes. This dataset was inspired by the Recipe1M+ dataset [19]. RecipeNLG piqued people's attention in the issue by having the most publicly available recipe collection at the time. Though there are no hard and fast rules for classifying global cuisines into genres, we can say that there is a distinct split of food market customers based on the components utilized or the nature of the meal patterns. The most prevalent distinction is between "fast food" and "slow food" marketplaces. According to our findings, the RecipeNLG [1] dataset's recipes are not classified into any genres. In this study, we split two million recipes into nine categories, each with its own set of justifications based on domain experts' judgments [22].

This study aims to contribute in this domain through: (1) constructing a recipe dataset that contains nine genres developed through domain experts, (2) applying active learning and ensemble-based techniques to semi-automate the annotation process of 2 million data using Human-in-the-loop approach. The outcome of this study is an annotated original dataset of two million culinary recipes (3A2M Cooking Recipes Dataset), as well as the possibility of new recipes being developed utilizing this information, allowing people to select food meals based on their favored categories. We began by collecting recipes from the RecipeNLG dataset. Three human experts were employed, whose trustworthiness score is higher than 86.667% to categorize 300K recipe by their Named Entity Recognition (NER) and assign it to one of the nine categories: bakery, drinks, non-veg, vegetables, fast food, cereals, meals, sides and fusion. The remaining 1900K recipes were then categorized using Active Learning and a query by committee procedure. The purpose of this study is to emphasize the diversity of the culinary genre in multi-class so that people may learn more about it and develop their abilities. It also tries to emphasize that the culinary genre comprises activities other than cooking, such as baking, pastry making, confectionery manufacturing, and beverage preparation. We believe that the research community can utilize this dataset to train more robust language models and can perform culinary related machine learning tasks such as recipe genre classification, recipe generation of a specific genre, new recipe creation, etc.

The rest of the paper is organized as follows. Some previous related works are presented in Sect. 2. Section 3 contains the description of the RecipeNLG dataset. In Sect. 4, we have discussed the 3A2M corpus annotation procedure and dataset validation procedure in detail. Section 5 concludes this study with some future research directions.

2   Related Work

Recipe datasets have been in the periphery of the research community's attention due to their richness in linguistic elements. Several research articles on recipe collection and preparation have been published in recent years. Though traditional tactics were beneficial in some studies, there is a lot of scope in this domain when it comes to resources and frameworks. Recipe1M+ dataset [19] is a pioneering work that inspired many culinary studies later on. Recipe1M+ is a large-scale, organized corpus containing over one million culinary recipes and 13 million food photos. It provided the opportunity to train high-capacity models on aligned, multi-modal data because it was the biggest publicly available collection of recipe data until 2020. Using this data, they trained a neural network to learn a combined embedding of recipes and photos, which produced outstanding results on an image-recipe retrieval test. They proved in that study that regularization with the addition of a high-level classification target both increases retrieval performance to rival that of humans and allows semantic vector arithmetic. A lot of works used the Recipe1M+ dataset to develop further resources. For example, using the Recipe1M+ dataset [19] and a language model, Lee et al. [17] developed a method for autonomously producing culinary recipes. Translation metrics were used to evaluate the model. They concentrated on two tasks: component development and instruction development. Their findings demonstrated that the language model was capable of producing recipes that were semantically comparable to the original recipes. Culinary research through data-driven methods has been hindered by a scarcity of publicly available culinary recipe datasets for machine learning models [19]. The RecipeNLG dataset [1], which includes both culinary recipes and named entities, might be viewed as a prominent contribution for attempting reduction of this scarcity. The corpus includes culinary recipes from various sources such as cookbooks, blogs, and recipe websites. The RecipeNLG authors have witnessed a significant increase in interest in utilizing culinary recipe datasets for deep learning studies. They were motivated by the release of the Recipe1M+ dataset, though it included both recipes and photos. They employed a Named Entity Recognizer (NER) to extract food entities from the dataset and feed them into the recipe generator through specific control tokens. This information is used to fine-tune a GPT-2 language model, which creates new recipes based on a given set of food things. On top of the Recipe1M+ dataset, the new dataset includes over 1 million fresh, preprocessed, and deduplicated recipes. They broaden the scope to allow normalization to a given number of servings. Another intriguing possible task may be the unification of primarily ambiguous units in relation to the item they are describing, which could have numerous applications in and outside of the culinary realm, and further unification using knowledge graphs. Though these recipe datasets made significant progress in culinary research through data-driven methods, there is a lack of large scale annotated recipe dataset based on genre which can help training robust machine learning models to foster research in this domain. When it comes to annotate unlabeled data, active learning is a commonly used method in multidisciplinary domain. Active learning is a supervised machine learning technique that trains a predictor iteratively and utilizes the predictor to pick the training instances in each iteration, boosting the predictor's odds of selecting better configurations and improving the prediction model's accuracy [26]. The Naive Bayes (NB) [10] classifier is commonly used as an active learning predictor. It is predicated on Bayes' theorem and strong (naive) independent assumptions about features. To categorize unlabeled data, supervised machine learning methods such as Support Vector Machine (SVM) [4], Logistic Regression [10], and Random Forest (RF) [11] are also employed as predictors. However, they are usually used to overcome classification problems. At each level, multi-layer perceptrons (MLP) [10] learn to abstract and mix data. The data is processed in several layers. Back propagation is utilized to train such neural network models with several layers [20]. Active learning is utilized in many different applications, such as image classification, speech recognition, and text categorization. Rather than assuming that all of the training examples are supplied at the start, active learning algorithms gather more instances on the fly, often by asking a human user questions. The query by committee (QBC) method is an example of an active learning algorithm since it picks a selection of training samples that are most likely to enhance the classifier's performance. Unlabeled data searches are usually a mix of semi-supervised and active learning scenarios. This method is used to classify unlabeled data and keep a high-quality training dataset [3]. In this study, we leverage the data from RecipeNLG dataset along with active learning and query by committee method to create a large scale annotated culinary dataset.

3   RecipeNLG Dataset

The RecipeNLG collection is the largest accessible dataset in the domain, with 2,231,142 different culinary recipes. One of the shortcomings of this dataset is that the genre of the recipes were discovered to be not categorized or unclassified. A culinary recipe's structure includes a title, a list of ingredients with quantities, and step-by-step directions. The title, the simplest component of the recipe, correctly identifies and explains the contents. Some examples from the RecipeNLG dataset are depicted in Table 1.

Table 1. Example samples from RecipeNLG dataset [1]

Title	Directions	NER
Chocolate Frango Mints	["Mix ingredients together for 5 minutes.", "Scrape bowl often. Last fold in chocolate chip mints.", "Bake at 350\u00b0 for 35 to 40 minutes or until done (cake mix directions)."]	["cake mix", "chocolate fudge pudding", "sour cream", "water", "Wesson oil", "eggs", "Frango"]
Cold Spaghetti Salad	["Cook noodles 1/2 done (do not rinse).", "Add all other ingredients; mix well.", "Marinate at least 3 hours.", "The longer it sits, the better it gets!!"]	["vermicelli", "bell pepper", "zucchini", "purple onion", "Salad Supreme seasoning"]
Chocolate Pie	["Mix dry ingredients; add milk.", "Beat in egg yolks.", "Pour on 1 cup boiling water.", "Mix and cook until thick.", "Cool.", "Pour in baked pie shell.", "Cover with meringue and brown in oven."]	["sugar", "milk", "cocoa", "flour", "egg yolks", "clump", "vanilla", "boiling water"]

All ingredients are proportionate to the serving size of the dish. The quantity is linked to the name of the unit. The processes involved in preparing certain food products are listed in the directions feature. Every ingredient on the list is utilized in the correct amounts. However, it was reported that the RecipeNLG dataset has a few limitations in terms of the validity of the recipe title structure [31]. The authors of RecipeNLG drew inspiration from the 1M+ Recipes dataset and contrasted it. They deleted duplicate recipes and translated them all into English. Though they did not discover the unified matrices, they did discover a list of substances known as Named Entity Recognition (NER), which is not exhaustive because the same item appeared in many recipes. It enables the employment of ensemble learning approaches by categorizing the data with suitable categories [1, 2, 19].

4   3A2M Dataset Construction

This section describes in detail the 3A2M corpus development, annotation, and assessment techniques. The overall dataset construction process is shown in Fig. 1.

4.1   Corpus Description

The 3A2M dataset is built on top of the RecipeNLG dataset and we have incorporated as well as utilized all the data along with their respective features. In terms of recipe name, cooking technique, ingredients, and recipe sources, all of the data are the same. 3A2M dataset has in total five attributes: *title, directions, NER, genre,* and *label* among which the data of *title, directions,* and *NER* attributes are directly incorporated from RecipeNLG dataset. Random 300K recipes are classified to one of nine categories by three human experts whose trustworthiness score is more than 86.667% based on the related Named Entity Recognition (NER): *bakery, drinks, non-veg, vegetables, fast food, cereals, meals, sides,* and *fusion.* The remaining 1900K recipes are automatically classified using active learning and a query by committee approach. As a result, there are more than two million recipes, each of which is classified into a certain genre and assigned a confidence score. The huge dataset's Fleiss Kappa score for the nine genres is around 0.56026. The techniques for evaluating corpora are covered in a subsequent section. To preprocess the original unlabeled data, Natural Language Processing (NLP) techniques such as unique word discovery, genre principle categorized word matching, and lowercase English letter conversion are employed.

4.2   Corpus Annotation Procedure

Predictors are data-driven algorithms that utilize data to forecast occurrences or infer a function. In a classification problem, we instead attempt to predict outcomes given a collection of distinct inputs. To put it another way, we are attempting to categorize input variables. Instead of delivering the intended result, we may transform the recipe data into a categorization challenge. In the 3A2M dataset, the recipes are organized into nine categories. Experts have identified nine separate genres, each with its own set of food entities or ingredient constraints. Food professionals determine the food specifications. Though we are familiar with the words "continental cuisine," "eastern cuisine," and "north american genre", several food sectors, however, create food zones based on their own preferences [13,14]. The working procedure of the dataset annotation is illustrated in Fig. 1. We have divided the corpus annotation into two steps. The first step is genre identification and initial data labeling by expert human annotators. The second step is to use active learning to automatically label the remaining unlabeled data using query by committee strategy and human in the loop approach. Each step is described in detail. First and foremost, we needed to determine the number of genres. To do this, we went through a large number of books and periodicals and determined that cuisines are typically classified by zone, such as Asian, South Asian, European, Arabian, Indian, Chinese, Japanese, Lebanese, or Italian [6,30]. With such a diverse range of cuisines in this type of genre, it might be difficult to establish which category a particular item belongs in. Food may become famous in one place, but its origins might be traced back to another. The French, for example, may be credited with inventing the hamburger, although the hamburger was created in the United States [25,32].

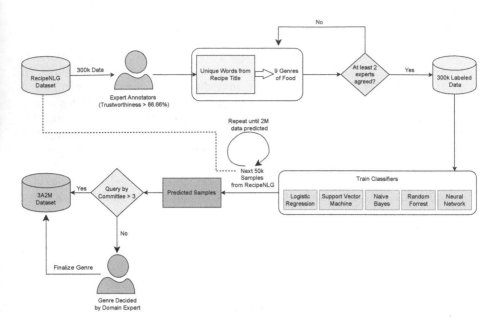

Fig. 1. Working Procedure of 3A2M Cooking Database

Taking into account these stressful scenarios, we took help from three expert annotators who have experience working with food recipes. We evaluated their trustworthiness score and all three of them have a trustworthiness score higher than 86.667%. Those three experts categorized meals in a novel way in the 3A2M dataset by forming nine unique genres, each with its own set of culinary goods or components norms. The genres are listed in Table 2. Initially, the experts intended to collaborate by using the NER associated with each recipe in the RecipeNLG dataset, but their significant expertise revealed that many ingredients had duplication in the same dish and that the same components were utilized in various genres. To address this, 100K data points were picked at random from a pool of 2231142. They utilized the food item's title and listed the unique phrases. They detected around 4329 unique terms. However, many of the terms in the unique word list are not related to food; others are proper nouns of restaurants, persons, chefs, or locales. So they had to examine a lexicon to determine whether these terms were related to food [5,28]. They specifically found 914 words that are directly connected to eating. To fit in with the provided words, a list of keywords with the appropriate genre is constructed. Following that, each expert voted on each of the genre classification recipes. Each dish earned one of three levels of confidence: 33.33%, 66.667%, and 100.00%. A perfect score was given to 68,236 of the 100K food titles. The remaining 28,729 titles received 66.66%, while the remaining 3035 titles received 33.33%. As a consequence, 3035 titles had to be re-evaluated and finalized by examining the cooking directions. Finally, 391 titles formed a new genre known as "fusion." Finally, the procedure

Table 2. Genre id, Genre Name and Facts and Instances in 3A2M Dataset.

Genre ID	Genre Name	Description	No. of instances
1	Bakery	This area mostly contains baked or fried foods that are served in the open or may be stored for a long period.	160712
2	Drinks	Drinks are in the liquid zone and can be blended with any chemical or ionic drink in this zone.	353938
3	NonVeg	This zone includes foods such as curries of poultry, beef, and fish, which can be self-serving or mixed serving.	315828
4	Vegetables	Foods cooked differently than the meats, seafood, and eggs found in this zone. This zone was built just for vegetarians.	398677
5	Fast Food	Only quick food is baked or fried food that cannot be kept for an extended period of time in an open or cold environment. Fast food may be produced by combining bakery and cereal goods.	177109
6	Cereal	Cereals are mainly foods made from corn, wheat, and rice. We have placed meals that are directly generated from grains in the corn zone.	340495
7	Meal	Some items may appear to be quick food, yet they might actually constitute a complete meal. Nonveg/vegetable products, like platters, can also be served with cereals to provide a full meal.	53257
8	Sides	The medicines, sauces, and toppings are basically sections in the side section.	338497
9	Fusion	Some food that can be properly sorted. Sometimes experts disagree on whether it belongs in a specific category known as fusion meals.	92630

was repeated, and a total of 300,000 sample points were initially categorized into 9 genres. The second step is presented in the following subsection.

4.3   Use of Active Learning

Machine learning methods are used to annotate 2 million recipes in order to grasp the current status of implementation. This study used traditional machine learning classifiers to classify items as bakery, beverages, non-veg, vegetables, fast food, cereals, meals, sides, or fusion. Three skilled annotators classified 300K dishes into genres in the first step. The remaining unlabeled data is labeled using active learning. To increase the efficiency of the data labeling process, changes are made to the active learning process. To categorize the remaining 1 million and 900K data points, we utilized five machine learning classifiers: Logistic Regression, Support Vector Machine (SVM), Naive Bayes (NB), Multi-layer Perceptron (MLP) and Random Forest (RF). It is conceivable for a learning method to perform well in one matrix while being sub-optimal in another. To avoid classifier bias, considering the accuracy, sensitivity, specificity, and precision parameters of classifiers might be a solution. An ensemble of classifiers can also be utilized to improve the performance of a single classifier. In the active learning process, the ensemble of classifiers may be utilized to decide on the class of a certain recipe, which is used as an input for the active learning process. In this scenario, we utilized the majority vote of all classifiers [12]. We first trained these five classifiers with 300K labeled recipe titles. After that, in each active learning iteration, we randomly chose 50K titles from the dataset and let the classifiers predict corresponding genres. The technique follows the Query by Committee procedure [26], so if the result indicated more than three classification algorithms categorizing a work in a given genre, that label was accepted and those 50K instances were added to the initial labeled dataset. That indicates that the confidence score is always greater than 60%. Otherwise, for the instances in which we could not fix the genre by following the query by committee procedure, we used the human in the loop (HITL) procedure to manually fix the genre of those specific instances and add them into the labeled training dataset. The whole procedure was repeated until all the unlabeled instances were labeled. After each iteration, the predictor models were trained using the updated labeled dataset.

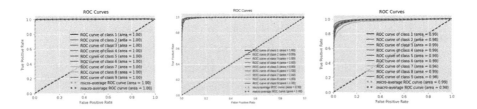

Fig. 2. ROC Curve for Logistic Regression, NB and RF

The optimum cutoff value for predicting new genres is determined using ROC (Receiver Operating Characteristic) curves. Instead of explicitly predicting classes, the precision recall curve shows versatility in evaluating the likelihood of an observation belonging to each class in a classification problem. Figures 2 and 3 show the ROC curve and the Precision Recall Curve of Logistic Regression, Naive Bayes, Random Forest classifiers, respectively.

A learning curve derived from the training dataset that indicates how effectively the model is learning. It is typical to generate dual learning curves for a machine learning model during training on both the training and validation datasets. The model's loss is nearly always lower on the training dataset than on the validation dataset. Figure 4 depicts how the fit is detected by a training and validation loss that reduces to a point of stability with a limited gap between the two final loss values.

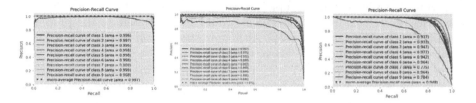

Fig. 3. Precision Recall Curve for Logistic Regression, Naive Bayes, Random Forest.

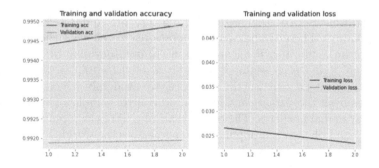

Fig. 4. Multi-layer Perceptron training and validation accuracy and loss graph

4.4   Corpus Evaluation

This section presents the statistical reliability measures to evaluate the quality of the annotated corpus .

Inter-Rater Reliability (IRR) [29]: The amount of agreement amongst experts is referred to as inter-rater reliability (IRR). We calculated the IRR value from 300K of expert-annotated data. If three experts agree, the IRR is 100%; if everyone disagrees, the IRR is 0%. We have simulated the agreement and found an IRR value of 50.3976667% for the 300K data over 9 genres. As there are multiple class levels, the IRR value is lower [21].

Fleiss Kappa [27]: Fleiss Kappa is a method of determining the degree of agreement among three or more raters when they are assigned category ratings to a group of objects. For example, if the raters were asked to rate the genre of a series of recipes, expert agreement would be evaluated as the proportion of recipes rated the same by each. Although there is no formal technique for interpreting Fleiss' Kappa, the values 0.20 = "poor," 0.20 = "fair," 0.41 = "moderate," 0.61 = "good," and 0.81 = "very good" show how the number is used to quantify the level of inter-rater agreement among raters. After computing over 300K annotated data by professionals, we identified the Fleiss' Kappa value of 0.4965 in the moderate zone. After processing the data over 300K, we identified a Kappa value of 0.5 in the strong zone since there are 9 genres. When the class numbers are large, the Kappa value of the strong zone is greater than that of the moderate zone [8].

Trustworthiness Score [7]: The quality of a categorized dataset is determined by the annotators. There are numerous approaches to calculate the trustworthiness score of an annotator. For example, the annotators may be asked to rate how well they found each sentence on a scale of 0 to 100. In this study, for calculating annotators' trustworthiness score, we randomly selected 470 labeled data samples from the dataset and created 30 control samples. Control samples are chosen by domain experts. The control samples were easy to understand and classify. For example, tea is a popular beverage across the world. The annotators were not aware of these control samples. We found the trustworthiness scores of the three annotators were 86.667%, 90%, and 96.667%, respectively, based on their responses to the control samples. As the set of classes was 9, domain experts felt that more than 80% would be adequate to qualify the annotators. In our case, the trustworthiness score of each annotator is above 80%, and the average trustworthiness score is 90%, which indicates that the annotators are qualified to annotate.

Confidence Score [18]: A confidence score is essentially a measure of annotative quality. A confidence score can be used to exclude low-quality annotations, but it is not a suitable overall measure of annotation quality. It depicts

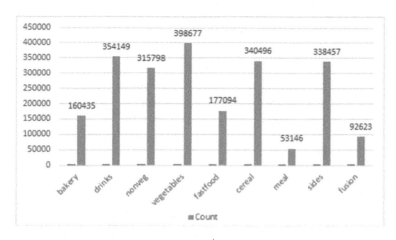

Fig. 5. 3A2M Dataset Distribution

the amount of agreement across numerous annotators; that is, weighted by the annotators' trustworthiness ratings; and it demonstrates our "confidence" in the result's validity. The aggregate result is determined based on the most confident response. In the event of a tie, we select the result with the most annotators. We calculated confidence scores of 100% for 89,378 recipes and 66.667% for 201,982 recipes across 300K entries. After conferring with the three annotators, the domain expert, a chef who has been cooking for more than 16 years, solved the ties. We then employed the domain experts to solve the remaining situations. The domain experts answered all of the remaining instances, and the overall confidence score for all of the recipes was 100%.

Anderson-Darling Test (AD Test) [23]: The Anderson-Darling test, which is dependent on the statistic, was employed for our dataset. It's similar to the t-value in t-tests or the F-value in F-tests. We do not usually interpret this statistic directly, but it is used by the program to generate the p-value for the test. We have an AD test Result on 100,000 data distribution. Figure !5 shows the distribution of the data on 9 genres by histogram reflection. Table 3 shows the AD test statistics of the Lower p-values indicate greater evidence against the null hypothesis. A p-value is the chance that the effect seen in our sample would occur if the null hypothesis for the populations were true. P-values are derived using our sample data and the null hypothesis. Lower p-values suggest more evidence against the null hypothesis, in contrast to our p-value with the degree of significance. If the p-value is less than the significance level, we reject the null hypothesis and conclude that the effect is statistically significant. In other words, the evidence in our sample is strong enough to reject the null hypothesis at the population level.

Table 3. Anderson-Darling Statistical analysis of the dataset.

Criterias	Values
Sample Mean	4.162
Sample Sigma	2.381
AD test statistic	2.5937
AD* test statistic	2.613899
P-value	<0.0005

4.5 Discussion

To automate the process of labeling the unlabeled data, we have used active learning with query-by-committee approach. For the committee, we have used five weak machine learning classifiers as the learners. Support Vector Machine (SVM) had "linear" kernel as the parameter and Multinomial Naive Bayes had the additive laplace smoothing parameter value of 1. Random Forest classifier was initialized with 100 estimators, gini impurity, and a max-depth of 50. The penalty and class weight parameters in Logistic Regression were set to "l2" and "balanced respectively". On the other hand, Mulit-layer Perceptron was initialized with 200 max iteration, hidden layer size was 100, learning rate parameter was set to "constant" and "adam" optimizer was used. The pre-trained model learns broad characteristics like language and context. As a result, the pre-learning model's embedding results lack adequate features differentiating the labels of downstream tasks. Therefore, data with the same label might have different features in a pre-trained model [15]. We could have incorporated large pre-trained language models like BERT by fine-tuning with the help of Transfer Learning, but due to resource constraints, the cost of training some layers of a such large model as a learner inside the active learning procedure, and for the sake of the simplicity, we did not consider BERT for labeling purpose in our study. The purpose of corpus assessment study is to obtain an overall measurement of the performance of a statistical technique and its data, which is the 3A2M dataset. Experts' assessments of circumstances and occurrences naturally differ. The IRR is mild, with the goal of minimizing subjectivity as much as feasible in our study. To ensure that the annotators were fit for this job, we measured trustworthiness score and calculated Fleiss Kappa score to measure the agreement among them. Our research demonstrates that corpus evaluation is moderate in the sense that the size of the data was greater than 2 million, and dependability demonstrates consistency of a measure by different methodologies such as confidence score, anderson-darling test.

5 Conclusion and Future Works

Construction of food recipe dataset is a kind of tedious job which requires careful inspection. Specially for nearly matched ingredients for two or more categories.

Taking help from domain experts and integrate their knowledge though machine learning approach is the worth things to do to generate a reliable dataset. Construction of food recipe dataset is a kind of tedious job which requires careful inspection. Specially for nearly matched ingredients for two or more categories. Taking help from domain experts and integrate their knowledge though machine learning approach is the worth things to do to generate a reliable dataset. Therefore, we have constructed the (3A2M) cooking recipes dataset, an annotated dataset of two million culinary recipes so that people can choose the food recipes according to their preferred categories. We built this dataset on top of the RecipeNLG dataset. First, we categorized 300K recipes into nine categories by human annotators and trained five machine learning classifiers to employ active learning for automatically labeling the remaining 1900K instances. We believe that in the future, unification of often ambiguous units (e.g. cups, pinch) might have a wide range of applications in and outside of the culinary world, as well as additional unification utilizing knowledge graphs, is another exciting future project. As the dataset is large and organized by genre, medical sectors, particularly those working with food nutrition, can recommend a variety of meals to the patients. If the recipe's portion can be estimated, a large area will open up, which is the components calories, which can be used to analyze food calories intake for various types of food analysis or nutrients. Finally, by training these massive datasets, an application can be created to build a new menu and generate buzz in the food market, giving consumers a new taste and direction to manufacture such delicacies, which may be a big contribution to the culinary sector.

References

1. Bień, M., Gilski, M., Maciejewska, M., Taisner, W., Wisniewski, D., Lawrynowicz, A.: RecipeNLG: a cooking recipes dataset for semi-structured text generation. In: Proceedings of the 13th International Conference on Natural Language Generation, pp. 22–28, December 2020
2. Buneman, P.: Semistructured data. In: PODS (1997)
3. Cohn, D.A., Ghahramani, Z., Jordan, M.I.: Active learning with statistical models. J. Artif. Intell. Res. 1(4), 129–45 (1996)
4. Cortes, C., Vapnik, V.: Support-vector networks. Mach. Learn. 20(3), 273–297 (1995)
5. Cuisine, S.: Food dictionary. Technical report, May 2022. https://www.soscuisine.com/food-dictionary/
6. eathappyproject: Types of cuisines. Technical report, May 2021. https://www.eathappyproject.com/types-of-cuisines-from-around-the-world-with-their-popular-food/
7. Elo, S., Kääriäinen, M., Kanste, O., Pölkki, T., Utriainen, K., Kyngas, H.: Qualitative content analysis: a focus on trustworthiness. SAGE Open 5, 4 (2014). https://doi.org/10.1177/2158244014522633
8. Falotico, R., Quatto, P.: Fleiss' Kappa statistic without paradoxes. Quality Quantity 49(2), 463–470 (2015)

9. Fisher, M.F.K.: The Anatomy of a Recipe, with Bold Knife and Fork. Counterpoint (1969)
10. Hastie, T., Tibshirani, R., Friedman, J.: The Elements of Statistical Learning Data Mining, Inference, and Prediction. Springer Series in Statistics, 2nd edn. Springer, New York (2009). https://doi.org/10.1007/978-0-387-84858-7
11. Ho, T.K.: Random decision forests. In: Proceedings of the 3rd International Conference on Document Analysis and Recognition, pp. 278–282, Montreal, Q.C. (1995)
12. Kalchbrenner, N., Grefenstette, E., Blunsom, P.: A convolutional neural network for modeling sentences. In: Proceedings of ACL, pp. 655–665 (2014)
13. Khodak, M., Saunshi, N., Vodrahalli, K.: A large self-annotated corpus for sarcasm. In: Proceedings of the Eleventh International Conference on Language Resources and Evaluation, LREC 2018 (2018)
14. Kiddon, C., Zettlemoyer, L., Choi, Y.: Globally coherent text generation with neural checklist models. In: Proceedings of the Conference on Empirical Methods in Natural Language Processing, Austin, Texas, pp. 329–339. Association for Computational Linguistics (2016)
15. Kim, G., Kang, S.: Effective transfer learning with label-based discriminative feature learning. Sensors 22(5), 2025 (2022)
16. LeCun, Y., Bengio, Y., Hinton, G.: Deep learning. Nature 521(7553), 436–444 (2015)
17. Lee, H.H., et al.: RecipeGPT: generative pre training based cooking recipe generation and evaluation system. In: Companion Proceedings of the Web Conference (2020)
18. Mandelbaum, A., Weinshall, D.: Distance-based confidence score for neural network classifiers. Technical report, 28 September 2017
19. Marin, J., et al.: Recipe1M+: a dataset for learning cross-modal embeddings for cooking recipes and food images. IEEE Trans. Pattern Anal. Mach. Intell. 43(1), 187–203 (2019)
20. Mitchell, T.M.: Machine Learning, p. 414. McGraw-Hill, Maidenhead (1997). International ISBN, Student edn
21. Phalippou, L.: The hazards of using IRR to measure performance: the case of private equity. SSRN 1111796 (2008)
22. Price, I., et al.: Six attributes of unhealthy conversation. Technical report, October 2020
23. Razali, N.M., YB., W.: Power comparisons of Shapiro-Wilk, Kolmogorov-Smirnov, Lilliefors and Anderson-Darling tests. J. Stat. Model. Analytics 1(2), 1 (2011)
24. Recipes, F.: food.com. Technical report, February 2022. https://www.food.com/
25. Salvador, A., et al.: Learning cross-modal embeddings for cooking recipes and food images. In: 2017 IEEE Conference on Computer Vision and Pattern Recognition (CVPR), pp. 3068–3076 (2017)
26. Settles, B.: Active learning literature survey (2009)
27. statology: Fleiss-Kappa. Technical report, March 2022. https://www.statology.org/fleiss-kappa-excel/
28. theodora: Culinary dictionary. Technical report, February 2022. https://theodora.com/food/index.html
29. To, S.H.: Inter-rater reliability IRR. Technical report, March 2022. https://www.statisticshowto.com/inter-rater-reliability/?fbclid=IwAR3nXWOlp0qN6PrdfR1fuURSjyKVsGim-0yVD4ccMqTKtWVZ0Nxcx69P2S4
30. wikipedia: List of cuisines. Technical report, July 2021. https://en.wikipedia.org/wiki/List_of_cuisines

31. Yagcioglu, S., Erdem, A., Erdem, E., Ikizler-Cinbis, N.: RecipeQA: a challenge dataset for multimodal comprehension of cooking recipes. In: Proceedings of the 2018 Conference on Empirical Methods in Natural Language Processing, pp. 1358–1368. EMNLP (2018)
32. Yang, Z., Blunsom, P., Dyer, C., Ling, W.: Reference-aware language models. In: Proceedings of the 2017 Conference on Empirical Methods in Natural Language Processing, pp. 1850–1859. EMNLP 2017 (2017)

The Impact of Data Locality on the Performance of Cluster-Based Under-Sampling

Ahmed Shabab Noor, Muhib Al Hasan, Ahmed Rafi Hasan, Rezab Ud Dawla, Afsana Airin, Akib Zaman, and Dewan Md. Farid(✉)

Department of Computer Science and Engneering, United International University, United City, Madani Avenue, Vatara, Dhaka 1212, Bangladesh
{anoor193024,mhasan191083,ahasan191131,rdawla191187, aairin191172}@bscse.uiu.ac.bd, {akib,dewanfarid}@cse.uiu.ac.bd
https://www.uiu.ac.bd

Abstract. Class-imbalanced classification is one of the most challenging issues in supervised learning. Traditional machine learning classifiers are generally biased toward to the majority class samples and ignore the minority class data. Although a good number of data-sampling methods have been introduced in the last decade, extracting patterns from biased data remains a problematic issue and a major research priority. In this paper, we have analysed the influence of cluster locality on various types of imbalanced datasets employing cluster-based under-sampling. Existing under-sampling methods removes a large portion of majority data to make the dataset balanced, so there is high chance that we may lose the instructive majority class samples. Cluster-based under-sampling technique addresses this issue and applies ensemble learning to boost-up the classification performance. This paper presents an extensive study on cluster-based under-sampling with ensemble learning using 31 imbalanced datasets to figure out which cluster locality is most important for data sampling.

Keywords: Class-imbalanced classification · Clustering · Data sampling

1 Imbalanced Data Classification

Classifying a class imbalance data in the machine learning field is a major issue [11]. Knowledge mining from imbalanced data has received substantial research attention in the last decade [9]. Many real-life applications face this class-imbalanced problem where the conventional algorithms of machine learning focus more on the majority class instances and overlook the minority class instances e.g., cancer detection, credit card fraud detection, and network intrusion detection [5,13]. For instance, data imbalance in fraud detection can go as low as 1 in 1000 and there have been reports of 1 in 100,000 instances in the real-world application. Conventional classification algorithms give accurate enough

Md. S. Satu et al. (Eds.): MIET 2022, LNICST 491, pp. 204–??, 2023.
https://doi.org/10.1007/978-3-031-34622-4_16

predictions for the majority class instances and perform poorly for the minority ones [3]. One of the ways to solve the class-imbalanced problem is the dataset sampling technique. Data sampling adds or removes instances from the dataset to make the dataset balanced [12]. Among the sampling techniques, over-sampling and under-sampling are the two types of sampling methods that are used on the training dataset. Over-sampling methods generate artificial instances to make the dataset balanced, but oversampling may provoke the model to overfit as the data tends to become dense and redundant [8]. On the contrary, under-sampling method decreases the majority class and keeps all the necessary information in the minority class and makes the dataset balanced [7]. As the under-sampling technique removes data, so it is very important to choose the right data. Exception of choosing the right data yields unsatisfactory results.

When it comes to under-sampling the majority class instances, there remains a question of how the majority class instances should be removed or selected. There are several cluster-based techniques for undersampling the unbalanced data, which use data points from various cluster locations, such as those close to the cluster centroid, those close to its edge, or even random instances selected across the cluster. However, all of these methods work differently for different types of datasets. This paper tries to understand which data point selection method from clusters is more informative for different types of datasets. On that note, we divide our datasets into five categories: (1) Continuous, (2) Discrete, (3) Nominal, (4) Continuous + Nominal, and (5) Continuous + Discrete. Then, we consider three types of data selection methods for cluster-based under-sampling: (1) random instances selection, (2) data points nearing the centre of the cluster, and (3) data points nearing the edge of the cluster. After applying the cluster-based under-sampling technique, we have built three ensemble models on the datasets: (1) Random Forest, (2) Bagging with decision trees, and (3) AdaBoosting algorithm. We have conducted an evaluation study with 31 imbalanced datasets (6 discrete, 9 continuous, 7 nominal, 6 continuous & nominal and 3 continuous & discrete) consisting of variable amount of imbalance ratio. The result demonstrates that random sampling from each cluster of majority samples yields better result than selective sampling from near the centroid or the edge of the cluster.

2   Literature Review

Since the majority of machine learning models are skewed in favor of the dominant class assumption, it might be challenging to work with imbalanced data in supervised learning today. Consequently, researchers conducted several studies to address the prevailing data imbalance problem using data-sampling techniques, ensemble methods, and cost-sensitive learning methods. LIUBoost is an approach proposed by Sajid et al. [2] designed to handle datasets with class imbalance. LIUBoost applies under-sampling for balancing the dataset yet retaining important information of each instance using the AdaBoost weight update equation expressed as cost terms. The novelty LIUBoost brings is, it creates an ensemble model which is cost-efficient and it does not suffer from information loss. Arafat et al. [6] introduced another under-sampling technique leveraging SVM for making imbalanced datasets balanced by making decision boundaries using cases from the majority and minority classes. To create a balanced dataset, it only takes into account the support vectors for the majority class and those closest to them when combined with cases from the minority class. When there are more instances, this model greatly outperforms other approaches. For handling multi-class, extremely imbalanced data, Arafat et al. [4] have suggested a cluster-based under-sampling technique leveraging the Random Forest algorithm. Here, informative majority class examples are chosen using cluster-based under-sampling, and informative instances near the cluster's center and border are also taken into consideration. In a similar note, Farshid et al. [15] developed MEBoost for imbalanced data handling a unique boosting algorithm which is a mixture of Decision Tree and Extra Tree, on the training instances. Instead of using a single base of learners, MEBoost uses both.

To categorize unbalanced data, Farshid et al. [14] demonstrated a novel method called CUSBoost, which combines the under-sampling and AdaBoost approaches. The imbalanced dataset is split using this approach into two groups: group of class with most instances and group of class with less instances. Using the k-means clustering technique, the majority classes are divided into many groups, and then specific examples of the class with most number instances are picked from every group to create a unbiased dataset. CUSBoost is considered as an efficient alternative algorithm to RUSBoost [16] and SMOTEBoost [8]. SMOTEBoost and RUSBoost are two hybrid algorithms that blend boosting and smote methods, respectively.

Farid et al. [10] proposed a clustering-based multi-class imbalance data handling method. By grouping the majority examples into several groups or clusters and choosing the most instructive examples in each balanced cluster, the suggested approach creates many balanced datasets from a large imbalanced dataset. This approach is compared with random under-sampling, random over-sampling, bagging, and boosting. This method outperforms the others since it does not suffer from over-fitting or the loss of potentially helpful information. Ahmed et al. [1] proposed two innovative solutions-ADASYNBagging and RSYNBagging-to address the issues associated with class imbalance. The most occurrences of the class are left unaffected by the ADASYNBagging, which applies an ADASYN-based oversample approach with a bagging algorithm on minority class instances only. The RSYNBagging method combines an oversampling technique based on ADASYN with random undersampling. The performance of the suggested methods is strongly encouraged after comparison with current bagging hybrid approaches.

Analyzing the prevailing studies, we have found that the under-sampling technique is certainly recognized with several successes in recent years. Several pieces of literature clustered the majority dataset and selected few instances from each cluster to create an updated majority class. Along with choosing random instances, instances near the centroid of the clusters and near the border of the clusters are prominent choices to select instances from the clusters. These techniques were widely used on various types of datasets (discrete, continuous, nominal, etc.) and were found to be effective. However, the comparison of the performance of these under-sampling techniques in mentioned variants of datasets is one of the under-explored areas. Thus, we develop our research framework to explore the performances of their prominent under-sampling techniques (Selection of instances near centroid, random location, or near borders) on various types of datasets.

3   Cluster-Based Under-Sampling

We have collected imbalanced datasets for binary-class classification with various degrees of features, instances, and imbalance ratios. We have segmented the dataset based on the characteristics of the features and divided datasets into five specific segments: (1) Discrete, (2) Continuous, (3) Nominal, (4) Continuous and Nominal, and (5) Continuous and Discrete. For example, a dataset that falls into the discrete segment only has features with discrete values. Similarly, a dataset that falls into the continuous and nominal segment has some features with continuous data and some with nominal data. The proposed research procedure is highlighted in Fig. 1.

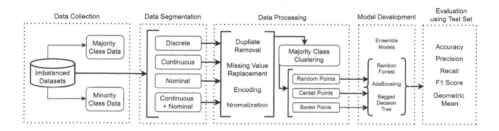

Fig. 1. Research Procedure

We have split up the instances of each dataset into majority and minority classes (Fig. 2a shows a visual representation of how the two class instances might reside in a biased dataset). We preserved the minority class and, using the k-means clustering algorithm, we created group of the majority class. We calculated the ideal number of clusters for k using the silhouette score. Here, $S(i)$ is data point i's silhouette coefficient. $a(i)$ is the average distance from every other point to data point i. And, $c_{min}(i)$ is the minimum average distance from data point i to every cluster except its own. After clustering the majority class instances with the optimal number of clusters, we sampled data points in three ways and discarded the rest. We took data points near the centroids of the clusters, along the boundary, and at random locations across the cluster (Fig. 2b shows a visual representation of these data localities). To take the centre and border data points, we sorted the examples based on their distance from the centroid and then took n examples from the head or tail respectively. Here n is selected in such a way, so that more examples are taken from larger clusters and the total number of examples that are taken are equal to the total number of minority examples.

$$S(i) = \frac{c_{min}(i) - a(i)}{max\{a(i), c_{min}(i)\}} \tag{1}$$

$$n = \frac{cluster\ size}{majority\ examples\ size} \times minority\ examples\ size \tag{2}$$

We took the under-sampled majority instances and all the minority instances as training data. Finally, Random Forest, AdaBoost and Bagged Decision Tree algorithms were used to develop the models and train using the training set.

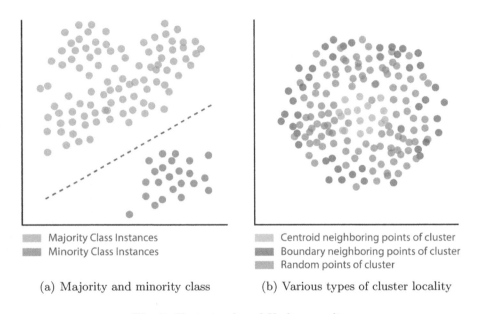

Majority Class Instances
Minority Class Instances

Centroid neighboring points of cluster
Boundary neighboring points of cluster
Random points of cluster

(a) Majority and minority class   (b) Various types of cluster locality

Fig. 2. Clustering-based Under-sampling

Random Forest (RF) is an ensemble learning technique which is customarily used to solve both regression and classification problems. It creates random decision trees with attribute bagging technique and uses majority vote technique for final prediction. The Random Forest Algorithm's prowess to deal data for both regression and classification is one of its main strengths. Adaptive Boosting or AdaBoost is a common boosting method that combines a number of weak identifiers to create a single powerful identifier. AdaBoost can be used to improve any machine learning algorithm's performance. It updates the weights of instances based on how they were classified by reinforcing the weights of wrongly predicted instances and decreasing the weights of correctly predicted instances. AdaBoost technique uses majority-weighted voting for making final predictions. Bagging is another accepted ensemble technique used to reduce the variance in corrupt data. Bagging is a process where random samples of data are selected from the original dataset with replacement, meaning each data point can be picked more than once. Then, using the collected data samples, these models are trained individually. Based on the kind of task, regression or classification for example, the average or majority of such forecasts yields a more accurate result.

4   Evaluation

4.1   Datasets

We collected 31 imbalanced datasets from the KEEL (Knowledge Extraction based on Evolutionary Learning) repository (http://www.keel.es). Table 1 shows the datasets with their category.

4.2   Experimental Setup

The experiments were carried out in Google Colab, or 'Colaboratory', which allows us to write and execute Python 3.10 codes in web browser (https://colab.research.google.com). We have used Python library scikit-learn (https://scikit-learn.org/stable/) for model building. The performance of the ensemble models are tested applying 10-fold cross-validation with the following standards:

- *F1 Score*: F1 Score unifies Recall and Precision by using the harmonic mean of the two. It is used to compare different classifiers more generally.

$$F1Score = \frac{precision \cdot recall}{precision + recall} \tag{3}$$

- *G-Mean*: Geometric Mean or G-Mean equals the N-th root of the multiplication of all the values, where N represents how many values were taken.

$$G - Mean = \sqrt[N]{item_1 \times item_2 \times item_3 \times ... \times item_N} \tag{4}$$

We have used the Jaccard similarity index to evaluate the difference of the undersampling techniques being tested.

- *Jaccard Similarity Index*: Jaccard Similarity Index or Jaccard Score shows us the similarity between two sets. Jaccard score is equal to 1 if the two sets are identical and 0 if they are mutually exclusive. Equation 5 shows the Jaccard score of two groups α and β.

$$J(\alpha, \beta) = \frac{\alpha \cap \beta}{\alpha \cup \beta} \tag{5}$$

Table 1. Imbalanced datasets collected from KEEL repository.

Discrete	Dermatology 6
	Poker 8 vs. 6
	Poker 8, 9 vs. 5
	Shuttle 2 vs. 5
	Shuttle c0 vs. c4
	Vehicle 0
Continuous	Led7digit 0, 2, 4, 5, 6, 7, 8, 9 vs. 1
	Segment 0
	Winequality red 4
	Winequality white 3, 9 vs. 5
	Yeast 0, 2, 5, 6 vs. 3, 7, 8, 9
	Yeast 0, 2, 5, 7, 9 vs. 3, 6, 8
	Yeast 4
	Yeast 5
	Yeast6
Nominal	Car good
	Car vgood
	Flare-F
	KR-vs-k-three vs. eleven
	KR-vs-k-zero vs. eight
	KR-vs-k-zero vs. fifteen
	KR-vs-k-zero-one vs. draw
Continuous + Nominal	Abalone 20 vs. 8, 9, 10
	Abalone 19
	Kddcup buffer overflow vs. Back
	Kddcup guess passwd vs. Satan
	Kddcup land vs. Satan
	Kddcup rootkit imap vs. Back
Continuous + Discrete	Page blocks 1, 3 vs. 4
	Page blocks 0
	Vowel 0

4.3   Results

From the experiment, We found various results regarding the impact of clustering locality while performing cluster-based under-sampling on the ensemble models. The summary of the results is highlighted in Table 3. In case of discrete data, random sampling techniques performs better than centre or border instances with an average f1-score of 0.82 and a g-mean of 0.882. Bagging of Decision tree contributed the most having a f1-score of 0.88. On a similar note, random sampling performs better on continuous, having an average f1-score of 0.756 and a g-mean of 0.805. AdaBoost performs well here for the f1-score and g-mean. Random sampling also performs well for the nominal data, with a f1-score of 0.87 and a g-mean of 0.919. In nominal data, there is no highest contributor. All models perform randomly here. If the dataset is combined with continuous and nominal values, random under-sampling gives a higher f1-score of having 0.905

and centre under-sampling gives a higher g-mean of 0.886. Random sampling again performs well if the dataset is combined with discrete and continuous values. The f1-score is 0.953 and the g-mean is 0.969. In summary (see Fig. 8a and Fig. 8b), Random under-sampling performs well in most datasets as it takes data points randomly from the whole bunch of the cluster acquiring the necessary diverse characteristics of all instances. On Contrary, taking instances near to the centroid and border demonstrates a lower performance metrics scores as it preserves a specific zone characteristics rather than the full set of instances.

Figures 3, 4, 5, 6, and 7 show the F1 score and G-Mean of the segments Discrete, Continuous, Nominal, Continuous+Discrete, and Continuous+Nominal respectively. Here the individual F1 score and G Mean score for all datasets can be seen in the aforementioned figures.

In Table 2, we show the difference of the data samples between different clustering methods using Jaccard Similarity Index. This indicates how the methods we are comparing are actually different from each other and not the same. We see that all the scores are below 0.5 meaning that the techniques are less than 50% similar. We have calculated this score for each dataset and averaged them according to their segment. We see Jaccard similarity index as low as 0.16 and no greater than 0.46 for the chosen datasets and undersampling techniques.

Table 2. Jaccard Score for different types of clustering methods.

Segmentation	Center vs. Border	Border vs. Random	Random vs. Center
Discrete	0.35	0.38	0.39
Continuous	0.16	0.19	0.2
Nominal	0.43	0.45	0.46
Continuous + Nominal	0.46	0.46	0.46
Continuous + Discrete	0.4	0.44	0.42

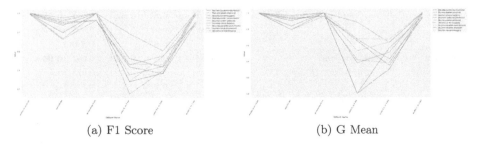

(a) F1 Score   (b) G Mean

Fig. 3. Discrete datasets

Table 3. Experiment results using cluster-based under-sampling techniques.

Type of Data	Cluster Based Under-sampling Technique	Models	F1 Score		Gmean	
			Unit	Average	Unit	Average
Discrete	Random	Random Forest	0.788	**0.82**	0.851	**.882**
		AdaBoost	**0.88**		**0.913**	
		Bagging	0.8		0.883	
	Center	Random Forest	0.785	0.774	**0.823**	0.817
		AdaBoost	0.75		0.805	
		Bagging	**0.787**		**0.823**	
	Border	Random Forest	0.736	0.749	0.688	0.713
		AdaBoost	**0.798**		**0.738**	
		Bagging	0.713		0.713	
Continuous	Random	Random Forest	0.74	**0.756**	0.815	**0.805**
		AdaBoost	0.738		0.777	
		Bagging	**0.79**		**0.825**	
	Center	Random Forest	0.655	0.671	0.741	0.759
		AdaBoost	**0.688**		**0.772**	
		Bagging	0.67		0.764	
	Border	Random Forest	0.602	0.615	**0.733**	0.72
		AdaBoost	**0.623**		0.697	
		Bagging	0.62		0.732	
Nominal	Random	Random Forest	**0.89**	**0.87**	**0.938**	**0.919**
		AdaBoost	0.86		0.912	
		Bagging	0.86		0.907	
	Center	Random Forest	0.69	0.698	0.821	0.822
		AdaBoost	0.685		0.811	
		Bagging	**0.72**		**0.834**	
	Border	Random Forest	0.63	0.643	0.747	0.747
		AdaBoost	**0.67**		**0.78**	
		Bagging	0.63		0.714	
Continuous + Nominal	Random	Random Forest	0.91	**0.905**	0.876	0.88
		AdaBoost	**0.93**		**0.898**	
		Bagging	0.875		0.868	
	Center	Random Forest	0.82	0.833	0.866	**0.886**
		AdaBoost	0.82		0.896	
		Bagging	**0.86**		**0.898**	
	Border	Random Forest	**0.67**	0.656	0.735	0.727
		AdaBoost	0.63		0.705	
		Bagging	**0.67**		**0.743**	
Continuous + Discrete	Random	Random Forest	0.933	**0.953**	0.956	**0.969**
		AdaBoost	**0.963**		0.973	
		Bagging	**0.963**		**0.98**	
	Center	Random Forest	0.74	0.741	0.836	0.843
		AdaBoost	0.72		0.83	
		Bagging	**0.763**		**0.863**	
	Border	Random Forest	0.713	0.759	0.806	0.838
		AdaBoost	**0.79**		0.853	
		Bagging	0.776		**0.856**	

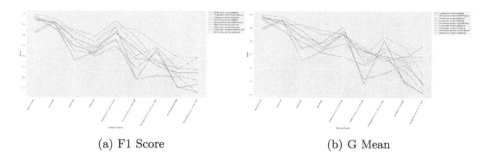

(a) F1 Score   (b) G Mean

Fig. 4. Continuous datasets

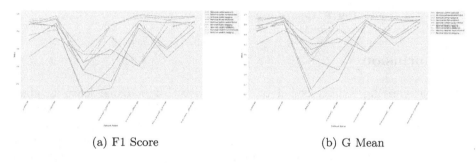

(a) F1 Score   (b) G Mean

Fig. 5. Nominal datasets

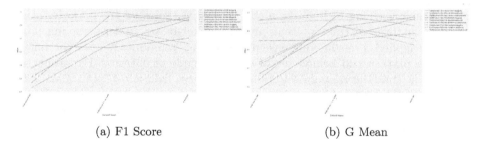

(a) F1 Score   (b) G Mean

Fig. 6. Continuous and Discrete datasets

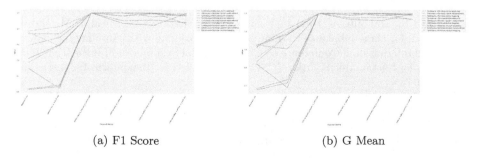

(a) F1 Score   (b) G Mean

Fig. 7. Continuous and Nominal datasets

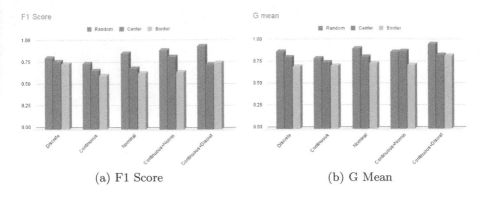

(a) F1 Score   (b) G Mean

Fig. 8. Comparative performance analysis

5   Conclusion

When categorizing imbalanced data, the majority of machine learning algorithms concentrate on the majority class instances rather than the minority class instances. Making a balanced dataset and accurately classifying examples from both the majority and minority classes is a difficult task. Combining sampling method with ensemble classifiers has grown in popularity recently as a means of addressing the challenges caused by class imbalance. The cluster locality in imbalanced classification was compared using cluster-based undersampling and ensemble learning techniques in this article. We selected the majority class instances in three distinct ways using the cluster-based under-sampling approach. We applied three different ensemble learning techniques in our experiment to find the pattern and behaviours of different kinds of datasets. Experimental results show that the random selection of instances from clusters to make balanced datasets performs better in most datasets. In future, we will apply different clustering algorithms and assign weights to the instances to select majority class instances.

References

1. Ahmed, S., Mahbub, A., Rayhan, F., Jani, M.R., Shatabda, S., Farid, D.M.: Hybrid methods for class imbalance learning employing bagging with sampling techniques. In: 2nd International Conference on Computational Systems and Information Technology for Sustainable Solution (CSITSS), pp. 126–131. Bengaluru, India, December 2017
2. Ahmed, S., Rayhan, F., Mahbub, A., Jani, M.R., Shatabda, S., Farid, D.M.: LIU-Boost: locality informed under-boosting for imbalanced data classification. In: International Conference on Emerging Technology in Data Mining and Information Security (IEMIS), pp. 1–12. Kolkata, India, February 2018

3. Ahmed, S., Rayhan, F., Mahbub, A., Jani, M.R., Shatabda, S., Farid, D.M.: LIU-Boost: locality informed under-boosting for imbalanced data classification. In: Abraham, A., Dutta, P., Mandal, J., Bhattacharya, A., Dutta, S. (eds.) Emerging Technologies in Data Mining and Information Security, AISC, pp. 133–144. Springer, Singapore (2019). https://doi.org/10.1007/978-981-13-1498-8_12

4. Arafat, M.Y., Hoque, S., Farid, D.M.: Cluster-based under-sampling with random forest for multi-class imbalanced classification. In: 11th International Conference on Software. Knowledge, Information Management and Applications (SKIMA), and IEEE Xplore Digital Archive, pp. 1–6, Colombo, Sri Lanka (December (2017)

5. Arafat, M.Y., Hoque, S., Xu, S., Farid, D.M.: Machine learning for mining imbalanced data. IAENG Int. J. Comput. Sci. **46**(2), 332–348 (2019)

6. Arafat, M.Y., Hoque, S., Xu, S., Farid, D.M.: An under-sampling method with support vectors in multi-class imbalanced data classification. In: 13th International Conference on Software. Knowledge, Information Management and Applications (SKIMA), pp. 1–6, Island of Ukulhas, Maldives, August 2019

7. Arafat, M.Y., Hoquef, S., Xuf, S., Farid, D.M.: Advanced data balancing method with SVM decision boundary and bagging. In: IEEE Asia-Pacific Conference on Computer Science and Data Engineering (CSDE), pp. 1–7. IEEE, Melbourne, Australia, December 2019

8. Chawla, N.V., Bowyer, K.W., Hall, L.O., Kegelmeyer, W.P.: SMOTE: synthetic minority over-sampling technique. J. Artif. Intell. Res. **16**, 321–357 (2002)

9. Farid, D.M., Nowe, A., Manderick, B.: Ensemble of trees for classifying high-dimensional imbalanced genomic data. In: Bi, Y., Kapoor, S., Bhatia, R. (eds.) IntelliSys 2016. LNNS, vol. 15, pp. 172–187. Springer, Cham (2018). https://doi.org/10.1007/978-3-319-56994-9_12

10. Farid, D.M., Nowé, A., Manderick, B.: A new data balancing method for classifying multi-class imbalanced genomic data. In: 25th Belgian-Dutch Conference on Machine Learning (Benelearn), pp. 1–2. Kortrijk, Belgium, September 2016

11. Farid, D.M., Shatabda, S., Abedin, M.Z., Islam, M.T., Hossain, M.I.: Mining imbalanced big data with Julia. In: JuliaCon. University of Maryland Baltimore (UMB), Baltimore, MD, USA, July 2019

12. Hoque, S., Arafat, M.Y., Farid, D.M.: Machine learning for mining imbalanced data. In: International Conference on Emerging Technology in Data Mining and Information Security (IEMIS), pp. 1–10, Kolkata, India, February 2018

13. Miah, M.O., Khan, S.S., Shatabda, S., Farid, D.M.: Improving detection accuracy for imbalanced network intrusion classification using cluster-based under-sampling with random forests. In: International Conference on Advances in Science. Engineering & Robotics Technology (ICASERT), and IEEE Xplore Digital Archive, pp. 1–5, Dhaka, Bangladesh, May 2019

14. Rayhan, F., Ahmed, S., Mahbub, A., Jani, M.R., Shatabda, S., Farid, D.M.: CUS-Boost: cluster-based under-sampling with boosting for imbalanced classification. In: 2nd International Conference on Computational Systems and Information Technology for Sustainable Solution (CSITSS), pp. 70–75. Bengaluru, India, December 2017

15. Rayhan, F., et al.: MEBoost: mixing estimators with boosting for imbalanced data classification. In: 11th International Conference on Software, Knowledge, Information Management and Applications (SKIMA), and IEEE Xplore Digital Archive, pp. 1–6, Colombo, Sri Lanka, December 2017

16. Seiffert, C., Khoshgoftaar, T.M., Van Hulse, J., Napolitano, A.: RUSBoost: a hybrid approach to alleviating class imbalance. IEEE Trans. Syst. Man Cybern.-Part A Syst. Humans **40**(1), 185–197 (2009)

An Analysis of Islamic Inheritance System Under Object-Oriented Paradigm

A. H. M. Sajedul Hoque(✉), Sadia Tabassum, Rashed Mustafa,
Mohammad Sanaullah Chowdhury, and Mohammad Osiur Rahman

University of Chittagong, Chittagong, Bangladesh
{hoque.cse,rashed.m,s.chowdhury,drosi}@cu.ac.bd

Abstract. The wealth of deceased should be distributed precisely and quickly according to inheritance laws in order to avoid the unrest situation in the society. A professional software solution can serve this purpose. The professional software can be developed through analyzing, designing, building and testing of the manual system. As the analysis is the first and crucial stage of software development life cycle, this paper focuses on the analysis of Islamic Inheritance System (IIS). This analysis can be performed employing either structured or object-oriented approach. The structured analysis depends on the functions of the IIS, while objects are the main part in the object-oriented analysis technique. The one demerit of structured analysis is that the IIS is modeled using Data Flow Diagram (DFD) which is not standard diagram in software engineering community. In addition, the structured analysis phase of IIS does not provide any knowledge of internal modules. In order to address these problems, this paper concentrates on the object-oriented analysis of IIS where standard UMLs are utilized describing the system. The object-oriented analysis is accomplished by generating use case diagram, activity diagram and domain class diagram of IIS which can be easily used in the design and implementation phase of software development process.

Keywords: Islamic Inheritance System · Object-Oriented Analysis · Activity Diagram · Domain Class Diagram

1 Introduction

People may be crazy for earning assets either in right or wrong way. This sort of tendency increases the crimes in the society. This problem is seriously visible after a man or woman is died. The way of distributing of the assets of deceased among relatives is a crucial task. The distribution laws vary from country to country or religion to religion. This article focuses on the Islamic Law. So, it is felt that a computerized Islamic Inheritance System (IIS) is necessary for easing the computation to avoid unrest in the society. In order to make a professional

Md. S. Satu et al. (Eds.): MIET 2022, LNICST 491, pp. 216–225, 2023.
https://doi.org/10.1007/978-3-031-34622-4_17

IIS, the system should be analyzed, designed, implemented and tested respectively. Among those phases, this article emphasizes on the analysis phase which determines all necessary requirements to build a robust IIS and this phase can be performed employing either structured or object-oriented technique. The structured analysis depends on developing Data Flow Diagrams (DFDs) over involved processes in IIS done by S. Tabassum et al. [10]. Those DFDs are transformed into structure chart as Architectural Design consisting of functions as module. However, the constructed DFDs in the structured IIS are not standard diagrams which may arise confusion among software engineering community. Secondly, although DFDs of IIS show the name of processes, a clear idea about its modules are not found. Finally, as the processes of IIS in DFDs cannot be extended, any types of changes or modifications on those DFDs are not easy. Considering these three problems, this paper focuses only on the object-oriented analysis phase for IIS. In this phase, the objects of IIS from its description are used to form a conceptual class diagram from which a class-based architectural design can be built in the Object-Oriented Design phase. This paper consists of five sections. The Sect. 2 describes the related works. The overall methodology of object-oriented analysis to determine the domain class diagram is illustrated in Sect. 3. Section 4 presents the result and discussion of the paper. Finally, the paper is concluded in conclusion section.

2 Related Works

Software makes the professional life of human being straightforward and it has become increasingly part of all aspect of daily life since 1960. From then on, it is a great challenge to produce a high-quality software being maintainable, usable, reliable and acceptable. Apportioning the shares of dead among live heirs according to inheritance laws is monumental business process in the society to prevent riots and the process of computation varies from religion to religion. This article basically focuses the Islamic Inheritance Law. In order to computerize the business process, software engineering techniques can be used to build the professional software solution named Inheritance system. So far, few works have been done on Islamic law. Firstly, H. Alshahad et al. presented a concept for calculating the shares of heirs in 2015 where a decision table having all inheritance related Islamic rules is employed [3]. Then, an expert system for the computation integrating 43 rules on Islamic law using CLIPS language was proposed by Alaa N. Akkila et al. (2016) [2]. In 2018, Zulkifli et al. applied Rapid Application Development (RAD) model for developing an android application of inheritance system [14]. Then, a family ontology based architecture of Islamic Inheritance System named AraFamOnto was provided by S. Zouaoui et al. where the ontology indicated family relationship [13]. Mathematical models for each heir should be developed for the business logic of each module of Islamic Inheritance System. In 2017, K. Babalola gave all mathematical models for computing the desired shares of live heirs of deceased [5]. But these expressions were not well-expressed for building the Inheritance system. In 2019, S. Tabassum et al.

presented well-expressed computational models for heirs [10]. Few prominent web applications for inheritance Calculators are found. Firstly, Halis Aydemir developed an inheritance calculator named "Division of Inheritance" where the results are displayed in percentage, fraction and bar chart [4]. In addition, a web application entitled ShariahStandards.org depicts the allocated shares of heirs in a circle with different shades of colors [9]. Moreover, the lubnaa is another inheritance calculator which is capable of computing shares of nine heirs in fraction [6]. Furthermore, the Access to Information (a2i) project of the office of the prime minister of Bangladesh is running a web application named Uttaradikhar based on the amended Islamic laws of Bangladesh constitution [11]. Over and above, Najeeb built another web application named Islamic Inheritance Calculator adding all Islamic laws considering 29 legal heirs over five generations of heirs [8]. Finally, the most comprehensive Islamic Inheritance System developed by Muhammad Waqas integrated all possible conditions of Islamic inheritance laws [12]. Although all aforementioned systems are available to use, their architectural designs are not published. Thus, the knowledge about the modules of those system is unknown which makes difficult to extend or maintain the system with extended rules. The precondition of developing an architectural design is to analyze the system for finding the requirements. Although S. Tabassum et al. [10] did the structured analysis approach for Islamic Inheritance System (IIS), there is no works for object-oriented analysis for IIS. For this reason, the main focus of the article is to analyze the IIS employing Object-Oriented paradigm.

3   Methodology

A very meticulous procedure of this work has to be followed in order to achieve the intended outcomes. The procedure will include several steps befitting to the objectives of this research. At the starting of the process, the context of the system is analyzed to find out the important services to be given to the user. According to the object-oriented technique, the determined services of the system are modeled using a UML diagram known as use case diagram. Then, the scenarios of those use cases are modeled where the sequence of interactions between system and user are described step by step. Next, the activities under the sequence of interactions are modeled using another UML diagram called Activity Diagram. After that, a conceptual class diagram using Unified Process methodology is built after finding the responsible autonomous agents or objects from the textual description of fixed use cases. The detail description of the methodology is presented in the following subsequent sections.

3.1   System Context Modeling

An application software without any useful service is meaningless to the user. Thus, every software system should have one or more services or use cases. In order to find those use cases, the context of the desired software system should be analyzed thoroughly. This paper focuses on one use case to distribute

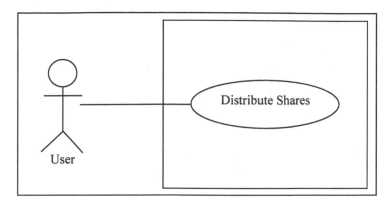

Fig. 1. Use Case Diagram

the wealth of deceased among live relatives illustrated in Fig. 1 using UML use case diagram. The distribution process varies from creed to creed. In Islam, the way of distribution is mentioned in the holy Quran and Hadith [1,7]. At the beginning of the process, the **Total Effective Shares** (**TES**) for allotting are computed by deducing his or her loan, will and funeral costs from the remaining shares. Then, the **TES** is distributed among the prescribed heirs: **Spouse** (**Husband** or **Wives**), **Daughter**, **Father**, **Mother**, **Grandfather**, **Paternal Granddaughter**, **Sister(full)**, **Paternal Grandmother** and **Maternal Grandmother** who are specified with their deserved portion in the Holy Quran. Among those relatives, **Spouse** and **Mother** must get shares without any condition, if they are alive. The rest of the prescribed relatives have one or more preconditions. For example, the **Father** will be considered for prescribed shares, if the deceased has no offspring. The Table 1 shows all preconditions of eligible prescribed heirs and their respective computational model for computing the portions [10].

The acronyms of computational model in Table 1 are as follows:

1. hNC() : hasNoChildren()
2. NW : number of Wives
3. hSD() : hasSingleDaughter()
4. ND : number of Daughters
5. hNMS() : hasNoMultipleSiblings()
6. hNMGM() : hasNoMaternalGrandmother()
7. hNF() : hasNoFather()
8. hPGM() : hasPaternalGrandmother()
9. hSGD() : hasSingleGranddaughter()
10. NGD : number of Grand Daughters
11. hSS() : hasSingleSister()
12. NS : number of sisters

Table 1. Summary of Prescribed Heirs

No	Heirs	Preconditions	Computational Model
1	Husband	Confirmed	$\frac{TES}{4}(1 + hNC())$
2	Wives	Confirmed	$\frac{TES}{8}(1+hNC())$
3	Daughters	Deceased has no son	$\frac{\frac{TES}{2} + \frac{TES}{6}(1 - hSD())}{ND}$
4	Father	Deceased has offspring	$\frac{TES}{6}$
5	Mother	Confirmed	$\frac{TES}{6}(1 + (hNC() \text{ AND } hNMS()))$
6	Paternal Grandfather	Deceased has no father and has offspring	$\frac{TES}{6}$
7	Paternal Grandmother	Deceased has no mother and father	$\frac{TES}{12}(1 + hNMGM())$
8	Maternal Grandmother	Deceased has no mother	$\frac{TES}{12}(1 + (1\text{-}(hNF() \text{ AND } hPGM()))$
9	Paternal Granddaughters	Deceased has no son, grandson and at most one daughter	$\frac{\frac{TES}{6} \cdot hSD()+ \frac{TES}{2}(1 - hSD())+\frac{TES}{6}(1 - hSGD())}{NGD}$
10	Sisters (full)	Deceased has no daughter, son, paternal grandson, paternal granddaughter, father, paternal grandfather and brother	$\frac{\frac{TES}{2} + \frac{TES}{6}(1 - hSS())}{NS}$

Every computational model has one or more predicates which return integer value 1(one) whenever those are true. However, the models for precondition of **Father** and **Grandfather** proposed by S. Tabassum [10] have not been covered completely. The modified models are shown in Table 1 where if deceased has offspring, the **Father** will be eligible for prescribed shares. Similarly, the condition for **Grandfather** is not to have **Father** and offspring. After distributing the prescribed shares, one out of four cases may happen. Firstly, the **Total Allotted Prescribe Shares(TAPS)** is equal to **TES**. Then, the earned prescribed shares will be final shares. Secondly, there are still some remaining shares. Then, the given list of heirs of deceased is checked if there are eligible residual heirs. The matching conditions for each eligible residual heir are illustrated in Table 2.

If the list of residual heirs is not empty, the remaining shares are distributed among male and female candidates employing the ratio 2:1. If the number of male and female candidates are **NM** and **NF** respectively, the portion of **Male Residual Shares (MRS)** and **Female Residual Shares (FRS)** are computed as Eq. 1 and 2 [10].

$$MRS = 2 \cdot \frac{TES - TAPS}{2 \cdot NM + NF} \tag{1}$$

$$FRS = \frac{TES - TAPS}{2 \cdot NM + NF} \tag{2}$$

Then, the individual earned shares in prescribed and residual category are summed and this is the final shares of heirs of deceased. Thirdly, in spite of having remaining shares, there is no residual heirs of deceased. In this case, the **Earned Prescribed Shares (EPS)** are proportionately increased except

Table 2. Summary of Residual Heirs

No	Relatives	Preconditions
1	Son	Confirmed
2	Daughter	Has Son
3	Paternal Grandson	Has no Son
4	Paternal Granddaughter	Has no Son AND Has Paternal Grandson
5	Father	Has no (Son AND Grandson)
6	Grandfather	Has no (Son AND Grandson AND Father)
7	Brother	Has no (Son AND Grandson AND Father AND Grandfather)
8	Sister	Has no (Son AND Grandson AND Father AND Grandfather) AND Has (Brother OR Daughter OR Granddaughter)
9	Brother's Son	Has no (Son AND Grandson AND Father AND Grandfather AND Brother AND Daughter AND Granddaughter)
10	Son of Brother's Son	Has no (Son AND Grandson AND Father AND Grandfather AND Brother AND Daughter AND Granddaughter AND Brother's Son)
11	Paternal Uncle	Has no Son AND Has no (Grandson AND Father AND Grandfather AND Brother AND Daughter AND Granddaughter AND Brother's Son AND Son of Brother's Son)
12	Paternal Cousin	Has no (Son AND Grandson AND Father AND Grandfather AND Brother AND Daughter AND Granddaughter AND Brother's Son AND Son of Brother's Son AND Paternal Uncle)

Spouse, whereas S. Tabassum considered **Spouse** in her model [10]. This situation is called **Radd** case [8]. Finally, the **TAPS** is greater than **TES** which is known as **Awal** case [8]. In this situation, the **EPS** are proportionately decreased. For both cases, the **Final Shares(FS)** of **heir** in the list of eligible prescribed heirs is determined using the Eq. 3, where **RS** and **TAPS** are **Remaining Shares** and **Total Allotted Prescribed shares** respectively.

$$FS(heir) = EPS(heir) \left(1 + (1 - isSpouse(heir) \cdot isPositive(RS)) \frac{RS}{TAPS} \right) \quad (3)$$

Here the function **EPS(heir)** returns the Earned Prescribed Shares of **heir** and **isSpouse(heir)** and **isPositive(RS)** are two predicates. The former predicate returns one if the **heir** is spouse, while the later predicate gives one for being positive value of **RS**. Otherwise, both predicate provides zero. It has been seen that when both predicates are 1, which indicates the heir is spouse and the sum of distributed prescribed shares is less than TES, the shares will not be increased. Otherwise, it will be increased. However, the whole scenario of the use case in Fig. 1 is structured in Fig. 2. This scenario consists of several activities. These activities and the flows among activities are shown in Fig. 3.

3.2 Domain Class Modeling

In object-oriented approach, domain modeling means finding the embodied autonomous agents or objects and their relationships from the scenario of use

UC1	:	Distribute Shares
Actors	:	User
Preconditions	:	The Home Screen of the system should be displayed
Main Success Scenario	:	1. Home Screen prompts user to select the live heirs and to enter the number of heirs, total shares and the bequest shares of the deceased 2. User selects the live heirs and gives the number of heirs, total shares and bequest shares of the deceased. 3. System takes the given information of deceased from the Home Screen. 4. System makes the list of heirs for prescribed shares measuring the eligibility of the heir. 5. System computes the portions of shares for all eligible heirs of prescribed shares from the total shares of deceased. 6. System sums all of computed prescribed shares. 7. System calculates the rest of shares subtracting the sum of prescribed shares from the total shares of deceased. 8. System makes the list of heirs for residual shares measuring the eligibility of the heir. 9. System computes the portion of residual shares for eligible heirs from the rest of the shares. 10. System computes the final shares of individual summing his or her got portions in prescribed and residual shares.
Post conditions	:	The Output Screen of the system shows the computed individual prescribed, residual and total final shares.

Alternative Courses	:	2.a. The number of Husband, Father, Mother, Paternal Grand Father, Paternal Grand Mother, Maternal Grand Mother is more than One
		    2.a.01. System will show a warning message as "The number is not possible".
		    2.a.02. Resume @ step 1
		2.b. The number of wives is more than four
		    2.b.01. System will show a warning message as "The number is not possible".
		    2.b.02. Resume @ step 1
		7.a. The rest of the shares is equal to zero
		    7.a.01. System will finalize the Computed Prescribed Shares as Final Shares
		    7.a.02. Resume @ step 10
		7.b. The rest of the shares is less than zero
		    7.a.01. System will be scaled down all Computed Prescribed shares under Total shares of deceased
		    7.a.02. Resume @ step 10
		8.a. The list is empty
		    8.a.01. System will be scaled up all Computed Prescribed shares under total shares of deceased
		    8.a.02. Resume @ step 10

Fig. 2. Use Case Description

cases. For this purpose, it is necessary to retrieve three types of classes: Entity Classes, Control Class and Boundary Classes. After analyzing the steps in Fig. 2, six entity classes, two boundary classes and one control class are modeled. The six entity classes are **DeceasedModel**, **PrescribedShares**, **PrescribedHeirs**, **ResidualShares**, **ResidualHeirs** and **FinalShares**. Among these entity classes, steps 1, 2 and 3 in scenario of Fig. 2 implies **DeceasedModel** class in order to deal the information of deceased including list of heirs, number of each heir and the total effective shares. The responsibilities of the **PrescribedShares** and **PrescribedHeirs** found from step 4 to 7 are to determine

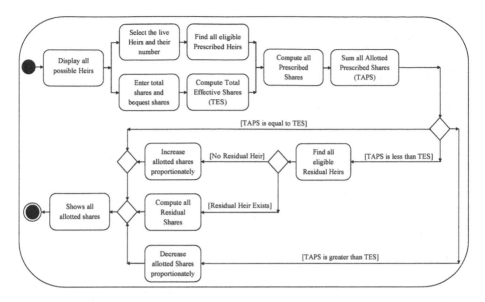

Fig. 3. Activity Diagram

the eligible prescribed heirs and the portion of those heirs. The **Prescribed-Shares** class holds the list of all eligible prescribed heirs of deceased and sum of distributed prescribed shares whereas the **PrescribedHeir** class includes type and number of heirs and respective portion of shares. Similarly, the step 8 and 9 hints about the two other entity classes named **ResidualShares** and **ResidualHeir** to find the eligible residual heirs and the portion of shares of those heirs respectively. The last final entity class called **FinalShares** having two attributes (list of heirs and list of shares) combines the earned portion in prescribed and residual category according to the special rules of Islamic Inheritance. Furthermore, two boundary classes named as **HomeScreen** and **OutputScreen** are seen in step 1 and precondition of Fig. 2 respectively. The object of **HomeScreen** class will take the list of heirs of deceased, their number and the amount of assets, whereas the **OutputScreen** type object shows the computed prescribed, residual and final shares of each heir. Finally, the whole business rules for distributing shares are conducted by a control class named **DistributeShares**. This class receives all necessary information of deceased from **Homescreen** type object, computes prescribed, residual and final shares employing six aforementioned entity classes and at the end shows those shares utilizing the object of **OutputScreen** class. The domain class diagram for distributing shares among heirs of deceased is shown in Fig. 4.

4   Result and Discussion

The purpose of the analysis phase for developing a professional software is to retrieve the required artifacts for design phase. S. Tabassum et al. used struc-

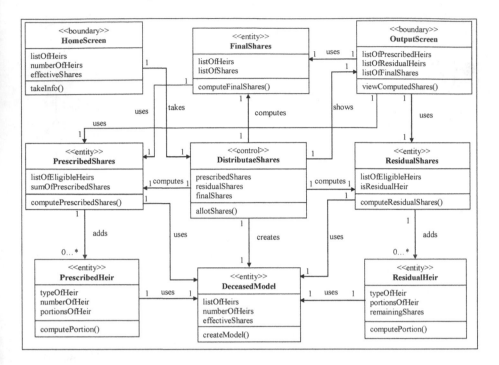

Fig. 4. Domain Class Diagram

tured analysis technique to analyze the Islamic Inheritance system employing
level 0,1 and 2 DFDs [10]. Compared to the structured analysis approach for IIS,
this work is more robust because of using object-oriented analysis technique. In
this analysis, some standard UML artifacts including **Use Case Diagram** in
Fig. 1, **Activity Diagram** in Fig. 3 and **Domain Class Diagram** in Fig. 4 are
produced, whereas the structured analysis phase generates only DFDs which are
not UML. So, this work is affluent in terms of diagram standardization. Secondly,
there is no way to get idea about the module of system in structured analysis
phase and we have to wait until design phase for structure chart having functions
as module. On other hand, the Domain class diagram in Fig. 4 in object-oriented
analysis phase consists of classes which are considered as modules for Architectural Design. Finally, classes in class diagram can be inherited to create new
classes and functions inside the classes can also be overridden which makes this
work very powerful. Therefore, it can be said that object-oriented analysis is
superior to structured analysis for IIS.

5   Conclusion

A professional software solution for Islamic Inheritance System (IIS) has great
demand to distribute shares of deceased among his or her heirs. The starting

phase of developing the professional software is analysis which is the main target of this work. In this paper, the analysis of the IIS has been done successfully by creating some artifacts including Use Case Diagram, Activity Diagram and Domain Class diagram. This work has valuable impact in the software engineering community, as the generated artifacts can be used to develop architectural design, detail design and build the desired IIS. In future, this work can be extended integrating other religions to build general inheritance system. The great limitation of this work is that complete object-oriented architecture of IIS is not developed. Thus, another future work is to develop the architectural design and detail design modeling sequence diagram, collaboration diagram and state machine diagram of the IIS from the produced domain class diagram.

References

1. Adelina Zuleika, N.P.D.: Islamic Inheritance Law (Faraid) and its economic implication. Tazkia Islamic Finance Bus. Rev. **8**(1), 97–118 (2013)
2. Akkila, A.N., Abu Naser, S.S.: Proposed expert system for calculating inheritance in Islam. World Wide J. Multidisciplinary Res. Dev. **2**(9), 38–48 (2015)
3. Alshahad, H.F., Abutiheen, Z.A.: Computation of inheritance share in Islamic Law by an expert system using decision tables. Q. Adjudicated J. Nat. Eng. Res. Stud. **1**(No. 1 and 2), 105–114 (2015)
4. Aydemir, D.H.: Division of Inheritance. https://kurandersleri.net/miras/en/Miras_en.html. Accessed 11 Aug 2021
5. Babalola, K.O.: The Inheritance of Legal Heirs: Mathematical Presentation. University of Ilorin, Department of Mathematics, September 2017
6. Lubnaa - Inheritance Calculator. https://www.lubnaa.com/money/InheritCalc.php. Accessed 10 Aug 2021
7. Muhammad, B.J.: The Islamic Law of Inheritance: Introduction and Theories. Abu Aisha Publishing (2020)
8. Najeeb: Islamic Inheritance Calculator (2014). https://inheritance.ilmsummit.org/projects/inheritance/home.aspx. Accessed 10 Aug 2021
9. ShariahStandards.org. https://www.inheritancecalculator.net/. Accessed 10 Aug 2021
10. Tabassum, S., Hoque, A.H.M.S., Twahura, S., Rahman, M.O.: Developing an Islamic Farayez system applying software engineering. Jurnal Kejuruteraan **31**(1), 25–38 (2019). https://doi.org/10.17576/jkukm-2019-31(1)-04
11. Uttaradhikar: Access to information (A2I), prime minister's office of Bangladesh (2016). https://xn-d5by7bap7cc3ici3m.xn-54b7fta0cc/index.php?lang=en. Accessed 10 Aug 2021
12. Waqas, M.: Islamic Inheritance Calculator (2017). https://www.inheritance-calculator.com/index.php. Accessed 11 Aug 2021
13. Zouaoui, S., Rezeg, K.: Islamic inheritance calculation system based on Arabic ontology (AraFamOnto). J. King Saud Univ. Comput. Inf. Sci. **33**(1), 68–76 (2018). https://doi.org/10.1016/j.jksuci.2018.11.015
14. Zulkifli, A.N., Batiha, Q.A., Qasim, M.M.: Design and development of M-Faraid: an Islamic inheritance mobile app. J. Adv. Res. Dyn. Control Syst. **10**(10 Special Issue), 1569–1575 (2018)

Can Transformer Models Effectively Detect Software Aspects in StackOverflow Discussion?

Nibir Chandra Mandal$^{(\boxtimes)}$, Tashreef Muhammad, and G. M. Shahariar

Ahsanullah University of Science and Technology, Dhaka, Bangladesh
nibir338@gmail.com, tashreef.muhammad@gmail.com, sshibli745@gmail.com

Abstract. Dozens of new tools and technologies are being incorporated to help developers, which is becoming a source of consternation as they struggle to choose one over the others. For developing web applications, they are continuously searching for all of the benefits and drawbacks of each API, framework, tool, and so on. One of the typical approaches is to examine all of the features through official documentation and discussion. This approach is time-consuming, often makes it difficult to determine which aspects are the most important to a particular developer and whether a particular aspect is important to the community at large. In this paper, we have used a benchmark API aspects dataset (Opiner) collected from StackOverflow posts and observed how Transformer models (BERT, RoBERTa, DistilBERT, and XLNet) perform in detecting software aspects in textual developer discussion with respect to the baseline Support Vector Machine (SVM) model. Through extensive experimentation, we have found that transformer models improve the performance of baseline SVM for most of the aspects, i.e., 'Performance', 'Security', 'Usability', 'Documentation', 'Bug', 'Legal', 'OnlySentiment', and 'Others'. However, the models fail to apprehend some of the aspects (e.g., 'Community' and 'Potability') and their performance varies depending on the aspects. Also, larger architectures like XLNet are ineffective in interpreting software aspects compared to smaller architectures like DistilBERT.

Keywords: StackOverflow · Software Aspects · Machine Learning · Transformers

1 Introduction

The information technology (IT) sector is leading the fourth industrial revolution and bringing about significant developments in the 21st century. The advancement of the sophisticated field is accelerating thanks to the concept of "open source". By deploying developed modules from various developers under a Creative Commons (CC) License [1] and the like, the opportunity to develop more and more over existing technologies has become quite simple. APIs are a popular technology these days. APIs enable third-party applications to easily access

Md. S. Satu et al. (Eds.): MIET 2022, LNICST 491, pp. 226–241, 2023.
https://doi.org/10.1007/978-3-031-34622-4_18

information while maintaining data security. APIs can now be found everywhere due to the widespread availability of various resources. It is challenging to identify the suitable API to get the task done. The "Opiner" [15] was proposed as a solution to this challenging problem. Opiner is a website that provides multiple summarized thoughts about APIs in an online search engine. Opiner's backend is powered by "Automatic Summarization of API Reviews" that employs the pattern recognition model Support Vector Machine (SVM) [16]. The model was trained using around 4000 sentences from *Stack Overflow*[1]. The advent of *Stack Overflow* has been a blessing to developers, as it has increased the frequency with which millions of engineers from various communities discuss the same subjects. This allows the newcomer's most welcoming environment to post their relatively unsophisticated difficulties. Furthermore, the cross-domain conversation is available here. "What are the better alternatives to pandas?" for example. One of the typical approaches is to examine all of the features through official documentation and discussion, which is time-consuming and can make it difficult to determine which aspects are the most important to a particular developer. Furthermore, most of the time, such conversations are ignored by the community. In addition, it is difficult to determine whether a particular aspect is important to the community at large. Despite these options, developers still find it difficult to choose the best solutions. This is due to the vastness and scarcity of posts. Each post may have several aspects, such as security and performance, or none at all. As a result, it is required to separate the portion that contains any aspects as well as the aspects linked with those. Thus, in this paper, we have concentrated on detecting aspects in textual developer discussion. As posts may contain multiple aspects, we analyze sentence level aspect detection. In summary, we make the following contributions in this paper:

- To increase the performance of the baseline Support Vector Machine (SVM) based model, we used four other Transformer models (BERT, RoBERTa, DistilBERT, and XLNet) and observed considerable performance improvement in most situations.
- We conducted a thorough performance comparison and discovered that transformer models completely fail to understand some aspects, and their performance varies depending on the aspects, through rigorous experiments. In addition, as compared to smaller designs like DistilBERT, bigger architectures like XLNet are inadequate at analyzing software aspects.

2   Related Work

2.1   Literature Review

Several recent papers have used SO posts to investigate various aspects of software development using topic modeling, such as what developers are talking about in general [8]. Mandal et al. [9] investigated at nearly 53,000 IoT-related posts on SO and used topic modeling [10] to figure out what people were talking

---

[1] https://stackoverflow.com/.

about. They intended to learn about the practical difficulties that developers experience when building real IoT systems. Recent studies [11,12] explored the connection between API usage and Stack Overflow discussions. Both research discovered a relationship between API class use and the number of Stack Overflow questions answered. But Gias Uddin [13] utilized their constructed benchmark dataset named "OPINER" [14] to carry out the study and noticed that developers frequently provided opinions about vastly different API aspects in those discussions which was the first step towards filling the gap of investigating the susceptibility and influence of sentiments and API aspects in the API reviews of online forum discussions. Uddin and Khomh [14] introduced OPINER, a method for mining API-related opinions and providing users with a rapid summary of the benefits and drawbacks of APIs when deciding which API to employ to implement a certain feature. Uddin and Khomh [15] used an SVM-based aspect classifier and a modified Sentiment Orientation algorithm [19] to comply with API opinion mining. Based on the positive and negative results emphasized in earlier attempts to automatically mine API opinions, as well as the seminal work in this field by Uddin and Khomh [15], Lin et al. [18] introduced a new approach called Pattern-based Opinion MinEr (POME), which utilizes linguistic patterns preserved in Stack Overflow sentences referring to APIs to classify whether a sentence is referring to a specific API aspect (functional, community, performance, usability, documentation, compatibility or reliability), and has a positive or negative polarity. Some other research works have concentrated on mining views in order to acquire knowledge about API usage. Wang et al. [20] mined Stack Overflow for brief practical and beneficial API use advice from developer replies. DEEPTIP, their suggested method, used Convolutional Neural Network (CNN) with a dataset of annotated texts (classified as "tip" or "non-tip") and achieved a high precision of 80%. Zhang and Hou [21] extracted Oracle's Java Swing Forum online conversations for problematic API features. The HAYSTACK technique they developed recognized negative statements using a sentiment analysis approach and analyzed these unfavorable comments using pre-defined grammatical patterns to reveal problematic characteristics.

2.2 Comparison

The main difference between the study of this paper to the existing studies is that the paper introduces usage of transformer type models. The study revolts around NLP and transformers are known for performing well in the sector of NLP. Hence, the main contribution of the study is introducing transformer which has not been done before.

3 Background Studies

3.1 StackOverflow

Stack Overflow (SO) is a question and answer website for programmers [2]. It is an open platform where many people ask questions and give answers related to programming. A typical Stack Overflow post contains a question, some number of answers, and some comments as shown in Fig. 1.

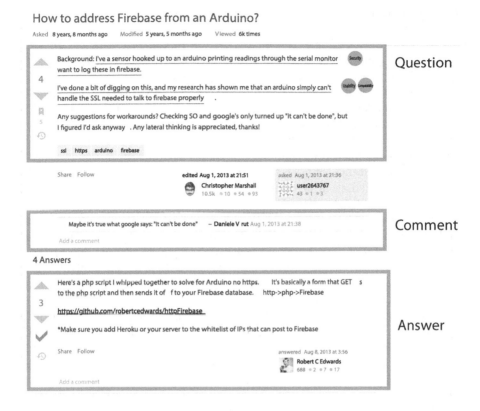

Fig. 1. Different Parts of a Stack Overflow Post

3.2 Software API

Application Programming Interface (API) is one of the most commonly used tools while developing software based services and products in recent times. It offers an easy accessibility (sometimes with enhanced security) of data very easily. Software developers use software APIs with appropriate category and architecture to get their job done easily. Some of the most popular APIs in RapidAPI include: *Skyscanner Flight Search, Open Weather Map, API-FOOTBALL, The Cocktail DB* and such [22].

3.3 Software API Aspects

An API may have multiple aspects associated with it, and developers choose their desired API based on those aspects and comparing them with their necessities. Following the survey and studies conducted by Uddin et al. [17], the study proposed a total of 11 aspects that are used for assessing a software API by coders or developers. Those aspects are as follows:

(a) **Performance:** This aspect includes comparison between two or more APIs in terms of speed, resource usages, etc. For example, a developer comments *'The alternative is to poll for changes at regular intervals, but that may create a delay in the event reaching a client.'* in SO question $A_{1728020}$. This sentence are related to the performance aspect of 'Java HTTP'.

(b) **Usability:** This aspect discusses the usages of an API, the difficulties of integrating an API, etc. are related to this aspect. For example, SO question, $A_{1728020}$, has a usability aspect related sentence as follows: *'All of this assumes we have a client that the server needs to be able to push data to.'*

(c) **Security:** This aspect is about how much security of data is ensured in the API. For instance, SO questions A_{992019} contains the following password encryption related security discussions: *'I have tried a 32bit one for 256bit encryption, but it did not work as expected.'*

(d) **Documentation:** This aspect is about how clear and thorough the official documentation is of the API. To give an example, the SO question $A_{2971315}$ can be considered where one of the answers *'From the API documentation: As of release JDK 5, this class has been supplemented with an equivalent class designed for use by a single thread, **StringBuilder**.'* is related to the documentation relating to 'StringBuilder'.

(e) **Compatibility:** This aspect is about how easily the API is compatible to the given framework environments. In the SO question $A_{5059224}$, the question regarding *Which is the best library for XML parsing in java* was answered by someone with *'JDOM would be another alternative to DOM4J'* is an example of compatibility for Java based XML parsing.

(f) **Portability:** This aspect is about how portable is the API in situations like being used in multiple Operating System environments. The SO question in $A_{1109307}$ has an answer saying *'These are standard on Linux, are generally available on Unix and can be run on Windows under cygwin, although you may be able to find windows-native apps that can do it as well'* is an example of portability.

(g) **Community:** This aspect is about how much active is the community of users who use the API for practice. In the SO question A_{326390}, the discussion contains *'And it seems to be the most wide-spread, at least in the sites I've visited'* is an example of community aspect.

(h) **Legal:** This aspect is about how much proper licensing and access is provided for using the API. In the SO question $A_{2129375}$ which is related to 'HTML/XML Parser for Java' an answer quotes the use of 'Apache Tika' as the best choice. One of the reasons behind his explanation includes a sentence *'Furthermore, it is open-source'* which directly indicates towards the legal aspects of the API that is being discussed.

(i) **Bug:** This aspect is about the presence or absence of bug or errors in the API overall. In the SO question A_{507391}, there is a discussion regarding comparison between 'Active MQ JBOSS Messaging' where the answer *'Feature-by-feature comparisons are all very well, but my experience of ActiveMQ (through various versions over the years) is that it is shockingly buggy, and no one seems inclined to fix those bugs'* clearly indicates the buggy features of 'Active MQ' that will make anyone think twice about using the API. This is an example of the bug aspect of an API.

(j) Only Sentiment: This aspect expresses only sentiment about an API without technical brief on the matter. The simple sentence of *'It's deeply frustrating'* in the SO question A_{507391} is a prime example of using sentiment only to express the aspect of an API.

(k) Others: The aspect that does not fall under all the other mentioned categories are stated in here. Even after specifying 10 concrete aspects, there are far too many types of sentences that are found in real-life relating to the performance of APIs. All those are gathered in this category. For example, the sentence *'I can manually change it, but I'd rather not have to remember to update it every time the jaxb files are regenerated'* can be considered as an example of such aspects. This example was taken from SO question $A_{15936368}$.

Developers primarily follow these aspects before selecting an API for their projects. They analyze the sentiment of these aspects and make a decision accordingly.

3.4   Transformers

A neural network that learns factors in sequential data is referred to as a transformer model. In natural language processing transformer models are used frequently as it tracks the meaning of consecutive data by tracking the relationships among them like the words in a sentence. Transformer models were first introduced by Google [3] and are one of the most powerful models till date in the history of computer science. We incorporated four different kinds of transformer model in our work which are RoBERTa, BERT, DistilBERT and XLNet. Bidirectional Encoder Representations from Transformers or BERT [4] was first established by Jacob Devlin et al. which is a transformer model to represent language. Yinhan Liu et al. introduced RoBERTa [5] as a replication study of BERT [4]. Authors showed that their model was highly trained than BERT overcoming the limitations and showed a good performance over basic BERT model. DistilBERT was proposed by Victor Sanh et al. [6] as a general purpose transformer model which is quite smaller than other language representation models. Authors showed that the size of a BERT model can be lessened by 40% by leveraging knowledge filtering at the time of pre-training stage. They also showed that their model is 60% faster than other transformer models. Zhilin Yang et al. introduced XLNet [7] which overcomes the constraints of BERT [4] using a universal auto-regressive pre-training technique. Maximum expected likelihood was taken into consideration over all arrangements of the factorization order. They have showed that their model beat BERT by a huge margin on a variety of tasks like sentiment analysis, language inference or document ranking etc. All these used models, RoBERTa, BERT, XLNet and DistilBERT have different architectures. The Table 1 contains details about these architectures.

Table 1. Architecture details of used Transformer variants

Architecture	Used Model	Layers	Heads	Hidden	Parameters
RoBERTa	distilroberta-base	6	768	12	82M
BERT	bert-base-uncased	12	768	12	110M
XLNet	xlnet-base-cased	12	768	12	110M
DistilBERT	distilbert-base-uncased	6	768	12	66M

4   Dataset

Previously, Uddin et al. [14] studied API aspects in SO. We follow the study and use benchmark dataset. The dataset was collected from SO posts, comments, and answers. It was primarily created for mining developers opinions. Thus, it includes varieties of opinions about multiple APIs. It contains 4522 sentences and each sentences are associated with one or more aspects. To keep the context of the dataset more concentrated on the textual data itself, some slight modifications were added. Initially the dataset consisted of some threads. Each thread was either a question, a comment or an answer of a SO post. It contained data wrapped with some HTML tags. These data were formatted for the above mentioned purpose of making it more concentrated on the textual format. For example,

- All hyperlinks were formatted by removing the HTML formats and appending a *URL_* in the prefix.
- Code examples were removed and replaced with *CODESNIPPET* and *CODE-TERM* as placeholders.

For example, the following sentences can be considered. **Example 1** contains two aspects, i.e., *Bug* and *Performance*. Again, sentences like in **Example 2** contains *Only Sentiment* aspect. Also, in Fig. 1 there are two underlined sentences. One sentence only contains the *Security* aspects whereas the other sentence contains *Usability* and *Compatibility* aspects.

> **Example 1:** *What HTML parsers have the following features: Fast Thread-safe Reliable and bug-free Parses HTML and XML Handles erroneous HTML Has a DOM implementation Supports HTML4, JavaScript, and CSS tags Relatively simple, object-oriented API What parser you think is better?*
>
> **Example 2** *This works fine for the following code: CODESNIPPET_JAVA2*

Table 2 shows the summary of our benchmark dataset. The dataset are clearly imbalanced and most of aspects have a positive rate below 5%. Others aspect has the highest number of samples (i.e., 1699 samples) followed by Usability aspect (1437 samples), Performance aspect (348 samples), Only sentiment aspect (348 samples), Documentation aspect (253 samples), Security aspect (253 samples), and so on. Legal aspect has the lowest number of samples- i.e., only 50 samples.

This distribution of topics in our benchmark dataset indicates that developers most frequently discuss about Usability aspect in SO and they rarely discuss about Legal aspects of APIs. As usability, security, and performance are the most widely used aspects of APIs in developer community, we find enough discussion about those in our benchmark dataset.

Table 2. Aspects distribution in the benchmark dataset

Aspects	# of Samples	Aspects	# of Samples
Performance	348 (8%)	Usability	1437 (32%)
Security	163 (4%)	Documentation	253 (6%)
Compatibility	93 (2%)	Portability	70 (2%)
Community	93 (2%)	Legal	50 (1%)
Bug	189 (4%)	Only Sentiment	348 (8%)
Others	1699 (38%)		

5   Methodology

The proposed system for aspect categorization is presented in this section. In this study, whole experiment setup is divided into five major steps. These key phases or steps of the proposed method for binary aspect classification (*considering Usability aspect as an example*) are summarized in Fig. 2 and are further detailed below.

Step 1) Input Sentence: Each raw sentence from the dataset is presented to the proposed model one by one for further processing. Before that each sentence goes through some pre-processing steps. For example, all urls and codes are removed and for some special entries are replaced by specific placeholders. These information actually do not contain any validation to the aspect considering the variation it creates in the sample inputs. Hence, they are summarized to reduce load on the model.

Step 2) Tokenization: Once the input sentence is gathered, each processed sentence is tokenized using the *BERT Tokenizer* [4]. This is a well known tokenizer that applies an end-to-end, text string to wordpiece tokenization. The system utilizes wordpiece tokenization after applying basic tokenization. Each tokenized sentence gets a length of 100 tokens and zero padded when required. In the event of length more than 100, we cut off after 100. In other words, for length greater than 100, it gets truncated to keep everything in synchronization. The output of this step is a tokenized sentence of size 100.

Step 3) Embedding: The tokenization step converts a complete sentence into tokenized list of sentences. However, it is not yet mathematically possible to compute it. In this regard, word embedding needs to be utilized. For word embedding, BERT [4] is used to turn each token in a sentence into a numeric value representation. Each token is embedded by 768 real values via BERT. The input to this step is a tokenized sentence of size 100 and output of this step is an embedded sentence of size 100 × 768. Now each of the sentences that were represented by list of tokens containing the length of 100 is now converted a 2D numeric list with each component of the list expressed by an array of 768 numbers.

Step 4) Pooling: To reduce the dimension of the feature map (100 × 768) for each tokenized sentence in step 3, max pooling is used. It provides a real valued vector representation of size 768 per sentence. The resultant of this step is a significant reduction of size (by a hundred) and yet keeping the integrity of the data intact.

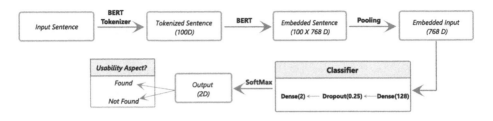

Fig. 2. Aspects Classification Process

Step 5) Classification: The data is currently ready for entering the training phase. Thus the current step is to prepare the classification model. Aspect classification is accomplished by the use of transfer learning [23]. In total the goal is to classify whether a sentence belongs to one of 11 categories or aspects or not. To detect 11 various aspects, a basic neural network with two dense layers (with 128 and 2 neurons) is utilized to fine-tune the pretrained four different transformer models one by one such as RoBERTa [5], BERT [4], DistilBERT [6], and XLNet [7] without freezing any of the previous layers of the existent pretrained model. The pretrained weights were initialized using *glorot_uniform* in the simple neural network. A dropout rate of 0.25 is employed between the dense layers. Throughout the scope of this experiment, there were a total of four pretrained models that were fine-tuned to serve the purpose of classification.

Step 6) Aspect detection: Because a sentence may have several aspects, we have employed 10-fold cross validation and binary classification. This helps evaluating the performance of the model more rigorously. On the output layer, the *Softmax* activation function is used. The final result of the model is to detect whether or not a specific aspect has been found on the provided input sentence.

6   Result Analysis

6.1   Experimental Results

We show our experimental results in Table 4. For the most part, we discovered that transformer models outperform baseline SVM. However, for Community

Table 3. Performance in different models

Aspect	Metric	Transformer Models				Baseline
		RoBERTa	BERT	XLNet	DistilBERT	SVM
Performance	P	**0.80**	0.76	0.78	0.78	0.78
	R	0.74	**0.77**	0.71	0.71	0.46
	F1	**0.77**	0.76	0.75	0.74	0.56
Usability	P	**0.68**	0.67	0.61	0.66	0.53
	R	**0.69**	0.67	0.65	0.67	0.75
	F1	**0.68**	0.67	0.63	0.66	0.62
Security	P	**0.81**	0.72	0.65	0.81	0.78
	R	0.74	**0.81**	0.73	0.74	0.58
	F1	0.72	0.75	0.68	**0.76**	0.60
Community	P	0.18	0.19	0.22	**0.33**	0.40
	R	0.13	0.11	**0.17**	0.16	0.24
	F1	0.15	0.13	0.15	**0.20**	0.26
Compatibility	P	0.17	0.10	0.10	**0.30**	0.50
	R	0.04	0.01	0.01	**0.09**	0.08
	F1	0.06	0.02	0.02	**0.13**	0.13
Portability	P	**0.67**	0.61	0.33	0.63	0.63
	R	0.45	0.49	0.15	**0.62**	0.63
	F1	0.49	0.51	0.19	**0.59**	0.61
Documentation	P	**0.69**	0.69	0.59	0.65	0.59
	R	**0.57**	0.50	0.50	0.54	0.43
	F1	**0.61**	0.56	0.53	0.57	0.49
Bug	P	0.64	**0.70**	0.59	0.65	0.57
	R	0.63	0.63	0.58	**0.66**	0.50
	F1	0.61	**0.63**	0.56	0.63	0.51
Legal	P	**0.72**	0.44	0.31	0.71	0.70
	R	**0.62**	0.39	0.42	0.61	0.46
	F1	0.61	0.38	0.35	**0.63**	0.52
OnlySentiment	P	**0.69**	0.69	0.69	0.65	0.61
	R	**0.51**	0.48	0.50	0.48	0.43
	F1	**0.58**	0.54	0.57	0.55	0.50
Others	P	0.77	0.74	**0.77**	0.74	0.61
	R	**0.71**	0.68	0.64	0.68	0.67
	F1	**0.73**	0.70	0.69	0.71	0.64

and Portability aspects, the SVM model still holds the highest performance. In addition, we found that the performance of each transformer varies across the different aspects. The results for each aspect are as follows:

(a) *Performance*. We found that RoBERTa offers the best results in terms of Precision and F1-Score, whereas BERT shows the best recall. In addition, RoBERTa's F1-Score of 0.77 beats baseline SVM's 0.56. This implies a huge improvement of 38% in terms of F1-Score. Besides this, our least performing transformer model, DistilBERT, offers an F1-Score of 0.74, which is also 32% higher than that of SVM.

(b) *Usability*. RoBERTa shows the best performance with a Precision of 0.68, Recall of 0.69, and an F1-Score of 0.68 among other deep and shallow models. Unlink the previous aspect (Performance), RoBERTa improves the baseline by only 10% in terms of F1-Score. Despite the fact that transformers outperform the baseline SVM, the F1-Score of XLNet and SVM is almost the same, i.e., 0.63 for XLNet and 0.62 for SVM.

(c) *Security*. Unlike the previous two aspects, DistilBERT shows the best F1-Score of 0.76 for security aspect detection, although RoBERTa has the best Precision of 0.81 and BERT has the highest Recall of 0.81. Our best performing model for security aspects, DistilBERT, increases the baseline SVM by 27% in terms of F1-Score. Other transformer models also show an almost similar improvement over the baseline SVM.

(d) *Community*. We found an interesting result for this aspect, as the expected transformer models fail to cross the performance line of baseline SVM. In fact, the best performing transformer model, DistilBERT, has a massive gap of 30% between the baseline SVM. In addition, we found that BERT records the lowest F1-Score of 0.13 among the transformer models.

(e) *Compatibility*. The transformer models perform poorly in detecting this aspect. At best, the DistilBERT achieves a maximum F1-Score of 0.13, which is exactly the same as the baseline SVM. Nevertheless, all the transformers and baseline SVM suffer from lower recall. Both BERT and XLNet record the lowest recall of 0.01.

(f) *Portability*. We observed that the baseline SVM narrowly beats the transformer models with an F1-Score of 0.61. Although RoBERTa offers better Precision (0.67) than SVM, the model unfortunately suffers from low recall. We also found that the XLNet model has the lowest precision (0.33) and recall (0.19) among all models for this task.

(g) *Documentation*. RoBERTa is the leading performer when it comes to detecting this aspect. It has the highest Precision of 0.69 and Recall of 0.57, which results in the best F1-Score of 0.61. It comprehensively outperforms the baseline SVM model by 25% in terms of F1-Score. Other transformers also shows similar results, but lower than the RoBERTa.

(h) *Bug*. We observed that both BERT and DistilBERT have the exact same F1-Score value of 0.63, which is also the highest among all models. However, both models have different Precision and Recall. DistilBERT has better Recall (0.66) whereas BERT has higher Precision (0.70). These models also outperform the baseline SVM by a long distance as well.

(i) *Legal*. We again found that DistilBERT, having an F1-Score of 0.63, appears to be superior over other transformers for this aspect detection. Although it has only a 3% higher F1-Score than RoBERTa, it thoroughly tops BERT's F1-Score of 0.38 and XLNet's F1-Score of 0.35. In addition, DistilBERT has better Precision, Recall, and F1-Score as well.

(j) *Only Sentiment.* For this aspect, RoBERTa offers the best F1-Score of 0.58, whereas BERT shows the lowest F1-Score of 0.54 among the transformer models. Nevertheless, all these models are able to beat the benchmark performance of the SVM model.

(k) *Others.* All the transformer models perform similarly when detecting these aspects. The best performing model, RoBERTa, has only a 5% higher F1-Score than the lowest performing model, XLNet. However, these models improves the F1-Score of the baseline SVM by more than 8%.

We therefore found RoBERTa as the best performer for Performance, Usability, Documentation, OnlySentiment, and Others aspects detection and DistilBERT for Security, Bug, Compatibility, and Legal aspects detection. This also implies that XLNet and BERT are not as useful as RoBERTa and DistilBERT for software aspect detection. In addition, no transformer models are as good as baseline SVM for detecting Portability and Community aspects.

6.2 Hyper-parameter Settings

The hyper-parameters associated with different models catalyze the performance of the model by a lot. Choosing the correct value of hyper-parameters for the best performance is not as easy task. In the conducted experiment many variation of hyper-parameters were tested in order to get good results in the experiment. Some of these values can be seen in Table 4. The other experiments have been conducted with different combinations quite similar to the ones seen in Table 4.

Table 4. Best performing models by precision with hyper-parameters

Metric	Best Model	Batch Size	Epoch	Learning Rate
Performance	RoBERTa	32	3	1.00E−05
Usability	RoBERTa	32	3	1.00E−05
Security	DistilBERT	16	2	1.00E−05
Community	DistilBERT	16	3	2.00E−05
Compatibility	DistilBERT	16	3	2.00E−05
Portability	DistilBERT	16	3	2.00E−05
Documentation	RoBERTa	32	2	1.00E−05
Bug	BERT	32	3	3.00E−05
Legal	DistilBERT	32	3	1.00E−05
OnlySentiment	RoBERTa	32	3	1.00E−05

6.3 Result Analysis

We described our experimental results in Sect. 6.1. We discussed the performance of each individual models and also showed a comparative analysis among them. We further investigated the results and found some interesting findings. In this section, we are focusing on these findings. We show a detailed analysis of our findings as follows:

1. *Transformer Models are more effective than baseline shallow models, such as, SVM and Logits.* Previously, Uddin at el. [16] showed that a shallow model can apprehend software aspects. However, our approach to detect software aspects is more effective. Our transformer models improve the performance of most of the aspects. Our best performing model for each aspect has higher precision and recall than baseline SVM. In addition, we find that our approach has a better balance between precision and recall, which indicates the stability of the model. For example, RoBERTa achieves a recall of 0.74 and a precision of 0.80 for 'Performance' aspect, which is around only 4.5% deviation from the F1 score. However, baseline SVM has a 21.8% deviation between F1-score and precision and recall. This indicates that our optimized transformer model is more effective and reliable than previous studies on aspects detection.

2. *Machine learning tools fail to apprehend 'Community' and 'Compatibility' aspects.* Although transformer models do a fairly good job of detecting software aspects, they completely go wrong when it comes to detecting 'Community' or 'Compatibility' aspects. An optimized model like RoBERTa has only 18% and 17% precision for Community and Compatibility aspect detection, respectively. One of the possible reasons for such low performance can be attributed to the low positive rates of these aspects in the dataset. However, the baseline model, SVM, which requires a lower training sample, shows similar performance. This indicates that these two aspects are difficult to comprehend for ML tools. This is because there are implicit contexts sparsely distributed in the dataset, which makes the classification task more challenging compared to other aspects. An extended dataset with more positive samples could be a fair attempt to improve the benchmark, which we left as our future work.

3. *Performance of transformer models varies depending on the aspects.* Transformer models perform fairly well despite a low positive rate of some software aspects, such as, 'Legal'. However, the performance changes when the targeted aspects have been altered, even for the same model. For example, RoBERTa does pretty well for 'Performance' aspect, but for 'Security' aspect, the performance drops a bit. A closer look at the results also indicates that there are no models that perform well across all aspects detection among the studied models. For instance, RoBERTa performs well for the usability aspect, whereas DistilBERT performs better for 'Security' aspects. This finding urges immediate research into multi-class aspects detection by ensembling all these models. In the future, we can explore this to learn the effectiveness of such blending for this aspect of the detection task.

4. *Larger architectures like XLNet are ineffective in interpreting software aspects compared to smaller architectures like DistilBERT.* An interesting finding of our studies is that larger or unoptimized architectural models perform lower than smaller or optimized architectural models. According to our background studies, BERT and XLNet have the largest architectures, where DistilBERT is a distilled version of BERT and RoBERTa is the most optimized model. Our experimental results imply that both BERT and XLNet models have lower performance metrics than RoBERTa and DistilBERT. Even though DistilBERT shares the same architecture, the performance shows huge improvement over BERT for all aspects. This finding could be attributed to the lower sample size for most of the aspects. However, for 'Others' aspect, which has enough samples, DistilBERT and RoBERTa also outclass BERT and XLNet. This result notes that huge parameter lists of larger architecture cause unnecessary intricacies in predicting software aspects, which eventually result in a partial drop in performance metrics. We believe this requires further investigation to identify the more literal cause of such behaviors. We left this work as a future avenue of improvements.

7 Conclusion and Future Work

The conducted experiments looked into how different transformer models performed on a benchmark dataset that had already been used with the SVM model. When it comes to predicting aspects of a text involving an API, the study found that different transformer architectures may outperform SVM. Despite the fact that there is no one architecture that can accurately categorize the text contexts of all sorts of aspects, the experiments yielded several ideas. The greatest issue that surfaced was the restriction of unbalanced data. Furthermore, the findings suggest that models with complicated large architecture have a decreased possibility of producing effective classification results in this experiment. By looking at the performance score, it's evident that there's still room for progress in this field of study. Though the study in this paper focuses on employing several types of transformer models, it does not evaluate all of the models available. There are many other sorts of models that may be employed to construct a system with higher prediction skills in the future. Furthermore, the dataset is rather unbalanced, and balancing it might considerably enhance the findings. Overall, because the necessity of precise API selection is so critical, subsequent research based on the results of the experiments has a lot of promise.

References

1. Creative Commons license - Wikipedia. https://en.wikipedia.org/wiki/Creative_Commons_license. Accessed 1 Apr 2022
2. Stack Overflow - Wikipedia. https://en.wikipedia.org/wiki/Stack_Overflow. Accessed 4 Apr 2022

3. Ashish, V., et al.: Attention is all you need. In: Advances in Neural Information Processing Systems, vol. 30 (2017)
4. Devlin, J., Chang, M.-W., Lee, K., Toutanova, K.: BERT: pre-training of deep bidirectional transformers for language understanding. arXiv preprint arXiv:1810.04805 (2018)
5. Liu, Y., et al.: RoBERTa: a robustly optimized BERT pretraining approach. arXiv preprint arXiv:1907.11692 (2019)
6. Sanh, V., Debut, L., Chaumond, J., Wolf, T.: DistilBERT, a distilled version of BERT: smaller, faster, cheaper and lighter. arXiv preprint arXiv:1910.01108 (2019)
7. Yang, Z., Dai, Z., Yang, Y., Carbonell, J., Salakhutdinov, R.R., Le, Q.V.: XLNet: generalized autoregressive pretraining for language understanding. In: Advances in Neural Information Processing Systems, vol. 32 (2019)
8. Barua, A., Thomas, S.W., Hassan, A.E.: What are developers talking about? An analysis of topics and trends in stack overflow. Empirical Softw. Eng. 1–31 (2012)
9. Mandal, N., Uddin, G.: An empirical study of IoT security aspects at sentence-level in developer textual discussions. Inf. Softw. Technol. **150**, 106970 (2022)
10. Blei, D.M., Ng, A.Y., Jordan, M.I.: Latent Dirichlet allocation. J. Mach. Learn. Res. **3**(4–5), 993–1022 (2003)
11. Kavaler, D., Posnett, D., Gibler, C., Chen, H., Devanbu, P., Filkov, V.: Using and asking: APIs used in the Android market and asked about in StackOverflow. In: Jatowt, A., et al. (eds.) SocInfo 2013. LNCS, vol. 8238, pp. 405–418. Springer, Cham (2013). https://doi.org/10.1007/978-3-319-03260-3_35
12. Parnin, C., Treude, C., Grammel, L., Storey, M.-A.: Crowd documentation: exploring the coverage and dynamics of API discussions on stack overflow. Technical report, Technical report GIT-CS-12-05, Georgia Tech (2012)
13. Uddin, G., Khomh, F.: Automatic mining of opinions expressed about APIs in stack overflow. IEEE Trans. Softw. Eng. **47**(3), 522–559 (2019)
14. Uddin, G., Khomh, F.: Mining API aspects in API reviews. Technical report (2017)
15. Uddin, G., Khomh, F.: Opiner: an opinion search and summarization engine for APIs. In: Proceedings of the $32^n d$ IEEE/ACM International Conference on Automated Software Engineering (ASE 2017), pp. 978–983. IEEE Computer Society (2017)
16. Uddin, G., Khomh, F.: Automatic summarization of API reviews. In: 2017 $32^n d$ IEEE/ACM International Conference on Automated Software Engineering (ASE), pp. 159–170. IEEE (2017)
17. Uddin, G., Baysal, O., Guerrouj, L., Khomh, F.: Understanding how and why developers seek and analyze API-related opinions. IEEE Trans. Softw. Eng. **47**(4), 694–735 (2019)
18. Lin, B., Zampetti, F., Bavota, G., Di Penta, M., Lanza, M.: Pattern-based mining of opinions in Q&A websites. In: 2019 IEEE/ACM $41^s t$ International Conference on Software Engineering (ICSE), pp. 548–559. IEEE (2019)
19. Hu, M., Liu, B.: Mining and summarizing customer reviews. In: Proceedings of the $10^t h$ ACM SIGKDD International Conference on Knowledge Discovery and Data Mining (SIGKDD 2004), pp. 168–177. ACM (2004)
20. Wang, S., Phan, N., Wang, Y., Zhao, Y.: Extracting API tips from developer question and answer websites. In: Proceedings of the $16^t h$ International Conference on Mining Software Repositories (MSR 2019), pp. 321–332. IEEE/ACM (2019)
21. Zhang, Y., Hou, D.: Extracting problematic API features from forum discussions. In: Proceedings of the IEEE $21^s t$ International Conference on Program Comprehension (ICPC 2013), pp. 142–151. IEEE Computer Society (2013)

22. Top 50 Most Popular APIs (Updated for 2022)—RapidAPI. https://rapidapi.com/blog/most-popular-api/. Accessed 11 Apr 2022
23. Raffel, C., et al.: Exploring the limits of transfer learning with a unified text-to-text transformer. arXiv preprint arXiv:1910.10683 (2019)

An Empirical Study on How the Developers Discussed About Pandas Topics

Sajib Kumar Saha Joy[✉], Farzad Ahmed, Al Hasib Mahamud, and Nibir Chandra Mandal

Ahsanullah University of Science and Technology, Dhaka, Bangladesh
`joyjft@gmail.com`, `farzadahmed6@gmail.com`, `{hasib.cse,nibir.cse}@aust.edu`

Abstract. Pandas is defined as a fast, easy open-source software library that is used for data analysis in Python programming language. It is rapidly used in different projects like software development, machine learning, computer vision, natural language processing, robotics, and others. Software developers show huge interest and discussions are becoming dominant in online developer forums, like Stack Overflow (SO) in pandas. Such discussions can help to understand the importance, prevalence, and difficulties of pandas topics. The aim of this work is to find the popularity and difficulty of pandas topics. In this regard, SO posts related to pandas are collected. Topic modeling is done on the textual contents of the posts. We found 26 topics which we further categorized into 5 board categories. We observed that developers discuss variety of pandas topics in SO related to error and excepting handling, visualization, External support, dataframe, and optimization. Also, a trend chart is generated according to the discussion of topics in a predefined time series. The finding of this paper provides a path to help developers, educators, and learners. For example, beginner developers can learn most important topics in pandas. Educators can understand the topics which seem hard to learners and make different tutorials that makes these topic understandable. From empirical study, it is possible to understand the preferences of developers in pandas topic by processing their SO posts.

Keywords: Pandas · Stack Overflow · Natural Language Processing · Empirical Software Engineering

1 Introduction

Pandas is an open source library where python package offers data manipulation and analysis in python programming language. As pandas has high performance and fast productivity for users, it's data analysis capability is utilized in

---

S. K. S. Joy, F. Ahmed and Al. H. Mahamud—Contributed equally to this research.

Md. S. Satu et al. (Eds.): MIET 2022, LNICST 491, pp. 242–255, 2023.
https://doi.org/10.1007/978-3-031-34622-4_19

different sectors of computer science like data visualization, machine learning, data driven software engineering, computer vision, natural language processing etc. Since 2008, the development of pandas has removed the distance between the availability of data analysis tools [4]. Pandas is considered for most suitable option for data analysis tool as it is written in python programming language and easy to understand for new beginner [5].

In the recent years, the utilization of pandas library is increased rapidly as pandas library has reduced the gap between scientific programming languages and database languages [4]. Pandas library is utilized in most of the sectors like machine learning, statistics, natural language processing, computer vision and others. Moreover, pandas library is easy to understand for a beginner and it is open source tool. For these reasons, most of the developers are now showing interest to utilize pandas tools in their projects. For the development of pandas library and it's utilization, a factor is observed that the discussions regarding pandas in online developers forums has increased, such as Stack Overflow (SO). From analysing these post, several findings can be achieved related to pandas library like it's popularity, difficulties, future scopes etc. To date, there are around 22.44 million questions are posted in SO [6]. Several research works are conducted based on SO posts in the field of IoT [8], blockchain [9], microservices [10], software engineering [8]. Some research works are also done based on the functionality, popularity, scope to development of pandas library [4,11,12]. According to the best of our knowledge, no research work is done based on the SO posts of pandas library to find the topics, popularity, scopes of pandas library.

In this research paper, total 236711 SO posts where user defined tags are related to pandas are analyzed to find the topics of pandas library. For topic modeling, Latent Dirichlet Allocation (LDA) is performed. Finally trend chart is generated to find the popularity's of the topics according to the discussions of the software development forums. In this empirical study, some major findings are shown. Among of the major findings, firstly we have found the topics and then we have categories pandas topics which are discussed most in the SO posts. According to the findings of this paper, there are total twenty six topics and these twenty six topics can be categorized into six categories. Among of the topics optimization is the most popular topic though SQL queries and Matplotlib support are the most difficult topics as SQL queries is having the lowest score and Matplotlib support is having the lowest accepted answer rate. Secondly, to make a closer look of the topics and categories, a trend chart is generated from the time slot July 2011 to February 2022. Some decline and arises are seen in the trend chart of the topics but the total number of posts are increased gradually as the total amount of pandas developers increased over time.

The next of the paper is organized in the following way: Sect. 2 discusses the background studies of this paper. Methodology is described in Sect. 3 where data collection, topic modeling and topic naming process are answered. Section 4 discusses implication of studies where several important expositions are described. Section 5 describes threats to the validity of our result. Section 6 describes results of our study where Sect. 7 answers the future scopes to work from the result. Section 8 concludes the paper.

2   Background Studies

2.1   Stack Overflow

Stack Overflow (SO) is considered as a question and answering sites which has become popular in recent times for software developers forum. There are some sites for programmers where programmers can ask questions, can answer other's questions and can share ideas. SO is one of them [4].

2.2   Topic Modeling

Topic modeling can be defined as unsupervised classification method which is similar to clustering data and it is usually used for finding groups of item [15].Though topic modeling is mostly used for textual data, it can be used for bioinformatics data, social science data and other source of data [10].

To apply topic modeling in the SO posts related to pandas, in this paper Latent Dirichlet Allocation (LDA) is used. In LDA, each document is considered as combination of topics and each topic is considered as combination of words [15]. Topic modeling is used in different papers of various fields where SO posts are utilized, specially in the aspects of software engineering development [8].

2.3   Pandas

Pandas is an open source data analysis tool which is built on Python programming language and it is considered as fast, flexible and easy tool [15]. Pandas works in structured dataset and can be leveraged in social science, statistics, finance and other fields [4]. Since the development of pandas in 2008, the main aim of pandas library development is to remove the distance between scientific programming languages and database languages [4].

2.4   Related Works

There are several works related to LDA Topic Modeling [8–10,18–21]. Uddin et al. [8] have done an empirical study based on the IoT discussions of IoT topic on SO posts. For this purpose, authors have gathered IoT posts from SO and have leveraged LDA to perform topic modeling. Four research questions are answered to find the discussion, evolve, question types, popularity and difficulties of IoT topics.

Stephen W. Thomas [16] has leveraged statistical topic modeling in mining software repositories to analyze unstructured and unlabeled data and has found structure in the textual repositories. Bavota et al. [17] have shown the opportunities of Move Method refactoring and have removed Feature Envy bad smells from source code and for this purpose Relational Topic Models are utilized.Nabil et al. [18] have utilized Topic modeling in cloud computing and to discover efficient cloud services, LDA is leveraged. To find the research trends, methodology and fields of further research in blockchain technology, Shahid et al. [19] have used topic modeling for literature analysis of the research. Mandal et al. [8] have utilized statistical topic modeling technique in software system and have found software concerns as topic. Ramage et al. [20] have utilized topic modeling in social sciences to find the barriers of adoption of topic modeling in social science field. Mei et al. [21] have utilized topic modeling in network regularization to explain the difficulties of topic modeling with network structure.

3   Methodology

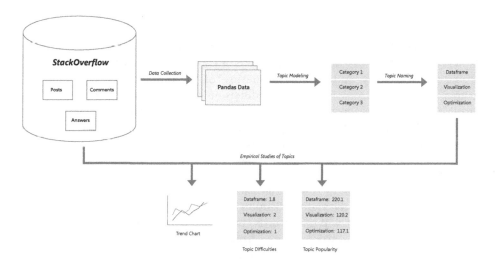

Fig. 1. Proposed Methodology

In this research work, we followed six steps to analyze pandas topic. As there has been no prior work, we began by collecting panda datasets from SO.We collected meta information such as post titles, creation dates, view counts, accepted answers, etc. for pandas posts from SO. Second, we applied LDA topic modeling to get all the discussed pandas topics in SO. From these steps, we only found categorized posts. However, LDA does not provide the topic name associated with each category. Thus, we followed the third step to name each category. In step four, we analyzed the topic using the collected meta information. We created a trend chart to understand how the pandas topic has evolved over time. In addition, we discovered the popularity and difficulties of pandas topics based on topic views, accepted answers, and score. We display an overview of our methodology in Fig. 1.

3.1   Data Collection

We performed our analysis on the dataset that we collected from the Stack Overflow (SO) dump relating to pandas library. We selected SO as it is a site that helps programmers receive facts quicker in the form of a Q&A site. Since

2008, Stack Overflow consisted over 18 million questions, 11 million users and 51 million different visitors monthly [7]. We downloaded the SO dump of July 2022 which is the newest during our analysis. We collected a total of 236711 titles of the post containing user-defined tags related to pandas library from the time period July 2008 to February 2022. The titles that were selected had around 144202 accepted answers related to it which is around 61% of the total titles. Each tuple in our dataset contains the following information: 1. Title of the post 2. Average Score (which is the difference between upvote and downvote of the posts) 3. Average View 4. Accepted Answer Percentage.

3.2 Topic Modelling Using Latent Dirichlet Allocation

Topic modelling can be defined as the function of recognizing topics that best depicts a collection of documents [3]. It is an unsupervised technique of identifying the topics by finding out the nature of the data, like clustering algorithms, which partition the data into different sections. Latent Dirichlet Allocation (LDA) [14] is the most widely used algorithm for Topic Modelling that generates topics based on word frequency in a document. We have used this technique to identify different topics that are present in our dataset. It generates a topic per document model and words per topic model, designed as Dirichlet distribution. The first step of this algorithm is to model each document as a multinomial distribution of topics and each topic as a multinomial distribution of words. Then it picks the right collection of data by assuming that every chunk of text that is fed into it will hold words that are connected to each other. It also deduces that documents are generated from a combination of topics and topics then produces words based on their probability distribution.

3.3 Topic Naming

LDA topic modeling provides topic distributions as the coherence score for each sample. As a result, each sample can be on any of the topics. As such, we select a topic for each sample based on the highest coherence value of the topics following O'callagha et al. [2]. Thus, each sample has a topic for which the sample has the maximum coherence score among all topics. Now, each topic has a set of samples. However, these topics have no definitive label as the LDA model only provides scores. Therefore, we label each topic manually by analyzing all the samples. To label these topics, the authors first virtually meet and analyze all the samples for each topic. Then we come up with their possible topic domains and share them with each other. We continue this until all authors unanimously agreed on the topic labeling. For example, a developer asks *'Matplotlib Axes legend shows only one label in barh'* in SO. As this post is related to a Python library that is used for data visualization, we label this post 'Data Visualization'. We finally group all of the labeled topics into larger groups by consulting with one another.For example, we find two topics labeled as 'Optimization' and 'Parallel Processing'. As these topics are related to optimization programming, we group them into a single category titled 'Optimizing'.

Sub Topics	Sample Title
Data Visualization Support	How do I plot subplots with different labels from pandas dataframe columns using matplotlib
Bar Chart Plotting	Pandas Bar plot, how to annotate grouped horizontal bar charts
Matplotlib support in Pandas	Show categorical x-axis values when making line plot from pandas Series in matplotlib
Error Handling: Floating Point Error	How do I overcome the TypeError: cannot convert the series to <class 'float'> error
Error Handling: Index Error	Python (Jupyter Notebook) : Pandas copying dataframe index causing length of value not matching length of index error
Error Handling: Import Error	Import Error: Cannot import name "IO" from typing" while importing pandas
Missing value handling	Get pandas.read_csv to read empty fields as NaN, and empty strings as empty strings
Pivot Table	Applying aggregate function on columns of Pandas pivot table
Dataframe Aggregation	Grouping columns of dataframe by other dataframe and calculate weighted average of aggregated columns
Dataframe Conversion	Convert nested dict containing nested list to pandas dataframe
Dataframe Sorting	Sorting a DataFrame such that NA values on the first sort column would be at the end regardless of the secondary sort columns
Dataframe Dimensionality	Pandas MultiIndex multi-dimentional intersection
Dataframe Concatenation	Join in Pandas similar to SQL Inner Join
Dataframe Update	Python. Update one dataframe with data from other dataframe (many columns) and exclude non-updated rows
Index Ordering	Pandas reset multilevel index order
Dataframe Filtering	Filtering dataframe based on items present in column
Time Series Analysis	Generating regular time series from irregular time series in pandas
Header	Converting specific column values to header and header to column values
Dataframe Slicing Operation	Select dataframe slice using condition on a separate dataframe
SQL Queries	Python - Conditional Word Frequencies in Dataframe w/ SQL style Search terms
File Operation	Python: How to copy Excel worksheet from multiple Excel files to one Excel file that contains all the worksheets from other Excel files
DateTime Functionality	Extract data from starting month and year to end month and year not working python pandas
Numpy supports in pandas	Replacing dash value from another dataframe on the basis of common user id Python Pandas Numpy
String Operation	Pandas dataframe replace the character in specific positions, without changing similar characters on other positions
Parallel Processing	How to parallelize the row wise Pandas dataframe's apply() method
Optimization	How to optimize code that iterates on a big dataframe in Python

Fig. 2. Sample post title for different categories

3.4   Empirical Analysis

Trend Chart. We used trend chart to illustrate the trend of our topics over time. It depicts the number posts that were made from July 2011 to February 2022 in Stack Overflow on the broad categories of the topics. We calculated number of posts created in each six months for each topics. We constructed line chart using those calculated values. By analysing the trend chart we can observe different characteristics of pandas topics. We can see at what time what specific pandas topic was popular. In short we can find the most trendy topics over different time periods. Also by inspecting the trend chart we can notice whether stack overflow changes with the real world events. We can directly correlate the change in curve of the line graph of the trend chart with change in the real world.

Topic Difficulties. Finding difficulties of each topic may help us to detect strenuous topics. By using the information about what topics are difficult, reason behind the difficulties can be investigated. Then by finding out the catalyst of laboriousness, developers can work on and can renovate the library in an easier way. This is why we preferred to measure topic difficulties. We explored the difficulties of the topics in our dataset. We analyzed the Score and Accepted Answer Rate of the titles in our dataset to find the difficulty of the titles in our dataset. The titles that have the lowest Score and the lowest Accepted Answer Rate is considered to be the most difficult topic in our dataset. We also further discussed the measures that can be taken to make the difficult topics more familiar to the programmers and developers.

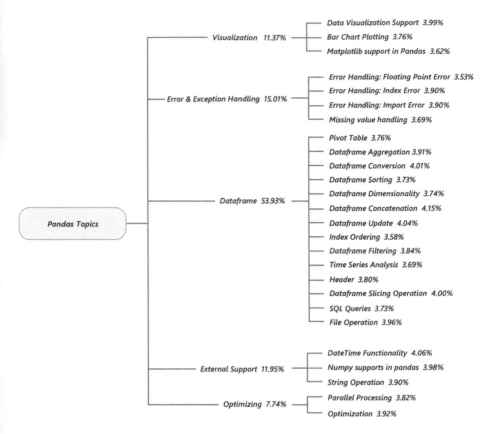

Fig. 3. Topic Distribution

$$Avg.\ View\ for\ Topic_i = \frac{Total\ \#\ of\ views\ for\ all\ posts\ in\ Topic_i}{Total\ Posts} \quad (1)$$

$$Score\ for\ Topic_i = \frac{Total\ Score\ of\ all\ posts\ in\ Topic_i}{Total\ Posts} \quad (2)$$

$$Accepted\ Answer\ Rate\ for\ Topic_i = \frac{\#\ of\ Accepted\ Answer\ in\ Topic_i * 100}{Total\ posts\ in\ Topic_i} \quad (3)$$

Topic Popularity. As pandas library is expanding day by day, some of the topics are being obsoleted while others are being used more frequently. These used topics or popular topics can give us insightful information, such as the community's demand for pandas topics. This is critical information for newcomers because they must begin with topics that are frequent, easy, and demanding. This helps them keep up to date with the community. Moreover, topic popularity is also useful for the research community to track user views for any new topics. Thus, we studied popularity. To study this, we followed the view count of each post, as there is no concrete formula to calculate popularity. Thus, we calculated Avg. View for each topic using Eq. 1. By finding the most popular topics, our model can encourage developers and programmers to focus more on the popular topics or start with the relatively easier topics.

4   Result and Discussion

We have divided the Result and Discussion section into 4 parts: Pandas Topic, Evolution of Pandas Topics, Trend Chart Interpretation and Analysing Topic Popularity and Difficulty. In Sect. 4.1, closer observation on each topic is discussed. About the growth of different pandas topics are discussed in Sect. 4.2 and in Sect. 4.3, we interpreted the trend of the topics over time with the help of trend chart. Lastly, in Sect. 4.4 we have analysed topic popularity and difficulty.

4.1   Pandas Topic

From Fig. 3 we can observe that the pandas titles were divided into 26 topics and these 26 topics were further categorized into 5 broader topics. Example titles of all the 26 topics have been shown in Table 2. Our observation on the 26 topics are described below:

o **Data Visualization Support:** We found that there exists enough discussion in SO related to data visualization supports, such as subplotting problems, labelling problems, etc. So all the titles that fall under this category were put in this topic. The titles under this topic make 3.93% of all the titles that we collected.

o **Bar Chart Plotting:** We have observed that 3.76% of all the titles that we have collected from SO were made on Bar Chart Plotting. Titles containing discussions relating to combining stacks to a Bar Chart, annotating barchart, coloring grouped barchat, etc. were put under this topic.

o **Matplotlib support in Pandas:** A lot of discussion relating to Matplotlib support in SO have been made, for example, discussion relating to grid, problems relating to drawing multiple graphs etc. These titles make up 3.62% of all the titles that we collected.

o **Error Handling: Floating Point Error:** Our SO dataset contained a lot of titles containing Error Handling of Floating Point Error specifically conversion error and retrieving error of floating point values. Posts containing these queries are put under this topic.

o **Error Handling: Index Error:** SO posts containing index error while using pandas library, such as length not matching index, were put in this category.

o **Error Handling: Import Error:** SO posts in our dataset containing queries relating to importing pandas library, csv files in pandas, data reader and many other import errors are put in this category.

o **Missing value handling:** Missing value handling is very important specially for machine learning models. Under this topic, users generally asked for support to fill missing values or drop rows which contains some missing values or NAN value.

o *Pivot Table:* This topic contains posts about aggregating and grouping data in the pivot table.

o *Dataframe Aggregation:* SO posts under this topic contained queries about executing operations on multiple columns in the dataframe to create new columns in the dataframe.

o *Dataframe Conversion:*JSON file to dataframe or dictionary to dataframe related queries are can be found under this topic.

o *Dataframe Sorting:* Sorting dataframe according to certain column, multilevel sorting related consultations are the most common title under this category.

o *Dataframe Dimensionality:* Dimentionality related discussions are assigned in this topic.

o *Dataframe Concatenation:* User queries related to concatenating two different dataframe with the help of a common column is sorted under this topic.

o *Dataframe Update:*Discussions related to updating dataframe, dropping row or column can be found under this topic.

o *Index Ordering:*Ordering index properly, multilevel index ordering, index mismatch related discussions can be found most in this category.

o *Dataframe Filtering:*Posts related to filtering data according to some criteria are assigned here.

o *Time Series Analysis:* Preparing dataframe to make it suitable for time series analysis was the main focus of this topic.

o *Header:*Modifying pandas dataframe header, setting column name, extracting column name these sort of discussions are assigned in this topic.

o *Dataframe Slicing Operation:* Discussions related to dataframe slicing are sorted in this topic. This topic contains 4% of all the posts.

o *SQL Queries:*How operations that are analogous to SQL queries can be applied to a pandas dataframe is the key theme of this topic.

o *File Operation:*Data of pandas dataframe can be saved in different file format like excel. This sort of posts are associated with this topic.

o *DateTime Functionality:*Formatting date and time from raw string, filtering data that exist within a given time interval are the keywords of this topic.

o *Numpy supports in pandas:*Numpy is a well known library in python for mathematical operations. A lot of users tried to apply different operations that can be done with numpy on pandas dataframe. This kind of posts lie in this category. This topic contains 3.98% of all the posts.

o *String Operation:*Posts related to modifying string of a particular column are assigned in this category.

o *Parallel Processing:*In this category the post of users, who were seeking help to take the advantage of processing data parallelly to make the best use of time, are sorted.

o *Optimization:*Same task can be performed by writing different code. In this category, users posted in SO to find optimized way to solve certain problems.

We further categorized this topics into five broad categories, i.e., 'Visualization', 'Error & Exception Handling', 'Dataframe', 'External Support', and 'Optimizing'. We found that most of the topics are under 'Dataframe' category which covers 53.92% posts. This categories includes all discussion related to 'Dataframe Aggregation', 'Pivot Table', 'Dataframe Conversion', 'Dataframe Sorting', 'Dataframe Update', 'Header', 'ataframe Dimensionality', 'Dataframe Concatenation', 'Time Series Analysis', 'Index Ordering', 'Dataframe Filtering', 'Dataframe Slicing Operation', 'SQL Queries', and 'File Operations'. The second largest category is 'Error & Exception Handling'. It covers 4 topics and 18.01% posts. Among the other three categories, 'Visualization' and 'External Supports' covers 3 topics and 2 topics are covered by 'Optimizing' category. We found that developers actively discuss 'External Support' while using pandas library. Moreover, we observed that those discussion includes compatibility of pandas library with external libraries, feasibility of using external libraries, performance of those libraries, etc. This indicates that the community should focus on these external libraries to facilitate the usages in pandas library. This requirements demands further investigation on 'External Support' in pandas which we left as our future work.

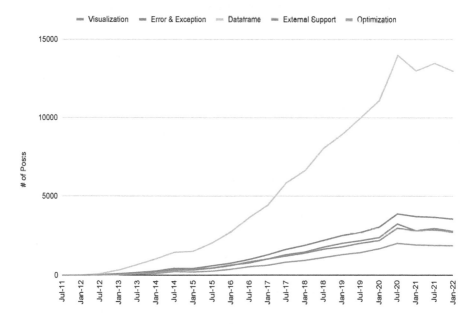

Fig. 4. Trend Chart

4.2   Evolution of Pandas Topics

From the trend chart in Fig. 4, it can be observed that the number of posts under different topics gradually increased over time. This behaviour is expected as the community is growing day by day. Dataframe category dominates the others by a large margin, and it continues to grow every year. The least discussed topic is 'Optimization'. The distribution of 'External Support' category and 'Visualization' category is nearly analogous over the given time frame. We also find the second ranked discussion topic is 'Error & Exceptions' which is also piling up as time passes by.

4.3   Trend Chart Interpretation

A closer look at the Fig. 4 notifies us that from January 2017 to July 2020, there is a massive upswing of pandas discussions. This indicates that pandas developers are adopting pandas library for their development work more than ever before. However, it can be noticed that after July 2020, the number of posts for all the categories tends to decline by a very small margin. We investigated this fall of pandas discussions. We find that a massive pandemic outbreak took place in early 2020, which shook the world [1]. This event forced the world to shut down for a while [1]. As such, the activity of the developer community reduced by this life threatening virus. As a result, pandas discussions were also hindered and had a downward slope. As a follow up to this event, we find an upward swing in January 2021, when the world get normal for a while [1]. However, this didn't last long as the virus continued to breakout again during 2021 [1]. This resulted in another lockdown, and developer activities were hampered as usual. As an immediate effect, we find another drop in pandas discussion in January 2022.

Topics	Sub Topics	Post Count	Average Score	Average View	Accepted Answer Rate
Visualization	Data Visualization Support	9433	2.23	2795	4.06
	Bar Chart Plotting	8909	2.24	3169	4.05
	Matplotlib support in Pandas	8577	2.01	2428	**2.96**
Error and Exception Handling	Error Handling: Floating Point Error	8357	1.86	2371	4
	Error Handling: Index Error	9220	1.86	2335	4.1
	Error Handling: Import Error	9230	2.2	2697	3.85
	Missing value handling	8732	2.32	3071	4.04
DataFrame	Pivot Table	8896	2.09	2609	4.2
	Dataframe Aggregation	9248	1.89	2377	4.13
	Dataframe Conversion	9482	1.87	2195	4.09
	Dataframe Sorting	8830	2.14	2520	4.11
	Dataframe Dimensionality	8852	2.05	2309	4.21
	Dataframe Concatenation	**9822**	2.03	2303	4.12
	Dataframe Update	9558	1.98	2307	4.08
	Index Ordering	8485	2.03	2275	4.11
	Dataframe Filtering	9088	2.24	2948	4.05
	Time Series Analysis	8740	2.1	2663	4.08
	Header	8985	2.18	2787	4.1
	Dataframe Slicing Operation	9465	1.92	2319	4.15
	SQL Queries	8826	**1.74**	2256	4.06
	File Operation	9372	2.07	2846	3.86
External Support	DateTime Functionality	9621	1.82	2273	4.1
	Numpy supports in pandas	9431	1.82	2388	3.97
	String Operation	9227	1.85	2397	4.16
Optimizing	Parallel Processing	9046	1.84	2075	3.93
	Optimization	9279	2.35	**3193**	3.99

Fig. 5. Topic Hierarchy Statistics

4.4   Analysing Topic Popularity and Difficulty

From Fig. 5 we can see that the most popular topic is Optimization as it has the most views. This means the programmer community is more concerned about how they can optimize their code while using pandas library. So, this shows that the developers need to emphasize more on the functionalities of optimization of pandas library to create a better coding experience for the programmers using this library. The researchers are also interested to make their research more optimized so that they can make their model more efficient, so the developers can collaborate with the researchers to make the optimization part of pandas library more handy for the research users. We can also see the that second most popular topic is Bar Chart Plotting as it has the second most views. The least most popular topic is SQL queries as it has the least amount of views. As SQL queries is a topic of database, it is not that important in the domain of pandas library. So developers show less interest in this specific topic.

From Fig. 5, we can see that the topic containing the highest Average Score of 2.35 is Optimization and the lowest Average Score of 1.74 is SQL Queries. The topic Matplotlib support in Pandas contains the lowest Accepted Answer Rate of 2.96 and Dataframe Slicing Operation contains the highest Accepted Answer Rate of 4.15. We can also observe from Fig. 5 that the most difficult topics in pandas library are SQL queries as it has the lowest Score and Matplotlib support in Pandas as it has the lowest Accepted Answer Rate. This means the general programmers struggle most in these topics. So the experts in pandas library can analyze these topics more to make the programmers use these topics more effectively.

5   Implication of Studies

Several important expositions can be observed from our work.

   o **Learner:** The enthusiastic learners who are trying to digest pandas library, can gain some idea about the popularity of different topics associated with pandas. This will paint a pathway for the learners to grasp pandas library in a more structured manner. To speed up their learning process they can learn relatively easier topics first. They can also prioritize their learning process according to the popularity of the topic if they want.
   o **Research Community:** Researchers, developers, marketers can analyze and decide what topics questions are frequently asked, and on what topics questions are frequently answered. Developers can see also which topics are popular for marketing purpose so that they can add new handy features on that. Rate of accepted answers can also be seen from our work by means of which the developers can work on the topics that has less accepted answers.
   o **Educators:** Instructors community of pandas can understand which topics need to be more focused based on the difficulty level of different topics. They can analyze the more difficult topics and make materials on it to better educate the learners on those specific topics. They can also contribute to the queries that has lower number of accepted answer.

o *Data science community* Those who are involved in data analysis can contribute more to the community by finding difficult problem and solve them in a easier convenient way. The community can also observe the trends of the evolving topics related to pandas.

6 Threats to Validity

There are certain factors that can impede the righteousness of our work. If any complementary library of pandas arises in future, our model will not be as impactful as it stands today. Then the study can be shifted to the another library analogous to pandas. Besides, we have considered the most upvoted posts while structuring our model. If this system changed, our model may not be valid anymore. Because with the change of scoring system our model could not relate to the new scoring system. Moreover, if some portion of data that we have used in our model is erased by Stack Overflow, our model will not be irrefutable. In addition, while modeling different topics, we assigned each title to a certain topic by manual observation. But there were cases where a single title might be categorized as multiple topics that avert our models purity.

7 Future Work

Our work could be expanded by investigating the popular and difficult topics further. We plan to break down the difficult topics to a greater extent so that we can understand the tendency of the general programmer, whether the reason for the those topics to be difficult is actually it's difficulty or reluctance of the general programmers to learn those topics.

8 Conclusion

In this study, we explored pandas library associated argument on Stack Overflow (SO) and employed topic modeling to institute different topics. We have added several findings about it. Pandas learners discuss a variety of topics in SO related to Visualization, Error and Exception Handling, DataFrame, External Support and Optimization. All these topics are exploding swiftly. Among them Dataframe is the most discussed topic because of its huge usage. Impactful factors like topic difficulties, topic usage, post count of different can be observed from our work which can act as the catalyst for the different pandas contributors to improve techniques, tools, and methods related to pandas.

References

1. Wu, Y.-C., Chen, C.-S., Chan, Y.-J.: The outbreak of COVID-19: an overview. J. Chin. Med. Assoc. **83**(3), 217 (2020)
2. O'callaghan, D., et al.: An analysis of the coherence of descriptors in topic modeling. Expert Syst. Appl. **42**(13), 5645–5657 (2015)

3. Brett, M.R.: Topic modeling: a basic introduction. J. Digital Humanities **2**(1), 1–2 (2012)
4. McKinney, W.: pandas: a foundational Python library for data analysis and statistics. Python High Performance Sci. Comput. **14**(9), 1–9 (2011)
5. Stepanek, H.: Thinking in Pandas: How to Use the Python Data Analysis Library the Right Way. Apress (2020)
6. Stack Overflow Questions, https://stackoverflow.com/questions/. Accessed 11 April 2022
7. Stack Overflow - a Winner at a Turning Point, https://digital.hbs.edu/platform-digit/submission/stack-overflow-a-winner-at-a-turning-point. Accessed 11 April 2022
8. Nibir, M., Gias, U.: An empirical study of IoT security aspects at sentence-level in developer textual discussions. Inform. Softw. Technol. **150**, 0950–5849 (2022) 106970
9. Wan, Z., Xia, X., Hassan, A.E.: What is discussed about blockchain? a case study on the use of balanced lda and the reference architecture of a domain to capture online discussions about blockchain platforms across the stack exchange communities. IEEE Trans. Softw. Eng. **01**, 1–1 (2019)
10. Bandeira, A., Medeiros, C.A., Paixao, M., Maia, P.H.: We need to talk about microservices: an analysis from the discussions on StackOverflow. In: Proceedings of the 16th International Conference on Mining Software Repositories (MSR '19). IEEE Press, 255–259 (2019)
11. McKinney, W.: Pandas, python data analysis library. https://pandas.pydata.org (2015)
12. Nelli, F.: Python Data Analytics: Data Analysis and Science using PANDAs. Apress, Matplotlib and the Python Programming Language (2015)
13. Chakraborty, P., Shahriyar, R., Iqbal, A., Uddin, G.: How Do Developers Discuss and Support New Programming Languages in Technical Q&A Site? An Empirical Study of Go, Swift, and Rust in Stack Overflow. Information and Software Technology (IST) (2021)
14. Blei, D.M., Ng, A.Y. and Jordan, M.I.: Latent dirichlet allocation. J. Mach. Learn. Res. **3**(Jan), 993–1022 (2003)
15. pandas. https://pandas.pydata.org/. Accessed 20 April 2022
16. Thomas, S.W.: Mining software repositories using topic models. In: 2011 33rd International Conference on Software Engineering (ICSE), pp. 1138–1139 (2011)
17. Bavota, G., Oliveto, R., Gethers, M., Poshyvanyk, D., De Lucia, A.: Methodbook: recommending move method refactorings via relational topic models. IEEE Trans. Software Eng. **40**(7), 671–694 (2014). https://doi.org/10.1109/TSE.2013.60
18. Nabli, H., Djemaa, R., Amous, I.: Efficient cloud service discovery approach based on LDA topic modeling. J. Syst. Softw. **146**, 233–248 (2018)
19. Shahid, M., Jungpil, H.: A Cross-Disciplinary Review of Blockchain Research Trends and Methodologies: Topic Modeling Approach (2020)
20. Ramage, D., et al.: Topic modeling for the social sciences. In: NIPS 2009 workshop on applications for topic models: text and beyond, vol. 5. (2009)
21. Mei, Q., et al.: Topic modeling with network regularization. In: Proceedings of the 17th International Conference on World Wide Web (2008)

BSDRM: A Machine Learning Based Bug Triaging Model to Recommend Developer Team

K. M. Aslam Uddin[1]([✉])(iD), Md. Kowsher[2](iD), and Kazi Sakib[1]

[1] Institute of Information Technology, University of Dhaka, Dhaka, Bangladesh
{mph003,sakib}@iit.du.ac.bd
[2] Department of Computer Science, Stevens Institute of Technology,
Hoboken, NJ, USA

Abstract. Bug triage assigns bugs to developers by mapping properties with past experiences. Without this process, many experienced developers may overwhelm with more assignments, whereas new developers are underwhelmed. Therefore, we propose a machine learning bug triaging approach called Bug Solving Developer Recommendation Model (BSDRM) to solve this issue by assigning developers. We first gather several datasets to combine and split them into train and test sets. Then, we create a sentence-embedded model from training set and generate a bag of developer's words. Instead, test set is transformed into a vocabulary list using an embedded model. BSDRM recommends some eligible developers by matching the developer's bag of words and vocabulary list of bug reports using K-Nearest Neighbour (KNN). A developer classification model categorizes these developers into experienced, newly experienced, and fresh graduate developers. It consists of Decision Tree (DT), Extra Tree (ET), AdaBoost (AdC), Bagging Classifier (BC), Gradient Boosting (GB), KNN, Nearest Centroid (NC), Bernoulli Naïve Bayes (BNB), Multinomial Naïve Bayes (MNB), Complement Naïve Bayes (CoNB), Gaussian Naïve Bayes (GNB), Logistic Regression (LR), Perceptron (Pr), and Multi-Layer Perceptron (MLP) produces individual outcomes of these classifiers. In this case, BC shows 96.59% accuracy to categorize developers with different experience levels. Based on these results, a developer team is recommended to solve testing bugs.

Keywords: Bug Triage · Machine Learning · BSDRM · Bug Report · Developer

1 Introduction

Bug triage is a process where each bug is prioritized based on its severity, frequency, risk etc. This procedure is helpful to justify different severities of bugs and assign appropriate resources for fixing them. It reduces time to enhance the quality of software. There are many software companies that continuously

Md. S. Satu et al. (Eds.): MIET 2022, LNICST 491, pp. 256–270, 2023.
https://doi.org/10.1007/978-3-031-34622-4_20

generate a massive amount of bug reports. When a new bug report is found, several skilled developers are worked on this bug to fix it. In this case, experienced developers are overwhelmed by the assignment of numerous bugs. Instead, new and mid-skilled developers do not get proper opportunities to fix sufficient amounts of bugs. Sometimes, many experienced developers come from other fields to perform this job. Therefore, it is required to assign bugs to different kinds of developers where they get knowledge and experience in bug solving.

We explore available information of bug reports such as severity, priority, source code, and commit logs to find appropriate developers for analyzing their issues. Recent commits are helpful to get the current activities of developers. Instead, previous records are used to define a developer's proficiency for a particular type of bug. Nonetheless, many fresh graduates (i.e., who have no experience in fixing any bugs) join in the company. In most cases, they are not used to doing such tasks before. On the other hand, some developers gather certain experiences to solve various types of bugs. Besides, developers who switch from another development project are assigned to fix received bugs. Both of these groups are treated as new experienced developers. However, they do not get more bugs to enhance their qualities. In these circumstances, experienced developers become overloaded and unable to fix numerous bugs in the expected time frame. Thus, freshers and new experienced developers are required to engage in the bug fixing tasks. If we build a developer team with experienced, new professionals, fresh graduates, all types of developers are got chance to solve recently arrived bugs. In addition, this team is more useful to solve newly arrived bugs in collaborative ways. As a result, skilled developers are overlooked more bugs and newly joined developers can learn how to solve them.

Numerous methods have been proposed in previous works to understand the impact of bug assignments. Baysal et al. [4] provided a bug triage method that combined different developers' proficiency. They identified expert developers to analyze historical records and suggested required distribution. However, this method is not considered for new fixers. Hu et al. [9] proposed a method called BugFixer, which built a Developer Component Bug (DCB) network using historical bug reports. To prioritize high relevance between the chronological list and new bugs, they recommended a developer list. However, their model does not provide any association of new developers. Zhang et al. [35] represented a team assignment approach called K-nearest-neighbor Search And heterogeneous Proximity (KSAP). This model creates an assorted network from previous bug reports and assigns a team based on their association. The critical drawback of this work is to over-prioritize individual developers' antique actions and does not recommend about new developers assign bugs. Khatun et al. [11] anticipated a Team Allocation technique to ensure bug assignment for both existing and new developers (TAEN). They generated a heterogeneous network from previous bug reports. It suggests a team of N developers based on TAEN score and current workloads. Nevertheless, they do not specify newly experienced developers in their work.

Machine learning is a study of algorithms that automatically improves to take a particular decision by investigating previous records. In this work, we propose a machine learning-based model called Bug Solving Developer Recommendation Model (BSDRM), which recommends a developer team combining experts, medium fixers or skilled developers of other domains, and fresh graduates to solve newly arrival bugs. In this model, all datasets are merged and created into a developer matrix. We divide this matrix into training and testing sets. Also, the training set is split into two parts. Then, we fit one part of this training set with a sentence embedding model that generates a bag of developers' words. Instead, a developer classifier is fitted with another training set that contains various classifiers like DT, ET, AdC, BC, GB, KNN, NC, BNB, MNB, CoNB, GNB, LR, Pr, and MLP. When we evaluate several new bug reports/testing instances, this embedded model generates a vocabulary list from them. Then, eligible developers are extracted by matching the bag of developers' words and testing the vocabulary list using an unsupervised KNN finder. The developer classifier is used to categorize these developers into Experienced Developer (ED), New Experienced Developer (NED), and Fresh Graduate (FG). Then, we combine these developer groups and make a bug-fixing team.

Eclipse, Mozilla, and Netbeans are used in a case study of open source projects to assess BSDRM. The data matrix is manually weighed and labeled with ED, NED, and FG. When a group of developers is identified, individual classifiers are employed to classify them as ED, NED, and FG. Thus, BC shows the highest accuracy (96.59%), and F-measure (96.59%) in this work.

2   Literature Review

Due to the significance of various bug assignment procedures, existing techniques are categorized into text exploration, tossing graph, cost-aware, activity, source, fuzzy, time, relevant search, and novice developer recommendation model. These models are briefly described as follows.

Text exploration approaches are investigated previous records and predicted the rank of developers [1,3,4,9,15,18]. Zhang et al. [34] suggested a BUg triage by topic modeling and heTERogeneous network analysis approach (BUTTER), which automatically assigns bugs to the developers. There are included both textual and structural data in bug reports. It employs Latent Dirichlet Allocation (LDA) to categorize texts into various topics. Also, a heterogeneous network is used to collect structural data for developers. Then, the RankClass model is trained based on the topic model and structural data. When a new bug report comes, LDA and RankClass are used to classify the final topics of the bug. This distribution provides a developer list to be assigned for a certain bug. However, this approach does not consider new developers. Hu et al. [9] proposed a bug triaging method called BugFixer that builds based on the past bug-fixing information. It creates a Developer-Component-Bug (DCB) network to connect developers, components, features, and related bugs. BugFixer computes the similarity between the new and existing bugs through the DCB network. Then, it depicts the ranked list of developers. Again, it does not consider new developers.

Tossy graph/length-based techniques recommend by developers for fixing bugs [2,5,10,27]. Jeong et al. [10] proposed a graph model which captures the tossing probabilities among developers from tossing history. It produces a low-qualified developer list and does not mention new developers. Yadav et al. [29] improved an algorithm for decreasing bug tossing length based on the Developer Skills Record (DSR). They created a two-step model where DSR is made for each developer from any five datasets. In the second step, they listed all competent developers who provide accurate predictions and effectively reduce bug tossing length. However, this model does not ponder new developers.

Park ct al. [19] developed a cost-aware developer ranking algorithm named CosTriage. The authors noticed a problem related to Content-Based Recommendation (CBR), which offers only experienced developers and solved associated bugs. For this reason, they are overloaded, and the bug-solving process becomes slower. In CosTriage, it optimizes performance (i.e., accuracy and cost) and combines a Collaborative Filtering Recommender (CFR) with CBR. It adopts content boosted collaborative filtering (CBCF) for ranking developers. The authors only considered previous bug history; thus, CosTriage fails to assign newly-appointed developers. Naguib et al. [17] proposed an activity-based bug triaging strategy which classifies existing bug reports into topics using LDA and creates an activity profile for each developer. When a new bug report has arrived, this strategy ranks the developer list based on the relevance between individual developer profiles and the topics of this bug report. Moreover, it does not consider new developers.

Source-based bug assignment techniques were proposed [6,12,15] to fix a new bug. Matter et al. [15] suggested a source-based expertize model called DEV-ELECT (i.e., a portmanteau word of developer and dialect) that parses source code and version history for recommending developers. It extracts a bag of words from each source code contributor. This model is trained with current vocabularies and created by a team-author matrix. It checks lexical similarities and developer keywords in a new report. However, this technique is hugely dependent on experienced developers. It also increases bug re-assignments, and delays and lessens recommendation accuracy. Mani et al. [14] used a Deep Bi-directional Recurrent Neural Network with Attention (DBRNN-A) which learns semantic and synthetic features from a long word sequence. Further, different bug reports are analyzed where DBRNN-A provides a higher rank-10 average accuracy using MNB, Cosine Distance, SVM [13], and softmax classifier. It preserves a word's order and semantic relationship in a more extended context.

Some researchers provided social network-based developer recommendations to accelerate this work [8,33]. Zhang et al. [32] proposed an integrated bug triage algorithm to improve the social network developer recommendation process. At first, a probability model analyzes its social network and determines candidate developers. Later, the experience model investigates a number of fixed bugs and solves each developer's cost as the estimated factor. It uses the smoothed Unigram Model (UM) and recommends appropriate developers for fixing a new bug. It suggests experienced developers but does not estimate new developers.

Xie et al. [28] proposed a topic-based approach called Developer REcommendation based on TOpic Models (DRETOM), which recommends developers to utilize their bug fixing history. The authors used the Topic Modeling Toolbox (TMT) to create a topic from existing bug reports. A probabilistic model calculates a developer's problem-solving probability based on interest and expertise. It determines the relationship between developers and bug reports. When a new bug report appears, different topics are determined by previous topic models. Then, DRETOM calculates the probability of each developer and ranks the developers in descending order. Finally, top K-developers are recommended to fix new bug reports. Again, this method does not consider new developers. Tamrawi et al. [25] proposed Bugzie which is fuzzy set-based modeling of developers for bug-fixing skills. The fuzzy set determines relevant developers who are suited to solve bugs. The membership function of a developer belongs to a fuzzy set. Also, it is computed with several terms derived from solved bug reports. When a new report is resolved, this function is updated. In this situation, these terms are extracted and recommended by a developer-ranked list based on their membership scores. This method urges developers to use past fixing history. However, it does not indicate newly appointed developers.

Time-based assignment techniques are proposed in the following [16,23]. Shokripour et al. [23] formulated a time-metadata method where all source code entities are parsed and connected with contributors to construct a corpus. When a new bug is found, several keywords are searched and provided weighted-based frequency with time metadata. Therefore, the high-scored developers are used at the top list. Khatun et al. [12] suggested a strategy called Bug fixing and Source commit activity-based Bug Assignment (BSBA). It contains three modules: source activity collection module, fixing history collection module, and developer suggestion module. The source activity collection module has constructed an index of the developer's source code activities. Besides, the fixing history collection module is built another index for connecting bug keywords with fixing time. Then, the developer suggestion module is employed to make queries into two indexes with new bug keywords. The top-scored developers are suggested as suitable fixers based on the query results.

Various types of techniques were used to suggest developers for solving different bugs. Most of them were trained by previous bug fixing histories. Besides, they extracted relevant topics/keywords by matching developer profiles and newly arrival bug reports. Then, they identified top experts for fixing bugs. In this case, many models are utilized a few information sources that provide shallow performance to identify suitable developers. When many newly generated bug reports arrive, experienced developers are overloaded with them. However, these models are not incorporated more instances of mid-level specialists, other domain experts, and newly graduated developers. As a result, this model represents less opportunity for them to learn about bug fixing.

3   Materials and Methods

This section explains how BSDRM recommends a qualified development team to fix bugs. Thus, the description of working bug reports and overall team suggestion procedure is given as follows.

3.1   Data Description

Eclipse, Mozilla, and Netbeans are widely used as large-scale open source projects in various bug triage studies. These datasets consist of source code, commit logs and bug reports of these projects from Bugzilla. They contain different types of variables namely severity, priority, fix status, platform or hardware, assignee, single developer, first assignee, developer comments, summary (title), and description. BSDRM uses this dataset to investigate and recommend developers for fixing bugs. We collect 13,7,147 bug reports between 2001 to 2020, 13,2,261 bug reports between 1999 to 2020, and 44,149 bug reports between 2001 and 2017 from Eclipse, Mozilla, and NetBeans, respectively.

3.2   Proposed Bug Solving Developer Recommendation Model (BSDRM)

In this section, we propose a machine learning-based bug triage approach called BSDRM which recommends a developer team with ED, NED and FG developers. Figure 1 represents the working steps of this model which is briefly described as follows.

– **Generating Developer Matrix:** We combine Eclipse, Mozilla, and NetBeans datasets where 56621 instances are gathered. This dataset is called the developer matrix. Each row represents each developer instance. However, they are not categorized/labeled according to their expertise. Thus, we consider three categories such as ED, NED, and FG to assess their skills. The brief description of these categories are defined as follows.

   1. **ED profile:** Developers who fix a large number of bugs as single developers, comment on various issues, assign as first developers into many bugs, and solve more prioritized and critical bugs are considered as ED. This work finds ED who fixes at least 200 bugs, comments on 1000 or more issues and assigns around 500 bugs as first developers.
   2. **NED profile:** If a fixer solves a moderate amount of bugs, comments on some issues, assigns as the first developer in some bugs, they are called NED. Again, some developers are experts in another software domain. If they are now working on bug fixing tasks, these developers are also

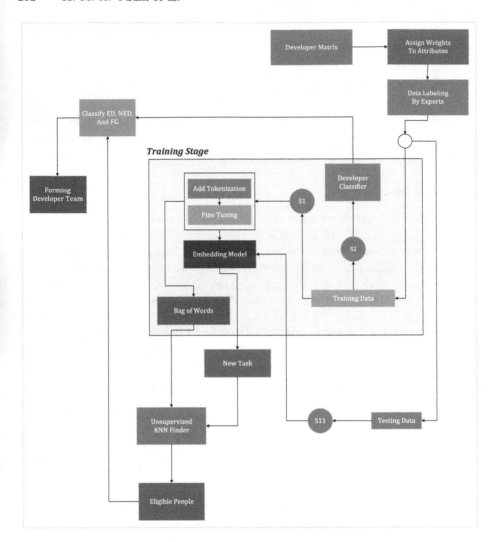

Fig. 1. The Workflow Diagram of BSDRM, Machine Learning based Developer Recommendation Model for Bug Triage

considered as NED. This work defines NED which solves almost 100–200 bugs, comments on less than 1000 bug reports, and is assigned less than 500 as first developers.

3. **FG profile:** Developers who have just passed from academia and started their career in bug fixing are taken as FG. In these circumstances, they do not have enough working experience.So, their histories are not available in the existing bug repository. The authority can give a predefined form to assess FGs skills such as academic knowledge, technical expertise, interests, developed projects, etc.

According to their importance, we manually assign weights to individual features and determined every developer's expert level [7, 24, 30]. We also emphasize more on human inspection rather than quantitative approaches. This labeled dataset is reviewed by some specialists to assess this manipulation. Then, it is split into 80% training and 20% testing sets for further analysis. In the training set, we divide it into two subsets, where one of them contains a summary and description of this dataset called Subset-1 (S1). Another subset includes the rest of the attributes- like severity, priority, fix status, platform or hardware, assignee, single developer, first assignee, commenter, and developers-called Subset-2 (S2). Besides, we extract another Subset-11 (S11) from the test set that contains a summary and description of this dataset.

- **Training Stage** In this section, we gather S1 and S2 to train sentence-embedded models of different classifiers. This stage is basically conducted different training processes that help to create a suitable developer team. Several steps of this session are briefly described as follows.

  - **Sentence Embedding:** At first, a fine-tuning process is employed on S1 by pretrained Bidirectional Encoder Representations from Transformers (BERT) and created a sentence embedding model. In this case, this model generates a bag of the developer's words by preserving word contexts of S1. If any unknown words are found on tokenizers, add them to the BERT tokenizer.

  - **Data Balancing:** S2 represents an imbalance condition where various types of developers are highly varied. Due to the overfitting issue, different machine learning models are not shown better outcomes. Therefore, we resample and balance this subset where each developer type contains 652 samples.

  - **Employing Different Classifiers:** Then, the following classifiers such as DT, ET, AdC, BC, GB, RF, KNN, NC, BNB, MNB, CoNB, GNB, SVM, SGD, LR, Pr, and MLP are trained with S2. These classifiers configure a developer classifier that categorizes new records based on the experience level.

- **New Task:** When a new bug report is received, it requires assigning several developers and solving this bug. In this section, we utilize S11 which are generated from 20% of testing reports. Then, we apply the pre-trained sentence embedding model into S11 and extract a vocabulary list for developers.

- **Exploring Eligible Developer** An unsupervised KNN finder is employed to match the vocabulary list of testing reports with the existing bag of developer's words. It identifies K nearest developers who are eligible to resolve this particular bug.

- **Classifying Developers:** In this step, we predict the experience level of K-relevant developers employing the developer classifier. The performance of this model is manipulated by the outcomes of its individual classifiers. These results are generated based on Accuracy (Accu), Precision (Prec), Recall (Rec), F1-Score (FS1), Hamming Loss (HL), Jaccard Score (JS), Matthews Correlation Coefficient (MCC), Area Under the Curve (AUC), Balanced Accuracy (BA), and Cohen's Kappa Score (CKS).

– **Forming Developer Team:** Each type of developer are gathered based on the outcomes of the best classifier. Thus, we create a developer team with eligible persons for solving different bugs.

3.3 Evaluation Matrix

We engender a confusion matrix to measure derived results and specify the number of accurate and inappropriate samples, respectively. However, this matrix is formulated with true positive (TP), false positive (FP), false negative (FN), and true negative (TN) values. Different evaluation metrics such as Accuracy, Precision, Recall, F1-Score, Hamming Loss, Jaccard Score, Matthews Correlation Coefficient, Area Under the Curve, Balanced Accuracy and Cohen's Kappa Score, are used to justify the classification results of individual classifiers. A brief description of these metrics is given as follows.

– **Accuracy (Accu)** measures the efficiency of classifiers using this following equation:

$$\text{Accu} = \frac{TP + TN}{(TP + TN + FP + FN)} \tag{1}$$

– **Precision (Prec)** represents the ratio of TPs and all positive predicted values.

$$\text{Prec} = \frac{TP}{(TP + FP)} \tag{2}$$

– **Recall (Rec)** provides the ratio of TP and all actual positive values.

$$\text{Rec} = \frac{TP}{(TP + FN)} \tag{3}$$

– **F1-Score (FS1)** manipulates the harmonic means of precision and recall which is defined as follows:

$$\text{FS1} = \frac{2TP}{2TP + FP + FN} \tag{4}$$

– **Hamming Loss (HL)** is the fraction of wrong labels and the total number of labels.

$$\text{HL} = \frac{\sum_{j=1}^{|L|} xor(I^j - p^j)}{|L|} \tag{5}$$

- **Jaccard Score (JS)** defines the intersection of the predicted and the true labels divided by the union of the predicted labels and the true labels.

$$JS = \frac{A \cap B}{A \cup B} \qquad (6)$$

- **Matthews Correlation Coefficient (MCC)** is a reliable statistical rate that provides a high score and predicts good results in all confusion matrix categories.

$$MCC = \frac{TP \times TN - FP \times FN}{\sqrt{(TP+FP)(TP+FN)(TN+FP)(TN+FN)}} \qquad (7)$$

- **Area Under the Curve (AUC)** characterizes how well positive classes are isolated from negative classes. It can be represented with TP rate (TPR) and TN rate (TNR) by the following equations:

$$AUC = \frac{TPR + TNR}{2} \qquad (8)$$

- **Balanced Accuracy (BA)** is evaluated for how good a binary classifier is. In addition, when the classes are imbalanced, it is beneficial.

$$BA = \frac{1}{2} \times \frac{TP}{(TP+FN)} + \frac{1}{2} \times \frac{TN}{(TN+FP)} \qquad (9)$$

- **Cohen's Kappa Score (CKS)** is used to manipulate the inter-rater reliability of qualitative items.

$$CKS = \frac{N \sum_{i=1}^{m} CM_{ii} - \sum_{i=1}^{m} Ci_{Corr}Ci_{Pre}}{N^2 - \sum_{i=1}^{m} Ci_{Corr}Ci_{Pre}} \qquad (10)$$

4   Experiment Result and Discussion

In this work, we implement pretrained Bidirectional Encoder Representations from Transformers (BERT) of Google employing for sentence embedding process [21,26]. Then, resample method is used to balance instances of S2 using the sci-kit learn package [20,22]. Numerous classifiers such as DT, ET, AdC, BC, GBC, RF, KNN, NC, BNB, MNB, CoNB, GNB, SVM, SGD, LR, Pr, and MLP are employed to identify different types of developers. Again, we utilize the sci-kit learn library to get these classifiers. All experiments are held in Google Colaboratory using Python. Table 1 shows the experiment results of individual classifiers. Here, we compare the performance of the different classifiers which are evaluated based on Accu, Prec, Rec, FS1, HL, JS, MC, AUC, BAC, and CKS.

After observing the results in Table 1, we observe that BC shows the best outcomes (i.e., except AUC) for individual classifiers. Besides, ET provides the best AUC among all classifiers. Moreover, RF and GBC obtain better accuracy

Table 1. Developer Classification Result

Classifier	Accu	Prec	Rec	FS1	HL	JS	MC	AUC	BAC	CKS
DT	95.74	95.75	95.77	95.75	4.26	91.90	93.61	98.85	95.77	93.61
ET	94.89	94.95	94.96	94.95	5.11	90.49	92.34	**99.23**	94.96	92.33
AdC	68.82	74.41	69.80	67.17	31.18	53.59	56.81	95.35	69.80	53.52
BC	**96.59**	**96.62**	**96.56**	**96.59**	**3.41**	93.42	94.89	98.73	**96.56**	**94.88**
GB	96.42	96.45	96.41	96.43	3.58	93.14	94.63	98.85	96.41	94.63
RF	96.42	96.48	96.40	96.43	3.58	93.15	94.63	98.99	96.40	94.63
KNN	88.93	88.92	88.90	88.82	11.07	80.12	83.47	94.24	88.90	83.39
NC	35.95	51.62	36.52	34.03	64.05	20.74	5.62	48.80	36.52	4.98
BNB	47.02	55.79	47.89	42.45	52.98	27.60	27.20	66.25	47.89	21.40
MNB	46.51	50.72	47.28	39.80	53.49	26.31	26.12	68.34	47.28	20.54
CoNB	44.97	31.75	45.65	34.58	55.03	23.56	24.31	67.50	45.65	18.16
GNB	79.39	83.12	80.13	79.06	20.61	67.78	71.55	99.00	80.13	69.19
SVM	69.85	74.62	69.86	70.52	30.15	54.76	56.35	83.60	69.86	54.84
SGD	83.65	85.64	83.53	82.27	16.35	71.02	77.18	95.71	83.53	75.41
LR	54.86	60.64	54.77	55.95	45.14	40.26	33.53	66.70	54.77	32.62
Pr	78.02	79.82	77.51	77.44	21.98	64.74	68.01	86.77	77.51	66.96
MLP	87.56	88.08	87.46	87.09	12.44	77.86	81.97	92.71	87.46	81.35

(96.42%) to classify developers. DT, ET, and AdC represent good outcomes (i.e., almost all of them are shown greater than 90% results). Also, KNN, SGB, and MLP show their all outcomes within 80%. GNB and Pr give their outcomes around 70%. Instead, the rest of the classifiers are not shown good outcomes in identifying developers. Finally, we determine BC as the best classifier to detect developer experience levels concerning all evaluation matrices.

However, several bug assignment works happened where they determined developer skills based on the previously solved bug reports [10,12,31]. A few studies were considered NED (i.e., mid-level, an expert in another domain) and FG for bug-solving tasks [11]. In this work, these types of developers are included along with ED and created a team to fix newly arrival bugs. NED and FG developers who engage in the bug triaging process fix and learn more about it. BSDRM automatically assigns bugs to the appropriate developers. So, it has the lower possibility to reassign the same bugs to similar developers. To compare this model with existing works, we check three criteria that distinguishes how BSDRM provides better outcomes than previous works. These criteria are given as follows:

– C1-Does BSDRM estimate the bug fixing history of a developer while assigning a new task?

- C2-Does BSDRM consider the interest of a developer in the task allocation scheme?
- C3-Does the assigned team consists of developers from all experience level?

Table 2. Comparison of BSDRM with Traditional Models

	Core Concept	C1	C2	C3
BugFixer [9]	Text exploration	Yes	No	No
Jeong et al. [10]	Tossing graph	Yes	No	No
Yadav et al. [29]	Tossing length	Yes	Yes	No
CosTriage [19]	Cost aware ranking	Yes	No	No
DEVELECT [15]	Source code based approach	Yes	No	No
Zhang et al. [34]	Social network based	Yes	Yes	No
DRETOM [28]	Topic model based approach	Yes	Yes	No
Shokripour et al. [23]	Time based approach	Yes	No	No
Khatun et al. [12]	Time based approach	Yes	No	No
TEAN [11]	LDA	Yes	Yes	No
BSDRM	**Proposed Model**	Yes	Yes	Yes

Table 2 shows the comparison of BSDRM with existing models. In this situation, we observe that BSDRM identifies experts based on their bug fixing histories (i.e., resolved C1) to assign a new task like previous models. Besides, many models [11,28,29,34] were considered developers interested to solve new bugs. Again, BSDRM identifies this matter and fixes C2. BSDRM and TEAN ensure a heterogeneous team formation with different types of developers [11]. However, TEAN does not esteem mid or other field experts of the different organizations (i.e., not properly fixed C4). In BSDRM, we consider three types of developer (i.e., ED, NED and FG) whose build a more robust and stable team to solve bugs based on experience level. Thus, this model also resolved C4. According to Table 2, BSDRM responses all of these criterias to fix a bug by creating a suitable developer team. Nevertheless, it is not always properly estimated how many ED, NED, and FG developers are classified by BSDRM.

5   Conclusion

In this work, we implement BSDRM to divide the developer matrix into training and test sets. The training set is split into S1 and S2. We generate a bag of words from S1 using the sentence embedding process. Various classifiers are used to build a developer classifier; then it is fitted with S2. Also, we extract a vocabulary list from S11 using the trained embedded model. Further, eligible developers are determined by matching bag of words of S1 and the vocabulary list of S11.

Using a developer classifier, we categorize this group into ED, NED, and FGs which creates a suitable bug-fixing team. Therefore, BSDRM recommends this team with mixed categorized fixers to solve newly arrival bugs in collaborative ways. After experimental analysis, BC is found as the most stable classifier to categorize different developers according to their experience label. It shows the highest 96.59% accuracy, 96.62% prec, 96.56% rec, 96.59 % FS1, 3.41 % HL, 93.42% JS, 94.89% MCC, 96.56% BA, and 94.88% CFS, respectively. Besides, GB and RF obtain very close outcomes to BC. Different criteria related to experience are investigated to assess the functionality of BSDRM. Thus, it reduces the abundant workload of ED where NED and FG are got the opportunity to learn deeply about bug solving.

In the future, we will balance task assignments of individual developers in the recommended developer team. Also, more bug repositories (i.e., large-scale software, open-source, and commercial projects) will be considered to evaluate this task and make this process more dynamic.

References

1. Anvik, J., Hiew, L., Murphy, G.C.: Who should fix this bug? In: Proceedings of the 28th International Conference on Software Engineering, pp. 361–370 (2006)
2. Baloch, M.Z., Hussain, S., Afzal, H., Mufti, M.R., Ahmad, B.: Software developer recommendation in terms of reducing bug tossing length. In: International Conference on Security, Privacy and Anonymity in Computation, Communication and Storage, pp. 396–407. Springer (2020)
3. Banitaan, S., Alenezi, M.: Tram: An approach for assigning bug reports using their metadata. In: 2013 Third International Conference on Communications and Information Technology (ICCIT), pp. 215–219. IEEE (2013)
4. Baysal, O., Godfrey, M.W., Cohen, R.: A bug you like: A framework for automated assignment of bugs. In: 2009 IEEE 17th International Conference on Program Comprehension, pp. 297–298. IEEE (2009)
5. Bhattacharya, P., Neamtiu, I.: Fine-grained incremental learning and multi-feature tossing graphs to improve bug triaging. In: 2010 IEEE International Conference on Software Maintenance, pp. 1–10. IEEE (2010)
6. Goyal, A., Sardana, N.: Feature ranking and aggregation for bug triaging in open-source issue tracking systems. In: 2021 11th International Conference on Cloud Computing, Data Science & Engineering (Confluence), pp. 871–876. IEEE (2021)
7. Grana, C., Bolelli, F., Baraldi, L., Vezzani, R.: Yacclab-yet another connected components labeling benchmark. In: 2016 23rd International Conference on Pattern Recognition (ICPR), pp. 3109–3114. IEEE (2016)
8. Hossain, M.B., Arefin, M.S., Sarker, I.H., Kowsher, M., Dhar, P.K., Koshiba, T.: Caran: a context-aware recency-based attention network for point-of-interest recommendation. IEEE Access 10, 36299–36310 (2022)
9. Hu, H., Zhang, H., Xuan, J., Sun, W.: Effective bug triage based on historical bug-fix information. In: 2014 IEEE 25th International Symposium on Software Reliability Engineering, pp. 122–132. IEEE (2014)
10. Jeong, G., Kim, S., Zimmermann, T.: Improving bug triage with bug tossing graphs. In: Proceedings of the 7th Joint Meeting of the European Software Engineering Conference and the ACM SIGSOFT Symposium on the Foundations of Software Engineering, pp. 111–120 (2009)

11. Khatun, A.: A team allocation technique ensuring bug assignment to existing and new developers using their recency and expertise (2017)

12. Khatun, A., Sakib, K.: A bug assignment approach combining expertise and recency of both bug fixing and source commits. In: ENASE, pp. 351–358 (2018)

13. Kowsher, M., Hossen, I., Tahabilder, A., Prottasha, N.J., Habib, K., Azmi, Z.R.M.: Support directional shifting vector: a direction based machine learning classifier. Emerg. Sci. J. **5**(5), 700–713 (2021)

14. Mani, S., Sankaran, A., Aralikatte, R.: Deeptriage: Exploring the effectiveness of deep learning for bug triaging. In: Proceedings of the ACM India Joint International Conference on Data Science and Management of Data, pp. 171–179 (2019)

15. Matter, D., Kuhn, A., Nierstrasz, O.: Assigning bug reports using a vocabulary-based expertise model of developers. In: 2009 6th IEEE International Working Conference on Mining Software Repositories, pp. 131–140. IEEE (2009)

16. Mohan, D., Sardana, N., et al.: Visheshagya: Time based expertise model for bug report assignment. In: 2016 Ninth International Conference on Contemporary Computing (IC3), pp. 1–6. IEEE (2016)

17. Naguib, H., Narayan, N., Brügge, B., Helal, D.: Bug report assignee recommendation using activity profiles. In: 2013 10th Working Conference on Mining Software Repositories (MSR), pp. 22–30. IEEE (2013)

18. Nagwani, N.K., Verma, S.: Predicting expert developers for newly reported bugs using frequent terms similarities of bug attributes. In: 2011 Ninth International Conference on ICT and Knowledge Engineering, pp. 113–117. IEEE (2012)

19. Park, J.w., Lee, M.W., Kim, J., Hwang, S.w., Kim, S.: Costriage: A cost-aware triage algorithm for bug reporting systems. Proc. AAAI Conf. Artif. Intell. **25**(1), 139–144 (Aug 2011), https://ojs.aaai.org/index.php/AAAI/article/view/7839

20. Pedregosa, F., et al.: Scikit-learn: Machine learning in python. J. Mach. Learn. Res. **12**, 2825–2830 (2011)

21. Prottasha, N.J., et al.: Transfer learning for sentiment analysis using bert based supervised fine-tuning. Sensors **22**(11), 4157 (2022)

22. Satu, M.S., et al.: Tclustvid: a novel machine learning classification model to investigate topics and sentiment in covid-19 tweets. Knowledge-Based Systems, p. 107126 (2021)

23. Shokripour, R., Anvik, J., Kasirun, Z.M., Zamani, S.: A time-based approach to automatic bug report assignment. J. Syst. Softw. **102**, 109–122 (2015)

24. Signal, B., Gloss, B.S., Dinger, M.E., Mercer, T.R.: Machine learning annotation of human branchpoints. Bioinformatics **34**(6), 920–927 (2018)

25. Tamrawi, A., Nguyen, T.T., Al-Kofahi, J., Nguyen, T.N.: Fuzzy set-based automatic bug triaging (nier track). In: Proceedings of the 33rd International Conference on Software Engineering, pp. 884–887 (2011)

26. Wolf, T., et al.: Huggingface's transformers: State-of-the-art natural language processing. arXiv preprint arXiv:1910.03771 (2019)

27. Wu, H., Liu, H., Ma, Y.: Empirical study on developer factors affecting tossing path length of bug reports. IET Software **12**(3), 258–270 (2018)

28. Xie, X., Zhang, W., Yang, Y., Wang, Q.: Dretom: Developer recommendation based on topic models for bug resolution. In: Proceedings of the 8th International Conference on Predictive Models in Software Engineering, pp. 19–28 (2012)

29. Yadav, A., Singh, S.K., Suri, J.S.: Ranking of software developers based on expertise score for bug triaging. Inf. Softw. Technol. **112**, 1–17 (2019)

30. Ye, Z., et al.: Lasdu: a large-scale aerial lidar dataset for semantic labeling in dense urban areas. ISPRS Int. J. Geo Inf. **9**(7), 450 (2020)

31. Zhang, T., Lee, B.: An automated bug triage approach: a concept profile and social network based developer recommendation. In: Huang, D.-S., Jiang, C., Bevilacqua, V., Figueroa, J.C. (eds.) ICIC 2012. LNCS, vol. 7389, pp. 505–512. Springer, Heidelberg (2012). https://doi.org/10.1007/978-3-642-31588-6_65

32. Zhang, T., Lee, B.: A hybrid bug triage algorithm for developer recommendation. In: Proceedings of the 28th Annual ACM Symposium on Applied Computing, pp. 1088–1094 (2013)

33. Zhang, T., Yang, G., Lee, B., Lua, E.K.: A novel developer ranking algorithm for automatic bug triage using topic model and developer relations. In: 2014 21st Asia-Pacific Software Engineering Conference. vol. 1, pp. 223–230. IEEE (2014)

34. Zhang, W., Han, G., Wang, Q.: Butter: An approach to bug triage with topic modeling and heterogeneous network analysis. In: 2014 International Conference on Cloud Computing and Big Data, pp. 62–69. IEEE (2014)

35. Zhang, W., Wang, S., Wang, Q.: Ksap: an approach to bug report assignment using knn search and heterogeneous proximity. Inf. Softw. Technol. **70**, 68–84 (2016)

A Belief Rule Based Expert System to Diagnose Schizophrenia Using Whole Blood DNA Methylation Data

Mohammad Shahadat Hossain[1], Mumtahina Ahmed[2]($\boxtimes$), S. M. Shafkat Raihan[1], Angel Sharma[1], Raihan Ul Islam[3], and Karl Andersson[3]

[1] Department of Computer Science and Engineering, University of Chittagong, Chittagong 4331, Bangladesh
hossain.ms@cu.ac.bd
[2] Port City International University, Dhaka, Bangladesh
mumtahina.ahmed.cs@gmail.com
[3] Pervasive and Mobile Computing Laboratory, Lulea University of Technology, Lulea, Sweden
{raihan.ul.islam,karl.andersson}@ltu.se

Abstract. Schizophrenia is a severe neurological disease where a patient's perceptions of reality are disrupted. Its symptoms include hallucinations, delusions, and profoundly strange thinking and behavior, which make the patient's daily functions difficult. Despite identifying genetic variations linked to Schizophrenia, causative genes involved in pathogenesis and expression regulations remain unknown. There is no particular way in life sciences for diagnosing Schizophrenia. Commonly used machine learning and deep learning are data-oriented. They lack the ability to deal with uncertainty in data. Belief Rule Based Expert System (BRBES) methodology addresses various categories of uncertainty in data with evidential reasoning. Previous researches showed the association of DNA methylation (DNAm) with risk of Schizophrenia. Whole blood DNAm data, hence, is useful for smart diagnosis of Schizophrenia. However, to our knowledge, no previous studies have investigated the performance of BRBES to diagnose Schizophrenia. Therefore, in this study, we explore BRBES' performance in diagnosing Schizophrenia using whole blood DNAm data. BRBES was optimized by gradient-free algorithms due to the limitations of gradient-based optimization. Classification thresholds were optimized to yield better results. Finally, we compared performance to two machine learning models after 5-fold cross-validation where our model achieved the highest average sensitivity (76.8%) among the three.

Keywords: BRBES · Scizophrenia · Dna methylation data · disjunctive BRBES

© ICST Institute for Computer Sciences, Social Informatics and Telecommunications Engineering 2023
Published by Springer Nature Switzerland AG 2023. All Rights Reserved
Md. S. Satu et al. (Eds.): MIET 2022, LNICST 491, pp. 271–282, 2023.
https://doi.org/10.1007/978-3-031-34622-4_21

1   Introduction

Schizophrenia is a hereditary acute mental disorder characterized by spasmodic psychosis and reduced cognitive function. Recent efforts to know the causes of schizophrenia have centered on explaining the disorder's genetic component. As a result, large-scale genome-wide association studies (GWAS) and genome sequences have made it possible to conduct hypothesis-free genetic risk factor research. [11]. The GWAS found 108 distinct genetic regions with a significant genome-wide connection with schizophrenia. According to one hypothesis, the majority of GWAS variations alter gene expression regulation. As a result, the relevance of epigenetic modification in the genetic pathogenesis of schizophrenia has aroused researchers' curiosity. The most well-studied epigenetic change is DNA methylation, which affects gene expression by disrupting transcription factor binding and recruiting methyl-binding proteins, which leads to chromatin compaction and gene silencing [12].

Recent developments in life sciences have allowed broad exposure to molecular features of living organisms, allowing researchers to investigate biological systems from a holistic perspective. The demand for new healthcare solutions and ongoing efforts to understand the biological origins of disease [20] necessitates substantial study in the life sciences. This has led to the development of reusable software tools that use machine learning (ML) -based algorithms to help with pattern identification, classification, and prediction in biological data [18]. Parkinson's disease (PD), Alzheimer's disease (AD), and schizophrenia (SZ) are three of the most prevalent neurological diseases causing a disturbance of normal brain activities. Hence, numerous neuroimaging techniques and deep learning-based analysis methods are being applied to the classification and early diagnosis of disorders to develop effective treatment strategies. Currently, Covid-19 is diagnosed utilizing a nucleic acid-based diagnostic method called RT-PCR. Nowadays, PCR is the most available technology with various clinical applications, including evaluating novel diseases, monitoring, advance detection of biothreat agents, and profiling of antibiotic resistance. Techniques based on PCR technology can be more economical than traditional evaluation measures [33].

Mendelian neurodevelopmental diseases are characterized by a wide range of symptoms that make clinical diagnosis difficult. Gene set analysis technologies widely use blood, phlegm, saliva, serum, etc., gene expression data to diagnose diseases due to the ease of sample collection. Gaining biological information from the collected data is the main challenge in achieving the potential of these technologies [21]. As a result of underlying genetic abnormalities, people with a growing number of rare diseases have distinct, disorder-specific DNA methylation patterns. These epigenetic patterns can be utilized as effective indicators for screening and diagnosing various illnesses, in addition to offering insights into the pathogenesis of these disorders [10].

Artificial intelligence techniques such as machine learning (ML) and deep learning (DL) can be used in smart diagnosis of such diseases. However, the underlying mechanism support explainability in the decision-making process [8, 19] have pointed out that the manifold transformation technique used by deep learning approaches do not work well, even for large datasets for data that have causal relationships. Also, neural networks are prone to mis-classifying data [23].

For these reasons, in this study we explored how DNA methylation data from blood samples could be utilized to identify Schizophrenia disorder using artificial intelligence systems that can reason under ambiguity. Knowledge-based approaches like the Bayesian approach [6], Fuzzy Inference Systems [32], Dempster-Shafer [5,27] theory, and MYCIN [29] can reasoning under uncertainty. However, Belief Rule-Based Expert Systems (BRBES), which is based on Dempster-Shafer theory, can handle a wide range of uncertainties, including ambiguity, imprecision, unpredictability, and incompleteness. The disjunctive BRBES was chosen as it can infer well in a variety of conditions of uncertainty, including imprecision, ambiguity, vagueness, incompleteness, ignorance, and randomness. As far as we know, BRBES has never been employed in the diagnosis of Schizophrenia disorder.

2 Related Work

Schizophrenia is a complicated psychiatric disorder influenced by several genes, some of which function as biomarkers for a more precise diagnosis [4]. Because epigenetic profiles can reflect environmental risk factors like stress and poor nutrition, new research reveals that epigenetic abnormalities like DNA methylation and histone alterations can be used to learn more about how schizophrenia develops [24]. Hence, the introduction of a readily available peripheral biomarker would greatly aid the diagnosis of this condition. However, the processes driving the onset, recovery, symptomatology, and therapy of schizophrenia remain elusive despite years of research. One of the explanations for this condition could be a lack of proper analytic methods to cope with the variety and complexity of schizophrenia [4].

Deep learning, a subfield of artificial intelligence (AI), has recently made complex, high-dimensional systems which are more accessible to model and analyze. [4]. Despite the promising findings produced utilizing deep architectures, the practical application of deep learning to health care still faces significant unsolved problems [22]. Deep learning is a type of computational model that necessitates the availability of large volumes of data. However, health care is a separate field. The world's population is only 7.5 billion people (as of September 2016), with the majority without access to primary health care. As a result, we won't acquire data from many patients to build a comprehensive deep learning model [22]. Although deep learning models have proved successful in various applications, they are frequently considered black boxes. However, in health care, not only is quantitative algorithmic performance important, but so is understanding why the algorithms function. Indeed, model interpretability is crucial for convincing medical practitioners to follow the predictive system's recommendations [22].

One study used an integrated approach to find variations that influence the methylation levels of adjacent genes and increase SCZ risk factors, and to investigate their potential role in SCZ pathogenesis. They combined GWAS and methylation quantitative trait loci data using the Summary data-based Mendelian

Randomization (SMR) approach. Therefore, they used blood and brain samples and reproduced 14 and one SNP methylation combination that were substantially linked with SCZ [36]. Based on blood gene expression data, several machine learning (ML) algorithms assist in identifying patients with SCZ. The messenger RNA expression level in peripheral blood was to distinguish SCZ patients from healthy individuals using machine learning algorithms such as artificial neural networks, extreme gradient boosting, support vector machine (SVM), decision tree, and random forest [37]. Another work used the regularization and dimension reduction capabilities of the sparse partial least squares discriminate analysis (SPLS-DA) algorithm. The supervised method presented SZ case-control data in a reduced 2-dimension space. They established a "risk distance" that allowed them to successfully identify a subset of those who were at the highest risk of SZ [9]. Sardaar et al. analyzed whole-exome sequencing (WES) data from patients with autism and schizophrenia using regularized gradient-boosted machines to determine major distinguishing genetic traits. They also developed a gene clustering strategy to emphasize the subsets of genes discovered by the ML algorithm are mutated in sick individuals and are crucial to each disease [26].

However, and we still don't know about the origin and progression of the majority of these diverse diseases [22]. Furthermore, health care data is highly heterogeneous, confusing, noisy, and incomplete, in contrast to other sectors where it is clear and well-structured. It's hard to train a good deep learning model with diverse data sets because of difficulties like data sparsity, redundancy, and missing values [22]. Deep learning methods do not take into account data uncertainty. It's a black box strategy that employs backpropagation and is prone to issues such as catastrophic forgetting. Therefore, authors of [25] explored the possibility of using artificial intelligence techniques that can draw inference in the presence of uncertainty to diagnose Parkinson's disease using various speech signal features. They utilized the disjunctive BRBES, which can reason efficiently under uncertain situations, including imprecision, ambiguity, vagueness, incompleteness, ignorance, and randomness. In another study, Raihan et al. used a BRBES to diagnose Covid-19 in pneumonia patients using blood and computerized tomography (CT) scan data of lung tissue infection. They used and variant of differential evolution inspired from BRBES called BRBaDE to optimize the system [28]. This study [2] presents the fusion of data-driven and knowledge-driven methodologies into a single framework to identify the survival chances of a Covid-19 patient. They trained state-of-the-art pre-trained neural network models with X-ray images to detect critical and noncritical cases of Covid-19. The study then conducted an assessment of the predictions and identified eight risk indicators associated with Covid-19 cases using BRBES. This research [1] proposes a conjunctive belief rule based clinical decision support system to distinguish critical and noncritical Covid-19 cases utilizing only three hematological markers. This research [16], on the other hand, offers a BRBES-based prediction model for predicting a data center's Power Usage Effectiveness (PUE). It outperformed other models such as Adaptive Neuro-Fuzzy Inference System (ANFIS), demonstrating the prediction model's robustness. The research done in [30] attempts to facilitate a novel optimal training strategy combining differential evolution (DE) and BRBES. Disjunctive BRBES can handle real-world data uncertainty without becoming exponentially complex, and it can be tuned using gradient-free techniques. Therefore , in the next section, we'll investigate how BRBES performs on a variety of gene expression data from Schizophrenia patients' blood samples.

3 Methodology

Although there's abundant brain tissue gene expression data for AD, this research utilized blood tissue gene expression data. This is due to the fact that blood tissue is comparatively easy and fast to collect compared to brain tissue. DNA methylation data obtained from the blood samples can then be input into the BRBES model to obtain diagnosis results. An overall work flow of the experiment is depicted in Fig. 1.

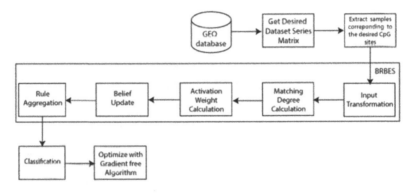

Fig. 1. Methodology of the Experiment

3.1 BRBES

The belief rule base (BRB) of a Belief Rule-Based Expert System operates as the knowledge base, whereas evidential reasoning operates as the inference engine. BRBES can render knowledge of imprecise nature, and evidential reasoning acquires knowledge from divergent and ambiguous information. The BRB contains two major components: the antecedent and the consequent. The consequent attribute deals with the distribution of degrees of belief, although each antecedent attribute has certain referential values. Evidential reasoning also comprises phases like input transformation (where the crisp input is transformed into fuzzy distribution), matching degree computation (where the extent by which the input matches a fuzzy referential level, is calculated), rule activation weight calculation (where the activation weights of the rules in the resulting rule base are calculated), belief update (where the degrees of belief of the consequent attribute are generated and modified based on completeness of antecedent information), and rule aggregation (where all the rules are aggregated to find the final belief degree distribution of the consequent attribute). A Belief Rule Base (BRB) can be represented with a BRB-tree. The brb-tree for our current research is shown in Fig. 2. Input transformation is used to distribute the input value of an antecedent attribute over the referential attributes correlated with that antecedent attribute; Eq. 4 of [13] is employed.

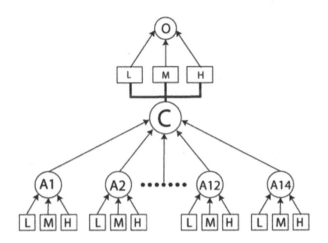

Fig. 2. BRB-tree. There are 14 antecedent attributes, each representing a CpG site along with the gene. The CpG IDs are according to GSE41037 dataset [31]. The attributes are A1 : cg27202708 - C1orf65, A2 : cg26020513 - GATA4, A3 : cg08395365 - MCCC1, A4 : cg10935723 - KCNK10, A5 : cg15452204 - CDX1, A6 : cg26581729 - NPDC1, A7 : cg18055394 - EPHA3, A8 : cg21342728 - MCHR1, A9 : cg03964111 - TMEM176B, A10 : cg23326689 - STMN2, A11 : cg07579404 - RAET1L, A12 : cg08961832 - NALP6, A13 : cg04991337 - MCCC1 and A14 : cg09614401 - ADRA1D. O is the crisp output.

Matching degrees are the terms used to refer to these transformed values. The rules are developed by multiplying or adding the various matching degrees together. Whether the BRB is conjunctive or disjunctive determines the operation type. Total matching degrees for each rule are obtained based on this operation. Total matching degrees for disjunctive BRBES are calculated using Eq. 4 of [38]. They each represent a rule from the rule base. The rules become active once matching degrees have been assigned. After that, according to Eq. 4 of [14], the rule's activation weight is computed using the matching degrees and relative rule weights. If a rule is not activated, its activation weight is set to zero. A rule base's rule activation weights should sum up to be one. Following these processes, an initial belief matrix is formed, which lists the degrees of belief associated with each rule's subsequent attributes. There may be a lack of data for any antecedent qualities due to ignorance. In this case, the belief degrees connected to each rule must be updated. It can help with the uncertainty that comes with ignorance. Therefore, evidential reasoning incorporates all of the rules and calculates the output for the input antecedent characteristics using Eq. 5 of [15]. The results of the input data calculation will be in a fuzzy form, spread over the referential values of the consequent. Equation 12 of [39] is then used to transform the fuzzy form to a crisp or numerical value. All of these processes are carried out in accordance with the processes outlined in [13,14].

3.2 Dataset

We used the methylation profiling dataset GSE41037 [31] from Gene Expression Omnibus (GEO) [3] for this research. The dataset contains whole blood DNA methylation data of 720 subjects (Control:394, Schizophrenia:325). The dataset had missing values corresponding to the sample ID GSM1007848 for the DNAm sites under consideration. Also, there was one sample diagnosed with bipolar disorder. These two samples were excluded from our experiment. Hence, our operational dataset contained 718 data points. We utilized the insight gained in the research of Liu et al. [17] for selecting the DNAm sites as features for our experiment. They too used GSE41037 dataset in their experiment and identified the following 14 CpG sites (on 13 Genes) correlated to methylation of Schizophrenia patients: cg27202708 - C1orf65, cg26020513 - GATA4, cg08395365 - MCCC1, cg10935723 - KCNK10, cg15452204 - CDX1, cg26581729 - NPDC1, cg18055394 - EPHA3, cg21342728 - MCHR1, cg03964111 - TMEM176B, cg23326689 - STMN2, cg07579404 - RAET1L, cg08961832 - NALP6, cg04991337 - MCCC1 and cg09614401 - ADRA1D where to the left of the hyphen is the CpG site ID and to the right is the Gene symbol. In the class field, Schizophrenia labels were replaced with '1', while control labels were substituted with '0'.

3.3 Model Training

BRBES requires predefined utility values for transforming the input into belief distributions. Since CpG data are percentage data and are available in the [0,1] range, we defined three utility values (Low:0.0, Medium:0.5, High:1.0) for our research. To check for model over-fitting, we conducted 5-fold cross validation. Five was selected as the number of folds due to better results seen in previous works [25,38]. Although BRBES is a knowledge based reasoning approach, that can take experts' knowledge into account during reasoning, it does not have an inherent learning mechanism that can optimize the model parameters such as belief degrees and rule weights. However, as briefly discussed in Sect. 2, the widely used back propagation algorithm has caveats owing to gradient-based searching of the solution space. Hence, we chose to optimize BRBES with gradient-free optimization algorithms. One such algorithm is the BRBaDE [16] which is a variant of the nature-inspired algorithm called differential evolution (DE). In traditional DE, the crossover and mutation factors remain constant. But this hinders the path to achieving a balance between exploration and exploitation in searching for the solution space. BRBaDE has been designed to overcome this limitation as it uses an additional BRB to facilitate variations in these two factors. In previous works, BRBaDE has shown promising results compared to other approaches [16,25]. Hence, we opted to optimize the BRBES with BRBaDE. The model was trained for 1000 iterations with a population size 10 times the length of the parameter. As an optimization algorithm, classification errors were chosen and minimized. The parameters optimized included rules weights, degrees of belief of the belief matrix, output utilities and classification threshold. We considered three output referential utilities here. The sum of products of the aggregated belief degrees and corresponding output utilities produced the final crisp output - a value in the range [0,1]. As mentioned, alongside BRBES parameters, classification thresholds were also optimized. If the aggregated consequent output was $\leq threshold$, it was classified as 0 (control) otherwise 1 (Scizhophrenia). There are various variants of differential evolution, which vary in their approach at creating the donor vector. The foundational paper of BRBaDE [16] utilized the basic DE/Rand/1/Bin scheme, represented in Eq. 6.6 of Chap. 6 in [35]. However, Raihan et al. found better results in [25] using the DE/Best/1/Bin scheme, depicted in Eq. 6.7 of [35]. In our experiments, BRBaDE/Best/1/Bin performed better than BRBaDE/r1/1/Bin scheme. So we selected the former for representing BRBES optimization in this research.

4   Results and Discussion

Multiple classification measures were used in this study to compare BRBES's diagnosis performance to that of other algorithms. The measure 'accuracy' can be used to determine the number of correctly identified samples. The metric 'precision' measures how accurate the model is. The 'sensitivity' or 'recall' of a model indicates its completeness. It is also known as true positive rate and is an important metric in disease diagnosis. Another important metric, 'specificity', represents the true negative (recognition) rate . The area under the curve (AUC) of a Receiver Operator Curve is the AUC (ROC). It assesses a classifier's ability to discriminate between classes. With an AUC of 50.

Previous research on BRBES has focused mainly on optimizing the various parameters of the BRBES model. But in our research, alongside the BRBES parameters, we have optimized the classification threshold as well. In binary classification, if the model output is probabilistic i.e., a real number in the range [0,1], by defining a threshold we can get crisp output. In this manner, values exceeding the threshold will be classified into one class, while those under it to another. An intuitive choice of thresholds can be 0.5. However, real world training datasets often have class imbalance, due to which the actual threshold may shifts from 0.5. To address this issue, we included the classification threshold value in our parameter list as well. The thresholds obtained for the five folds were respectively 0.5182, 0.2933, 0.3080, 0.8112 and 0.5898. According to this, fold 1 and fold 5 are closest to the intuitive threshold of 0.5. Table 1 depicts the performance of BRBES optimized with BRBaDE/Best/1/Bin relative to two

Table 1. BRBES and several optimization methods are compared in terms of performance. KNN is K-nearest neighour and NB is Naive Bayes classifier. The metrics are accuracy(Acc), precision(Prec), Sensitivity/Recall(Sens), Specificity (Spec), ROC Area under curve(AUC).

Algorithms	BRBES					KNN					NB				
Folds	Acc	Prec	Sens	Spec	AUC	Acc	Prec	Sens	Spec	AUC	Acc	Prec	Sens	Spec	AUC
Fold-1	0.570	0.573	**0.818**	0.277	0.548	0.620	0.615	0.608	0.731	0.629	0.648	0.651	0.630	0.808	0.716
Fold-2	0.615	0.606	**0.846**	0.339	0.592	0.608	0.602	0.597	0.709	0.624	0.671	0.668	0.661	0.760	0.708
Fold-3	0.566	0.5625	**0.829**	0.269	0.549	0.636	0.634	0.621	0.772	0.659	0.664	0.661	0.653	0.760	0.672
Fold-4	0.546	**0.610**	**0.602**	0.467	0.535	0.539	0.533	0.533	0.582	0.571	0.601	0.594	0.589	0.709	0.662
Fold-5	**0.622**	**0.615**	**0.747**	0.485	0.616	0.518	0.500	0.500	0.692	0.542	0.573	0.566	0.555	0.756	0.630
Average	0.584	0.593	**0.768**	0.367	0.568	0.584	0.577	0.572	0.697	0.605	0.631	0.628	0.6176	0.7586	0.678
Best	0.622	0.615	**0.846**	0.485	0.616	0.636	0.634	0.621	0.772	0.659	0.671	0.668	0.661	0.808	0.716

other models i.e., K-nearest Neighours and Naive Bayes. The metrics at which BRBES outperformed both of these models have been written in bold text. It can be observed that BRBES has a clear upperhand in sensitivity over the other two models. Also, it has gained better accuracy in fold 5 and better precision in fold 4 and 5, compared to the other two models. And overall it has performed better than KNN.

The limitations of our work can be seen in the specification and ROC-AUC. The other two models outperformed it in these metrics. However, in all 5 folds, our model scored more than 50%, indicating that BRBES indeed has skills for classification and is not random. Also, although naive bayes outperformed BRBES, the bayesian approach is characterized for committing degrees of beliefs to hypotheses based on negation, without taking into account whether evidence is present [7]. BRBES being based on the famous Dempster-Shafer theory and evidential reasoning [5,27,34]. Hence, it does not assign beliefs to a hypothesis, unless it has evidence. This facilitates reasoning with incomplete data and in situations of data ignorance. In BRBES, the absence of evidence is not the evidence of absence. Hence, the limitations of performance seen in BRBES might indicate a need for more features for a robust decision, supported with evidence.

5   Conclusion

In this research, we investigated the potential of BRBES system optimized with BRBaDE algorithm for diagnosing Schizophrenia patients based on whole blood DNA methylation data. Alongside the BRBES parameters, we optimized classification thresholds as well. The specification and AUC require much improvement. However, since the AUC has >50% performance, it can be suggested that BRBES has potential for smart diagnosis of Schizophrenia based on whole blood DNA methylation data. In future endeavors, possibilities will be explored to diminish performance limitations of BRBES. In [2], another variant of BRBaDE optimization has been employed with DL for inferring with BRBES which produced better outcomes. Hence, BRBES and deep learning can be utilized to complement each others' drawbacks in decision making.

Acknowledgement. We want to thank Mr Mahmud Shah Raihan and Miss Shagufta Mizan for their considerate suggestions on domain-specific issues.

References

1. Ahmed, F., Hossain, M.S., Islam, R.U., Andersson, K.: An evolutionary belief rule-based clinical decision support system to predict covid-19 severity under uncertainty. Appl.Sci. **11**(13) (2021). https://doi.org/10.3390/app11135810,https://www.mdpi.com/2076-3417/11/13/5810
2. Ahmed, T.U., Jamil, M.N., Hossain, M.S., Islam, R.U., Andersson, K.: An Integrated Deep Learning and Belief Rule Base Intelligent System to Predict Survival of COVID-19 Patient under Uncertainty. Cognitive Computation, pp. 1–17 (2021). https://doi.org/10.1007/s12559-021-09978-8
3. Barret, T., et al.: Ncbi geo: archive for functional genomics data sets-update. Nucleic Acids Res. **41**(D1), D991–D995 (2012)
4. Cortes-Briones, J.A., Tapia-Rivas, N.I., D'Souza, D.C., Estevez, P.A.: Going deep into schizophrenia with artificial intelligence. Schizophr. Res. (2021). https://doi.org/10.1016/j.schres.2021.05.018
5. Dempster, A.P.: Upper and lower probabilities induced by a multivalued mapping. In: Classic works of the Dempster-Shafer theory of belief functions, pp. 57–72. Springer (2008)
6. Duda, R.O., Hart, P.E., Nilsson, N.J.: Subjective bayesian methods for rule-based inference systems. In: Readings in Artificial Intelligence, pp. 192–199. Elsevier (1981)
7. Gordon, J., Shortliffe, E.H.: The dempster-shafer theory of evidence. Rule-Based Expert Systems: The MYCIN Experiments of the Stanford Heuristic Programming Project **3**, 832–838 (1984)
8. Grossberg, S.: A path toward explainable ai and autonomous adaptive intelligence: deep learning, adaptive resonance, and models of perception, emotion, and action. Front. Neurorobot. **14** (2020)
9. Gunasekara, C.J., et al.: A machine learning case-control classifier for schizophrenia based on dna methylation in blood. Trans. Psych. **11**(1), 142 (2021)
10. Haghshenas, S., Bhai, P., Aref-Eshghi, E., Sadikovic, B.: Diagnostic utility of genome-wide dna methylation analysis in mendelian neurodevelopmental disorders. International J. Mol. Sci. **21**(23), 9303 (2020)
11. Hannon, E., et al.: An integrated genetic-epigenetic analysis of schizophrenia: Evidence for co-localization of genetic associations and differential dna methylation. Genome Biol. **17**(1), 1–16 (Aug 2016). https://doi.org/10.1186/s13059-016-1041-x
12. Hannon, E., et al.: Dna methylation meta-analysis reveals cellular alterations in psychosis and markers of treatment-resistant schizophrenia. eLife **10**, e58430 (feb 2021). https://doi.org/10.7554/eLife.58430
13. Hossain, M.S., Ahmed, F., Andersson, K., et al.: A belief rule based expert system to assess tuberculosis under uncertainty. J. Med. Syst. **41**(3), 43 (2017)
14. Hossain, M.S., Khalid, M.S., Akter, S., Dey, S.: A belief rule-based expert system to diagnose influenza. In: 2014 9th International Forum on Strategic Technology (IFOST), pp. 113–116. IEEE (2014)
15. Islam, R.U., Hossain, M.S., Andersson, K.: A deep learning inspired belief rule-based expert system. IEEE Access **8**, 190637–190651 (2020)

16. Islam, R.U., Ruci, X., Hossain, M.S., Andersson, K., Kor, A.L.: Capacity management of hyperscale data centers using predictive modelling. Energies **12**(18), 3438 (2019). https://doi.org/10.3390/en12183438,https://www.mdpi.com/1996-1073/12/18/3438

17. Liu, J., Julnes, P.S., Chen, J., Ehrlich, S., Walton, E., Calhoun, V.D.: The association of dna methylation and brain volume in healthy individuals and schizophrenia patients. Schizophr. Res. **169**(1–3), 447–452 (2015)

18. Mahmud, M., Kaiser, M.S., McGinnity, T.M., Hussain, A.: Deep learning in mining biological data. Cogn. Comput. **13**(1), 1–33 (2020). https://doi.org/10.1007/s12559-020-09773-x

19. Mahmud, M., Kaiser, M.S., McGinnity, T.M., Hussain, A.: Deep learning in mining biological data. Cogn. Comput. **13**(1), 1–33 (2021)

20. Mahmud, M., Kaiser, M.S., Hussain, A., Vassanelli, S.: Applications of deep learning and reinforcement learning to biological data. IEEE Trans. Neural Netw. Learn. Syst. **29**(6), 2063–2079 (2018). https://doi.org/10.1109/TNNLS.2018.2790388

21. Maleki, F., Ovens, K., Hogan, D.J., Kusalik, A.J.: Gene set analysis: Challenges, opportunities, and future research. Front. Gen. **11**, 654 (2020). https://doi.org/10.3389/fgene.2020.00654,https://www.frontiersin.org/article/10.3389/fgene.2020.00654

22. Miotto, R., Wang, F., Wang, S., Jiang, X., Dudley, J.T.: Deep learning for healthcare: review, opportunities and challenges. Brief. Bioinform. **196**, 1236–1246 (2018)

23. Nguyen, A., Yosinski, J., Clune, J.: Deep neural networks are easily fooled: High confidence predictions for unrecognizable images. In: Proceedings of the IEEE Conference on Computer Vision and Pattern Recognition, pp. 427–436 (2015)

24. Nishioka, M., et al.: Comprehensive dna methylation analysis of peripheral blood cells derived from patients with first-episode schizophrenia. J. Hum. Genet. **58**, 91–97 (2013)

25. Raihan, S., Zisad, S.N., Islam, R.U., Hossain, M.S., Andersson, K.: A belief rule base approach to support comparison of digital speech signal features for parkinson's disease diagnosis. In: Brain Informatics : 14th International Conference, BI 2021, Virtual Event, September 17–19, 2021, Proceedings, pp. 388–400. No. 12960 in Lecture Notes in Artificial Intelligence (2021). https://doi.org/10.1007/978-3-030-86993-9_35

26. Sardaar, S., Qi, B., Dionne-Laporte, A., Rouleau, G.A., Rabbany, R., Trakadis, Y.J.: Machine learning analysis of exome trios to contrast the genomic architecture of autism and schizophrenia. BMC Psychiatry (2020). https://doi.org/10.1186/s12888-020-02503-5

27. Shafer, G.: A mathematical theory of evidence. In: A mathematical theory of evidence. Princeton University Press (1976)

28. Shafkat Raihan, S.M., Islam, R.U., Hossain, M.S., Andersson, K.: A brbes to support diagnosis of covid-19 using clinical and ct scan data, pp. 483–496. No. 95 in Lecture Notes on Data Engineering and Communications Technologies (2022)

29. Shortliffe, E.H., Buchanan, B.G.: A model of inexact reasoning in medicine. Math. Biosci. **23**(3–4), 351–379 (1975)

30. Ul Islam, R., Hossain, M.S., Andersson, K.: A learning mechanism for brbes using enhanced belief rule-based adaptive differential evolution. In: 2020 Joint 9th International Conference on Informatics, Electronics Vision (ICIEV) and 2020 4th International Conference on Imaging, Vision Pattern Recognition (icIVPR), pp. 1–10 (2020). https://doi.org/10.1109/ICIEVicIVPR48672.2020.9306521

31. Van Eijk, K.R., et al.: Identification of schizophrenia-associated loci by combining dna methylation and gene expression data from whole blood. Eur. J. Hum. Genet. **23**(8), 1106–1110 (2015)

32. Yager, R.R.: Approximate reasoning as a basis for rule-based expert systems. IEEE Trans. Syst. Man Cybern. **4**, 636–643 (1984)

33. Yang, S., Rothman, R.E.: Pcr-based diagnostics for infectious diseases: uses, limitations, and future applications in acute-care settings. In: The Lancet. Infectious diseases, pp. 337–48 (2004). https://doi.org/10.1016/S1473-3099(04)01044-8

34. Yang, J.B., Singh, M.G.: An evidential reasoning approach for multiple-attribute decision making with uncertainty. IEEE Trans. Syst. Man Cybern. **24**(1), 1–18 (1994)

35. Yang, X.S.: Nature-inspired optimization algorithms. Academic Press (2020)

36. Yu, H., Cheng, W., Zhang, X., Wang, X., Yue, W.: Integration analysis of methylation quantitative trait loci and gwas identify three schizophrenia risk variants. Neuropsychopharmacol.: Off. Public. Am. Coll. Neuropsychopharmacol. **45**(7), 1179–1187 (2020). https://doi.org/10.1038/s41386-020-0605-3

37. Zhu, L., et al.: The machine learning algorithm for the diagnosis of schizophrenia on the basis of gene expression in peripheral blood. Neurosci. Lett. **745**, 135596 (2021). https://doi.org/10.1016/j.neulet.2020.135596

38. Zisad, S.N., Chowdhury, E., Hossain, M.S., Islam, R.U., Andersson, K.: An integrated deep learning and belief rule-based expert system for visual sentiment analysis under uncertainty. Algorithms **14**(7), 213 (2021)

39. Zisad, S.N., Hossain, M.S., Hossain, M.S., Andersson, K.: An integrated neural network and seir model to predict covid-19. Algorithms **14**(3), 94 (2021). https://doi.org/10.3390/a14030094,www.mdpi.com/1999-4893/14/3/94

Network, Security and Nanotechnology

Reactive and Proactive Routing Protocols Performance Evaluation for MANETS Using OPNET Modeler Simulation Tools

Mala Rani Barman[1]([✉]) [ID], Dulal Chakraborty[2], and Jugal Krishna Das[3]

[1] Department of Computer Science and Engineering, Sheikh Hasina University, Netrokona,
Bangladesh
malabarman42@gmail.com
[2] Department of Information and Communication Technology, Comilla University, Comilla,
Bangladesh
[3] Department of Computer Science and Engineering, Jahangirnagar University, Dhaka,
Bangladesh
cedas@juniv.edu

Abstract. Ad hoc routing is utilized in MANET to provide effective wireless
communication between mobile nodes. The main issue with MANET is the frequent changes in network architecture. Different routing protocols come in various
forms. Here, the Dynamic Source Routing (DSR), Ad hoc On-Demand Distance
Vector (AODV), and Optimized Link State Routing (OLSR) protocols have all
had their performance assessed. The various protocols were simulated using the
OPNET Modeler simulator. As performance measures, we assessed the effectiveness of the routing protocols using three performance metrics. We can observe from
the simulation research that various procedures have various features. In certain
contexts, different protocols behave differently. Considering throughput, OLSR
performs better than DSR and AODV. DSR outperforms AODV and OLSR based
on end-to-end latency. Regarding normalized routing load, OLSR outperforms
AODV and DSR.

Keywords: DSR · AODV · OLSR · MANET · Throughput · OPNET Modeler

1 Introduction

Users in mobile ad-hoc networking seek to interact with one another via a temporary
network; centralized management is not required. The objective of every node is to
forward packets to other nodes. An autonomous group of mobile users that can interact
via wireless networks with limited capacity is referred to as a MANET (Mobile Ad-hoc
Network). It can be quickly and cheaply implemented as multi-hop packet networks.

Wireless computer devices like cell devices, computers, Personal Digital Assistants
(PDA), etc. make up MANET. These networks resemble that they are capable of self-
configuring route configuration and that additional connected host mobile nodes may

Md. S. Satu et al. (Eds.): MIET 2022, LNICST 491, pp. 285–293, 2023.
https://doi.org/10.1007/978-3-031-34622-4_22

be used to create any kind of wireless architecture [1]. The network's wireless topology may vary quickly and impredictably since the nodes are free to roam freely and arrange themselves anyway they see fit [2].

In later, the part II titled Literature Review describes the linked work. Section 3 contains a discussion of several routing protocols. In Sect. 4, the process to do this assignment is laid forth. In Sect. 5, the experimental findings analysis is discussed. Section 6 includes a picture of the resolution.

2 Related Works

Researchers have put forward a variety of methods for analyzing the effectiveness of this networks. For the comparison the effectiveness of AODV and GRP routing protocols, Haruskhpreet et al. [1] employed the OPNET Modeler simulator. In the scenario of Normalized Routing Load, AODV performs much better than GRP.

In some nodes, GRP performs better than AODV. AODV and DSDV routing protocols were compared by Deepak et al. [2] utilizing NS2's latency and throughput performance matrices.

Based on packet delivery fraction, DSDV outperformed AODV. On the other hand, AODV fared better than DSDV when considering latency from beginning to finish. Ahmed et al. [3] examined how mobility affected the DSDV, AODV, and DSR routing algorithms at different nodes and regions. NS2.35 has been used as a network simulator. DSR fared better than AODV and DSDV in defined as the ratio of packets that were successfully delivered. DSDV did better on average throughput. Besides, delivery from beginning to finish, DSDV did better.

Muawia and Yahia [4] assessed the throughput, packet delivery etc. ratio of the various routing protocols. With regard to having more nodes, AODV fared better. DSR, on the other hand, fared better in a network with lower density.

S. Xiang and J. Yang [5] assessed the MANET's transmission performance dependability. In this instance, the impact of interference on the dependability of the transmission was considered.

AODV, LAR, and DSR were all simulated by Satyam et al. [6] using Glomosim Simulator. Rate of packet delivery and throughput. Performance metrics included end-to-end latency and drop ratio where LAR1 fared better. When compared to DSR and AODV, LAR1 exhibited a smaller drop ratio and a larger latency.

Through simulation, Martin [7] examined how mobility models affected MANET performance and two mobility model were used. Diverse mobility models, speeds, and halt times result in different behaviors from MANET.

In a different publication, Anas et al. [8] used the OPNET 17.5 network simulator to test the various protocols. The protocols with various movement speeds and mobility models were compared.

Under different circumstances, Menaka et al. [9] simulated the DSR protocol's performance.

OLSR and AODV routing protocols were assessed by Al-Aiz et al. [10] using NS2 with different node counts, node speeds, and data rates. Both AODV and OLSR fared better.

3 Methodology

To assess the routing protocols' performance, we turned to the OPNET Modeler simulation tool. Numerous models of mobile behavior may be employed to simulate this situation and by default random way points are chosen. Mobile nodes operate as both clients and servers. For communication among these nodes, a protocol is required.

3.1 Routing Protocols

In networks like this, routing presents a significant difficulty because of the mobile nature of MANETs, which permits connections to change in a dynamic manner for nodes [4]. [Case in point] The establishment of a connection between two nodes is achieved via the use of ad hoc network routing protocols. Messages are sent and received along the path. Ad hoc networks are dynamic; therefore, they regularly change. In MANET, there are primarily three active routing protocols, which are described as follows.

Proactive Routing Protocols

These protocols ensure that routing tables are maintained up-to-date so that data may be sent from one node to another. All network destinations are included in the proactive protocol's routing tables, which are frequently updated to accommodate any network modifications that may occur [4]. There is a lot of overhead in the networks because of the constant communication between nodes. Communication is at a high level in this area because of the wide variety of routes. Table-driven or proactive protocols like as OLSR, FSR, DSDV, and CGSR (Cluster-head Gateway Switch Routing Protocol) are already in use. These include OLSR, FSR, DSDV, and CGSR.

OLSR Protocol

Among different proactive routing protocols, Optimized link state is a protocol which maintains a table for routing information and it provides available routes when necessary for the network. Without having central devices, OLSR performs in a distributed manner. In order to transmit data from one node to another, OLSR maintains a hop count by finding the best route. Hop count has a key benefit since it is easy to compute because it just considers the number of hops between nodes and does not take into account any other parameters [10]. HELLO messages and multipoint relays (MPRs) are two of its primary advantages [10].

Reactive Routing Protocols

Routing tables are not maintained by reactive routing systems. Data cannot be sent from one point to another unless a path is established. A path to a destination is required by all the nodes at any one time. They don't have as much overhead as proactive routing tables since they don't keep a routing table. Only a few instances of reactive routing systems exist.

AODV Protocol

AODV protocol doesn't maintain a routing table to identify routes in the network. For this reason, broadcasting and the overhead is minimized in this protocol. Routes are established when it is necessary and destination sequence number helps finding the best route. Rout request, route reply, and route error acknowledgement are all types of UDP messages in AODV [10]. A message called RREQ is sent to its neighboring nodes and if destination is not found then these nodes send the same message to their neighboring nodes. As a consequence, data is sent between nodes via the AODV protocol.

DSR Protocol
DSR protocol is used in various networks. Every node maintains caches and these caches contain information of destination and the corresponding nodes to reach the destination. Through this mechanism, messages of source node are transmitted to destination node. Because of this nature, a high overhead is resent in the network.

Hybrid Routing Protocols
Depending on the routing zone, it combines the greatest attributes from the previous two categories and Those nodes that are within a specific radius of the origin node, whether geographically or in terms of distance, are included in the routing zone. Table-driven approaches are used for routing inside the Routing Zone, while on-demand approaches are utilized to route external nodes. The Zone Routing Protocol (ZRP) and the Enhanced Interior Gateway Routing Protocol are two examples of EIGRP.

Performance Metrics
The throughput performance indicator is used to compare the utilized three routing protocols.

Average Throughput
Throughout total simulation time, the data packets received by the receiver is called average throughput. It can be measured in kilo bit per second (kbps).

– Throughput = Number of bits contained in accepted packet/total simulation time

Average End-to-End Delay
It refers to the typical amount of time needed for data packets to make their way across a MANET. This includes buffering during route discovery slowness, interface queueing, and MAC retransmission delays. Includes propagation and transmission times.

Normalized Routing Load
The typical count of data packets that are routed and sent out before one of those data packets is ultimately successful in being delivered to its intended location. Where NRL is determined by taking the sending packet and dividing it by the data packets delivered.

Simulation Tool
OPNET Modeler 14.5 has been used to simulate the two routing protocols. OPNET

Modeler is used to provide a commercial network simulation environment. It is used in the process of visually stimulating the network.

Mobile Ad hoc Network Set up for Normal Scenario

When applied to this scenario, the OPNET Modeler simulator is used to model a basic MANET. It is necessary to configure mobility in order to specify the mobility patterns for each and every node that will be utilized in the various situations. There are many other mobility models that may be simulated. The default random way point mobility is being utilized for this scenario, and the screen that corresponds to it is as follows (see Fig. 1):

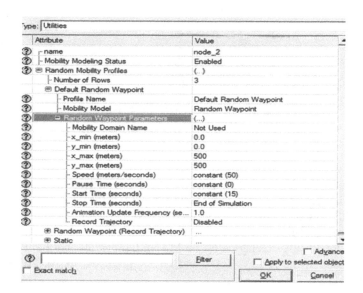

Fig. 1. Mobility Configuration

Once the fundamental network configuration has been completed, the relevant network will appear as indicated below (see Fig. 2):

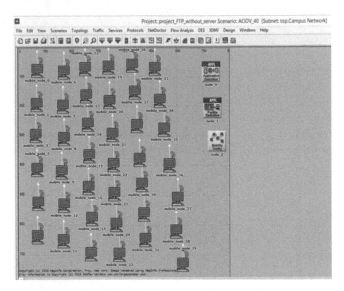

Fig. 2. MANET scenario for 40 nodes

4   Results

The number of nodes is varied in 10, 20, 30 and 40 to analyze the behavior of each MANET routing protocol. Simulation is run for 3600 s for each scenario. We were able to draw the graph for all of the specified MANET routing protocols by using the spreadsheet program Microsoft Excel.

There are total twelve scenarios of the MANET protocols. We have changed the number of nodes in the AODV, DSR, and OLSR protocols to 10, 20, 30, and 40 respectively.

The corresponding layout of the simulation scenario is depicted in Table 1.

Table 1. Simulation Scenario

Nodes	AODV	DSR	OLSR
10	A_10	D_10	O_10
20	A_20	D_20	O_20
30	A_30	D_30	O_30
40	A_40	D_40	O_40

From the following Fig. 3. we can see that according to our scenario, the best performance is found for the OLSR based on throughput. Here, DSR and AODV have almost similar throughput but DSR shows the least throughput. The throughput of OLSR is high because of MRP implementations which increases efficiency and reduces the transmission by controlling flooding. OLSR works better for large network.

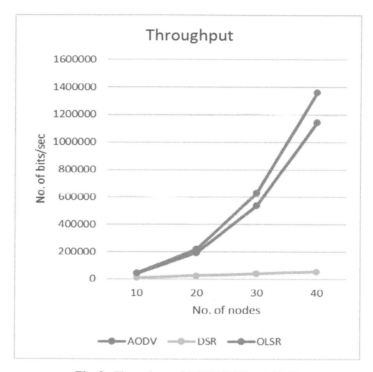

Fig. 3. Throughput of AODV, DSR and OLSR

From the following Fig. 4. we can evaluate the end-to-end delay of the protocols.

In comparison to AODV and OLSR, the end-to-end latency incurred by the DSR routing protocol is much longer than that of the other two routing methods shown in Fig. 4. On the other hand, even in the case of bigger nodes, the average latency from beginning to conclusion of an OLSR transaction is quite small.

According to Fig. 5, which was shown before, we are able to deduce that OLSR performs well. On the other side, concerning NRL, the performance of DSR is not good. AODV performs average compared to OSLR and DSR.

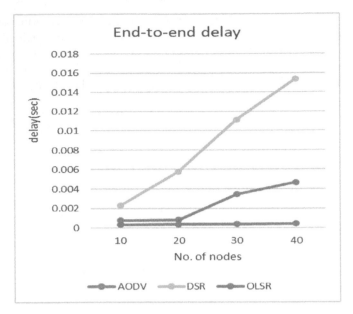

Fig. 4. End to end delay of AODV, DSR and OLSR

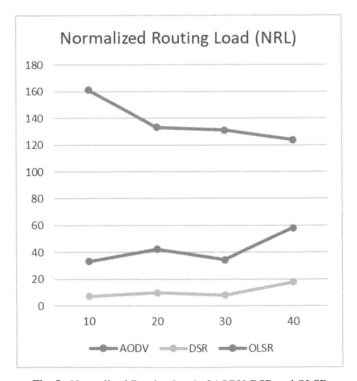

Fig. 5. Normalized Routing Load of AODV, DSR and OLSR

5   Conclusion

Three distinct routing protocols are designed with the use of a network simulator known as OPNET Modeler. All three of these protocols have been successful in their implementation. We have used three performance metrics. Other metrics we have considered include throughput on average and normalized routing load. We made the discovery that OLSR has a performance that is superior to that of AODV and DSR based on other two performance metrics. DSR, on the other hand, outperforms AODV and OLSR when it comes to the overall average delay that is incurred across the whole process. When it comes to NRL performance, OLSR outperforms both AODV and DSR.

In the future, one of our goals will be to estimate the other protocols performance. According to the results of our simulation research, the throughput of DSR is much lower when compared to that of AODV and OLSR. In the near future, we want to work on enhancing the throughput of DSR and decreasing the amount of time that routing protocols take.

References

1. Singh, H., Kaur, H., Sharma, A., Malhotra, R.: Performance investigation of reactive AODV and hybrid GRP routing protocols under influence of IEEE 802.11n MANET. In: 2015 Fifth International Conference on Advanced Computing & Communication Technologies, pp. 325–328 (2015)
2. Kumar, D., Srivastava, A., Gupta, S.C.: Performance comparison of pro-active and reactive routing protocols for MANET. In: 2012 International Conference on Computing, Communication and Applications, pp. 1–4 (2012)
3. Shantaf, A.M., Kurnaz, S., Mohammed, A.H.: Performance evaluation of three mobile ad-hoc network routing protocols in different environments. In: 2020. International Congress on Human-Computer Interaction, Optimization and Robotic Applications (HORA), pp. 1–6 (2020)
4. Elsadig, M.A., Fadlalla, Y.A.: Mobile ad hoc network routing protocols: performance evaluation and assessment. Int. J. Comput. Digit. Syst. 7(1), 59–66 (2018)
5. Xiang, S., Yang, J.: Performance reliability evaluation for mobile ad hoc networks. Reliab. Eng. Syst. Saf. **169**, 32–39 (2018)
6. Sainy, S.K., Chaudhary, R.R., Kumar, A.: Performance evaluation of routing protocols based on alternative models in MANET. In: 2016 IEEE International Conference on Recent Trends in Electronics, Information, and Communication Technology (RTEICT), pp. 1666–1670 (2016)
7. Appiah, M.: The impact of mobility models on the performance of mobile ad hoc network (MANET). In: 2016 International Conference on Advances in Computing and Communication Engineering (ICACCE), pp. 208–213 (2016)
8. AlKhatieb, A., Felemban, E., Naseer, A.: Performance evaluation of ad-hoc routing protocols in (FANETs). In: 2020 IEEE Wireless Communications and Networking Conference Workshops (WCNCW), pp. 1–6 (2020)
9. Menaka, R., Mathana, J.M., Dhanagopal, R., Sundarambal, B.,: Performance evaluation of DSR protocol in MANET untrustworthy environment. In: 2020 6th International Conference on Advanced Computing and Communication Systems (ICACCS), pp. 1049–1052 (2020)
10. Hashim, A.-A., Farhan, M.M., Alshybani, S.: Performance evaluation of OLSR and AODV routing protocols over mobile ad-hoc networks. In: 2019 First International Conference of Intelligent Computing and Engineering (ICOICE), pp. 1–8 (2019)

A Novel MIMO Antenna for 6G Applications

Umor Fasal[1]([✉]), Md. Kamrul Hasan[1], Ayubali[1], Md. Emdadul Hoque Bhuiyan[1],
Abu Zafar Md. Imran[1], Md. Razu Ahmed[1], and Ferose Khan[2]

[1] Department of Electronic and Telecommunication Engineering, International Islamic
University Chittagong, Kumira, Chattogram-4318, Bangladesh
{t173013,t173031,t173009}@ugrad.iiuc.ac.bd, imran@iiuc.ac.bd
[2] Department of Computer Science and Engineering, International Islamic University
Chittagong, Kumira, Chattogram-4318, Bangladesh
c173076@ugrad.iiuc.ac.bd

Abstract. This paper proposes a novel Antenna with many inputs and outputs 6G
MIMO (sixth generation) applications at a frequency of 300 GHz. The antenna
performance enhancement is studied by inserting different widths (very slight,
slightly noticeable, and hardly noticeable) of a decoupling structure between two
closely installed radiating elements with a very close together edges of 0.13 mm.
With 0.09 mm width decoupling structure, the highest performance (S21 $<$ $-$
26 dB, ECC $<$ 0.0003 and DG $>$ 9.99 dB) is attained. Therefore, MIMO antenna
design is suggested can be a good candidate for 6G technologies.

Keywords: MIMO · Terahertz · 6G · Decoupling Structure

1 Introduction

Nowadays, wireless technology is advancing at a rapid speed. The remarkable progression from 1G to 5G in such a short period of time suggests that 6G is simply the next logical step in the evolution of faster and better wireless communication. Every single improvement brought by 5G will be further enhanced in 6G. While 5G is still being evolved around the world, 6G is anticipated to be launched in early 2028 or be widely adopted around 2030. The University of Oulu in Finland made the announcement of funding for its 6G Landmark program in early 2018, which would research things such as software, antennas and more to be used for the implementation of 6G [1]. In mid-2021, the South Korean Ministry of Science and ICT (Information and Communications Technology) conducted a "6G Strategy Meeting". According to certain white papers, companies such as Samsung, LG, and others have initiated 6G research [2, 3].

In 6G, enhanced mobile broadband (eMBB) will offer a superior performance in terms of data usage and standards [4, 5]. 6G, according to the paper [6], is a robust information system powered by futuristic artificial intelligence (AI) technologies. Safe, highly dependable, low-delay communication (SURLLC) in 6G is an upgrade version of ultra-reliable and Communication between many machines with low latency (URLLC) and

Md. S. Satu et al. (Eds.): MIET 2022, LNICST 491, pp. 294–302, 2023.
https://doi.org/10.1007/978-3-031-34622-4_23

other types of heavy traffic (mMTC) in 5G, with more reliability (more than 99.9999999 percent) additional delay (less than 0.1 ms) paired in a security framework [7, 8]. 6G will allow for a variety of novel forms of communication, including 3D-InteCom, holographic, haptic, and human-bond connections. [7, 9]. 6G system will utilize a broader frequency band (THz Waves) to deliver a high data rate [10]. 0.1 to 10 THz is the frequency range of electromagnetic waves classified as terahertz (THz).

The channel capacity, dependability, and transmission data speed of a wireless communication system may all be improved via using MIMO antennas, which allow for simultaneous reception and transmission of data from a number of sources. Hence, MIMO approach can be said as a highly effective and reliable one for modern Technologies pertaining to wireless communication, In addition to WLAN, 4G, 5G, and 6G mobile networks are also available (6G).

In the paper [11], they describe how Dynamic Metasurface Antennas (DMAs) can be used as massive Multiple-Input-Multiple-Output (mMIMO) transceivers for 6G wireless communications and DMAs' operating model during transmission and reception, beamforming capabilities, and advantages and disadvantages in comparison to traditional arrays are discussed, among other crucial aspects of DMAs in the context of mMIMO systems. They conclude by providing some research directions for future researchers towards uncovering DMAs' potential for 6G wireless communication systems.

In the paper [12], they review some previous antenna designs for 6G applications such as a circularly polarized conical horn antenna at the frequency band (220 GHz- 330 GHz) [13], a low-cost PCB wideband antenna with common-mode current suppression at the frequency of 60 GHz [14], high-gain low terahertz (100 GHz-1.0 THz) antenna along with a wideband high gain resonant cavity antenna at the frequency of 300 GHz [15] and so on.

For 6G wireless communication, a tiny MIMO antenna at 300 GHz (THz band) is presented here. And antenna performance is enhanced by employing a technique of decoupling structure.

1.1 Methodology and Antenna Design

A very small MIMO antenna is designed by using CST studio software at the frequency of 300 GHZ because Electromagnetic waves in the THz range from 100 GHz to 10 THz in frequency. The THz wave is defined by the IEEE standard as 0.3 THz to 10 THz [16]. The suggested MIMO antenna dimensions are developed from the paper [12], where they designed a novel microstrip patch antenna for 6G application. Two patch antennas are created on a low-cost Fr-4 substrate and copper ground plane as shown in Fig. 1. The substrate has height (Subh = 25 μm), length (L = 0.484 mm) and width (W = 0.85 mm). The ground plane has a thickness of 100 nm and the ground plane's width and length are the same as the substrate. The patch is of width (Wp = 0.30 mm), length (Lp = 0.234) and 100 nm thick. The patches are fed by a width of 0.0469 mm microstrip line with a characteristic impedance of 50 Ω and having a length of 0.20 mm. It's worth noting that the patch antenna has a very small gap between its edges—just 0.13 mm (see Table 1).

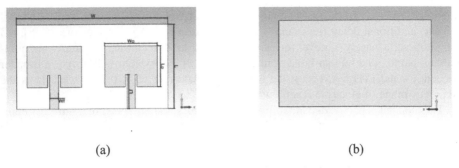

(a)   (b)

Fig. 1. Antenna Design, (a) font view, (b) bottom view

Table 1. Variables & dimensions of basic design

Variable	Dimensions	Variables	Dimensions
W	0.85 m	Wp	0.30 mm
L	0.484 mm	Lp	0.234 mm
Subh	25 μm	Wf	0.0469 mm
t	100 nm	Lf	0.20 mm

1.2 Antenna Performance Enhancement

The mutual coupling effect is inevitable in MIMO antennas due to the small spacing between the radiating elements and it has the potential to significantly degrade the antenna's performance [17]. As indicated in Fig. 2, a decoupling structure with varying widths (0.05 mm, 0.07 mm and 0.09 mm) is investigated to enhance isolation. The idea of inserting a decoupling structure is inspired by the paper [18]. In order to construct distinct shapes of decoupling structures, a deep study has been conducted in [18–20].

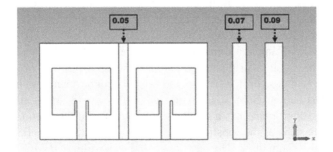

Fig. 2. Antenna design with decoupling structure

Figure 3 shows scattering parameter where the S11 is seen less than −10 dB at the operational frequency of 300 GHz without and with various widths of decoupling structure. Without decoupling structure, mutual coupling coefficient |S21| is −20.21122 dB. As illustrated in Fig. 3b, the highest mutual coupling coefficient |S21| achieved with the 0.09 mm wider decoupling structure is −26.56778 dB.

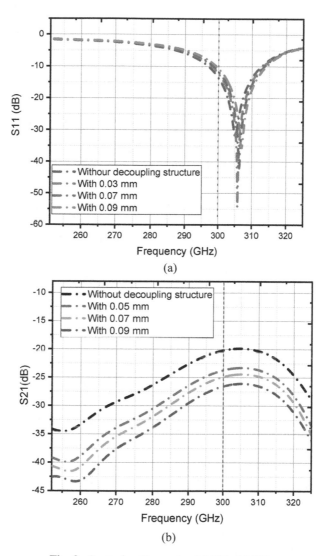

Fig. 3. Scattering Parameter, (a) S11, (b) S21

The two antennas' radiation patterns are examined and contrasted using the envelope correlation coefficient (ECC) [22]. The two radiation patterns are similar when ECC is one. This implies that both ports are receiving the same signal. When ECC is zero, the

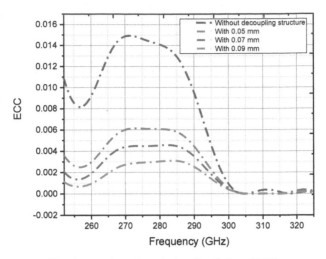

Fig. 4. Envelope Correlation Coefficient (ECC)

two radiation patterns do not overlap, and the single array element receives the incoming signal from any direction. A smaller value, ECC < 0.5 is recommended for acceptable performance. ECC is generated using two mathematical formulas. First formula based on the S-parameters [23] is

$$ECC = \frac{\left|S_{11}^* S_{12} + S_{21}^* S_{22}\right|^2}{\left(1 - |S_{11}|^2 - |S_{21}|^2\right)\left(1 - |S_{21}|^2 - |S_{12}|^2\right)} \tag{1}$$

Figure 4 illustrates the simulated results of ECC. Second formula utilizing far-field radiation patterns [24] is

$$ECC = \frac{\left|\iint_{4\pi}\left(\overrightarrow{F}_i(\theta, \varnothing)\right) \times \left(\overrightarrow{F}_J(\theta, \varnothing)\right)d\Omega\right|^2}{\iint_{4\pi}\left|\left(\overrightarrow{F}_i(\theta, \varnothing)\right)\right|^2 d\Omega \iint_{4\pi}\left|\left(\overrightarrow{F}_J(\theta, \varnothing)\right)\right|^2 d\Omega} \tag{2}$$

The simulation results of DG are shown in Fig. 5. The diversity gain (DG) of a MIMO antenna demonstrates whether or not the signal-to-noise ratio (SNR) of the calculated as the sum from several MIMO antennas is greater than that from a single antenna. The following expression can be used to compute DG [21],

$$DG = 10\left(\sqrt{1 - (ECC)^2}\right) \tag{3}$$

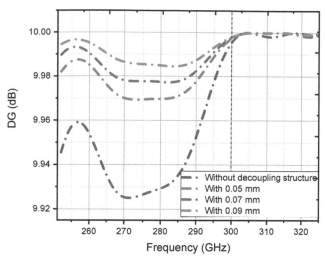

Fig. 5. Diversity Gain (DG)

2   Some More Antenna Results with 0.09 mm Decoupling Structure

At the frequency of 300 GHz, the power stimulated is almost 0.5 W, the power accepted by the port is about 0.46 W, the power radiated is nearly 2.4 and the power outgoing is 0.04 W as shown in Fig. 6.

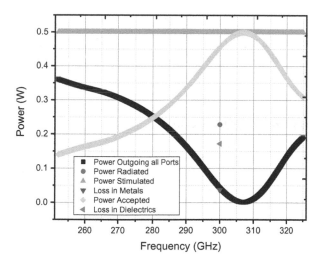

Fig. 6. Power Calculation of the proposed MIMO antenna with 0.09 mm decoupling structure

Directional (angular) dependence of radio wave power is shown by the radiation pattern [25]. The suggested MIMO antenna's decoupling structure is just 0.09 mm thick, and its 3D radiation pattern is seen in Fig. 7 where gain is 2.88 dB and directivity are

5.889 dBi. In Fig. 7, it also seen that radiated efficiency is −3.008 dB and total efficiency is −3.405 dB.

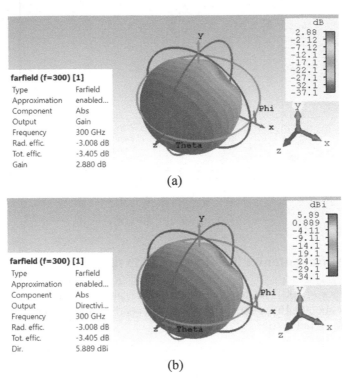

(a)

(b)

Fig. 7. 3D radiation pattern of the proposed MIMO antenna with 0.09 mm decoupling structure, (a) with gain, (b) with directivity

3   Result Analysis and Discussion

The recommended performances for a MIMO antenna are S11 < −10 dB and S21 < −20 dB, ECC < 0.5 and DG closed 10 dB according to the paper [26]. The results of our proposed MIMO antenna with 0.09 mm decoupling structure at the frequency of 300 GHz are S11 < −10 dB, S21 < −26 dB, ECC < 0.0003 and DG > 9.99 dB. As a result, for 6G networks, our suggested MIMO antenna satisfies the necessary MIMO system requirements.

4   Conclusion

This study describes a novel MIMO antenna for 6G application is presented at the frequency of 300 GHz. Some key characteristics of 6G are also highlighted, as well as when it will be adopted internationally. Previous works on 6G is studied in order to make a clear vision on antenna design requirements because 6G technology is still in its beginning phases and has yet to be established. To improve antenna performance, a decoupling structure with various widths (0.05 mm, 0.07 mm, and 0.09 mm) is examined. The highest isolation and diversity performance are achieved with a 0.09 mm width decoupling structure.

References

1. Pouttu, A.: 6Genesis–Taking the first steps towards 6G. In: Proc. IEEE Conf. Standards Communications and Networking. [Online]. Available: https://cscn2018.ieeecscn.org/files/2018/11/AriPouttu.pdf (2018)
2. Samsung Research.: 6G: The next hyper connected experience for all. Seoul. [Online]. Available: https://research.samsung.com/next-generation-communications (2020)
3. Rouse, M.: "6G," TechTarget. https://searchnetworking.techtarget.com/definition/6G Accessed 07 Sep 2020 (2020)
4. Gui, G., Liu, M., Kato, N., Adachi, F., Tang, F.: 6G: Opening new horizons for integration of comfort, security and intelligence. IEEE Wirel. Commun. 1–7 (2020)
5. Chen, S., Sun, S., Xu, G., Su, X., Cai, Y.: Beam-space multiplexing: practice, theory, and trends-from 4G TD-LTE, 5G, to 6G and beyond. arXiv 2020, arXiv:2001.05021
6. Letaief, K.B., Chen, W., Shi, Y., Zhang, J., Zhang, Y.J.A.: The roadmap to 6G: AI empowered wireless networks. IEEE Commun. Mag. **57**(8), 84–90 (2019). https://doi.org/10.1109/MCOM.2019.1900271
7. Dang, S., Amin, O., Shihada, B., Alouini, M.-S.: What should 6G be? Nat. Electron. **3**, 20–29 (2020)
8. Liang, Y.-C., Larsson, E.G., Niyato, D., Popovski, P.: 6G Mobile networks: emerging technologies and applications. China Commun. **17**, 1–6 (2020)
9. Chowdhury, M.Z., Shahjalal, M., Ahmed, S., Jang, Y.M.: 6G wireless communication systems: applications, requirements, technologies, challenges, and research directions. arXiv 2019, arXiv:1909.11315v1
10. Alsharif, M., Hilary, A., Albreem, M., Chaudhry, S., Zia, M.S., Kim, S.: Sixth generation (6G) wireless networks: vision, research activities. Challenges Potential Solutions Symmetry **12**, 676 (2020). https://doi.org/10.3390/sym12040676
11. Shlezinger, N., Alexandropoulos, G.C., Imani, M.F., Eldar, Y.C., Smith, D.R.: Dynamic metasurface antennas for 6G extreme massive MIMO communications. IEEE Wirel. Commun. **28**(2), 106–113 (2021). https://doi.org/10.1109/MWC.001.2000267
12. Hafizah Sa'don, S.N., et al.: The review and analysis of antenna for sixth generation (6G) applications. In: 2020 IEEE International RF and Microwave Conference (RFM), pp. 1–5 (2020). https://doi.org/10.1109/RFM50841.2020.9344731
13. Aqlan, B., Himdi, M., Le Coq, L., Vettikalladi, H.: Sub-THz circularly polarized horn antenna using wire electrical discharge machining for 6G wireless communications. IEEE Access **8**, 117245–117252 (2020). https://doi.org/10.1109/ACCESS.2020.3003853
14. Chi, L., Weng, Z., Qi, Y., Drewniak, J.L.: A 60 GHz PCB wideband antenna-in-package for 5G/6G applications. IEEE Antennas Wirel. Propag. Lett. **1225**, 1 (2020). https://doi.org/10.1109/LAWP.2020.3006873
15. Xu, R., et al.: A review of broadband low-cost and high-gain low-terahertz antennas for wireless communications applications. IEEE Access **8**, 57615–57629 (2020). https://doi.org/10.1109/ACCESS.2020.2981393
16. He, Y., Chen, Y., Zhang, L., Wong, S., Chen, Z.N.: An overview of terahertz antennas. China Commun. **17**(7), 124–165 (2020). https://doi.org/10.23919/j.cc.2020.07.011

17. Alibakhshikenari, M., Khalily, M., Virdee, B.S., See, C.H., Abd-Alhameed, R.A., Limiti, E.: Mutual coupling suppression between two closely placed microstrip patches using embandgap metamaterial fractal loading. IEEE Access **7**, 23606–23614 (2019). https://doi.org/10.1109/ACCESS.2019.2899326

18. Yon, H., Aris, M.A., Abd Rahman, N.H., Nasir, N.A.M., Jumaat, H.: A design of decoupling structure mimo antenna for mutual coupling reduction in 5g application. In: 2019 International Symposium on Antennas and Propagation (ISAP), pp. 1–3 (2019)

19. Baharom, B., Ali, M.T., Jaafar, H., Yon, H.: Dual-element of high-SHF PIFA MIMO antenna for future 5G wireless communication devices. In: Proceedings - 2018 International Symposium Antennas Propagation no. ISAP, pp. 151–152 (2018)

20. Qi, H., Xiaoxing, Y., Zhao Hongxin, W.J.K.: Mutual coupling suppression between two closely spaced microstrip antennas with an asymmetrical coplanar strip wall. IEEE Antennas Wirel. Propag. Lett. **1225**(c), 1–4 (2015)

21. Blanch, S., Romeu, J., Corbella, I.: Exact representation of antenna system diversity performance from input parameter description. Electron. Lett. **39**(9), 705–707 (2003)

22. Park, J., Rahman, M., Chen, H.N.: Isolation enhancement of wide-band MIMO array antennas utilizing resistive loading. IEEE Access **7**, 81020–81026 (2019). https://doi.org/10.1109/ACCESS.2019.2923330

23. Malekpour, N., Honarvar, M.A.: Design of high-isolation compact MIMO antenna for UWB application. Prog. Electromagn. Res. C **62**, 119–129 (2016). https://doi.org/10.2528/PIERC15120902

24. Sharawi, M.S.: Printed MIMO Antenna Engineering; Artech House: Norwood. MA, USA (2014)

25. Balanis, C.A.: Antenna Theory: Analysis Design. Third Edition, A John Wiles and Sons, Hoboken, New Jersey (2005)

26. Iqbal, A., Saraereh, O.A., Bouazizi, A., Basir, A.: Metamaterial-based highly isolated MIMO antenna for portable wireless applications. Electronics **7**, 267 (2018). https://doi.org/10.3390/electronics7100267

27. Distributed resource sharing. In: 10th IEEE International Symposium on High Performance Distributed Computing, pp. 181–184. IEEE Press, New York (2001)

28. Foster, I., Kesselman, C., Nick, J., Tuecke, S.: The physiology of the grid: an open grid services architecture for distributed systems integration. Technical report, Global Grid Forum (2002)

29. National Center for Biotechnology Information. http://www.ncbi.nlm.nih.gov

Modification of Link Speed Estimation Model for IEEE 802.11ac WLANs by Considering Shadowing Effect

Mohammed Aman Ullah Aman[(✉)] and Sumon Kumar Debnath

Begum Rokeya University, Rangpur, Bangladesh
aman922247@gmail.com, sumon.eee@brur.ac.bd

Abstract. In a wireless local area network (WLAN), 802.11ac protocol is commonly accepted due to its fast communication technology at 5GHz. For effective design of WLAN system, previously, we have studied link speed estimation model of 802.11n links that estimates the link speed among an AP and a client PC in the network field. However, it does not assume the shadowing effect which has great influence on the Received Signal Strength (RSS), especially in a complex network environment. In shadow fading, the RSS fluctuates due to the reflection, refraction, and scattering, which is characterized as small scale fading. Therefore, to achieve more accuracy in link speed estimation, it is crucial to consider shadow fading effect in link speed estimation model. In this paper, we present modification of link speed estimation model by considering shadow fading factor. First, we show the RSS and link speed measurement results of 802.11ac MIMO link to derive estimation model parameters including shadow fading factor. Then, by considering this shadow fading parameter we modify estimation model. Finally, we show the link speed estimation results which reveal that our modified model provides better accuracy than previous model.

Keywords: IEEE 802.11ac · Shadow fading · WLAN · Link speed estimation

1 Introduction

In today's world, several standards and protocols like 802.11a/b/g/n/ac are available for the deployment of wireless local area networks (WLANs). For its faster link features and new technology, the IEEE 802.11ac protocol is becoming more popular than other versions. These features include higher modulation and coding scheme (MCSs) up to 256 QAMs, wider bonded channel up to 160 MHz, beam-forming, Multi User multiple input and multiple output (MIMO) with up-to eight spatial streams etc. Multiuser MIMO facilitates users with more transmitters and receivers to increase data rates. As IEEE 802.11ac uses 5GHz, it has 24 non-overlapping channels available for the clients [1, 2].

In any complex network environment like school, college, Universities, or office buildings, the effective design of WLANs are very important which requires accurate link speed estimation between an access-point (AP) and a client. By designing WLANs

Md. S. Satu et al. (Eds.): MIET 2022, LNICST 491, pp. 303–316, 2023.
https://doi.org/10.1007/978-3-031-34622-4_24

with actual link speed estimation model, any client PC in the network field can achieve higher RSS and link speed performance. Link speed estimation greatly depends on RSS, shadow fading effect, antenna height of AP and client PC, interference, multipath effect etc.

To provide solution of the above stated problems, we have studied WLANS system and throughput estimation model [3, 4]. The model has two simple steps. At first, it estimates RSS at client PC side and in second step; the model maps RSS in to corresponding throughput. Although it can accurately estimate the throughput in simple network environment, its performance degrades for complex network environment because the model does not consider shadow fading effect.

The behavior of signal propagation is greatly influenced by the environment. In a complex network environment, reflection, refraction, and scattering effects are significant. Therefore, the received signal strength (RSS) at any particular point fluctuates more rapidly with time than the open space. This variation of RSS is occurred due to the shadow fading effect [5]. Hence, the link speed offered by the wireless link in such environment varies significantly due to the shadow fading effect. In order to estimate the link speed with higher accuracy in a complex network environment, it is essential to consider shadow fading effect in the link speed estimation model.

Based on our literature reviews, we have observed some issues of the link speed estimation models which are used for the deployment of WLANs. In [3, 4], Authors adopted a simple two-step approach to estimate the throughput of 802.11n MIMO/SISO WLAN system when only a client PC is communicating at a time with an access-point in the network field. First, they estimated RSS using log distance model and then converted this RSS into throughput by using the sigmoid curve. Besides, they proposed two modifications of the model for simultaneous communication by multiple clients with an AP [4]. Their model confirmed satisfactory accuracy in throughput estimation. Though, they considered wall loss factor, they did not assume shadow fading factor in their models. Authors proposed an analytical model in [6] to determine the throughput, delay, and fairness performance for IEEE 802.11 WLAN system with single hop. They estimated the throughput from the payload transmitted in a generic time slot which is achieved based on the state of time slots (idle, successful, or collision). They tuned three system factors like least contention window (CW_{min}), the maximum contention window (CW_{max}), and the retry limit (m) for optimizing link speed performance. Authors in [7] modified the log-normal distribution model and proposed an extreme value distribution model to estimate RSS fluctuations in their throughput estimation model for IEEE 802.11af WLAN system. Their model estimated RSS using modified log distance model and recorded the relationship between RSS and throughput using the exponential distribution which were further used in link speed estimation. Authors assumed a mathematical model to estimate throughput from the payload and the delay time in [8]. They also investigated the impacts of network variables such as size of packet and station count on throughput and delay. Their estimated results was based on the theoretical model which showed that by increasing the packet size, theoretical maximum throughput (TMT) and delay time can be raised. Again, by adding more stations in the network might improve the delay time which lowered TMT. The model considered an ideal environment where there is no packet loss, interference and collision. In practical WLAN scenario, delay time can be affected by parameters such as the reflection, refraction, and scattering of a signal. Authors in [9] implemented a two-phase estimation model of 802.11ac/n WLAN system to estimate throughput for holding AP assignment algorithm. Though their model confirmed its effectiveness by improving the total throughput performance through simulations, they did not assumed shadow fading parameters in their model. By considering shadow fading factor in the estimation model, the estimation accuracy can be improved which can make the network performance more realistic. In [10], authors compared throughput performance of 802.11n SISO/MIMO links by considering modulation and coding scheme (MCS) and power savings of MIMO link. They estimated the throughput by using capacity calculation considering system bandwidth, total transmit power and noise variance. But in practical scenario, it shows significant difference in predicted and measured values as wireless links are mostly affected by the environment. So, simply tuning the transmit power and SNR is not enough.

In this paper, we present modification of the link speed estimation model by considering shadow fading factor. First, we measure RSS and link speed to derive model parameters including optimized value of the shadow fading factor. Finally, we modify the previous estimation model by considering shadow fading factor and evaluate the efficiency of the modified model by comparing link speed estimation errors before and after using the modified model.

The upcoming portion of the paper is outlined as follows: Sect. 2 contains a review on previous link speed estimation model and background technology. Section 3 shows our proposed modification of link speed estimation model by examining shadow factor. We present the measurements of RSS and link speed for 802.11ac MIMO link in Sect. 4 for tuning the model parameters. Section 5 demonstrates the derivation of the modified model parameters for both line-of-sight (LOS) and non-line-of-sight (NLOS) situation and performance evaluation by comparing the estimation results with the previous model and error calculation. Finally, we conclude our work in Scct. 6 with a discussion of future works.

2 Review of Link Speed Estimation Model and Background Technology

We review previous link speed estimation model and technology related to our work in this section.

2.1 Review of Estimation Model

Here, we review the previous model used for throughput estimation [3]. The estimation process is carried out using two simple steps:

1. RSS estimation by log distance model.
2. Conversion of RSS into throughput using sigmoid function.

The flowchart of the model is presented in the Fig. 1.

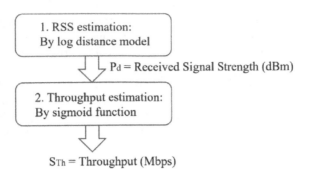

Fig. 1. Flow chart of estimation process

In first step, model estimates the RSS at client PC side situated any position in the field by using the following Eq. (1) [3]

$$P_d = P_1 - 10\,n\,log_{10}(d) - \sum_k n_k W_k \tag{1}$$

Here, P_d is the RSS at any distance d(m) from the AP, P_1 is the RSS at 1m distance from AP, n is the path attenuation or loss exponent of the network field. n_k represents total number of walls between the AP and client, W_k represents the wall attenuation factor.

In the second step, RSS is changed into corresponding throughput by using Eq. (2) [3]

$$S_{Th} = \frac{a}{1 + e^{-\frac{(P_d + 120) - b}{c}}} \tag{2}$$

Here, S_{Th} is the converted throughput (Mbps) with respect to the estimated RSS (P_d).

2.2   Overview of IEEE 802.11ac Technology

For the faster link features, the IEEE 802.11ac protocol is becoming more popular than earlier versions (802.11b/g/n).The protocol adopted modern technologies and offers higher link speed performance. The IEEE 802.11ac can only be deployed at 5GHz band [1] and it is less congested than 2.4GHz. 160 MHz channel bonding facility provides higher bandwidth to each 802.11ac client. 802.11ac also supports MIMO with up to eight spatial streams which enhance user experience. High-density MCS (up to 256-QAM) also provides higher data rates to the 802.11ac protocol [1, 2].

Considering those facilities, it is wise to use IEEE 802.11ac for deploying modern WLAN system.

2.3   Overview of Shadow Fading Effect for IEEE 802.11ac Technology

The rapid variation of the RSS caused by blocking large objects in the paths of propagation between the transmitter and the receiver is referred to as shadow fading. In this case, the transmitted signal is absorbed by the shadowing obstacles which introduce rapid variation in RSS at the client PC.

WLAN system uses electromagnetic signals that propagate to carry information to the client PC. In a complex network environment, where there more walls, doors, and other formations, offers more reflection, refraction, and scattering to the transmitted signal. As a result, fluctuations in signal become more severe than experienced in free space. This type of fluctuation of signal is termed as shadow fading [5].

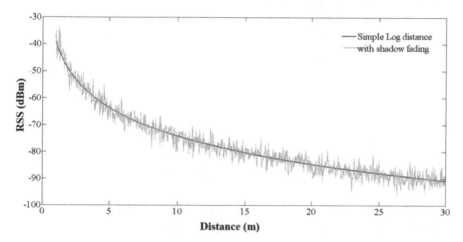

Fig. 2. Shadow fading effect on RSS

Figure 2 shows log distance path loss with rapid fluctuation of RSS caused by shadowing effect.

Due to the shadow fading effect, RSS maybe changed randomly from a predetermined level at a fixed client position over time or at different client distance with fixed time from the AP. Using Homedale [11] software, we can easily observe the shadow fading effect on RSS in practical WLAN environment.

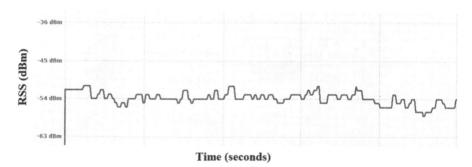

Fig. 3. Shadow fading effect on RSS at fixed position in different time

Figure 3 shows the variation of RSS at the client PC located at 7m distance from the AP for the duration of 0s to 50s. In this case, the RSS fluctuates between −52 dBm to −54 dBm. This deviation of RSS may cause for two different cases, such as 1) the line-of-sight (LOS) and 2) the non-line-of-sight (NLOS). As the transmitted signal is significantly affected by the shadow fading effect, we cannot estimate RSS accurately by using Eq. (1), because it did not consider the shadow fading effect in RSS estimation.

3 Proposed Modification of Estimation Model

To reflect the variations of RSS due to the shadowing effects, we include shadow fading parameter in Eq. (1) as follows

$$P_d = P_1 - 10\,n\,log_{10}(d) - \sum_k n_k W_k - X_\delta \tag{3}$$

Here, X_δ is the shadow fading factor. Then, we convert the estimated RSS into link speed by using in Eq. (2).

We tune several parameters of the modified model including shadow fading factor by fitting curve with measured results in the network field.

4 Measurement of RSS and Link Speed for 802.11ac MIMO Link for Tuning Parameters of the Modified Model

In this section, we carry out RSS and link speed measurements in the network field to tune several parameters of the modified model including shadow fading factor.

4.1 Measurement Setups

Here, we discuss about the essential devices, equipment, software and network architecture used in our measurement. Devices enabled with 802.11ac wireless standard are used in the measurement. We deploy wireless AP connected with a server PC via 1000 Mbps UTP cable with 802.3 protocol and a client PC via 802.11ac MIMO links.

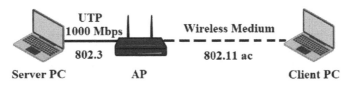

Fig. 4. Network architecture

Figure 4 demonstrates network architecture and link types. We run Homedale version 2.02 on the client PC to determine the RSS in dBm at different client positions. To obtain link speed of 802.11ac MIMO link, we run JPerf version 2.0.2 [12] on both server PC and client PC for 50s with an interval of 10 s.

Table 1. Briefs of device and software profiles.

Group	Specification
Server PC	Model: ASUS X510U, Processor: Intel Corei5-8250U, NIC: Realtek PCIe GBE family controller
Client PC	Model: ASUS X510U, Processor: Intel Corei5-8250U, Wireless Adapter: Intel Dual Band Wireless-AC 8265
Wireless AP	Model: Tenda AC2100, Mode: 802.11ac, 80 MHz, Antennas: 6
Software	Homedale version 2.02 [11], JPerf version 2.0.2 [12]

Table 1 presents the specifications of devices used in our measurement.

Using Homedale software tool, we continuously monitor and minimized interference and packet loss from the nearby AP using same channel to obtain actual RSS and link speed in the network field. We use 802.11ac MIMO link with 80 MHz channel width and 13 dBm transmit power. The heights of AP and client PC are set around 120 cm and 100 cm from the ground of floor respectively.

4.2 Measurement Topologies

We conduct our measurements on the 2nd floor in a three storied student hostel. Figure 5 illustrates the network field used for the RSS and link speed measurements considering LOS situation. We deploy the AP connected to the server PC on the left side of the corridor. Then, we connect the client PC with the AP using 802.11ac MIMO links and measure the RSS and link speed for a total distance of 18 m with an interval of 1 m.

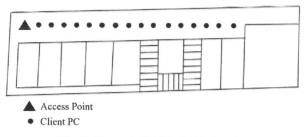

▲ Access Point
● Client PC

Fig. 5. Network field for LOS situation

For NLOS situation, we consider five random client PC positions for link speed estimation. The network environment is a complex one as it comprises several walls within a short distance. Figure 6 illustrates the network field where we deploy a commercial AP with 802.11ac on the left side of the corridor and measure RSS and link speed at those random client positions.

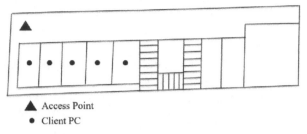

▲ Access Point
● Client PC

Fig. 6. Network field for NLOS situation

4.3 Measurement Results

From Fig. 7, we observe that the RSS attenuates at client PC with the increasing physical distance (0 m to 18 m) from the AP. In this case, the RSS drops from −38 dBm to −58 dBm. We also observe that this reduction of RSS is not uniform throughout the measured distances. It occurs because of the shadow fading effect on the transmitted signal. While propagating through the corridor, signal experiences reflection, refraction and scattering due to the network environment which are the three reasons for shadow fading.

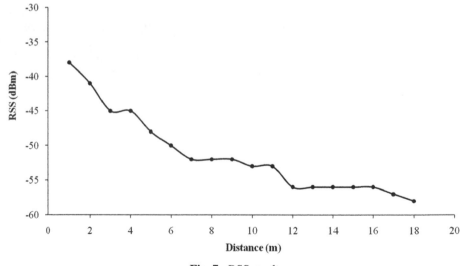

Fig. 7. RSS result

We derive the path loss exponent (n) of the network environment from the measured RSS using linear regression method [13]. In this scenario, the calculated optimum value of n is 1.52. The value may vary for different situations such as LOS (1.5–2) and NLOS (2–6).

The link speed measurement results of 802.11ac MIMO links is revealed in Fig. 8. We obtained maximum link speed of 450 Mbps in our measurement. In this case, the link speed does not decrease much. Because the corridor acts like a tunnel and link speed

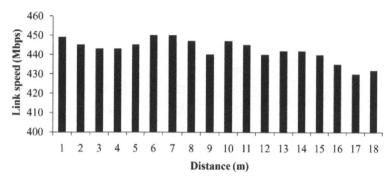

Fig. 8. Link speed result

escalate at some points due to multipath effect. In addition, we consider LOS situation and there is no obstacle between the AP and the client.

5 Link Speed Estimation Model Parameters and Performance Evaluation

In this section, we present link speed estimation by the modified model for both LOS and NLOS situation and compare the results with the previous model. We also calculate the error between the estimated and measured values.

5.1 Link Speed Estimation Model Parameters and Performance Evaluation Results for LOS Situation

The required parameters of the estimation model are derived and correlated from the field measurement.

To derive the shadow fading factor X_δ, we need to predict RSS at any distance (d = 10m) by using following equation

$$P_P = P_1 - 10 n \log_{10}(10) = -38 - 15.2 = -53.2 \, dBm \qquad (4)$$

Table 2 shows the values of measurements and calculations to derive standard deviation of RSS.

Here, P_P is the predicted RSS at d = 10 m and P_M is the measured RSS. Then, we derive standard deviation δ by using the data in Table 2 and the equation in (5)

$$\text{Standard deviation } \delta = \sqrt{\frac{\sum_{d=1}^{18}(P_M - P_P)^2}{N}} = \sqrt{\frac{632.72}{18}} = 5.92 \, dBm \qquad (5)$$

We determine the shadow fading factor X_δ by using Standard Normal Curve [13].

Figure 9 presents the standard normal curve considering zero mean with 60% probability. We need to tune the probability with respect to the network environment. In more complex network environments, there are more fluctuations in RSS due to the shadow

Table 2. Measured data for standard deviation.

Distance(m)	P_M (dBm)	(P_M-P_P)	$(P_M-P_P)2$
1	−38	15.2	231.04
2	−41	12.2	148.84
3	−45	8.2	67.24
4	−45	8.2	67.24
5	−48	5.2	27.04
6	−50	3.2	10.24
7	−52	1.2	1.44
8	−52	1.2	1.44
9	−52	1.2	1.44
10	−53	0.2	0.44
11	−53	0.2	0.44
12	−56	−2.8	7.84
13	−56	−2.8	7.84
14	−56	−2.8	7.84
15	−56	−2.8	7.84
16	−56	−2.8	7.84
17	−57	−3.8	14.44
18	−58	−4.8	23.04

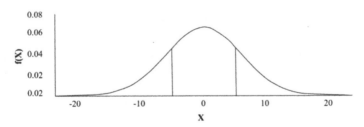

Fig. 9. Normal distribution curve

fading effect and we have to increase the probability so that the RSS does not go below the estimated level.

Then, X_δ is determined using Cumulative Density Function [13] as follows:

$$\phi(\frac{X_\delta - \mu}{\delta}) = 0.60 \, with X = 5 \, and \mu = 0$$

$$(\frac{X_\delta - 0}{5.92}) = 0.2$$

$$X_\delta = 1.184 \, \text{dBm}$$

In this case, the obtained value of the shadow fading factor is 1.184 dBm which indicates less fluctuation in RSS in our measurements as we considered LOS situation. The value of the shadow fading factor increases as the environment offers more reflection, refraction and scattering to the transmitted signal due to its complex nature.

Equation 6 and Eq. 7 shows the modified model by considering shadow fading factor with corresponding values of the parameters.

$$P_d = P_1 - 10 \, n \, log_{10}(d) - \sum_k n_k W_k - X_\delta \tag{6}$$

$$= -38 - 15.2 \, log_{10}(d) - 1.184 \tag{7}$$

Table 3 summarizes the estimation parameters for LOS situation derived from measurements and logistic curve fitting.

Table 3. Parameters of estimation model for LOS situation.

Parameter	P_1	n	X_δ	a	b	c
Value	−38 dBm	1.52	1.184 dBm	450	50	4.2

Figure 10 shows the link speed estimation results of the modified model and previous model. Here, we estimate link speed at different client distances from the AP with the modified and previous model. Then, we compare the estimated link speed with the measured link speed and calculate the error.

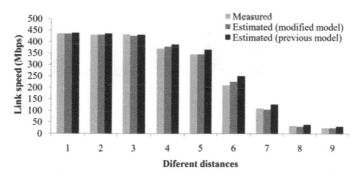

Fig. 10. Link speed estimation results for LOS situation

Estimated link speed by the modified model shows more correlation with the measured link speed than the previous model as it considered shadow fading factor in the estimation.

Table 4 presents the average, maximum and minimum of link speed estimation error.

In Table 4, results clearly show that estimation error is less noticeable in the modified model than the previous model.

Table 4. Error(Mbps) for both models.

Model	Average	Max	Min
Modified model	3.72	15	0.07
Previous model	6.80	40	0.00

5.2 Link Speed Estimation Model Parameters and Performance Evaluation Results for NLOS Situation

Table 5 summarizes the estimation parameters for NLOS situation derived from measurements and logistic curve fitting.

Table 5. Parameters of estimation model for NLOS situation.

Parameter	P_1	n	X_δ	a	b	c
Values	−38 dBm	1.52	2.5 dBm	450	62	7

Figure 11 shows the link speed estimation results of the modified model and previous model for each positions of the client PCs.

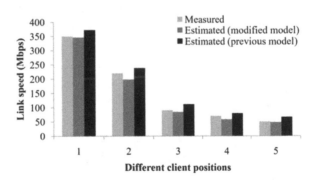

Fig. 11. Link speed estimation results for NLOS situation

In case of NLOS situation, estimated and measured data shows promising link speed estimation performance of the modified model.

Table 6 shows the average of link speed estimation error.

Results in Table 6 show higher error due to rapid fluctuations of RSS as we consider NLOS situation in the measurement. Results also confirm that estimation error is less significant in the modified model than in the previous model.

Table 6. Average Error (Mbps) for both models.

Model	Average Error (Mbps)
Modified model	9.2
Previous model	17.2

6 Conclusion

In this paper, we present modifications of the link speed estimation model for 802.11ac WLAN by assuming shadow fading effects to further improve the accuracy in link speed estimation. The effectiveness of the modified model is verified for both LOS and NLOS situations. In future, the estimation accuracy of the model should be enhanced more by introducing additional parameters in the model and test their effectiveness in several real network fields.

References

1. Gast, M.S.: 802.11ac: A Survival Guide: Wifi at gigabit and beyond. 1st edn. O'Reilly Media, Inc., USA (2013)
2. Banerji, S., Chowdhury, R.S.: On IEEE 802.11: wireless LAN technology. arXiv preprint arXiv:1307.2661 (2013)
3. Debnath, S.K., Funabiki, N., Sarker, P.K., Lwin, K.S., Saha, M.: Throughput Estimation of SISO and MIMO Links under LOS and NLOS Conditions in IEEE 802.11n WLAN. Computer Science and Engineering Research Journal 11, 19–27 (2018)
4. Debnath, S.K., Saha, M., Funabiki, N., Kao, W.C.: Throughput Estimation Model for IEEE 802.11n MIMO Link in Wireless Local-Area Networks. In: International Conference on Computer and Communication Systems 3, 327–331 (2018). https://doi.org/10.1109/CCOMS.2018.8463225
5. Rappaport, T.S.: Wireless Communications: Principles and Practice, 2nd edn. Prentice Hall, USA (2002)
6. Li, Z., Das, A., Gupta, A.K., Nandi, S.: Performance Analysis of IEEE 802.11 DCF: Throughput, Delay, and Fairness (2011)
7. Sawada, H., et al.: Path Loss and Throughput Estimation models for an IEEE 802.11af Prototype. In: IEEE 81st Vehicular Technology Conference (VTC Spring) 11, 1–5 (2015). https://doi.org/10.1109/VTCSpring.2015.7145995
8. Eyadeh, A., Jarrah, M., Aljumaili, A.: Modeling and Simulation of Performance limits in IEEE 802.11 Point Coordination Function. In: International Journal of Recent Technology and Engineering (IJRTE) 8(4), 5575–5580 (2019). https://doi.org/10.35940/ijrte.B2313.118419
9. Tajima, S., Funabiki, N., Higashino, T.: Application of IEEE802.11ac/n Link Throughput Estimation Model in Holding Access-Point Assignment Algorithm for Wireless Local-Area Network. Journal of Communications 15(1), 81–87 (2020). https://doi.org/10.12720/jcm.15.1.81-87
10. Chaudhari, S., Hu, J., Daneshrad, B., Chen, J.: Performance Comparison Between MIMO and SISO Systems Based on Indoor Field Measurements. arXiv preprint arXiv:1408.6587 (2014)
11. Homedale Wifi/WLAN monitor. https://the-sz.com/products/homedale/index.php, last accessed 28 July 2022

12. Jperf: https://jperf.soft112.com/, last accessed 28 July 2022
13. Ubom, E.A., Akpanobong, A.C., Abraham, I.I.: Characterization of Indoor Propagation Properties And Performance Evaluation For 2.4GHz Band Wi-Fi. International Journal of Wireless & Mobile Networks (IJWMN) **11**, 27–38 (2019). https://doi.org/10.2139/ssrn.339 1700

Electromagnetic Absorption Analysis of 5G Wireless Devices for Different Electromagnetic Shielding Techniques

Abdullah Al Imtiaz[1], Md. Saifur Rahman[1], Tanveer Ahsan[1],
Mohammed Shamsul Alam[1], Abdul Kader Mohammad Masum[1],
and Touhidul Alam[1,2(✉)]

[1] Department of CSE, International Islamic University Chittagong (IIUC), Kumira, Chittagong, Bangladesh
[2] Space Science Centre, Institute of Climate Change (IPI), Universiti Kebangsaan Malaysia, Bangi, Selangor, Malaysia
touhidul@ukm.edu.my

Abstract. The communication system has played an important role in human civilization from ancient smoke signals to wireless signals through electromagnetic signals. The wireless devices emit electromagnetic (EM) radiation during the active mode of operation. The human body absorbed the radiated EM waves up to a certain level. There are many short and long-term effects of EM radiation on human health. The active source of this radiation is the integrated antenna with the device. In this paper, EM absorption has been analyzed for multiband mobile communication. The human head and hand phantom models have been unitized to investigate the EM absorption towards the human body. Different types of shields to minimize the EM radiation have also been studied, and the results are tabulated to visualize the scenario.

Keywords: EM radiation · mobile communication · Specific absorption rate (SAR) · head phantom · hand phantom · 5G

1 Introduction

During the last few decades, the communication system has explored with various advanced technologies to benefit and enlighten human life. With the invention of the telephone, a revolutionary change was observed in human civilization. Later, the communication technology offered radio technology, by which a whole new level of communication system was introduced, such as cellular and satellite networks. The tremendous development of communication systems such as the second generation (2G), third-generation (3G), fourth-generation (4G), fifth-generation (5G) and upcoming sixth-generation (6G) mobile communications, global position system (GPS), WiFi, WiMAX,

Md. S. Satu et al. (Eds.): MIET 2022, LNICST 491, pp. 317–324, 2023.
https://doi.org/10.1007/978-3-031-34622-4_25

wireless Bluetooth, and Ultra-Wideband (UWB) systems have driven the wireless technology to the verge of revolutionary wireless communications. Antennas are indispensable elements of any wireless communication system, which radiates EM waves. Prolonged usages of the mobile phone could disrupt the biological condition of the human being. Several types of research have been performed on the long-term and short-term effects of EM radiation on the human body [1–3]. Moreover, there are various myths about the biological effect of using a mobile phone. Tissue heating is one of them. The principal reason for heat absorption by human tissue is due to the proximity of radiating devices and the human body[4, 5]. When the mobile phone is used, most of the energy is absorbed by the skin and other superficial tissues, which might increase biological tissues' temperature [6]. Extensive use of mobile phone has high risk on the brain [7, 8]. It had been ruled out that by more than 50% of the RF energy emitted from the mobile phone being absorbed at the side hemisphere of the brain where the mobile phone is usually held to [9]The side of the brain with the highest absorption of RF energy is known as the temporal lobe. RF radiation exposure from wireless devices is expressed in specific absorption rate (SAR). All wireless devices must comply the SAR safety guidelines. Currently, IEEE and ICNIRP [10, 11] have developed EM radiation exposure guidelines for general public and workers, except some special situation like, patients undergoing medical diagnosis or treatment [12]. The SAR guidelines for different countries are also different. Example, European countries follow the ICNIRP guidelines of 2.0 W/Kg in 10g tissue and Unites States follow the FCC guideline of 1.6 W/Kg in 1g tissue.

Lots of research is going on to minimize EM radiation toward the human body [13, 14]. Several methods have been investigated, where some achieved effective results, and some failed to achieve proper success. Increasing the distance between the human head and wireless devices is the easiest way to reduce the SAR values. However, this method has some constraints to ensure sound quality and effective communication. In 1998 Tay et al. proposed a new technique to reduce SAR by achieving 65–80% of peak value using an additional reflector. However, additional reflector required additional space was the major concern of this technique. In 1999, Wang et al. first proposed ferrite material attachment technique for SAR reduction [15]. In this technique, surface currents are reduced by the ferrite without degrading antenna efficiency [16]. Kitra et al. proposed another approach to reduce SAR using ferrite-loaded short monopole antenna [17]. In [18], magneto-dielectric Composites have been utilized to miniaturized antenna as well as SAR reduction. Recently, ferrite composite based reduced graphene oxide (rGO) coated meta structures have been developed for EM shielding [19]. Metamaterial, a special type of artificial EM structure known as electromagnetic bandgap (EBG), frequency selective surface (FSSS) [20] and artificial magnetic conductor (AMC) are employed to reduce SAR values without affecting the antenna efficiency [21], where high impedance surface technique is utilized to trap electromagnetic energy towards human body at resonating frequency [22]. This structure also required additional space to integrate with the antenna system [23–26].

In this research Specific absorption ratio (SAR) value of the mobile wireless device has been analyzed for two different frequencies and different EM shielding materials and conditions.

2 Methodology

A multiband patch antenna has been imported from Antenna Magus, shown in Fig. 1 and Fig. 2. The antenna is attached between the backplane and the mobile phone's battery. The shielding layer of 0.2 mm is attached behind the LCD screen to reflect the radiation towards the human body. The antenna reflection coefficient and efficiency of the antenna at 2.18 GHz and 3.66 GHz has been investigated and listed in Fig. 1, Table 1 and Table 2, respectively. CST microwave studio has been utilized to design and investigate the SAR values. This simulation used head and hand phantom with a cellular phone to investigate SAR values for different shield conditions.

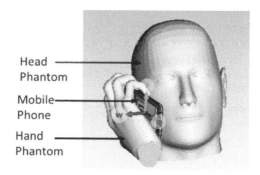

(a) Head and hand phantom with mobile phone

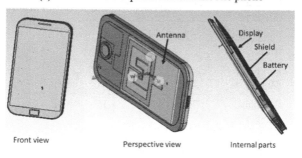

(b) Mobile device

Fig. 1. Simulation setup for SAR analysis

Table 1. Reflection coefficient for different shielding conditions

Shielding condition	S11 at 2.18 GHz (dB)	S11 at 3.66 GHz (dB)
Full plane (Copper)	−11.20	−23.2
Full plane (Silver)	−12.32	−24.0
Full plane (Brass)	−13.0	−23.0
Full plane (Zinc)	−11.0	−24.5
Full plane (Nickel)	−10.8	−24.6
Slotted shielding (Copper)	−13.9	−36

Table 2. Antenna radiation performances for different shielding conditions

Shielding condition	Efficiency at 2.18 GHz (%)	Efficiency at 3.66 GHz (%)
Full plane (Copper)	53	58
Full plane (Silver)	51	53
Full plane (Brass)	51.25	55
Full plane (Zinc)	52	54.5
Full plane (Nickel)	52.5	55
Slotted shielding (Copper)	54	59.5

3 SAR Analysis

The SAR analysis have been performed to investigate possible health risk by absorbing EM radiation. There are many important factors that has significant impact on EM absorption. Close proximity of the mobile phone with human head is one of them.

Moreover, the reference input power also has great influence on EM radiation. In this investigation, the input power was considered 0.5 W. The simulated 10g SAR values of the investigation are depicted in Fig. 2, where SAR analysis have been performed for three different conditions- (a) without shielding layer, (b) with slotted shielding layer and (c) with full plane shielding layer. It is shown from Fig. 2 that the highest SAR value is achieved without shielding conditions, and the lowest SAR is observed for full plane shielding with the copper substrate. Therefore, 95.8% and 92.2% of the SAR value reduction has been achieved with a full plane conductive shield at 2.18 GHz and at 3.66 GHz, respectively.

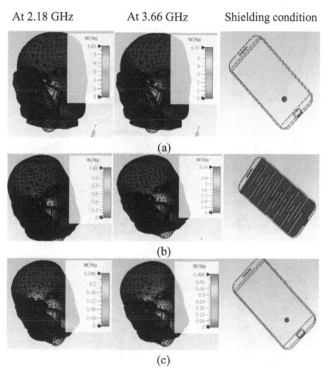

Fig. 2. SAR analysis for different shielding conditions

The SAR value has been investigated for different types of conducting materials, illustrated in Fig. 3. The red color in Fig. 3 indicates the maximum EM wave absorption at respective frequencies. It is shown from Fig. 3. That the lowest SAR value is found for Nickel materials, and the highest is observed for Silver materials. So, it can be concluded that any typed of a full layer of the conductive shield can minimize the SAR values with respect to the without using conductive shielding layers.

At 2.18 GHz   At 3.66 GHz

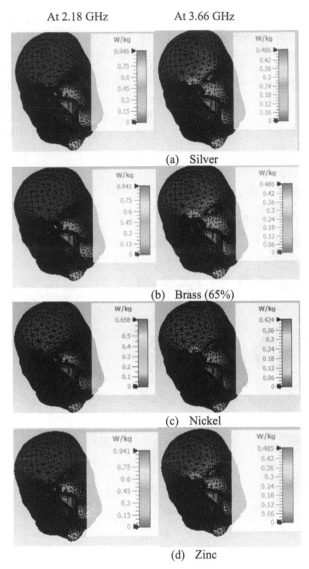

(a) Silver

(b) Brass (65%)

(c) Nickel

(d) Zinc

Fig. 3. SAR analysis for different materials.

4 Conclusion

The research is focused on investigating EM absorption reduction of wireless devices. Several shielding conditions have been investigated to achieve the EM absorption guidelines established by IEEE and ICNIRP without degrading other antenna performances. Moreover, the 95.8% and 92.2% of the SAR reduction at 2.18 GHz and at 3.66 GHz, respectively, has been attained with a conductive shield layer behind the LCD of the wireless devices.

Acknowledgments. This work was funded by the Universiti Kebangsaan Malaysia, research grant no: GGPM-2021-054.

References

1. Christopher, B., Khandaker, M.U., Jojo, P.: Empirical study on specific absorption rate of head tissues due to induced heating of 4G cell phone radiation. Radiat. Phys. Chem. **178**, 108910 (2021)
2. Priyadarshini, S.J., Hemanth, D.J.: Investigation and reduction methods of specific absorption rate for biomedical applications: A survey. Int. J. RF Microwave Comput. Aided Eng. **28**, e21211 (2018)
3. Hediya, A.M.: Reduction of Specific Absorption Rate: A Review Article. The Egyptian Intern. J. Eng. Sci. Technol. **39**, 80–96 (2022)
4. Gupta, S., Sharma, R.S., Singh, R.: Non-ionizing radiation as possible carcinogen. Int. J. Environ. Health Res. **32**, 916–940 (2022)
5. Zhang, H.H., Gong, L.F., Wang, J., Sha, W.E., Li, L., Wang, J.X., Wang, C.: Specific absorption rate assessment of fifth generation mobile phones with specific anthropomorphic mannequin model and high-resolution anatomical head model. International Journal of RF and Microwave Computer-Aided Engineering e23158 (2022)
6. Wang, H.: Analysis of electromagnetic energy absorption in the human body for mobile terminals. IEEE Open Journal of Antennas and Propagation **1**, 113–117 (2020)
7. Schüz, J., Jacobsen, R., Olsen, J.H., Boice, J.D., McLaughlin, J.K., Johansen, C.: Cellular telephone use and cancer risk: update of a nationwide Danish cohort. J. Natl Cancer Inst. **98**, 1707–1713 (2006)
8. Ahlbom, A., et al.: Epidemiologic evidence on mobile phones and tumor risk: a review. Epidemiology **20**, 639–652 (2009)
9. Cardis, E., et al.: Distribution of RF energy emitted by mobile phones in anatomical structures of the brain. Phys. Med. Biol. **53**, 2771 (2008)
10. ICNIRP: ICNIRP guidelines for limiting exposure to time-varying electric, magnetic and electromagnetic fields (up to 300 GHZ). Health Physics **74**, 494–522 (1998)
11. IEEE: IEEE standard for safety levels with respect to human exposure to radio frequency electromagnetic fields, 3 kHz to 300 GHz, IEEE Std C95.1. Institute of Electrical and Electonics Engineers, Incorporated (2005)
12. Kundu, A., Gupta, B., Mallick, A.I.: Contrast in specific absorption rate for a typical plant model due to discrepancy among global and national electromagnetic standards. Progress In Electromagnetics Research **99**, 139–152 (2021)
13. Alam, T., et al.: Specific absorption rate (SAR) analysis using plastic substrate based negative indexed metamaterial shielding. In: 2017 International Conference on Electrical, Computer and Communication Engineering (ECCE), pp. 619–622. IEEE (2017)
14. Alam, T., Faruque, M.R.I., Islam, M.T.: Study on EM absorption analysis of mobile handset antenna. J. Telecommun. Elec. Comp. Eng. (JTEC) **8**, 61–65 (2016)
15. Tay, R.-S., Balzano, Q., Kuster, N.: Dipole configurations with strongly improved radiation efficiency for hand-held transceivers. IEEE Trans. Antennas Propag. **46**, 798–806 (1998)
16. Wang, J., Fujiwara, O., Takagi, T.: Effects of ferrite sheet attachment to portable telephone in reducing electromagnetic absorption in human head. In: 1999 IEEE International Symposium on Electromagnetic Compatability. Symposium Record (Cat. No. 99CH36261), pp. 822–825. IEEE (Year)

17. Kitra, M.I., Panagamuwa, C.J., McEvoy, P., Vardaxoglou, J., James, J.R.: Low SAR ferrite handset antenna design. Antennas and Propagation, IEEE Transactions on **55**, 1155–1164 (2007)
18. Al-Sehemi, A., Al-Ghamdi, A., Dishovsky, N., Atanasov, N., Atanasova, G.: Miniaturized wearable antennas with improved radiation efficiency using magneto-dielectric composites. IETE J. Res. **68**, 1157–1167 (2022)
19. Parmar, S., Ray, B., Garg, S., Mishra, R.K., Datar, S.: Reduced graphene oxide (rGO)-Ferrite composite inks and their printed meta-structures as an adaptable EMI shielding material. Composite Interfaces 1–21 (2022)
20. Zhu, Y., Jiang, W., Zhang, T., Huang, H., Pang, B., Hu, W.: Design of low-specific absorption rate sticker using electric-field components optimization. International Journal of RF and Microwave Computer-Aided Engineering e23164 (2022)
21. Ejaz, A., Amin, Y.: Towards durable and efficient antenna with SAR reduction analysis for on-body applications. Frequenz (2022)
22. Kaharpardeshi, K.T., Ullah, S.U., Zafar, S.: Influence of circular patched EBG substrate on SAR and far-field pattern of dipole phase-array antenna. In: Electrical, Electronics and Computer Science (SCEECS), IEEE Students' Conference on, pp. 1–5. IEEE (2014)
23. Alam, T., Faruque, M.R.I., Islam, M.T.: Specific absorption rate analysis of broadband mobile antenna with negative index metamaterial. Appl. Phys. A **122**(3), 1–6 (2016). https://doi.org/10.1007/s00339-016-9692-8
24. Alam, T., Faruque, M., Islam, M.: Specific absorption rate reduction of multi-standard mobile antenna with double-negative metamaterial. Electron. Lett. **51**, 970–971 (2015)
25. Hannan, S., Islam, M.T., Soliman, M.S., Faruque, M.R.I., Misran, N., Islam, M.: A co-polarization-insensitive metamaterial absorber for 5G n78 mobile devices at 3.5 GHz to reduce the specific absorption rate. Scientific Reports **12**, 1–13 (2022)
26. Ramachandran, T., Faruque, M.R.I., Islam, M.T.: Specific absorption rate reduction for sub-6 frequency range using polarization dependent metamaterial with high effective medium ratio. Sci. Rep. **12**, 1–18 (2022)

ToothHack: An Investigation on a Bluetooth Dongle to Implement a Low-Cost and Dynamic Wireless Control-Signal Transmission System

Md. S. Shantonu[1]([✉]), Imran Chowdhury[1]([✉]) [iD], Taslim Ahmed[1] [iD], Al Imtiaz[2] [iD], and Md. Rokonuzzaman[3] [iD]

[1] Department of Electrical and Electronic Engineering (EEE), University of Information Technology and Sciences (UITS), Dhaka 1212, Bangladesh
uits.shaan@gmail.com, imranchd@outlook.com, taslimeee@gmail.com
[2] Department of Computer Science and Engineering (CSE), University of Information Technology and Sciences (UITS), Dhaka 1212, Bangladesh
al.imtiaz01@gmail.com
[3] School of Engineering and Advanced Engineering Platform, Monash University Malaysia, Bandar Sunway, 47500 Subang Jaya, Selangor, Malaysia
rokonuzzaman@uniten.edu.my

Abstract. Almost any electronic project that requires Bluetooth communication, relies on readymade Bluetooth Modules. These readymade solutions come with different models which are quite ready to be used with microcontrollers, but they have their tradeoffs depending on the use case. What if there is a way to set up a Bluetooth communication system with less setup time and more reliability while featuring some basic and important features like low cost, easy availability, and bi-directional communication for data transmission? In this paper, an investigative experiment is presented to find the solution for implementing such a Bluetooth communication system for microcontrollers, especially for development-oriented projects. This experimental solution of Bluetooth communication technique has the potential to allow wirelessly perform controlling tasks for other devices using simple interfacing, and fast prototyping for short-range wireless communication with popular platforms like Arduino or Raspberry-Pi, etc. in little to no time hassle-free. In the experiment, an attempt is carried out to replace traditional Bluetooth Modules for microcontrollers by hacking an easily accessible Bluetooth audio dongle. Transmitted 2V (peak-to-peak) sine and square signals from a laptop computer and a mobile phone with 100% media volume received as 3.28V signals by the audio dongle, meaning the experiment works and the system has a maximum gain of 1.64.

Keywords: Bluetooth · Wireless Communication · Control Signal · Radio Controller · Arduino Wireless Controller Module

Md. S. Satu et al. (Eds.): MIET 2022, LNICST 491, pp. 325–338, 2023.
https://doi.org/10.1007/978-3-031-34622-4_26

1 Introduction

Bluetooth is a wireless technology that allows short-range communication without any interference. Bluetooth uses UHF (Ultra High Frequency) in the ISM (Industrial, Scientific, and Medical) bands, from 2.402 GHz to 2.48 GHz radio wave frequencies [1, 2]. The most common usage of this technology includes wireless headphones, wireless computer accessories, wireless HCI (Human Computer Interaction) devices or modules, etc. Nowadays Bluetooth is used for IoT (Internet of Things) devices and low-power consumption devices like wireless sensors and microcontrollers [3–6]. Bluetooth technology was IEEE 802.15.1 standard but it no longer maintains the standard. Bluetooth has been the most famous communication technology since the early 2000s and still is an efficient protocol for short-range communication [1].

When one tries to develop an engineering project which includes wireless communication, there is no way around it except by getting the latest wireless communication module from the market and using it with microcontrollers [7, 8], and they come with their limitations. Since wireless communication techniques employ radio technology, it becomes tricky to work with them for beginners. That is why the wireless modules are developed with reliable wireless technologies such as WiFi or Bluetooth, the famous ones. WiFi modules are mostly used where in need of internet access to send or receive data, which includes other technology stacks to learn. On the other hand, Bluetooth modules are used when in need of short-range data communication between devices without access to the internet [9]. Most often, the modules are not tested, trusted, or certified to work reliably and have a tedious process to set up. Which is a waste of time and if damaged, is a loss of resources.

Over the years, a significant number of engineering research have been carried out that employed wireless communication techniques, especially Bluetooth. Some of the recent research utilizing Bluetooth technology have been conducted in [3–6, 9–29]. In [11, 26, 28], the authors incorporated Bluetooth technology for transmitting real-time traffic safety and vehicle detection data. In [3, 4, 10, 21], the authors employed Bluetooth technology for developing indoor positioning and localization systems. In [5, 13–16, 19], the authors utilized the technology for biomedical instrument design, and so on. The common thing among all is that they are using readymade Bluetooth Module for their respective microcontroller-based system. The current solutions that are available for wireless communication modules for microcontroller-based projects are often not found to be very easy to set up and often do not work as expected every time. There are several reasons for this scenario. Though they are available in the fast-growing tech market, most often the required electronics from trusted sources or providers are not found in every area. In addition, after getting the device, there is no easy way to test the device instantly or predict its performance capabilities. Setting up, testing, and maintenance takes a lot of time and continuous effort. On the other hand, using the best-suited software library for different microcontroller board support, performing basic tasks and user flexibility is very painful to find. Furthermore, troubleshooting these devices can be a nightmare sometimes.

1.1 ToothHack

Bluetooth technology is easily accessible in wireless audio systems. But it can essentially be hacked to send and receive other signals as well, which can be utilized to set up a reliable wireless data communication with a microcontroller. This will benefit the engineering students and hobbyists with the following features: (i) no need to purchase an expensive Bluetooth module, (ii) no need to set up extra connections, (iii) the development process will be faster, etc. After succeeding with the hack, this technique can be utilized to do various engineering experiments or projects, which will potentially provide the following advantages and application opportunities:

Easily Accessible. This technique is very easily accessible since one major part of the transceiver is dependent on any Bluetooth radio device. Meaning one only needs a Bluetooth receiver to make this module and use it. Since microcontrollers provide ADCs (Analog to Digital Converter) and other useful features, only a signal processing unit is needed to extract the data from the received signal.

Analog Computation. It provides analog signals as its outputs, which can be utilized to perform many interesting tasks and experiments with analog signals.

Dynamic Wireless Commands. Creating dynamic control with one Bluetooth device is doable, it can be done by only using a computer or mobile phone application's graphical user interface. Generating different tone frequencies is the hack here in the experimented technique.

User Control Flexibility. Users can control the device with an application either on a computer or on a mobile phone as a controlling device. The application can be hybrid, meaning the application can be programmed once and delivered to all the major platforms such as Android, Windows, Linux, macOS, iOS, and the Web.

2 Methods and Materials

2.1 Technology/Devices Used in the Experiment

To investigate and perform experiments on the discussed technique, various technology, devices, and tools are utilized, some of which are: a low-cost Bluetooth dongle (Fig. 1), laptop computer, mobile phone, Arduino Uno, etc. The total list of required technology, devices, and tools is provided in Table 1.

Table 1. Technology/devices used in the experiment.

Devices/Tools	Purpose	Technology
Audacity (software)	To generate necessary signal tones	Tone generation
Laptop computer	To transmit Bluetooth signals	macOS-based, Bluetooth 4.0
Mobile phone	To transmit Bluetooth signals	Android-based, Bluetooth 4.0
Bluetooth Audio Receiver (dongle)	To receive and analyze the Bluetooth signals	Bluetooth 4.0
DSO (Digital Storage Oscilloscope)	To analyze the quality and properties of the received signals	Signal processing
Arduino Uno CH340	To visualize the received signals with a built-in plotter	Microcontroller, HCI, ADC
Mobile Power Bank	To power the Bluetooth receiver and Arduino	Battery for power

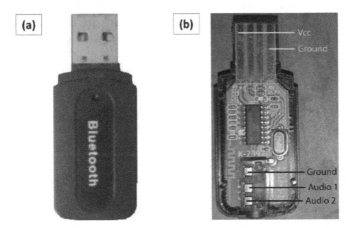

Fig. 1. (a) The low-cost Bluetooth audio receiver, and (b) the pinout diagram of the receiver used in the experiment to develop the technique.

2.2 System Model and Block Diagram

The system includes two major sides: transmission and reception in general for one-way communication in this experiment. The transmission side has two units: one is to generate the signals (Audacity) and the other one (computer/mobile phone) is to transmit them over Bluetooth wireless media. From the laptop computer, Audacity (open-source audio editing software) is used to generate the desired signals in.mp3 format and transmit (play) them over Bluetooth audio. A mobile phone is also used to transmit the same signals to observe if there is any difference at the receiving end. At the receiving end, a general-purpose audio receiver (Bluetooth dongle) is used as the receiving device that is plugged in with an Arduino Uno to sample and analyze the signal pattern and plot the signal values with Arduino's built-in plotter, which shows different responses for different signals. A DSO (Digital Storage Oscilloscope) is utilized to visualize the signal properties. A block diagram is presented in Fig. 2 to provide easy visualization of the entire system including its components.

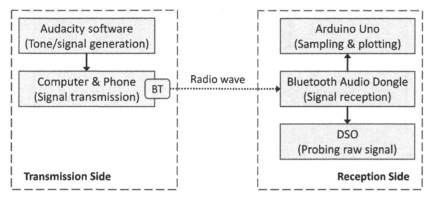

Fig. 2. Block diagram of the experimental system.

2.3 System Flowchart

For this experiment, first, the Audacity audio editing tool is used to generate tones with specific signal configurations. After pairing the sender device, in this case, a laptop or mobile phone with the Bluetooth receiver (dongle), the signal is simply transmitted by playing the audio tone file. The Bluetooth dongle receives the signal and outputs it to the Arduino Uno. With Arduino's built-in ADC (Analog to Digital Converter), the signal is visualized by plotting the values with respect to time. If no signal is transmitted over Bluetooth, the Bluetooth's general ping signal is observed in the oscilloscope. Figure 3 shows the flowchart of the experiment.

2.4 Experimental Setup

To perform the experiment, the devices and tools are set up in the lab with necessary apparatuses. The setup includes a Bluetooth audio receiver (dongle), an audio 3.5 mm jack is connected to probe it with the oscilloscope (DSO) and Arduino Uno. The ground pin of the Bluetooth dongle is connected to the ground of Arduino and the signal pin is connected to the "A0" pin. Both the Bluetooth dongle and Arduino Uno are connected to the mobile power bank for power. On the other hand, there is Audacity installed on the laptop which generates different signal tones. While the laptop is connected to a Bluetooth device via laptop Bluetooth settings, the connection ping is observed along with other Bluetooth standard signals being transmitted to the receiver device. Then, keeping the media volume of the laptop at 100% and 50% respectively, and probing all the devices carefully, the generated tones are played in Audacity from the laptop. This

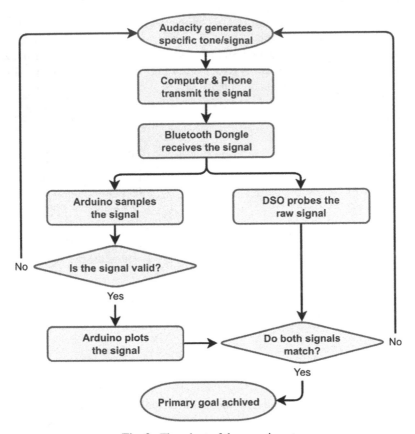

Fig. 3. Flowchart of the experiment.

transmits the tone signals to the Bluetooth dongle which can be observed in the DSO, as it is probed with the output of the Bluetooth dongle. Since the output of the Bluetooth dongle is also connected to the Arduino, voltage readings of the received signals can also be visualized at pin "A0" by plotting the voltage levels with the help of Arduino's built-in plotter to observe the signal pattern. If the signal pattern of the receiver matches the Arduino's plotter pattern, then it is considered that the same signals are being received which were transmitted over Bluetooth from the laptop computer (or mobile phone). Other properties of the signal, like frequency, delay, and amplitudes are observed from the DSO reading. After it is confirmed that the same signals are being received, some conditions can be tweaked depending on the signal patterns to reflect the response while transmitting the signals from the laptop. The built-in LED of the Arduino is used to respond to the received signal. Figure 4 shows an instance of the experimental setup of the investigation.

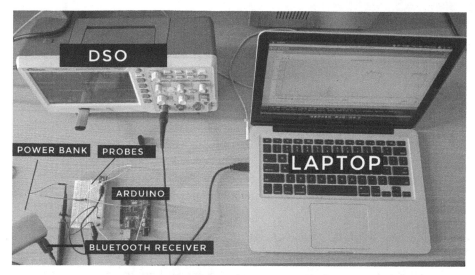

Fig. 4. Experimental setup of the investigation.

3   Results and Discussion

To verify the experiment, the quantitative data of the transmitted and received signals are being collected to match their properties, so that the quality of the received signals via the low-cost Bluetooth dongle can be compared. If the signals are received without any significant loss, this property can be used to detect the desired signal with a microcontroller or similar device, and use it for other purposes.

3.1   Results from the Experiment

Figure 5 shows the signal properties while generating a sine wave tone at 50 Hz for an hour. The square wave is also generated in the same fashion. Table 2 shows the Arduino sketch code to plot the signal with Arduino's built-in signal plotter, and Figs. 6 and 7 show the response in the Arduino plotter while receiving the signals (for sine and square wave respectively). It is to be noted that in the Arduino plotter the signals are referenced at 0 (zero) because Arduino samples the signal from 0 to 1023 ADC range and the voltage level is 0-5V DC. Figures 8 and 9 show the received signals – the sine wave and the square wave at 50 Hz respectively on a DSO. Tables 3 and 4 show the quantitative properties of the received signals for transmitted signals of 1V peak-to-peak voltage at media volumes of 100% and 50% respectively of the transmitting device (laptop and mobile phone).

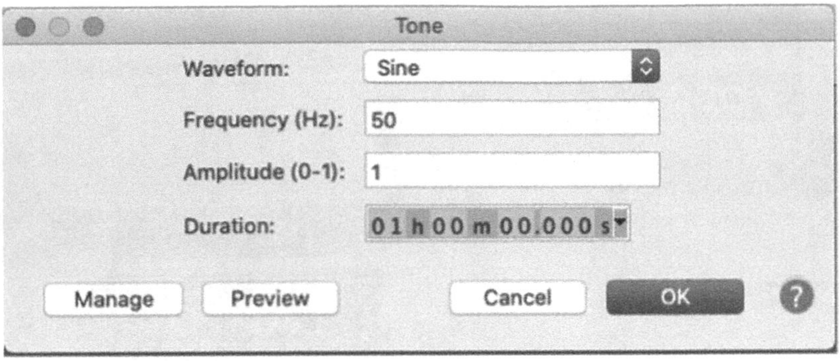

Fig. 5. Generating signal tone in Audacity software.

Table 2. Arduino Sketch (programming code) to investigate the received signals using the Arduino plotter.

```
void setup() {
  Serial.begin(9600); }

void loop() {
  int val = analogRead(A0);
//  int val = random(.5, 5);

  Serial.println(val);

  delay(100); }
```

3.2 Discussion

The match of Fig. 6 with Fig. 8 and the match of Fig. 7 with Fig. 9 signifies that it is possible to use a simple Bluetooth audio receiver as a signal receiver to use as a wireless controlling module with a general-purpose microcontroller like Arduino. Tables 3 and 4 signify that the voltage amplitude of the received signals depends on the media volume of the transmitting device regardless of the type of the signal, for a particular receiver. This means, that the received signals also depend on the output gain of the Bluetooth receiver since all the receivers are not designed in the same way.

Although all the receivers share a common property which is to amplify the Bluetooth signal to a certain level, generally within 5V. To handle this scenario, a signal conditioner needs to be employed so that signals can be received with a constant amplitude regardless of the output gain of the receiver. Furthermore, the codebase of the Arduino should be constantly developed till it can reliably detect the signal encodings, which is essentially the most significant thing for this dynamic device. These are the works in progress to perfect the presented technique.

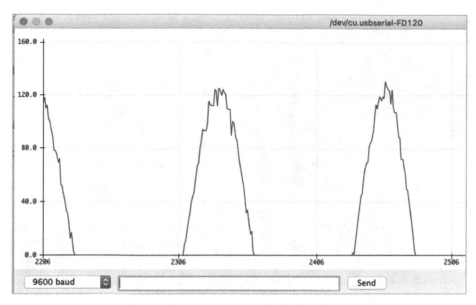

Fig. 6. Sine wave response in Arduino Plotter.

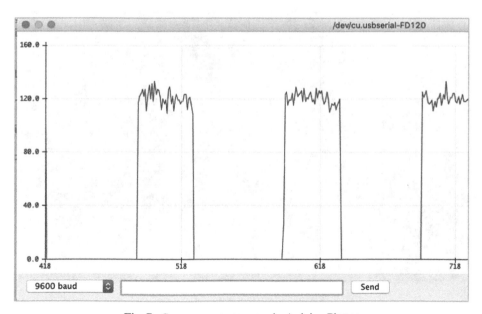

Fig. 7. Square wave response in Arduino Plotter.

Future development also involves the methods of control-signal generation. Initially, the desired signals are generated using open-source software called Audacity. But it is possible to generate different signals with different frequencies and patterns dynamically with the help of native software programming for both computers and mobile

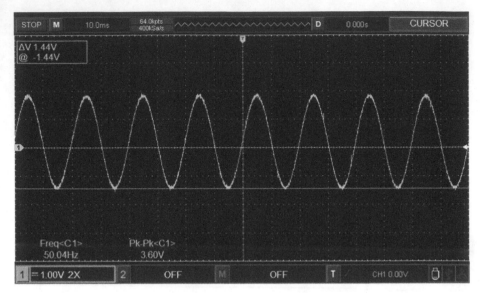

Fig. 8. Received sine wave response on DSO.

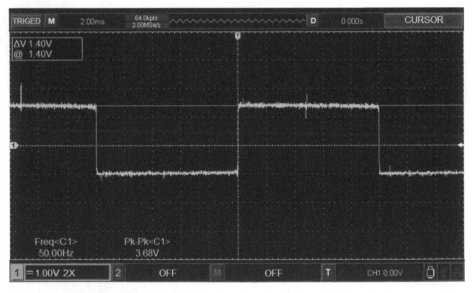

Fig. 9. Received square wave response on DSO.

phones. Current solutions of wireless controlling modules available in the market utilize Bluetooth functionality differently which provides a more low-level approach. But the significant disadvantage comes when one cannot be sure if the module will work or not and if one does not have low-level programming skills. But this approach uses a readymade Bluetooth audio receiver that works in sending signals wirelessly. The tricky

Table 3. Properties of the received signals when the transmitted signals are of 1V (amplitude) keeping the media volume of the transmitting device at 100%.

Media Volume (%)	Tone Frequency (50 Hz)		Receiving Voltage (+peak, − peak)	Receiving Frequency (Hz)
100	Tone Type	Transmitting Device		
	Sine	Laptop	+ 1.84V, − 1.44V	50
		Mobile	+ 1.84V, − 1.44V	50
	Square	Laptop	+ 1.84V, − 1.44V	50
		Mobile	+ 1.84V, − 1.44V	50

Table 4. Properties of the received signals when the transmitted signals are of 1V (amplitude) keeping the media volume of the transmitting device at 50%.

Media Volume (%)	Tone Frequency (50 Hz)		Receiving Voltage (+peak, − peak)	Receiving Frequency (Hz)
50	Tone Type	Transmitting Device		
	Sine	Laptop	+ 940mV, − 760mV	50
		Mobile	+ 940mV, − 760mV	50
	Square	Laptop	+ 940mV, − 760mV	50
		Mobile	+ 940mV, − 760mV	50

part however is to detect the signal parameters with a microcontroller and extract data from the signal dynamically.

The presented experiment in this paper is not about building some project with a readymade Bluetooth module as performed in the referenced papers [3–6, 9–29], but about trying to develop a new technique for Bluetooth control-signal transmission system. The presented technique could be beneficial for developers and students who need a wireless module for their Arduino or any other microcontroller-based projects.

4 Conclusion

This experimental technique of repurposing a low-cost (cheapest one found) Bluetooth audio receiver (dongle) as a control-signal receiver for a microcontroller is a tendency to develop a more raw and reliable Bluetooth solution for microcontroller-based engineering projects. In the experiment, transmitted custom signals from a laptop computer and mobile phone are shown to be received by the low-cost Bluetooth audio receiver and verified the received signals using DSO and Arduino plotter by sampling the signals with the interval of 100ms. According to Tables 3 and 4, transmitting 2V (peak-to-peak) signals (sine and square) from both a laptop computer and a mobile phone with 100% media volume turns out to be 3.28V (peak-to-peak) signals at receiving end using the audio dongle and 1.70V (peak-to-peak) signals with 50% media volume. That means the system has a maximum gain of 1.64. Upon employing a signal conditioner and developing an Arduino codebase, this raw technique of wireless control-signal transmission system has the potential to help developers and students significantly where readymade Bluetooth modules for a microcontroller are not available or applicable. Currently available Bluetooth modules like HC-05/06 require much technical skills to set it up with a project and make it work successfully. But this experimental solution can break the ice between uncertain issues with the microcontroller or the Bluetooth module itself. Since Bluetooth technology is still in use in almost all aspects of the modern digital era, this solution is expected to hold its value over time. The future scopes and improvements of the presented solution may involve: (i) improving the signal detection technique from the receiver end, (ii) signal conditioning before it is fed to a microcontroller system with discrete electronics, etc.

References

1. Arnau Soler i Recasens: Data capture and processing system to display a heat map. https://upcommons.upc.edu/bitstream/handle/2117/363254/163893.pdf?isAllowed=y&seq uence=1, last accessed 01 June 2022
2. Sairam, K.V.S.S.S.S., Gunasekaran, N., Redd, S.R.: Bluetooth in wireless communication. IEEE Commun. Mag. **40**, 90–96 (2002). https://doi.org/10.1109/MCOM.2002.1007414
3. Huh, J.-H., Seo, K.: An indoor location-based control system using bluetooth beacons for IoT systems. Sensors. **17**, 2917 (2017). https://doi.org/10.3390/s17122917
4. Duong, N.S., Trinh, V.T.A., Dinh, T.T.M.: Bluetooth low energy based indoor positioning on iOS platform. In: 2018 IEEE 12th International Symposium on Embedded Multicore/Many-core Systems-on-Chip (MCSoC), pp. 57–63. IEEE (2018)
5. Xia, K., Hou, R., Yang, J., Li, X.: A real-time spine orthopedic system based on bluetooth low energy and internet of things. IEEE Access. **9**, 153977–153984 (2021). https://doi.org/10.1109/ACCESS.2021.3128645
6. Kalanandhini, G., Aravind, A.R., Vijayalakshmi, G., Gayathri, J., Senthilkumar, K.K.: Bluetooth technology on IoT using the architecture of Piconet and Scatternet. In: AIP Conference Proceedings, p. 020121. AIP Publishing LLCAIP Publishing (2022)
7. Ahmed, T., Chowdhury, I.: Into the binary world of zero death toll by implementing a sustainable powered automatic railway gate control system. In: 2020 IEEE International Conference on Electronics, Computing and Communication Technologies (CONECCT), pp. 1–6. IEEE (2020)
8. Chowdhury, I., Ahmed, T.: Design and prototyping of sensor-based anti-theft security system using microcontroller. Int. J. Eng. Res. Technol. **10**, 58–66 (2021). https://doi.org/10.17577/ijertv10is030019
9. Derasari, P.M., Sasikumar, P.: Motorized wheelchair with bluetooth control and automatic obstacle avoidance. Wireless Pers. Commun. **123**(3), 2261–2282 (2021). https://doi.org/10.1007/s11277-021-09238-w

10. Soon, C.F., et al.: Bluetooth embedded digital ammeter with android app data logging. Indones. J. Electr. Eng. Comput. Sci. **18**, 1400 (2020). https://doi.org/10.11591/ijeecs.v18.i3. pp1400-1407
11. Yuan, J., Abdel-Aty, M., Wang, L., Lee, J., Yu, R., Wang, X.: Utilizing bluetooth and adaptive signal control data for real-time safety analysis on urban arterials. Transp. Res. Part C Emerg. Technol. **97**, 114–127 (2018). https://doi.org/10.1016/j.trc.2018.10.009
12. Guo, H., Zeng, Q., Chen, Z., Zhao, M.: Bluetooth door lock system based on smart mobile device. In: Proceedings of the 2nd International Conference on Computer Science and Application Engineering - CSAE '18, pp. 1–5. ACM Press, New York, New York, USA (2018)
13. Bernas, M., Płaczek, B., Korski, W.: Wireless Network with Bluetooth Low Energy Beacons for Vehicle Detection and Classification. In: Gaj, P., Sawicki, M., Suchacka, G., Kwiecień, A. (eds.) CN 2018. CCIS, vol. 860, pp. 429–444. Springer, Cham (2018). https://doi.org/10.1007/978-3-319-92459-5_34
14. Ranjitha, B., Nikhitha, M.N., Aruna, K., Afreen, Murthy, B.T.V.: Solar Powered Autonomous Multipurpose Agricultural Robot Using Bluetooth/Android App. In: 2019 3rd International conference on Electronics, Communication and Aerospace Technology (ICECA), pp. 872–877. IEEE (2019)
15. Astafiev, A.V., Zhiznyakov, A.L., Privezentsev, D.G.: Development of indoor positioning algorithm based on bluetooth low energy beacons for building RTLS-systems. In: 2019 International Russian Automation Conference (RusAutoCon), pp. 1–5. IEEE (2019)
16. Yin, Q., Zhang, J., Wang, X., Liu, S.: The video intelligent car based on wireless sensor. Clust. Comput. **22**(3), 5135–5150 (2017). https://doi.org/10.1007/s10586-017-1100-4
17. Tang, S., Fan, M., Ma, G.: Application of bluetooth in mine gas information transmission. IOP Conf. Ser. Earth Environ. Sci. **242**, 022014 (2019). https://doi.org/10.1088/1755-1315/242/2/022014
18. Khan, H.A., Islam, R.M.S.U., Attari, A.W., Mirza, S.I., Ahmed, M.: The economical design of a hand-gesture and bluetooth controlled wheel-chair by integrating indigenous components: mobility aid for the disabled. IOP Conf. Ser. Mater. Sci. Eng. **473**, 012004 (2019). https://doi.org/10.1088/1757-899X/473/1/012004
19. Janik, P., Pielka, M., Janik, M.A., Wróbel, Z.: Respiratory monitoring system using Bluetooth Low Energy. Sensors Actuators A Phys. **286**, 152–162 (2019). https://doi.org/10.1016/j.sna.2018.12.040
20. Chen, Q., Tang, L.: A wearable blood oxygen saturation monitoring system based on bluetooth low energy technology. Comput. Commun. **160**, 101–110 (2020). https://doi.org/10.1016/j.comcom.2020.05.041
21. Leith, D.J., Farrell, S.: Coronavirus contact tracing. ACM SIGCOMM Comput. Commun. Rev. **50**, 66–74 (2020). https://doi.org/10.1145/3431832.3431840
22. Alon, A.S., Susa, J.A.B.: Wireless hand gesture recognition for an automatic fan speed control system: rule-based approach. In: 2020 16th IEEE International Colloquium on Signal Processing & Its Applications (CSPA), pp. 250–254. IEEE (2020)
23. Amesimenu, D.K., et al.: Home Appliances Control Using Android and Arduino via Bluetooth and GSM Control. In: Hassanien, A.-E., Azar, A.T., Gaber, T., Oliva, D., Tolba, F.M. (eds.) AICV 2020. AISC, vol. 1153, pp. 819–827. Springer, Cham (2020). https://doi.org/10.1007/978-3-030-44289-7_77
24. Rodríguez-Jorge, R., De León-Damas, I., Bila, J.: Detection of the QRS Complexity in Real Time with Bluetooth Communication. In: Barolli, L., Takizawa, M., Yoshihisa, T., Amato, F., Ikeda, M. (eds.) 3PGCIC 2020. LNNS, vol. 158, pp. 429–439. Springer, Cham (2021). https://doi.org/10.1007/978-3-030-61105-7_43

25. Elser, H., Jongebloed, P., Buschmann, D., Ellerich, M., Schmitt, R.H.: Potentials of Bluetooth Low Energy Beacons for order tracing in single and small batch production. Procedia CIRP. **97**, 202–210 (2021). https://doi.org/10.1016/j.procir.2020.05.226

26. Tomažič, S., Škrjanc, I.: An Automated Indoor Localization System for Online Bluetooth Signal Strength Modeling Using Visual-Inertial SLAM. Sensors. **21**, 2857 (2021). https://doi.org/10.3390/s21082857

27. Bin, L., Xiaoyun, C.: Home intelligent sports action automation system based on bluetooth. Microprocess. Microsyst. **80**, 103335 (2021). https://doi.org/10.1016/j.micpro.2020.103335

28. Khalid, A., Memon, I.: Bluetooth-Based Traffic Tracking System Using ESP32 Microcontroller. In: Patnaik, S., Yang, X.-S., Sethi, I.K. (eds.) Advances in Machine Learning and Computational Intelligence. AIS, pp. 737–746. Springer, Singapore (2021). https://doi.org/10.1007/978-981-15-5243-4_70

29. Ngerem, E., Misra, S., Oluranti, J., Castillo-Beltran, H., Ahuja, R., Damasevicius, R.: A Home Automation System Based on Bluetooth Technology Using an Android Smartphone. In: Singh, P.K., Noor, A., Kolekar, M.H., Tanwar, S., Bhatnagar, R.K., Khanna, S. (eds.) Evolving Technologies for Computing, Communication and Smart World. LNEE, vol. 694, pp. 527–536. Springer, Singapore (2021). https://doi.org/10.1007/978-981-15-7804-5_40

Robustness of Eigenvalue-Spread Based Rule of Combination in Dynamic Networked System with Link Failures

Miss. Nargis Parvin[1]($\boxtimes$), Md. Saifur Rahman[2], Md. Tofael Ahmed[2], and Maqsudur Rahman[2]

[1] Bangladesh Army International University of Science and Technology, Comilla, Bangladesh
nargis@baiust.edu.bd
[2] Comilla University, Comilla, Bangladesh
{saifurice,tofael,mrrajon}@cou.ac.bd

Abstract. In this study, we investigate a dynamic wireless sensor network based on single-input multiple-output (SIMO) channels and attempt to estimate the transmitted signal blindly. The distributed blind equalization over networks follows the rule of combination among neighboring sensor nodes and it becomes more difficult for the different channel characteristics. In a dynamic context, the degree of noisy channel outputs, on the other hand, has a significant impact on performance. Eigenvalue-spread (EVS) based rule of combination is investigated in which the weights are inferred via surrounding channel outputs rather than just the node degrees. We consider a dynamic wireless sensor network to validate the robustness of the EVS based rule of combination. Through mean square error (MSE) performance, the simulation result demonstrates the robustness of the EVS-based rule of combination in comparison to conventional rule of combination.

Keywords: Blind equalization · Rule of combination · Dynamic network topology · Spread of eigenvalues · Wireless sensor network

1 Introduction

A network with wireless sensor (WSN) which is represented as the dispersed communication network made up of small, low-power sensor nodes that are geographically distant. WSNs can be used for a variety of tasks, including data collection, precision agriculture, environmental surveillance, target localisation, and more. [1,2]. In recent years, distributed estimation algorithms give attractive research attention in WSNs. Due to the sensor nodes' limited computing and communication capabilities in a large-scale network, these techniques are desired to coordinate the sensor nodes. In a distributed estimation system, these

© ICST Institute for Computer Sciences, Social Informatics and Telecommunications Engineering 2023
Published by Springer Nature Switzerland AG 2023. All Rights Reserved
Md. S. Satu et al. (Eds.): MIET 2022, LNICST 491, pp. 339–347, 2023.
https://doi.org/10.1007/978-3-031-34622-4_27

sensor nodes can work together to fulfill a complex task that a single sensor might find impossible or difficult.

The adaptive filter for each sensor is adjusted using the local observation and information collected from nearby nodes in the distributed estimate process. This method lowers latency and conserves communication resources. As a result, the distributed strategy outperforms the centralized approach in terms of robustness, privacy protection, ease of extension, and computing complexity. For this aim, several distributed estimating methods have been suggested, as in [3,4]. The majority of currently available distributed estimating methods are either training-based or non-blind. To estimate unknown parameters, training-based algorithms require knowledge of the broadcast sequence as well as the intended signal at the receiver [5]. However, there are certain disadvantages to training-based algorithms. Because the training signals lower the data rate, they cause considerable overhead costs and may be unreasonable or unworkable. As a result, system efficiency and precious channel capacity are lost. A blind algorithm is necessary in such circumstances. The standard blind method requires some prior knowledge of the transmitted sequence statistics.

The nodes share information with nearby nodes and utilize a rule of combination to fuse the data they acquire. Each node aggregates the data using the rule of combination's weights. The uniform rule, Laplacian rule, Metropolis rule, relative-degree rule, and others are examples of static rule of combinations [6]. The degrees of the nodes have a significant impact on the combination weight values of these rules. The methods discussed above do not take into account network noise or channel characteristics while transmitting the input signal. The combination weights are designed using the surrounding channel outputs in the rule of combination [7,8]. For a far-end common channel example in [9] and a time-varying (dynamic) network architecture with link failures in [3], the Metropolis rule performs better. When several channels are used for each node, however, the network performance suffers. The authors in [8] proposed the eigenvalue-spread (EVS) based rule of combination to fix this problem. They validated that the EVS based rule of combination provides better performance for different channel models and large-sized static network.

Due to the hostile environmental factors, the availability of information may be reduced if some network links become unstable. A link failure is the term we use to describe this event. The link is presumed to be broken and deleted from the network whenever this happens. In this paper, the robustness of the EVS based rule of combination is affirmed over a dynamic network topology with link failures. We alternately employ two separate topologies to be utilized at odd time indices and even time indices, respectively, to mimic the dynamic topology with link failures, the notion of which was discovered in [3]. With the EVS-based rule of combination, any distributed estimate technique may be modified. In a dynamic networked system with link failures, the EVS-based rule of combination has a lower steady-error rate and faster convergence speed than the traditional Metropolis and relative-degree rule of combinations.

The following is a breakdown of the paper's structure. The models for networks and channels are discussed in Sect. 2. The overview of the EVS-based rule of combination is included in Sect. 3. Section 4 examines the performance of the EVS-based rule of combination in a dynamic networked system with link failures. Finally, conclude of this paper is addressed in Sect. 5.

2   Network and Channel Models

One of the most significant aspects in WSN is network topology. In practical situations, the affiliated network links may fail due to the dynamic nature of sensor networks, the nodes may be failed to connect with the other nodes due to any reasons that include power depletion, environmental interference, circuit malfunction, processor failure, unreliable radio links, malicious attacks, and so on. We look into blind equalization in a dynamic network architecture with link failures in this paper.

In WSNs, the sensor nodes are connected by a specified communication topology. In this paper, we consider a collection of G nodes and $G \times G$ non-negative weight matrix for describing the topology. Two nodes are said to be neighbors if they are able to share information. The neighborhood of a node $k, k = 1, 2, ..., G$ is denoted by G_k, which is the set of nodes directly connected to it, including itself. All sensor nodes are interested to share the sender common message $x(n)$ through different finite impulse response (FIR) channels with impulse response $h_k(n)$ as shown in Fig. 1. The channel output is $x_k(n)$ at each sensor k, which is represented by

$$x_k(n) = \sum_{l=0}^{L-1} h_k(l)s(n-l) + o_k(n) \tag{1}$$

where $s(n)$ is the transmitted data signal and $o_k(n)$ is the additive white Gaussian noise for the k th sensor. In Eq. (1), it is presumpted that each $h_k(l)$ has an impulse response with L. In [8] considers the scenario in which the network architecture is static and all $h_k(l)$ are common. However, a more severe and realistic scenario is explored in this research, where all $h_k(l)$ are different and the network architecture is dynamic with link failures.

3   Overview of EVS Based Rule of Combination

The two components of the EVS-based rule of combination [7] are estimate of the distribution of eigenvalues and design of the weight matrix.

3.1   Estimation of Eigenvalue-Spread

The channel outputs' distribution of eigenvalues is crucial to the blind equalization process when many channel models are employed for the distributed estimating process. Channel's effect on the transmitted signal can be reflected

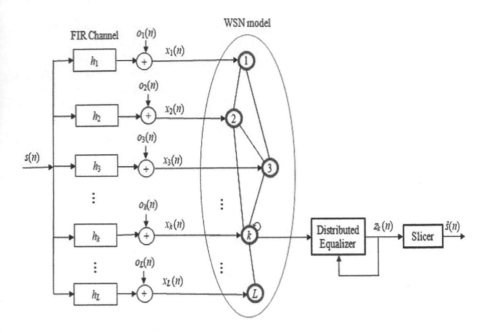

Fig. 1. System model

by the distribution of eigenvalues [10]. With large distribution of eigenvalues values, serious inter-symbol interference (ISI) happens. ISI, on the other hand, is minimal if the channel's distribution of eigenvalues is small. The matrix of correlation of $x_k(n)$ at the k th node, Γ_k, may be used to compute the distribution of eigenvalues. A matrix of Toeplitz is Γ_k. The distribution of eigenvalues is calculated as follows:

$$E(k) = \frac{\lambda_{k,max}}{\lambda_{k,min}} \qquad (2)$$

The maximum and minimum eigenvalues of Γ_k are $\lambda_{k,max}$ and $\lambda_{k,min}$, respectively. To obtain an accurate approximation, this procedure necessitates a long series of the received channel output $x_k(n)$, resulting in a significant computing complexity. The highest and lowest eigenvalues of the autocorrelation matrix of the input signal may be approximated using the maximum and minimum values of the corresponding input signal's power spectrum [11]. As a result, we calculate the power spectrum from $x_k(n)$, $n = 0, 1, ..., G - 1$, at the k th node, using spectral analysis techniques. We use the Welch technique [12] to do so, which offers a reliable and precise approximation.

The spectral estimate's highest and lowest values $\tilde{R}_k(\nu)$, where ν represents frequency bins, are calculated as $max(\tilde{R}_k(\nu))$ and $min(\tilde{R}_k(\nu))$, respectively.

The distribution of eigenvalues is therefore defined as follows

$$\hat{E}(k) = \frac{max(\tilde{R}_k(\nu))}{min(\tilde{R}_k(\nu))}. \tag{3}$$

In the WSN model, Eq. (3) is calculated for all k.

3.2   Design of a Weight Matrix

It is recommended to use all signals coming from nodes in G_k in order to converse near node k, G_k. This requirement can be fulfilled if the weights in G_k are positive rather than zero

$$c_{lk} > 0, \quad l \in G_k. \tag{4}$$

If this requirement is not met, the signal at around that point may not be used for connection in G_k. As a result, assuming that (4) is satisfied, the weights should be designed.

For accurate equalization to forecast the transmitted signal $s(n)$ from the channel output $x_k(n)$ at node k, the distribution of eigenvalues $E(k)$ at node k must be minimum [10,13]. This approach proposes that the node's weight k should be decreased when the distribution of eigenvalues $E(k)$ at node k is high. On the other hand, the node's weight k should be increased if the distribution of eigenvalues $E(k)$ is moderate. As a result, the opposite of the distribution of eigenvalues is used. The node's weight k is allocated $\frac{\beta_k}{E(k)}$, where β_k is a favorable constant that fulfills

$$\sum_{l \in G_k} \frac{\beta_k}{E(l)} = 1. \tag{5}$$

Here, we presum that the total of all the weights in Gk equals one. In reality, its estimate $\hat{E}(k)$ in (2) takes the place of $E(k)$ in (2). (6). To sum up, the EVS based matrix of combination wights are created as

$$c_{lk} = \begin{cases} \frac{\hat{\beta}_k}{\hat{E}(l)}, & \text{if } l \neq k \quad \text{are neighbors} \\ 1 - \sum_{l \in G_k} c_{lk}, & \text{if } l = k \\ 0, & \text{otherwise} \end{cases} \tag{6}$$

where $\hat{\beta}_k$ is a positive constant that fulfills the condition

$$\sum_{l \in G_k} \frac{\hat{\beta}_k}{\hat{E}(l)} = 1 \tag{7}$$

The coefficients $\{c_{lk}\}$ are non-negative coefficients that are used to aggregate estimates from various channel outputs. The coefficients $\{c_{lk}\}$ are used to create a $G \times G$ matrix C. The following requirements are met by C and its entries in this example.

$$c^T \mathbf{1} = \mathbf{1}, \quad \text{and} \quad c_{lk} = 0 \quad \text{if} \quad l \notin G_k \tag{8}$$

When the entries in each of the columns of C's matrix sum up to one, indicating that it is left-stochastic.

Smaller weights are allocated to nodes that are prone to greater distribution of eigenvalues values in the combination matrix C, which is a highly significant property. In other words, if the channel output has a wider distribution of eigenvalues, the inverse produces smaller weights. As a result, while performing distributed blind equalization, the more severe channel output is virtually completely disregarded. The EVS-based rule of combination may be used to update any of the distributed estimating techniques.

The coefficients of the rule of combination by which the nodes in the network topology communicate with each other impact the performance of the distributed estimation method. The distributed generalized Sato algorithm (d-GSA) [4] is used in the following part to estimate the transmitted signal blindly in a dynamic networked system with link failures, in order to evaluate the efficacy of the EVS-based rule of combination.

4   Simulation Results

We simulate the EVS-based rule of combination in this part and compare it to the traditional Metropolis (doubly stochastic) and relative-degree (left-stochastic) methods. In a dynamic WSN model with link failures that consists of five nodes ($G = 5$), we utilize non-minimum phase channels. The maximum communication range is 0.3 m, and the distribution of each node is random throughout a square rectangle $[0, 1.2] \times [0, 1.2]$. Between any two nodes, the Euclidean distance is equal to or less than this range, they are connected and recognized as neighbors with the capacity to communicate. If not, there is no connection between the nodes. For odd and even time indices, we assume two network topologies, as illustrated in Fig. 2.

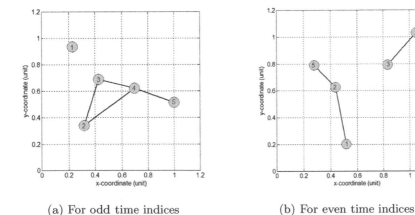

(a) For odd time indices   (b) For even time indices

Fig. 2. Network topology with link failures

Table 1. Metropolis combination weight matrices for odd and even time indices

1.0000	0	0	0	0
0	0.4167	0.3333	0.2500	0
0	0.3333	0.4167	0.2500	0
0	0.2500	0.2500	0.2500	0.2500
0	0	0	0.2500	0.7500

0.6667	0.3333	0	0	0
0.3333	0.3333	0	0	0.3333
0	0	0.5000	0.5000	0
0	0	0.5000	0.5000	0
0	0.3333	0	0	0.6667

Table 2. Relative-degree combination weight matrices for odd and even time indices

1.0000	0	0	0	0
0	0.3000	0.3000	0.2500	0
0	0.3000	0.3000	0.2500	0
0	0.4000	0.4000	0.3333	0.6667
0	0	0	0.1667	0.3333

0.4000	0.2857	0	0	0
0.6000	0.4286	0	0	0.6000
0	0	0.5000	0.5000	0
0	0	0.5000	0.5000	0
0	0.2857	0	0	0.4000

The robustness of the EVS-based rule of combination is validated using the mean square error (MSE) performance. The effectiveness of the EVS-based rule of combination is assessed using five FIR channels, each of which is assumed to be a channel with raised cosine [10], utilizing parameters determined by

$$h_k(i) = \begin{cases} \frac{1}{2}[1 + \cos(\frac{2\pi}{\theta}(i-1))], & i = 0, 1, 2 \\ 0, & \text{otherwise.} \end{cases} \tag{9}$$

We utilize the 4-QAM signaling constellation in our simulations. The tap coefficients of the equalizer are typically set to 1 for the center tap and 0 for the others. Through MATLAB simulations, the performance of the EVS-based rule of combination is assessed and compared to that of traditional rule of combinations. Tables 1 and 2 illustrate the Metropolis combination weight matrices and relative-degree rules for odd and even time indices, respectively. Each segment's length in a data set =100, DFT size = 128 and duplicating 50% are used to apply the Welch technique in the eigenvalue-spread computation for the EVS based rule of combination. Based on $N = 5000$ received channel outputs, the resultant distribution of eigenvalues values and associated EVS-based combination matrices for odd and even time indices are given in Tables 3 and 4, respectively.

Figure 3 compares the d-GSA method's averaged MSE convergence performance for the EVS based rule of combination to the d-GSA method's averaged MSE convergence performance for the traditional Metropolis and relative-degree rule of combinations. Equalizer length $M = 8$ and step size $\mu_k = 0.008$ for the kth node are frequently utilized for the aforementioned techniques. Figure 3 shows the average of 100 Monte Carlo runs for each convergence curve.

The d-GSA technique with the EVS based rule of combination converges quicker than the d-GSA method with the Metropolis and relative-degree rule of combinations, as shown in Fig. 3. In addition, as compared to traditional rule of combinations, the EVS-based rule of combination-based d-GSA obtains a lower MSE level in the steady state.

Table 3. distribution of eigenvalues values

$E(1)$	1.0624
$E(2)$	1.0760
$E(3)$	1.1352
$E(4)$	1.4033
$E(5)$	1.9804

Table 4. EVS based combination weight matrices for odd and even time indices

1.0000	0	0	0	0
0	0.3684	0.3684	0.3069	0
0	0.3492	0.3492	0.2909	0
0	0.2825	0.2825	0.2354	0.5853
0	0	0	0.1668	0.4147

0.5032	0.3962	0	0	0
0.4968	0.3912	0	0	0.6479
0	0	0.5528	0.5528	0
0	0	0.4472	0.4472	0
0	0.2126	0	0	0.3521

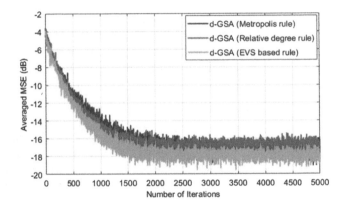

Fig. 3. Averaged MSE performance of d-GSA under EVS based, relative-degree and Metropolis rule of combinations with dynamic topology with link failures

5 Conclusion

A dynamic distributed network model with link failures is examined in this article. The transmitted 4-QAM data sequence has been estimated by the distributed blind equalizer where the transmitted channels are assumed to be unknown. To validate the robustness of the EVS based rule of combination under a dynamic topology with link failures, one of the distributed estimation algorithm, d-GSA, is adopted. The averaged steady state MSE performance of the d-GSA with EVS based rule of combination is reduced than that of the conventional rule based d-GSA. Also, the convergence speed of the d-GSA with EVS based rule of combination is faster than that of the conventional rule based d-GSA.

References

1. Pottie, G., Kaiser, W.J.: Wireless integrated network sensors. Commun. ACM **43**(5), 51–58 (2000)
2. Estrin, D., Girod, L., Pottie, G., Srivastava, M.: Intrumenting the world with wireless sensor networks, In: Proc. IEEE International Conference Acoustitcs, Speech, Signal Process. (ICASSP), pp. 2033–2036, May (2001)
3. Yu, C., Xie, L.: On recursive blind equalization in sensor networks. In: IEEE Trans. on Signal Process. **63**(3), 662–672 (2015)
4. Liu, Y., Cai, Y.: Distributed blind equalization in networked systems. In: Proceedings of the IEEE International Conference Acoustics, Speech, Signal Process, (ICASSP), pp. 4296–4300 (2017)
5. Abed-Meraim, K., Qiu, W., Hua, Y.: Blind system identification. Proc. IEEE **85**(8), 1310–1322 (1997)
6. Sayed, A.H.: Diffusion adaptation over networks. In: Academic Press Library in Signal Process., Elsevier, vol. 3, pp. 323–453 (2014)
7. Parvin, M.N., Shimamura, T.: New rule of combination over Wireless Sensor Networks. In: IEEE 2nd International Conference on Information Communication and Signal Process, (ICICSP) (2019)
8. Parvin, M.N., Shimamura, T.: Eigenvalue-spread-based rule of combination for distributed blind equalization in networked system. J. Signal Process. **23**(6), 243–256 (2019)
9. Liu, Y., Li, L.: Distributed blind estimation over sensor networks. IEEE Access **5**, 18343–18355 (2017)
10. Haykin, S.: Adaptive Filter Theory Prentice-Hall (1996)
11. Makhoul, J.: Linear prediction: a tutorial review. Proc. IEEE **63**(4), 561–580 (1975)
12. Welch, P.D.: The use of fast Fourier transform for the estimation of power spectra: a method based on time averaging over short, modified periodograms. In: IEEE Trans. Audio and Electroacoust., vol. AU-15, no. 2, pp. 70–73 (1967)
13. Itoh, K., Shimamura, T., Suzuki, J.: Prefiltering for blind equalization. Electron. Commun. Jpn., part 3, **78**(9) 1 11 (1995)

Blockchain Based Services in Education: A Bibliometric Analysis

Md. Shariar Hossain[1]([⊠]) and A. K. M. Bahalul Haque[2]

[1] Noakhali Science and Technology University, 3814 Noakhali, Bangladesh
`shmozumder2@gmail.com`
[2] Software Engineering, LENS, LUT University, Lappeenranta, Finland
`Bahalul.haque@lut.fi`

Abstract. Blockchain technology promotes immutability, transparency, integrity, and enhanced security. Recently blockchain-based applications and associated technologies have been noticeable in various domains such as finance, healthcare, education, transportation, supply chain, and access control. Blockchain in the education sector is a newly explored topic; the nature of research and the trend should provide useful directions for future research. Motivated by this factor, this work presents a bibliometric analysis of the blockchain in the education sector by investigating 512 research articles from the Scopus database. In particular, we had 335 Conference Papers, 150 Articles, and 27 Book chapters that were published between the year 2016 to 2022. This study provides a comprehensive visual analysis of research trends in subject areas, author contribution, citation, publication channels and venues, country-based research output, and other bibliometric data. To identify the gaps and expand the current scope of knowledge on blockchain technology in the education system, we have used the bibliometric data extracted from the Scopus database. Finally, the investigation concludes with guidelines for future research directions.

Keywords: Blockchain · Education · Bibliometric analysis · DLT

1 Introduction

Blockchain has untangled its application in different sectors in recent times. The network works without any middleman where the power of control is distributed among all the participants; being a distributed and immutable database, Blockchain is suitable for trustworthy and transparent record keeping. Each block contains hashed data and is added to the next block after approval through consensus [1, 2]. Blockchain is classified into Public, Private and Hybrid based on its decentralization principle [3, 4].

Though Blockchain technology was introduced globally with the launch of bitcoin in 2009, the scope of research and development has spread across various domains such as Fintech [5], Security [10, 50], Privacy, Healthcare [8], IoT [9], Supply Chain [11], Agriculture [7] and many other regions of the smart city [6]. However, the application of

Md. S. Satu et al. (Eds.): MIET 2022, LNICST 491, pp. 348–362, 2023.
https://doi.org/10.1007/978-3-031-34622-4_28

Blockchain technology in the Education system was a relatively less explored domain, but the literature has been increasing recently. Though a few review papers have been published to provide the recent status and challenges in the blockchain trends, to the best of the author's knowledge, there is no bibliometric analysis of the blockchain in the education system. Motivated by the above-mentioned factors, this work has used the Scopus database to analyze the published research trends, including works done in various regions, authors, and research institutions [12].

Our study differs from the existing research in two ways. First, we have concentrated on the research articles on applications of blockchain in education which has been less discussed relatively compared with other subject areas. Machado et al. 2019, discussed the scope of applications of blockchain technology in education for both learners and teachers on formative evaluation, learning activities design and implementation [13]. Bhaskar and Tiwari, 2020, contributed a systematic literature review on the understanding of present scenarios in terms of benefits and barriers of Education management. The authors have presented the potential of Blockchain in the education sector at large [14]. In addition, Rahardja et al. 2019, discussed the impact of Blockchain technology on higher education in Indonesia elaborately. Furthermore, they have extended the study to develop a Blockchain framework for Indonesia tertiary education using an AI platform [15]. Moreover, Sun et al. 2018, showed the integration of Blockchain technology is a growing trend in the development of online education [16]. Second, we have applied bibliometric analysis to discuss and address our research questions on the basis of some bibliographic approaches such as Subject areas and countries based on citation, Co-occurrences of Keywords, Co-Authorship among the countries, Bibliographic Coupling among the sources, and Author's impacts.

To identify and address these gaps and expand the current scope of knowledge on Blockchain technology in the education system, our study considers the following research questions (RQs) and discussion of their answers by analyzing the literature bibliographically. RQ1. What are the publication distribution and citation trends for Blockchain in education? RQ2. Which literatures are the most influential ones in terms of citation? RQ3: Which publication venues have published the most literature related to Blockchain in education? RQ4: What are the most explored research areas (subject areas) for Blockchain in education? RQ5. Who are the most influential authors in terms of citation and collaboration?

The remainder of this paper is organized as follows: Sect. 2 discusses the related works about Blockchain in education. Section 3 describes the research methodology, including the major steps. Section 4 presents the Bibliometric analysis and visualizations of this study. It provides a holistic perspective and focuses on the analysis in different subsections. Section 5 briefly discusses the study, which addresses the research question. Section 6 concludes this research and marks off future work.

2 Related Work

Blockchain technology is a combination of a decentralized linked list where the list contains blocks. This system was introduced globally with the introduction of cryptocurrency, mainly bitcoin, in 2009 [17]. Since its introduction, it has proved itself in the last decade that it can be an impactful technology in its different applications [18]. Karale et al. 2019, showed that the Education system is one of the useful applications of Blockchain technology where the scalability of the Blockchain can be effective for educational institutions [19]. Machado et al. 2019, appeared in applications of Blockchain innovation to education arrangement for learners and instructors on developmental assessment, learning exercises plan and execution [13]. Researchers tried to discuss the depth, significance and gaps of the existing studies on Blockchain technology in the education system by Bibliometric analysis such as Bhaskar and Tiwari, 2020, gives a systematic literature review on the understanding of the present situation in terms of benefits and boundaries of Education management. They attempted to explore the potential of Blockchain in the education sector at large by conducting a bibliometric analysis [14]. Rahardja et al. 2019, talk about their study around the impact of Blockchain innovation on higher education in Indonesia. They expand the study into developing a Blockchain framework for Indonesia tertiary education utilizing an AI platform [15]. Chen et al. 2018 discussed the benefits and challenges of using Blockchain technology for education and proposed some applications with advantages and features in their study [20]. Sun et al. 2018, showed the integration of Blockchain technology is a growing trend in the development of online education [16]. Albeanu, 2017, describe how Blockchain technology in education can be applied to a group of institutions, and they show a list of applications, including school records management, educator credentialing and tracking of school assets [21]. Juričić et al. 2019, proposed specific guidelines and upgrades in the area of Blockchain integration level in higher education [22]. Turcu et al. 2019, presented a literature review on the studies based on Blockchain technology in the educational field. [23]. The existing SLR papers, studies and bibliometric analysis differ from this study in the way of analyzing, visualizing and categorizing studies such as subject areas, co-occurrences, co-authorships, bibliographic coupling, impact factor and authors analysis on Blockchain or distributed ledger technology in the education system.

3   Methodology

We have used the Scopus database for extracting the search results for the bibliometric analysis. The search was conducted on January 10, 2022. The search results were modified to find our intended literature following the methodology outlined by Kitchenham and Charts, 2004 [24]. The methodology of this study is divided into six different steps. These are (1) Search, (2) Results, (3) Inclusion and Exclusion, (4) Categorizing (5) Analysis and visualization (6) Documentation. These steps are applied to the found dataset, respectively. We have used the Scopus database since it indexes peer-reviewed multidisciplinary articles from various publishers around the work.

3.1 Search: Based on the keywords "Blockchain", "Distributed Ledger Technology", and "Education System", the query on Scopus Database is – "((TITLE-ABS-KEY(Blockchain) OR TITLE-ABS-KEY(Distributed Ledger Technology) AND TITLE-ABS-KEY(Education) OR TITLE-ABS-KEY(Education System)) AND (LIMIT-TO (DOCTYPE, "cp") OR LIMIT-TO (DOCTYPE," ar") OR LIMIT-TO (DOCTYPE," ch")) AND (LIMIT-TO (LANGUAGE,"English")) AND (LIMIT-TO (SRCTYPE,"p") OR

LIMIT-TO (SRCTYPE,"j") OR LIMIT-TO (SRCTYPE,"k") OR LIMIT-TO (SRCTYPE, "b")))"

3.2 Results of search: After searching with the query, we found a total 512 documents in CSV format where 335 Conference Papers, 150 Articles and 27 Book chapters were included. There are a total of 87 different countries, 160 different authors, and 22 different subject areas on the dataset.

3.3 Categorizing: This study is bibliographically categorized into five major categories as Co-authorship, Co-occurrence, Citation, Bibliographic coupling and Co-citation. Combining these categories with the units of analysis like Authors, Countries, Organizations, Sources, Documents and Keywords, this study creates an organized way to implement the analysis on the dataset.

3.4 Documentation: After exporting datasets from Scopus, VOSviewer and Microsoft Excel were used for analyzing and exporting the visualized figures and tables. This study has made the documentation by collaborating all the data and their analysis with visualization.

4   Bibliometric Analysis

We have used VOSviewer as a software tool for constructing and visualizing bibliographic networks and density overlay [25]. Here we analyzed the type of categories where we selected documents depending on the minimum number of Documents per unit. For the Co-occurrences of terms, we considered Keywords from Author and Index [26]. As shown in Table 1, Co-Authorship among the Authors were found in 1453 documents, where with a minimum of two documents for a single author, the documents were 142 only. The number of documents among the Co-Authorship and the organizations was 965, and only 33 documents had a minimum of 2 co-authors. This amount has gone lower for co-authorship and country. A lot of keyword occurrences happened where 3403 co-occurrences were found for all keywords as units of the analysis, and only 168 were selected where there was a minimum of five co-occurrences. On this basis of a minimum of five co-occurrences, we have found 1313 and 2474 documents and selected 50 and 127 documents for co-occurrences of Author and Index Keywords, respectively. In the Citation category, we based on a minimum of one citation for each document and a minimum of two citations for sources, authors, organization and country. We found a very low number of documents for our Bibliographic coupling category. For Authors, the number of documents was quite high compared to other subcategories like Bibliographic analysis for documents, sources, organizations and countries. The number of Co-citations among the reference, sources and Authors is very high. Because co-citation among the research papers is very common for researchers. We can't even start our research without any previous research work for analysis, or study on that specific field, even if it is a very new topic, we need previous works for background analysis.

Further, the analysis is divided into five major different categories, which are: **Citation:** "Citation" contains analysis based on subject area and countries; **Co-occurrence:** "Co-occurrence" contains co-occurrences of all keywords and author keywords; **Co-authorship:** "Co-authorship" contains co-authorship among the countries; **Bibliographic coupling:** It contains the Bibliographic coupling among the sources and the

Table 1. Total Documents according to Type

Analysis Type	Unit	Total Documents	No. of Selected Documents	Minimum number of Documents per unit
Co-Authorship	Authors	1453	142	2
Co-Authorship	Organization	965	33	2
Co-Authorship	Country	106	58	2
Co-occurrence	All-Keywords	3403	168	5
Co-occurrence	Author-Keywords	1313	50	5
Co-occurrence	Index-Keywords	2474	127	5
Citation	Documents	512	272	1
Citation	Sources	307	62	2
Citation	Authors	1453	142	2
Citation	Organization	965	33	2
Citation	Country	106	58	2
Co-citation	Cited reference	13378	270	2
Co-citation	Cited sources	8241	201	5
Co-citation	Cited Authors	16822	182	15

Impact factor; **Authors:** "Authors" contains some analysis such as a number of citations, co-authorship among authors, co-citation among the cited authors and bibliographic coupling among authors.

4.1 Citation

Subject Areas and Countries Based on Citation. Figure 1. Depicts the subject area according to the number of documents. As we are seeing, computer science is getting more attention from researchers, which formed 375 involvements. After that, "Engineering" is the second most dominating area in the blockchain and education sectors. therefore, from the beginning, computer science and engineering stood out in the dominating region. later, the multidisciplinary domains came into the picture, as is seen in the figure [27]. The most interesting thing is that we can observe social science as one of the influential research domains for blockchain-based education services. It concludes the fact that blockchain has been a dominant technology in societal applications too. This fact has primarily triggered the multidisciplinary research in blockchain and now has a blended form of societal computing. From Fig. 2, we can make sure that blockchain technology is mostly cited by the researcher of the United States with 411 citations from our documents. India is in the second position with 346 citations and after that the United Kingdom with 328 citations. It's a clear message country are approaching blockchain technology for their socio-economic development.

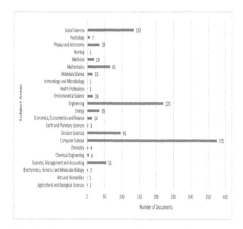

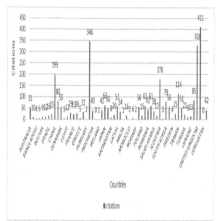

Fig. 1. Documents according to subject areas

Fig. 2. Number of Citation among the countries

In Fig. 1, the subject areas after social science are Decision Science, Mathematics and Business-management-accounting. All these subjects are connected to our daily life as we use our household things. So, we can come to the point that blockchain is going to be our next-generation dependency as we are seeing the subject area's rank. Our business, management and accounting are going to be based on blockchain technology as we analyzed. Mathematics is one of the leading subject areas for blockchain researchers. Algorithms that are followed are fully based on complex mathematical problems. Blockchain is a growing technology in every field of our subject area explained in Fig. 1.

Number of Documents Over the Years and Type. Research about blockchain technology started around 2016–2017, and gradually it was increasing over the years. In the years 2016–2017, according to our study, there were only a few documents. Interestingly, in the years 2019–2020, there was a lot of research on blockchain and distributed ledger technology. From our collection of documents, we can observe most of them were conference papers. The reason behind this is very clear. Researchers have to submit their papers before the conference. So that the reviewers can study, analyze and understand properly what the researcher actually tried to do on that specific paper. We included three types of documents in total 512 Where 335 conference papers, 150 Articles and 27 Book chapters.

4.2 Co-occurrence

Co-occurrence of Keywords. From Fig. 3, we can see the network visualization of Co-occurrence of all keywords. Researchers are trying to co-relate the research fields with blockchain technology where we can analyze the research trends among the fields based on blockchain. This network could analyze future trends of blockchain, research gaps and other correlations. Moreover, it's a clear message for future researchers that the development of Education, Artificial Intelligence, Information Management, the Internet of things, Smart contracts, Network Security, and Digital Currency like Bitcoin will be dependent on blockchain technology. From Table 2, there are 297 occurrences with 383 link strengths for the keyword "Blockchain". The next word is "education", with 58 occurrences and 102 link strengths. We can relate the research works for education based on Blockchain, which is very obvious because, in the near future, our education system will be evaluated by technology. Examinations, Grading, classes, courses, research and other related fields of education are already in the pipeline of technology at the time of the COVID-19 pandemic, which could be taken over by blockchain technology. Another Important keyword mentioned is "smart contracts", which is basically a program or something executable on a blockchain that runs on the basis of some predetermined conditions.

We have some more occurrences of keywords which are mainly related to cryptocurrency. "Ethereum", "Bitcoin", "cryptocurrency", and "decentralization" these words explain the relation between cryptocurrency and Blockchain technology. Besides these highly occurring keywords, we have some more important keywords. "Artificial Intelligence", "Machine learning", and "Internet of things" are the keywords which indicate to us that Blockchain is not only for cryptocurrency or transactions where it has a huge relation with these fields. Undoubtedly Artificial Intelligence is becoming the master of all technologies. We can consider blockchain as one of the biggest data sources for machine learning where we can train our AI systems with more realistic data so that both AI and Blockchain work cooperatively.

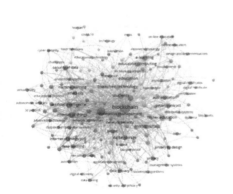

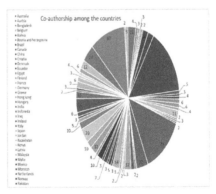

Fig. 3. Co-occurrence network among all Keywords

Fig. 4. Pie Chart of Co-Authorship based on documents among the countries

4.3 Co-authorship

Co-authorship Among the Countries. Co-authorship is making a significant contribution to another author of an article. All the co-authors share the responsibilities and accountabilities for the results. The main difference between author and co-author is that the author is the only individual who is responsible for research efforts, contributions, responsibilities and results. And co-author shares with other authors. we have the top 5 countries along with their documents, citations and total link strength, with the united states on the top with 67 documents, 411 citations and 40 link strength. Researchers from the United States, India and China are in the pipeline of developing research resources on the blockchain, where India is in the second position with 79 documents, 346 citations, and 24 link strengths. After the USA and India, There Are China, South Korea, and the United Kingdom with at Least 10 Documents, Respectively.

Table 2. Top 5 Bibliographic Coupled Sources Based on the Total Link Strength (TLS)

Sources	Documents	Citations	Total link strength
Acm international conference proceeding series	38	87	982
Advances in intelligent systems and computing	25	21	634
Communications in computer and information science	15	19	361
Lecture notes in computer science (including subseries lecture notes in artificial intelligence and lecture notes in bioinformatics)	8	201	353
Sustainability (Switzerland)	6	21	321

There are 106 countries where the minimum number of documents of a country or Total Link Strength (TLS) of a country is 2, and we found only 58 countries. In Fig. 4, we can see the visual representation of these countries by a Pie Chart. As expected, the United States is on the top, as the country of Satoshi Nakamoto China in the top three, but developing country like India is in the top three, this is representing the field of blockchain, and Distributed Ledger Technology (DLT) is growing equally all over the world.

4.4 Bibliographic Coupling

Bibliographic Coupling Among Sources. Bibliographic coupling is the inverse of co-citation. If two or more publications cite a publication, all of them are bibliographically coupled except the cited publication. The cited publication is common in the corresponding bibliographically coupled publications. The Total Link Strength (TLS) is the primary scale to measure the citation of a document which was cited by bibliographically Coupled publications. Figure 12 represents the Network overlay of Bibliographic coupling where all the documents were published in the period 2019.0 to 2020.5. According to Table 3 ACM international conference proceeding series has the most number of link strengths 982, the most number of documents 38, and the most number of network connections, respectively. As we know it is a Conference Proceedings source, where there are 335 conference papers out of our 512 documents. Advances in intelligent systems and computing are in the second position with 634 TLS, 25 documents and 21 citations, and 361 TLS, 15 documents, and 19 citations puts communications in computer and information science at one of the top 3 sources. Except for the Top 3 sources, the number of documents is less than 10 in all the sources.

4.5 Authors

The primary author is usually the person who has made the foremost noteworthy intellectual contribution to the work, in terms of planning the consideration, obtaining and analyzing information from experiments, and composing the manuscript. The author is responsible for any kind of data, analysis, visualization and representation of a document. Figures 7, 8, 9 and 10 represent the Documents and Total Link Strength (TLS) of authors, such as the number of citations, Co-Authorship, Co-citation and Bibliographic coupling of Authors. A co-author is a person who shares a contribution with another author of a document, where both of them are co-author of each other for that particular document. They both are equally responsible for that document.

Figure 8 illustrates the number of citations and Link strength of Co-Authorship for the authors. The more the Total Link Strength of a co-author, the more documents he contributed and shared responsibilities. Co-citation investigation includes the following sets of papers that are cited together within the source articles. When the same sets of papers are co-cited by numerous authors, clusters of inquiries start to make. The co-cited papers in these clusters tend to share a few common topics. It's a very useful research structure with authors where we can analyze the research trends among them and figure out the future research fields. Figure 9 illustrates the Co-citation of cited authors, where Satoshi Nakamoto is at the top with 169 documents and 2306 Total Link Strength. He is known for inventing bitcoin, implementing the first Blockchain and deploying the first decentralized digital currency. Figure 8 visualizes the Bibliographic coupling of authors. If two or more publications cite any publication, these two or more publications are bibliographically coupled. In Figs. 5, 6, and 7, we can see John Domingue is at the top with 177 publications, where TLS is 4, 2 and 36, respectively.

These authors evaluated in their publications the scopes of Blockchain in the Education sector and organized their research for the implementation of this technology on fields such as data security in the education system, online learning technologies, a ledger of records, student data storage, payment in a secure way, Transcripts analysis, Education Budgets, Securing Student identity and overall infrastructure of Education System.

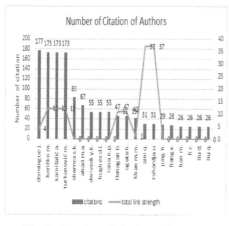

Fig. 5. Number of citation of Authors

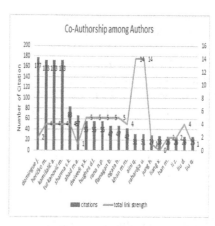

Fig. 6. Co-Authorship among Authors

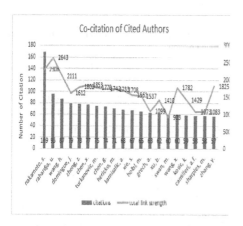

Fig. 7. Co-citation of cited Authors

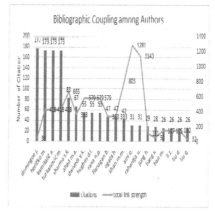

Fig. 8. Bibliographic Coupling among Author

5 Discussion

RQ1. What Is the Publication Distribution and Citation about Blockchain and Education Related Works?

This analysis can be found in subsections named "Subject areas and countries based on citation" and "Number of Documents over the years and Type" discussed in Sect. 4.1 (Citation). Total documents type shows the type variations of documents such as Articles, Conference papers, and Books. We found there are 335 Conference papers, 150 Articles and 27 Books, the number of documents over the years which are clearly indicating the publication distribution. As our search keywords, we selected only Blockchain in education-related works. Subject areas and countries based on citation illustrated in Fig. 2 the Blockchain and education-related works and their amount of citation.

RQ2. Which Literatures Are the Most Influential Ones in Terms of Citation?
Table 3 tabulated the top 5 cited papers based on Blockchain in education, which indicates the Conference paper titled "The Blockchain and kudos: A distributed system for the educational record, reputation and reward" is the top cited paper with 171 citations published in 2016 by Sharples M., and Domingue J as authors.

RQ3: Which Publication Venues Have Published the Most Literature Related to Blockchain in Education?
The subsection named "Bibliographic Coupling among sources" located in Sect. 4.4 shows the top 5 most popular publication venues for published literature related to Blockchain in education based on a number of documents and Total link strength. We found the ACM International Conference Proceeding Series on the top with 38 published documents, 87 citations and 982 Total Link Strength (TLS).

RQ4: What Are the Most Explored Research Areas (Subject Areas) for Blockchain in Education?
This analysis can be found in subsections "Subject areas and Countries based on citation" and "Co-occurrence of Keywords". Subject areas show the most explored regions and citation amount to decide the recent trends. Co-occurrence of keywords indicates related research areas to identify the gaps and density of areas where Blockchain and Education are the most occurring keywords. From the subject areas as expected from Fig. 1, Computer Science is the most explored research area and immediate next are Engineering and Social Science respectively. Among these broad domains, blockchain adoption in higher educational organizations has gained interest recently [33–35]. Furthermore, the use of blockchain for distance learning is another area that is being recently explored [36, 37]. Apart from these recent areas, blockchain is being thoroughly researched for certificate verification techniques. The use of blockchain and smart contracts [38] can effectively enhance educational certificate verification [39–41]. Moreover, permissioned blockchain-based educational certificate verification is also being explored [42].

RQ5. Who Are the Most Influential Authors in Terms of Citation and Collaboration?
In Sect. 4.5, the figures show and illustrate the number of citations, Co-authorship, and Co-citation of authors. These authors are the most cited and impactful in the field of Blockchain and education-based research. According to this study, Figs. 7, 8, and 10, John Domingue is at the top of co-authorship and number of citation lists. As shown respectively in Fig. 9, Satoshi Nakamoto is also one of the most influential authors in terms of citation and collaboration in Blockchain and Education-based research.

Table 3. Overview of top 5 cited papers based on Blockchain in Education.

Reference	Authors	Source	Year	Citations	Documents Type
[28]	Sharples M., Domingue J	Lecture Notes in Computer Science	2016	171	Conference
[29]	Turkanović M., Hölbl M., Košič K., Heričko M., Kamišalić A	IEEE Access	2018	162	Article
[30]	Radanović I., Likić R		2018	65	Article
[31]	Hoy M.B	Medical Reference Services Quarterly	2017	61	Article
[32]	Tanwar S., Bhatia Q., Patel P., Kumari A., Singh P.K., Hong W.-C	IEEE Access	2020	59	Article

6 Concluding Remarks

In this research, we displayed an intensive explanation of a bibliometric analysis of the existing studies of Blockchain and Distributed Ledger Technology in the education system domain. Overall this paper has made the following key contributions:

- Probably to the author's knowledge, this paper reports the first endeavor with the recent documents from the Scopus database, which has included an intensive bibliometric analysis in the Blockchain in Education system domain.
- Analysis, visualization and results of this study highlight the recent status, research gaps and corresponding proposed research themes to the interested researchers before pursuing advanced investigations in this field of research.

This study considers a few lines of research as future work. It would be worth investigating top listed sources, organizations and papers for the flexibility and applicability of Blockchain in the education system. Furthermore, it would be interesting to replicate the same bibliometric analysis on different literature databases such as Web of Science (WoB), PubMed, IEEE Xplore, and ScienceDirect with different inclusion and exclusion credentials. This domain of research could be applied for systematic literature review or meta-analysis with more detail-oriented analysis and limitations. Addressing the limitations and gaps of this research is also a potential future work for the researchers.

References

1. Haque, A.B., Islam, A.N., Hyrynsalmi, S., Naqvi, B., Smolander, K.: GDPR compliant Blockchains – a systematic literature review. IEEE Access (2021). https://doi.org/10.1109/access.2021.3069877
2. Haque, A.B., Bhushan, B.: Blockchain in a nutshell: state-of-the-art applications and future research directions. In: Blockchain and AI Technology in the Industrial Internet of Things, pp. 124–143. IGI Global (2021). https://doi.org/10.4018/978-1-7998-6694-7.ch009

3. Haque, A.B., Bhushan, B.: Emergence of blockchain technology: a reliable and secure solution for IoT systems. In: Blockchain Technology for Data Privacy Management, pp. 159–183. CRC Press (2021)
4. Bhushan, B., Khamparia, A., Sagayam, K.M., Sharma, S.K., Ahad, M.A., Debnath, N.C.: Blockchain for smart cities: a review of architectures, integration trends and future research directions. Sustain. Cities Soc. **61**, 102360 (2020)
5. Treleaven, P., Brown, R.G., Yang, D.: Blockchain technology in finance. Computer **50**(9), 14–17 (2017)
6. Haque, A.K.M.B., Bhushan, B., Dhiman, G.: Conceptualizing smart city applications: requirements, architecture, security issues, and emerging trends. Expert Syst. 1–23 (2021). https://doi.org/10.1111/exsy.12753HAQUEET AL.23
7. Pranto, T.H., Noman, A.A., Mahmud, A., Haque, A.B.: Blockchain and smart contract for IoT enabled smart agriculture. Peer J Comp. Sci. **7**, e407 (2021). https://doi.org/10.7717/peerj-cs.407
8. Haque, A.B., Muniat, A., Ullah, P.R., Mushsharat, S.: An automated approach towards smart healthcare with Blockchain and smart contracts. In: 2021 International Conference on Computing, Communication, and Intelligent Systems (ICCCIS), pp. 250–255. IEEE (2021)
9. Dorri, A., Kanhere, S.S., Jurdak, R., Gauravaram, P.: Blockchain for IoT security and privacy: the case study of a smart home. In: *2017* IEEE international conference on pervasive computing and communications workshops (PerCom workshops), pp. 618–623. IEEE (2017)
10. Zhang, R., Xue, R., Liu, L.: Security and privacy on Blockchain. ACM Comput. Surv. **52**(3), 1–34 (2019)
11. Korpela, K., Hallikas, J., Dahlberg, T.: Digital supply chain transformation toward Blockchain integration. In: Proceedings of the 50th Hawaii International Conference on System Sciences (2017)
12. Natarajan, H., Krause, S., Gradstein, H.: Distributed Ledger Technology and Blockchain (2017)
13. Machado, A.D.B., Sousa, M., Pereira, F.D.S.: Applications of Blockchain Technology to Education Policy, pp. 157–163 (2019)
14. Bhaskar, P., Tiwari, C.K., Joshi, A.: Blockchain in education management: present and future applications. Interact. Technol. Smart Educ. (2020)
15. Rahardja, U., Hidayanto, A.N., Hariguna, T., Aini, Q.: Design framework on tertiary education system in Indonesia using Blockchain technology. In: 2019 7th International Conference on Cyber and IT Service Management (CITSM), vol. 7, pp. 1–4. IEEE (2019)
16. Sun, H., Wang, X., Wang, X.: Application of Blockchain technology in online education. Int. J. Emerg. Technol. Learn. **13**(10) (2018)
17. Nakamoto, S.: Bitcoin: A peer-to-peer electronic cash system. Decentralized Business Rev. 21260 (2008)
18. Tasatanattakool, P., Techapanupreeda, C.: Blockchain: challenges and applications. In: 2018 International Conference on Information Networking (ICOIN), pp. 473–475. IEEE (2018)
19. Karale, A.S., Khanuja, H.: Implementation of Blockchain technology in education system. Int. J. Recent Technol. Eng. **8**(2), 3823–3828 (2019)
20. Chen, G., Xu, B., Lu, M., Chen, N.S.: Exploring Blockchain technology and its potential applications for education. Smart Learn. Environ. **5**(1), 1–10 (2018)
21. Albeanu, G.: Blockchain technology and education. In: The 12th International Conference on Virtual Learning ICVL, pp. 271–275 (2017)
22. Juričić, V., Radošević, M., Fuzul, E.: Creating student's profile using Blockchain technology. In: 2019 42nd International Convention on Information and Communication Technology, Electronics and Microelectronics (MIPRO), pp. 521–525. IEEE (2019)
23. Turcu, C., Turcu, C., Chiuchisan, I.: Blockchain and its potential in education. arXiv preprint arXiv:1903.09300 (2019)

24. Kitchenham, B.: Procedures for Performing Systematic Reviews, vol. 33, pp. 1–26. Keele University, Keele, UK (2004)
25. VosViewer. Available https://www.vosviewer.com/. Accessed 1 Oct 2021
26. Randhawa, K., Wilden, R., Hohberger, J.: A bibliometric review of open innovation: setting a research agenda. J. Prod. Innov. Manag. **33**(6), 750–772 (2016)
27. Haque, A.K.M., Rahman, M.: Blockchain technology: methodology, application and security issues. Int. J. Comput. Sci. Netw. Secur. **20**(2) (2020)
28. Sharples, M., Domingue, J.: The Blockchain and kudos: a distributed system for educational record, reputation and reward. In: European Conference on Technology Enhanced Learning, pp. 490–496. Springer, Cham (2016)
29. Turkanović, M., Hölbl, M., Košič, K., Heričko, M., Kamišalić, A.: EduCTX: a Blockchain-based higher education credit platform. IEEE Access **6**, 5112–5127 (2018)
30. Radanović, I., Likić, R.: Opportunities for use of Blockchain technology in medicine. Appl. Health Econ. Health Policy **16**(5), 583–590 (2018)
31. Hoy, M.B.: An introduction to the Blockchain and its implications for libraries and medicine. Med. Ref. Serv. Q. **36**(3), 273–279 (2017)
32. Tanwar, S., Bhatia, Q., Patel, P., Kumari, A., Singh, P.K., Hong, W.C.: Machine learning adoption in Blockchain-based smart applications: the challenges, and a way forward. IEEE Access **8**, 474–488 (2019)
33. Al Mansoori, S., Maheshwari, P.: A framework to implement Blockchain in higher education institutions. In: Al-Emran, M., Al-Sharafi, M.A., Al-Kabi, M.N., Shaalan, K. (eds.) ICETIS 2021. LNNS, vol. 299, pp. 244–254. Springer, Cham (2022). https://doi.org/10.1007/978-3-030-82616-1_22
34. Kumar, N., Singh, M., Upreti, K., Mohan, D.: Blockchain adoption intention in higher education: role of trust, perceived security and privacy in technology adoption model. In: Al-Emran, M., Al-Sharafi, M.A., Al-Kabi, M.N., Shaalan, K. (eds.) ICETIS 2021. LNNS, vol. 299, pp. 303–313. Springer, Cham (2022). https://doi.org/10.1007/978-3-030-82616-1_27
35. Miah, F., Onalo, S., Pfluegel, E.: Transforming Higher Education systems architectures through adoption of secure overlay blockchain technologies. In: Cybersecurity, Privacy and Freedom Protection in the Connected World, pp. 343–355. Springer, Cham (2021)
36. Liu, X.: Exploration and research on distance education system based on blockchain technology. J. Phys. Confer. Ser. **1769**(1), 12041 (2021)
37. Gajendran, N.: Blockchain-based secure framework for elearning during COVID-19. Indian J. Sci. Technol. **13**(12), 1328–1341 (2020)
38. Haque, A.K.M., Naqvi, B., Islam, A.K.M., Hyrynsalmi, S.: Towards a GDPR-compliant blockchain-based COVID vaccination passport. Appl. Sci. **11**(13), 6132 (2021)
39. Curmi, A., Inguanez, F.: BlockChain based certificate verification platform. In: International Conference on Business Information Systems, pp. 211–216. Springer, Cham (2018)
40. Ghazali, O., Saleh, O.S.: A graduation certificate verification model via utilization of the blockchain technology. J. Telecommun. Electr. Compute. Eng. **10**(3–2), 29–34 (2018)
41. Cheng, J.C., Lee, N.Y., Chi, C., Chen, Y.H.: Blockchain and smart contract for digital certificate. I0:n 2018 IEEE international conference on applied system invention (ICASI), pp. 1046–1051. IEEE (2018)
42. Cheng, H., Lu, J., Xiang, Z., Song, B.: A permissioned blockchain-based platform for education certificate verification. In: International Conference on Blockchain and Trustworthy Systems, pp. 456–471. Springer, Singapore (2020)
43. Chowdhury, N., Ramachandran, M., Third, A., Mikroyannidis, A., Bachler, M., Domingue, J.: Towards a blockchain-based decentralised educational landscape (2020)
44. Mikroyannidis, A., Third, A., Domingue, J., Bachler, M., Quick, K.A.: Blockchain applications in lifelong learning and the role of the semantic blockchain. In: Blockchain Technology Applications in Education, pp. 16–41. IGI Global (2020)

45. Mikroyannidis, A., Third, A., Chowdhury, N., Bachler, M., Domingue, J.: Supporting lifelong learning with smart blockchain badges. Int. J. Adv. Intell. Syst. **13**(3 & 4), 163–176 (2020)
46. Hsueh, S.-C., Zeng, J.-H.: Mobile coupons using blockchain technology. In: Pan, J.-S., Ito, A., Tsai, P.-W., Jain, L.C. (eds.) IIH-MSP 2018. SIST, vol. 109, pp. 249–255. Springer, Cham (2019). https://doi.org/10.1007/978-3-030-03745-1_31
47. Hori, M., et al.: Development of a learning economy platform based on blockchain. In: Pammer-Schindler, V., Pérez-Sanagustín, M., Drachsler, H., Elferink, R., Scheffel, M. (eds.) EC-TEL 2018. LNCS, vol. 11082, pp. 587–590. Springer, Cham (2018). https://doi.org/10.1007/978-3-319-98572-5_51
48. Hori, M., Ono, S., Miyashita, K., Kita, T., Terano, T.: Toward sustainable learning economy through a block-chain based management system. In: CSEDU, vol. 2, pp. 430–437 (2020)
49. Hori, M., et al.: Learning System based on Decentralized Learning Model using Blockchain and SNS. In: CSEDU, vol. 1, pp. 183–190 (2018)
50. Hossain, M.S., Riaz, M.H.: Android malware detection system: a machine learning and deep learning based multilayered approach. In: International Conference on Intelligent Computing & Optimization, pp. 277–287. Springer, Cham (2021)

An Approach Towards Minimizing Covid-19 Situation Using Android App and Drone-Based Technology

Robi Paul$^{(\boxtimes)}$, Junayed Bin Nazir , and Arif Ahammad

Department of Electrical and Electronic Engineering, Shahjalal University of Science and Technology, Sylhet, Bangladesh
robipaul01733@gmail.com, arif-eee@sust.edu

Abstract. The devastating effects of the novel Coronavirus (COVID-19) have been seen worldwide. It is comparable with influenza category viruses that cause concerns of its frightening transmission and intensity. The hotels, tourist, entertainment, transportation, and healthcare industries have been shattered. Despite their proximity to metropolitan and city centers, people's livelihood from remote areas is also being equally influenced by the worldwide pandemic. Due to ignorance and negligence, the acute pains of this pandemic are negatively affecting the livelihood of people from these isolated locations. Furthermore, the lack of high-quality hospitals and medical services in remote regions is a significant source of concern. Therefore, this system is designed in such a way that it can gather patient data with the help of Android-based applications and identify infected people as early as possible with an accuracy of up to 69%. Even when the system is unsure whether the person is infected, it suggests that the person might be infected and redirected to doctors accordingly. The system also commands Drones or Unmanned Aerial Vehicles (UAVs) to deliver necessary medicine to potentially infected patients which avoids human contact and has an accuracy of 6.3 m. The continuous stream of data collection, analysis, and contactless medicine transfer to isolated areas can indeed reduce the infection rate, which will maintain the safety of everyone.

Keywords: Coronavirus · COVID-19 · a worldwide epidemic · Drones · Unmanned Aerial Vehicles (UAVs) · contactless

1 Introduction

The Newly discovered Corona-Virus (COVID-19) is an infectious disease that has already created havoc worldwide [1]. The virus can be comparable to the influenza family and is causing concerns because of its frightening levels of transmission and intensity [2]. It has already infected around 250 million people globally in the last one and a half years (by October 2021) and killed over 5 million people and this number is increasing with each second [3, 4]. Due to the severe repercussion of the virus on day-to-day livelihood and economy, The World Health Organization (WHO) has already

© ICST Institute for Computer Sciences, Social Informatics and Telecommunications Engineering 2023
Published by Springer Nature Switzerland AG 2023. All Rights Reserved
Md. S. Satu et al. (Eds.): MIET 2022, LNICST 491, pp. 363–375, 2023.
https://doi.org/10.1007/978-3-031-34622-4_29

recognized the situation as a global pandemic [5–7]. Although the introduction of the Covid-19 vaccine has given some relief, the transmission rate of the virus is still considerable due to ignorance, insufficient medical services in rural locations, and much more.

The depreciation of the virus's spreading is one of the most critical matters human civilizations is dealing with right now. According to the researchers, the Novel Coronavirus or SARS-CoV-2 virus contains different strains ranging from 20 nm to 500 nm in size [8]. The virus is relatively massive compared to its neighboring family members, like influenza and some common colds [9, 10]. As a result, the virus can only be transmitted from one host to another by nasal secretions and cough vapors [11]. People in densely populated countries can quickly come into touch with one another, allowing the virus to spread at an alarming rate. On the other hand, emergency medical service is not being delivered to remote locations because of transportation problems and this is also responsible for the rapid escalation of the pandemic [12]. People who live in remote areas are deprived of proper vaccination and medication, resulting in insufficient identification of covid patients, increasing the virus spread [13, 14].

The importance of advanced technology involvement in pandemic response has been demonstrated by the recent outbreak. The use of digital technologies can support an effective healthcare response to the COVID-19 pandemic. They not only help to keep track of the worldwide cases but also facilitate the distribution of medical supplies and other supports, decentralization alerting, cashless digital transactions, etc. For the fastest response to COVID-19 and future pandemics, digitization of everyday processes has become unavoidable. Artificial intelligence (AI), the Internet of Things (IoT), drones, robots, 5G, and blockchain are just a few of the cutting-edge technologies being used to combat the COVID-19 epidemic [17, 18]. These innovative technologies are developing faster than ever before to build a safer planet. As a result, mitigation of the problems caused by the COVID-19 pandemic and ways to prevent further issues has become one of the burning topics of research. At times various researchers have taken different paths to address the situation in their way. Table 1 shows a comparative view of previously documented work with our approach. Jones et al. have incorporated Drone or Unmanned Aerial Vehicles (UAVs) to transfer medications to potentially infected patients to avoid human contact [19]. Ullah et al., in their system, tried to make use of an android app to develop a multilayer system where the patients can continuously contact doctors in need [20]. Their work has shown that involving modern technology can play a vital role in minimizing the outbreak as more people are being brought under proper medication.

In this study, the aim is to develop a system where users from remote locations can access high-quality medical facilities compared to smart cities. Here the system takes advantage of modern smartphones and requires less internet connectivity to collect symptoms and location of users via customized android applications. The system then automatically predicts patient conditions and redirects to doctors accordingly. The system then collects suggested medications from the doctors and sends them to the patient via drones with previously collected location data. The drones are also capable of spraying disinfection in public places both autonomously and under manual control. Implementing this system will surely increase the level of hygiene and deliver high-quality and emergency medical services to the doorstep which will reduce human contact and the spreading of the virus.

Table 1. Comparative analysis of the proposed approach with an existing systems

Authors	Year	System type	Features				
			A	B	C	D	E
Lum et al. [21]	2007	Drones/UAVs deployed for a surgical robot	×	✓	✓	×	×
Câmara [22]	2014	Drone-based Rescuers and disasters scenario system	✓	✓	×	×	✓
Kimet et al. [23]	2017	Drone-based healthcare services for patients with chronic disease	×	✓	✓	✓	×
Robert et al. [24]	2018	Drone-based system for medical services	×	✓	✓	✓	×
Ullah et al.[20]	2019	Drone-based multi-layered architecture with healthcare use-cases	×	✓	✓	×	×
Jones et al. [19]	2019	Drone-based system in medical drug supply	×	✓	✓	✓	×
Proposed Approach	2022	An Approach Towards Minimizing Covid-19 Situation Using Android App and Drone-Based Technology	✓	✓	✓	✓	×

Features: A: Monitoring, B: Data Collection, C: Medication, D: Delivery system, E: Other Application

2 Methodology

During the Pandemic, Government has imposed restrictions on any public meetings to prevent the epidemic. The system aims to reduce human contact while maintaining proper medical service in rural places. The designed system contains three sections. Following is a brief description of each level.

2.1 Android Application (E-Covid Care)

The android app is used to gather patients' data for further system analysis. Users can directly input their symptom data to the server through our custom app. Currently, we are using an Android-based application named "E-Covid Care" for this task. When the user initiates the app, it asks permission for gathering data regarding the user's condition, GPS data, etc. this is done to ensure user safety and government regulations. After getting user consent, the application goes through a series of questionnaires determined by medical professionals. When the users input their answers, it records them. The application sends a confirmation email for successful answer recording and submission to the server. Here Fig. 1 describes the working process of the developed Android application.

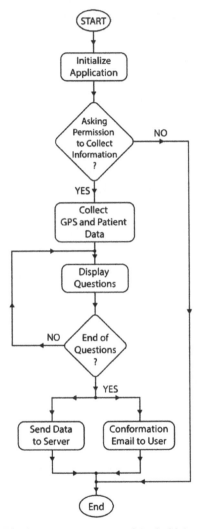

Fig. 1. Working process of Android App

2.2 Central Monitoring Server

The Central Monitoring Server is a crucial part of the overall system, which establishes continuous communication between the Android app, Doctor, and the Drone system. Instantaneous communication between each unit of the system is ensured to avoid unexpected delays between data transmission and analysis. For the Central Server, Google's

Firebase Realtime Database was used. This database supports a free service of around 1 GB of storage and 50 k reads per day. It also supports 20 k daily writes and 20 k daily deletes. This free service is quite enough for the developed system. When an end-user accesses the Android App, all data is sent to the central server with the user's permission. The server then runs an analysis for a potentially affected person from Covid-19 and assigns a doctor accordingly. The doctor can then access Patients' data and analysis answers collected previously for proper medication and input the medication list to the server. In this stage, the medicine is gathered by a medicine coordinated personnel and prepared as the Drone's payload to deliver. When the payload is ready, and everything is ok, the system then gives the Drone end-user coordinates for the delivery. Here, Fig. 2 represents the working process of the Central Monitoring Server system.

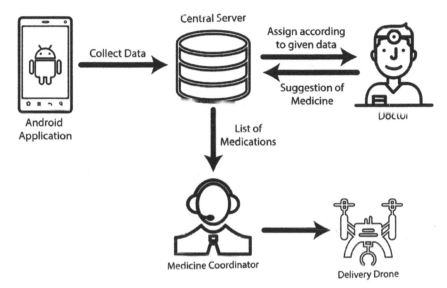

Fig. 2. Working process of Central server

2.3 Drone

The drone plays a significant role in delivering medicine without contact and maintaining hygiene in public places according to the needs. It can carry a payload, which includes medication and disinfecting fluid depending on tasks. In the case of the medicine delivery, when the shipment is attached according to the doctor's suggestion, the drone receives a set of GPS coordinates for the payload to deliver. After reaching the destination, the drone slowly positions itself with the onboard GPS and LiDAR sensor for a safe landing and successfully delivering the load. On the other hand, in the case of spraying disinfecting fluids, the drone supports two modes of operations. In manual control, the operator controls the drone containing disinfecting fluids in the payload chamber. But in Autonomous Control, a set of predefined coordinates is given to the drone by the server.

The drone then flies accordingly and sprays the disinfecting fluids. In all cases, the drone ensures the payload before taking off. If any command is given and the payload is missing, the drone immediately reports to the server and waits for further orders. Figure 3 represents the two working paths of the drone system.

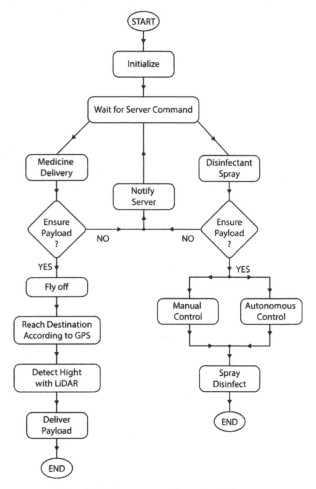

Fig. 3. Different control modes of Drone

3   System Description

In this section, a brief description of the overall system is given,

3.1   Software Interface

The software portion of the system includes the Android App and the Desktop Application, each having its own set of responsibilities. When the Android App is initiated via an

Android smartphone, the end-user is first asked for GPS credentials for future medicine delivery. The user scrolls and answers a set of yes-no questions according to their conditions. In the end, a mail is sent to the user conforming to the submission of answers. Here, Fig. 4. a) shows the Android app's interface where the users are intended to submit their responses by clicking on the options. Again, Fig. 4. b) shows the confirmation mail that the user will receive after successful submission.

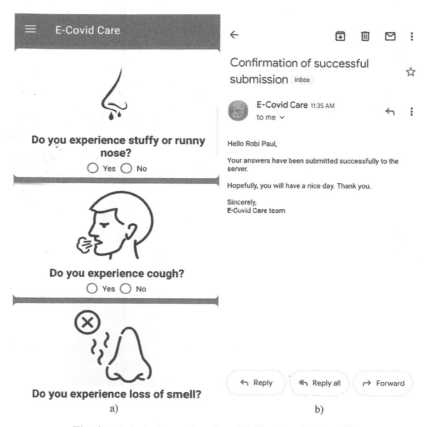

Fig. 4. (a) Android app interface (b) Confirmation E-mail.

When the system predicts a possible disease, it is then redirected to a doctor for further judgment and medications according to the analysis. The doctor has a desktop interface where they can see patients' information and the previously collected answers. Then the doctor gives medicines according to the symptoms and submits them back to the server. On the other end, a medical coordinator can arrange prescribed medications and transfer the payload to the drone. Then the drone delivers the payload to the GPS location provided by the system. Figure 5. a) and b) show the desktop interface from the doctor and medical coordinator end accordingly.

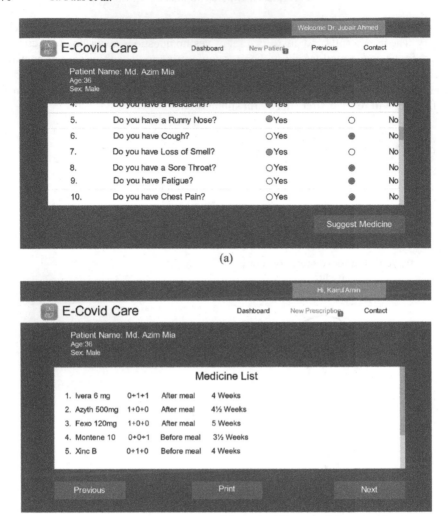

Fig. 5. (a) Doctor Interface (b) Medical Coordinator Interface

3.2 Hardware Interface

The Hardware Section for the system includes the drone. The drone receives the coordinates from the server and then delivers the payload. It uses an onboard LiDAR sensor for safe landing purposes. Again in manual disinfecting mode, the drone is controlled and navigated by an operator. When the drone is in autonomous disinfecting mode, the server gives a GPS path for the drone to follow and spray the disinfectants. Here Fig. 6 shows the different operating views of the drone. The specifications of the drone are represented in Table 2.

Table 2. Drone Specifications

Parameters	Value
Diagonal wheelbase	600 mm
Frame arm length	230 mm
Payload carrying capability	1500–1650 gm /4 rotor
Maximum thrust	3520 gm/4 rotor
Maximum power	724 W/4 rotor

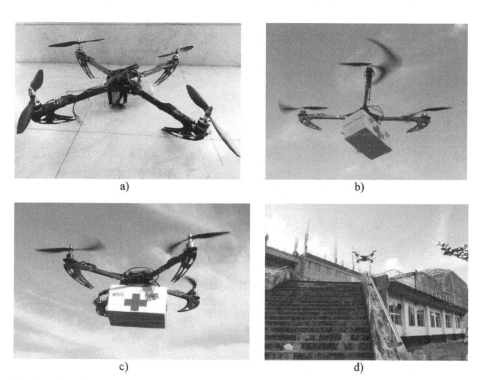

a)   b)

c)   d)

Fig. 6. (a) Designed System (b) Taking off scene (c) Payload Delivery (d) Spraying Disinfecting Fluid

4   Results

In this section, the results of the designed system are discussed. The data which are gathered from the system can be used to determine the system's performance and its effectiveness in reducing the virus spread.

4.1   Central Server Diagonosics

As Covid-19 patients start to show specific symptoms at the early stages of infection, the successful detection of the disease can play a vital role in preventing outbreaks in local areas. A correlation between different symptoms in a patient with the disease is represented in Fig. 7. The data was collected through various online surveys with the help of different stages of Covid-19 patients and Doctors. The End-User gives their physical condition data to the designed App, which sends it to the Central Server. The server defines the potential Carrier of the virus using the following set of relationships. Around 73% of the Covid-19 patient was correctly identified using the diagnostic method. The server then redirects the patient data to a doctor according to the diagnostics done for the final medication. This nullifies the possibility of false detection of potential Covid-19 patients and also ensures proper treatment from the specialized doctor.

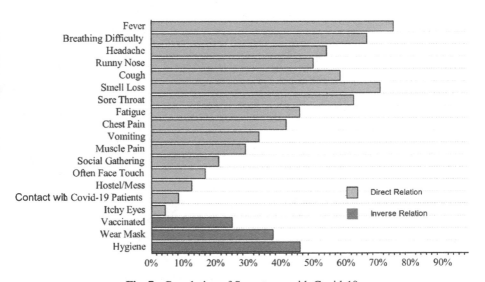

Fig. 7. Correlation of Symptoms with Covid-19.

4.2   Location Accuracy Versus Payload

The drone uses a GPS module to track and reach the exact GPS coordinate, retrieved from the End-user through the Android app. After getting to the destination, the drone uses a LiDAR sensor to measure the height underneath to land with the payload successfully and avoid unwanted hazards. The weight of the payload can also play a vital role in successful delivery and landing. Because the additional load can shift the center of mass and cause imbalance. Therefore, the system needs to adjust the thruster speed in order to compromise for the imbalance in the center of mass. Again added weight increases the inertia of the drone, which makes complications in maneuvering. When it has to handle highly complex calculations like holding or reaching a GPS coordinate, complexity increases even more. However, the problem can be minimized by fine-tuning the thrust of the propeller in real-life test situations. Here, Fig. 8 represents the GPS location accuracy of the payload attached in different scenarios. Here two possible weather scenarios are described by sunny and windy weather. The sunny weather had a minimal breeze, whereas the windy weather had some wind flow, corresponding to the higher error.

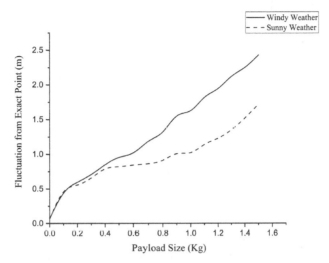

Fig. 8. Fluctuations from exact points with the corresponding Payload.

4.3 Expected Area Coverage Versus Reality for Disinfecting Spray

In some cases, the practically gathered results have come out slightly different from the theoretically calculated values. Many variables are responsible for this discrepancy. One of the significant aspects that are ignored when the values are theoretically calculated is the environmental effects. The speed of wind flow and the direction of the flow can significantly affect the performance aspect of the drone. If the direction of the wind flow is in the same direction as the drone, the drone's speed accelerates. This helps the drone to cover a larger area which increases its efficiency. Again, when the direction of the wind is opposite to the drone's direction, the wind slows the speed down, resulting in lower area coverage. This shows lower efficiency than theoretically considered. Here, Fig. 9 shows the area covered with disinfectant fluid for a specific flow rate of the spray pump. The graph shows when the drone sprays more frequently, it is more likely to cover less area. But when considering the environmental effects, sunny weather has less wind flow which corresponds to near theoretical results. But in the case of the windy weather, there is a difference. Depending on the direction of the wind flow, sometimes the drone has covered greater or less area than the theoretical result.

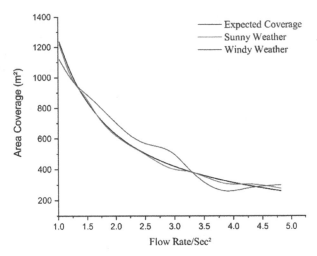

Fig. 9. Covered Area vs. Flow Rate.

5 Conclusion

Minimizing the COVID-19 situation from escalating to even worse is now the most challenging task in the world. This work is all about reducing a human to human contact while delivering a higher standard of medical treatment to rural areas. The use of Drone has also made the delivery possess much more accessible and time-saving. As it is a contactless delivery system, the implementation will nullify one of the most prominent viruses spreading mediums, which is human gathering. Hopefully, with further research and perfect refinement and tuning, the system will become one of the most effective and simplest ways to deliver medical goods to rural people while fighting against the deadly virus.

Acknowledgement. We would like to show our appreciation to all who have assisted us at different stages of this research. In addition, we would also like to express our gratitude to the Shahjalal University of Science and Technology Research Centre for providing financial support for our work.

References

1. Li, T., Lu, H., Zhang, W.: Clinical observation and management of COVID-19 patients. Emerg. Micro. Inf. **9**(1), 687–690 (2020)
2. Andreadakis, Z., Kumar, A., Román, R.G., Tollefsen, S., Saville, M., Mayhew, S.: The COVID-19 vaccine development landscape. Nat. Rev. Drug Discov. **19**(5), 305–306 (2020)
3. Hwang, J., Kim, H.: The effects of expected benefits on image, desire, and behavioral intentions in the field of drone food delivery services after the outbreak of COVID-19. Sustainability **13**(1), 117 (2021)
4. Ahmed, F., Paul, R., Amin, I.K., Ahammad, A.: Design and development of a disinfecting system for COVID-19. In: 2021 IEEE International Conference on Telecommunications and Photonics (ICTP), pp. 1–5 (2021)

5. Velavan, T.P., Meyer, C.G.: The COVID-19 epidemic. Tropical Med. Int. Health **25**(3), 278 (2020)
6. Hossain, M.: The effect of the COVID-19 on sharing economy activities. J. Clean. Prod. **280**, 124782 (2021)
7. Rigby, E.: The COVID-19 economy unemployment insurance, and population health. JAMA Netw. Open **4**(1), 2035955 (2021)
8. Mak, J.W., Chan, F.K., Ng, S.C.: Probiotics and COVID-19: one size does not fit all. Lancet Gastroenterol. Hepatol. **5**(7), 644–645 (2020)
9. Aabed, K., Lashin, M.M.: An analytical study of the factors that influence COVID-19 spread. Saudi J. Biol. Sci. **28**(2), 1177–1195 (2021)
10. Forni, G., Mantovani, A.: COVID-19 vaccines: where we stand and challenges ahead. Cell Death Differ. **28**(2), 626–639 (2021)
11. Khan, H., Kushwah, K.K., Singh, S., Urkude, H., Maurya, M.R., Sadasivuni, K.K.: Smart technologies driven approaches to tackle COVID-19 pandemic: a review. 3 Biotech. **11**(2), 1–22 (2021)
12. Koshta, N., Devi, Y., Patra, S.: Aerial bots in the supply chain: a new ally to combat COVID-19. In: Technology in Society, pp. 101646 (2021)
13. Canal, I., Reimbold, M., Campos, M.: Drone use to combat COVID-19: adaptive tuning proposal of the control system under variable load. IEEE Lat. Am. Trans. **19**(6), 901–908 (2021)
14. Jain, R., Gupta, M., Garg, K., Gupta, A.: Robotics and drone-based solution for the impact of COVID-19 worldwide using AI and IoT. In: Emerging Technologies for Battling Covid-19: Applications and Innovations, pp. 139–156 (2021)
15. Hwang, J., Choe, J.Y., Choi, Y.G., Kim, J.J.: A comparative study on the motivated consumer innovativeness of drone food delivery services before and after the outbreak of COVID-19. J. Travel Tour. Mark. **38**(4), 368–382 (2021)
16. Kumar, A., Sharma, K., Singh, H., Naugriya, S.G., Gill, S.S., Buyya, R.: A drone-based networked system and methods for combating coronavirus disease (COVID-19) pandemic. Futur. Gener. Comput. Syst. **115**, 1–19 (2021)
17. Paul, R., Ahmed, F., Shahriar, T.R., Ahmad, M., Ahammad, A.: Centralized power monitoring & management system of an institution based on Android App. In: 2021 International Conference on Automation, Control and Mechatronics for Industry 4.0 (ACMI). pp. 1–5 (2021)
18. Restás, Á., Szalkai, I., Óvári, G.: Drone application for spraying disinfection liquid fighting against the COVID-19 pandemic—examining drone-related parameters influencing effectiveness. Drones **5**(3), 58 (2021)
19. Jones, R.W., Despotou, G.: Unmanned aerial systems and healthcare: possibilities and challenges. In: 14th IEEE Conference on Industrial Electronics and Applications (ICIEA), pp. 189–194 (2019)
20. Ullah, H., Nair, N.G., Moore, A., Nugent, C., Muschamp, P., Cuevas, M.: 5G Communication: an overview of vehicle-to-everything drones, and health care use cases. IEEE Access **7**, 37251–37268 (2019)
21. Lum, M.J., et al.: Telesurgery via Unmanned Aerial Vehicle (UAV) with a field deployable surgical robot. Stud. Health Technol. Inform. 313–315 (2007)
22. Câmara, D.: Cavalry to the rescue: Drones fleet to help rescuers operations over disasters scenarios. In: IEEE Conference on Antenna Measurements & Applications (CAMA) pp. 1–4 (2014)
23. Kim, S.J., Lim, G.J., Cho, J., Cote, M.J.: Drone-aided healthcare services for patients with chronic diseases in rural areas. J. Intell. Robot. Syst., Theory Appl. **88**(1), 163–180 (2017)
24. Graboyes, R.F., Skorup, B.: Medical drones in the United States and a survey of technical and policy challenges. Mercatus Center Policy Brief (2020)

IoT and ML Based Approach for Highway Monitoring and Streetlamp Controlling

Mushfiqur Rahman$^{(\boxtimes)}$, Md. Faridul Islam Suny, Jerin Tasnim, Md. Sabab Zulfiker, Mohammad Jahangir Alam, and Tajim Md. Niamat Ullah Akhund[iD]

Department of Computer Science and Engineering, Daffodil International University, Dhaka, Bangladesh

{mushfiqur.cse,faridul15-1353,jerin15-2772,jahangir.cse, tajim.cse}@diu.edu.bd

Abstract. Excessive speed and violating traffic rules may cause dangerous road accident. Some reports show that around 3700 people die every day due to road accident. Controlling vehicle speed and proper automated street lighting system may mitigate this problem. This work implements an automated internet of things and machine learning based system to control streetlamps with vehicle speed tracking. The developed machine learning model is capable to guesstimate the speed of the vehicle on the highway and report if there is any excessive speed. The automated streetlamp is integrated with the system that can provide proper illumination considering the environment condition. The proposed system showed good results after practical implementation.

Keywords: Internet of Things (IoT) · Machine Learning (ML) · automated streetlamp · highway monitoring · vehicle detection · speed estimation

1 Introduction

Street lighting is the traditional energy recipient in metropolises. Up to 60% to 70% minimal money can be spent on street illuminating owing to lampposts [1]. The lights are turned on in the dark and switched off when it is adequately light outdoors.

The mechanism might also no longer be done remotely. Despite the fact that there are scant energy resources, the world's energy expenditure is climbing at the sharpest classify worldwide as a result of cohort increase and economic expansion. As a result, there are significant energy deficits since resource and energy gen consoles development cannot keep up with rising demand [11]. Streetlights are a vital element of every burgeoning metropolis. They can ever be revealed on all major highways including in the suburbs. Every day, from sunset to daybreak, lampposts are switched on at a high level, even when alone. These lamps cost far too much money each day to provide the required quantity of light energy on a world basis. Maintenance and replacement costs for mainstream incandescent bulbs are astronomically high. They produce a lot of heat and require a lot of electricity to operate. As a result, there is a greater need for electricity right now,

Md. S. Satu et al. (Eds.): MIET 2022, LNICST 491, pp. 376–385, 2023.
https://doi.org/10.1007/978-3-031-34622-4_30

which raises the amount of carbon dioxide that power plants emit into the atmosphere. As a result, this interaction hurts our environment in addition to producing excessive light pollution. The key goal of the venture is to create an energy-powered "Street Lamp-Post" for use at night. The lamppost is powered by the system, which considers the motion's trajectory of objects and supports them by lighting their path prior the next streetlight [14]. The embedded system can help pedestrians in faraway places with pressing supply constraints meet their objectives by consolidating with the street light system [13]. A convenient solution is to dim the lights during idol hours. When locomotion is perceived in the region, the lights in the surrounding will turn on in a predictable pattern [15]. This scheme would slash the cost of lighting while simultaneously preserving a significant amount of energy. Subsequently, we may leverage IoT to autonomously and in real-time monitor a system's status using the internet. This project's goal is to establish a speed camera without sensors and rely simply on neuroimaging of films using Python's OpenCV library [10]. A Doppler radar was eventually employed to measure the speed of vehicular traffic on highways. Then, fast cars were photographed using cameras. The speed of a passing vehicle is calculated by a Doppler radar using the frequency change of the approaching automobile [9]. Later, sensors were used by Traffic Radars to determine speeds. In order to detect traffic violators, traffic radars currently blend the use of sensors with image processing [16]. It is not sufficient to be speeding in order to commit a traffic infraction; other transgressions include the improper or reserved lane, running a red light, tailgating, overtaking out from wrong side, etc. Traffic radars may eventually be able to detect violations involving seatbelts and chatting while pursuing [9]. Wellas a piece is currently being researched and could be published soon. The streetlights gadget in Bangladesh remains manual. That suggests the road lighting fixtures gadget isn't automated, and technological innovation hasn't been assembled yet. There are three sorts of lighting fixtures hired in our country's streets: sodium, fluorescent, and energy-saving lighting. The city of Dhaka will deploy LED lights in all streetlamps to safeguard citizen reliability and give ample lighting on the streets for policy enforcement agents to do their jobs efficiently. Sensors and controllers are tied to construct an energy-saving lighting system, which is self-regulating, cost-effective, and acceptable for street lighting. Make a lighting system that is modular in order to allow for system expansion and customization. Our primary objective is to create a lighting mechanism that is scalable and compatible with various retail commodities and automated processes that can include more than simply lighting systems. And the project's initial focus is to build an IoT-based system for customizable street lighting that uses modern methods of technology, deliver an expedient lighting system that is totally based on biofuels, is long-lasting and durable, and saves energy.

As traffic steadily diminishes throughout the night, lights can be adjusted automatically until the morning to achieve power efficiency, and streetlamps switch on in the dark and then off in the sunlight [13]. In mild of the above goals, the task can pursue the subsequent effects:

- Most pivotal immediate advantage is that we've been able to tackle conventional switching until it's not necessary. As a result, a person's presence is not required while tapping on or off the streetlights.

- When the luminous flux drops due to bad weather, the lamp will automatically turn on and off in complies with the luminance. Consequently, we won't have to deal with turning on the lights.
- Monitoring the highway vehicle, track their speed and notify if high speed is found.

2 Literature Review

In many circumstances, IoT's positive impacts are evident [17]. An intelligent traffic and transportation system based on cutting-edge technology may be enabled feasible by the Internet of Things (IoT) [16]. Traffic jams, traffic accidents, and arrival delays will all be reduced because of this. A variety of studies were utilized to enhance the street lighting system. The illumination system was replaced or improved in the meantime to make it more user-friendly. In certain cases, the way things are happening was tweaked to generate a more reliable design. Today's street lighting system debuted vapor lamps with LEDs, protecting a significant amount of energy [2]. The system's linked research revealed a thorough review of several old lighting systems, their power consumption, and the aspects of new tech that is used to convert those customary lamps [3]. The country has adopted traditional lights after collecting data into the discrepancies in power efficiency, quality, and cost-savings compared to folklore bulbs and LED. Later work has explored using Wi-Fi to monitor the street light management system [5]. It lets cities have a more effective and affordable lighting control technique. The system consisted of a multiphase, digitally controlled LED lamp drive system and an LED light. A invention was made by including a transceiver inside the photoelectric circuit that regulates the ON/OFF of the High-Pressure Sodium bulbs [20]. Additionally, it enables the system's usage for a number of new municipal tasks. To alleviate the overload difficulties during peak hours, technology advanced. The street lighting system is mechanically generated, which allows for four disconnections during peak hours and optimizes the distribution of electrical energy [4]. Then a system for dynamically altering lighting based on pedestrian positions and safety zones was simulated using a gadget. The streetlamps are integrated with one using multi-hop relaying to reap commands of the cloud server [4]. The latter study concentrated on two areas: adopting the optimal protocol and looking for a network architecture that will support the prototype. The work focuses on anterior to this evaluating the effectiveness of mesh and tree community designs that might be used in conjunction with the ZigBee reliable wireless in the road lighting control structure [5]. A wi-fi tool with progressed handling and performance became implemented, giving stepped forward control performance, trendy interface, and manipulate architecture. Numerous sensors were employed to communicate data through ZigBee transmitters and receivers [5]. Assessing the device's condition and taking the appropriate action in the event of failure. An costly, high-performance LED module was created for favoured illumination. It has been developed and tested to be the 9-LED Module (9-LEDM). To extend longevity and improve induction therapy, an associate's degree harmonizing with a pair of frequencies has been devised. All three aspects—Three metrics—photometric, radiative, and electronic been presumed. Finally, experimental results based on the suggested method were acquired via lab measurements and a demonstration project. In terms of the pedestrian area and safety, an SSL device was proposed to explain a quick, stable, and powerful road light switching device [13]. A consolidated platform may be used to monitor the lane markers. The IRS2530D and a dimming control circuit may both change the lighting's brightness., which is a new dimming ballast control IC in a small 8-pin shape, and addressing the deployment of a sensor to detect the ambient light, A contraption emerges in which the microcontroller is intended to just control the rhythm and brightness of the lighting [14]. They incorporated a Real-Time Clock and an LDR that progressed into being connected to a microcontroller. LDR was incorporated to locate the mild extrude. The amended variant was provided to the analog to digital converter, which altered it into a voltage signal and forwarded it to the microcontroller (ADC), with the capability to control when the lighting should turn on or off. Then, when the ambient light intensity drops below an optimum criterion, the road lights are set up to turn on [15]. When the site visitors' depth is just too low, the RTC inside the device assessments the time and dims the mild among hours. Finally, mild Acceleration via way of means of Stimulated Emission of Radiation (LASER) gates come across motion and spark off positive avenue lighting fixtures to most depth for public use. Slightly less electricity is consumed. System and lamp spacing is optimal., the "Timer and Dimmer" project can optimize performance by up to 40% and can augment suction by up to 35% [19]. The lifespan of the burned-out lamps can be increased by this gadget by two times. A robust and durable road delicate manage device, which desires negligible maintenance, became delivered later. It works at the depth of mild, in which time sensing is used for deciphering the depth of mild A real-time clock, a microprocessor, and a driver circuit based on Metal Oxide Semiconductor Field Effect Transistors are employed in this plan to regulate the intensity of LEDs. It minimizes annual energy consumption per streetlight by 16.96 kwhr when compared to the standard regulating mechanism [12]. In comparison to wireless sensor networks, it is more dependable and needs less upkeep. The Mask R-CNN architecture is used for vehicle detection. Masking was used to highlight vehicle-accessible areas on the road video [6]. Equations are used to calculate the speed of a vehicle as it travels over a rectangular territory. The length of a road segment is calculated via Direct Linear Transformation [7]. Afterwards, a Gaussian mixture is used to calculate speed and Background Subtraction to estimate the vehicle's position [8]. Finally, camera calibration was employed to the 3D space segment stance of the vehicle. All of the aforementioned research indicates the necessity for a street lighting system that is more ecological [9] as well as convenient and adaptable to operate. Remote sensing is facilitated for individuals by IoT-based initiatives [22, 25, 29], patient management [23, 27, 28], medical management [34], poultry farm [24], agriculture [32], hotel management [26], Electronic voting [31], security management [30], solar panel monitoring [35] and so on in secure way [33]. So, we hope streetlamp management system can be maintained with IoT in an efficient way.

3   Proposed Methodology

Two fundamental parts of this proposed framework are artificial intelligence (AI) cameras and LED lighting, which integrate energy-saving technology and management to reduce carbon emissions and capture community actual traffic stats dissemination and observing of freight. The two primary components of this suggested approach are artificial intelligence (AI) cameras and LED lighting, which employ energy-saving technology and management to reduce carbon emissions and capture real-time traffic metrics for use in inspection and public release. To implement this system the requirements that include hardware, software, and online services are Arduino Uno, Breadboard, LDR Sensor, IR Sensor, Jumper wire, ESP8266, Camera-SQ11 Mini DV, Arduino IDE, ThingSpeak API, and PyCharm CE.

3.1 IoT Based Street Lamp

This flowchart (Fig. 1) will show the working procedure of IoT based streetlamp post of our proposed model. It will be operated in three modes. They are- Idol mode (When there's sufficient mild in the surrounding, at some stage in the daytime, the whole machine will transfer to the idol and the batteries might be charging), Active mode (When the ambient mild drops underneath a sure degree the machine mechanically activates and the sensors might be activated) and Operating mode (On the presence of a human, the sensors switch on and the machine will switch on the LED lighting fixtures. Following a while, these luminaires will turn off.).

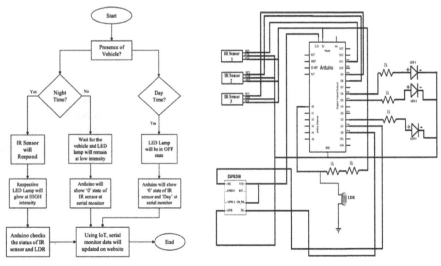

Fig. 1. Flowchart   **Fig. 2.** Schematic Architecture

This envisioned system's IoT-based streetlamp is exhibited by this schematic architecture (Fig. 2), which exhibits the circuit indicating the operations connection between various electrical components.

3.2 Highway Monitoring

Here Project model block diagram (Fig. 3) is showing the entire process of highway monitoring systems using IoT. Then, A low fraction of the original footage is taken up by Region of Interest (ROI). Image subtraction is used on this ROI to find moving vehicles. (Image subtraction aids in determining the distinction between two frames.)

Masking (Fig. 4) is used to make the background black and the moving vehicles appear white. The contours are recognized according to the area barrier of the number of pixels (Fig. 5). The threshold prevents the wrinkles of smaller moving objects that are not automobiles from being detected. Using the gap between two textures over frames as a premise, the object is tracked. Each contour is allotted an ID.

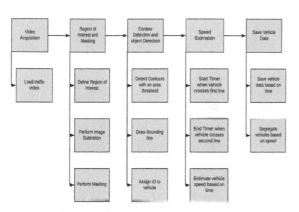

Fig. 4. Masked Image

Fig. 3. Project Model Block Diagram

Fig. 5. Contour Detection

3.3 Vehicle Detection and Speed Estimation

Image subtraction is used to detect moving cars because the background of the vehicles is immovable (due to the stationary nature of the speed camera) (Fig. 6). When a tracked vehicle travels a portion of the route, the speed of the vehicle can then be approximated. A formula is used to determine and anticipate the amount of time that will pass between a vehicle's position and speed. As immediately as the vehicle passes the first point, the timer begins, and it expires when it crosses the second line (Fig. 7). Thus, the speed is only shown when the car crosses both lines on top of the enclosing box [9].

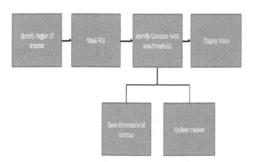

Fig. 6. Vehicle Detection Block Diagram   **Fig. 7.** Speed Estimation

382   M. Rahman et al.

4 Results

Along with the speed, a file is also recorded with a picture of the bounding box (the vehicle). Vehicles that exceed the speed limit are separated and placed in a different folder (Fig. 8). A text file contains the vehicle information. It is highlighted out which cars went over the pace seal. There is a summary of the handful of vehicles and the tailgaters (Fig. 9).

Fig. 8. Saved Vehicle Pictures   **Fig. 9.** Sample Summary

The streetlamp controlling system also worked properly.
The obtained features are as follows:

1. Can monitor the vehicles on the road and tack the speed.
2. If any excessive speed found it can notify.
3. Measure the sun light intensity and control the streetlamp illumination.
4. Can Detect human near the streetlamp with IR sensor and automatically illuminate if human found.

The system was tested for multiple times. Following Table 1 shows the results.

Table 1. System Results Analysis

Objectives	Test time	Original	System output	Success rate
Speed tracking and Vehicle monitoring	100 vehicles	28 were in high speed	25 found in high speed	$\frac{25}{28} * 100\% = 89.3\%$
Streetlamp controlling	100 times	35 times in day, 35 times in night, 30 times in present of human in night	Day time turned off 35 times, turned on 34 times in night, turned on 29 times in presence of human motion	$\frac{\left(\frac{35}{35}+\frac{34}{35}+\frac{29}{30}\right)}{3} * 100\% = 97.9\%$

5   Conclusion

The proposed system is quite effective. The automated IoT based system was able to control the illumination of the streetlamps in proper time which can save energy and help the drivers. The developed machine learning model was able to monitor the vehicle speed on the highway and notify. The system has certain constraints too. The mechanism cannot interpret the damaged streetlamps. Some features like number plate detection and driver's attention level detection can make the proposed system more effective in future. The success rate should be increased in future development.

References

1. Kodali, R., Yerroju, S.: Energy efficient smart street light. In: 2017 3rd International Conference on Applied and Theoretical Computing and Communication Technology (iCATccT). IEEE (2017)
2. Kulasooriyage, C., Namasivayam, S., Udawatta, L.: Analysis on energy efficiency and optimality of LED and photovoltaic based street lighting system. Eng.: J. Inst. Eng. Sri Lanka **48**(1), 11 (2015)
3. Cheng, Y.-K., Cheng, K.W.E.: General study for using LED to replace traditional lighting devices. In: 2006 2nd International Conference on Power Electronics Systems and Applications. IEEE (2006)
4. Denardin, G.W., et al.: Control network for modern street lighting systems. In: 2011 IEEE International Symposium on Industrial Electronics. IEEE (2011)
5. Lavric, A., et al.: A performance study of ZigBee wireless sensors network topologies for street lighting control systems. In: 2012 International Conference on Selected Topics in Mobile and Wireless Networking. IEEE (2012)
6. Grents, A., Varkentin, V., Goryaev, N.: Determining vehicle speed based on video using convolutional neural network. Transp. Res. Procedia **50**, 192–200 (2020)
7. Gunawan, A.A.S., Tanjung, D.A., Gunawan, F.E.: Detection of vehicle position and speed using camera calibration and image projection methods. Procedia Comput. Sci. **157**, 255–265 (2019)
8. Kumar, T., Kushwaha, D.S.: An efficient approach for detection and speed estimation of moving vehicles. Procedia Comput. Sci. **89**, 726–731 (2016)
9. Javadi, S., Dahl, M., Pettersson, M.I.: Vehicle speed measurement model for video-based systems. Comput. Electr. Eng. **76**, 238–248 (2019)
10. Vargas, M., et al.: A shadow removal algorithm for vehicle detection based on reflectance ratio and edge density. In: 13th International IEEE Conference on Intelligent Transportation Systems. IEEE (2010)
11. Festus, M.O., Ogoegbunam, O.B.: Energy crisis and its effects on national development: the need for environmental education in Nigeria. Br. J. Educ. **3**(1), 21–37 (2015)
12. Nunoo, S., Attachie, J., Abraham, C.: Using solar power as an alternative source of electrical energy for street lighting in Ghana, pp. 467–471 (2010). https://doi.org/10.1109/CITRES.2010.5619814
13. Ankalkote, T., Shere, V.B.: Modern LED street lighting system with intensity control based on vehicle movements and atmospheric conditions using WSN. Int. J. Innov. Res. Adv. Eng. (IJIRAE) **3**(05), 10–15 (2016)
14. Archana, G., et al.: Intelligent street light system. Int. J. Recent Adv. Eng. Technol. **3**(4) (2015)

15. Chen, P.-Y., et al.: Development of an energy efficient street light driving system. In: 2008 IEEE International Conference on Sustainable Energy Technologies. IEEE (2008)
16. Faridul Islam Suny, M., Monjourur Roshed Fahim, M., Rahman, M., Newaz, N.T., Akhund, T.M.N.U.: IoT past, present, and future a literary survey. In: Kaiser, M.S., Xie, J., Rathore, V.S. (eds.) Information and Communication Technology for Competitive Strategies (ICTCS 2020). LNNS, vol. 190, pp. 393–402. Springer, Singapore (2021). https://doi.org/10.1007/978-981-16-0882-7_33
17. Suny, M.F.I., et al.: Smart agricultural system using IoT. In: Nagar, A.K., Jat, D.S., Marín-Raventós, G., Mishra, D.K. (eds.) Intelligent Sustainable Systems. LNNS, vol. 333, pp. 73–82. Springer, Singapore (2022). https://doi.org/10.1007/978-981-16-6309-3_8
18. Louis, L.: Working principle of Arduino and using it. Int. J. Control Autom. Commun. Syst. (IJCACS) 1(2), 21–29 (2016)
19. Global LED & Smart Street Lighting Market (2015–2025). https://www.prnewswire.com/news-releases/global-led--smart-street-lighting-market-2015-2025-300277486.html. Accessed 01 Feb 2022
20. Ali Kumar, D.N.S.K.P., Au, T.W., Suhaili, W.S.: Smart LED street light systems: a Bruneian case study. In: Phon-Amnuaisuk, S., Ang, S.-P., Lee, S.-Y. (eds.) MIWAI 2017. LNCS (LNAI), vol. 10607, pp. 370–379. Springer, Cham (2017). https://doi.org/10.1007/978-3-319-69456-6_31
21. World Bank Publications: The World Bank Annual Report 2013. World Bank Publications (2013)
22. Akhund, T.M.N.U., Newaz, N.T., Rakib Hossain, M., Shamim Kaiser, M.: Low-cost smartphone-controlled remote sensing IoT robot. In: Kaiser, M.S., Xie, J., Rathore, V.S. (eds.) Information and Communication Technology for Competitive Strategies (ICTCS 2020). LNNS, vol. 190, pp. 569–576. Springer, Singapore (2021). https://doi.org/10.1007/978-981-16-0882-7_49
23. Akhund, T.M.N.U., et al.: Snappy wheelchair: an IoT-based flex controlled robotic wheel chair for disabled people. In: Kaiser, M.S., Xie, J., Rathore, V.S. (eds.) Information and Communication Technology for Competitive Strategies (ICTCS 2020). LNNS, vol. 190, pp. 803–812. Springer, Singapore (2021). https://doi.org/10.1007/978-981-16-0882-7_71
24. Akhund, T.M.N.U., Snigdha, S.R., Reza, M.S., Newaz, N.T., Saifuzzaman, M., Rashel, M.R.: Self-powered IoT-based design for multi-purpose smart poultry farm. In: Senjyu, T., Mahalle, P.N., Perumal, T., Joshi, A. (eds.) ICTIS 2020. SIST, vol. 196, pp. 43–51. Springer, Singapore (2021). https://doi.org/10.1007/978-981-15-7062-9_5
25. Akhund, T.M., Ullah, N., Newaz, N., Sarker, M.: Posture recognizer robot with remote sensing for virus invaded area & people. J. Inf. Technol. 9, 1–6 (2020). ISSN: 2227-1279
26. Akhund, T.M.N.U., Siddik, M.A.B., Hossain, M.R., Rahman, M.M., Newaz, N.T., Saifuzzaman, M.: IoT Waiter Bot: a low cost IoT based multi functioned robot for restaurants. In: 2020 8th International Conference on Reliability, Infocom Technologies and Optimization (Trends and Future Directions) (ICRITO), pp. 1174–1178 (2020). https://doi.org/10.1109/ICRITO48877.2020.9197920
27. Niamat Ullah Akhund, T.M., Jyoty, W.B., Siddik, M.A.B., Newaz, N.T., Al Wahid, S.K.A., Sarker, M.M.: IoT based low-cost robotic agent design for disabled and Covid-19 virus affected people. In: 2020 Fourth World Conference on Smart Trends in Systems, Security and Sustainability (WorldS4), pp. 23–26 (2020). https://doi.org/10.1109/WorldS450073.2020.9210389
28. Niamat Ullah Akhund, T.M., Mahi, M.J.N., Hasnat Tanvir, A.N.M., Mahmud, M., Kaiser, M.S.: ADEPTNESS: alzheimer's disease patient management system using pervasive sensors - early prototype and preliminary results. In: Wang, S., et al. (eds.) BI 2018. LNCS (LNAI), vol. 11309, pp. 413–422. Springer, Cham (2018). https://doi.org/10.1007/978-3-030-05587-5_39

29. Akhund, T.M., Ullah, N., Sagar, I., Sarker, M.: Remote temperature sensing line following robot with Bluetooth data sending capability. In: International Conference on Recent Advances in Mathematical and Physical Sciences (ICRAMPS), PID: 81302 (2018). https://doi.org/10.13140/RG.2.2.21258.77761

30. Sarker, M., Shah, M., Akhund, T., Uddin, M.: An approach of automated electronic voting management system for Bangladesh using biometric fingerprint. Int. J. Adv. Eng. Res. Sci. 3(11), 64–70 (2016)

31. Mesbahuddin Sarker, M., Akhund, T.M.N.U.: The roadmap to the electronic voting system development: a literature review. Int. J. Adv. Eng. Manag. Sci. 2(5), 492–497 (2016). ISSN: 2454-1311

32. Akhund, T.N., Newaz, N.T., Zaman, Z., Sultana, A., Barros, A., Whaiduzzaman, M.: IoT-based low-cost automated irrigation system for smart farming. In: Nagar, A.K., Jat, D.S., Marín-Raventós, G., Mishra, D.K. (eds.) Intelligent Sustainable Systems. LNNS, vol. 333, pp. 83–91. Springer, Singapore (2022). https://doi.org/10.1007/978-981-16-6309-3_9

33. Newaz, N.T., Haque, M.R., Akhund, T.M.N.U.T., Khatun, M.B., Yousuf, M.A.: IoT security perspectives and probable solution. In: 2021 Fifth World Conference on Smart Trends in Systems Security and Sustainability (WorldS4), pp. 81–86 (2021). https://doi.org/10.1109/WorldS451998.2021.9513997

34. Himel, A.H., Boby, F.A., Saba, S., Akhund, T.M.U., Ali, K.M.A.: Contribution of robotics in medical applications a literary survey. In: Nagar, A.K., Jat, D.S., Marín-Raventós, G. Mishra, D.K. (eds.) Intelligent Sustainable Systems. LNNS, vol. 333, pp. 247–255. Springer, Singapore (2022). https://doi.org/10.1007/978-981-16-6309-3_25

35. Rashel, M.R., Islam, M., Sultana, S., Ahmed, M.T., Akhund, T.M.N.U., Sikta, J.N.: Internet of Things platform for advantageous renewable energy generation. In: Mandal, J.K., Buyya, R., De, D. (eds.) Proceedings of International Conference on Advanced Computing Applications. AISC, vol. 1406, pp. 107–117. Springer, Singapore (2022). https://doi.org/10.1007/978-981-16-5207-3_10

Cyber-Attack Detection Through Ensemble-Based Machine Learning Classifier

Mohammad Amaz Uddin$^{(\boxtimes)}$, Khandaker Tayef Shahriar,
Md. Mokammel Haque, and Iqbal H. Sarker$^{(\boxtimes)}$

Department of Computer Science and Engineering, Chittagong University of
Engineering and Technology, Chittagong 4349, Bangladesh
amazuddin722@gmail.com, iqbal@cuet.ac.bd

Abstract. In this fourth industrial revolution era, cyber-attacks are
constantly increasing. A method called network traffic monitoring
blueprint has been used to detect these unusual suspicious activities in
the system. Fuzzers, Backdoors, DoS, Exploits, Reconnaissance, Shellcode, Worm, etc., are known as attacks that disrupt the functioning of a
system. This paper explores the performance of various machine learning (ML) algorithms and develops an ensemble-based model to detect
cyber-attacks. We first implement eight different machine learning models such as Support Vector Machine (SVM), Extreme Gradient Boosting
(XGB), Logistic Regression (LR), K-Nearest Neighbor (KNN), Decision
Tree (DT), AdaBoosting, Random Forest (RF), Naive Bayes by using
network intrusion dataset named UNSW-NB15 containing multi-type
data. Based on the performance of indiviaul machine learning models,
we construct an ensemble model by taking into account the top four
machine learning models. We also take into account a set of optimal
features while building our ensemble model. The experimental outcomes
demonstrate that our presented ensemble model produces good accuracy
of 98.48% while detecting diverse attacks.

Keywords: Machine learning · Cyber-attack · UNSW-NB15 dataset ·
Ensemble

1 Introduction

Nowadays, computer systems and networks are becoming more vulnerable to
many attacks and anomalies [1]. It is technically challenging and expensive to
ensure that a network system is not attacked by intruders exploiting those vulnerabilities. Due to the rapid evolution of technology, today's companies rely
on computer networks and the Internet to conduct their daily operations. As a
result, network attacks are increasing in parallel with the growth of the system.
By improving information system security, intrusion detection systems (IDSs)
can significantly contribute to preventing these incompatibility problems [2].

Md. S. Satu et al. (Eds.): MIET 2022, LNICST 491, pp. 386–396, 2023.
https://doi.org/10.1007/978-3-031-34622-4_31

IDS are security tools that detect evidence of malicious activity conducted on a network resource [3]. The main goal of IDS is to find unwanted or anomalous actions in a system or network, which is connected to a classification issue in the context of machine learning [4].

Anomaly-based systems look for anomalies from normal behavior and flag any abnormal behavior as malicious [5]. The benefit of abnormality detection in a network is the ability to detect new or undiscovered attacks. As the number of network-based attacks and anomalies increases, better approaches are needed to conduct network forensic investigations of attacks and anomaly detection [6]. However, many researchers have conducted many experiments using multiple models and datasets to detect anomalies and attacks [7]. They have created numerous effective attack and anomaly detection models and algorithms, most of which are based on typical machine learning, and deep learning methods. Furthermore, machine learning methods are highly adaptable to any type of automatic detection challenge [5]. It is able to learn from several data sources and create predictions using that information. Thus, we offer an effective attack detection approach in this paper utilizing the UNSW-NB15 [8] dataset, which contains both normal and unusual network activity data, and eventually build an ensemble learning model by taking into account a set of optimal features.

The remaining pieces of work are organized as follows. Section 2 discusses a review of various prior efforts in the literature. In Sect. 3, the dataset is described. The techniques, features, and application of ML models are the main topics of Sect. 4. The result analysis and discussion of the proposed work are described in Sect. 5. Finally, Sect. 6 concludes with some suggestions for further research in this area.

2   Literature Review

The task of attack and anomaly detection has been done many times by different researchers. They are still working on new techniques and algorithms to improve this field. In [6], a network forensics scheme was developed to monitor and evaluate network-based attacks in real-time testing. They completed their study by collecting network traffic data, using chi-square techniques to identify relevant features, and correntropy-variation techniques to investigate unusual phenomena. Shon et al. [9] developed a new SVM method called Advanced SVM to define a generic framework for detecting emerging attacks in traffic networks. This advanced SVM is the main contribution of their study. This enhanced SVM is a crucial part of hybrid machine learning algorithms for attack and anomaly detection. It combines supervised and unsupervised SVM. SVM, Self-organizing feature maps (SOFM), and GA are all used in this proposed technique for anomaly detection.

Mokhtari et al. [10] presented a strategy called Measurement Intrusion Detection System (MIDS) in which various machine learning models were applied to detect anomalies in datasets. Mostafa et al. [11] presented a beta mixing approach (BMM-ADS) for anomaly identification. Their BMM-ADS approach provided them a high detection rate and a low false rate on the UNSW-NB15 data set, which they used for their system. To find system vulnerabilities, many researchers have worked on IoT-based infrastructure [12]. For these tests, various machine learning algorithm types were employed, and the effectiveness of those algorithms was assessed using various metrics, including accuracy, precision, recall, and f1 scores. Nath et al. [13] proposed an ensemble approach combining Naive Bayes and SVM to detect network anomalies.

Elmrabit et al. [14] worked with three different cyberattack datasets: UNSW-NB15, CICIDS-2017, and Industrial Control Systems (ICS) to detect anomalous behavior with twelve ML algorithms. This study's primary goal is to identify the most effective ML algorithm among them by evaluating the performances. Panda et al. [15] applied the Naive Bayes algorithm for network intrusion detection. The KDD cup'99 dataset was used in this experiment and this dataset shows the novelty of their proposed technique. In [16], a behavior model for anomaly intrusion detection systems using Bayesian techniques was introduced.

The authors of ref [17] work with the UNSW-NB15 dataset to assess the performance of a deep binomial classifier for network intrusion detection systems (NIDS). The proposed method showed 98.99% accuracy compared to other existing methods. Baig et al. [18] developed a multi-class intrusion detection system utilizing an ensemble-based artificial neural network cascade. The experimental result of the proposed method was assessed using the KDD-CUP99 and UNSW-NB15 datasets, with the KDD-CUP99 dataset showing better results.

Zhang et al. [19] proposed a statistical neural network classifier that can successfully detect network-based attacks and UDP flood attacks. In [20], a intrusion detection system (IDS) based on a backpropagation neural network (BPN) with sample and attribute query was introduced. This approach can greatly reduce the amount of time spent on training, processing, and storage. Besides, it can easily analyze the complex attack behavior of electronic crimes.

The summary of the above works encourages us to build an effective and secure system to protect networks and hosts from malicious cyber attacks and thus reduce financial losses.

3   Dataset Description

In this work, we combine actual daily activities with simulated assault behaviour using the UNSW-NB15 dataset which prepared at the Cyber Range Lab of the Australian Center for Cyber Security. Analysis, Generic, Backdoor, Shellcode, Exploits, Reconnaissance, Fuzer, DOS, and Worms are among the nine attack types contained in this dataset. There are 49 features in this dataset, each with a class label. This data set creates two sets: the UNSW-NB15 training set and the UNSW-NB15 testing set. The training set contains 175,341 records, whereas the testing set contains 82,332 records from various attacks and normal data.

4   Methodology

This section explains the proposed method, including collection of data, pre-processing of those collecting data, feature selection from those processed data, and machine learning classification models. To run our experiments, we first collect the UNSW-NB15 dataset and then pre-process the data to apply machine learning methods to detect attacks and anomalies. In preprocessing steps, we remove the nan value and perform label encoding to solve the problem of multi type data. We also use the min-max normalization technique to normalize the data during pre-processing. After pre-processing, we perform the feature selection technique using the chi-square test to select highly influential features from the large amount of data which helps to reduce the execution time and increase the performance of the models. Finally, we evaluate the effectiveness of these features for attack detection using eight different classifiers [21], including NB, XGB, KNN, DT, SVM, LR, AdaBoosting, and RF. On the basis of performance indicators including accuracy, precision, recall, and f1-score, we select four machine learning classifiers for attack detection. By implementing these four classifiers such as Extreme Gradient Boosting (XGBoosting), Random Forest, Decision tree, and AdaBoosting we develop an ensemble model for cyber-attack detection. The proposed methodology of attack detection is shown in Fig. 1.

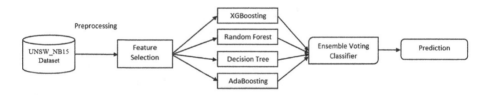

Fig. 1. Illustration of the Proposed Technique.

4.1   Preprocessing

Data preprocessing is a group of techniques that enhance the quality of the raw data to enhance the model's performance, such as missing value imputation and outlier removal [22]. In preprocessing steps, we try to solve the outlier problem of data in the dataset by following several techniques. We use the label encoding technique to convert categorical values into numeric values which help in solving multi type data problems.

One of the most prominent processes of data normalization is min-max normalization. We implement the Min-Max normalization for this detection problem. For each characteristic, the minimum value is set to 0 and the maximum value to 1, with all other values transformed to decimals between 0 and 1. Generally, this normalization technique improves the efficiency of machine learning models. The min-max value is calculated using Eq. (1).

$$value' = \frac{value - min(value)}{max(value) - min(value)} \tag{1}$$

4.2   Feature Selection

It is a technique for minimizing the number of dimensions, deleting irrelevant, noisy, or redundant features from the original dataset, and selecting the most relevant features [23]. A large number of non-essential features might increase training time and increase the risk of overfitting. This feature selection can help the model to improve learning performance, model interpretability, and lower computing cost. For this reason, we have utilized the Chi-square test [24] for the feature selection process. The Chi-square test is a statistical test for determining whether there is a difference between observed and predicted data. It is used to represent categorical features in a dataset. This Chi-square test is utilized in this paper to see whether it correlates with the categorical variables in our data. It is useful in determining if a difference between two category variables is the result of a simple chance or a significant correlation. We have utilized Eq. (2) for calculating the value of this test.

$$a_d^2 = \sum_{j=1}^{n} \frac{(O_j - E_j)^2}{E_j} \tag{2}$$

Here, O is the observed value, E represents the expected value and d represents the degree of freedom. The number of variables that can change without affecting the statistical output is measured by degrees of freedom. It is mainly used to confirm whether chi-square tests are valid or not. The degrees of freedom are calculated using Eq. (3).

$$d = (row - 1) * (col - 1) \tag{3}$$

where, row = number of rows and col= number of columns.

   In this experiment, we select a total of 25 features based on their importance using the Chi-square test. These selected features increase the performance rate of the model to detect attacks. Table 1 shows the 25 selected features.

4.3   Classifiers

There are two target categories of cyber-attack detection problems, normal and attacks. The main goal of our research is to classify the normal and attack with high accuracy and show the best model which performed well in this detection context. For this detection purpose, we have used SVM [25], Extreme Gradient Boosting (XGBoost) [26], Logistic Regression (LR) [27], KNN [28], Decision Tree (DT) [29], Random Forest (RF) [30], AdaBoosting [31]. NB [32] algorithms.

Table 1. 25 selected features for attack detection.

Feature Name	Feature Name
"id"	"dmean"
"dpkts"	"Ct_Srv_Src"
"dbytes"	"Ct_State_Ttl"
"rate"	"Ct_Dst_Ltm"
"sttl"	"Ct_Src_Dport_Ltm"
"sload"	"Ct_Dst_Sport_Ltm"
"dload"	"Ct_Dst_Src_Ltm"
"dloss"	"Ct_Src_Ltm"
"sinpkt"	"Ct_Srv_Dst"
"swin"	"Is_Sm_Ips_Ports"
"stcpb"	"service"
"dtcpb"	"state"
"dwin"	

4.4 Ensemble Classifier

The ensemble approach combines the predictions of numerous separate classifiers to obtain higher performance than a single classifier [33]. In this paper, we have used well performed algorithms into an ensemble voting classifier to create an efficient model. The ensemble voting model uses a collection of various machine learning models to predict a result with a high probability. Based on the high performance and low error rate we have selected four classifiers from eight machine learning classifiers to feed the ensemble voting classifier.

5 Result Analysis and Discussion

To detect attacks, we have trained the models using 175,341 records and tested the models using 77,302 records of the UNSW-NB15 dataset. For this purpose, we have used eight different machine learning algorithms. Among these ML algorithms, multiple algorithms perform well with good accuracy in detecting attacks. The performance comparison between these algorithms is shown in Fig. 2.

We also give a confusion matrix to show how well the algorithms performed. Table 2 displays the confusion matrix for the ML algorithms.

To assess the efficacy of ML algorithms, we examined precision, recall, and f1-score [34]. The "True Positive" (TP), "False Positive" (FP), "True Negative" (TN), and "False Negative" (FN) features of the confusion matrix must be used to determine the precision, recall, and f1-score.

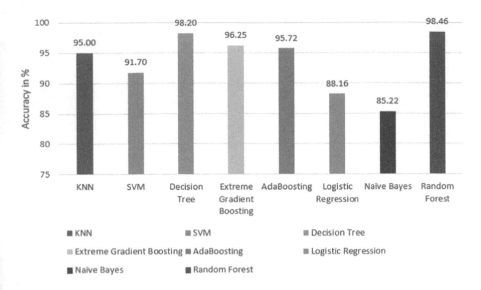

Fig. 2. Graphical Representation of Models Accuracy.

Precision: A precision indicator is the proportion of the anticipated positive observations to all positively anticipated positive findings.

Precision = (true_Positive)/(true_Positive + false_Positive)

Recall: Recall measures how many accurately anticipated positive observations were among all of the actual class's observations.

Recall= TP/(TP+FN)

F1-score: The weighted average of Precision and Recall is the F1 Score.

F1 score=2×(Precision×Recall)/(Precision+Recall)

The precision, recall, and f1-score of ML algorithms are shown in Table 3.

The efficiency of classifiers based on two parameters, such as "True Positive Rate" and "False Positive Rate", is depicted graphically using the receiver operator characteristic (ROC) curve. In Fig. 3, a ROC curve is depicted, with the x-axis and y-axis standing in for the "False Positive Rate" (FPR) and "True Positive Rate" (TPR), respectively. According to the ROC curve, the Random Forest (RF) performs better than other ML algorithms.

In this paper, we have tried to build an ensemble model using different ML algorithms based on their performance and detection rate. In Fig. 3, we can see that some algorithms are closer to the left corner of the ROC curve, indicating that they perform better. In this context, the Extreme Gradient Boosting (XGB), Random Forest, Decision tree, and AdaBoosting worked better than other algorithms. For this reason, we have selected these four models to build an ensemble model. In building ensemble models, we try to develop multiple ensemble models, although all ensemble models performed well. All models performing above 95% are used in the voting system. Table 4 presents the experimental outcomes of the ensemble models.

Table 2. Confusion matrix of all ML algorithms for UNSW-NB15 dataset.

Classifier Name		Normal	Attack
KNN	Normal	26272	1754
	Attack	2108	47168
SVM	Normal	22717	5309
	Attack	1107	48169
Decision Tree	Normal	27373	653
	Attack	735	48541
Extreme Gradient Boosting	Normal	26327	1699
	Attack	1198	48078
AdaBoosting	Normal	62065	1961
	Attack	1345	47931
Logistic Regression	Normal	21726	6300
	Attack	2850	46426
Naive Bayes	Normal	19352	8674
	Attack	2751	46525
Random Forest	Normal	27408	618
	Attack	575	48701

Table 3. Performance matrices for all ML attack detection algorithms.

Classifier Name	Precision	Recall	F-Score
KNN	0.9642	0.9572	0.9606
SVM	0.9007	0.9775	0.9375
Decision Tree	0.9867	0.9850	0.9859
Extreme Gradient Boosting	0.9658	0.9757	0.9707
AdaBoosting	0.9607	0.9727	0.9666
Logistic Regression	0.8805	0.9422	0.9103
Naive Bayes	0.8428	0.9442	0.8906
Random Forest	0.9875	0.9883	0.9879

Table 4. The experimental outcomes of the ensemble models.

Models used in ensemble	Accuracy
XGB, Random Forest, AdaBoosting, KNN	96.98%
XGB, Decision Tree, AdaBoosting, KNN	98.15%
XGB, Random Forest, Decision Tree, KNN	98.38%
Random Forest, Decision Tree, AdaBoosting, KNN	98.44%
XGB, Random Forest, Decision Tree, AdaBoosting	**98.48%**

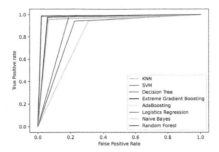

Fig. 3. ROC curve for model evaluation on experimental dataset.

Table 5. Comparison with existing works.

Year	Dataset	Algorithm	Accuracy
2011 [4]	KDD CUP 1999	varGDLF, KNN, Neural, SVM, TCM-KMM	85.2, 74.8, 76.9, 80.1, 83.5
2007 [9]	1999 DARPA IDS	Enhanced SVM	87.74
2021 [10]	HAI	KNN,DTC,RF	97.29, 99.37, 99.76
2018 [11]	UNSW-NB15	Beta mixture model (BMM)	93.4
This work	**UNSW-NB15**	**Proposed Ensemble-model**	**98.48**

The ensemble model constructed by XGB, Random Forest, Decision Tree, and AdaBoosting shows good accuracy from other ensemble models. The performance rate of this proposed ensemble model is also calculated where the precision, recall, and f1-score accordingly 0.98866, 0.98754, and 0.98810. The result of the developed ensemble method is displayed in Table 5 along with the comparison of different existing methods for cyber-attack or intrusion detection systems.

6   Conclusion and Future Work

The effectiveness of eight different machine learning models for cyber-attack detection has been compared in this study. Moreover, our proposed ensemble-based voting classification model is based on high-performance ML models. The UNSW-NB15 dataset, which includes nine attacks (analysis, exploits, backdoors, reconnaissance, denial-of-service, fuzzers, generic, worm, shellcode) and normal data, is used in this experiment. We effectively use a chi-square test technique to select features from large data that help the models perform better. Furthermore, we have selected well-performed models named XGB, RF, AdaBoosting, and Decision Tree based on the accuracy and error rate for the proposed ensemble model which produces 98.48% accuracy. In the future, we would like to enrich our work by applying deep learning, transfer learning, and unsupervised learning approaches.

References

1. Sarker, I.H.: Smart city data science: Towards data-driven smart cities with open research issues. Internet of Things **19**, 100528 (2022)
2. McHugh, J., Christie, A., Allen, J.: Defending yourself: The role of intrusion detection systems. IEEE Softw. **17**(5), 42–51 (2000)
3. Krügel, C., Toth, T., Kirda, E.: Service specific anomaly detection for network intrusion detection. In: Proceedings of the 2002 ACM symposium on Applied computing, pp. 201–208 (March 2002)
4. Fan, W., Bouguila, N., Ziou, D.: Unsupervised anomaly intrusion detection via localized bayesian feature selection. In: 2011 IEEE 11th International Conference on Data Mining, pp. 1032–1037. IEEE (December 2011)
5. Sarker, I.H.: Machine learning for intelligent data analysis and automation in cybersecurity: current and future prospects. Annal. Data Sci., 1–26 (2022)
6. Moustafa, N., Slay, J.: A network forensic scheme using correntropy-variation for attack detection. In: DigitalForensics 2018. IAICT, vol. 532, pp. 225–239. Springer, Cham (2018). https://doi.org/10.1007/978-3-319-99277-8_13
7. Sarker, I.H.: Cyberlearning: effectiveness analysis of machine learning security modeling to detect cyber-anomalies and multi-attacks. Internet of Things **14**, 100393 (2021)
8. Moustafa, N., Slay, J.: UNSW-NB15: a comprehensive data set for network intrusion detection systems (UNSW-NB15 network data set). In: 2015 Military Communications And Information Systems Conference (MilCIS), pp. 1–6. IEEE (November 2015)
9. Shon, T., Moon, J.: A hybrid machine learning approach to network anomaly detection. Inf. Sci. **177**(18), 3799–3821 (2007)
10. Mokhtari, S., Abbaspour, A., Yen, K.K., Sargolzaei, A.: A machine learning approach for anomaly detection in industrial control systems based on measurement data. Electronics **10**(4), 407 (2021)
11. Moustafa, N., Creech, G., Slay, J.: Anomaly detection system using beta mixture models and outlier detection. In: Pattnaik, P.K., Rautaray, S.S., Das, H., Nayak, J. (eds.) Progress in Computing, Analytics and Networking. AISC, vol. 710, pp. 125–135. Springer, Singapore (2018). https://doi.org/10.1007/978-981-10-7871-2_13
12. Hasan, M., Islam, M.M., Zarif, M.I.I., Hashem, M.M.A.: Attack and anomaly detection in IoT sensors in IoT sites using machine learning approaches. Internet of Things **7**, 100059 (2019)
13. Nath, M. D., Bhattasali, T.: Anomaly Detection Using Machine Learning Approaches
14. Elmrabit, N., Zhou, F., Li, F., Zhou, H.: Evaluation of machine learning algorithms for anomaly detection. In: 2020 International Conference on Cyber Security and Protection of Digital Services (Cyber Security), pp. 1–8. IEEE (June 2020)
15. Panda, M., Patra, M.R.: Network intrusion detection using naive bayes. International J. Comput. Sci. Netw. Sec. **7**(12), 258–263 (2007)
16. Puttini, R.S., Marrakchi, Z., Mé, L.: A bayesian classification model for real-time intrusion detection. In: AIP Conference Proceedings, vol. 659(1), 150–162. American Institute of Physics (March 2003)
17. Al-Zewairi, M., Almajali, S., Awajan, A.: Experimental evaluation of a multilayer feed-forward artificial neural network classifier for network intrusion detection system. In: 2017 International Conference on New Trends in Computing Sciences (ICTCS), pp. 167–172. IEEE (October 2017)

18. Baig, M.M., Awais, M.M., El-Alfy, E.S.M.: A multiclass cascade of artificial neural network for network intrusion detection. J. Intell. Fuzzy Syst. **32**(4), 2875–2883 (2017)
19. Zhang, Z., Li, J., Manikopoulos, C.N., Jorgenson, J., Ucles, J.: HIDE: a hierarchical network intrusion detection system using statistical preprocessing and neural network classification. In: Proceedings of IEEE Workshop on Information Assurance and Securitym, vol. 85, p. 90 (June 2001)
20. Chang, R.I., Lai, L.B., Su, W.D., Wang, J.C., Kouh, J.S.: Intrusion detection by backpropagation neural networks with sample-query and attribute-query. Int. J. Comput. Intell. Res. **3**(1), 6–10 (2007)
21. Sarker, I.H., Khan, A.I., Abushark, Y.B., Alsolami, F.: Internet of things (iot) security intelligence: a comprehensive overview, machine learning solutions and research directions. Mobile Netw. Appli., 1–17 (2022)
22. Fan, C., Chen, M., Wang, X., Wang, J., Huang, B.: A review on data preprocessing techniques toward efficient and reliable knowledge discovery from building operational data. Front. Energy Res. **9**, 652801 (2021)
23. Miao, J., Niu, L.: A survey on feature selection. Proc. Comput. Sci. **91**, 919–926 (2016)
24. Rana, R., Singhal, R.: Chi-square test and its application in hypothesis testing. J. Pract. Cardiovas. Sci. **1**(1), 69 (2015)
25. Wang, L., (ed.). Support vector machines: theory and applications, vol. 177. Springer Science & Business Media (2005). https://doi.org/10.1007/b95439
26. Chen, T., Guestrin, C.: Xgboost: A scalable tree boosting system. In: Proceedings of the 22nd Acm Sigkdd International Conference on Knowledge Discovery and Data Mining, pp. 785–794 (August 2016)
27. Uyanık, G.K., Güler, N.: A study on multiple linear regression analysis. Procedia. Soc. Behav. Sci. **106**, 234–240 (2013)
28. Guo, G., Wang, H., Bell, D., Bi, Y., Greer, K.: KNN model-based approach in classification. In: Meersman, R., Tari, Z., Schmidt, D.C. (eds.) OTM 2003. LNCS, vol. 2888, pp. 986–996. Springer, Heidelberg (2003). https://doi.org/10.1007/978-3-540-39964-3_62
29. Charbuty, B., Abdulazeez, A.: Classification based on decision tree algorithm for machine learning. J. Appli. Sci. Technol. Trends **2**(01), 20–28 (2021)
30. Breiman, L.: Random forests. Mach. Learn. **45**(1), 5–32 (2001)
31. Freund, Y., Schapire, R., Abe, N.: A short introduction to boosting. J. Japanese Soc. Artifi. Intell. **14**(771–780), 1612 (1999)
32. Rish, I.: An empirical study of the naive Bayes classifier. In: IJCAI 2001 Workshop on Empirical Methods in Artificial Intelligence, vol. 3(22), pp. 41–46 (August 2001)
33. Zhang, Y., Zhang, H., Cai, J., Yang, B.: A weighted voting classifier based on differential evolution. In: Abstract and Applied Analysis, vol. 2014, Hindawi (May 2014)
34. Goutte, C., Gaussier, E.: A probabilistic interpretation of precision, recall and F-score, with implication for evaluation. In: Losada, D.E., Fernández-Luna, J.M. (eds.) ECIR 2005. LNCS, vol. 3408, pp. 345–359. Springer, Heidelberg (2005). https://doi.org/10.1007/978-3-540-31865-1_25

A Stacked Ensemble Spyware Detection Model Using Hyper-Parameter Tuned Tree Based Classifiers

Nowshin Tasnim[1]($\boxtimes$), Md. Musfique Anwar[2], and Iqbal H. Sarker[1]($\boxtimes$)

[1] Department of Computer Science and Engineering, Chittagong University of Engineering and Technology, Chittagong, Bangladesh
tasnimnowshin95@gmail.com, iqbal@cuet.ac.bd
[2] Jahangirnagar University, Dhaka, Bangladesh

Abstract. Spyware is a type of malware that is designed to infiltrate a device or steal personal information. Over the last decade, the number of people facing such dangers has risen from 12.4 million to 812.67 million. Since the spyware target platform has been enlarged, additional strategies using non-detectable approaches have been noticed. Traditional detection approaches are ineffective in this instance since they can only detect known assaults. *Advanced behavior-based detection* can aid this problem as well as it can contribute to the detection of zero-day attacks. As a result, this study proposes an *ensemble stacking learning-based method* for detecting Spyware, which contains four conventional machine learning tree based techniques. To avoid biases and overfitting, we apply *grid search hyperparameter tuning approach*. Also, we perform an efficient feature selection technique that shows similar accuracy with less data dimension. At first in our proposed model, recursive feature elimination is used by utilizing a decision tree estimator to generate an optimized number for reducing data dimensions. Secondly, three different feature ranker selects K best features using the optimized number from the previous step. Finally, a union process is done avoiding redundancy to generate the resampled dataset. The experimental result shows around 88% accuracy with only a 0.35% error rate. The test accuracy is also around 96%, hence the model is not overfitted.

Keywords: Spyware · Ensemble learning · Behavior based detection · Cybersecurity

1 Introduction

Nowadays, the way people use the Internet and smart services has shifted considerably over time [17]. Cyber risks are gradually increasing as a result of the growth of web services. Cyber threats that aim to interfere with client data include malware, data breaches, zero-day attacks, identity theft, and other negative actions [4]. Spyware is one of the most frequent dangers faced by internet

Md. S. Satu et al. (Eds.): MIET 2022, LNICST 491, pp. 397–408, 2023.
https://doi.org/10.1007/978-3-031-34622-4_32

users. Once installed, it keeps track of login credentials, analyzes internet activity, and snoops on private information. The primary function of spyware is often to steal passwords, financial information, and credit card numbers. Bank robbers don't even need to enter the building, all they need is a computer and the correct software. According to a New York Times investigation, the digital security firm Kaspersky has been tracking a massive bank robbery that might have netted perpetrators up to $900 million.

As a result, protecting digital documents from infection is a significant concern. In order to protect against anomalies in a computer network, Sarker et al. [15] suggested a strategy utilizing ANN (Artificial Neural Network) and DL (Deep Learning) techniques. However, in this work, we emphasize the use of machine learning algorithms to effectively detect cyber-anomalies [14]. Machine learning can be used in security in a variety of ways, including behavior analysis, prediction, and clustering security incidents. It can also be used to identify new and unexplored attacks. In research, Bendovschi et al. [4] predict that by 2020, malware will have increased by 33% from 2019. As a result of the rise in malware assaults, it is crucial to properly identify attacks and reduce financial damage.

Anyway cybercriminals create novel forms of attacks and strategies to achieve undetectable property as information technology advances. Signature-based detection system is unsuccessful in recognizing malware since attackers might update and enhance the malicious program to evade the detection algorithms of anti-virus software [12]. Kruegel et al. pointed out the difficulty of retaining a large number of signatures of known abnormalities in a signature-based ransomware detection system [11]. The authors also proposed an approach for detecting anomalies by evaluating each web application and comparing it to standard log files. An overview was provided by Sarker et al. [15] based on the idea of Automation including the drawbacks of current approaches and emphasizing logical support in the further defense system against attacks.

In this research, we provide an effective spyware prediction technique. For the prediction analysis, we used a spyware dataset with 85 behavioral characteristics. Using a comprehensive feature selection method, we choose the 17 top features out of 85 characteristics. Moreover, we use a decision tree estimator in RFE with the repeated K fold to find out the threshold value for optimizing the feature selection process. The key benefit of this approach is that it concentrates on the dynamic prediction method rather than typical static ones. The primary contributions of this paper are given below:

- Our proposed approach performs a behavior-based analysis and acquires the ideal precision of spyware prediction by using a hybrid feature selection technique.
- The proposed approach effectively detects spyware anomaly by applying an ensemble stacking tuned Random Forest method with the implementation of four tree based ML classification techniques. To avoid the generic version of these techniques, it uses hyperparameter tuning with grid search space.
- The range of experiments presents a comparison of standalone models with the ensemble stacking tune RF model with various measurement units.

The remainder of the paper is structured as follows. Section 2 covers the relevant literature, and Sect. 3 provides a detailed explanation of how the suggested strategy actually operates. The outcome and performance analysis are found in Sect. 4. Finally, we wrap up the paper by summarizing the work in Sect. 5.

2 Related Work

Spyware is a harmful sort of software that spies on clients' private information and causes them great harm. He et al. [9] proposed a hybrid ensemble model with an effective feature generation technique. They applied a LightGBM based feature generation process for tree based classifiers and a CNN based feature generation process for Deep learning classifiers. Finally, they ensembled the result of both deep learning and machine learning models. Afzulpurkar et al. [1] offered a data filtration method at the network level to protect PC from spyware and bots. Mentioning the significance of behavioral analysis over pattern based and signature based analysis, the authors proposed a high level architecture to monitor outgoing packets and software solutions. Because of reliance on third-party sources, earlier approaches are difficult and complicated for real-time environments. To meet this research gap, Guptta et al. [8] employed a hybrid feature based anti-phishing technique using machine learning models. The most significant behavioral characteristics of malware, according to Pekta et al. [13], are file system, network, registry operations, and API requests. To distinguish malware families, they also employed N-gram displays rather than API calls. Daku et al. [6] mainly suggested two approaches: a collective method for highly linked behaviors and a repeated technique to detect behaviors for high-level classification performance. By using evasive and solicited tactics, Alaeiyan et al. [2] suggested another tier of trigger-based malware categorization. These two procedures dealt with defining the state of the environment. However, while eliciting practices highlight the advantages of malware for malicious demonstrations, evasive behaviors emphasize self-defense. Galal et al. [7] described malware structures that are statistically-based, graph-based, polymorphic, and metamorphic. Canfora et al. [5] and Bazrafshan et al. [3] offered various alternatives to signature-based detection, including obfuscation approach and heuristic methodology. Danial et al. [10] proposed an anti-spyware system with a specific and accurate classifier to detect spyware and ransomware. They acquired a 93% accuracy rate and a 7% error rate using Linear Regression, JRIP, and J48 decision tree algorithms. Furthermore, the proposed solution can disinfect an operating system from spyware infestation with an 82% strike probability.

In light of the aforementioned works, we concentrate on the behavior of anomalies in our study to address the growth of cybercrime and the issues with the conventional signature-based detection method. Additionally, our feature selection method offers a classification accuracy of about 88 percent, which is superior. The proposed method is built on a hybrid feature selection technique, which is then followed by an ensemble stacking model.

3   Methodology

Our proposed solution which executes the detection procedure on 3 various spyware classes, is presented in this part. We employ a hybrid feature ranker approach to dynamically choose the 17 top features from the 85 available features. Additionally, we use four well-known tree-based machine learning models-Decision Tree, Random Forest Classifier, XgBoost, and Extra Tree [16] to create a powerful ensemble classifier. Using the grid search hyperparameter tuning technique, our system automatically chooses the optimal parameters for the classifiers listed above. We conclude by comparing the ensemble model to individual models. In Fig. 1, we depict the whole workflow of the suggested ensemble model-based spyware classification technique.

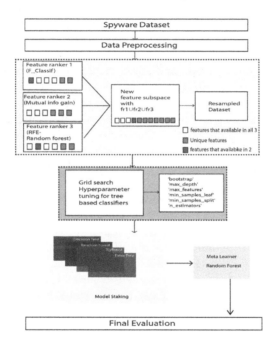

Fig. 1. Overview of the proposed approach.

3.1   Descriptive Analysis

The Federal Trade Commission characterizes spyware as 'programming that helps with getting data about an individual or association without their insight and that might misuse the data without client's knowledge' [18]. Spyware is programming that takes command over a client's PC without their consent. The most common types of spyware are adware, keylogger, trojan horses, and browser hackers. Our dataset is a collection of three types of adwares having 12410 instances. The datasets are collected from Canadian Institute for Cybersecurity. Figure 2 shows the number count of Adware Dowgin, Adware Ewind, and Adware Feiwo. The highest class in the dataset is Adware Ewind having 5915 instances whereas Dowgin and Feiwo classes have 2917 and 3578 data instances respectively. We applied SMOTE technique which over samples the lower classes with respect to the higher class to balance these class instances shown in Fig. 3.

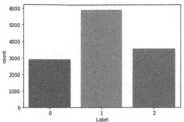

Fig. 2. Class values before applying SMOTE.

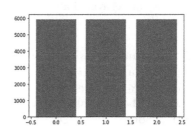

Fig. 3. Class values after applying SMOTE.

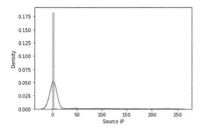

Fig. 4. Density of behavioral attribute 'Source IP'.

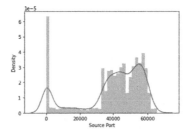

Fig. 5. Density of behavioral attribute 'Source Port'.

Adware is an undesirable software program intended to promote harmful advertisements on our screens, most frequently inside an internet browser. Key facts of Adware are-

- It can arrive on our PC through legitimate software inside which it's subtly covered.
- It keeps track client's web activity and sends designated ads to the client's work area in response to that browsing movement.
- Once adware seizes our gadget, it could do a wide range of unwanted tasks.

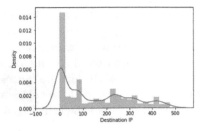

Fig. 6. Density of behavioral attribute 'Destination IP'.

Fig. 7. Density of behavioral attribute 'Flow ID'.

It is important to find out the density variance of the top-ranked features as they play a prime role in detection. Through our hybrid feature ranker, we select 23 features out of 85 features. Here, we have analyzed the density graph of 4 top-ranked behavioral attributes. Figure 4 to Fig. 7 present density plots for 'Source IP', 'Source Port', 'Destination Port', and 'Flow ID' respectively.

3.2 Diagnostic Analysis

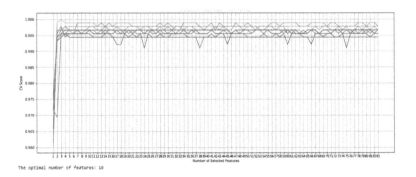

Fig. 8. Optimal number of Features for threshold generating.

Our spyware dataset is a high dimensional dataset with 85 behavioral attributes. To reduce high dimensionality, we follow a hybrid feature ranking method. In this process, we first find out an optimal number as the threshold using 10-fold cross validation in the RFE technique. Figure 8 presents the outcome of the threshold generating process. It depicts 10 as the optimal number of features. In the second phase, we pass this optimal number as a selection parameter to the other feature rankers. We use three popular feature ranker methods F classify, mutual information gain, and Recursive feature elimination technique with a decision tree estimator. As our final ensemble model mostly used tree based classifier, so it is required to use info gain and tree based estimator which helps to extract the most effective features.

In this stage of our approach, we have selected the 10 best features from every feature ranker. Table 1 shows best selected features from each ranker. Through this process, we discovered an interesting fact how different rankers prefer different behavioral attributes. Moreover, they are showing some unique attributes in their top 10 list. In Table 1, the colored rows signify those attributes which are seen only once. 'Destination IP' is the unique attribute that is seen in all three rankers.

Table 1. Top 10 ranked features of 3 rankers.

(RFE)	Ranker 2 (F Classif)	Ranker 3 (Mutual info classif)
'Source IP'	'Flow ID'	'Flow ID'
'Destination IP'	*'Destination IP'*	'Source IP'
'Flow Duration'	'Bwd Packet Length Mean'	'Source Port'
'Flow IAT Min'	'Flow IAT Mean'	*'Destination IP'*
'Subflow Bwd Bytes'	'Flow IAT Min'	'Flow Duration'
'act_data_pkt_fwd'	'Fwd IAT Mean'	'Flow Packets/s'
'min_seg_size_forward'	'Fwd IAT Max'	'Flow IAT Mean'
'Active Std'	'Packet Length Mean'	'Flow IAT Max'
'Idle Max'	'Average Packet Size'	'Fwd IAT Total'
'Idle Min'	'Avg Bwd Segment Size'	'Fwd Packets/s'

*Here, red blocks are used to indicate unique features in each ranker, bold text format is used to indicate that the features are available in all the three rankers and normal text format is used to indicate that the features are available in any two rankers.

Finally, we combine these three feature ranker sets to create a resampled dataset. The resampled dataset consists of 23 features. To avoid multicollinearity, we then dropped the features which have correlation values above 95%. Figure 9 shows the final 17 features having correlation values less than 95%. That means the resampled dataset is now free from multicollinearity.

3.3   Predictive Analysis

For predictive analysis, we used four different tree based machine learning classification techniques. Next, we followed the ensemble stacking method for the final analysis. However, we used hyperparameter tuned ML methods rather using the generic ones. Figure 10 presents the performance comparison between the optimized dataset of 17 features and the original dataset of 85 total features. We find that both feature subspace models provide almost similar accuracy. Thus, we can say our feature selection approach correctly identifies significant features.

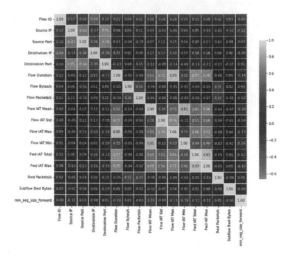

Fig. 9. Correlation value of finally selected 17 features.

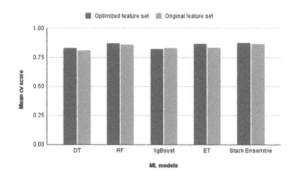

Fig. 10. Performance comparison between optimized and original feature set.

To accomplish predictive analysis, here we used tree based classifiers. Each technique has its own uniqueness. Notably, every one of them adds a better feature than the earlier one. We applied stacking ensemble using a decision tree, random forest, xgboost, and Extra tree as the base learners and random forest as the meta learner. Table 2 presents CV score as accuracy value, precision score, recall score for standalone models, and ensemble stacking model. The ensemble stacking shows the highest precision and recall value. So, it can be stated that our proposed approach returns the most relevant result. As we can see the Random Forest model and proposed ensemble stacking are showing almost similar results, so the important question arises why stacking is used here. In anomaly detection approaches, it is important to address even a little amount of compromise. Otherwise, the system may fall. Figure 11 shows that the proposed stacking ensemble exhibits the lowest root mean square error. We considered it as significant in our performance evaluation.

Table 2. Compare model with different measurement unit.

Tree based Classifier	Accuracy	Precision	Recall
Decision Tree	0.82	0.84	0.84
Random Forest	0.87	0.87	0.87
Extra Tree	0.86	0.87	0.88
XGBoost	0.82	0.80	0.81
Stack Ensemble	0.87	**0.88**	**0.88**

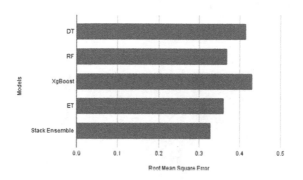

Fig. 11. Root mean square error of each model.

3.4 Prescriptive Analysis

We use Hyperparameter tuning for our traditional ML techniques.

Hyperparameter Tuning. When a model's argument or hyperparameters are chosen in advance of the learning process, then it is called hyperparameter tuning. Hyperparameter optimization is the core of machine learning algorithms. Additionally, it can be said that hyperparameter tuning is the process of determining the ideal set of hyperparameters to increase model performance.

Among different hyperparameter tuning methods, we particularly used the grid search method here. We build a grid of possible hyperparameter values when using the grid search method. Each iteration tries a certain order of hyperparameters. It fits the model to every conceivable hyperparameter combination and records the results. The best model with the best hyperparameters is then returned. Table 3 presents tuned and optimized hyperparameters of tree based models.

Table 3. Optimized Hyperparameter of tree based classifiers.

Tree based Classifier	Tuned Hyperparameters
Decision Tree	criterion='entropy', max_depth=3, min_samples_leaf=10, random_state=42
Random Forest	'bootstrap': True,'max_depth': 15,'max_features': 3, 'min_samples_leaf': 5, 'min_samples_split': 6,'n_estimators': 1350
Extra Tree	criterion='entropy', max_depth=3, min_samples_split=12
XgBoost	'colsample_bytree': 0.8831812755863229, 'gamma': 3.48678290749431, 'max_depth': 14.0, 'min_child_weight': 3.0, 'reg_alpha': 41.0, 'reg_lambda': 0.7123862610639354

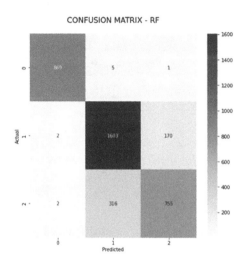

Fig. 12. Confusion matrix for Random Forest.

4 Experiment and Result Analysis

For experimental analysis, we proposed an efficient ensemble stacking model where we used 4 different ML tree based models with grid search hyperparameter tuning. The techniques we ensembled are Decision Tree, Random Forest, XgBoost, and Extra Tree. Figure 12 and Fig. 13 present the confusion matrix for the two best performed classifiers.

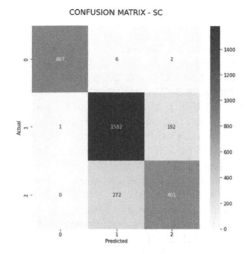

Fig. 13. Confusion matrix for Stacking ensemble.

These two figures visualize that the False positive value for class 0 in RF(Random Forest) is 4 whereas, in SC(stacked ensemble), it is 1. For class 1 Fp in RF is 321 and in SC, it is 280. Finally for class 2 FP in RF is 171 and 194 in SC. The overall performance of the stacked ensemble is also good in comparison to Random Forest with respect to the root mean square error value.

5 Conclusion

In this study, we present a novel ensemble stacking approach based on behavioral analysis as a prospective method of spyware family prediction. The most substantial outcomes are made possible by the behavior-centric detection system since attackers are always trying to get around security barriers. It might be difficult to choose the right characteristic to get the best accuracy. Using the recursive feature elimination approach with repeated K fold and a decision tree estimator, we construct an effective feature selection procedure to address this difficulty. Then three feature ranker selects k features individually and combines them avoiding redundancy. Performance comparison of the original dataset and resampled dataset presents how the proposed approach holds the accuracy same even after reducing the dimension significantly. The final evaluation follows an ensemble stacking method using a decision tree, random forest, XGBoost, and ExtraTree classifiers. Also, the importance of appropriate parameters in ML models is mentioned and the grid search hyperparameter tuning approach is followed to enhance the model's performance.

Acknowledgement. This work is accomplished under the project "Development of Chittagong University of Engineering & Technology".

References

1. Afzulpurkar, A., Alshemaili, M., Samara, K.: Outgoing data filtration for detecting spyware on personal computers. In: Barolli, L., Xhafa, F., Khan, Z.A., Odhabi, H. (eds.) EIDWT 2019. LNDECT, vol. 29, pp. 355–362. Springer, Cham (2019). https://doi.org/10.1007/978-3-030-12839-5_32
2. Alaeiyan, M., Parsa, S., Conti, M.: Analysis and classification of context-based malware behavior. Comput. Commun. **136**, 76–90 (2019)
3. Bazrafshan, Z., Hashemi, H., Fard, S.M.H., Hamzeh, A.: A survey on heuristic malware detection techniques. In: The 5th Conference on Information and Knowledge Technology, pp. 113–120. IEEE (2013)
4. Bendovschi, A.: Cyber-attacks-trends, patterns and security countermeasures. Proc. Econ. Finance **28**, 24–31 (2015)
5. Canfora, G., Di Sorbo, A., Mercaldo, F., Visaggio, C.A.: Obfuscation techniques against signature-based detection: a case study. In: 2015 Mobile systems technologies workshop (MST), pp. 21–26. IEEE (2015)
6. Daku, H., Zavarsky, P., Malik, Y.: Behavioral-based classification and identification of ransomware variants using machine learning. In: 2018 17th IEEE International Conference on Trust, Security and Privacy in Computing and Communications/12th IEEE International Conference on Big Data Science and Engineering (TrustCom/BigDataSE), pp. 1560–1564. IEEE (2018)
7. Galal, H.S., Mahdy, Y.B., Atiea, M.A.: Behavior-based features model for malware detection. J. Comput. Virol. Hacking Tech. **12**(2), 59–67 (2016)
8. Guptta, S.D., Shahriar, K.T., Alqahtani, H., Alsalman, D., Sarker, I.H.: Modeling hybrid feature-based phishing websites detection using machine learning techniques
9. He, H., Fan, Y.: A novel hybrid ensemble model based on tree-based method and deep learning method for default prediction. Expert Syst. Appl. **176**, 114899 (2021)
10. Javaheri, D., Hosseinzadeh, M., Rahmani, A.M.: Detection and elimination of spyware and ransomware by intercepting kernel-level system routines. IEEE Access **6**, 78321–78332 (2018)
11. Kruegel, C., Vigna, G.: Anomaly detection of web-based attacks. In: Proceedings of the 10th ACM Conference on Computer and Communications Security, pp. 251–261 (2003)
12. Patcha, A., Park, J.M.: An overview of anomaly detection techniques: Existing solutions and latest technological trends. Comput. Netw. **51**(12), 3448–3470 (2007)
13. Pektaş, A., Acarman, T.: Classification of malware families based on runtime behaviors. J. Inf. Sec. Appli. **37**, 91–100 (2017)
14. Sarker, I.H.: Cyberlearning: Effectiveness analysis of machine learning security modeling to detect cyber-anomalies and multi-attacks. Internet of Things **14**, 100393 (2021)
15. Sarker, I.H.: Ai-based modeling: Techniques, applications and research issues towards automation, intelligent and smart systems. SN Comput. Sci. **3**(2), 1–20 (2022)
16. Sarker, I.H.: Machine learning for intelligent data analysis and automation in cybersecurity: Current and future prospects. Annal. Data Sci. 1–26 (2022)
17. Sarker, I.H.: Smart city data science: Towards data-driven smart cities with open research issues. Internet of Things **19**, 100528 (2022)
18. Stafford, T.F., Urbaczewski, A.: Spyware: The ghost in the machine. Commun. Assoc. Inf. Syst. **14**(1), 49 (2004)

IoT Based Framework for Remote Patient Monitoring

Ifti Akib Abir$^{(\boxtimes)}$, Sazzad Hossain Rafi , and Mosabber Uddin Ahmed

Department of Electrical and Electronic Engineering, University of Dhaka, Dhaka 1000,
Bangladesh
iftiakib-2016815016@eee.du.ac.bd, iftiakibabir@gmail.com,
sazzadhossainrafi8@gmail.com, mosabber.ahmed@du.ac.bd

Abstract. Wireless technologies and body area networks are constantly growing with the help of IoT. Body Area Network has been widely applied for ubiquitous health monitoring under the IoT framework. This phenomenal expansion has significantly broadened the reach of the Remote Health Monitoring system. The implementation of an automated system for health monitoring using IoT sensors will improve patients' quality of life. In this paper, a real-time health monitoring system is proposed which comprises of a device and two android applications where IoT sensors (Temperature sensor, Pulse Sensor, and Oximeter) are incorporated to collect health data. The data measured by the sensors are evaluated by the microcontroller and then sent to the android application using a Bluetooth module. This system has a critical-circumstances alert that will be activated if the sensor value exceeds the predefined threshold value. The proposed system enables storing of measured data, which can be advantageous for future data analysis and will assist a doctor in making decisions based on the measured data. However, after evaluating the system on ten persons, we have discovered a maximum error rate of 1.93% for Temperature sensor, 8.82% for Pulse sensor, and 2.04% for Oximeter while assessing health data.

Keyword: IoT · Healthcare Application · Wearable · Real-time · Remote Monitoring

1 Introduction

Rapid expansion in medical services and wireless technologies have tremendously benefited in dealing with the pressing issue of minimal health care services during the recent decade. The integration of smartphone technologies with the wearable IoT sensors has greatly aided in the transition of medical services from clinic-focused to patient-focused which is termed as Telemedicine. This can be divided into two types in larger perspective [1]. They are as follows:

- Live communication in which both parties, patient and doctor must be present as well as high definition video quality, increased speed, and adequate data transfer rate.

© ICST Institute for Computer Sciences, Social Informatics and Telecommunications Engineering 2023
Published by Springer Nature Switzerland AG 2023. All Rights Reserved
Md. S. Satu et al. (Eds.): MIET 2022, LNICST 491, pp. 409–421, 2023.
https://doi.org/10.1007/978-3-031-34622-4_33

- Store and forward type, which refers to the collection of data related to some critical Health indicators and transmitting those data to relevant hospital professionals.

According to recent medical surveys, telemedicine is currently being implemented to treat individuals who have hypertension, hypotension, hypothermia, hyperthermia etc. Chronic diseases are one of the leading causes of human fatalities worldwide. Every year, nearly 2.8M individuals die as a result of being overweight or obese [2]. According to WHO projections, the global prevalence of chronic diseases could reach 23.3% by 2030 [3]. This poses a risk to human lives. As a result, for chronic diseases, uninterrupted and long-term monitoring has become essential in order to reduce this rate. Overall, it is critical to build an effective system, capable of collecting, storing, and transmitting crucial health data for monitoring patients' health conditions [4]. Furthermore, automating data gathering process and visualization on a gadget reduces the possibility of human error in manual data collection.

Around the world, the number of cell phone subscribers and internet users are growing rapidly which has been projected on below Fig. 1 [5]. To add, various services like SMS, WLAN, GPS etc. are present in the smartphones. Therefore, these mobile devices are perfect instrument for monitoring and visualization of patients' health data.

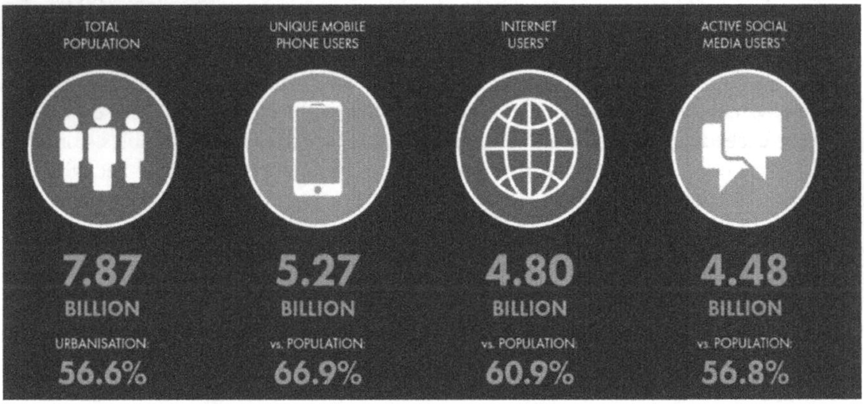

Fig. 1. Data Projection of Cell Phone Subscribers & Internet Users [5].

In this study, we have presented a framework that is sensor-based made up of both hardware and software, incorporated for health data measurement and it's visualization. The proposed system also includes certain unique features such as SMS triggering for critical circumstances, location tracking, health condition detection, and so on.

The remainder of the paper is structured as follows: Sect. 2 illustrates related works in the field of wearable sensor-based Remote Health Monitoring. Section 3 describes the proposed system's design and methodology. Section 4 presents the results of the implantation. Finally, Sect. 5 brings the paper to a conclusion.

2 Related Works

In recent years, human health has become one of the most important topics for scholars. Even if a person cannot afford to visit a hospital, many hours have been devoted to the development of medical gadgets to ensure that everyone has access to healthcare. Extensive research has been devoted to the exploration of diverse technologies. Widespread use of IoT has occurred in order to provide dependable, productive, and intelligent healthcare services. Healthcare mobile applications enable consumers to monitor their health state, take greater responsibility for their lifestyle, and increase the efficacy of care by giving health professionals with high-quality data. These medical data are frequently collected via wearable devices [6].

Literature illustrates several instances of health monitoring systems that are beneficial for the monitoring of physiological data recorded by the device. In the work of M. M. A. Hashem et al. [7], a device for detecting heart-rate and temperature was constructed using a wireless terminal for dispatching data and a wireless receiver for data reception. In another research work, N. Navale et al. [8] developed a telemedicine system consisting of a hardware device that continuously measures heart-rate and temperature, which are subsequently transmitted to a connected android application. Similarly, M. A. H. Akhand et al. [6] designed a system consisting of a microcontroller and a mobile application that gives heart-rate and temperature data acquired from the hardware device. Furthermore, K. K. Patil et al. [9] designed a system for the identification of the patient's current status that utilized many sensors such as temperature, heart-rate monitoring, and eye blink detecting sensors. The core component of the work is an android-based health monitoring system that is designed in such a way that, in the event that a patient is unable to talk or move his or her body, simply blinking five times will send a message to the caregiver outlining the patient's current condition, while also sending constant updates on the patient's heart-rate and body temperature to the server. Moreover, Tanupriya Choudhury et al. [10] introduced a solution in which temperature and heartbeat sensors were utilized for health monitoring.

In addition to continuous measurement and presentation of physiological data, our proposed system also retains real-time data for subsequent analysis and decision-making. Additionally, it offers flexibility to both the patient and doctor. The system also has an emergency notification function that captures the patient's current health condition along with the location.

3 Design and Methodology

3.1 System Design

This paper proposes a framework of wearable IoT sensors based Real-time Health Monitoring system which includes two parts: Hardware & Software. The hardware part comprises of one Microcontroller, one Bluetooth module and IoT sensors like Temperature sensor, Pulse sensor, Oximeter. The software part includes two Android applications and Firebase (Real-time database). The overall architecture of the proposed framework has been illustrated in following Fig. 2.

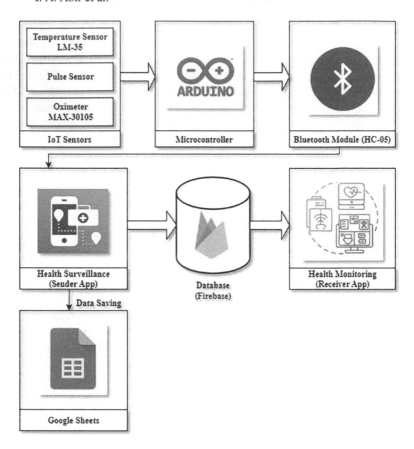

Fig. 2. High-level Overview of the Proposed Framework.

3.2 System Hardware

Hardware part of the proposed system comprises of the following three IoT sensors, one Bluetooth module and a microcontroller. The circuit diagram of the hardware has been depicted in the following Fig. 3.

- LM-35 is a temperature sensor which is an analog and linear sensor [11]. Instead of showing temperature in degree Celsius, it gives the value of the output voltage. The output voltage is directly proportional to the degree Celsius [12]. This increases 10 mV per degree Celsius rise in temperature (Scale factor = 0.01 V/°C) [13]. Temperature from −55 °C to +150 °C can be measured by this sensor. The temperature can be derived using the below mentioned Eq. 1 [14].

$$T(^{o}C) = \frac{V_{out}}{10\,mV} \tag{1}$$

where, V_{out} is the output voltage of the sensor and T is the temperature in °C.

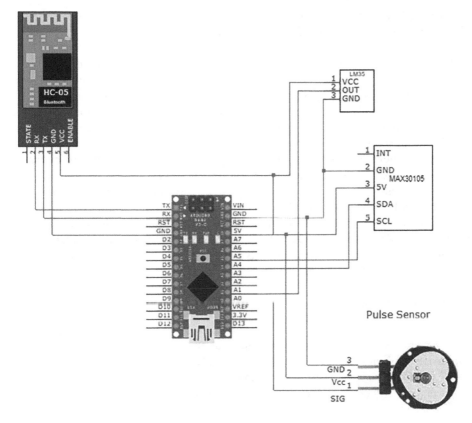

Fig. 3. Schematic Diagram of the Hardware.

- A Pulse sensor, additionally referred to as Heart Rate sensor, monitors the change in volume of the blood vessel that happens when the heart pumps blood. This sensor utilizes Photoplethysmography, one of four methods for detecting heart rate. This optical measurement method can be utilized to detect changes in blood volume inside the microvascular bed of tissue [15]. From the output signal of the PPG, heart rate can be simply determined. The signal's systolic peak signifies a heartbeat. Therefore, to quantify the heart rate in bpm, the time intervention between two systolic peaks needs to be defined. Heart rate in bpm can be derived using the below mentioned Eq. 2.

$$Heart\ Rate = \frac{60}{t}\ bpm \tag{2}$$

where, t (in seconds) is the time interval between two systolic peaks.
- MAX30105 is a multifunctional sensor authorizing anticipation of distance, heart rate, particle detection. This sensor is comprised of three LEDs and an optical detector. It can be employed as a wearable, biosensor for pulse oximeter and heart-rate calculation [16]. This sensor distinguishes the change in skin color using PPG technique when

it is placed over a fingertip. To use this sensor for Pulse Oximetry, small wires must be soldered to the circuit board to provide some movement when a finger is linked to the sensor [17].

- HC-05 Bluetooth module is designed for wireless communication which has multiple applications, including wireless keyboard, headset, and mouse. This sensor uses Frequency Hopping Spread Spectrum (FHSS) radio technology to transmit data over the air. This IEEE 802.15.1-standardized protocol [18] enables the formation of a wireless Personal Area Network (PAN) with the aid of this sensor. The range largely relies on the transmitter and receiver, the atmosphere, the terrain, and the metropolitan environment. This is a Bluetooth Serial Port Protocol module, indicating that it communicates serially with the microcontroller (USART).

- The microcontroller incorporated in this system is Arduino Nano v3.0. It is a very popular Arduino Development board, very much similar to Arduino UNO. Instead of UNO, Arduino Nano was preferred due to it's smaller size. In addition, Nano is more breadboard-friendly than UNO. Also, a standard USB cable is required for programming UNO, whereas a tiny USB cable is sufficient for programming NANO. Furthermore, both of them use the same processor: ATmega328P.

3.3 System Software

The software part of the proposed system comprises of two Android Applications and a real-time database (firebase). Both of the applications have been developed using MIT App Inventor which is basically a web application IDE. Furthermore, Firebase is cloud hosted NoSQL Database where data is stored as JSON. The software part employed in this proposed system has these following steps: data collection, visualization, data storing and monitoring.

Data Collection in Android Application. To collect the data, we need to use Bluetooth of a mobile phone. For this, we have developed the "Health Surveillance" app which will be resided with the patient for which this is termed as Sender app. For getting data in the app, Bluetooth needs to be turned on. We have used HC-05 Bluetooth module to receive data from Arduino. This Bluetooth module's range is about 10 m. So, if the user's android device is within 10 m, it can receive the sensors' data easily.

Age Selection. There is an option in the application for defining the user's age. As body temperature, heartbeat, oxygen saturation varies from age to age, this is necessary to define the age. The health condition will be determined based on the selected age and the measured data.

Location Tracking. Current location will be shown in the application. This is necessary to know the location of the person who will be monitored.

Data Visualization. Data measured by the sensors are visualized in the sender application "Health Surveillance". Figure 4(a) shows the state before taking data. This is why NULL is shown against the sensor values. The full view of the application during the data measurement is shown in Fig. 4(b).

Decision Making. Depending on the age and different sensors data, application will detect different health conditions. The decision-making criteria is given in Table 1 [2].

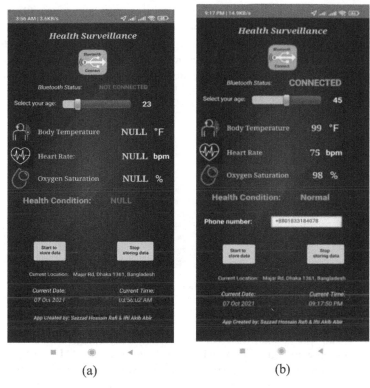

Fig. 4. Data Visualization (a) Initial View (b) Full View.

SMS Triggering. For emergency circumstances, SMS will be sent to a number which will be defined by the user. If any critical health condition is detected, then the SMS will be triggered which will contain both the current location and body condition. We have enabled this feature using the TextGroup component of MIT App Inventor for which we did not have to buy an extra GSM module for sending SMS.

Table 1. Criteria for Taking Decisions [2].

Decision	Age 18–35	Age 36–64	Age Above 64
Tachycardia	Heart Rate ≥ 110	Heart Rate ≥ 120	Heart Rate ≥ 100
Bradycardia	Heart Rate ≤ 55	Heart Rate ≤ 60	Heart Rate ≤ 65
Fever	Temperature ≥ 98.96 °F	Temperature ≥ 99.5 °F	Temperature ≥ 98.42 °F
Hypothermia	Temperature < 95.9 °F	Temperature < 95.18 °F	Temperature < 95 °F

Data Storing. The data which are coming to the application will be directly saved in Google Sheets containing the date, time, body temperature, heart-rate, oxygen saturation and health condition. Figure 5 shows a picture of the data stored in Google Sheets. These data can be observed from anywhere. If the person who will monitor cannot get into "Health Monitoring" application (Receiver App), then this can also be an alternative approach. These data can be used for further decision making. Sometimes unnecessary data may be stored. To avoid such data, there are two buttons given in the sender application: start to store data and stop storing data. Therefore, user can easily bound the level of data, he/she wants to store.

	A	B	C	D	E	F	G
1	date	time	temperature	bpm	spO2	Status	
2	05 Oct 2021	12:32:18 AM	99.1	78	98	Normal	
3	05 Oct 2021	12:32:19 AM	99.1	78	98	Normal	
4	05 Oct 2021	12:32:19 AM	99.1	78	98	Normal	
5	05 Oct 2021	12:32:20 AM	99.1	79	98	Normal	
6	05 Oct 2021	12:32:20 AM	99.1	79	98	Normal	

Fig. 5. Data Storing in Google Sheets.

Data Monitoring. The data from the real time database are being retrieved in the application of the person who will monitor, which has been named as "Health Monitoring". Figure 6 gives a glimpse of the data retrieved in Receiver's application. As firebase can store data within 1 ms, so the person who will monitor, will be able to monitor the real time value. This app can be handled by Doctor or Relative or the person who wants to monitor from any place.

3.4 End-to-End Summary of the Proposed System

The system proposed in this paper can be incorporated for both remote and real-time health monitoring. The system has low latency as we have used real-time database which can capture data within 1 ms. However, the user journey of the system has been given below:

Step 1. Patient/user has to connect the sensors of the device in appropriate places of his/her body.

Step 2. Need to turn on the Bluetooth of the android phone of the user where "Health Surveillance" application has to be pre-installed.

Step 3. Initially, app will show Null value against each field. After successful connection of Bluetooth, app will start to show the data measured by the sensors.

Step 4. These measured data will be stored in Google Sheets from this sender app. These data will also be sent to the database (Firebase).

Step 5. Data will be instantly captured in the receiver application "Health Monitoring" from the database. Doctor or individual who wants to monitor health will have to install this receiver app in their android phone.

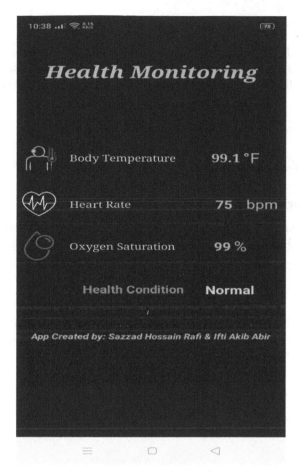

Fig. 6. Data Retrieved in Receiver's Application.

Step 6. The person who is monitoring need not be always concentrated in the app as the system has alarming feature where if any health parameter goes beyond the pre-defined threshold, the app will send SMS to the phone number which has been defined by the user. SMS will contain both the body condition and current location of the patient.

Step 7. Finally, data stored in Google Sheets can be analyzed for further decision making.

4 Result and Discussion

In this section, we have shown the measured data by our proposed system where we have compared these values with the market standard devices. We have taken those devices as a reference for the error calculation. For error calculation, the following equation has been used.

$$Percentage\ of\ Error = \frac{|Data_m - Data_{ref}|}{Data_{ref}} \times 100\% \tag{3}$$

where, $Data_m$ is the measured data by our device & $Data_{ref}$ is the reference data.

4.1 Body Temperature

We have taken data with our device from 10 persons. Then we have taken values using 'AirDoctor Digital Thermometer' from them and calculated percentage of error which is shown in Table 2. The maximum error was 1.93%.

4.2 Heart Rate

'AccuMax Advance Digital Blood Pressure' (BA-6310) has been used as a reference device and we have calculated the percentage of error from the measured data which has been shown in Table 3. The maximum error was 8.82%.

4.3 Oxygen Saturation

Due to Covid situation, pulse oximeter has become a common device for any family. Our pulse oximeter, however, has given satisfactory result with respect to 'Aeon Finger

Table 2. Body Temperature.

Person	Measured by Our Device (°F)	Measured by Digital Thermometer (°F)	Percentage of Error	Decision
01	99.1	98.2	0.9%	Normal
02	99.7	98.6	1.11%	Normal
03	99.3	100.0	0.7%	Normal
04	102.5	101.8	0.6%	Fever
05	103.4	102.1	1.27%	Fever
06	98.5	99.4	0.9%	Normal
07	98.7	99.3	0.6%	Normal
08	98.3	99.2	0.9%	Normal
09	100.4	98.7	1.7%	Normal
10	100	98.1	1.93%	Normal

Pulse Oximeter' (A320) which has been depicted in Table 4. The maximum error was 2.04%.

Table 3. Heart Rate.

Person	Measured by Our Device (bpm)	Measured by Digital BP Machine (bpm)	Percentage of Error	Decision
01	73	75	2.67%	Normal
02	70	68	2.94%	Normal
03	74	70	5.71%	Normal
04	79	83	4.82%	Normal
05	85	80	6.25%	Normal
06	68	72	5,56%	Normal
07	89	85	4.71%	Normal
08	111	102	8.82%	Tachycardia
09	73	78	6.41%	Normal
10	86	83	3.61%	Normal

Table 4. Oxygen Saturation.

Person	Measured by Our Device	Measured by Aeon Finger Pulse Oximeter	Percentage of Error	Decision
01	98	99	1.01%	Normal
02	98	99	1.01%	Normal
03	99	99	0%	Normal
04	96	98	2.04%	Normal
05	99	98	1.02	Normal
06	97	98	1.02%	Normal
07	98	98	0%	Normal
08	99	99	0%	Normal
09	98	98	0%	Normal
10	98	99	1.01%	Normal

5 Conclusion and Future Work

The primary objective of this research work is to remotely monitor health conditions. Here, we have evaluated three parameters: body temperature, heart rate, and oxygen saturation. These are essential health indicators. This approach will assist individuals in taking precautions and consulting a physician. Again, any busy individual who cannot constantly monitor a family member but wants to be alerted of a catastrophic body condition can use this system with ease. Although body temperature and oxygen saturation levels were pretty excellent, it was difficult to obtain precise data from the pulse sensor since it was constantly changing. The primary function of this proposed framework is based on software. Here, we are storing data, displaying data, tracking location, identifying health conditions, and sending Text messages in case of emergency. However, we have no limitation to store data as we do not need to use the internet or Wi-Fi to send data from the microcontroller to the android application. Additionally, Bluetooth modules are less expensive than other wireless modules. Other components are inexpensive as well. Overall, in terms of its characteristics, this proposed system is cost effective. Furthermore, the main limitation of our system is that it is basically a Threshold based system where threshold for each parameter has been hardcoded in the application. Moreover, only 3 parameters can now be defined with the current system. These are some of our limitations which will be improved in our next development phase.

However, we are storing the data captured in the application. This dataset can be employed to train a Machine Learning model which can be implemented in our proposed system. Then our application itself will decide the health condition with better accuracy in future. We will also design a PCB to reduce the size of the gadget for a better user experience. We will also enhance the number of sensors. ECG, blood pressure, and GSR sensor will also be utilized in future to define the health status with more precision. Thus, virtually all body symptoms of prevalent diseases can be detected, allowing the user to take extra precautions.

References

1. Ping, W., Jin-Gang, W., Xiao-Bo, S., Wei, H.: The research of telemedicine system based on embedded computer. In: 2005 IEEE Engineering in Medicine and Biology 27th Annual Conference, pp. 114–117. IEEE (2005)
2. Kakria, P., Tripathi, N.K., Kitipawang, P.: A real-time health monitoring system for remote cardiac patients using smartphone and wearable sensors. Int. J. Telemed. Appl. **2015**, 8 (2015)
3. Organization, W.H.: Global status report on noncommunicable diseases (2010)
4. Naddeo, S., Verde, L., Forastiere, M., De Pietro, G., Sannino, G.: A real-time m-health monitoring system: an integrated solution combining the use of several wearable sensors and mobile devices. In: Proceedings of the 10th International Joint Conference on Biomedical Engineering Systems and Technologies - SmartMedDev (BIOSTEC), pp. 545–552 (2017)
5. DataReportal: Digital Around the World. Global Digital Insights. https://datareportal.com/global-digital-overview. Accessed 10 July 2021
6. M, Miah, A., Kabir, M.H., Tanveer, M.S.R., Akhand, M.A.H.: Continuous heart rate and body temperature monitoring system using Arduino UNO and Android device. In: 2nd International Conference on Electrical Information and Communication Technologies (EICT), pp. 183–188 (2015)

7. Hashem, M.M.A., Shams, R., Kader, M.A., Sayed, M.A.: Design and development of a heart rate measuring device using fingertip. In: International Conference on Computer and Communication Engineering (ICCCE 2010), pp. 1–5 (2010)
8. Navale, M., Damare, S., Chavan, R., Dube, R., Patil, S.: Android based heart monitoring and reporting system. Int. J. Adv. Res. Comput. Commun. Eng. **3**, 6544–6546 (2014)
9. Indumathy, N., Patil, K.K.: Medical alert system for remote health monitoring using sensors and cloud computing. Int. J. Res. Eng. Technol. **3**(04), 884–888 (2014)
10. Krishnan, D.S.R., Gupta, S.C., Choudhury, T.: IoT based patient health monitoring system. Int. J. Adv. Eng. Res. Dev. **4**(06), 1–7 (2017)
11. ElectronicWings: LM-35 Temperature Sensor. Info, Design and Library. Components. https://www.electronicwings.com/components/lm35-temperature-sensor. Accessed 10 May 2021
12. Ali, Z.: Introduction to LM-35. https://www.theengineeringprojects.com/2019/01/introduction-to-lm35.html. Accessed 10 May 2021
13. Alaspure, S.: Arduino temperature Sensor using LM-35. https://www.instructables.com/Arduino-Temperature-Sensor-Using-LM35/. Accessed 10 May 2021
14. Corporation, N.S.: LM-35 Description. LM-35 Datasheet. https://pdf1.alldatasheet.com/datasheet-pdf/download/517588/TI1/LM35.html. Accessed 10 May 2022
15. In-Depth: Detect, Measure & Plot Heart Rate using Pulse Sensor & Arduino. https://lastminuteengineers.com/pulse-sensor-arduino-tutorial/. Accessed 10 May 2021
16. SparkFun: Photodetector Hookup Guide. https://learn.sparkfun.com/tutorials/sparkfun-photodetector-max30101-hookup-guide/introduction. Accessed 10 June 2021
17. SparkFun: MAX30105 Pulse Oximeter Sensor Hookup Guide. https://learn.sparkfun.com/tutorials/max30105-particle-and-pulse-ox-sensor-hookup-guide. Accessed 10 June 2021
18. ElectronicWings: Bluetooth Module HC-05. Sensors & Modules. https://www.electronicwings.com/sensors-modules/bluetooth-module-hc-05. Accessed 10 June 2021

Block-chain Aided Cluster Based Logistic Network for Food Supply Chain

Rahat Uddin Azad[1]([✉]), Khair Ahammed[1], Muhammad Abdus Salam[2], and Md. Ifthekarul Alam Efat[1]

[1] Institute of Information Technology, Noakhali Science and Technology University, Noakhali , Bangladesh
rahatuddin786@gamil.com, khairahmad6@gmail.com, iftekhar.efat@gmail.com
[2] Department of Management Information Systems, Noakhali Science and Technology University, Noakhali, Bangladesh
salam.mis@nstu.edu.bd

Abstract. Consumers are increasingly more concerned about the social and environmental food sustainability. Merchants, distributors, processors, and farmers are more worried about the traceability, safety, and sustainability of their products. Food supply chains are more responsive, and efficient regarding consumer demands and requirements. However, digitizing a food supply chain is difficult, resource-intensive, and time-consuming. The objective of this study is to conduct route analyses and increase the efficiency of the local food supply chain. Competitors need to work together with suppliers, distributors, and end-user to coordinate their businesses. Thus, we propose a Blockchain-aided cluster-based logistic network called BCLN to improve the efficacy of logistics, reduce the impact on the environment, and increase the potential market for food producers. We integrate blockchain technology to improve consumers' ability and trace the origin of food products. To map the locations of producers and Large Scale Food Distribution centers (LSFDCs), a location analysis was carried out using a Geographic Information System (GIS). Also, a cluster of producers was created, and the best product collection centers (CC) were identified. As a result, total pollution emitted by vehicles has decreased. This model is required for improving logistics efficiency and economic benefits, capturing the potential market, ensuring food and service quality, and traceability of food quality.

Keywords: Block-chain · Logistics Network · Traceability · Location Analysis · Clustering · Route Analysis

1 Introduction

Food safety and food quality are becoming important to consumers, they demand detailed knowledge and information about the origins of their food, as well as how it was handled and delivered. The revenue of food producers, the pricing of food products, and consumer satisfaction are all impacted by the effectiveness of logistics management.

© ICST Institute for Computer Sciences, Social Informatics and Telecommunications Engineering 2023
Published by Springer Nature Switzerland AG 2023. All Rights Reserved
Md. S. Satu et al. (Eds.): MIET 2022, LNICST 491, pp. 422–434, 2023.
https://doi.org/10.1007/978-3-031-34622-4_34

Environmental concerns have a direct impact on logistics efficiency. The transportation industry produces 25% of the world's greenhouse gas, and road transport is responsible for around 75% of those emissions [1]. Agricultural transportation is such an area where a reduction in emissions is likely to contribute to efforts to mitigate the danger of climate change. Due to disorganized and non-optimal food transportation methods, the local food supply chain is unable to meet the needs of the population [2].

There is a significant opportunity to increase the energy efficiency of the local food supply chain (LFSC) by reorganizing the food supply system, using vehicles with greater energy efficiency, introducing biofuel production in the local area, increasing vehicle operating efficiency, and preparing the most efficient routes for food distribution [3].

As the number of businesses grows, transportation and distribution get more sophisticated. Moreover, customer demands and satisfaction become more individualized, as well as supply chains are becoming increasingly complex. In a traditional food supply chain there contain socioeconomic, organizational, hygienic, and environmental components, and the deployment of specialized cognitive-based strategies is particularly important. It is critical to have faith in the product's quality and delivery in order to reach a win-win situation in the social and environmental domains.

In order to improve the efficiency of the logistics in the food supply chain, it is necessary to conduct precise location analysis and optimize routes through network integration. In addition, research in logistics is essential in the food and agricultural industries in order to analyze the effects of existing logistics networks on delivery performance and their impact on the environment [4].

Blockchain, an emerging technology, has sparked a lot of interest from a wide range of industries. Blockchain is a decentralized database that keeps a permanent record of all digital transactions. To ensure that all participants have access to real-time data, a blockchain network's decentralized and open architecture makes it possible for participants to share data in real-time with complete confidence. We use blockchain technology and integrate it with our proposed cluster-based logistic network to ensure supply chain traceability and real-time information exchange.

The primary objective of this study is to look into the characteristics of the Local Food Supply Chain (LFSC) and design a coordinated logistic network with the goals of improving production efficiency, reducing transportation burden, promoting sustainable development, expanding the global market for local food producers, and improving consumers' ability to trace the origin of food products.

2   Literature Review

In recent years, there has been conducted numerous research on food supply chain management. These studies concentrated on optimizing production, warehouse layouts, inventory levels, and transportation optimization. However, the majority of these studies concentrated on quality and safety in the food industry. But a few studies have attempted to enhance food supply chain information management via IT tools such as BIM, GIS, or IoT.

In 2004 a study was conducted where the researcher discusses possibilities of enhancing logistics and distribution supply chains within the food retail industry. It incorporates the ideas of logistics and supply chain as well as the emerging issues in the food business. The study derives that business-to-business and e-commerce are the ways of the future. The study covers the strengths and challenges of the sector [5].

Various Greek food retail enterprises are examined by Bourlakis et al to determine the strategic strategy they use for food transportation [6]. The findings highlight the critical role that storage plays in the logistical operations of multinational corporations and the importance of the logistics strategy of multinational retailers. International companies employ a deliberate logistics strategy that results in more efficiency than local companies employing an emergent strategy

Throughout Sweden, 19 large-scale food distribution centers (LSFDC) and 90 food producers supplied data to the study. GIS was utilized to map the locations of producers and LSFDCs, create producer clusters, and determine the ideal product collecting centers for each of these producer groups (CC). The Route Logix software took into consideration two different scenarios when determining the most efficient ways to transport food from farms to collection centers (CCs). The first scenario involved producers transporting their own products (without any coordination), while the second scenario involved CCs managing the collection of products, followed by distribution of products from CCs to potential markets [2].

Regulators have imposed a variety of laws, standards, and certifications on food producers in order to assure product integrity and consumer safety. According to numerous studies, standards and certifications are essential for ensuring the food supply chain is transparent and high-quality products are produced [7]. Food integrity should not only be the responsibility of a single company but of all those involved in the supply chain, [8].

All the phases in the supply chain, including materials, production, logistics, and delivery, can be inspected with RFID, as proposed by Yin et al [9]. Another study found that inventory and supply chain expenses were reduced by using information tracking technology such as barcodes and RFID [10]. We can also use Blockchain technology to manage IoT devices. In addition, blockchain technology will aid in the development of a secure communication platform in a smart city by integrating blockchain technology with smart gadgets. [11].

In 2020, a framework called Blockchain-enabled Vehicle Certification (BVC) was proposed[12]. This framework would connect the government body, the vehicle owner, the driver, and any other providers through a protected channel. The blockchain concept was implemented in the main business layer of the architecture as a result, all of the participants in the system are now able to communicate with one another and store data using an access method that is both confidential and safe. They claim that their framework will improve the existing car certification procedure and provides a safe network to store these certifications.

In the same year, Biswas et al. presented a solution to transition existing e-health systems to a unified Blockchain-based model, which allows access to large-scale medical data of patients to be achieved effortlessly by any service provider [13]. The demand for frequent updates to smart contracts was reduced as a result of this solution. As a component of its overarching architecture, the proposed system makes use of a centralized Trust Authority as well as decentralized off-chain storage.

In 2021, Again Biswas et al. presented GlobeChain, an architecture for the exchange of medical data that was based on Blockchain technology [14]. This was done in order to overcome the technical issues that were involved in the management of outbreak records. The proposed framework was able to address a wide variety of potentially vulnerable situations, such as a single point of failure, data leakage, access restriction, and so on. The architecture was suited for use in any medical data centers operating at the national level that are either based on blockchain technology or compatible with blockchain technology.

In 2022, Qi Tao explored the quality control system and assessed the risk factors for the rice supply chain using blockchain [15]. The paper also proposed the traceability management system for the rice supply chain. The consumer could easily get the information from the IoT devices and get details of the rice quality and supply chain.

To construct a decentralized network that can offer security, neutrality, and dependability of all operations in a supply chain, blockchain can be used in various supply chain management systems [16]. As with traditional databases, which are controlled by a central authority or administration (such as banks or government accountants) and responsible for all transactions, blockchain creates a distributed ledger consisting of a network of replicated databases that are synchronized via the internet and accessible to anyone within the network. A blockchain network can be public and accessible to everybody in the world, or it can be private and limited in membership [17]

3 Methodology

Local food producers and their distribution systems were the focus of our study. The primary tasks that were carried out were location analysis and route optimization, as well as attempts to enhance food supply chain traceability. The ArcGIS tool was chosen as the network analysis tool in this study [18]. Using ArcGIS, the locations of producers, CCs, and DCs were mapped. Basically, we divided the clustering process into six major steps. After that, we integrate block technology so that all the transactions between producers, suppliers, retailers, and customers are captured through smart contracts. This will ensure food traceability in the food supply chain. The general procedure followed in this study illustrates in Fig. 1.

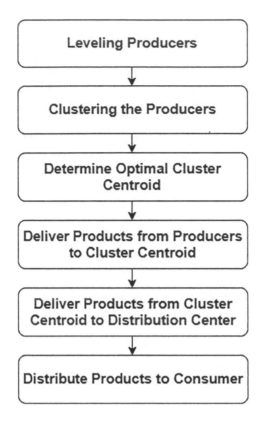

Fig. 1. Flowchart of the clustering process.

3.1 Leveling Producers

Producers' postcodes and extra info were first acquired from the Geographical data repository, and then respective locations were determined based on their postcodes and supplementary information. It was done by using ArcGIS to map and cluster local food-producing farms and existing food delivery sites [18].

3.2 Clustering the Producers

The producers were grouped together based on their geographical proximity to one another. During the clustering procedure, all producers within 100 km of one another were grouped together. Clusters of producers were constructed with the help of geographic information system (GIS) software, and the optimal location of the CC was found for each cluster. How a single cluster construct is illustrated in Fig. 2.

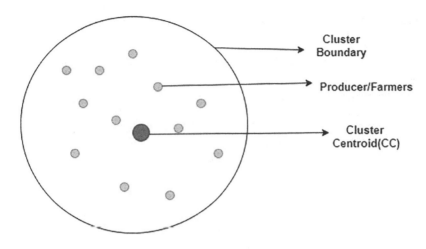

Fig. 2. A Cluster of Producers.

3.3 Determine Optimal Cluster Centroid

Producers distribute their own products to consumers and markets. According to our study, products from producers within a cluster will be transported in a coordinated manner to CC, where they could distribute their products to current and new consumers, as well as other markets. An optimal CC for each cluster must be determined in order to conduct a coordinated logistical operation.

3.4 Deliver Products from Producers to Cluster Centroid

CC will be used for more than just temporary storage; it will also serve as a distribution center for distributing products to customers and retailers in its immediate area as well as to potential markets, such as those in nearby towns and cities, which is pictorially described in Fig. 3. In order to comply with this requirement all producers of each cluster deliver their products to CC, and CC is responsible for the coordinated distribution of those products from CC to the distribution center.

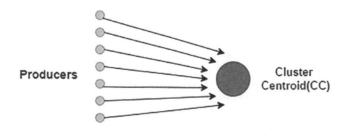

Fig. 3. Deliver Products from Producers to Cluster Centroid.

3.5   Deliver Products from Cluster Centroid to Distribution Center

As we clarify in the previous section that CC will be used for more than just temporary storage and serve as a local distribution center. But the local producers have difficulty contacting consumers who are located distant from their own local area, the process is displayed in Fig. 4 As a result, to extend the potential market for local food producers, the local food supply chain should be connected to the global food supply chain. Using ArcGIS software, the ideal distribution center for delivering products from the CC the determined to reach the targeted market.

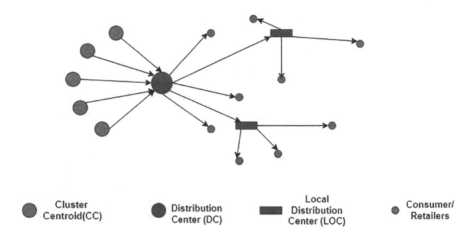

Fig. 4. Deliver Products from Cluster Centroid to Distribution Center.

3.6   Distribute Products to Consumer

Distributing foods to clients was handled in an integrated manner. Mostly data on consumer demands is being gathered and dynamic distribution plans being prepared. Local food distribution has been incorporated through the local food distribution hub.

3.7   Block Chain Integration

As a step in the Production process, food is packed in bags, given labels, and then added to the blockchain along with a digital profile. These computerized profiles contain the most crucial information about the food, including the soil, the water, the area, the season, the growth circumstances, the planting time, and the harvesting time, among other details. After that, farmers will utilize GIS routing techniques to locate the nearest cluster center or temporary storage, and then they will deliver their products. The product is then traded between the farmers and the distribution center using a handheld tag reader and a wireless network where the parties have later signed a digital contract (Smart contract) that is kept on the blockchain. How our complete BCLN framework operates is displayed in Fig. 5.

The information on logistics, storage, quality, and distribution is regularly updated on blockchain by the distributors at predetermined intervals after they have collected the products from the producers. This means that the blockchain is able to monitor the activities of all distributors as they supply products to retailers using a smart contract. After that distributors can deliver the foods to the nearest local distributors or retailers and then add the delivery information to the blockchain along with a digital profile. Moreover, a consumer can directly get the foods from the distribution center also.

The barcodes present on the packaging of food products can be scanned to reveal all information that a retailer might require concerning those products. As all of the food's information is maintained in its digital profile on the blockchain, the supply chain of a particular product may be accessed and audited by anybody who possesses software that is enabled with blockchain technology.

4   Implications of BCLN Framework

Considering networks and other organized forms of collaboration are techniques for improving a region's and country's competitiveness, so we think that the integration of the BCLN framework in the food supply chain will contribute to regional development. The process is displayed in Fig. 5

Listed below are some proper implementations of our proposed framework that will make a significant difference and radically improve people's daily lives.

4.1   Improve Logistics Efficiency

GIS is increasingly being used for location analysis because of its ability to display and manipulate geographic and spatial data [22,23]. When compared to the current food supply chain, improved coordination can lead to even more improvements. It is possible to improve service quality and economic benefits through the integration of a logistics network when cooperation and confidence are at a high-level [24]. A high-quality logistics service must ensure the delivery of the appropriate product, in the appropriate quantity, on time, and at a reasonable price. Transport distances in the food supply chain can be minimized with our BCLN framework. It is possible to reduce transportation distances by expanding the number of local suppliers and promoting production closer to the market.

4.2   Capturing Potential Market and Improve Economic Benefits

Producers in the local food chain have difficulty of reaching consumers who are far from the source of their food. The integration of logistic networks facilitates

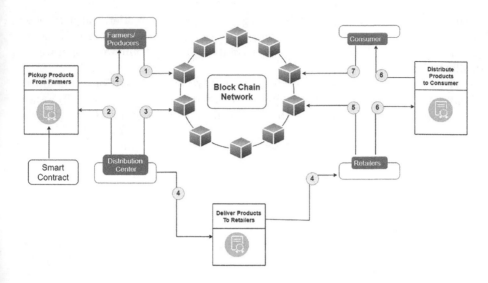

Fig. 5. BCLN Framework.

the distribution of local food to schools and restaurants, as well as the marketing of local items in supermarkets. Moreover, Logistics expenses might be reduced greatly by using this framework and gain more effective data processing.

4.3 Ensure Food and Service Quality

Enhancing logistical performance isn't enough to improve food quality and environmental sustainability in the supply chain. Biological variation, chronological variation, and environmental factors play a major role in determining food quality. Suppliers are responsible for ensuring that food and information about its quality and origin are properly regulated. It's possible that we'll use our framework in the future to make it easier for suppliers to track the movement of food goods and relevant information about their quality and provenance. In this way, they are able to satisfy the growing demand for locally produced food items in the global market, which in turn helps LFSCs become more sustainable. To do this, we must make it possible for local food producers to compete successfully in the global marketplace.

4.4 Ensure Traceability of Food Quality

When it comes to locally produced food, customers know exactly where their food comes from and who grew it. Consumers have a greater sense of trust in the local food producers since they rely on them to ensure that the food is safe. Basically, the traceability of local food products depends on how participants of the supply chain connect to each other. Incorporating blockchain technology into the food supply chain provides a solution that enables the traceability of product provenance. This information helps the building of trust amongst supply chain participants, including, producers, suppliers, manufacturers, transporters, and end customers. In addition, it offers precise product tracking, which helps predict various risks and enables all participants to act accordingly.

5 Discussion

According to the findings of our study, people want to know where their food comes from and have more access to locally sourced food. These concerns directly indicate both the quality and safety of food as well as the well-being of people. Local food systems facilitate the traceability of food products. As a result, customer preferences on the market are influenced by the price of locally sourced food. Because fraudulent food activity is widespread in today's food distribution networks, for this reason, the public places greater trust in local food manufacturers.

Customers enjoyed effective food delivery and fresh, locally produced foods. As a result, local food producers are being pushed to enhance the quality and amount of food. Manufacturers were interested in increasing their promotional strategies if they cut their manufacturing and delivery costs and increase their competency. Additionally, small-scale companies aim to lower their logistics costs, boost their production, and expand their markets. By considering all of these facts, the BCLN framework could be a robust solution.

However, by integrating the BCLN framework into local food systems, customers' satisfaction and local food producers' competitiveness could be improved. As a result of this effective logistical system, it will reduce the usage of packaging materials and reduce environmental impact. More people are likely to favor locally produced foods in the future if more research like this is done on the subject since they can provide important economic, social, and environmental benefits.

One of the most significant challenges that each possible scenario for the traditional food supply chain must deal with is the problem of traceability, safety, and sustainability. Each supply chain will face distinct digitalization difficulties and opportunities depending on the products and the requirements of the downstream customers/consumers.

By integrating digital platforms such as blockchain, which play a more vital role in authenticating all transactions and ensuring that they are carried out in a secure and efficient manner. The food supply chain becomes more transparent through the blockchain, which challenges its upstream operations to be truly sustainable.

Our proposed framework has the potential to reduce the overall number of transportation routes as well as the time and distance it takes to deliver goods. This suggests that there is significant potential for a logistics network, which might boost local producers' competitiveness and make local food supply structures more sustainable. Modern technologies like Route Logix and ArcGIS have made it simpler to conduct location and route optimization assessments.

As a result, it may be simpler to obtain a better understanding of food supply chains and also integrate this BCLN framework.

On the other hand, it is critical to situate the CC/DC in the best possible position when designing the BCLN framework for the food supply chain. In addition to selecting the optimum location for the CC/DC, determining the best food delivery routes offers a significant opportunity to enhance the existing local food supply chain. It is essential to a company's long-term performance to select an appropriate location for its headquarters because expenses are associated with transportation and distribution.

The absence of pilot projects was another limitation of this study, mainly because blockchain technology is still in the development phase in domains such as finance. There are a number of obstacles that may need to be overcome before the supply chain industry can successfully utilize blockchain technology. In addition, integrating blockchain technology in precast construction requires the full cooperation of almost all the stakeholders involved. However, our proposed model can improve supply chain management efficiency by enhancing real-time information sharing among various stakeholders.

6   Conclusion

Food traceability is a crucial component of the food logistics system because it makes it possible to manage the entire food supply chain in a more seamless fashion. Customers have a strong connection to local food suppliers. Therefore, a common central database for traceability information is needed for small manufacturers.

Clustering, coordination, integration, and optimization approaches can be used to tackle logistics issues in local food systems. When logistics networks are integrated with local food supply chains, then it can improve overall performance by lowering overstock, delivery delays, and end product prices and boosting product value, quality, and safety in addition to customer happiness.

The purpose of this study was to conduct location and route analyses in order to increase the efficiency of LFSC logistics. The cluster-based research allows the identification and clustering of regional food producers based on their location. All local food producers of each cluster will deliver their product to their own cluster centroid. After that foods will be delivered from cluster centroid to DC. Later DC will distribute products to retailers or directly to the end consumers.

The BCLN framework integration could result in vital improvements for the existing food supply chain such as a reduction in transportation costs and vehicle numbers. According to the findings of this study, our framework has various implications like enhancing logistical performance, ensuring food traceability, improving food quality, capturing potential market segments (and economic rewards), increasing supplier economic viability, and decreasing environmental impact.

Last but not least, this work presents a lot of novel ideas; as a consequence, future research can significantly take several different directions from this paper. From a methodological point of view, upcoming researchers might use the BCLN framework as a foundation for their studies. Moreover, in future, we will further evaluate or extend this framework by using real-time field data from the implementation of blockchain technology in the supply chain.

References

1. Määttä-Juntunen, H., Antikainen, H., Kotavaara, O., Rusanen, J.: Using GIS tools to estimate CO2 emissions related to the accessibility of large retail stores in the Oulu region Finland. J. Trans. Geography 19(2), 346–354 (2011)
2. Bosona, T.G., Gebresenbet, G.: Cluster building and logistics network integration of local food supply chain. Biosys. Eng. 108(4), 293–302 (2011)
3. Gebresenbet, G., Ljungberg, D.: IT-information technology and the human interface: coordination and route optimization of agricultural goods transport to attenuate environmental impact. J. Agric. Eng. Res. 80(4), 329–342 (2001)
4. Aronsson, H., Brodin, N.H.: The environmental impact of changing logistics structures. Int. J. Logist. Manag. (2006)
5. Aghazadeh, S.-M.: Improving logistics operations across the food industry supply chain. International J. Contemporary Hospitality Manag. (2004)
6. Bourlakis, M.A., Bourlakis, C.A.: Deliberate and emergent logistics strategies in food retailing: a case study of the Greek multiple food retail sector. Int. J. Supply Chain Manag. (2001)
7. Gharehgozli, A., et al.: Trends in global E-food supply chain and implications for transport: Literature review and research directions. Res. Trans. Bus. Manag. 25, 2–14 (2017)
8. Elliott, C.: Elliott Review into the integrity and assurance of food supply networks-Final report: A national food crime prevention framework, pp. 383–395 (2014)
9. Yin, S.Y.L., et al.: Developing a precast production management system using RFID technology. Autom. Const. 18(5), 677–691 (2009)
10. Du, J., Sugumaran, V., Gao, B.: RFID and multi-agent based architecture for information sharing in prefabricated component supply chain. IEEE Access 5, 4132–4139 (2017)
11. Huh, S., Cho, S., Kim, S.: Managing IoT devices using blockchain platform. In: 2017 19th International Conference on Advanced Communication Technology (ICACT). IEEE (2017)
12. Das, M., Azad, R.U., Efat, M.I.A.: Blockchain aided Vehicle Certification (BVC): A secured e-governance framework for transport stakeholders. In: 2020 23rd International Conference on Computer and Information Technology (ICCIT), pp. 1–6. IEEE (December 2020)
13. Biswas, S., Sharif, K., Li, F., Alam, I., Mohanty, S.: DAAC: Digital asset access control in a unified blockchain based e-health system. IEEE Trans. Big Data (2020)
14. Biswas, S., Sharif, K., Li, F., Bairagi, A.K., Latif, Z., Mohanty, S.P.: Globechain: An interoperable blockchain for global sharing of healthcare data-a covid-19 perspective. IEEE Consumer Electron. Mag. 10(5), 64–69 (2021)
15. Tao, Q., Cai, Z. and Cui, X.: A technological quality control system for rice supply chain. Food Energy Sec., e382 (2022)

434   R. U. Azad et al.

16. Bocek, T., et al.: Blockchains everywhere-a use-case of blockchains in the pharma supply-chain. In: 2017 IFIP/IEEE Symposium on Integrated Network and Service Management (IM). IEEE, (2017)
17. Zyskind, G., Nathan, O.: Decentralizing privacy: Using blockchain to protect personal data. In: 2015 IEEE Security and Privacy Workshops. IEEE (2015)
18. ESRI: ArcGIS desktophelp. Environmental Systems Research Institute, New York, USA (2008)
19. Smith, T.F., Waterman, M.S.: Identification of common molecular subsequences. J. Mol. Biol. **147**, 195–197 (1981). https://doi.org/10.1016/0022-2836(81)90087-5
20. Brimer, R.C.: Logistics networking. Logist. Inf. Manag. (1995)
21. May, P., Ehrlich, H.-C., Steinke, T.: ZIB structure prediction pipeline: composing a complex biological workflow through web services. In: Nagel, W.E., Walter, W.V., Lehner, W. (eds.) Euro-Par 2006. LNCS, vol. 4128, pp. 1148–1158. Springer, Heidelberg (2006). https://doi.org/10.1007/11823285_121
22. Beni, L.H., Villeneuve, S., LeBlanc, D.I., Delaquis, P.: A GIS-based approach in support of an assessment of Food Safety Risks. Trans. GIS **15**, 95–108 (2011)
23. Tavares, G., Zsigraiova, Z., Semiao, V., Carvalho, M.D.G.: Optimisation of MSW collection routes for minimum fuel consumption using 3D GIS modelling. Waste Manage. **29**(3), 1176–1185 (2009)
24. Daugherty, P.J.: Review of logistics and supply chain relationship literature and suggested research agenda. Int. J. Phys. Distribut. Logist. Manag. (2011)

Programmable Logic Array in Quantum Computing

Fatema Akter$^{(\boxtimes)}$ ⓘ, Tamanna Tabassum ⓘ, and Mohammed Nasir Uddin ⓘ

Computer Science and Engineering, Jagannath University, Dhaka, Bangladesh
fatema_akter@cse.green.edu.bd

Abstract. The field of computing known as quantum computing is devoted to creating computer technology that is based on the ideas of quantum theory (which makes sense of the way of behaving of energy and material on the nuclear and subatomic levels). These supercomputers are based on two aspects of quantum physical science: superposition and entanglement. As a result, quantum PCs can handle tasks at speeds that are significantly faster than those of traditional PCs and with a lot less energy consumption. On the other hand, Quantum logic gates are designed to empower this computing field. Programmable Logic Array is a type of PLDs (programmable logic devices) and is mainly used for designing combination logic mutually by sequential logic. It could be a general-purpose logic gadget that's programmable and a client can configure the gadget as a simple logic gate operation to complex systems on a chip. In this work, a PLA is designed using Quantum-based gates. The features of Quantum-based computing help Quantum-based PLA to perform billions of activities simultaneously and can give immense memory in small space.

Keywords: PLA · Quantum Computing · Qubit

1 Introduction

Quantum implies the littlest conceivable discrete unit of any actual property, like energy or matter. A branch of computing known as quantum computing aims to advance PC technology in accordance with the principles of quantum theory, which clarifies how to work on energy and matter at the nuclear and subatomic scales. Quantum figuring is an arising technique for calculation that vows to achieve computational assignments and calculations that are too challenging to even think about performing on existing processing standards [21]. Quantum and traditional processing are two equal universes for certain likenesses and numerous distinctions, for example, the utilization of qubits as opposed to bits.

- Quantum computers have a simpler architecture and they have no memory or processor. The equipment consists solely of a set of qubits that makes it run [17].
- Quantum computers can create vast multidimensional spaces in which to represent these very large problems [18].

Md. S. Satu et al. (Eds.): MIET 2022, LNICST 491, pp. 435–446, 2023.
https://doi.org/10.1007/978-3-031-34622-4_35

- Perform extremely complicated calculations easily such as extremely large systems of linear equations [19].
- Possible to simulate quantum systems not possible on traditional computers.
- Potentially thousands of times faster [20].

As quantum computer is basically reversible, Quantum mechanical cycles emerged as a promising candidate to build reversible gates, and these gates are known as quantum gates [3]. Following the introduction of quantum computation as a possibility, it has proactively been discovered that some quantum algorithms [15] which perform much more quickly than their classical counterparts. These processes, which present quantum computing as a superior future innovation, include quantum PLDs and quantum gates. The first steps in designing PLDs are quantum logic gates. Quantum logic gates is the initial steps to plan PLDs. Programmable Logic Array is a sort of PLD, which has both programmable Quantum AND array and programmable Quantum OR array. In a combinational circuit, all the minterms are not utilized because use of don't care conditions. Programmable Logic Array (PLA) is a fixed architecture logic device with programmable Quantum AND gates followed by programmable Quantum OR gates. PLA is essentially a kind of programmable logic device used to fabricate a reconfigurable digital circuit. PLDs have an undefined function at the time of manufacturing, but they are programmed before being made into use. PLA is a combination of memory and logic.

The rest of the paper is as follows: In Sect. 2, Quantum computing, the basis Quantum gates and Basic Quantum logic operation are described. In Sect. 3, the proposed Quantum PLA circuit is introduced. In Sect. 4, the algorithm of Quantum PLA is presented. Finally, Sect. 5 concludes the paper.

2   Background Study

In this section the basic of Quantum computing, Quantum basic Gate concept and Programmable Logic Array (PLA) architecture are discussed in details.

2.1   Quantum Computing

The field of quantum computing began during the 1980s. It was then discovered that certain computational problems could be tackled more efficiently with quantum algorithms than with their classical counterparts [4]. Quantum computing uses quantum bits or qubits. It outfits the remarkable capacity of subatomic particles that permits them to exist in more than one state (i.e., a 1 and a 0 at the same time) [5].

Quantum PCs process data in a different way. Old style PCs use semiconductors, which are either 1 or 0. Quantum PCs use qubits, which can be 1 or 0 at the same time. The quantity of qubits connected together expands the quantum processing power dramatically. In the meantime, connecting together more semiconductors just increments power straightly. Quantum processing could contribute enormously in the fields of materials science [6, 7], financial modelling [8], machine learning and artificial intelligence [9, 10]. One more fundamental field of quantum innovation is quantum control [11–14] whose objective is to control actual frameworks whose conduct is administered by the laws of quantum mechanics.

Quantum Basic Gates

The quantum gate, also known as a quantum logic gate, is a fundamental quantum circuit that uses only a few qubits. Based on the synthetization of the reversible logic circuits, there are three gates in Quantum Computing [16].

- CNOT (Controlled NOT)
- Controlled V
- Controlled V+ gates.

The input of NOT gate is only |A1> and |A0> is the gate control input that's why it is called CNOT gate [1] (Fig. 1).

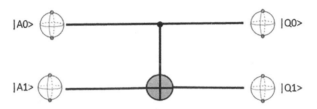

Fig. 1. Controlled CNOT gate

The output value |Q0> is always the same as the value of input |A0> because there is no operation through this line. When the control qubit |A0> is |0> then the gate will close and works as a buffer and when the control qubit |A0> is |1> it work as an inverter [2] (Table 1).

Table 1. Input-Output of Controlled CNOT gate

|A0>	|A1>	|Q0> = (|A0>)	|Q1>
|0>	|0>	|0>	|0>
|0>	|1>	|0>	|1>
|1>	|0>	|1>	|1>
|1>	|1>	|1>	|0>

The CNOT gate can be described as the gate that maps the basis states of input (|A0>, |A1>) to output (|Q0> = |A0>, & |Q1> = (|A0> XOR |A1>)).

Building a set of universal gates for the synthesis of reversible circuits (where the number of inputs and outputs is equal) requires the use of quantum V gates. The input of the V gate is only qubit |A1> and the qubit |A0> is the control input that's why it is called the Controlled V gate [3] (Fig. 2).

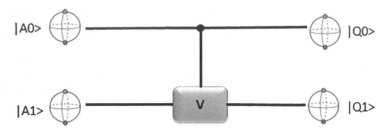

Fig. 2. Controlled V gate

The output values of the V gate are controlled by two intermediate inputs, |v> and |V>. Here, the |v> value is utilized to control the output of the V gate if it's input |A1> is |0> and the |V> value if it is |1> (Table 2).

Table 2. Input-Output of Controlled V gate

|A0>	|A1>	|Q0>	|Q1>(V)
|0>	|X>	|0>	|X>
|1>	|0>	|1>	|v>
|1>	|1>	|1>	|V>
|1>	|v>	|1>	|1>
|1>	|V>	|1>	|0>
|1>	|w>	|1>	|0>
|1>	|W>	|1>	|1>

Now, if |v> is the input to a V gate, then the gate's output is |1> (flip), as opposed to |0> for input to a V gate, which produces the value |v>. In the same way, the output of the gate is |0> if |V> is its input. When |w> is a V gate's input, the goal output is |0>, and when |W> is a V gate's input, the target output is |1>.

The conjugate transpose of the controlled V gate is the controlled V+ gate. Because qubit |A1> is the single input and qubit |A0> is the control input, the V+ gate is also known as the Controlled V+ gate (Fig. 3).

The two intermediate inputs |w> and |W> regulate the V+ gate's output values. In the V+ gate, the output is assigned the |w> value if the input |A1> is |0>, and the |W> value if the input |A1> is |1> (Table 3).

Now, if |v> is the input to a V+ gate, then the gate's output is |1> (flip), as opposed to |w> for input |0> to a V+ gate. Similar to the last example, the output of the V+ gate is |0> if |w> is its input. Again, if a V+ gate receives |v> as its input, its output is |0>, and if it receives |V> as its input, the target output is |1>.

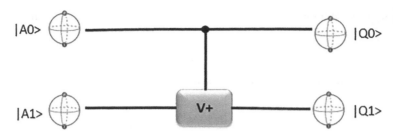

Fig. 3. Controlled V+ gate

Table 3. Input-Output of Controlled V gate

|A0>	|A1>	|Q0>	|Q1> (V+)
|0>	|X>	|0>	|X>
|1>	|0>	|1>	|w>
|1>	|1>	|1>	|W>
|1>	|v>	|1>	|0>
|1>	|V>	|1>	|1>
|1>	|w>	|1>	|1>
|1>	|W>	|1>	|0>

2.2 Quantum Logic Operations

Quantum AND Operation

The quantum gate, also known as a quantum logic gate, is a fundamental quantum circuit that uses only a few qubits. There is 2 variable input qubit (Control (open/close) the gates) and a constant input |0> (will go through gates on the target output line) in AND gate (Table 4).

Table 4. Truth Table of Quantum AND Operation

|A0>	|A1>	|Q>
|0>	|0>	|0>
|0>	|1>	|0>
|1>	|0>	|0>
|1>	|1>	|1>

Here, qubits |A0> and |A1> are used for the gate control and a constant input qubit |0> on the target output line produces desire output through quantum gates of target output line |Q>. When |A0> = |0> then the connected line 1 and 2 will not work (Fig. 4).

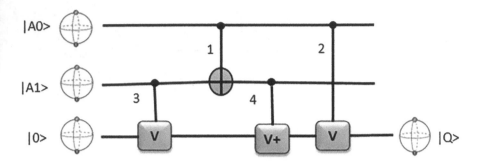

Fig. 4. Quantum AND Operation

So the connected CNOT(1) and V(2) gates will close. When |A1> = |0> then the connected lines 3 and 4 will not work. So the connected V (3) and V+ (4) gates will close. For AND gates, on the output line input qubit |0> is fixed. So this fixed value will go through all the closed quantum gates and produces |0> to target output.

Quantum OR Operations
There are 2 variable inputs (control (open/close) the gates) and a constant input |0> (will go through gates on the target output line) in OR operation. Here, qubits |A0> and |A1> are used for the gate control and a constant input qubit |0> is on the output line to produce desired output through quantum gates of the target output line (Table 5).

Table 5. Truth Table of Quantum OR Operation

|A0>	|A1>	|Q>
|0>	|0>	|0>
|0>	|1>	|1>
|1>	|0>	|1>
|1>	|1>	|1>

When |A0> = |0> then the connected line 1 and 2 will not work. So the connected CNOT and V gates will close. When |A1> = |0>, the connected lines 3 and 4 will not work. So the connected V(3) and V(4) gates remain closed. For OR operation, the constant qubit is |0>. This fixed value will go through all the closed quantum gates and produces |0> to target output (|Q>) (Fig. 5).

There are 2 variable inputs (control (open/close) the gates) and a constant input |0> (will go through gates on the target output line) in OR gate. Here, qubits |A0> and |A1> are used for the gate control and a constant input qubit |0> is on the output line to produce desired output through quantum OR gates of the target output line.

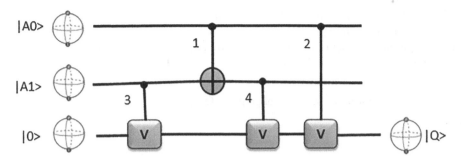

Fig. 5. Quantum OR Operation

3 Proposed System Architecture

3.1 General Organization of PLA Using Block Diagram

Quantum PLA is a programmable logic device that has both Programmable Quantum AND array & Programmable Quantum OR array. Hence, it is the most adaptable PLD. The block diagram of Quantum PLA is displayed in the following figure (Fig. 6).

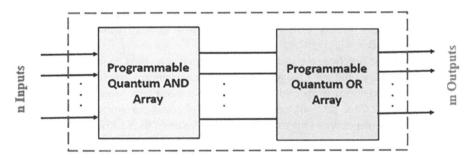

Fig. 6. Block Diagram of Quantum PLA

Here, the inputs of Quantum AND operations are programmable. That implies every Quantum AND activity has both ordinary and supplemented inputs of variables. So, based on the requirement, we can program any of those inputs. So, we can create only the required product terms by utilizing these Quantum AND operations. Here, Quantum OR operations inputs are also programmable. So, any number of required product terms can be programmed, since all the outputs of Quantum AND operations are applied as inputs to each Quantum OR operation. Therefore, the outputs of Quantum PAL will be in the form of a sum of products form.

3.2 Proposed Design Architecture of Quantum PLA

A Quantum PLA designed is proposed with three inputs ($|A>$, $|B>$, $|C>$) and three outputs ($|F1>$, $|F2>$, $|F3>$). The supplement of three inputs is acquired through Quantum

NOT operation. Thus, the realization has six input lines (input with its complement). The given expression has five product terms and so the fuses are placed in the relating literals to get the product terms. The input-output mapping of Quantum PLA is shown in Table 6

Table 6. Input-Output of proposed Quantum PLA Operations

IA>	IB>	IC>	IF1>	IF2>	IF3>
I0>	I0>	I0>	I0>	I1>	I0>
I0>	I0>	I1>	I1>	I0>	I0>
I0>	I1>	I0>	I0>	I1>	I1>
I0>	I1>	I1>	I1>	I0>	I1>
I1>	I0>	I0>	I0>	I1>	I1>
I1>	I0>	I1>	I0>	I1>	I1>
I1>	I1>	I0>	I1>	I0>	I0>
I1>	I1>	I1>	I1>	I0>	I0>

K map is used to reduce the function IF1>, IF2>, and IF3> that produced outputs IF1> = IA>.IB> + IA'>.IC>; IF2> = IA'>.IC'> + IA>.IB'> and IF3> = IA'>.IB> + IA>.IB'>.

The given three functions are in the sum of products structure. In the given Boolean functions IF1>, IF2>, and IF3> the number of product terms are two. IA>.IB'> product are use in both functions IF2> and IF3>. Thus, we need five programmable Quantum AND gates & three programmable Quantum OR gates for delivering those three functions. The corresponding Quantum PLA is displayed in the following Fig. 7.

3.3 Outputs of Proposed Quantum PLA

According to the proposed design of Quantum PLA, it produced following three output qubits for each combination of inputs qubits:

i. For input Qubits IA>, IB>, IC> = I0>, I0>, I0> function IF2> produce output I1> and IF1> and IF3> produce output I0>.
ii. For input Qubits IA>, IB>, IC> = I0>, I0>, I1> function IF1> produce output I1> and IF2> and IF3> produce output I0>.
iii. For input Qubits IA>, IB>, IC> = I0>, I1>, I0> function IF2> and IF3> produce output I1> and I IF1> produce output I0>.
iv. For input Qubits IA>, IB>, IC> = I0>, I1>, I1> function IF1> and IF3> produce output I1> and IF2> produce output I0>.
v. For input Qubits IA>, IB>, IC> = I1>, I0>, I0> function IF2> and IF3> produce output I1> and IF1> produce output I0>.
vi. For input Qubits IA>, IB>, IC> = I1>, I0>, I1> function IF2> and IF3> produce output I1> and IF1> produce output I0>.

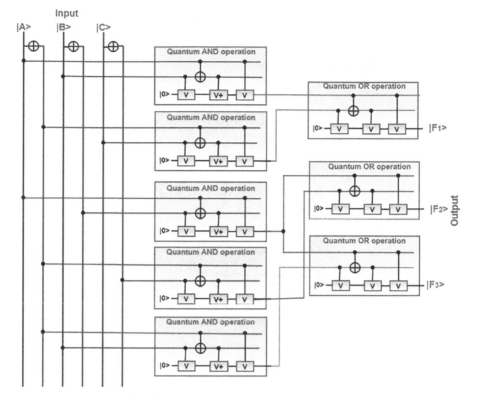

Fig. 7. Quantum Programmable Logic Array

vii. For input Qubits |A>, |B>, |C> = |1>, |1>, |0> function |F1> produce output |1> and |F2> and |F3> produce output |0>.

viii. For input Qubits |A>, |B>, |C> = |1>, |1>, |1> function |F1> produce output |1> and |F2> and |F3> produce output |0>.

4 Design Algorithm of Proposed Quantum PLA

The working procedure of the proposed Quantum PLA diagram is given "Algorithm-2". Two main functions are used to define the functionality of the Quantum PLA like DO_Quant_AND(| A>, | B>), 1. DO_Quant_OR(| A>, | B>).

Here, we use three main inputs (| A>, | B> and | C>) three output |F1>, |F2>, and |F3>. If the total number of inputs bits is n then O (n) is the run time complexity of this algorithm.

Algorithm: Quantum-based PLA

Input: | A >, | B>, | C>

Outputs: |F1>, |F2>, |F3>

1. *Begin*
2. *Procedure DO_Quant_PLA(| A >, | B>, | C>)*
3. $|A'> <- DO\_Quant\_NOT(|A>);$
4. $|B'> <- DO\_Quant\_NOT(|B>);$
5. $|C'> <- DO\_Quant\_NOT(|C>);$
6. $| P1> <- DO\_Quant\_AND (|A>,| B>);$
7. $| P2> <- DO\_Quant\_AND (|A'>,| C>);$
8. $| F1> <- DO\_Quant\_OR (|P1>, |P2>);$
9. $| P3> <- DO\_Quant\_AND (|A>,| B'>);$
10. $| P4> <- DO\_Quant\_AND (|A'>,| C'>);$
11. $| F2> <- DO\_Quant\_OR (|P3>, |P4>);$
12. $| P5> <- DO\_Quant\_AND (|A'>,| B>);$
13. $| F3> <- DO\_Quant\_OR (|P3>, |P5>);$
14. *end procedure*
15. *End*
16. *Procedure DO_Quant_AND(| A >, | B >)*
17. *if* $| A > and | B > both are | 0 >$
18. *return* $| 0 >$
19. *else if* $| A > is | 0 > and | B > is | 1 >$
20. $| P > <- PerformVPlusOp(| 1 >);$
21. $| Q > <- PerformVOp(| P >);$
22. $| R > <- PerformNOTOp(| Q >);$
23. *else if* $| A > is | 1 > and | B > is | 0 >$
24. $| P > <- PerformVOp(| 1 >);$
25. $| Q > <- PerformVPlusOp(| P >);$
26. $| R > <- PerformNOTOp(| Q >);$
27. *else if* $| A > and | B > both are | 1 >$
28. $| P > <- PerformVPlusOp(| 1 >);$
29. $| Q > <- PerformVPlusOp(| P >);$
30. $| R > <- PerformNOTOp(| Q >);$
31. *end if*
32. *end procedure*
33. *Procedure DO_Quant_OR(| A >, | B >)*
34. *if* $| A > and | B > both are | 0 >$
35. *return* $| 0 >$
36. *else if* $| A > is | 0 > and | B > is | 1 >$
37. $| P > <- PerformVOp(| 1 >);$
38. $| Q > <- PerformVOp(| P >);$
39. $| R > <- PerformNOTOp(| Q >);$
40. *else if* $| A > is | 1 > and | B > is | 0 >$
41. $| P > <- PerformVOp(| 1 >);$
42. $| Q > <- PerformVOp(| P >);$
43. $| R > <- PerformNOTOp(| Q >);$
44. *else if* $| A > and | B > both are | 1 >$
45. $| P > <- PerformVOp(| 1 >);$
46. $| Q > <- PerformVOp(| P >);$
47. $| R > <- PerformNOTOp(| Q >);$
48. *end if*
49. *end procedure*
50. **Procedure** *DO_Quant_NOT(| X >)*
51. *if* the value of $| X > is | 0 >$
52. *return* $| 1 >$
53. *else return* $| 0 >$
54. *end if*
55. *end procedure*
56. *End*

5 Conclusion

Quantum PCs address a better approach to handle data. They offer a method for breaking what are right now remembered to be unbreakable codes; model complex chemical processes, for example, the way that medications work in the body; reproduce molecule impacts; and answer many inquiries that lie past the capacity of current 'traditional' PCs. In this paper, a Quantum-based PLA is designed using Quantum logic Gates. Developing Quantum based PLA logic circuit might be a new direction of Nano scale computing with an extremely good possibility of implementation in the Quantum field. Quantum-based PLA logic circuits are not restricted to the decrease in the number of the gates based on the additional representation of an additional output state; it likewise empowers circuits to be compacted dependent on inputs. Simulation of quantum systems is possible that is not possible on traditional computers and a quantum computer is many times faster than a classical computer and even a supercomputer.

References

1. Thapliyal, H., Ranganathan, N.: Design of reversible sequential circuits optimizing quantum cost, delay, and garbage outputs. ACM J. Emerg. Technol. Comput. Syst. (JETC) 6(4), 14–29 (2010)
2. Feynman, R.P.: Quantum mechanical computers. Found. Phys. 16(6), 507–531 (1986)
3. Barenco, A., et al.: Elementary gates for quantum computation. Phys. Rev. A 52(5), 3457 (1995)
4. Steane, A.: Quantum computing. Rep. Prog. Phys. 61(2), 117 (1998)
5. Hey, T.: Quantum computing: an introduction. Comput. Control Eng. J. 10(3), 105–112 (1999)
6. Aspuru-Guzik, A., Dutoi, A.D., Love, P.J., Head-Gordon, M.: Simulated quantum computation of molecular energies. Science 309(5741), 1704–1707 (2005)
7. Hempel, C., et al.: Quantum chemistry calculations on a trapped-ion quantum simulator. Phys. Rev. X 8(3), 031022 (2018)
8. Ors, R., Mugel, S., Lizaso, E.: Quantum computing for finance: overview and prospects. Rev. Phys. 4, 100028 (2019)
9. Ciliberto, C., et al.: Quantum machine learning: a classical perspective. Proc. R. Soc. A: Math. Phys. Eng. Sci. 474(2209), 20170551 (2018)
10. Dunjko, V., Briegel, H.J.: Machine learning & artificial intelligence in the quantum domain: a review of recent progress. Rep. Prog. Phys. 81(7), 074001 (2018)
11. Wiseman, H.M., Milburn, G.J.: Quantum theory of optical feedback via homodyne detection. Phys. Rev. Lett. 70, 548–551 (1993)
12. Wiseman, H.M., Milburn, G.J.: Quantum Measurement and Control. Cambridge University Press, Cambridge (2009)
13. Nurdin, H.I., James, M.R., Petersen, I.R.: Coherent quantum lqg control. Automatica 45(8), 1837–1846 (2009)
14. Dong, D., Petersen, I.R.: Quantum control theory and applications: a survey. IET Control Theory Appl. 4(12), 2651–2671 (2010)
15. Kaye, P., Laflamme, R., Mosca, M.: An Introduction to Quantum Computing. Oxford University Press, UK (January 2007). eBook-LinG, ISBN 0-19-857000-7
16. Mohammadi, M., Eshghi, M.: Behavioral description of quantum V and V+ gates to design quantum logic circuits. In: 2008 5th International Multi-Conference on Systems, Signals and Devices, pp. 1–5. IEEE (2008)

17. Knill, E.: Quantum computing with realistically noisy devices. Nature **434**(7029), 39–44 (2005)
18. Ramezani, S.B., Sommers, A., Manchukonda, H.K., Rahimi, S., Amirlatifi, A.: Machine learning algorithms in quantum computing: a survey. In 2020 International Joint Conference on Neural Networks (IJCNN) (pp. 1–8). IEEE (July 2020)
19. DiVincenzo, D.P.: Quantum computation. Science **270**(5234), 255–261 (1995)
20. Van Meter, R., Horsman, D.: A blueprint for building a quantum computer. Commun. ACM **56**(10), 84–93 (2013)
21. National Academies of Sciences, Engineering, and Medicine. Quantum computing: progress and prospects. National Academies Press (2019)

QPROM: Quantum Nanotechnology for Data Storage Using Programmable Read Only Memory

Tamanna Tabassum$^{(\boxtimes)}$ ⓘ, Fatema Akter ⓘ, and Mohammed Nasir Uddin ⓘ

Jagannath University, Dhaka, Bangladesh
tabassum.csejnu@gmail.com

Abstract. Quantum computing has the features of parallel and fast processing capability that makes it unique from other conventional computing systems. It has various peculiar properties, like entanglement, that can be leveraged as a resource to build technology. It is a nanotechnology-based qubit programming where different types of electromagnetic interactions are performed for basic operations as qubits and process information as single photons by recreating the quantum state. Quantum computers are more powerful than classical Turing machines because of their coherent superposition of states. Quantum memories would make massive photonic quantum computing systems possible by allowing coherent manipulation, buffering, and retiming of photonic signals. Though traditional PROM (Programmable Read Only Memory) is a slower memory, quantum computing enables the creation of new types of computers capable of operating with qubits as input states, increasing storage capacity. In this paper, a Quantum-based PROM architecture is proposed using algorithms of quantum-based basic operations.

Keywords: Quantum Computing · Parallel Processing · Qubit · QPROM Architecture

1 Introduction

The smallest feasible discrete unit of any physical attribute, such as energy or matter, is called Quantum. Binary logic, in which everything is represented by the digits 0 and 1, is the foundation of modern computers, and in Quantum computational systems, computation is based on qubits [1]. Quantum computing (Qc) is a branch of computing devoted to developing computer technology based on quantum theory, which explains the behavior of energy and matter at the atomic and subatomic levels. In addition, Qc is a new way of computation that promises to solve computational jobs and algorithms that are too tough to solve using current computing paradigms [2]. Qubits, rather than bits, are used in quantum computing, a parallel world with some similarities and differences.

- Quantum computers have a simplified configuration and limited capacity and processing power. The only equipment that makes it work is a set of qubits [3].

© ICST Institute for Computer Sciences, Social Informatics and Telecommunications Engineering 2023
Published by Springer Nature Switzerland AG 2023. All Rights Reserved
Md. S. Satu et al. (Eds.): MIET 2022, LNICST 491, pp. 447–459, 2023.
https://doi.org/10.1007/978-3-031-34622-4_36

- Quantum systems can be simulated in ways regular computers cannot, perhaps thousands of times quicker [4].
- Easily do exceedingly tricky calculations, such as massive systems of linear equations [5].
- Quantum computers can represent these tremendous issues in enormous multidimensional areas [6].

Since quantum mechanics is reversible, quantum mechanical processes are an excellent option for creating reversible gates, referred to as quantum gates [7]. Following the introduction of quantum computation, it was discovered that some quantum algorithms [8] work significantly quicker than their classical equivalents. These processes, which establish quantum computing as a superior future technology, require quantum storage and gates. The earliest stages toward storing programmed read only memory are quantum logic gates. PROM is a form of Programmable Logic Array that includes a fixed Quantum AND array and a programmable Quantum OR array. Because of the don't care conditions, not all of the minterms are employed in a combinational circuit. Quantum AND gates are followed by programmable Quantum OR gates in the PROM logic device. PROMs are programmable logic devices that are used to create reconfigurable digital circuits. When PROMs are manufactured, they have no specific function but are programmed before use. In this work, PROM is introduced through the use of Quantum computing.

The rest of the paper is formed as follows. Section 2 discusses Quantum computing, Quantum basic Gates, and the structure of Quantum-based PROM (QPROM), the proposed Quantum PROM circuit is introduced in Sect. 3. Section 4 contains an algorithm to create a PROM logic block using Quantum computing. Section 5 brings paper closure.

2 Literature Study

In this section, the fundamentals of Quantum computing, Quantum basic gate concept, and Quantum Programmable Read Only Memory (QPROM) architecture are explicitly explained.

2.1 Quantum Computing

The field of quantum computing started in the 1980s, discovered that some computational issues could be tackled more efficiently with quantum algorithms than with their classical counterparts [9]. Quantum computing uses quantum bits or qubits. It harnesses the unique ability of subatomic particles that allows them to exist in more than one state (i.e., a 1 and a 0 at the same time) [10].

Quantum computers process information differently. Classical computers use transistors, which are either 1 or 0. Quantum computers use qubits, which can be 1 or 0 simultaneously. The number of qubits linked together increases the quantum computing power exponentially. Meanwhile, linking together more transistors only increases power linearly. Quantum computing could contribute significantly to the fields of materials science [11, 12], financial modelling [13], machine learning and artificial intelligence [14, 15]. Another essential field of quantum technology is quantum control [16–19], whose goal is to control physical systems whose behavior is governed by the laws of quantum mechanics.

2.2 Quantum Logic Gates and Operations

A quantum logic gate, called the quantum gate, is a basic quantum circuit operating on a small number of qubits. Based on the systemization of the reversible logic circuits, there are three gates (see Fig. 1) in Quantum Computing, CNOT (Controlled NOT), Con-trolled V and Controlled V+ gates [20].

The input of the NOT gate is only |A1>, and |A0> is the gate control input; that is why it is called the CNOT gate [21]. The output value |Q0> is always the same as the value of input |A0> because this line has no operation. When the control qubit |A0> is |0>, then the gate will close and works as a buffer, and when the control qubit |A0> is |1>, it works as an inverter [22]. The CNOT gate can be described as the gate that maps the basis states of input (|A0>, |A1>) to output (|Q0> = |A0>, & |Q1> = (|A0> XOR |A1>)).

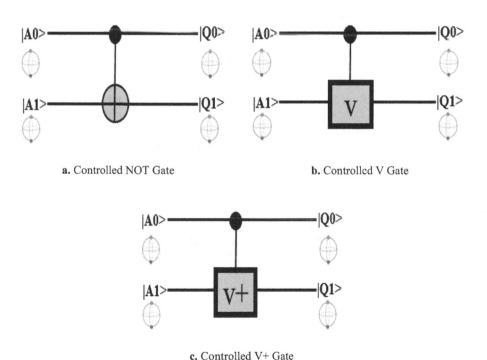

a. Controlled NOT Gate   **b.** Controlled V Gate

c. Controlled V+ Gate

Fig. 1. Quantum logic gates

The quantum V gates are necessary for constructing universal gates for synthesizing reversible circuits (the number of inputs and outputs are equal). The input of the V gate is only qubit |A1>, and the qubit |A0> is the control input; that is why it is called the Controlled V gate [23].

The Controlled V+ gate is the conjugate transpose of the controlled V gate. The input of the V+ gate is only qubit |A1>, and qubit |A0> is the control input; that is why it is called the Controlled V+ gate.

Quantum computing facilitates the execution of all fundamental operations, including AND, OR, NOT, XOR, and XNOR. "Algorithm 1" represents the basic OR operation using Quantum computing. While doing OR operation, CNOT and V gates need to be performed (see Fig. 2).

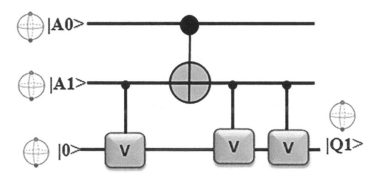

Fig. 2. Quantum based OR operation

In this OR operation, there are two variable inputs (control (open/close) the gates) and a constant input |0> (will go through gates on the target output line). Here, qubits |A0> and |A1> are used for the gate control, and a constant input qubit |0> is on the output line to produce desired output through the quantum gates of the target output line (Table 1).

Algorithm 1 Quantum-based OR Operation

1. *Begin*
2. *Procedure DO_Quant_OR(| A >, | B >)*
3.   *if | A > and | B > both are | 0 >*
4.   *return | 0 >*
5.   *else if | A > is | 0 > and | B > is | 1 >*
6.   *| P > <- PerformVOp(| 1 >);*
7.   *| Q > <- PerformVOp(| P >);*
8.   *| R > <- PerformNOTOp(| Q >);*
9.   *else if | A > is | 1 > and | B > is | 0 >*
10.   *| P > <- PerformVOp(| 1 >);*
11.   *| Q > <- PerformVOp(| P >);*
12.   *| R > <- PerformNOTOp(| Q >);*
13.   *else if | A > and | B > both are | 1 >*
14.   *| P > <- PerformVOp(| 1 >);*
15.   *| Q > <- PerformVOp(| P >);*
16.   *| R > <- PerformNOTOp(| Q >);*
17.   *end if*
18.   *end procedure*
19. *End*

Table 1. Truth table of Quantum OR Circuit

Input-1 (|A0>)	Input-2 (|A1>)	Output (|Q1>)
|0>	|0>	|0>
|0>	|1>	|1>
|1>	|0>	|1>
|1>	|1>	|1>

3 Proposed Quantum Based PROM Architecture

3.1 General Organization of Quantum Programmable Read Only Memory (QPROM)

Unlike traditional computer memory, the states saved in quantum memory can be in a qubit, providing far more practical flexibility in quantum algorithms than traditional information storage. A basic block diagram of Quantum 4-to-2 PROM is illustrated (see Fig. 3). Hence, QPROM is the most flexible PLA with a programmable Quantum AND array & Programmable Quantum OR array [24].

Quantum 4-to-2 PROM Block Diagram for functions |F1> and |F2>

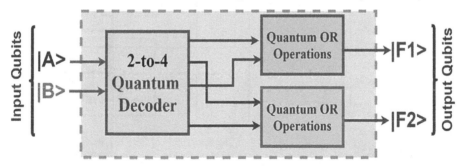

Fig. 3. General Organization of Quantum 4-to-2 PROM

Consider a Quantum 4-to-2 PROM general organization of block diagram (Fig. 3), and the unit consists of 4 words of 2 qubits (|A> and |B>) each. There are only two input qubits in quantum 4-to-2 PROM because $2^2 = 4$, and we can specify four addresses or minterms with two-qubit variables. To perform minterms of four addresses, a Quantum 2-to-4 decoder and Quantum OR operations for minterms |F1> = $\sum$ (0, 2) and |F2> = $\sum$ (1, 3) are required.

A Quantum 2-to-4 decoder is a combinational logic circuit illustrated (see Fig. 4). Illustrated in "Table 2" Quantum 2-to-4 decoder, the output |D0> = |A'>. |B'> evaluates |1> when the input sequences |A> and |B> are |0>. The output |D1> = |A>. |B'> evaluates |1> when the input qubit |B> is |0> and A is |1>. The output |D2> = |A>.

452   T. Tabassum et al.

|B'> evaluates |1> when the input qubit |B> is |1> and A is |1> and finally |D3>
evaluated |1> when both the input qubits are |1>.

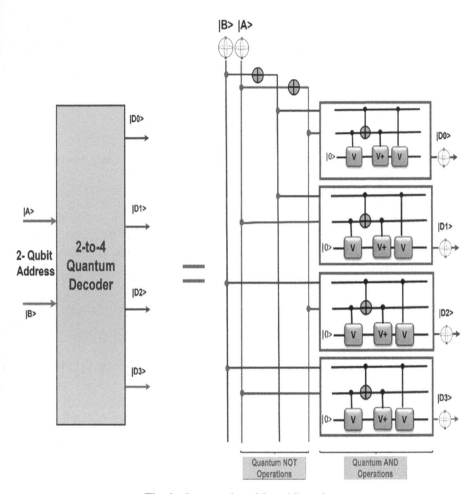

Fig. 4. Quantum based 2-to-4 Decoder

Table 2. Truth table of Quantum Decoder Circuit

IB>	IA>	ID0>	ID1>	ID2>	ID3>
I0>	I0>	I1>	I0>	I0>	I0>
I0>	I1>	I0>	I1>	I0>	I0>
I1>	I0>	I0>	I0>	I1>	I0>
I1>	I1>	I0>	I0>	I0>	I1>

Algorithm 2 Quantum-based Decoder Operation

1. *Begin*
2. **Procedure DO_ Quant _Decoder(|A>, |B>)**
3. |D0> <- **DO_Quant_AND(** |A '>, |B '>);
4. |D1> <- **DO_ Quant _AND(** |A>, |B '>);
5. |D2> <- **DO_ Quant _AND(** |A '>, |B>);
6. |D3> <- **DO_ Quant _AND(** |A>, |B>);
7. *end* Procedure
8. **Procedure DO_Quant_AND(| A >, | B >)**
9.   *if* | A > and | B > both are | 0 >
10.   *return* | 0 >
11.   *else if* | A > is | 0 > and | B > is | 1 >
12. | P > <- **PerformVPlusOp(** | 1 >);
13. | Q > <- **PerformVOp(** | P >);
14. | R > <- **PerformNOTOp(** | Q >);
15.   *else if* | A > is | 1 > and | B > is | 0 >
16. | P > <- **PerformVOp(** | 1 >);
17. | Q > <- **PerformVPlusOp(** | P >);
18. | R > <- **PerformNOTOp(** | Q >);
19.   *else if* | A > and | B > both are | 1 >
20. | P > <- **PerformVPlusOp(** | 1 >);
21. | Q > <- **PerformVPlusOp(** | P >);
22. | R > <- **PerformNOTOp(** | Q >);
23.   *end if*
24. *end* procedure
25. *End*

OR Operations. To perform the output qubits of F1 and F2 of Quantum 4-to-2 PROM, the Quantum decoder output qubits will operate in the sum of minterms form (see Fig. 5), where F1 and F2 will $\sum$ (0, 2), (1, 3) simultaneously.

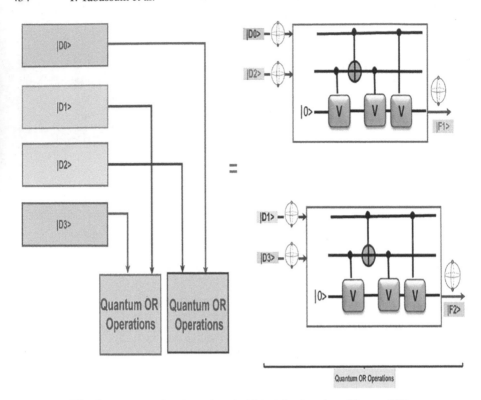

Fig. 5. Quantum OR Operations in PROM for functions |F1> and |F2>

To perform |F1> output qubit, first |D0> and |D2> will go through quantum OR operation, and for |F2> output qubit, |D1> and |D3> will go through quantum OR operation to generate the desired output qubit. The overall architecture of Quantum Based PROM is illustrated (see Fig. 6).

3.2 Working Procedure of Proposed QPROM

According to the truth table of Quantum 4-to-2 PROM (see in Table 3), it is necessary to do the following operations to perform desired output qubits:

[i] For input Qubits |A>, |B> = |0>, |0>, |D0> line will be open. So, the value of |D0> will 1 and |D1> to |D3> will |0>. For the output of |F1>, the quantum OR operation will perform between |D0> and |D2> that produces |1>, and for |F2>, perform quantum OR Operations between |D1> and |D3>and generates |0>.

[ii] For input Qubits |A>, |B> = |1>, |0>, |D1> line will be open. So, the value of |D1> will 1 and |D0>, |D2> and |D3> will |0>. For the output of |F1>, the quantum OR operation will perform between |D0> and |D2> that produces |0> and for |F2>, perform quantum OR Operations between |D1> and |D3>, generates |1>.

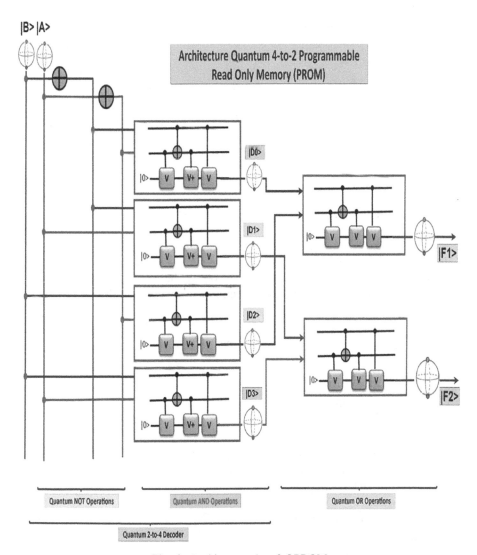

Fig. 6. Architecture 4-to-2 QPROM

[iii] For input Qubits |A>, |B> = |0>, |1>, |D2> line will be open. So, the value of |D2> will 1 and |D0>, |D1> and |D3> will |0>. For the output of |F1>, the quantum OR operation will perform between |D0> and |D2> that produces |1> and for |F2>, perform quantum OR Operations between |D1> and |D3>, generates |0>.

[iv] For input Qubits |A>, |B> = |1>, |1>, |D3> line will be open. So, the value of |D3> will 1 and |D0> to |D2> will |0>. For the output of |F1>, the quantum OR operation will perform between |D0> and |D2> that produces |0> and for |F2>, perform OR Operations between |D1> and |D3>, generates |1>.

Table 3. Truth table of Quantum 4-to-2 PROM

|B>	|A>	|F1>	|F2>
|0>	|0>	|1>	|0>
|0>	|1>	|0>	|1>
|1>	|0>	|1>	|0>
|1>	|1>	|0>	|1>

4   QPROM Algorithm

The working procedure of the proposed QPROM architecture is given (see in Algorithm 3). Here, we use two main inputs (|A> and |B>) and two outputs |F1> and |F2>. |A> and |B> contain qubits, and |F1> and |F2> also give the result in a qubit. If the total number of inputs bits is n, then O (n) is the run time complexity of this algorithm.

Algorithm 3 Quantum-based Read Only Memory (QPROM)

Input: |A>, |B>
Output: |F1>, |F2>;
The value of |A>, |B>, |F1>, |F2> can be |0> or |1>
   1. **Begin**
   2. **while** i equals to 1 to n **do**
   3. |P> = **DO_Quant_Decoder**(|Ai>, |Bi>); // Decoder generates |D0> - |D3>
   4. |F1> <- **DO_Quant_OR**(|D0>, |D2>);
   5. |F2.> <- **DO_Quant_OR**(|D1>, |D3>);
   6. **end while**
   7. Procedure **DO_Quant_Decoder**(|A>, | B>)

8. $|D0>$ <- **DO_Quant_AND(** $|A'>$, $|B'>$ **);**

9. $|D1>$ <- **DO_Quant_AND(** $|A>$, $|B'>$ **);**

10. $|D2>$ <- **DO_Quant_AND(** $|A'>$, $|B>$ **);**

11. $|D3>$ <- **DO_Quant_AND(** $|A>$, $|B>$ **);**

12. **end** *Procedure*

13. *Procedure* **DO_Quant_OR(** $|X>$, $|Y>$ **)**

14. **end** *Procedure*

15. *Procedure* **DO_Quant_AND (** $|A>$, $|B>$ **)**

16. **end** *Procedure*

17. *Procedure* **PerformVOp(** $|X>$ **);**

18.   *if the value of* $|X>$ *is* $|0>$

19.   **return** $|v>$

20.   **else if** *the value of* $|X>$ *is* $|1>$

21.   **return** $|V>$

22.   **else if** *the value of* $|X>$ *is* $|v>$

23.   **return** $|1>$

24.   **else if** *the value of* $|X>$ *is* $|V>$

25.   **return** $|0>$

26.   **else if** *the value of* $|X>$ *is* $|w>$

27.   **return** $|0>$

28.   **else if** *the value of* $|X>$ *is* $|W>$

29.   **return** $|1>$

30.   **end if**

31. **end** *procedure*

32. *Procedure* **PerformVPlusOp(** $|Y>$ **);**

33.   *if the value of* $|Y>$ *is* $|0>$

34.   **return** $|w>$

35.   **else if** *the value of* $|Y>$ *is* $|1>$

36.   **return** $|W>$

37.   **else if** *the value of* $|Y>$ *is* $|v>$

38.   **return** $|0>$

39.   **else if** *the value of* $|Y>$ *is* $|V>$

40.   **return** $|1>$

41.   **else if** *the value of* $|Y>$ *is* $|w>$

42.   **return** $|1>$

43.   **else if** *the value of* $|Y>$ *is* $|W>$

44.   **return** $|0>$

45.   **end if**

46. **end** *Procedure*

47. **End**

5   Conclusion

Quantum computers offer a new way to process information: they can crack what are currently thought to be unbreakable codes, model complex computational processes, simulate particle collisions, and answer questions beyond the capabilities of current 'classical' computers. This paper uses Quantum logic Gates to develop a quantum-based PROM for storage. Developing quantum-based PROM logic circuits could be a new avenue in Nanoscale computing, with a high chance of being implemented in the Quantum Storage sector. The proposed QPROM logic circuits enable circuits to be compressed depending on inputs and reduce the number of gates due to the added encoding of an additional output state. A quantum computer may simulate suggested quantum storage systems in ways that ordinary computers cannot, and a quantum computer is several orders of magnitude faster than a conventional computer or even a supercomputer.

References

1. Mohammadi, M., Eshghi, M.: Behavioral description of quantum V and V+ gates to design quantum logic circuits. In: 5th International Multi-Conference on Systems, Signals and Devices, pp. 1–5. IEEE (2008)
2. National Academies of Sciences, Engineering, and Medicine. Quantum computing: progress and prospects. National Academies Press (2019)
3. Saffman, M.: Quantum computing with atomic qubits and Rydberg interactions: progress and challenges. J. Phys. B: At. Mol. Opt. Phys. 49(20), 202001 (2016)
4. Van Meter, R., Horsman, D.: A blueprint for building a quantum computer. Commun. ACM 56(10), 84–93 (2013)
5. Ramezani, S.B., Sommers, A., Manchukonda, H.K., Rahimi, S., Amirlatifi, A.: Machine learning algorithms in quantum computing: A survey. In: 2020 International Joint Conference on Neural Networks (IJCNN), pp. 1–8. IEEE (2020)
6. Hempel, C., et al.: Quantum chemistry calculations on a trapped-ion quantum simulator. Phys. Rev. X 8, 031022 (2018)
7. Ors, R., Mugel, S., Lizaso, E.: Quantum computing for finance: overview and prospects. Rev. Phys. 4, 100028 (2019)
8. Ciliberto, C., et al.: Quantum machine learning: a classical perspective. Proc. R. Soc. A: Math. Phys. Eng. Sci. 474(2209), 20170551 (2018)
9. Dunjko, V., Briegel, H.J.: Machine learning & artificial intelligence in the quantum domain: a review of recent progress. Rep. Prog. Phys. 81(7), 074001 (2018)
10. Gambetta, J.M., Chow, J.M., Steffen, M.: Building logical qubits in a superconducting quantum computing system. npj Quant. Inf. 3(1), 1–7 (2017)
11. Wright, K., et al.: Benchmarking an 11-qubit quantum computer. Nat. Commun. 10(1), 1–6 (2019)
12. Barenco, A., et al.: Elementary gates for quantum computation. Phys. Rev. A 52(5), 3457 (1995)
13. Kaye, P., Laflamme, R., Mosca, M.: An Introduction to Quantum Computing. Oxford University Press (2006). Jan 2007eBook-LinG, ISBN 0-19-857000-7
14. Gibney, E.: Hello quantum world! Google publishes landmark quantum supremacy claim. Nature 574(7779), 461–463 (2019)
15. Hey, T.: Quantum computing: an introduction. Comput. Control Eng. J. 10(3), 105–112 (1999)

16. Aspuru-Guzik, A., Dutoi, A.D., Love, P.J., Head-Gordon, M.: Simulated quantum computation of molecular energies. Science **309**(5741), 1704–1707 (2005)
17. Travaglione, B.C., Nielsen, M.A., Wiseman, H.M., Ambainis, A.: ROM-based computation: quantum versus classical. arXiv preprint quant-ph/0109016 (2001)
18. Wiseman, H.M., Milburn, G.J.: Quantum Measurement and Control. Cambridge University Press, Cambridge (2009)
19. Nurdin, H.I., James, M.R., Petersen, I.R.: Coherent quantum LQG control. Automatica **45**(8), 1837–1846 (2009)
20. Thapliyal, H., Ranganathan, N.: Design of reversible sequential circuits optimizing quantum cost, delay, and garbage outputs. ACM J. Emerg. Technol. Comput. Syst. (JETC) **6**(4), 1–31 (2010)
21. Wang, C., et al.: Towards practical quantum computers: transmon qubit with a lifetime approaching 0.5 milliseconds. npj Quant. Inf. **8**(1), 1–6 (2022)
22. Dong, D., Petersen, I.R.: Quantum control theory and applications: a survey. IET Control Theory Appl. **4**(12), 2651–2671 (2010)
23. Hadzihasanovic, A., Ng, K.F., Wang, Q.: Two complete axiomatisations of pure-state qubit quantum computing. In: Proceedings of the 33rd Annual ACM/IEEE Symposium on Logic in Computer Science, pp. 502–511 (2018)
24. Blum, E., Castillo-Martin, M., Rosenberg, M.: Survey on the Security of the Quantum ROM (2019)

Analytical Modeling of Multi-junction Solar Cell Using SiSn Alloy

Tanber Hasan Shemanto$^{(\boxtimes)}$ and Lubaba Binte Billah

Military Institute of Science and Technology, Dhaka, Bangladesh
hasantanber519@gmail.com

Abstract. Modeling of Si_xSn_{1-x} alloy as a middle and bottom layer in a multi-junction solar cell requires the optical band gap of 0.81 eV and 0.64 eV respectively. MATLAB/Simulink is used to simulate an analogous circuit-based model, which aids in the presentation of a detailed study on the performance characteristics of Si_xSn_{1-x} p-n junction solar cell. From the simulation, a detailed analysis of the dependencies of short circuit current density (J_{sc}), open-circuit voltage (V_{oc}), fill factor (FF) and conversion efficiency (η) has been illustrated. It also shows the effect of energy band-gap, E_g on $P - V$ characteristics and $I - V$ characteristics of MJSC. The estimated results revealed that the p-n junction solar cell using $Si/Si_{0.88}Sn_{0.12}/Si_{0.81}Sn_{0.19}$ gives $J_{sc} = 35$ mA/cm^2, $V_{oc} =$ 1.38V and the maximum efficiency $\eta = 32.36\%$. With proper design and research, Si_xSn_{1-x} may be offered as a promising contender for future high-efficiency, low-cost solar cells to meet the forthcoming energy need.

Keywords: MJSC · Short circuit current density · Si_xSn_{1-x} · Conversion efficiency · Open circuit voltage · MATLAB/Simulink

1 Introduction

In the last decade, photo-voltaic industry has been rapidly developed and solar cells with high conversion efficiency have been implemented. Silicon (Si) has been studied extensively for quite a long time and is the most often utilized material for photovoltaic systems on a large scale. The material band-gap is 1.12 eV at 300 K, this makes Si transparent to low-energy photons while wasting surplus energy (above the band-gap) from high-energy photons which limits the conversion efficiency of silicon solar cells to 31% [1]. Because of this, only certain portions of the sun's spectrum are able to be absorbed, and the extra energy from higher-energy photons that are absorbed ends up dissipated as heat due to the action of electron phonon scattering. Furthermore, silicon has a low absorption coefficient for a considerable section of the solar spectrum owing to its indirect nature. One approach for increasing conversion efficiency is to combine semiconductor absorbers with numerous band-gaps that collect photons from

© ICST Institute for Computer Sciences, Social Informatics and Telecommunications Engineering 2023
Published by Springer Nature Switzerland AG 2023. All Rights Reserved
Md. S. Satu et al. (Eds.): MIET 2022, LNICST 491, pp. 460–471, 2023.
https://doi.org/10.1007/978-3-031-34622-4_37

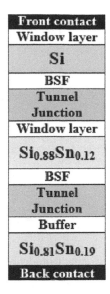

Fig. 1. Schematic illustration of the proposed $Si/Si_{0.88}Sn_{0.12}/$ $Si_{0.81}Sn_{0.19}$ MJSC.

various spectrum areas, thereby circumventing the Shockley-Queisser limit for single band-gap absorbent devices in the process [2].

In order to better utilize the solar spectrum and to achieve higher efficiency, multi-junction solar cells instead of single junctions were developed [3]. Indium phosphide (InP), gallium indium phosphide (AlGaInP) and gallium arsenide (GaAs) are good III-V materials for making solar cells and get up to 35 percent efficiency. This type of solar cell, however, is not cost effective for terrestrial applications due to the high production costs and lack of availability [4]. A key goal of photovoltaic researchers has been to minimize the levelized energy cost by developing high-performance solar cells that are also cost-effective (LCOE). Silicon based solar cells have practically saturated at an efficiency of 25%, but III-V compound semiconductor based solar cells have showed steady performance improvement at 1% (absolute) rise every year, with a recent record efficiency of 44.7 percent. As a result, the integration of high-efficiency III-V multi-junction solar cells on substantially cheaper and larger area Si substrates has recently emerged to meet future LCOE road maps.

A lack of III-V materials such as In and Ga, and the use of expensive substrates, has made material cost a major concern. CMOS substrates from Si have led to low-cost, industry-standard processing methods, which have led to silicon's rise to prominence. In contrast, Si has an indirect band gap, a weak absorption coefficient, and lattice mismatching with the majority of other semiconductors [13]. Addressing this issue, Yang et al. [14] proposed a three-terminal design where a quite thick AlGaAs buffer layer is to be grown over an active Si substrate. However, efficiency of this approach was found below 20% which pullbacks it's further development. Few years later, Taguchi et al. [15] implemented a four

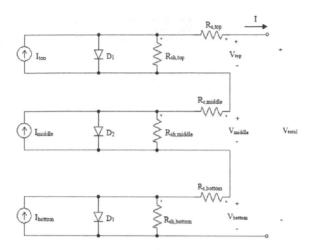

Fig. 2. Single diode equivalent circuit model of a triple-junction solar cell.

terminal design similar to the Yang et. al. [14] structure by growing high quality *GaAs* cell over GaAs substrate and then passed it on to a Si substrate. Unfortunately, this approach was also unsuccessful to attain more than 19% efficiency. Geisz et al. further investigated the two-terminal designs. A lattice-matched process using nitrides [16] and a lattice-mismatched approach were both used as well as graded buffers for strain relaxation that minimized bulk defect density [17]. Later that year, 17% efficiency under AM1.5G spectrum was attained by Lueck et al. [18] following similar approaches. Reasonable advancement was made by the aforesaid approaches. However, subjective to material quality considering high defect densities, there were some limitations that affected the overall efficiencies in a negative manner.

To overcome these limitations and to make a high efficiency solar cell, elements like Germanium (Ge) or Tin (Sn) can be used to make an alloy with silicon. Principally, it is not expected that the indirect nature of silicon will be changed by alloying silicon with tin [3]. Although, strained structures such as strained SiSn super lattices [5] or strained SiSn interfaces are observed to reveal direct transitions. However, as cited in [6], epitaxial tin deposition without a SiSn buffer layer results in lasing from the direct gap transition.

In addition, if it is possible to create a stable form of tin, this could provide an alternative to the materials currently used in solar cell production that is as effective as conventional solar cells based on silicon while also being non-toxic and safer, not requiring a significant amount of energy input, and being much cheaper and easier to manufacture on a mass scale. [7]. As an optically active material, $Si_xSn_{[1-x]}$ alloy makes a very good choice as its potential applications for optoelectronics and photo-voltaics which can be integrated with silicon technology. Using theoretical calculations, an energy band gap is predicted for binary silicon-tin compounds that is lower than that of silicon. It becomes direct with the tensile strain at 0.81 eV and a minimum of 0.46 eV [8].

Despite this, these models are mathematical in nature and so cannot be utilized directly in a circuit simulator. This is despite the fact that circuit simulation is now highly significant for a wide variety of applications, one of which is the investigation of PV systems. In order to accomplish this goal, this work presents a scalable model of a PV cell that is developed from a model with five parameters. After the mathematical model has been defined, the equations are interpreted from the perspective of a circuit, and then an electrical circuit is generated from that interpretation. In addition to this, it is possible to build it in a typical circuit simulator since it just makes use of fundamental analog components. The rest of the study follows Sect. 2, which discusses an analogous circuit for the suggested model. Following that, The analytical modeling of Si_xSn_{1-x} MJSC is articulated in Sect. 3. The outcomes of this study and the closing remarks are discussed in Sects. 4, 5 and 6.

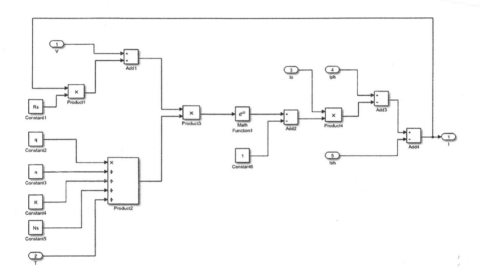

Fig. 3. MATLAB/Simulink model of the Load Current of a solar cell, I.

2   Equivalent Circuit of Proposed Model

Figure 1 represents the proposed schematic illustration of $Si/Si_{0.88}Sn_{0.12}/Si_{0.81}$ $Sn_{0.19}$ multi junction solar cell. With a view to attain the required band gap, middle and bottom layers are designed with different composition of Si_xSn_{1-x} alloy. Highly doped tunnel junctions are used to interconnect these sub-cells in series to eventually minimize electric resistivity and achieve a high optical transmission capability. It also helps to obtain a high peak tunneling current density between the sub cells. There is a stacking of junctions and the highest band-gap sub-cell is placed at the top of the solar cell so that the highest energy photons

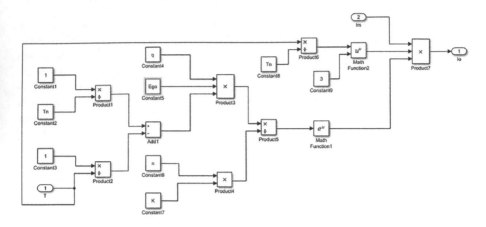

Fig. 4. MATLAB/Simulink model of the Saturation Current, I_o.

can be absorbed. The other sub-cells are placed in decreasing order of the band-gap in order to capture the photons with a lower energy level. As each sub-cell is optimized, the overall goal is to maximize light absorption from the incident spectrum. In addition, the buffer layer, the window layer and the back surface field layers are included in the sub cells so as to lessen the surface recombination velocity and the dispersion of charge carriers in the tunnel junctions. [9]. The thickness of the buffer layer and the window layer is presumed to be 6 nm [19] and [20] 5 nm respectively. As buffer layer, window layer, rear surface field layer, and front surface field layer, we may use $AlInP$, $InGaP$, $AlGaInP$, and $SiSn$ alloy respectively. It is important to consider lattice mismatch while choosing the material for these layers. For quick passage of carriers across these layers, it should be heavily doped. An equivalent circuit of the proposed multi junction solar cell which consists of current sources, diodes, shunt and series resistances is shown in Fig. 2. It can be considered as a series connection between three single junctions.

2.1   Tunnel Junction

In order to achieve a low electrical resistance, a high optical transmission, and a high peak tunneling current density, successive junctions are connected with each other by inserting a tunnel junction between them. Following is the voltage-current characteristic equation of a tunnel junction in a MJSC.

$$J_{total} = \frac{V_t}{V_p} J_p exp^{(1-\frac{V_t}{V_p})} + J_v exp^{A_2(V_t-V_v)} + J_s exp^{(\frac{qV_t}{KT})-1} \tag{1}$$

where J_p is the peak current density, V_t is the corresponding total voltage, V_p is the corresponding peak voltage, J_v is the peak valley current density, V_v is the peak valley voltage and A_2 is the excess current density.

2.2   Short Circuit Current Density (J_{sc})

All sub-cells in MJSC are in series connection and they act as a current source. The smallest current go through the sub cells is considered as the resultant current. The least current is produced by the sub-cell that has a lower bandgap. And it limits the overall current. So, MJSC's resultant current is defined by:

$$J_{sc} = min(J_{sc.i}) \tag{2}$$

2.3   Open-Circuit Voltage (V_{oc})

Open circuit voltage is regarded as the most significant amount of energy that can be recovered from a solar cell. The MJSC method of calculating open circuit voltage involves adding the open-circuit voltages of all of the junctions in the circuit.

$$V_{oc} = sum_{i=1}^{n}(V_i) \tag{3}$$

Here, n represents the Junction number.

3   Analytical Modeling of $Si_x Sn_{1-x}$ MJSC

Single junction solar cell's equivalent circuit contains a series resistance (R_s), a current source, a diode and a shunt resistance (R_{sh}). The load current of the circuit can be given by :

$$I = I_{ph} - I_o(exp^{\frac{q(V+IR_s)}{nKN_sT}} - 1) - I_{sh} \tag{4}$$

Here, I_{ph}, I, q, V, K, T, η and N_s represents photo-current, diode saturation current, the voltage across the diode, Boltzmann's constant, diode's ideal factor and the number of the cell respectively. According to Eq. 4, a single-junction solar cell's load current is shown in Fig. 3 by the MATLAB/Simulink model. This model contains several sub-systems. One sub-system is photo-current, I_{ph}. According to Eq. 5, it is dependent on the temperature & the solar radiation:

$$I_{ph} = \frac{G}{1000}[I_{sc} + K_i(T - 298)] \tag{5}$$

Here, I_{sc}= Cell's short circuit current at $25\,^{\circ}C$ and $1\,kW/m^2$, K_i = Temperature co-efficient of short circuit current (0.0032 A $^{\circ}C$), T= Cell's temperature (K) and G= Solar radiation (W/m^2).Another sub-system (Fig. 4) is saturation current density, I_0 according to the Eq. 6 [10].

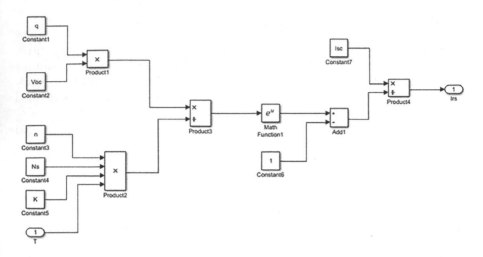

Fig. 5. MATLAB/Simulink model of Temperature dependent Reverse saturation Current, I_{rs}.

$$I_o = I_{rs}(\frac{T}{T_n})^3 exp[\frac{qE_{go}}{nK}(\frac{1}{T_n} - \frac{1}{T})] \tag{6}$$

In this equation, I_0 represents the diode saturation current, $I_{[rs]}$ represents the reverse saturation current, T_n represents the reference temperature, and $E_{[go]}$ represents the band-gap energy. In order to calculate reverse saturation current $I_{[rs]}$, we use Eq. 5.

$$I_{rs} = \frac{I_{sc}}{exp(\frac{qV_{oc}}{nN_sKT}) - 1} \tag{7}$$

where the open circuit voltage is V_{oc}. And also, I_{sh} in Eq. 4 which is the shunt current, is calculated as follows [11]:

$$I_{sh} = \frac{V + IR_s}{R_{sh}} \tag{8}$$

4   Result and Discussions

Following the design of all essential subsystems, all subsystems are linked in accordance with the design for simulation purposes. The suggested solar cell's MATLAB/Simulink model is shown in Fig. 6.

Table 1. Calculated Parameters From Theoretical Simulation.

Parameters	$E_g(eV)$	$I_{sc}(A)$	$V_{oc}(V)$
Si	1.12	3.5	0.6
$Si_{0.88}Sn_{0.12}$	0.81	7.7	0.48
$Si_{0.81}Sn_{0.19}$	0.64	7.7	0.3
Resultant	-	3.5	1.38

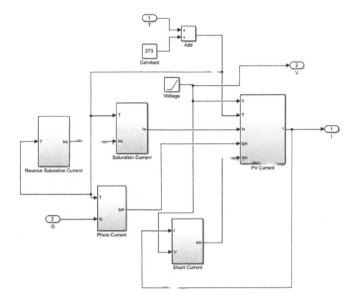

Fig. 6. MATLAB/Simulink model of the proposed Solar Cell.

For our designed solar cell, we simulated in MATLAB/Simulink for specific values such as solar radiation $(\beta) = 1000\ W/m^2$ (AM 1.5 one sun), shunt resistance $(R_{sh}) = 200\ \Omega$, cell temperature (T) = $25\,^\circ C$ and series resistance (R_s) = $0.2\ m\Omega$ to observe the P-V characteristic curves and I-V characteristic curves of different junctions.

As we proceed from the top to the bottom layer of our created solar cell, the energy band gap narrows. Short circuit current rises when the energy band gap narrows, as seen in Fig. 7. However, when the energy band-gap (E_g) grows, open-circuit voltage decreases, and vice versa.

Figure 8 shows that in our proposed cell, the maximum power of $Si/Si_{0.88}Sn_{0.12}/Si_{0.81}Sn_{0.19}$ based MJSC grows considerably. The results that are obtained from simulation are shown in Table 1. Table 2 compares the current work to previous work in order to indicate the uniqueness and contribution of the study. When compared to a triple junction solar cell $InAlAs/InGaAsP/InGaAs$ [21], it exhibits remarkable efficiency. It is designed

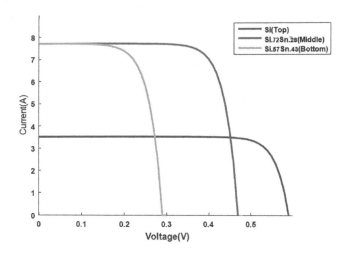

Fig. 7. I-V characteristics of $Si/Si_{0.88}Sn_{0.12}/Si_{0.81}Sn_{0.19}$ multi junction solar cell.

using high-quality materials. Despite its superior efficiency, it would be more expensive than ours. Additionally, the calculation of parameter values and generation of characteristic curves of our model is fairly straightforward and easy. We attempted to use a material that is readily available and affordable. Additionally, efficiency is greater. $SiSn$'s properties are quite close to what we need. And in contrast to previous MATLAB/Simulink models, our suggested model is fairly straightforward and unique. Based on the simulation, our designed multijunction solar cell has a maximum efficiency of 32.36%, and a maximum fill factor of 0.7. It is evident from these results that $SiSn$ alloy is a highly promising material for future high performance solar cells.

Table 2. Performance Comparison with other Existing Cells.

Categories	Technology	$\eta(\%)$	$V_{oc}(V)$	$I_{sc}(A)$
Crystalline silicon cells	Monocrystalline	24.7	0.5	0.8
	Polysilicon	20.3	0.615	8.35
Thin-film solar cells	Amorphous silicon	11.1	0.63	0.089
	CdTe	16.5	0.86	0.029
Multi-junction cells	MJ	40.7	2.6	1.81

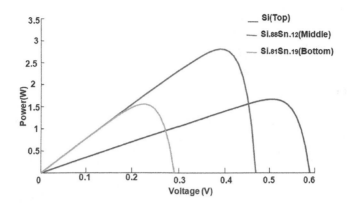

Fig. 8. P-V characteristics of $Si/Si_{0.88}Sn_{0.12}/Si_{0.81}Sn_{0.19}$ multi junction solar cell.

5 Conclusion

In order to study the performance, multi-junction solar cells based on Si_xSn_{1-x} have been designed and simulated in MATLAB/ Simulink. As a matter of fact, this model can be viewed as a tool for predicting and interpreting the behavior of MJSC solar cells. The generation rate and energy band gap of a layer have a significant effect on both the short circuit current density and the open circuit voltage. For $Si/Si_{0.88}Sn_{0.12}/ Si_{0.81}Sn_{0.19}$ solar cell, we observed $J_{sc} = 35.0$ mA/cm^2, $V_{oc} = 1.38$ V, $FF = 0.7$ and the maximum efficiency $\eta = 32.36\%$. Including additional layer of Si_xSn_{1-x} with variable band gap energy (E_g), the efficiency of solar cell increases significantly. Furthermore, Si_xSn_{1-x} material is widely available, it is a cost-effective choice for solar panels. Furthermore, Si_xSn_{1-x} shows direct band gap material properties which is very useful for PV cell. Again, it is both transparent and provides high mobility for carriers at the same time. Si_xSn_{1-x} is a semiconducting alloy that is compatible with silicon technology and ecologically benign, making it a good candidate for future solar cell architectures and technologies.

6 Limitation and Future Work

Future projects or studies should be implemented since there are many intriguing topics to focus on in this subject. The guidelines are as follows: – More wavelengths of the incoming spectrum will be conserved if we add more layers of similar or different semiconductor materials. The greater the absorption, the greater the efficiency. The efficiency, however, gets saturated after a given number of layers. Si is an indirect semiconductor that takes a significant amount of energy to form an electron-hole pair. Increased tin concentration in the SiSn alloy reduces the indirect property, perhaps improving performance. It would be extremely beneficial to employ SiSn alloy as a surface material since it preserves any building surface or aircraft design while also preserving solar energy.

A huge quantity of land is required for a solar plant, which raises the cost. If we can improve efficiency in a smaller cell area, solar plants will be an extremely cost-effective way to make energy in the future.

References

1. Bludau, W., et al.: Temperature Dependence of the Band Gap of Silicon. 1974. Semantic Scholar, https://doi.org/10.1063/1.1663501
2. Shockley, W., Queisser, H.: Detailed Balance Limit of Efficiency of P-n Junction Solar Cells. 1961. Semantic Scholar. https://doi.org/10.1063/1.1736034
3. Takehiko, N., et al.: Improvement of Photoconductivity in Silicon Tin (SiSn) Thin Films. Journal of Non-Crystalline Solids **358**(17), 2281–2284 (2012) ScienceDirect. https://doi.org/10.1016/j.jnoncrysol.2011.12.096
4. Solar Photovoltaic Technology Production - 1st Edition. https://www.elsevier.com/books/solar-photovoltaic-technology-production/sundaram/978-0-12-802953-4. Accessed 25 July 2022
5. Pearsall, T.P., et al.: Structurally Induced Optical Transitions in Ge-Si Superlattices. Phys. Rev. Lett. **58**(7), 729–32 (1987). APS. https://doi.org/10.1103/PhysRevLett.58.729
6. Liu, J., et al.: Ge-on-Si Laser Operating at Room Temperature. Optics Lett. **35**(5), 679–81 (2010). opg.optica.org, https://doi.org/10.1364/OL.35.000679
7. Lead out, Tin in for Cheap Solar Cell — University of Oxford. https://www.ox.ac.uk/news/2014-05-01-lead-out-tin-cheap-solar-cell. Accessed 25 July 2022
8. Jensen, R.V., et al.: Quasiparticle Electronic and Optical Properties of the Si-Sn System. J. Phys. Condensed Matter: An Inst. Phys. J. **23**(34), 345501 (2011). PubMed, https://doi.org/10.1088/0953-8984/23/34/345501
9. Cotal, H., et al.: III-V Multijunction Solar Cells for Concentrating Photovoltaics. Energy Environ. Sci. **2**(2), 174–92 (2009). pubs.rsc.org, https://doi.org/10.1039/B809257E
10. Bouzguenda, M.: MATLAB/Simulink Based Modeling of Photovoltaic Cell. International Journal, Jan. 2012. www.academia.edu, https://www.academia.edu/1976414/MATLAB Simulink Based Modeling of Photovoltaic Cell
11. Rustemli, S., Dincer, F.: Modeling of Photovoltaic Panel and Examining Effects of Temperature in Matlab/Simulink. Elektronika Ir Elektrotechnika **109**(3), 35–40 (2011). eejournal.ktu.lt, https://doi.org/10.5755/j01.eee.109.3.166
12. Untitled.   http://www.ijrer.org/ijrer/index.php/ijrer/article/view/157/pdf. Accessed 25 July 2022
13. Connolly, J.P., et al.: Designing III-V Multijunction Solar Cells on Silicon: III-V on Silicon Multijunction Solar Cells. Progr. Photovolt.: Res. Appl. **22**(7), 810–20 (2014). DOI.org (Crossref), https://doi.org/10.1002/pip.2463
14. Yang, M.-J., Soga, T., Jimbo, T., Umeno, M.: High efficiency monolithic GaAs/Si tandem solar cells grown by MOCVD. In: Proceedings of 1994 IEEE 1st World Conference on Photovoltaic Energy Conversion - WCPEC (A Joint Conference of PVSC, PVSEC and PSEC), 1994, pp. 1847–1850 vol 2, https://doi.org/10.1109/WCPEC.1994.520725
15. 3rd World Conference on Photovoltaic Energy Conversion. In: 3rd World Conference onPhotovoltaic Energy Conversion. In: Proceedings of, 2003, pp. 02-XXXVI (2003)

16. Nrel.gov (2022) https://www.nrel.gov/docs/fy04osti/35323.pdf. [Accessed: 25-Jul- 2022]
17. Geisz, J.F., et al.: Lattice-Mismatched GaAsP Solar Cells Grown on Silicon by OMVPE. 2006 IEEE 4th World Conference on Photovoltaic Energy Conference, IEEE, 2006, pp. 772–75. DOI.org (Crossref) https://doi.org/10.1109/WCPEC.2006.279570
18. Lueck, M.R., et al.: Dual Junction GaInP/GaAs Solar Cells Grown on Metamorphic SiGe/Si Substrates with High Open Circuit Voltage. IEEE Electron Dev. Lett. **27**(3), 142–144 (2006). DOI.org (Crossref), https://doi.org/10.1109/LED.2006.870250
19. Krajangsang, T., et al.: Study of an Amorphous Silicon Oxide Buffer Layer for P-Type Microcrystalline Silicon Oxide/n-Type Crystalline Silicon Heterojunction Solar Cells and Their Temperature Dependence. Int. J. Photoenergy **2014** 2014. cyberleninka.org, https://cyberleninka.org/article/n/1210551
20. Wafa HADJ, K., et al.: Window Layer Thickness Effect on Amorphous Silicon Oxide Solar Cell Performances. Algerian J. Renew. Energy Sustain. Develop. **2**(01), 67–74 (2020). ajresd.univ-adrar.edu.dz, https://doi.org/10.46657/ajresd.2020.2.1.10
21. Roy, S., Hossain, M.J.: Numerical Analysis of Lattice-matched InAlAs/InGaAsP/InGaAs based Triple-junction Solar Cell using MATLAB/Simulink. In: 2020 IEEE Region 10 Symposium (TENSYMP), 2020, pp. 1787–1790, https://doi.org/10.1109/TENSYMP50017.2020.9230890

Design and Fabrication of a Low-Cost Customizable Modern CNC Laser Cutter

Radif Uddin Ahmed$^{(\boxtimes)}$, Mst. Nusrat Yasmin, Avishek Das,
and Syed Masrur Ahmmad

Chittagong University of Engineering and Technology, Chittagong 4349, Bangladesh
radifuddinahmed@gmail.com, masrur@cuet.ac.bd

Abstract. In the modern era of research and development, fabricating prototypes of test setup and models is crucial. So much so that, the outcome of an experiment or product is highly dependent upon it. In order to prepare a prototype, the accuracy of the fabrication plays a crucial role both in industry and in research laboratories. Hence, to provide the most accurate results computer numerical machining provides the fastest and most accurate results while machining and fabrication. Among these computer numerical machining processes, LASER Cutting can provide a user with very precise geometrical cutting out of common prototyping materials vastly used for experimental setup preparation such as Wood, PVC board, Plywood, etc. However, these machines cost a lot more than any conventional machines due to their high accuracy and precision. Considering less funded research and development projects purchasing a state-of-the-art LASER Cutting Machine can be somewhat daunting or nearly impossible in some cases. Although In the local market, a person may find a plethora of these CNC Laser Cutting machines, these machines lack the precious attribute of accuracy. To solve this issue, this paper offers research done on the design, fabrication, and performance analysis of a low-cost CNC machine, which has been made out of widely available materials and requires very few technical skills to fabricate.

Keywords: CNC Machine · LASER Cutting · Low Cost · Performance Analysis

1 Introduction

In order to make a machine or any other part, it is essential for it to be cut to a specific dimension according to the design. For the machine to be manufactured properly this cutting process must be highly accurate. The accuracy of the final output of fabrication depends highly on the machining process. In this modern era of machining CNC (Computer Numerical Controlled) has become a buzzword. That is because of its ultra-precision and reliability. This is replacing the conventional machine tools that are hand-operated manually. The CNC machine tool is operated using a computer system. The design of a part is done

Md. S. Satu et al. (Eds.): MIET 2022, LNICST 491, pp. 472–485, 2023.
https://doi.org/10.1007/978-3-031-34622-4_38

using CAD (Computer Aided Drafting) software. This design specifies the cutting geometry of the part. But at this point, the CNC machine tool is unaware of the position where it will cut. For the machine to operate through a certain sequence of operations for a specific task the instructions must be converted to a machine language. This instruction lets the machine know which path it has to choose and there to do certain machining operations as well as automatic tool changing of the machine. This sequence of instruction is known as G-code. G-code stands for geometric code. Another computer program known as CAM (Computer Aided Machining) generates this G-code from the design file. It also sends this code to the CNC machine tool. The reason why a CNC machine is becoming so popular is that it is self-operated. It is capable of machining complex with very high precision. Every machine tool can be CNC operated. Out of its numerous kind, a type of it is a 2-axis CNC cutting machine. This cutting machine can perform the cutting operations by various methods such as oxygen gas cutting, arc cutting, plasma cutting, laser beam cutting, etc. But the key factor is the amount of energy focused on per unit area. From the above mentioned types laser delivers the highest available energy density up to 1013 kW/cm2. LASER cutting is suitable for almost all materials such as metal, plastics, wood, cardboard, and even ceramics and glass. LASER cutting of metals is a fusion cutting procedure. The energy causes the metal to melt and an inert gas blows the molten metal out of the gap. This process is known as LASER melt cutting. But this process is very costly hence in our case we have used a LASER diode of 2.5 W. This LASER cutting gives very high precision along with the highest possible surface finish. Combining this machine tool with CNC operation would give the highest possible accuracy.

2 Literature Review

Venkata Krishna Pabolu et al. (2008) proposed a machine tool of 3 axis. It is equipped with CNC control. The machine was controlled using a .NET based user control interface. The machine was built using PVC board [7]. F.Agalianos et al. (2011) proposed a work on industrial application of laser engraving. The experimentation was done using Al7075 as the main material. The engraving tests were performed using a Q-Switched 100 W Yb:YAG laser, with fundamental length $\lambda = 1064$ nm. The range of the frequency that can be used by the laser is between 4–50 kHz, the corresponding range in speed is between 50–1000 mm/s and the removal material thickness per layer can be between 1-15μm depending on the material. The laser system is controlled via a PC. Considering all the experimental data of the current experimental plan, the best surface roughness was achieved when using a frequency of 20 kHz, a scan speed in the range of 600–700 mm/s and a layer thickness of 4 and 6 μm [1]. Dharmesh K. Patel et al. (2014) did a research on laser engraving property on different materials. The laser variable properties such as spot diameter, laser power, frequency, different wavelength. To optimization of all these parameters with multiple performance characteristic based on the Grey relational analysis. Taguchi method of orthogonal array was performed to determine the best factor level condition. By analyzing Grey relational grade, it was observed that which parameter has more effect on responses of input parameter to the output parameter. It was found that the laser engraved depth became deeper for either higher laser power or a lower feed speed ratio. The color difference values increased under a lower feed speed ratio and higher power, and resulted in a brownish color in the engraved zone. The engraved depth and color difference values of Moso bamboo was predicted and estimated by regression analyses [9]. Dr.B.Jayachandraiah et al. (2014) fabricated a 3-axis CNC router. It had a drilling machine attached to the Z axis of the router. For the design cutting geometry CAD software were used. For the conversion of design file into machine language of G-code CAM software was used. The prepared G-code was sent to the machine using G-code sender application [3]. Dhaval B. Patel et al. (2014) did a review of the previous works that have been done on modern machining as well as CNC machining. The review was done on the following cases such as low cost CNC printer, open source hardware and software, basic requirement of building a CNC machine etc [12]. Mr. Ravi Patel et al. (2015) did a review work which described a variety of fundamental research of laser engraving of different materials which the authors have recently performed. Laser engraving is machining process where material is engraved by laser process. In this review the research and progress in laser engraving of different materials are critically reviewed from different perspectives. Basically many types of industrial lasers like, carbon dioxide (CO_2) laser and neodymium-doped yttrium aluminium garnet (Nd: YAG) laser, fiber laser, semiconductor laser which are used for laser engraving process. Some important laser processing parameters and their effects on MRR and surface roughness were discussed in this paper [10]. D. P. S. Pranav et al. (2016) researched on making an affordable CNC/3D printer using old computer parts that are easily accessible [11]. Harsh B. Panchal et al. (2017) did a research on fabricating a low cost CNC drilling machine from recycled CD/DVD drives [8]. Christine Marie J. Madrid et al. (2017) focused on a new concept of an Arduino-based Microcontroller wheeled laser cutting robot. This machine is consisted of a 2 axis mechanism. The X axis was consisted of two stepper motors. The Y axis was consisted of a single stepper motor. The driver for stepper motor was A4988. The control unit was made using an 8 bit microcontroller (Atmega328p) Arduino Nano. For the engraving a 2.5 W blue-violet laser diode was used. The robot was given mobility using four wheels. The controlling of the robot was done using Benbox 3.7.99 software [6]. R. Ginting et al. (2017) discussed the design and realization of complex 3-axis CNC machines based on microcontroller which combined with spindle drill. The cutting geometry was made using a computer. The cutting instruction was sent to the machine using serial communication. The machine was tested on wood, acrylic and PCB. It had 98.5% of carving accuracy and 100% of depth accuracy. This machine had a bed size of 20 × 20 cm [2]. The study of Štefan Koprda et al. proposed a CNC based Laser engraver prototype with a low cost of construction. This machine has 2 Axis for performing cutting operation and built using the H-bot configuration. With this configuration the machine produces horizontal and lateral movement using 2 stepper motors paired with belts. The machine has a bed size of 210 × 290 mm and a Laser diode of 2000 mw for performing cutting operations. Various 3D printed parts and wooded base has been used to reduce the fabrication cost [5]. Mohammad Nasir Khan et al. proposed a study of design of a CNC Laser Cutting machine based on Arduino. The machine has been designed with one axis being the bed itself controlled by a stepper motor and the Laser diode has been attached with the other axis also controlled using a stepper motor. The stepper motors have been controlled using DRV8825 stepper motor driver and an GRBL firmware flashed Aduino Uno R3 has been used as the GRBL controller [4].

3   Methodology

The machine design consists of the design of the structure and electronic section. While tailoring two of these sections specific steps have been taken, which have been given below as flowcharts in Figs. 1 and 2.

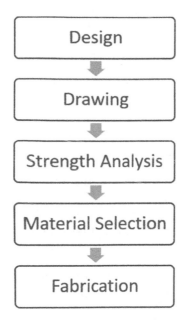

Fig. 1. Structural Design Flowchart.

After specifying structural and electronic design steps, the microcontroller of the machine needs to be programmed in order to establish communication of the machine with a computer. This will allow the machine to perform the desired cutting operation. This has been shown below as a flow chart in Fig. 3.

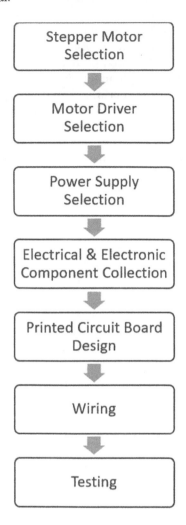

Fig. 2. Electronics Design Flowchart.

As soon as the machine is prepared with the aforementioned steps a performance analysis can be initiated. The process has been listed in Fig. 4 as a flowchart.

3.1 Design

Design of the CNC machine was done based on the structure and required electronics.

- Upon taking cost, longevity, availability Teak wood has been selected as primary fabricating material of the CNC machine. The machine was designed to have two axes one having bed which holds the job and another having

Fig. 3. Programming Flowchart.

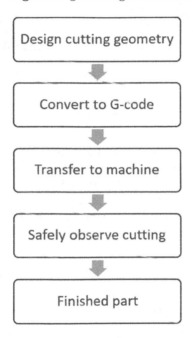

Fig. 4. Performance Analysis Flowchart.

carriage which holds the LASER cutting diode. The bed has a dimension of 1 square foot. Full machine dimensions have been described in Fig. 5.
- The machine bed and carriage has a weight of 756 gm and 820 gm respectively. Considering their weight stepper motors having a torque of 4.078 kg.cm has been selected. This motor has a rated current of 1.7 A. To control these motors A4988 motor driver has been selected, which is able to provide 2 A current per coil of the stepping motor. Moreover, A4988 has a 1/16 step microstep-

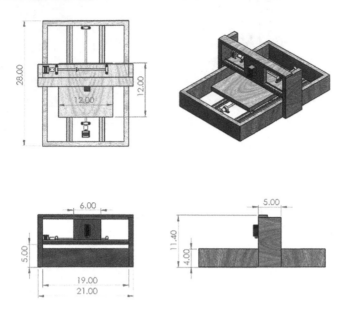

Fig. 5. Machine Dimensions.

ping resolution, which will let test if any noticeable accuracy improvement is possible using this feature. As the controller of the system, Arduino Nano is used, and to facilitate the electronics a GRBL shield is used which holds motor drivers, Arduino etc. As cutting tool a LASER diode of 2.5 W' power has been used. To power up the machine a 12 V 5 A power supply has been used. Figure 6 describes the electronic design block diagram.

3.2   Fabrication

Machine structure was fabricated first and then electronic parts were installed.

- Fabrication of the machine was divided into two parts. firstly, bottom portion of the machine was fabricated with the bed after that top part of the machine was fabricated with the carriage. Both the bed and carriage moving was based upon roller wheel and rail mechanism. Both the bed and carriage movement was facilitated using leadscrew and leadnut. Complete fabricated machine can be seen in Fig. 7.
- Motors of both axes, LASER diode, A4988, Arduino nano have been connected to the GRBL shield. GRBL shield is powered by 12 V 5 A power supply.

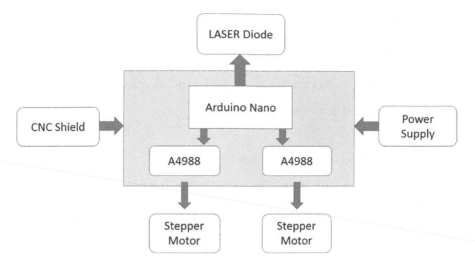

Fig. 6. Electronic Design Block Diagram.

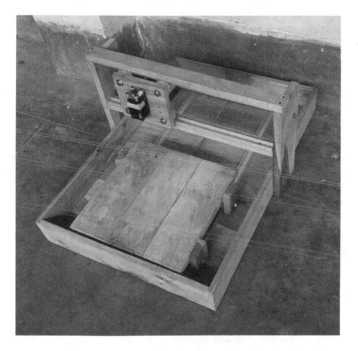

Fig. 7. Complete Fabricated CNC Machine.

3.3   Calculation

A4988 stepping motor driver has the feature of microstepping up to 1/16 of a step. This can deliver significant accurate output with the cost of speed of rotation. Arduino Nano coupled with A4988 working at 16 MHz clock speed has been used which can deliver upto 4000 steps per second while running a stepper motor. With this information in hand, the speed comparison can be done with microstepping.

Lead screw of our selection has below listed specifications.

- Lead Screw Diameter = 8 mm
- Lead Screw Pitch = 1 mm
- Number of Starts = 01
- Material of Construction = Stainless Steel

Based on these specifications the calculation of steps per millimeters can be calculated. It is to be mentioned that the calculations have been performed considering the leadscrew has directly been coupled to the stepper motor. Rotational steps required for a millimeter of linear travel can be calculated for below given equation.

Steps per Millimeter = Stepper Motor Steps*Micro Steps* Threads per Millimeter

The axial distance a leadnut will travel along the axes in one full revolution of the leadscew is known as lead distance. The lead distance can be calculated using following equation

Steps per Millimeter = Stepper Motor Steps*Micro Steps* Threads per Millimeter

The axial distance a leadnut will travel along the axes in one full revolution of the leadscew is known as lead distance. The lead distance can be calculated using following equation

Lead Distance = Pitch*Number of Starts

With every step of rotation of the stepper motor, the leadnut progresses in the axial direction of the leadscrew, which is known as lead per step. This can be calculated using below listed equations.

Lead per step = 1/ steps per millimeter

Lead per step = Lead Distance/ Steps per revolution

Calculated data of different parameter changes due to implementation of microsteps has been tabulated in Table 1.

Table 1. Calculated data of different parameter changes due to implementation of microsteps has been tabulated below.

Microstep/Fullstep	Steps Per Revolution	Steps per millimeter	Lead per step	Step Angle
1	200	200	1/200	1.8
1/2	400	400	1/400	0.9
1/4	800	800	1/800	0.45
1/8	1600	1600	1/1600	0.225
1/16	3200	3200	1/3200	0.1125

4   Result and Discussion

After the fabrication of the low-cost CNC laser cutting machine, the cutting accuracy of the machine needs to be tested to determine the performance of the machine. To facilitate this test 5 different shapes of unique dimensions need to be cut using the machine. After cutting the shapes using the Laser cutter dimension of the shape has been measured. The accuracy in this case, has been documented in terms of error percentage.

4.1   Square

Square shape having a dimension of 20 mm squared has been cut using the machine which is shown in Fig. 8.

Fig. 8. Complete Fabricated CNC Machine.

4.2   Rectangle

Square shape having a dimension of 20 mm*40 mm has been cut using the machine which is shown in Fig. 9.

Fig. 9. Complete Fabricated CNC Machine.

4.3   Equilateral Triangle

Square shape having a dimension of 20 mm*40 mm has been cut using the machine which is shown in Fig. 10.

4.4   Circle

Square shape having a dimension of 20 mm*40 mm has been cut using the machine which is shown in Fig. 11.

Fig. 10. Complete Fabricated CNC Machine.

Fig. 11. Complete Fabricated CNC Machine.

4.5   Grid Pattern

Square shape having dimension of 20 mm*40 mm has been cut using the machine which is shown in Fig. 12.

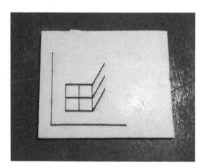

Fig. 12. Complete Fabricated CNC Machine.

After cutting the shapes dimensions have been measured and listed in Table 2. This table gives the comparison data of cutting accuracy against expected dimensions.

Table 2. PERFORMANCE ANALYSIS.

Shape	Expected (mm)	Actual (mm)	Deviation (mm)	Error (%)
▢	20.0mm (Length) 20.0mm (Width)	19.8mm (Length) 19.8mm (Width)	0.2mm 0.2mm	1%
▭	40.0mm (Length) 20.0mm (Width)	40.0mm (Length)19.8mm (Width)	0.0mm 0.2mm	1%
△	30mm 30mm 30mm	29.6mm 29.8mm 29.7mm	0.4mm 0.2mm 0.3mm	3%
◯	20mm (Diameter)	19.8mm (Diameter)	0.2mm	1%
(cube)	20mm (Horizontal Length) 20mm (Vertical Length) 90 Degree 45 Degree(Slope)	20mm 20mm 90 Degree 45 Degree	0.0mm 0.0mm 0 Degree 0 Degree	0%

After comparing the machine's accuracy against ideal condition using different shapes, now its performance has been compared with another same tier CNC machine named "Eleksmaker A3 Pro". This performance testing was facilitated into three categories namely, "horizontal cutting accuracy test", "vertical cutting accuracy test", "45 Degree slope cutting accuracy test". To perform the test 3 mm PVC board has been used as test cutting material. The accuracy of these machines has been compared in terms of error percentage and the result has been shown in Table 3.

Table 3. CUTTING ACCURACY COMPARISON.

Horizontal Cutting Accuracy Test				
Expected Length (mm)	Low Cost CNC Machine		Eleksmaker A3 Pro	
	Actual Lengt (mm)	Error (%)	Actual Length (mm)	Error (%)
40	39.5	1.25	39.8	0.5
100	99.8	0.2	99.9	0.09
160	159.7	0.19	159.9	0.06
230	230	0	229.9	0.04
280	279.8	0.07	280	0
Vertical Cutting Accuracy Test				
Expected Length (mm)	Low Cost CNC Machine		Eleksmaker A3 Pro	
	Actual Length (mm)	Error (%)	Actual Length (mm)	Error (%)
40	39.8	0.5	39.9	0.25
100	99.7	0.3	100	0
160	160	0.0	159.9	0.06
230	229.8	0.09	229.9	0.04
280	279.9	0.04	280	0
45 Degree slope cutting accuracy test				
Expected Length (mm)	Low Cost CNC Machine		Eleksmaker A3 Pro	
	Actual Length (mm)	Error (%)	Actual Length (mm)	Error (%)
40	39.6	01	39.8	0.5
100	99.8	0.2	99.9	0.09
160	159.5	0.3	160	0.0
230	229.4	0.3	229.8	0.09
280	279.6	0.14	279.9	0.04

5   Conclusion

The above calculations clearly show that the machine is not a hundred percent accurate. The reason being, the alignment of the lead screw and the stepper motor shaft wasn't perfect. The friction between the screw and the nut played a crucial role. Moreover, the whole construction was done using wood, and Wood construction has less accuracy than metal. The overall construction wasn't accurate either due to woodworking. Another noticeable error was in the carriages. The carriages didn't slide perfectly parallel they had some wobbling in them. All these errors add to the final product. If these errors could be reduced the machine would have been more accurate. This machine was built within $150 range of cost. Even though this machine could not outperform a rather expensive machine named Eleksmaker A3 pro giving an almost similar performance.

References

1. Agalianos, F., Patelis, S., Kyratsis, P., Maravelakis, E., Vasarmidis, E., Antoniadis, A.: Industrial applications of laser engraving: influence of the process parameters on machined surface quality. World Acad. Sci. Eng. Technol. **59**, 1242–1245 (2011)
2. Ginting, R., Hadiyoso, S., Aulia, S.: Implementation 3-axis cnc router for small scale industry. Int. J. Appl. Eng. Res. **12**(17), 6553–6558 (2017)
3. Jayachandraiah, B., Krishna, O.V., Khan, P.A., Reddy, R.A.: Fabrication of low cost 3-axis cnc router. Int. J. Eng. Sci. Invention **3**(6), 1–10 (2014)
4. Khan, M.N., Maheshwari, A., Verma, H.: Study and design of arduino based CNC laser cutting machine. IOP Conf. Series: Mater. Sci. Eng. **1224**(1), 012008 (2022). https://doi.org/10.1088/1757-899x/1224/1/012008
5. Koprda, Š, Balogh, Z., Magdin, M., Reichel, J., Molnár, G.: The possibility of creating a low-cost laser engraver cnc machine prototype with platform arduino. Acta Polytech. Hung **17**, 181–198 (2020)
6. Madrid, C.M.J., Saldua, R.S.: Paper and fabric cutting solution using automated cutting system
7. Pabolu, V.K., Srinivas, S.: Design and implementation of a three dimensional CNC machine. Int. J. Comput. Sci. Eng. **2**(8), 2567–2570 (2010)
8. Panchal, H.B., Mayur, S., Patel, P.D., Padia, U.N.: Arduino based cnc machine. Int. J. Res. Scie. Eng. P-ISSN, 2394–8280
9. Patel, D.K., Patel, D.M.: Parametric optimization of laser engraving process for different material using grey relational technique-a review. Patel et al. **3**(4) (2014)
10. Patel, R., Chaudhary, P., Soni, D.: A review on laser engraving process for different materials. IJSRD-Int. J. Sci. Res. Develop. **2**(11), 1–4 (2015)
11. Shahid, M.T., Khan, M.A., Khan, M.Z.: Design and development of a computer numeric controlled 3d printer, laser cutter and 2d plotter all in one machine. In: 2019 16th International Bhurban Conference on Applied Sciences and Technology (IBCAST), pp. 569–575. IEEE (2019)
12. Taufik, M., Jain, P.K.: Role of build orientation in layered manufacturing: a review. Int. J. Manuf. Technol. Manage. **27**(1–3), 47–73 (2013)

Hole Transport Layer Free Non-toxic Perovskite Solar Cell Using ZnSe Electron Transport Material

Rukon Uddin[✉] [iD], Subrata Bhowmik, Md. Eyakub Ali, and Sayem Ul Alam

Department of Electrical and Electronic Engineering, Noakhali Science and Technology
University, Noakhali 3814, Bangladesh
rukon2k13@gmail.com

Abstract. The demand for solar cells is increasing with the increment of the need for clean energy due to the rapid growth of environmental pollution. Perovskite, an abandoned material with supreme solar photovoltaic characteristics has come up to solve the problem. However, the cost of the perovskite solar cell is yet costlier due to costly Hole transport Material (HTM) and costly back contact material. A HTM free perovskite solar cell with low-cost back contact material can be a great solution for that as this is cost-effective, highly efficient, and stable. In this investigation, a HTM free perovskite solar cell with $MASnI_3$ absorber material and ZnSe electron transport layer is proposed. The cell is continuously simulated by varying different parameters including thickness, doping, defect density, metal work function of back contact, temperature, and series resistance. After optimizing the physical parameters mentioned earlier, the cell provides an efficiency of 24.08%, an open circuit voltage of 0.93 V, a short circuit current of 32.74 mA/cm^2, and a fill factor of 79.16%.

Keywords: Perovskite · SCAPS-1D · solar cell

1 Introduction

Due to the enormous amount of fossil fuel usage, different types of toxic gases are polluting the environment. This is also a prime reason for global warming. Hence, the importance of clean, efficient, low cost and easily attainable energy is increasing day by day and solar cells came with greater flexibility for their users by solving these problems. Perovskite is a third-generation solar cell material, which added a dimension to the energy harvesting field through its unique characteristics. Perovskite is cheaper, easily accessible, more efficient, can be easily fabricated and more tunable bandgap than other available solar cell materials. It was introduced with an efficiency of 3.81% by a Japanese research led by Kojima in 2009 [1], due to continuous research and development it has a got an efficiency of 25.8% by 2021 [2].

The perovskite crystal structure can be represented by AMX3, where A, M, and X are organic cation, divalent metal cation, and halide anions [3]. Perovskite has some

Md. S. Satu et al. (Eds.): MIET 2022, LNICST 491, pp. 486–498, 2023.
https://doi.org/10.1007/978-3-031-34622-4_39

superior characteristics over other solar cell materials. For instance, minimal excitation binding energy, higher absorption coefficient, a wide variety of bandgap for tuning, greater mobility of carrier, and diffusion length comparatively longer [4–8].

Although perovskite solar cells have a comparatively easy and low-cost production process but the cost of hole transport materials (HTM) and back contact materials is a major concern for perovskite solar cell design. Previous investigation reveals that, the Au (gold) back contact and HTM materials alone can cost up to 33.9% of the total cost of the cell [9]. Some common HTM and their cost are given in Table 1.

Table 1 indicates that HTM for highly efficient solar cells are very expensive. That is why we have removed the HTM from our proposed cell and doped the absorber layer to work as both absorber and HTM. Additionally, the price of back contact materials is also crucial for low-cost and highly efficient cell design. It is traced that Ni and Au back contact can provide similar efficiency but the price of commonly used Au back contact for perovskite solar cells is 106 times more than Ni back contact.

In this study, Hole transport materials are excluded as it is costlier and reduce the stability of the cell [10, 11], and expensive Au back contact is replaced with Ni back contact. The main of the study is to remove expensive HTM materials and replace expensive back contact materials with a cheap alternative to design an inexpensive and efficient perovskite solar cell.

Table 1. Common HTM for highly efficient perovskite solar cell and their cost.

Material Name	Material Type	Cost/gm(Euro)
Spiro-OMETAD	HTM	472
CuI	HTM	19.22
NiO	HTM	17.6
PCBM	HTM	1972
Graphene	HTM	956
P_3HT	HTM	669

*N.B: The price of each material is adopted from Sigma Aldrich (*https://www.sigmaaldrich.com*), 30/05/2022*

$MASnI_3$, which is a non-toxic perovskite absorber material, is used as absorber material and ZnSe is used as electron transport material. This structure is unique as there is no structure available with these materials. This study analyses most of the design parameters of a perovskite solar cell including the impact of thickness, doping, defect, temperature, series resistance, and work function of metallic contacts for enhancing the performance.

2   Device Physics and Simulation

In this battue, SCAPS-1D simulation software is utilized to perform the simulations. SCAPS-1D is introduced and moderated by the University of Gent, Belgium [11]. There are some basic layers including contacts for drawing power, transport materials for collecting carriers and absorber layer for producing electron hole pairs for simulating photovoltaic cells in SCAPS-1D simulator. For this study, the following structure is considered for simulation (Fig. 1).

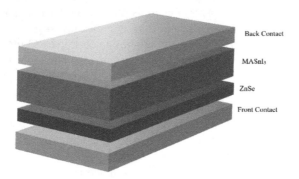

Fig. 1. Device structure for the proposed cell.

Here, the thickness of MASnI3 is higher compared to ZnSe because the generation of electron-hole pair for producing power is directly dependent on the thickness of absorber materials. The MASnI3 layer is graded to create an n^+-n-p structure of the cell as there is less barrier in this structure to flow electron-hole pair in this structure and it creates high mobility in the n^+ region of the cell to collect carrier in back contact. The ZnSe layer is kept smaller to reduce recombination and to increase the collection of charge at front contact.

In Table 2 E_g, χ, ε_r, Nc, Nv, μ_n, μ_p, N_D, N_A, and N_t denote bandgap energy, electron affinity, relative permittivity, effective conduction band density, effective valence band density, electron mobility, hole mobility, donor concentration, acceptor concentration, and defect density respectively.

Table 2. Basic parameters of MASnI3 and ZnSe.

Material	Thickness (μm)	E_g (eV)	χ (eV)	ε_r	Nc (cm^{-3})	Nv (cm^{-3})	μ_n (cm^2/Vs)	μ_p (cm^2/Vs)	N_D (cm^{-3})	N_A (cm^{-3})	N_t (cm^{-3})
MASnI3 [12]	0.75	1.3	4.2	10	1E18	1E18	1.6E0	1.6E0	0	Graded	4.5E16
ZnSe [13]	0.05	2.81	4.09	8.6	1.8E19	2.2E18	4E2	1E2	1E18	0	1E14

The band diagram of the cell indicates that the cell can be optimized to have higher efficiency (Fig. 2).

Here, The MASnI3 layer is graded to form the n^+n layer where the initial doping level is higher than the last region of absorber material. The graded doping concentration is given below (Fig. 3).

An intrinsic layer of the absorber layer is added later between MASnI3 and ZnSe layer to reduce the interfacial recombination. The simulation environment for simulation is considered as AM 1.5G with 300 K while illumination is considered as 1000 W/m^2.

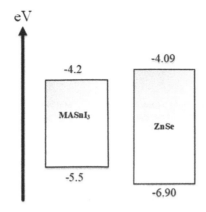

Fig. 2. Band diagram of the proposed cell.

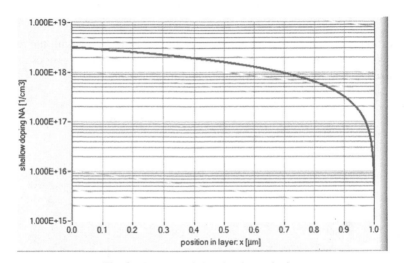

Fig. 3. Grading of absorber layer doping.

3 Result and Discussion

A solar cell's efficiency is contingent on the 4 basic distinct output variables i.e. short-circuit current density (Jsc), fill factor (FF), open-circuit voltage (V_{oc}), and input power P_{in} and the relation is drawn by the following equation.

$$\eta = \frac{FF * V_{oc} * J_{sc}}{P_{in}} \qquad (1)$$

The cell is simulated without including the interface layer and the following result is achieved (Fig. 4).

The figure exhibit that an efficiency of 22.32% can be acquired from the proposed cell without optimizing the parameters. Here, the quantum efficiency of the cell is lower than

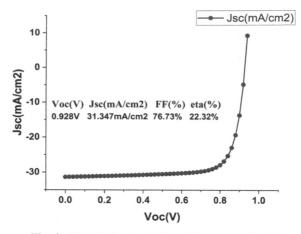

Fig. 4. The JV characteristics of the proposed cell.

the highest possible value of quantum efficiency and it is declining with the increment of the wavelength of the proposed cell. Hence, the parameters of the proposed cell can be optimized further to achieve maximum quantum efficiency (Fig. 5).

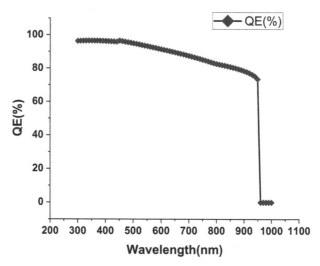

Fig. 5. Quantum Efficiency of the proposed cell.

The cell is simulated further by including the interface layer and the effect of different parameters is observed.

Effect of Thickness
The absorber layer has a pivotal function in solar cell efficiency as more electron-hole

pair is generated with the increment of thickness while current density is reduced. Hence, each layer of the cell is varied and the effect is observed.

Effect of Absorber Layer Thickness

To observe the influence of the absorber layer thickness, the absorber layer thickness is modified from 0.1 μm to 1 μm and the following result is achieved (Fig. 6).

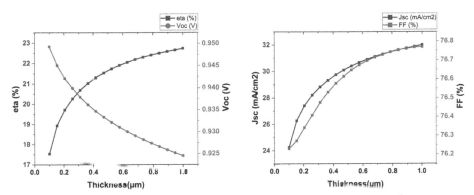

Fig. 6. Thickness of absorber layer vs Output Parameters (Voc (V), Jsc (mA/cm²), FF (%) and eta (%)) curve for the cell.

Here, efficiency (eta), open circuit short circuit current (Jsc) and fill factor (FF) is increasing but open circuit voltage (Voc) is decreasing by the increment of the absorber layer thickness and the maximum efficiency can be obtained when the layer thickness is 1 μm which is 22.72% .

3.1 Effect of interface Layer Thickness

The simulation for the interface layer is performed between 0.01 μm to 0.14 μm and the following result is gained (Fig. 7).

From the output of the simulation, it can be seen efficiency is increasing initially with the augmentation of the depth of the interface layer and then dropped again. Here, the optimized value for interface layer thickness is 0.02 μm where Voc is 0.91 V, Jsc is 32.70 mA/cm², FF is 76.95% and eta is 23.01%.

3.2 Effect of ZnSe Layer Thickness

The ZnSe layer is simulated between 0.01 μm to 0.14 μm and the following impact can be seen (Fig. 8).

The variation of thickness of ZnSe layer exhibit the same impact on each output parameter except exception in FF. Here, FF is increasing first accompanied by the enhancement of the thickness of ZnSe layer then diminishes again. The thickness for

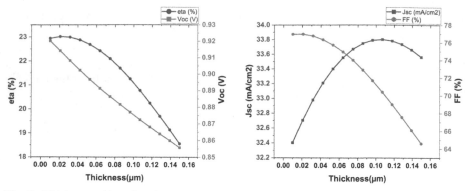

Fig. 7. Thickness of interface layer vs Output Parameters (Voc (V), Jsc (mA/cm2), FF (%) and eta (%)) curve for MASnI₃ based cell.

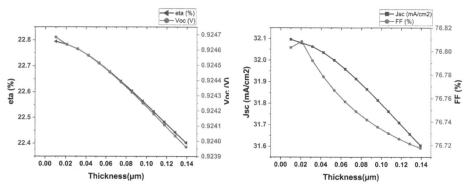

Fig. 8. Thickness of ZnSe layer vs Output Parameters (Voc (V), Jsc (mA/cm2), FF (%) and eta (%)) curve for MASnI₃ based cell.

further optimization of the cell is chosen as 0.01 μm due to the maximum efficiency that can be achievable at this point.

Effect of Absorber Layer Doping

The effect of doping concentration is one of the significant determining factors for solar cell efficiency. With the increment of doping concentration the electron-hole pair generation is enhanced, hence the performance is also increased. However, after a certain level the recombination of electron-hole pair is aggrandized, hence the efficiency is dropped. So, this study analyses the influence of absorber layer doping. As the absorber layer doping is graded. The first observation is done with a constant value of final length doping. Here, the value is 3.2E15 ($1/cm^3$).

The impact is given below (Table 3).

The simulation result indicates that an efficiency of 23.01% can be obtained when the initial length doping is 3.20E+18 ($1/cm^3$). Now, the final length doping of the grading is calculated by setting the initial length value as 3.20E+18 ($1/cm^3$) (Table 4).

Table 3. The variation efficiency according to doping variation.

$N_A(1/cm^3)$	eta (%)
3.20E+20	15.45
3.20E+19	19.71
3.20E+18	23.01
3.20E+17	22.53
3.20E+16	17.76

Table 4. The variation efficiency according to doping variation.

$N_A(1/cm^3)$	eta (%)
3.2E+14	23.01
3.2E+15	23.01
3.2E+16	22.96
3.2E+17	21.09

The result indicates that with the increment of doping level at final length the efficiency is decreasing. Hence, the final length grading value is taken as 3.20E+15 $(1/cm^3)$.

Effect of Absorber Layer Defect Density

The defect density of the absorber layer is important for designing an efficient cell as the diffusion length of the carrier is directly correlated with defect density. In this section of the investigation, the effect of defect density is studied (Table 5).

Table 5. The variation efficiency according to defect density.

$N_t(1/cm^3)$	eta (%)
4.50E+12	25.29
4.50E+13	25.29
4.50E+14	25.29
4.50E+15	25.26
4.50E+16	25.01
4.50E+17	23.07
4.50E+18	17.04

Here, the efficiency of the cell is decreased with the increment of defect density. The optimized value for the cell is 4.50E+14(1/cm^3) where the efficiency is 25.29%.

Effect of Back Contact Material
Before studying the effect of back contact the cell is simulated with a real front contact with a work function of 4 eV which exhibit an efficiency of 24.08%.In this segment, the influence of the back contact on the cell is studied. 5 back contact is chosen for study. Below is a list of the various back contacts' work functions (Table 6 and Fig. 9).

Table 6. Different back contact and their work function.

Back contact material [14]	Ag	Fe	Cu	Au	Ni
Metal work function, Φm (eV) [14]	4.74	4.81	5.00	5.10	5.50

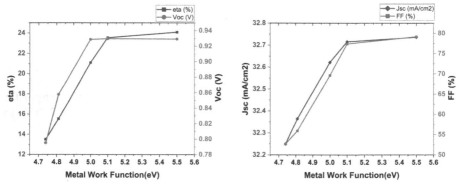

Fig. 9. Back Contact Metal Work Function (eV) vs Output parameters of the cell.

From the figure, it can be said that every output parameter is increasing with the increment of the metal work function of the cell, the maximum efficiency can be achieved with Ni back contact, and the efficiency is 24.08%.

Effect of Temperature
Temperature is another important aspect of solar cells, with the increment and decrement of the temperature the cell efficiency and output parameters are changed. Here, the effect of temperature on the proposed cell is studied (Fig. 10).

The output of the simulation indicates that the higher value of temperature improves the electron-hole pair generation rate but reduces the voltage and fill factor. Hence, the efficiency is also decreased proportionally with temperature. Therefore, the ideal temperature for the cell is around 250 K.

Effect of Series Resistance
In this part of the study, the effect of series resistance is studied from 0.5 Ω to 6 Ω and the output parameters are observed and analyzed accordingly.

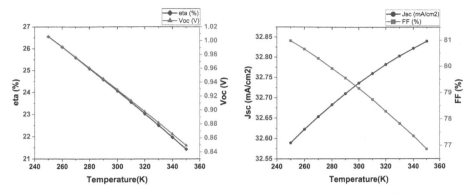

Fig. 10. Effect of temperature (K) vs Output parameters of the cell.

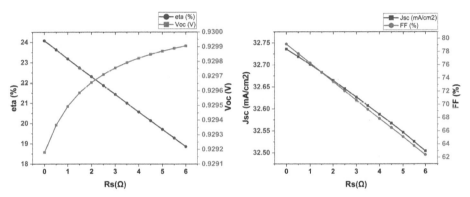

Fig. 11. Series resistance vs efficiency and open circuit voltage curve of MASnI₃ based cell.

Figure 11 clearly identifies that there is an inverse relationship between efficiency and series resistance as the open circuit current is decreasing with the increment of series resistance. Here, open circuit voltage is increasing with the increment of series resistance but the other three parameters are diminishing. Hence, it can be said that, the cell performs better with low series resistance value. We have chosen Rs value as 0.5 Ω where the efficiency is 24.08% which is achievable according to Shockley–Queisser Limit. The maximum achievable efficiency according to Shockley–Queisser Limit is 33.14% for a single junction cell [15].

Figure 12 indicates that there is an overall improvement between the initiatory cell and the optimized cell and the efficiency of the proposed cell has seen a 7.89% improvement for optimization of the cell parameters.

In the Fig. 13, the quantum efficiency of the cell is also increased significantly. Here the quantum efficiency of the final is have increased considerably in the initial and final range of wavelength. Hence, it can be said that both efficiency and quantum efficiency of the cell has increased due to the optimization of cell parameters.

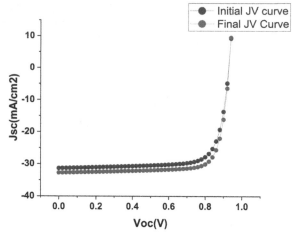

Fig. 12. Comparison of JV curve of initial cell and final cell.

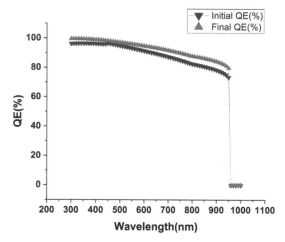

Fig. 13. Comparison of Quantum efficiency between initial cell and optimized cell.

4   Conclusion

In this investigation, we have proposed a HTM free perovskite solar cell with MASnI₃ as absorber layer and ZnSe as ETM, and all aspects of the proposed cell is studied, analyzed, and optimized. First, the cell is simulated without an interface layer, and then the interface layer is added to observe the effect. It is seen that the interface layer decreased the interface recombination. Hence, efficiency is increased slightly. After that, the influence of the thickness of each layer is observed and optimized by continuous simulation. In the next of steps of the design, the cell is gone through a simulation of absorber layer doping, absorber layer defect density, the effect of back contact, effect temperature, and effect of series resistance. It can be said from the observation of the simulation and analysis that, the cell efficiency is improved by n + n structural doping of the absorber layer and lower value of absorber layer defect density while the cell does not work efficiently with the increment if the temperature. The final section of the study indicates that the cell is efficient when the series resistance is lower and the metal the back contact work function is higher.

5 Contribution

The specific contribution of each author for this work is as follow:

- Rukon Uddin: Idea, Simulation, Figure Drawing, Paper Writing
- Subrata Bhowmik: Supervision
- Eyakub Ali: Figure Drawing, Reference Collection
- Sayem Ul Alam: Paper Revision

6 Future Work

There is a scope to increase the performance of the proposed cell by simulating and optimizing more parameters. In the future, we will simulate, analyze and optimize more parameters to reach the maximum output performance achievable by the proposed cell.

References

1. Kojima, A., Teshima, K., Shirai, Y., Miyasaka, T.: Organometal halide perovskites as visible-light sensitizers for photovoltaic cells. J. Am. Chem. Soc. 131(17), 6050–6051 (2009). https://doi.org/10.1021/ja809598r
2. Min, H., et al.: Perovskite solar cells with atomically coherent interlayers on SnO2 electrodes. Nature 598(7881), 444–450 (2021). https://doi.org/10.1038/s41586-021-03964-8
3. Habibi, M., Zabihi, F., Ahmadian-Yazdi, M.R., Eslamian, M.: Progress in emerging solution-processed thin film solar cells – part II: Perovskite solar cells. Renew. Sustain. Energy Rev. 62, 1012–1031 (2016). https://doi.org/10.1016/j.rser.2016.05.042
4. Zheng, K., et al.: Exciton binding energy and the nature of emissive states in organometal halide perovskites. J. Phys. Chem. Lett. 6(15), 2969–2975 (2015). https://doi.org/10.1021/acs.jpclett.5b01252
5. Kim, H.-S., et al.: Lead Iodide perovskite sensitized all-solid-state submicron thin film mesoscopic solar cell with efficiency exceeding 9%. Sci. Rep. 2(1), 591 (2012). https://doi.org/10.1038/srep00591
6. Noh, J.H., Im, S.H., Heo, J.H., Mandal, T.N., Seok, S.I.: Chemical management for colorful, efficient, and stable inorganic-organic hybrid nanostructured solar cells. Nano Lett. 13(4), 1764–1769 (2013). https://doi.org/10.1021/nl400349b
7. Leijtens, T., et al.: Electronic properties of meso-superstructured and planar organometal halide perovskite films: charge trapping, photodoping, and carrier mobility. ACS Nano 8, 7147–7155 (2014). https://doi.org/10.1021/nn502115k
8. Stranks, S., et al.: Electron-hole diffusion lengths exceeding 1 micrometer in an organometal trihalide perovskite absorber. Science 342, 341–344 (2013). https://doi.org/10.1126/science.1243982

9. Gong, J., Darling, S.B., You, F.: Perovskite photovoltaics: life-cycle assessment of energy and environmental impacts. Energy Environ. Sci. **8**(7), 1953–1968 (2015). https://doi.org/10.1039/C5EE00615E

10. Zou, H., Guo, D., He, B., Yu, J., Fan, K.: Enhanced photocurrent density of HTM-free perovskite solar cells by carbon quantum dots. Appl. Surf. Sci. **430**, 625–631 (2018). https://doi.org/10.1016/j.apsusc.2017.05.122

11. Hossain, M., Alharbi, F., Tabet, N.: Copper oxide as inorganic hole transport material for lead halide perovskite based solar cells of enhanced performance. Sol. Energy **120**, 370–380 (2015). https://doi.org/10.1016/j.solener.2015.07.040

12. Alam, I., Ashraf, M.: Effect of different device parameters on tin-based perovskite solar cell coupled with In 2 S 3 electron transport layer and CuSCN and Spiro-OMeTAD alternative hole transport layers for high-efficiency performance. Energy Sources Part Recov. Util. Environ. Eff. 1–17 (2020). https://doi.org/10.1080/15567036.2020.1820628

13. Bansal, S., Aryal, P.: Evaluation of new materials for electron and hole transport layers in perovskite-based solar cells through SCAPS-1D simulations. In: 2016 IEEE 43rd Photovoltaic Specialists Conference (PVSC), pp. 0747–0750 (2016). https://doi.org/10.1109/PVSC.2016.7749702

14. Anwar, F., Mahbub, R., Satter, S., Ullah, S.M.: Effect of different HTM layers and electrical parameters on ZnO nanorod-based lead-free perovskite solar cell for high-efficiency performance. Int. J. Photoenergy **2017**, 9 (2017). https://doi.org/10.1155/2017/9846310

15. Rühle, S.: Tabulated values of the Shockley-Queisser limit for single junction solar cells. Sol. Energy **130**, 139–147 (2016). https://doi.org/10.1016/j.solener.2016.02.015

A Novel ADI Based Method for Model Reduction of Discrete-Time Index 2 Control Systems

Mohammad-Sahadet Hossain[1] , Atia Afroz[1(✉)], Oshin Mumtaha[2], and Musannan Hossain[2]

[1] Department of Mathematics and Physics, North South University, Dhaka, Bangladesh
{mohammad.hossain,atia.afroz}@northsouth.edu
[2] Department of Electrical and Computer Engineering, North South University, Dhaka, Bangladesh
{oshin.mumtaha,musannan.hossain}@northsouth.edu

Abstract. An exclusive model order reduction (MOR) technique for a discrete-time (DT) index 2 dynamical structure is examined in this work. The power systems model can be considered a common model for control issues and controller design, and these models have relatively large dimensions. The cross gramian (CG) may be used to evaluate the key input-output characteristics of such systems CG. Computing the gramians using the traditional analytic approach can be time-consuming and next to impossible in certain cases. Hence, in the last few decades a lot of attention received on iterative approaches. The iterative approach proposed is focused on factored approximations of the CG, which are accomplished by alternating directional implicit (ADI) methods. We use the factors to derive a congruent reduced model of a discrete-time index-2 system. To demonstrate the effectiveness and correctness of our proposed approach, frequency response simulations are presented in a numerical example. Reduction of the structured model of discrete-time index 2 structures can now be accomplished using this method.

Keywords: Discrete-time system · Index 2 Dynamical system · ADI iteration · Model Order Reduction

1 Introduction

Linear discrete-time systems are challenging topics for research studies from their increasing application in engineering [1] fields. Large and complex models are required in real life applications and many of them are designed as discrete-time index 2 system [9]. We represent the discrete-time linear time-invariant (DT-LTI) of descriptor system in given form,

$$Ex(k+1) = Ax(k) + Bu(k),$$
$$y(k) = C(k), k \in \mathbb{Z}. \tag{1}$$

Supported by the North South University CTRG fund: CTRG-21-SEPS-06.

Here, the state of the above system is $x(k) \in \mathbb{R}^n$ and their input and output are $u(k) \in \mathbb{R}^n$ and $y(k) \in \mathbb{R}^p$. The matrices are $E, A \in \mathbb{R}^{n \times n}$, $B \in \mathbb{R}^{n \times m}$ and $C \in \mathbb{R}^{p \times n}$ subsequently.

Considering E be singular, we can write DT-LTI index-2 descriptor system as,

$$
\begin{bmatrix} E_{11} & 0 \\ 0 & 0 \end{bmatrix} \begin{bmatrix} x_1(k+1) \\ x_2(k+1) \end{bmatrix} = \begin{bmatrix} A_{11} & A_{12} \\ A_{12}^T & 0 \end{bmatrix} \begin{bmatrix} x_1(k) \\ x_2(k) \end{bmatrix} + \begin{bmatrix} B_1 \\ 0 \end{bmatrix} u(k),
$$

$$
y(k) = \begin{bmatrix} C_1 & 0 \end{bmatrix} \begin{bmatrix} x_1(k) \\ x_2(k) \end{bmatrix},
$$

(2)

defining $x_1(k) \in \mathbb{R}^{n_1}$, $x_2(k) \in \mathbb{R}^{n_2}(n_1 > n_2, n_1 + n_2 = n)$ are the states, $E_{11} \in \mathbb{R}^{n_1 \times n_1}$, $A_{11} \in \mathbb{R}^{n_1 \times n_1}$ is defining to be full rank and $A_{12} \in \mathbb{R}^{n_1 \times n_2}$, $B_1 \in \mathbb{R}^{n_1 \times m}$ and $C_1 \in \mathbb{R}^{p \times n_1}$. Here the matrix E_1 is symmetric positive definite and A_1 is defining to be full rank. The major purpose of using the MOR technique is to implant important system dynamics of higher-order model (2) in the derived smaller model. Balanced truncation (BT) is one of the most used methods for MOR which is highly preferred for producing stable reduced-order model [6]. Several research articles have been published in the last few decades focused on the BT method [7,8]. Previously, BT is processed for index-1 continuous and discrete-time systems [1,2,4]. Researches are successfully done based on BT of continuous-time index-2 LTI systems [10]. However, a limited number of articles are found that focuses on reducing models of discrete-time LTI systems in the form of index 2 structure.

This research presents an effective method for the MOR of index-2 discrete-time systems that do not require the use of a spectral projector. We elaborated on the necessary working details of the proposed implementation and theorem. The remainder part of the study is laid out as follows. We have discussed the MOR of index-2 systems in Sect. 2. In Sect. 3, we elaborate on the proposed MOR systems of index 2 followed by Cayley transformation so that we can get continuous-time Lyapunov equations from the generalized discrete-time systems. We discuss the ADI technique to find the transformed matrix equations and work out the factors of low rank for gramians. Section 4 covers the process of BT of reduced structure. The numerical outputs with the graphical representations discuss in Sect. 5. Lastly, we present the concluding remarks in Sect. 6.

2   Literature Review of MOR of Index 2 Systems

The model order reduction technique is used to minimize high computational expense and huge storage requirements while simulating and optimizing large and complex models [2,3]. MOR is an efficiently used tool that substitutes large models with congruent smaller models with maximum accuracy [4,5]. Model reduction is significant in a variety of applications of control space. For the linear time-invariant continuous-time descriptor system (LTI-CTDS), we scrutinize model reduction strategies. A balanced truncation technique is used in this method and are closely related to Gramians and Hankel singular values (HSVs).

Solving generalized Lyapunov equations can yield the Gramians and these are closely related to computing the HSV. When the MOR process is applied to a discrete-time linear time-invariant (DT-LTI) descriptor the system, the reduced model can be represented as follows,

$$\bar{E}\bar{x}(k+1) = \bar{A}\bar{x}(k) + \bar{B}u(k)$$
$$\bar{y}(k) = \bar{c}(k), \tag{3}$$

here, $\bar{E} \in \mathbb{R}^{l \times l}$, $\bar{A} \in \mathbb{C}^{l \times l}$, $\bar{B} \in \mathbb{R}^{l \times l}$, $\bar{C} \in \mathbb{R}^{p \times l}$ are defined for reduced matrices and l is the dimension of the reduced structures.

Several research works follow the idea proposed in [5] to reformulate the discrete-time index-2 of descriptor based system among a system, which is not singular, by manipulating the structure of the system's equations. The algebraic equations extracted from the matrix equations (2) have the following form

$$E_{11}x_1(k+1) = A_{11}x_1(k) + A_{12}x_2(k) + B_1u(k), \tag{4a}$$
$$0 = A_{12}^T x_1(k), \tag{4b}$$
$$y(k) = c_1 x_1(k), \tag{4c}$$

In many literatures, the above system is reformed as a generalized system by projecting it onto a $(n_1 - n_2)$ dimensional subspace by an oblique projector. The Ocean equations, spatial discretization developed by Stokes, or Navier-Stokes provide large-scale structured index-2 descriptor systems [12,14]. They play a dominant role to describe various problems in computational fluid dynamics and engineering applications.

BT method is used for design and control of Pezo mechanical system, specific CFD computation and simulation, structured circuit problem.

BT has been a preferred MOR approach for many researchers in recent decades, and it is a preferable alternative to generating stable reduced-order models [6,7]. In the recent two decades, the BT-based MOR method for index-1 descriptor systems has widely been prominent in both continuous and discrete settings, and it is a favored choice for many technical applications [12,14]. Model reduction for index-1 periodic systems using BT the technique has been proposed and successfully applied for both situations of continuous and discrete-time settings in [12]. There exist plenty of works that propose balanced truncation for MOR of index-2 LTI systems which can be found in [5,14]. However, the works focused on the continuous-time setting of index-2 LTI systems. But, there is very limited research that focuses on the discrete-time setting of index-2 LTI systems and the model reduction of them [9,10,15]. MOR of index 2 LTI system can be discussed for continuous and discrete cases by different methods such as Krylov, ADI, Smith iterative techniques, etc.

In this paper we have prepared the followings:

– The Smith iteration was slow because we do not have any provision for parameter choice to make it faster.

- Inversion of near singular matrices is required, which makes the computation difficult.
- Shift parameters of ADI ensure fast convergence.
- Use Cayley to avoid Smith because Smith is slow.
- Solve an equivalent continuous-time Lyapunov instead of the discrete-time Lyapunov equation. This ensures efficient computation.

Explicit computation of the projected system with an oblique projector is expensive. In this paper, the proposed projection free MOR method includes transformation of discrete-time system to continuous-time system, followed by Cayley transformation.

3   Proposed MOR of Index 2 Systems

The two Stein equations associated with the BT-based MOR process of structured DT-LTI index-2 descriptor system (2) are given by

$$EXE^T - AXA^T = P_l BB^T P_l^T, \quad X = P_r X P_r^T, \tag{5a}$$

$$E^T Y E - A^T Y A = P_r^T C^T C P_r, \quad Y = P_l^T Y P_l, \tag{5b}$$

where, spectral projectors P_l, P_r are defined on the sub-spaces to both the matrix pencil of $\lambda E - A$ analogous to finite eigenvalues. In the structured form of (2), they both are identity matrices. In the works of literature of control theory, solutions defined by X and Y of (5a) and (5b) are known as Controllability and Observability gramians and they are positive and semi-definite. Iterative solutions of them are proposed in [9,10] using the smith method. However, the Smith method is slow in convergence.

3.1   Cayley Transformed Matrix Equations

We do not use the Smith iteration approach to figure out the factors, Z_k of X or the L_k of Y of low rank according to our proposed model. The strategy of using oblique projector [2,10,11] is not suitable for our work. We use Cayley transformation to convert the Stein equations into the continuous-time Lyapunov equation. Now, the generalized Cayley transformation $\mathcal{C}(E_c, A_c)$ is defined here as follows

$$\mathcal{C}(E_c, A_c) = \lambda(A - E) - (A + E), \tag{6}$$

where

$$E_c = A - E = \begin{bmatrix} A_{11} - E_{11} & A_{12} \\ A_{12}^T & 0 \end{bmatrix}, \tag{7}$$

and

$$A_c = A + E = \begin{bmatrix} A_{11} + E_{11} & A_{12} \\ A_{12}^T & 0 \end{bmatrix}. \tag{8}$$

Projected continuous-time algebraic Lyapunov equations (PCALE) with (6) as follows

$$E_c X A_c^T + A_c X E_c^T = -B_c B_c^T,$$
$$E_c^T Y A_c + A_c^T Y E_c = -C_c^T C_c, \tag{9}$$

where $B_c := \sqrt{2}B$, and $C_c := \sqrt{2}C$. Also, the matrix pencil, that is Cayley-transformed, is $A_c - \lambda E_c = (A + E) - \lambda(A - E)$. The stable eigenvalues $A - \lambda E$ are mapped to stable eigenvalues of $A_c - \lambda E_c$. Infinite eigenvalues of $A - \lambda E$ are mapped to 1 in $A_c - \lambda E_c$. The PCALE of (9) becomes

$$(A_c^{-1} E_c)X + X(A_c^{-1} E_c)^T = -(A_c^{-1} B_c)(A^{-1} B_c)^T,$$
$$(A_c^{-1} E_c)^T Y + (A_c^{-1} E_c)Y = -(A_c^{-1} C_c)^T (A_c^{-1} C_c). \tag{10}$$

Now we consider the first equation of (10) and apply the ADI method to find a probable solution X_k of X. We impose the ADI in double sweep iterations form:

$$(A_c^{-1} E_c + p_k I)X_{k-1/2} = -B_c B_c^T - X_{k-1}((A_c^{-1} E_c)^T - p_k I)$$
$$(A_c^{-1} E_c + p_k I)X_k = -B_c B_c^T - X_{k-1/2}^T((A_c^{-1} E_c)^T - p_k I). \tag{11}$$

Simple substitution can help to write the two steps in a single iteration step as

$$((A_c^{-1} E_c)^T + pI)X(A_c^{-1} E_c + pI) - ((A_c^{-1} E_c)^T - pI)X(A_c^{-1} E_c - pI)$$
$$= -2Re(p)B_c^T B_c. \tag{12}$$

Hence, the ADI iteration stands with more mathematical manipulations

$$X_k = -2p_k(A_c^{-1} E_c + p_k I)^{-1}(A_c^{-1} E_c - \bar{p}_k I)X_{k-1}(A_c^{-1} E_c - p_k I)^T(A_c^{-1} E_c + \bar{p}_k I)^{-T}$$
$$- 4Re(p_k)(A_c^{-1} E_c + p_k I)^{-1}(A_c^{-1} E_c B_c)(A_c^{-1} E_c B_c)(A_c^{-1} E_c B_c^T)(A_c^{-1} E_c + p_k I)^{-T} \tag{13}$$

Since all the finite eigenvalues of $A_c - \lambda E_c$ have negative real parts, its guarantees that the ADI iterations proposed in (13) will converge to the exact solution after the limited number of iterations [5]. We find that (13) is symmetric. Considering $X_k = Z_k Z_k^T$ and $X_0 = 0$, we can write the iteration in terms of the factors Z_k, as

$$Z_1 = \sqrt{-2p_1}(A_c^{-1} E_c + p_1 I)^{-1}B_c,$$
$$Z_k = [\sqrt{-2p_1}(A_c E_c + p_k I)^{-1}B_c, (A_c^{-1} E_c + p_k I)^{-1}(A_c^{-1} E_c - p_k I)Z_{k-1}]. \tag{14}$$

At the k-th iteration of the ADI methods if X_k is the approximate solution of the Lyapunov equation, the error to the exact solution X is measured by

$$X - X_k = ((A_c^{-1} E_c)^T + pI)^{-1}((A_c^{-1} E_c)^T - pI)(X - X_{k-1})(A_c^{-1} E_c - pI)(A_c^{-1} E_c + pI)^{-1}. \tag{15}$$

Continuing the process at the k th iteration, the error bound can be measured by

$$X - X_k = \prod_{k=0}^{i}((A_c^{-1}E_c)^T + p_kI)^{-1}((A_c^{-1}E_c)^T - p_kI)\prod_{k=0}^{i}(A_c^{-1}E_c - p_kI)(A_c^{-1}E_c + p_kI)^{-1},$$

(16)

which measures the error of the Lyapunov solution at the k-th iteration of the ADI method, the Lyapunov residual can be reformulated as

$$
\begin{aligned}
R(X_k) &= (A_c^{-1}E_c)X_k + (A_c^{-1}E_c)^T X_k + B_c B_c^T \\
&= \prod_{k=0}^{i}((A_c^{-1}E_c)^T + p_kI)^{-1}((A_c^{-1}E_c)^T - p_kI)B_c B_c^T \prod_{k=0}^{i} d(A_c^{-1}E_c - p_kI)(A_c^{-1}E_c + p_kI)^{-1} \\
&= W_i W_i^T.
\end{aligned}
$$

(17)

3.2   Computation of Shift Parameters

The convergence rate of the ADI iteration (13) is extremely connected to the spectral radius of the matrix Z_k. Selection of suitable ADI parameters minimize the problem and leads to generalized minimax problem where spectral radius concerning the shift parameters. Because the spectrum of the pencil $\lambda E_c - A_c$ is unknown, the ideal ADI parameters are very difficult to determine in general, especially for large-scale situations. [13] proposes an alternate method for determining the sub-optimal parameters by substituting the Eigen spectrum with a collection of biggest and lowest values among the modulus Ritz values (MRV) and eigenvalues of A_c are mimicked by that.

It is evident that the pencil $\lambda E_c - A_c$ has a limited number of eigenvalues of negative real component, which is known to have stable eigenvalues, as well as an eigenvalue of $\lambda = 1$, a similar expression for finding the optimal shift parameters $p_1, p_2, \ldots, p_i$ can be found as

$$\{p_1, p_2, \ldots, p_i\} = \underset{p_1,p_2,\ldots,p_i \in \mathbb{C}^-}{\arg\min} \ \underset{t \in \mathrm{Sp}(E_c^{-1}A_c)\backslash\{1\}}{\max} \ \prod_{j=1}^{i} \frac{|(t - \bar{p}_j)|}{|(t + \bar{p}_j)|}, \quad (18)$$

here, $\lambda E_c - A_c$ is the spectrum to the matrix $E_c^{-1}A_c$ [13].

4   The BT-Based MOR

Using the BT-MOR approach, we can calculate the reduced order model (3) for the dimension l from system (2). The main system in BT must be brought into a balanced state, which is done when both of the Gramians X and Y

Algorithm 1: Low-rank ADI iteration for generalized.

Input: A_c, E_c, and B_c, $\{P_i\}_{i=1}^J$.
Output: $R = Z_i$, such that $P \approx RR^T$.

1: $W_0 = B$, $Z_0 = [\ \ ]$, $i = 1$.
2: $Z_1 = V_1$
    while $\|W_{i-1}^T W_{i-1}\| \geq \tau or i \leq i_{max}$ **do**
    Compute $V_i = (A_c + P_i E_c)^{-1} W_{i-1}$;
    if $Im(P_i) = 0$ **then**
        $Z_i = [Z_{i-1}\ \ \sqrt{-2P_i}V_i]$;
        $W_i = W_{i-1} - 2P_i E_c V_i$.
    else
        $\gamma = -2Re(P_i)$, $\ \delta = \frac{Re(P_i)}{Im(P_i)}$;
        $Z_{i+1} = [Z_{i-1}\ \ \sqrt{2\gamma}(Re(V_i) + \delta Im(V_i))\ \ \sqrt{2\gamma}\sqrt{(\delta^2 + 1)}Im(V_i)]$,
        $W_{i+1} = W_{i-1} + 2\gamma E_c(Re(V_i) + \delta Im(V_i))$.
        $i = i + 1$
    end
    i=i+1
    end

---

are diagonal and equal, also in BT, the main system should be allocated in a balanced state. The Cholesky factors Z_k and L_k satisfy $X = ZZ^T \approx Z_k Z_k^T$ and $Y = LL^T \approx L_k L_k^T$, based on a condition, which is, only if (E, A) the matrix pair is stable. The singular value decomposition (SVD) be calculated using the formula below,

$$Z^T EL = [U_1\ \ U_2] \begin{bmatrix} S_1 & \\ & S_2 \end{bmatrix} [V_1\ \ V_2]^T \qquad (19)$$

where $[U_1\ \ U_2]$ and $[V_1\ \ V_2]$ are orthogonal, and $S_1 = \text{diag}(\sigma_1, \sigma_2, \cdots, \sigma_l)$, $S_2 = \text{diag}(\sigma_{l+1}, \sigma_{l+2}, \cdots, \sigma_n)$, where $\sigma_1 \geq \sigma_2 \geq \cdots \sigma_{l+1} \geq \cdots \sigma_n$ are the HSVs. Following projection matrices can be created as

$$T_L = ZU_1 S_1^{-\frac{1}{2}}, \ \ T_Z = LV_1 S_1^{-\frac{1}{2}}. \qquad (20)$$

We generate the following reduced-order system by applying these projection matrices to the original systems matrices

$$\bar{E} = T_L^T E T_Z, \bar{A} = T_L^T A T_Z, \bar{B} = T_L^T B, \bar{C} = C T_Z. \qquad (21)$$

To verify the results, we check the reduced order system and original system they have closely similar approximation. Now we may consider the H_∞ norm of the error bound which is shown below,

$$\|G - \bar{G}\|_{H_\infty} = \sup \|G((j\omega) - \bar{G}(j\omega)\|_2 < 2 \star \text{trace}(S_2), \qquad (22)$$

where $G = C(j\omega E - A)^{-1}B$ and $\bar{G} = \bar{C}(j\omega \bar{E} - \bar{A})^{-1}\bar{B}$ are the transfer functions of the original and reduced order systems, respectively. S_2 denotes the Hankel singular values have been truncated from the system (2).

5   Numerical Findings

The developed algorithm is investigated by applying it to the discrete-time index 2 system. Following the system dynamics and criteria for the structure of an index-2 periodic descriptor system, the data was created.

In this reformulation, we consider $n = 10, n_1 = 8, n_2 = 2$, and,

$$r_1 = 0.5, \quad r_2 = 0.05, \quad r_3 = -0.02, \quad r_4 = 0.12,$$

$$A_{01} = \begin{bmatrix} r_1 \cos(\pi/3) & r_1 \sin(\pi/3) \\ -r_1 \sin(\pi/3) & r_1 \cos(\pi/3) \end{bmatrix}, \quad A_{02} = \begin{bmatrix} r_2 \cos(7\pi/5) & r_2 \sin(7\pi/5) \\ -r_2 \sin(7\pi/5) & r_2 \cos(7\pi/5) \end{bmatrix},$$

$$A_{03} = \begin{bmatrix} r_3 \cos(\pi/4) & r_3 \sin(\pi/4) \\ -r_3 \sin(\pi/4) & r_3 \cos(\pi/4) \end{bmatrix}, \quad A_{04} = \begin{bmatrix} r_4 \cos(\pi/10) & r_4 \sin(\pi/10) \\ -r_4 \sin(\pi/10) & r_4 \cos(\pi/10) \end{bmatrix},$$

$$A_{11} = (9/5) * \text{diag}(A_{01}, A_{02}, A_{03}, A_{04}),$$

$$A_{12} = \begin{bmatrix} 0 & 0 & 2 & 0 & 1 & s_1 & 0 & 1 \\ 0 & -1 & s_3 & -1 & 0 & -1 & 0 & 1 \end{bmatrix}^T,$$

$$A_{21} = A_{12}^T, \quad A_{22} = \text{zero}(n - n_1, n - n_1),$$

and

$$A = \begin{bmatrix} A_{11} & A_{12} \\ A_{12}^T & 0 \end{bmatrix}.$$

Furthermore, we consider

$$\theta = 10 * \pi,$$

$$s_1 = \sin(\theta), \quad s_2 = -0.3s_{1k}, \quad s_3 = 0.6s_1,$$

$$c_1 = \cos(\theta), \quad c_2 = 0.2c_1, \quad c_3 = 0.6c_1.$$

Also,

$$E_{11} = \begin{bmatrix} 1 & 1 & c_1 & s_1 & 0 & c_2 & 0 & 1 \\ 1 & 0 & -s_1 & c_1 & 0 & c_2 & 0 & -1 \\ c_1 & s_1 & 1 & 0 & c_2 & s_2 & 0 & s_3 \\ -s_1 & c_1 & 0 & 1 & -s_2 & c_2 & 0 & 0 \\ 0 & 0 & c_2 & s_2 & 1 & 0 & c_3 & s_3 \\ c_2 & 0 & -s_2 & c_2 & 0 & 1 & -s_3 & c_3 \\ 0 & c_1 & 0 & 0 & c_3 & s_3 & 1 & 0 \\ 0 & c_3 & 0 & 0 & -s_3 & c_3 & 0 & 1 \end{bmatrix},$$

and finally, form,

$$E = \begin{bmatrix} E_{11} & 0 \\ 0 & 0 \end{bmatrix}.$$

Now, the following matrices are the input form and output form,

$$B_1 = \begin{bmatrix} 4 & -1 & s_3+1 & 1 & 0 & -2 & 0 & 1 \\ 1 & 0 & s_1+1 & -2 & 1 & -1 & 0 & -1 \end{bmatrix}^T, B_2 = \mathrm{zeros}(n-n_1, m),$$

$$B = [B_1, B_2]^T,$$

and

$$C_1 = \begin{bmatrix} 5 & -2 & s_1+1 & 0 & 0 & 1 & -2 & -6 \\ 2 & 2 & s_3+1 & 0 & 1 & 0 & 1 & 1 \\ 0 & 2 & 0 & s_2+1 & 1 & 6 & 0 & 3+c_1 \end{bmatrix}, C_2 = \mathrm{zeros}(p, n-n_1),$$

$$C = [C_1, C_2]^T.$$

We consider here $n = 10$ and A and E the matrices have dimensions of 10×10, while, B is defined as input matrix and C as output matrix bearing 10×2 and 3×10, as dimensions. Lastly, A_{11} and E_{11} have the dimension 8×8, on the other hand B_1 and C_1 have the dimension 8×2 and 3×8, respectively.

We observe a similarity of the sparsity structures of the matrices E and A as (2) and they are depicted in Fig. 1.

We solved the Cayley transformed Lyapunov equation using the LR-ADI method. However, due to the Cayley transformation, all finite stable eigenvalues $\lambda A_c - \lambda E_c = A_c - \lambda E_c$ are imaged to the finite eigenvalues of $A - \lambda E$, and the eigenvalue of $A_c - \lambda E_c$ to the infinity is imaged to $\lambda = 1$. We have presented this transformation in Fig. 2.

We can obtain the reduced-order system with a dimension of $l = 6$ and a reduction tolerance 10^{-1}. $\bar{A}$ and $\bar{E}$ are the matrices of the system of reduced-order, have dimension 6×6 whereas the matrices defined as input and output, $\bar{B}$ and $\bar{C}$, have dimensions of 6×2 and 3×6, proportionately. We evaluate the low-rank Cholesky factor Z using Algorithm 1. And to obtain an appropriate Z, we executed the algorithm 8 times. Similarly, we evaluate L, the Cholesky factors of low rank, to determine the Observability Gramian.

We assessed the similarities of transfer functions of a reduced system and the original system in the domain of frequency. The transfer functions assigned to the reduction and the original systems in Fig. 3, we can notice that they have remarkable similarities between them. Despite the significant overlap between the transfer function of the original system and the transfer function of the reduced system, the errors have to be checked in evaluating the transfer function for the reduced structure. Figure 4 and 5 exhibits the absolute error and the relative error for the reduced transfer function. We observe that these errors are very negligible.

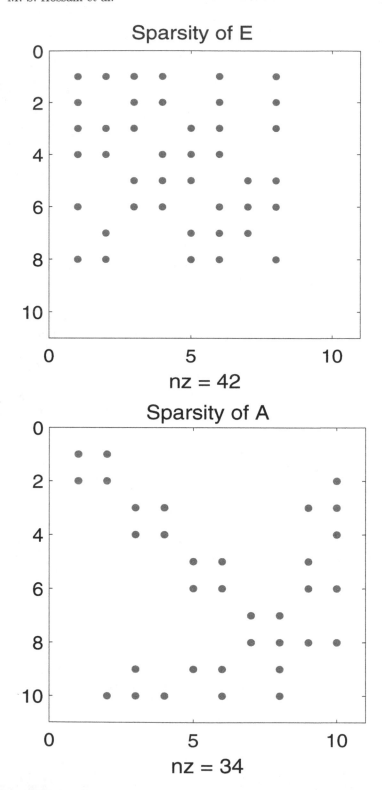

Fig. 1. Sparsity patterns of system's matrices.

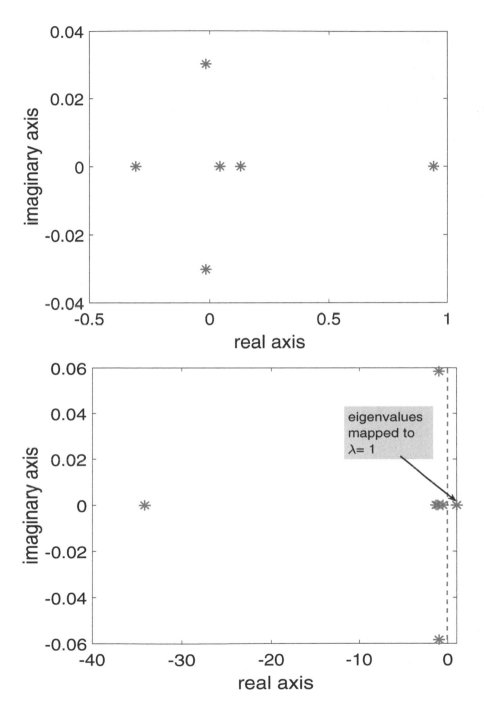

Fig. 2. Mapping of eigenvalues through Cayley transformation.

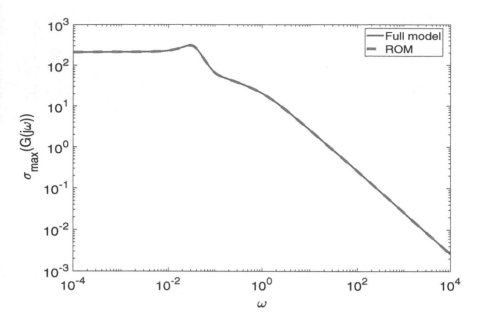

Fig. 3. Linear simulations.

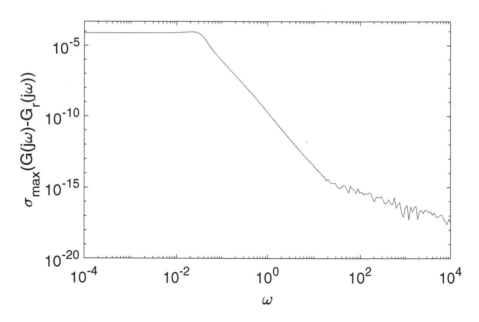

Fig. 4. Absolute error in reduced order MOR.

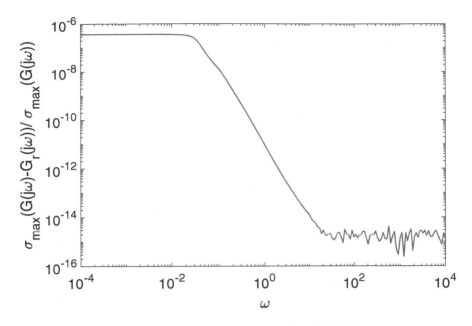

Fig. 5. Relative error in reduced order MOR.

6   Conclusion

We used the ADI method to solve the Cayley transformed Lyapunov equations that convert a discrete system into a continuous system of the DT-LTI index-2 descriptor system. The reduced-order system obtained by the MOR system is a reasonable approximation to the original system and it is confirmed by the mapping of eigenvalues under the Cayley transformation. We observe that after the first convergence, we can not ensure that the structure is preserved for the large model. We are working on it and using different techniques for making the problem faster preserving the structure.

References

1. Benner, P., Hossain, M.: Structure preserving iterative methods for periodic projected Lyapunov equations and their application in model reduction of periodic descriptor systems. Numer. Algor. **76**(4), 881–904 (2017)
2. Hossain, M., Omar, S., Tahsin, A., Khan, E.: Efficient system reduction modeling of periodic control systems with application to circuit problems. In: 4th International Conference on Advances in Electrical Engineering (ICAEE), Dhaka, Bangladesh, pp. 259–264 (2017)
3. Gugercin, S., Stykel, T., Wyatt, S.: Model reduction of descriptor systems by interpolatory projection methods. SIAM J. Sci. Comput. **35**(5), 1010–1033 (2013)
4. Hossain, M.: Numerical Methods for Model Reduction of Time-Varying Descriptor Systems, Ph.D. Thesis, Chemnitz University of Technology (2011)

5. Uddin, M.M.: Computational Methods for Model Reduction of Large-Scale Sparse Structured Descriptor Systems, Ph.D Thesis, Max-Planck Institute (2015)
6. Antoulas, A.C.: Approximation of Large-Scale Systems. SIAM, Philadelphia (2005)
7. Gugercin, S., Antoulas, A.C.: A survey of model reduction by balanced truncation and some new results. Int. J. Control **77**, 748–766 (2004)
8. Li, J.-R., White, J.: Reduction of large circuit models via low rank approximate gramians. Int. J. Appl. Math. Comp. Sci. **11**, 1151–1171 (2001)
9. Hossain, M.S., Khan, E.H., Omar, S.G.: An efficient algorithm for reduce order modeling of discrete-time index-2 descriptor control systems. In: 22nd International Conference on Computer and Information Technology (ICCIT), Dhaka, Bangladesh (2019)
10. Omar, G., Hossain, M.S., Khan, E.H., Tahsin, A.: An efficient model reduction strategy for discrete-time index-2 descriptor control systems. In: International Conference on Electrical, Computer and Communication Engineering (ECCE), Cox's Bazar, Bangladesh, pp. 1–6 (2019)
11. Benner, P.: Model reduction algorithm using spectral projection methods. In: Householder Symposium XV, Peebles, Schottland (2002)
12. Stykel, T.: Balanced truncation model reduction for semi-discretized Stokes equation. Linear Algebra Appl. **415**(2–3), 262–289 (2006)
13. Stykel, T.: Gramian-based model reduction for descriptor systems. Math. Control Signals Syst. **16**, 297–319 (2004)
14. Heinkenschloss, M., Sorensen, D., Sun, K.: Balanced truncation model reduction for a class of descriptor systems with application to the oseen equations. SIAM J. Sci. Comput. **30**(20), 1038–1063 (2008)
15. Yu, B., Fan, H.-Y., Chu,E.: Smith method for projected Lyapunov and Stein equations. UPB Sci. Bull. Series A: Appl. Math. Phys. **80**, 191–204 (2018)

Emerging Technologies for Society and Industry

Prevalence of Stroke in Rural Bangladesh: A Population Based Study

Md. Mashiar Rahman[1], Rony Chowdhury Ripan[2], Farhana Sarker[2,3],
Moinul H. Chowdhury[2], A. K. M. Nazmul Islam[2], and Khondaker A. Mamun[2,4(✉)]

[1] Palli Karma-Sahayak Foundation, Dhaka, Bangladesh
[2] CMED Health, Dhaka, Bangladesh
mamun@cse.uiu.ac.bd
[3] Department of CSE, University of Liberal Arts Bangladesh, Dhaka, Bangladesh
[4] AIMS Lab, Department of CSE, United International University, Dhaka, Bangladesh

Abstract. Stroke is one of the leading causes of mortality in Bangladesh. To create effective early prevention and interventions of stroke in Bangladesh, it is vital to comprehend the prevalence of stroke. To achieve this aim, we present a large-scale study to report the prevalence of stroke in a rural community in Bangladesh. We collected a total of 1 304 868 people's data from 50 unions in Bangladesh using the mHealth application. Among them, 51.34% were male and 43.66% were female. The overall prevalence of stroke patients was 1.04 (95% Confidence Interval [CI]: 0.98–1.1) per 1000 people. In addition, males had a significantly larger stroke prevalence rate (1.58 times larger than females). The prevalence of stroke patients increased as age increased. Moreover, the prevalence of stroke patients was higher (8.38 per 1000 people; 95% CI: 6.64–10.12) among " >= 80" age groups. Overall, this study will be helpful to understand the epidemiology of the stroke problem in the rural areas of Bangladesh.

Keywords: Prevalence of Stroke · LMICs · Cardiovascular disease (CVD) · Stroke & Heart Failure

1 Introduction

CVD, for instance, stroke, heart attack, abnormal heart rhythms, etc., is the primary cause of death and the main cause of long-term impairment [1]. CVD alone is responsible for 6.2 million (11% of global) deaths per year in worldwide [2]. Among CVD, stroke causes the greatest number of deaths worldwide [3]. For instance, ischemic heart disease and stroke combinedly responsible for 15.2 million deaths in 2015 [4]. In 2002, stroke was rated seventh among the main reasons for disability-adjusted life years (DALY) loss; by 2030, it will be the 2nd leading reason of death and the 6th major source of DALY loss worldwide [5]. Stroke survivors and stroke-related DALY are increasing day by day [3]. Globally, there are around 62 million stroke survivors [6] and up to five years following a stroke, 36% of victims are left with severe disability [7].

© ICST Institute for Computer Sciences, Social Informatics and Telecommunications Engineering 2023
Published by Springer Nature Switzerland AG 2023. All Rights Reserved
Md. S. Satu et al. (Eds.): MIET 2022, LNICST 491, pp. 515–523, 2023.
https://doi.org/10.1007/978-3-031-34622-4_41

As the number of stroke victims increases worldwide, so do stroke-related health care expenses. For instance, stroke accounts for around 3 to 4% of entire health care expenses in Western countries [8]. In 2017, Fernandez et al. calculated economic burden of stroke across Europe by collecting data from 32 European countries and they found each year around 1.5 million people are diagnosed with stroke, costing European societies around 60 billion euros [9]. In the United States, the average lifetime cost of an ischemic stroke is projected to be $140,048 per individual [10]. In 2009, Saka et al. took data from the South London Stroke Register and estimated that strokes were costing the UK a total societal cost of 8.9 billion per year [11]. In addition, Singapore spends around 0.65% of its GDP per capita on stroke management [12].

More than 75% of stroke-related deaths occur in low-middle income countries (LMICs) [13], but fewer studies have been done in those regions. For instance, Jones et al. in a systematic review stated that per year, the prevalence of stroke in India ranged from 0.26 to 7.57 per thousand people [14]. People in LMICs are at greater danger of stroke and other CVDs because there is no integrated primary healthcare system and no early detection and prevention of stroke-related risk factors like high blood pressure, smoking, diabetes, etc. [15]. The increasing burden of stroke on the economy and limited access to primary healthcare in LMICs are impeding the macroeconomic development of many countries [16]. Stroke and coronary heart disease (CHD) cost around $5000 per episode, and monthly treatment costs ranged between $300 and $1000 in LMICs [17]. Being a LMIC country, Bangladesh has a population of about 162.2 million and the majority (74%) of them reside in rural areas [18]; their health spending per capita is 123 US dollars [19]. One third of Bangladeshis are youths between 15 and 35 years old. People aged more than 60 years constitute around 14.6 million, which will increase to 55.7 million by the year 2061. As life expectancy is increasing, managing elderly people will create a burden on the economy, especially on the healthcare system [20] and stroke is prevalent among these adult people [18]. Few researches have been conducted showing the prevalence of stroke in rural areas of Bangladesh, although stroke is the 3rd biggest reason of mortality in Bangladesh, following coronary heart disease and infectious disease [18]. For instance, Saha et al. conducted a survey in Raiganj Upazila and found the prevalence of stroke at 1.96 per one thousand people [21]. Besides, Matin et al. did a study on 1250 stroke death data and reported related risk factors [22]. In addition, Islam et al. showed in a small-scale study that the prevalence of stroke is 3.0 per one thousand people, and male stroke patients are in greater number [18].

To create effective early prevention and interventions of stroke in Bangladesh, it is vital to comprehend the problem's prevalence. In this study, we present a large-scale study to report the prevalence of stroke in a rural community in Bangladesh.

The rest of the paper is designed according to the following: in Sect. 2, we provide the methodology of this study. Then, in Sect. 3, we analyze all the data and outline the findings. After that, we discuss our findings in Sect. 4. In Sect. 5, we provide recommendations and finally conclude this paper in Sect. 6.

2   Methodology

2.1   Data Collection

The epidemiological data were collected from 50 Unions of Bangladesh. Data was collected by community health workers (CHW) by visiting different households. Before collecting data, community health workers were trained for two weeks. In this study, we took data from a total of 24203 households that were visited during July 2018 to June 2021. For collecting data, the CHW used the "Enriched Sastho" mobile application (see Fig. 1). During data collection, a total of 104 data variables were collected, including socio-demographic, economic, environmental, and health-related data. Only stroke related data was considered for this study.

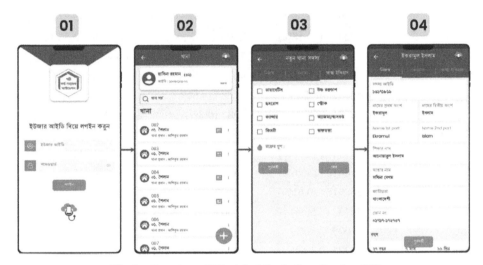

Fig. 1. Overview of "Enriched Sastho" application [27]

2.2   Statistical Analysis

First, we examined data for missing values and outliers [26]. Then, we used descriptive statistics to analyze the distribution of the population by age, gender, and education. Numerical variables were given as mean and standard deviation, and nominal variables were given as proportion. The prevalence of stroke was analyzed per 1000 people along with a 95% confidence interval (CI). The analysis was done with the help of Python's powerful libraries: Pandas, NumPy, Matplotlib, and Seaborn.

3   Results

3.1   Socio-demographic Information of the Studied Population

During this study, 1304868 people were surveyed. Among them, 669964 (51.34%) were male and 634904 (48.66%) were female. The mean age was 29.30 years (standard deviation: ± 18.99 years) and the maximum age was 99.00 years. Among studied population, maximum (44.6%) people was less than 25 years old and minimum (0.8%) people was greater or equal 80 years old. In addition, the number of male population members was greater in all age groups than the female population (see Fig. 2). Also, 557944 (42.76%) of the population completed primary level education and 316612 (24.26%) of the population were illiterate. A detailed socio-demographic distribution representation of the studied population is presented in Table 1.

Table 1. Distribution of socio-demographic information of the studied population

Characteristics	Overall	Male	Female
Age Groups			
<25	582027 (44.6%)	294981 (44.03%)	287046 (45.21%)
25–44	432936 (33.18%)	220087 (32.85%)	212849 (33.52%)
45–54	135275 (10.37%)	71615 (10.69%)	63660 (10.03%)
55–64	87372 (6.7%)	46516 (6.94%)	40856 (6.43%)
65–79	56757 (4.35%)	31383 (4.68%)	25374 (4.0%)
>= 80	10501 (0.8%)	5382 (0.8%)	5119 (0.81%)
Education			
PSC	557944 (42.76%)	290033 (43.29%)	267911 (42.2%)
Illiterate	316612 (24.26%)	151952 (22.68%)	164660 (25.93%)
Others	268918 (20.61%)	139026 (20.75%)	129892 (20.46%)
JSC	46432 (3.56%)	21367 (3.19%)	25065 (3.95%)
SSC	36008 (2.76%)	18599 (2.78%)	17409 (2.74%)
Honors	31225 (2.39%)	20764 (3.1%)	10461 (1.65%)
HSC	18227 (1.4%)	10546 (1.57%)	7681 (1.21%)
Literacy	13202 (1.01%)	6200 (0.93%)	7002 (1.1%)
Hafiz	3365 (0.26%)	3080 (0.46%)	285 (0.04%)
Masters	3301 (0.25%)	2295 (0.34%)	1006 (0.16%)
Dakhil	1997 (0.15%)	1321 (0.2%)	676 (0.11%)
Diploma	1964 (0.15%)	1533 (0.23%)	431 (0.07%)
Ebtedaye	1438 (0.11%)	782 (0.12%)	656 (0.1%)
Alim	1093 (0.08%)	679 (0.1%)	414 (0.07%)
Dawra-E-Hadith	1081 (0.08%)	605 (0.09%)	476 (0.07%)
JDC	984 (0.08%)	438 (0.07%)	546 (0.09%)
MBBS	412 (0.03%)	280 (0.04%)	132 (0.02%)
Fazil	303 (0.02%)	199 (0.03%)	104 (0.02%)
Kamil	298 (0.02%)	222 (0.03%)	76 (0.01%)
Engineer	64 (0.005%)	43 (0.01%)	21 (0.003%)

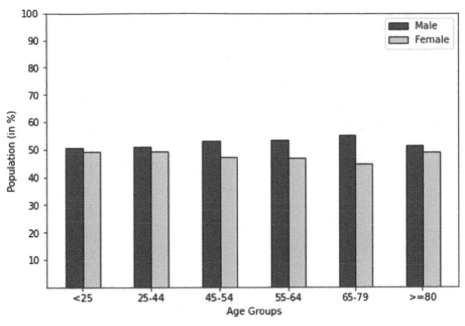

Fig. 2. Bar chart distribution of the studied population segregated into gender and age.

3.2 Prevalence of Stroke Patients

Among 1304868 studied population, 1368 (1.04 per 1000 people; 95% CI: 0.98–1.1) were stroke patients. Overall, males had a significantly larger (n = 857; 1.28 per 1000 people; 95% CI: 1.19–1.37) stroke prevalence compared with females (n = 511, 0.81 per 1000 people; 95% CI: 0.74–0.88). The prevalence of stroke patients' rates increased with age. The prevalence of stroke patients was higher (n = 88; 8.38 per 1000 people; 95% CI: 6.64–10.12) in the " > = 80" age groups. In addition, for "<25" age groups, females (n = 15; 0.05 per 1000 people; 95% CI: 0.03–0.08) were more prevalent than males (n = 11; 0.04 per 1000 people; 95% CI: 0.02 0.06). However, for the rest of the age groups, the male population was in higher numbers than their counterparts (see Fig. 3). A detailed distribution of stroke patients according to their age and gender is represented in Table 2.

Table 2. Population distribution of stroke patients according to age and gender

Age Groups	Overall	95% CI	Male	95% CI	Female	95% CI
<25	26 (0.04)	0.03–0.06	11 (0.04)	0.02–0.06	15 (0.05)	0.03–0.08
25–44	188 (0.43)	0.37–0.5	108 (0.49)	0.4–0.58	80 (0.38)	0.29–0.46
45–54	273 (2.02)	1.78–2.26	160 (2.23)	1.89–2.58	113 (1.78)	1.45–2.1
55–64	378 (4.33)	3.89–4.76	245 (5.27)	4.61–5.92	133 (3.26)	2.7–3.81
65–79	415 (7.31)	6.61–8.01	279 (8.89)	7.85–9.93	136 (5.36)	4.46–6.26
>= 80	88 (8.38)	6.64–10.12	54 (10.03)	7.37–12.7	34 (6.64)	4.42–8.87

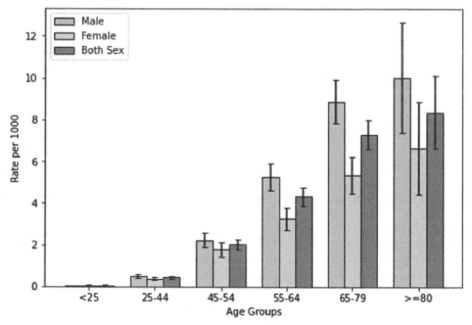

Fig. 3. Bar chart representation of prevalence of stroke per 1000 population among different age groups

4   Discussion

To our best knowledge, this is one of the largest population-based studies on the prevalence of strokes undertaken in rural Bangladesh. We collected data from 1304868 people from 50 unions in Bangladesh. Among them, 1368 stroke patients were found. The overall prevalence of stroke patients is 1.04 per 1000 people, which is slightly lower than these two studies [21, 23] conducted in Bangladesh in 2017 and 2011 respectively. We argue that the rate is lower because the total population size in our studies is bigger than in the first study; the second study collected data from urban and rural areas and only considered age groups above forty years. A study conducted in rural areas of India found the prevalence rate ranged from 0.8 to 2.44 per 1000 people [24]. However, another study conducted in urban Sri Lanka found a prevalence rate of 5.45 per 1000 adults [25], which is much higher than our study. Males had a significantly larger stroke prevalence rate (1.58 times larger than females), which is similar to this study [21]. However, for the "<25" age groups, females (0.05 per 1000 people) were more prevalent than males (0.04 per 1000 people). We are uncertain of the specific explanation behind it. The prevalence of stroke patients' rates increased with age, which is supported by these studies [18, 21]. The prevalence of stroke patients was higher (8.38 per 1000 people) in the ">= 80" age groups.

This study has some limitations. This study does not represent an urban scenario, since all the data was collected from rural areas of Bangladesh. Also, data was collected from only 50 unions (1.09% of total unions) in Bangladesh. Another limitation of this study was that we did not clinically justify the stroke events of the patients; rather, they were included based on their medical history.

5   Recommendations

As mentioned previously, one of the drawbacks of our study was that we lacked data from urban regions. We advocate collecting data from urban regions of Bangladesh so that future researchers can generate a stroke prevalence estimate for Bangladesh that is more generalizable. In addition, clinical justification of the stroke events is advised. Besides, to better comprehend the epidemiology of the stroke problem, it is necessary to gather risk factors such as tobacco use and family history of stroke in order to conduct risk factor association research.

6   Conclusion and Future Work

Not only is stroke a national health problem in Bangladesh; it is also a global health problem. To understand the stroke problem in depth, we believe it is important to understand the prevalence of stroke. To find out the prevalence of stroke in rural Bangladesh, we collected data from 50 unions and found the overall stroke prevalence rate was 1.04 per 1000 people. Male stroke patients were more prevalent than female stroke patients, and stroke prevalence was higher among adult people. Overall, this study will be helpful for future researchers to understand the epidemiology of the stroke problem in the rural areas of Bangladesh. In the future, we plan to design a stroke prediction model for early prevention and intervention of stroke in Bangladesh.

References

1. Malone, R.: The role of the physician associate: an overview. Ir. J. Med. Sci. https://doi.org/10.1007/s11845-021-02661-9
2. Engels, T., et al.: Socioeconomic status and stroke prevalence in Morocco: results from the Rabat-Casablanca study. PLoS ONE 9, e89271 (2014)
3. Katan, M., Luft, A.: Global burden of stroke. Semin. Neurol. 38, 208–211 (2018)

522   Md. M. Rahman et al.

4. Feigin, V.L., et al.: Global, regional, and national burden of neurological disorders during 1990–2015: a systematic analysis for the global burden of disease study 2015. Lancet Neurol. **16**, 877–897 (2017)
5. Mathers, C.D., Loncar, D.: Projections of global mortality and burden of disease from 2002 to 2030. PLoS Med. **3**, e442 (2006)
6. Strong, K., Mathers, C., Bonita, R.: Preventing stroke: saving lives around the world. Lancet Neurol. **6**, 182–187 (2007)
7. Hankey, G.J., Jamrozik, K., Broadhurst, R.J., Forbes, S., Anderson, C.S.: Long-term disability after first-ever stroke and related prognostic factors in the Perth community stroke study, 1989–1990. Stroke **33**, 1034–1040 (2002)
8. Struijs, J.N., van Genugten, M.L.L., Evers, S.M.A.A., Ament, A.J.H., Baan, C.A., van den Bos, G.A.M.: Future costs of stroke in the Netherlands: the impact of stroke services. Int. J. Technol. Assess. Health Care **22**, 518–524 (2006)
9. Luengo-Fernandez, R., Violato, M., Candio, P., Leal, J.: Economic burden of stroke across Europe: a population-based cost analysis **5**, 17–25 (2019). https://doi.org/10.1177/239698 7319883160
10. Johnson, B.H., Bonafede, M.M., Watson, C.: Short-and longer-term health-care resource utilization and costs associated with acute ischemic stroke. ClinicoEconomics and Outcomes Research. ncbi.nlm.nih.gov
11. Saka, Ö., Mcguire, A., Wolfe, C.: Cost of stroke in the United Kingdom. Age Ageing **38**, 27–32 (2009)
12. Wijaya, H.R., Supriyanto, E., Salim, M.I.M., Siregar, K.N., Eryando, T.: Stroke management cost: review in Indonesia, Malaysia and Singapore. AIP Conf. Proc. **2092**, 030022 (2019)
13. Checkley, W., Ghannem, H., Irazola, V., et al.: Management of NCD in low- and middle-income countries. Glob. Heart **9**, 431–443 (2014)
14. Jones, S.P., Baqai, K., Clegg, A., et al.: Stroke in India: a systematic review of the incidence, prevalence, and case fatality. Int. J. Stroke **17**, 132–140 (2022)
15. Islam, J.Y., Zaman, M.M., Moniruzzaman, M., Ara Shakoor, S., Hossain, A.H.M.E.: Estimation of total cardiovascular risk using the 2019 WHO CVD prediction charts and comparison of population-level costs based on alternative drug therapy guidelines: a population-based study of adults in Bangladesh. BMJ Open (2020). https://doi.org/10.1136/BMJOPEN-2019-035842
16. Islam, S.M.S., Purnat, T.D., Phuong, N.T.A., Mwingira, U., Schacht, K., Fröschl, G.: Non communicable diseases (NCDs) in developing countries: a symposium report. Glob. Health (2014). https://doi.org/10.1186/S12992-014-0081-9
17. Gheorghe, A., Griffiths, U., Murphy, A., Legido-Quigley, H., Lamptey, P., Perel, P.: The economic burden of cardiovascular disease and hypertension in low- and middle-income countries: a systematic review. BMC Public Health (2018). https://doi.org/10.1186/S12889-018-5806-X
18. Islam, M.N., et al.: Burden of stroke in Bangladesh. Int. J. Stroke **8**, 211–213 (2013)
19. Current health expenditure (% of GDP) - Bangladesh | Data. https://data.worldbank.org/ind icator/SH.XPD.CHEX.GD.ZS?locations=BD. Accessed 8 May 2022
20. Kabir, R., Kabir, M., Gias Uddin, M.S., Ferdous, N., Khan Chowdhury, M.R.: Elderly population growth in Bangladesh: preparedness in public and private sectors. IOSR J. Humanit. Soc. Sci. **21**, 58–73 (2016)
21. Saha, U.K., et al.: Epidemiology of stroke: findings from a community-based survey in rural Bangladesh. Public Health **160**, 26–32 (2018)
22. Mateen, F.J., Carone, M., Alam, N., Streatfield, P.K., Black, R.E.: A population-based case–control study of 1250 stroke deaths in rural Bangladesh. Eur. J. Neurol. **19**, 999–1006 (2012)
23. Mohammad, Q.D., et al.: Prevalence of stroke above forty years. Mymensingh Med. J. **20**, 640–644 (2011)

24. Pandian, J.D., Sudhan, P.: Stroke epidemiology and stroke care services in India. J. Stroke **15**, 128 (2013)
25. Chang, T., Gajasinghe, S., Arambepola, C.: Prevalence of stroke and its risk factors in Urban Sri Lanka: population-based study. Stroke **46**, 2965–2968 (2015)
26. Ripan, R.C., Islam, M., Alqahtani, H., Sarker, I.H.: Effectively predicting cyber-attacks through isolation forest learning-based outlier detection. Secur. Priv. **5**, e212 (2022)
27. Rahman, M.M., et al.: Implementation of a digital healthcare service model for ensuring preventive and primary healthcare in Rural Bangladesh. https://doi.org/10.1007/978-981-19-2445-3_37

Segmented-Truncated-SVD for Effective Feature Extraction in Hyperspectral Image Classification

Md. Moshiur Rahman⬛, Shabbir Ahmed⬛, Md. Shahriar Haque⬛,
Md. Abu Marjan$^{(\boxtimes)}$⬛, Masud Ibn Afjal⬛, and Md. Palash Uddin⬛

Hajee Mohammad Danesh Science and Technology University, Dinajpur, Bangladesh
{marjan,masud,palash_cse}@hstu.ac.bd

Abstract. Hyperspectral images (HSIs) are typically developed to obtain essential details about the land captured by hundreds of tiny and spectral bands. The classification does not achieve the desired performance using HSI dataset due to a large number of bands. Techniques for band reduction are utilized for the enhancement of classification performance. In this work, we propose an improved Truncated Singular Value Decomposition (TSVD), a classical feature extraction method, based on the supremacy of band segmentation in the HSI analysis. We call our method as Segmented-Truncated-SVD (STSVD), where the TSVD application extracts better local intrinsic and global properties from the HSI. Rather than applying the full dataset, we first segment the entire dataset into a number of strongly correlated spectral band subgroups and apply the TSVD on each subgroup separately. For Per-pixel classification by support vector machine (SVM) STSVD method, the classical PCA, Segmented-PCA (SPCA), SVD, and TSVD methods are applied to the mixed agricultural Indian Pines HSI dataset. The experimental results exhibit that the overall classification of STSVD (87.373%) remarkably outperforms all the other investigated methods: PCA (83.554%), SPCA (86.774%), SVD (83.986%), TSVD (83.526%), and the complete dataset without employing any feature reduction method (82.997%). The proposed STSVD also demands the least space complexities in different phases.

Keywords: Hyperspectral image classification · Feature extraction · Remote sensing · PCA · Segmented PCA · SVD · Truncated SVD · Segmented Truncated SVD

1 Introduction

Hyperspectral imaging (HSI) is a discipline with promising prospects that combines the benefits of optical spectroscopy as an analytical tool with the two dimensional objects viewing provided by spectral imaging. It is the simultaneous

Md. S. Satu et al. (Eds.): MIET 2022, LNICST 491, pp. 524–537, 2023.
https://doi.org/10.1007/978-3-031-34622-4_42

capture and integration of spatial and their resembling spectral characteristics in an image space. As such, it offers high spectral resolutions via hundreds of small and continuous spectral wavelength bands, which can be beneficial in a variety of applications, such as bettering the study of earth objects, agriculture, mining, geology, environment study, surveillance, food quality, pharmaceuticals and so on [1–4]. To acquire information about a given ground surface, the capturing wavelength range is commonly between $0.4\,\mu m$ to $3.0\,\mu m$, encompassing the spectrum of electromagnetic waves between visible light and near-infrared. To recognize characteristics of narrow absorption, the spectral resolution of HSIs is measured in nm in steps of contiguous wave-length ranges, allowing for data inspection discrimination [2,5,6]. HSI has a strong discriminating capacity in data analysis for a variety of categories like as vegetation classification, identifying if certain components exists or not in an object like- medicine, mineral resources, soil or field, lakes, changes of the earth's surface, etc. [7]. HSI data typically comprises two-dimensional spatial information with a third dimension within a hypercube that offers spectral features regarding the captured objects. Therefore, the complete HSI data contains $X \times Y \times F$, where X, Y and F is the HSI data's height, width and the number of bands respectively.

Information may not be equal across all HSI bands, while the neighboring bands holds highly correlated information from the data [8,9]. When the whole original HSI for practical applications is employed, the classification performance is not always adequate. Furthermore, for improved classification performance, the quantity of samples required is approximately exponentially related to the quantity of features. Practically, It is difficult to obtain a significant number of samples needed for training. Because of these reasons, feature reduction techniques, which are separated into feature extraction and feature selection methods, are applied in reducing the bands of HSI to improve the classification outcome [10,11]. The original data is used in feature selection algorithms in general and various searching criteria is applied to find the relevant bands [12]. These searching criteria are oftentimes challenging since the combinatorial exploration requires high computational costs [13]. On the contrary, feature extraction, a better alternative strategy for reducing dimensionality, obtains the most valuable details about the HSI after executing several statistical transformations on the dat [14]. Feature extraction methods are classified into two types: supervised and unsupervised. Both of them use linear as well as nonlinear transformations to extract appropriate and intrinsic characteristics from the HSI. The training data, which can be computationally demanding, is critical to the success of supervised feature extraction algorithms. Whereas, unsupervised feature extraction methods are used to extract relevant traits of the data without prior knowledge [15]. Supervised methods commonly uses spectral and spatial information for improved classification [16]. Seamise-CNN, generalized embedding regression, mixture of factor analysis etc. are used as supervised feature extraction methods for HSI classification [16–18].

Principal Component Analysis (PCA) is a commonly used unsupervised feature extraction method in hyperspectral imagery. However, unlike PCA, SVD does not require the data matrix to be centered and, therefore, it is capable of working with sparse data matrices without the requirement to densify them. To what follows, SVD substantially supersedes PCA in HSI context. TSVD, an enhanced version of the classical SVD, has been proved as an efficient unsupervised linear feature extraction method [19]. As such, we propose the STSVD feature extraction approach in this paper that segments the HSI dataset into some correlated band subgroups and then performs TSVD separately towards extracting HSI's global as well as intrinsic local characteristics for improving the classification performance. Moreover, we analyze the superiority of our proposed STSVD over the other well-known unsupervised linear feature extraction methods, such as PCA, SPCA, SVD, and TSVD. Therefore, this paper's primary contributions are outlined below:

- A correlation-based Segmented-TSVD (STSVD) feature extraction approach for effective classification of HSI,
- An empirical analysis using a series of experiments for validating the superiority of the proposed STSVD, and
- A theoretical analysis using the space complexities at different stages for illustrating the advantages of the proposed STSVD.

The following is how this paper is structured- Sect. 2 discusses the insights of PCA and it's variants, SVD and it's variants for HSI feature extraction. In Sect. 3, we provide the comprehensive idea and derivation of the proposed STSVD approach. Comparative result analysis and experimental setup are provided in Sect. 4, while summarizing conclusion of the investigations and findings are mentioned in Sect. 5.

2   Feature Extraction

2.1   PCA for HSI

PCA, as an unsupervised linear feature extraction approach, decreases the dimensionality of big datasets while keeping the majority of their information by turning a huge number of variables into a smaller set of variables. PCA determines the relationship among spectral bands via orthogonal transformation [20–22]. Let $\mathbf{x}_n$ be the spectral vector of a pixel in data matrix $\mathbf{D}$, which is stated as $\mathbf{x}_n = [\mathbf{x}_{n1}\mathbf{x}_{n2}....\mathbf{x}_{nF}]^T$, where $n \in [1, S]$ and $S = X * Y$ with X being the height and Y being the width of the HSI. In PCA operation, firstly the HSI data is converted into a 2D data matrix, denoted as $\mathbf{D}$, of size $F \times S$. Then, the image with zero-mean, $\mathbf{I}$ is obtained from the $\mathbf{I}_n$ as $\mathbf{I} = [\mathbf{I}_1\mathbf{I}_2....\mathbf{I}_n]$, where $\mathbf{I}_n = \mathbf{x}_n - \mathbf{M} = [\mathbf{I}_{n1}\mathbf{I}_{n2}...\mathbf{I}_{nF}]^T$ with $\mathbf{M}$, defined as $\mathbf{M} = \frac{1}{S}\sum_{n=1}^{S}\mathbf{x}_n$, as the mean image vector. The covariance matrix $\mathbf{C} = \frac{1}{S}\mathbf{II}^T$ is then produced for Eigendecomposition, where the core of PCA is represented by eigenvectors $(V_1V_2...V_F)$, known as principle components (PCs), and their corresponding eigenvalues $(E_1E_2...E_F)$. The new feature space's directions is controlled by the number of PCs whereas the eigenvalues control their amplitude or variance. If the corresponding $E_1E_2...E_F$ of $\mathbf{C}$ composes the diagonal matrix $\mathbf{E} = diagonal(E_1 E_2 ... E_F)$, and the matrix $\mathbf{V}$ contains all of the eigenvectors. Therefore,

$$\mathbf{C} = \mathbf{VEV}^T. \tag{1}$$

Now, q eigenvectors are chosen to build $\mathbf{w}$ matrix with $F \times q$ dimension, where $q \leq F$, and usually $q \ll F$. The traditional way for selecting the top q PCs is that the eigenvalues are ranked from the highest to the lowest. Finally, $\mathbf{Y}$, the projection matrix of $\mathbf{D}$ is obtained using $\mathbf{Y} = \mathbf{w}^T \times \mathbf{I}$.

2.2   SPCA for HSI

If the HSI bands are substantially connected, the standard PCA retrieves operative characteristics. PCA also generates a large covariance matrix with $F \times F$ dimension needs a high cost of computation [11,23]. PCA may omit certain subtle valuable information of the HSI that might be used for effective categorization because it considers global statistics. As a result, SPCA (Segmented PCA) is offered as a means to modify the use of standard PCA by removing low correlations between the blocks with high correlation for increased performance. L contiguous subgroup datasets are formed from the data matrix $\mathbf{D}$ depending on the bands' correlation. These data subgroups are used in the deployment of SPCA for HSI [23]. For extracting the dataset's local attributes, the strongly correlated bands are selected in a subgroup. After that, each subgroup dataset is subjected to traditional PCA. Let the matrices of segmented data be $\mathbf{D}_t$, where $t\epsilon[1, L]$ and for each segmented data matrix, n_t represents the number of consecutive bands. Then, $\mathbf{D}_1 = [\mathbf{I}_1' \mathbf{I}_2' ... \mathbf{I}_n']$, $\mathbf{D}_2 = [\mathbf{I}_1'' \mathbf{I}_2'' ... \mathbf{I}_n'']$, and so on, where $\mathbf{I}_j'$ includes the first n_1 rows of the corresponding $\mathbf{I}_j$ and $\mathbf{I}_j''$ includes the first n_2 rows by skipping initial n_1 rows of the corresponding $\mathbf{I}_j$ with $j, n\epsilon[1, S]$. The eigen-decomposition procedure is then applied to each $\mathbf{D}_t$ calculated covariance matrix. By sequentially combining the individual projection matrices of $\mathbf{D}_t$, the overall projection matrix is obtained.

2.3   SVD for HSI

Linearly independent rows or columns of the data matrix $\mathbf{D}$ is represented by rank r, where $S \geq F$ instead of compromising the consistency of data matrix, and thereby $r \leq F$. The transcriptional response of the ith pixel is formed by the components of the ith row of $\mathbf{D}$, which is represented by the F-dimensional vector g_i. Conversely, the components of $\mathbf{D}$'s j^{th} column can be combined to generate the S-dimensional vector a_j, which is denoted as the jth vector's expression profile. The following equation represents $\mathbf{D}$'s singular value decomposition [24]:

$$\mathbf{D} = \mathbf{U\Sigma V}^T \tag{2}$$

where $\mathbf{U}$ is an unitary matrix of $S \times F$ dimension, $\mathbf{\Sigma}$ is a diagonal matrix of $F \times F$ dimension, and $\mathbf{V}^T$ is an unitary matrix of $F \times F$ dimension. The left singular vectors, $\mathbf{u}_k$, are the columns of $\mathbf{U}$, and they construct an orthonormal model, with $\mathbf{u}_i \cdot \mathbf{u}_j = 1$ for $i = j$, and $\mathbf{u}_i \cdot \mathbf{u}_j = 0$ alternatively. The components of the singular vectors $\mathbf{v}_k$ are included in $\mathbf{V}^T$ rows. Solely the non-zero components on the diagonal are obtained in $\mathbf{\Sigma}$, which are denoted as the singular values. Therefore, $\mathbf{\Sigma} = diagonal(s_1 s_2 ... s_n)$. Moreover, $s_k > 0$ for $1 \leq k \leq r$, and $s_i = 0$ for $(r + 1) \leq k \leq n$. Ranking of the singular vectors is performed in the order from the highest to the lowest in terms of singular values. The highest singular value resides at the $\mathbf{\Sigma}$ matrix's top left position. Singular value decomposition is analogous to diagonalization, which is a solution to the problem regarding the eigenvalues of matrix $\mathbf{D}$ [24].

2.4 TSVD for HSI

TSVD performs linear feature extraction based on the truncated singular values. It is a variant of SVD that truncates the required information to provide the optimal low-rank matrix approximation of the data matrix. This estimator, unlike PCA, does not center the data before generating the SVD, which indicates that it can operate effectively with sparse matrices. In various applications, the rank r of the non-zero singular values might be huge, making SVD computationally problematic. In these kind of circumstances, the lowest singular values might require to be truncated so that only $t \ll r$ non-zero singular values are computed rather than r. TSVD only computes t largest singular values, where t is pre-defined [25]. The truncated SVD denoted as $\bar{\mathbf{D}}$, no longer represents a precise decomposition of the original data matrix $\mathbf{D}$, but instead offers the best low-rank matrix projection of $\mathbf{D}$ by any matrix of defined rank t.

$$\mathbf{D} \approx \bar{\mathbf{D}} = \mathbf{U}_t \mathbf{\Sigma}_t \mathbf{V}_t^T, \tag{3}$$

where $\mathbf{U}_t$ is an $S \times t$ matrix, $\mathbf{\Sigma}_t$ is a $t \times t$ diagonal matrix, and $\mathbf{V}_t^T$ is a $t \times F$ matrix. The t largest singular values $\mathbf{\Sigma}_t$ are computed from the t row vectors of $\mathbf{V}^T$ and the t column vectors of $\mathbf{U}$. If implemented, this can be lot faster and less costly than the SVD when $t \ll r$, but it necessitates an entirely different tool set of statistical methods. The lowest singular values of $\mathbf{D}$, which are more difficult to compute than the largest, are of importance in various applications that needs an estimation to the Moore-Penrose inverse of the data matrix $\mathbf{D}$.

3   Proposed Segmented-TSVD

HSI dataset comprises hundreds of bands. Correlations between the nearby bands are often higher than between those bands far distant. It has been noted that the high correlation between the bands appears in contiguous blocks. We term these contiguous blocks or band subgroups as segments and term the procedure as segmentation. Each segments comprises highly correlated bands that are similar in terms of their characteristics and attributes. Therefore, these band segments represent its local characteristics. The local intrinsic characteristics are neglected in the accumulation of the global characteristics when feature extraction is performed on the entire dataset without segmentation. Local characteristics as well

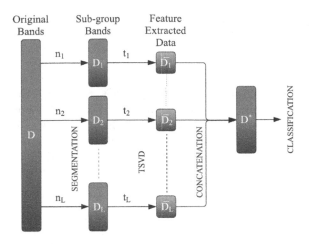

Fig. 1. Schematic diagram of the proposed STSVD.

as global characteristics offer more details regarding the original dataset, which might improve classification accuracy.

We propose STSVD in which feature extraction using conventional TSVD is performed on each of the band segments for better classification performance. To extract local intrinsic characteristics, STSVD applies the conventional TSVD to each highly correlated band segment of the HSI dataset. STSVD also accumulates the global structural characteristics of the dataset, because the segmented feature extracted data are concatenated as compressed data for classification. As STSVD is applied separately to each of the segments instead of the entire original data, low memory is required which is proportional to the number of t_i bands in a segment, where $i \in [1, L]$. Therefore, the upper bound of memory requirement for feature extraction is reduced. Figure 1 demonstrates the proposed STSVD's schematic structure.

To implement our proposed STSVD, the dataset is first partitioned into L segments according to the bands' high correlation. Let $\mathbf{D}_i$ be the ith band segment of the dataset $\mathbf{D}$, where $i \in [1, L]$ and n_i being the band's count in segment $\mathbf{D}_i$. Next, $\mathbf{D}_1 \approx \bar{\mathbf{D}}_1$ where, $\bar{\mathbf{D}}_1 = \mathbf{U}_{t_1}\mathbf{\Sigma}_{t_1}\mathbf{V}_{t_1}^T$ and t_i denotes the defined number of features to be extracted from $\mathbf{D}_i$ as stated in Eq. 3. Similarly, $\mathbf{D}_2 \approx \bar{\mathbf{D}}_2$ where, $\bar{\mathbf{D}}_2 = \mathbf{U}_{t_2}\mathbf{\Sigma}_{t_2}\mathbf{V}_{t_2}^T$ and so on, and the features from $\mathbf{D}_2$, ..., $\mathbf{D}_L$ can be extracted in the same way. Finally, the projection matrices of every $\mathbf{D}_i$ are concatenated into $\mathbf{D}^*$, the overall projection matrix which is used for classification.

4 Experimental Result

4.1 Description of the Dataset

Several experiments are carried out using the Indian Pines HSI dataset in order to evaluate the proposed methodology's efficiency. Collection of this dataset is obtained from the Purdue University Research Repository (PURR) through Grupo De Inteligencia (GIC) [26]. This dataset was originally generated by NASA's AVIRIS above Indiana's Indian Pines agricultural test site. This dataset's comprehensive information is demonstrated in Table 1.

Table 1. Indian Pines HSI dataset description.

No. of spectral bands, F	Range of wavelengths (nm)	Image height, X (piexls)	Image width, Y (pixels)	Ground classes	Spatial resolution (m)
220	400–2500	145	145	16	20

4.2 Experimental Setup

Indian Pines HSI dataset originally comprises 21025 pixels in total and 16 labels of class of ground truths alongside a huge number of pixels are unclassified. According to the matrix of band-to-band correlation, the dataset has been separated into contiguous set of bands as illustrated in Fig. 2. Correlation value 1.0, −1.0 and 0.0 indicates the perfect positive correlation, perfect negative correlation, and no correlation respectively. Based on the possible segments as shown in Fig. 2, SPCA and STSVD are used in 3 distinct fashions, each with 3, 4, or 5 segments of varied band subgroups, which are stated as STSVD3, STSVD4 and STSVD5, and SPCA3, SPCA4 and SPCA5 respectively. We provide the detailed segmentation information in Table 2. SPCA3 and STSVD3 indicates that for each of them the entire data has been segmented into 3 segments. Similarly, for SPCA4 and STSVD4, and, SPCA5 and STSVD5, the entire data has been segmented into 4 and 5 segments. Average correlation in diagonal of correlation matrix ≈0.50 has been chosen to separate the contiguous segments, which is calculated by taking the average of the values in the segment present in the correlation matrix [23].

The crucial challenge of the feature extraction approaches is finding the optimum number of Principal Components (PCs) for the optimum classification performance. We carry out thorough experiments to find out the optimal number of PCs for PCA, SVD, TSVD and STSVD. Based on the executed experiments demonstrated in Table 3, the optimal number of PCs are selected for the segments of SPCA and STSVD as shown in Table 2. All of the conducted experiments are executed and ranked based on the overall classification accuracy for

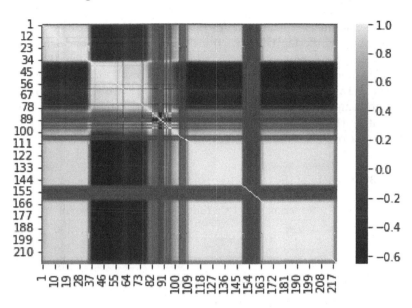

Fig. 2. Image representation of the band-to-band correlation matrix of the Indian Pines HSI dataset.

Table 2. Detailed band segmentation information for SPCA and STSVD on the Indian Pines dataset.

Segment	Factors	Number of Segments		
		3 (SPCA3 & STSVD3)	4 (SPCA4 & STSVD4)	5 (SPCA5 & STSVD5)
1	Band range	1–36	1–36	1–36
	No. of PCs	3	3	3
	Average correlation in diagonal	0.87312	0.87312	0.87312
2	Band range	37–102	37–79	37–79
	No. of PCs	6	1	5
	Average correlation in diagonal	0.54622	0.89601	0.89601
3	Band range	103–220	80–102	80–102
	No. of PCs	5	3	3
	Average correlation in diagonal	0.69487	0.43316	0.43316
4	Band range	N/A	103–220	103–162
	No. of PCs		5	4
	Average correlation in diagonal		0.69487	0.51454
5	Band range	N/A	N/A	163–220
	No. of PCs			6
	Average correlation in diagonal			0.93004

each of the experimented methods. All possible combinations of PCs from the three segments (considering 1-35 PCs from the first segment, and 1-50 PCs from the second and third segments) are conducted in the experiments for SPCA3 and STSVD3, and then we heuristically adopt the results for 4 and 5 segments, as provided in Table 3. The number of PCs for other feature extraction methods which do not employ segmentation is that PCA, SVD, and TSVD are selected by enumerating through all possible number of bands starting from 1 PC to the highest number of PCs by increasing it by one gradually [20].

Table 3. Summary of the conducted experiments to select the optimal PCs.

Method	Experimented PCs range	No. of experiments
PCA	1–220	220
SVD	1–20	220
TSVD	1–19	219
STSVD3 & SPCA3	1(1–5), 2(1–50) & 3(1–50)	87500
STSVD4 & SPCA4	1(1–8), 2(1–8), 3(1–7) & 3(1–8)	4096
STSVD5 & SPCA5	1(1–7), 2(1–7), 3(1–7), 4(1–7) & 5(1–7)	16807
Total no. of conducted experiments		109062

Support vector machine (SVM) with an RBF kernel from Scikit-learn python library is exerted for classification for computing the overall classification accuracy, precision score, recall score, and f1 score. SVM is usually accepted and used as classifier model by many researchers in the field of HSI classification [27,28]. However, overall classification accuracy is commonly considered as an objective parameter to quantitatively appraise the methods [22]. Per-pixel classification in SVM is used to classify each pixel individually [17]. The optimal values of C and *gamma* are determined using 10-fold cross-validation for SVM model's efficient training and testing. *MinMaxScaler* from Scikit-learn python library is used as a normalization technique on the training and testing samples for better classification performance.

4.3 Classification Performance

The dataset of 10249 pixels is divided into the training set that comprises 3074 pixels and testing set that comprises 7175 pixels. 30% of the dataset is used as training sets, and 70% is used as testing sets. Both the sets include samples of each 16 classes as demonstrated in Table 4. Datasets for training and testing are derived from the original dataset by splitting in stratified manner where the number of samples used for training and testing of each 16 classes are stratified. As a result, each of the 16 classes maintains the 30% and 70% train-test split. The train-test dataset split is performed using *train_test_split* method of Scikit-learn python library. Note that class imbalance problem is present in the dataset,

Table 4. Information of the training and testing samples.

No.	Class name	Training samples	Testing samples
1	Alfalfa	14	32
2	Corn (no-till)	428	1000
3	Corn (min-till)	249	581
4	Corn	71	166
5	Pasture grass	145	338
6	Grass (trees)	219	511
7	Pasture mowed grass	8	20
8	Windrowed hay	143	335
9	Oats	6	14
10	Soybean (no-till)	292	680
11	Soybean (min-till)	736	1719
12	Soybean	178	415
13	Wheat	62	143
14	Woods	379	886
15	Buildings-Drives	116	270
16	Stone-Towers	28	65
Total		3074	7175

since some of classes have large amount of pixels while some others have very small amount of pixels.

We provide the classification results in terms of aforementioned performance measure metrics in Table 5. Number of PCs achieving the best overall accuracy is applied to each investigated methods.

From Table 5 it can be observed that the proposed STSVD3 produces the highest classification performance among all the investigated methods in terms of all the aforementioned performance measures i.e. overall accuracy, precision,

Table 5. Classification performances using the proposed STSVD and some existing methods.

Method	No. of PCs	SVM (C, gamma)	Overall accuracy × 100	Precision score × 100	Recall score × 100	Kappa score × 100	Execution time (in seconds)
Original dataset	220	10, 0.11	82.997	83.117	82.997	80.500	6.92
PCA	72	10, 0.96	83.554	83.516	83.554	81.148	5.61
SVD	98	10, 0.53	83.986	83.982	83.986	81.635	19.20
TSVD	98	10, 0.79	83.526	83.475	83.526	81.115	6.61
SPCA3	15	10, 2.60	86.091	85.930	86.091	84.085	2.60
STSVD3	15	10, 2.22	**87.373**	**87.325**	**87.373**	**85.566**	2.43
SPCA4	12	10, 3.03	86.774	86.843	86.774	84.858	2.45
STSVD4	12	10, 2.10	87.038	87.094	87.038	85.171	**2.39**
SPCA5	21	10, 1.59	86.230	86.304	86.230	84.219	2.82
STSVD5	21	10, 1.18	86.997	87.050	86.997	85.104	2.72

Md. M. Rahman et al.

recall, Kappa score. The proposed STSVD4 and STSVD5 are the second and the third best performer in that comparison, respectively. Moreover, the proposed STSVD4 requires the least amount of execution time followed by the proposed STSVD3. STSVD3, STSVD4, and STSVD5 require only 15, 12, and 21 extracted features, respectively, to produce the best performances. The other feature extraction methods without segmentation i.e., PCA, SVD, and TSVD requires large number of PCs to produce optimal classification performance. In addition, each of the feature extraction methods generates better classification results than the experiment using original dataset (82.997% overall accuracy) without applying feature extraction. Segmented methods SPCA3, STSVD3, SPCA4, STSVD4, SPCA5, and STSVD5 outperform other feature extraction methods that do not use a segmentation methodology: PCA, SVD, and TSVD. The rationale for this is that segmentation methods extract both global and local intrinsic properties, whereas non-segmentation approaches simply extract global characteristics. It can be noticed that the non-segmentation approaches require large number of PCs to generate optimal outcomes compared to the segmented ones. Segmented approaches requires 12-21 PCs to achieve best performances, whereas non-segmented approaches requires up to 98 PCs. However, PCA requires lower number of PCs compared to SVD, and TSVD. Although STSVD3 supersedes SPCA4 in terms of all the performance measures, but SPCA4 requires less amount of PCs compared to SPCA3. STSVD4 takes 2.39 s which is the minimal execution time among the investigated methods. Moreover, STSVD3 has the second lowest execution time, which is 2.43 s. Finally, it is observed that proposed STSVD outperforms PCA, SPCA, SVD, and TSVD in terms of all the classification performance measurements.

We now provide the confusion matrix of the best classification performer STSVD3 in Fig. 3. The confusion matrix calculates the distribution of all expected responses and compares them to their correct classifications. Let the 2D confusion matrix be $\mathbf{C}$, where $\mathbf{C}_{ij}$ denotes the quantity of entries of class i that is projected as being of class j by the classifier model. $\mathbf{C}_{ij}$ where $i = j$ denotes the the value of true positives of class i.

4.4 Memory Requirement

We also consider memory requirement as the theoretical performance measure of the feature extraction techniques. Table 6 illustrates the memory requirements for the proposed and the investigated feature extraction methods. Here, n_i denotes the number of bands of ith segment, t stated as the number of extracted features, and, t_i stated as the number of extracted features of ith segment. As such, $n_i \leq F$, $t < F$ and $t_i < n_i$ always holds, it can be observed that STSVD requires the least memory for singular value matrix among the investigated feature extraction methods. SVD, TSVD, and STSVD generates singular value matrix, whether PCA, and SPCA generate covariance matrix. Furthermore, data matrix of SPCA and STSVD requires the least amount of memory. Therefore, STSVD requires the least amount of memory for both memory requirement criteria.

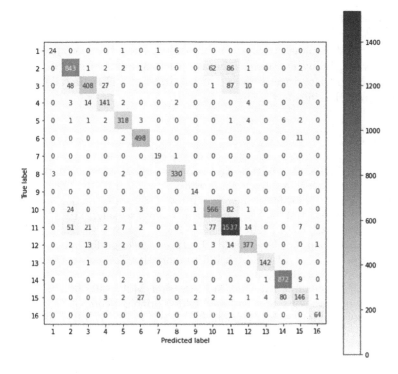

Fig. 3. Confusion matrix of the STSVD3 classification.

Table 6. Memory requirements of the proposed and the existing methods.

Method	Data Matrix	Covariance/Singular Value Matrix
PCA	$S \times F$	$F \times F$
SPCA	$S \times n_i$	$n_i \times n_i$
SVD	$S \times F$	$F \times F$
TSVD	$S \times F$	$t \times t$
STSVD	$S \times n_i$	$t_i \times t_i$

5   Conclusion

An improved and efficient feature extraction method using correlation-based segmentation and TSVD, called STSVD has been introduced in this paper. This
introduced method efficiently retrieves the global as well as the local intrinsic properties of the entire HSI dataset. STSVD has been compared to certain
commonly used feature extraction methods, including PCA, SPCA, SVD, and
TSVD according to all the mentioned classification performance measures, space
requirement as well. The comparative analysis demonstrates that the proposed
STSVD surpasses all of the experimented feature extraction approaches while

using a substantially less number of PCs, less execution time, and less memory requirement. Nevertheless, if the experimental setup such as the segmentation subgroups, SVM parameters, etc. are modified, then the classification performances may negligibly fluctuate. Increasing the amount of samples in training the classifier model and the removal of the dataset's class imbalance problem might enhance classification accuracy as well.

References

1. Richards, J.A., Jia, X.: Multispectral transformations of image data. In: Remote Sensing Digital Image Analysis: An Introduction, pp. 137–163 (2006)
2. Zabalza, J., et al.: Novel folded-pca for improved feature extraction and data reduction with hyperspectral imaging and sar in remote sensing. ISPRS J. Photogram. Remote Sens. **93**, 112–122 (2014)
3. Uddin, M., Mamun, M., Hossain, M.: Feature extraction for hyperspectral image classification. In: 2017 IEEE Region 10 Humanitarian Technology Conference (R10-HTC), pp. 379–382. IEEE (2017)
4. Uddin, M.P., Mamun, M.A., Afjal, M.I., Hossain, M.A.: Information-theoretic feature selection with segmentation-based folded principal component analysis (pca) for hyperspectral image classification. Int. J. Remote Sens. **42**(1), 286–321 (2020)
5. Uddin, M., Mamun, M., Hossain, M.: Segmented FPCA for hyperspectral image classification. In: 2017 3rd International Conference on Electrical Information and Communication Technology (EICT), pp. 1–6. IEEE (2017)
6. Mishu, S.Z., Ahmed, B., Hossain, M.A., Uddin, M.P.: Effective subspace detection based on the measurement of both the spectral and spatial information for hyperspectral image classification. Int. J. Remote Sens. **41**(19), 7541–7564 (2020)
7. Mohan, B.K., Porwal, A.: Hyperspectral image processing and analysis. Curr. Sci. **108**, 833–841 (2015)
8. Guo, B., Gunn, S.R., Damper, R.I., Nelson, J.D.: Band selection for hyperspectral image classification using mutual information. IEEE Geosci. Remote Sens. Lett. **3**(4), 522–526 (2006)
9. Uddin, M.P., Mamun, M.A., Hossain, M.A., Afjal, M.I.: Improved folded-pca for efficient remote sensing hyperspectral image classification. In: Geocarto International (just-accepted), pp. 1–28 (2021)
10. Uddin, M., Mamun, M., Hossain, M.: Improved feature extraction using segmented fpca for hyperspectral image classification. In: 2017 2nd International Conference on Electrical & Electronic Engineering (ICEEE), pp. 1–4. IEEE (2017)
11. Uddin, M.P., Mamun, M.A., Hossain, M.A.: Pca-based feature reduction for hyperspectral remote sensing image classification. IETE Techn. Rev. **38**(4), 377–396 (2021)
12. Jia, X., Kuo, B.C., Crawford, M.M.: Feature mining for hyperspectral image classification. Proc. IEEE **101**(3), 676–697 (2013)
13. Melgani, F., Bruzzone, L.: Classification of hyperspectral remote sensing images with support vector machines. IEEE Trans. Geosci. Remote Sens. **42**(8), 1778–1790 (2004)
14. Tsai, F., Lin, E.K., Yoshino, K.: Spectrally segmented principal component analysis of hyperspectral imagery for mapping invasive plant species. Int. J. Remote Sens. **28**(5), 1023–1039 (2007)

15. Fauvel, M., Chanussot, J., Benediktsson, J.A.: Kernel principal component analysis for feature reduction in hyperspectrale images analysis. In: Proceedings of the 7th Nordic Signal Processing Symposium-NORSIG 2006, pp. 238–241. IEEE (2006)
16. Shao, Y., Sang, N., Gao, C., Ma, L.: Spatial and class structure regularized sparse representation graph for semi-supervised hyperspectral image classification. Pattern Recogn. **81**, 81–94 (2018)
17. Liu, B., Yu, X., Zhang, P., Yu, A., Fu, Q., Wei, X.: Supervised deep feature extraction for hyperspectral image classification. IEEE Trans. Geosci. Remote Sens. **56**(4), 1909–1921 (2017)
18. Zhao, B., Ulfarsson, M.O., Sveinsson, J.R., Chanussot, J.: Unsupervised and supervised feature extraction methods for hyperspectral images based on mixtures of factor analyzers. Remote Sens. **12**(7), 1179 (2020)
19. Xu, P.: Truncated SVD methods for discrete linear ill-posed problems. Geophys. J. Int. **135**(2), 505–514 (1998)
20. Cao, L., Chua, K.S., Chong, W., Lee, H., Gu, Q.: A comparison of PCA, KPCA and ICA for dimensionality reduction in support vector machine. Neurocomputing **55**(1–2), 321–336 (2003)
21. Rodarmel, C., Shan, J.: Principal component analysis for hyperspectral image classification. Surv. Land Inf. Sci. **62**(2), 115–122 (2002)
22. Uddin, M.P., Mamun, M.A., Hossain, M.A.: Effective feature extraction through segmentation-based folded-pca for hyperspectral image classification. Int. J. Remote Sens. **40**(18), 7190–7220 (2019)
23. Jia, X., Richards, J.A.: Segmented principal components transformation for efficient hyperspectral remote-sensing image display and classification. IEEE Trans. Geosci. Remote Sens. **37**(1), 538–542 (1999)
24. Wall, M.E., Rechtsteiner, A., Rocha, L.M.: Singular value decomposition and principal component analysis. In: A Practical Approach to Microarray Data Analysis, pp. 91–109. Springer, Heidelberg (2003). https://doi.org/10.1007/0-306-47815-3_5
25. Hansen, P.C.: Truncated singular value decomposition solutions to discrete ill-posed problems with ill-determined numerical rank. SIAM J. Sci. Stat. Comput. **11**(3), 503–518 (1990)
26. Baumgardner, M.F., Biehl, L.L., Landgrebe, D.A.: 220 band aviris hyperspectral image data set: June 12, 1992 indian pine test site 3. Purdue University Research Repository 10, R7RX991C (2015)
27. Tu, B., Zhou, C., He, D., Huang, S., Plaza, A.: Hyperspectral classification with noisy label detection via superpixel-to-pixel weighting distance. IEEE Trans. Geosci. Remote Sens. **58**(6), 4116–4131 (2020)
28. Yan, Y., Ren, J., Tschannerl, J., Zhao, H., Harrison, B., Jack, F.: Nondestructive phenolic compounds measurement and origin discrimination of peated barley malt using near-infrared hyperspectral imagery and machine learning. IEEE Trans. Instrument. Meas. **70**, 1–15 (2021)

Effective Feature Extraction via Folded-Sparse-PCA for Hyperspectral Image Classification

Md. Hasanul Bari⬤, Tanver Ahmed⬤, Masud Ibn Afjal⬤,
Adiba Mahjabin Nitu, Md. Palash Uddin⬤, and Md. Abu Marjan$^{(\boxtimes)}$⬤

Department of Computer Science and Engineering, Hajee Mohammad Danesh
Science and Technology University, Dinajpur, Bangladesh
{masud,adiba,palash_cse,marjan}@hstu.ac.bd

Abstract. The remote sensing hyperspectral image (HSI) consists of hundreds of narrow and contiguous spectral bands. It conveys much significant information about the earth materials. However, use of all HSI bands leads to poor classification performance. To alleviate this, the reduction of the HSI bands is a must, where feature selection and feature extraction methods are commonly performed for the reduction of bands. One of the most extensively employed unsupervised feature extraction approaches is Principal Component Analysis (PCA). But it fails to extract the local intrinsic information from the HSI because it contemplates only the global variance of data. This problem can be partially overcome by the Folded PCA (FPCA) that considers both the global and local variance of the data using the folding trick mechanism. On the other hand, Sparse PCA (SPCA) provides the benefit of better interpretability and discriminative-ability of the features than the classical PCA. In this paper, we propose a feature extraction method, named Folded-Sparse-PCA (FSPCA), using the benefits of FPCA and SPCA together. The FSPCA is performed by applying SPCA on the folded spectral signature of the HSI data matrix. The efficacy of FSPCA is compared with PCA, FPCA, and SPCA for the Indian Pines dataset with support vector machine classifier. The experimental result shows that FSPCA (88.27%) outperforms PCA (84.37%), SPCA (84.76%) and FPCA (86.99%) over the all classes' samples.

Keywords: Remote sensing · Hyperspectral images · Feature extraction · PCA · Folded PCA · Sparse PCA · Folded Sparse PCA

1 Introduction

Hyperspectral images (HSIs) are recorded with the help of remote sensing techniques. Each HSI constitutes of several hundreds of narrow and contiguous spectral bands and is used to scrutinize the earth materials. The spectral wavelengths to capture the HSI bands usually vary from 0.4–3.0 μm [1–3]. HSIs come up with

Md. S. Satu et al. (Eds.): MIET 2022, LNICST 491, pp. 538–549, 2023.
https://doi.org/10.1007/978-3-031-34622-4_43

several conventional and new applications. Conventional ones include agriculture, geology, mining, and surveillance system of military, whereas the new ones comprise of analysis of skin cancer, pharmaceutical, quality assurance of food, security, and authentication of counterfeit goods [4–6]. Because HSI's spectral resolution is often scaled in nanometers, it offers increased discriminability in the inspection of data at the expense of huge computing complexity and big datasets [7]. Because the images are usually taken by satellite or aircraft sensors, they are susceptible to corruption. Therefore, further preprocessing needs to be conducted like geometric correction, radiometric correction or atmospheric correction [8–10]. Typically, HSI data is organized as a hypercube, where the first two dimensions define the information about of the spatial area while the last dimension describes the information of spectral area. The datacube can be denoted as $H \times W \times F$, where F represents the total quantity of spectral bands and H and W stand for the spatial height and spatial width, respectively.

As the number of bands extends, so does the processing complexity and time. Because of the existence of strong correlations between adjacent bands, a few bands may possess information which is less discriminant. It is possible that not all bands convey the same percentage of information [2,11,12]. On the other hand, because of the large dimensionality, HSI faces curse of dimensionality issue or Hughes consequence when there is an imbalance proportion between the training samples and the spectral bands [13]. For these reasons, dimensionality reduction approaches can be performed in order to filter the significant bands and retrieve intrinsic features to remedy the dimensionality problem. Different feature selection and feature extraction techniques are performed for dimensionality reduction. Feature selection picks a subset of relevant features discarding the less important ones from the original dataset. Several of the frequently used feature selection approaches are J-M and Bhattacharya distance measures. On the other hand, A non-parametric based mutual information method is used for multiclass feature selection [14,15]. Meanwhile, feature extraction lessens the number of features by re-purposing existing ones to create new ones. These extracted features summarize most of the information contained in the original dataset. Feature extraction can be implemented in supervised and unsupervised ways. In the supervised method, a priori information should be provided for the feature extraction whereas the unsupervised method need not any a priori information [16]. Examples of some linear feature extraction approaches are the unsupervised Principal Component Analysis (PCA), the supervised Linear Discriminant Analysis (LDA), and Independent Component Analysis (ICA) [17]. PCA is a broadly adopted unsupervised feature extraction technique [18]. PCA uses orthogonal projections to find the lower dimensional representation of the dataset that retains as much information as possible. The transformed features known as principal components (PCs) are linearly uncorrelated, which makes PCA one of the best adaptive techniques for the feature extraction of highly correlated HSI data [19]. Often, in contrast to the original number of features, the number of PCs is drastically decreased. PCA involves the calculation of covariance matrix which becomes more difficult to derive for large data. It struggles to extract the divergent contributions of the features as the global variance is considered [7,20]. There is another feature extraction technique named Folded PCA (FPCA) that is also unsupervised in nature. It overcomes the limitations of PCA. It brings out local information of the dataset in addition to the global characteristic. In this method, the features are folded to form a matrix for each sample. Then a partial covariance matrix is calculated for each of the matrices which adds up to the final covariance matrix. This covariance matrix is substantially smaller, which minimizes the cost of computation [7]. In PCA, a linear combination of all features makes up every principal component. And most coefficients of this linear combination, also defined as sparse loadings, are nonzero. It is difficult to explain the principal components. A modified PCA with sparse loading known as Sparse PCA (SPCA) overcomes this problem. SPCA is derived from the regression form of PCA [21]. As such, we propose Folded SPCA (FSPCA) feature extraction approach that combines the advantages of FPCA and SPCA. FSPCA is carried out by performing SPCA on the folded spectral signature of the HSI data matrix. Thus, the fundamental contributions of this paper are enlisted below:

- A thorough insightful study on the PCA based feature extraction approaches used for classification of HSI,
- A folding mechanism-based SPCA (FSPCA) feature extraction approach for effective classification of HSI,
- An empirical analysis using a series of experiments for validating the superiority of the proposed FSPCA, and

The remainder of this paper is organized as follows. Section 2 discusses the insights of the PCA based feature extraction techniques. Section 3, explains the overall idea and derivation of the proposed FSPCA approach. The experimental setup and result analysis are provided in Sect. 4 on the other hand, Sect. 5 summarizes and concludes our investigations and findings.

2   Feature Extraction for HSI

2.1   Principal Component Analysis

For the implementation of PCA [19,22,23], a 2D data matrix $\mathbf{D}$ is first constructed from the HSI datacube. The size of $\mathbf{D}$ is $F*S$, where F signifies the quantity of features and $S = H * W$ represents the quantity of samples. The spectral vector which uniquely identifies an object, expressed as $\mathbf{x}_n = [\mathbf{x}_{n1}\mathbf{x}_{n2}....\mathbf{x}_{nF}]^T$, where $n \in [1, S]$. Then, the F spectral bands are used to calculate the mean spectral vector $\mathbf{M}$ and can be expressed as:

$$\mathbf{M} = \frac{1}{S}\sum_{n=1}^{S}\mathbf{x}_n \tag{1}$$

Mean adjusted spectral vector I_n is computed by subtracting spectral vector from the mean spectral vector as $\mathbf{I}_n = \mathbf{x}_n - \mathbf{M}$. The mean adjusted data $\mathbf{I}$, can be defined as $\mathbf{I} = [\mathbf{I}_1 \mathbf{I}_2 .... \mathbf{I}_n]$. The covariance matrix $\mathbf{C}$ is then calculated from the equation:

$$\mathbf{C} = \frac{1}{S}\mathbf{II}^T \tag{2}$$

As PCA is based on the covariance matrix's eigenvalue decomposition, the covariance matrix is used to compute the eigenvector and eigenvalues from the following equation:

$$\mathbf{C} = \mathbf{VEV}^T, \tag{3}$$

where $\mathbf{E} = diag[E_1 E_2 .... E_F]$ contains the eigenvalues of $\mathbf{C}$ in the main diagonal that forms a diagonal matrix and $\mathbf{V} = [V_1 V_2 .... V_F]$ signifies the corresponding eigenvectors of $\mathbf{E}$. The eigenvalues are organized in the order of decreasing ($E_1 \geq E_2 \geq ... \geq E_F$) and the eigenvectors are reordered according to their respective eigenvalues. Thus, the first selected k ($k << F$) corresponding eigenvectors can be exploited to form an $F \times k$ matrix denoted as w. At last, the final projection matrix, denoted as $\mathbf{Y}$, is achieved from the following equation:

$$\mathbf{Y} = \mathbf{w}^T \mathbf{I} \tag{4}$$

2.2 Folded Principal Component Analysis

FPCA is executed by transforming each spectral vector $\mathbf{I}_n$ into a folded matrix $\mathbf{A}_n$ of size $P \times Q$ where $F = P \times Q$ [7]. $\mathbf{A}_n$ can be expressed as:

$$\mathbf{A}_n = \begin{pmatrix} \mathbf{a}_{n1} \\ \mathbf{a}_{n2} \\ \vdots \\ \mathbf{a}_{nP} \end{pmatrix}_{P \times Q}, \tag{5}$$

where $\mathbf{a}_{nj} = \left(\mathbf{I}_{n(1+Q(j-1))} \; \mathbf{I}_{n(2+Q(j-1))} \cdots \mathbf{I}_{n(Q+Q(j-1))} \right)$ and $j \in [1, P]$. A group of Q bands forms each row of the matrix, which results in total F bands to be folded into $P(< Q)$ groups. Then each folded matrix's covariance matrix $\mathbf{C}_n$ is calculated by

$$\mathbf{C}_n = \mathbf{A}_n{}^T \mathbf{A}_n \tag{6}$$

After that, individual covariance matrices are assembled together to determine overall covariance matrix in this way:

$$\mathbf{C}_{FPCA} = \frac{1}{S} \sum_{n=1}^{S} \mathbf{C}_n \tag{7}$$

It is obvious that the dimension of the $\mathbf{C}_{FPCA}$ is $Q \times Q$, while in the case of PCA, it is $PQ \times PQ$ or $F \times F$. Consequently, the time for calculating the covariance matrix, eigenvalues and eigenvectors is drastically reduced. In terms of data projection, first the eigenvectors and eigenvalues are obtain from $\mathbf{C}_{FPCA}$ by eigendecomposition. Then, top k eigen vectors are selected to construct a matrix z of dimension $Q \times k$, where the eigen vectors are arranged according to the descending order of corresponding eigen values. Finally, Each folded matrix $\mathbf{A}_n$ is multiplied with z to construct the projection matrix Y_n of size $P \times k$. Therefore, $f = P \times k$ features are extracted for all image pixels.

2.3 Sparse Principal Component Analysis

In the implementation of SPCA [21,24,25], the mean image spectral vectors $\mathbf{I}_n$ of $\mathbf{I}$ are used to derive the principal components in a self-contained regression form. For $\lambda > 0$ and first k principal components, let $\alpha = [\alpha_1, \alpha_2, ..., \alpha_k]^T$ and $\beta = [\beta_1, \beta_2, ..., \beta_k]^T$. Then PCA problem can be converted into a regression type problem with the following equation:

$$(\hat{\alpha}, \hat{\beta}) = \underset{\alpha, \beta}{\operatorname{argmin}} \sum_{n=1}^{S} ||\mathbf{I}_n - \alpha \beta^T \mathbf{I}_n||^2 + \lambda \sum_{j=1}^{k} ||\beta_j||^2, \qquad (8)$$

$$\text{subject to } \alpha^T \alpha = \mathbf{ID}_{kxk}.$$

The lasso penalty is added to Eq. (8) to achieve the regression coefficients or sparse loadings and the optimization problem becomes like the following

$$(\hat{\alpha}, \hat{\beta}) = \underset{\alpha, \beta}{\operatorname{argmin}} \sum_{n=1}^{S} ||\mathbf{I}_n - \alpha \beta^T \mathbf{I}_n||^2 + \lambda \sum_{j=1}^{k} ||\beta_j||^2 + \sum_{j=1}^{k} \lambda_{1,j} ||\beta_j||_1, \qquad (9)$$

The same value of λ is employed for all of the k components and for the penalization of the loadings of j principal components, different $\lambda_{1,j}$'s are provided. This optimization problem is also known as elastic net problem. The sparse vector β_j is attained by selecting suitable λ and $\lambda_{1,j}$. Generally a small positive number is used for λ. Finally, ridge regression is performed for the least squares projection of the data onto the sparse components.

3   Proposed Folded Sparse Principal Component Analysis

Folded PCA retrieves both the global as well as local intrinsic characteristics of the entire HSI datacube by representing each spectral vector of its in a two-dimensional matrix form. It also lessens the memory consumption and time cost [7]. On the other hand, SPCA uses regression type optimization problem to provide better interpretability and discriminating ability [25]. As such, it is clearly visible that, if the local along with the global intrinsic structure of the full dataset can be obtained with better discriminative ability and interpretability then it will provide useful information for the classification task. From this motivation, sparse loadings based FSPCA is proposed in which conventional SPCA is applied on each of the folded spectral vectors of the HSI with the intention of extracting local and global characteristics with better explicability as shown in Fig. 1.

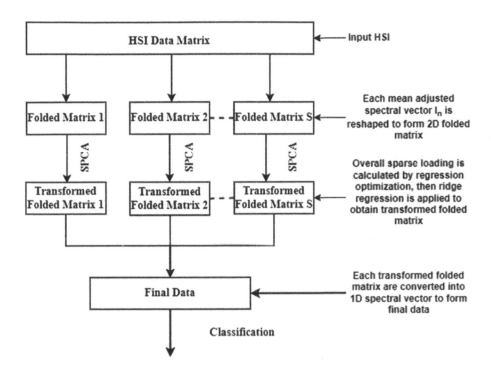

Fig. 1. Overall working procedure FSPCA approach.

In the implementation, first each mean-adjusted or mean image spectral vector $\mathbf{I}_n$ of the data matrix $\mathbf{D}$ is reshaped to form two dimensional matrix $\mathbf{A}_n$ of dimension $P \times Q$, where $F = P \times Q$ and $P < Q$. Then regression optimization problem is solved using lasso penalty as described in Eq. (9) to obtain the sparse loadings ($\mathbf{L}$) of each spectral folded matrix. Next, the overall sparse loadings is calculated as follows:

$$\mathbf{L}_{FSPCA} = \frac{1}{S} \sum_{n=1}^{S} \mathbf{L} \qquad (10)$$

Finally, ridge regression is applied with LARS (least-angle regression) method to project each spectral folded matrix onto the sparse components. Projected folded matrix are converted to 1D vector again to form the extracted data.

Table 1. Indian Pines HSI dataset's training and testing sample distribution.

No.	Class name	Quantity of training samples	Quantity of testing samples
01	Alfalfa	23	23
02	Grass-pasture	241	242
03	Oats	10	10
04	Wheat	103	102
05	Corn-notill	714	714
06	Grass-trees	365	365
07	Soybean-notill	486	486
08	Woods	632	633
09	Corn-mintill	415	415
10	Grass-pasture-mowed	14	14
11	Soybean-mintill	1227	1228
12	Buildings-Grass-Trees-Drives	193	193
13	Corn	119	118
14	Hay-windrowed	239	239
15	Soybean-clean	296	297
16	Stone-Steel-Towers	47	46
	Total	**5124**	**5125**

4   Experimental Outcomes and Analysis

4.1   Description of Dataset

The hyperspectral image of the Indian Pines in North-western Indiana, captured by AVIRIS sensor is used to evaluate the methods. The Indian Pines Dataset contains 220 spectral bands having 145×145 pixels each with 20 m of geometrical resolution. The spectral bands have a wavelength differing from $0.4 \mu m$ to $2.5 \mu m$ and the spectral resolution of the data is 10 nm. The dataset covers the information of 16 ground objects [26]. Some of the bands (104–108, 150–163, 220) cover the region of water absorption. These bands are removed, which results in 200 spectral bands [7]. For the evaluation of feature extraction methods, all 10249 pixels of all of the 16 different classes are considered. Total pixels or sample are split into 5124 training pixels and 5125 testing pixels (50:50 ratio). For each class, 50% pixels of that class are selected for training set and the rest for testing set. In Table 1, the detailed distributions of testing and training samples for all classes are presented.

4.2   Experimental Setup

The feature extraction methods are evaluated by considering classification accuracy, f1 score, recall and precision. Classification accuracy is calculated with

Table 2. Folding options for the proposed FSPCA.

Folding option	P	Q
FSPCA1	2	100
FSPCA2	4	50
FSPCA3	5	40
FSPCA4	8	25
FSPCA5	10	20

Table 3. Classification performance for the optimum number of PCs using the proposed FSPCA and baseline feature extraction methods.

Method	No. of PCs	c, γ	OA(%)	Precision	Recall	F1 score
Original Dataset	200	10, 0.05	83.53	0.8298	0.8353	0.8371
PCA	50	10, 1.371	84.37	0.8416	0.8437	0.8418
SPCA	55	10, 0.787	84.76	0.8450	0.8476	0.8462
FPCA	50	10, 0.391	86.99	0.8680	0.8698	0.8711
FSPCA1	48	10, 0.531	87.84	0.8767	0.8784	0.8793
FSPCA2	52	10, 0.493	87.18	0.8705	0.8718	0.8727
FSPCA3	45	10, 0.539	87.69	0.8753	0.8769	0.8784
FSPCA4	64	10, 0.416	**88.27**	**0.8815**	**0.8827**	**0.8833**
FSPCA5	50	10, 0.469	87.14	0.8697	0.8714	0.8722

the help of Support Vector Machine (SVM) via RBF kernel, based on LibSVM library [27]. The reasons for using SVM are that it is extremely resistant to the Hughes phenomenon and it can take advantage of margin-based criteria. Also, many scholars use SVM in the field of hyperspectral imagery. [7,28–31] The best values of the cost parameter c and kernel coefficient gamma (γ) are obtained using 10-fold cross validation in grid search. For the Indian Pines HSI dataset with 200 bands, we select $P = 10$ and $Q = 20$ for the folding operation as suggested in [7]. For our proposed FSPCA, we consider five possible folding combinations with various values of P and Q, as illustrated in Table 2.

4.3   Performance Evaluation

The majority of the dataset's information is found in the top PCs and obtained after applying the feature extraction method. We follow the following trick to attain the optimal number of PCs for achieving maximum classification results [1]. First, the overall accuracy (OA), precision, recall and f1 score using the

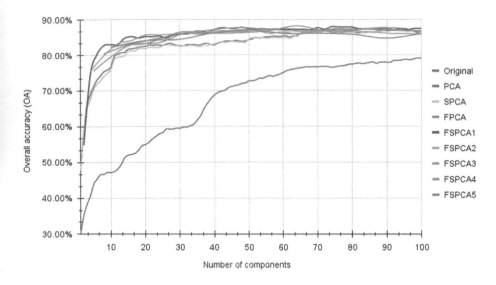

Fig. 2. Classification accuracy versus number of PCs.

baselines (PCA, SPCA and FPCA) and our proposed FSPCA are computed for the first PC and then this computation is repeated by increasing the PCs one-by-one upto 100 PCs. Note that we consider all five different folding options to calculate the classification performance for our proposed FSPCA method.

The OA, precision, recall and f1 score for the different feature extraction methods in terms of optimum number of PCs are provided in Table 3 while the classification accuracy plots are illustrated in Fig. 2 and the precision, recall and f1 plots are depicted in Fig. 3. From Table 3, it can be seen that all variants of our proposed FSPCA outperform all the investigated methods. In particular, FSPCA4 obtains 88.27% while PCA, SPCA and FPCA obtain 84.37%, 84.76% and 86.99%, respectively. The reason is as follows. As the folding technique is applied on the SPCA, it increases the overall accuracy of the SPCA via extracting both local and global information from the whole dataset. Figure 2 visually depicts the superiority of the proposed FSPCA over the baselines and the entire original dataset in terms of OA. It can also be observed from Fig. 2 that all the feature extraction methods outperform the original dataset and the SPCA gives almost similar performance to PCA. Finally, Table 3 and Fig. 3 illustrate that with regard to f1 score, recall and precision, FSPCA also produces better performance than FPCA, SPCA and PCA.

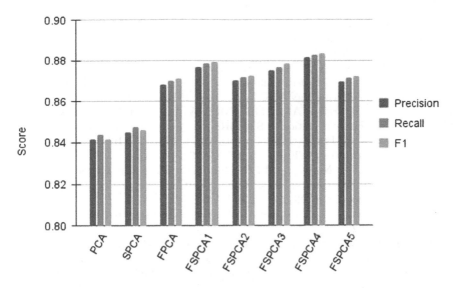

Fig. 3. F1 score, recall and precision for the optimum number of PCs.

5   Conclusion

The proposed feature extraction method FSPCA extracts the global and local intrinsic features of the HSI data. It also provides better interpretability and discriminative ability as it is obtained by applying SPCA on the folded matrix of the spectral signature of HSI data. The performance of FSPCA is evaluated by comparing with PCA, SPCA and FPCA in terms of overall classification accuracy, precision, recall and f1 score. The proposed FSPCA is proved to be fruitful as its classification performance outperforms PCA, SPCA and FPCA. There are several HSI datasets available, which could be used in future for analysis of the proposed methodology and to improve the accuracy of classification. Deep learning-based model or hybrid model could be introduced to make better analysis and contribute in the research field of HSI.

References

1. Uddin, M.P., Mamun, M.A., Afjal, M.I., Hossain, M.A.: Information-theoretic feature selection with segmentation-based folded principal component analysis (PCA) for hyperspectral image classification. Int. J. Remote Sens. **42**(1), 286–321 (2021)
2. Uddin, M.P., Mamun, M.A., Hossain, M.A., Afjal, M.I.: Improved folded-PCA for efficient remote sensing hyperspectral image classification. Geocarto Int. **37**, 9474–9496 (2021)
3. Afjal, M.I., Uddin, P., Mamun, A., Marjan, A.: An efficient lossless compression technique for remote sensing images using segmentation based band reordering heuristics. Int. J. Remote Sens. **42**(2), 756–781 (2021)

4. Afjal, M.I., Al Mamun, M., Uddin, M.P.: Band reordering heuristics for lossless satellite image compression with 3D-CALIC and CCSDS. J. Vis. Commun. Image Represent. **59**, 514–526 (2019)

5. Uddin, M., Mamun, M., Hossain, M.: Segmented FPCA for hyperspectral image classification. In: 2017 3rd International Conference on Electrical Information and Communication Technology (EICT), pp. 1–6. IEEE (2017)

6. Shimu, S.A., Aktar, M., Afjal, M.I., Nitu, A.M., Uddin, M.P., Al Mamun, M.: NDVI based change detection in Sundarban Mangrove forest using remote sensing data. In: 2019 4th International Conference on Electrical Information and Communication Technology (EICT), pp. 1–5 (2019)

7. Zabalza, J., et al.: Novel folded-PCA for improved feature extraction and data reduction with hyperspectral imaging and SAR in remote sensing. ISPRS J. Photogramm. Remote Sens. **93**, 112–122 (2014)

8. Mohan, B.K., Porwal, A.: Hyperspectral image processing and analysis. Curr. Sci. **108**, 833–841 (2015)

9. Richards, J.: Remote Sensing Digital Image Analysis, December 2013

10. Uddin, M., Mamun, M., Hossain, M.: Improved feature extraction using segmented FPCA for hyperspectral image classification. In: 2017 2nd International Conference on Electrical & Electronic Engineering (ICEEE), pp. 1–4. IEEE (2017)

11. Guo, B., Gunn, S., Damper, R., Nelson, J.: Band selection for hyperspectral image classification using mutual information. IEEE Geosci. Remote Sens. Lett. **3**(4), 522–526 (2006)

12. Uddin, M., Mamun, M., Hossain, M.: Feature extraction for hyperspectral image classification. In: 2017 IEEE Region 10 Humanitarian Technology Conference (R10-HTC), pp. 379–382. IEEE (2017)

13. Hughes, G.: On the mean accuracy of statistical pattern recognizers. IEEE Trans. Inf. Theory **14**(1), 55–63 (1968)

14. Hossain, M.A., Jia, X., Pickering, M.: Improved feature selection based on a mutual information measure for hyperspectral image classification. In: 2012 IEEE International Geoscience and Remote Sensing Symposium, pp. 3058–3061 (2012)

15. Hossain, M.A., Jia, X., Pickering, M.: Subspace detection using a mutual information measure for hyperspectral image classification. IEEE Geosci. Remote Sens. Lett. **11**(2), 424–428 (2014)

16. Fauvel, M., Chanussot, J., Benediktsson, J.A.: Kernel principal component analysis for feature reduction in hyperspectrale images analysis. In: Proceedings of the 7th Nordic Signal Processing Symposium - NORSIG 2006, pp. 238–241 (2006)

17. van der Maaten, L., Postma, E., Herik, H.: Dimensionality reduction: a comparative review. J. Mach. Learn. Res. - JMLR **10**, 13 (2007)

18. Dianat, R., Kasaei, S.: Dimension reduction of optical remote sensing images via minimum change rate deviation method. IEEE Trans. Geosci. Remote Sens. **48**(1), 198–206 (2010)

19. Rodarmel, C., Shan, J.: Principal component analysis for hyperspectral image classification. Surv. Land Inf. Syst. **62** (2002)

20. Siddiqa, A., Islam, M.R., Afjal, M.I.: Spectral segmentation based dimension reduction for hyperspectral image classification. J. Spatial Sci. 1–20 (2022)

21. Zou, H., Hastie, T., Tibshirani, R.: Sparse principal component analysis. Policy 1–30 (2004)

22. Shabna, A., Ganesan, R.: HSEG and PCA for hyper-spectral image classification. In: 2014 International Conference on Control, Instrumentation, Communication and Computational Technologies (ICCICCT), pp. 42–47 (2014)

23. Uddin, M.P., Mamun, M.A., Hossain, M.A.: PCA-based feature reduction for hyperspectral remote sensing image classification. IETE Tech. Rev. **38**(4), 377–396 (2021)

24. Mairal, J., Bach, F., Ponce, J., Sapiro, G.: Online dictionary learning for sparse coding, vol. 382, p. 87, January 2009

25. Wang, L., Xie, X., Li, W., Du, Q., Li, G.: Sparse feature extraction for hyperspectral image classification. In: 2015 IEEE China Summit and International Conference on Signal and Information Processing (ChinaSIP), pp. 1067–1070 (2015)

26. Baumgardner, M.F., Biehl, L.L., Landgrebe, D.A.: 220 band AVIRIS hyperspectral image data set: June 12, 1992 Indian Pine Test Site 3, September 2015

27. Chang, C.C., Lin, C.J.: LIBSVM: a library for support vector machines. ACM Trans. Intell. Syst. Technol. **2**(3) (2011)

28. Li, M., Zang, S., Zhang, B., Li, S., Wu, C.: A review of remote sensing image classification techniques: the role of spatio-contextual information. Eur. J. Remote Sens. **47**(1), 389–411 (2014)

29. Gualtieri, J., Chettri, S.: Support vector machines for classification of hyperspectral data. In: IGARSS 2000. IEEE 2000 International Geoscience and Remote Sensing Symposium. Taking the Pulse of the Planet: The Role of Remote Sensing in Managing the Environment. Proceedings (Cat. No. 00CH37120), vol. 2, pp. 813–815 (2000)

30. Waske, B., van der Linden, S., Benediktsson, J.A., Rabe, A., Hostert, P.: Sensitivity of support vector machines to random feature selection in classification of hyperspectral data. IEEE Trans. Geosci. Remote Sens. **48**(7), 2880–2889 (2010)

31. Melgani, F., Bruzzone, L.: Classification of hyperspectral remote sensing images with support vector machines. IEEE Trans. Geosci. Remote Sens. **42**, 1778–1790 (2004)

Segmented-Incremental-PCA for Hyperspectral Image Classification

Shabbir Ahmed[ID], Md. Moshiur Rahman[ID], Md. Shahriar Haque[ID],
Md. Abu Marjan[✉][ID], Md. Palash Uddin[ID], and Masud Ibn Afjal[ID]

Hajee Mohammad Danesh Science and Technology University, Dinajpur, Bangladesh
{marjan,palash_cse,masud}@hstu.ac.bd

Abstract. The Hyperspectral Image (HSI) through remote sensing contains crucial data about the land objects via adjacent cramped spectral wavelength bands. The classification performance does not appear to be adequate when all of the original HSI features (bands) are used. To mitigate this, band (dimensionality) reduction strategies via feature extraction and feature selection techniques are typically employed to enhance classification efficiency. Despite the widespread usage of Principal Component Analysis (PCA) for HSI feature reduction, it frequently struggles to assess the local beneficial properties of the HSI since it analyzes only the HSI's global statistics. Therefore, Segmented-PCA (SPCA) and Incremental-PCA (IPCA) are presented to supersede the classical PCA. In this paper, we propose the Segmented-Incremental-PCA (SIPCA) feature extraction approach to exploit the amenities of both SPCA and IPCA. In particular, SIPCA first segments the entire HSI into a number of strongly correlated bands subgroups and then apply the classical IPCA on each subgroup separately. We analyze the proposed SIPCA through experimenting utilizing a per-pixel Support Vector Machine (SVM) classifier over the Indian Pines mixed agricultural HSI classification. Based on the classification accuracy, we manifest that our proposed SIPCA technique (91.22%) outperforms the entire original bands of HSI (87.61%), PCA (88.78%), IPCA (89.171%) and SPCA (90.878%) feature extraction methods.

Keywords: Hyperspectral image · Feature extraction · PCA · Segmented PCA · Incremental PCA · Segmented Incremental PCA

1 Introduction

The hyperspectral images (HSIs) are remotely captured images that are typically acquired at a large amount of adjacent cramped spectral wavelengths to deliver high spectral resolutions for beneficial solutions in a variety of application regions. For obtaining the ground objects, the wavelength range for capturing HSIs usually ranges between 0.4 μm and 3.0 μm typically spanning from the visible light to the near-infrared portion of the EM-wave spectrum [1–3]. The

Md. S. Satu et al. (Eds.): MIET 2022, LNICST 491, pp. 550–563, 2023.
https://doi.org/10.1007/978-3-031-34622-4_44

Airborne Visible/Infrared Imaging Spectrometer (AVIRIS) and the Hyperspectral Digital Imagery Collection Experiment (HYDICE) are two spectrometers for imaging that are commonly utilized in remote sensing [4,5]. With the narrow absorption features of the HSIs represented by the spectral resolution in nm, HSIs have a strong discriminating capacity in the data analysis for different benefactor activities, for example, lake eutrophication, plantation discriminatory categorization, determining if a clay or stone has a certain ingredient or not etc. Generally, hyperspectral data is represented as a hypercube of the size $X \times Y \times F$, where the X and Y stand for the number of the rows and columns (width), respectively. Spectral data for ground surfaces is represented in the third dimension (F).

However, all of the HSI bands may not be beneficial in containing the same quantity of data and a minor amount of bands may retain less skewed data due to strongly correlated nearby bands [6,7]. Because of this reason, it is necessary to identify the appropriate bands and retrieve the implicit features by changing the features to obtain a satisfactory classification performance.

Consequently, feature selection as well as feature extraction methods as band reduction strategies are critical for resolving these challenges and ensuring effective classification [8–10]. The feature selection methods usually preserve the actual data while selecting significant bands on the basis of specific search parameters [11–13]. Nevertheless, these search-based approaches may be difficult at times due to the complexity caused by high processing cost and the local minima problem [14]. Alternatively, for extracting the appropriate features, linear and nonlinear transformations form techniques to feature extraction that are supervised as well as unsupervised. To excerpt the beneficial features, supervised methods require ground truth and information may be analytically fragile, and the training pixels have a significant impact on the efficacy of them. Unsupervised approaches, on the other hand, are used to extract beneficial features without any prior knowledge [15].

Principal Component Analysis (PCA) is the commonly utilized unsupervised feature extraction procedure in HSI perspective [3,16]. However, when the dataset to be decomposed is too vast to fit in memory, Incremental Principal Component Analysis (IPCA) is often employed in place of Principal Component Analysis (PCA) [17]. Unlike PCA, IPCA generates a low-rank approximation for the input data utilizing a fixed amount of memory disregarding the quantity of input data samples. It is still reliant on the characteristics of the input data, but modifying the batch size enables for regulation of the memory utilization. In order to enhance feature extraction by IPCA for delivering better classification performance. While only processing a few samples at a time, IPCA is able to identify a comparable projection of the data to PCA. In general, IPCA is meant for huge datasets that hardly fit in main memory and necessitate incremental techniques. On the other hand, although Segmented-PCA (SPCA) outperforms the classical PCA via segmenting the HSI dataset prior to apply PCA [18], it can still be prone to the pitfalls of the conventional PCA. As such, we propose the Segmented-IPCA (SIPCA) feature extraction approach in this paper to excerpt the whole dataset's global and local properties, as well as the segments of strongly correlated bands based on the amenities of both IPCA and SPCA. The classification performance using SIPCA is compared to that of using the original dataset, PCA, SPCA, and IPCA over the Indian Pines HSI. The main contributions of this paper are listed below:

- A correlation-based Segmented-IPCA (SIPCA) feature extraction approach for effective classification of HSI,
- An empirical analysis using a series of experiments for validating the superiority of our proposed SIPCA, and
- A conceptual assessment using the space complexities at different stages for illustrating the advantage of our proposed SIPCA.

The rest of this paper is organized in the following manners. Section 2 discusses the insights of the HSI feature extraction techniques based on PCA. In Sect. 3, there is description about the overall idea and derivation of our proposed SIPCA approach. The experimental setup and result analysis are provided in Sect. 4 while Sect. 5 summarizes and concludes the investigations and findings.

2 HSI Feature Extraction

2.1 PCA for HSI

PCA is a technique for HSI that uses unsupervised linear feature reduction and retrieves inherent information by determining the relationship between the HSI spectral wavelength bands via orthogonal adjustments. It is predicated on the assumption that continuous bands of HSIs are closely connected and generally provide the same information about land objects to function adequately [19]. Let $\mathbf{x}_n = [\mathbf{x}_{n1}\mathbf{x}_{n2}....\mathbf{x}_{nF}]^T$ be a pixel's spectral vector in the data matrix, $\mathbf{D}$, where $n \in [1, S]$ and $S = X \times Y$, where X and Y denote the height and the width of the HSI, accordingly. In PCA operation, the HSI hypercube data is initially transformed into a data matrix, $\mathbf{D}$, having the size of $F \times S$. The zero-mean image is denoted by $\mathbf{I}$ which is obtained from the $\mathbf{I}_n$ where $\mathbf{I} = [\mathbf{I}_1\mathbf{I}_2....\mathbf{I}_n]$. $\mathbf{M}$ represents the mean image vector defined as $\mathbf{M} = \frac{1}{S}\sum_{n=1}^{S}\mathbf{x}_n$. The covariance matrix $\mathbf{C} = \frac{1}{S}\mathbf{I}\mathbf{I}^T$ is then produced for Eigendecomposition, where the core of PCA is represented by eigenvectors $(V_1V_2...V_F)$, also called Principle Components (PCs), and their associating eigenvalues $(E_1E_2...E_F)$. If the diagonal matrix is represented by $\mathbf{E} = $ diagonal $(E_1E_2...E_F)$ and the matrix containing all of the eigenvectors is represented by $\mathbf{V}$, then $\mathbf{V}$ can be determined in the following way:

$$\mathbf{C} = \mathbf{V}\mathbf{E}\mathbf{V}^T \tag{1}$$

A dimensional matrix, $\mathbf{w}$ of size $F \times q$ is generated by choosing q eigenvectors, where $q \leq F$ and frequently $q \ll F$. The traditional way for selecting the upper q PCs is ordering eigenvalues from largest to smallest. Finally, $\mathbf{Y}$, the projection matrix of $\mathbf{D}$ is enumerated using $\mathbf{Y} = \mathbf{w}^T \times \mathbf{I}$.

2.2   IPCA for HSI

IPCA is generally employed, when the dataset to be decomposed is too big to fit in memory, as an alternative for PCA. Although it is still reliant on the features of the input data, altering the batch size results in improved memory usage. It supports sparse input and can be significantly more memory economical than PCA, relying on the size of the input data. The dataset is divided into mini-batches using this technique where each batch can fit into the memory and then feed it one mini-batch at a moment to the IPCA algorithm. Mathematically, an IPCA performs iteration, without apparently computing and storing the covariance matrix, and approximates the most notable PC for data arriving sequentially.

$$v^{(n)} = u^{(n-1)} + \beta^{(n-1)} \mathbf{D}_{(:,j)} \mathbf{D}_{(:,j)}^T u^{(n-1)}, \qquad (2)$$

$$u^{(n)} = \frac{v^{(n)}}{||v^{(n)}||_2} \qquad (3)$$

In the equations above, the jth column of the data matrix, $\mathbf{X}$ is $\mathbf{X}(:,j)$ and $\beta^{(n-1)} > 0$ is a step size. In the Eq. 2 and Eq. 3, $v^{(n)}$ represents nth step estimate of v, where $v = \lambda.x$. x and λ are such two corresponding eigenvalues of the covariance matrix $\mathbf{C}$ that satisfy $\lambda.x = \mathbf{C}.x$. For the problem of computing eigenvalues, it is possible to think of the IPCA method as a singular-vector algorithm in which the associated iteration, such as Eq. 2 and Eq. 3, only evaluates the eigenvector corresponding to the largest eigenvalue [20]. The data should be corrected by the projection of them onto the perpendicular counterpart space of the section of space covered by $u(n)$ before calculating the second-order eigenvector, where $u^{(n)}$ is calculated by diving $v^{(n)}$ by the Euclidean norm of $v^{(n)}$.

2.3   SPCA for HSI

If the HSI bands are substantially connected, the standard PCA retrieves operative characteristics. PCA retrieves efficient features when the elementary bands are strongly correlated and have a large covariance matrix having the size of $F \times F$, which needs a greater computing overhead [21]. Furthermore, correlations between contiguous HSI bands are frequently greater than correlations between bands that are farther away, where increased correlations emerge in blocks. Consequently, SPCA is offered to enhance performance of traditional PCA by eliminating weak correlation between strongly correlated blocks [22]. PCA may omit certain subtle valuable information of the HSI that might be used for effective categorization because it considers global statistics. As a consequence, the SPCA method is introduced as a way to tailor the usage of traditional PCA by eliminating weak correlations between blocks having strong correlations for improved performance [21]. The application of SPCA for HSI includes the whole zero mean data matrix of HSI is initially separated into L subsections of dataset [21], depending upon the correlation between the bands. Typically, the intimately correlated bands are frequently chosen to make up a subset of dataset for retrieving the dataset's local features. After that, each subgroup dataset is subjected to traditional PCA. Let $\mathbf{D_i}$ represent the segmented data matrices, in which $i \in [1, L]$ and n_i denotes the quantity of bands for each segmented data matrix in succession, respectively. The segmented data matrices are represented as $\mathbf{D_1} = [\mathbf{I'_1 I'_2} \ldots \mathbf{I'_n}]$, $\mathbf{D_2} = [\mathbf{I''_1 I''_2} \ldots \mathbf{I''_n}]$, and so on, where $\mathbf{I'_j}$ includes the initial n_1 number of rows of the corresponding $\mathbf{I_j}$ and $\mathbf{I''_j}$ contains the first n_2 number of rows and skips the initial n_1 number of rows of the corresponding $\mathbf{I_j}$ where $j, n\epsilon[1, S]$. Each generated covariance matrix denoted by $\mathbf{D_i}$ is then subjected to the Eigendecomposition procedure.

3   The Proposed Segmented-IPCA

On each of the dataset segments containing the highly correlated bands, SPCA executes conventional PCA to retrieve the global features of the segments. Conversely, IPCA supports sparse input and alters batch size that results in improved memory usage. This feature extraction approach discards the original data instantly after modifying the eigenspace, retaining just the data with reduced dimension [23]. Dimensionality reduction is done in this technique by taking use of the case that the system's eigenvector count is probably lower than the input vectors' dimensionality. Absolute restoration of the source data is obtained if all eigenvectors are retained in the system. This feature gives the user the ability to recreate the patches of the input image using the projected vectors which are preserved and clearly understand which environmental characteristics were learnt. Additional reduction in dimensionality can be accomplished by retaining just the greatest eigenvalues in the system at the cost of restoration losses (and possibly in the system's rate of comprehension). It is possible to choose the eigenvectors when computing the PCA batch at the time of learning. If the entire dataset's internal and external characteristics, in addition to the segments of the strongly correlated bands are acquired, it would provide the classification process with more information, the accuracy may improve. Furthermore, IPCA has the biggest advantage over other feature extraction methods that is the manipulation of the memory consumption. It is most useful when the input data is too large to fit in the main memory. In IPCA, the number of samples are separated into fixed size of batches where the batch size can be configured manually or automatically. This enables using the memory-mapped files which create memory-maps to the complete dataset for accessing small batches stored in memory. Proper manipulation of the batch size depending on the input data size provides a balance between prediction accuracy and memory usage. As such, we propose SIPCA in which traditional IPCA is applied on each of the dataset segments of the strongly correlated bands so that it can extract both global and local segment structures.

In the proposed SIPCA, as illustrated in Fig. 1, the original dataset ($\mathbf{D}$) used has F no. of features which is firstly segmented into L number of subgroups based on the strongly correlated bands of the dataset. In Fig. 1, the ith band segment of the dataset is denoted by $\mathbf{D}_i$ where, $i \in [1, L]$. These subgroups have $f_1, f_2, ..., f_L$ no. of features, respectively. When IPCA is applied on these strongly correlated

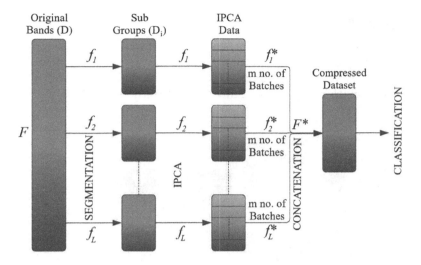

Fig. 1. Working procedure of the proposed SIPCA feature extraction approach.

bands' segment D_i, the segmented data is further separated into mini-batches of batch size m. These mini-batches are then fed to the IPCA algorithm incrementally to produce feature extracted data for each segmented data (D_i). After implementing feature extraction using IPCA on each of these strongly correlated segmented data, they extract $f_1^*, f_2^*, ..., f_L^*$ features respectively. Subsequently, the extracted features of the segmented data are concatenated into a compressed dataset having F^* extracted features as shown in the Fig. 1. Finally classification is performed on this feature extracted data.

4 Experimental Result

4.1 Description of the Dataset

The Indian Pine, which is a HSI dataset has been utilized in this study. It is collected from Purdue University Research Repository (PURR) through Grupo De Inteligencia (GIC) [24]. This dataset was originally constructed by NASA's AVIRIS-Airborne Visible/Infrared Imaging Spectrometer over the Indian Pines testing ground for agriculture in Indiana, USA in June 1992. Of the Indian Pines landscape, Two-thirds is agricultural, the remaining one-third is forestry or diverse organic long-living vegetation. There are a few low-density dwellings, a railway line, two major double-lane highways, other developed buildings, and tiny roadways. Because the image was taken in June, various of the crop plants visible like maize and soybeans seem to be in their initial phases of growth with not more than 5% covering. In this dataset, there are 220 spectral reflectance bands. Each band image has pixels 145×145 in size and has a geometric resolution of 20 m. There are 16 ground classes with a wavelength range from 0.4 μm to 3 μm, where the spectral resolution is 0.001 μm [24].

4.2   Experimental Setup

We consider the overall classification accuracy, precision score, recall score, kappa score, and space complexity as the performance measure metrics. However, overall accuracy (OA) is mostly considered as the objective measurement to quantitatively appraise the proposed and investigated methods [3, 25].

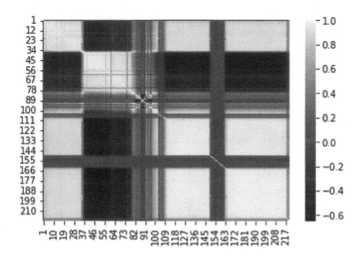

Fig. 2. Graphical Visualization of the band-to-band correlation matrix of the HSI dataset of Indian Pines.

The HSI dataset of Indian Pines includes in total $145 \times 145 = 21025$ pixels and 16 classes. 10776 pixels are not classified among 21025 pixels. These unclassified pixels are not used for the subsequent operations. The correlation matrices calculated band-to-band of the dataset are displayed in Fig. 2 are investigated by graphic representation to determine the number of ways to implement SIPCA and SPCA. To begin the implementation, the segmentation strategy needs separating the entire collection of bands in the dataset into multiple strongly correlated subdivisions. Having separated each subdivision, the singular-band distinguish-ability is utilized as a reference for feature selection. When compared to not employing segmentation, the approach greatly decreases the computational overhead which is beneficial to feature extraction. Less amount of features will greatly speed up the greatest probable classification procedure adequately. Correlation value 1.0 indicates highly positive correlation, 0.0 as no correlation and -1.0 as highly negative correlation in the band to band correlation plot. The entire dataset is separated into 3 distinct manners to perform SIPCA and SPCA. At first, the whole dataset is separated into 3 strongly correlated segments inj order to execute SIPCA and SPCA, which are designated as SIPCA3 and SPCA3 respectively. Likewise, the dataset is separated into 4 and 5 strongly correlated segments to carry out SIPCA and SPCA operations

Table 1. Segmentation of the bands of the HSI dataset of Indian Pines for proposed SIPCA and existing SPCA feature extraction methods.

Sub-group	Factor	Number of Segments		
		3 (SPCA3 & SIPCA3)	4 (SPCA4 & SIPCA4)	5 (SPCA5 & SIPCA5)
1	Band range	1–36	1–36	1–36
	No. of PCs	12	7	2
	Average correlation in diagonal	0.87312	0.87312	0.87312
2	Band range	37–102	37–79	37–79
	No. of PCs	7	4	6
	Average correlation in diagonal	0.54622	0.89601	0.89601
3	Band range	103–220	80–102	80–102
	No. of PCs	4	2	3
	Average correlation in diagonal	0.69487	0.43316	0.43316
4	Band range	N/A	103–220	103–162
	No. of PCs		4	3
	Average correlation in diagonal		0.69487	0.51454
5	Band range	N/A	N/A	163–220
	No. of PCs			5
	Average correlation in diagonal			0.93004

independently. These operations are denoted as SIPCA4 and SPCA4 for 4 segments; and SIPCA5 and SPCA5 in case of 5 segments. Table 1 represents the detailed information for 3, 4 and 5 segments of SIPCA and SPCA methods.

The performance measure indexes of all the investigated feature extraction approaches are analyzed using a per-pixel Support Vector Machine (SVM) classifier with Radial Basis kernel Function (RBF). To find the optimal value of C and $gamma$, we use GridSearchCV from Scikit-learn python package. 10-fold GridSearchCV has been performed to find the optimal parameters of C and $gamma$ for SVM classifier. The extracted features have been normalized for better tuning of classifier model to achieve better classification performances. This normalization converts all the samples into real values from 0.0 to 1.0. Then the feature reduced dataset is split into training datasets and testing datasets as 80% for training and 20% for testing split of the dataset. Table 2 illustrates information about the training datasets and testing datasets. In 80%:20% train:test split, 8199 samples are used in training and 2050 samples are used in testing, totaling 10249 samples. The batch size used in the implementations of IPCA and the proposed variants of SIPCA are specifically predefined. To achieve the optimum batch size balance for IPCA, SIPCA3, SIPCA4 and SIPCA5, all the possible batch sizes within 1000 have been experimented. Finally, the proper batch size found from the experiments are 902 for IPCA, 311 for SIPCA3, 105 for SIPCA4 and 191 for SIPCA5. These configurations mostly produce optimal overall accuracy for all investigated approaches with few exceptions. This

Table 2. Information about the samples for training and testing

No.	Class name	No. of samples for training	No. of samples for testing
1	Alfalfa	37	9
2	Corn-notill	1142	286
3	Corn-mintill	664	166
4	Corn	190	47
5	Grass-pasture	386	97
6	Grass-trees	584	146
7	Grass-pasture-mowed	23	5
8	Hay-windrowed	382	96
9	Oats	16	4
10	Soybean-notill	778	194
11	Soybean-mintill	1964	491
12	Soybean-clean	474	119
13	Wheat	164	41
14	Woods	1012	253
15	Buildings-Grass-Trees-Drives	309	77
16	Stone-Steel-Towers	74	19
Total		8199	2050

Table 3. Experimented no. of combinations for PCs for different methods

Methods	Range of PCs	No. of combinations for PCs
PCA	1–220	220
IPCA	1–220	220
SPCA3 & SIPCA3	1–35, 1–50, 1–50	87500
SPCA4 & SIPCA4	1–9, 1–9, 1–9, 1–9	6561
SPCA5 & SIPCA5	1–7, 1–7, 1–7, 1–7, 1–7	16807
Total		111308

classification environment is used to carry out classification of all investigated approaches for SIPCA. It has been found that a class imbalance problem exists in the dataset, as in certain classes, there are many pixels, whereas there are few pixels in other classes.

4.3 Classification and Evaluation

The primary issue with feature extraction approaches for classification is finding the ideal number of PCs. This study analyzes all possible number of combination for PCs within a suitable range are investigated for PCA and IPCA. The

Table 4. Optimal classification results.

Method	No. of PCs	SVM(kernel, C, gamma)	Overall accuracy × 100	Precision score × 100	Recall score × 100	Kappa score × 100
Original dataset	All bands	rbf, 10, 0.11	87.610	87.804	87.61	85.809
PCA	95	rbf, 10, 0.80	88.78	88.841	88.78	87.177
IPCA	84	rbf, 10, 0.64	89.171	89.246	89.171	87.624
SPCA3	23	rbf, 10, 1.82	90.878	90.965	90.878	89.575
SPCA4	17	rbf, 10, 1.83	90.439	90.48	90.439	89.075
SPCA5	19	rbf, 10, 1.77	90.878	90.935	90.878	89.579
SIPCA3	23	rbf, 10, 1.4	90.829	90.956	90.829	89.513
SIPCA4	17	rbf, 10, 1.53	**91.22**	**91.314**	**91.22**	**89.966**
SIPCA5	19	rbf, 10, 1.27	90.341	90.468	90.341	88.948

same experiment has been performed also for SPCA and SIPCA for 3 different segmentation approaches. In Table 3, the number of combinations for PCs for different feature extraction methods and their ranges are illustrated. Classification results in terms of aforementioned performance measure metrics are provided in Table 4. The ideal number of PCs for achieving the highest level of overall accuracy is applied to each investigated procedures.

Table 4 shows that SIPCA-4 (91.22%) outperforms all the other investigated feature extraction methods including SPCA (90.878%), IPCA (89.171%) and PCA (88.78%) in terms of all the performance measures i.e., overall accuracy, precision score, recall score and kappa score. Furthermore, the other SIPCA variations provide adequate accuracy. The reason for this is that by applying IPCA to each of the strongly correlated bands' segments, the strongly intertwined subgroup datasets and the entire dataset's local and global properties have both been effectively taken into account. Also, the batch sizes used in the experiments for IPCA, SIPCA offer a balance between prediction performance and memory utilization which stands out as a reason for IPCA to outperform PCA and also because of it, when it comes to memory efficiency and classification accuracy, SIPCA performs better than every other feature extraction strategies that have been investigated. Now, Fig. 3 illustrates the confusion matrix for the SIPCA4 which is plotted for the experiment's visualization of the feature extraction efficiency of SIPCA. The number of both correct as well as incorrect predictions is evaluated using count values and decomposed per class. It clearly visualizes the class by class accuracy of the classification using feature extraction by the SIPCA4.

Furthermore, every feature extraction approach outperforms the original dataset (87.610%) in terms of accuracy which explains the requirement of feature extraction for adequate HSI classification. Finally, it is found that SPCA and SIPCA aim to outperform PCA and IPCA in terms of performance since they handle the extraction of local features in different ways.

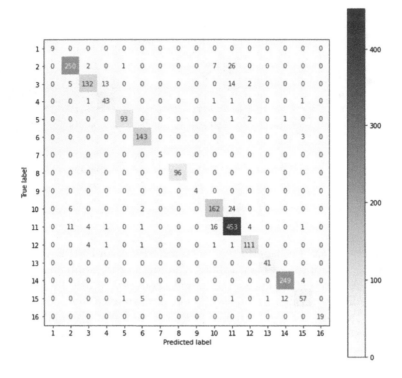

Fig. 3. Confusion matrix for SIPCA4.

4.4 Space Complexity

The most significant fact about the memory consumption of IPCA is that it splits the complete dataset into mini-batches and store them in memory-mapped files which enables it use a fixed amount of space irrespect to the complete data size. Conventional PCA requires more space to function as compared to IPCA. On the other hand, SPCA reduces the memory complexity as it divides the complete dataset into L subgroups. Let n_i refer to the quantity of the bands of the ith subdivision of dataset. In the proposed SIPCA, the data is firstly separated into L subdivisions which is similar to that in SPCA. Then the segments having strongly correlated bands, each of which has n_i number of bands, are divided into mini batches each having the size of m where the mini batch size m is predefined. Thus, SIPCA manages to consume a constant amount memory space that can further be manipulated. This advantage allows SIPCA to be significantly more memory efficient than any of the investigated feature extraction strategies in this paper as shown in Table 5.

Table 5. Memory requirements of the proposed as well as the existing methods.

Method	Data Matrix	Covariance Matrix
PCA	$S \times F$	$F \times F$
SPCA	$S \times n_i$	$n_i \times n_i$
IPCA	$S \times F$	$m \times F$
SIPCA	$S \times n_i$	$m \times n_i$

5 Conclusion

SIPCA, an enhanced feature extraction approach on the basis of the implementation of IPCA on the segmented datasets each of which has strongly correlated bands of the complete HSI dataset, is introduced for extracting local as well as global intrinsic characteristics within the complete dataset and the segmented datasets of it adequately in order to achieve enhanced classification performance. The proposed SIPCA is compared to PCA, SPCA, and IPCA in terms of classification performance measure metrics and space complexity. The comparison result demonstrates that SIPCA outperforms the analyzed feature extraction methods with comparably low number of features in terms of classification accuracy as it excels at extracting local structures within the dataset and also in terms of memory consumption. However, the accuracy of the classification may negligibly differ owing to changes in segmentation criteria, classifier optimization methods, kernel tricks, etc. Increasing the training sample number and addressing the problem of class imbalance in the dataset may boost the classification accuracy even more.

References

1. Hossain, M.A., Jia, X., Pickering, M.: Subspace detection using a mutual information measure for hyperspectral image classification. IEEE Geosci. Remote Sens. Lett. **11**(2), 424–428 (2013)
2. Uddin, M.P., Mamun, M.A., Afjal, M.I., Hossain, M.A.: Information-theoretic feature selection with segmentation-based folded principal component analysis (PCA) for hyperspectral image classification. Int. J. Remote Sens. **42**(1), 286–321 (2021)
3. Uddin, M.P., Mamun, M.A., Hossain, M.A.: Effective feature extraction through segmentation-based folded-PCA for hyperspectral image classification. Int. J. Remote Sens. **40**(18), 7190–7220 (2019)
4. Hossain, M.A., Jia, X., Benediktsson, J.A.: One-class oriented feature selection and classification of heterogeneous remote sensing images. IEEE J. Sel. Topics Appl. Earth Observations Remote Sens. **9**(4), 1606–1612 (2016)
5. Uddin, M., Mamun, M., Hossain, M.: Feature extraction for hyperspectral image classification. In: 2017 IEEE Region 10 Humanitarian Technology Conference (R10-HTC), pp. 379–382. IEEE (2017)
6. Guo, B., Gunn, S.R., Damper, R.I., Nelson, J.D.: Band selection for hyperspectral image classification using mutual information. IEEE Geosci. Remote Sens. Lett. **3**(4), 522–526 (2006)

7. Uddin, M.P., Mamun, M.A., Hossain, M.A., Afjal, M.I.: Improved folded-PCA for efficient remote sensing hyperspectral image classification. Geocarto Int. **37**, 9474–9496 (2021)
8. Zabalza, J., et al.: Novel folded-PCA for improved feature extraction and data reduction with hyperspectral imaging and SAR in remote sensing. ISPRS J. Photogramm. Remote. Sens. **93**, 112–122 (2014)
9. Hughes, G.: On the mean accuracy of statistical pattern recognizers. IEEE Trans. Inf. Theory **14**(1), 55–63 (1968)
10. Uddin, M., Mamun, M., Hossain, M.: Improved feature extraction using segmented FPCA for hyperspectral image classification. In: 2017 2nd International Conference on Electrical & Electronic Engineering (ICEEE), pp. 1–4. IEEE (2017)
11. Jia, X., Kuo, B.C., Crawford, M.M.: Feature mining for hyperspectral image classification. Proc. IEEE **101**(3), 676–697 (2013)
12. Uddin, M., Mamun, M., Hossain, M.: Segmented FPCA for hyperspectral image classification. In: 2017 3rd International Conference on Electrical Information and Communication Technology (EICT), pp. 1–6. IEEE (2017)
13. Chang, C.I., Du, Q., Sun, T.L., Althouse, M.L.: A joint band prioritization and band-decorrelation approach to band selection for hyperspectral image classification. IEEE Trans. Geosci. Remote Sens. **37**(6), 2631–2641 (1999)
14. Melgani, F., Bruzzone, L.: Classification of hyperspectral remote sensing images with support vector machines. IEEE Trans. Geosci. Remote Sens. **42**(8), 1778–1790 (2004)
15. Fauvel, M., Chanussot, J., Benediktsson, J.A.: Kernel principal component analysis for feature reduction in hyperspectrale images analysis. In: Proceedings of the 7th Nordic Signal Processing Symposium-NORSIG 2006, pp. 238–241. IEEE (2006)
16. Uddin, M.P., Mamun, M.A., Hossain, M.A.: PCA-based feature reduction for hyperspectral remote sensing image classification. IETE Tech. Rev. **38**(4), 377–396 (2021)
17. Qu, X., Yao, M.: Adaptive subspace incremental PCA based online learning for object classification and recognition. In: 2011 4th International Congress on Image and Signal Processing, vol. 3, pp. 1494–1498 (2011). https://doi.org/10.1109/CISP.2011.6100435
18. Tsai, F., Lin, E.K., Yoshino, K.: Spectrally segmented principal component analysis of hyperspectral imagery for mapping invasive plant species. Int. J. Remote Sens. **28**(5), 1023–1039 (2007)
19. Rodarmel, C., Shan, J.: Principal component analysis for hyperspectral image classification. Surveying Land Inf. Sci. **62**(2), 115–122 (2002)
20. Zhang, X., Teng, Z.: A subspace type incremental two-dimensional principal component analysis algorithm. J. Algorithms Comput. Technol. **14**, 1748302620973531 (2020). https://doi.org/10.1177/1748302620973531
21. Jia, X., Richards, J.A.: Segmented principal components transformation for efficient hyperspectral remote-sensing image display and classification. IEEE Trans. Geosci. Remote Sens. **37**(1), 538–542 (1999)
22. Mishu, S.Z., Hossain, M.A., Ahmed, B.: Hybrid sub-space detection technique for effective hyperspectral image classification. In: 2018 International Conference on Computer, Communication, Chemical, Material and Electronic Engineering (IC4ME2), pp. 1–4. IEEE (2018)
23. Neto, H.V., Nehmzow, U.: Incremental PCA: an alternative approach for novelty detection. Towards Autonomous Robotic Systems (2005)

24. Baumgardner, M.F., Biehl, L.L., Landgrebe, D.A.: 220 band AVIRIS hyperspectral image data set: June 12, 1992 Indian Pine Test Site 3. Purdue University Research Repository 10, R7RX991C (2015)
25. Camps-Valls, G., Bruzzone, L.: Kernel-based methods for hyperspectral image classification. IEEE Trans. Geosci. Remote Sens. **43**(6), 1351–1362 (2005)

Spectral–Spatial Feature Reduction for Hyperspectral Image Classification

Md. Touhid Islam, Mohadeb Kumar, and Md. Rashedul Islam$^{(\boxtimes)}$ (iD)

Computer Science and Engineering, Hajee Mohammad Danesh Science and Technology University, Dinajpur, Bangladesh
rashedul_cse@hstu.ac.bd

Abstract. Hyperspectral Image (HSI) has many narrow and continuous spectral bands. There are many problems with the original HSI. For example, the classification accuracy of the test data is affected by the curse of dimensionality problem because the image bands are highly correlated in both space and time. So, dimensionality reduction is done and improved the classification result. In this paper, a deep convolutional network is suggested to reduce the dimensionality of HSI classification by considering both spectral and spatial features. When combined factor analysis and mRMR are used, spectral features are reduced, while 2D wavelet CNN reduces spatial features. A wavelet CNN is an extension of a 2D CNN that can be used to classify high-resolution images. Wavelet CNNs also use layered wavelet transformations to pull out spectral features. A wavelet CNN is easier to calculate than a 3D CNN or a 2D-3D CNN. In the next step, the spectral features are connected to the two-dimensional CNN to get the spatial features, creating a spatial-spectral feature vector. It makes a model that can accurately classify HSI data at multiple resolutions. As part of the HSI classification, we used data sets from the Pavia University and Salinas Scene dataset to see how well the two methods work together. In two datasets, the proposed Expanded 2DNET did better than the handcrafted methods, according to the experiment.

Keywords: Factor analysis · minimum Redundancy Maximum Relevance (mRMR) · Wavelet CNN · Convolutional Neural Net (CNN) · hyperspectral image (HSI)

1 Introduction

Hyperspectral images are big, high-dimensional, remote-sensing images with information about space and color. Each band is a set of pixel values for a certain part of the spectrum. Hyperspectral imagery is becoming more and more important for monitoring the surface of the Earth in areas like agriculture, the environment, climate, the military, security, etc. [1, 2].

The manipulation of hyperspectral data is more complicated. Large-scale data collection may result in a dimension problem. From enormous data sets, just a few pieces

© ICST Institute for Computer Sciences, Social Informatics and Telecommunications Engineering 2023
Published by Springer Nature Switzerland AG 2023. All Rights Reserved
Md. S. Satu et al. (Eds.): MIET 2022, LNICST 491, pp. 564–577, 2023.
https://doi.org/10.1007/978-3-031-34622-4_45

of information with limited utility are recovered. In addition, the spectral bands of high-dimensional hyperspectral images are commonly interconnected. Consequently, the bulk of conventional algorithms suffers from the "curse of dimension" [3]. It is the phenomenon in which the accuracy of a machine learning model declines despite an increase in the number of features. However, the high-dimensional spectrum of HSIs can result in the Hughes effect, which diminishes categorization accuracy. Dimensionality reduction and feature extraction techniques are frequently used to provide a low-dimensional and discriminative HSI classification representation.

Traditional HSI classification techniques like SVM, KNN, and ANN depend only on spectral information and feature extraction and reduction procedures like principal component analysis (PCA) [4], independent component analysis (ICA), minimum noise fraction (MNF) [5], and factor analysis (FA) [6]. PCA selects features based on their differences. The original qualities of a dataset are isolated and then converted into linear combinations of the original characteristics known as principal components. The MNF data are aligned along decreasing signal-to-noise ratio (SNR) axis [7]. Inadequate band truncation might result in the exclusion of vital signals, which is a drawback of MNF. Another crucial part of machine learning's preprocessing is selecting relevant features to use. The key elements are determined by eliminating superfluous or irrelevant properties from the initial feature set. Popular feature selection strategies such as mutual information (MI) [8], normalized mutual information (nMI), and minimum redundancy-maximum relevance (mRMR) are used to retrieve the original features from datasets. The lack of spatial characteristics in hyperspectral images prevents them from being properly categorized by popular machine learning methods such as K-nearest neighbor (KNN) and support vector machine (SVM).

Hyperspectral pictures have been classified with greater accuracy using deep learning models such convolutional neural networks in recent studies that found both spectral and spatial information helped (2D-CNN, 3D-CNN). 2D CNNs have made great strides in using spatial information in images, while HSI classification uses both spatial and spectral information. Even though 3D Convolution is expensive to run, many different kinds of 3D CNN have been made to take advantage of these properties. Because of how well the two models worked on their own, hybrid 3D-2D CNNs [9] have been suggested in the literature [10]. Even though 3D-2D CNN models all the spatial and spectral parts of an HSI cube, the model doesn't seem to work well when applied to multiple datasets. In these methods, the spectral features are found and cut down based on how much they vary. High accuracy can't be reached by choosing features based on their differences. This point of view also looks at how to select features and how to extract features. But feature selection does not lead to new features. After evaluating the attributes with evaluation functions, it figures out which ones are the most important. In [11], Utkarsh Trehan and Tanmay Chakraborty proposed wavelet-based models that take into account both the spatial and spectral features of HSI cubes. It was shown that wavelet transform is an excellent way to classify HSI. The spectral-spatial characteristics of an HSI become apparent when a wavelet-based treatment is combined with a 2D convolutional neural network. After the features are put together, they are sent to the dense classification layers of the 2D CNN as inputs. Even though the models work well when applied to many different datasets, their accuracy is questionable.

In this study, we present a greedy hybrid technique for the reduction of spectral and spatial information in hyperspectral picture categorization. Using factor analysis and generating factors, the spectral properties are recovered. High-level characteristics are not necessary, to be precise. Instead of selecting the qualities with the most significant variance, the greedy technique selects the most relevant traits from a classification perspective. To remove additional duplicate information from the evaluation criteria, a popular technique called min-redundancy max-relevance (mRMR) is employed to make the selection. This strategy focuses on maximizing relevant information and minimizing redundant information. Before delivering the data to a deep learning model, the preceding procedures are executed (wavelet-CNN). The 2D wavelet CNN extracts spectral-spatial features by applying a wavelet transformation to the spatial input, which assists the perceptron in optimizing and eliciting spectral features. Two benchmark datasets are used to compare the model against alternative handcrafted or deep learning architectures (Pavia University, Salinas). Classification accuracy of the proposed network is shown to be superior to that of the current best practice.

The remainder of the piece is laid up like this. Section 2 focuses on related ideas in dimensionality reduction, traditional feature selection, and various algorithms relevant to machine learning and deep learning. In addition, we go into great depth about our proposed hybrid spectral-spatial feature reduction method in Sect. 2. Experimental designs and methods are discussed in detail in Sect. 3, as is an analysis of the data they produce. Section 4 of the article provides an overview of the content of the study.

2 Methodology

2.1 Spectral Feature Extraction

Factor Analysis

Factor analysis is a method for reducing the number of unseen variables responsible for a given level of variability in the observable variables or factors. This approach aims to redirect the variables so that many core variables can be comparatively compressed with a few factors that capture the most potential data variation from the original dataset. So, Factor analysis calculates that the data variability is due to common factors [12]. Suppose $Z = (Z_1, Z_2 \ldots \ldots Z_n)$ is a set of observable random variables with the mean vector $\mu = (\mu_1, \mu_2 \ldots \ldots \ldots \mu_n)$ [12, 13]. The factor analysis equation assumes as

$$Z = \mu + \lambda K + q \tag{1}$$

where λ is denoted as the matrix of factor loadings with a vector of latent factor scores, $K = (K_1, K_2 \ldots \ldots \ldots K_n)$ and $q = (q_1, q_2 \ldots \ldots \ldots q_n)$ stands for the list of hidden error terms. Under the factor analysis process, the covariance matrix of the observable random variable Z is estimated as follows:

$$Cov(Z) = \lambda \lambda' + \varphi \tag{2}$$

Here, φ is a diagonal matrix. The kth diagonal element of $\lambda \lambda'$, the addition of the values of the squared loading, is called the kth communality, which shows the percent of variability explained by the common factors. The kth diagonal element of φ is called the kth specific variance.

Mutual Information

Mutual information (MI) is the amount of information an individual can obtain about one random variable based on information obtained from another random variable [14]. It is a powerful criterion for selecting the best features [15]. To select the most relevant FA component, we can compute the MI measure between the newly generated features in M_i and the number of available classes in L. The most informative feature is the one containing the highest MI value and can be calculated using the following Eq. (3):

$$MI(M_i, L) = \int_M \int_L P(m, l) \log \frac{P(m, l)}{P(m)P(l)} dm dl \qquad (3)$$

Information-Based Feature Selection: Minimum Redundancy Maximum Relevance (mRMR)

The term mutual information (MI) refers to a measure of how much information a random variable contains about another random variable. We can compute the MI measure between the newly generated features in Mi and the number of available classes in L as described in the previous section Eq. (3).

In another concept [16], The mutual information formula measures the entropy drop under the condition of a target value. This formula (4) provides a summarized explanation of this concept:

$$MI(features; target) = Entropy(feature) - Entropy(features/target) \qquad (4)$$

We can select mutually dissimilar features yet have a high correlation to the classification variable [17]. This technique is known as Minimum Redundancy Maximum Relevance (mRMR). Concerning the target variable, mRMR can choose the feature which is the most relevant and which has the least redundancy in comparison to previous selections. The mutual information (MI) between the applicant and the predictor variable is computed in order to determine the relevance concept. The redundancy term is then determined by averaging the MI values of the applicant variable and the preselected variables [18]. The final features based on mRMR are obtained by removing the redundancy from relevant features. Let S be a set of features with an F number of features $\{F_i\}$ that should be considered highly correlated with class C. The equation of global relevance [19] concerning the S is as follows:

$$R_{max}(S) = \frac{1}{|S|} \sum_{F_i \in S} MI(C, F_i) \qquad (5)$$

Here, R_{max} is denoted as global relevance (Maximum Relevance) with mutual information $MI(C, F_i)$ of feature F_i. To obtain minimum redundancy in features [20]:

$$R_{min}(S) = \frac{1}{|S|^2} \sum_{F_i, F_j \in S} MI(F_i, F_j) \qquad (6)$$

$$mRMR_{max} \varphi (R_{max} - R_{min}) \qquad (7)$$

where minimum relevance is defined as R_{min} with mutual information $MI(F_i, F_j)$ of feature F_i with F_j. From the above two Eqs. 5 and 6, the simplest form of Minimum Redundancy Maximum Relevance $mRMR_{max}$ is obtained as the optimal subset of features.

2.2 Spatial Feature Extraction

Along with spectral features, the spatial features have almost similar effects on the latent classification accuracy of HSI. In [21], Gabor filtering is applied to the principal components derived by Probabilistic PCA (PPCA), which are taken advantage of while attempting to extract spatial characteristics. In this method, spectral characteristics are integrated with their spatial characteristics. 2D convolutional neural networks (2D CNNs) are able to extract spatial characteristics from images and merge them into greater features [22]. A simple example of the architecture of a CNN is presented in Fig. 1. In CNN, we have some images and initialize some filters or kernels to detect vertical or horizontal edges.

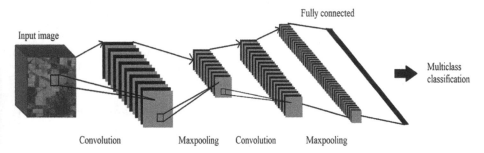

Fig. 1. Convolutional neural network architecture

A bias term particular to the feature map is included in each convolution sum. After one convolution operation, we apply the pooling layer with some pooling filters such as max-pooling or min-pooling to extract the spatial features and convert local spatial features into higher-order features [23]. A feature map is then created for the outputs. Then the rest of the CNN structure comes to take place in the classification operation.

2.3 Proposed Spatial-Spectral Feature Reduction

In the article paper, Fig. 3 illustrates the proposed HSI classification process. First, the input image cube having dimensions H × W × S is sent through a layer of Factor Analysis (FA) to extract all the spectral bands as features. The number of features remains the same number as the input image cube. Then the maximum relevant features were selected, except the redundant features using the minimum redundancy maximum relevance (mRMR) approach.

As a result, our spectral feature reduction is accomplished, and the resulting image has become in H × W × S dimension where only the bands are reduced from S to R.

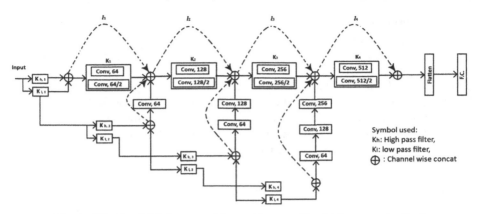

Fig. 2. Wavelet CNN decomposition architecture (Spatial feature extraction)

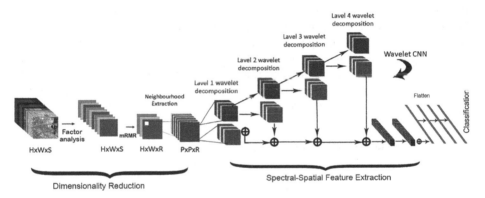

Fig. 3. The architecture of proposed Expanded 2DNET model

Training time is reduced almost by 60% when the dimension is reduced [24]. Factor analysis (FA) is a potentially powerful preprocessing step in HSI because it may capture the variation across the many correlated and overlapped spectrum bands [25], which makes the model classifier more effective. Besides, the additional mRMR algorithm selects optimal features avoiding redundancy. After the FA and mRMR step, we extract overlapping 3D patches of size P × P × R from the preprocessed HSI and send them into the wavelet CNN. We set the patch size to 24 × 24 according to the accuracy. The spectral feature extraction is done by the wavelet transformation. There is a four-level decomposition we've used in our proposed model. The decompositions of wavelet CNN are designed as Fig. 2. The input images for our Wavelet-based CNN experiment are decomposed into four levels. The spatial features are extracted using convolution and pooling operation in wavelet CNN. We have used convolutional kernels exclusively with 1 × 1 padding to ensure that the output is the same size as the input. Convolutional layers are used instead of pooling layers in order to minimize the size of feature maps. If one layer is added with padding of 1 × 1, and the stride is two, then the output layer shrinks in size by a factor of two. For each layer of decomposed photos in [26], Shin Fujieda and Kohei Takayama paired it with a feature map that is the same size as the layer's images. It is necessary to have the same size input pictures for Wavelet CNNs since they employ global average pooling. Thus, only 224 × 224-pixel pictures are used for training in our suggested model. To create these images first, scale the training images to 256 × 256 pixels, then conduct random cropping to 224 × 224 pixels, and flip each one. Various cropping options prevent the overfitting of the model. For further robustness, batch normalization [27] is used before activation layers during training. Instead of using Adam, we exploit the stochastic gradient descent (SGD) optimizer [28]. As the activation function, we use the Rectified Linear Unit (Relu) [29].

3 Experiment and Result Analysis

3.1 Data Set Description

Hyperspectral datasets from two well-known and freely available sources were utilized to show the comparison analysis often employed in hyperspectral image categorization. The Salinas Scene dataset was introduced by AVIRIS sensor over Salinas Valley, California, USA. This dataset has 224 bands (reduced to 204) and 512 × 217 pixels with 16 classes of surface objects [30]. The other one was gathered by ROSIS sensors and has 115 (reduced to 103) bands, ranging from 0.43 to 0.86 μm with a spatial resolution of 610 × 340 pixels with 9 classes from the University of Pavia [31].

3.2 Experimental Configuration

Due to the variability of factors in the input dataset, spectral analysis was applied to extract all the elements. The spectral bands in the input image have been selected to be extracted as features. Based on the minimum redundancy maximum relevance (mRMR) algorithm, only three features were selected, as shown in Table 1. Training and test samples were chosen randomly within each HSI dataset. Each experiment used 20% as training samples, while the remaining 80% was used as test samples to evaluate the performance of the proposed methods. The small number of samples in HSI makes it susceptible to overfitting. Low training samples result in the possibility of overfitting. Additionally, 3 × 3 convolution kernels and 1 × 1 padding is also used, as well as a stride of 2 in place of pooling layers throughout the model. Rectified Linear Unit (Relu) was selected as the activation function. Over 200 epochs have been performed with the stochastic gradient descent (SGD) optimizer. Based on the custom parameter tuning, learning rate and momentum were 0.01 and 0.9, respectively. A total of ten experiments were repeated to ensure stability, and the reported results are averages.

Table 1. Selected features from the dataset used for classification.

Datasets	Methods	Selected features
Salinas	mRMR-wavelet CNN	Bands: 88, 149, 1
	PCA-wavelet CNN	PC: 1, 2, 3
	Spectral-NET	Factors: 1, 2, 3
	Expanded 2DNET	Factors: **1, 4, 3**
Pavia University	mRMR-wavelet CNN	Bands: 21, 77, 54
	PCA-wavelet CNN	PC: 1, 2, 3
	Spectral-NET	Factors: 1, 2, 3
	Expanded 2DNET	Factors: **3, 2, 6**

3.3 Result Discussion

The proposed model is evaluated using the experimental configuration described in the previous section, based on different classification accuracy. The overall accuracy (OA) is measured by the total number of correctly classified labels out of all labels. Kappa Accuracy correlates ground-truth value with classification accuracy. Average Accuracy (AA) is the mean of classification accuracy when classes are compared. The experiments were run on the Colab cloud platform using GPUs. One of the main reasons for choosing Google Colab is that most sessions will come preloaded with 12 GB of RAM and an NVIDIA Tesla K80 GPU.

Table 2 and Table 3 represents the results in term of OA, AA, and kappa measures for two datasets. The results are compared with state-of-the-art methods like SpectralNET [11], SVM, wavelet CNN, etc. Based on the results above, SpectralNET standalone outperforms SVM and wavelet CNN in the SA dataset. There may be an increased spectral redundancy in the SA dataset compared to the rest. The performance of The Expanded 2DNET outperforms all three techniques, mRMR-wavelet CNN, PCA-wavelet CNN, and SpectralNET, throughout the two datasets. Even though it uses only 3 spectral bands, compared to the state-of-the-art models which use 15, and 30 bands, the Expanded 2DNET outperforms all spectral models. Although, for the selected 3 features as shown in Table 1, Expanded 2DNET has overall classification accuracy results of 99.92% and 99.99% for Pavia University and Salinas datasets respectively. The use of greedy selected spectral features combined with wavelet-based features shows the value of such an approach. According to our results, Expanded 2DNET performs better than all the current methods for HSI classification.

The categorization map also serves as a visual comparison tool between the suggested methodology and the existing one. Two separate HSI datasets' categorization maps are shown in Figs. 4 and 5. These maps are based on SVM, mRMR wavelet CNN, PCA wavelet CNN, SpectralNET, and the proposed Expanded 2DNET. In comparison with other methods, SpectralNET and Expanded 2DNET present far superior classification maps. SpectralNET and Expanded 2DNET are almost similar but Expanded 2DNET produces a little bit better maps in the small segment. Therefore, it is clear from the

Table 2. Classification results (%) were obtained using different methods for Salinas Scene.

Class Names	No. of samples			Classification methods			
	Train.	Test.	SVM	mRMR-wavelet CNN	PCA-wavelet CNN	Spectral-NET	Expanded 2DNET
Brocoli_green_weeds_1	402	2009	97.88	100.0	100.0	100.0	**100.0**
Brocoli_green_weeds_2	745	3726	99.53	99.93	100.0	100.0	**100.0**
Fallow	395	1976	97.72	99.93	100.0	100.0	**100.0**
Fallow_rough_plow	279	1394	98.89	100.0	99.82	100.0	**100.0**
Fallow_smooth	536	2678	96.17	99.71	99.72	99.58	**100.0**
Stubble	792	3959	99.81	99.87	99.97	100.0	**100.0**
Celery	716	3579	99.40	26.58	100.0	99.51	**100.0**
Grapes_untrained	2254	11271	88.62	99.98	99.70	99.88	**99.96**
Soil_vinyard_develop	1241	6203	97.24	99.93	100.0	100.0	**100.0**
Corn_senesced_green_weeds	656	3278	86.61	100.0	100.0	100.0	**100.0**
Lettuce_romaine_4wk	214	1068	93.21	99.18	99.88	100.0	**100.0**
Lettuce_romaine_5wk	385	1927	99.61	98.96	100.0	100.0	**100.0**
Lettuce_romaine_6wk	183	916	98.36	98.09	100.0	99.86	**100.0**
Lettuce_romaine_7wk	214	1070	93.46	100.0	100.0	100.0	**100.0**
Vinyard_untrained	1454	7268	46.33	100.0	95.60	100.0	**100.0**
Vinyard_vertical_trellis	361	1807	94.81	100.0	100.0	99.93	**100.0**
Overall Accuracy (OA)			88.35	95.57	99.39	99.92	**99.99**
Kappa coefficient (K)			86.98	95.08	99.33	99.91	**99.98**
Average Accuracy (AA)			92.98	98.45	99.97	99.93	**99.99**

Table 3. Classification results (%) were obtained using different methods for the University of Pavia.

Class Names	No. of samples			Classification methods			
	Train.	Test.	SVM	mRMR-wavelet CNN	PCA-wavelet CNN	Spectral-NET	Expanded 2DNET
Asphalt	1326	6631	87.07	98.93	97.00	99.62	**99.98**
Meadows	3730	18649	98.51	99.03	99.34	99.97	**99.97**
Gravel	420	2099	45.98	91.78	98.39	99.82	**99.64**
Trees	613	3064	83.45	99.43	98.20	99.76	**99.96**
Painted metal sheets	269	1345	98.89	100.0	99.34	100.0	**100.0**
Bare Soil	1006	5029	24.88	99.93	99.85	100.0	**100.0**
Bitumen	266	1330	68.70	95.39	97.37	99.62	**100.0**
Self-Locking Bricks	736	3682	83.33	95.15	97.39	99.80	**99.59**
Shadows	189	947	1.00	96.70	95.38	100.0	**99.47**
Overall Accuracy (OA)			82.23	98.58	98.81	99.87	**99.92**
Kappa coefficient (K)			75.47	98.13	98.43	99.82	**99.89**
Average Accuracy (AA)			76.76	97.78	98.34	99.84	**99.84**

classification table and the classification map that the proposed method outperforms than the method studied for spatial and spectral dimensionality reduction.

For the developed model, Fig. 6 shows the accuracy and loss curves averaged across 200 training epochs. Convergence is achieved in around 25 epochs, demonstrating the quick convergence of the suggested approach.

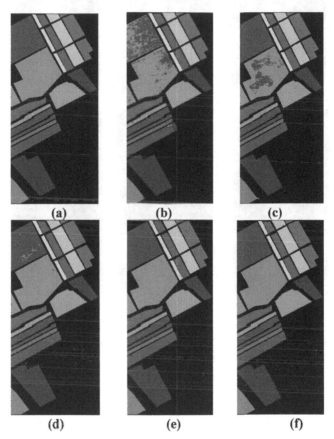

Fig. 4. Classification maps of Salinas dataset for different methods. (a) Ground-truth map (b) SVM, (c) mRMR-wavelet CNN, (d) PCA-wavelet CNN, (e) Spectral-NET (FA-wavelet CNN), (f) Proposed (Expanded 2DNET)

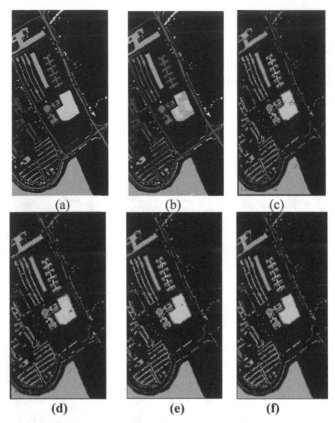

(a)   (b)   (c)

(d)   (e)   (f)

Fig. 5. Classification maps of University of Pavia dataset for different methods. (a) Ground-truth map (b) SVM, (c)mRMR-wavelet CNN, (d) PCA-wavelet CNN, (e) Spectral-NET (FA-wavelet CNN), (f) Proposed (Expanded 2DNET)

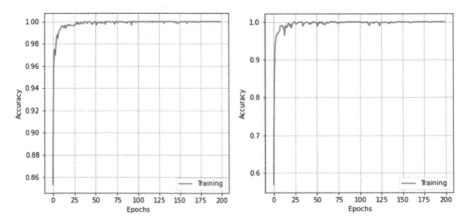

Fig. 6. Accuracy curve for the proposed methods on Salinas and Pavia university dataset

4 Conclusion

This study aimed to evaluate the proposed greedy hybrid technique for extracting spectral and spatial information from HSI data cubes. A mutual information-based feature selection approach, minimum redundancy maximum relevance (mRMR), was utilized to reduce the number of spectral features extracted using factor analysis (FA). These two processes are used for the HSI classification problem before passing the informative data via a deep learning model known as wavelet-CNN. Multiple layers of wavelet decomposition of the input data are used. In order to take into account both spectral and spatial information, these layers are then joined to the fully connected levels of the cube. Because spectral and spatial features are considered the extracted hybrid feature is very relevant to the classification's tasks. Additionally, the proposed model has a lower computational cost and a better classification accuracy than PCA and FA-based wavelet-CNN models. The future study focuses on altering existing feature reduction and selection strategies, reducing the running time of the algorithms utilized, and applying methods to various available variations of HSI datasets.

References

1. Chen, Z., Jiang, J., Jiang, X., Fang, X., Cai, Z.: Spectral-spatial feature extraction of hyperspectral images based on propagation filter. Sensors **18**, 1978 (2018). https://doi.org/10.3390/s18061978
2. Kong, Y., Wang, X., Cheng, Y.: Spectral–spatial feature extraction for HSI classification based on supervised hypergraph and sample expanded CNN. IEEE J. Sel. Top. Appl. Earth Obs. Remote Sens. **11**, 4128–4140 (2018). https://doi.org/10.1109/JSTARS.2018.2869210
3. Zhao, W., Du, S.: Spectral-spatial feature extraction for hyperspectral image classification: a dimension reduction and deep learning approach. IEEE Trans. Geosci. Remote Sens. **54**, 4544–4554 (2016). https://doi.org/10.1109/TGRS.2016.2543748
4. Ali, M.U., Ahmed, S., Ferzund, J., Mehmood, A., Rehman, A.: Using PCA and factor analysis for dimensionality reduction of bio-informatics data. Int. J. Adv. Comput. Sci. Appl. (2017). https://doi.org/10.48550/arXiv.1707.07189
5. Islam, R., Ahmed, B., Hossain, M.A.: Feature reduction based on segmented principal component analysis for hyperspectral images classification (2019). https://doi.org/10.1109/ECACE.2019.8679394
6. Salas-Gonzalez, D., et al.: Feature selection using factor analysis for Alzheimer's diagnosis using 18F-FDG PET images. Med. Phys. **37**, 6084–6095 (2010)
7. Islam, R., Ahmed, B., Hossain, M.A.: Feature reduction of hyperspectral image for classification. Spatial Science (2020). https://doi.org/10.1080/14498596.2020.1770137
8. Xu, Y., Jones, G., Li, J., Wang, B., Sun, C.: A study on mutual information-based feature selection for text categorization. J. Comput. Inf. Syst. **3**, 1007–1012 (2007)
9. Diakite, A., Gui, J., Xiaping, F.: Hyperspectral image classification using 3D 2D CNN. IET Image Proc. 15 (2021). https://doi.org/10.1049/ipr2.12087
10. Roy, S., Krishna, G., Dubey, S.R., Chaudhuri, B.: HybridSN: exploring 3-D-2-D CNN feature hierarchy for hyperspectral image classification. IEEE Geosci. Remote Sens. Lett. **17**, 277–281 (2019). https://doi.org/10.1109/LGRS.2019.2918719
11. Chakraborty, T., Trehan, U.: SpectralNET: exploring spatial-spectral waveletCNN for hyperspectral image classification (2021). Arxiv preprint Arxiv:2104.00341

12. Khosla, N.: Dimensionality reduction using factor analysis. Griffith University, Australia (2004)
13. Shrestha, N.: Factor analysis as a tool for survey analysis. Am. J. Appl. Math. Stat. **9**(1), 4–11 (2021). https://doi.org/10.12691/ajams-9-1-2
14. Shu, W., Qian, W.: Mutual information-based feature selection from set-valued data, pp. 733–739 (2014). https://doi.org/10.1109/ICTAI.2014.114
15. Zhou, H., Wang, X., Zhu, R.: Feature selection based on mutual information with correlation coefficient. Appl. Intell. **52**(5), 5457–5474 (2021). https://doi.org/10.1007/s10489-021-02524-x
16. Vergara, J.R., Estévez, P.A.: A review of feature selection methods based on mutual information. Neural Comput. Appl. **24**(1), 175–186 (2013). https://doi.org/10.1007/s00521-013-1368-0
17. De Jay, N., Papillon-Cavanagh, S., Olsen, C., El-Hachem, N., Bontempi, G., Haibe-Kains, B.: mRMRe: an R package for parallelized mRMR ensemble feature selection. Bioinformatics **29**(18), 2365–2368 (2013)
18. Kursun, O., Sakar, C.O., Favorov, O., Aydin, N., Gurgen, F.: Using covariates for improving the minimum redundancy maximum relevance feature selection method. Turk. J. Electr. Eng. Comput. Sci. **18**, 975–987 (2010). https://doi.org/10.3906/elk-0906-75
19. Aghaeipoor, F., Javidi, M.M.: A hybrid fuzzy feature selection algorithm for high-dimensional regression problems: an mRMR-based framework. Expert Syst. Appl. **162**, 113859 (2020). https://doi.org/10.1016/j.eswa.2020.113859
20. Billah, M., Waheed, S.: Minimum redundancy maximum relevance (mRMR) based feature selection from endoscopic images for automatic gastrointestinal polyp detection. Multimedia Tools and Applications **79**(33–34), 23633–23643 (2020). https://doi.org/10.1007/s11042-020-09151-7
21. Vaddi, R., Manoharan, P.: Probabilistic PCA based hyper spectral image classification for remote sensing applications. In: Abraham, A., Cherukuri, A.K., Melin, P., Gandhi, N. (eds.) ISDA 2018 2018. AISC, vol. 941, pp. 863–869. Springer, Cham (2020). https://doi.org/10.1007/978-3-030-16660-1_84
22. Vaddi, R., Prabukumar, M.: Hyperspectral image classification using CNN with spectral and spatial features integration. Infrared Phys. Technol. **107**, 103296 (2020). https://doi.org/10.1016/j.infrared.2020.103296
23. Wang, K., Cheng, L., Yong, B.: Spectral-similarity-based kernel of SVM for hyperspectral image classification. Remote Sens. **12**, 2154 (2020). https://doi.org/10.3390/rs12132154
24. Aparna, G., Rachana, K., Rikhita, K., Phaneendra Kumar, B.L.N.: Comparison of feature reduction techniques for change detection in remote sensing. In: Chowdary, P.S.R., Anguera, J., Satapathy, S.C., Bhateja, V. (eds.) Evolution in Signal Processing and Telecommunication Networks. LNEE, vol. 839, pp. 325–333. Springer, Singapore (2022). https://doi.org/10.1007/978-981-16-8554-5_30
25. Kong, F., Hu, K., Li, Y., Li, D., Zhao, S.: Spectral-spatial feature partitioned extraction based on CNN for multispectral image compression. Remote Sens. **13**, 9 (2020). https://doi.org/10.3390/rs13010009
26. Fujieda, S., Takayama, K., Hachisuka, T.: Wavelet convolutional neural networks (2018). arXiv preprint arXiv:1805.08620
27. Ghaderizadeh, S., Abbasi-Moghadam, D., Sharifi, A., Zhao, Na., Tariq, A.: Hyperspectral image classification using a hybrid 3D-2D convolutional neural networks. IEEE J. Sel. Top. Appl. Earth Obs. Remote Sens. **14**, 7570–7588 (2021). https://doi.org/10.1109/JSTARS.2021.3099118
28. Wang, C., Ma, N., Ming, Y., Wang, Q., Xia, J.: Classification of hyperspectral imagery with a 3D convolutional neural network and J-M distance. Adv. Space Res. **64**, 886–899 (2019). https://doi.org/10.1016/j.asr.2019.05.005

29. Li, X., et al.: A wavelet transform-assisted convolutional neural network multi-model framework for monitoring large-scale fluorochemical engineering processes. Processes **8**(11), 1480 (2020). https://doi.org/10.3390/pr8111480

30. Uddin, M.P., Mamun, M.A., Afjal, M.I., Hossain, M.A.: Information-theoretic feature selection with segmentation-based folded principal component analysis (PCA) for hyperspectral image classification. Int. J. Remote Sens. **42**, 286–321 (2020). https://doi.org/10.1080/014 31161.2020.1807650

31. Fu, H., Sun, G., Jaime, Z., Aizhu, Z., Ren, J., Jia, X.: A novel spectral-spatial singular spectrum analysis technique for near real-time in situ feature extraction in hyperspectral imaging. IEEE J. Sel. Top. Appl. Earth Obs. Remote Sens. **13**, 2214–2225 (2020). https://doi.org/10.1109/ JSTARS.2020.2992230

Predicting the Risk of COVID-19 Infection Using Lifestyle Data

Nafiz Fuad Siam, Mahira Tabassum Khan, M. R. Rownak, Md. Rejaben Jamin Juel, and Ashraf Uddin(✉) 🆔

American International University-Bangladesh, Dhaka 1229, Bangladesh
dr.ashraf@aiub.edu

Abstract. "Prevention is better than cure" is a well-known proverb that is more meaningful for contiguous diseases like COVID-19. During the coronavirus pandemic, people are advised to maintain a regulated and hygienic lifestyle to prevent mass transmission. But there is no effective way to inform them about the level of risk of infection based on their lifestyle to prevent the disease. There are several studies that have proposed the prediction of COVID-19 disease based on symptoms to help cure patients. This study has used a machine learning approach to analyze lifestyle-specific data to help prevent the disease. A public survey was done on lifestyle-related questions that resulted in a dataset consisting of 620 responses. A typical machine learning methodology has been followed that contains steps like data preprocessing, feature engineering, training, evaluation, etc. This study has used three machine-learning algorithms, including Neural Network. Relevancy of hygienic lifestyle habits in case of preventing such diseases has been found. The study has developed a system by evaluating and selecting a machine learning model that can predict if a person is prone to be affected by such a disease. The developed model has shown an accuracy of approximately 95% with an F1-score of 0.942.

Keywords: Covid-19 · Lifestyle · Machine Learning

1 Introduction

Covid-19 is a respiratory infection disease that can finally result in mortality. People have been suffering from this disease for the last two years, and it has turned out to be a great pandemic. A virus named Novel corona or SARS-CoV-2 is responsible for Covid-19. Coronavirus was first detected in Wuhan, China, in December 2019 [1]. This disease has infected more than 269 million people and killed above 5.3 million people worldwide [2]. All sectors were closed for several months in different countries worldwide, negatively impacting different aspects of life.

The disease continuously changes its genotype and comes in different waves in different countries. At present, the virus is showing its brutality by continuing the third wave worldwide. Specialists predict the virus will also come with a fourth wave. Statistics show this virus is more deadly than the previous century's Ebola virus, with the highest death rate [3].

In the above circumstances, the world will be benefited from the prevention method that can be implemented strictly besides helping infected people. If the risk of infection can be predicted by analyzing previous data, the most prone people can be identified. This research aims to predict the chances that a person will be affected by this disease by measuring their lifestyle data. The relevancy of lifestyle patterns with the disease can be determined using people's daily lifestyle data.

Although, the technical aspects of the work fall in regular machine learning tasks, the paper proposes a new solution to control Covid-19 spread by identifying the most likely persons to get infected. So, the main contribution of the paper is to help people to prevent infection by the proposed model. The second contribution is the dataset itself which has been collected through online campaign from various people. The dataset can be used by researchers for future research in the area.

2 Related Work

Similar studies have not been found in the literature, but some related research articles have been examined. Bhanu et al. represent an analysis [4], prediction, and evaluation of COVID-19 datasets to determine which age groups are most affected by COVID-19. They used Machine learning techniques to create various prediction models such as Random Forest, Support Vector Machine (SVM), KNN, Decision Tree Classifier, Gaussian Naïve Bayesian Classifier, Multilinear Regression, Logistic Regression, and XGBoost Classifier.

Wang et al. proposed a fully automatic deep learning system [5] for COVID-19 diagnostic and prognostic analysis by routinely used computed tomography. They used a large dataset and computed C.T. images from 5372 patients.

Ikemura et al. proposed automated machine learning to predict the mortality of patients with COVID-19 [6]. They presented Machine learning methods to forecast the severity of COVID-19 disease. To formulate the models, they used data from 4313 patients with 48 variables. Patients were examined for 30 days or until death. The best independent models were the gradient boost machine and extreme gradient boost models, and their accuracy rate is 0.803 and 0.793, respectively.

Raf et al. [7] used daily clinical and laboratory data to enhance RT-PCR's effectiveness and chest-CT for COVID-19 detection in patients hospitalized. They gathered data from 5196 patients to train the dataset but only used 536 suspected covid patients aged 18 or younger. They used three models to detect COVID-19: Binary Logistic Regression, Random Forest, and Artificial Neural Networks, each with 22 parameters.

Elaziz et al. present a new machine learning method for image-based diagnosis of COVID-19 [8]. They developed a novel machine-learning algorithm to distinguish between COVID-19 patients and non-COVID-19 patients, assigning each set of chest x-ray images to one of two categories. The accuracy of using the derived features without the feature selection approach is 0.901 and 0.9309, respectively.

Cabitza et al. used machine-learning models for detecting COVID-19 [9] based on regular blood tests. They collected 1624 patients' data from various hospitals, and the majority were positive for Covid-19. The dataset consists of up to 55 features. Their accuracy rate for the three datasets varies from 0.75 to 0.78. They used this approach to identify positive Covid-19 patients who require faster and cheaper testing.

Keeling et al. analyzed predictions of COVID-19 dynamics in the United Kingdom (U.K.) [10]. Using the information on positive samples of hospitals and death rates, they illustrate an observable age-structural concept that utilizes that data to calculate new predictions on the onset of an outbreak in ten U.K. regions. They ran multiple experiments to estimate the potential impact of various strategies to alleviate social distancing overtime on inpatient and acute care admissions and deaths.

Another study [11] represents an interpretable machine learning for COVID-19 on severity prediction task using a database of 92 patients who had confirmed SARS-CoV-2 laboratory tests, and the researchers trained the data to identify biomarkers indicative of infection severity prediction.

Watson et al. proposed a method [12] for forecasting COVID-19 in the United States with a machine learning & Bayesian time series compartmental model. They use an epidemiological compartmental model with a Bayesian time series model and a random forest algorithm to predict COVID-19.

Le et al. proposed IoT enabled depth-wise separable convolution neural network with deep SVM for COVID 19 diagnosis and classification [13].

There have been many studies conducted on Contagious diseases like COVID-19. Almost all the studies were conducted on clinical data regarding the physical factors of the patients. Most of the studies worked on predicting to identify the disease or the mortality by analyzing X-Ray/C.T. images, blood sample reports, etc. There seems to be no study exploring people's lifestyles to predict the chance or likelihood of getting affected by such diseases. We have found some other relevant studies [18, 19] where authors showed the performance of deep learning methods on biological data. This study focuses on that criterion, where peoples' daily lifestyle and hygiene levels will be analyzed rather than clinical data regarding physical conditions to predict whether a person is in danger of getting affected by the disease for their lifestyle.

3   Methodology

This section has been divided into two subsections: dataset description and machine learning approach.

3.1   Dataset Description

This study's approach required machine learning models to be trained with data depicting people's daily hygiene choices. A set of questions was prepared for the survey that reflects the lifestyle guidelines from the World Health Organization [17]. The survey was conducted using a google form with 25 questions anonymously, and 620 responses were received. The dataset is available on Mendeley[1]. Figure 1 shows one of the questions and the corresponding responses.

---

[1] https://data.mendeley.com/datasets/fc3dd2hp8b.

Have you ever been diagnosed With COVID Positive?
620 responses

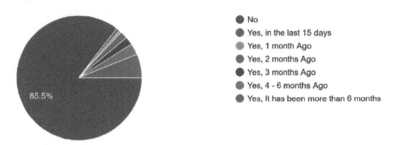

- No
- Yes, in the last 15 days
- Yes, 1 month Ago
- Yes, 2 months Ago
- Yes, 3 months Ago
- Yes, 4 - 6 months Ago
- Yes, It has been more than 6 months

Fig. 1. A sample question and responses

3.2 Machine Learning Approach

Several steps of the traditional machine learning approach were followed to develop this system. However, all the small steps can be categorized into two high-level abstract steps. The first one is Data Preparation, and the second one is Training and Evaluation. The high-level steps visualization can be seen in Fig. 2 below.

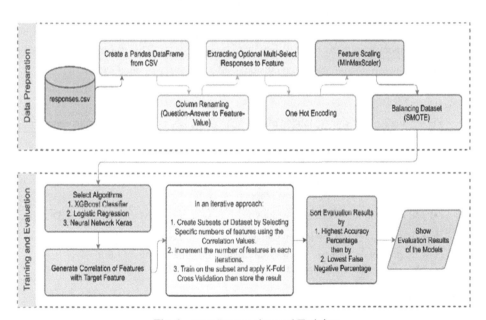

Fig. 2. Data Preparation and Training

Data Preparation. At the very beginning, right after creating a pandas dataframe from the responses, the column names were renamed into a 'feature-value form' from the 'question-answer form.' which can be seen in Table 1 below.

Table 1. Question-Answer to Feature-Value transformation

S.L.	Question	Feature
1	I am filling this form for –	FillingFor
2	Are you filling this form from Bangladesh?	FillingFromBD
3	Have you ever been diagnosed With COVID Positive?	CovidPositive
4	Have any of your family members / House-mates been diagnosed With COVID Positive?	RelatedCovidPositive
5	Have you taken any VACCINE for COVID-19?	Vaccinated
6	What is your living area type?	LivingAreaType
7	Your Profession	Profession
8	Your Job type	ProfessionType
9	Your Age (Years) [example: 25]	Age
10	Your Body Weight (K.G.) [example: 65]	Weight
11	Your gender	Gender
12	Tell us about your accommodation type	AccommodationType
13	How many people do live with you in your house?	HouseMateCount
14	Are you diagnosed with any of the diseases below?	Disease
15	Do you wear face masks?	WearingFaceMask
16	Do you uncover your mouth while talking to others?	UncoveringMouth
17	How frequently do you have to go outside?	GoingOutside
18	How frequently do your family members / House-mates go outside?	RelatedGoingOutside
19	For what reason do you go outside often?	GoingOutsideReason
20	Do you use hand sanitizer?	UsingSanitizer
21	How frequently do you wash your hands?	WashingHands
22	How frequently do you have to dine outside during pandemic? (restaurants, hotel, workplace)	DiningOutside
23	Do you maintain social distance when you go outside?	MaintainingSocialDistance
24	How frequently do you use public transport?	UsingPublicTransport
25	How frequently do your friends or family members come to your house for visiting purposes?	VisitByFnF

Checkboxes were used to receive multiple answers for two of the questions. Those multiple answers were stored in cells in a semicolon-separated manner. So, the next step was to extract them, and for this purpose, python's 'str.get_dummies' method was used. Then they were appended as binary columns in the dataframe. From below two tables, it can be understood where Table 2 represents the before extraction scenario, and Table 3 shows the after-extraction scenario.

Table 2. Before Extraction

	Disease
n	High Blood-Pressure; Allergy

Table 3. After Extraction

	Disease_High Blood-Pressure	Disease_Allergy
n	1	1

The response values (especially the responses submitted through radio buttons) were then transformed from categorical to numerical representation. The transformation process was One-Hot Encoding in this case. The reason for using One-Hot Encoding is that the values from those features are not ordinal. If they were ordinal, level encoding, or, to be specific, the 'integer encoding' technique could also be used.

Fig. 3. A sample question from the survey form for describing One-Hot Encoding

For example, if anybody responded with 'Male' for the question visible in Fig. 3, generated a row like Table 4, and preprocessing the data would convert it like Table 5.

Table 4. Before One-Hot Encoding

	Your gender
n	Male

Table 5. After One-Hot Encoding

	Gender_Male	Gender_Female	Gender_Prefer not to say
n	1	0	0

After that, the feature values of the dataset were scaled to keep them in a specific range. Min-Max Scaling was used in this approach. This scaling will ensure that the feature values be in the range of 0 to 1. The formula for this approach is as follows:

$$x' = \frac{x - \min(x)}{\max(x) - \min(x)}$$

The next step was to balance the dataset. The dataset created from the survey responses for this study had only 90 responses with covid positive diagnosis affirmative out of 620 responses. The visualization of this can be seen in Fig. 4 below.

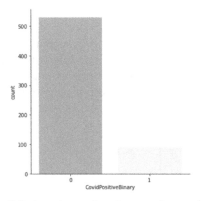

Fig. 4. Count of distinct observations in target feature after balancing.

Training and Evaluation. The beginning of this phase was started with selecting the algorithms for this study. Three popular machine learning algorithms were used to train models for this approach:

```
model = Sequential([
    Dense(16, (input_dim = input_dim), (activation = 'relu')),
    Dense(32, (activation = 'relu')),
    Dense(2, (activation = 'softmax')),
])
model.compile(
    Adam((lr = 0.001)),
    (loss = 'sparse_categorical_crossentropy'),
    (metrics = ['accuracy'])
)
```

Fig. 5. Code Snippet of Neural Network Model

- XGBoost Classifier
- Logistic Regression
- Neural Network Keras

Figure 5 represents a code snippet of the Keras Model. It was a sequential approach, stacking three tensor layers. The activation function ReLU was used for the first two layers, and the third or output layer, the Softmax function, was used [14, 15].

It was necessary to see how many features were needed to gain a specific level of accuracy to find out the most suitable algorithm and model combination for this study and similar machine learning jobs. Selection of features in such a manner was only possible if a ranking could be established for all the features against the target feature 'CovidPositiveBinary.' For this study, Correlation Matrix was used to analyze feature importance and rank them accordingly.

After generating the correlation matrix, a dictionary (python data structure) was created for storing the evaluation results. Initially, a 'subset' of the 60 most important features was selected according to the correlation matrix for the target feature. After that, a model was created for each of the three selected algorithms. Then those models were trained on the sub-dataset. After training each model with that supplied sub-dataset, K-Fold cross-validation was applied to each model, where the value of K was 10. The details step-by-step processes are shown in Fig. 6.

The size of 'subset' features used to specify the number of features included was incremented by 10 at each iteration. The full dataset had 100 features (excluding the target feature), and the iteration was repeated five times. Thus, the dictionary stores evaluation results of 15 models (3 algorithms trained with five different sub-datasets) by the end of 5 iterations. The performance metrics, including Accuracy, Precision, F1 Score, and Recall, were generated from cross-validation results for each model using the 'classification_report' function. The function is from the 'metrics' module from the 'sklearn' library for python [16]. Those values, alongside the confusion matrix values, were stored in the dictionary for every model.

Because of the stochastic nature of the neural network algorithm and the K-Fold evaluation procedure for the algorithm, the results can vary or show differences in numeric precision in each run [17]. It could affect the ranking as well. Hence, to stabilize the order to some extent, the K-Fold cross-validation was applied 10 times on each trained model, and the average was considered and stored as a result. Due to this step, some metrics value like true/false positive/negative count was stored in the dictionary as floating-point numbers instead of plain round integers.

After completing all the iterations, a pandas dataframe from the result storage dictionary was created. Then the dataframe was sorted by the models' 'Accuracy Percentage' and then by the 'False Negative Percentage.' After printing the dataframe, it was exported as a CSV file for future usage.

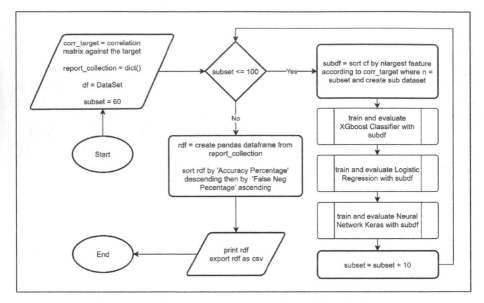

Fig. 6. High-level flow chart of iterative training and evaluation process

4 Result Analysis

The result summary can be seen in Table 6. Full forms of the used mnemonics are the following-

- NN 100: Represents the result for the Neural Network model with 100 Feature count.
- XGB 60: Represents the result for XGBoost Classifier with 100 Feature count.
- LR 100: Represents the result for Logistic Regression with 100 Feature count.
- TNP: True Negative Percentage.
- FPP: False Positive Percentage.
- FNP: False Negative Percentage.

Table 6. Performance Metrics Comparison

Metrics	NN 100	XGB 60	LR 100
Accuracy	0.942	0.926	0.855
TNP	0.445	0.471	0.415
FPP	0.054	0.028	0.084
FNP	0.0027	0.045	0.059
TPP	0.497	0.454	0.440
Precision	0.947	0.926	0.856
Recall	0.942	0.926	0.855
F1-Score	0.942	0.926	0.855

- TPP: True Positive Percentage.

Although a more detailed performance report was generated with nine-digit decimal point precision, the table above is constructed with three-digit decimal point precision and essential metrics for convenience. As described earlier, each algorithm was trained and evaluated with five subsets of features. But, here, the table compares the best models from each algorithm.

Now, it can be seen from the table that "NN 100" with 100 Feature count is winning almost every metric of the performance. The metric F1-Score is backing it up firmly, even though it has lost to XGBoost Classifier (XGB 60) in terms of true-negative detection and false-positive detection criteria.

XGB 60 could have been the best model if neural network models were excluded from the ranking. It outperformed the other non-neural algorithm, 'Logistic Regression (LR 100),' by a considerable margin. One noteworthy point about this model is that XGBoost Classifier performed best when feeding it 60 features only, which means it was doing its best when provided with 40% fewer features. This model's performance is impressive, keeping in mind that it is way less resource-hungry than any neural network model.

According to the performance of the top model, the main goal of this study seems accomplished with an acceptable accuracy level, which was to develop a machine learning system that will analyze people's daily lifestyle and hygiene levels and predict if they are prone to be affected by contagious diseases like COVID-19.

5 Conclusion

This study uses a deep learning neural network model on a dataset consisting of categorical and non-ordinal binary data. And another significant fact about this study is that features were not trimmed before training and evaluating the models; in fact, the study selected the best model for predicting the disease alongside determining the best subset of the primary dataset by selecting features to be included in the subset using an iterative approach.

References

1. Euro.who.int. About the virus (2021). <https://www.euro.who.int/en/health-topics/health-emergencies/coronavirus-covid-19/novel-coronavirus-2019-ncov> [Accessed 19 December 2021]
2. Worldometers.info. COVID Live - Coronavirus Statistics – Worldometer (2021). <https://www.worldometers.info/coronavirus/> [Accessed 19 December 2021]
3. Kortepeter, M.: Why is Covid-19 more deadly than ebola? An Infectious Disease Doctor Explains (2021). <https://www.forbes.com/sites/coronavirusfrontlines/2020/07/31/why-is-covid-19-more-deadly-than-ebola-an-infectious-disease-doctor-explains/?sh=2c1420a3f734> [Accessed 19 December 2021]
4. Prakash, K.: Analysis, prediction and evaluation of COVID-19 datasets using machine learning algorithms. Int. J. Emerging Trends Eng. Res. 8(5), 2199–2204 (2020)
5. Wang, S., et al.: A fully automatic deep learning system for COVID-19 diagnostic and prognostic analysis. Eur. Respir. J. 56(2), 2000775 (2020)

6. Ikemura, K., et al.: Using automated machine learning to predict the mortality of patients with COVID-19: prediction model development study. J. Med. Internet Res. **23**(2), e23458 (2021)
7. Gangloff, C., Rafi, S., Bouzillé, G., Soulat, L., Cuggia, M.: Machine learning is the key to diagnose COVID-19: a proof-of-concept study. Sci. Rep. **11**(1), 7166 (2021)
8. Elaziz, M., Hosny, K., Salah, A., Darwish, M., Lu, S., Sahlol, A.: New machine learning method for image-based diagnosis of COVID-19. PLoS ONE **15**(6), e0235187 (2020)
9. Cabitza, F., et al.: Development, evaluation, and validation of machine learning models for COVID-19 detection based on routine blood tests. Clin. Chem. Lab. Med. (CCLM) **59**(2), 421–431 (2020)
10. Keeling, M.J., et al.: Predictions of COVID-19 dynamics in the U.K.: short-term forecasting and analysis of potential exit strategies. PLoS Comput. Biol. **17**(1), e1008619 (2021). https://doi.org/10.1371/journal.pcbi.1008619
11. Wu, H., et al.: Interpretable machine learning for COVID-19: an empirical study on severity prediction task. IEEE Trans. Artif. Intell., 1–1 (2021)
12. Watson, G., et al.: Pandemic velocity: forecasting COVID-19 in the U.S. with a machine learning & Bayesian time series compartmental model. PLoS Comput. Biol. **17**(3), e1008837 (2021)
13. Le, D.-N., Parvathy, V.S., Gupta, D., Khanna, A., Rodrigues, J.J.P.C., Shankar, K.: IoT enabled depthwise separable convolution neural network with deep support vector machine for COVID-19 diagnosis and classification. Int. J. Mach. Learn. Cybern. **12**(11), 3235–3248 (2021). https://doi.org/10.1007/s13042-020-01248-7
14. Brownlee, J.: A gentle introduction to the rectified linear unit (ReLU). Machine Learning Mastery (2019). https://machinelearningmastery.com/rectified-linear-activation-function-for-deep-learning-neural-networks/. [Accessed: 27- Jul- 2021]
15. Brownlee, J.: Softmax activation function with python. Machine Learning Mastery (2020). https://machinelearningmastery.com/softmax-activation-function-with-python/. [Accessed: 27- Jul- 2021]
16. sklearn.metrics.classification_report — scikit-learn 0.24.2 documentation. Scikit-learn.org. https://scikit-learn.org/stable/modules/generated/sklearn.metrics.classification_report.html. [Accessed: 28- Jul- 2021]
17. Brownlee, J.: Why do I get different results each time in machine learning? Machine Learning Mastery. https://machinelearningmastery.com/different-results-each-time-in-machine-learning/. [Accessed: 28- Jul- 2021]
18. Mahmud, M., Kaiser, M.S., Hussain, A., Vassanelli, S.: Applications of deep learning and reinforcement learning to biological data. IEEE Trans. Neural Netw. Learn. Syst. **29**(6), 2063–2079 (2018). https://doi.org/10.1109/TNNLS.2018.2790388
19. Mahmud, M., Kaiser, M.S., McGinnity, T.M., Hussain, A.: Deep learning in mining biological data. Cogn. Comput. **13**(1), 1–33 (2020). https://doi.org/10.1007/s12559-020-09773-x

Forecasting Dengue Incidence in Bangladesh Using Seasonal ARIMA Model, a Time Series Analysis

Nur Mohammed and Md. Zahidur Rahman[(✉)]

Department of CSE, Britannia University, Cumilla 3500, Bangladesh
mzahidur.bd@gmail.com

Abstract. Dengue fever is now a serious problem for public health. The number of dengue affected cases has dramatically increased worldwide in recent years. There was an ongoing rise in the number of cases that were reported, particularly in Bangladesh. The objective of the study is to determine the best dengue prediction model using time series data and to forecast monthly dengue occurrence in 2022. The monthly data gathered from January 2017 to December 2021 have been validated using Seasonal Autoregressive Integrated Moving Average (SARIMA) models. Based on a number of factors, the SARIMA $(1,0,0)(1,1,1)_{12}$ model was selected as the best fit model and used to predict the next epidemic for the period from January 2022 to December 2022. The outcome indicates a rise in dengue fever cases during August 2022, with an anticipated 6,410 cases. The acquired model will be utilized as a tool for the forecast of dengue cases.

Keywords: Dengue · SARIMA · time series analysis · prediction

1 Introduction

Dengue fever is a serious public health concern affecting many countries, including Bangladesh. It is caused by a virus belonging to the *Flaviviridae* family and has four different variants. The principal vector for transmission of the disease in South-East Asia, including Bangladesh, is the *Aedes aegypti* mosquito. The severity of the disease and its increasing prevalence make it crucial for communities to be aware of the causes, symptoms, and preventive measures to curb its spread. Early diagnosis and prompt medical treatment are critical in reducing the risk of severe dengue and its complications [1]. Dengue fever is caused by different variants, leading to different types of fevers including Dengue Fever (DF), Dengue Hemorrhagic Fever (DHF), and Dengue Shock Syndrome (DSS) [2]. The disease causes a spectrum of sicknesses ranging from mild symptoms, for example, fever, body ache, joint agony, migraine, and body rashes, to serious hemorrhagic complications. There is no particular therapy for dengue or extreme dengue, yet early identification and admittance to legitimate clinical consideration brings casualty rates underneath down to 1% [3]. This viral illness transmitted to humans by the bite

Md. S. Satu et al. (Eds.): MIET 2022, LNICST 491, pp. 589–598, 2023.
https://doi.org/10.1007/978-3-031-34622-4_47

of an infected female Aedes mosquito, primarily *Aedes aegypti* and *Aedes albopictus.* *Aedes aegypti* is a highly competent epidemic vector of dengue virus and is the principal urban vector of the disease. These mosquitoes lay their eggs in artificial containers, and the females rest inside houses. On the other hand, *Aedes albopictus* females rest out-doors, where they lay their eggs in both artificial and natural containers. Understanding the behavior and habitat of these mosquitoes is important in controlling the spread of dengue and reducing its impact on public health. Effective mosquito control measures, such as removing breeding sites, using insecticide sprays, and utilizing bed nets, are essential in reducing the risk of dengue transmission [4]. Asymptomatic infection to potentially fatal shock and hemorrhage are all clinical signs of dengue. In a human host, it normally develops after a 4 to 7 day (up to 10 day) intrinsic incubation phase. The virus can be transmitted to mosquitoes during the viral period, which lasts for 4 to 5 days and can extend up to 12 days. After an 8-to-12-day extrinsic incubation period, the mosquitoes become infectious and can spread the virus to humans by biting. Once infected, the mosquito remains infectious for its entire lifespan, making it important to control its population and minimize exposure to mosquito bites to reduce the risk of dengue transmission. It's crucial for individuals to take preventive measures such as using mosquito repellent, wearing protective clothing, and using bed nets, especially during outbreaks [5]. Aziz and his colleagues first described dengue in Bangladesh as "Dacca fever" in 1964. Dengue was reported to occur periodically in Bangladesh between 1964 and 1999 [6], with the first epidemic of dengue fever being reported in the capital city, Dhaka in the year 2000. It is recorded an aggregate of 21,847 cases and 233 deaths (1.066%) in Jan 2000 to Dec 2007 timeframe; and 15,412 cases and 29 deaths (.188%) in Jan 2008 to Dec 2016 timeframe [7, 8]. Bangladesh has experienced multiple dengue outbreaks in recent years. In 2017, there were 2,769 cases and 8 deaths, while in 2018 the number of cases rose to 10,148 cases and 26 deaths. The outbreak in 2019 was the worst, with 101,354 cases and at least 179 deaths (0.162%). DENV-3 was identified as the predominant serotype in the 2019 outbreak [9]. While COVID-19 has been a global concern since early 2020 and the number of cases in Bangladesh has been increasing since May 2020, the country is also on the brink of another dengue outbreak. In 2020, there were 1,193 cases and 3 deaths reported. From January 2021 to November 2021, Bangladesh recorded over 27,368 dengue cases and 96 deaths, with 88% of the total cases occurring in Dhaka, according to the DGHS [10].

The remaining paper organizes as follows. Related works of this study are explained in section two. The proposed model and detailed discussions are provided in section three. Exploratory outcomes and discussions are provided in section four, and the conclusion and suggestions for future work are provided at the end.

2   Related Work

The spread of dengue patients can be examined using statistical models, which can also display the trend of how many patients will increase over the coming days. Recently, several authors explained the use of statistical tools like time series analysis to predict the quantity of dengue-affected people in a particular area. Box and Jenkins used a statistical method named Autoregressive Integrated Moving Average (ARIMA), which comprise three cycles, namely identification, parameter estimation, and diagnostic assessment. It is a famous model for forecasting dengue occurrence of epidemics [11, 12].

They proposed SARIMA in the 1970s expanding from ARIMA as per the season phases [12]. Additionally, they suggested using the Auto Correlation Function (ACF) and the Partial Auto Correlation Function (PACF) of the sample data as the primary tools to distinguish the order of the model [11]. In [13], Using the data from January 2000 to October 2007, Zamil Choudhury et al. developed a SARIMA model and forecasted the number of cases in the city of Dhaka between September 2006 and October 2007.

In [14], Shafia Shaheen found the relationship between the weather and the dengue incident in Dhaka. A time series analysis was completed by utilizing weather data from January 2009 to July 2019. In [15], Hashizume et al. analyze the impact of flooding on dengue epidemics. They used a general linear poisoning regression model to analyze a time series data of hospitalizations from 2005 to 2009.

The objective of this research is to create a SARIMA model to predict the outbreak for the monthly Dengue Fever cases in Bangladesh, based on reported cases available from January 2017 to December 2021. Many researchers have already worked with time series data for dengue forecasting. As we deal with Bangladesh perception, we will consider related papers published in Bangladesh. As we have discussed above, all the researchers considered only Dhaka city, whereas we will consider the entire country, which was never done before. Another difference in our study is that we will use RMSE (Root Mean Square Error), whereas other researchers used MAPE (Mean Absolute Percentage Error) values. The reason behind using RMSE is that it can use on any regression dataset. But, MAPE can't use on all datasets because when the true value is close to 0, it causes division by 0 error. This forecasting will help the government to understand the trend and make the right decision to deal with the next dengue outbreak.

3   Materials and Methods

3.1   Study Area

Bangladesh is situated in South Asia and is defined by its coordinates of 20°34' to 26°38' N latitude and 88°01' to 92°41' E longitude.

3.2   Data Collection

The data was obtained from the DGHS (Directorate General of Health Services) [16], Bangladesh and online news portals using web scraping techniques. The data collected covers the period from January 1st, 2017 to November 30th, 2021 and consists of information on Dengue Fever, Dengue Hemorrhagic Fever, and Dengue Shock Syndrome cases. It is important to note that the data is reported as Dengue Fever cases only.

3.3   Statistical Analysis

Initial Data Observation. At first, a simple data observation was led to figure out the fundamental pattern of the series. From Fig. 1, it is shown that the series is not stationary with the presence of the seasonal component.

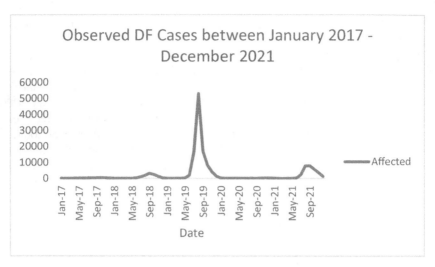

Fig. 1. Dengue Cases Observation.

Performing Seasonal and Non-seasonal Differencing. The series' stationarity was obtained using the seasonal and non-seasonal differencing patterns illustrated in Fig. 2 and Fig. 5 respectively.

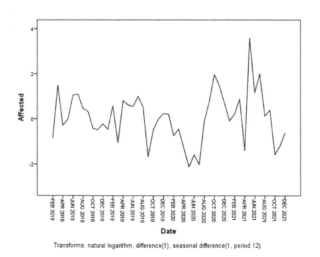

Transforms: natural logarithm, difference(1), seasonal difference(1, period 12)

Fig. 2. Time plot of Series in Seasonal Differencing.

The transformed series was analyzed using ACF (Auto-Correlation Function) and PACF (Partial Auto-Correlation Function) with seasonal difference 1 and period 12. The results were visualized in Figs. 3 and 4.

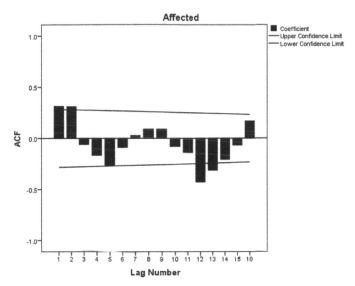

Fig. 3. Seasonal ACF.

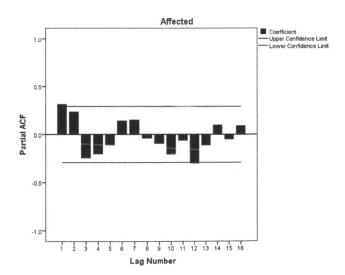

Fig. 4. Seasonal PACF.

The ACF and PACF were applied on the transformed series, which showed the pattern of the autocorrelation and partial autocorrelation of the series after adjusting for seasonality and non-seasonality. The results were displayed in Figs. 3 and 4 for the seasonal difference of 1 and period 12, and Figs. 6 and 7 for the non-seasonal difference of 1 and period 12.

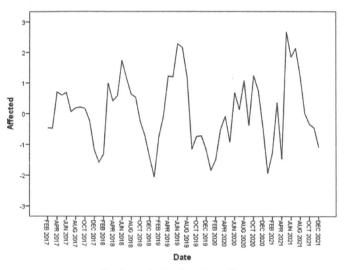

Transforms: natural logarithm, difference(1)

Fig. 5. Time plot of Series in the Non-Seasonal Differencing.

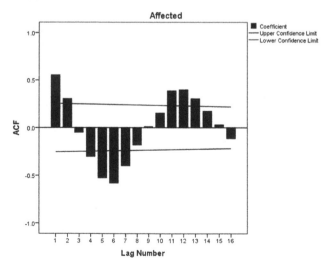

Fig. 6. Non-seasonal ACF.

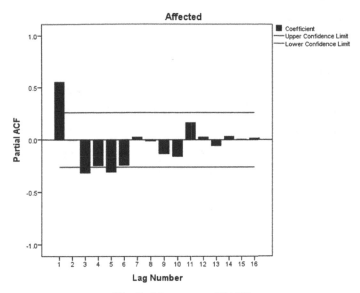

Fig. 7. Non-seasonal PACF.

Model Selection. SARIMA (p, d, q) (P, D, Q)$_S$ model, in which p & P indicate the order of auto regression and seasonal auto regression, respectively, d & D indicate the order of integration and seasonal integration, q & Q indicate the order of moving average and seasonal moving average, and s indicates the length of the seasonal period, can be used to analyze data and understand the pattern. Software such as SPSS 17 and MS Excel 2016 were used to conduct the analyses. The time series model was assessed using a SARIMA model on data gathered from January 2017 to December 2021. The optimal model was determined using normalized BIC and RMSE, where lower values were preferred. Then, we investigated a bunch of models based on Fig. 3, 4, 6, and 7 respectively and recorded those in Table 1 to choose the best model. In Table 1, the SARIMA $(1,0,0)(1,1,1)_{12}$ model has both minimal normalized BIC (18.549) and RMSE (9073.657) values and in this paper, In order to forecast values from January 2022 to December 2022, this model has been utilized. ACF residuals at various lag times were also tested using the Ljung-Box method to verify they weren't essentially distinct from zero ($Q_{18} = 15$ and $p > .05$). Each one of the coefficients of the proposed model was also significant (Table 2).

Table 1. Time Series Models: RMSE and Normalized BIC Values.

Model	RMSE	Normalized BIC
SARIMA $(2,1,1)(1,1,0)_{12}$	26546.531	20.783
SARIMA $(2,1,0)(1,1,0)_{12}$	27922.877	20.802
SARIMA $(1,1,1)(1,1,0)_{12}$	22477.758	20.368
SARIMA $(1,1,1)(1,1,1)_{12}$	20770.691	20.292
SARIMA $(1,1,0)(1,1,0)_{12}$	18955.171	19.945
SARIMA $(0,1,0)(1,1,0)_{12}$	16125.402	19.540
SARIMA $(1,0,1)(1,1,0)_{12}$	9309.588	18.600
SARIMA $(1,0,1)(0,1,1)_{12}$	10081.171	18.761
SARIMA $(1,0,0)(0,1,1)_{12}$	10295.642	18.721
SARIMA $(1,0,0)(1,1,1)_{12}$	9073.657	18.549

Table 2. Model Parameters.

Variable	β	SE	P value
AR (Lag 1)	.888	.081	0.000
AR, Seasonal (Lag 1)	-.275	.301	.366
Seasonal Difference	1.000	-	-
MA, Seasonal (Lag 1)	.986	16.346	.952

Forecasting Values Using the Proposed Model. Proposed model has been utilized to forecast the month-to-month dengue fever rate for every month of the year 2022. Figure 8 shows the observed dengue rate for the years 2017 to 2021, the forecasted month-to-month rate and the actual occurrence of dengue fever cases in 2022. The figure shows that the predicted model fits well with the real data.

4   Experimental Result

The SARIMA $(1, 0, 0) (1, 1, 1)_{12}$ model was used to predict the number of dengue cases from January 2022 to December 2022, as shown in the graph in Fig. 9. The graph shows that the monthly predicted incidents were low from January to May and began to increase from June. The peak occurred in July and continued to rise until November before starting to decline. This study indicated that dengue fever outbreaks were most likely to occur between August and November, with a seasonal peak in August 2022, when the predicted number of infected patients was 6,410.

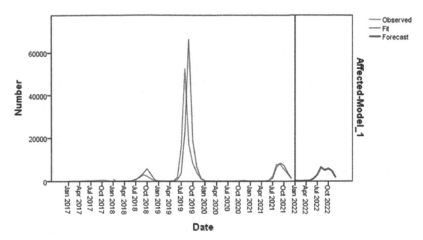

Fig. 8. Dengue rate: Observed values, fit values and anticipated values.

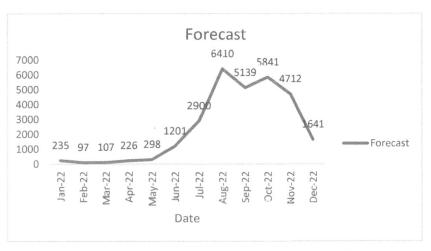

Fig. 9. Forecast of Dengue Incidence from Jan 22 – Dec 22.

5 Conclusion

The frequency of dengue fever turns into a constant threat for Bangladesh and a recurring issue for the health authorities. Moreover, every one of the natural circumstances that can set off an outbreak is available in Bangladesh. Predicting an outbreak on dengue can assist the government to deal with any unforeseen circumstances. SARIMA models are useful tools in epidemiological research that make precise predictions. The result uncovered that a seasonal rise in the dengue cases will be occurred in August 2022. Our research suggests that the impact of dengue will be much greater in 2022 and will help in better understanding the trend and being prepared for the year ahead.

References

1. WHO. Dengue and severe dengue. https://www.who.int/news-room/fact-sheets/detail/den gue-and-severe-dengue, last accessed 2022/05/10
2. Gupta, N., et al.: Dengue in India. Indian J. Med. Res. **136**(3), 373–390 (2012)
3. World Health Organisation. Fact sheet. Updated April 2017. https://reliefweb.int/report/ world/dengue-and-severe-dengue-fact-sheet-updated-april-2017, last accessed 2022/05/10
4. Bonizzoni, M., Gasperi, G., Chen, X., James, A.A.: The invasive mosquito species aedes albopictus: current knowledge and future perspectives. Trends Parasitol. **29**(9), 460–468 (2013). https://doi.org/10.1016/j.pt.2013.07.003
5. Centers for Disease Control and Prevention. Dengue 2010. http://www.cdc.gov/dengue/epi demiology/index.html, last accessed 2022/05/10
6. Aziz, M.A., Graham, R.R., Gregg, M.B.: Dacca fever -an outbreak of dengue. Pak. J. Med. Res. **6**, 83–92 (1967)
7. Rahman, M., et al.: First outbreak of dengue hemorrhagic fever, Bangladesh. Emerg. Infect. Dis. **8**(7), 738–740 (2002). https://doi.org/10.3201/eid0807.010398
8. Aziz, M.M., et al.: Predominance of the DEN-3 genotype during the recent dengue outbreak in Bangladesh. Southeast Asian J. Trop. Med. Public Health **33**, 42–48 (2002)
9. Dengue outbreak in 2019 crosses all previous records. https://bdnews24.com/health/2019/10/ 10/dengue-outbreak-in-2019-crosses-all-previous-records, last accessed 2022/05/10
10. Dengue outbreak shatters all records, Bangladesh. https://www.dhakatribune.com/bangla desh/2019/10/13/dengue-outbreak-shatters-all-records, last accessed 2022/05/10
11. Box, G.E.P., Jenkins, G.M.: Time series analysis: forecasting and control. Holden-Day (1970)
12. Martinez, E.Z., Silva, E.A., Fabbro, A.L.: A SARIMA forecasting model to predict the number of cases of dengue in Campinas, State of São Paulo, Brazil. Pub. MED **44**(4) (2011). Brazil
13. Choudhury, Z.M.A.H., Banu, S., Islam, A.M.: Forecasting dengue incidence in Dhaka, Bangladesh: a time series analysis. WHO Reg. Off. South-East (2008)
14. Shaheen, S.: Association between weather factors and dengue in Dhaka: a time-series analysis. J. Prev. Soc. Med. **39**(1), 43–49 (2021)
15. Hashizume, M., Dewan, A.M., Sunahara, T., et al.: Hydro climatological variability and Dengue transmission in Dhaka, Bangladesh: a time-series study. BMC Infect. Dis. **12**, 98 (2012). https://doi.org/10.1186/1471-2334-12-98
16. Bangladesh Health Observatory. Directorate General of Health Services (DGHS). https:// dghs.gov.bd/site/page/c5b78699-f2b9-4e05-a88b-d1dc73e2529b/-, last accessed 2022/05/10

The Impact of Social and Economic Indicators on Infant Mortality Rate in Bangladesh: A Vector Error Correction Model (VECM) Approach

Muhmmad Mohsinul Hoque$^{(\boxtimes)}$ and Md. Shohel Rana

Noakhali Science and Technology University, Noakhali 3814, Bangladesh
mohsinulhoque1698@gmail.com, shohel.stat@nstu.edu.bd

Abstract. In the last few years, infant mortality is getting more focused on the development and the results of action. Infant deaths have been reduced significantly in developed countries whereas developing countries such as Bangladesh are required substantial efforts to reduce infant mortality rates. The goal of this study is to evaluate different aspects of the high infant mortality rate in Bangladesh. It investigates the relationship between infant mortality rate and economic and social variables such as GDP per capita, female literacy rate, female labor force participation, current health expenditure, government expenditure in education, female primary school enrollment, and unemployment rate. Various econometric methods are used to validate this relationship. It was determined whether the series was stationary by employing the unit root test and cointegrated by determining the long-term relationship among variables. Using the Vector Error Correction Model, both long-term and short-term relationships of variables were identified. According to the findings, GDP, expenditure on education, and female labor force participation are associated with lower infant mortality rates. The unemployment rate and female school enrollment are also associated with higher infant mortality rates. According to the error correction term, the short-term shock restores equilibrium at a rate of 3.74%.

Keywords: Infant mortality · Socioeconomic variables · Bangladesh

1 Introduction

The demise of a baby before their first birthday celebration is characterized as infant mortality. The Infant Mortality Rate is an important thing to look at because it shows how healthy a society is [1]. MDG 4 seeks to reduce child and infant mortality rates by two-thirds between 1990 and 2015. The reliability of the infant mortality rate as a measurement of the health of a community has been called into doubt because it is derived from small sample size and frequently depends on projections and/or interpretations [2]. According to some critics [3], the infant mortality rate can be underestimated based on

© ICST Institute for Computer Sciences, Social Informatics and Telecommunications Engineering 2023
Published by Springer Nature Switzerland AG 2023. All Rights Reserved
Md. S. Satu et al. (Eds.): MIET 2022, LNICST 491, pp. 599–612, 2023.
https://doi.org/10.1007/978-3-031-34622-4_48

the live birth criterion, vital registration system, and reporting standards utilized in a particular nation. Despite the problematic concerns around Infant Mortality Rate measuring, we still utilize these as indicators of infant health, because a) there is data available on infant mortality, and are more dependable than other options. b) infant mortality is more responsive to changes in economic conditions than life expectancy conditions [4].

The rate of infant mortality is a factor that can be linked to the health of a community as a whole. Inadequate child care may be the cause of high infant mortality rates. A population of sick and un-healthy children impedes economic progress in a variety of ways: it reduces worker productivity; it harms future generations by lowering school enrollment; and it raises medical-care spending, resulting in inefficient resource allocation. Consequently, an enhanced state of health (as indicated by lower infant mortality rates) results in enhanced national economic performance [5].

Bangladesh has an estimated population of 161.4 million with a growth rate of 1.34. Around forty percent of the population is made up of children, which amounts to more than 64 million [6]. Almost half of the population of Bangladesh is female (81.3 million). The life expectancy at birth is 72.0 and the literacy rate is 72.3. Furthermore, the maternal mortality rate in Bangladesh ranges from 1.72 to 1.57 per 1000 live births [7].

In the course of the most recent 25 years, the decline in infant mortality (96/1000 in 1991 to 25/1000 in 2018) is slower than under 5 mortality rates (138/1000 in 1991 to 30/1000 in 2018) in Bangladesh. Infant mortality continues to decline from 96 in 1991 to 25 in the year of 2018. Just as neonatal passing has a critical part in infant mortality. As indicated by Health Bulletin 2017 of DGHS, for every 1000 live births neonatal mortality is 19 (SVRS 2016) and for every 1000 live births is 28 [8]. Long-term decreases in mortality rates have been supported by increases in nutrition, education, and especially female education. Improvements in social infrastructure such as water and sanitation, as well as advances in medical technology, have also contributed to these trends [9]. We're more interested in long-term changes in infant death rates, as well as their likely link to socioeconomic indicators.

Socioeconomic factors such as age at first marriage, general fertility rates, female literacy rates, and female agricultural activity all have an impact on infant mortality. Infant mortality is higher in agricultural districts where more women work [10]. According to [5] fertility rates, female labor force participation, per capita GNP, and female literacy rates all have a significant impact on infant mortality rates. Infant mortality rates are surprisingly unaffected by government health care spending as a percentage of GDP.

Leigh and Jencks [11] say that a higher GDP is linked to a lower death rate, and this effect gets smaller as the GDP goes up. Baird, Friedman, and Schady [12] have given us a new way of looking at the link between infant mortality and high health costs caused by female labor force participation. There is an association between a one percent drop in GDP per capita and an increase in the infant mortality rate of between 0.24 and 0.40 for every 1,000 live births, according to the study. It has been found that changes in monetary conditions have a smaller impact on male infant mortality than they do on female infant mortality, particularly when GDP growth is negative. Children under five make up about 30% of all deaths in poor countries, but less than 1% of all deaths in rich countries.

Immunization, breastfeeding, the mother's age at the time of childbirth, and the duration between births are the most important predictors of neonatal, post-neonatal, and child mortality. Children who have received immunizations have a 78.20% lower risk of death than children who have not received immunizations. In addition, the risk of infant mortality is 56.70% lower after a 36-month birth gap compared to an 18-month birth interval. Parental education and treatment locations are important indicators during the neonatal and childhood periods, whereas the father's occupation is important during the post-neonatal period. Mothers who have completed their primary education have a 31.40% lower risk of infant death, and mothers who have completed their optional and advanced education have a 52.30% lower risk of infant mortality, in comparison to women with no education [13].

Casarico, Profeta, and Pronzato [14] have embraced an exhaustive report on how changes in the surrounding context affect female education. The percentage of working women who have children under the age of five and the proportion of women in administrative or self-employment positions have a significant impact on the likelihood of women enrolling in postsecondary education. Their research suggests that policies that are often thought to promote female employment and career advancements, such as daycare services or affirmative action methods, may have positive feedback effects on younger generations' educational decisions.

Sackey [15] conducted a case study in Ghana and identified a correlation between the effect of education on female labor force participation. That is, a rise in female labor force participation shows a drop in fertility. The authors argue that, even though the gender gap in education has shrunk over time, government policies must assure the long-term sustainability of female educational achievements.

The primary objective of this study is to identify the key social and economic elements that contribute to Bangladesh's high infant mortality rate and to compare and contrast these aspects. This is the only study that we are aware of that attempts to analyze the precise consequences of these factors. We developed a comprehensive time series dataset containing Bangladesh's infant mortality rate and socioeconomic indicators from 1991 to 2018. In this study, the long-term relationship between socioeconomic variables and infant mortality rates is investigated. This study also evaluates the impact of socioeconomic determinants on short-term changes in infant mortality rate.

2   Methodology

The secondary data of Bangladesh has been collected for infant mortality rate (per 1000 live births), GDP per capita, female literacy rate (% of females ages 15 and above), female labor force participation (% of female population ages 15+), current health expenditure (% of GDP), government expenditure in education (% of GDP), female primary school enrollment (% gross), and unemployment (% of the total labor force) from the year 1991–2018. To fill up the missing data interpolation method have been used. The data source for all of the variables is World Bank. Econometric Views (EViews 10) and STATA 13 were used to test the result. The tables, figures, and results below are originally generated by us in this paper.

After collecting the above-mentioned data, the first step is a stationary check. Because of the inaccessibility of substantial data and variances in the data available, the variables are exposed to a unit root test to check for the absence or presence of stationarity. The Augmented Dickey-Fuller (ADF) unit root test was performed to determine whether the variables were stationary. Long-term co-integration was examined based on the order of variable integration in the second stage. The Johansen cointegration test was used for this purpose. In the final step, the relationship between the short-run and long-run dynamics was examined using the vector error correction method (VECM).

2.1 Unit Root Test

The fact that a series contains a unit root suggests that the series is not in a stationary state. To reduce the spurious regression performing unit root rest is vital [16]. By differencing the variables and estimating the equation of interest used in a regression it ensures that the variables are stationary [1]. In this study, every time series variable must be integrated in order 1. In this paper, to evaluate the stationary the Augmented Dickey-Fuller test was utilized. Given the notion of the components in this study, the null hypothesis under the Augmented Dickey-Fuller test consists of a unit root with a temporal trend and an intercept. The model for ADF is:

$$\Delta Y_t = \alpha + \delta t + \theta Y_{t-1} + \sum_{i=1}^{p} \lambda_i \Delta Y_{t-1} + \varepsilon_t \tag{1}$$

Here, $\Delta =$ difference operator

$\delta t =$ time trend

$p =$ number of lags

$\varepsilon =$ Error term

To select the lag, the Akaike Information Criterion (AIC) is applied. To determine whether the series contains a unit root, the t-statistic of θ is compared to the ADF critical values.

2.2 Johansen Cointegration

Cointegration takes place when several time series variables all have the same order of integration and when the linear combination of those variables results in a series that also has the same order of integration [17]. Cointegration is a statistical approach for detecting whether or not two or more variables have a stable long-term relationship. The method can be used for multiple variables at the same time. The socioeconomic variables and the infant mortality rate likely have a long-term link if they are integrated to order 1 and their combination results in a zero-order integral series. This would support the hypothesis that these factors are related. In this investigation, the Johansen cointegration test [18] is applied to determine whether or not there is a connection that exists between the variables over the course of time. The null hypothesis is used in this case.

H_0: No cointegration equation exists

H_1: H_o is not true

An n-variable generalized VAR model forms the basis of this test:

$$Y_t = \alpha + \sum_{i=1}^{p} \theta_i Y_{t-i} + \varepsilon_t \qquad (2)$$

After subtracting Yt-1 from both sides, the following equation is obtained:

$$\Delta Y_t = \alpha + \prod Y_{t-1} + \sum_{i=1}^{p-1} \eta \Delta Y_{t-1} + \varepsilon_t \qquad (3)$$

Here,

$$\prod = \sum_{I=1}^{p} \theta_i - I \ and \ \eta_i = - \sum_{j=i+1}^{p} \theta_j \qquad (4)$$

In the above equation, Y = n by 1 vector of the endogenous variable.

α = vector of parameters
θ = n by n matrix of parameters for endogenous variables
ε = vector of residuals
I = Identity matrix of dimension n

2.3 Vector Error Correction Model (VECM)

We use VECM to evaluate the short-run properties of the cointegrated series. The VECM model employed in this study is as follows:

$$\Delta Y_t = \alpha + \sum_{i=1}^{p} \beta_i \Delta Y_{t-i} + \lambda_i Z_{t-1} + \varepsilon_t \qquad (5)$$

Here, p = the number of lag differences

z = error correction term
ε = error term
λ = speed of adjustment
β = coefficient vector captures the variables' short-run dynamics

Many components need to be considered when choosing the number of lags—for example, setting the study, observational proof, and theory. Residual autocorrelation can occur if too few lags are selected, and loss of observations and forecasting errors is common when the lags are too many [19]. In this paper, the optimal lag duration was determined using the Akaike Information Criteria (AIC). The AIC, in general, is more exact with regard to Vector Auto Regression (VAR) models [20].

3   Empirical Results

3.1   Descriptive Statistics

For this type of analysis, descriptive statistics are beneficial. Table 1 displays the results. The empirical estimates declare the presence of negative skewness in infant mortality rate (IM), unemployment rate (UR), female school enrollment (FSE), female labor force participation (FLP), and expenditure on education (EE). GDP, female literacy rate (FLR), and health expenditure (HE) are positively skewed. The estimate provides positive kurtosis for all the variables. The Jacque-Bera statistic is used to perform the individual series normality test. The normality test findings confirm that the data is normally distributed for all variables in the investigation.

Table 1. Descriptive Statistics

	Skewness	Kurtosis	Jarque-Bera	Probability	Observations
IM	−0.1005	1.8073	1.17113	.4249	28
GDP	.5786	2.1431	2.4193	2982	28
FLR	.0385	2.1681	.8141	.6655	28
UR	−.5748	1.8888	2.9827	.2250	28
FSE	−.03272	1.9844	1.7030	.4267	28
FLP	−.0436	1.9655	1.2573	.5333	28
EE	−.7383	3.4173	2.7472	.2531	28
HE	.55655	3.0760	1.4523	.4837	28

3.2   Unit Root Test

The Augmented Dickey-Fuller (ADF) test is used in this study to discover the presence of unit root in the variables. The ADF tests are performed using a unit root with a constant and a time trend that was chosen based on the trending behavior of all the series.

Table 2 displays the ADF test results for Bangladesh's major social and economic factors. It proves that each variable has a unit root and is, therefore, a non-stationary process. The majority of the series' first difference, however, turns out to be stationary. This indicates that, except for the current health expenditures and the female literacy rate, all variables are integrated of order 0 in the first difference form but order 1 in level form. The cointegration test cannot be conducted on these variables since the index for current health expenditures and the female literacy rate are not integrated in either the level or first deference form.

Table 2. Unit root test

Variables	Level	First Difference(p-value)
Infant mortality rate	−0.6827 (.9635)	−3.8654** (.0340)
GDP per capita	−0.5118 (.9764)	−3.664434**(.0443)
Female Literacy rate	−2.9131 (.1783)	−1.6015(.7591)
Unemployment rate	−2.0680 (.5390)	−4.8604***(.0036)
Female School Enrollment	−2.2512 (.4438)	−4.6579***(.0054)
Female labor force participation	−1.4230 (.8302)	−5.6678***(.0005)
Govt. expenditure on education	−2.7870 (.2153)	−4.7038***(.0054)
Current health expenditure	−2.3463 (.3966)	−2.2305(.4543)

3.3 Cointegration Test

Given that all of the series, except for those indicating current health spending and Female literacy rate, is of order 1 in level but order 0 in initial differences. To determine whether or not there is a long-run link between infant mortality and socioeconomic variables, the Johansen cointegration test can be used. At the 5% level of significance, the critical value is evaluated based on comparisons with the trace statistic and the maximum eigenvalue statistic. Results from the Johansen cointegration test are displayed in Table 3 below:

Table 3. Cointegration Test

	Trace test				Max-Eigen test		
Rank	Eigenvalue	Statistics	Critical Value	Probability	Statistics	Critical value	Probability
0	0.934953	166.1038	95.75366	0.0000	71.04883	40.07757	0.0000
1	0.775005	95.05494	69.81889	0.0001	38.78361	33.87687	0.0120
2	0.642828	56.27133	47.85613	0.0067	26.76798	27.58434	0.0633
3	0.410215	29.50334	29.79707	0.0540	13.72794	21.13162	0.3878
4	0.359675	15.77540	15.49471	0.0454	11.59026	14.26460	0.1270
5	0.148680	4.185147	3.841466	0.0408	4.185147	3.841466	0.0408

The above table indicates the presence of cointegration between the infant mortality rate and the socio-economic variables. This suggests that there is a relationship that persists over the long run between the rate of infant mortality and the socio-economic variables.

3.4 VECM Models

Given that, all the social and economic variables have a cointegrating relationship with infant mortality rate, this study has employed Vector Error Correction models (VECM). Table 4, shows coefficients, standard errors, and the p-value. The equation for the long run is:

logIM = 13.79799 − .0774776logGDP − .0998003logEE + .1141932logUR + 1.593617logFSE − 2.182126logFLP.

Table 4. Long term equation

Variables	Coefficients	Standard Errors	t-statistics	Probability
Log(IM)	1	.	.	.
Log(GDP)	.0774776	.0287218	2.70	0.007
Log(EE)	.0998003	.0222194	4.49	0.000
Log(UR)	−.1141932	.0235478	−4.85	0.000
Log(FSE)	−1.593617	.1225313	−13.01	0.000
Log(FLP)	2.182126	.094271	23.15	0.000
Constant	−13.79799			

From Table 4, it is observed that the relationship of infant mortality rate is negatively significant with GDP, Expenditure on Education, and Female Labor Force Participation Rate which implies that a 1% increase in GDP, Expenditure, and Female Labor Force Participation decreases the infant mortality rate by .077%, .099%, and 2.18% respectively. The relationship positively significant with Unemployment Rate and Female School Enrollment. It suggests that a 1% increase in unemployment gives rise to an infant mortality rate of .114% and a 1% increase in Female school enrollment increases the infant mortality rate by 1.15%.

Table 5, displays the error correction model for all the variables from the table, we see that the error correction term is −.0374136 and its probability value is less than 0.05. So, the error correction term is significant. The error correction term shows that the short-term shock restores equilibrium at a rate of 3.74%.

Table 5. Error correction model

Variables	Coefficients	Standard Errors	Probability
CE of lag 1	−.0374136	.0178878	0.036
Log(IM)	.5346893	.1573554	0.001
Log(GDP)	.0002025	.0068531	0.976
Log(EE)	−.0000436	. 0059842	0.994
Log(UR)	.0091417	.0033416	0.006
Log(FSE)	.0202946	.0308538	0.511
Log(FLP)	.1336878	.0804811	0.097
Constant	−13.79799	.	.

4 Discussion

According to studies conducted in the past, countries with poor economies typically have high infant mortality rates. According to Dhrif (2018) [22], this condition is a significant problem because it is inextricably tied to human productivity, which is a component of production that contributes to economic development and well-being. As a result, the condition poses a significant threat to society. When infants and children have access to healthy food, quality education, and a safe environment, they are better equipped to become productive members of society and contributors to the economy. Earnings are an essential component to consider. If a family has a high income, they will have the financial means to buy goods of a higher quality, which will in turn improve their health and quality of life. Estimates suggest that Bangladesh's GDP per capita has a negative impact on the country's infant death rates. Every percentage point rise in GDP per capita resulted in a 0.077%age point decrease in the infant mortality rate. It has been shown in research carried out by Erdogan, Ener, and Arica (2013) [23] and Naveed et al. (2011) [1] that infant mortality rates and GDP per capita have a significant and negative effect on one another. As a direct consequence of this, the probability of death during infancy will drop as levels of affluence improve. According to Hosseinpoor et al. (2005) [24], socioeconomic disparity in Iran is the primary reason for the country's rising infant mortality rate. This rate is typically lower in regions that have a large amount of untapped economic potential. In addition, Rezaei, Mat-in, and Rad (2015) [25] found that the country's newborn mortality rate is only marginally affected by Iran's GDP per capita. While there was no significant correlation between the mother's degree of education and infant mortality rates in Italy, there was no correlation between household income and these rates [26]. When examining the risk of infant mortality from a socioeconomic vantage point, one must do so to establish a policy direction that is grounded in realism and to provide assistance to communities that are economically and socially disadvantaged.

To improve human growth and economic prosperity, as well as to lessen the burden of poverty in both developed and developing nations, governments need to commit enough and efficient resources to education and health ([27–30]). Using data from 111 countries,

Grignon (2008) [31] explores the relationship between education and health in countries with low and high levels of education. There are two categories for these nations: high education and low education. His findings provide support to the idea that the health benefits obtained by the two groups differ significantly based on their relative levels of education. The government covers the majority of the cost of university education in Bangladesh, making it one of the most affordable options globally [32]. Education in the public sector of Bangladesh is virtually free, and the country's average public expenditure on education in 2013 was only 2% of GDP (between 1991 and 2018). Bangladesh contributes the least to education investment compared to the other SAARC nations [33]. Bangladesh has not met the recommendations of different education commissions, which suggest that between 4 and 5% of the country's GDP should be given to education, since the country's independence in 1971. Government expenditures on education have a considerable influence on the infant mortality rate. The infant mortality rate decreases by 0.077%age points for every 1% increase in education spending, according to one study. According to the study undertaken by Ernest Simeon O. Odior [34], boosting the government's expenditure on educational services has a major impact on reducing poverty, which has a direct impact on the infant mortality rate.

Because the unemployment rate is a significant predictor of a region's economic success or failure, this study looked into the relationship between unemployment and infant mortality [35]. In Bangladesh, unemployment has a substantial impact on infant mortality rates. A 1% increase in unemployment is connected with a .114% increase in infant mortality, according to the findings. Several theories have been developed to explain the relationship between unemployment and poor health [36], as Janlert demonstrated (2009). Economic deprivation is the most effective intervention approach. Unemployed people, according to this sociological paradigm, have less money, and a lack of money makes it more difficult to maintain good health. As a result of its findings, the model suggests one possible solution: aiding the unemployed with subsistence expenses could help to alleviate the worst effects of unemployment [36].

In developing countries with a large female labor force, such as Bangladesh, the female labor force has a significant opportunity to contribute to the earnings of a family, increase the purchasing power of families, and increase collective spending. Regardless, women's labor-force participation had a considerable impact on infant mortality rates. Because a negative coefficient was found for female participation in the labor force, it may be deduced that the proportion of working mothers compared to the total number of mothers was adversely connected with the risk of infant mortality. On the other hand, the female workforce had a significant adverse effect on the situation. Furthermore, this influence was significant. An increase in the number of women in the workforce is associated with a 2.18% decrease in total infant mortality. The rate of female enrollment in school also had a significant correlation with a positive coefficient, indicating that each rise in the female enrollment rate caused an increase in the infant mortality rate. Poerwanto and colleagues (2003) [37] concluded that the mother's level of wealth and education influenced the Indonesian infant mortality rate. Numerous factors, including the maternal fertility rate, the use of contraception, birth spacing, and the amount of prenatal care received, had a significant impact on infant mortality rates. Low-income households tended to be more vulnerable. In addition, Naveed et al. (2011) [1] identified a negative association between female labor involvement and infant mortality rate in the near term. Additionally, there is a negative association between per capita income and female work participation. On the other hand, female labor force involvement and maternal education had a greater impact than per capita income over the long term. In contrast, a study conducted by Rezaei, Matin, and Rad (2015) [25] concluded that the presence of women in Iran's labor force does not affect whatsoever on the country's infant mortality rate. While this is occurring in Poland, the working environment is unsuitable, and the industrial sector's pollution affects the infant mortality rate [38].

5 Strengths and Limitations of the Study

This research has both strengths and weaknesses that should be taken into consideration. To begin the findings, confirm the overall situation in Bangladesh. A review of previous studies found that several socioeconomic and demographic factors could be used as predictor variables. As a result of the findings reflecting the national infant mortality rate, policymakers and the government will have more information with which to design effective plans and policies to minimize infant mortality.

The study has a number of limitations or limitations. The primary limitation is that the dataset is comparatively small. Additionally, the study analyzed only a subset of potential predictor variables. Following that, some variables had missing values, which could have influenced the results. Furthermore, several alternative variables were omitted due to a large number of missing cases.

6 Conclusion

Despite the fact that infant mortality is a micro-level phenomenon, its consequences can be felt on a macro-level. Infant mortality rates must be kept as low as possible because they are the primary indicator of a country's development. It has been demonstrated in the literature that health-related issues are significant determinants of infant mortality rates in any given country. Economic and social variables, on the other hand, have an indirect impact on these health indicators. The primary objective of this research is to identify the main aspects of the situation that lead to Bangladesh's alarmingly high rate of infant mortality. It investigates the relationship between infant mortality rate and economic and social variables such as GDP per capita, female literacy rate, female labor force participation, current health expenditure, government expenditure on education, female primary school enrollment, and unemployment rate. The model is estimated using standard time series econometric approaches, including a vector error correction model (VECM), after determining whether the data series is stationary and whether there is cointegration among the model variables. Based on data from Bangladesh collected between 1991 and 2018, the conclusion is that all factors have a significant impact on infant mortality rates. According to the findings, although GDP, expenditure on education, and female labor force participation are all related to reduced infant mortality rates, the unemployment rate and female school enrollment are associated with higher infant mortality rates. With the error correction term, we can see that the short-term shock is re-establishing equilibrium at a rate of 3.74%.

610   M. M. Hoque and Md. S. Rana

Children are seen as the future of a nation's population. A nation's well-being is therefore dependent on the well-being of its children [39]. Infant health, nutrition, and care are all reflected in the infant mortality rate, which also reveals the level of social, cultural, and economic development in a country. It is critical to secure the survival and healthy development of all children in order to have a productive nation with healthy citizens by 2022. The Government of Bangladesh should consider this issue very actively, and to minimize infant mortality as per aim, a sustainable correlating program for urban and rural areas must be ensured, as well as a twofold allocation in the health budget.

References

1. Naveed, T.A., Ullah, S., Jabeen, T., Kalsoom, A., Sabir, S.: Socio-economic determinants of infant mortality in Pakistan, 728–740 (2011)
2. Bhargava, A., Jamison, D.T., Lau, L.J., Murray, C.J.L.: Modeling the effects of health on economic growth. Econom. Stat. Comput. Approaches Food Heal. Sci. **20**, 269–286 (2006). https://doi.org/10.1142/9789812773319_0020
3. Anthopolos, R., Becker, C.M.: Global infant mortality: correcting for undercounting. World Dev. **38**(4), 467–481 (2010). https://doi.org/10.1016/j.worlddev.2009.11.013
4. Lee, H.-H., Lee, S.A., Lim, J.-Y., Park, C.-Y.: Effects of food price inflation on infant and child mortality in developing countries. Eur. J. Health Econ. **17**(5), 535–551 (2015). https://doi.org/10.1007/s10198-015-0697-6
5. Zakir, M., Wunnava, P.V.: Factors affecting infant mortality rates: evidence from cross-sectional data. Appl. Econ. Lett. **6**(5), 271–273 (1999). https://doi.org/10.1080/135048599353203
6. Children in Bangladesh | UNICEF Bangladesh. https://www.unicef.org/bangladesh/en/children-bangladesh (accessed Sep. 23, 2020)
7. BBS: Bangladesh Statistics 2018. Bangladesh Bur. Stat., 45 (2018)
8. Health Bulletin 2017. https://dghs.gov.bd/index.php/en/home/4364-health-bulletin-2017 (accessed Sep. 23, 2020)
9. Cutler, D., Deaton, A., Lleras-Muney, A.: The determinants of mortality. J. Econ. Perspect. **20**(3), 97–120 (2006). https://doi.org/10.1257/jep.20.3.97
10. Kalipeni, E.: Determinants of infant mortality in Malawi: a spatial perspective. Soc. Sci. Med. **37**(2), 183–198 (1993). https://doi.org/10.1016/0277-9536(93)90454-C
11. Leigh, A., Jencks, C.: Inequality and mortality: long-run evidence from a panel of countries. J. Health Econ. **26**(1), 1–24 (2007). https://doi.org/10.1016/j.jhealeco.2006.07.003
12. Baird, S., Friedman, J., Schady, N.: Aggregate income shocks and infant mortality in the developing world. Rev. Econ. Stat. **93**(3), 847–856 (2011). https://doi.org/10.1162/REST_a_00084
13. Mondal, M.N.I., Hossain, M.K., Ali, M.K.: Factors influencing infant and child mortality: a case study of Rajshahi District, Bangladesh. J. Hum. Ecol. **26**(1), 31–39 (2009). https://doi.org/10.1080/09709274.2009.11906162
14. Casarico, A., Profeta, P., Pronzato, C.: Great expectations: the determinants of female university enrolment in Europe. SSRN Electron. J. March 2012. https://doi.org/10.2139/ssrn.2014052
15. Sackey, H.A.: Female labour force participation in Ghana: The effects of education, September 2005
16. Phillips, P.C.B.: Understanding spurious regressions in econometrics. J. Econom. **33**(3), 311–340 (1986). https://doi.org/10.1016/0304-4076(86)90001-1

17. Pesaran, M.H., Shin, Y., Smith, R.J.: Bounds testing approaches to the analysis of level relationships. J. Appl. Econom. **16**(3), 289–326 (2001). https://doi.org/10.1002/jae.616
18. Johamen, S., Jtiselius, K.: Maximum likelihood estimation and inference on cointegration-with application to the demand for money. Oxf. Bull. Econ. Stat. **52**(2), 169–210 (1990)
19. Lütkepohl, H.: Vector autoregressions. A Companion to Theor. Econom. **15**(4), 678–699 (2007). https://doi.org/10.1002/9780470996249.ch33
20. Ivanov, V., Killian, L.: A practitioner's guide to a practitioner's guide to lag order selection for vector autoregressions. CEPR Discuss. Pap. **2685**, 1–22 (2001)
21. Granger, C.W.J.: Investigating causal relations by econometric models and cross-spectral methods. Essays Econom. vol II Collect. Pap. Clive WJ Granger **37**(3), 31–47, (1969). https://doi.org/10.1017/ccol052179207x.002
22. Dhrifi, A.: Health-care expenditures, economic growth and infant mortality: evidence from developed and developing countries. CEPAL Rev. **2018**(125), 71–97 (2018). https://doi.org/10.18356/02c1a26c-en
23. Erdoğan, E., Ener, M., Arıca, F.: The strategic role of infant mortality in the process of economic growth: an application for high income OECD countries. Procedia - Soc. Behav. Sci. **99**, 19–25 (2013). https://doi.org/10.1016/j.sbspro.2013.10.467
24. Hosseinpoor, A.R., et al.: Socioeconomic inequality in infant mortality in Iran and across its provinces. Bull. World Health Organ. **83**(11), 837–844 (2005). https://doi.org/10.1590/S0042-96862005001100013
25. Rezaei, S., Matin, B.K., Rad, E.H.: Socioeconomic determinants of infant mortality in Iranian children: a longitudinal econometrics analysis. Int. J. Pediatr. **3**(1), 375–380 (2015). https://doi.org/10.22038/ijp.2015.3760
26. Dallolio, L., et al.: Socio-economic factors associated with infant mortality in Italy: an ecological study. Int. J. Equity Health **11**(1), 1–5 (2012). https://doi.org/10.1186/1475-9276-11-45
27. Schultz, T.W.: Invest in human capital. Am. Econ. Rev. **51**(1), 1–20 (1961)
28. Barro, R.J., Lee, J.W.: International measures of schooling years and schooling quality. Am. Econ. Rev. **86**(2), 218–223 (1996). https://doi.org/10.2307/2118126
29. Devarajan, S., Swaroop, V., Zou, H.-f: The composition of public expenditure and economic growth. J. Monetary Econ. **37**(2), 313–344 (1996). https://doi.org/10.1016/S0304-3932(96)90039-2
30. Petrakis, P.E., Stamatakis, D.: Growth and educational levels: a comparative analysis. Econ. Educ. Rev. **21**(5), 513–521 (2002). https://doi.org/10.1016/S0272-7757(01)00050-4
31. Grignon, M.: The role of education in health system performance. Econ. Educ. Rev. **27**(3), 299–307 (2008). https://doi.org/10.1016/j.econedurev.2006.11.001
32. Islam, Z., Ahmed, S.U., Hasan, I.: Corporate social responsibility and financial performance linkage: evidence from the banking sector of Bangladesh. J. Organ. Manag. **1**(1), 14–21 (2012)
33. Chauhan, C.P.S.: Higher education : current status and future possibilities. Anal. Reports Int. Educ. **2**(1), 29–48 (2008)
34. Odior, E.S.O.: Government expenditure on education and poverty reduction: implications for achieving the MDGs in Nigeria: a computable general equilibrium micro-simulation analysis. Asian Econ. Financ. Rev. **4**(2), 150–172 (2014). aessweb.com/journals/5002/info/ci%0A ezproxy.lib.ucalgary.ca/login? url = http://search.ebscohost.com/login.aspx?direct=true& db=ecn&AN=1428299&site=ehost-live
35. Shaw, M.D.S.G., Galobardes, B., Lawlor, D.A., Lynch, J., Wheeler, B.: The handbook of inequality and socioeconomic position. Concepts and measures. Great Britain. In: The Policy Press (2007)
36. Janlert, U., Hammarström, A.: Which theory is best? Explanatory models of the relationship between unemployment and health. BMC Public Health **9**, 1–9 (2009). https://doi.org/10.1186/1471-2458-9-235

37. Poerwanto, S., Stevenson, M., De Klerk, N.: Infant mortality and family welfare: policy implications for Indonesia. J. Epidemiol. Community Health **57**(7), 493–498 (2003). https://doi.org/10.1136/jech.57.7.493

38. Genowska, A., Jamiołkowski, J., Szafraniec, K., Stepaniak, U., Szpak, A., Pająk, A.: Environmental and socio-economic determinants of infant mortality in Poland: an ecological study. Environ. Heal. A Glob. Access Sci. Source **14**(1), 1–9 (2015). https://doi.org/10.1186/s12 940-015-0048-1

39. Sen, A.: Mortality as an indicator of economic success and failure. Econ. J. **108**(446), 1–25 (1998). https://doi.org/10.1111/1468-0297.00270

Machine Learning Approaches to Predict Movie Success

Md. Afzazul Hoque and Md. Mohsin Khan$^{(\boxtimes)}$

International Islamic University Chittagong, Chittagong, Bangladesh
`ete.mohsin@gmail.com`

Abstract. The motion picture industry, commonly known as the film industry, is a huge investment sector. Furthermore, there is a massive amount of data related to movies on the internet. As a result, it became an interesting topic for research and analysis. Machine learning is a novel approach to data analysis. Our thesis presents a decision support system for the movie investing sector that employs various machine learning methods. In this context, our approach will assist film investment industries in avoiding investment risks. The algorithm evaluates historical data from numerous sources such as Rotten Tomatoes, IMDb, Box Office Mojo, and Meta Critics to calculate an estimated value of a film's success rate. The model will forecast movie success based on specific criteria such as the cast and directors, budget, month of release, runtime, several sorts of movie ratings, and movie reviews, and then process that data for categorization using machine-learning algorithms and a few other techniques.

Keywords: Film Industry · Machine Learning · Movie Success

1 Introduction

The motion picture industry, commonly known as the film industry, is a dominant market in the entertainment business. Each year more than 20 thousand movies are produced, distributed, and viewed worldwide in various languages, according to the Internet Movies Database (IMDB). These figures demonstrate the depth of the industry's impact on the market. In addition, to the cultural and socio-economic impact of the film, Motion Picture nowadays occupies a significant part of the business market, generating an average of 10 billion in annual growth, according to Boxofficemojo. The production houses invest much money in movie making every year. So, from this point of view, the film industry is a huge investment sector. However, larger business areas are more complex and difficult to choose how to invest. Big investments bring high risk. We cannot guess how a movie will do in the marketplace until the film opens in a darkened theatre. As film industry is getting competitive field and peoples are investing huge amount, so they need to are their film is going to gross or not. If we can predict them the result, it will help them a lot. As the film industry is expanding daily, a massive amount of data is now available on the web. Moreover, for this, it became an exciting area for data analysis. Predicting

Md. S. Satu et al. (Eds.): MIET 2022, LNICST 491, pp. 613–627, 2023.
https://doi.org/10.1007/978-3-031-34622-4_49

a movie, whether it is successful or flopped, is not an easy task to do. The concept of "movie success" is quite different here; some films are considered successful based on their worldwide gross income, while others may not perform well in terms of box office revenue yet receive positive reviews and popularity. Many films did not make a lot of money when they were first released but became popular after a few years. For example, in 1999, David Fincher directed "Fight Club," a widely popular film now. This film features actors such as Brad Pitt and Edward Norton. According to IMDb, however, this picture was a financial flop. The investment in "Fight Club" was 63 million USD. However, the global gross profit was only around 100 million USD, resulting in a net profit of only 37 million USD. That is not a very strong profit margin. However, "Fight Club" is a highly popular film right now, and every movie enthusiast is familiar with it. If profit is used as a criterion for success, then "Fight Club" is a financially flop movie. But if we look at other aspects, everyone can consider this film a successful film. As a result, it is a highly complicated issue for investors to make the right decision for these unforeseen circumstances of the film's success. Research studies say that nearly 25% of film revenue comes during the first and second week of release [22]. As a result, predicting a movie's success prior to its release is challenging.

In this research, we have attempted to construct a model that may enable investors to lower the risks in their investment. This research will be significant to the whole film business. A large portion of emerging artists can't create films for investment since no investor is willing to invest in them. Investors have their reasons as well; not every investor has the confidence to invest in a movie with a newbie filmmaker since he/she does not have any prior work or enough experience to demonstrate. However, they are tremendously talented and enthusiastic about film creation. The forecast will aid an investor in choosing whether he/she wants to invest in new artists. It would be wonderful for a new artist in the market. The film industry is contributing significant money to the worldwide market. Suppose any new artists can produce movies without difficulties. In that case, it will inspire more artists, and as a consequence, more films will be created, and thus, the film industry's contribution to the worldwide market will go up. Our purpose is to support young artists so that an investor can easily make investment decisions. However, our vision or significant goal is to do something for Bangladesh's film industry in the future. There are a lot of enthusiastic young artists in Bangladesh who are amazingly passionate and dedicated to making new films but cannot do anything because of money; no production companies are willing to invest money blindly for them. We expect this research will benefit the Bangladeshi film industry because there are few production houses in our country, and producers lack the courage and financial resources to work with young artists. It will be extremely beneficial to them if we can offer them an idea of how a movie can do business after its release. We focused on only foreign movies when we created our dataset because we do not have enough data on Bangladeshi movies available on the web. Managing the film data of our country will be time-consuming. Furthermore, that is our future goal to help the film industry of Bangladesh by collecting data and making a prediction model.

For 838 movies, we utilized two features in our proposed system: pre-release features and post-release features. We can only forecast upcoming films by looking at pre-release features. Both pre-release and post-release features will perform forecasting immediately after release. Five pre-release features and five post-release features are included. More features were included in this study to enable us to create a better and more standardized forecast. Instead of predicting flops and blockbusters solely, we will look at a variety of factors. [10]. However, we classify films into five categories depending on their box office revenue, from failure to blockbuster. Machine learning techniques such as Naive Bayes, Random Forest, Support Vector Machine (SVM), K-Nearest Neighbor (KNN), Decision Tree, and Logistic Regression are available for multiclass prediction. These classifiers are good enough for binary classification. We applied all the classification algorithms to our dataset for prediction. Among those, Random Forest showed 94.76% accuracy & Decision Tree showed the second highest accuracy of 93.33%. After cross-validation, accuracy for Random Forest was 96.05% & for Decision Tree 94.97%.

2 Literature Review

The success of a movie is largely determined by how it has been justified from various viewpoints. In the early days, many works have been done on this domain where they put gross box office revenue first. ([1–4]). Using IMDb data, a few earlier publications ([4–6]) have predicted the box-office gross of a film using stochastic and regression models. A handful of them used the revenue to determine if a movie was a success or failure and then used double classifications for forecasting. Its box office revenue does not solely determine the success of a movie. A movie's success is determined by various factors such as actors/actresses, directors, budget, release month, background story, and so on. Only a few individuals had developed a prediction model based on a few pre-released features. [7]. in most cases, only a few features are taken into account. As a consequence, their models were ineffective. They overlooked audience participation once again, even though the audience mostly determines the success of a film. Even though some peoples adopt numerous implementations of NLP for sentimental analysis ([8, 9]) and assembled movie reviews for their research purpose. However, the prediction accuracy is determined by the size of the test domain. A little domain is not good for estimation. Again, the majority of them ignored critics' reviews. Moreover, user reviews as fans of the actor/actress may be biased and fail to provide an unbiased opinion.

In their research, Latif & Afzal [14], used several features (MPAA Rating, Awards, Screenplays, Opening Weekend, Meta-score, and Budgets) to classify movies into four categories based on their IMDB user ratings: Terrible, Poor, Average, and Excellent. The authors used a variety of classifiers, including logistic regression, simple logistic, multilayer perceptron, J48, naive Bayes, and PART, to achieve a classification accuracy of 84.15%, 84.5%, 79.07%, 82.42%, 79.66%, and 79.52% respectively. But their data was inconsistent and highly noisy, as stated in their paper. For that, they have used Central Tendency to fill missing values for different attributes.

Lash, and Zhao's [10] main contribution was designing a decision support system based on machine learning techniques, social network analysis, and text mining. They get information from a variety of sources. A few examples are Twitter, YouTube comments, blogs, news stories, and movie reviews. They looked at motion picture success from three perspectives: audience, release, and movie. They used this system to predict movie productivity, not revenue. The authors used linear logistic regression to classify movies in order to forecast their profitability, which has a 77.1% accuracy rate. BoxOfficeMojo and IMDb were used to collect their original data. They only looked at movies released in the United States and left out any international films from their research.

To forecast a movie's box-office success, Mr. Sivasantoshreddy, Mr. Kasat, and Mr. Jain utilized a methodology called hype analysis [11]. For hype analysis, they mostly used Twitter data. The primary premise of hype analysis is that a film's success is mostly determined by its very first weekend earnings and the amount of hype it generates before its release. Firstly, they tried to find the total number of tweets. Here are a few factors to consider when measuring hype. The first step is determining the "number of relevant tweets per second." The second factor is "Find the number of posted tweets by different users." The third factor is to calculate "the reach of a particular tweet." The phrase "reach of a tweet" refers to the fact that the value of various people's tweets varies. They calculated the reach of a tweet by counting the number of followers of a certain user. They computed the number of linked tweets every second, and the second element is to "Find and Calculate a Tweet's Reach. In their investigation, they used the hype factor, the number of screens, and the average ticket price per show. No language processing technique was used to assess whether the tweet was good or negative. Before a movie was premiered in cinemas, a neural network was used to predict its financial success. [12]. This forecasting challenge was transformed into a nine-class classification task. The model was portrayed with only a few features.

Using Lydia's quantitative news data, Zhang and Skiena attempted to improve gross movie forecast using News analysis [13]. There are two models available (Regression and KNN models). However, they have only considered movies with a high budget. If a common word was chosen as a name, the model would fail, and it would be unable to forecast if there was no news about a movie.

Few researchers applied sentimental analysis to the social network to make their forecast [15]. Their study was focused on an intensity and positivity analysis of IMDb's Oscar Buzz sub-forum. Movie critics have been considered as their predictive perspective. When some words were used for negative meaning, however, the model produced an inaccurate result. In certain circumstances, neural network analysis was used to predict the success of a movie ([7, 18]).

Based on social media, social networks, and hype analysis, several studies calculated positivity and the number of comments associated with a certain movie ([16, 17, 19, 20]). In addition, few individuals predicted movie box office success based on Twitter tweets and YouTube comments. The forecast's accuracy will be uncertain in both cases, and the result will be unsatisfying. A limited domain is not a good concept for measuring. The majority of prior studies focused on features that were accessible either before or after the release of a film. Despite the fact that some studies considered both sorts of features, only a few were counted in that case. The probability of better prediction accuracy increases if the number of features increases.

3   Data Description and Methodology

In this chapter, we discussed the workflow, data extraction, cleaning, preprocessing, feature extraction, and several machine learning techniques we have used in our research.

3.1 Data Acquisition

Eight hundred thirty-eight films in our dataset were released between 2006 and 2018. We used the movies till 2018 because some fields of data were missing in latest films. Our primary data sources are Metacritic, IMDb, Box Office Mojo, and Rotten Tomatoes. The IMDbPy library in Python is used to collect IMDb ratings, IMDb votes, genre, directors, and casts. IMDb doesn't provide business data. We took movie budget value from Box Office Mojo and The Numbers. Another helpful aspect is the Metacritic rating, which may be found on the Metacritic website. In this dataset, we used two types of reviews. We used the Tomato rating from Rotten Tomato and the Audience Rating.

3.2 Data Preprocessing

Initially, we had 1764 films in our dataset. Then we recognized that several movies had no available data. The main issue was that most of the movies were missing budget data. First, we searched IMDB for the budget. IMDb does not have a budget for all films. Then we looked for a budget on Wikipedia, Box Office Mojo, Rotten Tomatoes, and The Numbers. We gathered budgets from Box-Office Mojo for some movies and The Numbers for others. We deleted any movie with an unknown year in addition to all the TV series and short movies (running time less than 60 min). After deleting the movies that did not have all of the information available, we finally had our dataset of 838 movies. The summary of our dataset is shown in Table 1.

A critical phase of data preprocessing is feature scaling. This approach normalizes the range of independent variables or data features. The algorithms can train quickly and avoid being stuck in local optima with the aid of feature scaling. In doing so, any data leaks throughout the model testing process would be avoided. We have scaled the data using machine learning techniques like logistic regression, neural networks, and others that usually utilize gradient descent as an optimization technique. Our chosen distance methods, KNN and SVM, are mainly influenced by the range of features. The scaling strategy of standardization has been applied. As a result, the attribute's mean is reduced to zero, and the distribution that results has a unit standard deviation (Fig. 1).

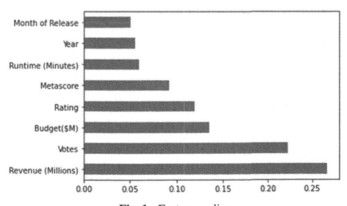

Fig. 1. Feature scaling

Missing information is a crucial component of the procedure. It's a serious problem for data analysis since it misrepresents the findings. Some characteristics in our dataset weren't accessible for all movies. As a result, we had to deal with the empty cells that were considered to be NaN. We used common-point data imputation methods to cope with missing data. In common-point imputation, the middle point, or the most frequently selected value, is used. Since this approach has three different middle values—mean, median, and mode—that are suitable for numerical data, we used mean values.

3.3 Feature Extraction

A dataset's features can be used to estimate a movie's rate of success. Most of the models taken into account in earlier research have a fairly small number of features. The majority of the features from the internet were included in this paper. Pre-released features and post-release features were the two distinct categories of features that we examined in this study. Pre-released features are used to assess the probability that upcoming movies will be a success. Pre-released features include the movie's budget, the month it will be released, the star power of the actors and actresses, and the star power of the director. After a few weeks after the movie's release, post-release features are helpful for increasing forecast accuracy. The post-released features in this study are the IMDb rating, IMDb votes, Meta Score, Run Time, and Gross Revenue.

Among all features genre plays an important role. Different audience have different choices. Some are fond of thriller; some are fond of action. Figure 2 shows the number of movies against each genre.

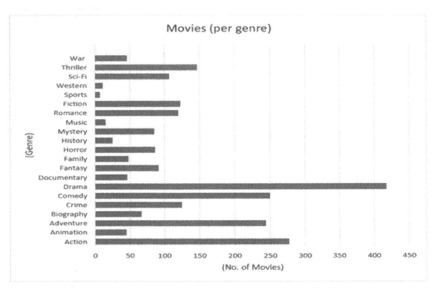

Fig. 2. Movies per Genre

Table 1. Dataset Summary

Features	Types	Mean	Min	Max	Std. Dev	Sources
Runtime (minutes)	Integer	114.661888	66.000000	187.000000	18.469466	IMDb
Rating	Float	6.816249	1.900000	9.000000	0.876500	IMDb
Votes	Integer	1.934572e + 05	1.780000e + 02	1.791916e + 06	1.931026e + 05	IMDb
Revenue ($)	Float	84.970550	0.010000	936.630000	104.857058	IMDb, BoxOfficeMojo, The Numbers
Budget ($)	Float	60.357918	0.007000	300.000000	61.860066	IMDb, BoxOfficeMojo, Wikipedia
Metascore	Integer	59.698925	11.000000	100.000000	16.949691	Meta Critic
Release Month (number)	Integer	6.672640	1.000000	12.000000	3.428753	IMDb
Cast Star Power	Integer	6.462313	3.500000	8.200000	4.986323	IMDb
Director Star Power	Integer	6.736406	4.300000	8.400000	5.334120	IMDb

We included the year as a part of the features in order to differentiate between movies having the same title but different years of release. Figure 3 shows the movies released in each year.

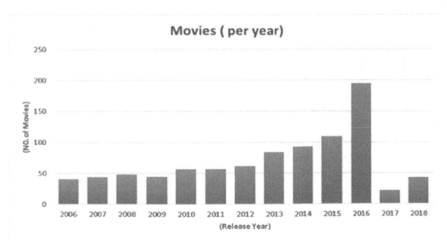

Fig. 3. Movies per Year

Film budgeting is, certainly one of the most essential aspects of the production process. Throughout the life cycle of a film, the budget plays a crucial role.

Another key aspect in the motion picture industry is the release date. For example, releasing a film in theaters at the beginning of summer permits the film to earn cash throughout the entire summer, which has a bigger demand than the fall season. Figure 4 shows the movies month of release.

Fig. 4. Movies per Month.

Most often revenue is the key to predicting whether a movie is succeed or not. For the creative industries, forecasting and analyzing these earnings is important, and it's often a source of interest for fans.

We considered audience votes and score from the websites like IMDb and Metacritic's. The number of votes reflects the number of individuals who enjoyed that particular film.

It's crucial that a film tells its story without being either too short or too long to be enjoyable. A comedy, for example, should never last longer than 110 min. Action/drama film with strong characters and a compelling story should be between 110 and 135 min.

3.4 Data Transformation

Table 2 shows the third phase, data integration, and transformation where we classify our target class into five classes. Rather than giving only two output "flop" or "blockbuster" [3], we make five classifications ranging from "Flop" to "Blockbuster."

Similarly, we have classified our other features such as budget, IMDb rating, Metascore, votes, cast star power, director-star power into different classes to predict our target model.

Table 2. Target class clssification

Class	Range ($)
A	Revenue <= 0.5M (Flop)
B	0.5M < Revenue <= 1Million
C	1M < Revenue <= 40Million
D	40M < Revenue <= 150Million
E	Revenue > 150 Million (Blockbuster)

4 Result and Analysis

In this chapter, we present the result of our experiment for movie success prediction and discussed the results of different machine learning methodologies. From this study the prediction of movie success is identified.

4.1 Support Vector Machine

We have used SVM for all the pre-release and post-release features in our dataset. And it produced an accuracy of 93.25%, which is shown in the figure with the confusion matrix.

We also applied K-fold cross-validation. The mean accuracy of K-fold cross-validation using SVM is 93.40% (Fig. 5).

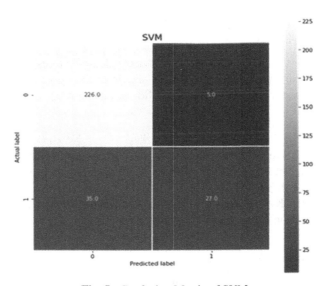

Fig. 5. Confusion Matrix of SVM

4.2 Random Forest

Again we used Random Forest for all the features in our dataset. And it produced an accuracy of 94.76%, which is shown in the figure with the confusion matrix. Random Forest is also used to perform K-fold cross-validation. The results of K-fold cross-validation with Random Forest with a mean accuracy of 96.05% (Fig. 6).

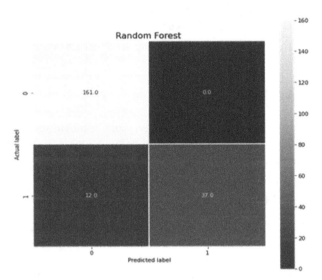

Fig. 6. Confusion Matrix of Random Forest

4.3 K-Nearest Neighbor

Used Random Forest for all the pre-release and post-release features in our dataset. And it produced an accuracy of 88.57%, which is shown in the figure with the confusion matrix. The mean accuracy of K-fold cross-validation using KNN is 88.66% (Fig. 7).

4.4 Naïve Bayes

We implemented Naïve Bayes for all the pre-release and post-release features in our dataset. And it produced an accuracy of 88.67%, which is shown in the figure with the confusion matrix (Fig. 8).

We also applied K-fold cross-validation for Naïve Bayes. The mean accuracy of K-fold cross-validation using Naïve Bayes is 89.60%.

4.5 Logistic Regression

We implemented Logistic Regression for all the pre-release and post-release features in our dataset. And it produced an accuracy of 89.04%.

We also applied K-fold cross-validation for Naïve Bayes. The mean accuracy of K-fold cross-validation using Naïve Bayes is 91.15% (Fig. 9).

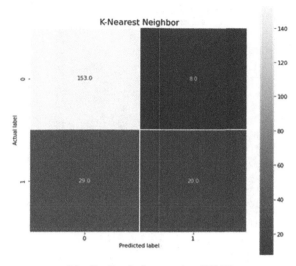

Fig. 7. Confusion matrix of KNN

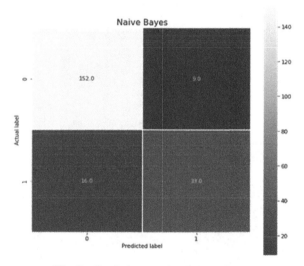

Fig. 8. Confusion matrix of Naïve Bayes

4.6 Decision Tree

We applied Decision Tree for all the pre-release and post-release features in our dataset. And it produced an accuracy of 93.33%, which is shown in Fig. 4.8 with the confusion matrix.

With Decision Tree, we performed K-fold cross-validation. K-fold cross-validation with Logistic Regression for each fold, with a mean accuracy of 94.97% (Fig. 10).

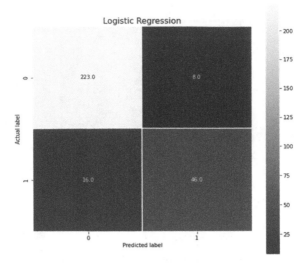

Fig. 9. Confusion Matrix of LR

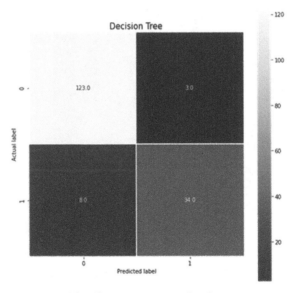

Fig. 10. Confusion Matrix of DT

4.7 Performance Analysis

A performance comparison among machine learning algorithms has been illustrated. It shows the accuracy of each algorithm used in your research. Some performed well and some showed less performance compared to others. We got accuracy for SVM: 93.25%, Random Forest: 94.76%, KNN: 88.57%, Naïve Bayes: 88.67%, Logistic Regression: 89:04% and Decision Tree: 93.33% (Fig. 11).

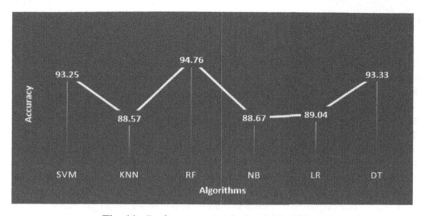

Fig. 11. Performance Analysis of Algorithms

After applying Cross Validation with each of algorithm, the performance increased surprisingly. Here K-fold cross-validation obtained accuracy of SVM: 93.40%, KNN: 88.66%, RF: 96.05%, NB: 89.6%, LR: 91.15% and DT: 94.97% which impacted our model significantly.

5   Conclusion and Future Work

The goal of this study was to develop a method for predicting movie success based on prior research. It wasn't a complete success, but it does demonstrate that other features are necessary for an accurate forecast. The number of theaters, the MPAA rating, or a film's sequel were not included in our assessment of features. It's difficult to predict a movie's sequel; some movies have generated a lot of money solely from their previous sequels. In a few other works, the sequel is likewise neglected [10]. Some research examined just pre-release features for prediction ([10, 12]), whereas others primarily examined post-release data ([1, 2]). However, while generating predictions in our research, we considered both features. In comparison to other methods, Random Forest produced the best accuracy of 94.76%. After cross-validation, Random forest once more has the highest accuracy of 96.05%. According to our research, some features have a bigger impact on a movie's success than others. Particularly affected were the budget and revenue. Furthermore, we have demonstrated that IMDB rating may be a reliable indicator of movie success.

Some aspects of the present research work can be further investigated and improved. Based on the literature reviews and studies conducted in this thesis, the following recommendations are proposed:

First, as additional features have an impact on performance rate, we intend to raise the number of features for future investigation. Second, we'll utilize more data for training, which should enhance the model's performance, and we'll use neural networks to increase performance.

References

1. Apala, K.R., Jose, M., Motnam, S., Chan, C.-C., Liszka, K.J., de Gregorio, F.: Prediction of movies box office performance using social media. In: Proceedings of the 2013 IEEE/ACM International Conference on Advances in Social Networks Analysis and Mining, Niagara Ontario Canada, pp. 1209–1214 (2014). https://doi.org/10.1145/2492517.2500232
2. Gopinath, S., Chintagunta, P.K., Venkataraman, S.: Blogs, advertising, and local-market movie box office performance. Manag. Sci. **59**(12), 26352654 (2013). https://doi.org/10.1287/mnsc.2013.1732
3. Mestyán, M.C.A., Yasseri, T., Kertész, J.: Early prediction of movie box office success based on wikipedia activity big data. PLoS ONE **8**(8), e71226 (2013)
4. Simonoff, J.S., Sparrow, I.R.: Predicting movie grosses: winners and losers, blockbusters and sleepers. Chance **13**(3), 1524 (2000)
5. Chen, A.: Forecasting gross revenues at the movie box office, Working paper, University of Washington, Seattle, WA (2002)
6. Sawhney, M.S., Eliashberg, J.: A parsimonious model for forecasting gross box-office revenues of motion pictures. Mark. Sci. **15**(2), 113131 (1996)
7. Sharda, R., Meany, E.: Forecasting gate receipts using neural network and rough sets. In: Proceedings of the International DSI Conference, p. 15 (2000)
8. Pang, B., Lee, L.: Thumbs up? sentiment classification using machine learning techniques. In: Proceedings of the Conference on Empirical Methods in Natural Language Processing (EMNLP), Philadelphia, p. 7986 (2002)
9. Chaovalit, P., Zhou, L.: Movie review mining: a comparison between supervised and unsupervised classification approaches. In: Proceedings of the Hawaii International Conference on System Sciences (HICSS) (2005)
10. Lash, M.T., Zhao, K.: Early predictions of movie success: the who, what, and when of profitability. J. Manag. Inf. Syst. **33**(3), 874903 (2016)
11. Sivasantoshreddy, A., Kasat, P., Jain, A.: Box-office opening prediction of movies based on hype analysis through data mining. Int. J. Comput. Appl. **56**(1), 15 (2012)
12. Sharda, R., Delen, D.: Predicting box-office success of motion pictures with neural networks. Expert Syst. Appl. **30**(2), 243–254 (2006)
13. Zhang, W., Skiena, S.: Improving movie gross prediction through news analysis. In: 2009 IEEE/WIC/ACM International Joint Conference on Web Intelligence and Intelligent Agent Technology (2009)
14. Latif, M.H., Afzal, H.: Prediction of movies popularity using machine learning techniques. National University of Sciences and Technology, H-12, ISB, Pakistan (2016)
15. Jonas, K., Stefan, N., Daniel, S., Kai, F.: Predicting movie success and academi awards through sentiment and social network analysis. University of Cologne, Pohligstrasse 1, Cologne, Germany (2008)
16. Duan, J., Ding, X., Liu, T.: A gaussian copula regression model for movie box-office revenue prediction with social media. In: Zhang, X., Sun, M., Wang, Z., Huang, X. (eds.) CNCSMP 2015. CCIS, vol. 568, pp. 28–37. Springer, Singapore (2015). https://doi.org/10.1007/978-981-10-0080-5_3
17. Doshi, L., Krauss, J., Nann, S., Gloor, P.: Predicting movie prices through dynamic social network analysis. Procedia. Soc. Behav. Sci. **2**(4), 64236433 (2010)
18. Rhee, T.G., Zulkernine, F.: Predicting movie box office profitability: a neural network approach. In: 2016 15th IEEE International Conference on Machine Learning and Applications (ICMLA) (2016)
19. Liu, T., Ding, X., Chen, Y., Chen, H., Guo, M.: Predicting movie Box-office revenues by exploiting large-scale social media content. Multimedia Tools Appl. **75**(3), 1509–1528 (2014). https://doi.org/10.1007/s11042-014-2270-1

20. Zhang, Z., Li, B., Deng, Z., Chai, J., Wang, Y., An, M.: Research on movie box office forecasting based on internet data. In: 2015 8th International Symposium on Computational Intelligence and Design (ISCID) (2015)
21. Valenti, J.: Motion Pictures and Their Impact on Society in the Year 2000, speech given at the Midwest Research Institute, Kansas City, 25 April 1978, p. 7 (1978)
22. Litman, B.R., Kohl, L.S.: Predicting financial success of motion pictures: the 80s experience. J. Media Econ. 2(2), 3550 (1989)
23. Hayward, S.: Genre/Sub-genre in Cinema Studies: The Key Concepts, 3rd edn., pp. 185–192. Routledge, Abingdon (2006)

Structure of Global Financial Networks Before and During COVID-19 Based on Mutual Information

Sheikh Shadia Hassan, Mahmudul Islam Rakib⃝, Kamrul Hasan Tuhin, and Ashadun Nobi⁽✉⁾ ⃝

Department of Computer Science and Telecommunication Engineering, Noakhali Science and Technology University, Sonapur, Noakhali 3814, Bangladesh
dashadunnobi_305@yahoo.com

Abstract. We investigate and perform a comparative study of the structure and network properties of global financial indices before and during COVID-19 using mutual information. We analyze the daily closing prices of 25 global stock markets from January 1, 2018, to March 31, 2021. We found that the dependence relationship among regional countries is enhanced during the pandemic. The network is constructed based on mutual information at different thresholds. At threshold 0.25, before the pandemic, the network was fragmented into two big clusters of Asian and European-Americans. At the same threshold, during the pandemic, the network forms a big cluster excluding New Zealand, which indicates strong dependence among indices in the pandemic. We observe different network properties of the threshold networks. A sharp drop in global efficiency is visible at threshold 0.25 before COVID-19 and at threshold 0.35 during the pandemic due to the network split into different isolated clusters at these thresholds. We construct the minimum spanning tree using the Kruskal algorithm and find a shallower tree during the pandemic. We found that the French, Canadian, and South Korean indices played an important role in their clusters before COVID-19, whereas during COVID-19, the hub of the European cluster was altered by Germany.

Keywords: COVID-19 · Financial Market · Mutual Information · Threshold Network · Network Properties · Minimum Spanning Tree

1 Introduction

COVID-19 is considered a global panic at the very beginning of 2020. It was first found in Wuhan (China). According to the report of WHO, on January 11, 2020, China reported the first death from the novel coronavirus up to September 1, 2020 [1]. On January 20, 2020, the WHO reported the first confirmed cases outside China (in Thailand, Japan, and South Korea [1]). On March 11, 2020, according to the director-general of WHO, there have been more than 118,000 cases in 114 countries, including 4,291 people who

---

S. S. Hassan and M. I. Rakib—Contributed equally to this work.

Md. S. Satu et al. (Eds.): MIET 2022, LNICST 491, pp. 628–643, 2023.
https://doi.org/10.1007/978-3-031-34622-4_50

have lost their lives [2]. As a result, on March 11, 2020, World Health Organization (WHO) declared coronavirus a pandemic in 2019–20. The evolution of COVID-19 and its economic impact on the regional financial markets are now highly uncertain. The COVID-19 pandemic has increased the rate of unemployment and also affected the trade and transportation system [3]. At the beginning of COVID-19, its negative effect on the real economy had already been shown [4]. Some studies showed that the outbreak of COVID-19 can greatly impact the world finance and economy [5, 6].

Since the financial markets of different countries in the world have been connected, the global spread of COVID-19 not only has a negative impact on social development and the economic status of the affected countries but also has a great impact on the financial markets. Some studies showed that the global spread of COVID-19 has a great impact on the volatility of the financial market [7–10], and the return of financial indices [11–15]. Hence, different statistical models and correlation methods have been applied to investigate and identify the impact pattern of COVID-19 on the local and global financial markets [16–20]. Compared with these statistical methods like the correlation coefficient, which can only measure linear correlation but cannot detect nonlinear dependence normally observed in stock markets [21, 22], the copula method, which can measure both linear and nonlinear dependence, but before using this method, certain copula functions need to be selected [23]; mutual information can measure both linear and nonlinear dependence [24–26]. Mutual information is completely independent of the model and does not perform any assumption among the variables which are in an underlying relationship [27]. Some studies showed that mutual information is a more effective approach than the correlation coefficient to measure the stock relationship in a stock market that may undergo large fluctuations in stock prices [28–30]. They also emphasized the usefulness of mutual information based network analysis for identification of Financial Markets features.

In this paper, we construct financial networks of global financial indices based on mutual information before and during COVID-19 at different thresholds. This research studies the dependence relationships among stock markets of countries that are severely affected by the COVID-19 pandemic and how these dependencies have changed with the arrival of the pandemic. Different network properties of the threshold networks are observed to understand the dynamical behavior of the global stock network in this epidemic time. We construct the minimum spanning tree (MST) to investigate a hidden hierarchical structure in global financial indices before and during the COVID-19 pandemic. Among all financial indices, this MST method selects the indices which have close interactions and finally constructs a visual presentation that shows the linkage relationship based on the selected interactions of the indices. The novelty of this work is to observe the global financial threshold networks and spanning trees based on mutual information and compare their structures around COVID-19, not done before.

2 Literature Review

Some studies focused on the operation of the financial markets in different countries and different sectors during the pandemic [19, 31, 32]. Mike et al. investigated the impacts of the COVID-19 pandemic on the connectedness of the Hong Kong financial market and found that during the COVID-19 pandemic, network density and clustering are higher in the partial correlation networks [19]. Baker et al. found that the impact of COVID-19 on US stock market volatility is much greater than that of previous pandemics including the Spanish Flu that occurred in the year 1900 [31]. Shehzad et al. compared the impact of the COVID-19 outbreak on the stock markets of different countries with that of global financial crises and found that the stock markets of the American region and European region were more seriously affected by COVID-19 [32].

In recent years, a certain number of studies have been done about the interdependence among stock markets [33–39]. In these studies, various models like Copula, Generalized Autoregressive Conditional Heteroscedasticity (GARCH), Dynamic Conditional Correlation (DCC), and different correlation methods are used to investigate the interdependence structure among various stock markets of different countries. Samitas et al. used the Asymmetric DCC and minimum spanning tree method to perform network analysis and examines the impact of the COVID-19 pandemic on 51 major stock markets [16]. Another study combined Copula and GARCH approaches to investigate cross-market linkages among six major stock markets during the COVID-19 pandemic [17]. Some studies implemented the feature ranking approach of machine learning to reconstruct the network structure of the local and global financial markets [40, 41]. Several articles applied Pearson correlation technique to analyze the impact of COVID-19 on the financial market [18–20]. The network properties of the minimum spanning tree constructed from the correlations of 58 world stock indices are observed to investigate the impact of COVID-19 on world stock markets [18]. Van Ruitenbeek et al. tracked 40 world stock indices and 74 raw materials and exposed relations between COVID-19, mobility, and the stock market from their correlations [20]. Guo et al. monitored 280 stocks from the Shanghai Stocks Exchange based on the Pearson correlation coefficient and mutual information and found that the network based on mutual information has a better power-law distribution for the degree of stocks, and also suggested that mutual information is a better approach to characterize the nonlinear dynamic relationship between stock markets with high frequency trading data [28]. Another article studied Brazilian equity networks during the governance of two different president using mutual information and correlation coefficient and concluded that mutual information based minimum spanning trees present higher degree of robustness and evidence of power law tail in the weighted degree distribution [29].

Previously, mutual information has already been applied in many studies including the financial sectors [42–46]. Mutual information technique was applied to measure the statistical interdependence between 23 industry sectors of the Shanghai stock market and analyzed the shock of financial crisis that happened in 2008 [42]. The network technique has become a useful tool for extracting information from the financial market [33, 47, 48]. The threshold method was used in many studies on financial indices to construct the financial network [49–51]. The minimum spanning tree (MST) has been applied in many studies [52–55] to understand the hierarchical structure of the financial indices.

3   Research Methods

3.1   Data Analysis

In this article, we analyze the daily closing prices of 25 stock markets around the world. We divide the stock markets into three groups like, Asia-pacific, Europe, and America based on their geographical location. All data were collected from Yahoo Finance [56]. The time range of the data is from January 1, 2018, to March 31, 2021. This range is further divided into before COVID-19 and during the COVID-19 period according to the different development status of COVID-19. The before COVID-19 period is from

Table 1.   Details of the 25 countries and their stock indices.

Continent	Country(region)	Index
Asia-pacific	Australia	AORD
	China	SSE
	Hong Kong	HSI
	Indonesia	JKSE
	Japan	N225
	Korea	KS11
	Malaysia	KLSE
	New Zealand	NZ50
	Philippines	PSI
	Taiwan	TWII
	Thailand	SETI
Europe	Czech Republic	PX
	Finland	IIEX
	France	FCHI
	Germany	GDAXI
	Netherlands	AEX
	Norway	OSEAX
	Spain	IBEX
	Sweden	OMXSPI
	United Kingdom	FTSE
America	Argentina	MERV
	Brazil	IBOVESPA
	Canada	GSPTSE
	Mexico	MXX
	United States	DJI

January 1, 2018 to December 31, 2019, and the COVID-19 period is from January 1, 2020 to March 31, 2021. The above time range is divided according to the development status of COVID-19; On December 31, 2019, Chinese authorities first reported COVID-19 to the World Health Organization [12]. Table 1 displays the names of the countries and their corresponding stock indices which we used in our research.

According to formula (1), we calculate the logarithmic return of each stock market for daily closing prices.

$$R(t) = \ln[P(t)] - \ln[P(t-1)] \tag{1}$$

where $R(t)$ is the logarithmic return of time t and $P(t)$ and $P(t-1)$ are the daily closing price at time t and prior time $t-1$, respectively.

3.2 Mutual Information

At first, we introduce Shannon entropy which is used to measure the uncertainty of a random variable in information theory. According to Shannon's entropy theory [57], for a random variable X, the entropy $H(X)$ of that variable is,

$$H(X) = -\sum_{x \in X} p(x)\log[p(x)] \tag{2}$$

where $p(x)$ is the probability of x. The joint entropy $H(X, Y)$ of two random variables x and y is given by

$$H(X, Y) = -\sum_{x \in X}\sum_{y \in Y} p(x, y)\log[p(x, y)] \tag{3}$$

where $p(x, y)$ is the joint probability of x and y. Assuming that $p(x)$ and $p(y)$ are the marginal probability distributions of two random variables x and y respectively and $p(x, y)$ is the joint probability distribution of x and y. The mutual information $I(X, Y)$ of x and y is defined by

$$I(X, Y) = -\sum_{x \in X}\sum_{y \in Y} p(x, y)\log\frac{p(x, y)}{p(x)p(y)} \tag{4}$$

After calculation according to formulas (2) and (3), the mutual information formula (4) can be rewritten as

$$I(X, Y) = H(X) + H(Y) - H(X, Y) \tag{5}$$

At first, we calculate the mutual information among the returns of 25 global financial indices before and during COVID-19. We further calculate normalized mutual information between the range 0 to 1 by using the following formula,

$$NMI(X, Y) = \frac{2I(X, Y)}{H(X) + H(Y)} \tag{6}$$

where $NMI(X, Y)$ denotes the normalized mutual information of X and Y.

Figures 1a and 1b show the color maps of normalized mutual information before COVID-19 and during COVID-19 respectively. Here, lighter color indicates higher dependence and darker color specifies the opposite. From Fig. 1a, before COVID-19 period, it can be seen that among the 25 financial indices, the normalized mutual information value is relatively small, especially in the indices of Asian and American regions. The financial indices of these regions have the smallest normalized mutual information with respect to the financial indices of European regions excluding the financial index of the Czech Republic, which indicates that they are less dependent. But also it can be seen that in the European region the financial indices of France and Netherland have relatively high normalized mutual information than other countries, which means that these two countries maintain a high dependence relationship. Germany also has a relatively close dependence relationship with France and Netherland.

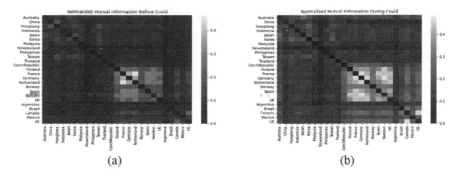

(a)   (b)

Fig. 1. Color map of normalized mutual information. (a) Before COVID-19 (b) During COVID-19.

On the other hand, during the COVID-19 period from Fig. 1b, it can be seen that the interdependence between the 25 financial indices has improved. The financial indices of the European region especially France, Netherland, Sweden have the greatest dependence on Germany. Spain, Sweden, UK have a relatively close dependent relationship with France. From both figures, the European cluster is clearly visible before and during the COVID-19 situation, which gets stronger during the pandemic shown by the white shaded area. In the American region, Canada and US have the greatest dependence relationship. These two American countries have a noticeable relationship with most of the European countries during the pandemic.

3.3 Network Construction

Let the set of vertices (V) of the network represents the set of global financial indices. We take a specific threshold value $\theta(0.1 \leq \theta \leq 1)$. At a specific threshold value θ, if mutual information I_{xy} is greater than or equal to θ then add an undirected edge that connects the vertices x and y. As a result, different threshold values construct networks with different sets of edges but the set of vertices remains the same [58]. In the graph $G = (V, E)$ the set of edges (E) which represents the global financial network of indices is generated by the following formula.

$$E = \begin{cases} e_{xy} = 1, x \neq y \text{ and } I_{xy} \geq \theta, \\ e_{xy} = 0, x = y. \end{cases} \tag{7}$$

3.4 Network Properties

Average Degree. In a network, the degree of a node is the number of connections that it has to other nodes. If e_{xy} is an undirected edge between node x and node y then the degree of node x can be defined as [58],

$$k_x = \sum_{y \neq x} e_{xy} \tag{8}$$

The average degree is based upon the degree and it shows the average number of neighbors per node in the network. It can be defined for all N nodes as,

$$\overline{K} = \frac{1}{N} \sum_{x=1}^{N} k_x \tag{9}$$

Average Clustering Coefficient. In a network, the clustering coefficient is a measure of the degree to which nodes in a network tend to cluster together. If node x has k_x neighbors and the number of edges between k_x neighbors of node x is n_x then clustering coefficient C_x of node x is defined by

$$C_x = \frac{n_x}{k_x(k_x - 1)} \tag{10}$$

which is the ratio of the number of existing edges n_x to the maximum number of possible edges $k_x(k_x - 1)$ in that cluster. Average clustering coefficient of the entire network is a measure of the total clustering coefficient for each node on average, can be calculated as,

$$\overline{C} = \frac{1}{N} \sum_{x=1}^{N} C_x \tag{11}$$

Clique Number. In an undirected graph, a clique is a subset of its vertices such that every two distinct vertices in that subset are adjacent. The clique number $\omega(G)$ of a financial network G is the number of nodes in a maximum clique in G, defined as follows,

$$\omega(G) = \sum_{x=1}^{N} \frac{1}{N - k_x} \tag{12}$$

Global Efficiency. In a network G, efficiency is inversely proportional to the distance, so in mathematical terms

$$\epsilon_{xy} = \frac{1}{d_{xy}} \tag{13}$$

where ϵ_{xy} is the pairwise efficiency of nodes x, $y \epsilon V$ in the network G. The efficiency of G is then defined as the average over all the pairwise efficiencies [59],

$$E(G) = \frac{1}{N(N-1)} \sum_{x \neq y \epsilon V} \frac{1}{d_{xy}} \tag{14}$$

where $N = |V|$ denotes the number of nodes in the network. Global efficiency $E_{glob}(G)$ is a measure of the exchange of information across the whole network where information is concurrently exchanged, so in mathematical terms,

$$E_{glob}(G) = \frac{E(G)}{E(G^{ideal})} \tag{15}$$

where G^{ideal} is the ideal graph of N nodes where all possible edges are present.

3.5 Minimum Spanning Tree

We construct the mutual information based network of financial indices by using the Kruskal algorithm. The distance between nodes in a mutual information based network is defined by,

$$d_m(X, Y) = H(X) + H(Y) - 2I(X, Y) \tag{16}$$

To construct a mutual information based network of financial indices, we used a normalized version which is defined by,

$$D(S_x, S_y) = 1 - \frac{I(S_x, S_y)}{H(S_x, S_y)} \tag{17}$$

where $D(S_x, S_y)$ is the distance of stocks x and y in the network. We construct an $N \times N$ distance matrix by using the formula (17) and construct the minimum spanning tree by applying the Kruskal algorithm.

4 Results and Discussions

4.1 Threshold Networks

We construct mutual information based financial networks of global indices at different thresholds (in the range 0.1 to 1). At threshold 0.1, the networks of global financial indices as shown in Figs. 2a before COVID and 2b during COVID are connected strongly. After increasing the value of the threshold, the network splits into different clusters. At threshold 0.25, before COVID-19, the indices are formed into different clusters as shown in Fig. 2c, European indices form a strong cluster with US and Canada while Asia-pacific indices form another cluster with disconnected nodes Indonesia, Malaysia, Philippines, Thailand and New Zealand. On the other hand, during COVID-19 at threshold 0.25, American, European and Asian indices form the same cluster with disconnected node

New Zealand as shown in Fig. 2d. If we further increase the threshold to 0.35, we can see that before COVID-19, European indices except the Czech Republic still form a cluster with US and Canada as shown in Fig. 2e. But at the same threshold during COVID-19, Fig. 2f shows that European countries form a strong cluster with American except Argentina while Asia-Pacific indices (Australia, Japan, Hong Kong, Korea, Taiwan) form another cluster. If the threshold is further increased to 0.5 as shown in Figs. 2g before COVID-19 and 2h during COVID-19, we find that only the European indices form a strong cluster except the Czech Republic. We observe that the networks are significantly connected during COVID-19 compared to the pre-COVID period implying the impact of the pandemic on the network structure. The indices are more likely to be connected with indices of the same continent while European indices show the most inter-continental dependency.

4.2 Dynamics of Network Properties

Average Degree. In a financial network, the degree of an index is the number of connections that it has to other indices. Figure 3a shows the average degree of the global financial network before and during COVID-19 at different thresholds (in the range 0.1 to 1). We can see that when the value of the threshold increases, the average degree decreases because, with the increase in threshold, more edges are filtered out from the network. We find that the average degree of the global market during COVID-19 is much larger than the pre-COVID situation for some smaller values of threshold. As we increase the threshold, the difference between the average degree during COVID-19 and pre-COVID situation increases and again decreases for $\theta > 0.2$. After that, a larger number of edges are filtered out from the global network during COVID-19 if we further increase the threshold and the average degree during COVID-19 is leading the average degree before the pandemic for $\theta < 0.6$. A larger value of the average degree in the mutual information based network of global financial indices indicates that more indices interact with each other during the pandemic.

Average Clustering Coefficient. The average clustering coefficient (ACC) starts with higher values for smaller thresholds as shown in Fig. 3b. As we increase the value of the threshold, the ACC decreases because a number of edges are filtered out from between neighbors of nodes at higher thresholds. We find that during COVID-19, the ACC possesses noticeably higher values than the pre-COVID period up to threshold 0.4 which indicates the higher dependence among financial indices during the COVID-19 period. From the curve, we observe that the ACC decreases successively except at threshold 0.35 during COVID-19 where we find an increasing trend. This is due to the strong formation of the American-European cluster and the cluster among five Asia-Pacific indices shown in the network structure at Fig. 2f. After that, we notice a sharp drop in the ACC during the pandemic compared to the pre-COVID period which indicates the rapid breakdown of the clusters at higher values of threshold. At thresholds from 0.45 to 0.55, the ACC remains almost similar in both periods, because only European indices are connected and they form a single cluster. If we further increase the threshold, the ACC decreases rapidly during than before COVID-19. For $\theta \geq 0.70$, no cluster formed in the network during COVID-19, so its ACC becomes zero. On the other hand, before

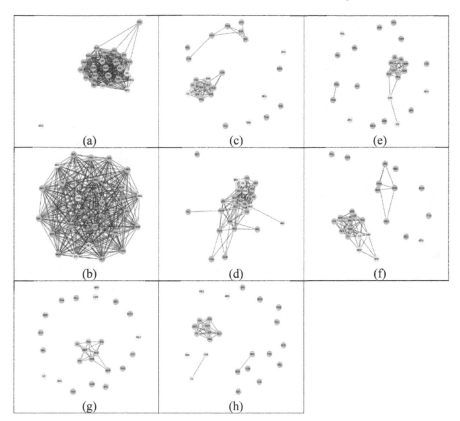

Fig. 2. The threshold networks. At threshold 0.1 (a) before COVID-19 (b) during COVID-19. The indices are connected strongly (c) At threshold 0.25, before COVID, the indices are formed into different clusters. (d) At 0.25 (during COVID), American (light yellow vertices), European (pink vertices) and Asian (light blue) form the same cluster with disconnected node New Zealand (e) At 0.35, European indices except the Czech Republic still form a cluster with US and Canada (f) At 0.35(during COVID), European countries form a strong cluster with American (g), (h) If we further increase the threshold and at 0.5, only European indices form a strong cluster except the Czech Republic.

COVID-19 the ACC becomes zero when $\theta \geq 0.9$. This implies that European indices interact strongly before COVID-19 even after the breakdown of all the clusters during the pandemic.

Clique Number. In a financial network, the maximum clique is one that finds the largest possible sized clique with the maximum number of indices that interact closely with each other. Figure 3c shows that at threshold 0.1, the maximum clique is formed with all the 25 indices that is the graph is a complete graph during COVID-19 where the maximum clique consists of 19 indices before the pandemic at the same threshold. But the clique number reduces in both periods if we increase the threshold value because large cliques split into smaller ones at higher thresholds. We find that during COVID-19 the clique number in the global financial network is greater than that of before COVID-19 up to threshold value 0.55 except at 0.35 to 0.4 where the clique number during and before COVID-19 remains the same because the maximum clique at these values of threshold is the European clique in both periods. At the higher thresholds, the clique number becomes 1 which means no edge remains in the network during COVID-19 where we find that the clique number is greater than 1 before COVID-19 at the same threshold which implies the existence of some strong connections in this period.

Global Efficiency. The global efficiency of the global financial network before and during COVID-19 at different thresholds (in the range 0.1 to 1) is shown in Fig. 3d. At the beginning, the global efficiency during COVID-19 is 1 which means every node is reachable from all other nodes directly in this period where, before COVID-19 we find a smaller global efficiency at the same threshold. After that, the global efficiency decreases with an increase in the threshold as edges are filtered out from the network by higher thresholds. A sharp drop in the global efficiency is visible at threshold 0.25 before COVID-19 and at threshold 0.35 during the pandemic which is due to the split of the network into different isolated clusters at these thresholds as shown in Fig. 2c and Fig. 2f respectively. We observe that the global efficiency during COVID-19 is greater than that of before COVID-19 for thresholds up to 0.55. After that, the global efficiency becomes almost similar in both periods as essentially the European indices are reachable from each other at higher thresholds.

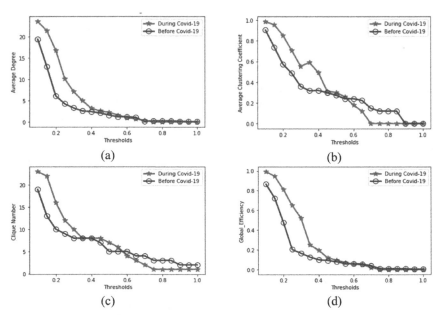

(a)   (b)

(c)   (d)

Fig. 3. Network properties of the threshold networks (a) Average degree before and during COVID-19 at different thresholds. (b) Average clustering coefficient at different thresholds. (c) Clique number at different thresholds. (d) Global efficiency at different thresholds.

4.3   Structural Change of the Spanning Tree

The minimum spanning tree (MST) of financial indices is constructed by using the Kruskal algorithm. From Fig. 4a, before COVID-19, we find a chain like MST where Asia-Pacific, European and American indices form their own clusters which are then connected via connector nodes to complete the tree. In the Asia-Pacific cluster, Korea and Hong Kong play an important role where Hong Kong is the hub node (maximum degree in Asia) and Korea acts as a connector node to the European cluster. France is a hub and connector node in the European cluster that connects with Canada of the American cluster. Sweden is another connector node that connects with Korea of the Asia-Pacific cluster. Now, consider the American cluster. This cluster is line-shaped where Canada is the connector node that interacts with France in the tree. The American and Asia-Pacific clusters communicate with each other via the European cluster in the MST. In this period, France is the hub node in the MST indicating the influence of this node in the network.

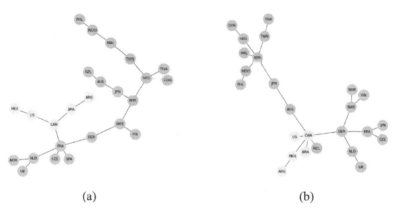

(a)   (b)

Fig. 4. The minimum spanning tree (MST) of the global indices. The MST is composed of the Asia-Pacific (light blue nodes), European (pink nodes), and American (light yellow nodes) clusters of indices. (a) Before COVID-19 (b) During COVID-19.

From Fig. 4b, during COVID-19, we can see that the continental clusters are reformed into a star-like network that ultimately results in a shallower tree. The Asia-Pacific cluster is arranged around Korea which is the hub node in that cluster. The depth of this portion of the tree reduces significantly compared to before COVID-19. This cluster is connected with the American cluster via the connector node Australia. New Zealand is detached from the Asia-Pacific cluster and connected with the American cluster. The American cluster is improved into a more compact form than before COVID-19 where Canada remains as the hub node in the cluster. Canada is also the hub node in the MST that connects the Asian, European, and American clusters together. The European cluster is formed around Germany which is a hub and also a connector node that connects the European cluster to the American cluster. The depth of this portion of the tree also reduces compared to the pre-COVID period. We find a more compact MST during COVID-19 which implies that the number of interactions among indices increases in this period.

5   Conclusion

The mutual information based analysis of global financial indices provides information about the dependence relationship among the financial indices of different countries in the period before and during COVID-19. We constructed networks of financial indices based on mutual information at different thresholds. At threshold 0.25, we show that the network is fragmented into two big clusters of Asian and European-Americans before the pandemic. At the same threshold, the network forms a big cluster excluding New Zealand which implies strong dependence among indices during the pandemic. If we increase the values of the threshold, the network splits into different clusters and the strong dependency is only retained among European indices at higher thresholds. We studied the topological properties of networks at different thresholds before and during the COVID-19 period. We construct the MST for both periods and find a shallower and dense tree during COVID-19. In conclusion, our studies show that the dependence relationship among stock indices is enhanced significantly during COVID-19 and the structure and topological properties of the financial networks are noticeably changed.

Acknowledgments. We would like to acknowledge the support of the ICT Division of Bangladesh (The tracking Number is 22FS15164).

References

1. World Health Organization: Novel Coronavirus (2019-nCoV): situation report, 1. https://apps.who.int/iris/handle/10665/330760
2. World Health Organization: Virtual press conference on COVID-19 (2020). https://bit.ly/3uYY2Tq
3. Malata, A.K., Pinshi, C.P.: Fading the effects of coronavirus with monetary policy. Theor. Pract. Res. Econ. Fields. **11**, 105–110 (2020)
4. Goodell, J.W.: COVID-19 and finance: agendas for future research. Financ. Res. Lett. **35**, 101512 (2020). https://doi.org/10.1016/j.frl.2020.101512
5. Akbulaev, N., Mammadov, I., Aliyev, V.: Economic impact of COVID-19. SYLWAN. **164**, 113–126 (2020)
6. Baig, A.S., Butt, H.A., Haroon, O., Rizvi, S.A.R.: Deaths, panic, lockdowns and US equity markets: the case of COVID-19 pandemic. Financ. Res. Lett. **38**, 101701 (2021). https://doi.org/10.1016/j.frl.2020.101701
7. Albulescu, C.T.: COVID-19 and the United States financial markets' volatility. Financ. Res. Lett. **38**, 101699 (2021). https://doi.org/10.1016/j.frl.2020.101699
8. Okorie, D.I., Lin, B.: Stock markets and the COVID-19 fractal contagion effects. Financ. Res. Lett. **38**, 101640 (2021). https://doi.org/10.1016/j.frl.2020.101640
9. Zaremba, A., Kizys, R., Aharon, D.Y., Demir, E.: Infected markets: novel coronavirus, government interventions, and stock return volatility around the globe. Financ. Res. Lett. **35**, 101597 (2020). https://doi.org/10.1016/j.frl.2020.101597
10. Bakas, D., Triantafyllou, A.: Commodity price volatility and the economic uncertainty of pandemics. Econ. Lett. **193**, 109283 (2020). https://doi.org/10.1016/j.econlet.2020.109283
11. Ashraf, B.N.: Stock markets' reaction to COVID-19: cases or fatalities? Res. Int. Bus. Financ. **54**, 101249 (2020). https://doi.org/10.1016/j.ribaf.2020.101249

12. Aslam, F., Aziz, S., Nguyen, D.K., Mughal, K.S., Khan, M.: On the efficiency of foreign exchange markets in times of the COVID-19 pandemic. Technol. Forecast. Soc. Change. **161**, 120261 (2020). https://doi.org/10.1016/j.techfore.2020.120261
13. Zhang, D., Hu, M., Ji, Q.: Financial markets under the global pandemic of COVID-19. Financ. Res. Lett. **36**, 101528 (2020). https://doi.org/10.1016/j.frl.2020.101528
14. Aslam, F., Mohti, W., Ferreira, P.: Evidence of intraday multifractality in european stock markets during the recent coronavirus (Covid-19) outbreak. Int. J. Financ. Stud. **8**, 1–13 (2020). https://doi.org/10.3390/ijfs8020031
15. Aslam, F., Awan, T.M., Syed, J.H., Kashif, A., Parveen, M.: Sentiments and emotions evoked by news headlines of coronavirus disease (COVID-19) outbreak. Humanit. Soc. Sci. Commun. **7**, 1–9 (2020). https://doi.org/10.1057/s41599-020-0523-3
16. Samitas, A., Kampouris, E., Polyzos, S.: Covid-19 pandemic and spillover effects in stock markets: a financial network approach. Int. Rev. Financ. Anal. **80**, 102005 (2022). https://doi.org/10.1016/J.IRFA.2021.102005
17. Alqaralleh, H., Canepa, A.: Evidence of stock market contagion during the COVID-19 pandemic: a wavelet-copula-GARCH approach. J. Risk Financ. Manag. **14**, 329 (2021). https://doi.org/10.3390/jrfm14070329
18. Memon, B.A., Yao, H.: The impact of COVID-19 on the dynamic topology and network flow of world stock markets. J. Open Innov. Technol. Mark. Complex. **7**, 241 (2021). https://doi.org/10.3390/joitmc7040241
19. So, M.K.P., Chu, A.M.Y., Chan, T.W.C.: Impacts of the COVID-19 pandemic on financial market connectedness. Financ. Res. Lett. **38**, 101864 (2021). https://doi.org/10.1016/j.frl.2020.101864
20. van Ruitenbeek, R.E., Slik, J.S., Bhulai, S.: On the relation between COVID-19, mobility, and the stock market. PLoS One. **16**, e0261381 (2021). https://doi.org/10.1371/journal.pone.0261381
21. Maccone, L., Bruß, D., Macchiavello, C.: Complementarity and correlations. Phys. Rev. Lett. **114**, 1–5 (2015). https://doi.org/10.1103/PhysRevLett.114.130401
22. Anagnostidis, P., Emmanouilides, C.J.: Nonlinearity in high-frequency stock returns: evidence from the athens stock exchange. Phys. A Stat. Mech. its Appl. **421**, 473–487 (2015). https://doi.org/10.1016/j.physa.2014.11.056
23. Chen, R.-B., Guo, M., Härdle, W.K., Huang, S.-F.: COPICA—independent component analysis via copula techniques. Stat. Comput. **25**(2), 273–288 (2014). https://doi.org/10.1007/s11222-013-9431-3
24. Kinney, J.B., Atwal, G.S.: Equitability, mutual information, and the maximal information coefficient. Proc. Natl. Acad. Sci. U. S. A. **111**, 3354–3359 (2014). https://doi.org/10.1073/pnas.1309933111
25. Dionisio, A., Menezes, R., Mendes, D.A.: Mutual information: a measure of dependency for nonlinear time series. Phys. A Stat. Mech. its Appl. **344**, 326–329 (2004). https://doi.org/10.1016/j.physa.2004.06.144
26. Hong, C.S., Kim, B.J.: Mutual information and redundancy for categorical data. Stat. Pap. **52**, 17–31 (2011). https://doi.org/10.1007/s00362-009-0196-x
27. Tourassi, G.D., Frederick, E.D., Markey, M.K., Floyd, C.E.: Application of the mutual information criterion for feature selection in computer-aided diagnosis. Med. Phys. **28**, 2394–2402 (2001). https://doi.org/10.1118/1.1418724
28. Yan, Y., Wu, B., Tian, T., Zhang, H.: Development of stock networks using part mutual information and Australian stock market data. Entropy. **22**, 773 (2020). https://doi.org/10.3390/e22070773
29. Barbi, A.Q., Prataviera, G.A.: Nonlinear dependencies on Brazilian equity network from mutual information minimum spanning trees. Phys. A Stat. Mech. its Appl. **523**, 876–885 (2019). https://doi.org/10.1016/j.physa.2019.04.147

30. Dionísio, A., Ferreira, P.: Using mutual information to analyse serial dependence: the effects of COVID-19. In: Teixeira, N.M., Lisboa, I. (eds.) Handbook of Research on Financial Management During Economic Downturn and Recovery:, pp. 411–427. IGI Global (2021). https://doi.org/10.4018/978-1-7998-6643-5.ch023

31. Baker, S.R., Bloom, N., Davis, S.J., Kost, K.J., Sammon, M.C., Viratyosin, T.: The Unprecedented Stock Market Impact of Covid-19. SSRN (2020)

32. Shehzad, K., Xiaoxing, L., Kazouz, H.: COVID-19's disasters are perilous than global financial crisis: a rumor or fact? Financ. Res. Lett. 36, 101669 (2020). https://doi.org/10.1016/j.frl.2020.101669

33. Qiao, H., Xia, Y., Li, Y.: Can network linkage effects determine return? evidence from Chinese stock market. PLoS ONE 11, 1–25 (2016). https://doi.org/10.1371/journal.pone.0156784

34. Long, W., Tang, Y., Cao, D.: Correlation analysis of industry sectors in China's stock markets based on interval data. Filomat. 30, 3999–4013 (2016). https://doi.org/10.2298/FIL1615999L

35. Sukcharoen, K., Leatham, D.J.: Dependence and extreme correlation among US industry sectors. Stud. Econ. Financ. 33, 26–49 (2016). https://doi.org/10.1108/SEF-01-2015-0021

36. Surya, A.C., Natasha, G.: Is there any sectoral cointegration in indonesia equity market? Int. Res. J. Bus. Stud. 10, 159–172 (2018). https://doi.org/10.21632/irjbs.10.3.159-172

37. Long, H., Zhang, J., Tang, N.: Does network topology influence systemic risk contribution? a perspective from the industry indices in Chinese stock market. PLoS ONE 12, 1–19 (2017). https://doi.org/10.1371/journal.pone.0180382

38. Alomari, M., Power, D.M., Tantisantiwong, N.: Determinants of equity return correlations: a case study of the Amman Stock Exchange. Rev. Quant. Financ. Acc. 50(1), 33–66 (2017). https://doi.org/10.1007/s11156-017-0622-4

39. Ji, J., Huang, C., Cao, Y., Hu, S.: The network structure of Chinese finance market through the method of complex network and random matrix theory. Concurr. Comput. Pract. Exp. 31, 1–15 (2019). https://doi.org/10.1002/cpe.4877

40. Rakib, M.I., Nobi, A., Lee, J.W.: Structure and dynamics of financial networks by feature ranking method. Sci. Rep. 11, 1–11 (2021). https://doi.org/10.1038/s41598-021-97100-1

41. Rakib, M.I., Javed Hossain, M., Nobi, A.: Feature ranking and network analysis of global financial indices. PLoS ONE 17, e0269483 (2022). https://doi.org/10.1371/JOURNAL.PONE.0269483

42. Yang, C., Chen, Y., Hao, W., Shen, Y., Tang, M., Niu, L.: Effects of financial crisis on the industry sector of Chinese stock market-from a perspective of complex network. Mod. Phys. Lett. B. 28, 1–13 (2014). https://doi.org/10.1142/S0217984914501024

43. Kharrazi, A., Fath, B.D.: Measuring global oil trade dependencies: an application of the pointwise mutual information method. Energy Policy 88, 271–277 (2016). https://doi.org/10.1016/j.enpol.2015.10.017

44. Aguilar, D., Oliva, B., Marino Buslje, C.: Mapping the mutual information network of enzymatic families in the protein structure to unveil functional features. PLoS ONE 7, 1–12 (2012). https://doi.org/10.1371/journal.pone.0041430

45. Lee, J., Kim, D.W.: Mutual Information-based multi-label feature selection using interaction information. Expert Syst. Appl. 42, 2013–2025 (2015). https://doi.org/10.1016/j.eswa.2014.09.063

46. Wang, J., et al.: Reconstructing regulatory networks from the dynamic plasticity of gene expression by mutual information. Nucleic Acids Res. 41, 1–8 (2013). https://doi.org/10.1093/nar/gkt147

47. Guo, X., Zhang, H., Tian, T.: Development of stock correlation networks using mutual information and financial big data. PLoS One 13, e0195941 (2018). https://doi.org/10.1371/journal.pone.0195941

48. Li, B., Pi, D.: Analysis of global stock index data during crisis period via complex network approach. PLoS ONE 13, 1–16 (2018). https://doi.org/10.1371/journal.pone.0200600

49. Kumar, S., Deo, N.: Correlation and network analysis of global financial indices. Phys. Rev. E - Stat. Nonlinear Soft Matter Phys. **86**, 1–8 (2012). https://doi.org/10.1103/PhysRevE.86.026101
50. Nobi, A., Maeng, S.E., Ha, G.G., Lee, J.W.: Effects of global financial crisis on network structure in a local stock market. Phys. A Stat. Mech. its Appl. **407**, 135–143 (2014). https://doi.org/10.1016/j.physa.2014.03.083
51. Nobi, A., Lee, S., Kim, D.H., Lee, J.W.: Correlation and network topologies in global and local stock indices. Phys. Lett. Sect. A Gen. At. Solid State Phys. **378**(34), 2482–2489 (2014). https://doi.org/10.1016/j.physleta.2014.07.009
52. Onnela, J.P., Chakraborti, A., Kaski, K., Kertész, J.: Dynamic asset trees and Black Monday. Phys. A Stat. Mech. its Appl. **324**, 247–252 (2003). https://doi.org/10.1016/S0378-4371(02)01882-4
53. Bonanno, G., Caldarelli, G., Lillo, F., Mantegna, R.N.: Topology of correlation-based minimal spanning trees in real and model markets. Phys. Rev. E - Stat. Phys. Plasmas, Fluids Relat. Interdiscip. Top. **68**, 4–7 (2003). https://doi.org/10.1103/PhysRevE.68.046130
54. Onnela, J.P., Chakraborti, A., Kaski, K., Kertész, J., Kanto, A.: Dynamics of market correlations: Taxonomy and portfolio analysis. Phys. Rev. E - Stat. Phys. Plasmas Fluids Relat. Interdiscip. Top. **68**, 1–12 (2003). https://doi.org/10.1103/PhysRevE.68.056110
55. Coelho, R., Gilmore, C.G., Lucey, B., Richmond, P., Hutzler, S.: The evolution of interdependence in world equity markets-evidence from minimum spanning trees. Phys. A Stat. Mech. its Appl. **376**, 455–466 (2007). https://doi.org/10.1016/j.physa.2006.10.045
56. Yahoo Finance: Major World Indices. https://finance.yahoo.com/world-indices
57. Kraskov, A., Stögbauer, H., Grassberger, P.: Estimating mutual information. Phys. Rev. E - Stat. Phys. Plasmas Fluids Relat. Interdiscip. Top. **69**, 16 (2004). https://doi.org/10.1103/PhysRevE.69.066138
58. Huang, W.Q., Zhuang, X.T., Yao, S.: A network analysis of the Chinese stock market. Phys. A Stat. Mech. its Appl. **388**, 2956–2964 (2009). https://doi.org/10.1016/j.physa.2009.03.028
59. Latora, V., Marchiori, M.: Efficient behavior of small-world networks. Phys. Rev. Lett. **87**, 198701-1–198701-4 (2001). https://doi.org/10.1103/PhysRevLett.87.198701

Employee Attrition Analysis Using CatBoost

Md. Monir Ahammod Bin Atique(✉), Md. Nesarul Hoque,
and Md. Jamal Uddin

Department of Computer Science and Engineering, Bangabandhu Sheikh Mujibur
Rahman Science and Technology University, Gopalganj 8100, Bangladesh
monircse@bsmrstu.edu.bd

Abstract. Almost everywhere, organizations or individuals can adopt technologies that can be supportive to make decisions and get insight from data: artificial intelligence (AI) is an advanced new technology which is used to aid organizations in their business procedures, organizational factors, and human resources management. Employees are the nucleus of the organization. When employees leave an institution of their own volition, the company suffers greatly from various dimensions. Nowadays, we have seen a huge change in companies due to COVID-19; employees are getting fired or resigning voluntarily. It is a big issue to keep the productivity constant of a company or individual as human resources (HR) has to spend a lot of time, from the selection process to the training process. In these circumstances, minimizing the attrition rate is one of the primary concerns of the Human Resource department, which deals with staffing, development, and compensation. From this point of view, more research projects have been done through statistical analysis and applying various types of machine learning (ML) and data mining techniques such as Extreme Gradient Boosting, Random Forest, Naive Bayes, decision trees, etc. In this paper, a state-of-the-art boosting method, CatBoost, and a feature engineering process have been applied for detecting and analyzing employee attrition. Our detection system shows the utmost performance compared to the other existing systems and sorts out the significant reasons behind the attrition. It reveals the best recall rate of 0.89, with an accuracy of .8945.

Keywords: Employee Attrition · Machine Learning · CatBoost

1 Introduction

Employee attrition is when an employee departs due to resignation, retirement, or other reasons. There are two types of attrition: voluntary and non-voluntary. In voluntary attrition, employees leave a company for personal reasons, but in non-voluntary attrition, an employer can fire an employee for any reason [2,13]. Attrition is a significant problem for the industry that negatively impacts organizational growth and reputation. This cannot be avoided when individuals leave

© ICST Institute for Computer Sciences, Social Informatics and Telecommunications Engineering 2023
Published by Springer Nature Switzerland AG 2023. All Rights Reserved
Md. S. Satu et al. (Eds.): MIET 2022, LNICST 491, pp. 644–658, 2023.
https://doi.org/10.1007/978-3-031-34622-4_51

their positions for personal and professional reasons. A high attrition rate creates many problems from different perspectives for a company, such as loss of experienced employees, recruitment costs, training, and administrative costs, unstable working environment, etc. Today, businesses need to cut down on attrition because it can be costly and hard to find out an exact match for a lost employee [15].

Employees are currently experiencing various issues at work and in their personal lives, which leads to early attrition. We should spend more additional time addressing what is the requirements for their advancement in their working place. After that, we can begin predicting who will depart in the next several years so that we can give them appropriate opportunities. These initiatives will motivate employees as well as assist the organization in retaining talent.

Nowadays, various machine learning algorithms play a significant function in predicting employee turnover. These forecast systems greatly support any organization's human resource (HR) department. If the HR department has previous information about employee attrition, then they have an option to take the necessary steps to resolve that issue in time.

Several machine learning algorithms like Extreme Gradient Boosting (XGBoost), Random Forest (RF), Naive Bayes (NB), Grey Wolf Optimisation (GWO), decision tree (DT), and so on have been developed in earlier studies to predict employee attrition automatically and reliably [14,16,18,23–25]. Even though their testing accuracy is satisfactory, there is still room for improvement. In most cases, researchers consider a huge number of features and do not focus on feature engineering [16,19]. In this study, we have analyzed the IBM HR Analytics dataset, available on the IBM dataset website or Kaggle[1]. We undertake some eminence feature engineering to enhance the prediction of employee turnover because there are many features in our dataset. In addition, we experiment with some novel models like CatBoost (Categorical Boosting) [8,20], XGBoost, RF, and some well-established classical models, such as Regression (LR), and Support Vector Machine (SVM) with Linear and RBF kernel for predicting Employee Attrition. One of them is the CatBoost, a gradient boosting technique that is highly useful for categorical features. Our dataset has many categorical features, and CatBoost works well for these features. As a result, in this research, we concentrated specifically on this boosting algorithm to reliably predict attrition to assist any company in improving alternative retention methods for crucial employees and enhancing employee satisfaction. The following are the primary goals of this research:

- Appropriate analysis of the features for employee attrition.
- Improve the system's detection accuracy.
- Suggest more essential features that are responsible for employee attrition.

This paper is organized as follows. Section 2 represents the Literature Review. Then, Sect. 3 outlines the methodology and presents a brief description of the

---

[1] www.ibm.com/communities/analytics/watson-analytics-blog/hr-employee-attrition/.

dataset, preprocessing tasks, feature engineering, and proposed models during the detection of employee attrition. Section 4 shows the results and its analysis. At last, Sect. 5 presents concluding statements of this study and mentions the direction of the future research.

2   Literature Review

Employee attrition is seen as an organization's capital loss [22]. Minimizing the attrition rate is one of the major challenges in any business organization. There are a number of studies on employee attrition that we have discovered. We have discussed these as follows:

Jain and Nayyar [16] applied one of the powerful decision tree-based boosting algorithms named XGBoost along with explaining some important features separately. Although they had achieved smart accuracy of 89.10%, they did not mention a comparative study with the other machine learning algorithms.

Another study was undertaken by Abhisek and Ajit [24], who performed fundamental exploratory data analysis before progressing to feature engineering and achieved 85% accuracy through the Random Forest classifier model.

Nilasha and Anil [14] worked on a balanced dataset of employees aged 20 to 39 years old. They revealed that the Random Forest classifier had a higher recall value but a lower precision value than Naive Bayes.

Usha and Balaji [25] showed in their study that there was a correlation between factors employed in the workplace and the decision to stay in business. They proved that clustering provides less accuracy than classification algorithms. They also showed the performance of several classification techniques and then clustering techniques utilising the open-source program (Waikato Environment for Knowledge Analysis).

Punnoose and Ajit [21] distinguished different types of machine learning methods in order to predict employee turnover by considering the accuracy, running time, and memory utilization. After the exploration, they clearly showed that the XGBoost technique outperformed the other predictive learning methods in the case of accuracy (86%) and memory consumption (12%). However, feature analysis or feature importance with respect to employee turnover is not mentioned throughout this research.

Yadav et al. [26] did the exploration on experienced employees and showed that salary was not only the main reason for the turnover, there had some others facts also like - job satisfaction, working hours and so on. In this paper, they had applied different machine learning techniques and given the comparative figures to each other in order to show the best one. However, only 11 features has been considered here to take a decision on the employee churn without showing the feature importance values with respect to the target attribute.

Sehgal et al. [23] reduced the processing time and consumption of memory during the prediction of employee attrition with the help of a data mining technique called Grey Wolf Optimisation (GWO) by comparing with Particle Swarm Optimisation (PSO) and a traditional decision tree-based method named C5.0.

In that paper, they experimented on only five selected features i.e. Home Distance, Education Area, Environment Satisfaction, Work-Life Balance, and Gender from the data set of IBM Watson Human Resource Employee Attrition 2, which is come from the Kaggle.

Previously, accuracy was used as the major assessment criteria for turnover prediction. Several ML algorithms have been tested and assessed on various data-sets. [18]. In our proposed system, we concentrate on feature engineering and choose a categorical feature-based classifier, CatBoost, to handle employee attrition issues.

3   Research Methodology

This section covered a detailed explanation of datasets, data preprocessing, feature engineering, and model classifiers. The overall process diagram is illustrated in Fig. 1.

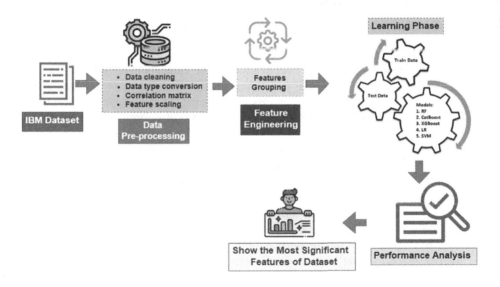

Fig. 1. System's Process Diagram.

3.1   Dataset

In this experiment, the dataset has been collected from the IBM HR Data Scientists who generated it in order to uncover the reasons behind employee erosion. Dataset contains 1470 entries where each one has 34 features and a target variable [See Table 1]. Table 1 represents a brief description with a p-value that indicates the features' significance. Our study performed a chi-square statistical test in which the threshold of significance is 0.05. A p-value of less than 0.05 means $p < 0.05$ is considered statistically significant. The target variable (Attrition) has two categories: yes and no. 237 employees are in the "yes" attrition group, whereas 1233 are in the "no" attrition group. Having an unequal distribution of records in the level class, like one class having a higher number of records than the other classes, then a dataset is called an imbalanced dataset. Therefore, this is not a balanced dataset. On the other hand, a balanced standard dataset has an equal number of distributions in the target classes. For example, we have a dataset of 1000 patients, out of which 500 are cancer patients, and the rest (500) are healthy patients.

- In this paper, a standard dataset is used. It is a binary classification problem.
- Gender, education, last promotion, work environment, and so on are some of standard HR attributes.
- The dataset had 1470 employee records having 35 attributes.
- Within the 1470 entries, 237 employees were in the "yes" attrition group, whereas 1233 were in the "no" attrition category.

3.2 Data Pre-processing

This subsection describes the following pre-processing tasks that will be used for subsequent processing, such as feature engineering and classifier implementation.

- **Missing value handling:** Since no missing values were detected in this dataset. Consequently, we skipped this step. But if any dataset contains missing values then we should handle missing values by following some strategies.
- **Data type conversion:** Before developing a detection model, it is necessary to transform categorical features into a numerical representation. In the case of boolean types of nominal categorical variables, a label encoding approach has been utilized to assign the value 0 or 1 to each data point. In the case of the "Gender" feature, the number 0 corresponds to "Female," whereas the value 1 corresponds to "Male
- **Show the correlation matrix** The correlation coefficient is the statistical measurement through which a linear relationship can be calculated between the variables. From the correlation matrix, we find an idea of dependencies, such as which features have strong dependencies and which features have weak dependencies. Figure 2 shows a diagrammatic view of the correlation matrix where the value ranges between −1 and +1. The value +1 means completely correlated, and -1 means the opposite. The white space means there is no relationship with other features.
- **Feature scaling:** A substantial difference between data points for a single feature can frequently slow down the algorithm's optimization procedures. Feature scaling may aid in the enhancement of classification performance.

3.3 Feature Engineering

Throughout the study of all the features, certain features are omitted, while others are included for this experiment. Below are specifics on feature exclusion and inclusion:

Table 1. Dataset with Explanation

Features	Data Types	Description	P-value
Age	Numeric	Age of the employees ranging from 18 to 60	2.57
Attrition	Categorical	An employee quits from the company (1=Yes, 0=No)	0.0
Business Travel	Categorical	(0 = Non Travel, 1=Travel Frequently, 2 = Tavel Rarely)	5.6
Daily Rate	Numeric	Salary levels ranging from 102 to 1499	0.62
Department	Categorical	(0 = Human Resources, 1 = Research and Development, 2 = Sales)	0.0
Distance From Home	Numeric	The Distance Between Work and Home	0.09
Education	Numeric	Education levels ranging 1 to 5	0.54
Education Field	Categorical	(0 to 5 different education label)	0.0
Employee Count	Numeric	Counted number of workers	-
Employee Number	Numeric	Employee's unique id	-
Environment Satisfaction	Numeric	Environmental Satisfaction	5.12
Gender	Categorical	(0 = Female, 1 = Male)	0.29
Hourly Rate Salary	Numeric	The hourly salary rate is between 30 and 100	0.41
Job Involvement	Numeric	Number of jobs involved	2.86
Job Level	Numeric	Level of job of an employee	6.63
Job Role	Categorical	(0 to 8 different job roles)	2.75
Job Satisfaction	Numeric	Workplace satisfaction	0.0
Marital Status	Categorical	(0=Divorced, 1=Married, 2=Single)	9.45
Monthly Income	Numeric	Monthly salary	0.70
Monthly Rate	Numeric	Monthy rate	0.65
Num. of Companies	Numeric	Total number of institutions have worked at	0.0
Over 18	Categorical	(1=Yes, 0=No)	-
Over Time	Categorical	(0=No, 1=Yes)	8.15
Percent Salary Hike	Numeric	Percentage increase in salary	0.49
Performance Rating	Numeric	Performance evaluation	0.99
Relationship Satisfaction	Numeric	Relations satisfaction	0.15
Standard Hours	Numeric	Standard hours	-
Stock Option Level	Numeric	Stock options	4.37
Total Working Years	Numeric	Total years worked	1.58
Training Times Last Year	Numeric	Time spent in training	0.01
Work Life Balance	Numeric	Time spent outside and at work	0.0
Years At Company	Numeric	Total number of years working in the company	2.84
Years In Current Role	Numeric	Years in current role	4.05
Years Since Last Promotion	Numeric	Year of last promotion	0.11
Years Under Present Manager	Numeric	Years paid to work under the present manager	-

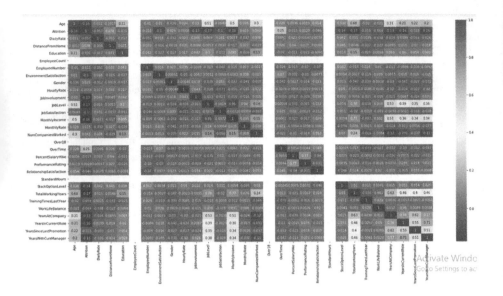

Fig. 2. Correlation of the feature variables.

Feature Exclusion: After analyzing the correlation matrix, it is evident that "Employee Count," "Over 18," and "Standard Hours" have no relationship with "Attrition", the target feature. Observing the "Employee Number" column revealed that each entry has a unique value, indicating that this column has no impact on predicting employee attrition. Thus, by eliminating these four attributes from the input features, the remaining 30 features and one target variable have been included.

Feature Inclusion: In our study, "feature inclusion" refers to the grouping of features and introduces new resulting features. The idea behind the inclusion of the features is that some of the features basically represent one feature. For example, in our dataset, "Environment Satisfaction", "Job Involvement", "Job Satisfaction", "Relationship Satisfaction", and "Work-Life Balance" features highly indicated a new feature that we named "Total Satisfaction". That's why we introduced the new features by eliminating the previous ones (such as "Environment Satisfaction", "Job Involvement", "Job Satisfaction", etc.) that were mentioned previously. The empirical study has resulted in the addition of the following two new features, which are also illustrated in Fig. 3:

- **Experience Less Than Three Years:** This new feature is the result of combining the "Total Working Years" and "Years At Company" attributes. People with less than three years of total work experience who have worked for any company will have a label value of 1, otherwise, it would be 0.
- **Total Satisfaction:** Employee satisfaction is comprised of "Environment Satisfaction", "Job Involvement", "Job Satisfaction", "Relationship Satisfaction" and "Work-Life Balance". Taking the average of all of these attributes into account, we've created another new feature.

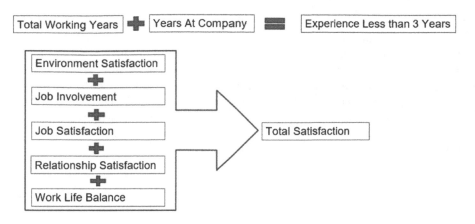

Fig. 3. Grouping of feature variables.

After completing the above exclusion and inclusion processes, we group all the features into two categories: Feature Engineering Type 1 (FET-1) and Feature Engineering Type 2 (FET-2). These two types are explained below:

- **FET-1:** Through the inclusion and exclusion process, we obtained 30 input features and one output feature. In FET-1, we are adding two new features ("Experience Less Than Three Years" and "Total Satisfaction") and removing seven features that are beneath the two new features. Finally, FET-1 includes 25 input features and one output feature.

- **FET-2:** After the inclusion and exclusion processes were the same as in FET-1, we obtained 30 input features. In FET-2 we are adding only one new feature, "Total Satisfaction", and removing five features that are beneath the one new feature. Finally, FET-2 includes 26 input features and one output feature.

3.4 Methods

Our dataset has two output classes, "Attrition" and "Non-Attrition", so we primarily work with classification models. Attrition is when an employee leaves the company, while Non-Attrition is when an employee stays with the company. Because of this, this work uses five different machine-learning classification models, including three ensemble models. Training data is used to train classification models on what to do, and test data is used to evaluate the model's performance. Five machine learning classifier techniques, including Random Forest (RF), Support Vector Machine (SVM) with Linear and RBF kernel, Extreme Gradient Boosting (XGBoost), Categorical Boosting (CatBoost), and Logistic Regression (LR), have been utilised in this study. The operating principle of these algorithms is explained below:

Random Forest: RF is the widely used machine learning algorithm. This model uses a method called ensemble-based bagging learning. The idea behind bagging is that from the original dataset, many subsets of the input features are made by choosing observations with replacements (called bootstrapping) for training different decision trees. The final decision is made by taking the majority vote from all of the prediction decision trees to get a solution. This method differs from ordinary trees in that it uses averaging to help reduce the overfitting problem of a single decision tree [3]. Each node is split based on the best split predictor [17].

Support Vector Machine: The most popular and widely used supervised machine-learning algorithm for implementing statistical learning theory concepts is the Support Vector Machine [6]. It can be used in both classification and regression problems. The basic principle behind SVM is to find the best maximum marginal hyperplane that separates the dataset into two or more classes. Its most popular kernel is SVC. When dataset samples are huge, it is the best choice [7,10,11].

Extreme Gradient Boosting: XGBoost is an abbreviation for the eXtreme Gradient Boosting package. This gradient-boosting framework implementation is scalable and effective. The package contains an efficient linear model solver, as well as a tree learning technique [4]. Numerous objective tasks, like regression, classification, and ranking, are among its capabilities.

Categorical Boosting: CatBoost is a recently open-source machine learning algorithm from Yandex. It can easily integrate with deep learning frameworks like Google's TensorFlow and Apple's Core. ML. This is a novel gradient-boosting approach that handles categorical features better [8,20]. To top it up, it provides best-in-class accuracy. Our dataset has many categorical features, and CatBoost works well for these features. However, the "CatBoost" name comes from two words "Category" and "Boosting". "Boost" comes from gradient boosting machine learning algorithm as this library is based on gradient boosting. Gradient boosting is a robust machine learning algorithm widely applied to multiple business challenges like fraud detection, recommendation items, and forecasting, and it performs well. It also employs a unique approach for computing leaf values when choosing the tree structure, which aids in the reduction of overfitting. As a result, the new approach beats prior methods including, gradient boosted decision trees (GBDT), XGBoost, and LightGBM.

Logistic Regression: Logistic regression is one of the simplest linear models. It uses the sigmoid function to make a map of the predicted values from 0 to 1. Logistic regression is often used when the target variable is categorical and has two class values, such as yes/no, win/lose, or leave/stay, as in the IBM attrition dataset [5]. The formula defines a simple logistic function:

$$Y = e^x/(1 + e^x) \tag{1}$$

In the above equation, x is the independent variable (input features) and Y is the conditional variable or the label ("Attrition"), and e is the Euler's number.

3.5 Evaluation Criteria for Model(s)

In this study, classifier performance was assessed using Confusion Matrix, Precision, Recall, F1 measure, and Accuracy.

Accuracy. Accuracy is defined as the number of accurate predictions divided by the total number of predictions [12].

$$Accuracy = \frac{TruePositive + TrueNegative}{TruePositive + TrueNegative + FalsePositive + FalseNegative} \tag{2}$$

Precision. Precision is the proportion of correctly classified positive records (True Positive) to the whole number of correctly classified positive samples [12].

$$Precision = \frac{TruePositives}{TruePositives + FalsePositives} \tag{3}$$

Recall. Recall is the ratio of the number of accurately identified Positive records to the whole number of Positive instances [1]. Recall assesses the model's capacity to identify positive samples.

$$Recall = \frac{TruePositives}{TruePositives + FalseNegatives} \tag{4}$$

F1 Score. The F1 is the balance between accuracy and recall for any classifier [1]. The F1 score is essential when the dataset is imbalanced.

$$F_1 = (\frac{2 * Precision * Recall}{Precision + Recall}) \tag{5}$$

4 Results and Discussions

We have experimented with five classifier models (CatBoost, XGBoost, RF, LR, SVM with Linear and RBF kernel) over two feature engineering types: FET-1 and FET-2. Before applying the models, we performed the dataset-splitting process. Using the "train_test_split" method, We divided the IBM dataset into two parts for training: 80% data for training and 20% data for testing. The parameter "stratify" is used in this method to return training and test subsets with the same distribution of class labels as the input dataset. Firstly, the model learns the relationship among the input data samples using the training dataset.

Then the testing dataset is used to evaluate the model to see how well it predicts the new dataset and calculates the errors.

CatBoost outperforms the other classifier by adding two additional features, "Experience Less Than 3 Years" and "Total Satisfaction", as FET-1. It enhanced accuracy over the other models, increasing it to .8945 as shown in Table 3. Precision and recall value reveals that CatBoost is the best performer in this feature engineering type. CatBoost also outperformed the previous studies in terms of specificity (greater than 84.00%) and error rate (less than 11%). In FET-2, we focused on 26 features. It also enhanced accuracy, raising it to .8843, as displayed in Table 3. Precision and recall values are decent and high enough, revealing again that CatBoost performs well in this feature engineering type.

IBM datasets contain categorical features for prediction. Categorical features have discrete, non-comparable values (e.g., user ID or name of a city). Before training gradient boosting, categorical features are converted to numbers. We introduce a new gradient-boosting technique that handles categorical features automatically during preprocessing. The algorithm's improved schema for computing prediction.

In summary, in terms of accuracy and error rate, the CatBoost model outperforms its counterpart, XGBoost. CatBoost and XGBoost classifiers outperform the other classifiers during training, but CatBoost surpasses XGBoost considerably during testing. The CatBoost classifier beats the other classifiers if we consider precision, recall, and f1-score. When we have a large dataset with categorical variables, then CatBoost is the best choice. It can convert categories into numbers without explicit preprocessing. This conversion is done by looking at different statistics. It is the only boosting algorithm with a very short prediction time. While predicting, it is 8 times faster than XGBoost. It has been discovered that our model and feature engineering beat the other techniques, as indicated in Table 2 below. A comparison with the previous studies is presented in the Table 2.

On the other hand, Random Forests is an algorithm that utilizes randomness to generate significant generalization. However, it is still insufficient to avoid the over-fitting problem in this scenario. On the other hand, XGBoost tries to make new trees that go well with the ones that are already there [21]. Boosting improves training for difficult-to-classify data points

The importance of the best classifier of the two FE types is shown in Fig. 4. So, we focused on the feature importance of CatBoost only. After exploring feature importance, we can conclude that the key ten features (MonthlyIncome, OverTime, Age, Total Satisfaction, Distance From Home, Job Role, Hourly Rate, Stock Options Level, Marital Status, and Number of Companies Worked for) lead to employee attrition. We can highly claim that our included new feature 'Total Satisfaction' has a significant impact on predicting employee attrition.

In comparison to the previous study, we found very few studies in which the authors focus on feature engineering or selection. Jain and Nayyar did a study on this topic. They added three additional features to this dataset using feature engineering. Based on what they found, the XGBoost performs better than the

Table 2. A comparative overview of (IBM Dataset) relevant research works

Authors	Recommend Model(s)	Evaluation Metrics
Najafi-Zangeneh, Saeed, et al. [19]	LR	Accuracy(.8100), F1 Score(0.56)
K. K. Mohbey [18]	LR	Accuracy(.8600), F1 Score(0.83)
Fallucchi, Francesca, et al. [9]	LSVC	Accuracy(.8790)
Qutub, Aseel, et al. [22]	LR	Accuracy(.8843), F1 Score(0.57)
Jain and Nayyar [16]	XGBoost	Accuracy(.8910), F1 Score(Not mentioned in the paper)
Abhisek and Ajit [24]	SVM	Accuracy(.8844), F1 Score(Not mentioned in the paper)
Proposed	CatBoost	**Accuracy(.8945), F1 Score(0.88)**

Table 3. Model Performances

Feature Engineering Types	Model	Accuracy(%)	Precision	Recall	F1-score
FET-1	RF	.8707	0.86	0.87	0.84
	CatBoost	**.8945**	**0.89**	**0.89**	**0.88**
	XGBoost	.8843	0.87	0.88	0.87
	LR	.8911	0.88	0.89	0.88
	SVM (Linear kernel)	.8877	0.88	0.89	0.87
	SVM (RBF kernel)	.8809	0.87	0.88	0.86
FET-2	RF	.8742	0.87	0.87	0.85
	CatBoost	**.8843**	**0.88**	**0.88**	**0.87**
	XGBoost	.8809	0.87	0.88	0.87
	LR	.8775	0.86	0.88	0.87
	SVM (Linear kernel)	.8775	0.88	0.88	0.85
	SVM (RBF kernel)	.8877	0.88	0.89	0.87

random forest, the decision tree, and other classifiers. In their extensive analysis, XGBoost achieved .8910 accuracy.

Najafi-Zangeneh, Saeed, et al. conducted more research on this dataset. They also emphasized feature selection in their research methodologies. Logistic Regression had the highest accuracy in their study, with an accuracy of .81. The

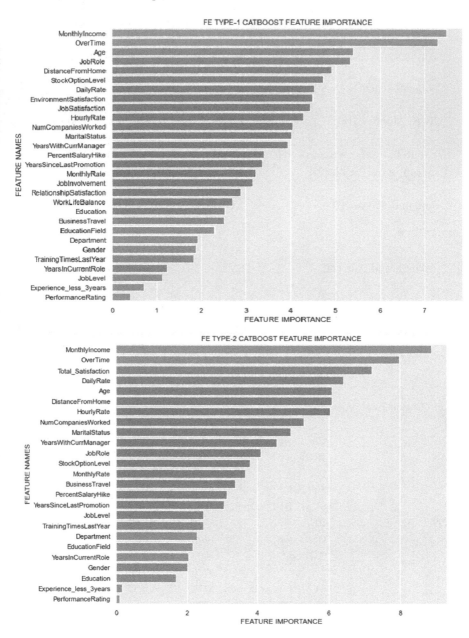

Fig. 4. Features Importance of CatBoost

rest of the study did not highlight feature engineering and instead concentrated solely on the classification method.

Finally, we can say our feature engineering techniques add a new dimension to this IBM dataset and increase the predictive model's accuracy.

5   Conclusions

The suggested technique has the greatest detection accuracy and F1-score for employee attrition, with .8945 and 0.88 respectively. Following a rigorous evaluation of the given features, we propose additional features and apply the CatBoost model to the newly proposed features. Therefore, we can enhance the performance of the current detection system. At the same time, we have outlined the key ten factors directly responsible for the attrition. Our proposed approach will be of considerable assistance to the company's HR department in managing attrition. The company will take the necessary steps for vulnerable employees who are more prone to attrition. In that way, a company can retain its positive work atmosphere and save time and money by avoiding the new recruitment process. In the future, we will further study the 34 features and experiment with various cutting-edge models to improve the accuracy.

References

1. Agarwal, R.: The 5 classification evaluation metrics every data scientist must know. towardsdatascience. com 17 (2019)
2. Allen, D.G.: Retaining talent: A Guide to Analyzing and Managing Employee Turnover. SHRM Foundations Alexandria, VA (2008)
3. Breiman, L.: Random forests. Mach. Learn. **45**(1), 5–32 (2001)
4. Chen, T., et al.: Xgboost: extreme gradient boosting. R package version 0.4-2 **1**(4), 1–4 (2015)
5. Chomas, J.E., Dayton, P.A., May, D.J., Ferrara, K.W.: Threshold of fragmentation for ultrasonic contrast agents. J. Biomed. Opt. **6**(2), 141–150 (2001)
6. Cortes, C., Vapnik, V.: Support-vector networks. Mach. Learn. **20**(3), 273–297 (1995)
7. Debole, F., Sebastiani, F.: An analysis of the relative hardness of reuters-21578 subsets. J. Am. Soc. Inform. Sci. Technol. **56**(6), 584–596 (2005)
8. Dorogush, A.V., Ershov, V., Gulin, A.: Catboost: gradient boosting with categorical features support. arXiv preprint arXiv:1810.11363 (2018)
9. Fallucchi, F., Coladangelo, M., Giuliano, R., William De Luca, E.: Predicting employee attrition using machine learning techniques. Computers **9**(4), 86 (2020)
10. Hasan, R.A., Mohammed, M.A., Salih, Z.H., Ameedeen, M.A.B., Țăpuș, N., Mohammed, M.N.: Hso: a hybrid swarm optimization algorithm for reducing energy consumption in the cloudlets. Telkomnika **16**(5), 2144–2154 (2018)
11. Hasan, R.A., Mohammed, M.A., Țăpuș, N., Hammood, O.A.: A comprehensive study: Ant colony optimization (aco) for facility layout problem. In: 2017 16th RoEduNet conference: networking in education and research (RoEduNet), pp. 1–8. IEEE (2017)
12. Hossin, M., Sulaiman, M.N.: A review on evaluation metrics for data classification evaluations. Int. J. Data Mining Knowl. Manage. Process **5**(2), 1 (2015)
13. Igbaria, M., Greenhaus, J.H., Parasuraman, S.: Career orientations of mis employees: an empirical analysis. MIS quarterly, pp. 151–169 (1991)
14. Jadhav, A., et al.: Churn prediction of employees using machine learning techniques. Tehnički glasnik **15**(1), 51–59 (2021)

15. Jain, P.K., Jain, M., Pamula, R.: Explaining and predicting employees' attrition: a machine learning approach. SN Appl. Sci. **2**(4), 1–11 (2020)
16. Jain, R., Nayyar, A.: Predicting employee attrition using xgboost machine learning approach. In: 2018 International Conference on System Modeling & Advancement in Research Trends (smart), pp. 113–120. IEEE (2018)
17. Liaw, A., Wiener, M., et al.: Classification and regression by randomforest. R news **2**(3), 18–22 (2002)
18. Mohbey, K.K.: Employee's attrition prediction using machine learning approaches. In: Machine Learning and Deep Learning in Real-Time Applications, pp. 121–128. IGI Global (2020)
19. Najafi-Zangeneh, S., Shams-Gharneh, N., Arjomandi-Nezhad, A., Hashemkhani Zolfani, S.: An improved machine learning-based employees attrition prediction framework with emphasis on feature selection. Mathematics **9**(11), 1226 (2021)
20. Prokhorenkova, L., Gusev, G., Vorobev, A., Dorogush, A.V., Gulin, A.: Catboost: unbiased boosting with categorical features. In: Advances in Neural Information Processing Systems, vol. 31 (2018)
21. Punnoose, R., Ajit, P.: Prediction of employee turnover in organizations using machine learning algorithms. Algorithms **4**(5), C5 (2016)
22. Qutub, A., Al-Mehmadi, A., Al-Hssan, M., Aljohani, R., Alghamdi, H.S.: Prediction of employee attrition using machine learning and ensemble methods. Int. J. Mach. Learn. Comput **11** (2021)
23. Sehgal, K., Bindra, H., Batra, A., Jain, R.: Prediction of employee attrition using gwo and pso optimised models of c5. 0 used with association rules and analysis of optimisers. In: Innovations in Computer Science and Engineering, pp. 1–8. Springer (2019)
24. Sethy, A., Raut, A.K.: Employee attrition rate prediction using machine learning approach. Turkish Journal of Physiotherapy and Rehabilitation 32, 3
25. Usha, P., Balaji, N.: A comparative study on machine learning algorithms for employee attrition prediction. In: IOP Conference Series: Materials Science and Engineering, vol. 1085, p. 012029. IOP Publishing (2021)
26. Yadav, S., Jain, A., Singh, D.: Early prediction of employee attrition using data mining techniques. In: 2018 IEEE 8th International Advance Computing Conference (IACC), pp. 349–354. IEEE (2018)

Readiness Towards Industry 4.0 of Selected Industrial Sector

Choudhury Abul Anam Rashed$^{(\boxtimes)}$, Mst. Nasima Bagum, and Mahfuzul Haque

Shahjalal University of Science and Technology, Sylhet, Bangladesh
{rashed-ipe,nasima-ipe}@sust.edu

Abstract. Technology and innovation are the driving forces behind any company's long-term success. Industry 4.0 targeted to achieve the standard level of operational effectiveness and productivity. In this study work, it aims to determine the adoption level of technology and innovation management and the barriers to implementation in the manufacturing sector. Data value was collected through a semi-structured questionnaire. The respondents were chosen based on their relevance to the management of technology in their respective sectors. Both face-to-face and online interviews were performed. Analysis was performed using SPSS 25 and Microsoft Office Excel 2016. Obtained results showed that around 37% of the organizations small scale digitization as 25% of their products and services are digitized. Approximately 46% of organizations use medium digitization & integration at the life cycle phase of the product digitization. At the adoption level, 80% of the manufacturing industries want to transform their factory into a digital model through digitization and 72% of the industry's responses are instantaneous with the change of situation. 27% of the organizations realized that customer data are relevant to their business. Based on the overall results, two of the hypotheses were generated to testify the relevance of the Internet of Things (IoT) and information sharing with the implementation of industry 4.0 (I4.0).

Keywords: Technology · innovation · Industry 4.0 (I4.0) · IoT · Information Sharing

1 Introduction

Technological adoption is alarming task for small and medium-sized enterprises (SMEs) due to lack of resources. when passing through the next level of automatization, Industry 4.0 need to attain the complicated level through effectiveness and productivity. Industry 4.0 is a new stage of the industrial value chain which is known as the 4th industrial revolution.

Bangladesh's export-oriented RMG and manufacturing industry began as a modest non-traditional export sector in the late 1970s. The industry deserves special recognition for at least three reasons: (a) it is the single largest earner, accounting for approximately 77% of the country's annual foreign exchange earnings; (b) it has been the fastest growing industry in recent years, and (c) it employs approximately 4.2 million people. The

Md. S. Satu et al. (Eds.): MIET 2022, LNICST 491, pp. 659–673, 2023.
https://doi.org/10.1007/978-3-031-34622-4_52

Manufacturing industry's contribution to Bangladesh's economy is well-known, well-appreciated & well-respected. This paper trying to show the combined effect of IoT, Information sharing, and visibility on the Implementation of Industry 4.0.

2 Objectives of the Research

The objectives of study-

- Studying the readiness of particular manufacturing sectors towards Industry 4.0.
- To develop hypothesises and testify to the relation among IoT, Information sharing with the implementation of I4.0.

3 Literature Review

I 4.0 is totally important for the development of a country as it automates and exchange data in technologies related to manufacturing [1–3]. Countries with high technological integration along with innovation can improve their production capability as well as productivity.

The fundamental element of the 4th industrial revolution is the IoT and services. In developed nations, IoT and services are essential part of manufacturing, particularly in high-tech manufacturing and service industries, such as automobiles, aircraft production, logistics, insurance, and the field of communications [4–6].

The manufacturing sector of the world gaining many advantages throughout the Information and Communication Technologies (ICT), which is now acting as the driver of automation (Industry 3.0). IoT, cyber-physical systems, cloud computing, and virtual reality which are the ingredients of industry 4.0 has transformed manufacturing and services throughout whole supply chains [7].

SMEs implementation of technology is a difficult job because of the deficiency of resources. The main objective of fourth industrial revolution is to achieve innovative operational efficacy and productivity along with higher level of automatization. Elements of I4.0, such as IoT, data analytics, smart factory has a significant impact on sustainable business performance as well as on implementation of Information Technology (IT) [8].

Choi et al. [9] empirically examined the connection of innovation performance in manufacturing SMEs in metropolitan areas of Korea utilizing the structural equation modeling (SEM). Giotopoulos et al. [10] identified the probable determinants of ICT adoption in SMEs. Specific accentuation is put on the role of firms' mechanical capabilities, human resources of labor force and internal organization in ICT adoption estimated by five indicators alluding to the firms' expectations toward ICT implementation, ICT infrastructure, internet integration, e-sales and e-procurement.

Damanpour et al. [11] contributed on their study by inspecting double part of inward and outer wellsprings of information and data on the appropriation of administrative developments, a type of non-mechanical advancement considered fundamental for organizational effectiveness but not examined sufficiently.

Schniederjans [12] addressed on his study using three of the research inquiries. (1) Top-management adoption classification on 3D-printing speed in manufacturing (2) main drivers of 3D-printing in manufacturing from the view of top-administration on the innovation and, (3) discernments contrast based on adoption category with regards to 3D-printing adoption.

Chiu et al. [13] focused on their study by exploring the basic components for enterprises to embrace broadband mobile applications. This study examined the Technology-Organization-Environment (TOE) framework and Innovation Theory to set up comprehensive view of understanding.

New period of technological advancement and business intelligence (BI) frameworks have attracted to provide complex and competitive data contributions through choice interaction. In this study, Ul-Ain et al. [14] utilizing a systematic literature review, and present extensive information of business intelligence (BI) system achievement.

Research into the construction industry's adoption of equipment technology has been dismissed to contrast the adoption of information technology. Sepasgozar et al. [15] addressed on their research the gaps in information by wandering the role of customers and suppliers in the modern equipment technologies.

The adoption and deployment of IoT innovations prompting structural changes to Industrial Automation and Control Systems (IACS), including grater network to industrial frameworks. Boyes et al. [16] showed on their study to build up a meaning of IIoT and analyzed related halfway IoT scientific classifications.

Canetta et al. [17] proposed on their study, an Industry 4.0 system that is showing each conceivable activity towards the total digitalization of an organization both thinking about key and innovative perspectives.

Castelo-Branco et al. [18] studied on their research by estimating the presence of the variables that describe the I4.0 in manufacturing across European countries.

4 Methodology

Current research is survey-based research. In primary step the research problem was formulated. Appropriate research area was formulated. At the same time all available literature was examined to get acquainted with the selected area. Mainly state-of-the art conference, journal papers, books, web presentations and case study-based literature was reviewed.

The second step is to prepare the research design. In this step the research design was conceptualized and the questionnaires was formulated. The developed questionnaire was validated through consultation with the experts from both academics and industrial arena.

In third step data was collected in two phases. At first, an on-site visit was conducted in the manufacturing organizations to collect data. Data was collected through in-depth interviewing (face-to-face), consulting subject matter experts and related employees. In this study, engineers, production managers, planning managers, administrative officers, owners etc. of organizations interviewed from the various industries like as agro-processing industry, automotive industry, cement industry, consumer goods, electronics, plastic product manufacturing industries, pharmaceutical, RMG etc.

The secondary data was collected through the annual reports of Bangladesh Garment Manufacturers and Exporters Association (BGMEA), newspaper articles, journals and so forth.

5 Analysis and Result

To identify the readiness towards Industry 4.0, semi-structured questionnaire developed by the researchers was presented to the targeted factories. About four hundred questionnaires were dispersed through face-to-face interview and email. Among the distributed questionnaire one hundred and twenty-five factories responded.

Readiness (Strategy Level)

Degree of the Average Products Portfolio Digitization
In the studied organization degree of the average products portfolio digitization was showed up in Fig. 1. 36.7% of the organizations showing that, 25% of their products and services are digitized and portfolio is limited extent which was totally based on digitized services.

Current research is survey-based research. In primary step the research problem was formulated. Appropriate research area was formulated. At the same time all available literature was examined to get acquainted with the selected area. Mainly state-of-the art conference, journal papers, books, web presentations and case study-based literature was reviewed.

On the other hand, 19.2% of the organizations showing that, 50% of their products and services are digitized. 18.3% of the organizations products & services are fully digitized.

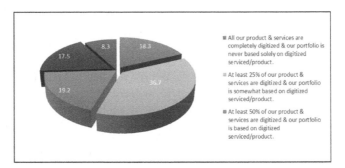

Fig. 1. Degree of the average products portfolio digitization. (MS Excel 2016)

Degree of life cycle phase of product digitization
Degree of the life cycle phase is represented in Fig. 2. About 45.8% organizations use medium digitization & integration for the products digitization, 25% organizations are using low digitization & integration for the products digitization & 21.7% organizations are using high digitization & integration for the products digitization.

It means that most of the organization are going through to digitized their products by using the medium digitization & integration process.

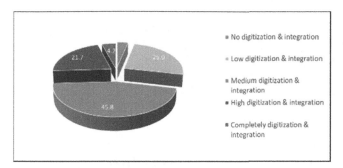

Fig. 2. Degree of the life cycle phase of the product digitization. (MS Excel 2016)

Importance of the Usage & Analysis of Data

The importance of the usage & analysis of data for the business model has been shown up in Fig. 3. About 21% of the customer's data, machine-generated data is relevant to business, 26% of the Customer data, machine-generated data is somewhat relevant to business, 25% of the data values are crucial and the customer data, machine-generated data is strongly relevant to business.

It means that one-fourth of the organizations feel the importance of the use of data analysis.

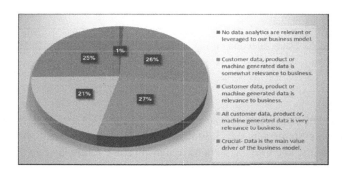

Fig. 3. Importance of the usage & analysis of data. (MS Excel 2016)

Readiness Level (Scheme)

Digital Model of factory

Digitization of manufacturing plant to create a digital model of factories responses is represented in Fig. 4. 80% responses were about yes and they collect their machine & process data during production i.e., most industries want to transform their factory into a digital model through digitization.

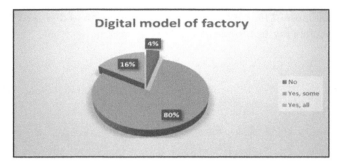

Fig. 4. Digital model of factory. (MS Excel 2016)

Data Collection Throughout the Manufacturing Process
Figure 5 depicts data collection through the manufacturing for processes, and products. Majority of the responses of data systems are following the manual processing system.

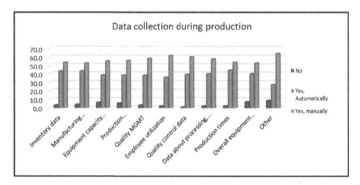

Fig. 5. Data collection during production system. (MS Excel 2016)

System of Use
Figure 6 represent the system of use & interface to the leading system. Most of the responses of the systems was yes. It indicates that the industries use those systems in their production line and every system have the interface to the leading system.

Integrated Cross-Departmental Information Sharing System
Figure 7 depicts an integrated cross-departmental inforamtion sharing system for smart operations. Most of the responses are positive through the internally between departments and externally with customers.

Production Process to Change the Production Condition
Figure 8 depicts the production process which response automatically to changes in production conditions. 52% of responses were yes only in selected areas, 5% of responses were about only in the test & pilot phase, 15% of responses were cross-enterprise for the

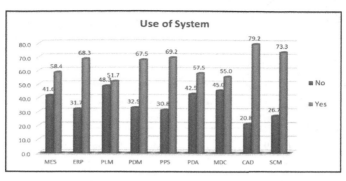

Fig. 6. System of use. (MS Excel 2016)

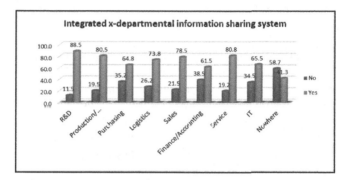

Fig. 7. Integrated x-departmental information sharing system. (MS Excel 2016)

manufacturing process that responds to changes in production conditions. Overall, 72% of industries can automatically change the production condition in real-time as long as they want to process the production.

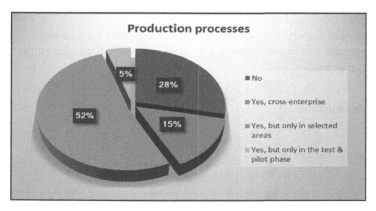

Fig. 8. Production process to change the production condition. (MS Excel 2016)

Hypothetical Analysis

Figure 9 illustrates the link between Implementation of industry 4.0 with IOT and information sharing.

Fig. 9. The Conceptual Model. (MS word 2016)

In this research work we have 3 variables. These are: 1. IOT, 2. Information sharing & visibility, 3. Implementation of Industry 4.0 for Value creation/Competitiveness Here, dependent variable is (no.3) Implementation of Industry 4.0, and the other two variables are the independent variables.

Hypothesis 1:

IoT initiatives look promising and attractive, but its significantly more complicated to implement.

IoT improves or, helps to increase the competitiveness of the business strategy. It is a logical step of using IoT technologies to improve performance and enable greater integration with organizational operations. The deployment of extensively used IoT technologies will also reduce implementation hardware, software, and labor costs, much as the PLC (Programmable Logic Controller) did years ago.

H1: IoT is strongly connected with implementation of Industry 4.0.

From hypothesis 1 where IoT is the independent variable. Here have,

- Portfolio digitization for the average products.
- Degree of life cycle phase for product digitization.
- Add-on functionalities based on ICT.
- Evaluation of equipment infrastructure based on machine-to-machine communications, machining system & integrating the machining system.
- Evaluation of adaptability of equipment infrastructure based on machine-to-machine communications, machining system & integrating the machining system.
- Digitization of factory that can create the digital model of the factory.
- To change the production condition in real time which can create an impact in production process.

Model Fit Information

Model Fitting Information

Model	Model fitting criteria	Likelihood ratio tests		
	-2 log likelihood	Chi-square	df	Sig.
Intercept only	296.632			
Final	4.734	291.897	132	.000

The model fit was assessed by using the chi-square statistic. The p-value is the probability of a statistical hypothesis test. Null hypothesis will be rejected when p-value is less than 0.05 and when p-value is greater than 0.05 then null hypothesis will be accepted.

Goodness of Fit

Goodness of fit

	Chi-square	df	Sig.
Pearson	.000	224	1.000
Deviance	.000	224	1.000

From the table it seems that the model is fit. Since the p value is greater than 0.05 then test are not statistically significant.

Pseudo R-square

Pseudo R-square

Cox and Snell	.914
Nagelkerke	.992
McFadden	.963

The model accounts for 96.3% to 99.2% of the variance and represents relatively decent-sized effects.

Likelihood Ratio Test
The Likelihood Ratio Test proves that the independent variables of hypothesis 1 was significant.

Hypothesis 2:
Information sharing & visibility improve or, help to increase the competitiveness of the business strategy.

H2: Information sharing and visibility are required for the implementation of Industry 4.0.

From hypothesis 2 where Information sharing & visibility is the independent variable. Here have,

- Importance of customers, products & machines data for the business model.
- System which can follow to use in Industry 4.0.
- Integrated system for sharing information across departments.

Model Fit Information

Model Fitting Information

Model	Model fitting criteria	Likelihood ratio tests		
	-2log likelihood	Chi-square	df	Sig.
Intercept only	217.659			
Final	1.391	216.268	160	.002

The model fit was assessed by using the chi-square statistic. The p-value is the probability of a statistical hypothesis test. Null hypothesis will be rejected when p-value is less than 0.05 and when p-value is greater than 0.05 then null hypothesis will be accepted.

Goodness of Fit

Goodness of fit

	Chi-square	df	Sig.
Pearson	.002	148	1.000
Deviance	.005	148	1.000

From the table it seems that the model is fit. Since the p value is greater than 0.05 then test are not statistically significant.

Pseudo R-square

Pseudo R-square

Cox and Snell	.917
Nagelkerke	.997
McFadden	.987

The model represents relatively respectable-sized effects and accounts 98.7% to 99.7% of the variance.

Likelihood Ratio Test
The Likelihood Ratio Test proves that the predictor variables of hypothesis 2 was significant.

6 Discussion

The whole analysis is based on Bangladesh's Manufacturing Industries.

Degree of the Average Products Portfolio
And degree of the average products portfolio digitization showed that 36.7% of samples

organization showing 25% of their products and services are digitized. Not only that it also showed that portfolio is somewhat based on digitized products.

Life cycle Phase of Product Digitization
45.8% of the responded organization are use medium digitization and integration for their product digitization, which is almost 50% of the collected sample size.

Importance of the Usage & Analysis of Data
If we going through the importance of the data for the business model here, we see that 27% of the responses from the collected sample size of the customer's data, product data and machine generated data are relevance to business.

Smart Factory
Smart factory projects are most of times known as digital factory. Here we see that, industry 4.0 systems of the organization can be controlled through IT and the integration of the possible systems have some positive context. On the other hand, the evaluation of the adaptability of the equipment infrastructure through the smart factory concepts we see that there has the machine-to-machine communication. By moving through the digitization of the factories, here 80% of the responses of the organization was positive. That means a large number of industries wants to build up their factory into a digital model through digitization.

Smart Operations
The smart operations are a term that refers to the wide concept that encompasses the use of technology-enabled and automated connectivity and intelligence to efficiently deliver improved insights and predictability through sophisticated analytics, resulting in autonomous operations. In this research work here the integrated cross-departmental information sharing system for the smart operations are showing that most of the responses are positive through the internally between departments and externally with customers. Here it means that every industry positively integrates cross-departmental information sharing system in every store of their production line. And on the smart operations phase here the graphical data shows that 72% of the responded industries can automatically change the production condition in real-time which they wants to process in the production.

7 Conclusion

From the obtained results it can be concluded that,

i. elements of readiness like degree of the average products portfolio digitization, importance of the usage & analysis of data, digital model of factory, data collection during production system, system of use, integrated cross-departmental information sharing system, production process to change the production condition indicates that the selected industrial sector is not yet ready.
ii. IoT and Information sharing are two utmost ingredients for the adoption of Industry 4.0. The developed hypothesis was used to test it.

Appendix

Company Name:	
Address:	
Capital:	
Contracted, part-time and temporary employees:	
Yearly income:	
Answerers dept. Name:	
Answerers name:	
Address:	
e-mail:	
Contact number:	

Industry Type

RMG	Agro processing	Furniture/Wood
Consumer Goods	Electronics	Seafood Processing
Construction	Packaging	Pharmaceutical
Toiletries	Automation	

Estimate the size of your company's domestic workforce (employees)

1–19	20–99	100–249
250–499	500 to more	

1. How much of the average product portfolio is digitized?
   - Products and services are digitized.

     • All of the products and services are totally digitized and the portfolio is never solely comprised of digitized services/products.
     • 25%
     • 50%
     • 75%
     • All product and services are completely digitized.

2. How much of product's life cycle phase is digitized?
   - digitization and integration

     • No

- Low
- Medium
- High
- Completely

3. How important is data use and analysis to the business model of company?

   – digitization and integration

   - There have no data analytics.
   - Consumer data, product information is somewhat relevance to business.
   - Customer data and product data is relevance to business.
   - All customer data, product data is highly relevant to business.
   - All customer data, product data are highly relevant to the company.

4. During production does your company use machine data and product data?

Yes, to all	
Yes, to some	
No	

5. Which type of data is acquired on your machinery, process, production process?

	Yes (manually)	Yes (automatically)	No
Inventory data	<25% 25–50% 51–75% ≥76%	"	"
Throughput times in manufacturing	"	"	"
Capacity utilization of equipment	"	"	"
Residues at the production/ WIP	"	"	"
Quality management	"	"	"
Usage of employee	"	"	"
Quality control data	"	"	"
Process condition data	"	"	"
Production time	"	"	"
Overall equipment effectiveness	"	"	"
Other	"	"	"

6. Do you utilize any of the following systems?

Modern tools like- Collection of data with the use of machine, acquiring data of production, products management information etc.	Existent		Interface through the system	
	Yes	No	Yes	No

7. Where in your system have you implemented x-departmental information sharing?

System of use- Research and development, manufacturing, logistics, finance, IT, service etc.	Internally between departments		Externally with partners	
	Yes	No	Yes	No

8. Is the manufacturing process of your company able to respond automatically to changes in the production condition?

- cross-enterprise
- only in selected areas
- only in the test and pilot phase

References

1. Lasi, H., Fettke, P., Kemper, H., Feld, T., Hoffmann, M.: Industry 4.0. Bus. Inf. Syst. Eng. 6(1), 239–242 (2014)
2. Buhr, D.: Social innovation policy for Industry 4.0. Friedrich-Ebert-Stiftung, Division for Social and Economic Policies (2015)

3. Berawi, M.A.: Utilizing big data in industry 4.0: managing competitive advantages and business ethics. Int. J. Technol. **3**(1), 430–433 (2018)
4. Trappey, A.J., Trappey, C.V., Govindarajan, U.H., Chuang, A.C., Sun, J.J.: A review of essential standards and patent landscapes for the Internet of Things: a key enabler for industry 4.0. Adv. Eng. Inf. **33**(1), 208–229 (2017)
5. Hofmann, E., Rüsch, M.: Industry 4.0 and the current status as well as future prospects on logistics. Comput. Ind. **89**(1), 23–34 (2017)
6. Witkowski, K.: Internet of things, big data, industry 4.0-innovative solutions in logistics and supply chains management. Procedia Eng. **182**(1), 763–769 (2017)
7. Srivastava, S.K.: Industry 4.0. BHU Engineer's Alumni, Lucknow (2016)
8. Haseeb, M., Hussain, H.I., Ślusarczyk, B., Jermsittiparsert, K.: Industry 4.0: a solution towards technology challenges of sustainable business performance. Social Sci. **8**(5), 154 (2019)
9. Choi, Y.S., Lim, U.: Contextual factors affecting the innovation performance of manufacturing SMEs in Korea: a structural equation modeling approach. Sustainability **9**(7), 1193 (2017). https://doi.org/10.3390/su9071193
10. Giotopoulos, I., Kontolaimou, A., Korra, E., Tsakanikas, A.: What drives ICT adoption by SMEs? evidence from a large-scale survey in Greece. J. Bus. Res. **81**, 60–69 (2017). https://doi.org/10.1016/j.jbusres.2017.08.007
11. Damanpour, F., Henriquez, F.S., Chiu, H.H.: Internal and external sources and the adoption of innovations in organizations. Brit. J. Manag. **29**, 712–730 (2018). https://doi.org/10.1111/1467-8551.12296
12. Schniederjans, D.G.: Adoption of 3D-printing technologies in manufacturing: an empirical analysis. Int. J. Prod. Econ. **183**(Part A), 287–298 (2016). https://doi.org/10.1016/j.ijpe.2016.11.008
13. Chiu, C.Y., Chen, S., Chen, C.L.: An integrated perspective of TOE framework and innovation diffusion in broadband mobile applications adoption by enterprises. Int. J. Manag. Econ. Social Sci. (IJMESS) **6**(1), 14–39 (2017). ISSN 2304–1366
14. Ul-Ain, N., Giovanni, V., DeLone, W.H., Waheed, M.: Two decades of research on business intelligence system adoption, utilization and success – a systematic literature review. Decis. Supp. Syst. **125**, 113113 (2019). https://doi.org/10.1016/j.dss.2019.113113
15. Sepasgozar, S.M.E., Davis, S., Loosemore, M., Bernold, L.: An investigation of modern building equipment technology adoption in the Australian construction industry. Eng. Constr. Arch. Manag. **25**(8), 1075–1091 (2017). https://doi.org/10.1108/ECAM-03-2017-0052
16. Boyes, H., Hallaq, B., Cunningham, J., Watson, T.: The industrial Internet of Things (IIoT): an analysis framework. Comput. Ind. **101**, 1–12 (2018)
17. Canetta, L., Barni, A., Montini, E.: Development of a digitalization maturity model for the manufacturing sector. In: IEEE International Conference on Engineering, Technology and Innovation (ICE/ITMC) (2018)
18. Castelo-Branco, I., Cruz-Jesus, F., Oliveira, T.: Assessing industry 4.0 readiness in manufacturing: evidence for the European Union. Comput. Ind. **107**, 22–32 (2019). https://doi.org/10.1016/j.compind.2019.01.007

Estimating Energy Expenditure of Push-Up Exercise in Real Time Using Machine Learning

Md. Shoreef Uddin[1(✉)], Sadman Saumik Islam[1], and M. M. Musharaf Hussain[2]

[1] Department of Computer Science and Engineering, Daffodil International University, Dhaka, Bangladesh
`shoreef.cse.diu@gmail.com`

[2] Department of Computer Science and Engineering, University of Creative Technology Chittagong, Chittagong, Bangladesh
`musharaf@uctc.edu.bd`

Abstract. The Covid-19 pandemic has nearly brought the globe to a standstill. However, we were able to adjust to the circumstance with the aid of computer technology by working remotely from home. Health and fitness have grown to be top priorities during these tumultuous times when people are confined to their homes. By completing certain easy physical activities that don't require any special equipment and can be done at home, a person can maintain good health and fitness. Furthermore, the detection and recognition of human body motions or gestures is not a new concept when using artificial intelligence. Analysis of human body movement is now quicker and easier because of the development of real-time detection and identification technologies like YOLO. In this study, we have employed YOLO V4 as an AI helper to detect and identify push-ups from a real-time video stream recorded from a webcam or a smartphone camera that may be used to aid with push-ups. In order to keep the system affordable, we are recommending an approach that can identify pushups and estimate energy usage in real-time without the use of additional sensors or other wearable gadgets.

Keywords: Health and Fitness · Push-up Exercise · Energy Expenditure · Home-Based Exercise Program

1 Introduction

Exercise is essential for maintaining good health and a clear mind. Regular physical activity and exercise can benefit us in a number of ways, including improving our sleep patterns, managing weight issues, lowering the risk of heart failure, maintaining hormone balance, and strengthening our mental and creative thinking capabilities [1]. Simply said, regular exercise raises the likelihood of living longer. There are many different ways to exercise, such as aerobic activity, strength training, stretching, and balance exercises. One exercise for strength

© ICST Institute for Computer Sciences, Social Informatics and Telecommunications Engineering 2023
Published by Springer Nature Switzerland AG 2023. All Rights Reserved
Md. S. Satu et al. (Eds.): MIET 2022, LNICST 491, pp. 674–686, 2023.
https://doi.org/10.1007/978-3-031-34622-4_53

training that is more usual and well-liked is the push-up exercise. Without any special equipment, push-ups can be performed anywhere. Push-ups can be extremely beneficial for building strength and flexibility since they strengthen a variety of critical human muscles, such as the Anterior Deltoid, Upper and Lower Pectoralis Major, Bicep Brachii, Tricep Brachii, External Oblique, Gluteus Maximus, Gluteus Medius, Quadriceps, Tensor Fasciae Latae, Sartorius, among others. When a soldier is being recruited into the military, push-ups are also used to gauge their strength. The benefits of health tracking gadgets are driving the popularity of health-related applications today. Therefore, it will be extremely helpful in the field of health and fitness to estimate energy costs in real-time while executing push-ups. There are over 60–70 different variations of push-ups, and every single one is done to target a certain muscle [2]. There is one thing that all push-up variations have in common: they always begin with the body in a prone posture, and then the arms are used to raise and lower the body. In light of this, by identifying the common attribute, a real-time push-up exercise detection system can be constructed. We divided the shared characteristic into two areas. We divided that shared common attribute into two sectors. the former is the body in the rising position, and the latter is the body in the lowering position while performing a push-up. The conflict between accuracy and speed must constantly be considered when developing a neural network for a particular use case. The model selection determines the right balance between speed and precision. The chosen model's purpose in object detection is to display bounding boxes around predicted classes in the image frame. Single-shot detection (SSD) and two-shot detection are two widely used and accepted methods for object detection. You Only Look Once (YOLO) [3] is a single-shot strategy that is quicker but somewhat less accurate than the two-shot detection method, which uses R-FCN [5] and Fast-RCNN [4]. Ren et al. originally launched YOLO in 2016. They merged Region Proposal Network (RPN) and Faster R-CNN features in their study such that the same network could detect objects. The goal of our project is to provide a hassle-free, more precise, and quicker system for estimating the amount of energy expended when performing push-ups. We employ the YOLO v4 [6] network in this research, a fully new and improved form of YOLO that allows us to obtain the mAP of 96%. The following is the prepared framework for this study. There is a review of the literature in Sect. 2. Section 3 explains the structure of our study methodology, including the network architecture and dataset. We analyze the outcome of our study in Sect. 4. Finally, a general conclusion is reflected in Sect. 5.

2   Related Works

Artificial intelligence (AI) was not widely used in the fitness and health industries in the past. Tracking bodily mobility formerly included using electrical and wearable sensors. The fitness and health sector has recently undergone a transformation thanks to AI. Recent advances in computer vision for exercise detection have produced some excellent approaches for classifying and localizing various activity types as well as estimating energy expenditures. In their invention, M. Kodama et al. [7] employed a motion sensor to detect motion while the load difference was being computed, a load measurer to periodically measure the load on the device surface, a calculating system to compute the local maximum and minimum in the load changes over time. By first sensing forward motion and then a comparable backward motion, the gadget subsequently identified and tallied push-ups. A. Muzakir et al. [8] discussed a desktop program linked with two motion sensors to track push-ups. Their tests had two flaws: first, participants had to calibrate the devices before using them, and second, the results were disappointing since each user's weight and height numbers influenced the output. A multi-parameter integrated wearable system with real-time posture detection, heart rate (HR) monitoring, and quantitative activity monitoring was created by E. Prawiro et al. [9]. The electrocardiogram (ECG) sample rate 200 Hz, while the accelerometer sample rate 50 Hz on the device. To identify push-ups and other workouts, the system first calculated the scaled signal vector magnitude (SVM) and then passed the results into an algorithm. F. Nurwanto et al. [10] developed a technique in which smartwatches and cellphones were used simultaneously to capture time-series data from the accelerometer. They classified the input according to a pattern in the database using the k-Nearest Neighbor technique and the dynamic time warping algorithm. Although their efforts produced some excellent outcomes, people found it uncomfortable to wear equipment or sensors while working out. In a study, Jia Lu et al. [11] developed the YOLO-v3 model architecture for real-time human behavior detection. 120 photos were used for testing, and 1078 images were annotated for use in the study's five training classes. As a result, their trained model was able to recognize the following human behaviors: walking, skipping, running, jacking, and jumping. They were able to achieve a mean average precision of 98%. Although the results of their study were astoundingly impressive in principle, the system was underperforming in practice due to the subpar training dataset. H. -J. Park et al. suggestion's [12] of identifying appropriate and inappropriate pushup actions is a solid alternative. Using Openpose [13], a real-time 2D video imaging system, scientists retrieved numerous joints and linkages of a human body from each frame. The system consequently selected and managed eight crucial body parts. The angle of the elbow, wrist, and knee angles as well as the separation between the midpoints of both wrists and both shoulders were also determined using a parametric classification model. Their suggested method had a 90% accuracy rate. The system could only recognize standard push-ups, which limited their ability to do their job. To distinguish between many push-up variations, including diamond push-ups, broad arm push-ups, single hand push-ups, shoulder tap push-ups, and others, the model needed to undergo a few minor adjustments. We suggest an entirely different methodology that is more precise, more cost-effective and requires no equipment or sensors to be worn in order to address all the shortcomings of the current method for identifying push-ups and estimating energy expenditure.

3   Proposed Methodology

The proposed methodology is subdivided into two parts; the first section's goal is to count the repetition frequency of push-up exercises, and the second section's purpose is to estimate the cost of energy. In order to count the repetition frequency, Our project's initial objective is to train a neural network model to be able to classify and localize push-up exercises in real-time. We underwent a number of procedures in order to succeed and fulfill our goal. The workflow of our study includes data gathering, pre-processing, splitting, choosing of anchor boxes, model building, training, and testing. Additionally, we executed several tests in various training stages on the testing dataset using the trained weights to evaluate the performance of the proposed study. Finally, we estimated the cost of energy by applying logistic regression to the detection data. Figure 1 demonstrates the process diagram of our proposed research.

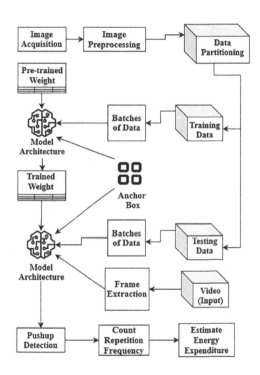

Fig. 1. Process Diagram.

3.1   Data Collection

The more images we can include into our system while training, the more accurate it will become. We adhered to the general rule of thumb which is 1,000 images per class. The system must be able to recognize both the rising and lowering positions of the human body in order to recognize a complete push-up.

Therefore, we can state that two classes are required in order to detect push-up exercises: "pushup_up" for recognizing rising body posture and "pushup_down" for recognizing lowering body posture. We picked images for the dataset in three different manners, including from the gymnasium, the internet, and film footage. While extracting frames from films, snapping pictures at the gymnasium, or downloading images from the web we made sure to wrap every aspect of the human body's posture for each variety of push-ups. However, we gathered almost three thousand images for two classes in which more than two thousand pictures were used for training for testing 712 images were utilized.Table 1 reflects the dataset's information.

Table 1. Data set

	Image	Object	Pushup_up	Pushup_down
Training	2081	2141	1175	966
Testing	712	782	452	330
Total	2793	2923	1627	1296

3.2   Data Preprocessing

A strong and informative dataset is essential in order to achieve higher accuracy in detection. Hence, Data preprocessing is fundamental to ensure the dataset's quality. Our dataset contained images of various sizes thus we downsized each picture to the constant size of $416 \times 416 \times 3$ pixels. Next, we manually annotated each image in the dataset by drawing a rectangle around the class object along with assigning the class name with the help of the Microsoft Visual Object Tagging Tool [14]. An annotated file contains the normalized value of the bounding box: height, width, center (x,y), and corresponding class id. Later, we used both images and their corresponding annotated files for training. Figure 2 depicts the annotation of an image.

3.3   Anchor Box Selection

Since object detection combines both classification and localization tasks, It is compulsory to provide the training network with both classification and localization data. We can reduce localization difficulties in prediction by choosing more anchor boxes for training. Unfortunately, we can not choose a large number of anchor boxes since doing so would make the model more complex and would increase the size of the feature filter in the detector, and would rise the training time. As a result, we used the K-Means clustering technique to choose three anchor boxes (tiny, moderate, and large) using the normalized height and weight. By computing the intersection over union [15], Formula"(1)" is utilized

Fig. 2. Image Annotation

to determine the distance matrix of the K-Means algorithm. Figure 3 displays the clustering depiction.

$$box - (w_1, h_1), \ centroid \ box - (w_2, h_2) \ as \ follows,$$
$$Intersection - min(w_1, w_2) \times min(h_1, h_2)$$
$$Union = (w_1h_1 + w_2h_2)$$
$$Iou(box, centroid) = \frac{Intersection}{Union - Intersection} \tag{1}$$
$$Distance \ matrix, d = 1 - Iou$$

3.4 Model Architecture

All previous neural network models were straightforward and linear. Neural network models have undergone rapid evolution in order to improve accuracy and performance. An enhancement over the YOLO V3 [16] is the YOLO V4 model architecture [17], which has undergone a complete makeover. The backbone, neck, and head are the three building components that make up the YOLO v4's architecture. The model's backbone processes the input picture first in order to compress its features. Second, the outputs from the backbone are mixed using a Neck block. The detection eventually happens in the head block.

Backbone. The Backbone is where the formation of feature layers occurs. A 53-layer deep convolutional neural network with the properties of densenet [18], is employed as the backbone of YOLO v3 [18]. On the other hand, YOLO v4 employs CSPDarknet-53, a hybrid of darknet53 and the Cross-Stage Partial Network [19]. Multiple Dense blocks are combined with convolution and pooling-based transition layer to form a densenet. In a Densenet, each layer's output is combined with the output of the one before it, and its features are then passed on

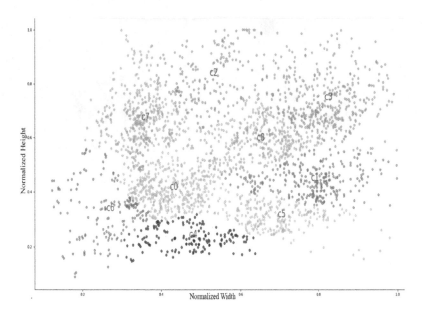

Fig. 3. Visualization of Clustering

to all succeeding layers. In opposite, the input feature of DenseBlock is divided into two portions in CSPDarknet53. A portion of the input will be processed using a block of convolutions similar to the densenet, and the remainder will be combined with the output. Because of this, the final three layers of CSPDarknet-53 hold the most useful information, which is then utilized as the neck's input. CSPDarknet-53's module structure is displayed in Fig. 4.

Neck. Initially, the convolutional neural network's end had a fully connected network attached for detection. Therefore, a fixed-size input picture is needed for the fully connected network, which can only be obtained by using cropping, resizing, and wrapping procedures that result in object missing or other distortion issues. Thereafter, to resolve the issues the Feature Pyramid Network (FPN) [20] is launched. Depending on the size of the input picture, the output feature layers of the backbone can have a variety of sizes. Due to this, the neck network In YOLO v4 uses spatial pyramid pooling [21], which creates fixed-size features regardless of the size of the backbone's output. In addition, A modified Path Aggregation Network (PaNet) [22] is used in the neck network to cope with the vanishing localization information problem. In conclusion, The Neck network secures the versatility of input sizes and gives the Head network additional useful information for further processing.

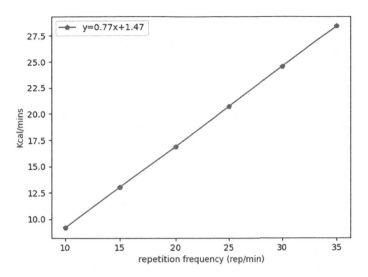

Fig. 6. Estimating Energy Expenditure

4 Result Analysis

Our system must first be able to correctly count the repetition frequency in order to estimate energy expenditure during the push-up activity. For achieving precise classification and localization, we trained our constructed model with the training dataset at Google Collab for up to six thousand iterations. Our proposed system generated a trained weight file every thousand steps. We calculated the values of four information measures based on the testing dataset using this weight file, maintaining the confidence threshold value once at 0.5 and at another time at 0.75. The six weight files we collected in this manner were saved, and the best ones were used later for push-up detection. The values of the information measures that were generated to assess the best-trained weight files are provided in Table 3. The average map value of our model is 96% illustrated in Table 4, which is very satisfactory for push-up detection. Regarding real-time detection, the detection time is another issue of concern. The more quickly the system can classify and localize push-ups, the more useful and effective it will be. Our model processed each picture in the testing data set on average in 77 milliseconds since we used virtual machines for training and testing. We achieved 15 frames per second when processing real-time or pre-recorded footage. However, it is possible to reduce the detection time and increase the number of frames per second if we use a local machine with high computational power. Since on a powerful GPU, YOLO v4 can maintain an FPS of 60–70. Figure 5 displays the outcomes of push-ups localization and detection produced by our proposed approach. We fed our system pre-recorded videos of push-ups being performed by a 180 pounds man at frequencies ranging from 10 to 35 repetitions and by using the formula "(3)" the system estimated energy expenditure. Additionally, we also calculated the energy expenditure by using the traditional method "(2)". The comparison between the proposed approach and the existing method is reflected in Table 2. The linear relationship between estimated energy expenditure and repetition frequency of our study for the push-up exercise is shown in Fig. 6 (Table 3).

Table 2. The output difference between proposed approach and the existing method.

Effort	Repetition Frequency	Results of the proposed Method	METs Value	Results of the Traditional Method
Moderate	10	9.17	3.8	5
Moderate	15	13.02	3.8	5
Moderate	20	16.87	3.8	5
Vigorous	25	20.72	8	11
Vigorous	30	24.57	8	11
Vigorous	35	28.42	8	11

Table 3. The four information measures

Confident Thresh	Precision	Recall	F1-Score
0.5	0.90	0.94	0.92
0.75	0.93	0.90	0.91

Table 4. Detection results on the test set.

Class	AP	Threshold 0.5			Threshold 0.75		
		TP	FP	FN	TP	FP	FN
Pushup-down	0.9855	315	13	20	304	06	27
Pushup-up	0.9444	420	68	27	396	45	55
mAP = 0.96495		735	81	47	700	51	82

5   Conclusion and Future Work

At present days, people are very concerned about their health and entirely rely on technology to keep track of it. The usage of wearable devices for monitoring health and tracking daily activities is going downward. In contrast, people demand a hassle-free solution for keeping tabs on one's health and regular activities. The novelty of our study is to develop a simplistic solution for detecting and counting push-ups exercise in real-time aiming to calculate total burned calories. This study was just the start of more beneficial work that can be done in the field of health and nutrition sectors in the near future. In our future study, We will add some more exercises to this work, while also focusing on a more efficient way to calculate the total burned calories for different exercises. A smart IoT-based gymnasium can be built with the help of the methodology that contains different exercise detection in real-time as well as calculating estimated energy. Furthermore, such technology can also be implemented in sports and the armed forces so that sportsmen and soldiers can track their activity in order to maintain their physical fitness.

References

1. Kramer, A.: An overview of the beneficial effects of exercise on health and performance. Adv. Exp. Med. Biol. **1228**, 3–22 (2020)
2. English, N.: 82 Push-Ups You Need to Know About. https://greatist.com/fitness/bodyweight-push-up-variations. Accessed 6 Nov 2021
3. Redmon, J., Divvala, S., Girshick, R., Farhadi, A.: You only look once: unified, real-time object detection. In: Proceedings of the IEEE Conference on Computer Vision and Pattern Recognition (CVPR), pp. 779–788 (2016)
4. Girshick, R.: Fast R-CNN. In: Proceedings of the IEEE International Conference on Computer Vision (ICCV), pp. 1440–1448 (2015)
5. Dai, J., Li, Y., He, K., Sun, J.: R-FCN: object detection via region-based fully convolutional networks. In: Advances in Neural Information Processing Systems, pp. 379–387 (2016)
6. Bochkovskiy, A., Wang, C.-Y., Liao, H.-Y. M.: YOLOv4: optimal speed and accuracy of object detection. arXiv preprint, arXiv: 2004.10934 (2020)
7. Kodama, M., Ku, I.: Exercise Detection Apparatus. United States Patent 7901324 B2, 3 March 2011
8. Muzakir, A., Kusmindari, C.D.: Push-up detector applications using quality function development and anthropometry for movement error detection. Sci. J. Inform. **5**(2), 248–257 (2018)
9. Prawiro, E.A.P.J., Chou, N.-K., Lee, M.-W., Lin, Y.-H.: A wearable system that detects posture and heart rate: designing an integrated device with multiparameter measurements for better health care. IEEE Consum. Electron. Mag. **8**(2), 78–83 (2019)
10. Nurwanto, F., Ardiyanto, I., Wibirama, S.: Light sport exercise detection based on smartwatch and smartphone using k-Nearest Neighbor and Dynamic Time Warping algorithm. In: 2016 8th International Conference on Information Technology and Electrical Engineering (ICITEE), pp. 1–5 (2016)
11. Lu, J., Yan, W.Q., Nguyen, M.: Human behaviour recognition using deep learning. In: 2018 15th IEEE International Conference on Advanced Video and Signal Based Surveillance (AVSS), pp. 1–6 (2018)
12. Park, H.-J., Baek, J.-W., Kim, J.-H.: Imagery based parametric classification of correct and incorrect motion for push-up counter using OpenPose. In: 2020 IEEE 16th International Conference on Automation Science and Engineering (CASE), pp. 1389–1394 (2020)
13. Cao, Z., Hidalgo, G., Simon, T., Wei, S.-E., Sheikh, Y.: OpenPose: realtime multi-person 2D pose estimation using part affinity fields. IEEE Trans. Pattern Anal. Mach. Intell. **43**(1), 172–186 (2021)
14. Solawetz, J.: Getting started with VoTT annotation tool for computer vision. https://blog.roboflow.com/vott/. Accessed 3 Nov 2021

15. Subramanyam, V.S.: IOU (Intersection over Union). https://medium.com/analytics-vidhya/iou-intersection-over-union-705a39e7acef. Accessed 3 Nov 2021
16. Redmon, J., Farhadi, A.: YOLOv3: an incremental improvement. arXiv preprint arXiv:1804.02767 (2018)
17. Rugery, P.: Explanation of YOLO V4 a one stage detector. https://becominghuman.ai/explaining-yolov4-a-one-stage-detector-cdac0826cbd7. Accessed 3 Nov 2021
18. Huang, G., Liu, Z., Maaten, L.V.D., Weinberger, K.Q.: Densely connected convolutional networks. In: Proceedings of the IEEE Conference on Computer Vision and Pattern Recognition, pp. 4700–4708 (2017)
19. Wang, C.-Y., Liao, H.-Y.M., Wu, Y.-H., Chen, P.-Y., Hsieh, J.-W., Yeh, I.-H.: CSP-Net: a new backbone that can enhance learning capability of CNN. In: Proceedings of the IEEE/CVF Conference on Computer Vision and Pattern Recognition Workshops, pp. 390–391 (2020)
20. Lin, T.-Y., Dollar, P., Girshick, R., He, K., Hariharan, B., Belongie, S.: Feature pyramid networks for object detection. In: Proceedings of the IEEE Conference on Computer Vision and Pattern Recognition, pp. 2117–2125 (2017)
21. He, K., Zhang, X., Ren, S., Sun, J.: Spatial pyramid pooling in deep convolutional networks for visual recognition. IEEE Trans. Pattern Anal. Mach. Intell. **37**(9), 1904–1916 (2015)
22. Liu, S., Qi, L., Qin, H., Shi, J., Jia, J.: Path aggregation network for instance segmentation. In: Proceedings of the IEEE Conference on Computer Vision and Pattern Recognition, pp. 8759–8768 (2018)
23. Hosang, J., Benenson, R., Schiele, B.: Learning non-maximum suppression. In: Proceedings of the IEEE Conference on Computer Vision and Pattern Recognition, pp. 4507–4515 (2017)
24. Ainsworth, B.E., et al.: 2011 compendium of physical activities: a second update of codes and MET values. Med. Sci. Sports Exerc. **43**(8), 1575–1581 (2011)
25. Nakagata, T., Yamada, Y., Naito, H.: Estimating energy cost of body weight resistance exercise using a multistage exercise test. J. Strength Cond. Res. **36**(5), 1290–1296 (2022)
26. Hatamoto, Y., Yamada, Y., Fujii, T., et al.: A novel method for calculating the energy cost of turning during running. Open Access J. Sports Med. **4**, 117–122 (2013)
27. Hatamoto, Y., Yamada, Y., Higaki, Y., Tanaka, H.: A novel approach for measuring energy expenditure of a single sit-to-stand movement. Eur. J. Appl. Physiol. **116**, 997–1004 (2016)
28. Hatamoto, Y., Yamada, Y., Sagayama, H., et al.: The relationship between running velocity and the energy cost of turning during running. PLoS ONE **9**, e81850 (2014)

Cross-Layer Architecture for Energy Optimization of Edge Computing

Rushali Sharif Uddin$^{(\boxtimes)}$, Nusaiba Zaman Manifa, Latin Chakma,
and Md. Motaharul Islam

Department of Computer Science and Engineering, United International University,
Dhaka, Bangladesh
{ruddin201144,nmanifa201155,lchakma201232}@bscse.uiu.ac.bd,
motaharul@cse.uiu.ac.bd

Abstract. As the scope of edge computing keeps expanding, the energy demand grows as well, and ensuring apt management will be essential in kick-starting the next stage of edge computing. More attention needs to be paid to the cross-layer architecture to scale the energy output as well as the optimization of more comprehensive performance. But a very limited endeavor has been made until now to explore the potential of edge computing after optimizing each layer incorporated with green and easily procurable renewable energy. As we are moving towards the future the applications that are emerging are latency-salient, bandwidth-demanding, and privacy-yearning. Cross-layer energy management is the kernel for the proper function of these features to safeguard the Quality of Service (QoS) and Quality of Experience (QoE) of the applications. An overall system framework modification is required to channel the necessitated technical unit of power. This paper proposes a cross-layer energy architecture model which cascades optimized energy from each layer, thus yielding the power required to manage the whole edge computing system. A mathematical model is devised to study the aftermath of the cross-layer architecture and performance evaluation is executed based on the model which generates 50% power savings.

Keywords: Cross-layer Architecture · Energy Architecture · Optimization · Edge computing · Power Savings

1 Introduction

Even though the cloud is providing on-demand services, the desire for geographically aware computing is felt which resulted in the rise of the popularity of edge computing. Edge and cloud are confidants in providing computing as a ubiquitous utility [1]. Edge-of-Things (EoT) has materialized in the world to provide exclusive storage and processing services at the edge. The growing trend in this technology craves more energy-efficient systems which are not fulfilled by the Internet of Things (IoT). But integrating cloud and fog/edge computing catapulted efficient data storage and resource management [2]. So the architecture of these infrastructures becomes an issue.

© ICST Institute for Computer Sciences, Social Informatics and Telecommunications Engineering 2023
Published by Springer Nature Switzerland AG 2023. All Rights Reserved
Md. S. Satu et al. (Eds.): MIET 2022, LNICST 491, pp. 687–701, 2023.
https://doi.org/10.1007/978-3-031-34622-4_54

The bloom of futuristic applications' demands as well as unending end-users expectations gave rise to huge industry investments and research areas on the edge with the only goal to unleash the full potential of IoT. Even though it has been proved through various ongoing researches that cross-layer architecture is energy-efficient for wireless networks, the scope of cross-layer architecture in edge computing is still widely unexplored. But due to some constraints on the cross-layer architectural design of edge computing, it gets harder to harness the utmost performance. Edge computing system architecture encapsulates layers like edge devices, edge networks, edge servers, and the cloud itself. All these parts are interdependent. The proper synergy of all these layers will help us to get our desired optimized result.

Power is used in every layer. To make the whole cross-layer model energy-efficient, the power consumption of every layer has to be focused on. Only cascading optimized power from every layer will boost ideal power usage. For the edge device layer, the hardware design where most power is used is centered and worked on. To capture the whole hardware framework the power management, storage devices, processors, and energy resiliency are made epicenters. For power management, we have applied Dynamic Voltage Frequency Scaling (DVFS) on both CPU and memory modules to adjust the CPU frequency and voltage according to real-time workloads which are efficient in energy saving. A high-energy storage-intensive battery, Zinc-Nickel (Zn-Ni) battery, is used as a storage unit to stock surplus energy from production. As CPUs are bad at parallel processing, so different kinds of processors like GPU, FPGA, ASIC, and TPU are suggested to be used along with CPUs creating a heterogenous chipset [3]. For the energy resiliency of the hardware, we have incorporated a microgrid with local renewable energy sources with brown energy as backup [4].

For edge network layer optimization we will be using Affinity Propagation (AP) algorithms to create a prediction model of the edge servers with Virtual Network (VN) embedding [5] for the task to resource distribution function. The algorithms will predict how much resource is to be allocated to the required edge servers to reduce the energy consumption by keeping unnecessary servers idle thus also reducing communication latency. Dynamic Speed Controller (DSC) will be implemented on the active edge servers as well as the IoT applications to reduce the workload solely on the servers. This will enable us to keep power wastage to a minimum thus optimizing the edge server layer [2]. Edge Content Delivery (ECD) framework is used to optimize the cloud by reducing its workload. Now the cloud doesn't have to use bandwidth and CPU for processing the same request as the previously calculated data is stored in the ECD and sent back. The ECD will send the data directly to the edge devices. That way energy will be saved since the path of data flow becomes shorter.

Our paper will include improving the energy architecture on every layer so that we can harness the maximum possible outcome from all these layers maintaining sustainability.

The significant works of this research paper are summarized below:

- We have proposed a cross-layer architecture for energy optimization at different layers of edge computing.
- We have introduced mathematical models to measure the impact of our methodologies on each layer.
- Our model performs better than single-layer optimization.
- We have generated graphs calculating energy savings over time for each layer using our proposed architecture.
- Using our proposed architecture, cross-layer power savings can be increased by 50%.

The structure of the paper is as follows: Sect. 2 presents Related Works. The Proposed Methodology and its impact expressed mathematically are discussed in Sect. 3. Performance Evaluation is analyzed in Sect. 4 and Sect. 5 concludes the paper.

2   Related Works

Edge computing is an emerging paradigm in the case of latency-critical and time-sensitive computation; many works have been put forward focusing on making different aspects of the layers efficient.

In this paper, the researchers have pointed out different problems in edge computing along with their solutions. The researchers have addressed performance constraints of devices, privacy issues, latency problems, the performance of the coding environment, and drawbacks in a centralized system. To overcome these problems solutions such as ECD devices, a Multi-source Transmission Protocol, Dynamic Edge-Fabric Environment, etc. were introduced [6]. On the other hand, this paper put forward the idea of incorporating edge computing with renewable energy sources to make it more sustainable and improve the quality of service by proposing an energy management framework. The framework proposed by the authors uses a microgrid instead of a centralized grid system. Experimental data reveal the prototype system to have a 94.8% success rate [4]. Highlighting the optimization problems of a Wireless Optical Broadband Access Network (WOBAN), [7] proposes a green survivable virtual network embedding for collaborative edge computing in smart cities. The researchers formulated the problem mathematically and determined the effectiveness of the algorithm using simulations. This paper presents the possibilities of Edge Computing in building a sustainable future. The researchers in this paper applied the DFasWB method to generate two integrated sustainable EC fictions - a user interface or 'dashboard' titled InterNET ZERO and an Internet-connected fruit bowl called the Fruit Sentry [8].

The authors of this article propose an ECIoT architecture that focuses on admission control, computational resource allocation, and power control in edge computing for IoT. A cross-layer dynamic stochastic network optimization based on the Lyapunov stochastic optimization approach is used to enhance the system performance of ECIoT [9]. While in this paper, concern over efficient virtual node mapping and virtual link mapping in VN embedding is raised. In light of this, the researchers have proposed VN embedding algorithms to have efficient coordination between the two mapping phases onto the substrate network resources [5]. The increasing data traffic and the drawbacks of a centralized system in providing real-time data analysis is addressed in [10]. To cope with the problems the authors are proposing an SDN-based distributed layered network architecture, namely the SoftEdge Net model. SDN-based secure fog node architecture was applied at the fog layer to overcome security issues. A flow rule partition and an allocation algorithm at the network edge were also proposed. The researchers in this paper focus on the energy consumption at the edge of the network. A linear power model was proposed for the EdgeCloudSim simulator. It is used to assess the energy consumption of edge network servers. They also presented a simple effective power control model used to minimize power consumption in the edge network [11].

In [3] the researchers survey the research work on energy-aware edge computing and identify related research challenges and trends which includes architecture, operating system, middleware, applications services and computation offloading. [12] proposes a two-phase immersion cooling system and smart resource allocation via Deep Reinforcement Learning for edge computing scenarios. Through these energy-aware optimizations respectively, around 23% energy savings and 24% reduced energy consumption was achieved. Similarly, this paper discusses the cross-layer optimization required to associate deep learning with edge computing. The current trends of such optimization are surveyed and challenges are investigated. The authors propose optimization on different layers of both hardware and software to overcome the challenges [13]. The researchers in this paper analyze ways to support cross-layer pacing to enhance energy efficiency in edge computing. They have proposed X-Leep which is a run-time system that detects the pace of the system and supports IoT and edge computing [14].

This paper analyzes the possibilities of edge computing operating in dynamic and resource-constrained environments. An architecture for energy aware cluster based edge computers supporting portability and usability in fieldwork has been proposed by the researchers in [15].

3   Proposed Cross-Layer Architecture Design

To achieve energy efficiency on every layer it is important to acknowledge the power usage on every layer. As a huge amount of data is being processed and computed as well as traveling back and forth a lot of power is needed for efficient management of these actions. It is seen that more power is being used than needed in some cases which does not help us to achieve the ultimate less-power-more-work agenda. As a result, we need to focus on using the right amount of power on every layer so that we can reduce power wastage. Figure 1 shows each layer that comprises our cross-layer architecture and proposed frameworks. Our cross-layer model is targeting to increase cumulative power savings by 50%. Our aim is to save energy in all layers thus achieving our ultimate goal which is to reduce power usage. The optimization of each layer is discussed below:

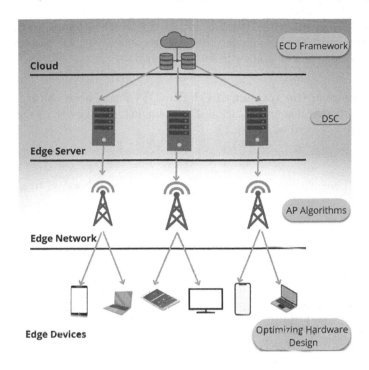

Fig. 1. Cross-layer architecture of edge computing with proposed frameworks

3.1 Edge Devices Layer

For an energy-efficient architecture for edge devices, we have focused on the overall hardware design where most power is being used. Modifying the hardware design can make it more power-efficient. The number of edge devices is increasing day by day. Proper management of these devices will ensure QoS and QoE of real-time applications. However, these devices are constrained by the limited power supply. Moreover, they have the less computational power and storage resources which are not capable of performing huge computing-intensive tasks. Energy awareness at the hardware level can save huge energy consumption. We aim to render hardware design by fine-tuning the process via the following techniques:

3.1.1 Power Management

Power Management becomes an important part in the case of proper energy management of edge devices. The idea of power management encapsulates powering up every part of the edge device efficiently which includes not using unnecessary power when it is not needed. It will consist of a technique called Dynamic Voltage Frequency Scaling (DVFS). But applying DVFS only on the CPU will not be efficient as we are using heterogeneous chips. Studies show applying DVFS on CPU will enhance energy saving greatly. So we will apply these techniques to both CPU and other components [3]. DVFS is one common technique that provides the capability to adjust the CPU frequency and voltage according to real-time workloads which are efficient in energy saving.

Measurement of the Impact of DVFS: DVFS uses both voltage regulation as well as CPU frequency regulation. For a single CPU, Power Usage, and Max Power Usage is described in Eq. (1).

$$P_{max} = CV_{max}^2 f_{max} \tag{1}$$

Equation (2) calculates the power usage after voltage is lowered to x%.

$$P_{vx} = C(V_{max}\frac{x}{100})^2 f_{max} \tag{2}$$

Again, Eq. (3) shows the power usage after lowering the frequency to x%.

$$P_{fx} = CV_{max}^2 f_{max}\frac{x}{100}\% \tag{3}$$

From this, we can calculate the overall power savings in a day of a single CPU formulated by the Eq. (4).

$$Ps_{t0} = \frac{tP_{max} - \sum_i^t Pi}{tP_{max}} * 100\% \tag{4}$$

In Eq. (1), t is the amount of time the CPU was active for. P_i stands for the power usage at i-th second.

3.1.2   Storage Devices

A hybrid model of Zn-Ni battery (High energy storage intensity) and micro-grid is used to improve energy resiliency. Many storage devices have appeared over the years, such as Lithium-ion batteries are of low expense but have low capacity. The zinc battery in this case is safe but it has poor rechargeability. Si-nanolayer-embedded graphite/carbon hybrids (SGC) have high coulombic efficiency, enhanced capacity, and excellent capacity retention. But since we will be using the storage units to store surplus energy, we require one that has high energy storage intensity. Hence we are using a Zn-Ni battery.

3.1.3   Processors

We have suggested heterogeneous chips like CPU, GPU, FPGA, ASIC, and TPU for multifarious reasons. The traditional processors used in cloud computing have high computing performance. But these cannot cope with big data processing in edge computing where billions of edge devices are involved. And also it takes hundreds even thousands of instructions to complete one unit processing which is not compatible with edge computing. So specially designed hardware is needed for data processing in edge computing. GPU can support high parallel programming which is needed for big data analysis on edge devices. Therefore harnessing powerful GPU cards can give us satisfactory power consumption in parallel computing. FPGA is more flexible than CPU and GPU and it can support a variable depth pipeline structure that provides a large number of parallel computing resources. CPU, GPU, and FPGA work differently based on the environment they are deployed in. TPU is used for processing machine learning data/FAST matrix multiplication [3]. Heterogeneous chip design means that a chip will contain different types of processors. Such as CPU, GPU, and TPU in a single chip. So we can divide the computation according to its type. For example, CPU should be used for floating-point calculations, GPU should be used for parallel computation of matrices and positional vectors, and lastly TPU for processing tensors that are used in machine learning. This way all the workload doesn't need to be processed by the generalized processor which will be slow.

3.1.4   Energy Resiliency

Energy resiliency refers to the energy security and energy efficiency under changing and unpredictable demands such as power outages and power scarcity. Since edge devices are powered by either the external power supply or the energy buffer battery, energy resiliency is of importance when the external power supply sources are discontinuous, or the battery is drained out to non-working conditions. That is why we propose a renewable-energy-driven system, which aims to integrate edge computing with the microgrid to incorporate a highly volatile renewable energy supply and maximize its usage to reduce carbon emissions. Renewable energy sources will be the primary source of energy but to combat the unpredictable nature of renewable energy we will use non-renewable energy such as nuclear energy, biomass, etc. as a secondary source or backup. Storage profiles will be used to accumulate the surplus energy produced during off-peak hours to maximize power supply according to power demand. This method will work best for stationary edge devices. For example, edge devices that are monitoring harvest, temperature, humidity, etc. But it will not work with portable devices, such as Phones, Laptops, Tablets, etc.

For the portable edge devices or in specific terms mobile devices, we will be using rechargeable batteries and recharge them using the extra energy generated from the peak hours of the renewable sources.

3.2   Edge Network Layer

The Edge network is the network consisting of all the edge devices and servers connected through virtual links and virtual nodes in a substrate network. VN embedding is the process of finding optimal network resource distribution for each virtual node in the network. This is an NP-hard problem. So, it could be said that it needs exponential time complexity for solving the problem. Instead, we will limit the problem space to different dimensions and solve it in polynomial time using R-ViNE and D-ViNE algorithms which have better performance than most other algorithms [5].

Resource allocation on demand is a possibility but one of the key problems of this is latency. If we allocate resources when a command for a task arrives and then run the task it will create a huge bottleneck because it will have to wait till the resource allocation is done. And sometimes the amount of resources allocated in the virtual machine is higher than the amount needed. Thus wasting the resources of the edge server. We will be using Affinity Propagation (AP) algorithms to create a prediction model of the edge servers for the task to resource distribution function. By doing so we will be able to predict the amount of computational and networking resources needed beforehand and allocate it according to the substrate network generated by the previous two algorithms. Thus it solves the problem of energy consumption, as we can keep unnecessary edge nodes in an idle/energy-saving state while making no compromises in latency.

Measurement of the Impact of AP Based Prediction Model with VN Embedding: As this is a substrate network of virtual nodes with many edge devices, we will be using n as the number of Processing Units in the substrate network. We calculate the total energy saving by the substrate network in Eq. (5),

$$P_{f_n} = \frac{\sum_i^n Ps_{t0_i}}{n}\%$$ (5)

In a substrate network, there will be many computational units. So, to get the total energy savings we need to add up the energy savings percentage of all the units in a single substrate network. To get the average power savings of a single substrate network in a single day, total power saving has been divided by the number of computational units. Power saving has been calculated for the whole network. But the whole network will not be running at the same time. Virtual Embedding is used to allocate the necessary amount of computational resources depending on the workload. We assume the amount of computational resources needed for computing the necessary resource allocation is Pc. So, Eq. (6) is the computational resource needed for computing resource allocation.

$$P_c = P$$ (6)

In Eq. (6), P is the power usage described in the first layer. AP-based prediction models will not always give correct predictions, so we need to recompute the data if that happens. So, let x be the percentage of predictions that are correct and t be the number of seconds the nodes were active, and n be the number of nodes, then the total power usage,

$$P_t = P_c * \frac{100 - x}{100} * t + \sum_i^t \sum_j^n P_{i,j}\%$$ (7)

Equation (7) computes the total power usage of the n nodes over t seconds. The total energy saving from the second layer is the weighted average of Eq. (5) and the correct prediction percentage. So, Eq. (8) gives us the total energy saving from the second layer,

$$Ps_{t_1} = \frac{x * w_1 + P_{fn} * w_2}{w_1 + w_2} * 100\% \tag{8}$$

Here w1 and w2 denote the weight of these variables.

3.3   Edge Servers Layer

Edge servers refer to servers (compute resources ex.EoT/IoT applications) that does the processing work at an edge, which can be anywhere along the edge spectrum. As discussed in the previous layer we will be using AP algorithms to predict the amount of computational and networking resources needed beforehand and allocate it according to the substrate network generated using R-ViNE and D-ViNE algorithms. After allocating it properly to the respective devices we will implement DSC on both EoT/fog servers and IoT applications so that more data is not processed on servers only. Servers now need to monitor only half of the workload as the other half is sent to IoT applications whereas previously DSC sent workload to the fog servers irrespective of it being light, medium, or heavy workload which used to create a lot of computational problems. Those computational problems cause a lot of unnecessary power wastage. But now as we are not only changing the whole hardware structure of edge devices but also allocating the feasible amounts of workloads using our algorithms to both the edge devices and servers, it is reducing the computational pressure on both of them and thus we can minimize power usage.

Measurement of the Impact of DSC in Edge Servers: DSC will monitor half of the workload depending on the priority of the tasks. So, The total workload on the edge server is the summation of the workload divided by two, as it halves the workload.

$$W_t = \frac{\sum_i^n W_i}{2} \tag{9}$$

So, the amount of energy consumed on this layer is the multiplication of energy consumed per second per task with Eq. (9). So, Eq. (10) computes the power consumption,

$$P_c = W_t * P \tag{10}$$

Equation (11) calculates the total energy consumption in a single day is,

$$P_t = \sum_i^t P_{ci} \tag{11}$$

In Eq. (12) we get the total energy savings of a single day.

$$Ps_{t_2} = \frac{t * W_t * 2 * P - Pt}{t * W_t * 2 * P} * 100\% \tag{12}$$

3.4 Cloud Layer

Cloud computing can process and analyze heavy data that requires more complex operations (e.g., big data processing and predictive analysis), which exceeds the edge computing capability. A plethora of data is processed in the IoT applications, and this data puts a lot of burden on the Cloud. "The Cloud" refers to servers that are accessed over the Internet, software and databases that run on those servers. Cloud servers are situated in data centers around world. These data centers become overly heated and need constant cooling due to processing and analyzing complex operations. A lot of energy is necessary for this purpose. So to reduce the load on the cloud servers, an Edge Content Delivery (ECD) framework is proposed. ECD is a framework that has a cache that stores mapped data for repeating requests. We can use ECD to lower the burden on the servers with unnecessary computation that has already been calculated. Then we will send the data to the requested device from the ECD. Thus the main server that is the cloud does not have to process the redundant requests reducing the burden on itself.

Measurement of the Impact of ECD: Due to the usage of ECD, the number of clock cycles is reduced to the number of types of requests. As such Eq. (13) calculates the number of clock cycles reduced for the n type of requests,

$$Cr_p = \sum_i^n C_{qi} * ki - \sum_i^n C_{qi} \tag{13}$$

Here, Cqi stands for required clock cycles and ki stands for the number of requests. So, Eq. (14) calculates the amount of energy saved by this model,

$$E_s = \frac{\sum_i^n C_{qi} * K_i * P - \sum_i^n C_{qi} * P}{\sum_i^n C_{qi} * K_i * P} * 100\% \tag{14}$$

Here, P stands for Power usage for each clock cycle.

4   Performance Evaluation

Evaluating the performance of the cross-layer model is a must to understand how much impact it has on the energy optimization scheme. We have done the necessary calculations below for the overall performance analysis. Table 1 shows the tools used to simulate and generate the graphs.

Table 1. Tools Used

Sl	Name	Version	Description
1	Python	3.9.12	Python is a high-level, interpreted, general-purpose programming language
2	NumPy	1.21.5	NumPy is a library for the Python programming language, providing assist to large, multi-dimensional arrays and matrices. It also has a large stack of high-level mathematical functions to operate on these arrays
3	Matplotlib	3.5.2	Matplotlib is a plotting library for the Python programming language and its numerical mathematics extension NumPy. It administers an object-oriented API for embedding plots into applications using GUI toolkits for example Tkinter, wxPython, Qt, or GTK

$$TE_s = \frac{W_1 * \frac{Ps_{t_1}}{100} + W_2 * \frac{Ps_{t_2}}{100} + W_3 * \frac{E_s}{100}}{W_1 + W_2 + W_3} * 100\% \qquad (15)$$

In Eq. (15) we get the overall energy savings of the model by the weighted average of Eq. (8), Eq. (12), Eq. (14).

As Eq. (8), Eq. (12), Eq. (14) gives the overall energy savings of each layer, to calculate the overall energy savings of the cross-layer model we need to understand how much impact does each of these layers provide to the cross-layer model. That is why we have used some weights that will be used as the measure of impact for each layer. W_1, W_2, W_3 are the weights that were used in this model. The values used as the weights are 25, 25, and 50. The weights need to be adjusted according to the user's needs.

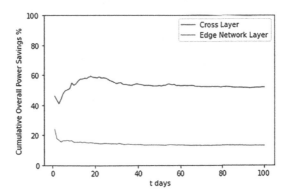

Fig. 2. Cumulative power savings percentage: cross-layer vs edge network layer

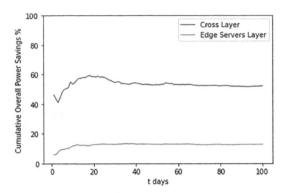

Fig. 3. Cumulative power savings percentage: cross-layer vs edge servers layer

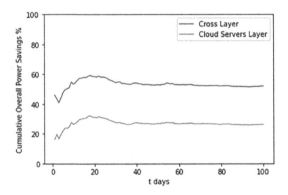

Fig. 4. Cumulative power savings percentage: cross-layer vs cloud servers layer

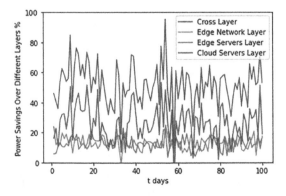

Fig. 5. Overall power savings over different layers

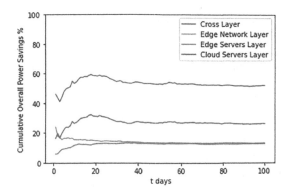

Fig. 6. Cumulative power savings over all layers

Figure 2 shows the cumulative performance of using the Cross-Layer model vs the Optimized Edge Network Layer. The X-axis and Y-axis denote the time period in days and Cumulative Overall Power Saving achieved after t-days respectively. In Fig. 2 we can see that the cumulative overall power savings percentage achieved by the Cross-Layer model reaches around 50%, whereas the Edge Network Layer only could come up to around 19%.

Figure 3 compares the cumulative overall power savings between the Cross-Layer model and the Optimized Edge Servers Layer. In the graph, we can see that the cumulative overall power savings percentage achieved by the Optimized Edge Servers layer is around 15% to 16%. Which is far lower than the 50% achieved by the Cross-Layer model.

Figure 4 shows the cumulative overall power savings of the Cross-Layer model against the Optimized Cloud Servers Layer. As we can see, the Cross-Layer model still beats the Optimized Cloud Servers layer by around 20%.

Figure 5 shows all the layers in a single graph for comparison between different layers. Here X and Y axes denote time in days and power savings on each of the days. We can see that the cross-layer model has an advantage over all the layers respectively. We can see that power saved by the cross-layer model hovers around 40% to 80%. Whereas optimized edge network and edge servers layer hover around 20% and optimized cloud servers layer hovers around 20% to 50% mark which is lower than the cross-layer model. As the amount of workload may vary significantly each day the overall power savings varies as well.

Figure 6 shows cumulative performance over t days of all the layers in a single graph against the Cross-Layer model. Here X and Y axes denote time in days and cumulative power savings in t days respectively. Each of the layers starts with random peaks as the amount of power savings hasn't been calculated at this point. But as time progresses we can see that the amount of cumulative overall power savings mark is diverging into a single point instead of having any peaks/slopes etc. which implies that the cumulative power savings over t days are the point at which the line is approaching. Here in Fig. 6 we can see that the cross-layer has reached around 50% mark whereas the optimized edge network layer and edge servers layer has reached about 15%. On the other hand, the optimized cloud servers layer has ultimately achieved 30% energy efficiency. In the end, our Cross-layer model has outperformed all the other layers as it combines all the optimizations mentioned in each of the layers.

5 Conclusion

In this paper, we have proposed a cross-layer architecture to cascade optimized power from every layer to power up the whole architecture. The cross-layer architecture generates about 50% power savings which are better than optimizing a single layer where we used to get around 15%–20% power savings. Power Management is very crucial for the inclusive performance of edge computing services. Edge computing is emerging as a victorious paradigm for providing ubiquitous services so the synergy between different layers becomes important for providing these services. Only optimizing a single layer cannot be beneficial in the long run as it cannot assure whether the other layers are performing at their maximum potential. A proper system is required that monitors the power sector. So it becomes significant to unleash the full potential of each layer which can be done by making sure that every layer is using its required power which the cross-layer architecture does.

References

1. Varghese, B., et al.: Revisiting the arguments for edge computing research. IEEE Internet Comput. **25**(5), 36–42 (2021)
2. Toor, A., ul Islam, S., Ahmed, G., Jabbar, S., Khalid, S., Sharif, A.M.: Energy efficient edge-of-things. EURASIP J. Wirel. Commun. Networking **2019**(1) (2019)
3. Jiang, C., et al.: Energy aware edge computing: a survey. Comput. Commun. **151**, 556–580 (2020)
4. Li, W., et al.: On enabling sustainable edge computing with renewable energy resources. IEEE Commun. Mag. **56**(5), 94–101 (2018)
5. Chowdhury, N.M.M.K., Rahman, M.R., Boutaba, R.: Virtual network embedding with coordinated node and link mapping. In: IEEE INFOCOM 2009, pp. 783–791. IEEE (2009)
6. Udeen, H., Abbas, S., Mumtaz, A., Hussain, F., Kousar, K.: Critical analysis of edge computing. In: 2020 IEEE 5th International Conference on Signal and Image Processing (ICSIP). IEEE, October 2020
7. Hou, W., Ning, Z., Guo, L.: Green survivable collaborative edge computing in smart cities. IEEE Trans. Industr. Inf. **14**(4), 1594–1605 (2018)
8. Stead, M., Gradinar, A., Coulton, P., Lindley, J.: Edge of tomorrow: designing sustainable edge computing, August 2020
9. Li, S., et al.: Joint admission control and resource allocation in edge computing for internet of things. IEEE Network **32**(1), 72–79 (2018)
10. Sharma, P.K., Rathore, S., Jeong, Y.-S., Park, J.H.: SoftEdgeNet: SDN based energy-efficient distributed network architecture for edge computing. IEEE Commun. Mag. **56**(12), 104–111 (2018)

11. Daraghmeh, M., Al Ridhawi, I., Aloqaily, M., Jararweh, Y., Agarwal, A.: A power management approach to reduce energy consumption for edge computing servers. In: 2019 Fourth International Conference on Fog and Mobile Edge Computing (FMEC), pp. 259–264. IEEE (2019)
12. Pérez, S., Arroba, P., Moya, J.M.: Energy-conscious optimization of edge computing through deep reinforcement learning and two-phase immersion cooling. Futur. Gener. Comput. Syst. **125**, 891–907 (2021)
13. Marchisio, A., et al.: Deep learning for edge computing: current trends, cross-layer optimizations, and open research challenges. In: 2019 IEEE Computer Society Annual Symposium on VLSI (ISVLSI). IEEE, July 2019
14. Reif, S., et al.: X-Leep: leveraging cross-layer pacing for energy-efficient edge systems. In: Proceedings of the Eleventh ACM International Conference on Future Energy Systems, pp. 548–553 (2020)
15. Rausch, T., Avasalcai, C., Dustdar, S.: Portable energy-aware cluster-based edge computers. In: 2018 IEEE/ACM Symposium on Edge Computing (SEC). IEEE, October 2018

Energy Consumption Issues of a Data Center

Nabila Islam, Lubaba Alam Chhoa, and Ahmed Wasif Reza$^{(\boxtimes)}$

Department of Computer Science and Engineering, East West University, Dhaka, Bangladesh
wasif@ewubd.edu

Abstract. Nowadays, local or private data centers are a revolution that is developing rapidly. Many companies and educational organizations are building local data centers for security reasons. However, the energy consumption issues of data centers are rapidly increasing which needs to be addressed to develop green data centers. Many methods and techniques had been developed for minimizing the energy consumption of data centers. In this paper, an energy-efficient proposed model has been suggested for East West university's local data center for upgrading to a green data center. It is found that approximately 20% to 30% of energy will be saved after redesigning the data center.

Keywords: Green data center · energy consumption · cooling system · virtualization

1 Introduction

Green Data Center is also another way to promote green computing. The new generation is rapidly evolving through technology. These are the Internet of Things, Cloud computing, Data and artificial intelligence, and information technology. At present, the use of technology is increasing at a tremendous rate, as a result of which the amount of data is increasing at an average rate every year. Data centers consume more power and pollute the environment and produce more CO_2. Green computing can reduce environmental pollution and high power consumption. Green ensures that the increase in computing of resources in data centers will not harm or impact our environment as the design will be eco-friendly. Carbon emission/footprint is also a major problem in today's world. Lowering carbon emissions is also the goal of the Green data center. This is ongoing research about computing methods that are eco-friendly and cost-efficient. But despite the challenges faced, only a significant number of benefits of using green data center techniques are witnessed [1].

Energy consumption is a crucial factor in global warming difficulties since the more electricity consumed, the more carbon footprint is produced. If data centers lower their energy consumption, efficiency for climate-related issues would improve. As a result, energy conservation can improve system productivity and reliability, and it is one of the primary concerns in in-service distribution [2].

Md. S. Satu et al. (Eds.): MIET 2022, LNICST 491, pp. 702–714, 2023.
https://doi.org/10.1007/978-3-031-34622-4_55

The energy usage of data centers and their attached emissions of greenhouse gases (GHGs) is an alarming topic that should receive much attention. The energy requirements of cloud data centers are less than local data centers. However, there are a lot of issues related to energy consumption faced by data centers. There is a lack of knowledge about the issues and concerns caused by energy consumption in the data center [3]. In most cases, data centers utilize a drastic quantity of electricity and produce huge amounts of greenhouse gas (GHG) emissions. So, data centers are consuming major energy worldwide. The cloud infrastructure devoured nearly 623 terawatt-hours (TWh) of energy in 2007. After a few years in 2020, the energy consumption of the cloud infrastructure is about 1963.74 TWh. As a result, the energy cost is rising rapidly [4].

Energy usage accounts for 50% of data center operational costs, according to figures [5]. As a result, rising energy use necessitates large-scale power generation, putting enormous strain on the environment. High energy consumption can be attributed to two factors. For starters, when little operations take a lot of resources, a resource scheduling strategy is required and secondly, the data center's recent refrigerating technique produces energy wastage and an increase in cost. The paper [6] stated that the performance and energy consumption of systems are dependent on a variety of factors and that some of the basic approaches for conserving energy include turning on and off servers as needed, use of Dynamic Voltage/Frequency Scaling (DVFS), enable sleep mode while the servers are in an idle period, and rational/smart use of docker containers or virtual machines (VM).

The targets and goals were to determine and introduce a sustainable Green data center where the energy consumption issues are reduced which helps us take a step further on making our planet green and low/zero carbon emission.

- At first, thirty papers have been summarized.
- Techniques have been proposed for achieving a green data center at East West University.

The goal of this study is to interpret the challenges of a local data center, analyze energy consumption issues of data centers, summarize effective solutions for a sustainable data center and propose a method for sustainable improvement of East West University.

1.1 Problem Statement

According to [6], a huge amount of approximately 70 billion kilowatt-hours of electricity has been consumed by US data centers, which is accounting for about 2% of overall energy usage in the country. Furthermore, between the years 2014 to 2020, energy consumption is predicted to increase by 4%. As a result of this increase, a massive amount of greenhouse/harmful gas is generated, which is impacting the environment negatively and increase in global warming day by day. Moreover, as a result, many important research projects on data center energy usage have been started in recent years but, the main problem lies in the inefficient usage and underutilization of the resources. Server resources being utilized are between 10% and 50% and up to 70% when used at full capacity, according to data collected from over 5000 servers, which could result in a massive increase in costs.

Furthermore, because a considerably large amount of energy is consumed by data centers, they face the challenges of a sustainable energy economy, and as the demand for cloud-based services grows, so does the demand for data centers [7]. By 2030, data centers will consume 8000 TeraWatt hours (TWh) of energy if demand continues to rise [8].

All potential providers of datacentre services are trying to reduce their infrastructure's carbon footprints so that they can provide services without any emissions of harmful gas and use eco-friendly resources in their data centers [9].

1.2 Research Questions

The research questions based on the problem statements of this research are given below:

(i) How to develop a Green Data Center?
(ii) What are the issues of energy consumption in data centers?
(iii) What are the most effective methods for reducing energy use and waste?

2 Related Work

The authors of [10] created energy consumption methodologies for assessing overall energy usage in a system, suggesting that up to 20% energy savings are attainable. Using a data center with confinement which index can be improved to 0.99 and servers may be encased in shipping containers to enhance 30 percent energy efficiency. The authors of [10] found some new technologies to minimize both energy and cost. One of these energy-saving approaches is the use of heuristic algorithms. This algorithm is widely used for the optimization of energy consumption in wireless access networks. Total power consumption by the factors are– servers 53%, cooling systems 23%, power 19%, and others 5%.

Paper [11] proposed an algorithm which is VS placement algorithm. According to the author, this method aims to lower a data center's energy use. The authors of the paper [12] discussed the energy consumption contour analysis method. They found two layers of energy consumption management mechanisms. They are Virtualized Layer Energy Consumption Management and Cloud Computing Layer Energy Consumption Management. Moreover, a virtual machine provides an efficient solution and improvements. The authors of the paper [13] proposed an energy efficiency evaluation plan for the operational data center. Using computational equations and measurements for validation, this method will identify the sustainable opportunities for improvements for efficiency gains. By 2025, renewable energy consumption will increase by 30 percent taking a step further toward green IT.

The study in [9] discovered various reasons for energy waste in cloud data center services. Unfortunately, data centers need a substantial amount of electricity, accounting for 3% of global electrical energy usage. He discovered that data centers can squander up to 90% of the electricity they consume from the grid.

To balance trade-offs between the power consumption, the number of migrations, host performance, and the total number of shut-down hosts, the author of [14] developed a MuMs dynamic VM selection algorithm. Consolidates virtual machines from an overburdened or under burdened host in preparation for migration to a more appropriate host. Idle hosts/servers are also moved to energy-saving mode. According to statistics, by 2019, the number of customers for private and local data center services will increase drastically.

The VMR (Virtual Machine Replacement) method for QoS and Energy Awareness in Data Centers was presented in this paper [15]. Clients of data centers often have four major concerns: energy cost, peak power dissipation, cooling mechanisms, and carbon emissions. The major goal of this algorithm is to improve the energy-aware allocation of resources techniques and processes for data centers by solutions formed such as turning off idle PMs and reducing the number of active PMs. The comparison, shows the number of using active PMs is 15.29%, using the FF1 algorithm is 28.23%, and using a random algorithm is 56.47%.

The authors of [16] proposed Energy-Efficient and SLA-aware algorithms for Dynamic Virtualization Aggregation in data centers. Service providers can optimize resource use while lowering data center power consumption by using VM consolidation. Data centers consumed about 1.5 percent of global electricity usage in 2010, and this amount has risen to 3 percent in 2016. On the other hand, 30% of servers, on average, use 10–15% of their resource availability most of the time.

The authors of [17] outline how cloud computing can help to minimize energy consumption. The energy expenses of software and hardware are decreased by using VM (visualization technique) in data centers. Improving load balance. Excess wire usage is being reduced, eliminating GHG gas and CO2 and protecting the environment.

In [18], the author talks about using cloud computing instead of server in a data center which is playing a role in energy saving. Using cloud computing prevents excess CO2 emissions and reduces environmental pollution. VM and Task schedule algorithm is being used which is saving more energy in cloud computing data center.

The authors of [19], mention the use of cloud computing instead of servers for saving energy in data centers. Using VM and scheduling algorithms in the cloud computing data center is saving a huge amount of energy on that server and networking device. In [20], the author mentions the use of cloud computing in data centers. Powerful ICT equipment used in the data centers a lot of energy consumption. Using a Cloud data center will reduce energy consumption by 20% and with it co2 emissions. In [21], the author mentions the use of cloud computing instead of servers for energy saving in the data center. A genetic algorithm has been used in a virtual machine for green cloud computing. The author also mentions VM migration. A virtual machine for migration and a policy for spreading it. It depends on the idea that transferring VMs and hosts with minimal CPU consumption is preferable to overloading and blocking the host. This results in relatively low power consumption.

The author designed an infrastructure for controlling a VMS data center that is optimized for power usage in a research paper [22]. Using VMs in cloud computing does not result in additional energy loss.

The authors of [23] develop a neural network architecture that examines actual operation data from model plant performance and 0.4 percent errors for PUE forecasts of $0.004 + /0.005$ or PUE of 1.1. On Google DCs, this model has been well tested.

The authors' findings suggest that machine learning is a DC performance model and an effective technique to increase energy efficiency using existing sensor data.

In [24], the usage of a supporting facility level for an actual analysis of the IT system level and cross-layer optimization, according to the author, optimizes data energy-saving potential. This research focuses on optimizing cross-layer energy consumption and having all the modules implemented in the data center. The author of [25] discusses data center architecture as well as power consumption. By modifying the architecture of the data center, it is also possible to save a significant amount of energy. Also mentioned in this paper is 4%-12% power consumption through a three-tier hardware network.

The related works and literature review are given in the following Table 1.

Table 1. Related Work

Ref. No.	Approach	Techniques	Solutions/Aim
[26]	Design of Green Data Center	1. Reduces Data Centre Hot Spots	• Thermal systems must be enabled to identify data center equipment cooling and decrease data center hot spots
		2. Consolidate Storage	• Estimation of the upcoming data storage capacity and its routine involvement • Consolidated NAS (network-attached storage) could also help to decrease costs of cooling and power
		3. The appliance of virtualization schemes	• Virtualization technique used to full utilization of processors capacity • physical and virtual servers can use a similar configuration • It can serve to iterate hot plugs minus troubling the applications • high speed of network with low cost of the technology by more than 30% • raising the operation of the current plantation from below 10% to over 40%

(*continued*)

Table 1. (*continued*)

Ref. No.	Approach	Techniques	Solutions/Aim
		4. Design the Accurate Infrastructure	• Use of domestic stone and brick • The entire structure should have insulation as it increases energy productivity • Qualified services for virtualization techniques
[27]	Cooling Management System	1. Minimize the energy CRAC consumes	• natural cooling technique • Build-in fortification (bunkers) like underground area • using low power server • Optimizing airflow in the data center
		2. Direct Clean Power	• Use offset direct techniques for sustainable power • hydroelectric generated locations, or doing on-site clean energy production
[28]		1. Use of Renewable Energy, 2. Thermal-aware Scheduling, 3. Future resource capacity Planning, 4. Use of renewable Energy, 5. Heat/Cold Utilization	• decrease carbon footprints • the energy efficiency of power infrastructure/management and cooling devices increases
[29]		1. Workload Scheduling	• Power will be saved and better server utilization will be maintained

3   Materials and Method

For this research paper, the data collection method that has been selected is the literature review study. Energy consumption issues of a data center are a fundamental topic. For this study various research papers, articles and journals were collected. The focused part of this literature review was the energy consumption issues of data centers and how they can be reduced.

Step 1: Recent research papers related to energy consumption issues of data centers from high-impact journals are collected and summarised. Identifying and listing the methods/algorithms mentioned for reducing energy consumption issues.

Step 2: Summarization of the several methods (e.g, VM scheduling and migration, cooling, DVFS, and DENS) selected from the related works section as they are the recent techniques used for energy consumption in data centers. Gain in-depth knowledge about these eight techniques to propose a method with the combination of all the techniques together.

Step 3: Design a proposed model for reducing energy consumption in East West datacenter.

3.1 Data Collection Method

Thirty research papers had been collected and read for summarizing all the methods and algorithms available. For document study, the research papers and journals were collected using the Mendeley library to find eligible documents from reputed online databases. For conducting the systematic literature review, topics and keywords such as energy efficiency and energy consumption issues, and data center were focused on. The selected papers were published between the years 2015 to 2021 and written in English.

Surveys, on-site visiting, and interviews had been conducted at East West University premises for collecting data about the local data center.

3.2 Data Analysis

In this study, thirty paper was summarized to gain insights into the issues of energy consumption faced by data centers and the target of this study was ied to determine the difficulties with energy/power consumption. The data collected from the interview and surveys had been sorted out to determine the issues found in the data center that needs to be addressed.

The data collected from the East West University premises (Fig. 1) are summarized below:

a) The data center consists of four racks which currently hold twenty-seven servers of which fourteen are outdated and one server is used as a VM.
b) Cooling equipment: It is built on a raised floor (one foot above), the ceiling is sealed with insulation, cold and hot aisle, and has two precision air conditioning units.
c) The energy consumption of each server is approximately 700 to 800 w.

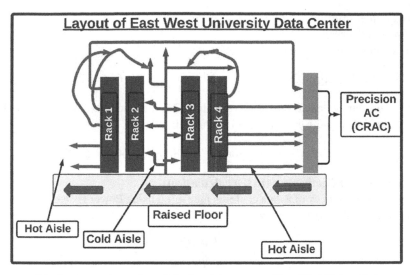

Fig. 1. Layout/overview of the local data center (East West University)

The proposed methods for reducing the energy consumption of East West University premises data center are given in the following Table 2:

Table 2. Proposed method

No.	Components	Methods	Aim
1	Cooling equipment	1. The cold aisle must be covered with a glass wall surrounding the racks so that the cold air stays intact on the glass box	• This will reduce a huge amount of energy consumption as it will take less power and time to cool the racks • This method will also reduce the amount of energy consumed by the precision air conditioner by **20% - 30%** as it can be replaced with a low-powered AC
2	Cabling Management System	2. Wiring should be changed to low energy power cables and must be neatly organized so that the air can flow freely through and fro	• Optimizing airflows in the data center
3	Servers	3. Servers should be converted to virtual servers using VMR so that the servers required are fewer 4. Idle or old unutilized servers must be turned off or replaced with VM	• To minimize the amount of energy consumed by unused/idle servers • Energy/power consumed by half of the servers will be reduced and it becomes easier for resource management
4	Power Source	5. More solar panels can be installed	• It saves energy and costs up to more than **20%**
5	IT equipment	6. UPS can also be replaced with a low configuration and energy-efficient certification so that a power-saving mode can be enabled	• Power will be saved and better server utilization will be maintained

Power consumption calculation for servers:
Total no. of servers $= 27$
per server energy consumption $= 800$ w

$$\text{Total energy consumption} = 27 \times 800 = 21,600 \, w/21.6 \, kw$$

10 servers can be replaced by 2 servers plus VM, if the servers are reduced to 5 to 7 servers with VM then the energy consumption will be:

$$\text{Total energy consumption} = 7 \times 800 = 5,600 \, w/5.6 \, kw$$

Power Usage Effectiveness (PUE) calculation:
The energy efficiency of a data center is measured using Power Usage Effectiveness (PUE) and it is computed as follows:

$$PUE = \frac{Total \, facility \, power}{IT \, equipment \, power} \tag{1}$$

Total Facility power includes servers, IT equipment, lighting, cooling, etc. and IT equipment power includes servers and IT equipment alone.

For the current 27 servers, the approximate PUE calculation where,
Total Facility power $= 21.6$ (server) $+ 10$ (IT) $+ 100$ (cooling) $+ 5$(lighting).
IT equipment power $= 21.6$ (server) $+ 10$ (IT) [approximate values]

$$PUE = \frac{21.6 + 10 + 100 + 5}{21.6 + 10} \tag{2}$$

$$PUE = 4.32 > 3.0(Very \, inefficient) \tag{3}$$

For the current 7 servers, the approximate PUE calculation where,
Total Facility power $= 5.6$ (server) $+ 10$ (IT) $+ 100$ (cooling) $+ 5$(lighting).
IT equipment power $= 5.6$ (server) $+ 10$ (IT) [approximate values]

$$PUE = \frac{5.6 + 10 + 100 + 5}{5.6 + 10} \tag{4}$$

$$PUE = 7.73 > 3.0(Very \, inefficient) \tag{5}$$

For the current 7 servers plus CRAC, the approximate PUE calculation,

$$PUE = \frac{40.6}{5.6 + 10} \tag{6}$$

$$PUE = 2.5 < 2.60 < 3.0(inefficient) \tag{7}$$

By making these changes, the energy consumption will be reduced and more resources can be allocated to fewer servers.

3.3 Research Ethics

The energy consumption issues of data centers that have been summarized in this paper are all collected from dependable and credible sources. The collected data received from the selected papers were qualitative. The data were assigned into categories based on their functions and roles. The data was further analyzed to determine the methods and algorithms along with the percentage improved, efficiency, cost consideration, and space for each data. The targets and goals were to determine sustainable Green data centers where the energy consumption issues are reduced which helps us to take a step further on making our planet green and low/zero carbon emission.

4 Results and Discussion

The redesigned layout according to the proposed method for the cold aisle for reducing the energy consumption of East West University premises data center is shown in Fig. 2.

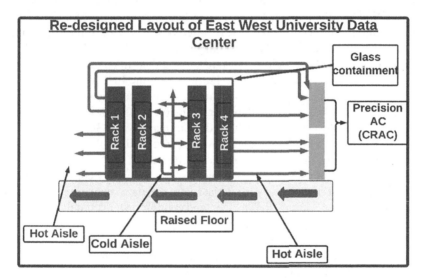

Fig. 2. Redesigned Layout/overview of the local data center (East West University)

After evaluation of the proposed method mentioned above in Table 2, the approximated calculation has been found to show the reduction in energy consumption, the values taken into consideration are less compared to the real values for simplification of the calculation and results analysis. The result above in Table 3, shows a comparison between the approximated calculation of the proposed method and the current method which is calculated using an online calculator [30]. If the servers are being utilized according to the resources required and all the unutilized idle servers are turned off, the efficiency will increase by 15%. The power consumption of 27 servers is reduced to 5,600 w from 21,600 w by replacing the servers with virtualization. Moreover, the cold aisle should be covered with a glass container so that no cold air can escape and

Table 3. Result analysis/comparison of the energy efficiency between the proposed model and the existing model.

Technique	Existing model	Proposed model
Servers replacement	21,600 w	**5,600 w**
PUE (servers)	4.32	7.73
DCiE (servers)	23.13%	12.94%
Annual power uses (kw/h)	1,196,616 kw/h	**1,056,456 kw/h**
PUE (servers + CRAC)	4.32	**2.60**
DCiE (servers + CRAC)	23.13%	**38.42%**
Annual power uses (kw/h)	1,196,616 kw/h	**355,656 kw/h**

no hot air can enter the cold aisle. The time and power required to cool the whole room and maintain a fixed temperature are excessive. The annual power uses reduces from 1,196,616 kW/hr to 1,056,456 kw/h after servers had been reduced from 27 to 7 servers plus virtualization. Thus, cooling only the required portion requires much less time and power, and as well as the high-powered/voltage precision AC can be replaced with a low-powered precision AC which shows a tremendous fall in annual energy consumption from 1,196,616kw/h to 355,656kw/h. Furthermore, the PUE value increases from 4.32 to 7.73 after reducing servers making it more inefficient as the total facility power is much more compared to IT equipment power. To increase efficiency, the cooling power has been reduced, so the new PUE is 2.60, and DCiE increased to 38.42% from 23.13%. Furthermore, the use of virtualization and power-saving mode will also increase energy efficiency tremendously and carbon footprint will decrease.

Moreover, the cooling systems are the major source of energy consumption issues. Usually consume most of the energy. To initiate a green data center energy consumption issues of servers, power, cabling, IoT devices, and cooling systems should be reduced as they are the main source of power consumption. Initiatives like low-powered CRAC, cold aisle covered in glass containers to minimize the mixing of hot and cold air, insulation, cable management, power-saving IT equipment, and visualization mentioned in Table 3, is a fundamental approach toward developing a green data center as it can be seen that 20% to 30% energy efficiency is increased.

5 Conclusion

Recently, due to the increase in demand for data center services, the energy consumption issue has become both ecological and economical. The necessity for energy-saving and identifying concerns with data centers has been summarized in this document for thirty papers from accessible research on the subject.

It has been reported that several components of data center design, such as servers, nodes, and memory, utilize more energy than the CPU. Moreover, data center equipment and servers produce a lot of heat and because of that, a large portion of the energy is needed for cooling all the equipment and servers which is a major issue for consuming more energy. Another major issue is zombie/idle servers because although there is no use, still the servers are running and consuming more and more energy. Moreover, it can be seen that the consumption rate of energy in data centers is high which increases the operational cost.

In this study, the proposed methods and the techniques mentioned in the related work section are cost efficient as the proposed method requires a low-powered AC, and will reduce and save approximately 20% to 30% of the energy required. If implemented accordingly, the local data center of East West University will take a step further towards green IT and achieving a green data center.

The future work of this study will include, further research on how a green data center can be achieved in a cost-effective way and surveys may be taken from the on-premises data centers present in Bangladesh so that an overall energy issue can be identified. Many technologies and services have become essential for creating an eco-friendly environment using clean and green energy.

References

1. Cholli, N.G.: Green Cloud computing: redefining the future of cloud computing. Int. Res. J. Adv. Sci. Hub 3, 12–19 (2021)
2. Depavath, H., Ramesh, K.B., Chithra, B., Ramana, M.V.: Green computing-an efficient eco friendly computing, vol. 2, no. 08, August 2015
3. Atrey, A., Jain, N., Iyengar, N.: A study on green cloud computing. Int. J. Grid Distrib. Comput. 6(6), 93–102 (2013)
4. Managing and Understanding On-Premises and Cloud Spend. https://www.softwareone.com/en-ie/downloads/global/research-report-on-premises-and-cloud-spend. Accessed 11 Jan 2022
5. Yang, J., Xiao, W., Jiang, C., Hossain, M.S., Muhammad, G., Amin, S.U.: AI-powered green cloud and data center. IEEE Access 7, 4195–4203 (2018)
6. Yadav, A.K., Garg, M.L, Ritika: The issues of energy efficiency in cloud computing based data centers. Oryzae. Biosc. Biotech. Res. Comm. 12(2) (2019)
7. Diouani, S., Medromi, H.: Survey: an optimized energy consumption of resources in cloud data centers. Int. J. Comput. Sci. Inf. Secur. (IJCSIS) 16(2) (2018)
8. Buyya, R., Gill, S.S.: Sustainable cloud computing: foundations and future directions. arXiv preprint arXiv:1805.01765 (2018)
9. Derdus, K.M., Omwenga, V.O., Ogao, P.J.: Causes of energy wastage in cloud data centre servers: a survey (2019)
10. Helfert, M., Desprez, F., Ferguson, D., Leymann, F. (eds.): CLOSER 2013. CCIS, vol. 453. Springer, Cham (2014). https://doi.org/10.1007/978-3-319-11561-0
11. Diaconescu, D., Pop, F., Cristea, V.: Energy-aware placement of VMs in a datacenter. In: 2013 IEEE 9th International Conference on Intelligent Computer Communication and Processing (ICCP), pp. 313–318. IEEE (2013)
12. Li, L.: Energy consumption management of virtual cloud computing platform. IOP Conf. Ser. Earth Environ. Sci. 94(1) (2017)
13. Dumitrescu, C., Plesca, A., Dumitrescu, L., Adam, M., Nituca, C., Dragomir, A.: Assessment of data center energy efficiency methods and metrics. In: 2018 International Conference and Exposition on Electrical And Power Engineering (EPE), pp. 0487–0492. IEEE (2018)
14. Yadav, R., Zhang, W., Chen, H., Guo, T.: Mums: energy-aware VM selection scheme for cloud data center. In: 2017 28th International Workshop on Database and Expert Systems Applications (DEXA), pp. 132–136. IEEE (2017)

15. Ali, R., Shen, Y., Huang, X., Zhang, J., Ali, A.: VMR: virtual machine replacement algorithm for QoS and energy-awareness in cloud data centers. In: 2017 IEEE International Conference on Computational Science and Engineering (CSE) and IEEE International Conference on Embedded and Ubiquitous Computing (EUC), vol. 2, pp. 230–233. IEEE (2017)
16. Khoshkholghi, M.A., Derahman, M.N., Abdullah, A., Subramaniam, S., Othman, M.: Energy-efficient algorithms for dynamic virtual machine consolidation in cloud data centers. IEEE Access **5**, 10709–10722 (2017)
17. Berl, A., et al.: Energy-efficient cloud computing. Comput. J. **53**(7), 1045-1051 (2010)
18. Adhikary, T., Das, A.K., Razzaque, M.A., Sarkar, A.J.: Energy-efficient scheduling algorithms for data center resources in cloud computing. In: 2013 IEEE 10th International Conference on High Performance Computing and Communications & 2013 IEEE International Conference on Embedded and Ubiquitous Computing, pp. 1715–1720. IEEE (2013)
19. Babu, G.P., Tiwari, A.K.: Energy efficient scheduling algorithm for cloud computing systems based on prediction model. Int. J. Adv. Network. Appl. **10**(5), 4013–4018 (2019)
20. Basmadjian, R., Meer, H.D., Lent, R., Giuliani, G.: Cloud computing and its interest in saving energy: the use case of a private cloud. J. Cloud Comput. Adv. Syst. Appl. **1**(1), 1–25 (2012)
21. Singh, S., Sharma, P.K., Moon, S.Y., Park, J.H.: EH-GC: an efficient and secure architecture of energy harvesting Green cloud infrastructure. Sustainability **9**(4), 673 (2017)
22. Madani, N., Lebbat, A., Tallal, S., Medromi, H.: Power-aware virtual Machines consolidation architecture based on CPU load scheduling. In: 2014 IEEE/ACS 11th International Conference on Computer Systems and Applications (AICCSA), pp. 361–365. IEEE (2014)
23. Gao, J.: Machine learning applications for data center optimization (2014)
24. Wang, J., Zhou, B., Liu, W., Hu, S.: Research progress and development trend of cross-layer energy efficiency optimization in data centers. SCIENTIA SINICA Inf. **50**(1), 1–24 (2020)
25. Pries, R., Jarschel, M., Schlosser, D., Klopf, M., Tran-Gia, P.: Power consumption analysis of data center architectures. In: Rodrigues, J.J.P.C., Zhou, L., Chen, M., Kailas, A. (eds.) GreeNets 2011. LNICSSITE, vol. 51, pp. 114–124. Springer, Heidelberg (2012). https://doi.org/10.1007/978-3-642-33368-2_10
26. Rais, M.Z.: Design of green data center. Int. J. Res. Eng. Technol. (IJRET) **03**(05) (2014)
27. Kass, S., Ravagni, A.: Designing and building the next generation of sustainable data centers. Sustain. Dev. Goals, 1–21 (2019)
28. Mukherjee, D., Chakraborty, S., Sarkar, I., Ghosh, A., Roy, S.: A detailed study on data centre energy efficiency and efficient cooling techniques. Int. J. **9**(5) (2020)
29. Peoples, C., Parr, G., McClean, S., Morrow, P., Scotney, B.: Energy aware scheduling across 'green' cloud data centres. In: IEEE International Symposium on Integrated Network Management, pp. 876–879 (2013)
30. https://www.42u.com/measurement/pue-dcie.htm

Trade-Offs of Improper E-waste Recycling: An Empirical Study

Md Shamsur Rahman Talukdar[1], Marwa Khanom Nurtaj[1], Md Nahid Hasan[1], Aysha Siddeka[1], Ahmed Wasif Reza[1], and Mohammad Shamsul Arefin[2,3]([✉])

[1] Department of Computer Science and Engineering, East West University, Dhaka, Bangladesh
wasif@ewubd.edu
[2] Department of Computer Science and Engineering, Daffodil International University, Dhaka, Bangladesh
sarefin@cuet.ac.bd
[3] Department of Computer Science and Engineering, Chattogram University of Engineering and Technology, Chattogram, Bangladesh

Abstract. The term "E-waste" refers to any electronic equipment that has been abandoned and discarded or reached the end of its service life. As electronics is one of the largest growing industrial sectors, the recycling of E-wastes has evolved into a serious global issue. E-waste contains both metals and chemicals. A growing country like Bangladesh is now estimated to create 2.8 million tons of E-waste every year. Around 15–25% of it gets recycled, while the remaining end up in open soil, farmland, and water. Many hazardous elements from improper E-waste disposal can cause health diseases for workers and their families like breathing problems, skin infections, and stomach problems. Also, improper disposal of E-waste can harm the environment and have a negative impact on our climate. In this paper, we analyze the environmental effects and health issues of electronic waste. We found that there is a significant lack of understanding on how to reuse, rescale, and refurbish electronic equipment. People everywhere may avoid health and environmental problems by managing E-waste effectively, collecting E-waste properly, and raising awareness about the dangers of improper e-waste disposal can save people all over the world from challenges.

Keywords: E-waste · Environmental Impacts · Health Impact · Improper Recycling · Disposal

1 Introduction

E-waste is a general term for electronic equipment that has achieved the end of its lifespan or has been thrown away because newer and better technology has come out [1]. Improper E-waste disposal is causing a considerable loss of something rare or expensive precious metals and other raw materials like Indium (essential for flat-panel televisions), Nd (used in motor magnets), and Co (for batteries) [2]. It is estimated that E-waste accounts for more than 5% of municipal solid waste across the world. In developing nations,

Md. S. Satu et al. (Eds.): MIET 2022, LNICST 491, pp. 715–729, 2023.
https://doi.org/10.1007/978-3-031-34622-4_56

where E-waste is recovered, it is typical for metals to be extracted and sold in unsafe, inefficient ways [3]. Electronic waste is recognized as a valuable resource on every continent because it can be used to get back precious materials like Fe, Cu, Al, Ag, Au, etc. [4]. Abandoned electronics are considered a global resource since they can be recycled for valuable materials. So, proper E-waste disposal seems to be an important subject to take into consideration.

Personal electronics such as displays, mobiles, PCs, and televisions account for half of all E-waste. The other half comes from large-scale home electronics equipment. Every year 40 million tons of E-waste are thrown away into landfills, fired, or sold cheaply and poorly handled [2]. Though, only 12.5% of electronic trash is recycled currently. E-waste is mainly a problem in developing and emerging countries because they don't have the right infrastructure in place to deal with it or, sometimes, it is not there at all. For this reason, many unauthorized and informal vendors handle most of the E-waste. Nowadays, E-waste is frequently mishandled which harms workers and the health of children, who spend their time near the places where E-waste is disposed [1].

Again, improper E-waste disposal increases global warming. If the materials from electronics garbage are not recycled, these scraps will not be able to substitute primary materials or reduce carbon emissions caused by the extraction and refinement of raw equipment. Also, some temperature exchange equipment uses refrigerants, which are greenhouse gasses. If discarded refrigerators and air conditioners are not properly disposed of, they can release approximately 98 million tons of CO_2 into the atmosphere, which is equivalent to 0.3% of the world's 2019 energy-related emissions (IEA) [1].

In improper E-waste systems, batteries are holding a large portion. Most batteries have at least one of the nine metals listed below: Li, Co, Cd, Pd, Zn, Mg, Ni, Ag, or Hg. The fastest-growing category, lithium-ion batteries, is expected to reach $100 billion by 2025 [2]. Lithium-ion batteries consist of many harmful materials which are toxic to people and the environment. Li-ion batteries are more frequently found in the environment as E-waste because most electronics are becoming easier to throw away [5]. One electric vehicle lithium battery can contain the same lithium as 1000 smartphones [2].

By 2030, it is assumed that over 11 million tons of old lithium-ion batteries would have been dumped [6]. The absence of necessary information regarding the treatment of this expired electronics equipment, as well as the improper disposal, does not raise concerns about human health only. It can also be harmful to our environment. The study's findings would give us an essential understanding of the increasing crisis of E-waste and assist us in gathering the necessary information.

1.1 Background

Electronic products which have concluded their respective time are known as E-waste [7]. E-waste is a toxic brew of metals and other substances. A new item enters the market and quickly replaces older ones, often even before they reach the decline stage [8]. This kind of generated E-waste is increasing quickly, with estimates indicating that 72 billion tons are created globally each year [7]. Economically depressed countries rely on informal electronic waste recycling to generate cash flow. The problem is that in developing countries, it is often handled and disposed of in unsafe ways, resulting in poll uncontrolled processing methods exposing vulnerable populations, such as women and children, to harmful chemicals [1].

According to the EPA, about 18% of the hazardous and valuable electronic waste can be integrated and properly processed. However, no initiative can achieve its full potential even in the absence of active participation and appropriate lessons for consumers. According to the ITU, E-waste is the most extensive and difficult to manage waste stream in the world. In the year 2019, the globe produced 53.6 metric tons of electronic garbage, of which only 9.3 metric tons or 17% were recycled. Electronic trash comprises both valuable materials and hazardous substances, recycling in a way that is both efficient and safe is becoming more significant for the economy, the environment, and also for human health. The difference between how much E-waste is made and how much is properly recycled shows how important it is for everyone, including young people, to work on this problem [9].

As Bangladesh rapidly moves closer to its goal of being a middle-income nation, IT infrastructure is being constructed and the usage of electronic devices in homes, offices, and several other government and non-government sectors is growing daily. Every year, Bangladesh generates approximately 2.8 Metric Tons of electronic waste. An unknown quantity of electronic garbage is dumped in open soil, farmland, and water. People in Bangladesh are not following the rules for the proper disposal of these products. In Bangladesh, there is no definite amount of E-waste created each year. As technology advances, more new electronic devices are produced, and disposing of old computers, phones, and TVs becomes more common [8].

E-waste is one of the most harmful sources of contamination in the environment [10]. But the lack of awareness and inappropriate electronic garbage disposal may lead to environmental contamination. People can get sick if they don't know how to properly handle or reuse expired products. Electronic trash poses a threat to the health of humans. E-waste contaminants can be inhaled, eaten, or absorbed through the skin. A Bangladeshi study found that over 15% of children die because of improper recycling of E-waste. More than 80% get sick from toxic chemicals and chronic illnesses. Also, the E-waste collecting process in Bangladesh is managed in a harmful way. Because the process of collecting E-waste is mainly dependent on "Vangari" (Local vendors) Shops. They do not follow any rules or regulations while collecting or recycling E-waste. For this reason, the toxic chemical from the E-waste can mix with the environment easily. In illegal E-waste collection and recycling, approximately 50,000 children are involved [8]. The main ideas of our study are to identify, describe, analyze, and assess E-waste damage patterns. Our research will investigate the current state of E-waste in Bangladesh and deliver better ideas for safe and secure E-waste recycling by raising public knowledge about the dangers of improper E-waste recycling.

1.2 Problem Statement

The significance of E-waste management is becoming more challenging as technology use increases. In this recent pandemic situation of COVID, people have started online education and work-from-home tasks. For this, the use of electronic devices increased by a large amount among average people. Unfortunately, most of these technologies end up in the trash, resulting in E-waste. The majority of E-waste is still dumped in an open area, as a result of which valuable resources are lost as well as the release of harmful chemicals and pollutants into the water, soil, and atmosphere. These toxicities can cause harm to the human health system and also can create skin problems.

According to our research, general people are not concerned about the hazardous effects of improper E-waste Handling. In the large or small recycling industry, management and workers do not pay enough attention to hazardous electronics wastes that are imported for reprocessing. In a human sense, the absence of an appearance of hazardous material contained in E-waste leads them to believe that these items are toxic-free. There is a huge knowledge gap between shop owners and workers [11]. As far as the authors' knowledge goes, no scientific paper describing IT waste processing and dealing with its dangerous impact of improper disposal in Bangladesh could be located [9]. In addition, neither a systematic review nor a case study has been conducted in Bangladesh about improper E-waste recycling and its effects on health and the environment.

1.3 Aim

This study explores the E-waste scenario, the E-waste recycling system, and industrial actions in Bangladesh, which represent impediments to proper E-waste recycling, and finds solutions to remove the Inappropriate E-waste Management structures.

1.4 Objectives

The study's aims are as follows:

- To illustrate the current E-waste management company initiatives in Bangladesh
- To describe the practices of IT waste disposal in Bangladesh.
- To investigate the health consequences of poor E-waste disposal in Bangladesh.
- To analyze the effect of improper electronics waste recycling in Bangladesh.
- To analyze the awareness level of the shop owners and workers and general people in Bangladesh.

1.5 Scope of the Study

This research focuses on the trade of inappropriate E-waste treatment in growing nations such as Bangladesh. It has explored and analyzed the situation in Bangladesh and described the health and environmental damages. All other waste management is out of our scope. Also, the study is based in Bangladesh. The research will be focused on observations of the E-waste disposal scenario in Bangladesh.

2 Related Work

Apparently, in accordance with the Step Initiative of 2014, "Electronic waste" is a phrase that is used to include objects of all different sorts of EEE and a component of the item that the owner no longer needs and is so disposed of as garbage without any intention of reusing it. Bangladesh purchases roughly 3.2 million electronics items each year, according to the Bangladesh Electrical Merchandise Manufacturers Association (BEMMA) [12].

According to a survey done by ESDO (2016), in Bangladesh, totally broken or unusable electronic devices are 50% disposed of, whereas partially damaged equipment is fixed 90% of the time. The author also suggested that E-waste must be treated carefully since many of these goods include poisonous and dangerous materials, posing a huge environmental concern as well as a major danger to employees' health in the workplace. In order to establish an efficient method for managing electronic trash, it is essential to have a solid understanding of the journey that electronic trash takes from the point at which it is produced until it reaches its final destination [13].

The author conducted a poll of the employees at the recycling center, and the results showed that the average monthly salary for these workers is BDT 3000, even after working twelve-hour per day. When compared to those in other fields, the individuals that are involved in recycling electronic garbage are receiving lesser salaries. A day worker in this town may expect to earn at least BDT 200 for putting in an average of eight to nine hours of work per day [11]. The lower salary rate indicates that there are a lot of infrastructure problems in Bangladesh's E-waste recycling system.

According to the first proposal, The GEA would allow the E-waste industry to be rebranded from its present polluting image to a greener potential that reflects Bangladesh's economic progress. The second proposal is to construct nationwide electronic trash databases alongside a decision-making tool, to gather, maintain, and disseminate information and statistics on electronic waste. The third option is to establish a stepwise national E-waste register for the unorganized sector with the intention of publicly recognizing and observing the unorganized sector [14].

The environment can be protected by recycling, reusing, or rehabilitating electronic trash [1]. Reuse decreases the amount of human- and environmentally harmful chemicals by 71% and 40%, respectively. Refurbishment/Upgrading decreases the number of harmful toxins by 61% for individuals and 31% for the environment. From Recycling/Secondary production, the scientific recycling procedure eliminates human and environmentally harmful pollutants by 11% and 14%, correspondingly [15]. The primary manufacturing of these metals would have created 1.28 million tons of carbon dioxide (or 17.1 tons of carbon dioxide per ton of metal). The comparative analysis demonstrates that secondary production generates less CO2 [16].

Young people in the country of Bangladesh, numbering in the vicinity of fifty thousand, are actively engaged in the recovery and sorting of electronic waste. About 40%, or 20,000 minors, are employed in shipbreaking yards [8]. In our nation, 15% of child laborers die due to improper E-waste handling. Moreover, 83% of children workers in this industry suffer from illnesses [17, 18]. There are about 120,000 Vangaries (E-waste recycling workers) who will be much more badly affected by their exposure to the chemicals found in E-waste [19].

3 Methodology

3.1 Data Collection Methods

This chapter specified the study methods and procedures for achieving its research objective. The design and data sources have been designed here for the study. This study was conducted in a few recycling industries in Bangladesh. We also collect data from various online resources because Bangladesh, as a developing country, is quite new in its E-waste recycling culture.

3.2 Research Process

The study aims at finding the problem that is created by improper E-waste recycling in Bangladesh. The study used qualitative data collected from surveys, case studies, and field observations. The data is about the collection, disassembly, disposal, E-device users, and the generation of E-waste.

- Identifying environmental and health hazards while disposing of the E-wastes in an improper way
- Exploring the current state of the electronics waste recycling practice in Bangladesh.
- Collecting and analyzing data from different places (Experts, industry, vendors, public opinions).
- Designing solutions to recycle E-waste in a non-hazard way.

The following diagram (Fig. 1) is referring to the process flow of the research.

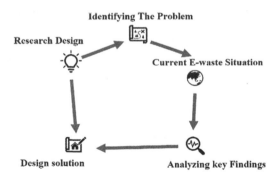

Fig. 1. Research Process

3.3 Research Ethics

In this study, we visited a few well-known E-Waste recycling companies, and also for research purposes we met with some entrepreneurs and researchers who are doing research on opening a new E-waste recycling industry. For the collection of data from individual interviews, a consent form describing the goal of this study was issued. The anonymity of the participants was maintained. Participants in the offline survey were required to read the informed consent form, and interviews were conducted only if they agreed to the conditions.

4 Result and Discussion

4.1 Recycling System in Bangladesh

From our research and analysis, we can assume a scenario where very few people in our country are concerned about improper E-waste disposal which has so many hazardous effects. There are some E-waste recyclers that exist in our country, but they are facing many kinds of barriers to collecting e-waste and recycling them in a proper way.

Basically, people are concerned about using good electronic devices, but they are not aware of the situation when the technology becomes E-waste. Some people throw them in the dustbin, and some sell them to second-hand device users or vendors in exchange for a small amount of money. There are very few well-known companies that collect their perished products to reuse or recycle the E-waste in a proper way to reduce its harmful effects. The recycling process of E-waste in general in Bangladesh follows the process which is attached below:

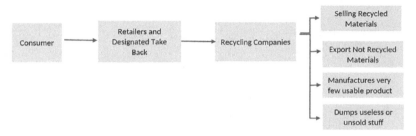

Fig. 2. E-Waste Recycling procedure in the Bangladeshi recycling industry.

Thus, from the diagram (Fig. 2), we can see that very few recycling companies collect electronic devices from retailers and designated take back which comes from consumers, and then sorts them and divides them into 4 segments:

- Selling recycled materials.
- Exporting not recycled materials.
- Manufacturing very few usable products.
- Throwing the rest of the parts in an improper way.

Though, the E-waste recycling system of Bangladesh is not maintained in a proper way. But our research finds that there are few well-known E-waste companies in Bangladesh who are aiming to recycle E-waste in an efficient technique. They try to follow the rule and regulations of considering environmental and health issues which strictly follow international standards and satisfy most of the government policies of Bangladesh.

A summary of possible E-waste recycling pathways is provided in Fig. 3. The chain for reusing and recycling electronic scrap has many steps, such as inventorying, assessing, collecting, shipping, reselling, recovering electronic parts, disassembling, shredding/pre-processing, and final processing of the different materials and metals.

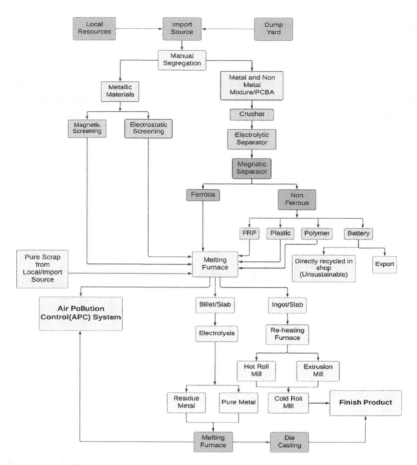

Fig. 3. Overview of possible E-waste recycling pathways.

Pre-processing is one of the most crucial phases following the collection of electronic waste equipment. Most of the time, E-waste is sorted by type before it is processed. This is because some parts of E-waste, namely batteries, cathode ray tubes, and lamps where mercury is used, need extra steps to be taken to reduce risks. Heating electronic parts above the threshold at which solder (around 250 degrees Celsius) typically used in construction would melt is another method for reducing their size and then hitting, shearing, or vibrating the material. Using this method, it is possible to get the maximum disassembly rate.

On the other hand, the research found that shipping the waste does not result in the burden that comes with recycling operations and the issues that come with them [20]. However, it benefits the exporter financially. Importers of E-waste are typically from developing countries, and they process the E-waste in informal recycling circumstances, which can cause harm to the environment [21].

As a developing country, the recycling process of batteries is not started since there is no appropriate technology are not available in Bangladesh. For instance, batteries require pretreatment to control accidental disposal that may result in combustion. More waste is handled wrongly in growing countries, where most companies are informal and there are few health and safety regulations in effect to protect employees.

The existing companies in Bangladesh do not recycle all kinds of E-waste because they face many different types of barriers. The drawbacks should be overcome to establish a recycler company that will be able to recycle all kinds of hazardous products (Fig. 4).

Fig. 4. Necessary steps to establish a recycler company to recycle all kinds of hazardous products.

From investigating current barriers, we can summarize that if government policy issues, general people awareness, and fund initiatives are taken seriously and also if the worker community works together to collect E-waste from the district wise and maintain safety measurements and concerns about proper import-export ways then Bangladesh can go forward to go green in IT waste management situation.

4.2   E-waste Generation Scenario

The study investigated and examined the present scenario of E-waste in Bangladesh. Bangladesh is well-known for being one of the leading electronic waste import nations. Aside from that, the country generates 2.81 million metric tons of these scrap materials each year [18]. Dhaka and Chattogram are the two most important stakeholders in the collection and management of electronic scraps [22]. Workers may be exposed to health risks as a result of dermal contact with harmful components in E-waste. Despite the fact that this employment poses several health risks, workers do not receive either health benefits or recompense for the harm done to their health. In Bangladesh, the labor force associated with collecting and dismantling electronic garbage lacks a strict legal framework. The study reveals that the workforce involved in managing E-waste earns only 3,000 takas per month, works 12 h per day, and does extremely dangerous tasks. Moreover, any analysis to analyze this possibility could not be done due to a lack of essential data. Again, no scientific articles or supporting documentation were found to justify the risks posed by toxic element interaction through the skin [13].

4.3 Impact of Improper Recycling

The release of dangerous compounds into the surrounding environment is one of the consequences of inefficient management of electronic waste throughout the collecting, sorting, reprocessing, and open dumping processes, including aquatic areas, as well as reservoirs that mix into the atmosphere.

E-waste is the major source of several heavy metals (e.g., Hg, Pd, Cd, Cr, Zn, etc.) [23]. When heavy metals are left untreated and exposed to the elements, they become toxic and cause numerous human diseases like cancer, sight problems, damage to kidneys, and damage to other tissues (Table 1) [24].

If these heavy metals are not cleaned up and are left out in the environment, they can cause many diseases, such as cancer, nerve damage, asthma, hearing problems, infant mortality, kidney problems, birth problems, brain disorders, liver damage, and lung damage. The following table provides a summary of the many elements that are produced by electronic waste and the risk they bring to human health.

Most of the people who are associated with recycling waste in developing nations like Bangladesh are women and children, making them the most vulnerable because they breathe in the dust, eat it, or touch it. The most obvious health problems are related to exposure at work or in a local area. E-waste and associated contaminants can be exposed to people outside of the workplace in a variety of ways. Children who work in E-waste recycling are in danger as well, getting sick from their parents' clothes and skin, and relatively high contamination if recycling is carried out in their houses. We observe that the children who live near recycling sites have health problems like breathing problems, skin infections, and stomach diseases.

Electronic waste has negative consequences for the atmosphere, hydrosphere, lithosphere, and biosphere. Personal computers (PCs), notebook computers (notebooks), and laptop computers (laptops) emit CO_2 during their mining, manufacturing, use, and disposal as E-waste. Cyber Warming refers to CO_2 emissions from the information technology and computer industries. In electronics equipment, one of the most common materials is PVC (Polyvinyl Chloride) also when hydrogen chloride is mixed with water, it produces hydrochloric acid, which causes lung issues when inhaled. Furthermore, as it covers copper wires and plastic computer casings, PVC emits highly toxic dioxins and furans when burned [24].

Table 1. Health and Environmental Hazard

E-waste category	Some examples of products	Hazardous Elements	Health and Environmental Hazard	Source
Temperature exchange equipment	Refrigerators, Freezers, Air conditioning equipment	Pb Ba	Pb, Ba, and hazardous phosphors discharge into the soil Damage kidney and digestive system. Cause children's slow mental development	Kaushik (2018) [26]
Display equipment	Screens, Televisions, LCD photo frames, Monitors, Laptops	Hg Cd	Loss of mental ability, annoyance, and IQ drop CH_3Hg can slow down maturation, and reproduction	Ramachandra and Saira (2004) [27]
Large equipment	Washing machine, Dishwashing machine, Cooker, Electric stove, Musical equipment, Large printing machines, Large medical devices	Sb Be	Loss of sensation and control in the limbs for Se. Respiratory tissue that has aged. Blood pressure elevation, migraines, and diarrhea	Wu & Ikerionwu (2010), ATSDR (2003) [28]

(continued)

Table 1. (*continued*)

E-waste category	Some examples of products	Hazardous Elements	Health and Environmental Hazard	Source
Small equipment	Vacuum cleaner, Carpet sweeper, Microwaves, Iron, Toaster, Calculator, Toys, Smoke detectors	Brominated Flame Retardants BPA	Cd accumulates in the kidneys and damages the liver, breathing, and joints From Arsenic Allergic reactions, nausea, vomiting - A decrease in blood cell production, Absurd heart rhythm	Dyrud (2007) [29] Schmidt (2002) [30]
Lamps	Straight fluorescent and Compact fluorescent lamps, Strong density discharge lamps, Na lamps, LED	DPB Phathalas PVC	Br cause vomiting, breathing issues and stomach pain, diarrhea	The US. National Library of Medicine [31]
Small IT equipment	Mobile phones, Routers, Personal computers, Printers, Telephones, IC, switches, cables		PVC produces dioxins which can damage reproductive and immune systems	

By exploring categorizes E-waste by dividing it into six waste categories [25] and other sources, we designed a collective table (Table 1) where health and environmental hazards are pointed focused on category-wise created hazardous elements.

5 Conclusion

Bangladesh imports electronic trash from advanced nations and manufactures its own. However, this electronic garbage is gathered, handled, and recycled outside in the open air without proper protection for the workers, resulting in difficulties for both the environment and workers' health. When electronic garbage is burned, it produces smoke containing toxic gasses and heavy metals (lead, cadmium, and mercury).

- These toxic elements can be inhaled by people who work with E-waste, take it apart, and recycle it. This can cause cancer and other health problems.
- Because there is no strong regulatory framework for E-waste disposal, the labor force in Bangladesh involved in collecting and recycling E-waste works for very low salaries and is exposed to health risks.
- When workers eat lead, they put their health at risk because it can cause cancer. Chromium and cadmium, on the other hand, do not pose any health risks when eaten.
- People who work in the informal sector, especially children, recycle without any safety measures or protective gear.
- The environment is at risk when E-waste isn't recycled and thrown away in the right way. Weathering and chemical reactions speed up the release of dangerous elements from electronic waste into the air, water, and soil, which is very bad for the environment.

The recycling of old electronic equipment is very important, but the process must be carried out in a secure and consistent way. However, there should be age-related differences in the allowed limits for children and adults because their bodies are different, and they are more likely to be hurt. It is non-negotiable to improve working conditions for every employee of E-waste companies and eliminate child labor. Every year, tons and tons of E-waste are dumped, and the problem keeps getting worse.

6 Recommendations

Recycling, reusing, or refurbishing E-waste can help save the environment. The following recommendations are based on the findings and discussions of the research.

- There must be a distinct infrastructure for gathering, sorting, and disposing of E-waste in order to adequately manage it., recovery, and disposal (at least for chosen goods).
- Workers' health and safety must be protected during recycling processes.
- To stimulate the establishment of collection and disposal facilities, the administration may provide financial incentives to industry and businesses in the nation.
- Harmful objects need to be covered or protected properly so that any harmful chemical or gas cannot mix with their surroundings.
- After recycling all the industrial equipment needs to be cleaned properly.
- One of the simplest methods to reduce electronic waste footprint is to sell or donate our devices to others who can use them.
- Maintaining your gadgets properly to extend their life is also a great way to save money and reduce E-waste.

Therefore, social engagement, events, workshops even curriculum implementation in our education system may raise awareness of the E-waste problem.

Acknowledgment. The Authors thank Abdulla Al Mamun, Business Development senior executive officer, Azizu Recycling and E-waste Company ltd, and also Yosuf Enterprise, Array Consortium, and 3R Future (in a process of opening a new recycling industry).

References

1. Devika, S.: Environmental impact of improper disposal of electronic waste. In: Proceedings of the International Conference on "Recent Advances in Space Technology Services and Climate Change - 2010", RSTS and CC-2010 (2010)
2. World Economic Forum: A New Circular Vision for Electronics Time for a Global Reboot. World Economic Forum (2019)
3. electronic waste, Britannica. https://www.britannica.com/technology/electronic-waste. Accessed 13 May 2022
4. Heacock, M., Kelly, C.B., Asante, K.A., Birnbaum, L.S.: E-waste and harm to vulnerable populations: a growing global problem. Environ. Health Perspect. **124** (2016)
5. Reasons Lithium Ion Batteries in E-Waste Require Careful Recycling. https://www.1green planet.com/general/5-reasons-lithium-ion-batteries-in-e-waste-require-careful-recycling/. Accessed 13 May 2022
6. Richa, K., Babbitt, C.W., Gaustad, G., Wang, X.: A future perspective on lithium-ion battery waste flows from electric vehicles. Resour. Conserv. Recycl. **83**, 63–76 (2014). https://doi. org/10.1016/j.resconrec.2013.11.008
7. Kudrat-E-Khuda: Electronic Waste in Bangladesh: Its Present Statutes, and Negative Impacts on Environment and Human Health. Pollution 2021, 633–642 (2021). https://doi.org/10. 22059/poll.2021.321337.1056
8. Islam, M.N.: Bangladesh GB E-waste management of Bangladesh. Int. J. Innov. Hum. Ecol. Nat. Stud. **4**, 1–12 (2016)
9. The Growing Environmental Risks of E-Waste. https://www.genevaenvironmentnetwork.org/ resources/updates/the-growing-environmental-risks-of-e-waste/. Accessed 13 May 2022
10. Babu, B.R., Parande, A.K., Basha, C.A.: Electrical and electronic waste: a global environmental problem. Waste Manage. Res. **25**, 307–318 (2007). https://doi.org/10.1177/073424 2X07076941
11. Riyad A.S.M., Mahbub Hassan K.H., Jabed Iqbal M., Abdur M., Wasi Uddin R.S.M.: E-waste recycling practices in Bangladesh (2014)
12. Doan, L., Amer, Y., Lee, S., Phuc, P.: Strategies for E-waste management: a literature review'. World Academy of Science, Engineering and Technology, Open Science Index 147. Int. J. Energy Environ. Eng. **13**(3), 157–162 (2019)
13. Final Report Assessment of Generation of E-Waste, Its Impacts on Environment and Resource Recovery Potential in Bangladesh (2018)
14. Alam, M., Bahauddin, K.M.: Electronic Waste in Bangladesh: evaluating the situation, legislation and policy and way forward with strategy and approach, p. 9 (2015). https://doi.org/ 10.1515/pesd-2015-0005
15. The Risk of E-Waste at Your Company. https://www.securityinfowatch.com/home/blog/104 74774/the-risk-of-ewaste-at-your-company. Accessed 13 May 2022
16. Howard, S.: Minerals, metals and materials society, EPD Congress 2009.: Proceedings of sessions and symposia sponsored by the Extraction and Processing Division (EPD) of The Minerals, Metals & Materials Society (TMS). Warrendale, Pa: TMS (2019)
17. Masud, M.H., et al.: Towards the effective E-waste management in Bangladesh: a review. Environ. Sci. Pollut. Res. **26**(2), 1250–1276 (2018). https://doi.org/10.1007/s11356-018-3626-2

18. Hossain, S., Sulatan, S., Shahnaz, F., Akram, A.B., Nesa, M., Happell, J.: Environment and social development organization-ESDO, 2010 study Team leader Produced by Environment and Social Development Organization-ESDO Supported by International POPs Elimination Network-IPEN and Toxics Link Study Report; E-waste: Bangladesh Situation, 3 Study on E-waste: Bangladesh (2010)
19. Sadeque, F.R., Fazle, A., Ahmed, R.S.E.: E-waste management waste management scenario in Bangladesh scenario in Bangladesh Government of Bangladesh
20. Wiesmeth, H.: Stakeholder engagement for environmental innovations. J. Bus. Res. **119**, 310–320 (2020). https://doi.org/10.1016/j.jbusres.2018.12.054
21. Alblooshi, B.G.K.M., Ahmad, S.Z., Hussain, M., Singh, S.K.: Sustainable management of electronic waste: empirical evidence from a stakeholders' perspective. Bus. Strateg. Environ. (2022). https://doi.org/10.1002/BSE.2987
22. Abdur, M., Khan, R., Saadat, A.H.M., Motalib, M.A.: Status of electronic waste generation in bangladesh: a review (2019)
23. Sthiannopkao, S., Wong, M.H.: Handling e-waste in developed and developing countries: initiatives, practices, and consequences. Sci. Total Environ. **463–464**, 1147–1153 (2013). https://doi.org/10.1016/j.scitotenv.2012.06.088
24. Meem, R.A., Ahmed, A., Hossain, Md. S., Khan, R.A.: A Review on the environmental and health impacts due to electronic waste disposal in Bangladesh. GSC Adv. Res. Rev. **8**, 116–125 (2021). https://doi.org/10.30574/gscarr.2021.8.2.0174
25. Baldé, C.P., Forti, V., Gray, V., Kuehr, R., Stegmann, P.: International Telecommunication Union, United Nations University, International Solid Waste Association The global e-waste monitor 2017: quantities, flows, and resources (2017)
26. Kaushik, M.V.:E-waste and its management. Int. J. Res. Appl. Sci. Eng. Technol. **6**, 170–178 (2018). https://doi.org/10.22214/ijraset.2018.6031
27. Ramachandra, T.V., Saira Varghese, K.: Environmentaly Sound Options For E-wastes Management (2004)
28. Ikerionwu, C., Oliver, O.: E-cycling E-waste: the way forward for nigeria IT and electro-mechanical industry. Int. J. Acad. Res. **02**, 142–149 (2010)
29. Dyrud, M.A.: Not in our backyard: computer waste and engineering ethics (2007). https://doi.org/10.18260/1-2--1564
30. Schmidt, C.W.: Unfair Trade e-Waste in Africa (2006). https://doi.org/10.1289/ehp.114-a232
31. The US. National Library of Medicine. https://www.nlm.nih.gov/. Accessed 13 May 2022

A Hybrid Cloud System for Power-Efficient Cloud Computing

S. M. Mursalin, Md. Abdul Kader Jilani, and Ahmed Wasif Reza[(✉)]

Department of Computer Science and Engineering, East West University, Dhaka, Bangladesh
akzilani875@gmail.com, wasif@ewubd.edu

Abstract. Around our world clients needs services that are informative and technologically advanced. Advanced technologies like cloud computing allow the clients or the consumer to pay an efficient amount of money according to the service that they are getting. It permits any application for being hosted in a research or corporational structure. The included networked computers, cables, power supply, etc. in the data center is the main bone of cloud computing. The data centers consume a great amount of power to fulfill their work process which increases the cost and also affects the environment of the work by increasing the carbon footprint. To keep the carbon emission to check it is very necessary to check the electricity and power consumption. Keeping the energy in check we have solved the issue of efficient cloud computing.

Keywords: Efficient Energy · Power Usage · Policy · Cloud Computing · Algorithm

1 Introduction

The utilization of the network and data in our day-to-day lives has dramatically risen as a result of global technological improvement. These network applications, data storage, and computing capacity have ushered in a new era of computing known as cloud computing. Cloud computing allows us to access data on-demand via the internet and shared computing resources. It processes and stores data using the internet. Though it is mostly used for data processing and storage, it can also deliver bandwidth on demand via the internet in some circumstances. It can share resources by storing all of them in the cloud and retrieving them as needed. Using this method, several users can access the same data or resources through a cloud service. There are three delivery models for cloud computing:

1. Using SaaS means for the users to get access to the apps that the providers have stored in the cloud.
2. Platform service is another name for this service. Users can utilize this service to distribute their apps to the cloud and serve them to everyone.

© ICST Institute for Computer Sciences, Social Informatics and Telecommunications Engineering 2023
Published by Springer Nature Switzerland AG 2023. All Rights Reserved
Md. S. Satu et al. (Eds.): MIET 2022, LNICST 491, pp. 730–738, 2023.
https://doi.org/10.1007/978-3-031-34622-4_57

3. Infrastructure service: is another name for this service. Users can access SPC's cloud data storage with this service [1].

A data storage system is required for cloud computing. The data centers are where this system is constructed and managed. Energy usage in data centers is a major source of worry these days. Cloud computing is becoming more popular. To address this, cloud service providers are increasing the computing power in their data centers by adding more servers. As a result, 3% of total electricity in the world is used by the data center. This has a high operational cost as well. Because data centers consume a significant amount of energy, they contribute to carbon emissions in the environment. According to some research, the technological sector gives roughly 2% of CO_2 emissions around the globe. As a result, this has become a global problem [2, 3].

The data centers that are utilized for cloud computing take a lot of energy to run. According to a survey, a data center consumes enough energy to power 25,000 homes. As a result, lowering data center power usage has become a global issue. We investigated numerous ways for reducing data center power consumption in this article. We've developed certain techniques that, if implemented, can cut data center power consumption [4].

We have attempted to reduce power consumption in this area. We've come up with a few ways to use the algorithms in conjunction with the workload comprehensions. We've learned that the CPU is a server's primary power user. Power is consumed by other components as well. As a result, all of them should be taken into account. We used an energy-efficient hybrid method to lower cloud computing's energy use.

The remaining portions of this study are organized into five sections: Sect. 2 discusses relevant research, Sect. 3 discusses methodology, Sect. 4 discusses results and discussion, and Sect. 5 provides concluding remarks.

2 Related Work

A great chunk of research effort is being given to some processes in cloud systems, such as job scheduling, virtualization, and so on, throughout the previous decade. Lowering energy consumption has become a priority when it comes to constructing and running cloud datacenters.

To improve total system energy efficiency [5], suggested a VM scheduling strategy. It uses the facts of consuming less energy metric to support a system working characteristic of apps deployed with Virtual Machine on various CPUs. Grid users' security methods are used to monitor energy usage in various grid circumstances. Multi-level scheduling of grids may be thought of class with difficult enhancement, planning, and problems during the making of a decision involving many, A few times competing requirements, rendering several quality initiatives less effective. For virtualized heterogonous multicore systems, the method performs better.

In [6], Schedules for Quasi where EDA-NMS is an algorithm for Energy and Deadline Aware was proposed. It's a task scheduling algorithm that uses heuristics. EDA-NMS takes advantage of the slackness of function time limit to delay its operation for activities within the slack time limit intending to keep away from starting up new PMs. To respond as rapidly as feasible to user requests with variable priorities. Genuine importance is a notion that is also presented in this strategy, which aids in the scheduling of high-priority projects with short deadlines.

In [7], developed an algorithm for VM Scheduling those results in a high utilization level while consuming the least amount of energy and maintaining a defined QoS. Giving attention to raising task acquiescence rates while neglecting workloads that impair the scheduling algorithm's QoS guarantee, such as time-based and non-time-based jobs working in virtual machines. If a host's current utilization falls below a particular level, its VMs will be merged on other machines, and the host will be switched off, according to this procedure. As a result, to limit the number of migrations, which incurs considerable costs not only on the server but also on the Cloud's network architecture.

DVFS enabled Efficient-energy [8] Workflow Task Scheduling was proposed as a power-saving technique in (DEWTS). The quantity of energy consumed in total is separated into two categories: dynamic and static energy consumption. Consumption of powerful energy refers to the additional electricity used while it is occupied. This DEWTS algorithm assigns the minimum amount of CPU resources to each operation intending to reduce dynamic as much consumption of energy as feasible. When compared to previous studies, the algorithm saves a significant amount of energy. It also looked at the aspects that influence the algorithm's performance.

In [9], he suggested a VM choosing method lies on network RAM and bandwidth utilization. They simulated a difficult condition, and the results showed that it may reduce cloud data center energy use. This method resulted in a 19% reduction in energy expenses. However, by boosting SLATAH, it is possible to save 94 percent on VM migrations.

Michael et al. proposed [10] a solution for dealing with topology-aware dynamic VM allocation and SLA-aware application autoscaling. It's an integrated type that can aid with both allocation and autoscaling, allowing clients to make judgments. Autoscaling decisions are made with the user's best interests in mind, and the implementation of these decisions is managed in such a way that dynamic VM allocation needs are met.

3 Proposed Work

From previous works, we have found out that there are some lackings in terms of energy efficiency and getting optimal performance. We have tried to solve this issue with our proposed method. Two rules were implemented in our proposed study to reduce energy usage and increase efficiency in virtual data centers. The proposed work provides a better option configuration for the VM that has to be reallocated, as well as a mechanism for choosing which host will be chosen for the virtual machine's relocation. The hybrid virtual machine selection technique and the low usage host selection policy will decide which virtual machines will be migrated and which will not. A host will be chosen to reallocate the virtual machine. In the selection policy for hybrid virtual machines, the algorithm looks through the list of virtual machines to choose the best virtual machine to transfer from the host. If the VM is migrated from the host, The difference between the higher threshold and the new utilization should be the smallest of all the VMs' values, and its utilization should be more than the difference between the host's total usage. If no virtual machines fulfill the upper criteria, the algorithm selects the virtual machine with the max utilization and removes it from the virtual machine list, then begins the process again. Workload Consolidation on cloud energy consumption and reduced power usage was another strategy we implemented. Although the CPU consumes the most power in a server, other components such as storage, memory, and network interface swallow power as well and must be taken into account before workload consolidation.

4 Methodology

Here we will be showing two methods to achieve our goal where one is a hybrid VM recruitment technique and the other one is the low electricity consumption of hosting VMs.

4.1 Algorithm for Hybrid Virtual Machine Recruitment Policy

Step 1: Analysis of Virtual machines on the end of the host.

Step 2: Determine whether or not the virtual machines on the host can be migrated. Return null if no VMs are migratable.

Step 3: Set the first virtual machine's CPU use and RAM to the bare minimum.

Step 4: Determine the amount of CPU and RAM used by the virtual machine on the host. Compare CPU and memory usage using the previously saved VM if CPU utilization is higher than the minimum. If the CPU and RAM utilization of the selected Virtual machine are both lower than the stored Virtual machine, then pick Vm for migration.

Step 5: Step 3 should be repeated until all Vms have been evaluated.

4.2 Algorithm for Hosting Regulation with Low Consumption

Choosing the virtual machines to be replaced, the second procedure is to pick up a host to which the virtual machines may be up for relocation. To our analysis, migrating VMs to hosts with low CPU utilization is preferable since migrating VMs to hosts with high CPU use risks overloading the host and causing it to fail. The risk of host overload is decreased by transferring Vms to a low-utilization host.

Step 1: Getting a schedule of hosts to whom a virtual machine may be relocated.

Step 2: Determine the host's total utilized amount.

Step 3: Record the utilization data for the first host on the list; this data will be used as a benchmark against which other hosts will be assessed.

Step 4: Compare the host's utilization to that of the prior host; if the host's utilization is less than the previously stored utilization information, the previously stored utilization information will be replaced.

Step 5: Compare how much each host is used. At the end of the day, we'll have the host having the lowest load.

Step 6: If you return this host, it will be picked for virtual machine relocation.

4.3 Designing the Algorithm

The proposed algorithm is presented in Fig. 1.

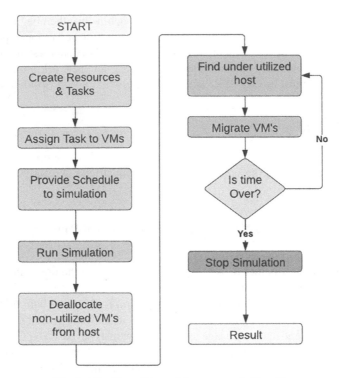

Fig. 1. The Flow-Chart of the proposed Algorithm

5 Result and Discussion

As indicated in Table 1, when compared to awareness of power Cloud computing and energy conservation Cloud, Our energy-efficient hybrid Cloud consumes less energy (0.02 KWh). Energy consumption, virtual machine migration, and Service Level Agreement(SLA) degradation (percentage) are all highly tuned measures [11].

As shown in Table 2, it is evaluated that our dynamic VM reallocation technique uses lower energy while maintaining a good degree of Quality of Sevice(QoS). Dynamic reallocation of VMs based on current CPU use saves more energy than policies of fixed allocation. The most energy-efficient policy is the MM policy. MM policy is a technic for lowering energy consumption. When compared to the ST strategy, the MM technique resulted in over 10 times fewer VM migrations [12].

Table 1. Hybrid Clouds with Low Energy Consumption vs. Other Clouds

Parameters	Energy Efficient Cloud	Power Aware Cloud	Hybrid Cloud with energy efficiency
Experiment Name	Energy Efficient Cloud	Power Aware Cloud	Hybrid Cloud with energy efficiency
No. of Hosts	5	5	5
No. of VM's	10	10	10
Simulated Time in total	1440.00 S	1440.00 S	1440.00 S
Consuming of energy	0.03 kwh	0.05 kwh	0.02 kwh
No. of VM migrations	3	11	3
SLA degradation	0.09270%	0.01246%	0.00158%
SLA time per active host	52.22%	8.01%	1.94%
No. of host shutdowns	4	4	4

Table 2. Power consumption with different policies

Policy	Energy (KWh)	SLA	Migr.
NPA	9.15	-	-
DVFS	4.4	-	-
ST 50%	2.03	5.41%	35.226
ST 60%	1.5	9.04%	34.231
MM 40–80%	1.27	2.75%	3.241
MM 50–90%	1.14	6.69%	3.12

As demonstrated in Table 3 its goal is to develop a viable approach for allocating resources to physical hosts based on the krill algorithm. The three algorithms (krill, GA, and MBFD) are explained separately in the following sections, with the results given in charts and tables, utilizing the IQR and MAD algorithms in both cases. Energy consumption and contract violations are depicted in Table 4. In ten experiments, the recommended technique that we have given was found to lower energy usage by 35% and 17%, respectively, when compared to genetic and MBFD algorithms with IQR and MAD as overloaded host detection and random selection approaches for virtual machine selection [13].

Table 3. Viable method for allocating resources

Policy	MAD/MMT	MAD/RS	IQR/MT	IQR/RS
GA	0.027	0.019	0.023	0.019
MBFD	0.02	0.023	0.023	0.018
Our	0.011	0.011	0.011	0.015

While the CPU consumes the most power in a server, other components such as RAM, disk, and network card also consume power and must be considered before workload consolidation. It summarizes virtual machine workload performance and power consumption (Table 4). It has been established that when single VMs are run on a physical server, the performance of executing a workload is better than when several Virtual Machines are run on an identical realistic server [14].

Table 4. The average power consumption

	Average Power consumption (W)			
	CPU	Memory	Hard disk	Network
Executing each of the 4 workloads in 1 VM running on a physical server separately	23.39	23.99	11.71	15.36
Executing homogenous workloads in 4 VMs	46.48	19.00	10.36	15.39

In this research, they used DVFS in conjunction with a modified MM Migration algorithm for migration (Table 5). DVFS stands for dynamic voltage and frequency scaling. When compared to the best available method, the comparative result reveals that energy usage has decreased by 60%, although SLA breaches have increased marginally.

Table 5. Power consumption with DVFS and MM Migration algorithm

Policy	Energy (kWH)	Energy (kWH)/105	Average SLA Violation (%)
NPA	3013.50	28.69	0
DVFS	803.91	7.64	0
MAD-MMT	177.50	1.68	9.77
LRR-MMT	159.66	1.51	9.51
LR-MMT	159.16	1.51	9.51
DVFS-MMT	95.47	0.90	14.34

When we compare all of the existing or modified algorithms [15-20], we find that they all perform worse than our proposed approach. The energy usage of all of those approaches, as well as their modified (suggested) approaches, are shown. In terms of low energy use and lesser SLA violation, the hybrid approach outperforms the others.

6 Conclusion

In this paper, We propose a hybrid energy-efficient technique to reduce cloud computing's energy usage. In addition to achieving the energy conservation objectives, we will also stop any SLA violations to guarantee that the user receives a high-quality service. Green cloud computing, which offers strategies and methods for reducing energy waste by embracing its reuse, has grown in significance since energy has recently been a major concern. Because energy use and CO_2 emissions are both bad for one's health, the study's objective is to find a way to lessen them.

In the virtualization business, the power usage of various desktop components often underappreciated. Although the CPU in a server uses the most power, other parts like memory, storage, and the network interface also use power and must be taken into account before workload consolidation. Additionally, it has been demonstrated that a good workload mix can increase power efficiency without sacrificing performance. We will be able to examine various Cloud situations in the future and propose unique optimization policies to reduce CO_2 emissions in the Cloud. We will include an energy cost rate in our new models to maximize overall energy cost in various environmental effects. Additional properties, such as network bandwidth, could be used as an example. More research into energy-saving optimization for live VM migration policies could be done in the near future. Apps can now be supplied to hardware that doesn't normally support them thanks to virtualization. The opportunities and challenges that virtualization may present are evident when evaluating the potential of virtualization technology in high-performance computing.

References

1. Deiab, M., El-Menshawy, D., El-Abd, S., Mostafa, A., El-Seoud, M.S.A.: Energy efficiency in cloud computing. Int. J. Mach. Learn. Comput. 9(1), 98–102 (2019). https://doi.org/10.18178/ijmlc.2019.9.1.771
2. Shree, T., Kumar, R., Kumar, N.: Green computing in cloud computing. In: Proceedings - IEEE 2020 2nd International Conference Advanced Computing Communication Control Networking, ICACCCN 2020, pp. 903–905 (2020). https://doi.org/10.1109/ICACCCN51052.2020.9362822
3. Mosoti, K., Oteke, V., Job, P.: The effect of cloud workload consolidation on cloud energy consumption and performance in multi-tenant cloud infrastructure. Int. J. Comput. Appl. 181(37), 47–53 (2019). https://doi.org/10.5120/ijca2019918353
4. Kumar, S., Kalra, M.: A hybrid approach for energy-efficient task scheduling in cloud. In: Krishna, C.R., Dutta, M., Kumar, R. (eds.) Proceedings of 2nd International Conference on Communication, Computing and Networking. LNNS, vol. 46, pp. 1011–1019. Springer, Singapore (2019). https://doi.org/10.1007/978-981-13-1217-5_99
5. Kołodziej, J., et al.: Security, energy, and performance-aware resource allocation mechanisms for computational grids. Futur. Gener. Comput. Syst. 31(1), 77–92 (2014). https://doi.org/10.1016/j.future.2012.09.009

6. Zhang, Y., Cheng, X., Chen, L., Shen, H.: Energy-efficient tasks scheduling heuristics with multi-constraints in virtualized clouds. J. Grid Comput. **16**(3), 459–475 (2018). https://doi. org/10.1007/s10723-018-9426-6
7. Hosseinimotlagh, S., Khunjush, F., Samadzadeh, R.: SEATS: smart energy-aware task scheduling in real-time cloud computing. J. Supercomput. **71**(1), 45–66 (2014). https://doi. org/10.1007/s11227-014-1276-9
8. Tang, Z., Qi, L., Cheng, Z., Li, K., Khan, S.U., Li, K.: An energy-efficient task scheduling algorithm in DVFS-enabled cloud environment. J. Grid Comput. **14**(1), 55–74 (2015). https:// doi.org/10.1007/s10723-015-9334-y
9. Akhter, N., Othman, M., Naha, R.K.: Energy-aware virtual machine selection method for cloud data center resource allocation **2018** (2018). http://arxiv.org/abs/1812.08375
10. Tighe, M., Bauer, M.: Topology and application aware dynamic vm management in the cloud. J. Grid Comput. **15**(2), 273–294 (2017). https://doi.org/10.1007/s10723-017-9397-z
11. Goyal, Y., Arya, M.S., Nagpal, S.: Energy efficient hybrid policy in green cloud computing. In: Proceedings 2015 International Conference Green Computing Internet Things, ICGCIoT 2015, pp. 1065–1069 (2016). https://doi.org/10.1109/ICGCIoT.2015.7380621
12. Beloglazov, A., Buyya, R.: Energy efficient allocation of virtual machines in cloud data centers. In: CCGrid 2010 - 10th IEEE/ACM Internationl Conference Cluster Cloud, Grid Computing, pp. 577–578 (2010). https://doi.org/10.1109/ccgrid.2010.45
13. Soltanshahi, M., Asemi, R., Shafiei, N.: Energy-aware virtual machines allocation by krill herd algorithm in cloud data centers. Heliyon **5**(7), 3–8 (2019). https://doi.org/10.1016/j.hel iyon.2019.e02066
14. Kumar, N., Kumar, R., Aggrawal, M.: Energy efficient DVFS with VM migration. Eur. J. Adv. Eng. Technol. **5**(1), 61–68 (2018)
15. Sharifi, M., Salimi, H., Najafzadeh, M.: Power-efficient distributed scheduling of virtual machines using workload-aware consolidation techniques. J. Supercomput. **61**(1), 46–66 (2012). https://doi.org/10.1007/s11227-011-0658-5
16. Khattar, N., Sidhu, J., Singh, J.: Toward energy-efficient cloud computing: a survey of dynamic power management and heuristics-based optimization techniques. J. Supercomput. **75**(8), 4750–4810 (2019). https://doi.org/10.1007/s11227-019-02764-2
17. Kenga, D.M., Omwenga, V.O., Ogao, P.J.: Autonomous virtual machine sizing and resource usage prediction for efficient resource utilization in multi-tenant public cloud. Int. J. Inf. Technol. Comput. Sci. **11**(5), 11–22 (2019). https://doi.org/10.5815/ijitcs.2019.05.02
18. Patel, Y.S., Mehrotra, N., Soner, S.: Green cloud computing: a review on Green IT areas for cloud computing environment. In: 2015 International Conference on Futuristic Trends on Computational Analysis and Knowledge Management (ABLAZE), pp. 327–332 (2015). https://doi.org/10.1109/ABLAZE.2015.7155006
19. X. Chen, L. Rupprecht, R. Osman, P. Pietzuch, Franciosi, F., Knottenbelt, W.: CloudScope: diagnosing and managing performance interference in multi-tenant clouds. In: Proceedings - International Symposium on Modeling, Analysis and. Simulation of Computer and Telecommunication Systems, MASCOTS, vol. 2015, pp. 164–173 (2015). https://doi.org/10.1109/ MASCOTS.2015.35
20. Kaur, T., Chana, I.: Energy efficiency techniques in cloud computing. ACM Comput. Surv. **48**(2), 1–46 (2015). https://doi.org/10.1145/2742488

A Sustainable E-Waste Management System for Bangladesh

Md. Shahadat Anik Sheikh, Rashik Buksh Rafsan, Hasib Ar Rafiul Fahim, Md. Tabib Khan, and Ahmed Wasif Reza[✉]

Department of Computer Science and Engineering, East West University, Dhaka, Bangladesh
wasif@ewubd.edu

Abstract. The use of electronic devices is increasing rapidly as it is an essential part of our life in today's world. Shown in numbers, it has grown from zero to 7.2 billion in only three decades. There is a 5–10% annual rise in the quantity of used electronic equipment, which, if not correctly disposed of, can result in environmental dangers that harm human health, marine life, and soil fertility. For developing countries like Bangladesh, managing this massive stream of electrical and electronic garbage is challenging due to the lack of solid organizational and governmental e-waste management infrastructure. Lack of public knowledge, policies, and funding in waste management are only a few of the significant causes driving this situation. In this study, a majority of the adopted E-waste management systems and their limitations, along with the proposal of a new and sustainable E-waste management system, have been discussed. The implementation gap of government rules and policies has been highlighted here. The successful application of these recommended strategies could improve Bangladesh's E-waste management capability.

Keywords: E-waste Bangladesh · E-waste collection · Effective E-waste Management

1 Introduction

E-waste is used to describe all sorts of electrical and electronic equipment (EEE) and its parts that have been dumped as wastes by the owner with no intention of re-use [1, 2]. And those expired products are then thrown away or dumped into the environment as people are unaware of their harmful effects [3]. Hazardous substances like lead, mercury, cadmium, barium, and lithium, among others, can be found in e-waste. As a result, the worldwide E-waste management system is a crucial topic to consider, particularly in poor and emerging countries such as ours. Recently, Bangladesh has been approaching rapidly to digitalization with the developing world. Therefore, the use of electronic equipment is increasing rapidly, and these products are also expiring. But those e-wastes are not appropriately managed and hamper our environment, health, etc. Also, in Bangladesh, there is no active policy from the government for e-waste management, but some third-party organizations of Bangladesh are trying to manage these e-wastes sustainably. This

Md. S. Satu et al. (Eds.): MIET 2022, LNICST 491, pp. 739–753, 2023.
https://doi.org/10.1007/978-3-031-34622-4_58

is a significant issue affecting nature's ecosystem and human health and should be addressed accordingly.

During this time of globalization, Bangladesh has been working on industrial transformation to become a middle-income country. However, in the name of E-waste, it has its drawbacks. E-waste is increasing proportionally as more IT platforms are formed in Bangladesh, and the use of electronic gadgets in households rises daily. It could have long-term harmful implications if it is not dealt with quickly. As the world advances toward a greener future, E-waste policies are being implemented to aid in this goal. Proper management systems are being discovered to ensure a better and healthier world.

1.1 Background

Electronic waste has the potential to seriously harm the environment and its sustainability. As a result, it must be appropriately controlled and disposed of. In recent years, the amount of e-waste has gone over the roof due to excess use and easily broken products. E-waste represents 5% of municipal solid trash generated globally, as emerging countries invest more in electronics [4]. Bangladesh produces around 2.81 million metric tons of E-waste each year. In the north-eastern area of this country, 36.3% of women who live near recycling sites have lost a child. Because of E-waste mishandling, around 15% of child workers die, and 83% of child laborers are seriously exposed to E-waste pollutants and struggle with long-term health issues [5].

Every electronic equipment is made up of different materials and compositions, with different use and functions, characteristics, structure, and prices. As a result, conventional waste disposal procedures should not be utilized to dispose of e-waste. Being made from various hazardous and reactive materials such as lead, sulfur, and plastic, among others, combining those components with other wastes may cause significant harm to the environment and ecosystem, as well as be highly hazardous to human life [6]. For better e-waste management, collection schemes need to be aggregated from the product users before throwing away or sending those waste products to treatment in facilities. Landfilling, dumping, and other traditional waste disposal methods cannot be utilized to appropriately diagnose and manage e-waste and prevent adverse environmental consequences [5].

Several wealthy countries have built infrastructures and technology to effectively handle and re-use E-waste while minimizing environmental and health hazards. Bangladesh, on the other hand, as a developing country, lacks access to such E-waste processing processes as well as the legislative framework to ensure efficient E-waste management [7]. Digitalization of Bangladesh is mostly done thanks to the use of technology and science. These technologies are developing our country in a lot of ways, but the lack of proper waste management of these electronic devices is a serious setback that can be very dangerous and damaging. As electronic devices can't be burned or dismantled due to toxicity, so they are often subjected to unsafe re-use, recycling, or dangerous waste disposal. As a result, e-waste has raised serious concerns on a national and even global level. In this study, a good idea about E-waste and its efficient management method has been thoroughly discussed.

1.2 Problem Statement

We live in an age of science and technology. Computers and mobile phones have become widely available and inexpensive to purchase for individuals of all ages. A few people only think of recycling them or re-using them after repairing them. Apart from them, everyone buys new products and discards the old ones, resulting in a massive amount of e-waste in our environment. As a result, the necessity of E-waste management is becoming challenging. However, the world's developed countries are taking steps to dispose of the garbage created by electronic gadgets. Developing and underprivileged countries, according to the author, are falling far behind. Bangladesh, being a developing country, has a knowledge gap in terms of regulations and processes for dealing with E-waste. However, we were unable to locate any systematic review or case study in this field to our knowledge [8].

1.3 Aim

In Bangladesh, there is a lack of managing e-waste appropriately, which causes a significant impact on our environment. This research aims to propose a sustainable way to manage e-waste. The authors are going to collect data, compare existing models, and propose an effective model by visiting different organizations.

1.4 Objective

The objectives of this study are:

- To find out the government's e-waste management policies' effectiveness.
- To compare the policies and practices of e-waste management organizations in Bangladesh with government policies.
- To develop an efficient method of managing e-waste.

1.5 Scope of the Study

This research looks at the management of e-waste in Bangladesh. It is a discussion on how various organizations handle wastage caused by worn out/used/expired electronic equipment such as computers, machinery, and electronic devices. We are not in charge of any other waste management. Furthermore, the research is focused on Dhaka, Bangladesh. The study will be based on observations of the Bangladesh E-waste management scenario.

2 Related Works

The authors of the paper [9] explained the current situation of e-waste management and showed how e-waste management works in Bangladesh. From Fig. 1, we can see that "Repairing," "Recycling," and "Dumping parts which cannot be recycled or repaired" are the methods of informal sectors of Bangladesh. The authors also mentioned that at that time, there were no governmental initiatives on e-waste management. That's why people were not aware of the harmfulness of e-waste. Also, the author mentioned that A 5–10% annual rise in the quantity of used electrical and electronic equipment that is properly disposed of could lead to environmental dangers that harm human health, destroys marine life, pollutes groundwater, and reduces soil fertility. Insufficient public knowledge, policies, and a lack of funding in the field of waste management are only a few of the significant causes driving this situation. As a result, the authors identified the issue and recommended an e-waste management system. According to the authors, integrating with current e-waste systems will address e-waste management difficulties.

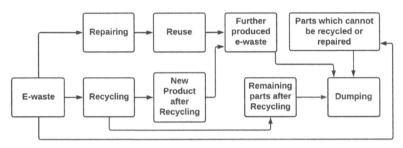

Fig. 1. Informal Scenario of Bangladesh's E-waste Management System [9].

The authors of the paper [10] have mentioned various laws, regulations, and standards for managing e-waste in Bangladesh [11]. The paper, electronic items, and electrical wastes are defined in the law, as well as the responsibilities of manufacturers, consumers, buyers, stores, repairers, collection centers, recyclers, and the ministry. Not only that, but the authors also analyzed the consumer WTP (Willingness to pay) for recycling costs in their research. For analysis, the author gathered information by doing a questionnaire-based survey. By doing that, the author found out that consumers 5–10% WTP will cover the recycling cost of e-waste in Bangladesh. But participants of the survey also mentioned the government's initiatives in e-waste management. For that reason, the author suggested increasing environmental awareness and educating the public about the harmfulness of e-waste to make recycling more convenient. Also, the author mentioned that environmental education is essential for promoting environmental awareness and increasing the WTP of consumers [10].

In the paper [11], The goal was to examine the current state, concerns, and challenges facing Asia Pacific countries, as well as to recommend a path forward for environmentally sound management (ESM) of e-waste [11]. Besides, the author thoroughly explained the regulations and current practices of e-waste in almost every country in the Asia Pacific Region.

The authors of the article [12] evaluated India's e-waste management system to that of other industrialized countries throughout the world. As per a United Nations Environment Program estimate, the volume of e-waste in India might rise by 500% every ten years. In this research, practical recommendations relating to the Indian context, such as financial system sustainability, implementation, legislation and regulation, and monitoring, will play a vital role in the e-waste management system [12].

The author of the paper [13] is developing a new method for estimating the cost and life-cycle effect of e-waste management. Some process models might be investigated to improve recycling and categorize e-waste while minimizing system costs and carbon emissions (such as consumer drop-off, Interfacility Transportation, and System Net Cost, where the cost, energy use, and emissions are associated). A Washington study case based on a process-level life-cycle model is also offered for modeling e-waste collection, transportation, processing, and disposal [13].

The author of the paper [14] analyzed e-waste management in Switzerland and Australia. The government of Switzerland has made e-waste recycling a high contribution. In 2017, 122,800 tons of e-waste were collected in Switzerland for recycling. This adds up to a significant volume of e-waste gathered. By recycling the gathered e-waste, the country achieved tremendous success in e-waste management. This program aims to recycle e-waste rather than landfilling it. As a result of the corresponding section, Australia has had a lot of success with e-waste management.

2.1 Research Questions

- What are the policies of e-waste management of the government of Bangladesh?
- What are the differences in the policies and practices of the e-waste management process in Bangladesh by different organizations?
- What are the hindrances of managing e-waste effectively?

3 Methodology

3.1 Data Collection Method

There are two types of research from a broad perspective. The first is qualitative, whereas the second is quantitative. Qualitative research is descriptive and non-numerical, whereas quantitative study is more concerned with numbers, algorithms, and statistics [15]. Words are used to acquire qualitative information. The nature of the data generated by the research defines the sort of research, not the techniques employed to acquire it. Qualitative data may be obtained using a variety of research methods [16].

There are five different approaches to doing research. Surveys, case studies, simulations, subjective/argumentative research, and action research are the types of research. Surveys, a popular research technique, is helpful for gathering current information and learning about people's latest activities, and by this, we access a large amount of data. A case study can be used to try to describe links between various topics and theoretical ones. Those who wish to investigate a unique circumstance of a present situation or research, where solving issues analytically is difficult, approach the simulation technique. Subjective/argumentative research is used to develop new hypotheses and concepts that may later be evaluated. Action research is the most productive technique because it allows authors to uncover practical answers to real-world issues while still adding theoretical value [17].

Case studies, grounded theory, ethnography, and phenomenology are the most often utilized qualitative research methods. These strategies include a variety of research methodologies. Sampling is one of the approaches. There are several types of sampling, including simple random sampling, systematic sampling, stratified sampling, cluster sampling, multi-stage sampling, Quota Sampling, Haphazard sampling, and so on [16]. Interviews, which are extensively utilized in qualitative research, are another approach included in these methodologies. Taking interviews is more appropriate for qualitative research. Interviews can be conducted in a structured, semi-structured, or unstructured manner. Structured interviews have well-defined questions and responses. In a semi-structured interview, the questionnaire might expand from its root as the interviewer progresses. An unstructured interview is a free-form conversation [16].

There are two kinds of data gathering: Primary and secondary. Primary data collection refers to information gathered from sources by the investigators themselves. Secondary data collection refers to data obtained from secondary sources such as a database or data pre-collected by other people [17].

Authors have collected data in both ways, primarily and secondarily because authors have interviewed a few e-waste management companies and also collected data from research papers, journals, and so on.

3.2 Interview

It may appear simple at first glance because the conversation is already a strength that the interviewers possess, but it is essential to remember that an interview is not a conversation. The investigator is responsible for passively controlling the conversion flow and ensuring that all relevant data is obtained. When the participant is asked about any vital information, the situation might get a bit odd. A similar situation occurred when one of the authors questioned a participant from "Azizu Recycling & E-Waste Company" about the company's annual income. The participant replied that this information was confidential [16]. But other than that, they have shared all the information related to the research which had been asked. Authors have asked about their strategy to collect, process, and manage e-waste by their company. The participant willingly shared their strategy and showed their types of machinery and how they work and process to dismantle e-waste components.

The interview was semi-structured. The authors have a clear list of topics and questions to discuss and answer during semi-structured interviews. In semi-structured interviews, however, authors have more freedom with the replies and question sequence. The participants are free to answer in their style and can add more information to the initial ones, and the interview can grow from there [16]. So, the authors of this study asked the participants the pre-prepared questions but then allowed them to explain so that more information could be gained from the session.

To be concerned about e-waste management, a country's organizations and industries that employ electrical equipment must first be concerned since they are responsible for a significant portion of overall e-waste. This is a qualitative study since the primary goal is to find out a sustainable way to manage e-waste [17]. The information was gathered in the form of words. The authors collected data for this study using interviews, which is a scientific approach for collecting data for qualitative research [16]. They also gathered information by interviewing persons who collect and handle E-waste from large organizations and businesses. By conducting the interviews, themselves, the investigators were able to acquire primary data [17].

3.3 Data Analysis

The authors conducted interviews with IT officials from notable Bangladeshi firms since interviewing is a scientific approach to conducting qualitative research. The information gathered from the conducted interviews will be presented scientifically and systematically in this study. The whole e-waste management practices of organizations where the investigators conducted interviews are described. Flow charts are used to depict the entire process since they may represent a complicated process simple.

3.4 Research Ethics

The consent form was provided for collecting data from individual interviews that outlined the purpose of this research project. The participants' anonymity was protected. Participants in the offline survey had to read the informed consent form, and only if they accepted the conditions, their interviews were taken. They had the option to deny giving an opinion. The phone conversations in which the author contacted participants described the context of the study and acquired permission to record the call.

4 Materials and Method

4.1 Data Collection and Analysis

In this study, the authors gathered information by interviewing experts on this subject. The authors were divided into two groups. One group was interviewed at "Azizu Recycling & E-Waste Firm Ltd." in Narayanganj, and the other at "Yousuf Enterprise – Electronic waste recycling company" in Badda. The authors created an informed consent form and questionnaire before beginning the interviews. The interviewees' consent was obtained verbally or in writing. The information was gathered through handwriting and recording. The information gathered is qualitative. After gathering the data, the authors analyzed it and utilized the online tool Lucid Chart to build flowcharts of the procedures reported by the interviewees.

4.2 Policies of E-waste Management of the Government

The relevant goods manufacturers, traders, dealers, transporters, repairers, collection centers, recyclers, dismantlers, and others must register with the DOE using a prescribed form. They must provide a WEEE management strategy with their registration application. According to the Bangladesh Environmental Protection Rules, 1997, registered producers, recyclers and others must acquire environmental clearance. Manufacturers must set up individual or collaborative collection facilities and budget for WEEE management. WEEE traders, dealers, and collectors are required to collect WEEE from customers at authorized locations and transfer it to collection facilities [18].

4.3   Policies of E-waste Management of Different Organizations

The authors went to some e-waste management organizations to collect data and learn how the e-wastes are managed at their organizations. The company's name was "Azizu Recycling & E-Waste Company Ltd" (Fig. 2), where the authors went to interview the participants of the company. Azizu Recycling & E-Waste Company Ltd. Was formed in 2006 as an importer of computer parts and accessories. In 2008, the company started working with "Tes-Amm," a Singapore recycler company. But in 2013, the company started e-waste management instead of importing electronic parts.

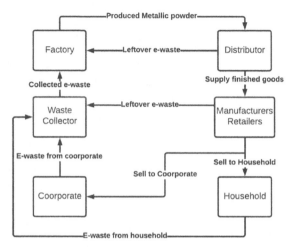

Fig. 2.   Azizu Recycling & E-Waste Company Ltd Recycling Process.

The authors asked the participant what e-waste means in their company. The participant replied that any kind of electronic component is considered e-waste, and they recycle all kinds of electrical components. As for collecting e-wastes, the participants mentioned that telecom company, office, garments, and street vendors are their sources of e-wastes. About their recycling techniques, the participant mentioned that they have recycling techniques that are different based on the components. First, they dismantle the component and then sort the dismantled component according to recycling techniques. They have five recycling processes by which they separate metals, plastics, glasses, etc., which were later shown and explained by the participant. The researcher asked about is the company's techniques were adapted from an overseas company. The participant talked about the Tes-Amm company, from where they adapted their techniques. However, the company is not getting enough e-wastes to recycle from the mentioned sources. For that reason, their profit from recycling is relatively lower. As for following governmental regulations, the government published a direction for managing e-waste on June 22, 2021, and they are following those regulations. The researcher asked about the cost of e-waste management and recycling. The participant replied that the cost varies on the components they are recycling. They not only recycle the components in Bangladesh but also receive products from overseas to recycle those components. As per their participant, by recycling, they get 90% copper and 5% or less gold, and others are mixed metals which are later separated by a sorting machine. The researcher also asked what the company would do with those recycled metals. The participant said they often sell it to manufacturing companies or export it overseas.

Another company, the authors, visited was "Yousuf Enterprise" which is also an e-waste management company. The mobile, laptop and sim companies give tenders to them to collect their e-waste. Yousuf Enterprise mainly targets those tenders and collects e-wastes from those companies. After collecting that e-waste, they dismantle the products, send the components like PCBs (Printed Circuit Board), and export them to overseas companies, mainly in Japan or Malaysia. As for other e-wastes, they collect metals from those and sell them to mills based on the metal they get. Before dismantling e-wastes, they take permission from BTRC (Bangladesh Telecommunication Regulatory Commission), BEDS (Bangladesh Environment and Development Society), and other organizations.

From an interview with a local vendor, the authors found that the local vendors don't get enough e-waste from people to send to a recycling company. The main reason is that people do not get enough money selling their unused e-products as the vendor buys them based on their weight. Another reason for the local vendors not getting enough e-waste is that they cannot sell them to recycling companies at the expected price. As a result, most of the e-waste remains un-recycled.

4.4   Design and Framework for Bangladesh and Other Countries

The author of the paper [9] mentioned a framework of e-waste management in Bangladesh, including repairing, recycling, and parts that cannot be repaired or recycled (Fig. 1). These initiatives were encircled in one framework, later divided into two frameworks by the author (Figs. 3 and 4).

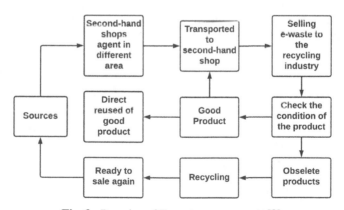

Fig. 3. Re-using of E-wastes components [9].

In Fig. 3, the author mentioned how the re-using would occur depending on the condition of the received product. So, if the product quality is good enough, it will be sent to a secondhand shop, which they will sell, and eventually, the products will be re-used. If the quality is not good, then it will be sent for recycling. After recycling, the product will be re-manufactured by the manufacturing company and be ready to sell again in the market.

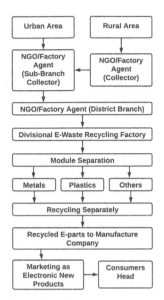

Fig. 4. Recycling of E-wastes components [9].

In Fig. 4, the author mentioned how recycling works. The author also designed the after products of module separation should be recycled separately because the metals are mixed products, and those cannot be dumped. Still, these products can be used for making other electrical components. That's why metals should be recycled separately. As for plastics, things are the same. After recycling the elements, these metals and plastics are sent to the manufacturer.

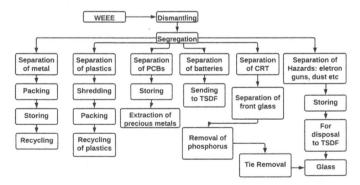

Fig. 5. Recycling operation of a company in India [9].

Bangladesh's neighboring country India also has some initiatives for managing e-waste. Figure 5 is showing a company's recycling operation. It represents the company's recycling techniques are different based on the components. Also, it gives the company a complete framework for what they will do after separating the elements. Like after the metal separation, they will pack the metal, store it and recycle the component for re-manufacturing other electrical products or sell it to a manufacturing company.

Other nations worldwide have already introduced a law and begun implementing electronic recycling and take-back schemes. Switzerland was the first country to develop and implement a comprehensive framework for e-waste recycling and disposal [19]. The WEEE guideline governs European nations, requiring IT equipment providers to back up their outmoded equipment and provide protocols for safely disposing of it. The legislative framework of the country is founded on the concept of Extended Producer Responsibility (EPR) [20, 21].

The US e-waste management framework consisted of re-use programs, recycling, domestic landfill discharge, and many more characteristics within the Circular Economy concept. Furthermore, while Brazil and Canada have signed the Basel Convention, which intends to stress hazardous chemical management, uniform regulation, and limited control of the illicit e-waste trade, their regulatory scopes differ [22]. Furthermore, several countries manufacturing IT equipment, such as China, Vietnam, and Japan, have adopted ISWM's (Integrated Sustainable Waste Management) global best practice guideline for e-waste management [23].

4.5 Proposed Model

To solve the issues of e-waste collection and management, the authors proposed a model (Fig. 6) that is expected to change toward effective e-waste management significantly.

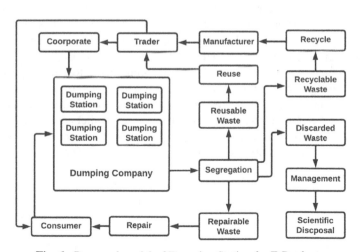

Fig. 6. Proposed model of Dumping Station for E-Products.

The authors propose a model that includes a Dumping Company for managing e-waste. There will be several dumping stations throughout the country which will trade unusable e-products from people with reasonable prices based on products condition.

Then the dumping company collects all products from dumping stations and sorts them. Also, the dumping company collects e-waste from Corporates through tenders or contracts. The Dumping company will segregate the collected e-waste. After that, reusable products will be sent to the traders, repairable products to the consumers after repairing, recyclable products to the recyclers, and the rest of the products will be sent for scientific disposal. The recycling company recycles the products into raw materials and sells them to the manufacturer. Manufacturers produce a finished product and individual components. Manufacturers sell the individual components to repair companies or shop and finished products in the market, from where the corporate and general public buys the product. Repair companies refurbish the repairable e-waste and sell the refurbished product in the market.

5   Result and Discussion

In this research, the authors discussed the policies and processes of different organizations and countries' e-waste management systems. The summary is given in this table (Table 1):

In terms of the segregation of e-waste, there is a similarity in plastic, metal, PCB, and CRT recycling techniques of "Azizu Recycling & E-waste Company" with an Indian recycling company. In paper [5], the authors proposed a model which includes an e-waste collection factory, but the government or any other NGOs took no initiative. As a result, recycling companies must collect e-waste on their own or look for local vendors. Two European Union policies are the waste electrical and electronic equipment (WEEE) directive and the Restrictions of hazardous substances (RoHS) directive. Another strategy is extended producer responsibility, in which the producer bears partial liability for product return [11]. Along with WEEE, RoHS, and EPR, China has enacted the 3R (Recycle, re-use, reduce) rule, which significantly reduces the environmental effect of e-waste and increases resource efficiency [24]. Under the WEEE law, users in Japan must drop off their old products and pay a collection charge to cover the expenses of collecting, shipping, and recycling. Used household appliances are meant to be collected by retailers, and manufacturers are required to recycle them with government funding. Previously owned electrical products must be returned to retailers or municipalities [25].

The authors found out that collecting e-waste is a significant concern in these policies. For that reason, the authors proposed a model which is effective for managing e-waste. To recycle e-waste, recycling companies must first collect e-waste from the general people who have electronic devices. To do that, the authors proposed making some "Dumping Stations" across the country where people can sell their useless electronic devices reasonably. Now people can only sell their e-products according to their weight, giving them very little money. But as Dumping Stations will provide them with a price based on product condition, people will get a reasonable price for their e-products and will be encouraged to recycle them at Dumping stations. Then the Dumping Station can send those e-products to the Dumping Company, where repairable products will be sent to repair shops, non-repairable products will be sent to the recycling company, and reusable products will be sent to traders. Big organizations can also tender out their e-products to Dumping companies to recycle or re-use them.

Table 1. Different organizations and countries' e-waste management policies and practices.

Serial	Country or organization	E-Waste Management Policies and Practices
1	Azizu Recycling & E-Waste Company Ltd	Collects e-waste from Street vendors, Telecommunication Companies then process the e-waste to form metal plates then sell it to Manufacturing companies or factories
2	Yusuf Enterprise	Collects e-waste from Mobile, Laptop, Sim then dismantles those e-wastes and exports them to Japan or Malaysia
3	An Indian Company	After collecting e-waste, they dismantle and segregate the e-waste using different techniques and sell those recycled products to a manufacturing company
4	Japan	Drop their old product, and pay the collection charge for recycling under WEEE law. Also, household appliances are collected by retailers and manufacturers to recycle with government funding
5	China	Adapted 3R rules, which reduced the environmental effect of e-waste
6	Other Nations	Introduced law and implemented electronic recycling techniques and take-back schemes

A survey conducted by the researchers found that 65% of people use scrap shops to dump their e-waste. According to 77% of people, scrap shop buys e-product according to weight and 66% of people keep storing their e-product to them without recycling them as the money scrap shop offers is not sufficient. Therefore, the researchers asked if their proposed model will be able to solve this problem and the rate of positive response was 87%. From the research, the authors found different ways to manage e-waste in Bangladesh by different organizations. The authors also found the government's approach to managing e-waste. This indicates lacking e-waste collections, so the authors introduced a model to fill the knowledge gap. This model is expected to make a significant change in e-waste collections and management. Local vendors don't get enough e-waste nowadays. This also makes local vendors jobless. As people of all stages can trade any unnecessary electronic devices at a reasonable price, they will be encouraged to recycle, which will solve the issue of e-waste collections. Then the recycling company can get enough e-waste to recycle. Local vendors can work in Dumping stations and Dumping companies, which will solve their employment problem.

752 Md. S. A. Sheikh et al.

6 Conclusion

The sole purpose of this research was to find a sustainable way to manage e-waste in Bangladesh and to compare the proposed model with the existing ones. The existing models have many drawbacks. Some models were designed for other countries and were not entirely compatible with Bangladesh. Also, the current e-waste collecting and managing system were not appropriate, thus, causing recycling companies not to get enough e-wastes. Through the model, the authors can solve the issues regarding the existing models by proposing a proper e-waste collecting and managing system.

Acknowledgment. We want to express our gratitude to "Azizu Recycling & E-waste Company" and "Yousuf Enterprise" for cooperating with us. We want to thank Rashedul Amin Tuhin, Senior Lecturer, East West University, and Abdulla Al Mamun Asif from "Azizu Recycling & E-waste Company" for guiding and helping through our research.

References

1. Chaudhary, K., Vrat, P.: Optimal location of precious metal extraction facility (PMEF) for E-waste recycling units in National Capital Region (NCR) of India. Opsearch **54**(3), 441–459 (2016). https://doi.org/10.1007/s12597-016-0287-0
2. Solving the E-Waste Problem (Step) White Paper One Global Definition of E-waste 1 Solving the E-Waste Problem (Step) Initiative White Paper One Global Definition of E-waste (2014)
3. Karim, R.T., Bari, N., Amin, M.A.: E-waste management in Bangladesh. In: 2014 2nd International Conference on Green Energy and Technology, ICGET 2014, pp. 104–109 (2014). https://doi.org/10.1109/ICGET.2014.6966673
4. Encyclopedia Britannica: Electronic waste. https://www.britannica.com/technology/electronic-waste. Accessed 3 Aug 2022
5. Meem, R.A., et al.: A review on the environmental and health impacts due to electronic waste disposal in Bangladesh. GSC Adv. Res. Rev. **8**, 116–125 (2021). https://gsconlinepress.com/journals/gscarr/sites/default/files/GSCARR-2021-0174.pdf. https://doi.org/10.30574/GSCARR.2021.8.2.0174
6. Irthiza, A.: Environmental Policy Instruments Use-design for Improving E-waste Management in Bangladesh (2021)
7. Rahman, M.A.: E-waste Management: A Study on Legal Framework and Institutional Preparedness in Bangladesh (2016)
8. Herat, S.: E-waste management in Asia Pacific Region: review of issues, challenges and solutions. https://doi.org/10.46488/NEPT.2021.v20i01.005
9. Masud, M.H., et al.: Towards the effective E-waste management in Bangladesh: a review. Environ. Sci. Pollut. Res. **26**(2), 1250–1276 (2018). https://doi.org/10.1007/s11356-018-3626-2
10. Ananno, A.A., Masud, M.H., Dabnichki, P., Mahjabeen, M., Chowdhury, S.A.: Survey and analysis of consumers' behaviour for electronic waste management in Bangladesh. J. Environ. Manage. **282**, 111943 (2021). https://doi.org/10.1016/J.JENVMAN.2021.111943
11. Herat, S., Agamuthu, P.: E-waste: a problem or an opportunity? Review of issues, challenges and solutions in Asian countries. Waste Manage. Res. **30**, 1113–1129 (2012). https://doi.org/10.1177/0734242X12453378

12. Wath, S.B., Vaidya, A.N., Dutt, P.S., Chakrabarti, T.: A roadmap for development of sustainable E-waste management system in India. Sci. Total Environ. **409**, 19–32 (2010). https://doi.org/10.1016/J.SCITOTENV.2010.09.030

13. Jaunich, M.K., DeCarolis, J., Handfield, R., Kemahlioglu-Ziya, E., Ranjithan, S.R., Moheb-Alizadeh, H.: Life-cycle modeling framework for electronic waste recovery and recycling processes. Resour. Conserv. Recycl. **161**, 104841 (2020). https://doi.org/10.1016/J.RESCONREC.2020.104841

14. Islam, M.T, Dias, P., Huda, N.: Comparison of e-waste management in Switzerland and in Australia: a qualitative content analysis. World Acad. Sci. Eng. Technol. **12**(10), 610–616 (2018). http://scholar.waset.org/1307-6892/10009626

15. Jackson, R.L., Drummond, D.K., Camara, S.: What is qualitative research? **8**, 21–28 (2007). https://doi.org/10.1080/17459430701617879

16. Denscombe, M.: The Good Research Guide: For Small-Scale Social Research Projects (2010)

17. Igwenagu, C.: Fundamentals of Research Methodology and Data Collection, pp. 4–5. LAP Lambert Academic Publishing (2016)

18. Bangladesh Government: E-waste Management Rule of Bangladesh. https://www.dpp.gov.bd/upload_file/gazettes/40075_81487.pdf. Accessed 3 Aug 2022

19. Premalatha, M., Tabassum-Abbasi, Abbasi, T., Abbasi, S.A.: The generation, impact, and management of E-waste: state of the art. Crit. Rev. Environ. Sci. Technol. **44**, 1577–1678 (2014). https://doi.org/10.1080/10643389.2013.782171

20. Shumon, M.R.H., Ahmed, S.: Sustainable WEE management in Malaysia: present scenarios and future perspectives. IOP Conf. Ser. Mater. Sci. Eng. **50** (2013). https://doi.org/10.1088/1757-899X/50/1/012066

21. de Oliveira, C.R., Bernardes, A.M., Gerbase, A.E.: Collection and recycling of electronic scrap: a worldwide overview and comparison with the Brazilian situation. Waste Manage. **32**, 1592–1610 (2012). https://doi.org/10.1016/J.WASMAN.2012.04.003

22. Xavier, L.H., Ottoni, M., Lepawsky, J.: Circular economy and e-waste management in the Americas: Brazilian and Canadian frameworks. J. Clean. Prod. **297**, 126570 (2021). https://doi.org/10.1016/J.JCLEPRO.2021.126570

23. Ignatuschtschenko, E.: Electronic waste in China, Japan, and Vietnam: a comparative analysis of waste management strategies. Vienna J. East Asian Stud. **9**, 29–58 (2018). https://doi.org/10.2478/VJEAS-2017-0002

24. Liu, L., Liang, Y., Song, Q., Li, J.: A review of waste prevention through 3R under the concept of circular economy in China. J. Mater. Cycles Waste Manage. **19**(4), 1314–1323 (2017). https://doi.org/10.1007/s10163-017-0606-4

25. Chung, S.-W., Murakami-Suzuki, R.: A comparative study of e-waste recycling systems in Japan, South Korea and Taiwan from the EPR perspective: implications for developing countries (2008)

Machine Learning Algorithms on COVID-19 Prediction Using CpG Island and AT-CG Feature on Human Genomic Data

Md. Motaleb Hossen Manik[✉], Md. Ahsan Habib, and Tanim Ahmed

Department of Computer Science and Engineering, Khulna University of Engineering and Technology, Khulna, Bangladesh

{mh.manik,mahabib}@cse.kuet.ac.bd, ahmed1507113@stud.kuet.ac.bd

Abstract. A pandemic has broken out throughout the world since December 2019 and later it has been named COVID-19. The flow of normal life has collapsed due to this pandemic, especially in the economic, public health, and education sectors. The number of infected people is increasing daily. So, the identification of COVID-19 patients is a crying need in the health sector to stop the spread of this virus. Recently, Machine Learning algorithms have shown fascinating results in the prediction of medical data. In this study, we have proposed an approach to predict COVID-19 on human genomic data using the CpG Island feature and the newly introduced AT-CG feature by Machine Learning algorithms. Our proposed system produces an impressive result of the highest 99.91% accuracy on the Naïve Bayes algorithm.

Keywords: Coronavirus · Prediction · Machine Learning · CpG Island Feature · AT-CG Feature

1 Introduction

Coronavirus (COVID-19) is a recently discovered virus that was initially spotted in Wuhan, Hubei, China [1]. Among different viruses, it has the longest genomic length of 30,000 bps and it is a single-strand RNA virus [2].

Severe Acute Respiratory Syndrome Coronavirus (SARS-CoV) is a beta variant coronavirus among four discovered variants namely alphacoronavirus, betacoronavirus, gammacoronavirus and deltacoronavirus. Initially, the virus appeared with the symptom of Pneumonia later revealed breathing problems, fever, and loss of taste symptoms. A new diverged disease from SARS-CoV has been considered a sub-variant of beta coronavirus referred to as SARS-CoV-2 [3].

A study suggests that different methods have a hypothesis that DNA sequences possess common features [4]. These methods have been applied to classification tasks, and the results are noticeable. BLAST and FASTA can be mentioned of that type. Though direct sequence alignment algorithms perform well on sequence classification, their usage may be costly sometimes in the long sequence alignment. Instead, sequence

Md. S. Satu et al. (Eds.): MIET 2022, LNICST 491, pp. 754–762, 2023.
https://doi.org/10.1007/978-3-031-34622-4_59

alignment-free methods have been introduced later [5, 6]. Among different classification tasks, the virus classification task is one of the critical ones. But recent studies have revealed that Machine Learning algorithms can successfully classify viruses based on their internal features [7] whereas, for COVID-19, Forecasting, Diagnosis, Environmental Dependencies, Surveys, and Screening are the most common uses for Machine Learning-based models [8, 9]. Reyes et al. [10] proposed a method for subtyping HIV-1 sequences. Their supervised alignment-free model was based on open-source k-mer that achieved 97% accuracy and conclude that their model could be adaptable for other types of viruses. A combinational method of supervised learning and Digital Signal Processing has been introduced by Randhawa et al. [7] that works on the intrinsic genomic signature of coronavirus. They have used the KNN algorithm on 7396 full mitochondrial genomes and achieved an accuracy of 97% but failed to cross the accuracy of the Benchmark dataset while validating with a small dataset. Berlian [11] proposed a new method with optimized Machine Learning algorithms that can predict COVID-19 patients. The optimization occurred on Discriminant Analysis, K-Nearest Neighbor, Decision Tree, and Support Vector Machine algorithms. These algorithms have been applied to isolated DNA of infected patients and achieved a result of 98.3%, 100%, and 100% accuracy with Decision Tree, K-Nearest Neighbor, and Support Vector Machine, respectively. But the limitation of this model is not using the different variants of coronavirus data that are trending currently. Another research on COVID-19 by the Machine Learning approach has been conducted by Yousef et al. [12] on infected and non-infected patients' DNA tests. The study has been applied to find the clinical elements that are affecting the DNA sequencing most and found that fever, headache, and cough were the initial causes. They have attained an accuracy of 0.84 and an AUC value of 0.92 with the Random Forest algorithm. They have used sampled data rather than a population that included unjustified cases to be tested thus questioning its usability. Zhang et al. [13] have proposed a comparative method that has included the application of feature extraction without a feature extraction model in Machine Learning algorithms. They have used COVID-19, Influenza, AIDS, and Hepatitis C virus dataset incorporating three algorithms, namely Convolutional Neural Network, Neural Network, and N-gram probabilistic model. Their finding indicates that the newly developed feature extraction model proposed by them showed excellent results on smaller COVID-19 datasets while traditional models lead the accuracy curve. Though their proposed feature extraction model performed well but failed to outperform the traditional methods.

Wang et al. [14] have conducted a study on the COVID-19 DNA sequence that has concluded that COVID-19 has a low CG content abundance. Arslan [15] used the CpG Island feature in COVID-19 prediction, but the main disadvantage of using the CpG Island feature only is that the lack of CG content in genomic sequence generates a lower value thus generating almost the same value for all sequences. In this case, the presence of rich AT content in the COVID-19 genomic sequence can be a remedy for the prediction task. Considering these findings, we have proposed a new model in this paper that encompasses the following contributions:

- Introduced a new feature, namely AT-CG content
- Applied the CpG Island feature along with the AT-CG feature to increase the usability of DNA sequence in COVID-19 prediction

- Collected DNA sequence of different variants of Coronavirus
- Outperformed the previously developed models *i.e.* [10, 12, 13]

Our approach comprises a collection of Machine Learning algorithms on Human Genomic data, available on the National Center for Biotechnology Information website [16]. We have used the CpG Island and AT-CG features for the algorithms and found the highest accuracy of 99.91%.

The rest of the paper is designed as follows. Section 2 describes the materials and methodology in brief. Section 3 explains the results found in this study. The discussions and future work have been included in Sect. 4. Finally, Sect. 5 concludes the paper.

2 Materials and Methodology

In this section, three subsections have been included. The extraction of genomic data, feature selection, and Machine Learning algorithms have been described briefly in this section. Moreover, Fig. 1 shows the pictorial view of the full system architecture.

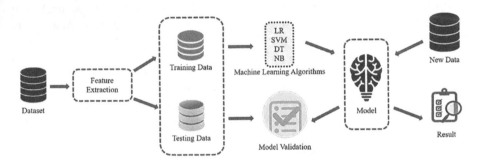

Fig. 1. Pictorial view of system architecture

2.1 Dataset Collection and Data Labelling

It has been a long time since the coronavirus has been discovered. Since then, different organizations are collecting data on infected patients from different sources. Though initially there was a lack of appropriate data, now data is almost accurately available. In this research, the data has been collected from the National Center for Biotechnology Information website [16] which contains 45,000 genomic data of humans. Among these genome sequences, half have a corona positive sequence and the rest half have a corona negative sequence. Data of different variants of COVID-19 has been included in the dataset to increase the usability of the models. The positive cases have been marked as 1 and the negative cases have been marked as 0. From the dataset, 80% of the data has been treated for training purposes while the rest 20% has been used for testing the models. Table 1 summarizes the data with different variants of coronavirus.

Table 1. Summary of collected data

Data type		Amount	Label
Non-COVID		22500	0
COVID	Alpha Variant	10125	1
	Beta Variant	6750	1
	Gamma Variant	5625	1

2.2 Feature Extraction

Any Machine Learning algorithm's working procedure starts with the feature that the algorithm utilizes to perform prediction or classification. The algorithm sets its parameter values based on the features that it uses. Thus, the accurate feature selection task plays a vital role in accepting the model. Since studies have found that COVID-19 has a strong absence of CG content in its genomic sequence [14, 17], the CpG Island feature is used as the first feature in this study. Moreover, to consider the relative presence of CG with C and G, another feature has been used namely feature. Since, the absence of CG content generates lower values for the CpG Island feature, in this study a new feature extraction material has been introduced namely the AT-CG content. The following three equations describe those processes for extracting the features.

$$CpG = p(C) + p(G) \tag{1}$$

$$CpGo = \frac{p(CG)}{p(C) * p(G)} \tag{2}$$

$$AT - CG = \frac{p(AT)}{p(CG)} \tag{3}$$

Here p(C), p(G), p(CG), and p(AT) are the percentage of C, G, CG, and AT in the DNA sequence, respectively. Using these three equations, the corresponding features are extracted and provided to the Machine Learning algorithms. However, Fig. 2 illustrates the feature extraction process with an example.

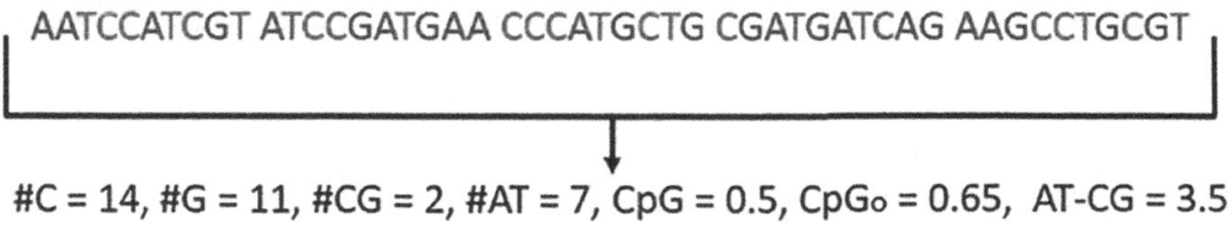

AATCCATCGT ATCCGATGAA CCCATGCTG CGATGATCAG AAGCCTGCGT

#C = 14, #G = 11, #CG = 2, #AT = 7, CpG = 0.5, CpGo = 0.65, AT-CG = 3.5

Fig. 2. Feature extraction from a genomic sequence

2.3 Machine Learning Algorithms

This section describes the Machine Learning algorithms applied in this research to classify human genomic data either as COVID-19 positive or negative. Four different Machine Learning algorithms have been used to conduct this study in classifying the data, namely Logistic Regression (LR), Support Vector Machine (SVM), Decision Tree (DT), and Naïve Bayes (NB).

Logistic Regression: LR is a pre-trainable Machine Learning algorithm. This algorithm can be used for predicting the probability of the target variable. Normally a Logistic Regression model is binary in nature, which means the target variable can have only two classes, either 0 (no/failure) or 1 (yes/success). The value of the target variable is determined by the Sigmoid function where if the value ≥ 0.5, then the output is 1 otherwise 0. In our research, the dataset has two states of the target attribute. Thus in this study Binary Logistic Regression (BLR) model has been used. Other than this, there are two types of Logistic Regression named Multinomial and Ordinal Logistic Regression that works on more than two classes of the target attribute.

Support Vector Machine: SVM is one of the remarkable Machine Learning algorithms that can do regression and classification based on purpose. The main process of the algorithm to classify data is drawing hyperplanes. Data points are put based on their axis values. The more the gap between the two hyperplanes will be, the more accurately the algorithm will classify data points. The hyperplanes will separate the data points into their desired classes. An idea of kernel trick is applied for higher dimensional data to view them in a usable format. In this research, the dataset has been classified as 0 or 1 for a negative result and positive result, respectively and three features have been used which are mentioned in Eqs. 1, 2, and 3.

Decision Tree: DT is another frequently used Machine Learning algorithm that can be mentioned as a tree-structured classifier. Since it is a tree-like structure, the internal nodes act as the features and the joining branches are the rules for choosing the decision on which path the algorithm should proceed to select the class. The leaf nodes are the decisions that follow the path through the decision branches starting at the root to the leaf nodes. Multiple methods are available to build a decision tree where the main idea is the same which is calculating the entropy and information gain or Gini index. In a particular node, the path is selected either with higher information gain or a lower Gini index. In this study, the generated Decision Tree obtained 10 leaf nodes. Figure 3 illustrates the built Decision Tree by the algorithm.

Naïve Bayes: Based on the theorem of Bayes, the NB algorithm has been developed. This algorithm is a commonly used Machine Learning algorithm for the classification task. This is one of the probabilistic classifiers that calculates the probability of the hypothesis based on the value of prior knowledge. The algorithm can handle multidimensional training datasets. Our dataset has three attributes as prior knowledge (Eqs. 1, 2, and 3). Based on these feature values, the output class of the genomic sequences is generated.

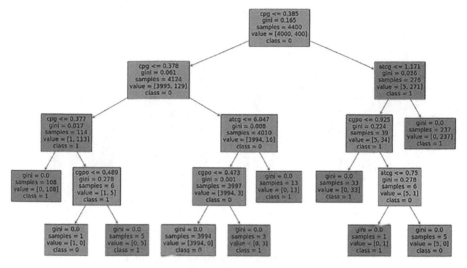

Fig. 3. Decision tree built by the algorithm

3 Result Analysis

The authors were enthusiastic about the applied CpG Island feature along with the AT-CG feature in the coronavirus classification task. The feature values have been calculated by using Eqs. 1, 2, and 3. Then the feature values have been provided to four Machine Learning algorithms which are Logistic Regression (LR), Support Vector Machine (SVM), Decision Tree (DT), and Naïve Bayes (NB). The result analysis section summarizes the performance of the algorithms featuring four performance measuring elements, namely Precision, Recall, F1-Score, and Accuracy.

The experiment has been carried out on the Kaggle platform in a Windows operating system configured laptop with a configuration of 4GB RAM, Intel Core i3 Processor, and 1.20 GHz clock speed. In our study, maximum accuracy has been obtained by the Naïve Bayes algorithm which is 99.91%. Since the Naïve Bayes algorithm is known as the probabilistic algorithm and works well on low features, this algorithm has performed well enough on our three features. Figure 4 exhibits the measuring elements of four algorithms as a pictorial view.

Figure 4 notifies that Decision Tree and Naïve Bayes are providing almost similar results and higher than the rest of the two algorithms. Again, a comparative study has been shown in Table 2 where the proposed methods have higher accuracy in predicting genomic sequences.

Figure 4 and Table 2 declare the competency of this research hence the proposed method.

Moreover, since a new feature, namely AT-CG content has been introduced in this study, a comparative study has been also been shown in Table 3 to indicate that without the AT-CG content feature, the COVID-19 classification accuracy is demoted.

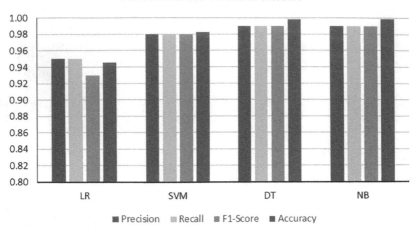

Fig. 4. Performance measurement of algorithms

Table 2. Performance comparison with existing methods

Sl	Author [Ref]	Methods used	Highest accuracy
1	Yousef et al. [12]	Random Forest	84%
2	Zhang et al. [13]	CNN, Neural Network, N-gram Probabilistic model	92.90%
3	Reyes et al. [10]	KAMERIS	97%
4	Proposed model	LR, SVM, DT, NB	99.91%

Table 3. Comparative analysis of using and not using AT-CG content feature

Algorithms	Without AT-CT content				With AT-CT content			
	Precision	Recall	F1-Score	Accuracy	Precision	Recall	F1-Score	Accuracy
LR	0.93	0.93	0.93	0.932	0.95	0.95	0.93	**0.951**
SVM	0.97	0.99	0.99	0.963	0.98	0.98	0.98	**0.982**
DT	0.98	0.98	0.99	**0.998**	0.99	0.99	0.99	**0.998**
NB	0.98	0.98	0.97	0.988	0.99	0.99	0.99	**0.999**

Naïve Bayes has been our first choice for performing the task. But still, other algorithms have been discussed in this paper considering that they would perform better while applied to other available datasets.

4 Discussions and Future Work

In this research, human genomic data has been used as a use case and Machine Learning algorithms have been applied to that data for screening out patients with COVID-19. The models have shown fascinating results on human genomic data with different variants of coronavirus. The proposed feature selection approaches have overcome the previously developed models where they did not solve the zero value and lower value of feature problem. This is another reason for the achievement of a better result. The achieved result suggests that there is an effect of low CG and high AT content in COVID-19 affected patients. Again, the used algorithms have classified the provided genomic data almost accurately while the probabilistic algorithm shows better performance which indicates the finding that the length of genome sequence affects the classification task.

Though in this study we have tried to recognize the patients with coronavirus, still some limitations have been traced including not covering the latest variants' data, environmental effects, and health condition analysis. Again, there is still some risk in a misclassification case. In future studies, these limitations will be overcome with newly appeared variants data and other associative data incorporated with the existing models.

5 Conclusions

In this peak time of COVID-19, the identification of infected patients is the major task that can prevent further propagation of coronavirus. In this research, we have tried to develop a way by which the task can be resolved. We have used human genomic data available on the NCBI website [16] which includes different variants' data of COVID-19. By using Eqs. 1, 2, and 3, the feature of the Machine Learning algorithms has been extracted. Then Logistic Regression, Support Vector Machine, Decision Tree, and Naïve Bayes algorithms have been applied to that data to predict the existence of COVID-19 in a patient. Finally, the proposed approaches show an impressive result of the highest 99.91% accuracy on the Naïve Bayes algorithm.

References

1. COVID-19 - Wikipedia. https://en.wikipedia.org/wiki/COVID-19. Accessed 21 July 2022
2. Sohrabi, C., et al.: World health organization declares global emergency: a review of the 2019 novel coronavirus (COVID-19). Int. J. Surg. **76**, 71–76 (2020). https://doi.org/10.1016/J.IJSU.2020.02.034
3. Wu, Y., et al.: SARS-CoV-2 is an appropriate name for the new coronavirus. Lancet **395**(10228), 949 (2020). https://doi.org/10.1016/S0140-6736(20)30557-2
4. Pinello, L., lo Bosco, G., Yuan, G.C.: Applications of alignment-free methods in epigenomics. Briefings Bioinf. **15**(3), 419–430 (2014). https://doi.org/10.1093/BIB/BBT078
5. Kari, L., et al.: Mapping the space of genomic signatures. PLoS ONE **10**(5), e0119815 (2015). https://doi.org/10.1371/JOURNAL.PONE.0119815
6. Karamichalis, R., Kari, L., Konstantinidis, S., Kopecki, S.: An investigation into inter- and intragenomic variations of graphic genomic signatures. BMC Bioinf. **16**(1), 1–22 (2015). https://doi.org/10.1186/S12859-015-0655-4/COMMENTS

7. Randhawa, G.S., Hill, K.A., Kari, L.: ML-DSP: machine learning with digital signal process-ing for ultrafast, accurate, and scalable genome classification at all taxonomic levels. BMC Genomics **20**(1), 1–21 (2019). https://doi.org/10.1186/S12864-019-5571-Y/FIGURES/9

8. Rahman, M.M., Islam, M.M., Manik, M.M.H., Islam, M.R., Al-Rakhami, M.S.: Machine learning approaches for tackling novel coronavirus (COVID-19) pandemic. SN Comput. Sci. **2**(5), 1 (2021). https://doi.org/10.1007/s42979-021-00774-7

9. Rahman, M.M., Manik, M.M.H., Islam, M.M., Mahmud, S., Kim, J.H.: An automated system to limit COVID-19 using facial mask detection in smart city network. In: IEMTRONICS 2020 - International IOT, Electronics and Mechatronics Conference, Proceedings, September 2020. https://doi.org/10.1109/IEMTRONICS51293.2020.9216386

10. Solis-Reyes, S., Avino, M., Poon, A., Kari, L.: An open-source k-mer based machine learning tool for fast and accurate subtyping of HIV-1 genomes. PLoS ONE **13**(11), e0206409 (2018). https://doi.org/10.1371/journal.pone.0206409

11. al Kindhi, B.: Optimization of machine learning algorithms for predicting infected COVID-19 in isolated DNA. Int. J. Intell. Eng. Syst. **13**(4), 423–433 (2020). https://doi.org/10.22266/IJI ES2020.0831.37

12. Yousef, M., Showe, L.C., ben Shlomo, I.: Clinical presentation of COVID-19 - a model derived by a machine learning algorithm. J. Integr. Bioinform. **18**(1), 3–8 (2021). https://doi.org/10. 1515/JIB-2020-0050

13. Zhang, X., Beinke, B., al Kindhi, B., Wiering, M.: Comparing machine learning algorithms with or without feature extraction for DNA classification (2020). https://doi.org/10.48550/ arxiv.2011.00485

14. Wang, Y., et al.: Human SARS-CoV-2 has evolved to reduce CG dinucleotide in its open reading frames. Sci. Rep. **10**(1), 1–10 (2020). https://doi.org/10.1038/s41598-020-69342-y

15. Arslan, H.: Machine learning methods for COVID-19 prediction using human genomic data. Proceedings **74**, 20 (2021). https://doi.org/10.3390/PROCEEDINGS2021074020

16. SARS-CoV-2 Resources - NCBI. https://www.ncbi.nlm.nih.gov/sars-cov-2/. Accessed 21 July 2022

17. Dinka, H., Milkesa, A.: Unfolding SARS-CoV-2 viral genome to understand its gene expres-sion regulation. Infect. Genet. Evol. **84**, 104386 (2020). https://doi.org/10.1016/J.MEEGID. 2020.104386

Statistical and Bioinformatics Model to Identify the Influential Genes and Comorbidities of Glioblastoma

Nitun Kumar Podder[1,2] and Pintu Chandra Shill[2(✉)]

[1] Bangladesh Institute of Governance and Management (BIGM), Dhaka, Bangladesh
[2] Department of Computer Science and Engineering, Khulna University
of Engineering & Technology, Khulna, Bangladesh
pintu@cse.kuet.ac.bd

Abstract. Glioblastoma (GBM) is the most common fatal cancer whose median survival time is estimated to be 12 to 18 months. GBM occurs in the frontal and temporal lobes of the brain and spread quickly. It's necessary to trace down GBM because people who are affected by GBM have a great risk to occur comorbidities like Arteries, Leukemia, Pancreatic Neoplasms, Sudden cardiac death, Autism, etc. We chose the Cancer Genome Atlas(TCGA) dataset to identify influential genes (IFGs) of GBM, which are linked with comorbidities. Drug designing for cancer as well as comorbidities would be more practical and easier if we can identify the IFGs. After some preprocessing, we have used the Kruskal-Wallis (K-W) test and Bonferroni Correction (BC) to select IFGs. We have successfully identified 26 dysregulated IFGs from 16261 genes. We performed PPIs, PDIs, comorbidity and phylogenetic analysis on IFGs. This study provides a basis to identify the IFGs and perception about the influences of GBM on comorbidities progression.

Keywords: Glioblastoma · Arteries · Leukemia · Pancreatic Neoplasms · Heart Rate · Autism · Comorbidities · PPIs Network · PDIs networks · Phylogenetic Tree

1 Introduction

GBM is one kind of brain tumor and the abnormal growth of this tumor tissue may be the cause of GBM [1]. Some IFGs mediate the influences of GBM on comorbidities progression that's why there is a very high scope to be affected with other diseases that can parallelly occur when the patient has GBM. Still, we are learning how IFGs affect the influences of GBM on comorbidities. Tissue Plasminogen Activator (TPA) is a type of clot-dissolving enzyme that can make help dissolve blood clots. Whenever TPA can't work properly it's may possible to occur a stroke in the human body caused by a blood clot. In U.S TPA is the drug approved by Food and Drug Administration for stroke. In recent

Md. S. Satu et al. (Eds.): MIET 2022, LNICST 491, pp. 763–774, 2023.
https://doi.org/10.1007/978-3-031-34622-4_60

times TPA is being studied for cancer treatment. So, a patient with a stroke has a chance of GBM. We recognize that there are many types of blood vessels present in the human body and arteries are one of them. Arteries carry oxygenated blood away from the heart to our body. Atherosclerosis is caused by the poor work of arteries that can affect the human brain. Pancreatic Neoplasms treats as pancreatic tumors that can occur anywhere in the pancreas. These neoplasms have a form of cancer when the cells of the pancreas growth in the human body are out of control. Pancreatic cancer has many several signs and symptoms such as-abdominal ache, weight loss, blood clotting, itchy skin, dark-colored urine, and these several symptoms may affect the glioblastoma that exists in the human brain. Normally Leukemia is a cancer that forms in the blood cells such as Red blood cells, White blood cells, and Platelets. But in general, Leukemia refers to cancer of the WBCs. Leukemia is similar to glioblastoma because Leukemia mostly affected people who are age over 55 years. Autism is a long-lasting affliction that affects the thinking, communicating and interacting capability of humans. Analysis many research some autism genes might be influences on glioblastoma. Sudden cardiac death (SCD) is a circumstance in which the function of the heart stops suddenly. Mostly sudden cardiac death happened due to glioblastoma is a rare incident [2].

In this exploration, we have developed a statistical and bioinformatics model to identify the IFGs and comorbidities of GBM [3]. We have used these differentially expressed IFGs for comorbidity analysis and successfully identified significant comorbidities (Arteries, Leukemia, Pancreatic Neoplasms, Sudden cardiac death, Autism, Heart rate etc.) of GBM [4]. We have successfully performed phylogenetic analysis on these comorbidities to identify the evolutionary relationship between GBM and comorbidities [5]. We performed protein-protein interactions (PPIs) analysis and protein-drug interactions (PDIs) analysis for proving the macromolecule interactions of our investigations [6]. We constructed IFGs diseasome network, comorbidity network, phylogenetic tree, PPIs network, and PDIs network. Our identified IFGs of GBM would be more efficient for gene therapy, drug design, and comorbidity identification. This investigation provides a basis of evidence for IFGs that mediate the influences of GBM on comorbidities progression [1].

2   Methodology

2.1   Working Principle and Datasets

In this model, K-W test and BC methods have been used on TCGA datasets of GBM to identify IFGs. Usiung the identified IFGs we have performed comorbidity analysis, phylogenetic analysis, PPIs analysis, Protein-drug interactions (PDIs) analysis. Proposed working principle of our study is described in Fig. 1.

For exploration one real dataset of mRNA median Zscores datavalues was used which is free and available e.g. Glioblastoma Multiforme (TCGA, Firehose Legacy). We have utilized this datasets from cBioPortal (www.cbioportal.org), delete the null value, replace the gene name and attribute by the nominal value to make it easier to import the dataset into RStudio for analysis [7].

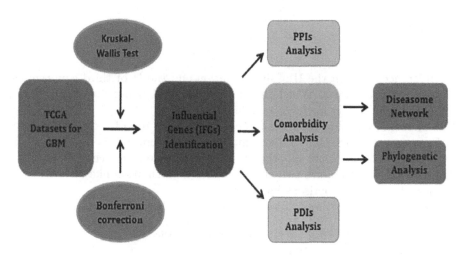

Fig. 1. Analytical approach of this investigation.

2.2 Analysis Method

K-W test is a non-parametric test that can be used instead of one-way annova and used to compare numerous independent random samples. Population samples are chosen randomly and self-contained in this approach. Each sample has its own independence and measured in ordinal scale [3].

If samples are not equal, the K-W test statistic is defined as Eq. 1:

$$H = \frac{12}{M(M+1)} \sum_{i=1}^{c} \frac{R_i}{M_i} - 3(M+1) \tag{1}$$

In the Eq. (1), C represents number of samples, Ri denotes the sum of the rankings in the I-th sample, Mi denotes the number of observations in the I-th sample, and M denotes the total number of Mi, which denotes the total number of observations in all combined samples.

When the value of H is big, the null hypothesis rejects the test result. The hypothesis H0 assumes that all C groupings are descended from the same population. Because this is an actual dataset, no tie can be guaranteed. Tie is a natural fit for this type of real-world dataset. If ties occur, each observation is given the average of the ranks for which it is tied. The H is then calculated using Eq. (1) and divided by the flowing Eq. (2),

$$1 - \frac{\sum T}{M^3 - M} \tag{2}$$

In Eq. (2), $T = (t-1)t(t+1) = t^3 - t$ for each group of connections. The number of tied observations in the group is given by t. The total is calculated over all tie groupings. As a result, H's final equation is defined as Eq. (3).

$$H = \frac{\frac{12}{M(M+1)} \sum_{i=1}^{c} \frac{R_i}{M_i} - 3(M+1)}{1 - \frac{\sum T}{M^3 - M}} \tag{3}$$

The difference between the H of first equation and the H of third equation can be quite small at times. When the ties are handled using mean ranks, H is distributed as $X^2(\text{C-1})$ for large samples [8].

Bonferroni inequality theory is the base of BC and used for confidence interval. For counteracting the multiple comparisons problem, BC is the easiest solution. To reject a false null hypothesis, BC gives greater chance of failure than other methods, as it ignores potentially valuable information like distribution of p-values across all comparisons [9].

The selecting algorithm to identify IFGs is as followed [3]:

- Preprocess the TCGA datasets for applying tests.
- Select the α value as significance level.
- For each existing gene
  - For each class make vectors with TCGA datasets
  - Scale the class vectors
  - Calculate 'P-value' by implementing K-W test.
- Calculate 'P-adjustment value' by implementing BC.
- Select the IFGs of which adjusted p value is less than or equal to 0.05 (p-adjusted <= 0.05).

We have used gold benchmark databases (OMIM and dbGaP) for comorbidity analysis with the help of gene enrichment tools Enrichr [9]. We have used neighborhood topological approach (multilayer) for constructing IFGs diseasome network and comorbidity network. In these networks each node represents either IFGs or diseases and there exists association between them by sharing edges [4,10].

Phylogenetic analysis for the entire sequence was obtained by MEGA based on aligned nucleotide sequences, which is obtained by ClustalW multiple alignment program [5]. Proportional distance method was used for genetic distance calculations. For phylogenetic tree building, various genetic distance matrices were used for the neighbor-joining method, where the bootstrap confidence interval is 500 [11].

Markov clustering algorithm is used to analyze the PPIs and PDIs. STRING database has been utilized with medium confidence score to calculate the interactions between macromolecules. For the constructions of PPI and PDI networks we have used Cytoscape and NetworkAnalyst [12].

3   Result and Discussion

3.1   Influential Genes (IFGs) Identification Analysis

We have analyzed TCGA dataset for GBM from cBioPortal. After preprocessing we have seen that there were total 16261 features. We have applied Kruskal's Wills H test and Bonferroni correction to select influential features (IFGs). We have successfully calculated p-values and adjusted p-values by applying those test. To select the IFGs we have kept the adjusted p-value is less than equal to 0.05. We have successfully identified 26 IFGs from 16261 genes of GBM. These 26 IFGs would reduce the complexity of our work. These 26 IFGs are DEGs and either it is up-regulated genes or down-regulated genes. We have constructed a IFGs diseasome network, as shown in Fig. 2 and the identified IFGs are represented in Table 1 [1,3].

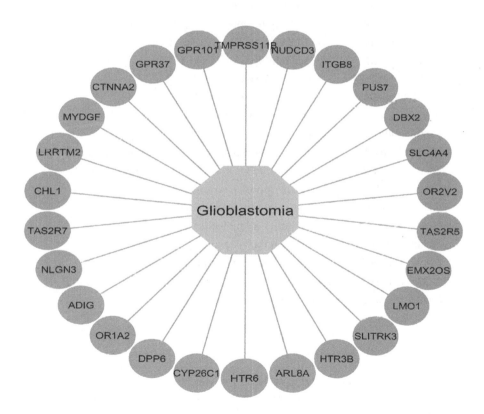

Fig. 2. IFGs diseasome network of GBM. The green circles represent the IFGs. There exist a connection between IFGs and GBM. (Color figure online)

Table 1. Identified 26 IFGs of GBM. Blue colored 06 IFGs are the reason of association between GBM and its comorbidities.

Gene ID	Symbol	Gene name
285659	OR2V2	olfactory receptor family 2 subfamily V member 2
83550	GPR101	G protein-coupled receptor 101
54413	NLGN3	neuroligin 3
127829	ARL8A	ADP ribosylation factor like GTPase 8A
8671	SLC4A4	solute carrier family 4 member 4
2861	GPR37	G protein-coupled receptor 37
149685	ADIG	adipogenin
9177	HTR3B	5-hydroxytryptamine receptor 3B
440097	DBX2	developing brain homeobox 2
1496	CTNNA2	catenin alpha 2
26189	OR1A2	olfactory receptor family 1 subfamily A member 2
22865	SLITRK3	SLIT and NTRK like family member 3
54517	PUS7	pseudouridine synthase 7
56005	MYDGF	myeloid derived growth factor
1804	DPP6	dipeptidyl peptidase like 6
4004	LMO1	LIM domain only 1
3696	ITGB8	integrin subunit beta 8
26045	LRRTM2	leucine rich repeat transmembrane neuronal 2
340665	CYP26C1	cytochrome P450 family 26 subfamily C member 1
196047	EMX2OS	EMX2 opposite strand/antisense RNA
23386	NUDCD3	NudC domain containing 3
10752	CHL1	cell adhesion molecule L1 like
3362	HTR6	5-hydroxytryptamine receptor 6
54429	TAS2R5	taste 2 receptor member 5
132724	TMPRSS11B	transmembrane serine protease 11B
50837	TAS2R7	taste 2 receptor member 7

3.2   Comorbidity Analysis

We have used glodbenchmark databases for the comorbidity analysis of GBM. Database for Genotypes and Phenotypes (dbGaP) and Online Mendelism Inheritance for Men (OMIM-diseases and OMIM-expand) has been utilized for this analysis with the help of online gene set enrichment tools (Enrichr). We have used our identified 26 IFGs for comorbidities analysis. We have collected information from Enrichr and filtered the information with necessary conditions to reject null hypothesis. On the basic of these information and literature study we have successfully identified some diseases which are associated with GBM. These are

Heart rate, Sudden cardiac death, Arteries, Hemoglobin A- Glycosylated, Pancreatic neoplasms, Tissue plasminogen Activator, Autism, and Leukemia. We have identified these comorbidities with the help of the IFGS of GBM. Some literature also proved that these identified comorbidities are really associated with GBM. Here, we also identified 6 shared IFGs, which are created link between GBM and its comorbidities. These 6 genes are also common in our identified 26 IFGs (which are blue marked in Table 1). These 6 IFGs are the reason of association between these comorbidities and GBM [4]. We have constructed a comorbidity diseasome network as shown in Fig. 3.

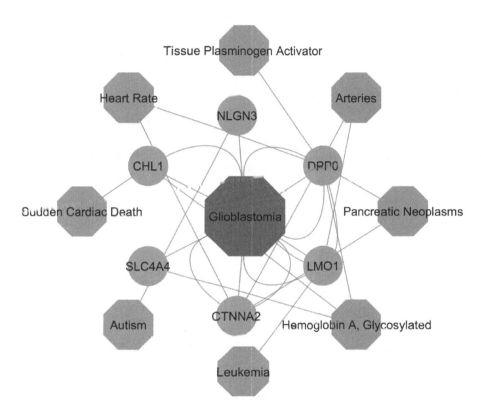

Fig. 3. Comorbidity diseasome network. Yellow colored octagon represents the comorbidities of GBM. Green colored circular shapes represent the shared IFGs between GBM and comorbidities.

3.3   Phylogenetic Analysis

Phylogenetic analysis is very important because it describes the understanding of how genes, species, and proteins are originated. This phylogenetic tree is a diagram or tree structure that shows the evolutionary connection among diseases. For the construction of phylogenetic tree we have used Molecular Evolutionary

Genetics Analysis (MEGA) computer software and chose FASTA sequences for this analysis [5]. We have collected FASTA sequences from NCBI for each comorbidities and GBM and constructed phylogenetic tree for each diseases which is shown in Fig. 4. By analyzing our derived tree, we can see that GBM and Autism are very much associated i.e., their evaluation can be occur from same species. If we want to brunch out the diseases, we can conclude that Sudden cardiac death, Arteries, Tissue plasminogen Aativator, Leukemia, and Hemoglobin A-Glycosylated are in one branch and Pancreatic neoplasms, Autism, Heart rate, GBM are in anonter brunch. These brunching represent the association degree among diseases [11].

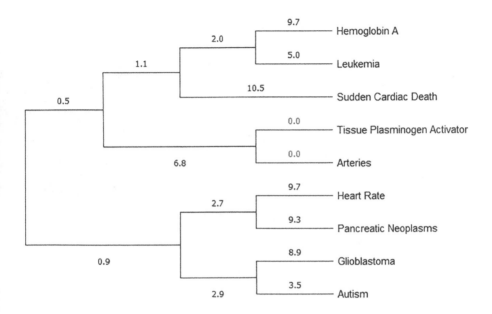

Fig. 4. Phylogenetic tree between GBM and Comorbidities.

3.4 Protien Protien Interactions (PPIs) Analysis

PPIs analysis are the presentation of physical association between proteins, molecules in cell [13]. This interaction is a major biological operation to predict the basis of target protein. For the formation of the PPIs network we have used NetworkAnalyst, Cytoscape and String database with medium confidence score. The PPIs network is represented in Fig. 5. We have successfully identified some hub-proteins during the observations of PPIs [4,10].

These hub proteins can be associated with comorbidities of GBM. The hub proteins information which we have identified through PPIs analysis is listed in Table 2.

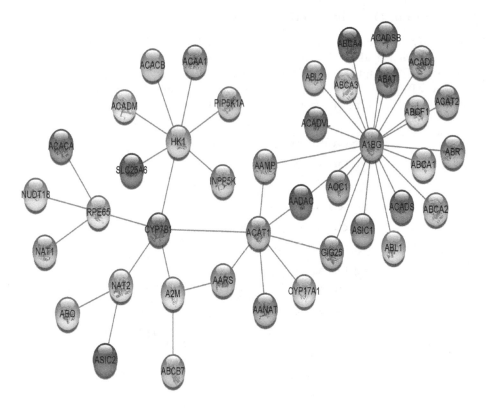

Fig. 5. PPIs network for the IFGs of GBM.

Table 2. Hub-proteins information from PPIs of GBM.

Hub Protein	Degree	Betweenness Centrality
HTR6	19	207
HTR3B	2	20
ITGB8	20	596.5
GPR37	8	280
CTNNA2	7	536.5
PUS7	6	205
UBC	5	573
ARL8A	3	52
NUDCD3	3	85
ACTN2	2	144
ACTN4	2	144
ACTN1	2	144

3.5   Protein Drug Interaction Analysis (PDI)

To identify significant drug particles for IFGs, Protein-drug analysis is a must. Using the identified IFGs, we have successfully identified 20 drug particles for the IFGs HTR6 and HTR3B. Our constructed PDIs network has been prepared with DrugBank [6]. The whole network has been clustered with NetworkAnalyst and Cytoscape. These are represented in Fig. 6.

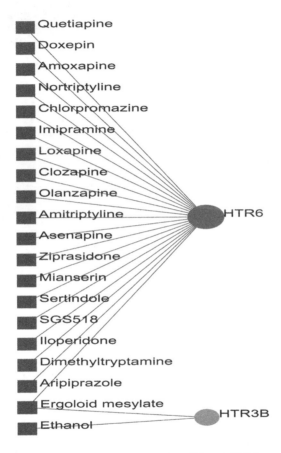

Fig. 6. PDIs network for the IFGs of GBM.

4   Conclusion

Nowadays cancer is the largest threat for humans. GBM is one type of cancer that can occur in the frontal and temporal lobes of the brain and their quick growth and invasion of nearby tissues. We have developed a model to identify the IFGs, which are responsible to occur GBM [1,2]. In TCGA datasets there are a lot of genes with different parameters [7]. To reduce the computational complexity for various analyses like gene therapy, drug design, etc. IFGs identification is a must. That is why we feel motivated to do this type of investigation [3]. First, we have preprocessed the TCGA datasets for analysis. Then we have used the K-W test and BC to select IFGs for GBM [8,14]. We have successfully identified 26 dysregulated IFGs from 16261 genes of GBM. These IFGs will reduce the complexity of computation and various bioinformatics analyses. From various research papers and literature, we knew that people who are affected by GBM have a great risk to occur comorbidities like Arteries, Leukemia, Pancreatic Neoplasms, Sudden cardiac death, Autism, etc. For comorbidity identification, we have performed drug and diseases analysis [4]. We have utilized gold benchmark databases for these purposes and successfully identified comorbidities (Heart rate, sudden cardiac death, Arteries, Hemoglobin A- Glycosylated, Pancreatic neoplasms, Tissue plasminogen Activator, Autism, and Leukemia.) of GBM [10]. We have successfully identified the evolutionary relationship between comorbidities and GBM by phylogenetic analysis [5]. The phylogenetic tree represents the degree of association between comorbidities and GBM. We have identified that GBM and Autism are mostly associated and Hemoglobin-A is less associated with GBM [11].

To identify the macromolecule interactions among cellular components we have performed the analysis of the protein-protein interactions. We have successfully identified 12 hub proteins with a degree and betweenness centrality from PPIs. For the identification of drug molecules of identified IFGs, we have performed protein-drug analysis. We have successfully identified 20 drug molecules for IFGs [6]. PPIs and PDIs networks suggest a significant link between comorbidities and GBM at the molecular level. Our findings prove that GBM has a strong association with Heart rate, sudden cardiac death, Arteries, Hemoglobin A- Glycosylated, Pancreatic neoplasms, Tissue plasminogen Activator, Autism, and Leukemia on the genetic level. Their evolutionary relation represents the level of association among them. Our identified 26 dysregulated IFGs will reduce the computational complexity. Our identified hub proteins and drug molecules will be helpful for drug design and gene therapy. This study would be helpful for accurate comorbidities identification also. It will also be useful for raising awareness about the threatening consequences of GBM among people [4].

References

1. Rahman, M.H., et al.: Bioinformatics and machine learning methodologies to identify the effects of central nervous system disorders on glioblastoma progression. Briefings Bioinf. **22**(5), bbaa365 (2021)
2. Villani, V., et al.: Comorbidities in elderly patients with glioblastoma: a field-practice study. Future Oncol. **15**(8), 841–850 (2019)
3. Das, U., Hasan, M.A.M., Rahman, J.: Influential gene identification for cancer classification. In: 2019 International Conference on Electrical, Computer and Communication Engineering (ECCE), pp. 1–6. IEEE (2019)
4. Podder, N.K., et al.: A system biological approach to investigate the genetic profiling and comorbidities of type 2 diabetes. Gene Rep. **21**, 100830 (2020)
5. Moni, M.A., Liò, P.: Genetic profiling and comorbidities of zika infection. J. Infectious Dis. **216**(6), 703–712 (2017)

6. Nain, Z., Rana, H.K., Liò, P., Islam, S.M.S., Summers, M.A., Moni, M.A.: Pathogenetic profiling of COVID-19 and SARS-like viruses. Brief. Bioinform. **22**(2), 1175–1196 (2021)
7. Tomczak, K., Czerwińska, P., Wiznerowicz, M.: The cancer genome atlas (TCGA): an immeasurable source of knowledge. Contemp. Oncol. **19**(1A), A68 (2015)
8. Kruskal, W.H., Wallis, W.A.: Use of ranks in one-criterion variance analysis. J. Am. Stat. Assoc. **47**(260), 583–621 (1952)
9. Podder, N.K., et al.: A bioinformatics approach to identify the influences of diabetes on the progression of cancers. In: 2022 International Conference on Advancement in Electrical and Electronic Engineering (ICAEEE), pp. 1–6 (2022)
10. Datta, R., Podder, N.K., Rana, H.K., Islam, M.K.B., Moni, M.A.: Bioinformatics approach to analyze gene expression profile and comorbidities of gastric cancer. In: 2020 23rd International Conference on Computer and Information Technology (ICCIT), pp. 1–6. IEEE (2020)
11. Smith, S.A., Beaulieu, J.M., Donoghue, M.J.: Mega-phylogeny approach for comparative biology: an alternative to supertree and supermatrix approaches. BMC Evol. Biol. **9**(1), 1–12 (2009)
12. Podder, N.K.: Network-based approach to identify pathways and macromolecule interactions that mediate influences of covid-19 on the progression of respiratory system diseases. In: 2022 International Conference on Advancement in Electrical and Electronic Engineering (ICAEEE), pp. 1–6 (2022)
13. Podder, N.K., Shill, P.C., Rana, H.K., Omit, S.B.S., Al Shahriar, M.M.H., Azam, M.S.: Genetic effects of covid 19 on the development of neurodegenerative diseases. In: 2021 5th International Conference on Electrical Information and Communication Technology (EICT), pp. 1–6. IEEE (2021)
14. Bonferroni, C.: Teoria statistica delle classi e calcolo delle probabilita. Pubblicazioni del R. Istituto Superiore di Scienze Economiche e Commericiali di Firenze **8**, 3–62 (1936)

Protein Folding Optimization Using Butterfly Optimization Algorithm

Md. Sowad Karim$^{(\boxtimes)}$, Sajib Chatterjee, Ashis Hira, Tarin Islam, and Rezanul Islam

North Western University, Khulna, Bangladesh
sowad1990@gmail.com

Abstract. Protein folding optimization (PFO) is an NP-hard problem. The Butterfly Optimization Algorithm (BOA) is a recently invented meta-heuristic algorithm that has outperformed current algorithms on a variety of issues. Figure out the structure of a protein is a hard task. Many biomedical operations depend on it. Its already tried by many types of calculation but no one gets the appropriate result. For protein figure analysis but steel have a plethora of place to do some task. That's why we are going to use the BOA algorithm. And we get enough good results regarding this problem. The three operators of the BOA are (1) Initialization phase, (2) Iteration phase, and (3) Final phase. We have also created a mechanism to obtain the proper structure which is a repair mechanism. Test results show that it works well when the BOA performs in the PFO problem which is better than many other calculations.

Keywords: 3D HP lattice model · Protein folding optimization · Butterfly Optimization algorithm · Propagate to best butterfly · Get the best butterfly · Repair direction operator

1 Introduction

Proteins are polymers made from combinations of amino acids that are accessible in various sorts and expect more parts in existing animals. From the beginning, a protein is an immediate combination of amino acids. Proteins cross-over, impacted by a couple of mixtures and natural factors, into the three-layered (3D) structures that choose their inherent limits and properties. In best protein structure estimate (PSP), a cross-segment model has been utilized for imploding spine examining at the most elevated mark of an ever-evolving system. The protein falling issue is defined as the assumption for a protein's tripartite plan given its amino destructive strategy [1]. Protein shape is an NP-hard (non-deterministic polynomial-time) issue, which has drawn the attention of several examiners.

Researchers have found numerous facility strategies to be specific x-ray crystallography and nuclear magnetic resonance (NMR) that decide the local shape of proteins. In spite of the fact that these strategies give productive comes about they are not continuously enforceable. Since these strategies are exorbitant and time-consuming.

© ICST Institute for Computer Sciences, Social Informatics and Telecommunications Engineering 2023
Published by Springer Nature Switzerland AG 2023. All Rights Reserved
Md. S. Satu et al. (Eds.): MIET 2022, LNICST 491, pp. 775–787, 2023.
https://doi.org/10.1007/978-3-031-34622-4_61

There have been numerous advancements in the field of protein collapsing. There is still a lot of work yet not done in reenacting proteins for many combinations. Calculations of this type stay infeasible with running handling innovation. The problem is enhanced by the Hydrophobic-Hydrophilic (HP) lattice-based model protein with maintaining conduct relevance. As of not long ago, the 3D HP model has been generally overlooked due to the ease of the hunt space and the 2D HP model and simpler perception. Worked on HP models have been demonstrated to be NP-complete [2] and along these lines are ideal for assessing and further developing heuristic-based calculations that will help future advancement of extended protein collapsing issues. Ill protein is the reason for many fatal diseases. So, if we can optimize the protein folding it will help us to treat those ill proteins.

Protein Folding Optimization (PFO) can be an issue where a course of action of The input of amino acids enables us to determine the local three dimensional structure along with the precise value. A structure with the first diminished vitality relates to the first persistent position, following the rule of thermodynamics.

HP Lattice Model
The HP model relies upon the view of hydrophobic association in two amino destructive buildups [2, 3]. This is the primary stage for protein falling and the improvement of a nearby protein position. The most un-troublesome model is for the examination of protein The HP model, which may be found in 2D or 3D, describes falling [2, 3]. The more exact HP bend Determine the sample amino acids into types which are both hydrophobic and hydrophilic [2].

The calculation for free energy: The mathematical methodology can be used to power the calculation [2]:

$$\varepsilon_{ij} = \begin{cases} -1.0 & the\ pair\ of\ H\ and\ H\ residues \\ 0 & other \end{cases} \quad (1)$$

$$E = \sum_{i,j} \Delta_{rij}\varepsilon_{ij} \quad (2)$$

where the parameter,

$$\Delta_{r_{ij}} = \begin{cases} 1 & S\ is\ adjacent\ but\ not\ connected\ amino\ acids \\ 0 & others \end{cases} \quad (3)$$

There are two types of sights in the HP lattice model: H (hydrophobic) and P (phobic) (hydrophilic). H-H is the first in the amino acid sequence. Affiliations are most noteworthy. In the HP model, the optimum change is the one with the greatest number of H associations and the minimum power value.

The issue of advancement of protein collapsing may be changed into the estimation of the base proteins' free power collapsing adaptation. This is the easiest model to understand the protein structure adequately with good visualization.

A Plot of the HP 2D Lattice Model

Fig. 1. 2d off-lattice model

In Fig. 1 we have a picture of a 2d off-lattice model. In this image, all the blue nodes are represented as the P monomer and the gray ones are represented as the H monomer. As well as the picture's format is PHPPHPPHHP. The H-H covalent link is represented by the black line in between the H monomer.

A Plot of the 3D HP Lattice Model

Fig. 2. 3D HP lattice model

In Fig. 2, we have a picture of a 3d off-lattice model. In this image, all the blue nodes are represented as the P monomer and the gray ones are represented as the H monomer.. As well as the picture's format is PHPPHPPHHP. The H-H covalent link is represented by the black line in between the H monomer.

The value of the power technique declines as the count of HH contact rises. A perfect construction would minimize energy use by requiring the least amount of labor. The proteomics projection challenge is also regarded as an NP-hard optimal solution with just this show.

2 Related Work

In this zone, we have overviewed a couple of metaheuristic calculations that were utilized to light the protein collapsing optimization issue.

2.1 Chemical Reaction Optimization

Lam and Li proposed the CRO optimization algorithm [4]. It is One population-based meta-heuristic algorithm that mimics the process of a chemical process. In addition, CRO is a way closely linked to chemical reactions [5]. The function of the CRO is based on two parts of thermodynamics. The very first part discloses that; energy is then converted from one type to the next and moved from one creature to another; it cannot be easily broken. Chemical reactions produce chemicals and their surroundings. As a result, the first thermodynamics low has been applied. It has many positive sides like having multifarious features of simulated Algorithms for annealing and particle swarm optimization The CRO algorithm is grouped into three categories: startup, iteration, and finalization. The search area is provided and critical parameters are initialized in the beginning stages. That's one of four molecular reactions chosen by almost everyone in the repetitive stage. The algorithm is finished. The algorithm work like a searching process for minimum energy (optimal solution). It's time-consuming, it can't provide better minimum free energy for all sequences.

2.2 Genetic Algorithm

The HP framework just on a cubic lattice has already been properly linked to formative and swarm algorithms. The designers of [6] built a GA algorithm with an assortment of conformations. Confirmation is changed utilizing transformation, within the shapes of the ordinary Monte Carlo process, and hybrids, in which bits of the specified orientation sequence are swapped among conformations Dual genetic operators repeat till confirmable results are obtained. GA calculations are prevalent in customary Monte Carlo strategies. This task for updated in [7] where the creators appeared that GA is active in deciding protein folding shape. In this study, untenable configurations have been used in the activity is great, and the energy of these residues was determined using disciplinary work. Also, a swarming mechanism was used for keeping up with the population's diversity. The think about [8] considered where the two operators of multipoint hybrid and a neighborhood irritation are required for any GA to be completely successful. An orderly crossover look is offered in [9] that employment data almost differ between two objects. In connection with GA, this device dramatically better visual effectiveness Another concern [10] contrasted relative and absolute structural encoding. The appearance space is various as a result of encoding, which is typically why the GA illustrated in [11] is preferred over the GA displayed in [12]. In this case, the creators also proposed altered vitality importance that facilitated the GA look and recognized shortcomings within limitation administration techniques. It's difficult to implement and time-consuming, it can't provide the best minimum free energy in less time.

2.3 Artificial Bee Colony and Pigeon-Inspired Optimization

The artificial bee colony algorithm (ABC), like other bionic intelligent algorithms, mimics the operation of a bee colony harvesting honey. The tentacles of a bee are the organ of smell in nature. Bees can detect the scents of various frothers and use them to discover nectar. Circular dance and figure-of-eight dance are Bee's communication tools; these dances are used to express distance and direction. The efficiency with which bees find nectar inspires researchers. D. Karaboga, a Turkey professor, proposed ABC in 2005. The normal mechanism is that all bees hunt in a random range with their tentacles [4]. Their dance to deliver the knowledge after some time. The honey-seeking bees.

will then lead the non-rewarding bees. As a result, the bees will focus on a honey source. The traditional ABC divides bees into 3 types: working bees, observation pollinating insects, and scout bees. Their jobs are different. Employed bees go on odd honey hunts and contact each other. Before taking over the duties of hired bees, onlooker bees learn a lot from them. If the Scout bee observes that any spectator bees have been unable to access the honey in a fair length of time, an employment bee will be dispatched to take their place. Duan and Qiao created pigeon-inspired optimization (PIO) in 2014. This one was motivated by pigeons' homing instinct. The height of the sun, the oscillations of the force field, and the depth of familiarity with the terrain are the three key characteristics that govern the pigeons' behavior, according to scientists. The first two elements have a stronger impact when a pigeon is flying at a high altitude, and the third component has a larger effect when it is flying near the ground. The landmark method and the map and pointer operator are two aspects of the original PIO procedure.

For the aim of protein optimizing, we will employ the "Butterfly Optimization Algorithm" (BOA), a brand-new meta-heuristic algorithm because none of these possess the precision that has been demonstrated to be useful.

3 Protein Folding Optimization Using (BOA)

Arora and Singh presented the Butterfly Optimization Algorithm (BOA), a recently designed conceptual estimate, in 2009. It reenacts the scrounging and mating qualities of butterflies. The Butterfly Optimization Algorithm (BOA), it is patterned like the butterfly purchase behavior, is also another environmental metaheuristic technique for global simplification. This way of behaving of the beneficial growth of butterflies forward towards the meat source position can be demonstrated. The butterflies detect for analyzing the scent in the air to major the likely location of a source of food or mate. To discover the optima in the vast solution space, BOA mimics this behavior. When conducting innovations like protein folding direction, BOA are used as search specialists. A butterfly's ability to strongly create odor is a hypothesis developed in BOA. Additionally, its scent is related to the butterfly's health.

Three processes in BOA: The entire BOA calculation will work to get the best direction set for the amino acid sequence where it will get the minimum energy value. The characteristics of butterflies mentioned above are exalted as follows in order to demonstrate all the talks mentioned above as lengthy as a calculation [13]:

1. Butterflies are about to emit some smell that allows the other butterflies to connect.
2. Every butterfly takes place normally or will move to the best one by spending more smell as compared to amino acid sequence moves for the optimum direction.
3. The environment of the target function affects or decides the perceptual acuity of a butterfly-like ascertain the power amount of the amino acid.

There are three processes in BOA: (1) Initialization phase, (2) repetition phase, and (3) Finalization phase.

Algorithm 1 **BOA**PFO (Butterfly Optimization Algorithm)

1: **procedure** BOA$_{PFO}$ (sequence)
2:　　**Calculate Energy** f(x), x=(x$_1$, x$_2$, x$_3$, ..., x$_{dim}$) dim = no of dimensions
3:　　Set, pop Size, sequence, new Direction
4:　　population = **GIB** (sequence, length(sequence))
5:　　or energy is determined by f(x) or Calculate Energy
6:　　Define the terms sensor (c), power (a), and probability (p)
7:　　**While** stopping criteria are not met **do**
8:　　　　**For** each bf in each population **do**
9:　　　　　　Fragrance = **CFEB** (sequence, Direction)
10:　　　　**end for**
11:　　　　　　bf = **FBB**(sequence, Direction)shown
12:　　　　**for** each bf in each population
13:　　　　　　Create a random number r using [0, 1]
14:　　　　　　　　**if** r < p **then**
15:　　　　　　　　　　**MTBB**(sequence, Direction)
16:　　　　　　　　**else**
17:　　　　　　　　　　Move randomly
18:　　　　　　　　**end if**
19:　　　　**end for**
20:　　　　Update the value of a
21:　　**end while**
22: **end procedure**

3.1 Populace Initialization and Algorithmic Portrayal

The initialization is chosen by giving each sequence in a randomized direction. For the BOA problem, the population is set as an individual set of directions for amino acid sequences, which are individually termed butterflies. The quantity of the produced population will be in l if the length of the sequencing of amino acids is in l. of the direction(butterflies) has the length of size l - 1. Cause In a lattice structure, the first location is already established at the center (0, 0, 0). R, L, U, D, F, and B are the six potential directions, with R denoting right, L denoting left, U denoting up, D denoting down, F denoting forward, and B denoting backward. Every array-based answer is defined through the number between 1 and 6 generated at random. The cubic lattice's matching orientation is chosen at random from the array. The generation process of the amino acid sequence {H, P, P, H, H} is shown in Fig. 3.

We could see that the initial position is specified in the first step, hence no direction is formed. The right direction was chosen at random in the second phase, and the route value was placed in the orientation array. This process continues until the sequence set is completed. And then generate a valid or invalid output array or vector. After all of the processes have been completed, a full structure is created. The an amino acid's chain sequence is classified according to its energies after obtaining a complete solution. As

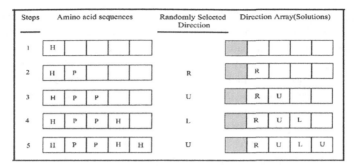

Steps	Amino acid sequences					Randomly Selected Direction	Direction Array(Solutions)				
1	H										
2	H	P				R		R			
3	H	P	P			U		R	U		
4	H	P	P	H		L		R	U	L	
5	H	P	P	H	H	U		R	U	L	U

Fig. 3. Initial Generation of Population

well as the top five of both the ordered route are chosen to proceed to the following steps.

3.2 Get the Best Butterfly Sequences Operator

Steps	Randomly Generated Direction (sorted)				Energy
1	R	U	R	U	0
2	R	U	R	D	0
3	R	U	L	U	1
4	L	D	R	D	1
5	L	D	R	R	1

Best N Selected

Fig. 4. Get the Best Butterfly Sequence

The find best butterfly sets of operators takes two parameters. One is the order of the amino acids and the other one is the population size of the butterfly orders that we want. So when the operator is called the operator takes two parameters, one is the sequence and the other one is the population size. After the initial variables are defined the main procedure of the algorithm is started. Which is to generate a random butterfly population direction and store it in the array. After that, it calculates the energies of each butterfly population and then sorts them in ascending order. After the sorting is finished it returns the best 5 butterfly population to the next operator. The working procedure is shown in Fig. 4.

3.3 Calculate the Fragrance of Each Butterfly Operator

In this section, the H-H amino acid bond has formed. In the figure, the H-H covalent bond has been shown with deep blue color. And the processor labels the covalent link as a cluster everywhere it occurs, then evaluates the scent of that region based on its frequency. All the cluster in the monomer group has the same way of calculation. It tries to compensate for the modality sense in a bit different way. The first step is to set the initial position of the butterfly population to the cubic lattice center which is {0, 0, 0} and a set of positions { }, which is supposed to store the visited butterflies. There's also an array that's utilized to gather every butterfly's scent. The algorithm takes two parameters, the amino acid sequence seq, and a mutated sequence dir which is merged and repaired after taking the best five sequences. Then the algorithm takes each butterfly from the population and changes the position x of the butterfly. Now if the changed position p is valid then the algorithm stores the fragrance and repeats the step. After all the steps are finished the algorithm returns the fragrance array FA = {f1, f2, f3 ...., fn} (Fig. 5).

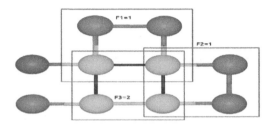

Fig. 5. Find Fragrance Operator

3.4   Propagate to the Best Butterfly Operator

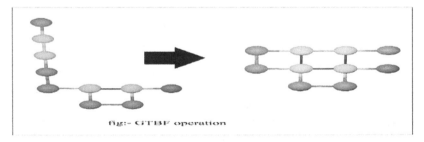

Fig. 6. Propagate To Best Butterfly Process

In Fig. 6 we can see that the initial position of the monomers in structure 1 is a bit odd. The 7th monomer in the structure is a P monomer. The 8th atom formed an H-H covalent connection with the 4th and 2nd monomers following the spread. Thus, the framework is maintained.

However, the PTTBB algorithm concentrates simply on the butterfly's scent, or more precisely, the fragrance among each near group of butterflies. The algorithm takes two parameters as input {seq, dir}. Where the seq is the initial amino acid sequence, and direction is the mutated direction or butterfly population in this context. In the algorithm, it first gets the Fragrance of the butterfly population $F = \{f_1, f_2, f_3, ..., f_n\}$. Now after that, it shifts the butterflies to a new state according to the fragrance. After that, a new direction is generated. So after comparing the newly generated sequence and the previous sequence the best one is returned.

3.5 Mutate Best N Butterfly Population Operator

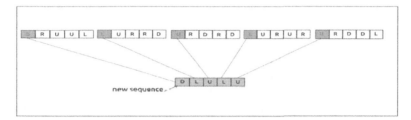

Fig. 7. Mutation of Best N Butterfly Population

The mutation Algorithm used in this paper is quite simple and forward. It takes the top five generated sequences and divides them along with a determined length. And connect those sequences. The working principle of the mutation algorithm is shown in Fig. 7. We can see in the figure that we have five sequences respectively. Which are {PRUUL, LURRD, URDRD, LURUR, URDDL}. In this algorithm, then each of the sequences is divided respected to its size. And then recombined to a new order s = {DLULU}.

3.6 Repair Sequence Direction Operator

In our Proposed method Algorithm 4, MBNBP takes N number of the direction of number sequences and merges them with a stride-based method, and returns a single direction sequence of length(sequence) - 1. However, the MBNBP algorithm's fundamental flaw is that the generated pattern can overrun. Which is also referred to as an invalid sequence. So to move forward we need to repair the sequences.

In Fig. 8 we can see that the left amino acid structure consists of blue, gray, and red monomers. However, there is no third atom within the HP structure model. In the structure the blue monomer is P and the Gary monomer is H. But the red section has two monomers at the same position. However, well after correction, the lattice or framework in Fig. 3.5 has now become the correct shape.

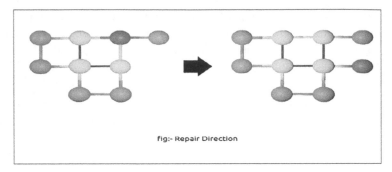

Fig. 8. Repair Direction Operator

4 Results After Experiments

All of the previously shown operators have been implemented in c++ language which is compiled and run on an Intel Core i5 processor with 4 × 1.6 GHz Speed and 8 GB of RAM. We used 10 protein sequences as shown in Table 1 and Table 2.

4.1 Setup of Experimental Parameter

In the algorithm that we have proposed, here we have utilized a considerable parameter setup. Population Size = 1000, c = 0.05,alpha = 0.3. These values have been selected randomly. When the Population size index reaches the maximum the program ends. To justify our output, we have considered and justified the Best Energies for each sequence E_{best}, Mean Energy E_{mean}, and best level of deviation E_{std}. We have examined our result with Advanced Mechanisms (GAAM [13], CRO [20], MO + FR [15]) which is one of the most proficient metaheuristic algorithms utilized to figure out the PFO problem.

Table 1. TEST SEQUENCE OF PROTEIN 48 LENGTH

Label	Sequence
T48.1	HPHHPPHHHHPHHHHPPHHPPHPHHHHPHPHHPPHHPPPHPPPPPPPPHH
T48.2	HHHHPHHPHHHHHPPHPPHHPPHPPPPPPHPPHPPPHPPHHPPHHHHPH
T48.3	PHPHHPHHHHHHPPPHPHPPPHPHHPHPHPPPHPPHHPPHHPPHPHPPHP
T48.4	PHPHHPPHPHHPPHHPHHPPPHHHHHPPHPHHHHPHPHPPPPHPPPHPHP
T48.5	PPPHPPHPHHPPHHHHHPHHPHHHHPPHPHPHPPHPPPPPPHHPHHPH
T48.6	HHHPPPHHPHPHHPHHPHHPHPPPPPPPHPHPPHPPPHPPHHHHHHHPH
T48.7	PHPPPPHPHPPPPHPHHHHHPHHPHHPPPHPHPPPPHHHPPHHHPPHHPPPH
T48.8	PHHHPHHHPHHHHHPPHHHHPPPPPPHPHHHPPHHPHPPPHHHPHPHPHHPPP
T48.9	PHPHPPPPHPHPHPPHPHHHHHHHPPHHHHPHPPHPHHPPHPHHHHPPPPH
T48.1	PHHPPPPPPPHHPPPHHHHPHPPHPHPHHPPHPPHPPHPPHHPPHHPPHH

This Table 1 is Containing 10 of 48 length Amino Acid Sequence which is used as a dataset [8].

Table 2. Test sequence of protein 8 different length

Label	Sequence
T20	HPHPPHHPHPPHPHHPPHPH
T24	HHPPHPPHPPHPPHPPHPPHPPHH
T25	PPHPPHHP4HHPPPPHHP4HH
T36	PPPHHPPHHPPPPPHHHHHHHPPHHPPPPHHPPHPP
T48	PPHPPHHPPHHPPPPPHHHHHHHHHHPPPPPPHHPPHHPPHPH2HHHHH
T50	HHPHPHPHPHHHHPHPPPHPPPHPPPPHPPPHPPPHPHHHHPHPHPHPHH
T60	PPHHHPHHHHHHHHPPPHHHHHHHHHHPHPPPHHHHHHHHHHHHPPPPPHHHHHHHPHHPHP
T64	HHHHHHHHHHHHHPHPHPPHHPPHHPPHPHPPHHPPHPPHHPPHPPPHHPPHHPPHPHPHPHHHHHHHHHHHHH

Table 2 is containing 8 various lengths of Amino Acid Sequence which is also used as a dataset [8].

4.2 Results

We can observe that after evaluating and implementing, Our proposed algorithm provides an acceptable result for these given sequences compared to the GAAM [12], CRO [15], and MA [16] Algorithm and the result is quite good for a length of 48. The result is in Table 2.

Table 3. Results of 48-length protein sequence

Seq.	BOA			GAAM			CRO			MA	
	E_{best}	Emean	Estd	E_{best}	E_{mean}	E_{std}	E_{best}	E_{mean}	E_{std}	Ebest	S R
T48.1	32	32.00	0.00	32	31.82	0.38	32	32.00	0.00	32	0.23
T48.2	34	33.25	0.56	34	33.08	0.77	34	34.00	0.00	34	0.03
T48.3	34	33.87	0.23	34	33.26	0.44	34	34.00	0.00	34	0.03
T48.4	33	33.00	0.00	33	32.22	0.54	33	33.00	0.00	33	0.13
T48.5	32	31.25	0.88	32	31.58	0.49	32	32.00	0.00	32	0.23
T48.6	32	30.14	0.69	32	31.18	0.38	32	22.00	0.00	32	0.10
T48.7	31	31.00	0.48	32	30.62	0.56	32	22.00	0.00	31	0.00
T48.8	31	30.42	0.53	31	30.38	0.48	31	21.00	0.00	31	0.07
T48.9	34	33.85	0.56	34	33.02	0.08	34	34.00	0.00	33	0.00
T48.10	33	32.71	0.45	33	32.28	0.56	33	33.00	0.00	33	0.07

Our proposed algorithm provides quite an efficient result for all the given sequences in Table 2 compared to the GAAM [17], CRO [15], & MO + FR [14] Algorithm and the result are quite good for up to length $<= 50$. Its in Table 3 (Table 4).

So, all over our result was quite good as compared to that algorithm for both 48 and different lengths of the protein sequence.

Table 4. Results of 10 different proteins swquence.

Seq.	BOA			GAAM [38]			CRO [20]			MO + FR [12]	
	E_{best}	Emean	Estd	E_{best}	E_{mean}	E_{std}	Ebest	Emean	Estd	Ebest	Emean
T20	11	11.00	0.0	11	11.0	0.0	11	11.00	0.00	11	11.00
T24	13	13.00	0.0	13	13.0	0.0	13	13.00	0.00	13	12.96
T25	9	9.00	0.0	9	9.0	0.0	9	9.00	0.00	9	9.00
T36	18	18.00	0.0	18	18.0	0.0	18	18.00	0.00	18	16.84
T48	31	30.50	0.54	31	31.0	0.0	31	31.00	0.00	31	27.39
T50	33	31.20	0.44	33	31.66	0.57	33	31.00	0.00	32	27.40
T60	53	50.16	1.16	53	50.84	0.67	53	50.84	0.00	50	44.45
T64	57	54.14	1.95	58	55.52	1.0	58	55.52	0.00	51	45.63

5 Discussion

We have got many good results as compared with GAAM [12], CRO [20], and modified MO + FR [12] for multiple lengths of amino acid sequence. Especially in terms of 48 lengths, there was a magnificent out for the BOA algorithm. Besides it, we have got some good results for varieties of lengths like T20, T25, T36, T50, T60, and T64.

6 Conclusions

We have presented one of the most important and well-known NP-Hard problems. Which is called the Protein Folding Optimization Problem (PFO). We used the Butterfly Optimization Algorithm to address this particular problem (BAO). Which is Particle Swarm Optimization (PSO) Algorithm. We've also been able to employ the BAO to fix at least several of these issues. We designed three operators to use the BAO algorithm and were also able to apply the operator respective to our problem. The butterfly Optimization Algorithm is relatively new. So our main task was to find that how well the algorithm goes with the problem. That would be the scene for our paper.

In the Future, we can acquire better results than we are getting right now if we can solve the limitations of our current algorithm. For example, if we alter the algorithm architecture of the system, we will achieve better results across the board. Furthermore, if the memory leaks are resolved, we will be able to operate the program more times, yielding a better result than we currently have. As a consequence, valid results for even more than 64 amino acid sequences were obtained. Even bigger amino acid sequences can yield good outcomes.

References

1. Zhou, C., Hou, C., Zhang, Q., Wei, X.: Enhanced hybrid search algorithm for protein structure prediction using the 3D-HP lattice model. J. Molec. Model. **19**(9), 3883–3891 (2013)
2. Mansour, N., Kanj, F., Khachfe, H.: Particle swarm optimization approach for protein structure prediction in the 3D HP model. Interdisc. Sci. Comput. Life Sci. **4**(3), 190–200 (2012)

3. Lin, C.-J., Su, S.-C.: Protein 3D HP model folding simulation using a hybrid of genetic algorithm and particle swarm optimization. Int. J. Fuzzy Syst. **13**(2), 1–8 (2011)
4. Garza-Fabre, M., Rodriguez-Tello, E., Toscano-Pulido, G.: Constraint-handling through multi-objective optimization: the hydrophobic-polar model for protein structure prediction. Comput. Oper. Res. **53**, 128–153 (2015)
5. Islam, M.K., Chetty, M.: Clustered memetic algorithm with local heuristics for ab initio protein structure prediction. IEEE Trans. Evol. Comput. **17**(4), 558–576 (2012)
6. Zhang, X., Cheng, W.: Protein 3D structure prediction by improved tabu search in off-lattice AB model. In: 2008 2nd International Conference on Bioinformatics and Biomedical Engineering, pp. 184–187 (2008)
7. Custódio, F.L., Barbosa, H.J.C., Dardenne, L.E.: Investigation of the three-dimensional lattice HP protein folding model using a genetic algorithm. Genet. Molec. Biol. **27**(4), 611–615 (2004). https://doi.org/10.1590/S1415-47572004000400023
8. Palu, D., Alessandro, A.D., Pontelli, E.: Heuristics, optimizations, and parallelism for protein structure prediction in CLP (FD). In: Proceedings of the 7th ACM SIGPLAN International Conference on Principles and Practice of Declarative Programming, pp. 230–241 (2005)
9. Li, T., Zhou, C., Wang, B., Xiao, B., Zheng, X.: A hybrid algorithm based on artificial bee colony and pigeon inspired optimization for 3D protein structure prediction. J. Bionanosci. **12**(1), 100–108 (2018)
10. Arora, S., Singh, S.: Butterfly optimization algorithm: a novel approach for global optimization. Soft Computing **23**(3), 715–734 (2018). https://doi.org/10.1007/s00500-018-3102-4
11. Bošković, B., Brest, J.: Genetic algorithm with advanced mechanisms applied to the protein structure prediction in a hydrophobic-polar model and cubic lattice. Appl. Soft Comput. **45**, 61–70 (2016)
12. Cutello, V., Nicosia, G., Pavone, M., Timmis, J.: An immune algorithm for protein structure prediction on lattice models. IEEE Trans. Evol. Comput. **11**(1), 101–117 (2007)
13. Bazzoli, A., Tettamanzi, A.G.B.: A memetic algorithm for protein structure prediction in a 3D-lattice HP model. In: Raidl, G.R., et al. (eds.) EvoWorkshops 2004. LNCS, vol. 3005, pp. 1–10. Springer, Heidelberg (2004). https://doi.org/10.1007/978-3-540-24653-4_1
14. Custódio, F.L., Barbosa, H.J.C., Dardenne, L.E.: A multiple minima genetic algorithm for protein structure prediction. Appl. Soft Comput. **15**, 88–99 (2014). https://doi.org/10.1016/j.asoc.2013.10.029
15. Chatterjee, S., Smrity, R.A., Islam, M.R.: Protein structure prediction using chemical reaction optimization. In: 2016 19th International Conference on Computer and Information Technology (ICCIT), pp. 321–326. IEEE (2016)
16. Angela, U., Sylvester, Adetayo: Protein secondary structure prediction using deep neural network and particle swarm optimization algorithm. Int. J. Comput. Appl. **181**(28), 1–8 (2018). https://doi.org/10.5120/ijca2018918070
17. Islam, M.R., Smrity, R.A., Chatterjee, S., Mahmud, M.R.: Optimization of protein folding using chemical reaction optimization in HP cubic lattice model. Neural Comput. Appl. **32**(8), 3117–3134 (2019). https://doi.org/10.1007/s00521-019-04447-8
18. Chatterjee, S., Shill, P.C.: Protein folding optimization in a hydrophobic-polar model for predicting tertiary structure using fruit fly optimization algorithm. In: 2019 10th International Conference on Computing, Communication and Networking Technologies (ICCCNT), pp. 1–7 (2019)

Author Index

rinted in the United States
y Baker & Taylor Publisher Services